The Baby and Child Book

Andrew & Penny Stanway

·

The Baby & Child Book

PEERAGE BOOKS

Dedication
To our own children Susannah, Amy and Ben
and to our stillborn son
who have taught and given us so much.

First published in Great Britain in 1983 by
Pan Books Ltd

This edition published in 1988 by
Peerage Books
59 Grosvenor Street
London W1

ISBN 1 85052 114 X

Printed in Czechoslovakia

50682

Contents

Acknowledgements

We should like to thank all those who have helped us to build our knowledge and understanding of baby and child care over the years. They are too numerous to mention but our special gratitude is due to two people whose valuable comments on the final draft have so enriched the book.

First to Heather Welford, herself a gifted writer and journalist, who read through the book wearing two hats. One, as a young mother of two and another as deputy editor of *Parents* magazine. Her experience at *Parents* of several years of handling the readers' letters pages fitted her uniquely to the task of ensuring that the book contains information that parents of young children really want to know.

Second, we are indebted to one of the country's leading paediatricians, himself a grandfather, and until recently head of the Department of Child Health at a major London teaching hospital. He has seen all the fashions come and go in half a century of baby and child care and was a great help as a result.

Last, we should like to thank our editors, Kyle Cathie and Harriet Thistlethwaite, at Pan, whose careful work on the manuscript did so much to improve it.

About the authors

Drs Andrew and Penny Stanway qualified in medicine in 1968 and 1969 respectively and were married soon after. They have had four children, one of whom was stillborn. At the time of writing the book they had three children under the age of seven.

Dr Penny Stanway MB, BS, MRCS, LRCP worked in two hospitals as a houseman, then spent a year in general practice, where she tended to see mostly women and children. After this she joined the largest Area Health Authority in London as a medical officer and carried out routine school medical examinations and sessions at baby clinics. She spent a year at the Wolfson Centre, attached to the Institute of Child Health, in London during which time she studied developmental medicine and the assessment and care of physically and mentally handicapped children. She became a senior medical officer before she was thirty and helped start and run an assessment unit to serve the area. At this stage of her career she also carried out assessments of handicapped children in their homes and in special schools, and examinations of newborn babies in hospital.

Since she has had children she has chosen to stop working away from home and has become a full-time mother. Even with her busy life as a mother she has not stood still professionally, but has taken care that her work has not interfered with her children's well-being.

Her main professional interest is in the field of breast-feeding in which she has become a world expert. She wrote the best-selling book *Breast Is Best* with her husband and this has now sold over 250,000 copies worldwide. She is on the National Childbirth Trust's panel of advisers and professional advisory board of La Leche League International, the world's foremost breast-feeding self-help group which is active in fifty-five countries.

For ten years she wrote widely for the mother and baby magazines, professional journals and the national press and she answered readers' letters for Britain's *Parents* magazine for several years. In this capacity she kept closely in touch with the very real problems parents have today in coping with bringing up their children.

Penny Stanway has also written the *Pears Encyclopaedia of Child Health* and *The Breast Book* with her husband. She believes that those writing about baby and child care should ideally have had recent experience in caring for their young children, simply because the world changes so fast and valuable details are forgotten so quickly that it's the best way to produce a truly useful book for parents in the same position.

She has done a good deal of lecturing to large audiences and speaking to small groups both in Great Britain and the USA about breast-feeding and the prevention of illness.

As well as these professional activities she has carried out research into the causes of spina bifida and anencephaly. She is active in the local community, runs a mother and toddler group with a regular attendance of about forty mothers and their children and spends a lot of time telephone counselling on breast-feeding problems. She is a member of the National Childbirth Trust, the Association for the Improvement of Maternity Services, the National Association for the Welfare of Children in Hospital and the Birth Centre.

Dr Andrew Stanway MB MRCP practised medicine in the Professorial Medical Unit at King's College Hospital in London before leaving to edit a leading medical magazine. He then spent three years editing journals for doctors and in 1974 started his own medical film company making educational and documentary films for doctors, dentists, health care professionals and television around the world. He has written twelve books including *A Dictionary of Operations*, *Taking the Rough with the Smooth*, *The Boots Book of First Aid*, *Overcoming Depression*, *Why Us?* – a guide for infertile couples, *Alternative Medicine* – a guide to natural therapies, and the three titles with his wife mentioned above.

He was instrumental in helping launch the UK edition of *Parents* magazine, wrote for it for some time and acted as an editorial consultant for several years. He is deeply involved with his wife in her paediatric interests and travels the world with her lecturing on breast-feeding and other baby and care subjects.

Drs Andrew and Penny Stanway look after their children themselves with occasional help from a local person who has virtually become part of the family. They are committed Christians and active in their local church. They try to give medical advice and advice on family matters that they know works from personal and professional experience. Much of their time is spent in trying to give parents confidence in their task of bringing up children in our society today.

SECTION ONE

Some thoughts on baby and child care

Some thoughts on baby and child care

People have been telling others how to bring up their children and how to look after them for centuries, but it was not until this century, with the printed word so readily available to so many, that there was an explosion of advice on child care.

That parents and others are ready and willing to seek and to follow advice is obvious; bookshops can't sell enough of such books. Cynics say that this is a reflection on today's parental inadequacy and lack of confidence. However, it may be simpler than that. Parents have always sought advice but used to get it from relatives and friends living in tightly-knit communities. Today, advice comes from trained 'authorities' in amounts limited by the time such people have for each individual parent and child. Health professionals have historically been primarily involved in saving life and promoting health – a vital role until quite recent times because so many babies died or were ill. Today, baby and child survival is taken for granted and everything within reason is done to promote it. Child care advice, however, is a very poor second priority. As a result, lots of parents feel that they simply don't know enough about it.

With smaller families made up of children born close together, children don't learn how to care for younger brothers and sisters, and by the time most parents are beginning to feel more confident about caring for children, their children are no longer young and they have finished their childbearing. Their accumulated expertise is thus wasted and by the time their grandchildren come along, most useful day-to-day hints will have been forgotten or deemed inappropriate in our fast-changing society.

Many professionals – health visitors, general practitioners and paediatricians – are often called upon to advise on problems for which they have little – if any – training. The commonest subject we had letters on in our years with *Parents* magazine was sleep difficulties, yet neither of us had had any training in how to handle such problems by the day we qualified as doctors. What so many health professionals do, with the best will in the world, but not always with good results, is to enrich their professional knowledge with their personal experience as parents (or as children). However, this simply perpetuates the sort of care currently accepted by our society and doesn't widen anyone's horizons. It's also unrealistic for a lot of parents because most such health professionals are middle class, white, articulate, and better off than most financially. This makes it difficult for some parents to be really open with them and creates a barrier to communication on far too many occasions.

The other possible sources of advice, books on children and child care, are usually written by individuals who naturally have individual viewpoints on how to look after children. If that viewpoint is based on experience of many families and on reading about many different ways of bringing up children, and if the author is accustomed to seeing the results of different sorts of upbringing, then there may be much that is useful in the book. However, even 'experts'' viewpoints can alter over the years. The brave ones admit their initial mistakes but that doesn't help the thousands of parents who will have been (mis)guided by them. Anyway, child care patterns reflect the mood of the times to a great extent and as times are changing so fast, new approaches become appropriate.

What we've done is to look at methods of child care in other cultures and tried to apply the many things we've learnt to life in our society in the '80s. We have been fortunate in being involved in the subject of baby and child care professionally at a time when we have young children ourselves and mix with a large number of families of all types with young children. We've been closely involved with groups of people who have had the courage not to follow the experts blindly but to bring up their children in their own more instinctive way. That many of these methods work perfectly well made us want to share them with our readers in a book.

A right and a wrong way? We feel that far too much advice today gives the impression that there is only one 'right' way to bring up children. In fact there are many different ways of raising well-adjusted children, all of which work with some children, for some parents, and in some situations. However, it seems to us that lots of parents are trying to bring up their children in a way which they have been *told* is right yet which they don't feel *is* right. Lots of mothers fail to breast-feed for as long as they set out to; lots of babies cry a good deal; and many babies and young children keep their parents up at night. Post-natal depression is common, as indeed are all kinds of psychiatric problems in our society; and of the increasing numbers of divorces many are among parents of young children. It seems too that many parents are slavishly adhering to principles of child rearing which are not suitable for them and their families and as a result end up paying a heavy price.

In our work with children and their parents it has become apparent that we are saying some very different things compared with most other people. Most of the existing advice on baby and child care seems to be based on the principle that, however parents bring up and handle young children, it should be done in a way that changes their life-style as little as possible. In other words, most advice is adult-centred rather than child-centred. This has led to unrealistic expectations of babies and young children which simply aren't borne out in practice. This in turn causes frustration and a sense of failure in many well-meaning but harassed parents who do everything 'by the book' yet are still up half the night, have a faddy eater, a clinging or aggressive child, or a baby who always seems to be crying. Parents need help to accept their children as they *are*, not as they were led to believe they *should* be.

Of course, parents have rights too and child care can't be totally child-centred or the couple will suffer, which in turn will harm their child. Children need caring, stable parents so as to grow up to be emotionally and psychologically stable and well-balanced themselves. Any form of child care that makes the mother (or the father for that matter) into a tired drudge is bound to affect the parental relationship adversely. So it's a matter, as with so many other things in life, of keeping a sense of proportion. By hoping (or even trying) to run your lives as you did before you had a baby you'll make your life and that of your child unhappy but to become a twenty-four-hours-a-day parent can be just as damaging to your marriage. Many men complain to marriage guidance counsellors that their wives 'go off' them after the birth of their first (and even subsequent babies). There are lots of reasons for this, most of which needn't be gone into here, but one of the most important for the couple is the feeling the man has that his wife's love, affection, time and energy are now totally devoted to someone other than him. This should never be allowed to happen, of course, but the fact is that it does, and very commonly. In a society in which the new mother is indeed often lonely, tired and involved in very heavy mothering commitments almost twenty-four hours a day, especially in the early days, it takes a real effort to keep the marital relationship – and by that we don't just mean sex – going happily. Knowing in advance that this can be a trying time for a couple helps, but there's no substitute for making a positive effort to maintain the close, loving relationship you had before. Many men tell us that they fear that their share of their wives' love and affection will be smaller after the birth of a baby, but many couples find that this isn't so. In fact for many the amount of love and affection increases – leaving more for everyone.

It is a shame that advice on baby and child care in industrialized societies has lost sight of the time-honoured and successful methods still practised in many parts of the world. So far twentieth-century parents have been very sheep-like and seem to have lost their natural ability to decide how to care for their own babies. They expect to be told that there is one right way to behave in any given situation, regardless of their personality and that of their child, their personal circumstances, their upbringing and their expectations. Thankfully things are changing.

Because there actually is no one right way, baby books and other sources of advice say different things and parents can become confused. When a baby, brought up by one or other of these methods, cries for much of the time, for example, and doesn't seem happy, they are even more confused. Parents need to be led gently back to a more natural, basic and instinctive way of behaving, and then supported and encouraged to do what *they* feel is best for *their* child.

Experience in many other areas of medicine and health has shown that a return to a simpler and more 'natural' way of life has a lot to recommend it for the health of both mind and body. Such a return in the field of baby and child care seems to pay off handsomely even in an industrial society such as ours.

Simple, straightforward scientific research to evaluate different ways of bringing up children isn't possible because you can't take one group of children and bring them up in one predetermined way and then repeat the process with the same children in another way. You'll never know for sure whether your child would have turned out differently if you'd treated him differently. However, such research as there is on various groups of children who have been brought up in specific circumstances can teach us something. It's not a totally uncharted sea.

Children deprived of their mothers or stable mother figures in their early life tend to have certain personality and behaviour problems. People who care for their babies and young children in a way which means they rarely have to cry but always have their needs met seem to rear happy, contented, generous children with very few aggressive tendencies. Some children brought up by a succession of nannies report years later their mixed emotions, including anger, towards their mothers for voluntarily separating themselves from them, or their unrealistic idealization of their mothers whom they scarcely knew. Any parent can tell his or her own story of how certain circumstances have affected their child, temporarily or permanently. There is now no doubt that what is done to a child and to his surroundings can affect his developing personality and behaviour for ever.

Of course each child is born with his own personality and this is apparent immediately from the way he behaves even as a newborn baby. You could not alter your child's basic personality, even if you wanted to, but you can accept it and then try to bring him up so that his attractive character traits are encouraged and others suppressed. You won't always be successful but it helps to remember that if you are loving towards your child, and other people, he'll learn to be loving; if you respond generously to his needs for your time and attention, he'll learn to respond in the same way to others; if you allow him to be with you as much as he needs you, he'll grow up to be trusting and secure and (perhaps surprisingly to some people) more adventurous and independent, not less.

Lots of mothers who have brought up their first child according to conventional western practices, with rigid feeding schedules, allowing them to cry themselves to sleep, leaving them alone for long periods and so on, and have then brought up subsequent children in a far more instinctive way, responding generously and more continually to their needs, comment on the very noticeable differences in their children's personalities and in their own increased enjoyment of their later babies as a result. These differences go far beyond those usually seen between first and subsequent children all brought up the same way. These mothers can't all be wrong, but the few doctors who have steered child-rearing practices this century towards their present state, in which so many parents no longer feel that what they are doing seems right or enjoyable, may well have been wrong.

Children inherit certain personality traits from their families but are also heavily influenced in childhood by their parents' personalities. An outgoing, optimistic parent who is never serious or unhappy for long will inevitably raise a different child from a quiet, introspective or pessimistic parent. Besides looking at how you bring up your child, it makes sense to look at yourself and how your behaviour and personality affect your child. It's quite possible to alter yourself to some degree and to grow in maturity, common sense, kindness, curiosity and tolerance, for instance. Many parents grow as people partly because of the experience of having children and partly because they have a wider experience of life as they get older and this is inevitably good for their children. Coming to terms with your life and with yourself as a person will help you settle down to your role as a parent.

Expectations of parenthood People's attitudes to having children and bringing them up have changed enormously over the last twenty years or so mainly because of the changing roles and expectations of women in western society. These changes have taken place regardless of the fact that babies and young children haven't gone through a similar revolution. Nobody has told the under-fives that their mothers think differently from mothers twenty years ago.

Babies and young children haven't changed. They still need total, committed, long-term, stable care and love and for the vast majority this is best and most easily supplied by their mothers with back-up from their fathers.

Parenthood is the most important and time-consuming undertaking we ever make in our lives. It starts the day a woman becomes pregnant and ends only when we (or our children) die. Yet the preparation we have for it in our society is almost non-existent. With today's average family of two children born close together, few children have the chance to watch younger brothers or sisters being brought up and so fall in at the deep end when they become parents themselves. The learning about child care and parenting that takes place within larger, more spaced-out families is one enormous advantage of such families that is often overlooked. Parentcraft classes at school and in the antenatal period can't possibly do anything more than scratch the surface of the subject.

The average young couple today get married in their twenties, often with completely unrealistic ideas about babies and family life in general. It's unfashionable to think of having a baby as anything other than 'lovely' but this 'roses round the door' attitude to babies is a long way from the reality experienced by most parents at some time and for some parents all the time. Numerous studies have shown how unrealistic parents' attitudes and expectations are when embarking on family life. Why? Who has led them astray? Why won't other parents or experts, or whoever is responsible, tell the truth? We have tried to be truthful throughout this book. A lot about baby and child care is hard work and there are lots of negatives to having children. For some parents these unfortunately outweigh the positives and in their private moments they wish they hadn't had children at all. But even though most people have some black patches, they agree that, overall, having children is enjoyable and worthwhile, and for some it is the most important and fulfilling thing they ever do.

Having a baby changes your life *for ever* – yet it is fashionable to treat the whole event as though you were buying a new car or TV. Many women who have told us that they didn't realize how they'd feel when they had a baby. They imagined they would want to get back to work for the adult contact or to carry on earning but for many this doesn't work out. They find to their surprise that they want to be with their baby, in spite of the fact that they've been conditioned into thinking of themselves as workers first and mothers second. Of course, some mothers feel very strongly that they should be at work, are miserable if they stay at home as full-time mothers and should probably be true to themselves so that they can give of their best to their children. More job sharing and part-time work would greatly help and such opportunities are slowly increasing.

Today's young mother has been conditioned into thinking that once her 'baby' is out of her arms she is free to live her normal life again. This *can* work well for the few women who can cope with separation from their children and who can afford good, loving and consistent substitute child care but it can also be an unattainable dream which creates dissatisfaction and an unwillingness to enter into motherhood as a full-time, enjoyable and fulfilling job. The difficulty is that in order to enjoy her new-found role for what it is a woman has to adjust to a totally new way of life. Far too few women are willing to take this step to accept themselves as full-time, whole-hearted mothers and as a result see motherhood as a kind of failure instead of the triumph it really is. How much better for mother and child is a relationship in which the mother doesn't feel constantly torn between work and home.

But the social conflicts are enormous. There are ever-present pressures to organize family life so that the children interfere with their parents' life as little as possible. Many fathers are somewhat resentful of what they imagine to be their wife's 'cushy' life at home with young children. Many mothers can't help but look back longingly at their working life (before they had children) and on top of all this, bringing up babies according to current advice doesn't seem to work out a lot of the time.

We have found that the quality of life of many young families can be improved if the parents' ideas of baby and child care are broader and in general more child-centred. This way of bringing up children has been ignored by our society for too long a time.

Back to Nature? It has been fashionable in modern medicine and anthropology to study the 'noble savage' and to put him on a pedestal. Whilst it is obviously nonsense for us to expect to live our lives along the lines of pre-industrial peoples (either those alive today or those who lived in the past) it is equally nonsensical to ignore what they do entirely, because they have a lot to teach us. In our hasty Western development we have thrown the baby out with the bath water in more ways than one. Instead of combining the best of the new with the best of the old, we have too often thoughtlessly scrapped tried-and-tested concepts and replaced them with gleaming new ones which soon tarnish. Have such cultures ruined their health with refined and synthetic foods? They have not. Are they permanently constipated and dying prematurely of incurable diseases such as strokes, cancer and heart attacks? They are not. Are their societies ridden with the mental and emotional stress that now fills more hospital beds in the West than all other diseases put together? They are not. *So perhaps they may just have something to teach us, even if we are reluctant to listen.*

When we look at the child-rearing patterns of such cultures we often find that the parents seem to cherish and enjoy their children more than we do. Cynics in the Western world say that this is because so many babies and young children die in these cultures that the live ones are especially valued. In many societies that rely on children as a source of cheap labour to survive they also assume great financial importance. There may be some truth in these arguments but it still doesn't detract from the fact that their children are brought up in a different way.

In pre-industrial societies child care was and still is the responsibility of the women but this doesn't mean that the men don't take any interest at all. In some cultures they don't, but this is rare. Men in most non-Western cultures see their role as protectors and providers to a group of women who look after their children between them. In such close communities it's easy to see how children can enjoy the friendship, love and care of many adults other than their parents. We are a long way from this in most Western families but things are changing slowly.

One good thing in the West today is that caring for children is more than ever a *two* person affair. Many modern fathers are involved with baby and child care and are often the envy of previous generations, generations that substantially excluded men from baby and child care, often to the detriment of both father and child.

Perhaps the most important thing we can learn from other cultures is that we should trust our instincts more than we do. Many women have told us that they knew instinctively what to do about baby and child care but because of the pressures from society (or one particular group within society), they were led astray and they and their children suffered as a result. Parents often instinctively know how to behave yet are torn between these instinctive feelings and what they are told they *should* do to please and fit in with everybody else. Perhaps the best example of this is the subject of babies in bed. People tend to confess that their babies are allowed in their bed somewhat shamefully and reluctantly because they fear it's unnatural, dangerous or otherwise wrong. In most pre-industrial societies families sleep together and have probably always done so. We are behaving differently from all other mammals if we shut our babies away out of sight and earshot in another room. The babies don't like it and many parents don't either – so why do we do it? One answer is that over the last century or so children have become nuisances: a chore to be endured. The Victorian saying 'children should be seen and not heard' is still much adhered to but the reason they're not seen or heard today is because they're stuck in front of a TV set, sleep apart from their parents and are sent out to playgroup or nursery school as soon as possible.

Nature has organized things for the human race so that babies and young children are dependent on their parents for several years. No other mammalian offspring are as helpless as human babies or as totally reliant for every need on their mothers. Even after a nine-month pregnancy, a baby needs yet another nine months at least before he can do the most basic things for himself, such as crawl and feed himself at all reliably. Anthropologists call man a 'continuous contact' species: a baby given the chance will want to be at the breast for much of the time early on, sometimes feeding little and often and at other times, a lot and often! If left to himself the average newborn baby will suck at the breast on and off for much of the day and night. Because of the close physical contact that breast-feeding necessitates, the baby gets a great deal of comfort and warmth (both emotional and physical) at the same time as obtaining food and of course if there is the slightest thing wrong with him his mother will know immediately. Even once he is weaned from the breast the human child is still incapable of coping with the hostile world and needs twenty-four-hours-a-day care and attention for years if he is to survive and thrive.

Many cultures regard all children under five as babies and we share this view. We cannot and should not expect too much of them even if in our so-called sophisticated society they seem to be so grown up. It only takes the slightest thing to go wrong (an illness in either child or parent, an absence of one parent, a domestic crisis of some kind, or a host of other common trigger situations) to prove just how vulnerable and helpless an under-five really is.

What to aim for The most universal aim in our society today, in which children are by and large well cared for materially, is probably that children should do at least as well in the world as their parents have done. 'Do as well' usually means 'earn as much money'. However, there are many ways of judging personal success other than by monetary achievement. By all means try to bring up your children so that they are better than yourselves in other ways – have more rounded personalities; have fewer hang-ups; are more generous; more understanding; better educated or whatever, but any aims centred purely on worldly success are bound to be frustrated at least some of the time, making the child feel a failure because he can't live up to his parents' expectations.

The main aim of parenting must be to provide a loving, secure home in which a child can grow and develop to his full potential and from which he can safely explore the world with its joys and problems. The provision of this secure home starts with a loving relationship between the parents.

The cycle of life Providing the best possible environment for a child starts even before he is conceived. Parents have the best chance of producing a normal, healthy baby if they are both healthy themselves and if the mother takes adequate care of herself during pregnancy. By doing this you'll give your baby a good physical and emotional start in life. Thousands of babies are harmed unnecessarily because of inadequate antenatal care or because the mother has had a poor diet or has smoked or drunk too much during pregnancy.

It's worth making a real effort to have your baby in a hospital that'll let you (and even preferably encourage you to) have him with you all the time right from the moment of birth. Ideally, the hospital will give you and your husband time alone with your baby as a threesome immediately after the birth, will allow your husband to be with you during the birth if you want and will encourage you to breast-feed right from birth.

Once out of hospital, if you allow yourself to behave instinctively, you'll probably want to be with or near your baby all the time in the early weeks. He'll sleep in your bed or in your room at night. You'll take him with you everywhere you go and never leave him to cry or to be lonely. You and he will virtually be an indivisible unit. Going out to places where a baby would be unwelcome or unhappy will be put off until he's old enough to stay happily with a baby-sitter.

Towards the end of the first year, or whenever he becomes mobile, your baby will still spend most of his time with you. As he grows he'll gradually be introduced to the outside world but never in such a way as to shatter his faith in you as a provider and loving mother for him.

Children brought up like this tend to be secure, friendly, happy and outgoing and naturally assume that the world is a pleasant place. Why should they not: they have never experienced anything unpleasant? The fact that a lot of it isn't all that pleasant doesn't need to concern him at this age – he's only a baby and shouldn't have to bear such burdens before he can cope with them.

What we're suggesting is that there is a way of bringing up babies and children which doesn't involve pushing them towards independence before they are ready and which will bring you and your children more joy than conventional methods. Bringing up children in this way is demanding only if you make it so by never really accepting your role as giver and provider.

However you raise your children you'll have some sleepless nights and times when things can get you down. There'll be worries, illnesses, insecurities, job problems, marital problems, and a host of other things to rock your boat. You'll also find that you'll have much less time for yourself than before. But underneath it all you'll have the loving, caring bond between you and your children to knit things tightly together.

By the age of five or six your child will be itching to go his own way, to start becoming independent and living his life (with your guidance) the way he wants. This is perfectly natural and what we all want for our children. The one-to-one demands of a child on his parents begin to diminish around this age. You'll have helped mould his personality and behaviour and he'll be on his way to becoming a fully-fledged member of society. The Jesuits boast 'give me the child till he's seven and I'll give you the man'. What we do and how we behave to our children in their early years is vitally important, as any teacher or psychologist will agree. Unfortunately, many parents act as if they didn't believe this.

Children are not their parents' chattels. They don't *belong* to their parents: they are individual human beings with their own minds and their own potential for a future which holds things we can't dream of let alone adequately plan for. We as parents have the responsible task of nurturing our children through the early years of life when their basic attitudes, personality and behaviour patterns are formed and conditioned until they can respond to and cope with the world alone. No one will ever ask you to do anything more important in your life than to create and bring up another human being. That seems to us to be well worth five years of serious effort.

The modern family One of the commonest myths today is that of the 'happy family'. Young couples about to start a family have all kinds of unrealistic expectations about family life just as they do about the 'perfect baby'. How sad it is that so often reality comes nowhere near their expectations. The modern family unit of a man and a woman living in a home with their two children, with few relatives around on whom to call for help and advice (not to mention for baby-sitting or other practical help with child care), can be terribly isolated. Many a father helps with family life as much as he can but he often commutes to work or travels a lot and finds he has little time to be at home except when his babies or young children are asleep. This means he sees his children at weekends only and can be of very little practical help to his wife. Is it any wonder then that so many young mothers get run down physically and mentally and become bored and depressed? This is no basis for a loving relationship with either their husband or their child.

There are ways around these problems though. It's virtually essential for young mothers at home most of the time to create a social life for themselves if they are to remain happy and effective mothers and wives. Physical and mental isolation is unhealthy and abnormal, as human beings are social animals. Now is probably the first time in the history of the human race that a woman and her young children have been cooped up alone so much. Many women's social interactions are fleeting ones with their husbands at either end of the day, and superficial ones with others to whom they will never become close. Life doesn't have to stop because you have a baby – in fact many women find they're more active socially than they've ever been before. Babies and young children can form a bridge to other people, and if you allow it you'll find that this period of your life is in fact one of the easiest in which to make good friends.

Just because our philosophy of child care is more child-centred than most doesn't mean for a moment that we think children should ride roughshod over their parents. We're certainly not suggesting that children should be brought up without discipline – loving, firm guidance – or that they should be overindulged. Unfortunately, too many parents have one set of rules for themselves and another for their children. They let their babies cry for hours on end, for example, yet would hate anyone to behave in the same way to them. Our children should be able to expect very much better and more considerate behaviour from us than they are capable of returning.

The modern family is made up of individuals who have rights, needs and feelings, all of which have to be taken into consideration. Just as in a good marriage there's no question of either party being more important, so family life is a team effort with the most experienced people – the parents – acting as guides and referees. Inevitably there will be clashes of interests from time to time. Sometimes the parents' needs will have to be put first and sometimes those of the children. With their age and experience behind them parents are more able to cope with adverse situations than babies. Usually it's not a question of looking to the needs of the baby *or* the parents but rather of the parents doing their best for their baby within their own prescribed yet flexible limits. Fashions and baby books come and go; parents must in the end decide for themselves how to raise their families, using common sense mixed with intuition, compassion and a liberal sense of proportion. When deciding how to behave, it's worth remembering that whatever you do to your children, they'll tend to thrive in a happy, loving home.

Bringing up a family is a long job, if only because it goes on day after day for years. What a shame it is then that so many parents don't enjoy it as much as they could and spend years regretting how they did it. Bringing up children is also a responsible job. Like any job, you get out of it what you put in and it brings its own rewards and problems.

Can you bring up children in any way you choose and still be sure of success? Whenever parents ask us this we find it helpful to reduce the question to the absurd for a moment. 'Would you agree,' we ask, 'that to lock a child in a cupboard every day, to starve him, or to give him no affection at all would probably produce lifelong problems?' Most people readily agree that it would. 'Where then would you be happy to draw the line?' we ask. 'To shut him in the cupboard once or twice a week only; to give him just enough food to stay alive; to kiss and cuddle him once a week and to ignore him for the rest of the time?' 'No,' they say, 'that wouldn't be right either.' Slowly they come to accept that there must be some rules that can be applied when bringing up children even though at first they'd thought this unlikely.

We feel there *are* some quite definite and unassailable rules. A child must never be physically or emotionally abused, for example. He should ideally always be treated as you yourself would wish to be treated. We should never make unthinking, unreasonable demands of our children. We should treat them with dignity as human beings who have rights and needs. Lastly, we should bear in mind at all times that our young children not only look to us in their helplessness to be their examples but also put their trust in us absolutely. How can we ever betray that trust?

Lots of people say, 'Surely most children turn out all right in the end, so why worry about what happens in the first few years of life – it can't be that important.' Although it is true that children are very adaptable we would definitely not agree with this sentiment. Mental hospital beds are more numerous than any other; more tablets that alter the mind are prescribed than any other except for simple pain-killers; and marital and emotional disharmony surround us on all sides. How can anyone possibly claim that most people 'turn out all right in the end'? Certainly one can't blame *all* these problems on poor parenting but current research and thinking is that the way a young child is brought up can permanently affect the way he behaves and feels as an adult. His life's computer is programmed in the first few years and thereafter he tends to act and respond within the confines of that programming. Certainly the programme can be modified but it becomes increasingly difficult as the years go by and is almost impossible past middle-age.

Parents who have had several children often comment that they made their mistakes – often unknowingly at the time – on their first child and learnt more with each child they had. Of course as they learn more and become more mature as parents and as people, their first child benefits as well as the subsequent children. This first child's programming can be adjusted or modified by his parents' current behaviour and by their behaviour towards his younger brothers and sisters, which in turn will affect the way he behaves as a parent to his children.

Anyway, what is 'success' in the context of child upbringing? We think this is easy to define. A 'successful' adult is one who can fit into society; is at ease with himself; can help others; and can run a family and bring up children effectively and enjoyably. Millions of people in the West today feel so insecure and have such a poor sense of self-esteem that they cannot hope to run happy and successful lives for themselves, let alone for their children. Many of them were programmed as children, through insecurity and a lack of love and attention, in such a way as to make them incapable of leading successful lives.

Bringing up children 'by the book' Most advice about baby and child care is about children of all ages but we have found that parents most need help and guidance with their under-fives. After this they seem to gain confidence in themselves. Also, most children over five behave in a more 'adult', less baffling, and more reasonable way, and this helps their parents to understand and therefore to cope better than they did before. Ailments and illnesses become more adult-like too after the age of six or so, but before this age children seem to the average man and woman in the street to be very different creatures from older children and adults . . . and indeed they are, and usually need to be treated accordingly. A child under five isn't simply a small adult.

While writing this book we have been aware of our responsibilities because for some parents it will be all they have to turn to when the going gets tough. We realize that not all our suggestions will work in every family. However, we make no apology for this because the more conventional 'separatist' methods certainly don't work for everyone either. At least by airing our more child-centred approach many parents will feel more confident about behaving more naturally.

Some one-parent families and immigrant families and those in which the mother chooses to work outside the home, have particular needs or problems and we have tried to take many of these into account when writing the book.

Reading a book such as this can have a negative effect on some parents as well as, we hope, a positive one for most. Our work constantly reminds us that many parents feel guilty about things they wish they had done with previous children. This is especially sad to see (but is inevitable occasionally) when the parents have changed their ways with a later child and have seen the benefits both to themselves and to the child. There's nothing to be gained from blame because if you did your best at the time that was all you could have done. If you now realize that you missed out on a form of child care you would have preferred, don't be disheartened but ensure that your child has plenty of love, attention and security. It's never too late to start being unselfish and it always pays dividends.

About the book and how to use it If you've read this far you've read much of the philosophy about child care. The main part of the book (Section two) is arranged alphabetically but there is also an index. Where appropriate, at the end of an entry is a list of related topics that could be of interest. There is also a list of any organizations or self-help groups that could be useful; these can be found in Section four.

If your child is ill or has something specific wrong with him (for example, he's passing dark-coloured urine) you can use Section three – the medical action chart. In this you can look up the area of the body involved and then by running down the list of possible things that commonly go wrong you can see whether or not to get help or advice from your doctor or what action to take yourself. Often, more details on the topic are available elsewhere in the book. In this section words that appear in headings in the main part of the book have an asterisk against them.

Section four is a list of most of the useful addresses you might need when looking for help and advice in the baby and child field. There's a potted history of each organization, what it can offer, how you can join and what useful literature it publishes.

Last, but by no means least, there are three points we'd like to make which apply throughout the book:

1. We have stuck to the conventional use of the word 'he' as the neuter pronoun for the baby.
2. Often we have referred to a 'mother' where it is implicit that this could equally well refer to 'mother and father' or 'mother or father'. While more and more fathers today are involved in the care of their babies and young children, the bulk of this care is still carried out in our society by mothers and this is why we have tended to address many remarks to them.
3. We know that some babies are cared for by a mother figure rather than by their mother. To avoid ugly repetition we have used the word 'mother' all through the book but this could nearly always equally well refer to 'mother figure'.

take yourself. Often, more details on the topic are available elsewhere in the book. In this section words that appear in headings in the main part of the book have an asterisk against them.

Section four is a list of most of the useful addresses you might need when looking for help and advice in the baby and child field. There's a potted history of each organization, what it can offer, how you can join and what useful literature it publishes.

Last, but by no means least, there are three points we'd like to make which apply throughout the book:

1. We have stuck to the conventional use of the word 'he' as the neuter pronoun for the baby, just to keep the book uncomplicated.
2. Often we have referred to a 'mother' where it is implicit that this could equally well refer to 'mother and father' or 'mother or father'. While more and more fathers today are involved in the care of their babies and young children, the bulk of this care is still carried out in our society by mothers and this is why we have tended to address many remarks to them.
3. We know that some babies are cared for by a mother figure rather than by their mother. To avoid ugly repetition we have used the word 'mother' all through the book but this could nearly always equally well refer to 'mother figure'.

Abdominal pain Pain in the abdomen (tummy). A very common symptom in children which can be difficult to sort out – the tummy ache may be secondary to a disorder elsewhere. Pain in the abdomen can be caused by infection, inflammation, a change in bowel activity, obstruction or distension of the bowel and lots of other causes (see page 736).

Unless the pain is accompanied by vomiting, diarrhoea, weight loss, or pain on passing water, or is very severe, the chances are that it will turn out to be nothing serious and will pass. However, you should always take abdominal pain seriously in an under-five until a doctor has put your mind at rest.

Some abdominal pains seem to come back time and again in certain children. Such recurrent abdominal pains are usually caused by emotional and psychological upsets. Other pains are present, on and off, for months or years.

Get medical help for: any pain of sudden onset bad enough to make a child lie down; any pain lasting for more than six hours; and any pain bad enough to make a child vomit.

Things your doctor will want to know include: how long the pain has been there; is it like anything the child has had before?; is it getting better or worse?; where did the pain first start?; what is the pain like (e.g. knife-like, gnawing, aching, dull, comes and goes); where is it worst now?; did anything particular bring it on?; does anything make it better?; and are there any other things wrong with the child as well as the pain? Having answers to these questions ready will greatly help the doctor to make a diagnosis.

A much more extensive look at abdominal pain and its possible causes can be found in the medical action chart on page 681. *Related topics* Appendicitis; diarrhoea; intestinal obstruction; mesenteric adenitis; pain; periodic syndrome; recurrent abdominal pain; vomiting; weight loss.

Abrasion Most abrasions aren't serious and bleed very little. Deeper ones may ooze tissue fluid and blood and will need treatment.

Gently wash the area with plain water. Apply an antiseptic cream and cover with an adhesive dressing if deep. Minor abrasions heal best if left open to the air and need no creams.

If the abrasion is serious or has dirt embedded in it, it may have to be cleaned up by a doctor who will also ask whether your child has been immunized against tetanus. If he has not, then a course of anti-tetanus immunization can be started at once. *Related topics* Cuts; tetanus.

Abscess A localized collection of pus in any part of the body. Abscesses may produce symptoms of inflammation, swelling, generalized body symptoms (such as fever and feeling unwell), pain or tenderness. Some abscesses, especially those that are deep in the body, produce no symptoms at all. An abscess in the skin is called a boil.

The treatment for an abscess is to let the pus out, usually by making a small incision over the most prominent part of the abscess. This is a job for a doctor. Never poke about in an abscess yourself. Very rarely a child may have un underlying condition that produced the abscess in the first place. A doctor will look for such conditions and rule them out. *Related topics* Boils and pimples.

Accident prevention However thoughtful you are and however much you protect your child, accidents will always happen, so be prepared.

The problem for most parents is striking the balance between over-protection and allowing their child to be free to explore and experiment in the world. If we bear in mind that a timid child who is over-protected will eventually stop experimenting and may even be shunned by his friends, then we can more easily strike a reasonable balance between our fears as adults and allowing him to learn how to cope with new and potentially dangerous situations. He must be able to learn how to cope with danger but these lessons should be under the watchful (though not too obviously so) eye of a parent or other adult.

When bigger children are encouraging young ones to overstretch their physical abilities it's time for an adult to step in because young children are so easily carried away with their enthusiasm and don't have an adult's wisdom or experience to see the dangers. Over-excitement is a real cause of danger and is a sign to step in and control things firmly.

It makes sense to ensure that your home is as safe as possible. As soon as you have a baby you should start thinking 'safety'. Even before a baby is mobile he can knock a cup of hot tea over himself or someone else. Once he is on the move, the potential for accidents is even greater. He is too young to see the dangers but soon becomes frustrated if he is cooped up in a confined space or has things repeatedly snatched away from him. Most accidents occur in the kitchen (16%) and living room (16%), with the seemingly more dangerous garden next (11%), so pay special attention to these areas. Here are some useful tips room by room.

Kitchen Turn saucepan handles sideways; fit a safety guard round the top of your cooker that prevents young children from pulling saucepans off it; keep all poisons, domestic cleaning fluids and disinfectants high up out of a child's reach; keep sharp knives out of reach; wipe up all spills at once; don't polish floors highly while you have little children; check the safety of all plugs and sockets; have a fire extinguisher or fire blanket handy and know how to use it; teach children to respect kitchen machinery; never leave the flex of the electric kettle overhanging the edge of the worktop; never give young children peanuts or tiny sweets and never let them play with them because if they go down the wrong way and end up in a lung they cause terrible trouble.

Bathroom Keep all drugs and medicines locked away out of children's reach; place a medicine chest high on the wall; flush all old or surplus medicines down the lavatory or – better – hand them in to the pharmacist at your chemist's shop; choose non-slip flooring; have a non-slip bathmat in the bath; run cold water before hot when filling a child's bath; never take electric fires into a bathroom – any electric fires should be wall-mounted and high up; keep razors and blades well out of children's reach; never leave a child under five alone in the bath; and be careful not to burn a baby against a hot tap.

Shed, garage and workshop Keep tools safely away from children; keep garden chemicals and weedkillers well out of reach; *never* put chemicals or any noxious fluids in old soft-drink bottles or children may drink them; check a child's bicycle for safety at least twice a year; and when chopping wood or doing other household chores, ensure that the children watch at a safe distance because in one third of DIY accidents it is a watching child who is hurt.

Garden Supervise young children all the time on swings and other garden equipment; make water butts safe; keep ponds fenced; learn which shrubs and trees are poisonous and either get rid of them or inform older children; never allow a child under five near a swimming pool alone (and ideally keep swimming pools covered or fenced); never leave a mower running unattended if children are around; keep septic tanks properly covered; check garden furniture every year for safety; and put a cat net over the pram if you leave your baby in the garden (or even in the home, if you have a cat yourself).

Living room Keep fires guarded (it is illegal to leave a child under twelve in a room with an unguarded fire); never put a mirror over the mantelpiece as clothes could catch fire while the child looks at himself; keep pins, needles and scissors away from young children; never let children play with doors; make sure bookshelves can't be pulled over; replace flexes immediately if they are worn; keep all plastic bags away from children (including the inner sleeves of records); never leave windows open where children are playing; don't let children play with sash windows; don't leave small objects lying around as a child may swallow them or put them in his ear or nose; stop using tablecloths as babies and small children can so easily pull them off, bringing knives or hot drinks over themselves. Children like to poke things in electric sockets so buy special covers or keep plugs in them to prevent this. Never leave matches around and always choose non-inflammable materials when making or buying children's clothes.

Bedrooms, halls and stairs Fix oil heaters so that children can't knock them over; fit safety catches to all upstairs windows; never leave bottles of medicine or pills on your bedside table; never let a child get into bed with an electric blanket on; clear up things from the stairs on every trip – they can be lethal to children and adults; ensure that the stair carpet is fixed and has no holes to trip up on; when carrying a child up or downstairs always leave a hand free to hold the rail or banister. Don't use a pillow at all for your baby in the first year of life as it is unnecessary and could possibly suffocate him. Once your baby is on the move, use a stair gate at the bottom to stop him climbing up and at the top when he is upstairs to stop him falling down. As he grows older, teach him to go downstairs backwards (resting on his tummy). Walking forwards will come when he is confident and safe enough on the stairs.

Toys Safety regulations are now so strict that the vast majority of toys are made to be safe. Always look out for small parts that might be detachable and then swallowed; avoid toys with sharp edges and don't buy old toys that are painted with lead paint. Hanging loops on toys can get twisted round a child's finger. Older children's toys can be dangerous for babies and small children, so be especially vigilant about this.

Locks and bolts are always fun for young children, but are dangerous because they can so easily lock themselves in. The safest thing is to place bolts high up on doors or to remove the handle parts while the children are small. Front doors are a real danger because a small child can lock himself in while you are outside. Make a habit of putting the safety catch on whenever you leave the front door open.

Fireworks The main rule is never to let an under-five have anything to do with fireworks, except to hold a sparkler, supervised. Always keep young children well away from the lighting-up area, and have plenty of adults to supervise them. Keep stored fireworks out of the reach of young children and of course never let an under-five have matches. *Related topics* Accidents; road safety. *Useful organizations* The Royal Society for the Prevention of Accidents.

Accidents Accidents are very common in young children, and nearly half of all under-fives' accidents occur at home. Boys tend to be involved in more accidents than girls. The best cure is prevention as outlined above but when an accident occurs, here are some basic rules.

Keep calm yourself. Pain and fear feed on each other but if you are calm the child will feel less fearful and will in turn be less distressed.

Don't be panicked into attempting heroic first aid procedures. Stop bleeding (see page 76) or start breathing again (see artificial respiration, page 34) if necessary but otherwise get medical help. Remove the child from the source of danger if you can do so safely, and await professional help. If the child complains of pain in his back or cannot move his legs, don't move him as he may have damaged his back. A child who is unconscious or has straw-coloured fluid leaking out of his nose or ears after a fall *must* receive immediate professional attention, so call an ambulance.

Never leave your child alone after an accident until professional help comes.

Ensure that you, the parent, stays all the time. When it comes to going to hospital, stay with the child. Your presence will help keep him calm and will reduce his fear of going into hospital. Make arrangements with a neighbour or close friend to look after other children. *Related topics* Abrasions; bites and stings; bleeding; burns; electric shock; first aid; fractures; head injuries; kiss of life; poisoning; scalds; shock. *Useful organization* The Royal Society for the Prevention of Accidents.

Achondroplasia A rare condition, usually inherited, affecting the growth of cartilage in the body, that produces the classical circus dwarf. The condition affects the limb bones most severely so that the child becomes shorter in comparison with his peers as he grows older. The head is relatively large, the forehead prominent and the bridge of the nose flattened. The child's intelligence is usually normal. There is no cure. Parents should ask their GP to arrange genetic counselling.

Activity kits Kits of play and 'educational' materials for parents to use at home with their pre-school children. They can be fun as well as educational, but if a child has plenty of opportunities to play with his parents and other children they are unnecessary as well as being expensive. A child who is at a play-group or nursery school will similarly get plenty of stimulation without activity kits.

The main problem with activity kits is that they can become an end in themselves if you're not careful. Remember they are meant to be fun and a guide to stimulating and educating your young child, not a series of hurdles to be overcome at all costs. There is no need to finish all the projects if your child is not enjoying himself. You'll probably end up doing a lot of the work yourself, but if your child enjoys watching and helping, this is no bad thing. *Related topics* Play, toys. *Useful organization* Pre-School Playgroups Association.

Adenoids These are collections of infection-fighting lymphoid tissue in the upper part of the space at the back of the nose and mouth (the naso-pharynx). The adenoids usually enlarge, together with the tonsils, when fighting infection, and they may almost fill the nasopharynx, interfering with the passage of air through the nose and obstructing the Eustachian tubes. A child with chronically enlarged adenoids breathes through his mouth some or all of the time and has a runny nose. Snoring, chapped lips, smelly breath, impaired taste and smell, a nasal, muffled tone to the voice and a sore throat may be noticed. There may be a cough caused by breathing air that hasn't been warmed by passing through the nose. Inflammation of the middle ear (otitis media) may be associated with blockage of the Eustachian tube(s) by enlarged adenoids. Normally once the infection is over, the adenoids shrink to their pre-infection size but in some children repeated infection causes long-term enlargement. Adenoidal enlargement has been reported to be related to cows' milk hypersensitivity in some pre-school children. The adenoids can be removed by an operation but this is usually only considered if the child has more than three episodes of acute otitis media a year or if there is glue ear, and if the surgeon thinks that the adenoids are blocking the Eustachian tube on one or both sides. Snoring and mouth breathing alone usually clear up without an operation.

Adoption A system through which a child in need of a home legally and permanently becomes a member of a family other than his own.

When most couples think of adoption they think of getting a lovely little healthy baby. The reality is rather different, there being a considerable shortage of young, normal, healthy babies for adoption (under 2,000 in 1980).

Preparation for adoption is a serious business and don't forget that adoption is a legal commitment and is for ever. The child becomes part of your family. It's also important to bear in mind that adoption is all about finding homes for babies and *not* finding babies for couples. This is why the agencies have to be so careful about choosing the right adoptive parents. If it goes wrong it can be a problem for all concerned.

If you are thinking of adopting, write to or telephone the British Agencies for Adoption and Fostering, 11 Southwark St, London SE1 (tel. 01-407 8800), and ask for their booklet 'Adopting a Child'.

Aggression A type of behaviour normal in all children as they learn to cope with or avoid problems in life. We all have inborn aggressive tendencies which are essential for self-preservation, but harnessing them is an important lesson we all have to learn in childhood.

Babies are aggressive from birth and even young babies show it when their natural desires or needs are thwarted. A hungry baby, for example, will become aggressive if these urgent needs aren't met at once. Babies have very few ways of communicating their aggression and screaming and throwing their arms and legs about are their ways of letting you know that they are angry at you for ignoring their earlier messages. There's no point at all in making a baby wait for things he needs; if they are met at once he soon learns that the world is a pleasant place and resorts to aggressive behaviour less frequently when frustrated. Some babies, if left to scream turn their aggression inwards once they realize that it has no effect. This can lead to a variety of emotional and physical ailments including failure to thrive and depression.

Young children often resort to aggression when you prevent them from doing something and the next stage from furious crying or kicking may be a temper tantrum. Never return aggression – loving firmness is the best answer.

Young children of two or three often go through a stage (sometimes provoked by something not entirely to their liking at home such as a new baby) of being aggressive to other children. They may bite, kick, push, spit or pinch, much to your horror. This doesn't mean to say that their basic personality is unduly aggressive or otherwise unpleasant, just that they are not old enough to understand that this sort of behaviour is unacceptable.

A young child rarely plays *with* other children, though he may play alongside them, so he cares little about the other children's reactions to what he does. It's not until later that he'll want to please them. At this age his naked emotions are unharnessed and the only way for a parent to cope is by calmly but firmly telling him that this behaviour is unacceptable. It's not a good idea though to threaten your child that you won't love him if he goes on being aggressive. Such a child needs extra love and security, not less.

An older child who is frequently and persistently aggressive needs help as this behaviour may be caused by problems in his day to day life. Your health visitor or family doctor will help you to sort out what it is that is disturbing your child. Family problems are usually at the root of the child's aggressive behaviour. As the children grow, their aggression can be channelled into healthy competitive activities with other children. We all need to release aggression throughout our lives. The problem for a parent is how to harness and control aggression so that it becomes a positive force and not a negative one.

If your child has trouble with a child who is aggressive to him or actually bullies him, try and sort things out straight away. If another child is playing at your house, make it obvious that such behaviour is unacceptable to you. If you explain this gently but firmly, it may have a more helpful and lasting effect than if you simply pull the child away or shout at him. If the problem is at play-group, talk to the play-group leader about it without delay, or your child may be put off going to play there.

Children have to learn to cope with the inevitable aggression they will encounter from other people during their lives. While they must stand up for themselves, fighting back is not a good approach to teach. If your child is brought up with the advice, 'Do as you would be done by', it will stand him in good stead. *Related topics* Anger in children; behaviour problems; discipline; jealousy, temper tantrums.

AIDS Auto-immune deficiency syndrome – AIDS – is thought to be a new disease and is caused by infection with the AIDS virus. Only one in ten people infected with the AIDS virus go on to develop the disease and it seems that the incubation period can be many years. The AIDS virus is spread at present mainly among homosexual men by sexual contact, and by infected blood entering the body either from a blood transfusion or by using shared needles to inject drugs, as some drug addicts do. Increasing numbers of women are now getting the disease. This can happen because they are the sexual partners of bisexual men, because they are drug addicts and share needles, because they are the sexual partners of drug addicts, or because they have received blood transfusions or treatment with blood products. It is known that the AIDS virus can be passed from mother to child before, during or after birth, though this doesn't of course necessarily cause AIDS in the child. If the mother was known to be infected with the AIDS virus before the birth of her child, then it's likely that her child will already have acquired the infection and there is no reason why she should not breastfeed. The difficulty is if a mother is exposed to AIDS after the birth of her child. If she is infected, then some doctors would advise against breastfeeding unless the baby is already infected too, in which case the mother must weigh (with her doctor's help if necessary) the possible harm of adding viruses to the baby's body with the disadvantage of removing all the immunity factors that breast milk provides.

Albino A child with blonde, silky hair, fair skin and red pupils in the eyes. This condition is caused by an absence of colouring in the hair, skin and retinae. It is an inherited condition and occurs in about one child in 20,000. Albino children may also be short-sighted, have a squint and be sensitive to light. The only treatment available is avoidance of exposure to sunlight, the use of sunglasses and an ultraviolet screening skin cream.

Allergy A child is said to be allergic if his immune system (the body system that produces protective antibodies in response to foreign proteins entering his body) over-reacts and causes bodily symptoms. We have an immune system to protect us from the proteins we inhale, eat, or come into skin contact with and most children experience no problems as their body deals with the intruders.

About one in five children develop allergies very easily, though. They produce bodily reactions whenever they come into contact with proteins to which they are sensitive. They are more likely to have repeated infections than other children and are also likely to have a family history of asthma, eczema and hay fever. Such children (and indeed their families) are said to be atopic.

When the body over-reacts to the proteins that it comes into contact with it can produce a variety of signs and symptoms. Eczema affects the skin; asthma the lungs; hay fever the nose and eyes; conjunctivitis the eyes; diarrhoea and colic the gut; and dermatitis the skin. Allergic reactions to food are numerous and commonplace. Some children are allergic to drugs and even to insect stings and bites. Many other diseases, such as migraine and coeliac disease (defective digestion of fats), may also have an allergic basis.

Even though a baby is born with a working immune system to protect him from foreign proteins, it is not mature until about six months of age by which time he can make enough antibodies to cope with onslaughts from the outside world. In the first six months, therefore, he has to have 'immune' cover from some other source. This other source is breast milk. Repeated research has shown that solely breast-feeding babies produces more allergy-free children. If the baby's immune system was sensitized to a particular protein in his early months, it may be primed to react adversely (and so develop allergies) to other foreign proteins later. It is thought that one bottle of cow's milk (the commonest allergen babies come into contact with) can prime the immune system in this way and increase the likelihood of future allergic problems. *Related topics* Antihistamines; asthma; breast-feeding; bottle feeding; coeliac disease; desensitization; hay fever; milk intolerance; patch test. *Useful organizations* Asthma Society and Friends of the Asthma Research Council; The Coeliac Society; National Eczema Society.

Amniocentesis The removal of a small amount of amniotic fluid from around a baby while it is still in the womb.

Having an amniocentesis is much like having an injection. The doctor takes an ordinary syringe with an ordinary blood-taking sized needle and inserts it in the midline between the navel and the pubic hair line. The skin is sterilized first to ensure that no bacteria are introduced into the baby's world. A local anaesthetic may be used. Although it is not essential, many doctors prefer to scan the abdomen with an ultrasound machine so as to localize exactly the greatest area of amniotic fluid and so be able to insert the needle into that and not into the baby or placenta. This is especially important in early pregnancy, when there is little fluid, and in mothers with rhesus-negative blood in whom any bleeding in the baby (caused by the needle) could provoke rhesus disease.

Amniocentesis does not hurt much and there is no leakage of amniotic fluid as the needle hole is so small. There is a small (one per cent) risk of the mother miscarrying if the procedure is carried out early in pregnancy but the later it is done, the less the risk. The main danger is that the placenta may be punctured. This is unlikely to occur if the doctor has ascertained (by ultrasound) the position of the placenta before inserting the needle.

There are many ways in which a sample of amniotic fluid can help doctors help mothers. Perhaps one of the best publicized is that of foetal abnormality detection. Many pointers can make a mother or a doctor suspect that a foetus may be abnormal. If it is likely to be, the parents may wish to have the pregnancy terminated. Ideally an abnormal foetus should be aborted as early as possible, so the earlier the amniotic fluid sample can be obtained, the better. This is difficult before fourteen weeks, but the sample needs to be taken as soon as possible after this.

Amniocentesis can help doctors diagnose an abnormality in several ways. The fluid extracted contains cells that have been shed from the body of the foetus. As each body cell contains a replica of all the genetic material of the body, doctors can tell from one cell if the foetus has a major chromosomal abnormality such as mongolism (Down's syndrome). This can be useful if the mother has already produced such a baby, or in older mothers, because it is known that women over the age of thirty-five are more likely to produce Down's babies than are younger women.

Haemophilia is known as a 'sex-linked' disease because it is only seen in males. Females act as carriers but do not suffer from the disease. If there is a family history of a sex-linked genetic disease, it helps to know the sex of the foetus. Cells from the amniotic fluid can be examined to tell the sex of the foetus. A male foetus will have a 50–50 chance of suffering from such a disease. The parents are asked to decide before the amniocentesis whether they want the foetus aborted if it is a male, on the understanding that it would have a 50–50 chance of suffering from the disease if they do not.

Disorders such as spina bifida and anencephaly can also be detected early by measuring the level of substance called alphafetoprotein in the amniotic fluid.

The rhesus-positive foetus of a rhesus-negative mother who has rising levels of rhesus antibodies during her pregnancy is in danger of becoming severely ill even before birth. Amniocentesis enables the amount of bilirubin in the amniotic fluid to be measured, giving doctors a guide as to whether to induce labour early.

Amniocentesis is, however, relatively expensive and at present it is only justifiable when there are medical reasons for suspicion about the outcome of the pregnancy.

If you have an amniocentesis to rule out a certain condition (such as Down's syndrome) and the answer proves to be negative, it does not necessarily mean that there is nothing else wrong with the baby. Many parents are shocked when they have a baby with an abnormality after having a 'normal' result from an amniocentesis but it is important to remember that the sample of fluid the doctors remove is not – and cannot be – tested for every abnormality. *Related topics* Anencephaly; blood groups; Down's syndrome; genetic counselling; haemophilia; spina bifida.

Anaemia A condition in which there are either too few red blood cells, too little haemoglobin in each red blood cell, or both.

Your child will seem quite well if he is only mildly anaemic. If the anaemia develops slowly, the body adapts to the smaller amount of haemoglobin. This means that even severe anaemia – if it is of gradual onset – may cause no symptoms. What you'll probably notice first is that the child is abnormally tired. He may be pale – the colour of his lips, fingertips and insides of the eyelids are a better guide than the cheeks. He may also have a poor appetite or be irritable. If the anaemia is caused by a sudden loss of blood, as in an accident or in certain blood disorders, then there may be some breathlessness, a fast pulse and even heart failure if treatment isn't begun.

The many possible causes fall into three main groups. A lowered red blood cell production in the body; excessive breakdown of red blood cells by the body; and blood loss.

Iron deficiency anaemia is the commonest blood disorder in children. Because breast milk usually contains plenty of easily-absorbed iron, young breast-fed babies don't often suffer from it. Some premature babies are born with low body stores of iron and so have blood tests to check for anaemia from time to time. The young child who doesn't eat a varied diet containing iron-rich foods may become anaemic. The main sources of iron in our diet are meat, bread (especially wholemeal), flour, cereals, potatoes and vegetables.

About one child in three with iron deficiency anaemia has slight, continual bleeding from the gut after drinking cows' milk. This can be prevented by heating cows' milk before it is drunk or by reducing the amount of cows' milk drunk by the child. Large amounts of cows' milk may also reduce the amount of iron absorbed by the body and reduce the child's appetite for other foods.

Anaemia (other than iron deficiency anaemia) can be caused by blood loss (a severe nose bleed, an accident or an operation); certain drugs which damage bone marrow or red blood cells; abnormalities in the red cells themselves (thalassaemia and sickle cell disease are two examples) or by leukaemia. Rhesus babies usually suffer from anaemia due to red cell abnormalities (see Blood groups, page 79).

The vast majority of children whose cheeks look pale aren't anaemic at all. In those that are, iron deficiency anaemia is the commonest condition by far. **Related topics** Blood groups; iron; sickle cell disease; thalassaemia.

Anal fissure A crack in the skin of the anus (back passage) that produces pain and possibly bleeding when a child opens his bowels. Fissures occur because straining to pass a hard motion tears the delicate mucous membrane in the anus. Because opening his bowels is painful the child is reluctant to do so and becomes more constipated, so adding to the vicious circle. Bleeding from an anal fissure is never serious.

Thankfully, treatment is simple. Lubricate the anus with a little petroleum jelly or a similar substance just before the child opens his bowels. Your doctor might prescribe a mild laxative to keep the motions soft while the fissure heals itself. The most important treatment is to ensure that the child has plenty of dietary fibre in his diet so that his stools remain soft. A recurrence of the anal fissure is then very unlikely. **Related topics** Constipation.

Analgesic A drug or medicine that relieves pain without causing a loss of consciousness. The most commonly used analgesics are aspirin and paracetamol, of which millions of tablets are taken daily in the UK. Recent evidence suggests that aspirin is unsafe for children under 12 because of the possibility of developing a rare, and even more rarely fatal, condition known as Reye's syndrome. Because young children rarely complain of the pains that adults most often use such medicines for (headache, toothache, period pain) they are not often used in young children. When a child complains of pain it usually means a medical opinion is worth seeking. Certainly analgesics should *not* be used for tummy aches or as sleeping medicines, or placed against the gum for a toothache. Tummy aches usually need other investigations and treatment.

Analgesics, like all drugs, should be kept out of the reach of children and should only be given according to the dosage suggested on the container. Always keep analgesics in child-resistant containers or in their original foil packaging until use. Because aspirin is so commonplace it is often taken in overdose by children. This is very dangerous because children can appear to be quite well immediately after taking aspirin in overdose and can then become ill very suddenly without warning. If your child takes three or more aspirins, take him to a doctor or casualty department at once.

Paracetamol is a pain-reliever and fever-reducer, just like aspirin, but if taken in excess can be very toxic to the liver. It is very difficult to treat an overdose of paracetamol and the effects can be lethal, so be especially careful with this medicine. *Related topics* Abdominal pain; fever; headache; medicines; pain; sleep problems; toothache.

Anencephaly A congenital abnormality in which the skull is not completely formed, part of the brain is exposed and part of the brain is absent. Babies with this condition die at or very soon after birth and it is responsible for about one in eight of all stillbirths. It is more common among girls than boys and is seen more often in Ireland than any other country.

Anencephaly and spina bifida have a related cause and a mother who has had a baby with either condition is more likely to have a subsequent affected baby than are other women. Ultrasound can detect anencephaly early in pregnancy, as can other tests of the mother's blood and amniotic fluid. Parents with an affected foetus may decide to have the pregnancy terminated. *Related topics* Amniocentesis; ultrasound.

Anger in children Anger is a perfectly normal feeling in children and our main job as adults is to try to understand the reasons behind it. A baby may cry because he is frustrated or angry at, for example, being left alone, having a dirty nappy, having to wait too long for a feed, being taken off the breast or bottle before he is ready, or being put down when he would prefer to be held.

A toddler gets cross for a variety of reasons such as not being able to make his hands do what he wants them to do, or being prevented by his mother from doing something he wants to do. Temper tantrums are an obvious expression of anger at this age. Fatigue always makes frustration worse and a child who can accept his tower of bricks falling over in the morning may be very cross about it at night. You can help prevent some of his frustration at objects and at his lack of dexterity by helping him when necessary. If you are the cause of his anger, because you are frustrating his desire to do something you don't want him to do or making him do something he doesn't want to do, it's not so easy to help. Explanations are of little use at this age and the best solution is to distract his attention.

As the child grows older, explanations and sympathetic discussion help him cope with his anger at things or at people. Some children act out their angry feelings in imaginative play by themselves or with other children. If your child does something wrong, certain parental reactions are likely not to make the child sorry for what he has done, but angry at the parent for disciplining him in such a way. Being smacked or being shouted at lengthily are two prime examples of how to make a child angry. What you need to do is first to make the child understand that he has done something wrong, then to explain why it was wrong. If he sees that your displeasure is reasonable, he's less likely to do it again and certainly won't harbour any anger towards you.

Anger in a child is best expressed rather than suppressed, because only then can you help him understand it and cope with it. Some ways of expressing it are more acceptable than others, however. Hitting or biting you is unacceptable, whereas shouting, crying or kicking the floor are all right. As he grows older he'll be able to release his anger by telling you about it or just by thinking it over himself. *Related topics* Aggression; behaviour problems; discipline; temper tantrums.

Anger in parents Feelings of annoyance or rage over some aspects of their child's behaviour are so universal among parents as to be considered normal. The amount of anger you'll feel will depend entirely on your personality, your expectations of your child, and your state of body and mind at the time. Some people are naturally quick to anger, while others are more easy going, and everyone knows that physical fatigue or emotional stress make it more difficult to be patient.

If your child's behaviour often seems to make you angry, it's worth asking whether your expectations are too high. Maybe it's unrealistic to expect a baby to settle down and sleep after a feed: perhaps the baby's need for you to cuddle him even though he's clean, fed and comfortable is reasonable, and you should just try to enjoy a time of sitting down with him instead of getting on and doing the cooking or whatever. Maybe you could start getting your child ready to go out ten minutes earlier than usual, so his slowness doesn't irritate you and make you late.

If you find you are often angry with your children the chances are that *your* life needs looking at. Talk to your doctor about what could be making you edgy and irritable – perhaps you are depressed but hadn't realized it. Don't wait for things to get desperate before seeking help. *Related topics* Child abuse; swearing.

Anorexia The medical word for a loss of appetite for food. Young children often go off their food and the cause is usually simple and harmless. Many children go through phases of eating very little or of only eating a few favoured foods. As long as the food they are offered is as attractive and nutritious as possible, and as long as the parents don't make a 'thing' of the child not eating, the phase will eventually pass.

Sometimes though there may be more serious causes. By far the commonest of these is an infection. Children often have a lot of infections in their pre-school years, with colds and the common childhood infections and so on, so if your child goes off his food it's worth thinking about one of these first.

If a child has an infection the most important thing is to keep his fluid intake high. Fluid is essential for the body to function and to heal and if the child has a temperature he'll be losing a lot more fluid than usual in the form of sweat.

In general, however, as far as food is concerned the principle should be never to force food down a child who doesn't want to eat. A previously well-nourished child will eat if he is hungry. Unless a child is ill there is almost no danger of him starving himself, so don't get locked into a battle over a loss of appetite.

Diseases of the thyroid gland, kidney, liver and intestine can produce anorexia and these will need to be sorted out by your doctor. *Related topics* Appetite.

Antenatal care Baby care begins as soon as pregnancy does because a mother's body provides nourishment, oxygen, warmth, and protection from the outside world, as well as the removal of waste products from the developing baby, for the next nine months. Some babies are born with the odds stacked against them from the beginning simply because they weren't looked after well enough during this vital time. It's sensible to try to be in the best possible state of health before conceiving. Experts now accept that the pregnant woman should ideally not smoke at all, as babies of smokers tend to weigh less than their optimum weight and it is now known that low birth weight carries the risk of several complications to the newborn baby's health.

It has also been shown that excess alcohol and the consumption of certain drugs can prevent optimum development of the unborn baby. Because of the difficulty of determining the 'optimum', some experts recommend no alcohol at all during pregnancy.

Attendance at an antenatal clinic will give the pregnant woman the benefit of skilled dietary and medical advice. She will have a physical examination, blood tests, special diagnostic tests such as an ultrasound scan or an amniocentesis, if necessary, and regular checks of her blood pressure, weight, urine, abdominal size and general wellbeing. Anything wrong can be spotted quickly and treatment can be given in order to give the baby the best possible chance of a safe delivery. *Useful organizations* Association for Improvements in the Maternity Services; The Birth Centre; The National Childbirth Trust.

Antibiotics A family of drugs that is used to kill bacteria in the body. If you are given a course of antibiotics for your child, give him the medicine exactly as prescribed, in the full dosage for the full time. Many parents, finding their child better after a couple of days of the antibiotic, stop giving it. This then leaves a half-killed population of bacteria which may cause a new or more virulent infection in the child or in someone else.

By far the commonest widely-used antibiotic is penicillin in one of its many forms. Unfortunately, most penicillins in use today can cause side-effects, including diarrhoea, skin rashes and allergies. Allergic reactions to penicillin are fairly common in children who have a family history of asthma, eczema or hay fever. Penicillin applied to the skin (in an ointment) is especially likely to cause a reaction but such preparations are now rarely used.

If your child gets a rash, itching or indeed any new symptom when taking an antibiotic, tell the doctor at once. If the doctor thinks this is an allergic reaction then your child should be closely watched if he is ever given that antibiotic (or its close relatives) again. There are many alternatives to penicillin so don't worry that the child's condition might be incurable if he can't take penicillin. Remember to tell any new doctor you come into contact with about this sensitivity and be sure to have it written across his hospital notes if ever he has to go into hospital.

Very few children today reach school age without having had a course of antibiotics. Used properly and with respect by both the medical profession and the child's parents, they are useful tools in fighting infections. Remember though that the majority of the common childhood infections (including colds, 'flu, sore throats, and childhood ailments like measles, mumps and chickenpox) are not caused by bacteria but by viruses. In these conditions antibiotics are a waste of money and can even do the child harm. Under no circumstances should you keep antibiotics around the home 'just in case'. Once a child (or even an adult) has finished with a course of antibiotics, dispose of any excess safely. If the child has taken all the antibiotics and the amount prescribed was exactly right, there should be none left over. Never use your medicines for your children and never give the odd antibiotic tablet, capsule, or syrup dose hoping it will do some good. It certainly will not and could be harmful by producing resistant bacteria, which then become difficult to eradicate.

Some children on antibiotics have diarrhoea and a sore tongue and may even develop thrush. All of these are well-recognized side-effects of antibiotics as they kill off the normal resident populations of bacteria in the body. Eating plain, live yoghurt seems to help re-colonize the large bowel with useful organisms but thrush in either the mouth or the vagina will have to be treated by a doctor.

For all their dangers and potential problems, antibiotics can be life-saving and certainly prevent a lot of unnecessary suffering. If your child seems to be getting no better with a particular antibiotic, tell your doctor after a few days' trial. If necessary he can take a swab of the infected area and have sensitivity tests carried out on the bacteria at the local hospital. This will then enable him to prescribe just the right antibiotic to be sure to kill the bacteria.

Antihistamines Medicines taken to block the effects of histamine release in the body. Histamine is a natural body chemical made by specialized cells in the body and is released in response to an allergic stimulus. In the skin histamine causes reddening, the appearance of a wheal (a raised white area) and itching. A nettle sting is a classic example of histamine release. Histamine also has effects in many other areas of the body; for example, in the lungs it causes asthma.

Antihistamines are usually taken as syrups or tablets and can be applied to the skin as a cream. Some children become allergic to the cream itself if it is used repeatedly.

The main side-effect of antihistamines is drowsiness. This property has been harnessed to good effect in the treatment of children who have itchy conditions that stop them sleeping. Some children are made more excitable by antihistamines and this is especially likely in pre-school children. Never exceed the dose on the packaging.

Probably the commonest everyday use of antihistamines is in travel sickness medicines. Most motion sickness preparations are antihistamines. They are also used in anti-hayfever preparations. *Related topics* Bites and stings; motion sickness; urticaria.

Antiseptics

Antiseptics Chemicals produced commercially to kill bacteria on the surface of the body or on clothes, floors, drains and children's toys, for example. Antiseptics are *not* drugs and should never be taken internally as they can cause dangerous poisoning. Disinfectants are strong household antiseptics used for cleaning non-living things.

Disinfectants have a dubious place in the home unless there are animals around. The obsession many households have with disinfecting everything in sight is understandable given the publicity disinfectant manufacturers have put out over the years but there is little evidence that children and babies catch any fewer diseases if all their surroundings are cleaned with disinfectant.

Mild antiseptic creams can be useful on grazes and small spots but are by no means essential for healing to occur and bathing children in antiseptic solutions has nothing to recommend it at all.

Anxiety

Anxiety A state of apprehension or worry about possible future misfortune. To some extent this is a perfectly normal emotion which can be felt at any age, but young children, unlike adults, are unable to cope with anxiety or to avoid frightening things. Certain situations such as being left with a stranger are likely to make children anxious, but the degree felt depends on the child's personality, on his past experience and on his current emotional and physical state.

Anxiety is only a problem if it interferes with a child's normal developmental progress. Sometimes a parent's anxiety can be transmitted to a child and problems with toilet training are a prime example of this. If a mother is worried that her young child won't use the pot or lavatory to open his bowels, for example, her threats, bribes or attempts at explanation and persuasion may make the child concerned too much about his bowel motions. He may be so frightened of opening his bowels, because he knows that when he does it in his nappy it makes his mother angry, that he becomes constipated.

Many young children are anxious about going to bed at night. They worry in advance because they know their mother will leave them in a room alone and in the dark. Many toddlers show anxiety in front of other people by clinging or being shy. Others feel anxious when confronted with a plate of food if they have previously been made to eat everything up.

Anxiety can be the cause of physical symptoms such as recurrent abdominal pain or vomiting, though these are more likely to be seen in older children.

As with any emotional problem, the first thing to do is to try – perhaps with professional help – to understand the cause. *Related topics* Behaviour problems; development – emotional; insecurity; leaving a baby; potty training; separation anxiety; shyness.

Apgar score A measurement of the extent, if any, of lack of oxygen in a newborn baby. It is a scale of assessment used routinely by doctors and midwives at one minute after birth and a second time at five minutes after birth to see how the baby is progressing. The lower the score, the less likely is the baby to be breathing completely normally. Marks from 0 to 2 are given for each of five signs of life: the heart rate, respiratory effort, muscle tone, the response to stimulation by a catheter in the nostril and the colour of the baby's trunk. A baby in the best possible state has a score of ten. A score of under seven alerts the birth attendant to the fact that there may be something wrong, and a score of less than four suggests that the baby's life is in danger and that assistance to start him breathing is urgently needed.

One of the most common reasons for a low Apgar score is a depression of the urge to breathe caused by pain-killing drugs given to the mother in labour and then passed into the baby's body. Some babies have a low Apgar score because they have been short of oxygen during labour. This is one reason why a baby's heart rate is monitored so carefully during labour and why some labours are interrupted by a Caesarean section, or speeded up by, for example, a forceps delivery. *Related topic* Asphyxia.

Appearance – child's A baby may be branded as 'happy', 'extrovert', 'serious', or 'difficult', simply because of his expression. People rarely take into account that the baby's emotions are at this time greatly influenced by the way he is cared for. It is widely held that a baby who is breast-fed on an unrestricted basis, carried round by his mother, allowed to sleep with her at night, and given lots of love and attention smiles more often than a conventionally reared baby. Already the environment is influencing the child's personality, facial expressions, and therefore the way others react to him. Everyone loves a smiling baby and the baby who smiles more is smiled at more. Over the years this trend may continue and the child's sense of self-esteem will inevitably be heightened by the interest shown in him by others.

Whatever looks a child is born with, he can be very attractive if he is outgoing, smiles and laughs a lot, takes an interest in what is going on, and is sympathetic to others. Children with conventionally attractive looks start off with an advantage in life but an attractive personality is worth more every time than good looks alone and what people do with their lives is far more important than how they look.

Appendicitis Inflammation of the appendix. The appendix is a small, tubular organ that lies in the lower right part of the abdomen. It opens at one end into the first part of the large bowel and is shut off at the other. The function of the appendix isn't known but it is probably not the useless organ it has been made out to be. The wall of the appendix is rich in antibody-producing tissue and this may be important.

It isn't known why the appendix becomes inflamed as often as it does but small pellets of hard food residue can obstruct its narrow opening into the bowel. Inflammation then occurs in the stagnant fluid in the blind end of the appendix and infection sets in. Although the cause of appendicitis is uncertain it is definitely less commonly seen in people who consume a lot of dietary fibre as part of their diet. If these same people change their diet to one low in dietary fibre they start to get appendicitis.

The main symptom of appendicitis is abdominal pain. This can be worrying for many parents who wrongly assume that any tummy ache is going to end up being appendicitis. Having said this, if your child has a tummy pain which lasts for more than two hours, if his temperature is slightly raised and if he vomits, call your doctor at once. While awaiting the doctor don't give any food, drink or tablets at all.

The pain of appendicitis is variable in its position and character in children, and the younger the child the less likely signs are to be typical. The pain frequently starts in the centre of the tummy around the umbilicus and then settles in the lower right part. There may be diarrhoea, constipation, vomiting or no bowel upset at all. There is often a low grade fever. It is rare in children under one year old.

When the appendix is inflamed it can easily burst, shedding pus and infection around the inside of the abdomen. This causes peritonitis, which can kill. Because this is so serious a condition, the doctor may want your child to go into hospital for observation while the situation becomes clearer. No one wants to operate unnecessarily on a pre-school child so every opportunity will be taken to ensure that what is wrong is in fact appendicitis. Sometimes it's impossible to be sure and the surgeon will have to look and see just in case he's missing a case of appendicitis.

At one time there was a lot of talk about the so-called 'grumbling appendix'. This was thought to be a condition in which the appendix become repeatedly inflamed over months or years. Such a complaint is now considered to arise from constipation, wind, anxiety, or inflammation of the lymphatic tissue around the intestine (mesenteric adenitis). *Related topic* Abdominal pain.

Appetite It isn't known why we feel hungry but the emptiness of the stomach and a low blood sugar are probably two mechanisms.

Anyone who has had several children will know how different their appetites are right from the earliest days of life. Not only do children vary enormously in their appetites but any one child's appetite can differ considerably from day to day. From the very beginning many mothers make the mistake of believing that breast-feeding their babies regularly every four hours has some sort of magic to it. Nothing could be further from the truth. Experience with large numbers of babies shows that a few do indeed do well with four-hourly breast-feeds but that the vast majority do not and need feeding more often, especially in the early days. This is the whole basis of 'demand' or unrestricted breast-feeding. When the baby is hungry, he asks for more and should get it. This is what nature intended because human milk passes through the infant's stomach much more quickly than does cows' milk, which therefore can be given less frequently.

Babies eat a lot for their size compared with older children because they are growing so fast. From time to time they have an appetite increase, usually coinciding with a growth spurt. By six months the growth rate slows and so does the appetite.

It's during the second year of life that babies most often lose their appetite, if indeed they do so at all. The growth rate falls right off (compared with the first year) and many one-year-olds need comparatively less food than before. So if a toddler goes off his food but is otherwise well, don't be alarmed – he won't starve.

There are probably more battles over meals than almost anything else with toddlers. This is unnecessary and can build up a complex about food if allowed to carry on. Be guided by what your child feels like eating. Provided he's being given good food and things that he likes he'll eat when he's ready. If he uncharacteristically goes off his food for more than a couple of days or so, seek your doctor's help as there could be something wrong.

Lots of children seem to like only a very few foods and sometimes change to another collection of equally restricted tit-bits. This can be frustrating for a mother determined to impose her idea of a balanced diet at all costs but again, the battle really isn't worth fighting as no toddler or older child will come to harm on a diet of one food for a few days. Some children really *do* dislike certain foods. No one knows why but it is probably wrong to force a child to eat any food he says he dislikes. Current research is finding that certain avoided foods cause food allergies and it is quite possible that when a child refuses a food he is doing so because he gets some kind of bodily reaction from it that he can't explain, or isn't even aware of. No doubt research will soon clarify some of these dietary mysteries.

Patterns for eating are set for life in the early years and many an adult has been conditioned into eating far too much by being forced in his early childhood into eating everything up when his appetite told him he was full. Eating then becomes imprinted in his mind as a sign of parental approval and he eats more to receive more approval – even though he doesn't need the food. This sets the pattern for excessive eating throughout life and this is proven to be dangerous. **Related topics** Anorexia; eating habits; feeding schedules; food; mealtimes; underfeeding.

Arguing Arguing must be one of the most widespread habits in children, especially among brothers and sisters, and is certainly one of the most annoying to parents. Children often aren't interested in leading a peaceful life but want to assert their own ideas. This goes for a lot of adults too, of course. Give and take is something that has to be learned and accepting the fact that there can be different points of view on any subject is something that the young child finds hard to understand. He knows what his point of view is and wants to make sure that things happen the way he wants. Put two or more three-, four- or five-year-olds together, and they'll sometimes bicker endlessly, especially if they are left alone without adults. It's often sensible to intervene and explain both points of view, and then to act as the referee. Doing this helps them to learn how to cope with playing and doing things together in a peaceful way, and prepares them for dealing with other children when they go to school.

Children may argue about things you ask them to do. Rather than tell them that they must obey you just because you say so, it's worth explaining why you want the child to do something. Time spent on this helps the child understand the basis on which your requests are made and the reasons for them. Sometimes you might even be persuaded to go back on what you said and that is in itself a good way of teaching children the value of discussion. There are occasions when arguments are completely out of place, such as when crossing the road, when 'stop' means 'stop right now'. Children soon learn to accept when you mean business and when discussion is permissible. When asking a young child to do something that he is reluctant to do, always take time to consider whether your request is reasonable. *Related topics* Anger in children; contrariness; discipline; temper tantrums.

Arthritis Young children by and large don't get 'arthritis' in the way that adults do – their arthritis gets better because it is almost always caused by a short-lived condition and not by degeneration, as is the case in adults. Some children, for example, get aches and pains in their joints when they have an infectious fever – but such arthritis is almost never serious.

Growing pains are felt in the muscles between the joints (particularly in the calf or thigh) and not in the joints themselves.

Arthritis can also be caused by an injury to a joint. *Related topics* Rheumatic fever; rheumatoid arthritis. *Useful organization* The British Rheumatism and Arthritis Association.

Artificial respiration ('kiss of life') A severely ill child, one involved in an accident, one who has taken poison, had an electric shock, or has drowned may become unconscious. Get someone to ring immediately for a doctor or ambulance.

What to do if he's unconscious
1 Put your cheek against his mouth and feel for breaths.
2 See if there is anything in his mouth (vomit, a toy or other inhaled object). If there is something obvious, remove it and lie him on his back.
3 Pull his chin upwards so that his head is bent backwards. With one hand pulling his chin up, push the top of his head down with your other hand.

This simple procedure opens up the throat and he may start breathing spontaneously. Once he does, lie him on his tummy with his head to one side and one leg pulled up and bent at right angles at the knee and hip. Stay with him while awaiting the arrival of professional help.

If breathing doesn't restart at once
1 Place his head in the position described above.
2 Pinch his nose shut.
3 Make sure his mouth is open.
4 Take a shallow breath yourself.
5 Apply your mouth to his, ensuring there is a good seal all round.
6 Breathe gently into his mouth, watching for his chest to rise.
7 Take your mouth away and repeat the procedure.

Watch carefully for spontaneous breathing to restart and stop as soon as it does. Try to blow a breath into the child's mouth once every six seconds but be guided by common sense on this timing.

Other hints
1 Don't blow too hard as this can send air into his stomach and make the child vomit, which is unpleasant for you and dangerous for him because the vomit could cause irritation in his lungs.
2 If the child is much under five, seal your lips over both nose and mouth and *blow gently*. In babies only blow the amount of air you can hold in your cheeks – don't blow from your lungs as this could over-inflate and damage the baby's lungs.
3 If the tummy starts swelling you'll know that you're blowing air into the stomach down the gullet. Stop what you are doing, turn the child to one side and expel the air by pressing firmly over his stomach.
4 From time to time check the child's heartbeat by feeling the pulse at the wrist or in the neck. Sometimes whatever was wrong that stopped his breathing can also stop his heart (see heart massage, page 293).

How long should I continue? Either until the child starts to breathe spontaneously or until professional help comes. *Never* breathe into a child who is breathing on his own.

All other methods of artificial respiration are unsuitable for use in children and should not be used. They are also very much less effective than the kiss of life.

Artistic activities Even though we live in a technological age and it would seem that many (especially older) children are more likely to be interested in mechanical toys bought from shops, many young children also enjoy artistic and creative activities.

Every child needs to express himself whether in words, music, make-believe, dance, painting or in a host of other creative pursuits. It's not talent that's important (though a talented child will get more positive feedback from adults, which may make him enjoy the activity more than would a non-talented child) but the fact that the effort is his alone. Early on a child will change his artistic activities every few minutes. At this stage little supervision is required because his creativity is self-motivated and needs little structure. He'll like it if you keep him company and, preferably, join in, but he won't want you to take over what he's doing.

As the child grows though he'll welcome more help and guidance in his creative pursuits and this may help him enjoy the activities more. The help doesn't need to come from an adult. Very often ideas flow more readily and enjoyably between children than between parents and children and they get pleasure from presenting their parents with something ambitious created without the parents' knowledge or help.

Perhaps the single most valuable thing to remember is not to impose one's own adult ideas on a young child's creativity. Your stereotyped concept of a train, for example, may be totally different from his and his idea of a dance quite amazing to you. The discovery of what looks and feels good and what gives other people pleasure is what artistic activities are about at any age, perhaps even more so because children have no 'goals': they simply enjoy themselves. *Related topics* Creativity; dancing; painting; play; rhythm and music.

Asphyxia The medical name for a condition resulting from a lack of oxygen (anoxia) when a child suffocates or chokes.

Asphyxia can occur before or during birth if the baby suffers from a lack of oxygen or immediately afterwards if the onset of breathing is delayed. Because the brain's cells are so sensitive to any shortage of oxygen, action has to be taken to restore the baby's oxygen supply at once.

Many parents quite understandably worry when their baby doesn't start breathing as soon as he is born but many children grow up to be perfectly normal even after as long as two minutes without breathing at birth and some develop normally even after much longer periods of asphyxia. If the umbilical cord is still attached to the baby he'll be getting oxygen-rich blood for a few minutes until the placenta separates, just as he did in the womb. *Related topics* Breathing difficulties; choking.

Asthma A common condition in which breathing is difficult because the air passages in the lungs are narrowed temporarily. Breathing out is more difficult than breathing in and the distress this causes is unpleasant both for the child and his parents. About one in twenty children suffers from asthma, twice as many boys as girls.

Asthma tends to get better spontaneously as the child grows older. Half of all asthmatic children of seven years of age will be clear of attacks by eleven. About a fifth of asthmatic children go on to become wheezy adults.

In asthma the lining of the airways in the lungs seems to be especially sensitive to certain stimuli. As a result, the muscles in the walls of the airways contract, so making the airways narrower and the linings are stimulated to produce excessive amounts of mucus.

Asthma is produced by two main stimuli, allergy and infection. Allergy can manifest itself in many different ways, and children who have an allergic family history (eczema, hay fever or nettlerash) are more likely to suffer from asthma than other children. This allergic (or atopic) asthma tends to occur more in the spring and summer. Complete and exclusive breastfeeding for several months significantly reduces the likelihood (by more than threefold in one study) of a baby from an atopic family suffering from this type of asthma, so it's certainly well worth doing, especially if you have a family history of allergy.

The commonest cause of allergic asthma is the house dust mite. Unfortunately, it is almost impossible to free a house from these mites but damp dusting, the use of synthetic bedding materials and careful attention to domestic cleanliness can all help reduce the mite population. Other causes of allergic asthma include grass pollen, pets and certain foods. Some children get asthma after eating foods to which they are allergic, for instance nuts, cows' milk, fish, wheat, chocolate or eggs and avoidance of the food in any form often cures them completely.

Emotional stress, whether pleasant or unpleasant, produces asthma in some children, a few of whom get better when they are away from their stressful domestic or school environment. Exercise, fumes and extremes of temperature can also produce asthma in an asthma-prone child and asthma is usually worse at night.

Respiratory infections commonly provoke asthmatic attacks, especially in susceptible individuals, but the way that they do so isn't known. Bacterial vaccines have been used to try to reduce a child's sensitivity but with little success. Some viruses, though, do seem to provoke asthma in young children in a sufficiently reliable way to be able to consider making vaccines against them.

An asthmatic attack is a very distressing thing both for the child and his parents but a calm, caring atmosphere can do much to improve the child's breathing. Panic makes the breathing worse and reassurance improves it. In an acute attack when the child is fighting for breath there is little you can do except help to keep him calm and reassure him. He may need emergency medical help, unless you are used to dealing with the situation yourself and have the drugs to hand.

Treatment involves eradicating any infection and giving drugs that increase the diameter of the airways in the lungs. An anti-allergy drug, sodium cromoglycate, is useful in between attacks because it tends to prevent them happening. This and several other anti-asthma drugs are taken via an inhaler and even quite young children can usually learn to use one reliably. Some doctors think that inhalers (other than those containing sodium cromoglycate) should not be used for children.

Asthmatic children used to be treated as 'special' or 'delicate'. Today, with good preventive drugs, better treatment of the acute attack and the increasing use of breathing exercises, most asthmatic children lead normal lives. ***Related topics*** Allergy; desensitization. ***Useful organizations*** Asthma Society and Friends of the Asthma Research Council.

Athlete's foot

A fungal infection of the skin between the toes that occurs more commonly in older children and teenagers but can occur in young children. The infection is picked up at a swimming pool or from going barefoot where an infected person has been.

In the commonest form of the condition there is severe cracking and peeling of the skin with red raw areas underneath. Itching is the main symptom and picking and scratching make it worse. The skin between the little toe and its neighbour is most commonly affected.

Prevention is the best cure. Keep your children's feet covered in public places and treat any infection you have straight away so as not to spread it around the family. Shoes with composition soles are bad for children's feet because they encourage the feet to sweat and this produces just the conditions that the fungus likes. Unfortunately, it's very difficult to get shoes that don't have these soles. Cotton socks and leather soled shoes are helpful in curing and preventing the condition.

The mainstay of treatment is to keep the feet dry, especially between the toes, until healing is complete. Dusting powders and sprays containing a fungicide can also be very effective.

Because the condition is so contagious an infected child should have his own towel and bathmat and shouldn't go barefoot in the presence of other children (in paddling pools and swimming pools, for example). Change his socks every day and boil them to kill the fungus. Unless you do all these things athlete's foot can be very difficult to eradicate from a family.

Attachment

A baby must be cared for in order to survive. Like other animals, human beings are genetically programmed to respond to their offspring's behaviour. A baby continually tries to attract his mother's (and, later, his father's) attention and makes sure that she is aware of his needs. As she cares for him in response to these needs, she'll talk to him, smile, cuddle and play. In return he'll stop crying, listen intently, gaze at her face, keep quite still or sometimes kick in a certain way, and smile at her.

At around three months, it's clear that the baby recognizes his mother. He has an extra special smile for her and within a few months will cry when she leaves him, or if a stranger approaches. The baby is said at this stage to be 'attached' to his mother and treats her in a special way, clearly liking her more than anyone else.

If his mother doesn't look after him, he'll become attached to whoever does. Whoever brings him up, he'll form an attachment to one person in particular by between six and twelve months. Babies brought up in institutions with lots of caretakers can become confused and even emotionally deprived. This is why it's always best for one person in particular to be responsible for a baby for much of the time. It's well known that a baby can become attached to people other than his mother. Babies can, in fact, form multiple attachments. However many people a baby is attached to, though, there's always a favourite (usually the mother). When a baby or young child is with several people to whom he is attached, he'll automatically choose to base himself with the one he is most attached to. One thing is certain and that is that a stranger will not do. A baby doesn't become instantly attached to someone new but takes time to get to know them. It is the emotional aspects of the baby's attachment experience that are most important. One person may take physical care of him – feeding, washing and keeping him warm, for example, but if another person spends even a short time each day reacting to him in a loving way, he will become attached to that person. Active and responsive interaction with a baby is what counts and sensitive responsiveness is the one quality most likely to foster attachment. Usually, of course, the person who gives a baby this also meets his physical needs besides comforting him through anxiety, fear, illness and tiredness.

It is through a baby's first love that he learns to love other people. The more adequately his emotional needs are met, the better able he will be to respond to others in turn.

Later, a baby also becomes attached to his father or other people closely involved with him who offer a loving relationship.

An older baby may show his attachment to his mother by wanting to be held or cuddled. As the child becomes mobile, he'll wander off but returns often, to reassure himself of his mother's presence. The child who is secure in his attachment to his mother (or the one whom he can rely on to be there and to respond to his needs) will explore more confidently than the one who always thinks that his mother will leave him alone.

A child can become attached to someone even though they may treat him very inconsistently. This explains why a baby or young child who is sometimes physically or emotionally hurt by his mother will still cling to her when in the company of others. It seems that it's better for a child to have someone to be attached to, however they treat him, than no one special to call his own. *Related topics* Bonding; dependence; love; mothering; mother substitutes.

Attendance allowance An allowance payable by the state to the parents or guardians of severely disabled children over the age of two. In order to qualify, the child has to have been severely ill for at least six months and must need a lot of looking after. Even if the child lives away from his parents yet spends weekends or holidays at home the parents can claim the allowance for when he is with them. Forms can be obtained from your local social security offices and the allowance is tax free. There are two sets of allowances: a higher one for those with children who need care twenty-four hours of the day and a lower one for the child who needs only day or night care. If you have any questions about the attendance allowance, ask at your local social security office or talk to your health visitor or social worker.

Attention Adults vary a lot in their ability to pay attention to something and babies and young children are no different. Though an older child can learn to concentrate or pay attention to what he is doing (or what someone else is doing), a young child simply reacts according to his innate personality and his developmental level, which depends largely on his age. To some extent, a child's ability to pay attention can be helped along by his parents. For example, if a child is used to being read to and enjoys sitting with and listening to his mother in this way, he's more likely to pay attention to a book than a child whose interest and attention have never been fostered.

A baby has a relatively short attention span. From birth he can stare at an object and follow a moving object with his eyes for a short distance. Because the focal length of his eyes is about twelve inches (30 cm), he spends a lot of time looking at his mother's face while he's at the breast. Experiments have shown that babies are fascinated by faces and choose to look at them rather than at other things. They pay more attention to patterned things and prefer some patterns to others. Many mothers have noticed that babies are interested in the patterns made by a tree blowing in the wind for example. They also like bright colours and lights.

Sounds can also catch a baby's attention and by the time he is three weeks old, a voice interests him more than other sounds. Two weeks later, his own mother's voice is the one most likely to make him coo and smile.

Babies and one-year-olds are 'distractable' – their attention can easily be shifted away to something new. This is useful if you want to divert your baby's attention from something you'd rather he didn't play with: you simply offer him something new and he'll forget the first thing. The attention span in a one-year-old is not very long, as any mother knows. You can't put a baby on the floor with some toys and expect him to amuse himself for half an hour while you get on with something else because he'll soon become uninterested in them and will want to move on to pastures new! If you want to keep him happy, you'll have to talk to him and give him new things to look at at least every couple of minutes or so. By two, a child may play for up to fifteen or twenty minutes before he becomes bored but most are bored before this.

As a child grows older, he'll be more and more able to amuse himself and his attention span will gradually increase. Parents have a vital part to play in encouraging their children to take an interest in their environment. If you give your young child lots of your attention now, you'll reap the dividends later when you see him concentrating with delight on what interests him.

Attention seeking Wanting attention from other people is quite normal and the younger the child, the more attention he will seek. Babies signal their needs for attention by being restless or by crying and the natural response of the person taking care of them – usually their mother – is to find out what is wanted straight away. As a child grows older, he demands attention by asking. Often a child is not really concerned about getting what he has asked for but simply wants attention from the parent. Whenever practicable, the best solution is to stop doing whatever it is that one is doing and give the child some time to talk, play or cuddle.

Some young children find it hard to share their mother or father with other people and continually interrupt conversations. Telling them off is not the answer and a compromise situation of less conversation and more attention to the child is sensible. It's worth at this point assessing whether the child is getting enough time with you and whether you only really come to life when you are talking with other people.

If a child seems to demand more than his fair share of attention, he may be feeling insecure emotionally and will benefit from a more obviously loving relationship with his parents, or – if he is old enough – a discussion about anything that is worrying him. *Related topics* Boredom; conversation; insecurity; jealousy.

Audiometry The measurement of hearing, often using a special instrument called an audiometer. This produces pure tones of different frequencies and of variable loudness. Very young children's hearing is tested simply by watching whether they turn towards the source of a sound of known loudness and frequency from an audiometer.

Once a child can register that he is hearing a given sound (for example by putting a bead in a box each time he is able to hear a sound through his earphones) a graph (audiogram) is plotted of the levels of sound that he can hear. Such a graph can show any hearing loss at each sound frequency tested and can be useful in helping doctors decide what sort of deafness – if any – the child has.

Audiometry shouldn't be done if a child has recently had a cold or earache because these can produce false readings. *Related topic* Hearing.

Au pairs Young (usually foreign) girls who come to live with your family in order to see the country, learn the language and get a taste of English life. They are untrained, in terms of babycare, and only expect to work for a few hours a day for up to six days a week. In return they expect board and lodging and a small amount of pocket money. Although you are not officially acting *in loco parentis,* you may in effect be. All of these terms should be worked out well in advance of the au pair starting to ensure that both parties to the agreement know exactly where they stand. Although some au pairs stay for a year or more this is unusual and most stay for only a few months.

While there are several advantages to having an au pair (notably that they'll do things around the house as well as look after babies and young children) there are many disadvantages. Most of them are young (in their late teens); many have little English and so may be a negative influence on your child's language development; and some are frankly uninterested in children. If the au pair is given responsibility for your child but doesn't bother to amuse him, this can lead to your child feeling very frustrated and lonely. Don't think that just because an au pair is only with you for six months the effects she'll have on your child will be minimal. This need not necessarily be the case at all. Six months is a very long time in the life of a pre-school child.

Many children, if left for long periods with an au pair, become very attached to them and grieve when they go. Even this can be harmful, especially if the child is cared for by a succession of short-term mother substitutes. Continuity of mothering has been shown to be important to the development of a child and au pairs simply cannot provide such continuity. Ideally an au pair should be used not as a surrogate mother but as an older sister or friend. Used in this way an au pair can enrich a child's life and be of great help to the mother. *Related topics* Attachment; mother substitute.

Autism Between four and five children in every ten thousand are affected by this condition which is classified as a childhood psychosis. More boys than girls are affected.

Autistic children cannot seem to make sense of what they experience. They are unable to communicate normally in any way and become with-drawn and unable to form proper relationships. The first signs that some-thing is wrong may be a lack of awareness of what is going on around them, a feeding problem, a lack of attention, or overactive behaviour. The child is slow to talk and one in three such children don't learn to talk at all. Words may be repeated meaninglessly or used wrongly. Some children seem to enjoy pointless repetitive movements. Autistic children are likely to be less intelligent than average and about half of them are severely mentally retarded.

The cause of autism is not clear, though often there are associated problems such as epilepsy. There is often a history of a complication during pregnancy or childbirth.

The treatment is non-specific. An autistic child should ideally be taught by a skilled teacher with back-up from a team of experts including a child psychiatrist, psychologist, psychotherapist and social worker.

Though care and sheltered work may always be necessary, some children with this condition become less socially withdrawn as they grow older. *Useful organization* The National Society for Autistic Children.

Baby alarm A piece of electrical equipment (often battery operated) that amplifies your baby's noises and relays them to another room to be heard by yourself or the baby-sitter. Ideally sleeping babies should be near their mothers all the time in the first year or so of life, in which case a baby alarm is unnecessary. However, if you prefer your baby to sleep alone, it's far better to have an alarm so that he isn't left screaming for long before being attended to.

We feel that babies should never be left out of earshot anyway and certainly should never be left in the house with the baby alarm on while you go next door to neighbours. No noise could mean the baby has died in a fire, yet you'd be none the wiser.

Baby-bouncer A piece of equipment consisting of a canvas (or other type of material) sling with leg holes and safety straps, suspended from either a collapsible tubular metal frame or from a door frame by elastic. The idea is that a baby sits in the sling and bounces up and down by kicking with his feet on the ground. The height of the sling should be adjusted so that the baby's toes only just touch the ground, otherwise he may jar himself by hitting the ground with too much momentum once he starts bouncing enthusiastically.

Babies are usually ready to enjoy a bouncer by six months. Younger babies must be able to support their heads confidently in order to be safe in one.

As with any baby equipment, a bouncer should be examined carefully before use for signs of danger due to faulty parts or simply wear and tear. The baby must be securely fastened into it. If suspended in a doorway, make sure everyone in the house knows the baby is there so there is absolutely no chance of anyone accidentally closing the door on him.

There is no danger of a baby harming his joints, bones or muscles by bouncing like this: he'll only bounce if he likes it anyway. If a baby is left in the bouncer for longer than he wants, he'll probably learn to dislike being put into it because he'll associate it with being unhappy. If used wisely, a bouncer is a source of great pleasure for your baby. **Related topic** Bouncing chair.

Baby bath A baby bath is frequently listed as being an essential piece of equipment but can in fact easily be done without. Babies can be bathed in a plastic washing up bowl when they are small and in the family bath when they outgrow the bowl. However, some parents like having a plastic baby bath because its contours are more rounded than those of a bowl; it holds less water than the family bath does (even if filled only with a few inches of water); and either on the floor or in a special metal stand it is more comfortable for the mother, who can sit on the floor or on a chair and not have to lean over the family bath.

One disadvantage of baby baths is that they have to be lifted to empty them, and even a small amount of water is heavy. Some baby baths have a plug in the bottom through which the water can be drained into a bucket. Filling must be done either with another container or by using a bathtap and then lifting the baby bath out of the bath. Putting the baby bath inside the family bath makes filling and emptying easier, but means that the mother has to bend over the bath rather awkwardly.

It's sensible to put a rubber, non-slip mat in the bottom of a baby bath because small, wriggly, soapy babies are very slippery, however securely you may be holding them.

Baby care   There's much more to caring for a baby than simply feeding, clothing and washing him. Some people suggest that baby care starts before conception by ensuring that both prospective parents are in the best possible state of health. Certainly a pregnant woman should care for her unborn baby by taking advantage of all our society has to offer in the way of antenatal care.

The need for adequate care during childbirth goes without saying, as the day a baby is born is statistically the most dangerous day of its life. A growing number of experts believe that the safest way to care for a baby during normal labour is to allow the mother to assume whatever position she feels most comfortable in, instead of laying her down on her back.

Nowadays more and more babies are handled gently and considerately immediately after delivery, instead of being slapped on the feet and held upside down to start them breathing, then weighed, washed and labelled, even though they are screaming, before being handed to their mother. Obviously medical care for a baby takes utmost priority, but most babies can be introduced to our world in a welcoming way. Caring for a baby in such a way that he grows up secure, contented and trusting can start from the moment of birth.

Methods of baby care are not always based on 'science' or accurately-observed fact. They often correspond to fashion, or to current philosophies on life – orderly and regimented or lax and pleasure-seeking, for example. As a result, there are few real laws of baby care but many systems which may appeal or not to parents and their advisers.

There are lots of books and people to tell new parents how to take care of their baby but because there are also many different ways of bringing up children, it pays to compare ideas before embarking on any one. Very many parents will recount how ill at ease they were with their first baby, and how they learnt a little more with each one and enjoyed the last most of all. Very often this is because they suppressed their own instincts when it came to looking after their first, and simply did what they thought they ought to do, or what a book or expert told them was correct. Many such ideas are alien to parents who allow their natural 'animal' instincts to overrule, and their babies – when observed by anthropologists – seem to grow up happier, more secure and needing to cry far less (if at all) than babies reared in the conventional Western way.

Having a baby alters the life of his parents irrevocably and in these days of contraceptive choice it's sensible to have a baby only if both partners feel that they're going to enjoy looking after one and bringing it up. Parents content in their role are more likely to rear a child who feels that he is good and that life is good, simply because they'll take more pleasure in every aspect of baby and child care and their feelings will be transmitted to their child.

Caring for a baby can be a pleasure if one is not bound by rules and schedules, but it can sometimes be a chore for a mother who is lonely or depressed. There is very little help today for a mother with young children and she owes it to herself to try to alter her circumstances so as to make her life as pleasant as possible. For some women whose husbands are away for much of the day, this means finding congenial adult company by making friends or acquaintances. For others it may mean making time to read, sew or enjoy a hobby. Some women prefer not to be with their baby all day for various reasons and leave the baby with a minder of some sort so that they can work. If this means that they are happier when they do spend time with their baby, this may be the best solution, provided the minder is well chosen, loving and reliable. There is no doubt that babies need relative consistency in mothering for optimal healthy growth in mind and body.

The way a baby or a child is brought up affects the way he or she in turn will bring up his or her children. Similarly, older brothers and sisters will learn from the way their parents behave to a younger child. Specific actions will be forgotten, but general attitudes towards baby care will be remembered when it comes to caring for the next generation.

Babies grow up quickly, as any grandparent will agree. The period of absolute dependence is relatively short and it's all too easy to be so busy looking after a baby's physical needs that one misses out on playing with him, lying down with him and cuddling, tickling or talking, and just enjoying having him. A love affair with a baby is a wonderful experience and stands both parents and baby in good stead for the rest of their lives.

What makes baby care so controversial and anxiety-producing for many parents is the widely-held belief that one can do just about anything to babies and young children and they'll 'come out all right in the end'. It's true that babies are very adaptable and given average loving care will grow up to be mentally and emotionally balanced, and it's also true that in baby and child care there are few absolute 'rights' and 'wrongs', but there can be little doubt that a system which ensures the baby's happiness in the short term is just as valid as one which looks only to the long term. No caring parent would want a miserable child today against the promise of possible long term happiness. We feel sure that the two are inextricably interlinked. A child who is brought up to feel loved, happy and secure in his first five years will stand a better chance of future mental and physical health than one who is not.

Baby carriers Throughout history babies have been carried by their mothers. The modern baby sling or back-pack is no new-fangled invention: it's simply a modification of a very old idea. A sling is made of strong material and can be worn on the front, back or side. Some are only suitable for wearing on the side as they need the mother's arm to help support the baby. These are much less useful than the ones that can be worn at the front or back. With a young baby, it's better to wear a sling in front because if his head lolls back, it can easily be supported by the parent's hand. The more cleverly made slings have an adjustable inside pocket to hold the baby when he is very young so that he is neither buried too deep within the sling's outer pocket so that he can't see over the top, nor is he sitting so high in it that his neck and head are unsupported. As the baby grows, the inside pocket can be lowered in the sling and eventually dispensed with altogether.

Some slings come with a detachable headpiece which seems to be virtually useless in its supposed role of supporting the head. This is because as soon as the baby's head lolls back, the headpiece bends back too! Older babies are capable of supporting their own heads unless they are asleep, when their mother's hand can gently hold their head as she bends forwards.

Quite heavy babies and young children can be carried in a sling because the weight is taken on the shoulders and thence vertically down the spine. Carrying a baby in a sling makes life much easier for the mother on many occasions and babies (if used to a sling from early on) seem to enjoy the closeness of their mother's body, with its sounds, motion and warmth, and are much less likely to cry than if put in a pram or cot when they're not asleep. An older child will fit into a lightweight back-pack (often made with a metal alloy frame) and such back-packs are nowadays very easy to put on and take off, with a simple loop to go over the shoulder each side. Slings are slightly less easy to use but are lighter, less bulky and more adjustable in most cases.

Patterns are available from various sources if you want to make your own sling. Some mothers use a heavy or even waterproof material for the winter and a lightweight but strong cotton for the summer. Slings can be readily washed and some are made with a detachable dribble bib where the baby's head rests. Some slings don't leave enough room for the baby's thighs, while others haven't a good enough 'seat'. Have a good look at several slings before you buy one and remember that the more expensive ones often have more to offer. Waterproof macs are available to put over your baby when he's in a sling or carrier, or you could easily make one yourself. *Related topics* Swaddling; temperature.

Baby chair There are several chairs other than bouncing chairs and high chairs which are specially made for babies to sit in. One that is widely available is made of moulded plastic and the angle of the back is adjustable. There are often straps to go round the baby's waist and between his legs, so he can't fall out unless he is strong and mature enough to push the whole chair over with his legs while he is sitting in it. If he can do this, he is too old for this sort of chair and shouldn't sit in it again until he is old enough to sit on his own without a safety strap. It's probably safest to do as some manufacturers suggest and use a detachable safety harness too.

A baby chair may have a detachable tray and some are convertible to a high chair by attaching it to a stand.

There are baby chairs which can be attached safely to an ordinary adult chair so that the baby can sit at the table. If you are thinking of buying one, make absolutely sure that your particular chairs will be stable with such a device attached. *Related topic* Baby-bouncer.

Baby clinic Baby clinics (child health or well baby clinics) come in two forms: those run by the local health authority and those run by some family doctors (general practitioners). The health visitor who comes to see you and your new baby at home after you have had your baby will tell you about your local baby clinic. If your doctor runs his own clinic, you can choose to go either to his or to the nearest health authority one. We all pay for the baby clinic's services in our taxes and it's up to us to make the best use of them.

The baby clinic is there to check whether your child under five is developing normally, to answer your questions on baby care and child health and to give you any advice you may want. They also offer a routine immunization service and can refer your baby or child for specialist medical advice if necessary. If a health authority baby clinic doctor decides to refer your child for specialist advice, the doctor will contact your family doctor before an appointment is made to make sure that he is in agreement with the referral.

Children who are ill should not be taken to the baby clinic as it is there for *healthy* children and is actually sometimes known as the well baby clinic. If your child is unwell you should consult your family doctor, not go to the clinic.

When you visit the baby clinic for the first time, the receptionist (or the health visitor or clinic nurse) will take all your baby's details and ask about your pregnancy and birth. Of course, your health visitor may already have all these details, having obtained them when you were at home. Your baby's record card will remain at the clinic until he is at school. If you move out of the area, your new clinic will write off for the record card.

Your baby will be weighed if necessary or anyway if you would like it and then you can see the health visitors. This is the time to bring up any queries you have about your baby's development or health.

At regular intervals your baby or young child will be seen by the clinic doctor for a routine developmental check. However, if there is anything you want to discuss with the doctor, you don't need to wait until it is time for a routine check up. The developmental examinations are usually very thorough and include a physical examination besides questions and observations of the baby's hearing and eyesight, coordination and fine movements, vocalization and social ability.

Immunization courses are recorded on a card for you to keep.

You may go to the baby clinic as often as you like and can also phone the health visitor for advice during non-clinic hours.

Baby foods Ideally, breast milk should be the only food your baby receives for the first four to six months. Modified cows' milk and other milks are available, usually as dried milk, for babies who aren't breast-fed.

When starting solids, give your baby only one new food at a time and wait a couple of days before introducing another. This is so that you can spot the culprit if any one food is going to make him sick or give him tummy ache, diarrhoea, or a rash, and so avoid it for a few weeks.

As far as possible don't give him food which is different from what your family eats, or he may have trouble when he has to give up his 'baby food'. Babies enjoy a wide variety of food and as long as they have the security of their familiar milk, they'll gradually eat more and more of what everyone else at home eats. It is said that commercial baby foods are easier for mothers but in practice they are expensive and unnecessary. Nothing could be easier than giving a little of the food you are eating to the baby, and there is no reason to give your baby foods that you normally wouldn't have for the rest of the family.

Babies – like everyone else – benefit from a diet high in dietary fibre (roughage) which means using unrefined cereal (whole grains, 100% wholemeal flour and wholemeal flour products such as wholemeal bread), peeling and cooking fruits and vegetables as little as possible and choosing brown rice and wholemeal pasta. Unfortunately, many commercial companies use refined flour for their baby cereal products though there is no good reason for this. Give your baby cereal, by all means, but try mashed up Weetabix, well-cooked porridge made from whole oats or mashed up wholemeal bread, rather than pappy, refined cereal which has been shown to pave the way to a variety of health disorders when eaten over a long period. Sieving fruit and vegetables removes much of their fibre, so liquidize or mash instead. Don't be alarmed when you see the fibrous residue of fruit and vegetables in your baby's nappy – this is what should happen.

It's sensible to avoid commercially prepared foods which contain additives in the form of colourings, flavourings, emulsifiers, stabilizers, preservatives and so on. Though these additives are all 'permitted' some have not been adequately tested as far as side-effects go, and some are banned in other countries. Anyway, the effects of these additives are not always known in growing children. If you prepare your own food you know exactly what goes into it. Some commercial baby foods are advertised as 'gluten free' but this is of no advantage to the average healthy baby.

The order in which you give new foods is unimportant. A six-month-old baby can digest many foods but may have individual likes and dislikes. Some babies find it hard to digest egg white, for example.

Avoid adding sugar and salt to your baby's food. Sugar provides 'empty' calories with no other food value and can cause dental decay. Many commercial baby foods are very sweet. Salt can cause illness in a young baby, especially if too much is added, not enough fluids are given, and the baby also gets diarrhoea or a fever, leading to dehydration. Babies' taste buds don't need the flavourings many adults are accustomed to, so don't sweeten or salt their food to *your* taste.

Baby foods can be given as 'finger foods' such as a wholemeal rusk or a scrubbed carrot to chew on, but don't leave your baby alone when eating these in case a small piece breaks off and makes him choke. Babies of four to six months need their food sieved, liquidized or mashed, by itself or with milk or water, while older babies like gradually more lumpy food until they are eating normal family consistency food.

While you should use hygienic precautions such as washing your hands when preparing your baby's food, there's no need to sterilize cooking pans, bowls or cutlery. It is most important to store food in a cool place, to reheat cooked food thoroughly and to cook poultry well. Gastroenteritis, especially in a bottle-fed baby, can be dangerous and special care should be taken when preparing food on holiday abroad.

As your baby eats more and more foods other than milk, give him extra drinks of water or well-diluted fruit juice to allay his thirst, as well as his breast or bottle feeds. Beware of fruit squashes which contain little, if any, fruit juice but do contain sugar or other sweeteners, flavourings, colourings and other additives. If you dilute real fruit juice with lots of water, you'll find it doesn't cost very much. **Related topics** Blender; cooking for children; feeding equipment; food; rusk; spoon-feeding; vitamins.

Baby-sitters Common sense and the law dictate that a baby or young child should not be left alone without a responsible person to take care of him. If both parents want to go out at the same time and there is no one left to look after their baby or children, they'll have to find a suitable baby-sitter. The ideal person is someone who is known and liked by the child, besides being trustworthy and able to cope in an emergency. Baby-sitters are frequently used in the evenings and this may mean that the child will either be put to bed by the sitter or may wake up while she (or he) is there. Babies and young children nearly always prefer their parents to other adults when they are tired, and are likely to object if a stranger appears. If at all possible, let your baby-sitter meet your child beforehand so that when the evening comes round, he or she won't be completely strange. Many parents try to make sure that babies and young children are asleep before they leave home, which makes their departure easier for everyone. It's doubly important then for the child to know the sitter, just in case he wakes up and is afraid.

Make sure your sitter has the phone number or address of the place you are going to, together with your doctor's phone number just in case of an accident. Let him or her know roughly what time you intend coming home and, if the sitter has no transport, arrange to give a lift home afterwards if possible.

Baby-sitting circles or clubs have been formed in some areas and members sit for each other's children or you can advertise for a baby-sitter, in which case you should find out what the going local rate for payment is.

Good bets for sitting are teenagers who have studying to do in the evenings and don't mind where they do it as long as they are comfortable, or nurses from the local hospital. Remember not to be too late back for them. In cities there are baby-sitting agencies.

The pressure will be on you as soon as your baby is born to leave him behind and go out and enjoy yourself. Don't be brainwashed into believing that you can't enjoy yourself with your baby there too. It's far less of a worry to take a baby who doesn't sleep through the evening along with you if you are going to a friend's house, as you can feed him as soon as he wakes if he is with you, and he can sleep in a carrycot or on your lap. It's possible to leave a bottle of expressed breast milk for a sitter to give if you *have* to go out alone, but you'll probably have to express milk after each feed for a couple of days in order to get enough. The bottle-fed baby can be more easily left behind. Since babies don't understand that your absence is temporary, it's not surprising that some are inconsolable with a baby-sitter.

Do tell your sitter what to do with your child in the way of changing nappies, reading stories, bedtime routines, drinks and so on. If the child wakes and is inconsolable without you, it is kindest for the sitter to contact you and for you to come home, both for the baby's sake and for the sitter's. *Related topic* Leaving a baby.

Baby talk A baby spends a lot of time watching other people move their mouths at the same time as making sounds. He experiments with similar movements and is delighted to find himself making sounds such as 'oooh oooh'. He'll progress to a variety of sounds such as 'awah' and 'ba' and can be greatly encouraged by your pleased response to his vocalization. As he grows older, he is continually listening to your voice and the pattern it makes. He'll hear the different tones of voice you use at different times and the different facial expressions that go with them. Around six months or so he'll start making repetitive sounds such as 'da-da'. This babbling is at first meaningless but at around a year, he'll gradually start to use words with meaning.

Babies vary greatly in the speed at which they learn new words. However, speech itself is secondary in importance to understanding what words mean. Without understanding, speech is meaningless. As the baby learns to associate sounds with objects ('da-da' for his father, for instance), he'll store up the information in his mind so that one day when you mention 'da-da', his eyes will light up and he'll look round for his father. Not only can he name his father when he sees him, but he can also conjure him up in his imagination when he's not there.

Totally deaf babies progress as far as the babbling stage but no further unless special teaching techniques are used.

There's been some controversy over whether parents should talk to their babies in 'baby talk' or whether they should always speak as they would to an adult. However, parents the world over talk to babies with a certain tone of voice, looking the baby closely in the eye as they do so, and can be seen to carry on a 'conversation' with their baby by making a sound, smiling, moving the head in a certain way and waiting for the baby to respond with a sound and – usually – a delighted smile. The baby's vocalization in turn produces a response in the parent. The baby may imitate the parent or vice versa. This sort of behaviour can be seen even in very young babies. *Related topic* Languages.

Baby walker A metal frame with legs on wheels. A sling of canvas or plastic is suspended from the frame. The baby has the sling between his legs so that when he is tired or stumbles, he's automatically supported and can hold on to the metal frame as he pushes it along with his feet on the floor. A baby-walker gives the baby confidence on his feet and is usually much enjoyed because it allows him to be mobile far sooner than he would otherwise be. Some babies get so good at it that they can go quite fast. As they become more mobile you'll have to look out for new dangers that were previously out of his reach. It is a bulky piece of equipment and one that will only be used for a few months. For both of these reasons many parents don't bother to buy one.

Babies who can walk often like to push a large toy on wheels with a handle. A baby who is only just learning to walk won't like such a push-along because of the feeling of insecurity it gives him as it starts moving – he'll be unable to move his feet fast enough to keep up with it. Once he gets the hang of walking, though, a pusher toy like this gives him something to hold on to and helps him travel further than he otherwise might.

The best way of helping a baby to learn to walk is to spend time encouraging him and holding his hands. Equipment, however good, can only be of secondary value.

It has been suggested that baby-walkers might retard the rate at which a baby learns to walk on his own but as far as we know there is no evidence for this and even if it were true the child is mobile sooner and gets so much pleasure from this that it would be unreasonable to prohibit baby-walkers on these grounds. *Related topics* Baby equipment; walking.

Back Back problems are uncommon today in young children, but rarely there may be a backwards curve (hump back) which is called a kyphosis, or a sideways curve, called a scoliosis.

The main problem that worries parents of young children is whether encouraging their baby to sit up and to walk early might damage his back. There is no evidence that either of these things is harmful and certainly baby slings and baby buggies will do no harm. Women have been carrying babies around in soft-backed pouches of cloth for thousands of years and no harm seems to have been done. As soon as your baby wants to sit up, let him. Similarly, baby-bouncers and walkers can do no harm to a child's back, assuming that he's ready to go in them anyway. *Related topic* Sitting up.

Balanitis An inflammation of the end of the penis occurring mainly in uncircumcised boys who have material trapped under their foreskins. Rarely the inflammation can be so bad that the foreskin can't be pulled back at all, and there may be a discharge. The only treatment needed is to improve personal hygiene (seeing that the foreskin is pulled back as far as it will easily go and then washed thoroughly and dried).

If there are repeated infections under the foreskin your doctor may suggest that the boy be circumcised to prevent further trouble but an operation is not usually necessary. A tight foreskin is not a sufficient reason for doing a circumcision. *Related topics* Circumcision; smegma.

Baldness Everyone accepts that many newborn babies have very little hair but once it has grown, its disappearance – either totally or in patches – is worrying and looks unpleasant.

By far the commonest cause of hair loss in young children is ringworm but some children pull out hair as a nervous tic or habit. Both these conditions produce patchy hair loss. Hair loss caused by ringworm has a characteristic appearance. There are bald patches and the skin is pink and scaly with stubbly hairs. The diagnosis, which can only be made with certainty by a doctor, involves looking at the area under illumination with an ultraviolet lamp. The hair stumps then fluoresce a greenish-blue. Ringworm spores can also be seen under a microscope. The condition is easily treated with the drug griseofulvin.

Young babies, especially if left alone a lot, may rub their scalps against the bedclothes and produce quite large bald patches. These look unpleasant but can often be prevented by never leaving your baby to cry for long periods in his cot.

Your baby can also get a bald patch simply by sitting in a fabric baby bouncing chair. Don't worry about this though, it soon grows back.

Bandaging Bandages are used for keeping dressings in place; for giving support to an injured part of the body; and to apply pressure over dressings so as to stop bleeding. In general, those for covering dressings are lightweight and made of gauze and those for supporting muscles or joints are elasticated and firm.

When applying a bandage over a wound it should be put on just firmly enough to keep the dressing in place unless there is also considerable bleeding, in which case it can be applied more firmly. However, do remember to keep an eye on the bandaged part if you have applied the bandage very firmly because any changes in colour of parts distant to the bandaged area mean you've put it on too tightly, and should undo it and put it on less tightly.

An elasticated support bandage should be applied firmly but again, any tingling, pins and needles or skin colour changes indicate that the bandage is too tight. Elastic bandages need careful instruction before use because it is easy to put them on seemingly well only to find that after a few minutes of moving the part they have fallen off or become so loose as to be useless. Your doctor or district nurse will show you how to apply a bandage properly if necessary.

Bandages are not used nearly as often as they were. Adhesive strapping and self-adhesive dressings have replaced old-fashioned dressings and bandages and tubular gauze bandages put on with a special applicator are increasingly used instead of crêpe bandages. If your child breaks a limb he may well come across another sort of bandage – the plaster of Paris bandage. This is made of muslin impregnated with plaster of Paris which when soaked in water becomes ready to apply to an injured part of the body. Once dry (within a few minutes) the bandage sets hard and supports the broken bones while they heal. *Useful organization* The British Red Cross Society.

Baptism In the Church of England a child can be baptized at any age but the ceremony is commonly performed on babies. The baby is welcomed into the church family and the parents and godparents make promises on his behalf that he will set aside evil, believe and trust in God, and serve him. The baby is named after these promises have been made and the sign of the cross is made with water on his forehead.

It's customary for a boy to have two godfathers and one godmother and for a girl to have two godmothers and one godfather. Parents can act as godparents if they wish. Godparents have no statutory duties but some parents discuss the possibility of their acting as guardians if anything should happen to the parents. Some children have a special relationship with their godparents all their lives.

Some Christians choose to have their baby dedicated to God instead of baptized, choosing to leave the choice of baptism to the child himself when he is able to understand the promises and to make them for himself, rather than have them made for him.

Before being confirmed into the Roman Catholic Church or Church of England, it is necessary to have been baptized. However, if a person hasn't been baptized as a baby there is no reason not to be confirmed as a teenager or an adult, because one can be baptized at any time. *Related topics* Development – spiritual; godparent; religion.

Bare feet It is generally agreed by doctors and chiropodists that it is healthier for a child's feet to be bare most of the time than to be encased in shoes. A baby's feet certainly need no shoes until he is walking out of doors.

Shoes are only really necessary for young children to protect their feet when walking on rough or dirty ground or when out of doors in our cold, wet climate. Were it not for this and the fact that parents like to see their children in shoes, children could safely and happily go about without shoes altogether. Bare feet are safer than socked feet because they are less slippery.

However, if you'd rather your child wore something on his feet to keep them warm while playing around the house, socks made of natural fibres are a good second best to bare feet.

If your child or any other member of the family has a plantar wart (verruca) or ringworm (athlete's foot) no one should go around barefoot until it is healed. *Related topic* Shoes.

BCG vaccination A vaccination against tuberculosis (TB) which is offered to children in their early teens if they are found not to have any natural immunity to TB (as judged by the results of a simple skin test). It is only ever given routinely to young children if they come from areas of the world where TB is still common. If there is active TB in the family newborn babies should be vaccinated. A special BCG vaccine with an isoniazid-resistant strain of TB bacteria is used if a baby or his breast-feeding mother is taking the drug isoniazid.

Bedding

Mattress The first types of mattress necessary for your baby depend on what he is sleeping in. A *pram* is well-insulated against the cold and may also have a padded base, so an expensive, thick mattress is not essential, especially if the pram is well sprung. A *carrycot*, however, is much colder to sleep in as the sides and base are so thin. Also the ride in most models of carrycot and transporter is rough. The mattress should therefore be a thick, comfortable one, to withstand the cold and the jolts. A thick mattress is a necessity if the baby is ever put to sleep in a carrycot placed on the ground, as the cold can strike upwards. Similarly, if a baby is allowed to sleep in a *Moses' basket* on the floor, a thick mattress will prevent him from getting too cold, especially if his clothes and bedding are wet. *Cradles* vary in the thickness of their walls and base and because a baby is likely to spend a fair amount of time there, the mattress should be thick and comfortable. The popular 'cocoons' have only a thin mattress built in and if he is to be placed on the ground, the baby should be well insulated with several layers of blanket. There is no room inside for a thick mattress. It seems surprising that a baby could need three mattresses, but if you plan to use a carrycot (perhaps when you use the car), basket or cocoon, a pram and also a cradle, then three mattresses will save you having to switch bedding around. If you plan to economize by switching bedding, make sure before you buy the baby's carrycot, pram and cradle that they will take the same sized mattress. If you make your own mattress, don't make it soft because a baby could theoretically asphyxiate himself if his face was turned towards the mattress and his nose and mouth were blocked.

Cot mattresses should be firm, comfortable and provide insulation. They are often sprung and may come with a waterproof covering. Mattresses for your child's *bed* come in many prices depending on their quality and construction. Your individual preference as to the degree of firmness, whether or not it has a sprung edge, and the type of springs it has will help determine your choice.

Waterproof sheet This is essential to protect the mattress (unless what your child is sleeping in has a waterproof cover of its own) for any child still likely to wet or dirty his nappy at night. Plastic pants or disposable nappies often leak, and the urine or bowel motion not only stains but also makes the mattress smell unpleasant. Waterproof sheets are easiest to put on and to keep smooth if they are fitted with elastic at the corners. However, a sheet of polythene or some other soft plastic can be tucked in just as you would use a sheet. Fitted waterproof sheets are made in all sizes. A relatively cheap waterproof sheet with ties to pass under the mattress is available for a bed. Waterproof sheets need washing and drying well and you'll find it easier if you have at least one spare one. There is no need to wash them each time they are wetted; a wipe down with a nappy or some kitchen or toilet paper will usually suffice.

Underblanket This is not essential but a baby is more comfortable – and warmer – with an underblanket between the bottom sheet and the waterproof sheet, especially if the bottom sheet is wet. However, having an underblanket means there is more washing should the bedding get wet.

Sheets Bottom sheets are available in plain or fitted versions. The fitted ones are preferable as they don't ruck up, but they are more expensive. They come in all sizes. A top sheet is unnecessary for a baby as he can be wrapped in a sheet, shawl or blanket and placed directly on the bottom sheet, then covered with one or more blankets. Sheets for cradles, carrycots, prams, etc. can be made from old full-size sheets, cut down to size. The material for sheets is a matter of individual preference. Ordinary smooth cotton needs ironing to look attractive, but is very comfortable. 'Polycotton' is practical and also comfortable. Nylon is slippery and not very warm unless it is brushed, and a child may become sweaty as the nylon tends not to let water evaporate through it. Perhaps the best is flannelette (cotton), which needn't be ironed. Cheaper, synthetic versions of flannelette are widely available. Don't necessarily buy cot sheets *and* pram sheets: cot sheets doubled can be used in a pram and the same goes for blankets.

Blankets These can be made of whatever you like. Cellular blankets are light and warm. White cotton cellular blankets last well, feel pleasant and can be laundered with the nappies. Fluffy blankets should be edged with sateen to prevent tickling of the baby's face. How many blankets you put on your baby depends on the room temperature and the draughts in the room. The same number of blankets you have on your bed and then one more is a good guide to start with, but check by putting your hand under the bedclothes to see how warm your baby feels after a while. Don't go by his hands as they are a poor guide to body warmth.

Duvets These were popular for a time but have lost favour now for babies because parents worry that a baby might accidentally be smothered under one. They are certainly quite suitable for children over the age of two and make bedmaking much easier.

Quilts/eiderdowns These add extra warmth but are not essential: extra blankets will do just as well.

Pillows These are available in all sizes and can be made of various materials, pure down being the softest and most expensive. Pillows with synthetic fillings may be washable and are suitable for allergic children who are sensitive to feathers. A pillow is unnecessary for a baby and there is a theoretical risk that he might be smothered by one, so it's sensible not to have one.

Sheepskin This is very warm and comfortable and doubles as a bottom sheet/underblanket/waterproof sheet. It's also very suitable as a buggy lining.

Bed – keeping child in

Many is the toddler or older child who has climbed out of his cot or bed and either come downstairs to be with his parents in the evening or gone into their bedroom at night. Few young children like to be left alone and their loneliness, together with their anger at their mother or father for having put them to bed and, perhaps, a fear of the dark, make it imperative to them that they should escape from the confines of their bed and bedroom and find someone to be with. Babies in particular prefer to be with or near someone when they go to sleep and when they wake up. However, as they can't get out of their cots, keeping them there is no problem if the parents are content to let them scream! Many children are afraid of the dark, especially if they sleep in a room alone, and their vivid imaginations conjure up all sorts of ghosts, wolves, witches, etc. A dim light by the bed, the landing light left on, the bedroom door open and a teddy bear to cuddle are poor substitutes to the child who is lonely or afraid and wants human contact and company.

Another reason why children escape from their beds is that they are not tired because they have been sent to bed too early. Because they are not ready to sleep, they lie awake and get bored unless they are mature and motivated enough to play or read alone. Though our society expects children to sleep a lot longer than their parents do, some children need relatively little sleep, and a few need less than their parents at night, especially if they have a sleep during the day. It may seem a good idea to put the children to bed early so that you can spend some time together or get on with whatever you want to do, but keeping a child in bed against his will can make him at best resigned and lonely and at worst angry and afraid.

If a child keeps getting out of bed, consider whether it is because he is lonely, not tired, bored, or afraid and, if necessary, make his bedtime later or let him sleep downstairs with you until you go to bed. Also it's worth considering whether – if you have other children – he could share a bedroom or even a bed with another child. This can work well. When several members of the family sleep near each other, there is no problem keeping the young child in bed because that is where he will want to be – with the others.

If you have decided that your child needs to go to bed at a certain time, but he won't stay in bed, try lying down with him to read him a story, then putting the light out and cuddling him until he falls asleep. If he isn't used to this, it'll take several days or more for him to get used to the new idea, but he'll almost certainly like it. The disadvantage is that it may be half an hour or so before you can slip away and you may go to sleep yourself. The advantages are that you'll have a chance to relax physically and that your child will undoubtedly feel more secure and loved. It's also a chance to enjoy being close to your child. *Related topics* Bed sharing; bedtime; sleep.

Bed – keeping a child in when ill

As any adult knows, when you're feeling really unwell, bed or, at any rate, somewhere to lie down, is the most attractive place to be. There may come a time when the only thing you can do is to lie down and rest because you're feeling too weak and ill to be up. Whether or not lying down before it becomes essential helps shorten the illness or prevents it from worsening isn't clear, but it's certainly more pleasant to give in and rest rather than to struggle on. Children, especially young ones, usually flop when they feel unwell. They aren't concerned with carrying on running the house or earning a living, and so find it easier to respond to what their bodies are telling them. If your child is ill enough to want to lie down and you don't know what's the matter with him, ask your doctor's advice.

It doesn't matter where your child lies down, though most children, unless they are very ill, want to be near their parents, so the kitchen or sitting room is probably best. If there's room in the kitchen, a mattress or several firm chair cushions on the floor with a sheet folded over to form a top and bottom layer and some blankets on top will suffice. If there's no room, you could try making up a 'bed' like this just outside the kitchen door in the hall, providing it's draught free. The sitting room is much easier as a 'bed' can be made on the sofa or on the floor.

The older child may be quite happy to retire to his bed when he's ill and may enjoy the peace of his bedroom, especially if he has a headache with a fever.

As for getting out of bed to go to the lavatory or for meals or play, be guided by your child. The one who is so ill that he shouldn't get up because he is too weak will prefer to stay in bed anyway. A potty by the bed can be very useful in this case. If you get your child out of bed for a bath, then be sure to stay with him all the time as he may be too weak to climb in and out of the bath, and a hot bath may make an unwell child feel faint.

A child too ill to have a bath can be freshened up in bed if necessary, putting a towel underneath him while washing him. Be careful not to let him get cold. The sickroom should be kept warm (about 65°F, 18°C) but not hot, as this will encourage further fluid loss through sweating excessively. Cleaning his teeth can be done in bed and will make his mouth feel more pleasant.

You can warm a child by putting on more clothes, or bedding, giving him hot drinks and food, a hot water bottle (suitably protected and well stoppered to prevent burning), or by warming the room. If your child has a temperature, cool him if necessary by sponging him with lukewarm water, giving him aspirin in the recommended dose, removing clothing and bedding, and cooling the room. *Related topics* Illness; invalidism.

Bedroom sharing In some societies there is only one bedroom for the whole family, and that is how it used to be in this country too. Today, bedroom sharing is very much a matter of personal preference within the family and is obviously also affected by the number and size of bedrooms in the house. Many parents in our society keep a baby in a cot or in their own bed in their bedroom for much of the first year or so, if only because they can keep an eye on him better and because the mother doesn't have to go so far to feed him at night.

If your children share a bedroom and are relatively near each other in age, it's easier to put both to bed at the same time to avoid any jealousy and to avoid waking up the sleeping child.

One disadvantage of bedroom sharing is that if one of the children – usually the younger one – wakes at night, he may wake the other. This can also happen even if the children are in separate rooms.

Though older children may like to have a room of their own, the under-fives are not usually concerned about privacy or having their own territory, so there is no real benefit to giving each one his own bedroom. As for letting a boy and girl share a room, it doesn't matter at all at this age.

The under-fives are not usually concerned with how tidy their bedroom is and so it won't matter if one child makes more mess with his clothes and toys than the other. It's later, and especially in the teenage years, that quarrels over the room's appearance arise if the two children have different temperaments and notions of tidiness.

Even a small bedroom can be shared if bunk-beds are used. If you have two children and two available bedrooms, you might like to let them share a bedroom and use the other as a playroom.
Related topics Bed sharing; bedtime.

Beds Choose your child's first bed as carefully as you would your own. The priority when buying a bed is comfort. It's difficult for an adult to test a bed for a child because of the weight difference, but a very firm bed is unlikely to be necessary. Individual preference and what you can afford will determine whether you choose an ordinary sprung mattress, one with pocketed springs or a foam one. Similarly, there are many sorts of bed base, including a wooden slatted one, a sprung edge divan, a firm edge divan and a raised platform built on the floor.

You might like to consider having a rail down the side of the top half of the bed for a young child. This may make the child who has come from a cot feel more secure and will certainly help to stop him falling out.

Bunk-beds are a way of saving space and are enjoyed by many children, particularly older ones. However, a restless child can easily disturb the sleep of the other child. Fitted bottom sheets and duvets are the easiest sort of bedding for bunks. Some sort of rail is essential if a young child is to sleep in the top bunk.

Beds which slide under each other when one is not in use, beds built at right angles to each other and beds with storage space built in underneath are available.

Unless a child is allowed to jump on his bed, the bed is unlikely to need to be replaced during his childhood, so it's sensible to buy a full size bed straight away, even for a toddler just out of his cot.

Bed sharing Babies and young children like to sleep with their parents just as any other baby mammals do and it's certainly less hassle for the breast-feeding mother if she can feed her baby in bed at night rather than having to get out of bed to do it. The idea that babies sharing their parents' bed are in danger of suffocating is only true if one parent is drunk, drugged or very obese.

Most parents take their babies and young children into bed with them from time to time and some do so regularly. Many of them don't tell anyone because they feel it may be deemed improper or that it might even be thought a sign of poor parenting. We feel that on the contrary, done wisely, it is a sign of sensitive parenting. Many babies and young children are not ready for a bed of their own, let alone a room of their own as soon as many adults would like them to be. We in the Western world are most unusual in banning our babies and children from our beds and historically it is a very new development in human behaviour.

The pleasures of cuddling up to a baby at night or simply lying next to him are difficult to beat. Lots of breast-feeding mothers quickly get used to feeding their babies lying down in the dark and simply roll over with the baby on their tummy to change breasts. In the early weeks you may have to sit up in bed to hold the baby upright to 'wind' him or to change a nappy, but it's possible to sit a baby up for a minute or two while lying down and if you're clever with the baby's nappies there's no need for a change at night (unless the skin is sore). Bed sharing and easy night breast-feeding go hand in hand and it's possible to learn to doze through feeds so that however often the baby wakes, you aren't exhausted the next day.

Young children vary as to the age at which they are ready to leave their parents' bed. The time will come, though, when a child prefers his own bed. There is no set age for this: it will depend on the family circumstances, the personality of the child and the feelings of all concerned. If your baby is accustomed to sleeping in your bed from birth onwards, he'll naturally think of your bed as his bed too. It's unfair to expect him to make the change to a bed of his own quickly: he's unlikely to choose to leave your bed for a long time to come. If you're not prepared to let him share your bed for as long as he wants to (which may easily be for a couple of years or more), then make the changeover as easy and happy as you can for him. Be prepared for some natural resistance to the idea and accustom him to his new sleeping arrangements gently. If there is an older brother or sister the child may be happy to decamp to their bed one day. It's been noticed that children who share a bed often seem to be particularly friendly and even to argue less during the day. It's important to make sure that the younger child can't fall out of bed.

If you decide to let your baby share your bed until he is old enough to be happy to sleep separately or with a brother or sister, your bed must be large enough for each person to sleep well. Some parents have built a 'sleeping platform' in their bedroom and put mattresses and bedding on top so as to get a wide enough bed. Others put a double bed at right angles to its original direction and then put a single bed along the new base of the bed. The crack between the beds surprisingly is not uncomfortable, and the legs of the two beds can be tied together. Yet others put a cot or a single bed alongside the double bed and just slide the baby into bed with them (or slide into the baby's bed) when necessary. Large conventional beds can be bought but are expensive.

If parents find that their sexual relationship is hampered unacceptably by having a baby in bed, and they can find no ways round the problem such as making love in another place, then it may be best for him to have his own bed but to come into his parents' bed if he wakes during the night. Usually, making love with a baby asleep in the bed is not a problem. You can always keep a cot in your bedroom near the bed and put the baby into it when making love and then bring the baby back in afterwards or when he wakes.

Parents who try having their baby or young child in their bed to solve problems such as night waking may find that they never really get used to sharing their bed. Similarly, the baby or child may react by being excited or unsettled, or may spend much of the night kicking. Children like familiarity and don't much like chopping and changing. If you find that your family plays 'musical beds' at night, pause to reconsider whether you aren't making problems for yourselves by expecting your children to start off the night in a bed that they obviously aren't going to end up in.

Some children are such restless sleepers that sharing a bed with them is most uncomfortable. Bed sharing is not for every family, but more and more families are discovering and enjoying it. **Related topics** Bedroom sharing; bedtime.

Bedtime Of all the topics we get letters on and hear most anxious comments about from parents, sleeping comes very near the top of the list. Many of these problems are self-made and are therefore easily remedied.

Babies usually have fairly irregular sleeping habits at first and the easiest way to cope is simply to let them go to sleep in your arms after a feed, then to put them somewhere warm and safe to sleep if you don't want to hold them. Some mothers lie down with their babies on their bed, breast-feed them until they go to sleep, then creep away. If your baby sleeps with you,

you can join him in bed once he's asleep. Otherwise, you can transfer him to his cot when he's sound asleep. Some babies are happy to be put into their cot when they're sleepy and well-fed, but others wake up and cry at the sight of the cot, probably because they associate their cot with the absence of their mother. Such babies need the reassurance that they won't be left alone. You could put the cot in the room where you'll be, or you could let your baby sleep on the sofa next to you. *Whatever you do, don't leave an unhappy baby before he has gone to sleep.* Most babies are happiest to go to sleep in their mother's arms.

As your baby passes the six-month mark, you may see some sort of sleep pattern emerging. Your baby may have one or more periods of sleep (or catnaps) during the day, then be ready for a longer period of sleep starting some time in the evening. To encourage this, start making bedtime a recognizable part of the day. You could give him a bath now and change his clothes, for instance. Afterwards, a time of play, followed by feeding, should get him off to sleep happily. Obviously this only works if he's tired. Nothing will induce a baby who isn't sleepy to go to sleep!

Some one- to five-year-olds are happy to lie down and go to sleep by themselves after the bedtime ritual, while others are clearly not happy to be left alone and prefer their mother (or father) to stay with them until they drift off to sleep. Many a mother finds that a breast-feed is a sure way of getting a child off to sleep happily and peacefully. Often a child will show no interest in the breast at all during the day but will want it at night. This is one excellent reason for carrying on for months or even years with breast-feeding, because it's such a good way of helping a child to go to sleep at night. Whether or not you feed your child, you may enjoy lying down in bed next to him as he goes off to sleep.

You'll probably get used to your child's sleep requirements. The number of hours sleep needed by different children varies enormously, as does the number of times they wake each night. Comparing your child with others will teach you nothing about what he needs but will just make you disgruntled, especially if he seems to need less sleep than everybody else's child or others that you've had. Getting your child to bed in the evening in order to give you some time alone inevitably means in this case that the child will wake up a long time before you do in the morning. It's unlikely that a very young child will be content to play quietly on his own for long in the morning, so you will soon feel very tired and sorry for yourself if you allow this to go on. Even if you let your child come into your bed in the morning, he'll have you properly awake fairly soon. Some parents find that by discouraging daytime naps, their child sleeps better at night, especially if the nap usually happens late in the afternoon. Others find that lots of fresh air and exercise make a child sleep better. Others simply allow their children to stay up until they are really tired, which gives the parents a longer sleep overall.

Many children feel happy and secure with a regular bedtime ritual and look forward to it as a time when they get uninterrupted attention from one or both parents. If a child is accustomed to look forward to bedtime for these reasons, he'll be much more positive towards going to bed than if he thinks he's going to be lonely and upset there. Never ever use bed as a threat to a child – you'll make him resentful about going to bed. His bed should be thought of as an attractive haven of comfort, warmth and rest. If he goes to bed happy, evening after evening, as a young child, you're unlikely to have problems with bedtime when he's older.

Some young children, especially if they have brothers and sisters, love to put off bedtime by playing about and end up getting more and more excited. If you are keen for your child to go to bed, be firm. Most four- or five-year-olds understand rules and in fact prefer it if you tell them what you expect at bedtime. If you let your child stay up late when you know he's got to get up in the morning to go to play-group, for example, you're doing him a disfavour because he'll be tired and cross the next day. Try to arrange the day so that there's plenty of time for stories, games, or whatever it is that your child likes to do before bed. It's up to us as parents to work out how much sleep our children need and to try to see that they get it. *Related topics* Bed – keeping child in; bed sharing; bed-wetting; bedroom sharing; rituals; sleep; sleep problems.

Bed-wetting Even after a child is potty trained during the day he may still wet the bed at night for a variety of reasons. Usually, it's because a full bladder is simply not a strong enough stimulus to wake him once he's asleep. If he does wake, he may be too tired and sleepy to cry out for his mother, or he may be too young to cope with getting out of bed and on to a potty by himself. If there's any chance of bed-wetting, most mothers keep their children in a nappy at night to save themselves the work of washing sheets and an underblanket and to save their child the unpleasant feeling of being in wet bed linen that will inevitably become cold. It may also save the parents from being woken up as a cold, wet child is highly likely to cry! A potty by the bed is some incentive to get out of bed because it's much preferable in a child's eyes to finding his way down a dark landing to the lavatory. However, it only works if the child has no nappy on. A nappy is a straightforward invitation to wee in bed. A soft light from a twenty-watt bulb left on in the child's room at night may encourage him to use the potty.

While most children become dry at night (with only occasional accidents) when they are two or three, others take very much longer, especially if they are heavy sleepers. One in two two-year-olds is wet at night, one in four three-year-olds, one in ten five-year-olds, and one in twenty eleven-year-olds. Some children become dry suddenly, while others have gradually more and more dry nights. All children become dry eventually, unless there is some underlying medical problem (see below).

Bed-wetting occurs regardless of intelligence but may begin or happen more often if the child is emotionally upset. Parental rows, jealousy of a new baby, anxiety over going to play-group, moving house or fear of the dark can all spark off bed-wetting in a previously dry child. Reassurance and removal of the stress, if possible, should ease the problem in time. Telling a child off for wetting the bed *never* helps, though it would be silly to pretend that you wouldn't be pleased if he were dry. What you do about bed-wetting depends on whether your child has ever been dry at night. If he hasn't, the odds are in a young child that he hasn't reached the necessary level of developmental maturity of the nerves and muscles operating his bladder to keep himself dry at night. Some anxious doctors recommend that if a four-year-old isn't yet dry at night, he should be checked over in case he has some medical condition such as diabetes, a hidden infection of the urine, or a structural abnormality of the urinary system. These conditions usually cause trouble in the day, such as an increased need to urinate if not actually to wet himself. However, there must be many parents who are content to wait longer than this before consulting a doctor. If a doctor is consulted, make sure that your child isn't made to feel that he's doing something abnormal by wetting his bed, because he's not. It's easy for a child to feel that his parents and the doctor think he's naughty. Brothers and sisters can also lower his sense of self-esteem if they tease him. If you keep calm about his bed-wetting and don't make an issue of it, he'll grow out of it in his own good time. It's extremely rare for a child to wet the bed on purpose.

If your child has been dry at night and starts wetting the bed, it is worth seeing a doctor just in case there is a medical problem that could be helped or an emotional one that could do with being aired.

If your child wets the bed every night or more often than not, it's simplest to put a nappy on him at night. A double terry nappy inside plastic pants works well for most children and also seems to keep them warm even if the nappy is wetted in the middle of the night. A large size disposable nappy, perhaps with an extra pad inside, may be absorbent enough.

A plastic sheet can be put either beneath the bottom sheet or beneath the underblanket. If it's beneath the sheet, it means less washing but isn't nearly as comfortable to sleep on as the child will inevitably get hot and sweaty. A plastic sheet saves the mattress from being spoilt. If your child's wet nappy leaks in the middle of the night, you can avoid stripping the bed by putting a large, folded bath towel beneath him. With his wet nappy off, that'll keep him warm until the morning.

Some children are more prone to bed-wetting when they are cold, so keep them as warm as you can by putting them in warm nightwear with a jumper on top if they are in the habit of lying outside the bedclothes. Remember that the stuffing inside a duvet migrates to one end over the weeks, so shake it down every so often. Though a duvet is supposed to be enough on top of the bed, lots of people need more on top of them.

Some parents avoid the problem of bed-wetting by lifting their child out of bed when they go to bed, and putting him on the potty or lavatory to pass water. Some children will apparently remain asleep throughout, while others wake a little and immediately go back to sleep once they are in bed. Some children obligingly walk to the lavatory once they are woken. This isn't always a good idea though as you may find that your child wakes properly and finds it hard to go back to sleep, or he may be annoyed and difficult to control on being woken and so might refuse to be taken out of his bed. You may feel that it isn't fair to disturb his sleep and that you would rather launder a nappy than wake him.

Should you limit fluid intake in the afternoon and evening if your child wets the bed? The answer is to use some common sense over the matter. Just let him have what would seem to be enough to satisfy his thirst.

Bed-wetting treatments used for some older children, such as the 'star' system of reward for a dry night, or treatment with drugs are really inapplicable for the under-fives. Rather than thinking of your child as a bed-wetter, think of him as a person who simply hasn't grown up enough to be dry. As long as you're not worried, he won't be, and that's the important thing.

Don't forget that a child who has wet the bed or been in a wet nappy may smell badly. If he goes to a play-group, it's possible that other children may shun him or tease him so give him a wash in the morning before dressing him. *Related topics* Anxiety; behaviour problems; bladder control; imagination.

Behaviour A child's behaviour or conduct towards and treatment of others is influenced by his basic inborn temperament and by the way in which he is brought up. Each society's code of conduct is learned by imitating other children and grown-ups and is often regulated by unspoken rules. There are two ways you can teach a child to behave 'well' – that is, in a manner pleasing to you and the rest of society. Firstly, you can help him positively by telling him what to do and how to do it in a way which will please you; by encouraging him in his efforts and by praising him when he's done it; by setting a good example yourself and expecting a certain basic standard of behaviour from other people who visit your house and from other members of your family; and – when the child is old enough – by discussing other people's behaviour with him, so that he learns why you disapprove of some sorts of behaviour and approve of others.

Secondly, you can alter his behaviour by correcting him when he has done something wrong. It's difficult to be positive when doing this but if you're clever you can twist what might have been a negative 'telling off' into a constructive lesson. For example, 'Don't run into the house with all that mud on your shoes!' becomes 'Let's practise wiping our feet on the doormat'. If you then wipe your feet at the same time, the child will see the lesson as a game with Mummy and will be more likley to remember next time. Even if he doesn't remember it's a lot more pleasant, keeps the atmosphere brighter and avoids confrontation.

Whichever way you choose, and most parents use both ways from time to time, your child is unlikely to get everything right the first time. Part of the job of being a parent is to teach your child how to behave and any teacher knows that repetition is essential with young children. They simply don't remember after being told only once.

It's important not to expect a child to do something you don't do. If you go outside without a coat on a cold day, your child will quite naturally want to follow your example. It's totally unreasonable to expect your children to behave in a way which is contrary to your behaviour.

Standards of behaviour vary from society to society, from social group to social group and from family to family. What constitutes 'good' behaviour in one family may not be seen as such by another and the same is true for bad behaviour. Perhaps our aim when bringing up children should be to help each child behave as an individual within the framework of his own character, but in such a way as to fit in with other people, not to upset them or to disrupt their lives and – if possible – to behave in a way that improves the quality of their lives.

A normally well-behaved child may act out of character and training if he's over-tired, unwell or brewing up for something. As grown-ups we should try to make sure that our expectations are realistic. If a mother takes her child to a tea party at three o'clock in the afternoon after a busy day with no time for an adequate nap, she shouldn't expect him to be all sweetness and light. A child's behaviour can be affected by unusual tension in the family as well. Many's the child who suddenly starts to behave differently because his parents have separated, because they are quarrelling in front of him at home or because of some other domestic upheaval such as a move, or a bereavement. Any change in a child's behaviour is worth investigating to see if there is a remedial cause. If you are too close to your child to do this, ask for help from someone who can advise you from outside the family. Your family doctor or health visitor may help or can put you in touch with professionals who can. **Related topics** Behaviour problems; copying; development – emotional; development – social; profile (of appropriate age).

Behaviour problems If your child's behaviour is unacceptable you'll naturally want to try to modify it. Behaviour modification varies from sophisticated psychological ploys to a simple telling off if a child does something wrong. If you feel incapable of coping with your child's behaviour, whether or not you know what's causing it, ask for help from your family doctor or health visitor. Chatting about a problem often clears the air and may help and you may need encouragement to carry on behaving just as you have been. Some children are naturally more aggressive or jealous than others, for instance, and it may be that the parents need help in coming to terms with their own normal child. Of course you'll want to change any unpleasant behaviour traits, but it may need weeks, months – or even years – of patient example and repetitive teaching before a child learns to behave differently by controlling his natural instincts.

Perhaps one of the most difficult aspects of a child's behaviour problem is parental guilt. Over the last half century or so we've become conditioned into thinking that everything that goes wrong with our children is a direct reflection of how we've brought them up. Of course this isn't always so. A child's environment is certainly extremely important, but a parent with a large family knows that character and behaviour traits are to a certain extent inborn as well as learnt. All the parents can do is their best in bringing up their children. If something seems to have gone wrong, then they can perhaps improve on their best by getting outside help. If you do this, there's no need ever to feel guilty because you will always have done your best.

Any child, however well brought up and however lovingly treated, can develop a temporary behaviour problem. By responding in a loving and carefully considered way, you'll be helping your child overcome it as quickly as he can. The essence of preventing or avoiding behaviour problems lies in praising a child when he behaves well rather than ignoring good behaviour and complaining about bad behaviour. If a child is aware that his good behaviour pleases you and that you think well of him because of it, he's more likely to try to live up to your expectations and his own image of himself, which is partly a reflection of what you think of him.

Often, behaviour problems develop because we expect a child to do something he is not yet developmentally ready for. Young children have neither the intellect nor the conversational fluency to be able to explain to their parents how they feel and a behaviour problem may be the result of frustration at being made to do something they're not yet ready to do.

If your child has a behaviour problem of some sort, you'll probably be inundated with advice from everyone you know about what to do. There are usually several ways of dealing with any such problem, so listen to the advice and then decide what to do for yourself and your child. You may need to try several ways of altering your child's behaviour, but try not to confuse him too much.

It's important not to label every slight 'imperfection' as a behaviour problem. *All* children are jealous, aggressive, clinging, whiny and so on at times.

It's much more rewarding for a child if his behaviour is such that his parents and others around him like him and think that he's 'good'. All the more reason then to understand that a child with a behaviour problem needs help. The quality of his life and his self-esteem are diminished by the way he behaves because he elicits an unfavourable response from others. To prevent a vicious circle from starting up, try and nip any problem in the bud. Time and care spent early on will save hours of worry later. **Related topics** Aggression; bed-wetting; blinking; breath-holding attacks; cheating; contrariness; dirt eating; discipline; habits; jealousy; lead poisoning; lying; maladjustment; nail biting; obsessions; overbreathing; stealing; temper tantrums.

Bereavement Children under five are very self-centred and are in general affected by bereavement only when their own lives are disrupted. The loss of a parent – especially the mother, if she was the child's prime caretaker, obviously changes the child's whole life. A father's death may be less disruptive in absolute terms to a young child, though the effect of his death on his wife will indirectly have an important effect on the child. The loss of other family members will disturb a child in proportion to how close they were to the child both emotionally and physically, as well as by the effect the loss has on the parents.

A young child may be very accepting of a loss in the family. In years to come he'll be unable to remember the person except when the memory has been kept alive by conversation. This is one reason why it's so important to talk about a dead person. Another is that it helps a child understand what happens to people when they die if you answer his questions about where the person is and why the body has been taken away, and so on. Faith in God makes such a discussion easier and some parents, themselves agnostics, use concepts of God and an afterlife as devices to smooth the way for their children in such circumstances. Children are very direct and open in their questions when someone has died and you must be prepared for questions such as 'why do they bury people under the ground?' and comments like 'our baby is under the earth in that cemetery', after a stillbirth or the death of a sibling.

Grieving is a natural human response to the death of a loved one. A child old enough to realize that someone close to him has gone will inevitably miss that person. If that person played an important part in his life, he'll mourn his loss in much the same way as an adult would, feeling sadness and depression as a natural and necessary grief reaction. Even a baby can mourn the loss of a loved person, though it is the loss of the baby's mother that inevitably produces the most marked response.

Some young children respond to the death of someone close with feelings of guilt as though they had in some way caused the person to die. Children don't understand the extent of their power and if they have at any stage wished a person were dead and gone, or if they have wished them ill in any way, and then that person dies, the coincidence may be too much for them to cope with and they may believe that in some way they caused the death. It's wise to talk at a very simple level, depending on the age of the child, about why the person died to allay any such worries on the child's part.

If there has been a stillborn baby or if a baby has died soon after birth, the next time the mother is pregnant or has a baby, a child may be consumed with fear that that baby will die too. Again, the wise parent will talk about such worries and bring them out into the open rather than let them smoulder subconsciously.

A child may mourn for dead pets too. Birth, life and death are all part of a child's experience and there is no point in shielding him from the sad parts of life and exposing him only to the happy parts. It's much more helpful to explain happenings such as death as you see them so that he can come to terms with his feelings gradually as he grows up. If someone in the family died and you were so keen to avoid involving your child in the grief that you hid your own feelings, he might think that you didn't care that the person had died. Let him share in the bereavement and it'll help the whole family through its loss.

Berries, poisonous

Berries, poisonous Several domestic and countryside plants have poisonous berries in the UK. The commonest are bryony; cotoneaster; daphne; deadly nightshade; honeysuckle; laurel; pyracantha; yew; mountain ash (rowan); ivy; solanum (Christmas cherry); and the arum lily.

There are several different ways of handling the poisonous berry problem. Either you teach your children that they must never eat anything out of doors without first asking you or another adult (and this is what we recommend) or you can remove all poisonous trees, flowers and shrubs from your garden so that the danger cannot arise. The latter action is rather drastic but many parents only feel completely safe by doing this.

If your child eats literally one or two berries, don't worry but keep a close eye on him and get him to a doctor or casualty department if his condition changes at all for the worse. Anything over two berries should be reported to your doctor at once or the child should be taken to hospital just in case he has in fact eaten a lot more than you realize.

It's probably wise to discourage older pre-school children from playing with berries of any kind when they are out of doors, even if they don't actually eat them. Be very sure when you're out in the country picking blackberries or whatever from the hedgerows that your children don't wander off and pick other things in their enthusiasm.

Bibs

Bibs Bibs are used to keep a child's clothes from getting wet or soiled when he eats, drinks or dribbles. There is a wide variety, from the stiff plastic 'pelican' bib with its little tray to catch things in, to the conventional fabric one that ties at the back of the neck. Some have sleeves incorporated, while others have detachable plastic inside the top. Some are short, others are more like overalls. Whether or not you like the look of them, bibs can save a lot of washing, especially in the early stages when your baby is learning to feed himself with a spoon.

Bicycles and tricycles

Bicycles and tricycles These can be a source of hours of pleasure for your young child. Toddlers will enjoy a push-along tricycle and can graduate to a pedal tricycle as an intermediate stage to a real bicycle. The age at which any one child can cope with a bicycle or tricycle varies enormously, some being quite competent several years before others. Stabilizers (additional small wheels on a frame each side of the rear bicycle wheel) give a child the pleasure of riding a bicycle younger than he would otherwise be able to and also mean that he'll learn balance and stability sooner than if left to ride a tricycle. As he becomes more stable and confident, one and then both stabilizers can be removed.

No child under the age of five should ever cycle on the road, unless perhaps it's in a quiet cul-de-sac supervised all the time by an adult. A child of this age, even if very intelligent, simply hasn't got the sense of danger one has to have to go on public roads. Always keep young children to paths, pavements, parks and gardens.

While a child won't hurt himself so much if he falls off his bike on to grass, it is easier for him to ride on a pavement or tarmacked area. This is because it will go more smoothly and acceleration will be better, enabling him to start off more easily. The answer is to let him learn on whatever surface is readily available and to supervise him at first by running along by the bike so you can save him if he does fall.

Even though a young child's bike is a relatively simple thing in engineering terms, do look after it and give it an overhaul at least twice a year. The brakes will need regular attention and tyre pressures and lubrication should also be checked. A bicycle can be a real milestone in the development of the child's independence. For the first time he can go somewhere without his parents taking him. This does mean that limits have to be set. Always tell your children how far you'll allow them to go on their bicycles.

There is no need to spend a lot of money by buying a new tricycle or bicycle. Look in the small ads, in your local newspaper, or in the news-agent's window for a second-hand one, which will be a good deal cheaper.

Bilingual child The vast majority of children grow up speaking one language but with intermarriage so common and with the flow of people around the world to work, increasing numbers of children are brought up speaking two languages.

The way that individual children respond to this varies greatly, as you'd expect, but in general it has been found that one language tends to predominate in the child's mind and that most of these children take longer to become proficient in either language than their single-language contemporaries. Some children may appear to be backward in their language development because of this, whereas in fact they are simply confused.

There is controversy over the best thing to do in such circumstances. Some people believe that it's best to get the child speaking confidently in one language before introducing the second. There really are no rules though, as so much depends on the amount the child hears and on the child himself. If his parents talk to him a lot, he'll get more experience of language than if he only hears a few words a day. It's sensible to use one language at a time and perhaps for each to be used in specific circumstances. Perhaps the mother could speak one language when she is alone with the child, and another when the rest of the family or other people are there, for instance.

Immigrant children sometimes start school not speaking the language of their new country and inevitably, therefore, fall behind academically. It may be difficult for them to catch up even when they have a good grasp of English. Bright children tend to learn a new language more quickly but all children find it easier if they know at least some English words before starting school. In areas with high immigrant populations there are classes for teaching mothers English. They in turn can then teach their pre-school children.

English families working abroad in large cities can usually find a suitable

English-speaking school for their child. Elsewhere their children have to learn the native language of the country or be taught at home. Most children find it easy to learn a new language especially if encouraged at home, so they may be better off going to the local school.

Knowing more than one language is always an asset. If your child learns two when he is young, it's worth keeping both up because a language is all too easy to forget when it is not used. *Related topic* Language.

Birth certificate A certificate issued at a Register Office to parents of all newborn babies – even if they are stillborn.

Wherever your baby is born you must, by law, register his birth with the Registrar of Births and Deaths in the area where your baby was born. If you have your baby in a large maternity home or hospital the Registrar may visit and this makes the whole thing very easy. If the baby is born at home or if you didn't register the birth in the hospital, you or your partner will have to go to the Register Office to do so within forty-two days (twenty-one days in Scotland) of the baby's birth. In very exceptional cases someone other than the baby's parents can register the birth.

The Registrar will give you a shortened form of the birth certificate there and then and will charge you nothing. This is fine for most uses but a full version can be produced if you need it. At the time of receiving your baby's birth certificate or shortly after, you'll be given a card to give to the doctor on whose NHS list you want your baby to be. You'll also be given DHSS tokens so that you'll be able to get children's vitamin drops and baby foods if you are on a low income; have a handicapped child or are an approved child minder or playgroup organizer. When you take the birth certificate home, put it in a safe place because you're likely to have to show it from time to time in the early years.

Certifying your baby's birth is different from notifying it. Every birth has to be notified to the area medical officer within thirty-six hours. This is usually done by the hospital or nursing home staff. If your baby is born at home, the midwife will do it. If you deliver the baby with no medical help you must notify the area medical officer yourself.

Birthdays Children love joining in celebrations and particularly enjoy their own birthdays if it's the custom to make birthdays special days. Celebrations can include cards, presents, having friends or relatives or both round for a special birthday lunch or tea, a party, or a treat such as going to the zoo or the seaside. Take care not to get so involved with the production of the day that you neglect your child. He will prefer more of your time and attention and less organized activity.

If your child has set his heart on a particular toy, try to get it for him as his birthday present because he may be very disappointed otherwise, even with a much more 'suitable' or more expensive present. If it's out of the question because it costs too much, warn him beforehand that he won't be getting it and explain why.

When the day arrives, try to make it special in every way for your child.

Remember that a young child in particular can all too easily get tired or over-excited, so make some time during the day to sit quietly and read, play, or watch television. If friends or relatives are coming round, encourage your child to act as host or hostess and to make the guests comfortable and welcome. A traditional birthday cake with candles and the child's name on it, or a fancy-shaped cake are much appreciated, together with the singing of 'Happy Birthday'. **Related topics** Birthday parties; celebrations.

Birthday parties Birthday parties are usually a source of enormous pleasure, anticipation and delight to the under-fives and, with a little care, need not be much trouble or hard work for their parents.

A baby's first birthday party doesn't need to be a great production. His family, perhaps a guest or two, a 'Happy Birthday' song, a little help blowing out the candle, and the cake itself are all that are needed to celebrate the event.

As a child gets older the anticipation becomes more important than the event. The planning of who is to be invited, the food, what sort of cake to have, the day, the location and so on all give more fun than the event and may go on for months.

Ideally, try to hold the party on the birthday itself or choose a day very close to the day. Send out invitations – perhaps handmade by you and your child. Give people two to three weeks notice and be sure to say whose party it is, give a return address, your phone number, the date, place and the time of start and finish. Two hours is plenty for a 'formal' party for three- or four-year-olds and means that the children don't get overtired. A party doesn't have to be in your house or garden. You could take the children for a picnic or for an outing instead, though this is easier if some other parents help. Never invite so many children that you can't manage to make the party run smoothly and ensure that each child is looked after and enjoys himself.

Young guests of two and three nearly always prefer it if their mother (or father) stays at the party with them. Some three-year-olds are happy to stay alone, especially if they know the family well. Most four-year-olds can be left happily.

As children arrive get them involved in something fairly quickly so as to keep the momentum going. Have a few games (with little prizes – preferably not all sweets). If the guests bring gifts, ensure that your child thanks them but also get across in your manner that what is important is the arrival of the person and not only what he or she has brought. Young children often brush aside the welcome with their eagerness to see if they've been brought a present. You'll have to make up for this by welcoming the child and his parent warmly yourself. About half an hour's games is enough before most under-fives are ready for the food.

A party doesn't have to be in the afternoon. Sometimes a lunch party is appreciated more because the children will be fresher. It's all too easy for a child to become frustrated by waiting around till three o'clock for his party.

At lunchtime you could serve something like fish fingers and chips with a few peas and tomato ketchup, followed by ice-cream or birthday cake and fresh fruit. For a teatime party you can make the traditional party fare attractive by putting colourful food in pretty bowls or doilies on plates. A bright tablecloth together with paper plates looks pretty and makes clearing up easy.

Don't make the mistake of offering only sweet foods. Children often prefer savoury things. Few under-fives have big appetites but most eat with the eye, so take trouble to make the food look delicious. Make sandwiches from thinly sliced wholemeal bread, cut into simple shapes with a cutter. Cakes are often left at this age, though tiny sponge cakes in paper cases with a spot of icing and a Smartie on top are popular, as are tiny meringues. Crisps are evergreens, as are whole satsumas in winter. Lots of children – perhaps surprisingly – like peeled raw carrots and clean, fresh sticks of celery. Little sausages or sausage rolls go down well. Have plenty of orange juice (or water or milk) to drink from paper cups.

After the food there'll be time for more games, some tricks or entertainment by a parent or friend or even a professional entertainer (though a professional will be expensive) and then it's time for home.

Some parents give each child a small present to take away with them as well as a balloon. You'll need several extra balloons because some always burst.

Safety is something to be very aware of at birthday parties. Probably the greatest form of safety is to have enough helpers – you can't be everywhere and extra, young, excited children need a lot of supervision. Guard all fires and ponds; don't have peanuts for young children who might choke on them; remove keys from doors; don't allow playing on the stairs or unsupervised upstairs; and put away anything you don't want broken. Never run a party without at least one other adult person – if you get into trouble of any kind they can then take over. *Related topic* Celebrations.

Birthmarks

Birthmarks Marks on the skin, usually present at birth. None are serious or dangerous but large ones can be unsightly and if in a prominent place can cause embarrassment or even real mental suffering. Fortunately most birthmarks disappear in time.

Being born can itself cause temporary marks but not true 'birthmarks'. All such marks go within a few days, including the marks on the side of the head made by obstetric forceps. The commonest birthmarks – the so-called 'stork's beak marks' – are transient. These are small red or salmon pink discolorations on the forehead above the nose, on the eyelids or on the back of the neck at the hairline and can take a year or more to disappear.

The next most common birthmark is a strawberry naevus (cavernous haemangioma) which is not necessarily present at birth and can take several days to appear. It is raised from the surrounding skin and may look like a squashed strawberry. Most strawberry birthmarks disappear within two years though some last longer. They often enlarge over the weeks or months just before they start to disappear. Enlargement at this time is therefore a good sign. As they go they lighten in colour from the middle outwards. Bleeding after a cut or other injury is the biggest problem with this sort of mark but is usually not severe and can be stopped by firm pressure over the area and a sticking plaster with the adhesive part well clear of the birthmark. Any treatment used to get rid of the mark is likely to leave a scar whereas left alone it will disappear eventually anyway.

A birthmark known as a port wine stain (a capillary haemangioma) is the least common and the worst because it is permanent. It is flat and dark purplish-red. Special cosmetics are available to cover up such marks. These are only available from specially trained consultants and not over the counter. Write for information to Covermark, Medexport Limited, PO Box 25, Arundel, Sussex, or to Keromark, Innoxa Limited, 202 Terminus Road, Eastbourne, Sussex. Young children with birthmarks on their faces may be teased or even shunned by their contemporaries though this is unusual before school age. If this is happening, covering up the mark with cosmetics is an alternative to helping the child learn to cope with unkind remarks or behaviour, and may make his life easier. Treatment with new laser techniques is enabling some to be obliterated almost without trace. Ask your doctor to refer you to a hospital unit that uses this technique. Sometimes a birthmark may be a mixture of a strawberry mark and a port wine stain. Some of this sort of mark will disappear in time. *Related topics* Moles; haemangiomas.

Birth – questions children ask

Most young children are interested in knowing where babies come from but the mistake most parents make (because of their own embarrassment and insecurity) is in assuming that this question is any more important to the child than 'why is a tomato red?' When answering questions on babies and birth, keep the answers simple. The child under five doesn't want a mini-lecture. He just wants to know that there is an explanation and that you, his parents, know it. Simply saying that Daddy put a seed in Mummy's tummy and that made a baby grow is often quite enough for the first question. As the child gets older he'll want to know how this happened and how the baby will get out but these questions don't need in-depth sex-education lessons to answer them to the *child's* complete satisfaction. These would be wasted on even the intelligent under-five. However, just because he is content with a simple answer is no excuse to brush off the questions. Treat such questions just as you do those on any other subject and you'll have a child with balanced views on the subject who is brought up from his earliest days to think of childbirth as a normal part of life, not as something rude or unmentionable.

If you are expecting a baby, your young child of one, two or three may not be aware that your tummy is getting bigger until you point it out to him and tell him that there is a baby inside. If your baby is wriggling, let your child look at or feel your tummy. By doing all this and involving him in the anticipation of the birth, he'll begin to accept and look forward to the arrival of the new baby.

A few mothers today allow their older child or children to be present when their baby is born, if the labour is going normally. Children given this experience take it very well and seem to 'bond' to the new baby easily.

Birth weight The average weight of a newborn baby in the UK is between 7 and 7½ pounds (3200–3400 g). Over the last fifty years this has altered very little – there has only been a rise of some 3 ounces (85 g). A baby whose weight is below 5½ pounds (2500 g) is classed as 'low birth weight'. About seven per cent of all babies come into this category. The majority of babies weigh between 6½ and 8 pounds. Heavier and/or taller women tend to have heavier than average babies and women who put on more weight than average during their pregnancy have heavier than average babies. However, if you were fat before you became pregnant, this is unlikely to influence your baby's weight. Babies also tend to be heavier as the mother gets older and she's likely to have her heaviest baby when she's thirty-five. The more babies a woman has, the heavier they're likely to be as well. On average, boy babies are likely to weigh about 5 ounces (140 g) more than girls.

Can you influence how heavy your baby will be? The only sure way of doing this is by smoking. Statisticians and obstetricians are agreed that it is unwise for a mother to smoke during pregnancy, or to breathe in smoke-filled air from other people's cigarettes for more than short periods, because this can reduce her baby's birth weight by reducing the supply of blood to the womb. Low birth weight can be associated with disadvantages to the baby and is well worth preventing.

Women in higher socio-economic classes tend to have heavier babies. The reason for this isn't known for sure but may be to do with their better diet, more rest and better antenatal care during pregnancy.

It's quite usual for a baby to lose weight after birth. This is because of the low volume feeds of colostrum and the loss of meconium from the bowel. This loss of birth weight takes a very variable time to be replaced. Frequent, uncurtailed breast-feeds by night and day are the most likely to nourish the baby well, but even so some quite normal, healthy babies may take up to three weeks to regain their birth weight. A few take even longer and still appear to suffer no ill effects.

If your baby is born early, his weight will depend on his state of health and on the length of your pregnancy. A baby born after 28 weeks of pregnancy is likely to weigh about 2 pounds (900 g); a 32-week baby will weigh about 3½ pounds (1500 g); and a 36-week baby about 5½ pounds (2500 g). In the last month of pregnancy, the baby puts on about an ounce (28 g) a day.

Birth weight has assumed rather too much importance in our technological age although it's easy to understand how women felt historically because large, sturdy babies would have stood a better chance of survival. *Related topics* Weighing; weight gain; weight loss.

Bites and stings

We are fortunate in the UK in not having many biting and stinging creatures. Insect bites and stings are discussed elsewhere as are dog bites and jellyfish stings.

Snake bites are uncommon in the UK and there is only one native type of poisonous snake – the adder. This snake lives in clearings, on the edge of woodlands, on moors, hills, railway cuttings or mountains. It is grey, yellow or reddish-brown, about thirty inches (75 cm) long, has a broad head and a black zig-zag mark down its back. Adder bites are painful and may produce sweating, vomiting and diarrhoea, stomach pains and even a loss of consciousness. The bites rarely cause death. It's sensible for your child to wear Wellington boots when walking through areas of long grass or knee-high scrub where there may be snakes.

If your child is bitten by a snake that you think may be an adder, 1) make him rest, 2) immobilize the bitten part, 3) reassure and comfort him, 4) give painkilling tablets in the correct dose and 5) get him to hospital at once. *Never* suck out the venom; never apply a tourniquet; and never cut the bite or put any chemicals on it at all.

Apart from dogs, other pet animals such as guinea pigs and cats can bite and scratch. Such events are usually completely harmless (even though they may be frightening to the child) and need only the simplest of treatment. Clean the area gently with plain, warm water and put a light, dry dressing on it. If it is deep see a doctor. If there is bleeding a sticking plaster will usually be all that is needed. Any bite or scratch that causes bleeding that cannot be easily controlled by a sticking plaster needs medical attention.

Plants can sting children and cause unpleasant problems. Stinging nettles are the commonest stinging plants but their stings are easily treated with soothing lotions such as calamine. Rubbing a dock leaf on to the sting is the time-honoured way of relieving a nettle sting. Dock leaves are usually to be found growing in the wild near nettles. If the child's skin becomes really inflamed, has large weals (white raised areas) and is very itchy, anti-histamine tablets or syrup can work wonders and will allow him to sleep at night. Any reaction as serious as this should be seen by a doctor. Some plants, especially those of the primula family, don't actually sting but produce allergic skin reactions in susceptible people. Such dermatitis may need medical treatment. If in doubt ask for your doctor's advice. Children who are sensitive to any plants should not be allowed to come into contact with them again. *Related topics* Dog bites; fleas; insect bites and stings; jellyfish stings; pets; rabies.

Bladder control

A child's bladder grows as he does and is gradually able to hold more and more urine. During the first year urine is passed less and less frequently and by the time the average child is eighteen months old, he is dry for about two hours at a time. This is most likely to be when he's asleep because a smaller amount of more concentrated urine is made by the kidneys during times of quiet sleep.

Babies and young children can't control their bladder opening until they reach a certain stage – at a different age in each child – when the bladder's nervous system is mature enough to signal to them in time that it is full and needs to be opened. When a child shows signs that he is ready to be potty trained (staying dry for longer periods, holding his pants or crossing his legs, telling you that he wants to pee and so on) this is the time to help him to become dry. This can be at any time from eighteen months onwards, but can't be forced. If you sit your child on the potty before that, you may be lucky enough to catch some urine by coincidence, but that's all, unless your child is exceptional. Children usually learn to recognize when they need to pee at about the same time as they learn to recognize their need to open their bowels. Because it's easier for them to control the opening of their bowels, than the opening of their bladder, they usually become clean before they become dry. This is why lots of children use a potty to open their bowels but still wet their nappies. However, sooner or later they'll open their bladder at the same time as their bowels, into the potty, and this will help them understand that the potty can be used to pee in as well as a nappy. Few children are reliably dry during the day before they're two.

A child usually manages daytime dryness before night-time dryness, though one per cent of babies are spontaneously dry at night when they're a year old and before they have any bladder control during the day. Night-time dryness comes when a child's bladder is mature enough to hold all the urine produced during the night and again, the age for this varies widely, with the average at about three years.

Boys tend to be later in developing bladder control than girls, especially at night. Bladder control may disappear temporarily at times of emotional stress, such as after the birth of a new baby.

Potty training ideally needs sensitivity and skill on behalf of the parents, especially if it is to be fast. If you can give your child the idea that while it would be lovely for you and for him if he were dry, but that you'll still love him just as much if he can't always manage it, you'll do no harm. When he does become dry, it'll be one more step towards his independence. *Related topics* Bed-wetting; potty training.

Bleeding

Bleeding Bleeding can occur from any of the blood-carrying channels in the body. Arteries are thick-walled and bleed profusely with high pressure, bright red blood; veins are thin-walled and ooze dark purplish-blue blood and capillaries bleed a little bright red blood (as from a graze).

Capillary bleeding stops on its own in a few minutes and usually needs no further treatment but arterial and venous bleeding can be more serious. Most often, simple pressure over the bleeding area (through a clean handkerchief or similar) stops even quite severe bleeding in a few minutes. Bleeding that doesn't stop in ten to fifteen minutes or seems to be too serious to control using pressure over the area should be attended to by a doctor urgently.

If your child is bleeding severely and cannot be moved safely to a doctor, call an ambulance and in the meantime lay him down, preferably with his feet raised, loosen any tight, constrictive clothing and try to stop the bleeding by pressing hard on the area. Once such serious bleeding has stopped, don't remove the pad you were pressing over or you'll disturb the clot and start the bleeding off again. If the blood oozes through the first cloth, add more and press hard for longer until professional help arrives.

After some injuries there may be no obvious signs of bleeding yet bleeding may have or may even still be taking place inside the body. A broken bone can cause considerable internal bleeding as can a ruptured internal organ. If ever a child becomes pale, sweaty, feels faint and has a weak, thin pulse, get medical help urgently. These are all signs of shock.

Children often fall over and hit their heads but usually there is no serious damage. A scalp cut will bleed, just as a cut on any other part of the body, but is more likely than a similar cut elsewhere to need stitches to stop the bleeding. Any blood loss or loss of clear fluid from the nose or ears must receive urgent medical attention. *Related topics* Abrasions; bandaging; cuts; graze; shock.

Blender Electrical kitchen equipment that breaks solid foods down into particles. Some mothers, when starting their babies off on solid foods, like to liquidize some of the family's foods so as to make them easy for a baby to eat from a spoon. However, a blender is a waste of time and money if used only for this purpose as babies' food can quite easily be mashed with a fork in far less time and at a fraction of the cost of a blender. Also, there's no reason to believe that babies like to eat uniformly mushy food. Many babies today aren't given foods other than milk until they are at least three months and often not till six months or more – and this is the ideal. By six months small, soft lumps can usually be managed well, though a baby should never be left alone when eating. *Related topics* Baby foods; cooking for children; food.

Blepharitis Inflammation of the edges of the eyelids, often associated with seborrhoea. The eyelids are pussy and the eyelashes matted together with dried pus. The edges of the lids are red and itchy and the child may rub the affected eye repeatedly. Apart from this infective type of blepharitis there are allergic causes, and exposure to dust, smoke and fumes can also cause it.

If the blepharitis is due to infection, treatment with antibiotic drops helps cure it. Frequent eye-bathing will remove the discharge. If the condition is left untreated it can become very longlasting and can even cause permanent loss of the eyelashes and scarring of the lids.

Blindness Although total blindness in a child is rare, many children have poor eyesight that requires artificial help in order that they can read even large print. Such children are called 'partially sighted' and there are special schools all over the country that are geared to helping them. Some ordinary primary schools are capable of helping these children too.

The causes of blindness are many, and certain conditions (such as cataracts caused by German measles) that produce blindness are apparent at birth. Some blind babies have wandering eye movements or flicking of the eyes and others rhythmically rub their eyes with the backs of their hands. Sometimes parents will notice that their baby can't follow things with his eyes, even in the first few months of life. Early diagnosis is important because in some children treatment (for example the removal of a cataract or a brain tumour) can enable the brain to regain some of its lost vision.

Congenital glaucoma (buphthalmos) occurs in the first year of life if there is defective drainage of the natural fluid inside the eyes. Pressure builds up in the eyeball and makes the eyes appear large and bulging. Expert treatment can often save the sight.

A retinoblastoma is a rare tumour that occurs inside the eye. It sometimes runs in families. If the diagnosis is made very early in life and the eye removed, the child's life may be saved.

Other causes of blindness in young children are due to certain drugs (for example, thalidomide) taken by the mother in pregnancy; infections during pregnancy such as toxoplasmosis; eye injuries; retinal detachment; infestation with the worm toxocara (caught from dogs and cats); and severe eye infections. Blindness in one eye can occur if a squint is left untreated as the brain suppresses the image from the 'lazy' eye.

If you havè a child who is partially sighted or totally blind you'll need lots of help. Start with your own doctor or the specialist who is treating your child and make full use of the excellent facilities available through the Royal National Institute for the Blind. *Related topics* Cataract; squint; toxoplasmosis; toxocara. *Useful organization* Royal National Institute for the Blind.

Blinking Repeated blinking is a nervous tic or habit which can be very annoying to the adults around a child. The temptation is to tell the child to stop doing it. However, many children only start blinking repetitively when they are worried about something, so telling them to stop is less helpful than finding out what the root of the problem is and doing something to put that right. If you simply tell your child to stop blinking and he does so (which is possible even though many such habits work at an almost unconscious level, not on purpose) then his unease will almost certainly show up in some other way.

Blinking can also be a sign of allergic conjunctivitis (as occurs with hay fever). If you are worried about your child's blinking, see your doctor, but usually it does no harm and disappears as the child grows older. *Related topics* Anxiety; behaviour problems; glasses; habits; hay fever.

Blisters Raised, fluid-filled areas on the skin surface or on the mucous membranes. The commonest cause of blisters is repeated rubbing of the area, for example, by shoes. A burn or scald can also cause blistering.

Such blisters are easily treated. Simply cover them with a sticking plaster for a day or two while the fluid is reabsorbed by the body. Never burst a blister with a needle or other instrument unless it is sterilized first by passing it through a flame or boiling it for ten minutes. Make sure the needle then touches nothing before you let the fluid out. Cover the area with a sticking plaster.

Chickenpox is a well-known cause of blistering and the appearance of the classical blisters makes the diagnosis of the rash easy.

If ever your child gets multiple blisters for no apparent reason, tell your doctor.

Blocked tear duct If your baby's eyes water persistently it's possible that the duct that takes tears from the eyes to the nose is blocked. Such a blockage usually clears spontaneously before the age of six months but probing can easily widen the duct if the blockage persists. This is usually done by a specialist.

Blood groups At least fourteen blood groups have now been discovered but the majority of people belong to one of the four commonest groups, A, AB, O and B. Blood is grouped or typed according to the antigens and antibodies present in the red cells and plasma.

The rhesus system was discovered when red cells from a rhesus monkey were injected into a rabbit. An understanding of this system is important to parents who are having babies because the presence of a baby with rhesus positive blood in the womb of a rhesus negative mother can lead to the production of antibodies by the mother. These can pass into the baby via the placenta before or during birth and damage or even destroy his red blood cells. The condition this produces in the baby is called haemolytic disease of the newborn and in its most severe form can be fatal if not treated. This is why a woman is always tested early in pregnancy to find out if there is any danger of rhesus incompatibility. Should the mother be rhesus negative the level of rhesus antibodies in her blood is checked both then and later on in the pregnancy and the mother and foetus carefully watched if the level rises. First rhesus positive babies of a rhesus negative mother are usually not affected (unless the woman has had a miscarriage – unknown to her perhaps) but later-born rhesus positive babies can be at risk from the disease unless the woman was immunized after the birth of the first rhesus positive baby. This immunization has greatly reduced the incidence of haemolytic disease of the newborn.

A baby who suffers from the condition may need medical treatment for the anaemia and the jaundice it produces. His blood can be exchanged for rhesus negative blood and phototherapy (light treatment) can help lower the raised bilirubin levels that cause the jaundice. Incompatibility of other blood groups is rarely such a problem but can produce similar symptoms.

Before a child needing a blood transfusion (after an operation or an injury, for example) is given blood, his blood will be grouped by the pathology laboratory, then cross-matched with the blood to be given, to make sure that it is compatible with his. *Related topics* Blood transfusions; exchange transfusion.

Blood in motions

This is almost always caused by an anal fissure and disappears when the condition is treated. Large amounts of blood in the stools can be caused by a rare malformation of the intestines, by severe diarrhoea and by an intussusception. Any serious loss of blood in the stools (anything more than blood specking) requires expert medical attention. *Related topic* Intussusception.

Blood in vomit

This is very rare in children and when it occurs is usually secondary to very severe and persistent retching. The many causes of vomiting of blood in adults don't apply to the under-fives. If your child ever vomits more than a few specks of blood, get medical help urgently. If you have a cracked nipple your breast-fed baby may have flecks of blood in his vomit. Once you know that this is the cause there is no need for alarm.

Blood tests

One of the first things that happens to babies after they are born is that they have a tiny amount of blood taken from a needle prick in the heel to test for an uncommon disease called phenylketonuria. Apart from this the average baby should need no blood tests under the age of five. If a little blood is needed for investigations it can be obtained from a quick finger prick, from which a drop or two of blood is squeezed. If more blood is needed, then it can be taken from a vein using a syringe and needle just as in an adult. It's wise to stay with your child while this is being done because your presence will reassure him.

Blood transfusion

The giving of blood to one person from another. Children are not allowed to be blood donors but do receive blood in certain situations. Major accidents or other trauma (including operations) may call for a blood transfusion in a child just as in an adult and in children with haemolytic disease of the newborn it may be necessary to exchange some of the child's damaged blood for donated blood. Children with haemophilia also benefit from whole blood or from special fractions of blood when they bleed.

Before a child can receive donated blood his own group has to be ascertained. Blood to be given is then matched in a laboratory so that the chances of any adverse reactions occurring are reduced to a minimum. Once the correct match of blood has been obtained it is given into a suitable vein. *Related topics* Blood groups; exchange transfusion; haemophilia.

Blue babies

If your baby looks blue when he's born, the odds are that as soon as he starts breathing his natural colour will return and he'll be perfectly well. The blueness of his skin is caused by a lack of oxygen in his blood. An unborn baby receives his oxygen supply from his mother. Her blood vessels carry oxygenated blood to the placenta where the oxygen passes across into the blood vessels of the umbilical cord and hence to the baby's circulation. A baby can become short of oxygen even before labour begins if the placenta stops working properly. This is one reason why electronic foetal monitoring may be done in hospital in some women towards the end of pregnancy: a machine records the baby's heartbeats so that if there is any shortage of oxygen getting to the baby the rise in the baby's heart rate can be spotted and, if necessary, labour induced or a Caesarean section performed as an emergency.

During labour, a shortage of oxygen may occur because of a knot in the umbilical cord pulling tight or by compression of the blood vessels in the cord. It is thought by increasing numbers of experts that the position in which a woman labours may have important effects on the amount of oxygen reaching the baby. If she labours on her back, the weight and shape of the contracting uterus compresses her aorta – the main blood vessel carrying oxygenated blood. This means that there is less available oxygen for the baby. However, if she is upright (in a kneeling position, standing, squatting or on all fours), then the blood supply is uncompromised. Women labouring in an upright position tend to have shorter labours, so any compression of the blood vessels of the cord that may occur will be of shorter duration and so less hazardous to the baby.

Once the baby is born, if the placenta hasn't been working properly, the medical team will help the baby to start breathing as quickly as possible so that he can get oxygen into his lungs. It may be necessary to pass a tube into the baby's windpipe so that oxygen can be gently blown into the lungs if he is unable to start breathing on his own.

If the blueness was caused by mechanical compression of the cord, then once the compression is relieved by the expulsion of the baby from the birth canal, the blood can flow freely again from the placenta to the baby. In case the baby doesn't breathe spontaneously, the doctor or midwife may wait until there is evidence that the placenta has separated from the wall of the uterus before cutting the cord. This is because the baby then has the benefit of a few more minutes of oxygen from his mother to tide him over until his lungs start working.

Blueness may be caused by problems such as a hole in the heart, in which deoxygenated blood from the right side of the baby's heart is forced through a hole between the two sides of the heart. Arterial blood from the heart is therefore poorly oxygenated and the baby looks blue, especially round the lips and the fingers. Another congenital defect involves the main blood vessels coming from the heart and allows blue, deoxygenated blood to mix with red oxygenated blood. If your baby's blueness is thought to be caused by such a defect, special tests and x-rays will be carried out to enable the doctors to decide on the best course of action. Sometimes it is best for a baby to have an immediate operation but for other babies the operation can be deferred.

An oxygen lack has nothing to do with the blueness of the fingers and toes so commonly seen in newborn babies even when they are well wrapped up. This blueness is caused by a relative immaturity of the capillaries (tiny blood vessels) in the baby's skin and is in no way serious. **Related topic** Heart diseases and abnormalities.

Boasting

Boasting Boasting or bragging is something children do openly and grown-ups do discreetly. It's one thing to be proud of what one has or what one has achieved and quite another to belittle someone else because they haven't got it or done it. The chant '*I've* got a bigger doll's pram than *yours*' or '*My* daddy's more important than *yours*' is all too often to be heard among four- and five-year-olds. As parents we should teach by example that it's all very well to take a delight in something but it's not acceptable to be pleased that someone else hasn't got it.

You might think that a child with few possessions might be more inclined to boast when he has something but sometimes it's the other way round. The child on whom everything but love and attention is lavished may in fact be more boastful. Possessions mean a lot to him because he has so little of the more important things in life. He gradually learns that in his family, things are more important than human relationships. Perhaps he is unhappy because subconsciously he realizes he's being done down; and his unhappiness is reflected in his boasting.

Of course, many quite happy and much loved children go through a phase of boasting. School will soon knock such behaviour on the head but it might be kinder to help your child understand that boasting is not socially acceptable before he goes to school. **Related topics** Emotional deprivation; jealousy.

Body contact

Body contact Newborn babies, including premature babies nursed in incubators, are more likely to thrive if they have plenty of physical contact. A baby in the womb is accustomed to almost continual movement and pressure on all parts of his skin. He can also hear the sounds of his mother's body and listen to her voice. Suddenly to be placed in a motionless, quiet crib is an enormous change for a baby and many babies are obviously happier if the change from intra-uterine to extra-uterine life is not so abrupt. If they can be cuddled, held, or allowed to lie next to their mother for much of the time, she can respond more quickly to their needs and for that reason too they'll tend to be more contented.

Lots of mothers find that a sling gives them the chance to be close to their babies and yet allows them to have their hands free. As a baby grows older and starts to become more independent, he spends less and less time in physical contact with his mother. However, he comes back for a cuddle when he's tired, hungry, bored or upset for some reason and the physical presence of his mother's body serves to reassure and comfort him.

Many peoples in the world touch their babies much more than Westerners do. Some carry out a type of massage, often using oils to make the stroking movements even more gentle. Babies love this, as do older children.

Anthropologists believe that as a species humans were meant to be in touch with their young babies almost all the time. The amount of protein in breast milk is so low that babies prefer to feed very frequently and this necessitates being close to their mothers. Humans are classified as a 'continuous contact species'.

Physical contact is a very basic and easy way of demonstrating love and affection. We do all too little of this with our children and the slogan 'have you hugged your kid today?' perhaps serves to remind us to overcome our cold, sophisticated, no-touch twentieth century Western reserve. Touching is pleasant, not only for the child but for the adult too, but it's very easy to forget to do it. **Related topics** Bonding; cuddling; massage; mothering.

Boils and pimples A boil is a raised, reddened area of skin containing pus. The body is covered with hairs, each of which reaches the skin through a channel or follicle. A boil often starts at the root of a hair follicle when it becomes infected by bacteria. The commonest places for boils are when the skin is rubbed by clothing, such as the neck or the buttocks. A pimple is a small boil.

Boils should never be squeezed because it's all too easy to squeeze the infection deeper into the tissue and so encourage the infection to spread. Let a boil come to a head and burst on its own. You can encourage it to do so by soaking the area in the bath or by applying a hot cloth or a covered hot water bottle to it. Be careful though when doing this in small children not to have the source of heat too hot.

Boils are infectious so be careful not to spread them around the family. Most healthy children aren't susceptible to boils but those with a chronic illness or malnutrition can get crops of boils that are difficult to cure.

Once a boil has burst, simply cover it and leave it alone. It will heal in a few days. A boil in a difficult place (on the face, in the ear or in the armpit, for example) will probably need medical attention to be on the safe side. This also applies to really large boils anywhere.

If your child has a boil, don't give him any antibiotics you may have around the house. Unless the boil is very serious it will heal itself and the misuse of antibiotics could actually make it worse.

Bonding Bonding is defined as 'a phenomenon whereby adults become committed (by a one-way flow of concern and affection) to children for whom they have cared during the first few months and years of life'. In a way it is the opposite of attachment. A child becomes attached to its mother; the mother becomes bonded to her child. We say 'mother' but if someone else cares for the baby, that person can become bonded to the child as well or instead.

Bonding is not necessarily the same as loving your baby. It's well known that although many mothers feel an immediate surge of love for their newborn babies, some have no positive feelings at all. These feelings almost always grow with time, especially if the mother is able to and is allowed to care for her baby herself without interference from other people. When helping a new mother, it's best to let *her* actually care for her baby and to give her help in other ways. Bonding involves reciprocal interaction between a baby and his mother in which each plays an active role. The period immediately after birth seems to be an especially important one for the mother–baby relationship to take root. This means that mothers and babies should ideally be together right from birth and parted only when medically essential. Babies who are apathetic for whatever reason (such as illness or prematurity) don't interact as actively as full-term, healthy babies and bonding may be temporarily impaired.

You're more likely to bond easily and well to your baby if the conditions surrounding the birth are right. It's best if your baby stays with you all the time – day and night – after the birth instead of being taken to a nursery. In some hospitals premature babies who need to be in an incubator only to keep them warm are allowed to be nursed in their incubators by the mother's bedside to avoid separation.

Although sometimes essential, the separation of mother and baby is best avoided because it can occasionally lead to problems with their relationship later. If the early stress of separation is combined with other continuing problems, difficulty in bonding is more likely. It's not just the separation *per se* that can affect the development of a mother's relationship with her baby, but also the possible associated factors such as actually being denied access to the special care baby unit, her natural anxiety over her baby's condition or her fear of the equipment surrounding him, and the commonplace restriction of spontaneous interaction between a mother and her baby which is so common in maternity wards. Free access of mothers to special care units should always be allowed.

Studies around the world have shown that mothers separated from their newborn babies are more likely to batter them later and that the babies are more likely to fail to thrive. Forward-thinking planners now build premature baby units with enough room for mothers to live in close proximity to their babies.

When the conditions for optimal bonding are right, it has been shown that the mother is not only more likely to breast-feed, but is also more likely to breast-feed successfully. Researchers have also found that mothers who are allowed to be with their babies all the time behave differently towards them even up to two years later and that their babies' language development is more advanced than would be expected.

Once a bond has been formed, it persists in spite of separation. However, from the point of view of the child, separation is best avoided until he is able to cope with it and willing to accept it. The Department of Health in the UK has recommended that when children under five have to go into hospital their mothers should be allowed to stay with them.

Deep bonds can be formed later, for instance to children adopted when they are several years old.

Some women cannot be with their babies all the time perhaps because they, or their babies, are too ill. If this happens to you try to see as much as possible of your baby, have a Polaroid photograph taken to keep with you and cuddle him and stroke him as much as the medical and nursing staff will allow. Separation certainly doesn't mean that bonding cannot occur, only that it may be more difficult or take longer. *Related topics* Attachment; body contact; mothering; rooming in.

Books for children In a world increasingly dominated by TV and electronic forms of communication the book still reigns supreme as a ready source of enjoyment and education for children.

Because of the tremendous amount of fun and learning to be had from books (not to mention magazines, newspapers, comics and so on), it's sensible to lay the foundations for a love of reading in early childhood. As with most other things, a child will learn best by example. If other family members obviously enjoy reading, the child is likely to think that reading must be an enjoyable thing to do and will show interest in doing so himself. If books are looked on as important and valuable things to be used and cherished, the child will gradually think that way too.

Books are expensive if you read them once and then give them away but most families keep books for years and pass them from child to child. Jumble sales are a cheap source of children's books, though if a book is too battered a child may be reluctant to take an interest in it. Some play-groups have a small library from which a child can borrow a book. Local lending libraries are very valuable and more and more librarians are making positive efforts to encourage children to look at and read their books and to enjoy coming to the library. Don't forget to allow your child to choose for himself sometimes. Most children enjoy having some books of their own and such books are likely to be read and read again. Children delight in old favourites being repeated and this is fine, provided they also have new material to look at and read. Reading to a child has been proven to be the best way to get him reading early – and lots of children greatly enjoy being able to read on their own. Don't stop reading to your child just because he can read himself. Being read to is one of childhood's pleasures and it's a shame to cut it short unnecessarily. *Related topic* Reading.

Booster A follow-up dose of a vaccine which boosts a child's immunity to a particular disease.

Young children in the UK are routinely offered immunizations against whooping cough, diphtheria, tetanus, polio and measles. The first three are usually combined in a triple vaccine given in the first year as a course of three injections. The polio vaccine is given orally each time.

A booster is given against polio, tetanus and diphtheria when the child is about five. Whooping cough vaccine is no longer necessary at this age because the chances of a five-year-old getting the disease are small and the danger, even if he does get it, is minimal. **Related topic** Immunization.

Boredom Some children are never bored because their environment is full of things to do and because they have ample opportunity to talk to other people and play. Certain groups of young children may quite justifiably feel bored and their boredom is no reflection on their personality. Take, for example, a baby left in a cot in a quiet room on his own. His mother may want him to sleep but, if he doesn't want to sleep or if he wakes up earlier than expected, he may be left there in order to give his mother a break. Even if there are toys in the cot, a mobile over it, pretty wallpaper and an activity centre on the cot side, all these things can become very dull when seen or played with day after day. It's not surprising then that the baby bangs his head and rocks the cot or simply cries from sheer frustration at having nothing attractive with which to occupy himself.

Mentally handicapped children are another boredom-prone group because they tend to need even more stimulation than children of greater ability. Such children need to be helped to be interested in things and need a lot of time and attention during their play.

First or only children may be bored because they have no playmates unless their mothers really make an effort to entertain them or get friends in for them. A play-group for the over-threes may help here. Younger children tend not to play *with* other children but rather alongside them. Even so, they appreciate company.

Most children are bored when they are with adults talking to each other for long periods. Seen from the child's point of view, his mother, who usually spends lots of time talking to him and seems to consider him an important person, suddenly has no time for him and brushes him away with 'go away and play and I'll listen to you later'. The situation can be made more palatable for the child if the mother has the sensitivity to make time for him so as not to leave him out in the cold. Conversations between adults with young children around are inevitably punctuated by pauses while the child demands his mother's attention. Anyone with young children understands this and won't think you're impolite if you break off from what you were saying to look at what your child is showing you or to attend to his needs temporarily.

Any young child will be bored sooner or later if you give him a pile of toys and expect him to amuse himself. And children between about seven months and two years bore very quickly. Children enjoy company if they are to play for more than short periods. If you have to get on with other things, try to keep your child amused by involving him in your jobs instead of expecting him to amuse himself. For example, your toddler could 'help' with a cloth or duster when you are cleaning.

After the age of about two a child, although needing company, will usually enjoy getting immersed in activities for increasingly longer periods. You can combat periods of boredom by trips to the shops, to see a friend or simply by a change of scene. ***Related topics*** Attention; companionship; creativity; loneliness; play; play-group.

Bossing Personality differences show themselves from an early age and being bossy can be the forerunner of being a leader in later childhood and adult life. Some children quite naturally and instinctively seem to want to tell others what to do. Unfortunately, they don't yet know how to handle people successfully and end up by instructing them in what is often an overbearing manner! A tiny two-year-old is quite capable of bossing others much older and bigger than he; being bossy is no function of age or size, though, of course, it's often easier to get results if size and age are on the child's side.

Should you stop a child from being bossy? Perhaps the answer is gently to get it across to him that there are other ways of getting people to do things. This is a fairly sophisticated concept and not one that he will learn in a hurry. Don't forget that if you are in the habit of bossing by asking or ordering him to do things in an unnecessarily abrupt manner, he will copy you. 'Please' is something that comes from hearing other people use the word in context, not from being told to say it when it apparently means nothing.

Just as some children are happy to follow, others like to lead. Leadership is a valuable personality trait and one that parents should encourage. Bossiness is a young child's way of leading other people but because the older a child gets, the more unattractive it is to be led by someone bossy, the child needs to be helped to tell others what to do in a more acceptable way or he'll lose friends. ***Related topics*** Aggression; behaviour; development – social; manners.

Bottle feeding If you are one of the few women who can't produce enough breast milk for her baby; or if you try breast-feeding and decide that it's taking up more of your time than you are prepared to give up or that it has some other disadvantage inconsistent with you carrying on, then bottle-feeding is a very practical alternative. If you are encountering difficulties with breast-feeding but would really like to continue, try hard to get good and informed advice before putting your baby on the bottle – it's all too easy to stop unnecessarily.

It's important to come to bottle-feeding with a positive frame of mind even if you think of it as a second best to breast-feeding. We're extremely lucky today to have a safe alternative to breast-feeding. In centuries past most babies whose mothers couldn't feed them died unless another woman breast-fed them instead.

In this country most women choose to give their bottle-fed babies feeds prepared by mixing dried cows' milk powder with water. If you prepare feeds from anything other than a milk preparation made for babies, check with your doctor or health visitor first that it's suitable. Each animal's milk is different and breast milk has its own unique composition suited perfectly to human babies. Any other milk (including soya bean milk) has to be specially modified to make it safe for a baby; it is no longer considered safe for a young baby if you dilute cows' milk from the milkman's bottle, boil it and add sugar. The modification to make it more like breast milk is more complex than this.

Whatever milk preparation you choose to make up your baby's milk formula, it's important that the milk he drinks and the bottle and teat he drinks it from are as bacteria-free as possible. It's difficult to make a feed absolutely sterile in the domestic setting but feeds should be prepared as hygienically as possible to prevent the risk of gastroenteritis. Bottle-fed babies are more prone to this infection than are breast-fed babies because of the lack of live cells, antibodies and other protective factors in bottle milk, but with adequate hygiene the risk in this country with its clean water supplies is minimal.

Make up your baby's feeds either once a day or before each feed. There is little advantage in doing them all at once and storing them in the fridge because today's dried milk powders are so easy to prepare with boiled water from a kettle. If you make up each bottle as it's needed, you'll need to cool the milk. If you take a ready-made bottle from the fridge, you'll probably want to warm it up. Babies seem to be quite happy with cold milk if they usually have it, but most mothers prefer to give it warm. This seems sensible for a small baby because the heat supplied by the warm milk will help maintain his body temperature.

Follow the manufacturer's instructions precisely and don't add an extra scoop or pile the scoop high because this will make the milk too concentrated. Always use the scoop provided in the can and add the powder to the water, not the other way round. Shake the bottle really thoroughly because if the powder isn't properly dissolved it will clog up the hole in the teat. Once the feed is made up, either give it straight away or store it in the fridge or in a cool box. If your baby only wants a little of the milk you've made up, put the bottle back in the fridge and keep it till he's hungry again, but don't do this more than once in case bacteria multiply in the milk each time you warm it.

At night-time, make up feeds in the bottle in your bedroom or in the baby's room by adding milk powder to boiled water from a thermos flask. If you're clever, before filling the flask before you go to bed you'll wait until the boiled water in the kettle cools off a bit. If it's too hot when you prepare your baby's milk, cool the bottle under running cold water in the bathroom, or in a bowl of cold water if you don't want to make too much noise at night. The faster you can prepare a feed at night the better, to avoid your baby's cries waking the rest of the household. Keep the thermos flask well cleaned and rinse it before each use with boiling water. If your flask is not suitable for boiling liquids, sterilize it daily with a commercial solution for this purpose. Bacteria are not as likely to thrive in boiled water as they are in warm milk, but it's best not to take any risks. Some mothers take an electric kettle upstairs and boil some water as they are going to bed. By the time their baby wakes up, this water may be at just about the right temperature. This method avoids having to sterilize the thermos flask.

One very important difference between bottle-feeding and breast-feeding is that the breast can be given just to comfort the baby and as a source of pleasure as well. It doesn't have to have any milk in it for a baby to enjoy sucking. This means that a breast-feeding mother has a ready way of quietening her crying baby most of the time. However, although a baby can get comfort and pleasure from sucking at a bottle, once it's empty he can't go on sucking at it because he'll suck in air as soon as he has released the vacuum inside the bottle. Let your bottle-fed baby suck at something else if he hasn't had enough sucking when he's finished his bottle. A dummy or his fingers may be just what he needs.

Don't let your baby miss out on being cuddled, looked at and talked to just because he's being bottle-fed. This is an important part of giving him a feed and helps make feeding a very special part of his day.

If you're giving your baby some bottle milk and some breast milk, you'll probably find that fairly quickly he'll start to want the bottle first and will reject the breast if you try to give it first. This is because the milk comes out of the bottle so much more easily and he has to work less hard to get it. Also, once he has learnt to bottle-suck, he won't be as adept at getting milk from you, so breast-feeding won't be as rewarding for him. If he does want the bottle first, let him satisfy his hunger there, then put him to the breast. Even if he gets most of his milk from the bottle and simply sucks for pleasure and comfort at the breast, you'll have the pleasure of satisfying some of his needs.

If you're thinking of giving complementary bottle feeds because you don't seem to have enough breast milk, get some really sound advice on increasing your milk supply before you give the first bottle. The odds are very high that you can manage without bottles at all if you want to.

When you give a bottle feed, make yourself comfortable and hold the bottle so that there's no air in the teat. Touch the baby's cheek with your finger and he'll turn towards you, then if you touch his mouth with the teat he'll open it and you can slip the teat in. Some babies soon learn to let a little air into the bottle as they drink, in order to prevent a vacuum developing which would make it harder to suck the milk out. If your baby doesn't get the hang of this and tends to suck so hard to get the milk that he collapses the teat, just remove the bottle a little way from his mouth to release the suction every now and then. You may need to put a fingertip into his mouth alongside the teat in order to pull the bottle out.

As with breast-feeding, your baby will be happier if you feed him when he's hungry and thirsty than if you let him cry till it's time for a feed. This means that within reason, every time he cries in the early months you'll offer him a bottle. The most common cause for crying at this age is a need for milk. Babies are very different in their temperaments and needs from birth onwards, and you may have a baby who is erratic in his sleeping and feeding pattern or one who quickly falls into a recognizable pattern. Most babies fall somewhere between the two and you'll be able to predict roughly when they're likely to want a feed for at least a part or parts of every day. If your day follows a regular routine, for instance, if you wake up at the same time each day and leave the house to take the children to school at the same time, your baby will probably adopt some sort of pattern sooner than he would if all your days are different. Lots of babies behave erratically at weekends and during school holidays because the family's living pattern changes.

Bottle-fed babies are just the same as breast-fed babies in that they take different amounts of milk at different times of the day. Their behaviour changes too at different feeds. At one feed your baby may want to concentrate on gulping down his milk single-mindedly, scarcely pausing once, while at another he may take half an ounce then lose interest, perhaps because he wants to play or wants to snooze, only to come back for more twenty minutes later. There are many variations on this theme and as long as you know that this behaviour is perfectly reasonable and normal, you won't worry about it. Few babies take a full feed in twenty minutes each time. When you think about it, adults eat their meals at different rates and take longer at some mealtimes than others, for various reasons, and babies are no different. Let your baby have as much or as little as he wants to at each feed. If he takes only a little, don't try to force him to take more – you can't make him drink and he knows what he needs. When you make up your baby's feed, make up two ounces more than he usually takes, in case he has a large appetite for that particular feed.

A few parents are determined to make their babies adopt a regular feeding and resting pattern and are inflexible over feed times from birth onwards. They may well succeed in forcing their babies into their pattern, but unless they happen to have a naturally regular baby whose timing fits in with theirs, they'll also have a very unhappy baby, especially in the early days. A baby whose needs aren't met by people looking after him soon comes to lack confidence in them and because he can't seem to control his caretakers by his desperate signals, he gradually loses his self-confidence along with his trust in them. It's all very well to say he'll soon learn that he has to wait, but babies have no concept of time or of waiting. If they are left to cry, all they know is that no-one is there to satisfy their aching tummy. Loneliness, anger and fear are added to their hunger and thirst and this is the way to create a feeding problem. Once such a baby is fed, he may be so hungry and so beside himself that he can't take the feed; he may be too tired by all his screaming to suck; or he may bolt his milk along with a lot of air and then be sick afterwards.

Some mothers try to encourage a baby to adopt some sort of a routine by stretching out the gap between feeds by carrying their hungry baby around until he can wait no longer. It's certainly sensible to feed your baby as you go to bed rather than be woken an hour or so after you've fallen asleep. If you have a newborn baby who is exceptionally sleepy or apathetic or sucks weakly, you'll need a lot of patience as feeds will be long drawn-out affairs in the early days. Wake him at least every four hours, and more often if he is small or if he isn't putting on enough weight.

When your baby is about six months old, it's safe to give him pasteurized milk from the milkman. If the bottle has been opened for more than a day in the fridge, boil the milk before giving it. In the early days of the changeover from dried milk formula to bottled whole milk, you might like to dilute the milk a little because it is a lot stronger than dried milk. Carry on sterilizing the bottle and teat because bacteria can easily multiply in bottles which aren't scrupulously clean. When you stop giving your baby a bottle is up to you. You can introduce him to a cup (or a teacher beaker) at any time from six months, and because babies like to suck you'll probably find that he'll continue to want his bottle at certain times of the day, especially at night. **Related topics** Baby feeding; breast-feeding; breast-feeding problems; comforters; demand feeding; dummies; feeding equipment; feeding schedules; milk; sterilizing bottles; sucking; weaning.

Bottom shuffling Some children in the second half of their first year learn to move around on their bottoms. They may never crawl but progress from their sitting position to standing and walking. A bottom shuffler usually tucks his legs to one side, leans forward on to one or both hands and moves his bottom up towards his hands. Such a child can move around very fast and is no worse off than a conventional crawler. It's interesting that bottom shuffling seems to run in families to some extent! A child usually starts bottom shuffling at about ten months (the average age for crawling as well). Walking is usually slightly later compared with children who crawl, but there is no problem in learning to walk. About one child in ten bottom shuffles instead of crawling and a few learn both methods of getting about. *Related topic* Walking.

Bottom, sore This is usually caused by a nappy rash but can be caused by other things too. Diarrhoea or very frequent motions in a baby in nappies can cause soreness around the anus (back passage). Certain spicy foods can also cause soreness around the anus. Stopping the foods cures the condition.

The skin in the creases of the buttocks can become inflamed and sore, as can the vulva, if a baby's bottom isn't washed thoroughly and often enough. A young child's bottom and genitals should be washed every day at least once if the child is still in nappies or wets the bed and babies need their bottoms washed even more frequently.

To avoid a sore bottom, wash your baby's skin each time he soils a nappy, then rinse it well to get rid of the soap and dry him thoroughly. If he has a sore bottom, change his nappy more frequently and put on some suitable cream to protect his skin. Sunshine, or at least fresh air, heals a sore bottom quicker than anything.

When three- or four-year-olds begin to wash themselves, there's often a chance that they won't wash their bottom properly. Keep an eye on how

well the washing is being done and throw in a casual reminder if necessary.
Related topics 'Topping and tailing'; washing children.

Bouncing chair A bouncing chair can be used from very early on and
takes the form of a piece of material slung on a tubular metal frame. The
baby is put into it in a half-lying, half-sitting position and there is a strap to
help keep him in position. Sooner or later the baby will find that he can
make the chair bounce by moving his body. One danger with this sort of
chair is that at some stage the baby will lean forwards and tip the whole
chair forward so that he lands on his nose. If you think that your baby is
getting to this stage, stop using the chair. Many mothers put their bouncing
chair on a table, kitchen worktop, etc. This is terribly dangerous because a
baby can easily push the chair off.

If you are busy and your baby is happy not to be held but doesn't want to
lie down in a carrycot, you could put him in this sort of chair as an
alternative to propping him up in a sitting position in a carrycot or
somewhere else safe. It's easy to dismantle and take with you on a journey,
and the material of the seat is washable. When your baby is in the chair,
take care that other young children or dogs don't molest him. **Related topic**
Baby-bouncer.

Bowel motions Young babies by and large open their bowels several
times a day but older ones usually do so less often.

In children of all ages and in adults the bowels tend to want to move after
a meal. This is because a reflex (the gastro-colic reflex) stimulates the large
bowel to empty when food enters the stomach. This reaction occurs most
obviously after the first meal in the day (breakfast for most people) because
the stomach is nearly empty beforehand. Some breast-fed babies open
their bowels after each feed.

A baby's first bowel motions consist of a material called meconium. This
is greenish-black, smooth and sticky. Most babies open their bowels for the
first time in the first forty-eight hours. If this doesn't occur, see your doctor
or tell someone in the hospital. As the days go by the meconium changes to
the usual yellow semi-liquid bowel motion of a young baby.

Breast-fed babies usually pass large numbers of light yellow motions in a
very loose form (like diarrhoea). At first every nappy will have a buttercup
yellow stain on it. This is completely normal. If the breast-fed baby
sometimes doesn't open his bowels for a day or two, don't worry. This
again is perfectly normal and is because breast milk is so well digested and
absorbed. Even after a day or so the stools still come out soft or even liquid.
If a breast-fed baby seems to have an unusually large number of dirty
nappies (for him) look at what you've been eating and cut out possible
culprits one by one by trial and error to see if you can cure the condition.
Quite a lot of foods taken by mothers (especially spicy foods and cabbage)
can cause an increased frequency of bowel motions in their breast-fed
babies. There is no harm in this but it is extra work for you and may make
your baby's bottom sore.

Bottle-fed babies have fewer bowel motions than do breast-fed ones because cows' milk is digested very differently by the bowel. There are usually anything from one to four movements a day in the early days and one or two a day as the baby grows older. It doesn't matter how many times a day your bottle-fed child opens his bowels though as long as he does so without straining. Many normal babies and young children make grunting or straining noises but produce soft stools effortlessly. Cows' milk stools are very different from breast milk ones. They are thicker and browner or even tan coloured. Some babies have stools like scrambled eggs. Bottle-fed babies can become constipated. If sugar is added to the milk feed the stools tend to be looser and may be green.

When a baby is first put on to food other than milk, some of it may come through into his nappy undigested. This is most noticeable as he grows older and is given food of a lumpier consistency. Far from being undesirable, it simply means that the high-fibre food is helping the bowel move.

Although we as a nation tend to worry a lot about our bowel movements there is no need to worry about your baby if he is healthy and growing well. What *is* important is any change in bowel movements. A bottle-fed baby may develop hard stools suddenly because of dehydration but this is not always so. With gastroenteritis, of course, the motions are much looser.

Mucus is sometimes seen in a child's motions, especially when he has diarrhoea. Mucussy stools are also seen in a newborn baby who is perfectly healthy, in a child with a cold, a sore throat, or an infection of the lower respiratory tract (if he coughs up phlegm and then swallows it), or if undigested food passes straight through, irritating the bowel on the way.

If your baby or young child consistently has strange coloured or abnormally smelly stools, ask your doctor's advice. **Related topics** Blood in motions; constipation; dietary fibre; potty training.

Bow legs

Bow legs It is quite normal for a newborn baby to have bowed legs but this becomes less noticeable as he grows. The vast majority of all bow-legged children have normal legs by the age of five but fat children stay bow-legged for longer than slim children.

Severe bow legs are sometimes seen in rickets (vitamin D deficiency) but this is uncommon today except among certain racial groups who keep their children indoors out of the sunshine and feed them restricted diets.

Playing in a baby-walker or bouncer won't make a child's legs bow, nor will allowing him to push with his legs on your lap or encouraging him to stand up early. A bulky nappy can make a baby's normal bow-leggedness look worse than it is but almost certainly doesn't *cause* it. If nappies are consistently too bulky between the legs (as can happen if two nappies at once are used) a child can develop the habit of throwing one foot round the other as he walks. This looks uncomfortable but is his way of relieving his discomfort! The solution is to put on the nappy in a more suitable way.

If you are worried about your child's bow legs or if one leg only is bowed, see your doctor.

Brain damage A baby's brain can be damaged before, during or after birth and the outcome depends upon the type of damage, its timing, its severity and the part of the brain affected. Various things can damage the brain, including infections, injury, a lack of oxygen, jaundice and low blood sugar.

During pregnancy the baby's brain can be affected by trans-placental infection with German measles, the cytomegalovirus, listeriosis, toxoplasmosis and, rarely, syphilis. A failing placenta can so diminish the baby's oxygen supply from the mother's blood that the baby's brain may be damaged.

During birth itself it is a lack of oxygen that is the biggest culprit. This can occur because of a poor birth position (oxygen shortage is less likely if the woman is upright – standing, squatting, kneeling, or crouching during labour – than if she is lying on her back) or if the placenta isn't working well. If the umbilical cord has a knot in it which pulls tight, or if a loop passes round the baby's neck and tightens, the baby's brain may be affected because of insufficient oxygenated blood reaching it. A good obstetrician will look for signs of foetal distress caused by too little oxygen and will speed up the delivery or even deliver the baby by Caesarean section if necessary in order to prevent his brain from being damaged.

Many babies don't start breathing the moment they emerge into the world and the baby whose mother has been given large doses of pain-killing drugs shortly before delivery is more likely to have difficulty with his breathing. Some babies have a lot of blood or amniotic fluid in their breathing passages and this has to be sucked out to get their breathing started. If there is any concern that the baby may be short of oxygen, it can be given to the baby via a mask, a tube passed down the windpipe, or – in extreme emergency – by the kiss of life. For a few minutes after birth, before the placenta separates from the wall of the mother's womb, the oxygenated blood in the umbilical cord continues to supply the baby with oxygen just as it did throughout pregnancy so it makes sense not to cut the cord immediately, unless the baby needs to be taken away to be resuscitated. When the placenta has separated, the cord is seen to have stopped pulsating and can be tied and cut at leisure.

A baby's Apgar score reflects his condition at birth but there is little direct relationship between this score and the likelihood of brain damage.

Rhesus haemolytic disease used to be a serious cause of brain damage in babies but with the immunization of rhesus negative mothers and much better treatment this is no longer such a danger. Very high levels of jaundice in this condition can cause mental retardation and deafness or strange writhing movements in surviving babies.

A newborn baby's brain is sensitive to low blood sugar and this is why babies should be fed soon after birth. Colostrum and mature breast milk supply the right sugars in the right concentration and amounts. Glucose water is rarely necessary if adequate help with breast-feeding is given to women from day one. Premature or ill babies do best on their own mother's colostrum and milk.

Brain damage can produce many different signs and symptoms, depending upon how bad the damage is and which part of the brain is affected. Cerebral palsy, epilepsy, clumsiness, mental retardation and behaviour problems can all be the result of such damage. The outlook for the brain-damaged child is dependent to some extent upon his environment but it's very difficult even for an expert to predict any one child's future capabilities, partly because the effects of any brain damage often aren't apparent for some time.

Only the most severely affected brain-damaged children will need special schooling, the type of school depending upon the nature of the main disability. *Related topics* Behaviour problems; cerebral palsy; clumsiness; coordination; epilepsy; mental handicap. *Useful organizations* British Institute of Mental Handicap; National Association for Mental Health; National Society for Mentally Handicapped Children and Adults; Voluntary Council for Handicapped Children – National Children's Bureau.

Brain tumour Although many parents worry about brain tumours, they are very uncommon. Having said this, tumours of the brain and urinary systems are the commonest tumours of young children, three-quarters of all cancers affecting one of these two body systems.

The symptoms produced by a brain tumour are very varied, depending upon the part of the brain affected by the growth, but vomiting and headaches are often seen. In older children, a headache first thing in the morning, or on changing head position can be symptomatic of a tumour. Young children rarely complain of headaches so when they do they are worth taking seriously, especially if they do so repeatedly. (Keep a sense of proportion though, as very few headaches are caused by a brain tumour!) As a tumour grows the child becomes lethargic and drowsy.

Unfortunately, many brain tumours are difficult to treat. Any persistent pain in the neck or head in a young child should be reported to your family doctor, as early treatment can sometimes improve the outcome. *Related topics* Cancer; dying child.

Bras When you are pregnant or have just had a baby it's sensible to wear a firm, well-fitting bra so that your breasts, made heavy by pregnancy, don't sag and become uncomfortable. Many women worry about the effects of breast-feeding on their breasts but research suggests that it is pregnancy that affects the breasts and not breast-feeding. Women fall almost equally into three groups on this. Those who say that pregnancy and feeding has had a beneficial effect on their breast size and shape; those who notice no difference; and those who complain that their breasts are less attractive.

Whether or not you wear a bra is really up to you from this point of view but it probably makes very little difference to the long-term outcome of your breast shape.

Specialist nursing bras that open at the front or flap down to allow the baby to get at the nipple are widely available and some women like them. Many women, however, manage perfectly well with an ordinary bra, pulling the cup down when the baby wants to feed. Too tight a bra can reduce your milk duct in the breast and cause the painful swelling of a blocked duct. *Related topics* Breast-feeding.

Bravery

Bravery is the ability to show courage in the face of some kind of unpleasantness or danger. You may want your child to be brave if he is to have an injection or if he is frightened by a dog, for example, and this is an important part of growing up because lots of things in life are frightening but have to be coped with. When asking your child to be brave be sure to let him know that you realize he is scared and anxious and even tell him that you don't like such situations either. Knowing that you as a parent have fears too doesn't take anything away from your authority but simply makes you more human in his eyes and proves that he isn't abnormal.

There is a difference between bravery and fearlessness. Fear is a normal and essential part of survival and forcing a child to do something he's scared of will be no answer to the problem and could well produce problems in later life. It's unkind to make a young child fight the battle between trying to please you (which he desperately wants to do) and trying to preserve himself from the danger he sees as so real.

If a thing that produces fear *has* to be done (such as going into hospital for an operation) then you can help your child overcome his fear by staying with him. If it doesn't have to be done (such as climbing a tree) let him find his own way round the fear, perhaps with the help of his playmates or family. *Related topic* Fears.

Breast enlargement in babies

Newborn babies, boys as well as girls, are often noticed to have enlarged breasts and these are thought to be caused by hormones which have passed from the mother to the baby across the placenta before birth. If the baby's breasts are squeezed gently, milk comes out and this is known as witches' milk. The breast swelling virtually always disappears on its own and there is no need to do anything about it at all.

Breast-feeding

Breast-feeding is recommended as the best method of feeding babies by both the Department of Health in the UK and by the World Health Organization. This is because the unique composition of breast milk provides babies not only with an unrivalled source of nourishment but also confers many other health benefits. Some of these health benefits are thought to be important not only during infancy but in later life as well, long after breast-feeding has finished.

It's interesting that the word 'breast-feeding' has probably done quite a lot of harm in itself, because it's generally assumed that putting a baby to the breast is simply a form of getting nourishment into babies. It takes an instinctive or experienced breast-feeding mother or adviser to understand that breast-feeding is much more than this and that a baby allowed the breast whenever and for as long as he needs it gets much more than milk. He gets comfort, pleasure and reassurance, quite apart from the physical benefits of the jaw, mouth and tongue action during breast-feeding that is so different from that of a baby sucking at the bottle. The breast-fed baby also learns that he can control the flow of milk in several ways, whereas when bottle-feeding all he can do is suck harder or not so hard. The breast-fed baby has to 'milk' the breast as well as exerting some suction. He also has to learn how to encourage his mother's let-down reflex, which doesn't work just once during a feed but can work up to eight times in any one session at the breast. He has to work harder for his milk and there is of necessity much more of a two-way interaction between him and his mother during a feed, both physical and emotional. The fact that breast milk tastes much better than cows' milk formula is a fact that's nearly always ignored. It's noticeable that babies breast-fed on an unrestricted basis are happy and also seem to become independent early, which is usually a good indicator of inner emotional stability and security.

Because breast-feeding has been unfashionable for much of this century, the skill of helping women to breast-feed successfully (that is, for as long as they want to) was found to have been largely lost. Everyone seemed to take it for granted that breast-feeding usually failed and it took a great deal of hard work to explain that the reason for breast-feeding failure was that women were attempting to use their breasts as if they were bottles, and this doesn't usually work as the 'milking' action is different for a bottle teat.

More and more women are nowadays choosing to breast-feed but there is nevertheless a widespread body of ignorance about breast-feeding which conspires to hinder some women who start off with the best of intentions. Even today in some hospitals women are prevented from breast-feeding their newborn babies at night and their babies are given bottles of cows' milk formula. Usually in these same hospitals three- to five-hourly schedules and limited feed times are recommended and breast-feeding is forbidden at visiting time or when doctors are doing their ward rounds. Complements of cows' milk formula are advised without bothering to increase a mother's milk supply first. Until these customs change, many women will leave hospital already on the pathway to breast-feeding failure, for failure it surely is in the eyes of any woman who wants to breast-feed and finds her milk running dry.

Unlike bottle-feeding with cows' milk formula, breast-feeding works basically on a demand and supply system. The experience of thousands of mothers shows that the more a baby stimulates the milk supply by suckling at the breast, the more milk there is. This stimulation can be increased by the baby spending more time at the breast, either by feeding more frequently, or by staying there for longer at each feed, or both. If a breast-feeding mother copies a bottle-feeding one and schedules her baby to a set number of feeds a day, she's very likely to find that her milk gradually runs dry. Breast milk is absorbed much more quickly than cows' milk formula from the baby's gut because it is so easily and completely digested. This is why breast-fed babies need frequent feeds. If you take breast-fed babies off the breast before they have finished, it's the same as if an adult were dragged away from his meal while he was still hungry. One expert has found that if a breast-feeding baby is given five or fewer feeds in twenty-four-hours, it's unlikely that the milk supply will satisfy him for long. Babies fed on an unrestricted basis by day and night are not only contented but also stimulate their mothers' milk supply so that there is an increasing amount of milk for them as they grow older.

Breast-feeding is convenient for the mother and most mothers find that they enjoy feeding their babies. Researchers are now suggesting that breast-feeding on an unrestricted basis and for longer than just the first few months is not only good for babies but is also good for mothers, as the hormones circulating in their bodies are different from those in their non-breast-feeding sisters and may possibly protect them from certain disorders of their reproductive systems in later life. *Related topics* Breast-feeding problems; breast milk; demand feeding; feeding schedules; jealousy; let-down reflex; milk teeth; nipple care in mother; overfeeding; sucking; sunshine; underfeeding; weaning. *Useful organizations* La Leche League of Great Britain; The National Childbirth Trust.

Breast-feeding problems

Not enough milk This is by far the most common breast-feeding problem and the one responsible for the largest number of mothers stopping before they want to. Women produce different amounts of milk for the same sucking stimulus (the amount of time a baby spends at the breast during a day, together with the strength with which he sucks) and while some women can produce enough milk for their babies on a four-hourly, ten-minutes-a-side regime, the majority can't and need the stimulus of much more frequent feeding, for longer times, to produce enough milk. Unrestricted breast-feeding by night and day from birth onwards is the way to ensure that a baby will stimulate enough milk. If your baby isn't thriving, or if he seems unhappy or cries a lot, increase your milk supply by letting him feed as often and for as long as he wants. If you're already doing this, fit in extra feeds and express any remaining milk at the end of a feed to stimulate your milk further. Don't give complements of cows' milk formula because this will reduce your baby's hunger and thirst and his desire to suck from your breast, and will cease to stimulate your milk supply. For a few women, the amount of time they'd have to spend with their babies at the breast in order to produce enough milk is unacceptable. A few women in every thousand will find it impossible to produce enough anyway. The vast majority of women *can* make enough milk for their babies and the 'not enough milk' syndrome is often the result of mistaken advice on giving three-to-five-hourly, ten-minutes-a-side feeds – suitable for bottle-fed babies but not breast-fed ones.

Engorgement A possible problem of the early days of breast-feeding which can be avoided almost always simply by not letting too much time elapse between feeds. If the breasts overfill, they'll become swollen, hard, tense, lumpy, painful, tender and hot. The mother may feel hot and shivery and may sweat a lot and feel weepy.

If your baby won't suck properly, express your milk frequently to keep your breasts from overfilling. Express them before they are at all tender and remember to do it several times at night too if necessary. If you do get engorged, use ice packs or hot or cold compresses to relieve the pain; soften the areola by expressing some milk before the baby is put to the breast; and feed more often and for longer periods.

A blocked duct This is often mistaken for mastitis. Any abnormal tender or non-tender lump or area of lumpiness in your breast is probably caused initially by a blocked milk duct. If this happens, check that your whole breast is emptied thoroughly at each feed: express afterwards if your baby doesn't want much milk. Feed your baby often enough to avoid lumpiness due to overfilling. Give the lumpy breast first because it will then stand the best chance of being emptied well. Change the position in which your baby feeds several times within a feed and massage the lump towards the nipple during and after a feed to try to clear it. Check that your bra or clothing isn't pressing anywhere, and avoid sleeping on your stomach at night. Relieve any pain with hot compresses or a hot water bottle. If the symptoms improve, it'll probably be several days before the lump goes completely. If it gets worse, consult your doctor because mastitis due to infection can easily occur in the stagnant milk behind a blocked duct. You shouldn't stop feeding but make sure you get plenty of rest.

Mastitis This usually starts off as a blocked duct which isn't treated properly. You'll need an antibiotic from your doctor to clear it up but there's rarely any need to stop breast-feeding. Poorly treated mastitis can become a *breast abscess*. One survey showed that an abscess was highly likely if a woman stopped breast-feeding when she got mastitis. If you have an abscess, don't feed the baby from the affected breast: express and discard the milk temporarily, and be sure to take the full course of antibiotics.

Breast-feeding problems in the early days can be caused by a baby who is a difficult feeder. Some babies suck poorly or weakly following the use of pain-killers by the mother in labour; others, because they are pre-term, jaundiced, mentally handicapped, have a cleft lip or palate or are tired because they have been crying, may need patience and skilled help to get them sucking adequately. Your expressed or pumped milk can be given by spoon if necessary. If you know about this problem beforehand, you can avoid having pain-killers in labour – especially pethidine late in labour.

Remember that your milk supply depends on frequent and adequate stimulation, so express or pump your breasts frequently (two- or three-hourly) if your baby isn't doing the job for you. Insist on your right to feed your baby in hospital whenever he cries. It's ridiculous for a baby to tire himself out by crying because 'it's not time for a feed'. With patience, perseverance and common sense, together with skilled advice and support, you'll be able to keep your milk supply going until.your baby sucks more strongly.

A poor feeding position is the basic cause of many babies' difficulty with breast-feeding. Experiment with different positions and ask an experienced midwife to help you help your baby to take enough of the breast in his mouth. Don't press on the back of his head while he's at the breast because he'll automatically push back. Too full a breast may make it difficult for a baby to suck and milk the nipple and part of the areola. Soften if before a feed by expressing a little milk, and don't let too much time elapse between feeds. If you have inverted nipples, use a breast shell for a few minutes before a feed.

Babies exhibit all sorts of different behaviour at the breast: some gulp their milk down and others take ages over feeds. Some babies fight at the breast before the milk is let down, through impatience. Make sure your breast isn't smothering him; get your milk flowing before a feed; and try feeding him in a different position.

Some babies are overwhelmed by the force of the let-down milk. You may have to collect the fast-flowing milk early in a feed and give it to your baby later by spoon, otherwise he may cough, splutter, swallow a lot of wind, or refuse the breast altogether. You could try giving only one breast per feed if you have too much milk.

If your baby bites you, take him off the breast and say 'no' firmly. Most mothers get over this problem with ingenuity and patience. Some use a rubber nipple shield to protect their nipples until their baby learns not to bite.

Unfortunately, far too few health professionals understand how to deal with common breast-feeding problems. Probably the best sources of readily-available help are the nationwide self-help groups such as the National Childbirth Trust and La Leche League (addresses on pages 774 and 770 respectively). **Related topics** Appetite; breast-feeding; cleft lip and palate; feeding schedules; nipple care in mother; overfeeding; sleepy baby; underfeeding; weaning. **Useful organizations** La Leche League of Great Britain, National Childbirth Trust.

Breast milk Scientists of all sorts are agreed that breast-feeding is the best way to feed babies. The milk of each mammal is specific for its young and humans are no exception. Breast milk is like no other milk from any other animal: its contents are unique in their proportions and concentrations and cannot be reproduced by the manufacturers of baby milk formula no matter how hard they try. For one reason, breast milk contains live cells and active enzymes. Virtually any form of treatment of cows' milk (the main constituent of milk formula) kills the live cells and inactivates the enzymes, both of which are valuable to the baby when present in their natural, unadulterated form in breast milk. For another, breast milk contains specialized proteins – the immunoglobulins – which carry antibodies conferring protection against certain infectious diseases. The antibodies in cows' milk formula are no use to a baby because not only have they been altered by the processing of the milk, but also they would only have been active against the diseases affecting cows.

Milk contains proteins, fats, carbohydrates, minerals, vitamins, hormones, enzymes, various anti-infective substances and live cells, not to mention traces of some foodstuffs the mother has eaten, together with certain medicines she may have taken and alcohol and nicotine if she drinks and smokes.

Breast milk looks different from cows' milk formula: it is thinner looking and, apart from colostrum (the first milk made after birth), is not as creamy-looking as cows' milk formula and may even be bluish-white. Early on in a feed the drops of milk at the nipple are more watery than towards the end, when their higher fat content makes them look richer and more creamy. No matter what it looks like (and both appearance and content alter during a feed), breast milk is always more valuable to a baby than cows' milk.

Colostrum can be expressed from the breasts even before a baby is born. The baby needs very little of this valuable milk but even the few millilitres he drinks each time at the breast are precious. There is no need for a baby to be given anything in the first few days of life other than colostrum except in a few special circumtances. His body contains enough water to tide him over until larger quantities of breast milk are produced within a day or two. Colostrum is rich in proteins (especially antibodies), cells, minerals, vitamins A, E and B_{12}, and has less fat and sugar than later milk. Its composition is perfectly suited to the needs of a newborn baby.

The volume and composition of breast milk alter throughout the day according to a mother's eating and sleeping patterns. Breast milk produced by mothers whose babies are premature differs in composition from the milk of mothers of full-term babies. This pre-term milk fits an immature baby's needs perfectly.

Breast-fed babies are statistically healthier than bottle-fed babies. They are less likely to suffer from infections – particularly various sorts of infectious diarrhoea and certain respiratory infections. They are also less likely to have allergic problems, to die from a cot death, or have dental decay later. Research suggests that ulcerative colitis and Crohn's disease may also be less common in adults who were breast-fed as babies, as may heart disease causing angina and heart attacks. **Related topic** Breast-feeding; milk. **Useful organization** La Leche League of Great Britain.

Breath-holding attacks
A child who has breath-holding attacks is often intelligent, easily frustrated and reacts in a dramatic way to get

attention. The attack begins with a deep breath in as if he were about to scream but instead he holds his breath and his face goes redder and redder and eventually blue. Most attacks end at this stage but a severe one can end with a convulsion or a short period of unconsciousness from which he quickly recovers. There is no permanent damage to the brain. Such attacks rarely occur when the child is alone.

Slapping the child rarely makes him stop but putting your finger over the back of his tongue and hooking it forwards usually starts the breathing again. This has to be done early in an attack though before he clenches his teeth.

Such manoeuvres are a poor second best to trying to prevent such attacks which can be difficult. Try to avoid situations in which you know he becomes frustrated and handle the attacks sensitively rather than with punishment and he'll stop them in time. Almost all children who have such attacks grow out of them before the age of five. *Related topics* Behaviour problems; temper tantrums.

Breathing difficulties These are usually caused by a blockage or impairment in the breathing system, but may be caused by a heart problem. Laryngitis, bronchiolitis, croup, pneumonia, a foreign body stuck in the nose or throat, food allergy, and irritant fumes can all cause difficulties in breathing. In the prematurely newborn the respiratory distress syndrome can be a cause. Repeated breathing difficulties, especially with wheezing, should make you think of asthma.

Whatever the cause, the child who has difficulty in breathing is a distressing sight. His neck muscles stand out prominently and there are dips and gullies between the ribs. Feeding is especially troublesome for such a baby because whilst feeding he becomes even more breathless and may even be unable to feed at all. If your baby ever seems to become exhausted during a feed, tell your doctor at once.

Always call a doctor urgently if your baby or young child becomes breathless or has noisy breathing. Don't wait until things become more serious but act quickly. The only exception to this is if your child is an asthmatic and you are quite confident that this attack is as usual. *Related topics* Allergy; asthma; bronchiolitis; croup; foreign body; humidifier; laryngitis; pneumonia; respiratory distress syndrome; vaporizer; wheezing.

Broken homes Children in our society ideally need two parents to bring them up so that they have the best chance of living secure and emotionally stable lives. Homes that deprive children of a male and a female 'model' undoubtedly leave the child poorer for it. Deprivation (especially of a mother in the first few years of life) has widespread and far-reaching effects. A young child under five is too immature to cope with all the emotions stirred up by a broken home and lots of research has shown that such deprivation early in life does affect the child's future. *Related topics* Divorce; one-parent families; separation of parents. *Useful organizations* Gingerbread; One Parent Families.

Bronchiolitis A viral infection of the bronchioles (the smallest air passages in the lungs) seen most commonly in babies between two and six months of age in the winter and spring.

Most of the babies that get the condition have been exposed to an adult or an older child with a respiratory infection. The baby's bronchioles fill with mucus and his breathing is impaired. He may wheeze or cough and can go blue. If ever you think your baby has bronchiolitis, tell your doctor at once. He will assess the baby's condition and send him to hospital if necessary. There, the staff will put the baby in an oxygen tent or incubator and keep his nose and throat clean by sucking out the mucus. They'll also watch his intake of fluids and food and may even have to feed him intravenously. Antibiotics are not used routinely for bronchiolitis.

More than half of all babies with bronchiolitis caused by the commonest virus go on to have recurrent episodes of mild wheezing during childhood. *Related topic* Pneumonia.

Bronchitis An inflammation of the linings of the main air passages in the lungs (the bronchi). The condition is usually caused by viruses but can also be bacterial in origin. In children especially, the main airway from the larynx to the lungs (the trachea) is also affected, so giving rise to the more accurate term tracheo-bronchitis. It is uncommon in the under-fives.

It isn't known why some children are so prone to bronchitis but it is thought that climate and air pollution play a part. Children with tonsillitis, sinus infections, congenital heart disease or a chronic condition such as cystic fibrosis are more prone to bronchitis. Some parents use the term 'bronchitis' to describe the bubbly noise that some babies make when they have a cold. This is not bronchitis. Teething doesn't cause bronchitis, though bronchitis *can* occur coincidentally during the long period of a child's life when he is teething.

Some children with bronchitis wheeze but by no means all such children have asthma. Wheezy bronchitis is more common in fat children and tends to disappear by the age of seven.

The treatment of bronchitis includes physiotherapy and postural drainage of the child's chest. This can be performed by the parents after a demonstration. No cough medicines are of any use and antibiotics are not used routinely. In young children what seems like 'bronchitis' sometimes turns out to be the early stage of measles, 'flu, whooping cough or scarlet fever. *Related topics* Wheezing.

Bruises Darkened areas of skin caused by the accumulation of blood. Bruises are usually caused by a knock which was hard enough to break blood vessels but not strong enough to break the skin. A bruise starts off as a dark, blackish-brown area and then lightens and changes colour as the blood cells that have leaked out are absorbed by the body. This takes about seven days for a medium-sized bruise.

It can be difficult to know whether a child has broken a bone if there is a big bruise but in general bruises get better with time and fractures get worse. If you are in any doubt, see your doctor who may have an x-ray taken of the area.

Emergency first-aid for bruises isn't effective unless it's done very soon after the event. The most effective is an ice pack. Get a polythene bag, fill it with ice cubes and place it over the area for ten to fifteen minutes. Apart from this first-aid treatment, never do anything else to bruises, no matter how large they are.

If your child seems to bruise very easily he may have a serious blood condition such as leukaemia or haemophilia but as these are very uncommon, there's no need to worry unnecessarily.

Bruising, especially in babies, can have another significance – it is often the only outward sign that the child is being physically assaulted ('battered'). The NSPCC will respect your confidentiality and by reporting the incident you might save the child further damage or worse. **Related topics** Child abuse; violence against children. **Useful organization** National Society for the Prevention of Cruelty to Children.

Burns Burns are fairly common injuries in children, especially in young ones who have no sense of the danger of hot things and fires. The aim of every parent must be to prevent trouble occurring by having fires guarded (it is illegal to leave a child under twelve in a room with an unguarded fire) and to foresee dangers from other hot surfaces well in advance.

Because a burn is a raw area of the body it can leak tissue fluid and also become infected. Anything other than the smallest burn must receive medical attention because of these dangers.

If your child burns himself: 1. Remove the source of burning; 2. cool the affected area at once; 3. treat the shock if the burn is severe, and 4. get medical help if you're at all worried. Don't put cotton wool or other fluffy dressings on the area as they can become stuck to the burn and are difficult and painful to remove. Don't put grease, oils or creams on the wound. Leave blisters alone – to burst them encourages infection.

Place the burned part under running water for several minutes or until the pain goes but don't do this if the skin is charred. If you can't do this, splash the area with water but not iced water, as this can be painful in itself. Don't pull off any clothing that's burned on to the area: pulling off adherent clothing from burnt flesh is a job for experts. If a chemical has caused the burns, douse the area thoroughly with plenty of water and be sure not to burn yourself on the chemical-soaked clothing.

By and large medical attention will be needed for any child who has anything but the tiniest of burns and will certainly be essential if the child is shocked.

If the burn is small, dry the area carefully, applying a dry dressing (preferably a non-adhesive burns dressing from your first-aid box), bandage the area lightly to hold the dressing in place, keep the burnt part elevated to reduce swelling and give the child a pain-relieving tablet (in the correct dose) if the pain is bad. If a burn becomes red, pussy, weeps, or is increasingly painful, get medical help. Infection may produce scarring later.

All electrical burns should be seen by a doctor. Scalds in the mouth can be relieved by sucking ice. Treat severe friction burns just like other burns. *Related topics* Accident; accident prevention; fires; scalds; sunburn.

Burping In the Western world many mothers seem to want to 'burp' their babies. This is a cultural phenomenon that is not seen in many other areas of the world.

There is no doubt that some babies, whether breast-fed or bottle-fed, seem to swallow more air than others and that this sometimes makes them cry or be restless until it comes up (or goes down). When the child is put into an upright position (such as over the mother's shoulder or sitting up on her lap), the release of the air as a burp often seems to relieve him.

Burping a baby does no harm, provided that it doesn't interfere with a feed. There are many mothers who stop their baby while he is still feeding happily and poke and jiggle him about until they get the ritual burp, by which time the baby is crying because he wants to carry on feeding. Others wake their baby to burp him at the end of a feed. Neither practice is necessary nor very nice for the baby. At the end of a feed, if you can easily hold your sleeping baby in a semi-upright position without waking him, do so, if he is normally a windy baby. Otherwise don't bother. Hold him like this for a minute or so and if he hasn't brought up any wind by then he probably won't, so you can put him down to sleep.

Our experience teaches us that young babies in particular want cuddling after a feed and that most mothers naturally cuddle their babies in an upright or semi-upright position. If you do this then any wind that is there will come up on its own and you won't need to pat your baby's back or do anything else at all unless you enjoy doing it anyway. *Related topic* Wind.

Caesarean section An abdominal operation to deliver a child from the uterus in a woman in whom a vaginal delivery is impossible or dangerous, either to the mother or the baby.

The main problems with this sometimes life-saving operation arise post-operatively. The abdomen is sometimes very painful and you'll probably need really effective pain-killing drugs during the first day or two. Though the pain gradually improves as the scar heals, you won't be pain-free for several weeks.

After about a day in bed most women are up and about, going to the lavatory, walking up and down the ward or corridor, sitting in a chair – albeit cautiously – and eating a light diet. Because of the soreness and the after-effects of the anaesthetic some women don't 'bond' to their babies as easily as if they had had an uncomplicated delivery. This problem is lessened to some degree if the Caesarean section is carried out under epidural anaesthesia because the woman will be able to hold her baby as soon as he is born if he is breathing well and won't feel tired and 'woozy' as she might after a general anaesthetic. Mothers allowed to hold their babies immediately post-operatively have been found to feel less pain than those whose babies are kept from them.

It usually takes at least six weeks for women delivered by Caesarean section to feel as fit as a vaginally-delivered woman. Most women are in hospital for seven to ten days.

The key to successful breast-feeding after a Caesarean section is to find a comfortable position in which to feed and this means help from the nurses. Don't be embarrassed to spend time experimenting with the feeding position. If the baby is not put to the breast often enough, and if a mother is not encouraged to breast-feed at night, the milk won't come in as soon as it might. The very fact of having an operation and an anaesthetic may also delay the appearance of the milk (other than the still valuable colostrum). Perseverence and knowledgeable help enable a mother to breast-feed successfully. Initiating breast-feeding is more difficult in those hospitals which keep babies apart from mothers who have had Caesarean sections. Insist on keeping your baby with you all the time unless he is ill.

The scar from the most commonly performed incision is usually completely invisible under the pubic hair within a few months. A return to sexual activity is possible just as early (or even earlier) than after a vaginal delivery and fertility isn't altered in any way. Most women are going about their normal lives four to six weeks after a Caesarean section though it's best to do nothing but the lightest lifting or housework for the first month.

Just because a woman has once had a 'Caesar' doesn't mean another will be essential next time. Each pregnancy is different. *Useful organizations* Association for Improvements in the Maternity Services; Association for Post-natal Illness; National Association for Maternal and Child Welfare; The National Childbirth Trust.

Calamine lotion
A soothing, pink lotion for use on the skin. It contains zinc oxide and ferric oxide and can be bought without a prescription. It is useful for any itchy condition, especially bites, stings and prickly heat. It is best applied liberally and frequently with a piece of cotton wool and dries to a white or pink crust or powder (depending on the thickness of the lotion) but this does no harm to the skin. Keep it well out of the reach of children when you are not actually applying it. Having said this, there is no danger from a child licking the dried lotion on his skin.

Camping
Holidays under canvas can be great fun, even with young children and for many city children they offer a real taste of the countryside in the raw. Many campsites today, especially on the Continent, are very sophisticated. Such places have shops, lavatories, washing facilities and play areas for children. Whether you choose this sort of campsite or something more rural is up to you.

When camping ensure that everyone has meaningful jobs to do, even the under-fives. They hate to sit around watching others being busy. It's a good idea to plan at home what needs doing and to allot jobs to the family accordingly. Having a dress rehearsal in the garden at home can be great fun and means you know what to do when you arrive at the site. A five-year-old will enjoy, and can be very useful with, even quite grown-up jobs, so don't underestimate his abilities. A four-year-old can help assemble tent poles and a two-year-old can help lay them out. Two-year-olds will love zipping up the tent and fetching and carrying.

If you're taking a baby you'll need all your normal baby care things. A very young baby is easiest to take camping if he is breast-fed and sleeps in his mother's sleeping bag. You could also take a collapsible canvas travelling cot. Disposable nappies will free you from hours at the launderette. Older children will need rubber boots and some warm and waterproof clothing in case it's chilly or wet as well as all the usual changes of clothes you'd normally take on holiday.

Water is the main problem when camping with young children. If they get wet, it's very difficult to dry things out unless you are in a hot country. Take plenty of changes of clothes and ensure that everyone has one really waterproof outfit. If you'll be on a boat, don't forget you must have life-jackets for the children. These can usually be hired.

If the lavatories on a camp site are primitive or dirty, your children may sometimes be reluctant to go and may become constipated. Counter this by choosing a site with clean and well-maintained lavatory and washing facilities or by taking your own portable toilet. Take your own lavatory paper with you if necessary.

Cancer A rare condition in young children but because deaths from other childhood illnesses are now so uncommon cancer has become a leading cause of death in the under-fives. The two most commonly affected areas of the body are the brain and the urinary system. Leukaemia is a cancer of certain blood-producing cells.

Treatments have greatly improved in recent years and are better tolerated by children than by adults. Cure rates are improving too with, for example, more than half of all children with acute leukaemia alive five years or more later and some even appearing to be totally 'cured'.

The trend today is to tell the child with cancer much more than ever before. Telling the child about the possible complications of anti-cancer treatment actually seems to reduce their number and severity, so it's well worth doing but clearly many under-fives won't be in a position to understand. The decision will have to be made on an individual basis. There is a tremendous burden on the family of a child known to be dying from a cancer but the child himself is often remarkably happy, and parents usually cope better with their grief if they share in the management of their child. The heartening thing about cancer in young children is that the outlook *is* improving for many of them and in the next ten years we shall undoubtedly see even greater advances. **Related topics** Bereavement; dying child.

Caput A harmless swelling usually on the back of a baby's head caused by the pressure of the head against the opening of the cervix and walls of the birth canal as he is being born. The swelling is caused by a leakage of tissue fluid into the deep layers of the skin and usually disappears within a day or two at the very most. Even if a caput is on a baby's face no treatment is necessary and no harm is done. *Related topic* Cephalhaematoma.

Cardiac massage A procedure to restore the heartbeat when it has stopped. In children the heart only stops beating after drowning, electrocution, drug overdose or other poisoning, or some other major threat to life. This is a very different picture compared with adults in whom the heart usually stops (if and when it does so) because of some underlying heart disorder or disease.

Before starting to do anything about a stopped heart you have to be able to recognize that it has in fact stopped. The child whose heart has stopped is unconscious, looks pale or grey, has very large pupils (the black areas in the centre of his eyes), no pulse in his neck, his heart can't be felt beating in the left side of his chest and there is no audible heartbeat when you listen with your ear to the left side of his chest.

If by these criteria you are sure that his heart has stopped, get the child to the ground and lie him on his back. Give one sharp, hard, blow to the chest with the side of your hand just to the left of the breast bone, and see if the heart re-starts. If it does, a pulse can be felt in the neck, the heart will be heard in the chest and the child will quickly regain his normal colour.

If the heart doesn't restart, take the heel of one hand and press firmly (not sharply) and rhythmically (at about 80 times/minute) on the lower end of the breastbone so that the centre of the chest moves inwards about one inch each time you press. In a baby, use two fingers and press at about 100 times/minute. When doing heart massage on a baby, press higher up the breastbone so as not to damage the liver, which is large and easily ruptured.

While you are pumping the heart by pressing on the chest wall in this way get someone else gently to blow breaths (using only very small breaths) into the child's nose and mouth, making sure that his head is pulled back so that his nostrils point directly upwards. Get the helper to do one breath for every five heart compressions you do and in babies be sure to use only the amount of breath held in the cheeks – don't breathe from the lungs. Keep on doing this until the child's heart restarts or until professional help comes. *Once the heart has restarted, stop the cardiac massage at once*, as it is dangerous to continue. Always stay with the child until professional help arrives and keep a close eye on his condition.

Car pools A system of sharing the transportation of children around a neighbourhood. Instead of each mother driving to take her child to play-group, nursery school, school, dancing lessons and so on, a group of mothers arranges to share the ferrying of children so that they each do it less often. This saves petrol as well as time.

Experience shows that there are some basic rules that are worth adhering to. The first is to have a pool of a size such that the smallest car can ferry all the children safely. This means in the back seat or back of an estate car. Each child must be ready to go at exactly the agreed time so that when the driver of the day knocks at the door or 'beeps' her horn outside the house the child is ready to hop in. If your child is ill, cancel in plenty of time to save the driver a wasted journey. If you are the driver, do be punctual. Keep the children well disciplined and secure as many as possible in seat belts or harnesses. When you drop a child off stay there until you actually see him go into the house.

If your child is being picked up by someone different, make sure he knows who it will be beforehand. If the arrangement has been made some time ahead, it's worth checking so that your child isn't left stranded.

If you stick to these few rules car pools are a good idea, provided you are happy about other people driving your children. This means knowing the other members of the pool fairly well and ensuring to your satisfaction that their driving comes up to your standards. A mother who's feeling off colour physically or mentally must realize that she's responsible not only for her children but for other people's too and shouldn't drive if she's unwell or over-tired.

Only arrange a lift for your child if you know he will be able to cope with leaving you.

Carrycots A carrycot is a useful piece of equipment though by no means an essential one. It provides a snug place for a baby to lie and when used with a hood and an apron can be made waterproof. In the smallest, most basic sort of carrycot there is no mattress and little room to put one, but a sheepskin or a soft blanket folded several times will provide a comfortable base. Most carrycots can be fitted into a transporter to turn them into a pram. The ride is bumpy as there is no suspension or springing system, but babies probably don't mind. A transporter folds easily, which makes a carrycot and transporter combination very suitable for the mother who travels a lot by car or bus.

For a little more money you can buy a carrycot-transporter duo which looks more like a conventional pram, with a small, lightweight pram top with carrying straps and a well-sprung but collapsible chassis. This will last your baby through to toddlerhood and is a more comfortable ride, but is heavier and often larger than the basic carrycot and transporter.

In spite of the carrying handles provided, a carrycot is fairly awkward to carry far, especially with a heavy baby inside. With two people, though, carrying it is much easier. Some carrycots have rings inside to which a safety harness can be attached, but many mothers stop using a carrycot before their babies are in any danger of falling out simply because they are too small for comfort.

In a car, a carrycot can be secured to the back seat with specially fitted safety straps. When a baby is old enough to sit up, he is probably best put in a child's safety seat on the back seat of the car.

Take care to check your baby's carrycot every so often for signs of wear and tear. The straps in particular are not very strong.

One relatively new idea in baby equipment is the pram buggy. This is basically a carrycot which fits into a wheeled base. When you want to turn the 'pram' into a buggy, the buggy seat material is simply fitted on to the wheeled base and the carrycot or pram top is put away.

Car safety The modern child spends quite a lot of time in cars. Unfortunately, many parents don't take car safety very seriously. This can end tragically. Each year about 1,300 children under thirteen are killed or seriously injured in cars and another 7,000 are slightly injured in the UK. Many of these tragedies could have been prevented.

In a car, safety is basically a simple matter. Never let children under five ride in the front seat. Adult seat belts cannot adequately restrain children when a car is going at even a modest speed and has to stop suddenly. Adult seat belts *can* be used in conjunction with seat wedges (booster cushions) made by at least one Continental car manufacturer but very few under-fives are large enough or heavy enough for these to be useful.

At the time of going to press, there are no laws that say your child must travel in the back of a car but there is rising pressure to introduce such laws.

Many parents foolishly expose their young children to terrible dangers by carrying them on their lap in the front seat. Even if a car just has to stop suddenly a baby or young child can be crushed between the adult's body and the windscreen. If you need to carry your baby or child always make sure you sit in the back.

Babies should be in a secured carrycot or strapped into a baby's car safety seat. A baby won't be able to use such a seat much before six months because until then he's too small and can't keep his head steady enough. As children get too old for baby seats in cars (some time in their third year usually), they enter a difficult phase when they're too small for adult seat belts yet aren't safe 'free' in the back. The answer is to use a special child harness, though the child will feel more restrained than in an inertia seat belt. Carrycot restraining straps, baby seats and child harnesses all need to be properly anchored to the car and this is a professional job.

Many modern cars have child safety locks on their back doors to stop children opening them from the inside. It's best always to keep the child lock on even if it's annoying for adults who sit in the back to have to be let out. It's safer than forgetting to put them on again.

One of the greatest dangers in cars with the under-fives is that they get bored and tired and become a serious distraction to the driver. This can be dangerous, especially for a mother who is already short of sleep or worn out by a demanding toddler. Whatever you do, never drive with so much noise or distraction in the car that you feel unsafe. It might not only be your life but those of your child and innocent parties who could suffer if you do.

Never leave your children alone in a car with the engine running, with the key in the ignition, or parked on a slope or hill. Babies can become dangerously overheated if left in a car on a hot or sunny day with the windows closed. In fact, with the increase in baby snatching, it's best not to leave your baby or child alone in a car at all.

The fumes from clothes just picked up from the dry cleaner have proved overwhelming in some cases in a closed car. Remember to open windows when you carry your freshly-cleaned clothes home. *Related topics* Car seats; road safety. *Useful organization* The Royal Society for the Prevention of Accidents.

Car seats Children under five should always be restricted in special car seats made for the purpose or be strapped in using child harnesses or the adult seat belts and sitting on specially-made wedges ('booster cushions').

There are lots of different models and makes of child car seat, each claiming to provide easier, more effective protection for your child. Babies, once out of restrained carrycots, need extra protection around their necks in addition to that supplied by older children's car seats. Children between 20 (9kg) and 40 pounds (18kg) (approximately nine months to four years) need extra protection around the rib cage because this is small and more susceptible to injury than an adult's). Children of these ages should therefore be carried in properly designed seats that are high enough to support the head and preferably with an in-built harness.

Ideally, you should only buy a car seat with the BSI 'kitemark' on it because such seats have been tested and proven to be safe. A well-designed car seat should have shoulder straps and a strap in the crutch. The crutch strap prevents the child from 'submarining': slipping under the straps on collision. When buying a car seat make sure that the buckle or clip that secures the harness is not too awkward for you to do up and undo repeatedly yet is not so simple that the child himself can undo it. Some newer designs of car seat are made to face backwards for added safety but these can often be difficult to fit into British cars.

All car seats need to be fitted to the car securely. Some are fixed using existing adult seat belts but most need special anchorages to be made on the car. This is a professional job but is not expensive.

If you have car seats make sure your children use them for *every trip*.

Cataract An opacity of part or all of the lens in the eye. It may be visible to the naked eye of an observer as a whiteness in the pupil but is usually only visible with a special instrument.

Babies can be born with cataracts when the mother has had German measles during pregnancy, or has been poorly nourished, or the baby has galactosaemia. Congenital cataracts may develop in Down's syndrome. Cataracts that develop later in childhood are usually caused by eye injury or inflammation.

Cataracts can be operated upon but the operation is rarely done in babyhood unless the condition is causing blindness in both eyes. A child from whom the lenses have been removed will need to wear glasses or contact lenses for life. *Related topics* Eyes; vision. *Useful organization* Royal National Institute for the Blind.

Catarrh An increase in the normal amount of mucus produced by the membranes lining the nasal passages, throat, ears and sinuses. The catarrh so produced may trickle down the back of the child's throat and make him cough. It is then usually swallowed and passes through his bowel with the food he eats. Some catarrh is thick and tends to make a child speak with a nasal intonation.

The commonest causes of catarrh are the common cold, sinus infection, inflammation of the adenoids and allergies.

Catarrh usually produces nasal stuffiness or snuffliness and a cough but there can also be deafness (if the openings of the Eustachian tubes are blocked), bronchitis, or even vomiting and diarrhoea if a viral infection affects the intestine too.

The treatment of catarrh is to cure the cause if possible and nasal sprays and antihistamine medicines can be useful to relieve troublesome symptoms. Antibiotics are used only if there is evidence of an infection with bacteria. Catarrh caused by the common cold needs no treatment, other than to treat the cold. *Related topics* Colds; glue ear; hay fever; sinusitis.

Cat net A specially made net that keeps cats off a baby left in a pram or carrycot. It fits between the hood and the body of the pram and if made of a very fine mesh material will double as an insect net for the summer too. Even if you have no cat yourself it's worth having a cat net, because cats love sleeping on or next to a warm baby and could theoretically scratch or suffocate them. Some children are also allergic to cats and wheeze or get a rash when a cat is close by.

Celebrations Amid the hustle and bustle of modern family life it's sometimes easy to miss the opportunity to celebrate special occasions. Celebrations need not be hard work for you, though, and children appreciate the simplest and cheapest of attempts to set the scene. In some families not only are children's birthdays marked with a party of some sort but so also are those of the adults. It's a good idea to make your children aware that they are not the only ones who have birthdays or who get presents at Christmas. Involve them in choosing and packing presents and sending cards to relatives, friends, neighbours and so on. This will be more fun if they make their cards (or even sometimes presents) to give away. The joy of giving is learnt to some extent by your example and in these acquisitive times it's all too easy to forget that even the most expensive gifts are not necessarily as highly valued as carefully and lovingly home-made ones.

Most of the religious festivals give cause for a celebration, often with a special theme. Easter, for instance, is much loved by children who thoroughly enjoy the fluffy yellow chickens on the cake and the Easter egg hunt in the garden. Don't be so involved in the material side of the celebrations that you forget to teach your child the true significance of the festival. *Related topics* Birthdays; birthday party.

Cephalhaematoma A harmless swelling on a newborn baby's head that is really like a large bruise of the scalp. The normal process of being born puts great pressure on the head and can cause a collection of blood between the skull bones and the scalp (a cephalhaematoma). It doesn't connect with or have anything to do with the brain and may or may not be present at birth. Some children develop one a few days after birth. Unlike a caput which can occur anywhere on the head and is caused by tissue fluid, a cephalhaematoma is more localized, is a collection of blood, and never spreads over the midline to the other side of the head. It subsides on its own over a few weeks and causes no trouble. *Related topic* Caput.

Cereals Foods made from grains. There is no special order in which non-milk foods should be introduced into a baby's diet but commonly the first foods given are some kind of cereal. In many ways this is a pity because highly refined cereals (with all their fibre and therefore many of their vitamins and minerals removed) are neither tasty nor particularly nutritious. There is no reason why a baby's first food *should* be cereal of any kind but if it is it should be made from whole-of-the-grain cereal.

A baby is not ready to digest cereal until he is several months old and making the necessary enzymes. Whatever form of cereal food you start with, it can be given dry or wet. To get a baby used to feeding from a spoon the cereal needs to be wet. This is often the stage at which some parents start to introduce cow's milk into their breast-fed baby's diet but this isn't necessary or even desirable. It's best only to introduce one new food at a time into a baby's diet. Try wetting cereal with water. Your baby will probably like it just as much.

The vast majority of cereal products made especially for babies are highly-refined and costly. They are fortified with vitamins and minerals but this is only necessary because the manufacturers have taken out most of the vitamins and trace elements when refining the cereal in the first place. Many packeted cereals also have added salt and sugar which are quite unnecessary for a baby. Wholegrain cereal such as Weetabix or whole oat porridge can be given as your baby's first food.

If there is a history of allergy in the family it's possible that your baby could be allergic to wheat and its products. If this is so try him on cereals of other kinds (oats, corn, rice, or barley) and omit wheat from his diet altogether for several months.

Babies vary greatly in their enthusiasm for cereal. Start off by offering it once a day only and if the child doesn't like it, don't worry.

As a child grows he'll be influenced by TV advertising and his friends and may want to have breakfast cereals which have sugar or malt added. Sugar and malt are both fattening sugars which also encourage tooth decay and are better eaten only occasionally. **Related topics** Food; sugar.

Cerebral palsy The term cerebral palsy covers several conditions including spasticity, paralysis, involuntary movements, incoordination of movements, and sensory loss involving balance, each of which is caused by non-progressive damage to a part of the brain. The type of condition depends on the extent and the site of the damage to the brain. Children may be affected in varying degrees and many children with mild cerebral palsy carry on a perfectly normal life with only very minor disability. Others are severely affected and have to live out their lives in wheelchairs. Brain damage has many possible causes and it's sometimes difficult to know exactly how the damage was done. Before birth, a baby's brain can be harmed by an infection of the mother with cytomegalovirus, toxoplasmosis, or German measles. Some babies are not adequately nourished in the uterus and a few suffer from brain damage as a result. During labour, events such as a shortage of oxygen to the brain or a haemorrhage can cause brain damage. Even after a baby is born, infection, oxygen lack or bleeding into the brain can all cause cerebral palsy.

Spasticity is the most usual form of cerebral palsy. The child's arms and legs are stiff even when he is asleep, though often only in one direction of movement. One side of the body only may be involved, or just the legs, or all four limbs. Convulsions sometimes accompany this sort of cerebral palsy.

Other forms of cerebral palsy include athetosis (with its characteristic involuntary movements) which can follow very severe, untreated jaundice in a baby; ataxia (unsteadiness); and a loss of balance.

Cerebral palsy may come on gradually over the first year or so of life. This means that a diagnosis may not be able to be made with certainty for some reason. Some parents find that not knowing what is wrong with their baby for several months is on balance a good thing, because had they been given a label of 'cerebral palsy' early on, they feel they might have panicked, thinking that all cases of cerebral palsy were equally severe. Others feel very frustrated during the time of waiting for a diagnosis, sometimes because they feel they are not being told the truth about their child or because they feel that not enough is being done to 'cure' their child's illness. In fact, there is no cure for cerebral palsy although there is plenty that can be done to treat the child and to help the parents adjust emotionally.

The first thing to do when coping with a baby who is suspected of having cerebral palsy is to prevent the gradual joint damage that can be produced by the abnormal pull of the muscles on them. This can be done with a suitable exercise programme recommended by an expert physiotherapist. Second, the baby needs expert medical assessment to make sure that there are no associated problems such as a hearing loss, a speech impediment, or a lower than normal level of intelligence (as is the case in roughly half of cerebral palsied children). If the child has other problems, then early diagnosis and treatment may be useful. Third, the whole family may need practical and emotional support to come to terms with looking after a child with multiple problems.

If your child has cerebral palsy, your family doctor, clinic doctor or paediatrician may refer him to an assessment centre, whose specialist staff will help ensure that everything possible is done for him. It's worth remembering that even if your child is moderately or severely handicapped, he needs you to relate to him as a loving parent and not as a nurse. He will grow up knowing only what it's like to be handicapped. The last thing he'll want is to be treated as abnormal by the people closest to him.

When intelligence and movement are both severely limited the question of eligibility for an Attendance Allowance should be discussed with your doctor. **Related topics** Attendance Allowance; brain damage. *Useful organization* The Spastics Society.

Changing mat A changing mat simply provides a clean, soft and waterproof place on which to lay your baby while you change his nappy. Some have slightly raised edges, presumably to reduce the risk of the baby rolling over the edge if the mat is put on a table. It's always safer to put the mat on the floor, because even though your baby may not yet have rolled over, one day he'll do it for the first time.

Cheating The under-fives don't get much opportunity to cheat. Sometimes an enthusiastic four-year-old will suddenly change the rules for a board game to suit himself, or will start running a race before 'go' has been said, but the intention is so obvious and the 'cheating' done with such huge enjoyment that it's hard to keep a straight face.

It is important to help a child understand that some activities are governed by rules, though, because when he gets to school there will be more and more competitive situations in which he wants to do well and may be encouraged to cut corners unless he knows that this is wrong. Even a young child can be taught that he has to take it in turns when playing ludo, but if you get cross with him for making too large a move when in fact he does this because he can't really count accurately, you may put him off board games for a long time. You have to strike a balance between telling him what should 'officially' be done and letting him enjoy the game as he chooses to play it. Half the fun of playing this sort of game is the working out of the ever-changing rules.

It can be worrying if a child cheats and then lies about what he's done when asked about it. Rather than make him confess it's infinitely preferable simply to say that games are much more fun if the rules are kept. Try to help him understand that he doesn't always have to win.

Cheating in older children is usually a sign that they are worried that they can't do whatever it is they're supposed to be doing. The cheat lacks confidence and needs help. **Related topics** Lying; self confidence.

Chewing gum There is no dietary harm in chewing gum provided that it doesn't contain any sugar. Sugar-free gum is now widely available and may have the added bonus of cleaning a child's teeth in areas a toothbrush can't get to.

There is potentially only one real danger with chewing gum and that is that it may be inhaled accidentally with serious results. It's wise to insist that your children don't do vigorous activities or run around while chewing gum.

There have been instances when a child's small intestine has been blocked by a piece of chewing gum, so teach your child not to swallow his gum but to put it in a rubbish bin.

Chickenpox A highly infectious viral illness mainly affecting children under the age of ten. It is spread by contact with an infectious person or in droplets of saliva spread around when he speaks, coughs or sneezes. The most infectious time is on the day before the spots appear and the child remains infectious until all the spots are scabbed over and dry. This usually takes about six or seven days from the first sign of the rash.

Chickenpox is caused by a virus very similar to that which causes shingles and children who come into contact with an adult with shingles can get chickenpox, though an adult rarely gets shingles from a child with chickenpox. Pregnant women who have been in contact with chickenpox and who are not immune should inform their doctor.

The incubation period is about two weeks (thirteen to seventeen days) and the illness starts with a headache, a fever, a general feeling of being unwell, swollen lymph nodes and a blotchy rash which disappears as the classic chickenpox rash appears.

Classically the spots are little pimples at first but soon become oval blisters. The clear fluid in these blisters becomes cloudy and then slowly the spots scab over. Scabs fall off after about ten days. There is no way of knowing which particular spots will scar permanently but certainly ones which are scratched are likely to do so. Small spots are just as likely to scar as large ones and spots whose scabs stay on a long time are just as likely to scar as those whose scabs fall off sooner. Itching can be a real problem and the child's hands may have to be put in mittens to prevent scratching which might produce scarring when the spots have gone. Simple lotions such as calamine are effective for soothing the irritation and a mild sedative may be needed at night to enable the child to sleep if the itching is really bad.

The spots are usually seen on the body, face, scalp and palate (roof of the mouth), the arms and legs being relatively little affected. Spots come out in crops over three to four days which means there are spots at several different stages at any one time.

There are two possible complications. Scratching can produce a bacterial infection of the skin which can lead to impetigo, conjunctivitis or boils which will need treating. Rarely the virus causes encephalitis between the fourth and tenth day after the appearance of the rash. If your child becomes abnormally drowsy, has a headache or vomits, ask for your doctor's advice.

As with so many childhood infections there is no specific treatment and most children aren't ill enough to be in bed. Be sure to warn friends and relatives if you have the illness in your family before exposing their children to it. Quarantine for chickenpox contacts is today not commonly advised, partly because the illness is so much more unpleasant if a person gets it when adult that it is considered better to have it while young. If you know that your child has been in contact with chickenpox, it's considerate to warn friends so they can keep their children away when your child is about to develop his most infectious stage (about twelve to seventeen days after contact) – if he is going to get the illness at all.

Certain children (including those with diseases of the immune system, those with chronic renal disease and those on anti-cancer drugs) should avoid contact with chickenpox. *Related topics* Itching; virus.

Child abuse Child abuse is a term that is usually used to describe baby battering and other direct physical assault. More subtle types of abuse include mental and emotional cruelty and neglect, such as ignoring the obvious dangers around the house to the extent that the child hurts or poisons himself. The 'abuser' is usually a parent but can be any adult who cares for the child. Such adults are often at the end of their tether emotionally. Some were abused themselves as children – research shows that at least half and probably nearer three-quarters of battering parents have had an unhappy, rejecting, cruel, or violent upbringing (though only a tiny number of children brought up against this sort of background in fact end up battering). Others find that the stress of being out of work or in bad housing, for example, together with having a noisy or demanding young child, is simply too much to cope with. They end up behaving irrationally or uncontrollably to the detriment of the child. Some child abusers drink too much, or take drugs, and this is usually symptomatic of some other problem.

Physical assault on children may start off as a punishment which then gets out of hand, especially if the child doesn't stop doing whatever was annoying the adult or if he does it repeatedly. Once a child has been assaulted by a parent, it's likely to happen again. The more often it is done, the more 'acceptable' it becomes and the less guilt there is about it. Children can be extremely annoying and a person with an inadequate personality, emotional, housing, financial, or work problems, inadequate parenting himself, and who is tired, may find himself lashing out indiscriminately at the children.

Other less obvious but probably more common forms of child abuse include incest, emotional deprivation and neglect. The neglect may take the form of not giving the child enough to eat, not having enough warm clothes to wear or not giving him suitable medical treatment.

It's not uncommon for one child in a family to be made the scapegoat for the wrongdoings of the others. Other adults in the family may not have the power or authority to stop the abuse, or may fear for the consequences to themselves or to the child if they ask for outside help. Some children are not openly abused but instead suffer from repeated emotional rejection, tellings off or blame. Many children abused in this way grow up with· personality problems and some find it difficult or impossible to be good parents themselves later, simply because they've been set such a poor example during their own childhood.

The social services and certain voluntary organizations inevitably only see the tip of the iceberg of this problem. However, now more people are aware of the damage that can be done to children virtually under their noses, they are more ready to point out families that may need help.

Frequent bruises, black eyes, a failure to grow in height or weight, a general appearance of misery, repeated crying and running away are suspicious circumstances that neighbours can notice. Parents of such children tend to prefer isolation and to reject visitors so an affected child may go unnoticed for months or even years.

If ever you suspect that a child is being abused, never ignore it. Tell the local social services department, the National Society for the Prevention of Cruelty to Children or telephone Parents Anonymous who'll ell you what's best to do. Parents Anonymous really exists for parents who feel they might batter (or who already have battered) their children. These organizations will protect your identity so no one will know who reported the trouble. *Related topics* Anger in parents; crying; emotional deprivation; fretful baby; incest; smacking. *Useful organizations* National Society for the Prevention of Cruelty to Children; Parents Anonymous.

Child benefit A state benefit paid to parents, tax-free and irrespective of their National Insurance payments or their income, for each child in the family. The money is paid to the person who is responsible for the child whether this is a parent or a guardian. It is payable monthly at a nominated post office but does not necessarily have to be collected each month. You can opt for weekly payment if you wish – ask at your local post office.

When you have a new baby or adopt a child ask your social security office for a claim form and index slip. These should be completed and sent to the local office together with the child's birth certificate. There is a special form and a special rate for one-parent families.

Childbirth Preparation for childbirth should start even before you get pregnant, by making sure that you are well-nourished and generally in a good state of health. If you smoke, try to stop before you become pregnant as smoking has definitely been shown to affect unborn babies adversely. As soon as you know you are pregnant, book an antenatal clinic appointment and decide where you would like to have your baby. Regular attendance at an antenatal clinic or at your doctor's surgery is sensible as some conditions might not be noticed by you yourself, but might be serious enough to warrant investigation, treatment or early obstetric intervention.

Recently there has been much discussion among the medical and nursing professions, not to mention among parents, as to whether some forms of obstetric intervention (inductions, episiotomies, forceps, etc.) are being used too readily, causing unnecessary distress to mothers, yet not always offering any real advantage to babies. Although childbirth is usually an entirely natural process culminating in the birth of a live, healthy baby, some women do need obstetric intervention such as the induction of labour before the end of the pregnancy, a Caesarean section, or a forceps delivery. Some hospitals use electronic equipment to monitor the unborn baby's heartbeat before and during labour, especially if problems are suspected. If the baby seems to be 'in distress', perhaps because of an insufficient oxygen supply, then a Caesarean section can be done as an emergency, or labour can be induced if the baby's condition is not that serious.

There is interest in obstetric and midwifery circles over the apparent increase in safety to a baby if his mother is in labour for most of the time in an upright (squatting, kneeling or on all-fours) position. Being upright takes the weight of the heavy, contracting uterus off the main oxygenated-blood carrying blood vessels to the uterus and is thought to increase the blood flow to the baby during labour. It also shortens the length of labour in many women and makes it less painful or even pain-free for some women.

Preparation for childbirth may include learning relaxation exercises to assist a woman during labour. Some obstetricians find that it helps if a woman has learnt to 'listen' to what her body tells her to do during labour. By concentrating on her feelings, she can move her body to alleviate pain and can put herself in the most advantageous position for the baby to come down the birth canal. Anything that makes a mother feel good after delivery is worth promoting, because it's important that as little as possible should interfere with the mother–baby bonding process.

Most obstetric units now make it possible for the father to be present at the delivery. This can be a great source of comfort to the woman but not all fathers want to be present. This is something that should be discussed by the couple before labour starts. *Related topics* Antenatal care; episiotomy. *Useful organizations* Association for Improvements in the Maternity Services; The National Childbirth Trust.

Child guidance A National Health Service system of medical and paramedical specialist care for children whose problems are emotional and psychological rather than physical. Child guidance clinics are usually run by a psychiatrist (a doctor specializing in diseases of the mind and the emotions) and or a psychologist (a non-medical professional who tends to deal with *disorders* rather than *disease* of the mind).

The psychiatrist working in a child guidance clinic is trained to get to know a child with a problem, to use tests of his mental function (often carried out by a psychologist) and to assess how the child fits in with his family and society generally. He can then suggest to the parents what the child most needs so as to see that his happiness and development are safeguarded and promoted.

If your child has behaviour problems or emotional disturbances of any kind do ask your general practitioner, clinic doctor, or the medical officer who visits your child's day nursery or nursery school about your local child guidance clinic. Many parents quite understandably feel that anything wrong with their child's behaviour or personality is attributable to their mishandling of him. This can, of course, be the case but isn't always so. Anyway, even if it is true, most parents' first concern is for their child's well-being, so facing up to the problem is a hurdle that has to be jumped at some stage.

If you decide to get help at a child guidance clinic don't think for a minute that your child will be taken away from you. Unless you are abusing him this is almost never suggested. Modern child guidance clinics often like to see each member of the family because so often a personality or behaviour problem is caused by friction of some sort at home. *Related topics* Behaviour problems; child psychiatry. *Useful organization* National Association for Maternal and Child Welfare.

Child-minders
A child-minder is a person who is paid to look after children in her own home, usually while their mothers are at work. She may have her own children to look after as well. The hours of care she can offer are by arrangement and may be long. Some child-minders will pick a child up from school and look after him until his mother comes home. Regulations enforced by the social services departments of local authorities exist to control child-minding. It is illegal to be paid to look after children unless you are registered with your local authority.

Anyone who applies to be registered as a child-minder is visited by a social worker who decides whether the house and garden are suitable (whether there is enough space; whether the heating is adequate; whether the toilet and washing facilities are adequate); how many children can be minded (generally only a maximum of three under fives); and for how long and how many days a week they can be minded (nine hours daily and six days a week is the usual maximum). The social worker also advises about additional safety and fire precautions necessary before children can be minded; gives the minder details about which infectious diseases have to be notified and what to do if a child becomes ill; and makes sure that there are enough toys and play materials. A register of the children minded has to be kept and the minder has to know the child's doctor's telephone number and whether or not the child has been immunized against tetanus. Meals are supposed to include a suitable amount of protein and fresh vegetables. A minder must complete a health declaration and must have had a satisfactory chest x-ray within the last two years before starting, and three-yearly thereafter.

A child taken to a minder needs sympathy and attention to help him settle. It helps if any routine he is used to is followed and if he takes a familiar toy or other possession with him. The minder's own young children (if any) may react adversely to new children at first and their needs must be remembered as well.

If you are considering becoming a minder yourself, remember that few jobs are more demanding than looking after young children, so take care to look after yourself and not to get over-tired. Child-minders can take out a suitable insurance policy arranged by the National Child-minding Association against injury to children in their care or damage caused to other people's property by children in their care. Some minders never bother to get themselves on the register of approved child-minders, and there have been occasional reports of minders 'looking after' far too many babies in very poor conditions, with little or no social stimulation. Use a minder whose reputation you are sure of, preferably as a result of personal recommendation from another mother who was happy with her child being there. Official registration is mainly concerned with the practicalities of minding: it is impossible for a social worker to judge after one visit how suitable a person is psychologically for the job of minding other people's children.

Most minders enjoy looking after children and make a good job of it. There are sometimes opportunities in the form of TV programmes or local lectures for them to learn more about child development so that they can get more fulfilment out of their work.

If you are considering whether or not to take your child to a minder while you work, first of all consider the alternatives: a nanny living in or on a daily basis; a mother's help (who may also be resident or not); a friend who might look after the child; or a place in a local authority or private day nursery. Local authority day nursery places are often kept for families which have problems that make it essential for the mother to go out to work. Some places of employment run crèches, but these are few and far between in the UK. A child-minder, other than a relative who might well look after your child for love alone, is usually the cheapest option. Your child will be out of his familiar surroundings and if the minder looks after other children you'll have no choice over his companions.

Because your child could end up spending a lot of time with the minder, choose her carefully. Your child will inevitably learn some of her values, habits and ideas, so try to find out what sort of a person she is. Find out whether she likes children or whether she's doing it just for the money. Looking after other people's children isn't always the easiest of jobs, and if she's unhappy, this will reflect on your child. Find out what sort of food she gives the children, what she does about sleeping arrangements, whether the children play outside, whether she takes them shopping, to the park, or to a toddler or play-group, and – most important – whether she spends time playing, reading or talking with them. If the TV is on all the time, it's unlikely that your child is in the best place. It's important that you should like the minder yourself because if you don't you won't feel happy about leaving your child with her. ***Related topics*** Mother substitute; nannies; play-groups; toddler groups. ***Useful organization*** The National Child-minding Association.

Child psychiatry A branch of medicine which specializes in mental and psychological diseases of children. It is closely allied to child guidance and may be run from the same clinic and even by the same staff.

True psychiatric disease is uncommon in the under-fives but behaviour disturbances are very common. If your general practitioner suggests a child psychiatrist for your child, don't jump to the conclusion that the child is 'mental' or imbalanced in some way, as this is usually not so at all. ***Related topic*** Child guidance.

Children – how many? 'How many children should we have?' is a question that every couple asks in these days of comparatively reliable contraception.

As soon as you have one child, life becomes quite different from what it was before. Many women, before they have their first baby, kid themselves that having a baby will make little or no difference to how they run their lives. Lots want to go back to work and employ someone to look after the baby, or will rely on granny, a neighbour, or a baby-minder. Once the baby arrives, some realize, however, that they really want to look after their baby themselves.

Looking after one baby, being totally responsible for another person, can involve a far greater change in lifestyle than you had imagined, and when the second arrives many women find that the amount of work more than doubles. Some parents find that the jump from two to three is much less of an effort than that involved in going from one to two, though others don't notice this relative easing off of the increase in work until they go from three to four children. So much depends on how old your other children are and on whether or not they can help you with the new baby. If they are very young themselves, a new baby will appear to be much harder work than if you have one or two willing helpmates to play with or hold the baby for you sometimes. It also helps enormously if your other children are old enough to wash, dress and do things for themselves without much parental help. Of course, not all older children are interested in helping with a new baby.

These days a prime factor in deciding how many children to have is the family's income and expectations. Each child costs more money in terms of feeding, clothing and housing him and also by delaying the mother's return to work once all her children are at school.

Return to work is commonplace in our society, to earn money or because some women want the stimulus of a job. If you enjoy having children around, you may feel that the pleasures of adding to the family will far outweigh the disadvantages of less money to go round.

Many people have fixed ideas on how many children they want, based on their experiences of their own families and of those they have known. It's well worth talking about how many children you and your partner want before you even get married because if you have very different ideas you may end up with one of you always dissatisfied, which can ultimately break up a relationship. Once you have started your family you may find that one or even both of you changes your mind about how many children you want. The realities are different from the theories and even the most strong-minded child-lovers may decide to call it a day after one.

A child's position in the family affects his developing personality for good and bad. A new baby means that parents have less time for the other children, but the number of members of the family to relate to and to love is increased. In a large family, the oldest child sometimes describes his feelings of resentment as each extra child takes away some of his share of his parents' time. The youngest child also sometimes finds that as the older children grow up and move away from home, he feels progressively more lonely, especially by contrast with having so many children around before.

It's entirely up to you how many children to have. Whether you decide to have more depends on many factors, not the least of which is how much you enjoy your existing children. Perhaps you agree with the person who said that modern contraception makes life more difficult because now the decision is largely in our hands. *Related topics* Family planning – age gaps; large families.

Child's special allowance A state benefit paid to a woman whose divorced husband has died without making any provision for the main tenance of the child. It is not paid if the mother remarries. You have to claim within three months of your former husband's death or you might lose some benefit. Ask your social security office for the correct form.

Choking Choking is a fairly common event in babies and young children and needs urgent action as a child can become short of oxygen if his breathing is obstructed for more than a minute or so.

Babies often choke on pieces of lumpy food as they are getting used to eating solids but this can easily be prevented by giving small pieces and ensuring that the baby can chew them up completely before swallowing them. If he can't do this, then he'll need to have skins removed from fruit and have other foods mashed. A sharp pat on the back is usually all that is needed but if the child doesn't immediately start breathing turn him upside down and pat him firmly on the back.

An older child quite often finds that a piece of food has gone down the wrong way. The best thing to do is to turn him upside down at once and slap him firmly on the back. This dislodges the lump of food and all is well almost immediately. Choking on things other than food is a common emergency in childhood. Beads, small toys and the like are a real danger and it's wise to keep these away from young children and to discourage older ones from putting them in their mouths. If a child chokes on something, see if you can easily and quickly remove it from his mouth or throat and if you can't, put him over your knees with his head down and smack him firmly on the back. This will usually dislodge the foreign body.

Another good way of getting a child to expel an inhaled foreign body is called the Heimlich manoeuvre. Stand behind the child with your arms around his upper abdomen, make a fist with one of your hands, clasp it with the other hand and then press firmly and sharply inwards and upwards over the upper part of the child's abdomen. By so doing you force the air out of the lungs and the object flies out with it.

If your child's inhaled object can't be dislodged by one of these self-help methods (and usually it can be), get medical help at once. Call an ambulance. *Do not* give the kiss of life because this can force the object further down into the lungs.

One of the most common causes of suffocation today is a plastic bag. Children often put them on their heads, perhaps pretending to be spacemen. Even record sleeve linings are lethal in this respect. Always keep polythene bags away from children. Other ways that children and babies can be suffocated are with talcum powder (it clogs their lungs if inhaled) and during 'prop' feeding. Never prop up a bottle of milk and leave a baby to feed on his own. Climbing into disused refrigerators is another way some children die of asphyxia. Either lock or remove the doors of old refrigerators.

It's best not to give a baby a pillow in his first year. Although he probably wouldn't suffocate on it, he doesn't need it and it'll give you peace of mind. Many mothers feel happier if their babies sleep on their sides rather than on their backs, so that if they vomit or regurgitate some milk, it'll simply run out of the corner of their mouth.

Cholesterol A natural chemical building block of the body, essential for its normal function. It is obtained in two ways; from food sources and from the body itself. The controversy over cholesterol has arisen over the last twenty years or so when it has repeatedly been suggested that coronary heart disease (including heart attacks) could in some way be attributed to excessive amounts of this substance in the diet and thus in the bloodstream. The evidence is by no means clear and the cholesterol story is currently being hotly disputed as a cause of heart attacks.

Breast milk has higher levels of cholesterol than does cows' milk and it has been suggested that this is an important factor in the baby's acclimatization to cholesterol in his diet later in life. We have been eating cholesterol-containing foods for many thousands of years and are probably well adapted to them, especially if breast-fed. There is no doubt that children who are totally breast-fed have fewer harmful cholesterol deposits in the lining of their arteries than do bottle-fed children and this could be important because we know that such areas can cause heart attacks in later life.

Chorea Rapid, jerky movements of the face and limbs performed involuntarily and continuously. It is generally a symptom of rheumatic fever – itself rare. This sort of chorea is called St Vitus' dance and is more common in girls. It usually lasts about two months and disappears spontaneously. There is no special treatment other than that for the accompanying rheumatic fever. *Related topic* Rheumatic fever.

Chromosomes The human body is made up of cells and each cell contains a nucleus with chromosomes inside. The chromosomes are parts of the cell that programme (via the genetic material of the genes they carry) the growth, development and basic activity of the body. They also pass on inherited characteristics from one generation to the next. In each cell, except sperms and ova, there are twenty-three pairs of chromosomes, including two sex chromosomes. In males each cell contains an X and a Y chromosome and in females, two X chromosomes. Sperms and ova have only twenty-three single chromosomes each. Ova carry an X chromosome while sperms carry either an X or a Y chromosome. If an egg is fertilized by an X sperm it will produce a girl (XX) and if by a Y sperm, a boy (XY). A child's father is therefore responsible for its sex, though local conditions in the mother's vagina and uterus at intercourse may influence whether a boy or a girl is conceived. A baby receives twenty-three chromosomes from his father and twenty three from his mother, that is, half of his genetic programming material comes from each. Some genes are said to be dominant, that is, their programming instructions are recognized and acted on by the body in preference to those on the corresponding gene from the other parent. Similarly, some genes are recessive: unless a baby inherits two corresponding recessive genes (one from each parent), the material carried is not used. Some illnesses or conditions are passed on by dominant or recessive genes and it is possible with an understanding of its type of inheritance, to work out what the chances are of an affected parent having an affected child. If a person has only one recessive gene for a particular condition, he or she is said to be a carrier and this genetic material may or may not show up in the next generation. There are some conditions which are only present in males but which can be passed on by females.

The transfer of genetic information from generation to generation is usually trouble-free but on occasions an abnormality occurs. Haemophilia, Down's syndrome, muscular dystrophy, colour blindness and various metabolic disorders are all examples of genetic abnormalities. It is possible to get help from a genetic counsellor if you are worried about the possibility of having a genetically abnormal baby. Your family or clinic doctor can refer you to such a specialist. *Related topic* Genetic counselling.

Cleft lip and/or palate During early pregnancy separate areas of the face and head develop individually and then join together. If the parts of the upper lip and/or the roof of the mouth don't join properly, the baby is born with a cleft (or 'split') lip and/or palate. A cleft occurs in about 1 in 700 babies born in the UK. Twelve per cent have a relative with a cleft palate but it isn't an inherited condition as such. The cause is unknown, though X-rays, German measles, steroid drugs and other factors during pregnancy have been implicated.

A cleft palate is usually noticed at birth when the baby is examined but some aren't noticed until later. Most babies with a cleft lip and/or palate feed very well but some don't suck well and sitting them up to feed helps. Breast-feeding is possible but can be difficult especially without expert advice and the best thing if there seem to be insuperable difficulties is probably to express your milk and give it from a bottle with a special teat, or from a spoon. Special orthodontic 'feeding' plates are sometimes made to fit over the cleft palate in the baby's mouth. These close over the deficit in the palate and make sucking easier. A cleft lip, although more obvious, doesn't usually cause insuperable breast-feeding problems because the soft breast can be moulded around the cleft in a way which a bottle teat can't.

A cleft lip is easier to repair than a cleft palate and can be done before the baby is three months old. Sometimes a further cosmetic operation is advised when the child is older. The timing of the cleft palate repair depends on its size and shape and on the health of the baby and it is not usually done before six months of age. Doctors vary in their opinions and full discussion with your doctor is advisable.

After the repair children with a cleft lip end up with just the faintest hairline scar on the upper lip. After a cleft palate repair about one in five children may have a problem with speech – in particular finding it difficult to pronounce consonants (K, P, T, G, B and D). Such a child will benefit from long term speech therapy. There may also be hearing and dental problems. About one in ten children with a cleft palate has other developmental abnormalities such as a visual defect, mental retardation and hydrocephalus. *Related topic* Talking. *Useful organizations* Association for All Speech Impaired Children; The Cleft Lip and Palate Association.

Climbing Some babies start climbing as soon as they can crawl. If a child tries to climb out of his cot at night it can be dangerous because he might fall. Even if he gets out all right he could then fall downstairs. The answer isn't to harness him in or lock the door because this will only frighten him. The main way around this problem is to understand why it happens. A child climbs out of his cot because he wants to be with his mother (or father), not by himself. He may not be sleepy and he may be afraid to be alone or afraid of the dark. Some parents never put their child in a cot awake but lie down with him on a bed or cuddle him till he is asleep, then transfer him to the cot (if a cot is used at all). If your baby cries when he's in his cot, go to him at once because he needs you – he's not being 'naughty'. If he wants to be with you, let him be. Some toddlers want to be where the action is and will later either go straight back to sleep in their cot or even in your arms downstairs.

Children sometimes climb without any fear for their safety. When a baby or toddler first attempts the stairs, stay with him and show him how to come down on his tummy or sitting down. Most parents don't allow a child to go up or down stairs unsupervised until they can do it easily and safely. Fixing a removable stair gate will mean you don't have to worry about falls. If you have only one gate put it at the bottom when you are downstairs and at the top when you are upstairs. It is easier to have two safety gates and this will be essential if you have the type that fixes to the wall.

On cold wet days when children are cooped up indoors, or if you live in a flat, climbing over the furniture may be an important (to the child) part of his physical activity for the day. You'll make your own decisions about whether beds can be jumped on and chairs and sofas climbed over. Children love doing this but you may feel you can't afford to replace mattresses with broken springs and chairs which look tatty.

Climbing on to window sills upstairs must be discouraged unless you have safety bars at the window.

People are good for climbing over when you are little. Experiment with your child but hold him tightly! A rope, tree or frame in the garden will provide a lot of fun for young children and a hill or bank to climb and roll down will be enjoyed. *Related topic* Climbing frames.

Climbing frames Strongly constructed structures for use outdoors or indoors to be climbed over by young children. They are made of metal or wood and some indoor ones can be folded away when not in use. Tubular steel is probably best for the garden-sized frames but it should be galvanized or painted regularly because the roughened surface of rusty steel is unpleasant for children's hands and stains their clothing. Both metal and wooden climbing frames should be checked at least once a year for safety, and if you can find one second-hand you'll have to be even more careful about safety.

When buying a climbing frame get the biggest you can afford and can fit into the space available. As children grow, their demands soon outstrip a small unambitious climbing frame. Many frames have optional extras such as ladders, swinging ropes, slides and nets and these can be enormous fun for years on end. By blocking off parts of the frame with a sheet or an old blanket it can be transformed into a tent.

Climbing frames are safe for children of all ages from toddlers upwards but it makes sense to see that they aren't allowed to push each other about or get over-excited when climbing. Children rarely fall off climbing frames and if you site a frame on grass they won't hurt themselves seriously even when they do fall.

Most toddler groups and play-groups have some sort of climbing equipment which the children very much enjoy.

Clinging child It's all too easy to mistake the normal behaviour of a young child at various stages of his development for abnormal behaviour if you don't know what makes children tick. For example, babies of around six to twelve months go through a mummyish stage when they are really only happy if their mother is in sight all the time unless they are asleep. She has only to leave the room for a moment before her baby cries inconsolably, and she may feel that she has made some dreadful mistake in how she has been bringing him up. Relatives may tell her that she must start leaving the baby in order to teach him that he can't always have his mother but, if she follows their advice, he may become abnormally anxious, whereas up till now he had been only *normally* anxious. If separation is enforced in this way, the next time he's given to someone else to be held or looked after, he's very likely to cry and be suspicious, even if his mother is right there by him.

Leaving a baby when he's obviously unhappy to be left does him no good at all and certainly doesn't foster his independence or liking for other people. A baby of this age realizes that his mother (and/or whoever looks after him regularly for long periods of the day) is the most important person in the world to him and is actually frightened if she disappears. Babies have no concept of time and don't understand the difference between an absence of a minute and one of hours. Because they can't yet understand what you say, you can't tell them that you're coming back or when you're coming back, so it's understandable that they think that to all intents and purposes you've gone for good.

Instead of fretting over your baby's dependence on you, try to enjoy it. It's generally agreed by psychologists and many parents that by allowing a baby to be as dependent as he wants when he wants, you're setting the scene for his natural independence to develop at its own rate. However, if you try to force a baby or young child to be independent in the adult sense, he'll lag behind his own normal developmental rate and may, ironically, end up being dependent on you emotionally for very much longer.

In effect, by trying to push your baby or child away from you before he's ready, you're making a rod for your own back. Unfortunately, most parents have so little opportunity to see the results of both types of parental behaviour that they find this hard to believe if they haven't experienced it at first hand.

There's a world of difference, however, between pushing your child away before he's ready and encouraging his natural independence to develop. If you have a baby of seven months, for example, it's sensible to give him to other people with whom he is familiar for a cuddle every now and then. If an unfamiliar person wants to hold him, stay close and smile and talk to him so that he gains confidence in this new situation. If you seem happy about it, he's more likely to be happy, but he'll want to come back to you fairly soon anyway because you're the reference point of his world. As he becomes happy to be held by or to stay with other people you can happily retreat and let them talk to and play with your baby. Stay around though so that you can take over if he becomes upset. Unless you have to, or unless he is extremely familiar with the person, it's not wise to leave your baby with someone else for long. Babies love their mothers and develop a taste for other people at their own pace.

When it comes to older children, if you force them to stay away from you before they're ready, or on a day when they want to be with you for some special reason (they may not be feeling well or may be tired or generally mummyish), then you're laying up trouble for the future. Many's the mother who has tried to get her child to stay at a play-group before he's ready and has later had to take him away for some months or even longer. A child who's not ready to go it alone will try his hardest to keep you with him and may actually cling to your legs or skirts to stop you going. If this happens every time you try and do something without him, even if it's just going to the loo, your child will soon be branded as a clinging child and that's a label that's difficult to shake off. A clinging child is often one whose mother has tried to force independence too soon but this is by no means invariably the case. Some children are naturally clinging despite their upbringing. Your child will be independent all too soon and it seems silly to make him stay away from you if he doesn't want to.

There are some exceptions. A mother can be at her wits end and getting away from her child for a time may seem to her to be the only way she can cope. If there is anyone willing to keep her company, though, she may find that with that person at home she can cope with her child much better than she thought. Separation isn't the only answer. Another exception may be the child who has got into the habit of clinging but is in fact secretly longing to be off playing with other children. The great difficulty is in distinguishing this sort of child from one who is truly not ready to leave his mother. Simple rules relating to age are no good because while some three-year-olds are ready for a play-group, for example, by no means all are and some will benefit by staying at home with their mothers for at least another year. If this is your problem, try staying at the play-group with your child: you may be able to decide whether he is ready for it by watching his behaviour there. You may be advised to leave your child even if he screams when you go. If you can stomach this (most of us have to grin and bear this for a few days but you won't be alone if you can't), then make sure from the play-group leaders that he stopped crying soon after you went and that he quickly joined in with the play. If your child was miserable, quiet or thumb-sucking while you were away, then perhaps he simply isn't yet ready to leave you. Not being ready to be left at three is *not* a bad reflection on you or your child. It's simply a reflection of your child's developmental stage and personality. **Related topics** Attachment; dependence; development – emotional; development – social; independence; separation anxiety.

Clothing Children's clothes (especially more formal clothes) are relatively expensive to buy, simply because the amount of work involved in making, for example, a little girl's dress is very little less than in making a woman's dress even though there is obviously less material. Many women pass children's clothes round between them because with the average family size of two children, clothes are often nearly new when one family has finished with them. Baby clothes get very little wear until the baby starts crawling, though they do need to be washed frequently. They can often be passed on in good condition. Older babies' clothes get much more wear on the knees but once children start to walk the clothes again are usually in good condition when they're outgrown.

If you can do your laundry in a washing machine and have a tumble drier, then you need fewer clothes than if you have to rely on a washing line and elbow grease. Some parents are much more clever at protecting their children's clothes during mealtimes and during messy play than others, so make much less work for themselves. A bib is far easier to wash out than a jumper! Overalls with sleeves will save on laundry when your child paints or plays with glue. You can buy plastic sleeve covers which are even more protective.

All children dislike having clothes put on if the neck opening is tight. Choose envelope-necked vests for babies and not ones with ribbons which knot. If necessary, slit a neckline, bind it, and put on snap fasteners, or put buttons and buttonholes in. Some young children won't wear anything tight round their waists, perhaps because they don't really have waists and so anything that's going to stay up has to be too tight for comfort. Get around this by buying dungarees or dresses instead of trousers and skirts. Braces will hold loose-waisted garments up.

One of the banes of a parent's life is buttons on children's clothing. A baby or young child will rarely keep still for long enough for the buttons to be done up in the first place, and often large buttons, snap fasteners, velcro or zips are easier.

Children keep warmer if you put them in several light layers of clothing rather than one thick one. It's no use expecting a child to keep warm in a vest and a long-sleeved dress in the middle of winter. Instead, put her in a vest and long-sleeved T-shirt under her dress, then put a cardigan or jumper on top as well if necessary. Wearing lots of clothes also means that you can save money on heating at home!

Tights can be useful for boys as well as girls if you can find ones that fit properly. You can buy 'pull-ups' with shoulder straps which are exactly like tights but look less girlish.

Choose clothes that need little or no ironing. With today's modern fabrics your children can wear fabrics such as wool and cotton without you having to spend ages doing careful laundering. Anoraks and macs should be easily washable so that you don't have to worry every time your child falls over in the mud or gets splashed by a passing car. A zip-in snowsuit is better value than an expensive winter coat. It can also be washed and dried quickly (coats need dry cleaning) and as it's unisex can be passed around the family.

Some children take a great interest in what they're going to wear and have very definite ideas about what they like and look good in. It's up to you whether or not you let children go out in unusual combinations of clothes but certainly it makes sense to let them have some say when it comes to choosing the colours of new clothes. You may feel this isn't on. though, because children are so fickle! Last week's favourite garment is soon replaced by this week's. **Related topic** Dressing.

Club foot A congenital deformity of the foot in which it points abnormally downwards or upwards and may also be twisted so that the sole faces inwards or outwards.

Because of the way babies lie in the womb, many of them are born with odd-looking feet. The vast majority of these correct themselves with or without the help of exercises but if one foot only is affected or if simple measures fail, then specialist medical care is needed. The main problem for the child with a club foot is that he can't put it flat on the ground to walk. If the condition is left untreated irreversible deformities can develop and he may never walk properly.

Clumsy child Children vary a good deal in their natural abilities to do physical tasks and even within a family there can be striking differences. Some children seem hamfisted early but develop considerable dexterity later whilst others go on to become clumsy adults.

A child who is very clumsy will need medical assessment. Such children often can't distinguish right from left and find difficulty in judging distances accurately. Clumsy children are likely to be of normal intelligence but minor brain damage can be a cause of clumsiness. If you are really worried about your child's clumsiness, see your doctor.

Coeliac disease A disease in which a child's gut is sensitive to the protein gluten, which is found in wheat, rye, barley and oat flour. Such a child will be symptom-free until flour is introduced into his diet. Although the condition cannot be called common it is more so in certain parts of the world. In Ireland, for example, 1 in 300 people are affected. There is no need to give cereal as your baby's first food and by avoiding it for the first few months of his life, the (unlikely) possibility of coeliac disease developing is postponed. Very few babies need solids before three months; many do well without them until around six months; and some thrive on milk alone for eight months or more. There is some evidence that breast-feeding protects babies against developing coeliac disease.

The first signs of coeliac disease that a parent will notice are that the child doesn't want to eat, becomes irritable, passes pale, bulky, smelly stools and may vomit. Because of the poor absorption of his food the baby fails to gain weight and his abdomen swells up. He then gets anaemia and other nutritional deficiencies unless the condition is treated.

The treatment is relatively straightforward. All foods containing gluten are removed from the diet and any existing nutritional deficiencies put right. The absence of gluten from the gut allows it to function properly and the child thrives as he should. He may have to stay on a special diet recommended by your doctor, or by the hospital, for a long time. Various gluten-free foods including bread are now commercially available and available on prescription from your doctor. *Useful organization* The Coeliac Society.

Coffee Parents often ask if it is safe for children to drink coffee. It does contain various stimulants but there is no reason to believe that an occasional cup of tea or coffee is harmful in reasonable amounts. A child may be sensitive to these stimulants though and if a lot of tea or strong coffee is drunk he may not sleep, may become overactive and will pass lots of urine.

There are so many other alternative drinks, that coffee is simply unnecessary rather than undesirable. Most children don't even like it very much but they are likely at least to want to try it if they see you drinking a lot.

Colds Infections with one of several common cold viruses which affect the mucous membrane lining the upper respiratory system (nose, ears, throat and sinuses). The infection can produce a sore throat, nasal discharge, sneezing, sudden fever (especially in children from three months to three years) and irritability and restlessness in babies. Some babies vomit and have diarrhoea but older children have symptoms more like those seen in adulthood (a cough from the postnasal discharge or 'drip' tickling the back of the throat, aching muscles, headache, loss of appetite and general malaise).

The average pre-school child has three to six colds a year. Colds last for up to ten days unless there are complications. These can occur if the child's resistance to infection is low. The commonest complication is a secondary infection with bacteria. This produces a greenish-yellow pussy discharge from the nose and can cause otitis media, sinusitis, a sore throat, or pneumonia.

Just why some children seem to get so many colds isn't known, and all kinds of remedies have been tried from large doses of vitamins to removing the tonsils and adenoids. There is no way of preventing a cold as far as is known. Antibiotics neither prevent nor cure uncomplicated colds and shouldn't be taken unless prescribed by your doctor.

Young babies can be upset by a cold, mainly because they normally breathe through their nose while sucking, yet can't if their nose is stuffed up. They slowly learn to break off after every few sucks to breathe through their mouth.

It's wise not to expose young babies unnecessarily to other people with colds because even a simple cold can be distressing, and can cause sleepless nights. Considerate visitors will either stay away or else keep their distance. Some babies benefit from nasal decongestant drugs just before a feed to help them suck easily.

Bed rest is usually unnecessary but if the child's temperature is very high he may want to lie down anyway. With a child who has a high temperature (over 101°F/38°C), vomits a lot, can't hear or complains of painful ears, has a sore throat, or seems too unwell for a simple cold, ask your doctor's advice. Babies need very careful watching because they may feed poorly and become dehydrated because of this and because of the fluid loss they experience with the fever.

While your baby should be kept comfortably warm, don't overheat him by putting the heating up high. At this time (as at any time) it's best to put on extra layers of clothes if necessary and have a source of gentle heat along with some fresh air. An open fire provides heat and fresh air by drawing in air from outside through doors and windows but central heating with no open windows can cause a dry atmosphere which isn't ideal.

Runny noses need continual wiping but take care not to add to the child's discomfort by making his nose and lips sore. Put a layer of zinc and castor oil cream or petroleum jelly round his nostrils and on his upper lip for protection. Encourage an older child to blow his nose gently so as not to blow pus into his ears, and teach him to put his hand over his mouth when sneezing or coughing. **Related topics** Bed – ill child in; damp; fever.

Cold sores Tiny blisters around the lips caused by a reactivation of the herpes simplex virus (subtype HSVI) which normally lies dormant in the body following a 'primary' infection. The blisters usually break and crust over before they heal.

In two out of three children the primary infection is unnoticeable and in most of the rest it causes only trivial symptoms, especially in young children. Infection with this virus is extremely common (one in three people throughout the world are said to be infected) and mainly occurs after kissing an adult with cold sores, hence the term 'viruses of love'. The lips and mouth are the most common sites for the first infection with the virus and because the reactivated viruses affect the site of the first infection, cold sores are the commonest signs of reactivation.

The first infection is very different from subsequent ones. In it there are small blisters followed by ulcers inside the mouth and on the lips together with inflamed gums which can be so painful that eating and drinking are difficult. A few young children have a fever, feel unwell, have a heavily coated tongue, smelly breath, and swollen lymph nodes in their neck. In this case it is worth seeing a doctor. The infection clears up by itself within a few days. Next time the child gets the infection he doesn't have ulcers in his mouth but has cold sores around his lips.

The dormant viruses live around the sensory nerves supplying the site of the first infection and are reactivated sporadically by a wide variety of stimuli including a fever, cold, sunlight and physical or emotional stress. Often no cause can be pinpointed.

The treatment for a primary infection is careful oral hygiene, which means wiping the inside of the mouth with moist cotton wool swabs and cleaning the teeth gently. Ice cold drinks and food which doesn't need chewing are most likely to be taken. The only topical application which might be helpful for cold sores is a solution of IDU, which is too expensive for routine use. Gamma globulin is occasionally used.

A child with cold sores or any other known herpes virus infection should be kept away from a child with eczema because of the risk of infection of the eczematous skin.

Cold sores burn or itch and, if scratched, can become infected with bacteria, causing impetigo. Normally cold sores disappear within a week or two.

Cold sores are uncommon before school age. ***Related topic*** Herpes.

Colic Colic is the word used to describe a pain in the abdomen that comes and goes and is caused by spasm of one of the abdominal organs (such as the intestine). In children intestinal colic is commonly caused by certain foods – 'green apple colic' is the best-known example. The treatment is simply to wait for the spasm of the intestines to pass, which it will in a few hours at the most. A hot water bottle (safely covered) held against the tummy may help relieve the pain sooner. Because of the danger of overheating or burning, a hot water bottle must be closely supervised and is best avoided for a baby.

'Three month colic' is a term used to describe the periods of crying and discomfort suffered by some babies in the first few months of life. It usually – but not always – disappears by three months of age. Because it so often happens in the evening, it is also known as evening colic. Many babies with so-called colic don't have abdominal pain at all. It's not always possible to discover the cause of the baby's discomfort. It is traditionally called colic because such babies often pass wind from the back passage while they are crying. However, crying often makes babies pass wind, and there hasn't been shown to be any extra air in the intestine in these babies. (All babies have some air in their intestine which gets there by being swallowed along with gulps of milk.)

Recently, some researchers have suggested that traces of undigested foods (and drinks) such as cows' milk in the mother's breast milk may produce colic in susceptible babies. This may be more likely to happen if the baby comes from a family in which one or more members have allergic problems such as eczema, asthma or hay fever. Also, if the mother eats an excess of the food in question, her baby may be more likely to be affected. More than 300 ml (half a pint) of cows' milk a day for a breast-feeding mother, for instance, represents quite a large proportion of her daily calorie intake in the form of one food. If you think that it's worth trying, avoid one food at a time completely for four or five days. If your baby's colic disappears, then try the food again in the same amounts you were eating it in before. If the colic reappears, you'll be fairly sure that that food was the culprit and will be able to avoid it or have much less of it until your baby is older and more able to tolerate it. When your baby goes on to foods and drinks other than breast milk, be wary of the food that seemed to affect him via your breast milk and give it in small amounts until you are happy that he is not affected by it.

Other foods that the breast-feeding mother eats (or drinks) may affect her baby even though they are digested by her first, and even if there is no allergic family history. Onions, Chinese food, beans, cabbage and other green, leafy vegetables, and alcohol, for example, may make the young breast-fed baby cry unconsolably for long periods. Green, leafy vegetables and pulses can also make the breast-fed baby very windy: he'll have a distended abdomen and he will pass a lot of wind from his back passage. Each baby is different though and many babies don't react at all when their mothers eat these foods. Get to the bottom of the problem by avoiding the food you think is the culprit, seeing if the 'colic' disappears, then eating the food again a few days later to see if the baby has colic again. This sort of colic usually begins within a few hours of the mother eating the food in question and may last for two or three hours.

If your baby cries for long periods, run through a check list of possible solutions: Is he hungry? This is the commonest cause of crying and hunger is often misdiagnosed as colic. He may well be protesting because his tummy has been left empty for too long.

Some breast-feeding mothers have nothing to eat for several hours at a time and their babies may cry because the quality or quantity of milk may be reduced. Try eating little and often to counteract this. Lots of babies want the comfort of sucking at the breast on and off all evening from time to time in the first few months. Try and accept this because if you fight the idea of sitting with your baby on your lap for several hours, you'll have to put up with a screaming baby instead and it's fairly obvious that it's more pleasant for the whole family – not to mention the baby – if you sit down with him at the breast. If your baby wants this, it certainly doesn't mean that there's anything wrong with him or how you're bringing him up. It's perfectly normal behaviour, as millions of mothers of young babies will agree.

The other possible causes of crying in a young baby are loneliness, the desire to have physical contact with you, and simple things like being too cold or hot and having a dirty nappy. 'Wind' in the tummy will come up fairly soon if you try holding your baby upright, if you gently prop him up in a sitting position and lean him forward over your hand, or if you lean him facing against your shoulder. Even the most experienced mother sometimes has to cope with an inconsolable baby and just has to comfort him as best she can. Babies vary and some cry more easily than others.

Babies cry for a reason and leaving them alone will be no help. When you are at your wits end because you can't seem to help your baby, get in a neighbour or friend if you are alone, just for moral support. Don't blame yourself but calmly tell yourself that you are the one person in the world whom your baby most wants to be with when he is upset like this. Even if you have to spend several hours sometimes walking round doing the 'Chinese jiggle' (a fairly rapid – about two a second – but gentle, up and down movement with your baby in your arms) and sometimes sitting with your baby on or off the breast, there's nothing better you could do for him.

Bottle-fed babies are just as likely to get colic and cows' milk formula actually causes colic in some babies.

The irritability of some teething babies may be mistaken for colic. If your baby wants to bite on something, rub his gums firmly but gently with your thumb or finger. A teething baby may not produce teeth for months but his gums may seem to bother him all the same.

If your colicky baby has any other problems such as vomiting or diarrhoea, if he goes very pale, or if anything else is abnormal, see the doctor. *Related topics* Abdominal pain; crying.

Colour blindness
A condition in which a child cannot distinguish colours normally. It is about twenty times more common in boys than girls. About eight per cent of boys are colour blind and this can be a real disadvantage because they are often wrongly thought to be backward.

Colour blindness is easily tested for at the clinic before your child goes to school, or routinely at the school medical examination, with specially created colour cards. Normally-sighted children can see pictures, numbers and letters on the cards but colour-blind ones can't. The commonest problem is in distinguishing red from green.   Even if a child is colour blind there are very few jobs that will be absolutely closed to him and many children learn to distinguish shades of the colour in question. *Related topic* Sight testing.

Coma
A state of unconsciousness in which a child cannot be aroused at all. It is a serious medical state and requires urgent medical attention. Children can become deeply unconscious in this way after a fall, after asphyxiating themselves, as a result of a severe shock, from taking an overdose of drugs or household poisons, after an electric shock, during an epileptic fit, after convulsions with a fever, or if they are diabetic.

If your child becomes unconscious and cannot immediately be aroused, lay him on the floor on his side with his uppermost leg drawn up to stop him from rolling over. If there is an obvious cause for the condition remove it but always call a doctor anyway. If he's not breathing you may have to try the kiss of life, and if his heart has stopped, heart massage.

Never attempt to give a child in a coma anything to eat or drink. *Related topics* Heart massage; kiss of life.

Comfort habits
Head banging, rocking, hair twiddling, thumb (or finger) sucking, nail biting and nose rubbing are some of the comfort habits commonly seen in young children.

No one knows for sure why some children start these habits. It may be because the child feels a need for comfort which isn't being met in other ways. Perhaps he is being left for long periods to amuse himself when he hasn't the inner resources of an older child to be left alone. In other words they can be a manifestation of boredom. There are other possible explanations too. Perhaps he has been weaned when he would ideally have liked to have gone on sucking at the breast until he was older. Perhaps he is upset or worrying about something you aren't even aware of.

Each child and each home environment is different. Adverse circumstances may make a child begin one of these habits which can then be difficult to break even though the circumstances improve. If your child has a comfort habit and you are worried about it, ask for advice from your health visitor, baby clinic or family doctor. *Related topics* Behaviour problems; comforters; cot rocking; head banging; nail biting; rocking; thumb and finger sucking; weaning.

Comforters A comforter is any object that makes a child feel happier and more secure in times of stress, boredom or tiredness. Common comforters are a soft toy, a dummy, a piece of cloth or a cot blanket. The comforter becomes valuable and important to the child and is irreplaceable. A cot blanket ('security' blanket) may become torn to ribbons and yet the child won't allow you to replace it. The look, feel and smell of the object is well-known and loved and nothing else will do instead. Some mothers interchange two identical blankets so they get a chance to wash out one every so often.

A comforter is hugged and sucked and is usually taken to bed. Invariably it has to accompany the child on outings and there may be trouble if it gets left behind. It becomes almost like an old friend and can assume a seemingly unreasonable (to adults) importance.

If you have a child who can't go anywhere without his comforter, and who spends much of his day clinging on to it, you should think whether the child may feel insecure. While many perfectly normal, happy children use a comforter when they're tired, others seem to need theirs almost all the time. Though not proven statistically, the impression is that children who feel insecure and anxious tend to have a greater need for comforters.

Never stop a child from using a comforter, but think what made him take to it in the first place. You may like to get an outsider's opinion from your family doctor or the baby clinic doctor because they are experienced at sorting out this kind of problem and are sufficiently distant from your family to be able to see things objectively.

Comics The under-fives don't usually *read* the words in comics but they may enjoy being read to, looking at the pictures, colouring them, or cutting out characters and sticking them into paste-up books. All these activities are enjoyed even more when done with an adult, as are most things when you're under five. Comics are not a good way of keeping a young child amused on his own and will probably be discarded largely unlooked at unless you take an interest. There are special comics with pages of things for young children to do.

In an age in which many parents start pushing their children academically even before they go to school, it's no bad thing to encourage them to enjoy 'escapist' comics. After all, many adults enjoy the adult equivalent.

The main fears parents have about comics are either that they will give their children bad ideas or that they are such rubbish that they'd rather they didn't waste their time reading them at all. There is no evidence though that comics harm children – on the contrary they probably foster their quite natural sense of the dramatic.

Companionship
Babies and young children need other people with them to develop normally emotionally, socially and intellectually. For a long time, mothers fit the bill completely – indeed, a baby could develop normally with only his mother for company. Other people also enrich a child's experience and help him to develop his attitudes, behaviour and personality. It's never too early for a child to have other people around and even a very young baby will show signs of appreciation when other people take an interest in him, or if he can watch them playing or doing things. Social interaction isn't something that suddenly begins when a child is ready for play-group but develops gradually over the years and is influenced by his mother's and father's attitudes towards other people. If you have prepared him for his growing independence by encouraging him to like other people, you'll have done well for him. A basic sense of trust and liking for other people is worth fostering and will mean that your child enjoys the company of others from an early age.

When one- and two-year-olds are together, they usually play alongside each other, stopping every now and then to see what the other is doing. Three- and four-year-olds play increasingly *with* each other, relying on each other's interactions in games. Even good companions may hit each other out of curiosity to see what happens, or out of rage. This is why you need to be near, to be a referee, and to try and instil a basic sense of right and wrong into the playmates. Children can have very strong likes and dislikes of other children even as young as four or five. These feelings are fickle, though, and opinions can change overnight. If your child has one or more brothers and sisters and if he sees other children at play-group, toddler group, or at your friends' or neighbours' houses, then it's unlikely that he'll lack for companionship. But if you have an only child you might try to make friends with other mothers who have young children just so he has some experience of other children before he has to go into the maelstrom of school when he's five. **Related topic** Development – social.

Competition between parents
One of the reasons that competition is so rife among parents stems from the fact that we are anxiously trying to learn about their children so as to understand our own; this invariably ends up creating a false atmosphere of competition. We also live in a competitive society in which a person's achievements determine to a large extent what job he is going to be able to do and how much money he is going to make. Our educational system often conditions even very young children into thinking they are clever (or not, as the case may be) and even very young children may find themselves competing in exams and other tests.

The 'can your baby smile yet?' becomes 'can your baby sit up/crawl/stand/walk/talk yet?' and the parent whose child lags behind can feel that his child is a 'failure' even before he reaches the ripe old age of one! Babies develop at their own individual pace and there's a wide age range for any one achievement. Early physical progress is by no means always associated with, for example, early speech or with high intellectual achievements later. In any case, it's obviously much more important that you enjoy your child, however quickly or slowly he does things. If someone comments on how slow he is, counter the comment with a positive remark about your child's personality or how clever he is with a ball or bricks, for instance.

Competition means that someone loses and someone wins. In an ideal world we would all do our best and yet not compete with each other. Comment by all means on the natural and essential differences between your child and others, but don't let it fool you into believing that your child is instrinsically a better person if he does something earlier or more competently than another child. Take a pride in your child's achievements and encourage him where he could do better, but also take notice of and praise other children's achievements. A shared delight in what children do should be the aim of any balanced society.

Complementary feeds Feeds of cows' milk formula given after a breast-feed to add to the amount of breast milk given. The formula should be made up in the normal way with sterile precautions and given either in a bottle or with a spoon. The commonest reason for giving these 'top-up' feeds is when a mother's milk supply is failing but they are almost always unnecessary. They are also sometimes given routinely from birth but this is almost never necessary if breast-feeding is managed properly.

The most usual times for starting complements are immediately after coming home from hospital with a new baby, and when the baby seems unsatisfied with the breast – perhaps when having a 'growth spurt'. The mother who is partially breast-feeding is highly unlikely to carry on doing this for long as the combination of the two methods is so time-consuming. Also, the longer she gives complements, the less breast milk she'll produce because the baby simply won't stimulate her milk supply by sucking enough.

If you think you have insufficient milk for your baby, you can increase your milk supply, for example by letting him feed for longer and more often. In the few days after your baby is born, the small amounts of colostrum you produce are quite sufficient for him. If you feed your baby on an unrestricted basis by day *and* night (and give extra feeds if your baby is sleepy, drugged, jaundiced, ill, or premature and doesn't demand feed) then your milk will come in quickly. *Related topics* Bottle-feeding; breast-feeding; breast-feeding problems; breast milk; underfeeding.

Concussion An injury to the brain from a fall or a bang on the head by a blunt object. The skin of the scalp may or may not be broken. The damage is done inside the head and may at worst involve leaking of blood into the brain itself.

Children are forever banging their heads during early childhood.

especially toddlers who are learning to walk, but usually a bang leaves a red mark and nothing more. A child who has banged his head badly might cry, have a headache, look pale, may vomit once or twice, have a lump on his head and get sleepy. This is not concussion but your child still needs medical attention in case he has a fractured skull.

The child with concussion becomes temporarily unconscious at the time of the injury; may vomit persistently; may have pupils of different sizes which don't contract when a light is shined into them; and may have a squint, blood oozing from his ear or nose, a severe headache which gets worse, a stiff neck, a slow pulse and even abnormal breathing. When he regains consciousness he is confused and may have lost his memory for the time immediately preceding the incident and for the incident itself. Walking may be unsteady for a while afterwards.

Get the child to lie down and rest completely *even if only a few of these signs are present*. In any case, if concussion is suspected, call the doctor. Someone must stay with him to ensure that he gets no worse. Get help urgently (call an ambulance) if the child loses consciousness and can't be aroused; if there is a depression in the skull at the point of impact; if the breathing changes; or if the pulse slows to less than fifty to sixty beats a minute.

The hospital may do some skull x-rays, and other tests if necessary. Only the most serious cases will need treatment other than is widely available in accident and emergency departments and neuro-surgery is rarely required.

Most concussed children are better after a few hours' rest. **Related topics** Head injury; unconsciousness.

Congenital malformations
Abnormalities present at birth. When one considers the complexity of human development from two cells (the egg and sperm) to such a sophisticated being as a baby, it is hardly surprising that things go wrong from time to time.

If a foetus is very abnormal it will usually be naturally aborted early in pregnancy. Man is unusual in the animal kingdom in having a very high foetal wastage rate, with about one in ten pregnancies ending in this way. About ninety-six per cent of all babies born are perfectly normal and of the four per cent with abnormalities many of these are trivial or easily corrected. Inherited diseases are discussed elsewhere.

The causes of congenital malformations are often not known but it *is* known that German measles, certain drugs, toxoplasmosis, herpes simplex, cytomegalovirus and x-rays during pregnancy can all produce abnormal babies. Of course this doesn't mean to say that they always do.

Some congenital disorders are known to be influenced by the parents' age, the time of year, the geographical location and the social environment into which the baby is born.

Undoubtedly the best way to be sure of having a normal baby is to aim for two parents in good health and not taking any drugs or having x-rays when they conceive; to look after the mother during pregnancy, especially with regard to her drug intake (which should ideally be nothing at all), and her exposure to the known hazards mentioned above.

The outlook for many of the quite severe congenital malformations is now very good. Holes in the heart, dislocated hips and blocked intestines, for example, all have a very good outlook. *Related topic* Inherited disorders.

Conjunctivitis An inflammation or irritation of the conjunctiva – the delicate membrane that lines the inside of the eyelids and the exposed parts of the eye. In children the commonest causes are local infections, (which sometimes occur in epidemics) and generalized illnesses such as measles or a local infection. A foreign body in the eye and certain allergies can also cause it.

In conjunctivitis the white of the eye is pink, the child complains of grittiness and stickiness (especially on waking in the morning) and some children can't stand the light. There may be excessive production of tears and pus can stick the eyelids together.

Antibiotic eyedrops, creams or ointments cure infective conjunctivitis very quickly. Sunglasses can be useful with severe sensitivity to light.

If your child has infective conjunctivitis wash your hands thoroughly after touching his eyes and make sure that other children don't use his pillow, towels and so on, to prevent the infection from going round the family.

Constipation Difficulty or delay in passing bowel motions. Constipation is the commonest disorder of the bowel in the Western world yet it is totally preventable. We now know that the cause of constipation is almost always a faulty diet and our modern Western diet contains far too little dietary fibre (roughage). It is easy to ensure that your child gets enough. Simply increase the amount that he eats of the following foods and his constipation should disappear within a few days: wholemeal flour (found in wholemeal bread); bran-containing or whole-grain breakfast cereals; and fresh fruit and vegetables. Cut down on foods made with white flour and added sugar in all forms.

It's a tragedy that many older children and adolescents have signs of bowel disease because they have had to put up with a totally abnormal diet for so long. The best possible thing you can do for your child's present and future bowel health is to ensure that his fibre intake is high.

Constipation doesn't just cause bowel disease but can also produce a painful, bleeding anal fissure, which in turn makes the child afraid to open his bowels because of the pain and hence he gets more constipated.

Laxatives can be dangerous for young children and shouldn't be used as they gradually damage the bowel's natural ability to work properly and so in time become essential for the bowel to function.

There's nothing magic about a child opening his bowels once a day and many children eating a really high fibre diet open their bowels twice a day or more. Opening the bowels after breakfast is a frequent routine, but try to make sure that children have enough time and that you aren't rushing them.

Lavatories away from home can be off-putting, especially for the toddler, and this makes it unlikely that a child will open his bowels, which can lead to constipation. So too can an over-insistent parent when potty training a toddler. Such children may refuse to open their bowels even in their nappies and so become constipated.

Breast-fed babies usually only open their bowels once a day, or less after the first few weeks, and they never have to strain. Bottle-fed babies can become constipated if they are not having enough milk. *Related topics* Dietary fibre; food; potty training.

Contraception The only reason for including this subject at all in a book about child care is to discuss the need for contraception as soon as you start intercourse again after having had a baby. If you are totally and solely breast-feeding on an unrestricted basis your ovulation will be suppressed for an average of fourteen months. However, as some fully breast-feeding women ovulate as early as ten weeks, this obviously cannot be relied upon as a safe means of contraception. You should only use lactation contraception as your sole method if you wouldn't be heart-broken if you became pregnant. The chances of becoming pregnant with on-demand breast-feeding are slim but an unusual break in the frequency of breast-feeds such as if your child is unwell and doesn't want the breast or if he happens to sleep for a long time can let ovulation occur. It's up to you what additional precautions you take if you are breast-feeding but the sheath or diaphragm are both suitable. Remember to ask for a prescription for a new diaphragm at your post-natal examination. Your old one may have perished during the months it has been put aside and there is a chance that you may need one of a different size after the birth. The 'mucus' or 'Billings' method of contraception is increasingly widely used today and is suitable for the breast-feeding woman. The sheath, diaphragm and mucus method are all safer when used with contraceptive jelly or foam. It's probably wiser not to take the pill. Some types have been shown to suppress milk production; and others cause a decrease in the protein, fat and mineral content of breast milk. One study, uncon-firmed as yet, showed a correlation between prior contraceptive use of these hormones and breast milk jaundice. The effects of the newer pills, including the progestogen-only pill, on breast-fed babies have not yet been fully evaluated. For some women a coil (IUD) is best – talk to your doctor.

Parents of a bottle-fed baby should of course take full contraceptive precautions as soon as they start to be sexually active after the birth. *Useful organizations* British Pregnancy Advisory Service; Family Planning Information Service; Pregnancy Advisory Service.

Contrariness Between the ages of two and three especially many children are occasionally awkward and contrary. The two-year-old is learning how to make decisions but often he finds it difficult to make up his mind and changes it often and easily. He may become annoyed when people interfere with *his* way of doing something and he's loath to be shown how to do something. Some two-year-olds become almost obsessed with doing things their way and will hear of no other.

It's a bad time for parents who are themselves busy and who don't have the patience or – perhaps – the maturity to face the fact that it is just a phase that will pass. The secret is patience on behalf of the parents and the other children in the family. If the two-year-old wants to dress in *his* own way, for example, let him, and don't rush him into doing things your way. If you have to hurry him along for some reason, try to divert his attention from the task in hand and then quickly do it yourself. It's wise always to start getting ready to go out, for example, much sooner than you think necessary.

If your child always wants to do the opposite of what you want to do, there's no need to insist on your way every time unless it's important or necessary. Your child is flexing his intellectual muscles to find out what his limits are and you can help him by giving him alternatives instead of telling him to do something. For example, instead of saying 'hold my hand while we cross the road' (at which point some children will refuse point blank, sit down, run away or have a tantrum!) try saying 'would you like to sit in the buggy or hold my hand', or 'either hold this hand or the other one'. The child won't feel he's being told what to do and will enjoy the importance of the choice. Of course, there are many variations and you'll have to decide your own methods of dealing with contrariness. Just don't squash it too hard: it's certainly not done with the intent of annoying you even if it feels like this sometimes. **Related topics** Defiance; temper tantrums; visiting.

Convalescence As soon as any disease affects the body, a person's natural defences start to combat it. However a disease is treated, the body – once over the acute phase of an illness or operation – needs time to get back to normal. This time is known as the convalescent period. Children, unlike adults, seem to bounce back to health very quickly but even so it's sensible to be prepared for a child to feel unwell and off-colour for some days after an illness has actually finished. Convalescence used to be a much talked of necessity after almost any illness but today children tend to get back to their normal lives very soon after an operation or an illness because today they're well nourished and generally healthy before they become ill.

But don't expect a child to be completely back to normal soon after an illness. He may be irritable, short-tempered, tired, whiney, clinging or even actually weak for some days or weeks after certain conditions, especially viral illnesses. A child may be clingy and whiney as a result of his hospital stay rather than because of the illness itself. This can occur even if you were able to stay with your child almost all the time. Extra love and cuddling usually overcome this problem within a few days. There are no hard and fast rules on convalescence for children, so be guided by what your child seems to need and if you are at all worried that he's not getting better as quickly as he should or if he develops any new symptoms, tell your doctor. If you push your child back to play-group or expect him to cope with long outings before he feels well again, he'll be tired and irritable, so it's sensible to let him get back to normal at his own pace.

A young child recovering from an illness will benefit from extra attention; nourishing, attractive food that he likes (though he may not be hungry, so give him small portions); fresh air; and as much gentle exercise (walks, playing on the swings or in the garden) as he can enjoy. If he wants extra rest let him have it. Some children want to go back to daytime sleep and others have disturbed sleep. Sometimes the first sign that they are better is that they have a sound sleep at night. **Related topics** Bed – ill child in; illness.

Conversation Making conversation is a necessary and pleasant human skill that has to be learnt. It's as much a matter of listening to what the other person says as it is of talking oneself. Children learn by copying what other people do. It's important that you should listen to what your child wants to communicate to you as well as talk to him. If you listen to him, he'll learn to listen to you. If you show an interest in what he says, he'll learn to take an interest in what you and other people say. Learning to listen is more important and more difficult than many people realize. Young children often seem to be 'turned off': they simply don't hear what is being said to them because their mind is on something else. As they grow older, they learn to listen at the same time as doing something else. Eventually they get to the stage where they can do several things, and make conversation at the same time.

Conversing calls for considerable language skills. The child has to be able to think of what he wants to communicate and then find the right words to say it. Early conversations often consist of just one word, combined with actions or facial expressions. To encourage a young child when he is learning to talk, respond to what he says encouragingly, perhaps repeating the word and then adding to it. If, for example, he says, 'dog', pointing to the dog as he says it, then you might reply 'Yes, that's Sandy, let's pat Sandy', patting the dog as you say it. Try and understand what the child is saying even if it's fairly incomprehensible, otherwise he will feel that there's no point in attempting to converse as you don't understand what he's saying and don't seem to be interested either.

If you are with other people as well as your baby, take the trouble from time to time to give the baby some attention. This is just as important with older under-fives who often feel very frustrated because they can't get a word in edgeways when their mother has someone with her. It's all too easy to ignore a child completely when you are talking to someone else simply because he can't participate as an equal and also because you don't want to be interrupted. Obviously it would be wrong for a child to prevent you having conversations with other people, and wrong to teach him to interrupt rudely. How you cope with this situation depends on the child's age. With babies and under-threes, you'll probably just have to break off your conversation every now and then to give them some attention when they need it. However, as your child gets older, he'll gradually be able to understand that he may have to wait for your attention before he can tell you something. Sometimes he'll be too tired or bored to wait, in which case it's better for everyone if you break off your conversation temporarily. At other times, he'll wait until you've finished talking.

Don't forget that children aren't born knowing how to behave politely but need to be taught patiently and tactfully. If you tell your child off for interrupting, you're acting in a negative way. To be constructive, tell your child what you expect him to do and be prepared to repeat this advice next time, as any teacher would do.

If your child is talking to a friend, don't butt in when you want to say something, but wait for a natural pause. We adults have no right to be rude and unfeeling to our children. They'll learn best how to behave from our example.

Making conversation is an art that can be acquired from early on. Children who are talked *with* rather than *to* are much more likely to acquire the art. **Related topic** Talking.

Convulsions A convulsion (fit or seizure) is a sudden muscular spasm which can occur repeatedly over a short time span and is caused by a spontaneous outburst of electrical activity from the brain. Convulsions are not at all uncommon, especially in babies, and can easily be divided into two main groups – those with a fever and those without a fever. Epilepsy is the commonest cause of a convulsion in a baby or young child who has no fever, but epilepsy is uncommon.

By far the commonest cause of fits in babies and very young children is a high fever. The commonest age for such fits is between three months and three years. They are rarely seen after the age of five. For a fever to produce a convulsion it has to be very high. Febrile (fever) convulsions can be caused by any common childhood infection. This is one reason why every household should have a clinical thermometer and know how to use it: young children often don't seem very hot or even really ill right up to the time when they have a convulsion. Such children often have a family history of febrile convulsions in childhood so perhaps they've inherited a brain which is particularly sensitive to temperature changes.

A fit of any kind has four main stages. First, there is an aura, during which the child feels frightened, has strange sensations or has a headache. This stage is rarely obvious in young children, and is usually unreported. Stages two and three are the muscle spasms with stiff limbs and then repeated jerky movements. This stage lasts less than ten minutes if fever is the cause. Stage four is the recovery phase during which the child sleeps.

Obviously fits are very frightening for all concerned and many parents are afraid that their child will die, though of course he won't. All you can do is lay him down somewhere safe so that his limbs aren't damaged while jerking. Leave his mouth alone (don't force anything between his teeth or you may break them). Wait until he stops fitting. He may wet himself but this doesn't matter. If you are used to fits you'll be less alarmed than if it's the first time. If it is the first time call a doctor and certainly do so if the child has repeated fits in a short time. A baby may have none of these signs but may simply stare fixedly ahead, stop breathing for a short time (in which case he'll go blue), or have periods of rapid breathing.

If the child has a fever of more than 102°F (38·9°C), lower it by giving paracetamol in the correct dose and sponging him. Keep this up until his temperature is down below 100°F (37·8°C).

The treatment of febrile convulsions is controversial. Some experts, fearing that repeated convulsions when he has a fever might harm the child's brain, suggest that he goes on to a preventive drug to suppress any possible convulsions when he has an infection. Only five to ten per cent of these children ever has another fit so this is difficult to justify. True epilepsy requires very different treatment.

A child having a fit for the first time in his life may well be sent by the family doctor to hospital to establish the cause. Apart from observation and a thorough medical examination, various tests may be done, including a lumbar puncture because of the risk of meningitis first showing up as a fit.

If your baby has ever had a convulsion, your doctor will advise against whooping cough immunization and also possibly against measles vaccination. **Related topics** Epilepsy; fever.

Cooking for children
It's quite possible to raise a healthy child without ever cooking his food because lots of food can be eaten raw. However, it's essential to cook most meats and fish, many vegetables and some fruit and grains. In our society, a relatively large proportion of the day-to-day diet is cooked and most children are brought up eating the same food as the rest of the family, some of which is cooked and some not.

The easiest way to wean a baby on to mixed foods is to give him a little of what you are eating, suitably mashed up and moistened if necessary. This means that no special food preparation is needed. If you tend not to eat much for breakfast or lunch but want to cook for your child, only cook very small amounts. If you have a freezer, you can freeze small portions and take them out one at a time to re-heat. Be sure to do this thoroughly though as food poisoning could be a hazard. There's nothing worse than cooking a delicious lunch for a young child and watching it all being left, so batches of favourites stored in tiny portions in the freezer can work very well.

On the whole, most children prefer different foods kept apart from each other on the plate and some are very pernickety about where they want their gravy or tomato ketchup to be put. Presentation is even more important for children than it is for adults. Attractive-looking food with eye appeal is more likely to be eaten than a plateful of food which looks boring.

Contrasting colours on the plate together with foods of varying textures and shapes will appeal to most children. Some children are naturally suspicious about foods they haven't tried before and many don't like 'messes' of foods. They may be concerned that you will make them eat a new food up even if they don't like it. Only put a tiny amount of a new food on the child's plate. He can always have more if he likes it and he won't be intimidated by a small helping.

Easily recognizable and familiar food is most likely to tempt young visitors. Bread and butter, chicken, peas, chips, sausages, beefburgers, fish fingers and fresh fruit, for example, are winners with most children.

Don't forget that whatever you cook, if your children are already full up with between-meal snacks they won't want the meal you have prepared. If the children are so hungry that they can't wait for you to cook their meal, then don't fight them but serve them a meal which doesn't need so much time spent on preparing it. Uncooked food can be just as attractive, nutritious and appetizing as cooked food though some young children don't feel that they have had a 'proper' meal unless it's something cooked. **Related topics** Appetite; eating habits; food; weaning.

Cooking with children

Cooking with young children around is not always the easiest of tasks. Babies are soon bored without your full attention; crawling babies get under your feet; toddlers need careful, constant supervision unless in a play-pen (and they soon start to object if left there for long); and older pre-schoolers clamour to help. All this means that every meal takes far longer to prepare than ever it did before and you may have to settle for cooking stage by stage, having a break between each few lines of the recipe. Some mothers start getting the evening meal ready in the morning and do a little bit every so often throughout the day to avoid the misery of trying to cook against a background of whining or various demands.

Another way round the problem with a baby is to put him in a sling so that he can enjoy being close to you as you cook. If you're using the hob then it's safer to put the baby in the sling on your back in case he gets splashed. An older baby might enjoy sitting in his high chair near you (but not too near the cooker) so that he can watch what you're doing. Being at floor level is very boring when there are fascinating things going on overhead. Give him something to play with on the high chair tray; a peeled carrot to bite on or a few pastry cutters to play with and throw on the floor will keep him amused for a time.

As for older children, you'll find that their help will make your jobs take twice as long but it's fun for them and ensures that the job gets done without tears or fuss. Even a two-year-old can scrub a potato: make sure he's dressed for the job though. Children of any age will thoroughly enjoy playing with a small piece of your pastry and making jam tarts to cook, however awful they look.

Do bear in mind that when you are busy around the kitchen there is a danger that your child could be getting into trouble elsewhere. This is especially true of toddlers who'll take the opportunity of your being engrossed in cooking to empty your bedroom drawers or drown the cat!

Coordination The ability to make your body do what you want it to by transmitting messages via the nervous system which make the muscles move. Every day a baby's movements become more coordinated and less haphazard. Soon he'll be able to grasp something with his hand, roll over, sit up, crawl and walk. Each of these skills requires a complex set of movements or muscular contractions.

Anything wrong with a child's nervous system can interfere with the coordination of his movements and make them jerky or uncoordinated. Even though the child knows what he wants to do, he finds he can't do it easily and sometimes can't do it at all. Many brain-damaged children with cerebral palsy have poorly-coordinated movements. When combined with weakness or stiffness of the muscles, poor coordination makes every movement difficult and time-consuming.

There is a wide variation in how well-coordinated normal children are and in the speed at which they learn to do things. Every parent soon learns that there will always be some children who are better and some who are worse at all the physical skills a child learns. A child's degree of coordination is no reflection of his general intelligence.

Minor degrees of clumsiness or poor coordination can be signs that a child had a difficult birth with some lack of oxygen to his brain. As the child grows older they don't get worse – in fact they often appear to get better as the child learns to compensate for and disguise his very slight handicap. *Related topics* Clumsy child; chorea; development – physical; hands; nervousness.

Copying Watching what other people do or listening to what they say and then trying to do or say exactly the same is how babies and older children learn all the many skills they need. It's interesting that even walking upright is a skill that doesn't necessarily come naturally. There are several reports of 'wolf children' – human babies who were lost or cast aside as babies and reared by wolves – who walk on all fours because they have copied the only models they had available.

Copying is easiest and most effective in a one-to-one relationship. During the early months of a baby's life he and his mother enjoy a sort of social interaction that involves reciprocal movements, expressions and sounds. Babies learn to smile, coo, blow bubbles, and wave goodbye because their mothers spend hours responding to them, encouraging them and showing them what to do. Repetition is the essence of teaching babies and young children and they love it. It's no good showing a baby or young child how to do or say something once and then expecting him to copy it. It may not be until you've shown him lots of times that he'll do the same. Mostly in this early interaction a mother is imitating her baby, not the other way round, but the baby is learning that he can provoke a response by doing or saying something in a certain way and, most important, that if he smiles, she'll smile back. In time he'll begin to imitate her and later other people.

Older babies and toddlers love to do what their mother, father, brother or sister is doing. If someone is building a tower of bricks, the baby will want to play too. If someone is writing, the baby will want to use the pen. He wants to join in and prefers to copy than to initiate play most of the time. Copying other children is also an important part of growing up and, eventually, joining a peer group. Some children learn more readily from other children than they do from their parents. Babies in particular often take a delight in copying older brothers and sisters and toddlers will often do what the other children are doing – for example, sitting down properly at the meal table – whereas they wouldn't do it for their parents.

Pre-school children of between three and five love to do things together and imitate each other in play, dress, speech and so on. They also like to help their parents by doing the same as they are doing. Imitation is a very good way of learning and a child apprentices himself to whoever is nearest. Out of copying grows competition, though it's not usually until later that this becomes fierce. Among pre-schoolers competition usually amounts to an interested comparison of each other's skills.

Imitation may be the sincerest form of flattery but sometimes older brothers or sisters don't see it that way and simply get annoyed when a little one copies everything they do and wants to join in all the time. Tactful and patient intervention is necessary to calm the situation down, to make sure the older ones get a little peace and to encourage them to include the would-be participant. Point out that the younger one wants to learn from them because they are older, cleverer and more experienced. Some older children are very good with their younger siblings and will let them play with them often, whilst others simply prefer not to and have to be coaxed or cajoled into spending time with them. The worst situation is often when the older child has a friend with him and they want to play alone. Try to invite a friend for the younger child as well if this happens often in your house.

There are many things that parents do which won't be imitated for years. Imitation of all the skills and attitudes involved in parenting is a very important pastime which goes on, largely unnoticed, throughout childhood. Your children will tend to behave to their own children, for example, in a way similar to the way you behave to them. During their childhood they will have absorbed and learnt how to be a parent and all this will come out into the open when it's needed. Especially if a child has much younger brothers or sisters, he or she will be picking up your ways of looking after and teaching your younger children. If you watch when games of mothers and fathers are being played, you'll see your own style of parenting being copied right in front of your nose! Even the way you punish your child will probably be copied by him with his children years later. Smacking, for instance, has been found to run in families and is learnt by years of patient observation. Similarly, the way you cope with or respond to any given situation is inwardly noted. If you keep calm in an emergency, for example, your child is likely to copy you when the same thing happens to him. Not everything will be copied from you alone, of course. Your children's personalities together with their experience of other people and other situations will influence how they behave, think, speak and so on, but you are, initially at any rate, the most important person.

Children learn most things by imitation. They learn how to walk upright, how to talk, how to draw, read and write, how to cook, sew and do carpentry, how to play, ride a bicycle and eat with a knife and fork. The way your child does things will have been influenced largely by how you do things. If you want him to sit up straight at the table, you'll have to set a good example. If you don't want him to shout at you, you shouldn't shout at him. The basis of all the most important things in his adult life such as how he relates to other people and whether or not he is kind and loving to his family will be laid now: it's up to you to give your child something worth imitating.

Cot A baby's bed with high sides to stop him getting out or falling out. One or both sides can usually be let down so the bedding can be straightened or changed and the baby or young child put in or taken out. Safety precautions to watch out for are: that the cot shouldn't be painted with old lead-containing or flaky paint; the bars should be close enough together so that the baby can't get his head stuck between them; the cot should be stable even if the baby stands up in it and tries to tip it over by rocking or by pushing against a wall; the base should be secure so he can't hurt himself or get his fingers or toes stuck; and any pictures or transfers should be properly fixed so that the baby can't take them off and eat them.

Mobiles and toys may amuse a baby left in a cot for a short time but they soon become boring. However attractive your baby's cot is to look at, he'll be much more attracted by the prospect of going to sleep in your arms or on your lap.

Most babies soon get used to noise, so you could leave your baby's cot (pram or carrycot) in the room where you are while he sleeps. Wherever it is though, make sure that it's within earshot. If your baby sleeps in a cot in your bedroom at night, put it close to your bed so you don't have to get up to pick him up and feed him when he cries. Some parents cut the legs off the cot so that the mattress is at the same level as that of their bed.

A few parents harness their children into their cots if they are in the habit of getting out in the evening or at night. This would seem by any reckoning to be a sure way of producing neuroses and insecurity in a child whose need to be with his parents is, after all, quite normal and understandable.

A baby may be moved from his cot to a bed for a variety of reasons: a new baby may take it over; the cot may be too small for him; or his mother may find that he goes to sleep more easily if she lies next to him in a proper bed, and leaves him there when he's asleep.

A collapsible travelling cot is useful for a baby too big for a carrycot. This item of baby equipment is relatively expensive and is perhaps worth sharing between a few friends – unless you do a lot of travelling yourself. *Related topics* Bedding; carrycot; sleep.

Cot death The sudden loss of an apparently healthy baby must be one of the cruellest things that can happen to parents. Every year in the UK one in every five hundred babies suddenly dies from an unknown and inexplicable cause. In 1980 there were 1021 cot deaths in England and Wales. In fact, this sudden infant death syndrome, or cot death, is the commonest label given to babies dying after their first week of life and before they are two years old.

The average age for a cot death to occur is at four months, and the commonest age range is between three and eight months. Half of the babies that die in this unexpected and inexplicable way are apparently quite well beforehand. The other half have had some minor symptoms of illness – often a respiratory infection – and the respiratory syncytial virus is found in one in three of all babies dying from a cot death. The usual story is that the parents put their baby to sleep in his cot and when they next go to him – perhaps because they think he has been asleep for longer than usual – they find him lying lifeless.

Research has found that babies are most at risk if their mothers are young; if there are several children in the family and if the family is poor. Low birth weight babies and those whose mothers smoked in pregnancy also seem to be at greater risk, as are babies who aren't fully breast-fed. Some of these babies have an abnormal conducting system in their hearts which may be the root cause of the death. Others don't breathe normally.

The grief and guilt felt by parents who have lost a baby in this way takes years to get over. The guilt is unjustified yet is almost universal, and it isn't helped by the many curious questions the parents are asked by all and sundry.

There isn't an answer to the cause of cot death as yet. There may not even be one answer. In order to run the lowest risk of losing a baby in this way mothers should take full advantage of antenatal care facilities offered and should stop smoking in pregnancy and stay away from smoke-filled places. Both parents should avoid smoking with a young baby in the house and should avoid taking the baby to smoky places. At the slightest sign of the baby being unwell it would seem sensible to keep him within sight and sound. A baby alarm is not good enough. This may seem ridiculous, but given that researchers think that some cot deaths can be avoided, it is surely worthwhile. Babies with a temporarily abnormal heart rate or breathing can sometimes be set right again just by being picked up and cuddled. There's no absolute need to have a baby wired up to expensive apparatus for this – if you can see him (or hear his breathing and movements), you'll have a good chance of telling if his circulatory system fails. His breathing may become laboured or obviously different and he may become very restless, flailing his arms and legs about. Keep your baby by you day and night (and in, or just by, your bed at night) if you're not entirely happy with his condition. Many mothers prefer not to be separated from their babies anyway, well or ill. Another precaution is to take your baby to the doctor even sooner than you would have thought necessary if he is slightly unwell in the high risk time of between three and eight months of age.

Some researchers have suggested that one cause of cot deaths may be a sudden overwhelming allergic reaction. Full and unrestricted breast-feeding for the first four to six months at least, with no cows' milk formula feeds, no vitamin drops or fluoride drops, no orange juice, and with the breast-feeding mother taking care not to eat an excess of any one food, especially if she has ever had allergic symptoms herself from that food, or if there is a family history of allergy, all go towards making a cot death less likely. When the baby starts a mixed diet, ideally he should continue to be breast-fed as well. No food should be given in excess and if he has any allergic symptoms after eating a particular food, it's best avoided thereafter until he's much older and more able to cope with it. Babies can be allergic to inhaled matter as well as to food. Cats' fur can cause problems, as can house dust mites and being near horses, for instance. If you suspect allergy, try to analyse its cause (though this is difficult) and then avoid the offending circumstances.

A cot death is unlikely to strike in a family more than once. Allow yourselves reasonable time to mourn the loss of your child before starting another pregnancy.

Advice about the death certificate, post mortem, funeral, burial and other practical arrangements will be given by your family doctor. If you need further help about these or if you want to talk about your grief and the marital and personal problems such a loss often causes, try talking to a member of the self-help group formed to do just this. See page 768 for address. **Related topics** Allergy; bereavement; overlaying. **Useful organization** Foundation for the Study of Infant Deaths.

Cot rocking
A habit some babies develop. It may be done for sheer amusement once a baby or young child has discovered he can do it. This is especially fun if he finds the cot moves around the room as it's rocked. There's no danger to this as long as the cot is stable.

Other babies develop the habit of cot rocking as a source of comfort rather like head banging. Such babies are usually bored because they are spending too much time alone and awake in their cots. **Related topics** Comfort habits; cots; rocking.

Cough
In a child infection of the nose, throat and sinuses – such as occurs in a cold – is the commonest cause of a cough because the catarrhal or pussy discharge trickles down the back of the throat and tickles it.

Coughing is nature's way of removing irritating material from the windpipe and respiratory passages and shouldn't be routinely damped down with cough medicines containing codeine unless the cough is 'dry' – that is with no catarrh or phlegm to be coughed up. Children don't get rid of coughed-up phlegm when they have a chest infection, but swallow it, unlike most adults who spit it out. This can give them tummy ache and can make them vomit or have diarrhoea. Bouts of coughing (such as in whooping cough) sometimes make a child vomit.

Asthma and wheezy bronchitis, measles, whooping cough, German measles, cystic fibrosis, an inhaled foreign body, bronchitis or tracheo-bronchitis, croup, pneumonia, bronchiolitis and a smoky atmosphere can all cause coughing. A longstanding cough can be caused by a smoking parent and it is well proven that children with a smoker in the house have more bronchitis and pneumonia than do those of non-smokers. Thanks to antibiotic drugs and to public health measures, including immunization, TB tests and mass x-rays, tuberculosis is rarely seen today, except among families of immigrants who arrive in the UK with the disease.

Cough linctus can be helpful to suppress an irritating cough that is keeping a child awake at night but home remedies (such as hot lemon drinks) can be just as good. Antibiotics should never be used without medical advice. They are only of any benefit for a bacterial infection and most coughs are of viral origin. If your child's cough is caused by anything other than a simple cold, ask for your doctor's advice.

Some children cough noisily during the night while remaining asleep. Others have attacks of noisy coughing which wake the household. Allergy or emotional stress should be suspected and discussed with your doctor.

Cradle cap

Cradle cap is caused by seborrhoea. It consists of yellowish-brown crusts, worst on the top of the head and especially over the soft spots (fontanelles).

Although it is most often seen in babies, as the name suggests, it can be seen in children up to the age of three years. It can occur in the cleanest babies and children and is no reflection of the parents' care.

Children with cradle cap may have seborrhoeic dermatitis (red, scaly areas) on their ears, foreheads, behind the ears, on the nose, eyebrows, eyelids, and folds of the tops of their thighs. It can look very like atopic eczema but goes quickly with treatment, unlike most eczema.

If you don't mind the look of cradle cap, you can leave it alone. As the natural tendency of the young child's scalp to produce a lot of oil disappears with time so will the cradle cap. If you want to get rid of it, the treatment is straightforward. Crusts can be removed in several ways. Rub olive oil or liquid medicinal paraffin into the scalp before the baby goes to bed and gently remove the softened crusts next morning with a comb. If they aren't very thick they'll be softened if a solution of one teaspoonful of sodium bicarbonate in a pint of water is used to wash the scalp. Shampooing alone rarely clears the condition but special shampoos can be bought which are effective. A solution of cetrimide used as a shampoo on its own without soap is also useful. Some mothers quite simply gently and carefully scrape the crusts off with a comb or a clean fingernail.

If these simple measures don't work or if your child has seborrhoea elsewhere, tell your doctor or health visitor. **Related topics** Hair care; seborrhoea.

Crawling The way in which most babies move around on the floor on all fours before they learn to walk. Most babies can sit more or less steadily before they first crawl.

While most babies learn to get about by crawling before they start to walk, by no means all do. Some perfectly normal babies go straight from sitting to standing and then start walking, missing out any intermediate stage of mobility. Others develop the knack of bottom shuffling – getting along on their bottoms with the help of one hand, one knee and both feet.

Crawling is done on hands and knees. Some babies get along on all fours but on hands and feet (with their bottoms in the air) which is known as 'walking like a bear'. Sometimes this is a progression from straightforward crawling.

When babies first crawl, some go backwards and they find this very frustrating when trying to get to something interesting. Crawling is hard work early on and progress is slow, with the head held low so that the baby can scarcely see where he's going. Within a few weeks though he'll be moving around much more smoothly and quickly and with his head held high so he can see better what he's aiming at. He'll also learn to get into and out of his crawling position easily.

The average age for crawling is around ten months, but there is a wide range, as there is for sitting and walking. Once a baby can get about, he'll be less easily bored because there'll be so much more for him to explore. Now is the time to put away breakable ornaments on coffee tables or low shelves; to move books up higher; to secure low drawers or cupboard doors with magnetic latches or bolts; to put a gate at the stairs (and to remember to move it to the top or bottom of the stairs, as appropriate); to do away with tablecloths for the time being; never to leave small objects lying around that might be swallowed; to store household chemicals, cosmetics, shampoo and so on somewhere safe; to shut the outside doors unless he can safely go outside, and to put pets' food and drink bowls out of reach. The time has come, in other words, to 'toddlerproof' your home even though your baby is not yet toddling!

Crawling children get dirtier than immobile ones, so dress your baby in easily washable clothes. Girls will wear out trousers less quickly than comparatively expensive tights. Clothes should be easy to move in: put your baby in a restrictive boiler suit and you'll soon notice how his crawling is impaired.

Most babies take a delight in crawling and seem very proud of their achievement. Because they can move around, they seem to grow overnight. Don't be under any illusions though: your crawling baby is still a baby and you'll need to watch him wherever he goes. 'No' is a word he can't yet understand and for the next few months at least you'll have to be even more than usually patient as he satisfies his curiosity about his surroundings. *Related topic* Accident prevention.

Creativity A child's ability to invent and make things depends on his natural intelligence, his environment and the possibilities it opens up, and on the encouragement he gets from his parents and others around him. Even a very young child can be creative. 'Creative' play includes elements of invention as well as imagination. Parents can't make a child creative but they can provide opportunities for him and an environment in which he can be creative.

When encouraging a child to be creative, we as parents have to remember that there are lots of ways of doing most things in life. Your way may not be your child's if left to himself. His method may actually be better because he hasn't been influenced by 'experience'. Try not to give out ready-made ideas to your children but let them find their own ways of doing things. By all means help a child achieve his goal but let him decide what to do and how to do it. Young children can't be creative in a vacuum in the same way that an older person can because they lack the necessary intellectual skills to think things through. They need materials, perhaps an exchange of ideas and above all encouragement in a loving environment in order to make the most of their potential. *Related topics* Artistic activities; boredom; drama, imagination; play; storytelling.

Crèches Nurseries where babies and young children can be supervised while their mothers are elsewhere. They range from crèches run in church halls while a church service is in progress, to those run by employers for the staff, and to crèches run by mothers in homes, at club sessions, or at meetings where the presence of children and babies would disturb the proceedings.

Crèches such as those run for women at their place of work are strictly controlled by local authority social services departments as to the number and the health of the people who are looking after the children, the size of the room, the lavatory and cooking facilities and the number of children they can take. Such crèches are run like local authority day nurseries and are funded either by the employer, by the mothers, or both.

With the increasing impact of the women's movement, and with more mothers working outside the home than in recent years, there has been an increased demand for day care for babies and young children. Day nurseries run by social services departments of local authorities generally reserve their places for children from families with problems, such as one-parent families, those where there is no one at home able to look after the child, or those in which the mother is overstretched and needs some rest. Because of this and because there are so few crèches at places of work, the demand for such places is generally very large.

In many EEC countries it is easier for working mothers with young children to arrange care for them in a crêche or nursery than in the UK. Some mothers go back to work when their babies are still being breast-fed and because the crêche is close to where they are working, they can carry on breast-feeding successfully.

When a baby is looked after in a crêche it is best if there is one particular person who cares for him on a regular basis. Babies can become confused, upset and even slow to develop if they have constantly changing caretakers. They prefer one familiar person and whoever is in charge of the crêche should make it a priority that this continuity is organized as effectively as possible within the limits of staff illnesses, holidays, changes of staff and so on.

Ill children should stay at home, so unless there is back-up care at home, a working mother may sometimes have to stay away from work.

Taking your child to a crêche at work is obviously easier for you than taking him to a private or local authority one some distance away and it's better for the child because he is with you for longer and you can be called if anything happens to him. You'll find that a place in a crêche is expensive, though, (unless it's provided free by your employer) and may eat into your salary quite a lot. Some mothers decide that even if they have access to a crêche while they are at work, they would prefer to take their child to a minder, or spend more and employ someone to look after their child in his own home.

If using a crêche on an occasional and non-essential basis such as at church, while shopping, or at a meeting, be aware of your child's feelings. Though some children stop crying after a few minutes, they may be unhappy while you are away. Others cry on and off all the time. What you are doing while your baby or young child is in a crêche needs to be very important to make it worth leaving him if he isn't happy. Ask the person in charge what your baby was like while you were away but be sure you get an honest answer. Some people are more eager to please the mother by saying her baby or young child was happy than to tell the truth. It's an unusual baby or young child who doesn't prefer to be with his mother. Children like a one-to-one relationship and a crêche can provide that for only a tiny proportion of the time.

Some children have the sort of personalities that adapt well to being in a crêche. If this is so and if the crêche is well run and there are plenty of interesting things to do, your baby or young child will settle in well. *Related topics* Childminders; day care; day nurseries; separation anxiety.

Cretinism or hypothyroidism

A condition resulting from a lack of thyroid hormone and affecting more than 1 in 5000 babies. A screening test is done in some areas which uses the same blood (obtained from a heel prick) as is used for the Guthrie test for phenylketonuria. This latter test is routinely done on all newborn babies. A lack of thyroid hormone is often not diagnosed at birth, because the mother's thyroid hormone production is adequate for both herself and her baby when he is still in the uterus but as the weeks go by the baby slows down, becomes cold, sluggish and constipated and cries very little. His skin becomes thick, yellow and coarse, his tongue seems too big for his mouth and his abdomen blows out. He may have an umbilical hernia. His growth is stunted and he may also have dry, thin, brittle hair with sparse eyebrows and a hoarse, deep cry. Blood tests confirm the lack of thyroid hormone.

Thyroid or thyroxine is given as soon as the diagnosis is made and the improvement is dramatic. Unfortunately, many children have already suffered irreversible brain damage by the time treatment is begun and will never be as intelligent as they could have been. The dose of thyroid hormone varies from child to child and has to be continued for life. Never take your child off his thyroxine just because he looks better.

Cretinism can also be caused by a deficiency of iodine in the diet of the pregnant mother and by such a deficiency in the baby's diet. Deafness, uncoordinated movements, epilepsy and mental retardation are seen in this disorder. It is rare in the Western world and is preventable by adding iodine to food.

Croup A type of laryngitis seen in young children. It is characterized by difficult breathing and a high-pitched croaking wheeze on breathing in. Croup is usually caused by a viral or bacterial infection but can also be due to an allergy or an inhaled foreign body. By far the commonest type is associated with catarrh caused by a viral infection of the upper respiratory passages and the crowing noise together with the difficult breathing can be alarming to a parent.

Most children with croup aren't seriously ill. If your child has difficulty in breathing, stay calm because anxiety is infectious and if he is alarmed by you, he may find his breathing even more difficult. Sit him up and get a kettle boiling in a safe corner of the room. The steam will help his breathing. Keep the room warm, but not hot, and open a window. If these simple measures don't help, call the doctor. If your child has inhaled a foreign body and the techniques outlined on page 158 have no effect, you'll need to get medical help fast. *Related topics* Hoarseness; laryngitis; wheezing.

Crying Crying is an expression of sadness, fear, loneliness, frustration, anger, boredom, pain, discomfort, or – most often in a baby – hunger. Babies prefer frequent breast-feeds because breast milk passes through the stomach relatively quickly. This means that they need feeding much more often than bottle-fed babies do, so they tend to cry more often as a signal to their mothers to put them to the breast. A crying breast-fed baby can almost always be pacified by putting him to the breast, which acts as a comforter whatever else is wrong. A bottle-fed baby will suck in air if you let him suck on an empty bottle teat for comfort, so give him the crook of your little finger or a dummy if he can only be pacified by sucking.

Sometimes, though, you'll have to search further to find out what is wrong: a baby may be crying from colic, because his gums are swollen and itchy for teething, because he's too hot or cold, has an earache, or because he's developing an illness. Lots of babies are unhappy as an illness such as a cold or other minor infection is developing, perhaps even before they have any obvious symptoms, and the same goes for toddlers and pre-schoolers.

pre-schoolers. After a day or so of crying on and off for no apparent reason, they suddenly start a runny nose, a cough or one of the common childhood infections, for instance. As your baby grows older, you'll slowly learn to tell what's making him cry – you'll know his tired times, expression and behaviour and you'll know when he's wanting to be at the breast or sucking at a dummy on and off for some time (often in the early evening).

It makes it easier to comfort a crying child if you know what's wrong but until your child can talk well enough to explain what it is that's upsetting him, you'll have to use detective work to find out, if obvious measures like feeding and cuddling don't work. Children are always more likely to cry when they're tired or if the atmosphere at home is strained.

Besides sucking, just being cuddled or gently and rhythmically rocked helps calm a crying baby down if he's not hungry. Motion of any sort is appreciated, in fact, and many parents know the trick of taking a baby out for a ride in the car or pram to quieten him down. A fast, jiggling motion sometimes soothes a baby more than a slower swaying rock in your arms, and many babies stop crying if you show them things as you walk round with them in your arms.

Never leave a baby crying because 'it's good for him', 'it'll exercise his lungs', 'he's got to learn that he can't get his own way all the time', or 'it's not time for his feed yet'. You can't spoil a baby by responding to his need for you. Babies and young children left to cry time after time soon become apathetic and sad, losing their sense of fun. Many become more demanding than before. Instead of thinking that the world's a good place to be in, they grow up learning that even if they're in trouble, its unlikely that anyone will be kind to them. If you love your child, he'll learn to be responsive to other people in need. You are his example of how to behave and he'll subconsciously accept your sort of behaviour as a parent and then treat his own children or even other people the same when he in turn becomes a parent.

If you find it hard to be altruistic, even towards your own child, just consider how you would feel if you were unhappy, unwell, or hungry, and you couldn't put things right for yourself.

If one day you find that your baby won't stop crying in spite of your doing all the right things, and as long as you're sure he doesn't need medical attention, just take comfort in the knowledge that you are doing all you can. If you feel you're at the end of your tether, ask your husband or a relative, friend or neighbour to look after the baby for you for a while, just to give you a break. Babies sometimes sense when their mothers are het up and cry even more. Another person might have the magic touch necessary to calm your baby down for a while.

Some babies do seem especially prone to crying, however they are handled. Take heart that if the only way your young baby will stop crying is if you cuddle or feed him for most of the time, you and your baby are not alone, and this stage will pass, however draining and hopeless it may seem to you when you are tired out. Parents of first babies are usually much more anxious and upset when their babies want constant attention than are parents of subsequent babies. By the time the third or fourth baby comes along it seems second nature to have the baby on your lap in the evening or on your hip as you unpack the shopping, whereas with the first you might have expected him to sleep a lot and to lie quietly in his pram or cot between feeds, and been very agitated when he obviously didn't agree with this idea.

Inevitably there will be occasional times when your crying baby will have to wait for you to comfort him and no harm will come to him from this. Having said this though, it's usually possible to pick your baby up even if you can't attend to his dirty nappy, for example, immediately, and just being in your arms or being put to the breast may quieten him as you finish your phone call or whatever.

What happens if your baby starts crying in the middle of the supermarket and you're stuck in the check-out queue? This has happened to most mothers and it's not much fun because of all the disapproving glances you'll get. You're most likely to avoid such outbursts if you give your baby a feed as late as possible before starting out from home; if you make sure he has a clean nappy on; if you carry him round the supermarket in a sling (provided he likes this form of transport; and if you don't tempt providence but do your shopping as quickly as you can.

The day you can hear your baby crying and are not concerned, ask yourself what's gone wrong with your relationship with your child. Few mothers can carry on with what they are doing for long if their baby is crying , if they try to, they'll be hurrying so much that they'll drop things or make mistakes. Nature has designed things so that a baby's cry is a powerful signal to his mother – one that really can't be ignored. The natural response is to stop the crying by giving the baby what he needs.

If you are a parent who is irritated when your baby wakes sooner than expected and cries for attention, or who cries on and off for long periods at certain times, try a bit of positive thinking. Instead of allowing yourself to be irritated and flustered, especially if you have a lot to do, try to remember that the baby will only be this demanding for a relatively short time (even though a few months may seem like ages at the time), and that you can't expect a baby to grow up and be independent overnight. Most important, decide if you can to let yourself enjoy cuddling and calming your baby. Let everything else wait if at all possible.

Babies who are attended to promptly end up crying less. Babies who are allowed to go on crying so as not to 'spoil' them end up crying a lot more of the time. If you want your baby to cry as little as possible for his sake and yours, respond quickly and don't stop trying to find out what he needs until he stops crying. **Related topic** Child abuse; fretful baby.

Cuddling Cuddling is a natural form of behaviour in most animals: even young fish get as close to their mothers as they can. Nestling into a warm body must be pleasant for a baby or young child if our adult experience is anything to go by. A baby stands to gain even more from close physical contact with his mother – particularly if he gets her breast milk and the chance to suck at her breast simply for comfort when he needs to. Bottle-feeding mothers are sensibly advised to cuddle their babies as they give the bottle so that their babies don't lose any more physical contact than they have to.

Cuddling a baby keeps him warm. Many pre-industrial societies living in cold climates wrap the baby up inside the mother's clothing so that as much of her body heat as possible reaches her baby. It's easier to tell when a baby is warm enough if he's in your arms rather than if he's in a cot. It's also easier to tell if he's too hot, which can be just as bad.

Babies who are cuddled or held in a sling (which gives the baby approximately the same feeling) for much of the time cry less. They are lulled by their mother's movements, her body's noises and its warmth. The comfort of being held firmly but gently must be similar to that felt in the womb. Perhaps that's why swaddling a baby often calms him and helps him sleep as well. Often when a baby is sleeping in his mother's arms, if he starts twitching in his periods of light sleep, she can hold him firmly and let him drift back to sleep, whereas otherwise his movements would have wakened him.

Cuddling a child is a parent's natural response if the child is unhappy. Even as an adult you will have probably been cuddled from time to time to cheer you up and will know that it works. A hug is worth a thousand words when it comes to comforting another human being or simply to demonstrate love and affection. The British are relatively undemonstrative as a race and tend not to hug or kiss each other very much. It's surprising though how quickly you can get used to being more physical with other people, and not even just with those you love, if you try. Parents say that babies brought up with lots of physical contact, unrestricted breast-feeding and perhaps sleeping with the parents in their bed tend to be much more cuddly than other children brought up more conventionally at arms length.

Cuddling doesn't have to be done sitting in a chair. Try cuddling your baby naked in a warm room, in the sunshine, or when you have a bath. You'll enjoy yourself just as much as he will. Make the most of having a baby or young child to cuddle.

As your child gets older and his days get fuller, you'll find there's still always time for a cuddle at bedtime, after the bedtime ritual of teeth cleaning, story, and so on. You might like to lie on your child's bed and let him talk as you have a cuddle and you'll find this is often the time when you learn a surprising amount about what makes him tick.

Don't reserve open physical affection just for the children in your family but let them see you cuddle each other, your own parents and other people who are important to you. They love watching their parents hug or kiss each other and it will reinforce the fact that even if you sometimes quarrel or get cross with each other, you still love each other. That's an important thing to learn and it'll also give them a real feeling of security within the family.

Cups You can choose your baby's first cup from a variety of shapes and sizes and the choice will depend to some extent on his age when you give him his first drink other than from the breast or bottle. There's no need for a baby to drink from a cup at all while he's being completely breast- or bottle-fed, though some mothers want to get their babies used to the skill of drinking like this from early on and so introduce a cup from time to time even before their baby is six months old.

If you're going to hold the cup for him, then you can give your baby a drink from your best bone china if you like because you won't drop it and you can control the rate at which the fluid in it goes into his mouth. However, if he's going to hold it – and most babies have a good try after six months or so – then choose a baby cup made from an unbreakable plastic. There are lots available but one of the best to start with is smaller than the rest (just over three inches (8 cm) high and two inches (5 cm) in diameter), has a lid with a spout to drink from, and no handles. It is small enough and light enough for a young baby to grasp with both hands to put to his mouth and most mothers say that their babies find it easier to hold than a cup with a handle or handles. Other suitable cups have one or two handles and either a lid with a spout with a row of holes in it or a depressed lid with a row of holes for the baby to drink from.

Some people don't like the look of a spout on a baby's cup but it does serve two useful purposes. The drink is much less likely to be spilt accidentally or on purpose, though a baby can have fun showering the carpet if he holds his mug upside down without being noticed; and because the baby's natural reaction is to suck, he'll learn to drink from such a cup quickly with only a minor change in the position of his mouth and tongue. Holes in a spout or a lid can be blocked by orange juice or by milk if they aren't thoroughly rinsed clean each time. It may be worth sieving orange juice to let it flow freely. Unblock the holes with a needle or pin if necessary.

If you want to take your baby's familiar drink with you when you go out, make sure the cup doesn't tip up in your bag and perhaps put it in a polythene bag with a wire tag around it first. Some mugs have secure lids which are useful for travelling. Your baby may be one of those who only drinks from his own cup, so remember always to take it with you or you may have a thirsty child on your hands.

Young children often don't notice full cups and it's up to you to make sure you don't put a cup of hot tea, for example, somewhere where your child could knock it over and scald himself.

Your child will enjoy having his very own cup to drink from. When he graduates to having a breakable one, you might like to get him one with his name on or one with a picture on it. Old-fashioned mugs with a frog or other surprise at the bottom are now being made again and make each drink more fun.

Curiosity Young children are naturally curious. Curiosity is an essential part of growing up and learning about the magic of the world around them. A child's curiosity should be encouraged because it's a good basis for learning to live a full and enjoyable life. Many adults have lost their child-like curiosity and this is a sad loss.

Closely associated with curiosity is a child's imagination. This turns the mundane into the marvellous. A bright child can be brilliant when he uses his imagination and even a slow child becomes a special source of delight at such times. Never make the mistake of putting a child down in his imaginary world and only intervene with adult views if there is danger in what he is doing.

As he grows, your baby will explore the smell, taste, sight, sound and feel of the things he comes into contact with. It's often easy to forget as he's sitting there banging away at something or chewing some totally inappropriate object that he's learning and that it is his curiosity that drives him. When he becomes mobile he can indulge his curiosity much more easily, which in turn takes the pressure off you to provide him with new sources of interest. If you take an interest in everything around you and enjoy exploring new places, ideas and things, your child will take his cue from you. Enjoy your child's curiosity and foster it. It's a wonderful gift that should be encouraged to stay with him all his life. ***Related topic*** Creativity.

Curly toes Many babies are born with curly toes and these often straighten out on their own. If a child still has curly toes when he wears shoes, make sure that there is adequate space for his toes in the vertical plane of the shoe as well as from side to side. If one toe actually rubs over the other, a callus or corn may form at the pressure site. If you are concerned that your child's curly toes are causing problems ask your clinic or family doctor's advice. An operation can be performed if necessary to straighten the toes but no movement of the toes will be possible afterwards.

Cuts These are very common in toddlers, who are into everything, and in older children as they explore and play rough games out of doors.

Small cuts usually heal perfectly well if the edges are brought together and kept there with a sticking plaster. You may have to apply pressure to the area through a clean handkerchief if the bleeding is profuse before you can put the sticking plaster on. Don't bother to wash small, clean cuts and don't use antiseptic as this can delay healing.

Larger cuts, cuts on the face, and deep ones on the hands or feet should always be seen by a doctor. Jagged cuts may leave a nasty scar unless they're stitched up professionally and so should be seen by a doctor. Whilst on the way to the casualty department simply keep pressure over the area through a dressing or a freshly-laundered handkerchief to stop the bleeding. Cuts on the scalp almost always need stitches to control the bleeding but all except the most serious of cuts on other areas of the body stop bleeding within ten to fifteen minutes of pressure.

Even large cuts heal well and with careful stitching will be invisible in about a year. ***Related topics*** Bleeding; grazes.

Cystic fibrosis An inherited disorder affecting about two babies in every thousand. The main problem in this condition is an over-production of mucus by many of the mucus-producing glands in the body, especially those in the lungs, the pancreas, the bowel and the sweat and salivary glands. The mucus produced is more sticky than normal. This can produce a blockage of the intestine caused by sticky bowel contents (meconium ileus) in affected newborn babies, which needs an operation to cure it. Most cystic fibrosis babies develop a swollen abdomen, have pale, bulky, offensive stools and don't gain weight properly. The rectum may prolapse too. Cystic fibrosis is the commonest cause of rectal prolapse in children.

As the disease progresses the lungs become permanently affected through repeated infections.

Treatment involves giving a special diet including extracts of pancreatic enzymes to enable the child to grow; antibiotics and inhalations to make lung secretions less sticky; and physiotherapy to help drain the lungs. Children with this condition benefit from being breast-fed but should also receive all their immunizations and should, if possible, be kept away from people with infections. Even though they may have repeated illnesses over many years, they need to be treated as normally as possible so that they don't grow up to regard themselves as cripples.

The treatment of cystic fibrosis has greatly improved and the outlook today is much better than it used to be. ***Useful organization*** The Cystic Fibrosis Research Trust.

Cystitis An inflammation of the bladder, usually as part of a generalized infection of the urinary tract. The condition is commoner in girls than in boys, possibly because they have a shorter urinary passage (urethra) which bacteria can go up more easily.

The diagnosis in babies and young children can be difficult to make because they can't tell you that it hurts to pass water (usually a major symptom in older children and adults). The other symptom – passing water frequently – is usually normal in young children anyway. Inflammation of the vulva or penis is a more common cause of painful urination than is an infection of the urine. Urinary infections in babies often show up as a loss of appetite; poor weight gain; a pale face; crying and generally seeming unwell; and occasional vomiting.

The only way to be sure of the diagnosis in a young child is for a fresh specimen of urine to be examined for bacteria. Your doctor will tell you how to collect the urine sample using a simple, pain-free method.

Prevention is better than a cure. Your baby's bottom should be kept clean, perferably by being washed in plenty of warm water each time the nappy is dirty, so as not to encourage infection, and girls should be taught to wipe their bottoms from front to back so as not to transfer bacteria from around the opening of the back passage to the urinary opening in front of the vagina.

Antibiotics will usually cure a urinary infection within a few days but the recommended course *must* be finished. Your doctor will ask you to bring a second sample of your child's urine to see if the bacteria are killed. One in three children with a urinary infection has another within a year. Recurrent urinary infections can be troublesome and will need long-term treatment. A child with recurring infections may need to have special x-rays of the urinary system to see if there is an abnormality.

Cytomegalovirus A type of virus that can cause severe problems if acquired before birth. The affected baby may be of low birth weight and may have jaundice, anaemia, an enlarged liver and spleen, deafness, and calcium deposits in the brain. If he survives he could be left with hydrocephalus, blindness, or mental retardation.

Some babies are symptom-free 'shedders' of this virus following infection during birth from a mother with an infected cervix. They can infect other babies and so need to be isolated from them.

Older babies and young children can also be infected with cytomegalovirus. They may be symptom-free or may have liver involvement, inflammation of their lungs, and inflammation of their bowels with poor absorption of food.

Generally the outlook for future pregnancies for the woman who has had a baby with the condition is very good. It's wise, however, not to get pregnant again too quickly after such an infection.

There is no satisfactory treatment for cytomegalovirus infection as yet.

Damp It is often said that wearing damp clothes or living in damp conditions causes illnesses, especially colds. There is no evidence that this is true but living in damp housing certainly can reduce a child's resistance to infections and is generally considered to be unhealthy. Damp homes also enable house dust mites to flourish and this can be a major aggravating factor in certain children with asthma.

Preventing damp can be difficult in much poorly constructed or old housing but often the problem arises simply from poor ventilation. Remember too that paraffin heaters produce a lot of water vapour when they are working and that this could add to the problem of damp.

One answer is to heat your home to the temperature you like but to leave a window slightly open so that damp air can escape. If you are troubled with damp get the local council (if you have a council property) or a builder to come and suggest ways of overcoming the problem.

Dancing Dancing has always been and still is practised by virtually every society in the world. It's an art form as well as a form of personal amusement, entertainment for others, exercise, courtship and, sometimes, part of a ritual of celebration, worship or even war. Sometimes a dance is done in sheer high spirits, unstructured and free-form; at other times each step, each expression on the dancer's face and even the position of each finger is carefully laid down, learnt, adhered to and passed down from generation to generation. Dance is often a form of expression of feelings or of stories. It can be aesthetically beautiful or it can be fierce and horrific. Any form of behaviour and any emotion can be mirrored and enlarged on if necessary in dance.

In the West children first learn to dance by watching others, for example their parents or older brothers and sisters dancing for fun at home, and dancers on television or at a pantomine or other show. Once they get the idea of moving around, even quite young children can invent their own dances. Music is a help, though not essential, and it can be of any kind.

Dancing lessons for young children are mostly a preparation for classical ballet, but more and more teachers are enrolling pre-schoolers, both boys and girls (but still mostly girls), for modern dance sessions. The aim of any dancing lesson must be enjoyment. Given that so few children will be any good at classical ballet, for example, there is absolutely no point in pushing a child into learning steps or sequences that she doesn't want to learn. If there is interest and ability, then that can be fostered as the child grows older. As with learning anything, if the parents take an interest, the child will be eager to please. Taking an interest doesn't only mean asking the child to show you what she's done in her lesson that week! It means getting up and doing it with her, for fun. Once she sees you enjoying yourself doing what she's been doing, or doing your own dances as well, she'll be half-way towards learning the main importance of dancing. Dancing to please an audience is something that comes later than dancing for the sheer pleasure of it.

If you don't want to or can't afford the uniform (usually a leotard and ballet shoes) for your child's dance class, buy second hand or ask the teacher if she has any hand-me-downs from mothers whose children have grown out of their clothes. Leotards stretch but can be uncomfortable if too tight in the crutch. They aren't very warm and if your child tends to get cold, put a vest underneath even if it shows. An old-fashioned bolero looks attractive and is quick to knit, but a cardigan will do as well unless there are strict regulations about the uniform. Shoes are another matter. They are very expensive for the amount of use your child will get out of them. They are also flimsy and wear out fairly quickly. You'll be advised to buy fairly tightly-fitting ones as this is how they should traditionally fit for ballet dancing. However, use your own discretion and choose ones which are roomy and will therefore last longer. There'll be plenty of time to have tighter ones when she comes to doing exams, if ever. With a little elastic round the ankle, the shoe will stay on and be very comfortable. To sew on the elastic, bend the back of the shoe down on to the inner. Where each side of the shoe is folded at right angles is the place to attach the elastic. Don't forget to name the shoes as they can easily get lost in the mêlée of the changing room.

You needn't be a trained dancer to teach your children to dance. Put on some music and dance to it at home and your child will soon join in. If you're self-conscious, he or she could be too because your attitude is their example. Suggest that they do some dancing at the toddler group or play-group you take them to. Organize slightly more formal dances like oranges and lemons or very simple square dances. There's no end to the possibilities. Dancing is a very good way to teach your children to enjoy exercise.

Although it may seem unnecessary for an under-five to go to a dancing class because you may feel you can do just as well on your own at home, there is no doubt that most children enjoy the fact that it involves an outing and that it is a social event which involves teamwork, learning from others, and making new friends. *Related topic* Exercise.

Dawdling Toddlers and pre-schoolers have little sense of time nor of all the many things a busy parent has to do in a day. They have no urgency in their life but make the most of each thing they do, enjoying it (or otherwise) to the full. Getting dressed quickly is beyond them, as is eating their breakfast fast. As for hurrying when walking somewhere, who wants to hurry when there are so many interesting things to look at?

You'll just have to accept that your aims are sometimes different from those of your child and then organize your day so that the inevitable dawdling will fit in without you having to nag and hurry him. Get up half an hour earlier so that there's time to spare in the morning before you take older children to play-group or school. Start putting your child's outdoor clothes on ten minutes before you otherwise would. Lay breakfast the night before so you've got a five-minute headstart in the morning. If the early morning isn't your best time, put out all the clothes for you and the children the night before. In other words, if your child's dawdling is worrying you, inject some calmness into your life by giving yourself more time.

Sometimes a little dawdling doesn't hurt us parents either. Lots of adults tend to pile too many things into a day and end up racing against time and not enjoying anything they do. With little children around it's difficult to start any job and follow it through. If you dawdle through your day, you'll probably find that everything gets done in the end just the same and you don't finish the day exhausted and frustrated.

Day care The term 'day care' generally implies that a child is being looked after in a day nursery or a crêche during the working week. Some children of working parents are looked after by child-minders in the minders' homes, while others go to a friend, relative or neighbour. Yet others are looked after in their own home by a nanny.

Day nurseries and crêches tend to open five days a week only, but they generally start their day early enough for mothers or fathers to drop the child off before work and finish at the end of the working day. Minders, on the other hand, are much more flexible about their hours and will fit in day care to suit the parent's individual needs. Some will even mind a child at night if the parent is on a night shift.

The staffing, space and hygiene of nurseries and crêches are monitored carefully by local authorities. Child-minders who are paid to look after children are also vetted to make sure that the children are being looked after in suitable surroundings and to check that the minder is not looking after too many children.

Day care facilities vary widely from area to area and the number of places is often inadequate. Each form of care has its own advantages and disadvantages. Perhaps the sort of care that most nearly replaces the mother is when the grandmother or another female relative takes over. The child has a one-to-one relationship with a familiar and (hopefully) loved and loving person, and the sort of care he gets is more likely to be as the mother wishes than if he were in a more institutional setting. However, not everyone has a willing and able granny at hand and will have to choose from whatever facilities are available. Whatever you arrange, make sure that it's as stable as possible. Too many changes of caretaker are upsetting even for the most phlegmatic of children.

Day care can usually be arranged by the local council for young mentally and physically handicapped children both to give their mothers a break and to provide extra stimulation. Sometimes this is in an ordinary day nursery and for pre-schoolers it may be in a class in a special school. *Related topics* Child-minders; crêches; day nurseries. *Useful organization* The National Childminding Association.

Day nurseries Places run either by a local authority or privately where children under the age of five go on a daily basis. Most parents using a day nursery for their child are at work. Local authority day nurseries are usually greatly oversubscribed and the places are allocated according to need. One parent families, families in which the mother is ill or in hospital and there is no one else to look after the child, families in which the mother is overburdened and families with a mentally or physically handicapped child are usually given priority. Payment is usually according to means, whereas with a private nursery there is a fixed scale of charges. Private day nurseries at places of work are commonly known as crêches.

If your child is to go to a day nursery, tell the nursery supervisor about his sleep pattern during the day, any special toy or cuddly he likes to have with him, whether he's reliably dry and clean, and his likes and dislikes when it comes to food. Tell her on a daily basis if you're not happy about his behaviour or health. If there are particular family problems it also helps to tell her because if he reacts by behaving in an unusual way during the day, she'll know why and will be able to help her staff cope better with him. If you're going to be early or late in picking him up, mention it on the day, and if you're delayed on the way home, be sure to telephone to put her mind at rest that he hasn't been forgotten.

It goes without saying that a child with an infectious illness shouldn't go to a day nursery. Recommended periods of isolation for infectious illnesses are well worth adhering to. You'll find that if your child has infectious diarrhoea the nursery will want to be especially sure that he's clear before he's allowed back. Regulations about the children's health are clearly laid down by the area health authority and the nursery supervisor has ready access to advice when necessary. Often a visiting doctor carries out periodic developmental and medical examinations on the children in the nursery. You'll be notified and invited to attend.

Day nursery staff today are trained to be aware of the importance of play to young children. Some of the staff are permanent and others are there on a temporary basis as part of their nursery training. As far as possible the nursery supervisor will try to allocate one member of staff to a small number of children so that they can get to know her and she them. This person will do everything for her charges during the day as a mother would. The children's day will be made up of meal and sleep times, play, music, and a time outdoors on most days.

Children in day nurseries are adequately cared for physically but may miss out emotionally by not having a one-to-one relationship with an adult as they would have had with their mother for much of the time, (unless she had a large number of children). Also, however much the staff may be fond of a child, they can never love him in the way his mother can. Some children do very well in a day nursery but others quite obviously miss their mothers a lot and never really settle down in such a large group of children.

Partly because of the family problems which may account for a child being in a day nursery and partly because of the separation from the mother, the staff see a lot of behaviour problems. These are best sorted out as well as possible for the good of the child by sympathetic discussion between the supervisor and the parents.

Many children, especially as they grow older, enjoy playing with the other children at the nursery much as they would at a play-group. Nursery staff are encouraged to give the children plenty to do and to talk to them just as their mothers would if they were with them.

Better a good day nursery than a bad minder, and the nursery staff may give a child more stimulation than a minder can simply because they are trained to and a minder has a home to run as well. On the other hand, being with a capable and caring minder is much more like being at home with mum, and therefore is often preferable. *Related topics* Child minders; crêches; nannies; play-groups; separation anxiety.

Deafness A moderate degree of deafness is not at all uncommon in many under-fives, mainly because there are several childhood conditions that can cause it. A very few babies are born with a congenital malformation of the hearing nerve or of the middle ear; a mother who has German measles while pregnant can have a deaf child; severe jaundice in the newborn can cause it, as can brain damage due to a shortage of oxygen at birth, otitis media, mumps, meningitis, encephalitis and a blockage of the outer ear canal by wax or a foreign body.

By far the commonest of all of these (once a child is past the first few weeks) is otitis media. This usually causes temporary deafness only and then only on the affected side. A common complication of the condition (called glue ear) can lead to a more serious or even permanent hearing loss, and it has been estimated that one in ten children in the UK are partially deaf as a result of this condition.

As with so many other problems in childhood the sooner it is discovered the better. This is especially important with hearing because a child who is even partially deaf will have problems with learning to talk. A deaf baby doesn't babble in the second half of the first year, he doesn't turn towards sounds or jump at a loud noise and will only know you are there if he sees you. If ever you notice any of these things tell your family doctor or clinic doctor, who'll do some simple tests to find out if it's really deafness that's the problem.

The vast majority (ninety-eight per cent) of deaf children are not completely deaf and slight degrees of hearing loss are easy to miss unless you're an expert at recognizing them. This is especially the case when only one ear is affected. Some children hear some sound frequencies and not others, which results in a distortion of what they hear. Speech is greatly delayed and disturbed because of this type of loss yet the child may not seem obviously 'deaf'.

Today there's no need for a child to be untreated for even slight degrees of deafness. Hearing aids can be used by the very young if necessary and you can learn to speak close to your child's ear, repeating the sounds so that he learns how to distinguish them. There are lots of experts on hand to help. Only if your child is very deaf will he have to go to a special school for the deaf and some ordinary schools today have special classes for partially deaf children. *Related topics* Glue ear; hearing testing; otitis media; wax in ears. *Useful organizations* National Association for Deaf/Blind and Rubella Handicapped; National Deaf Children's Society; The Royal Institute for the Deaf.

Decisions – learning to make

Decisions – learning to make Part of the process of becoming independent from one's parents is learning to make decisions. Even a baby makes conscious decisions. He decides what he wants to pick up and what he likes to eat. He decides when he's had enough to drink. He lets you know when he's finished his meal by throwing the food on the floor or by playing with his spoon. Sooner or later he'll show his temper at being thwarted in what he has decided to do and one day may throw a tantrum. Each child has to learn not only to make some decisions for himself but also how to behave if someone else decides the opposite! For the naturally self-centred young child, as all young children are, it is often difficult to accept that he is not in fact in control of his life, and that someone else – usually his mother – will make many of the day-to-day decisions about what he wears, eats and does.

Being able to make good decisions is a valuable asset in life.

While it's important to weigh up the pros and cons each time, it's often far more useful to make a decision and stick to it than to shilly shally around and change your mind frequently. Help your child to learn how to take various factors into consideration before making up his mind and then to stand by his decision. Choosing what to wear is something that many young children take seriously. They'll look at all their clothes and then decide. Sometimes such a decision takes a long time, but the fact that he is taking the trouble to choose carefully is what is important. If you encourage your child to make certain decisions, be sure to let him carry them through when he's made them. It's no good telling a child that he can choose whether to go for a walk to the shops or a walk to the swings if you're going to say no when he chooses a walk to the swings. If *you* want to make the decision, don't offer the choice to your child in the first place, though by all means let him in on the discussion so you can take into account what he wants to do.

From making very few decisions in babyhood your child will slowly make more and more decisions for himself and if encouraged by you will be sufficiently independent to enjoy making decisions for himself most of the time when it comes to going to school.

Defiance A defiant child is one who is testing you out to see how you'll respond to his rudeness or other forms of bad behaviour. He may be copying other children he's seen being defiant at play-group or elsewhere; he may just be going through a stage where he wants to pit himself against you to see who'll win – he wants to know what the limits are; he may be resentful of the way you treat him, thinking it unfair; he may be tired out or sickening for something and not behaving in his usual way; or he may be sad or unhappy about something that has gone wrong for him during the day and showing his unease by being defiant. Defiant children may have a poor self image and – perhaps surprisingly – they often lack confidence.

Children of all ages are likely to defy their parents' intentions and wishes at some stage but it's most likely to happen with older toddlers between eighteen months and 2½ and – surprisingly, perhaps – with four-year-olds. Whatever you suggest, they'll want to do something else. This is the classical 'Mary, Mary, quite contrary' stage.

The way to handle the situation, especially if it's important that the child does what you say, is to *tell* him to do something rather than to *ask*. Saying 'will you . . .' gives the child the chance to say no. If you can give him a choice of what to do, wear, or whatever, he'll appreciate being involved in the decision-making and will probably forget his usual habit of going against whatever you suggest. When you feel strongly about something simply make the decision, announce it and see it through. If the subject is of no importance to you or the family (for example, what dress to wear), don't be dogmatic about it but let the child choose. It's a lot easier than creating a fuss over issues which really don't matter anyway. Many parents tell how they won such battles yet lost the war. And there is little point in that.

A toddler who seems defiant needs guidance in what to do, and how to do it. If you let him go all his own way every time he'll feel insecure and certainly not pleased with himself. It's at this stage that your child learns what you are like as parents and whether you have the strength to stand up for the things you believe in. If you constantly back down in the face of his defiance it's he who'll suffer though you may think you're buying an easy way out. Sticking to your guns doesn't mean being violent (either physically or emotionally). Be firm and convincing and, most of all, be consistent. He needs to be able to rely on your doing what you say you will whether it's to his advantage or disadvantage in the short term. The under-fives are still very immature as people and rely on a consistent response from their parents – after all it's often all they have to build on.

Sometimes three- or four-year-olds are defiant when their mother seems to be occupied a lot of the time with a younger brother or sister. It probably appears to them that they are always being told off and that they never get their share of attention. If they're told to do something which they don't really want to do, for example, they may refuse in a defiant way. Previously their mother would have realized what was happening and asked in a different way or helped them do whatever she had asked, much as she would before the new sibling came on the scene. However, because she's tired and upset that her child is behaving less well than he used to, she gets cross and this sets the scene for more defiance.

Countering defiance with punishment doesn't often work because it makes an unhappy child more unhappy and it does nothing positive to help him through this stage. Try to find out why he's behaving like this and then talk it over with him. Understanding, loving firmness, and never asking too much of a child who has had his nose put out of joint work best. While you shouldn't put up with rudeness, there are ways of showing him how you would like him to behave that are more constructive than telling him off, sending him to his room, or smacking him. Instead of running your child down by constantly criticizing him for his behaviour, boost his confidence by praising him when he behaves well. Positive reinforcement of good behaviour makes a child feel that he is 'good' in both your eyes and his own. Once he thinks of himself as being good he'll want to live up to his – and your – expectations of himself and defiance will be seen as letting both himself – and you – down. Sometimes a child uses defiance simply as a way of getting attention, perhaps because when he behaves well you tend to ignore him. Counter this by remembering to talk to him and do things with him from time to time throughout the day: it would be a shame if the only attention you gave your child was anger provoked by his defiance.

Often a bright young child will play one parent off against the other – if his mother says no to a TV programme, for instance, he may get permission from his father instead and defiantly confront his mother with this. Parents must agree to cooperate if this sort of behaviour is to be discouraged. All too easily arguments can ensue between them simply because one parent doesn't want to back down in front of the child.

Be prepared for this stage to last for some time and be prepared for your patience to be sorely tried. *Related topics* Attention seeking; rivalry between siblings; temper tantrums.

Dehydration A medical term for a condition in which a person's tissues become short of water. so that the normal processes of metabolism cannot occur. It can be caused by too small an intake or too great a loss of fluid, or both and unless prevented or properly treated is dangerous to life.

Because two-thirds of our body weight is made up of water both within and outside the cells, it's important to keep the body's water balance within certain fairly fine limits. Water is also important as the carrier for essential salts necessary for the healthy functioning of the body.

Children usually become dehydrated as a result of vomiting or diarrhoea or when they have a high fever and lose a lot of sweat. A child with a fever of over 100°F (38°C) can lose pints of fluid a day and this must be replaced. In fact replacing fluid is about the most important thing a parent can do when his child has a fever. When adults lose a lot of fluid they feel thirsty but babies and very young children can become dangerously dehydrated and yet not want to drink. They have to be especially carefully watched. One way of telling if your baby is dehydrated is to look at the soft spot on his skull. This is usually flat but becomes sunken if he is dehydrated.

Getting fluids into a child who is becoming dehydrated can be a problem but is worth doing because he'll feel so much better just for being rehydrated. Plain water or diluted fruit juice are the best but if he won't take these, then give anything he will take rather than nothing.

If your bottle-fed baby becomes dehydrated because of diarrhoea or vomiting, be sure that the milk you are giving him is made up to the correct strength and no stronger. An extra scoop of milk powder in each bottle can cause severe problems in an already dehydrated baby. If he wants more to drink, give cooled, boiled water and not more formula.

The breast-fed baby needs unrestricted time at the breast if he is short of fluid. If you are drinking according to your thirst and there has been no problem with your milk supply, then you'll produce more milk to cope with his increased demands within two or three days. If you are at all worried that your breast-fed baby isn't having enough to drink in spite of unrestricted time at the breast, extra fluids in the form of cooled, boiled water can be given by spoon or (if breast-feeding is well established) by bottle.

If your child won't drink, if he vomits what you give him, or if he develops sunken, glazed eyes, a dry mouth and dry or just damp nappies, call your doctor at once. Dangerously dehydrated babies and young children need urgent hospital treatment.

Delicate children An out-of-date term that used to be used to describe children who were socially and educationally backward as a result of repeated ill health. Such children had diseases such as TB, polio, rheumatic fever, asthma and whooping cough – all now uncommon or far less serious than they were. Severely malnourished children too were often included in the term 'delicate' but such malnourishment is rare today in the UK.

There are still about 3,500 children in special schools who are classified as 'delicate', with asthma being the biggest single diagnosis today but there are also a few children with TB or difficult to control diabetes for whom such schools are advised.

Demand feeding A term used to describe the sort of feeding that involves feeding a baby whenever he asks for a feed by crying. Sensitive mothers can often tell when their babies want to feed simply by the way they move their bodies and before they have to cry. Some young babies make mouthing movements as they wake and it's obvious then that they want to suck. The problem with the term demand feeding is that it implies that the baby is being imperious and this gives a slightly negative feeling to the whole business. A better term is unrestricted feeding or, as one expert called it, 'ask feeding', that is, feeding a baby for as long as he wants at each feed and giving him as many feeds as he wants by day and night.

Demand feeding can be done with bottle-fed as well as breast-fed babies. A bottle-fed baby can be given a bottle whenever he seems to want one but you'll have to be careful not to overfeed him if you do this. Give him the same number of scoops of milk powder in twenty four hours that you'd be giving him on a rigid schedule but put fewer scoops in each bottle of water, so making his milk more dilute. Unrestricted feeding can't be done with bottle-feeds because if a bottle-fed baby goes on sucking for as long a time as he wants to suck, the milk will run out and unless his mother makes up another bottle, he'll be sucking on an empty one and may get windy if he lets air into the bottle by relaxing his mouth. You can make his bottle last longer and so give him more time to suck if you use a teat with a smaller hole so that the milk comes out more slowly. If he wants to suck still more, you could let him suck his fingers or thumb or a dummy. A breast-fed baby can quite safely suck as long as he wants to on a breast which is virtually empty. From time to time he'll get a few drops of milk because milk is made continuously by the breasts.

Unrestricted breast-feeding is a good way of keeping a baby happy because he can always be comforted at the breast at any time – the breast is there for pleasure, reassurance and solace as well as for food. The American term 'nursing' is better than 'breast-feeding', especially when breast-feeding is done on an unrestricted basis, because it doesn't imply that the baby is always *feeding* when he's at the breast. Babies 'fed' on demand actually spend a relatively small proportion of their time at the breast getting nutrients.

The mother who demand feeds or feeds on an unrestricted basis will usually feed her baby when he wants. Occasionally, it may not be convenient for her to give her baby as much time as he would like and at times like this she'll stop before he would really like to stop. He's unlikely to cry if she takes him wherever she's going or if someone else amuses him. Occasionally she won't be able to feed him immediately when he wakes for a feed. Impatience for a feed is something seen much more often in very young babies. As they grow older they can more easily wait a little while until their mother is ready. Also, there will be many times when she wants to feed her baby before going out or before doing something time-consuming at home, just to make sure that he doesn't get hungry when she's unable to feed him. Occasionally she'll even wake him to feed him. This sort of feeding isn't only for the baby's benefit: it is so flexible that it can be geared to his mother's needs too.

Demand breast-feeding, and particularly unrestricted feeding, is more successful than schedule feeding because it stimulates the milk supply more efficiently. Not only does the milk come in quicker but it is highly unlikely ever to be inadequate in amount. *Related topics* Bottle-feeding; breast-feeding; breast-feeding problems; feeding schedules.

Dental caries (dental decay) A disease mainly seen in the Western world probably caused by eating too much highly-refined food, especially sugar and white flour products. Only three in a thousand people in the West have a mouth free of caries.

In Britain, for example, by the age of five, the average child has several decayed, missing or filled teeth and dental decay causes more pain and suffering among children than does any other disease.

Caries starts as a layer of sticky protein called plaque which is deposited on the teeth. This is teeming with micro-organisms which thrive on sugary foods. The bacteria produce acids which eat into the enamel of teeth and dental decay starts. Once the decay has gone through into the nerves at the core of the tooth there is pain.

It has been shown that sweets eaten in one 'binge' a week have far fewer adverse effects on the teeth than the same amount eaten over the whole week. It's perfectly possible to hide the fact that sweets exist from young children, who won't clamour for them until the full force of advertising or the example of older children hits them.

Sweets which remain in the mouth being sucked for long periods and chewing gum with sugar are especially bad for the teeth. A particularly bad practice from this point of view is the giving of a dummy dipped into honey, rose hip syrup or other sweet substances to a baby. It is now known that teeth are most susceptible to decay immediately they appear above the gum. There is no need to add sugar to any of your baby's foods – this too can start his teeth rotting at a vulnerable time.

Toothbrushing should start when the teeth come through completely. Brushing at least once a day with a fluoride toothpaste is of proven value in cutting down tooth decay. Get your toddler interested in brushing his teeth and then check up to ensure that he's doing it properly. A child under three is unlikely to be able to brush his teeth properly, however intelligent and well-meaning he is. Most children forget the big back teeth so be sure to pay special attention to these.

When your baby's teeth first come through clean them with a cloth wrapped around your fingertip and when most of the milk teeth are through you can start with a brush. Encouraging a child to play with a toothbrush is a good way of getting him interested and soon tooth cleaning will be seen as fun and not a chore.

Fluoride tablets or drops have been shown to reduce dental decay in areas with low concentrations of fluoride in the water but there is violent controversy as to whether fluoride should routinely be added to drinking water.

Lastly, don't forget your dentist. He'll help with suggestions about the prevention of caries and will want to see your child from about three and a half onwards, every six months. The milk teeth are well worth looking after as they help ensure the correct growth and positioning of the second teeth.

Today's child need never lose a tooth – he can keep his teeth for life. It's exciting to find that dental decay is actually much less common among children than it was even five years ago. Things are improving but there is still a long way to go. **Related topics** Dentist; fluoride; teeth; toothbrushes; toothpaste.

Dentist A professional who looks after teeth. Statistics show that most children don't go to the dentist at all or, if they do, they go far too infrequently. As a result dental caries and other tooth conditions are often caught too late when they could have been totally prevented. Children should go to the dentist every six months from the age of three or four.

When you first go to the dentist he'll show your child how the chair works and will let him play around with things so he feels as relaxed as possible. Today's dentistry is almost always pain-free and there are even methods of doing small fillings that don't need any drilling. Children pick up parental anxiety so try to be as relaxed as possible. If you play dentists or read about visiting the dentist before you go it helps to take the strangeness out of the occasion. If your child has seen you or an older brother or sister in the dentist's chair, he's less likely to object when it's his turn.

Try to encourage your child to listen carefully to what the dentist says and then make sure that his advice is implemented at home. You and the dentist should be working as a team to keep your child's mouth healthy.

Specially skilled dentists called orthodontists have a particular interest in the straightening out of crooked teeth.

Dental treatment for children under five is completely free. **Related topics** Dental caries; orthodontist; teeth.

Dentures A complete or partial set of artificial teeth which take the place of lost natural ones. There are twenty-two million people in the UK with some sort of denture and even the under-fives have to have them sometimes. Teeth are lost by this age almost always because of dental caries which is a preventable disease. Much more rarely a child will have a denture to replace teeth lost in an accident. This produces a pleasant, cosmetic effect and helps the other teeth come through straight while awaiting the permanent teeth. *Related topics* Dentist; dental caries; orthodontist.

Dependence Without someone to protect him, move him around, keep him at the right temperature and feed him, a baby would die. Unlike some newborn animals that are independent right from birth, a human baby is dependent on others for many years. For the first nine months or so he is actually immobile, though he will be able to roll over around the age of three months. He can suck if the breast or a bottle teat is given to him, but he can't search for food or even pick it up if it's put before him. He certainly can't put anything round himself to keep warm and he can't even hold on to his mother's body to be carried round by her to keep warm, as can some young mammals. In view of all this it's not surprising that some anthropologists call a baby in the first nine months of life after birth an 'exterogestate foetus' (an extra-uterine foetus). It's only after nine months of complete dependence that a baby even starts to be able to move from one place to another or feed himself.

While a child of several years old might survive for a short while without someone to look after him, it wouldn't be for some time that he'd be independent and capable enough to find food, shelter and warmth. Parents are legally and financially responsible for their children for a long time – this isn't just socially desirable but virtually essential.

Babies allowed to be as dependent as they like have been found to become more independent as young children than those constantly being pushed away from their mothers in an attempt to give the mothers more freedom and to make the babies more independent. Never make the mistake of thinking that you're spoiling a baby or young child by allowing him to be as dependent as he wants. Let him be with you constantly until he's ready to explore without you, hold him when he needs it, give him the breast if he's hungry or thirsty or wants comfort, and don't pressurize him into sleeping alone in a room away from you if he's obviously unhappy. The natural place for a baby is with his mother. By tampering with his normal dependence you'll create problems for both of you. *Related topics* Attachment; clinging child; independence.

Depression in children This is a very controversial subject and some doctors don't believe that children get depressed in the way that adults do. It is certainly a fact that a baby over the age of about four months when separated from his mother becomes anxious, apprehensive and miserable. Older children become angry and frustrated and later apathetic and undemanding if they don't get enough of their mother's attention.

A considerable amount of research has shown that young children of depressed mothers are more likely to become depressed as children and that depressed adults, when asked about their childhood are more likely to report poor parenting because of mental ill health in their parents (usually the mother).

The trouble with all of this is that there is no accepted definition of childhood depression and much of what undoubtedly is depression masquerades as other things. Symptoms of depression in young children include irritability, a short attention span, sleep difficulties, colic, temper tantrums, bed-wetting, certain allergies and forgetfulness. The classical adult pattern, including sadness, is very uncommon. Sadness can occur of course in childhood but it is difficult to know whether it is 'real' depression. Tense, miserable children lash out when provoked and often find themselves in trouble with other parents and eventually with teachers when they go to school. Children with learning problems, hyperactivity and even behaviour problems have been shown to have a low level of self-esteem very often and to feel sad a lot of the time.

Bereavement, separation from parents and illness in a parent can all cause depression in a child and some children become very sad when they move away from a close friend.

Just how childhood depression should be treated isn't known. Some experts are convinced that anti-depressant drugs are the answer and others feel they should be forbidden. Almost certainly the best treatment is some form of family therapy, because most of these children need more love, security, stability and attention than they are getting. The first step to getting help for your child is to contact your family doctor who may refer him to a child psychiatrist. *Related topics* Anxiety; behaviour problems; child guidance; child psychiatry; depression in mothers.

Depression in mothers Many studies have shown that mothers of children under five are especially likely to suffer from true depression, particularly if they have other psychological or social problems to bear.

Babies can be a potent source of stress and depression in our society. 'Post-natal' depression is a term commonly used to describe the experience of weepiness on the one hand to full blown depression on the other, experienced soon after having a baby. If the condition is mild, it is called the 'baby blues'. At least half of all recently-delivered mothers suffer from the blues, but the condition usually only lasts for a day or two. Some studies have found that up to eighty per cent of women have mild depressive feelings in the month or so following the birth, so perhaps it should be seen as normal in our society.

Post-natal depression itself is a term used to describe a depression which, although unpleasant for the woman, isn't usually severe enough to prevent her from functioning properly. The symptoms are much like any other depression but there are other factors too. Such a woman feels she can't cope with her baby, cries at the slightest provocation, is critical of her husband, feels guilty about not loving the baby enough, goes off sex, loses her appetite, can't sleep, has nighmares, and may have anxious panic attacks. Very few women suffer from all of these problems but it's quite possible to be severely depressed and be affected by only a few of them. About one woman in ten is found to suffer from this more serious type of depression which classically begins at any time from three weeks to six months after the birth. Puerperal psychosis is a much more serious depressive condition still, occurring only in one in five hundred newly-delivered mothers. Emergency hospital admission may be necessary.

The law officially recognizes that some women become mentally disturbed after having a baby and the Infanticide Act of 1938 states that a woman can't be found guilty of the murder of her child within 12 months of its birth provided 'the balance of her mind was disturbed by reason of not having fully recovered from the effects of giving birth'.

The vast majority of women who become seriously clinically depressed after having a baby get better quickly either with the help of drugs or electro-convulsive therapy (ECT). Psychotherapy (talk therapy) can be useful but as most psychatrists are men it is quite possible that a lot of the underlying problems will not get the airing they deserve. Women psychotherapy counsellors are available all over the country and more are needed for such work. There is only one place that is run solely for women by women and that is The Women's Therapy Centre, 5 Manor Gardens, London N7 6LA (telephone 01 263 6200). They will help if they can or will tell you the name of a therapist who could.

Many mothers become depressed with babies and young children because of social isolation. It can help if you join or get in touch with a group such as Meet-a-Mum Association, your local mother and toddler group or even with other mothers at the baby clinic. *Useful organizations* Association for Postnatal Illness; Meet-a-Mum Association; National Association for Mental Health; Parents Anonymous; The Samaritans.

Dermatitis A broad term used to describe inflammation of the skin due to many causes. Skin affected by dermatitis is red, swollen and itchy. There may also be blisters. Scratching makes the skin thicken and can introduce infection.

Dermatitis can be caused by irritant chemicals, in which case the treatment is avoidance. It can also be caused by an allergy, when it is called allergic contact dermatitis or contact eczema. It may not occur after one exposure to a substance but repeated exposure may sensitize a child. Once the child is sensitized, inflammation starts a few days after subsequent contact with the chemical. Chemical culprits can often be run to ground using patch testing on the skin. Such eczema in children can be caused by primula plants, certain chemicals in toys, shoes and clothing, and some drugs and creams (notably local anaesthetics and antihistamines). Some foods cause eczema too.

Nappy rash is a dermatitis usually caused by frequent or prolonged contact of the skin with a rough, chafing, wet nappy. Some foods in the child's diet can make the skin more likely to be irritated by contact with bowel motions. *Related topics* Eczema; nappy rash.

Desensitization A form of treatment carried out by a family doctor or specialist for children with asthma and hay fever (types of allergy or sensitivity) aimed at reducing or preventing the symptoms. The child is usually patch tested to find out what he is sensitive to and a vaccine made which is specific to the child's individual sensitivities. The vaccine is given over a period of weeks or months during which the child becomes gradually less reactive to the substances to which he is sensitive. Young children don't much like repeated injections but if the allergic symptoms are really disabling then desensitizing injections are the lesser evil. Desensitization is rarely recommended unless a child's symptoms are very troublesome and can't be controlled in other ways. *Related topic* Allergy.

Development – emotional Normal, healthy emotional development comes naturally to a child brought up in a loving, caring, relatively unrestricted environment. If a baby perceives his mother as being a 'good' person who responds willingly and generously to his needs for food, comfort, reassurance and physical contact, then he'll be on the way to being a loving and giving person himself.

Children learn a lot by example and if the parents are happy with their lot in life and content with each other and with their child, then the child will grow up feeling at ease with his family and his surroundings. On the other hand, lots of negative input to a young child such as occurs if his parents are constantly criticizing other people adversely, or if they row for much of the time, will teach him to be critical and quarrelsome. Because he feels unhappy, he'll grow up thinking that the world is a 'bad' place to be in and that people aren't to be trusted.

There's a lot to be said for bringing children up to expect that others will be loving, pleasant and polite towards them. A positive attitude like this tends to produce an equal response in others and brings out the best in them.

However a child is brought up, he'll still have to live within the framework of his own personality which is built as much on his genetic make-up as on his environment. If your child tends to be naturally nervous, over-excitable, quiet or shy, for example, help him to live with his feelings and not let them get out of hand or bottled up. If he seems aggressive, unhappy, suspicious, unusually quiet and inward looking, or if he cries a lot and loses his temper, there's almost certainly something wrong with his environment. Most often it's something to do with the way in which the most important people in his life – his parents – are behaving, to him or to each other. Of course people outside the family or at play-group could be the cause of the problem. If you can't work out what's wrong, discuss the problem with your health visitor or doctor.

Vast numbers of people in the West don't realize their full potential in life because of emotional problems. Gone are the days when we could assume that because of their natural resilience children would withstand all the emotional knocks that come their way. Obviously, any family will have set-backs, arguments, worries and financial problems from time to time. But it's the way in which the parents cope with these and relate to each other and to their children that's important. It would be quite unrealistic to suggest that a child should never be exposed to negative feelings from his parents. But the child should see that his parents can experience such difficulties, discuss them and then find a way of coping with or overcoming them.

Many children feel guilty when anything bad happens to their family even though they obviously (from an adult's viewpoint) had nothing to do with it. Whatever happens, remember to let your child know that you love him and want the best for him. The emotional security this produces will help him through the rest of his life. *Related topics* Anxiety; behaviour problems; emotional deprivation.

Development – intellectual
Some children are more clever than others in the accepted academic sense but there is no point in worrying about this because there is no evidence that such children enjoy life any more. All we as parents can do is to provide the right environment for our children to be able to develop intellectually to their full potential. A good brain may mean that a child succeeds in areas in which he is not necessarily particularly gifted, simply because he is able to work out how to do things well. Some bright children develop fast as babies, walking and talking earlier than average, for example. But this doesn't of course mean that every child who walks and talks later than average will be slow intellectually. Parents frequently report that their bright children sleep less than their less intellectually able children, both during the day and at night and that this reduced need for sleep continues throughout childhood. Bright children also tend to need a lot of attention in the early years because they are so easily bored. These things can make intellectually bright children a real handful.

Mentally handicapped children usually reach developmental milestones a little later than average, and even sometimes much later. Psychologists and doctors tend to assess such children's abilities by comparing them with what children of 'normal' intelligence would do and then arriving at a mental age. If a mentally handicapped child of twelve has a mental age of three, for instance, that means that he is capable of doing what the average three-year-old could do. A parent's main aim when bringing up a mentally handicapped child should be to fit him for everyday life. If he can look after himself to some extent, there will be more avenues open to him in the future. *Related topics* Developmental testing; intelligence; school – preparation for.

Development – physical
From the day an egg and a sperm fuse to start an embryo, physical growth and development continue until the

person is about twenty-one years old. Birth is really only a developmental milestone along the way.

Most of the truly miraculous physical developments of a child have ended by the time he is born. There's no doubt that knowledge of foetal development will take enormous strides forward in the next decade or so and that this could lead to all kinds of medical advances – and problems.

As children grow in size they also become more able (because of the growth and development of their brains) to do more complex things. In the first year or so a baby makes formidable progress physically. After this the rate of physical development slows considerably.

There are tremendously wide variations in the ages at which children achieve various 'milestones' in their physical development and parents are often very concerned (though usually unnecessarily) in case their child is falling behind others. This is partly because we live in a highly competitive society in the West, and partly because, with fewer children to learn from, they get carried away with textbook 'normals' for these times and forget that they are the parents of an individual and not a textbook statistic. Provided that you are taking your child to the clinic or to your doctor for regular developmental testing there's very little likelihood that anything wrong with his physical development will go unnoticed. After the age of five or so the school medical system takes over this surveillance of your child's physical progress, so from birth until he leaves school he will be well covered. If at any time over these years you have a particular concern, ask your family doctor. *Related topics* Coordination; crawling; developmental testing; grasping; hands, use of; head control; height; 'milestones'; sitting up; walking. (Also see profile entries for ages: three months; six months; one year; two years; three years; four years and five years).

Development – psychosexual The word psychosexual refers to the mental aspects of sexuality. Combined with the physical aspects of genitality it's the way the species survives. A newborn baby can do little more than breathe, cry, suck and excrete, and ideally needs parents who love each other and him and who are capable of caring for themselves and him. A satisfying sexual and emotional relationship between the parents is an important basis for the continuation of the bond between them – at least for most people. Such a relationship protects the bond from disruption by the child who later seeks an exclusive relationship with the opposite sex parent. It also protects the child from exploitation by a dissatisfied parent who may look to the child for some of the satisfactions not available in his adult relationship. The newborn baby over the next two decades or so, develops the capabilities to fulfil these reproductive roles and this process is what psychosexual development is all about.

The forces behind this process are thought to be both instinctual and part of the child's basic genetic make-up. Even before birth hormonal and probably other influences can, some experts consider, affect later psychosexual attitudes and behaviour and may, for example, be a cause of later homosexuality, but by far the most important influences on psychosexual development occur after birth.

Parents unconsciously transmit their attitudes on sexuality to their children, attitudes which in turn are stored in the child's unconscious mind later to affect his sexual and psychosexual behaviour. Our culture is basically anti-sexual and even if parents have reasonable attitudes towards sexuality those of others around their child can still affect him adversely.

Psychosexual development is thought not only to affect attitudes towards sex and sexuality but also to exert an influence on personality development generally as well as on masculinity or femininity. This makes the subject one of considerable personal and social significance.

Although not everyone agrees, psychosexual development up to the age of five probably consists of three stages. The first is the oral stage. It is widely held that a baby obtains intense erotic pleasure from his mouth. If feeding is relaxed and pleasurable (and some experts believe the pleasure is enhanced if there is extensive skin contact between mother and baby), the baby will feel secure and will later regard the world as friendly. If it involves too much frustration, for example by not being fed when he is hungry or if the process is accompanied by tension, or is unsatisfying, the baby may become distrustful and may later be prone to depression or other emotional ailments. In this oral stage a baby begins to love his mother and starts to learn how to please and manipulate her.

Eventually, he begins to test everything he encounters through his mouth and it is at this stage that some parents start to impose control over his orality. But, whatever they do, oral drives persist and later form an important component in adult sexuality, more for some than others, perhaps related to frustrations in this oral stage.

Around the age of one year the primary focus of erotic interest shifts from the mouth to the anus as potty training becomes important. Mothers expect children to control their excretion in order to please them and so to retain their love. Opening his bowels only when required and 'allowed' to do so provides a child with the first 'gift' he has to give, namely his faeces. Also, he learns that he can control his mother by performing or not depending on how he feels emotionally towards her. Over-strict potty training can later lead, it is claimed, to untidyness and rebellion. Many later personality characteristics, for example, sadism, frugality and even certain artistic interests, are attributed to problems with this stage.

A young child discovers erotic pleasure in controlling and relaxing the muscles responsible for urination and defaecation. These pleasures persist, usually in a diminished form, as part of adult sexuality but most mothers eventually oppose their child's natural interest in excretion and his pleasure in the appearance and smell of his faeces. This probably helps the third stage in infantile psychosexual development to assert itself. This is the phallic stage. In this, the penis or clitoris now become the chief focus of erotic pleasure and interest. This is not to say that they were unimportant earlier but simply that they were not predominant. Suckling boys may have an erection and girls may roll their thighs together but at that stage (the oral stage), the mouth was the main source of pleasure. As soon as children can control the activities of their hands they suck their thumbs and may stimulate their genitals. Children of just a few months of age have been observed to masturbate to orgasm but until the phallic stage is reached the genitals are of lesser interest than the mouth or anus.

Such activities produce anxiety in many parents because of their inhibited attitudes and such parents become tense and try to distract the child from his genital stimulation. Under-fives can, in this stage, become involved in showing and looking at the genitals of other children and this can get them into trouble from adults – trouble which frightens them because they can't understand why their parents seem to over-react to such a seemingly harmless pursuit. This stage is, emotionally, one in which love for the opposite sex parent figures importantly and the handling of this relationship has implications not only for later psychosexual capacities but also for the child's self-confidence. Conscience and guilt begin to develop at this stage too and gender identity becomes more firmly established. So-called transitional love objects (comforters) may be important. These take the form of a cuddly toy from which the child will not peacefully be separated. They give a sense of security as well as being the recipients of sexual and aggressive feelings. **Related topics** Comforters; masturbation; Oedipus complex; sex education; sex awareness.

Development – social

It's essential that children are brought up knowing how to get along with people other than their family because they'll have to live, work and play in society for the rest of their lives.

Relationships with members of his family provide a child with models for his future relationships with others. If his parents bring him up in a warm, loving atmosphere, trying to bring out the best in him and if they act in a generous, loving or friendly way to other people, he'll follow their example and – within the limits of his personality – will find it easy to develop relationships.

During the first few months he takes his cue as to how to behave from his mother. If she smilingly introduces a person to him, for instance, he's going to be delighted to meet that person. After about six months, he'll enter a developmental stage in which he begins to be shy of other people (even familiar ones) and may bury his head against his mother or crawl or walk to her as quickly as possible if someone makes overtures to him. Provided he is not repeatedly made to go to someone he would rather not be with, he'll pass through this stage after a few months and will soon become increasingly curious about other people.

Some one- and two-year-old children are happy to be looked after for a few hours by a familiar person whom they like, and it's usual during the toddler years for a child to become increasingly independent and socially confident. Some time between two and a half and four, most children are ready to join in at a play-group and, once they are settled in, will enjoy playing there. It takes a certain amount of maturity for a child to play *with* other children rather than simply alongside them. Although many children know whom they like (and dislike) at four or even three, they don't usually have a best friend until they are of school age, but are happy to play with many children.

Most pre-school children are not particularly bothered about the age of their playmates and get along well even though there may be several years' difference. It's not until school age that most children begin to identify with their peer group and even this is often artificially encouraged by the restricted age range they mix with in their class.

Some children are naturally quiet and shy and prefer to play by themselves. Others are more ebullient and confident, like to play with others, and seem more attractive to others as a result. If your child has emotional problems and is aggressive towards other children, try to sort out what is wrong – it's often something at home.

A child who is frequently criticized and told off at home will not be as self-assured as he should be. If you encourage him to think well of himself and of others, he'll take his place in the world more easily and confidently, relating well to both adults and children. **Related topics** Aggression; shyness.

Development – spiritual It's an historical fact that virtually every culture in the world believes in the existence of spirits, a god or gods, or at least a higher plane of existence. Whatever your beliefs, your child might one day think it rather strange if you'd never mentioned such things to him as a young child. Some peoples in the world have their spiritual beliefs at the very centre of their lives and their children are brought up with all their religion's stories, ideas, rituals, celebrations and ways of praying, meditating and worshipping. Even in our somewhat half-hearted, though basically Christian, society in the UK, the faith of some parents forms part of the fabric of their family life.

Children are ready to accept that there is a god. They ask all sorts of questions about Him just as they do about everything else. Some people feel that it's wrong to instil religion into a child, believing that this is somehow a form of brainwashing and that he should make up his own mind when he's capable and ready. Many who have spent a long time thinking about the subject say that it's best for a child to be exposed to religious beliefs. If later the children find they can't accept them, that's up to them, but at least they'll have had a chance to learn about spiritual matters.

Many faiths put great stress on the value and sanctity of children but they vary greatly as to their attitudes on how meaningful a part children can and should play in religious life.

It is quite possible to be a spiritual person yet not be very religious. Religion is the formalized, man-made way in which we show our spiritual beliefs. However, most cultures lay stress on the communal nature of spiritual life and worship together is an essential part of many spiritual sects and religions. *Related topic* Religion.

Developmental testing Psychologists, audiologists, ophthalmologists, paediatricians and others have over the years worked out many ways of testing a child's physical and mental development. The tests are used to make sure that a child's developmental level is within the expected range for his age for any particular ability. If it is not, then he can be referred for special help if necessary, or the parents can be advised on the situation and what they can do to help the child. Developmental testing as carried out in local authority baby clinics, general practice baby clinics or surgeries, hospitals, day nurseries and special schools can give the doctor and parent an idea of whether a child is able to see and hear properly, and whether he is developing normally in other ways (physically, mentally, emotionally and socially).

The most commonly used tests involve simple observations and examinations and are used in conjuction with information about the child obtained from his parents. Sometimes a game is used to test a child's ability. Any developmental testing session uses materials and methods specially designed for young children and if the child can't do something, then an easier form of test is used. If the child is too tired or not in the right mood to be tested or examined, the session can be rearranged for another time. Intelligence testing is just another sort of developmental testing but is carried out within the NHS by specially trained doctors and psychologists.

Routine medical examinations at baby clinics include developmental testing but standard intelligence tests are only carried out if considered necessary – mainly because they are so time-consuming. Parents are asked to bring their babies and young children to the clinic to be examined and tested at certain ages, which vary slightly from clinic to clinic, but if you ever have cause for concern between clinic appointments, don't hesitate to get a medical opinion. *Related topics* Development – emotional/intellectual/physical/social.

Diabetes mellitus (sugar diabetes) A disease of metabolism in which the pancreas doesn't produce enough of the hormone insulin. This results in a high blood sugar with the loss of excess sugar in the urine. No one knows what causes it but the tendency to get it can be inherited.

Diabetes isn't common in childhood and the type that does occur is different from that which affects the majority of adult diabetics. Only one in ten of the diabetics in this country are children.

If your child becomes thinner (loses weight rapidly), drinks more than before and passes a lot of urine, diabetes must be suspected. Rarely, the first sign of diabetes is a coma caused by a very high blood sugar level. This needs urgent medical attention, so call an ambulance.

The diagnosis of diabetes is made by blood and urine tests and, once confirmed, the child is started on insulin by injection. It has to be given by injection because as a protein it would be digested in the intestine if taken orally. Most parents soon become expert at injecting their under-fives and older children inject themselves quite happily. Today the outlook for such children is excellent and there are improvements around the corner in insulin therapy that could revolutionize the life of the diabetic child. Insulin doesn't cure diabetes but it does replace the missing hormone and so prevents the symptoms occurring. Many parents are taught to monitor their child's blood sugar and urine sugar levels and alter the insulin regime accordingly.

Diabetic children should carry a few sugar lumps around with them just in case they develop a low blood sugar (a 'hypo') suddenly. If a child is conscious but feels faint he can be given a spoonful of jam or a sugar lump. Never give anything by mouth to an unconscious child but call an ambulance at once. *Related topic* Hormones. *Useful organization* British Diabetic Association.

Diarrhoea   The frequent passage of loose or watery bowel motions. There are many causes of diarrhoea in children. Breast-fed babies' stools are normally unformed and bright yellow in colour. Every nappy may be stained yellow and this is normal. Many young children have soft stools containing pieces of undigested food and this is quite natural and harmless. Intolerance to lactose (milk sugar), commoner in some black races, also causes diarrhoea. A tummy upset caused by a viral or bacterial infection (gastroenteritis) is another cause.

Children sensitive to cows' milk protein get diarrhoea from milk and this is cured by removing it from their diet.

A common cause of diarrhoea today is an antibiotic given for an infection somewhere else in the body. Sometimes the infection itself causes diarrhoea (middle ear infections, for example). Until recently it wasn't known what organism caused infective diarrhoea in young children but a virus called the rotavirus has now been isolated. Bottle-fed babies are much more susceptible to diarrhoea caused by infections than are breast-fed babies because they receive no immunity from their mother's milk.

Food poisoning is an increasingly common cause of diarrhoea in people of all ages and children are no exception. This condition is caused by the swallowing of toxins produced by certain bacteria or by swallowing the bacteria themselves. There is usually vomiting too and sometimes a fever.

Diarrhoea can be dangerous for young children if it goes on for more than a day or so because the loss of so much fluid in the watery motions can easily cause dehydration. If you are at all worried, ask your doctor for advice. Help may be needed sooner for small babies who become dangerously dehydrated more quickly than for older children. The bottle-fed baby will need extra drinks of *water* and your doctor may suggest a specially made glucose-salt solution instead of milk, which may not be tolerated well by a child with diarrhoea. The chances of dehydration are increased if feeds are made up too strong – only add to the measured amount of water in the bottle the number of scoops of powder recommended on the can of milk powder. Once the diarrhoea has stopped you can re-introduce milk and solids if the child was previously on them. Breast-fed babies with serious diarrhoea should be fed more frequently and possibly given water too by bottle or by spoon.

A child with persistent large stools that are also loose may be suffering from a disease such as cystic fibrosis or coeliac disease, so do get help if your child's diarrhoea is persistent.

Strangely enough diarrhoea can sometimes be a sign of constipation as the fluid bowel motions ooze around the craggy masses of hard motions in the rectum, sometimes producing soiling.

Some children start to pass unformed stools or liquid motions as certain new foods are introduced into their diet or when they have had a lot of one particular food. Often the cause is obvious but if it isn't, discuss it with your doctor. *Related topic* Dehydration.

Dietary fibre A valuable fraction of food formerly known as roughage. It is composed of the cell walls of plants and cereals and acts in the intestine to absorb water and make the motions soft, bulky and easy to pass.

Foods containing dietary fibre include all cereal products (if they contain all the grain), fruits and vegetables. The fibre in cereals is known to be the most valuable. Most modern foods are highly refined and have had all their fibre removed. This not only makes them less pleasant to eat but also means that very large numbers of calories can be too easily consumed because fibre-free foods are not as filling as those with their fibre intact. If you give your family wholemeal bread, use only wholemeal flour in your cooking, eat bran-containing or whole-of-the-grain breakfast cereals and plenty of fresh fruit and vegetables, your family will be healthier and you'll never suffer from constipation. For children up to about a year it makes sense to peel fruit, not because the roughage in the skin does any harm to their bowel but because they can choke on it.

Many claims are being made for the disease-preventing properties of foods rich in fibre but only time will tell how many of these claims will be proven to be realistic. *Related topic* Constipation.

Dieting This is rarely necessary for the under-fives and if it is done, should be supervised carefully by a doctor. Dietary control in a fat child should produce a slowing of weight gain as the child grows rather than an actual weight loss.

There is no place in a book like this to discuss dieting for a mother, but it is worth mentioning dieting during pregnancy which could be harmful, especially if taken to extremes. There is no doubt that a certain amount of fat is usually laid down during pregnancy to act as a food store for breast-feeding. If you are breast-feeding you'll probably notice that your figure gets back to normal quicker than your non-breast-feeding friends because you are using up your fat stores to make milk. It is wise not to slim drastically while breast-feeding as the amount of milk you produce may diminish. *Related topics* Fat; obesity.

Diphtheria An uncommon but serious disease caused by bacteria spread by droplet infection from person to person. All babies are now offered immunization against diphtheria. This means that the disease has virtually disappeared from the community. Diphtheria immunization is almost always combined with the immunizations against whooping cough and tetanus as a 'triple' vaccine first given at about three months of age. For a mother who decides not to have her child immunized against whooping cough there is a special vaccine which is active against the other two diseases.

Dirt eating This is a quite normal pursuit for many babies and toddlers who put dirt into their mouths out of curiosity and even sometimes actually eat it. Earth, sand, plants, flaky paint, grass and coal are all possible culprits, but it is usually simply a part of exploring their surroundings and doesn't amount to an obsession or compulsion. Some neurotic or mentally retarded children, however, eat unsuitable things repeatedly.

The average dirt-eating child isn't likely to suffer from this practice provided he's not eating lead-containing paint which can cause lead poisoning if prolonged. This is really only a danger in old houses and other buildings as lead has been kept out of paints for some years now.

Some children eat hair from their own or their doll's head or from their blankets and this usually passes through the bowel easily. If any child eats odd things repeatedly it's worth seeking advice because it can be a sign of an underlying neurosis or simply of severe boredom or unhappiness. **Related topics** Behaviour problems; hair eating.

Dirtiness Most of us like to see our children clean and tidy but small children often want to do things that make them dirty. They love to dig in earth and sand and to splash paint and glue all over themselves. All of this is fun and is a harmless way of enriching their lives. Although it's tough on parents to allow children to make a mess of themselves all the time there should be times when they can do so, either protected so that their clothes aren't soiled or ruined, or naked in the summer to make cleaning up easier. An old adult-sized tee-shirt makes a good coverall for toddlers while painting, glueing and so on. Making a mess is an enjoyable pastime for adults too. Join in with your children sometimes and they'll be delighted. **Related topic** Play; sandpit.

Disability – physical There are so many physical disabilities that it's difficult to generalize about them. Whatever your child's physical disability though, local social services departments, health visitors, occupational therapists and self-help groups can all be useful in different ways. There will almost certainly be a self-help group that will be helpful. They will give invaluable practical advice on living with a disabled child and will be able to put you in touch with others who have the same problems so that you don't feel alone with your child's difficulties. The addresses are to be found from pages 759–91.

If you have a physically handicapped child in need of a great deal of attention and supervision you may be able to get an Attendance Allowance. Your social worker will help you get all the state aid you are entitled to. Don't forget that as your child's condition changes for better or worse, you'll need to re-appraise his needs. Again, the self-help groups are a great asset with this. *Related topic* Attendance Allowance; physical handicap. *Useful organizations* The British Rheumatism and Arthritis Association; Centre on Environment for the Handicapped; The Disabled Living Foundation; Invalid Children's Aid Association; The Spastics Society.

Discipline A rather difficult word to define coming from the Latin *disciplina* – teaching. It's a word that means different things to different people. Some of the commonly accepted definitions are: 'systematic training in obedience to regulations and authority'; 'punishment'; 'a system of rules for behaviour, methods of practice, etc.' and, lastly, 'training or conditions imposed for the improvement of physical powers, self-control, etc.' Most parents see discipline as a mixture of most of these,

Many schoolchildren today seem to have had little discipline in their lives and meet it at school too late. One well known animal trainer says that children should be trained like dogs, with clear instructions, firmness, constant repetition and praise when they do something right. Lots of dog owners go to training classes in dog management. How many parents though bother to get their approach to their children's training for life sorted out?

To some extent what is meant by discipline varies according to the personalities, attitudes and expectations of parents, the way they themselves were brought up, and the personalities and behaviour of the children. There is by no means always a *right* way of behaving in any particular situation but most parents tend to adopt one particular form of discipline.

A useful way of thinking of discipline is as loving guidance. You as the parent are your child's guide through the early years and often beyond and because you love him, you will want to guide him gently, carefully and lovingly, supporting him when he fails instead of blaming him and getting cross. Perhaps the easiest way to explain this sort of discipline, which is based on the principle of 'do as you would be done by', is to give some examples of how differently any one situation can be handled. Suppose your three-year-old child is sitting down at the tea table and though he has been told not to touch the teapot, he reaches across the table for it and knocks it over. One parent would smack him hard and send him up to his room. The next time there was a teapot on the table, he might be warned sternly not to touch it and threatened with another smack if he does. Another parent would handle the situation differently. After checking he wasn't scalded, he would use the incident as a teaching exercise, explaining gently that if he had done what he was told, he wouldn't have messed up the table and run the risk of being scalded. Later, he might play a game with

him, using a doll or two and a tea set. He would have the job of managing
the teapot and telling his child (the doll) why he mustn't touch it. Almost
certainly the child would enjoy the game, learn the lesson well (there's
nothing like teaching someone else – the doll – to learn it yourself), and
would harbour no ill feelings.

The first parent's reaction might sound a reasonable one, after all, the
child had been told not to touch. However, young children are essentially
curious and need to be told things lots of times before they remember what
to do. They also like to copy their parents and this child was probably trying
to copy an adult in pouring out the tea rather than being naughty for the
sake of it.

If it's essential that your child obeys you, such as when crossing the road,
you must have a fail-safe net for when he forgets what he's supposed to do.
Young children can't be trusted to do what they're told, not because they
are naughty but because they don't understand the consequences of their
actions. A good and loving parent constantly points out pitfalls.

A feature of this sort of discipline based on loving guidance is that
children are only ever asked to do what they're capable of doing. It's no
good expecting a baby to wait five minutes for a feed when he's yelling his
head off, and getting cross with him because he's hurrying you. That's
unreasonable. Similarly, a tired four-year-old will almost certainly not
want to put his toys away at the end of the day when he's asked to. A more
sensible request would have been for him to help you put them away an
hour earlier. He would then enjoy doing something with you, especially if
you made a game of crawling round the floor picking up bricks or whatever,
and he wouldn't feel naughty for having disobeyed you. In fact, he would
end his day feeling good because you would have thanked him for helping
rather than telling him off.

If children are to behave well, they need to be praised for good behaviour
so they realize what your standards are. Children who are constantly told
off for not doing things in the right way or for behaving badly, and who are
never encouraged or told that they're doing something right, end up feeling
lousy failures and expecting that they'll never please anyone. On the other
hand, children who are regularly hugged or encouraged in other ways for
doing what they're told or for behaving well spontaneously will have every
reason for continuing to behave in such a way.

Children like to know that there are certain limits to behaviour laid down
in the family. No child wants to be able to behave badly unchecked. Being
constantly naughty isn't much fun in the long term because it makes the
child feel bad. What happens in some homes is that no limits of behaviour
are set and the child doesn't know where to stop because his parents
haven't told him what their expectations of him are. Try to be consistent in
the limits you set, explain them if necessary, and then help your child to
stick to them.

Try not to think of discipline as a battle *against* your child, taming him
and breaking his spirit. Think of it instead as a mountain pathway. You as

guide are walking along with him. It's not his fault that the world is filled with dangers and rules he didn't make and can't understand or cope with. To be a safe mountaineer, your pupil will have to learn to obey rules about being on mountains. However, if he should put a foot wrong, you'll instinctively save him and then show him where he went wrong so he can learn from his mistake. The parent who bases his discipline on punishment may indeed be teaching his child a lesson, but it won't be in a loving way. Put yourself in his place and ask yourself how you would like another adult to behave to you in the same situation. Ten to one, you'll opt for loving guidance rather than stern punishment.

One of the ultimate aims of disciplining a child must be to teach him self-discipline. As he learns this, so he'll become more independent and able to cope with himself and by himself. A child whose parents have never really bothered to help him understand what discipline is will find it difficult, if not impossible, to run his own life effectively or to follow society's rules as he grows up. *Related topics* Guilt in children; guilt in parents; permissiveness; provocative behaviour; punishment; rules; threats.

Dislocations A dislocation is a serious sprain that not only tears the supporting ligaments of a joint but actually displaces the bone-ends. The commonest joints to be dislocated are the fingers, the jaw, the shoulder and the elbow. The joint usually looks fairly obviously deformed but x-rays may be necessary to be sure of the diagnosis.

If your child has dislocated a joint it'll look deformed and he'll be reluctant to move it. Treat it as you would a fracture. Never try to replace the joint yourself or you may damage nerves or blood vessels that sometimes get trapped in the dislocation. Get medical help.

Most dislocations in children go back very easily, often without the need for an anaesthetic, but it is a skilled job. *Related topic* Fractures.

District (community) midwife A midwife employed by the local health authority to look after women who have their babies at home and those who have returned home from hospital. They have a statutory duty to visit every day during the first ten days after the birth if the mother is at home and can continue to visit or be called on at any time up to twenty-eight days after the birth. Normally, the health visitor takes over from the midwife at about ten days and sometimes these two professionals work together in parallel.

District (community) nurse A nurse employed by the local health authority to work in the community. She deals with patients of all ages and can be called in by your family doctor if your child needs to be nursed yet doesn't need to be in hospital.

Divorce Unfortunately, approximately one in four marriages ends in divorce so a lot of children are going to be affected by it and some will end up living with an adult who is not their natural parent but a step-parent. It's difficult to explain the breakdown of a marriage to a young child and he'll find it hard to understand why the two adults in his life won't live together any more. The idea that love can end will be alien to him and frighten him because, he may think unconsciously, if his parents can stop loving each other it's just as likely that they might stop loving him.

However bad family life was when you were married and however smoothly your divorce went, the first year or so afterwards will be very hard on your child. He'll mourn the loss of the parent who has gone and may show a variety of behaviour disorders including depression, tantrums and periods of confusion and inattention.

Though you won't be able to give an under-five any really convincing reasons for the break-up, it's worth trying with a child old enough to listen because he's so self-centred at this age that otherwise he'll probably imagine that it was something to do with him. Guilt feelings may then make it difficult for him to adjust to his new life and relationships. If you try to keep open hostility between the adults down to a minimum in front of the children it'll be less destructive to them.

If the mother has custody of the child (as is so often the case) it makes sense from the child's point of view to encourage regular visits to or from the father. It is all too easy for the child to have unrealistic views and fantasies about the absent parent, either idealizing or putting him down in his mind, and anyway a child needs adults of both sexes to relate to and love (and who love him) so as to develop normally emotionally. When you're single your children will miss the presence of the other parent but there are ways around this (see one-parent families, page 438).

Despite the many disadvantages to children of one-parent families they may be better off than in a home with two deeply distressed parents who may be constantly bickering. However, the most important thing for a couple whose relationship is faltering must be to renew their feelings for each other somehow. Marriage guidance counselling, discussions with good friends or respected acquaintances, and plenty of time to talk through grievances constructively are all worth pursuing. If divorce is decided upon, what can the parents do to ensure that the children suffer as little as possible?

The prime objective must be to let them know that although you don't want to live with each other any more you still love *them*. Show by your lack of open hostility that you are still responsible human beings even though you can't go on living together, and never use the children as weapons of war. It's easy to do this because only an insensitive fool wouldn't be hurt by such behaviour and this makes it a powerful weapon against your partner. Agree about access and stick to it. Some parents are trying longer periods of continuous child care rather than the often-used arrangement whereby the mother has the child all week and the father at weekends. One or two weeks with each parent can work well but inevitably disrupts the child.

The remaining parent after a divorce can all too easily become overworked, overtired, lonely and thoroughly stressed. Depression is not at all uncommon and needs to be taken seriously if the children are not to suffer. It's important in these circumstances to get all the help you can and to call on the 'absent' parent to take some sort of responsibility for the children. Don't wait until you're at rock bottom before doing anything but see your doctor and get help quickly.

By and large it's fair to say that the younger a baby is when his parents divorce the less he'll be affected by it. A baby under a year will miss his father when his parents divorce but because he's so mother-centred he won't feel the loss very acutely. A child of four or five, however, will sorely miss his opposite sex parent because children at this stage are identifying strongly with the parent of the opposite sex. It would be foolish to assume that the under-fives are too young to be harmed by a divorce. Research has shown that the loss of a parent (for whatever reason) during these crucial years predisposes to an increased likelihood of emotional problems later in life, especially depression. *Related topic* Remarriage; separation of parents. *Useful organizations* Gingerbread; The National Marriage Guidance Council; One Parent Families.

Dog bites These are much more common than people imagine and a recent study has found that some of the most popular pet dogs are the worst when it comes to biting people. Teach your children to respect dogs and not to tease or torment them. If you let a young child treat a dog as if it were a toy the dog may not put up with it for long. One day he may snap and bite the child.

Although a dog bite can lead to tetanus the vast majority of children under five have excellent immunity to the disease because of their routine immunizations. The other great fear is that the dog may have rabies but the UK is still free of this disease, thanks to stringent quarantine regulations at ports and airports.

Treat small dog bites as if they were small cuts but if you are at all worried, go to the local casualty department. Serious bites with torn flesh or serious bleeding will, of course, need cleaning by a doctor and possibly even stitching. What you do with your dog after such an incident will be up to you. Discuss the matter with your vet. *Related topic* Rabies.

Dolls Children in every society, both in the past and today, have played with dolls. Boys and girls use them in their make-believe play and they're as popular now as they ever were.

If you watch children playing with dolls, you'll notice that the games they play are reflections of their own experiences. Often the acted out events help them accept or understand things that have happened to them. A child who's been in hospital, for instance, will endlessly play hospitals with dolls as patients. The child who has just started at a play-group will pretend to be the play-group leader. Interestingly, in the role play the child often takes the part of the adult and the doll is given the role of the child. A new doll sometimes helps a child who has just had a new baby brother or sister to come to terms with it. He or she can look after the doll just as her mother is looking after the baby, whilst realizing that the doll is second best to the baby.

A good supply of dolls' clothes, a doll's bed, a pram, and all the many accessories that some commercially made dolls can have will be greatly enjoyed. Many such toys can be home-made by a keen DIY parent and are very much cheaper than shop bought equivalents. However, with strong brand images today many children really want what they see on TV or at their friends', so home-made (once a sign of being 'special') need not necessarily mean 'most desirable' from the child's point of view. Lots of day-to-day toys can be made for dolls though and older pre-school children will get a lot of fun out of helping make them. A cardboard box lined with soft material makes a good bed for a doll, for example. If you have enough room at home or in your garden, your own buggy can do its duty as a doll's buggy when it's not being used for a child.

Your child will enjoy helping you to make a doll from cut-out material stuffed with foam chips or old tights. Bits and pieces of wool make realistic hair, and the face can be painted on with felt-tip pens. Cardboard dolls are fun to make as well, and can be dressed in paper clothes. Try folding a piece of paper into quarters, then with the folded corner at the top right, draw half of the front of a dress, with the centre front on the fold and the collar at the folded corner. Cut it out, leaving part of the top fold for the shoulder of the dress, open it out, put a slit down the centre back, and you can dress the cardboard doll by inserting its head in the slit and twisting.

Many children have a favourite doll which they take everywhere but inevitably you'll find that they'll be given lots of dolls they're not very keen on. If a doll isn't ever played with, how about discussing giving it away to a charity at Christmas or to a less fortunate family you know. You'll find that your child will love this and it's a good way of encouraging your children to be generous. *Related topic* Drama; play.

Domestic help Few families these days can afford paid domestic help, however much they might like to. People are also less willing to work in other people's houses nowadays, perhaps partly because they feel it is demeaning, especially as the work to be done is usually the hardest or dirtiest, and partly because there are other, more attractive ways of earning money. Home helps can be supplied by the social services department of your local authority in some situations, for example, if you have just had a baby and have no one at home with you.

If you can't manage your housework, there are several points worth thinking about. First, are you aiming at an unnecessarily high standard? Dusting and vacuuming doesn't have to be done every day. The only essentials are keeping the kitchen and bathroom clean. Second, have you turned down any offers of help from family or friends? It's all too easy to turn your nose up at offers of help, thinking you can do everything, only to find that you can't cope with the house and the children after all. Third, why not try what some women have found successful. Ask a friend in to help you perhaps once a week and do the work together, breaking off to look after your children when they need you. Do the same thing for her and you may find that sharing the work makes it more enjoyable.

If you decide to pay someone to help you, first ask round to find out whether anyone you know already has a help who is looking for more work. At this stage, you'll find out what the going rate is and how much it's all going to cost you. Don't forget that some domestic helps will want bus fares or travelling expenses too so this will add to your bill. Failing this, put an advertisement in a shop window or in your local paper, or ask the local job centre to send you applicants. References are helpful and you must interview the person beforehand. Tell your help exactly what it is you'd like her to do before she starts so there are no misunderstandings later.

Some mothers find that if they have a really good domestic help she can slowly do things other than cleaning and may even occasionally help out with the children. Each situation like this has to be worked out on a one-off basis but it can be a satisfactory and good way of getting occasional child care. You may find that as your domestic help gets to know the family well you'll be happy to ask her to baby-sit for you. Play it by ear and see how it goes.

Down's syndrome (Mongolism) A condition present at birth, affecting about one in six hundred babies in the UK.

Down's children have certain physical characteristics that usually make the condition easy to spot, though the diagnosis may not be easy in the first few days of life. The children have small slanting eyes; there is a fold of skin at the inner corner of each eye; the bridge of the nose is low; the head small and round; the mouth small and straight; the hands have abnormalities of the crease lines; and the little fingers are often curved inwards. They are nearly all mentally handicapped to some degree and a large proportion of children in special schools for the educationally subnormal are Down's children. The level of intelligence varies widely and some can lead near-normal lives as adults in the community.

Down's babies are more likely than other children to have additional congenital abnormalities, to get respiratory infections, to develop cataracts later, and are three times as likely to suffer from leukaemia at some time when compared with normal children. They used to have a short life expectancy but today with good treatment they can and do live to middle-age and beyond.

The basic abnormality in Down's syndrome is that instead of having two number twenty-one chromosomes in each body cell, the child has three. The extra chromosome can be detected antenatally by removing amniotic fluid from the uterus and examining the cells in it. This procedure is called an amniocentesis. As older women are more likely to have a Down's baby, many doctors advise that all pregnant women over thirty-five should have an amniocentesis. This is only worth doing, of course, if the woman will consent to an abortion if the foetus is affected.

Having a Down's baby changes the lives of everyone in the family. Caring for such children can be very time-consuming (depending on the level of handicap) and some families find they cannot cope. Many Down's children have to have some kind of institutional care in later childhood but ideally they should start life at home. More help is given nowadays, though, to enable a family to keep a Down's child at home, perhaps with occasional institutional care to tide the family over bad patches, holidays, times when the mother is in hospital and so on.

A positive attitude towards the situation, looking for all available help and deciding to do everything possible to help the child enjoy his life and achieve his full potential, helps parents come to terms with their child. Some families say that their lives have been positively enriched by having a Down's child. **Related topic** Mental handicap. *Useful organizations* British Institute of Mental Handicap; Down's Children's Association; National Association for Mental Health; National Society for Mentally Handicapped Children and Adults.

Drama Under-fives love make-believe play and will play in imaginary worlds quite unprompted by adults. Organized drama is also appreciated by this age group.

It's easy to make a simple puppet theatre from an old fashioned clothes horse; dressing-up clothes (perhaps bought from jumble sales) provide hours of fun; dolls can act out endless different situations; and four- or five-year-olds can produce their own plays.

When creating plays with children, be guided by their imagination and go along with it – try not to impose your ideas on the drama as it unfolds. We all love make-believe and it doesn't have to be as sophisticated as a James Bond movie to be entertaining. Use television drama and books as a sparking-off point to fire your children's imagination. Most children enjoy acting and especially so if they have an audience, so be prepared to be appreciative.

Acting out stories is a way in which children can learn to accept and come to terms with various events and aspects of human behaviour. Their stories are therefore just as likely to have unhappy endings as are real life ones!

Dreams There are two types of sleep: quiet or deep sleep and the less deep 'rapid eye movement' (REM) sleep. If you watch your baby you'll be able to tell which state he is in. In deep sleep the baby's breathing is regular and his body is still. In REM sleep he is restless, perhaps has flickering changes of facial expression, his eyes move under their lids and his breathing becomes irregular and shallow. This is quite normal and occurs in adults too. It is during this type of sleep that dreaming occurs.

No one knows for sure why we dream or what the functions of dreams are. It has been suggested that while we're dreaming, information is being shifted around our brain from place to place to clear pathways for new inputs the following day. Babies spend a large proportion of their sleeping time (up to seventy per cent) in REM sleep but no one knows why.

As your child grows he'll begin to tell you about his dreams if you are interested. The age at which a child does this varies enormously but by about four when the imagination is especially active he'll be keen to tell you all his dreams, at least all those he can remember. We only remember a tiny fraction of all our dreams.

Try to be interested in your child's dreams and tell him about yours so that he feels it's normal to dream. Sometimes the dream account will get muddled up with what you know to be reality but don't bother to labour the point – just let it all come out. If a child has a recurring dream that troubles him it makes sense to talk about it and if possible to try to find an explanation. There is absolutely no doubt that certain foods such as cheese make people dream more and these can be isolated and removed from the child's diet if they are causing bad dreams.

Most children have occasional nightmares and need to be comforted at night. **Related topic** Nightmares.

Dressing Dressing a baby or a young child isn't always easy but a little thought can help you avoid a lot of trouble. Children hate clothes that are awkward or painful to put on. It's surprising how many manufacturers make jumpers or tee-shirts which have inadequate openings at the neck; boiler suits or stretch suits which mean you virtually have to bend your baby's limbs in half to get them in; and blouses, shirts, cardigans, coats and dresses with buttons so tiny that they are difficult to undo or with holes too big for the buttons, so they keep coming undone. Look carefully at clothes before you buy them and ask yourself whether they are going to be easy to put on and comfortable for your child to wear. Do the same with paper patterns or knitting patterns.

When you're dressing a baby, stop if he cries and put him to the breast or cuddle him until he feels better. If you always carry on dressing him regardless, he'll come to associate being dressed with crying and you could have long-term problems. Try to make the sequence of dressing as easy as possible so that you don't have to keep laying the baby down and sitting him up – new babies in particular aren't very fond of that. When you put a young baby's arms into a sleeve, put your fingers and thumb 'backwards' through the cuff first, roll the sleeve back on to your hand, then take hold of the baby's hand and pull it gently through the cuff. This way you can protect his fingers and thumb from getting caught up.

You don't have to change a baby into night clothes. One set of clothes, changed when wet or dirty during the day or night, will do until he starts having a mixed diet, crawling or bottom shuffling, when you'll almost certainly prefer to change him. When going out, always allow yourself more time than you think you'll need to get the baby ready. This goes for toddlers and pre-schoolers too.

When you have a baby or young child in nappies, choose clothes that make nappy changing as little of a hassle as possible. If you have to undress the child's top half as well as his bottom half, you're making more work than necessary. If you're away from your familiar nappy changing place at home in particular, you'll want the baby's clothing to be as easy as possible to undo.

If you're going out later in the day or expecting visitors and you want your child looking smart, don't expect him to keep his clothes clean until then. Bank on changing him beforehand and think yourself lucky if you don't have to.

As children pass their second or third birthday many begin to have very definite ideas as to what they want to wear. It's not a bad idea to let your child choose what he's going to wear: it'll help him learn to make decisions and what's more, he'll enjoy it. However, it's sensible to put away any clothes that are unsuitable for the time of year, special clothes that you'd like to keep for best, clothes that are too small or too big, and clothes that need mending, otherwise you'll have trouble when he wants to wear them. Make the time to help him choose and accept the fact that the choosing is the most enjoyable part of dressing and may take a long time. Discuss colours with him and which clothes would be suitable for what he's going to do that day, then help him put them on. Many's the young child who gets everything on then changes his mind and wants to take it all off and start again. If you have the time, treat this as a game and go along with it. If you're trying to get an older child to school, you'll have to explain firmly that though you would like to take your time, you can't because it'll make his brother or sister late. Some mothers choose clothes for the next day the night before with their child.

It takes a long time for a child to learn how to get dressed. Some three-year-olds attempt it while other children still want their mothers to dress them at four or five. If you're trying to encourage your child to dress himself, put all the clothes he needs out on his bed so he can see at a glance what he needs to put on. Buttons and laces are difficult to do even for many five-year-olds. Try to teach your pre-schooler how to do them but if he can't or doesn't want to, don't worry. He'll learn soon enough when he sees others doing them at school. Slip-on shoes with elastic to keep them on, and shoes with buckles are both easier than lace-ups. *Related topic* Clothing; footwear.

Dressing-up

Dressing-up One of many children's favourite pastimes from the age of two or three onwards. If you have room, get a large cardboard box from a supermarket or grocer's shop, or some other suitable container such as a chest, a cupboard or a large basket, and keep the clothes in there so they are easily accessible. Some play-groups keep the dressing-up clothes on coat hangers hanging on a low clothes rack and this is even better as the children can see what there is and the clothes don't get scruffy so quickly. Dressing-up clothes need occasional washing and renovation if the children are to enjoy playing with them. In the haste of play, fastenings and seams easily get broken.

Make a collection of dressing-up clothes by adding some of your discarded clothes to ones chosen from jumble sales. Ask your friends and family for contributions. Children like anything unusual, glamorous or funny and also enjoy having lots of accessories. Gold high-heeled evening sandals, old feather boas, sequinned or lamé evening dresses, velvet jackets, hats, belts and scarves are just a few of the things you might acquire. If clothes are too long, show your child how to pull them up over a belt or shorten them with deep hems if necessary. The needlework doesn't have to be exquisite! ***Related topics*** Drama; play.

Drinking We all have to drink in order to keep our body fluid level up to normal: more than two-thirds of the body is composed of water.

The breast-fed baby normally needs nothing other than breast milk to drink for the whole time he is being totally breast-fed. If the weather is exceptionally hot or if he gets a fever, give more breast feeds and remember to drink more yourself.

Bottle-fed babies can be given boiled water or diluted fruit juice if they get thirsty between feeds. There is no need to boil the water you give to your baby whether he's breast or bottle-fed once you have started him on solids.

As milk gradually ceases to be the sole source of fluid, give your baby drinks of water or fruit juice (diluted with water to make it cheaper) as well as breast milk or cows' milk formula.

It's not essential for children past babyhood to drink milk – all its nutrients are present in other foods or drinks and vast numbers of people in the world are quite healthy without it. If your child likes it though, let him have some milk every day but remember that because milk is high in calories he may fill himself up on it if allowed to drink it freely, and so may not have any appetite for his meals.

Most commercially made drinks contain added sugar, colourings, flavourings or other additives and a child simply doesn't need them. Water is just as delicious to a thirsty child and isn't fattening, addictive or harmful in any way. By all means have vitamin C drinks, fizzy pop and milk shakes at parties or on special occasions but not as a routine.

Remember when you go abroad on a sunny holiday or go to live in a hot climate that your children will need more fluid than at home in Britain. If you notice that their urine is very concentrated (dark yellowish-orange) make sure they have more to drink.

If your child has three meals a day, offer him a drink at each mealtime and between meals as well. If he asks for a drink at other times, always let him have one.

It's best for an under-five to drink sitting down properly to avoid spills and choking. Children vary as to the age at which they learn the skill of drinking from a cup, or cup with a lid and a spout (or holes), or from a straw. If you go out, take your child's cup with you if he can only drink easily from a spout, for example. A small cup held with two hands is easier for a young child to hold than a cup held by the handle, which is usually tipped too far and the drink spilt. *Related topics* Dehydration; feeding equipment; thirst.

Drowning

Drowning If a child falls into water or gets into trouble while swimming and inhales water into his lungs, the first priority is to get him out of the water at once. Don't worry about emptying water out of his lungs and don't wait until actually getting to dry land. As soon as your feet are on the bottom or you can hold on to a boat you can start mouth-to-mouth resuscitation (page 34). A drowned child can be revived after a lot longer a period of absent breathing than is the case when breathing stops for other reasons.

Once breathing has restarted get him to hospital at once for observation. It's probably best to ask someone else to get an ambulance or medical help at once while you get on with mouth-to-mouth resuscitation. The professionals can then take over when they arrive.

Drowning can be prevented on many occasions by ensuring that all children, even those that can swim, wear life jackets whenever they are near or on water.

Swimming with the under-fives must always be supervised by a responsible adult swimmer. *Related topics* Artificial respiration; heart massage. *Useful organizations* The Royal Society for the Prevention of Accidents.

Dummies

Dummies A dummy is a specially shaped object designed for a baby to suck. It has a handle on it for the mother to hold when she gives it to her baby or for the baby to hold himself if he is old enough. The most popular type of dummy has a rubber teat which is prevented from being swallowed by a plastic flange between the teat and the handle. Dummies are nowadays usually made of plastic and are non-toxic, washable and sterilizable.

A dummy is used to keep a baby quiet and happy and to encourage him to go to sleep. Babies breast-fed on an unrestricted basis never need a dummy. The reason some mothers find dummies necessary is because they choose not to let their babies suck at their breast for comfort, enjoyment and to help them go to sleep. There is no absolute right or wrong in this, but increasing numbers of mothers are finding that they are quite happy to put their babies to the breast whenever they want.

Some women choose to give their babies absolute priority while others use a dummy from time to time if they want to give attention to other children or finish a job for instance. Sometimes it is quite impossible to comfort a crying baby at the breast – when walking, or driving, for example. A dummy can then bring peace to an otherwise fraught situation. However, even young babies become accustomed to the idea that when they are in their pram or the car, their mother isn't available as usual. By starting off with a dummy in such circumstances your baby probably won't want to give it up for a long time.

The more sucking a breast-feeding baby does (whether it is 'nutritive' – when the baby is actually getting milk as a result – or 'non-nutritive'), the more milk the mother will make, so sucking for comfort, enjoyment or to go to sleep is not only pleasant but essential for any baby who isn't yet gaining enough weight. A woman whose baby isn't happy or isn't gaining weight should never use a dummy if she is breast-feeding but should put the baby to the breast whenever he or she (the mother) wants.

Mothers who give their babies dummies instead of the breast miss out on the special feeling they could get by knowing that they can satisfy all their baby's needs themselves. For the baby, sucking at the breast in his mother's arms must be quite a different emotional and physical experience from sucking a hard, plastic-smelling, unresponsive dummy while lying in a pram or cot. The dummy is a poor substitute for the breast, though it's one that a baby will get used to.

If you are unhappy that your breast-fed baby is getting too fat because he is sucking at the breast so much and you have a lot of milk and if you're sure he's not wanting to suck in a desperate attempt to be allowed to stay with you, then a dummy might be useful to satisfy your baby's sucking needs. First try carrying him around with you for much of the time, as you may find that his need to suck so much diminishes because he gets all the physical contact he needs just by being next to you.

If you give your baby a dummy, make sure it's clean and regularly washed. Some mothers like to sterilize them in solution every so often and they have an extra dummy while one's being sterilized. It's not a good idea for a young baby (particularly a bottle-fed one who has less protection against infection than a breast-fed baby) to suck a dummy that's been on the floor or pavement. At least wash such a dirty dummy. Older babies take a great delight in throwing their dummies on to the floor. Try tying the dummy on to the pram or cot side or on to a button on the baby's clothes. Take care though that the ribbon can't harm the baby – ribbons have been know to get twisted round a baby's neck or to be partly swallowed.

Babies who have a dummy regularly become very attached to it and hate to be without it. Keep an identical one somewhere safe to avoid trouble if the first one is lost, and remember always to take the dummy with you on outings.

If a baby likes to go to sleep sucking a dummy, he may be upset when he wakes at night to find it's fallen out of his mouth. Try leaving several dummies in an older baby's cot so that he has a good chance of finding one, or secure it safely to his clothing so that it can't get lost. If you take the dummy out of his mouth when he's nearly asleep, he won't become dependent on it in order to sleep.

Some dummies have built-in containers for a drink and are known as comforters. One great hazard with them is that they can be filled with a sweetened fluid such as a blackcurrant drink, sweetened orange juice, orange squash or sugar syrup to make the child more willing to suck them and thus to keep him quiet for longer. The first teeth can decay as soon as they've come through because of this slow trickle of sugar solution and the same can happen if you dip a dummy's teat into honey or syrup to encourage the baby to suck. The first teeth are very important and are well worth looking after. There is no evidence however that dummies cause crooked teeth.

Some people suggest that babies automatically give up the dummy at about three or four months but it seems likely that this is because they are encouraged to do so, and babies who aren't still being breast-fed will be likely to start sucking their fingers or thumb instead. *Related topics* Breast-feeding; comforters; milk teeth; sucking; thumb and finger sucking.

Dying child Coping with a dying child, especially if it's your own, is never easy but it is sometimes made worse for a child who knows that something must be very wrong by parents who, quite innocently, keep up a brave face and try not to talk about it. Even doctors and nurses keep up the façade in hospital, sometimes changing beds around in the ward hoping that the other children won't notice when one is empty. Of course they do and it's hard to imagine what they think about the adults' performance. Many very young children don't understand the concept of death yet still understand very well that they're causing their parents distress and will be worried about protecting them.

A young child who doesn't know he is dying is probably best left uninformed especially when there is a chance he'll get better. There's no point worrying him with talk of death when he can have little idea of what it means. But if death is certain and your child is obviously uneasy, there can be a positive value in sharing his fears and concerns. Parents (and children) who have a deeply held religious faith often cope far better when this happens and a child who knows about heaven will often be quite happy to accept that he'll see his family and friends there one day when they die. If possible, try to talk to the hospital staff so that they know what your child's views are. The last thing you'll want is to have conflicting messages for the child to cope with at such a time.

Both parents and children generally have an over-dramatized view of actually dying, believing it will be frightening and painful. This comes about as a result of watching death in films. Most people (and children are no exception) die quietly, peacefully and without pain and knowing this and saying it if necessary to the child will put his mind at rest.

Few things can be worse for a parent than when a child dies. Unexpected death such as after an accident is shattering because there has been no time for the parents to prepare themselves emotionally. When a child has a long terminal illness, at least the loss is expected and to some extent the mourning is begun even before the child has died.

In your grief don't forget to help the brothers and sisters of the dying child with all the feelings they inevitably have. Some will feel guilty because if they have wished that their sibling hadn't ever been born, they may think that they have in some magical way caused the death. Others feel extremely sad and may even become depressed. *Related topic* Bereavement. *Useful organization* The Compassionate Friends.

Dyslexia A term used to describe specific reading retardation (not just a general slowness in reading) often found in children with other learning problems. Three times as many boys as girls are affected. Some people use the term loosely (and wrongly) for a child who is just slow at reading.

Children with dyslexia can be clever or dull. They can't seem to recognize whole words even if they can write down the individual letters perfectly competently. Sometimes they also write the actual letters wrongly. Bright children are especially at a disadvantage because adults have great expectations of them which they cannot attain. This can produce emotional dilemmas and problems for the child. Such a child often becomes aggressive or withdrawn and it can be these symptoms that take him to the doctor. Unfortunately, unless dyslexia is specifically looked for it can be missed in the effort to find an answer to the more obvious behaviour problems. Also, the picture can be further complicated by the child unconsciously producing physical symptoms such as abdominal pain, asthma, or cyclical vomiting which are just more red herrings.

Many dyslectic children eventually learn to read fairly well but some have spelling problems for the rest of their life. Some schools can arrange for special reading lessons for a dyslectic child. Other children can be helped by specialist teachers at home.

A thorough assessment including a medical examination (to check eyesight among other things) and intelligence tests is necessary before anyone jumps to the conclusion that a child has dyslexia. The diagnosis of dyslexia is rarely made or even considered for children under five. *Related topic* Reading.

Earache The major cause of earache in young children is otitis media but infections of the outer ear canal, glue ear, cold winds, and inflammation of the eardrum (seen in measles and German measles) can also cause it. Sometimes the pain in the ear has nothing to do with the ear at all but is 'referred' from some other affected part to the ear because they share a nerve. Serious dental caries of the lower molar teeth, disorders of the jaw joint (that lies in front of the ear) and a sore throat can all produce earache in healthy ears. Children whose tonsils have been removed often complain of pain in their ears between the third and sixth days after the operation. Swallowing something rough (a crust of bread for example) can irritate the back of the throat and also produce earache.

The best treatment for earache is to hold a covered hot water bottle against the ear and to give the child paracetamol in the correct dose while awaiting medical advice. If ever your child rubs or pulls at his ears repeatedly and doesn't seem well, ask for your doctor's advice. He may prescribe pain-killing drugs to put in the ear. *Related topic* Otitis media.

Ear drops These are usually used for one of two quite different purposes. Oil (often warmed cooking oil but preferably a special wax-softening oil) drops are used to soften hard wax in the ear so that it will either run out on its own or can be syringed out by a doctor. Antibiotic or antifungal drops can be used to cure infections of the skin in the ear canal. The latter drops should only ever be used on the recommendation of a doctor.

If your child has otitis media (inflammation of the middle ear) and an unperforated eardrum, then eardrops are of no curative value. Warm oil run into the affected ear may ease the pain slightly, but paracetamol and warmth over the ear are probably more effective. *Related topics* Otitis externa; otitis media; wax in ears.

Eating habits Babies develop their own individual feeding habits, whether at the breast or at the bottle. Some like to suck as fast as they can and finish their milk very quickly. They tend to wave their arms and legs around as they drink and nothing can distract them. Others take their time, perhaps drifting off to sleep every so often and doing little fluttering sucks as they doze. They like to stay at the breast or with the bottle teat in their mouths for a long time and they don't mind if a feed is interrupted before they've had enough as long as they can go back to it in half an hour or so. Yet others are very easily distracted from sucking. This is most often seen in older, alert babies who are interested in what the rest of the family is doing. They bob up at the slightest noise, completely ignoring the breast in full flow!

Often a breast-fed baby's feeding habits are formed because of the way the milk comes from the breast. Some mothers' milk takes several minutes from the start of a feed before it is let down and a baby can become very frustrated if he finishes the foremilk present in the reservoirs and ducts beneath the areola before the hindmilk from the milk glands themselves is let down. During a feed the milk can be let down several times and you'll notice that the baby's sucking and swallowing pattern and frequency follows the let-down pattern and frequency. In some mothers the milk flows much faster than in others and their babies, particularly if they are young, can sometimes be overwhelmed by the flow, coughing and spluttering and needing to come up for air.

When it comes to mixed feeding, babies again differ in their eating habits. Some soon get the hang of being spoon-fed while others are happier from the beginning if allowed to feed themselves with the spoon or with their fingers. Playing with food is as much fun as eating it, as is a game of 'give and take' with the spoon.

Just like adults, some children prefer many small meals while others are content with the traditional three meals a day. It's easy to fit in several small meals. Breakfast, elevenses, lunch, a three o'clock snack, tea and something before bedtime are the meals many children like to have. From lunch until a 5.30 tea is too long for most young children to go without food. Eating a large proportion of their day's food at one meal is common and there's nothing wrong with this unless you start bullying the child into eating because you happen to have cooked more than he wants at his least favourite mealtime. Drinks should always be drunk sitting down properly to avoid spills. But spouted cups reduce spills anyway.

Some children eat with a spoon for a long time while others – particularly if they are copying older brothers and sisters – attempt to eat with a knife and fork quite young. It doesn't matter what they eat with at first.

Eating with fingers is only considered acceptable for a very few foods in our society. Sooner or later you'll have to teach your child how to behave at the table but again patient example over the years will teach him better than getting cross will.

Some children become attached to their own mug and make a fuss if they don't get it. The easiest way round this is always to put it on the table at his place for him. You can run into problems though if he won't drink from anything else and you forget to take it with you when you go out to eat.

Lots of children have set ideas about how they like their food to be presented to them. Some like each food separately on the plate and others vehemently avoid any 'messes'. Others like anything savoury covered with tomato sauce, or they may like their sauce placed in one particular position such as on the peas but not touching the sausages. Go along with all these likes and dislikes because they probably won't last long – as your child grows his eating habits will change and probably come to resemble those of the rest of the family. *Related topics* Eating out with a baby; table manners.

Eating out with a baby Facilities for eating out with a baby in the UK are by and large very poor. Few restaurants have high chairs, and changing facilities are not usually adequate. In the US and on many parts of the Continent restaurants are very different. Children and babies are not only catered for but are positively welcomed. In Europe, particularly in southern Europe, babies often accompany their parents out in the evenings, to the delight of the other diners. In Britain babies are considered to be all right as long as they stay at home!

Of course, one reason for this is that babies are thought to cry a lot and the management thinks that crying would upset other customers. Unfortunately, this is – or can be – true in our society. However, it needn't be: if babies were accustomed to eating out with their parents; if breast-feeding were not frowned upon in public; if life were made easier for mothers with high chairs and decent changing facilities were installed; and if smoking were outlawed in all but very well-ventilated areas of restaurants, then babies would be much happier in restaurants and would never cry or would easily be consoled when they did.

If you take your baby to a restaurant, try to take him at the time of day when he is not usually fractious. It helps if he has a sleep beforehand. Wear clothes that won't reveal everything when you breast-feed, and choose a seat that is not facing people who aren't sitting at your table. If your baby will have something to eat, remember his bib and take a moistened flannel in a polythene bag to wipe him clean afterwards. If he throws a lot of food on the floor, pick up as much as you can so the waiters don't tread it into the carpet. If your baby does create a rumpus, perhaps because he objects to keeping still for so long, take him outside to avoid disturbing other people. There is more than one chain of family restaurants in the UK now which really do make babies welcome (by supplying high chairs and special toddler seats for example), so things are looking up.

As for the baby's food, breast-feeding is obviously easy as long as you are discreet. If you are bottle-feeding the waiter will warm your baby's bottle if you explain exactly how you want it done. A few restaurants keep jars of baby food but if your baby likes these and you aren't sure whether the restaurant will have them, take your own jar and ask for it to be warmed if necessary. If your baby usually eats whatever you are eating, simply choose something you know he likes for your meal and give him a little of it from a saucer.

With the coming of fast food outlets to the UK it has become a lot easier to eat out with babies and very young children.

Eczema An itchy dermatitis that has an allergic basis and may run in families. There is reddening, itching and swelling of the inflamed skin. Tiny blisters may form and if these are scratched or otherwise broken they weep and then form crusts. After this acute phase the skin becomes dry, scaly and thick as it heals. If the eczema is long-standing or if it frequently recurs, the skin cracks and bleeds.

Eczema can be the first sign of atopy (a group of allergic conditions which run in families, consisting of eczema, asthma and hay fever). About three per cent of children get eczema of this kind early in life. Many children with eczema go on to get asthma later in life, especially if they have a family history of atopic conditions.

Eczema is more common in bottle-fed babies than in those who are breast-fed. Experts recommend that babies with a family history of asthma, eczema or hay fever should be exclusively breast-fed for at least three months and that they should *never receive a single bottle of cow's milk formula* during this time. Research suggests that even one bottle of cows' milk formula can set off the body's immune responses in susceptible children. In children from atopic families, half develop eczema if they are bottle-fed, whereas only eight per cent do if they are totally and solely breast-fed.

Proteins other than cows' milk protein (eggs and wheat especially) can also produce eczema in susceptible children. Some babies have a very quick reaction to the offending food with nettlerash (urticaria), colic and flushing of the skin followed by scratching and the development of eczema, while in others the response is less clear-cut. The link between food allergy and eczema is no longer disputed.

Atopic eczema usually comes on in the first two to three months of life and tends to disappear between the ages of three and five years. It often occurs first on the face and nappy area and spreads to the neck, wrist, hands and fronts of the legs and arms. Eczema in the nappy area may be complicated by a monilial infection.

Treatment isn't very satisfactory. A warm, humid climate seems to suit most children with eczema best. Sweating seems to make matters worse, so never put synthetic clothes next to the skin of your eczematous child. Wool makes itching worse, so cotton underclothes are best. The dryness of the skin can be a troublesome problem and very irritating. Never use soap and detergents but add baby oil to the bath after the child has soaked for some time to seal water into the skin, and possibly use creams and lotions after a bath too. Emulsifying ointments can be used in the bath or directly on the skin.

Scratching is a problem because eczema can be excruciatingly itchy. Try to stop your child's scratching by keeping acute, angry skin lesions covered with moist dressings and ensure that his fingernails are kept short. Your doctor may suggest antihistamines to help control the itching.

The development of steroid creams and ointments has revolutionized the treatment of eczema in recent years but they don't answer all the problems by any means. They are absorbed through the skin and can build up in the body to produce important and harmful effects if an excess of certain types is used. These drugs should only be used exactly as prescribed.

A baby with eczema is in danger of developing a very unpleasant complication if he is vaccinated with smallpox vaccine so neither the child himself nor any member of the family should be vaccinated if a baby in the family has eczema.

Atopic eczema can be a very distressing condition for any child and can disrupt family life for years, often seriously. Sleep is disturbed, the child scratches pathetically, tends to grizzle with discomfort, may be ostracised by his young friends and acquaintances, and can find life scarcely bearable. Such families need a lot of practical help if they are to cope. Self-help groups can be very useful.

A less common type of eczema (contact eczema or allergic contact dermatitis) can occur in the under-fives just as in adults. This is usually triggered by contact with something to which the child is allergic. The condition disappears on avoidance of contact with the substance. Rubber in exposed elastic in the waist and thigh holes of plastic pants may cause this, as may the glue in the sticky tabs of disposable nappies, and disposable nappy liners.

Some children get an eczematous rash round their mouths and on their cheeks because of the dribble that runs out at night. Treat this by putting a barrier cream on the affected skin. *Related topics* Allergy; antihistamines; desensitization; food allergy. *Useful organization* National Eczema Society.

Educational subnormality A term used to describe a child who is intellectually unable to cope with education at an ordinary school. You may know that your baby is bound to fall into this category if he has an easily recognizable form of mental subnormality, but for many children the decision as to what sort of schooling they'll need is a difficult one and is only made after careful, and sometimes repeated, assessment. Schools available for these children are those for the mildly educationally subnormal (ESN(M)) and those for the severely educationally subnormal (ESN(S)). If you think that your child will definitely need special schooling of this kind one day, or if you are concerned that he is slow, get in touch with your family doctor, clinic doctor, or health visitor, who will put you in touch with the hospital or community paediatrician for a thorough assessment of your child, including a physical examination, hearing and vision tests, developmental tests and an intelligence test.

Teachers, doctors and psychologists are only too well aware that it is difficult to assess a young child and if it seems at any time that a wrong decision has been made about schooling, the mistake will be put right as soon as possible. *Related topics* Mental handicap; special schools. *Useful organization* British Institute of Mental Handicap.

Eggs Eggs, like milk, have attained an almost mythical value in many parents' eyes. Certainly they have good food value and can be cooked in a variety of ways to please children but they're not essential in any way. Egg yolk is rich in iron but this can be obtained by eating wholemeal cereals and fruit and vegetables just as easily.

When starting a baby on eggs, introduce them gently because of all foods they are amongst those most likely to produce allergic reactions, especially in children of allergic families. Watch out for eczema or diarrhoea after eggs and if either develops, stop giving eggs in any form (even in cakes and pastries). Since it is almost always the egg white that causes the trouble, you may still be able to give the yolk. *Related topic* Food allergy.

Electric blanket Electric blankets shouldn't be used for any child who is at all likely to wet his bed because this can be dangerous. Once a child is apparently reliably dry then such a blanket is safe to warm the bed but should never be left on when he is in bed just in case he wets it. Low voltage overblankets are safer and can be left on all the time but again, not if your child might wet the bed.

Electric shock Electricity is dangerous because as it passes through the body it can harm the tissues. It causes clotting in blood vessels, injures the brain and nervous tissues and can paralyse the breathing and heart muscles.

The domestic electric current makes the muscles contract at 50 cycles per second – the frequency of this current – and this means that if a child grasps a faulty electric appliance or live wire his hand muscles will grip the object until the current is switched off or his hand is forcibly removed.

Electricity can kill instantly or knock someone unconscious.

If a child is in contact with an electrical appliance or is being electrified by it, switch off the supply at the wall or pull the cord so hard that the plug flies out. Whatever you do, don't touch the child yourself until he's clear.

Once he's free from the source of electricity see if his breathing is still going. If it isn't, do mouth-to-mouth resuscitation (see page 34). Check if his heart is going, if it isn't, restart it if possible (see page 293). If either of these two main systems have stopped get someone else to call an ambulance and continue with life-saving methods yourself.

Prevention is the best cure for electric shock. Keep all electrical appliances safely serviced; never allow a lead to become worn or bare; keep safety covers over wall sockets; and never take electrical apparatus into the bathroom. Take out plugs and switch off any sockets after using an appliance; buy equipment made to British safety standards; and never overload adaptors with too many plugs. **Related topics** Accident prevention; artificial respiration; heart massage **Useful organization** The Royal Society for the Prevention of Accidents.

Emotional deprivation Babies can do without toys, expensive prams, new nappies and beautiful homes to live in but they can't do without love and affection. Depriving a child of these essential commodities is to his mind what starving him is to his body. Ironically, emotional deprivation can in itself make a child so unhappy that he goes off his food and starves anyway and older pre-school children who are emotionally deprived can fail to grow properly too. Emotional deprivation isn't an all-or-nothing phenomenon but there are varying degrees and for any one child there is an optimum amount of loving responsiveness which will fill that child up to the full. Anything less than the child could ideally do with is a form of emotional deprivation, though most children who are given a certain amount of love manage to compensate and adjust well emotionally. Many children bury the loss of the love they need (but don't get) in their unconscious minds, maybe to reappear years later as the result of a trigger factor, in the form of depression, for example. Others are well aware even as young children that they are not loved as they know they should be by their parents.

To onlookers who are aware of the problem, the signs of emotional deprivation in a child are often all too obvious. Such a child may actually seem sad. He may have one of many behaviour problems, be apathetic or abnormally dependent on his mother past the first few years. Interestingly, an emotionally deprived child often sticks up for his parents if they are criticized and glosses over the poor way they have treated him. It is as though he were unconsciously idealizing them because he can't bear to think of them as they are, only as he wishes they were. Another explanation is that he is trying to cling on to any shred of love they show him and can't bear to accept the fact of his loveless, or comparatively loveless upbringing.

Researches have repeatedly found that babies and young children thrive best emotionally if they have a one-to-one relationship with one loving, caring person. That person for almost every baby is his mother. Babies need to be given love in order to learn to love others. Obviously the baby who is happy to be occasionally looked after for a short time by someone well known to him won't suffer emotional damage, even though he might prefer it if his mother were there constantly. However, somewhere in between these two extremes there is a line to be drawn, a line that will be different for each child and which will depend on his personality, on the age at which his mother first leaves him with someone else, on how often and for how long she leaves him, or whether that person is well known to the baby before he is ever left with her, on whether he is left with more than one other person, on whether the other person is loving and caring towards him, on whether his mother leaves him even though he is obviously unhappy to be left, and on whether if he is unhappy, she is able to return at once to look after him. Sometimes a baby is better off being cared for by someone other than his mother if that person is more loving and caring for him than his mother would be.

In many cultures babies automatically stay with their mothers all the time, even when the mothers are working or when they go into hospital. In this country we are probably treading a dangerous course by continually trying to push our babies away from us. Babies like to be with their mothers all the time until they are ready to explore and even then they like a safe base to return to when they want. Only when a baby is ready should he be left with someone else.

Often for no fault of their own some mothers are incapable of providing a loving and secure background for their babies. Such mothers often experienced an unhappy home life themselves as children and never had a chance to learn how to be a good mother from their own mothers. Their babies may be adequately dressed and fed, but may not get the emotional stimulation and feedback which are essential for optimal emotional development. It's likely that they will grow up with one of a variety of behaviour problems well known to teachers in infant schools, and will proceed to mother their children in the same inadequate way in their turn. This cycle of emotional deprivation needs a great deal of help by the community and its helping agencies if things are to improve.

Fathers are not to be forgotten in this area. A loving relationship with his father may be the saving factor for a child. One reason why having two parents is important is that if one feels incapable of reacting normally to the children at any one time, the other can take over temporarily. Many a depressed mother's children have been saved from emotional deprivation by their loving father.

Some mothers do everything they can to cater for the material needs of their children and forget that their emotional needs are more important than having material luxuries. These mothers go out to work to earn extra money for the family, leave their children with a minder, and return in the evening to cook, clean and put the children to bed. This can work well if the minder is a kind and loving person and if the mother tries to make some time to forge a relationship with her children in the short times she has with them. However, some minders – often unregistered and unmonitored by the local authority – virtually ignore their charges, either because they are too busy doing other things or because they have illegally taken on too many children. The children are fed but little else. Also, some mothers work such long hours that they see little if anything of their children at either end of each working day. If the children don't get their share of love from their minders, they may end up being emotionally deprived.

When young children who are cared for by minders while their mothers work first realize that they are different from other children whose mothers or loving caretakers are with them most of the time in the first five years, they may wonder whether they are somehow at fault and that the reason their mothers leave them is because they are unlovable.

A healthy and caring society needs to understand the reasons for emotional deprivation and try to prevent it from happening rather than merely criticize one or both parents. *Related topics* Mothering; separation.

Employment Protection Act If you have been in one job for two years or more and were working for more than sixteen hours a week when you became pregnant under the above Act you can be sure that your employer will keep your job (or something very similar) open for you if you return to work within twenty-nine weeks of the birth. If he should refuse to take you back you can appeal to an industrial tribunal. Your employer is also bound to pay you a proportion of your normal wage or salary for the first six weeks of your maternity leave whether you return to work or not. All of these rights are set out in a leaflet (No. 4) available from Jobcentres, Employment Offices and Unemployment Benefit Offices.

Encephalitis An inflammation of the brain caused by viruses, bacteria, a particular type of allergy or, rarely, by an immunizing injection. Several childhood infections can spread to the brain, including measles, whooping cough, polio and mumps but fortunately this happens rarely. When it does occur it can be serious because between five and twenty per cent of all children with encephalitis die and a further twenty per cent are left with mental disorders, memory loss, personality changes or paralysis. Having said this, fewer than one in a thousand children with measles, for example, get encephalitis.

There has been considerable debate over the danger of whooping cough immunization with respect to encephalitis but the evidence is confused.

Certain children should definitely *not* be immunized against whooping cough or measles but your doctor should know or will ask you questions to find out if your child is one of these.

There is no specific treatment for encephalitis and the severity and outcome depend upon the cause.

Enemas An enema (fluid given into the rectum to promote bowel opening) and suppositories used to be commonly used for constipated children at a time when constipation was thought to cause all kinds of illnesses. Today it is realized that there are simpler and more pleasant dietary ways of overcoming constipation and enemas are no longer used for healthy children. *Related topics* Constipation; dietary fibre.

Epilepsy A disorder affecting the brain characterized by fits or convulsions caused by abnormal bursts of electrical activity. Epilepsy may also cause repeated transient losses of consciousness. Certain types of epilepsy don't produce fits but have other bodily manifestations.

Epilepsy isn't a disease in itself but a collection of signs and symptoms that arise as a result of one of many underlying disorders of the brain. In the majority of children who have epilepsy there is no known cause for their condition. Not every fit is caused by epilepsy. By far the most common cause of a fit or convulsion in a young child is a high fever. A small proportion of children who have such febrile convulsions go on to become epileptic.

Epilepsy can start at any age but fequently it begins in infancy. A child may have only one fit ever or many fits per hour. All but the most severely affected can lead a normal life, helped by today's drugs.

There are two main types of fit. Petit mal is the mild kind in which the child loses consciousness for a split second or so but not for long enough to make him fall down. He comes to at once and carries on as if nothing has happened. Such attacks can occur very frequently throughout the day.

The more classical type of epilepsy that the public recognizes is called grand mal epilepsy. The child loses consciousness, wets himself, shakes, goes rigid, clenches his teeth and falls to the ground. Such fits usually occur for no apparent reason but can be prompted by flashing lights, stress, sleep loss, and infections. When a child has such an attack, never try to force anything between his teeth or you may break a tooth. Bitten tongues heal but broken teeth don't. Never restrain a child who is fitting or you could damage his muscles. Do make sure he can breathe though and pull him away from furniture or other things he could damage himself on. Many children sleep after a fit. If you are used to all this, there's no need to call a doctor but the first time it happens it's wise to get a medical opinion.

Today's drug treatment, usually in the form of tablets regularly taken, ensures that most epileptics can lead a normal life with few fits and there is no longer such a social stigma attached to the disorder. *Related topics* Convulsions; fever. *Useful organization* British Epilepsy Association.

Episiotomy A surgical incision (cut) in the perineum (the tissues between the openings of the vagina and the back passage) made during the second stage of labour (when the baby is being pushed down the birth canal) in order to make the birth quicker, less painful and to avoid serious tearing. Unfortunately, in recent years in the West this cut has been done with increasing frequency and often quite unnecessarily. Mothers are very rarely warned about the after-effects of an episiotomy and in fact are not usually even asked whether they mind having it done, let alone told! If they knew what to expect afterwards, many might choose to have a slightly longer labour, as long as the health of their baby was not compromised, of course.

In order to enlarge the opening of the birth canal (the vagina) so as to accommodate the baby's head (or bottom in a breech delivery) more easily, quite a deep and long cut has to be made. Because the cut extends into the wall of the vagina and into the muscles of the perineum, stitching up after the birth is fairly complicated and unless the area is anaesthetized with a local anaesthetic the stitching is painful.

In the days and weeks after the birth, the tissues around the stitched area swell and can sometimes become inflamed. Healing is often delayed, partly because the area is sat upon and partly because the sewing-up material isn't properly absorbed or pushed out. But, worst of all, the area is extremely painful for a lot of women. So painful can it be that a woman may not be able to sit down without a rubber ring on the chair and walking becomes a comical waddle with every step painful. When she and her husband are ready to resume lovemaking, the stitched area may be so painful that she is very reluctant to have intercourse. What's more, all this can go on for some months and will certainly do so for several days – contrary to what some doctors promise. She needs a very patient and understanding husband to be able to cope with all this.

Unless a mother is feeling well and painfree, she won't be as relaxed and happy as she should be, and that will reflect badly on how she behaves to her baby. Women have often told us that given any difficulties with breast-feeding, for example, if they have a painful episiotomy scar too they are less inclined to persist with the breast-feeding. *Useful organizations* Association for Improvements in the Maternity Service; The National Childbirth Trust.

Equipment for a baby Unless you're going to bottle feed, you really need very little equipment for your newborn baby. If you decide to have your baby in bed with you at night you don't even need a cot or crib, though you may like to have one anyway because it looks pretty and you can put your baby there when he sleeps during the day to keep him warm, safe and draught-free.

The single most useful piece of equipment is a baby sling to carry your baby in and yet leave your arms free. Millions of women all over the world carry their babies in this way and babies accustomed to them from the start are quite happy and cry less than babies kept in prams, cots and so on. A sling will give you more time to get on with cooking, shopping, walking, and housework while your baby is kept happy, so it's a good investment for both of you.

Next on the list comes some form of transport for the baby. At some stage – perhaps when your baby gets too heavy for you to carry him a lot, or if you have long distances to cover on foot – you'll want to put your baby in a pram, a carrycot and transporter, a lie-back buggy or a pram buggy. Which you choose depends on whether you travel a lot with the baby in a car (when a carrycot and transporter or a pram buggy would be a good buy) or whether you tend to walk with your baby everywhere (in which case a comfortable, well-sprung pram would be the answer). If you cover only short distances and don't need a carrycot to put the baby into in the car, then a lie-back buggy will do. Some mothers buy or are given more than one form of transport. All these items are bulky and have to be kept somewhere dry if they are not to rust.

Buckets with lids for soaking nappies are essential. How many you need depends on how often you intend to wash nappies. Two is a reasonable number, if you have a washing machine. You will also need the sanitizing products to soak the nappies in while they wait to be washed. Of course, if you use disposable nappies you won't need any of these. A changing mat for putting your baby on is a wise buy but isn't necessary.

If your baby has a lot of hair, you'll need a brush and comb. There's no need to buy special towels for the baby, but a rubber non-slip suction mat to put in the bath is a sensible buy. You may like to have a baby bath (with a rubber suction mat inside) and a stand, but neither is essential. One of the easiest and most pleasant ways of bathing a baby is to have him in the bath with you, especially if your husband is there to give him to you and take him out afterwards. It's quite possible to bath even a newborn baby in the family bath even if you're not in it yourself. The main reason people have a baby bath is so that they don't have to lean over and don't have to use a lot of expensive hot water. However, if the room is warm you only need an inch or so of water in the bath and even if you have more, the money it costs to heat the water would have to be spent on buying a baby bath anyway! If you're fairly supple, you won't mind kneeling on the bathroom floor to wash your baby as he sits or is held in the bath. For hundreds of years mothers have bathed their babies in a large bowl or even in the kitchen sink or a hand basin, though you must take care not to burn him on the hot tap if you use either of these.

A high chair is a very useful piece of equipment because it leaves the mother's lap free at mealtimes so she can feed the baby, serve the family's meal and eat her own at the same time.

A harness is useful to keep a baby from climbing out of a high chair or pram. It can be moved from one to the other if there are anchorage points. It should only ever be used for short periods when you are going to and fro and a child shouldn't ever be left in it if he is crying and struggling and doesn't want to be there. Some mothers buy a set of reins to attach to the harness for when their baby walks, doesn't want a hand held, and would either disappear completely or would step into the traffic if she didn't somehow control his wanderings.

A car seat is useful for a baby who is old enough to sit in one and must be specially fixed to anchorage points on the car. Until a baby is large enough for a car seat, he'll be safe harnessed into a carrycot which is in turn kept safe by straps attached to anchorage points on the car.

So much for what you need for a young baby. Whether or not you buy a baby-walker, a baby's chair, a baby-bouncer, a swing, a play-pen, a baby alarm or any one of the many other available items of equipment, is up to you but none of them is essential. When a baby is mobile, certain safety items are very useful: a stair gate, magnetic catches for kitchen cupboard doors and safety window latches are all worth considering.

Some families equip themselves for a baby as though it were a creature from outer space. Unless money is no object, only buy what you think will be really useful and if you aren't sure, discuss it first with friends who are experienced mothers. Many things can be borrowed or bought second hand to keep costs down. **Related topics** Baby bath; baby-bouncer; baby carrier; baby chair; baby walker; carry-cot, cot, harness; high chair; pram; push-chair; reins; second-hand equipment; transporter.

Exchange transfusion A life-saving procedure in which blood of a suitable group is given to a child in equal volume to that removed from his body. It is not a common procedure but is used to remove the damaged blood from a baby with haemolytic disease of the newborn. Blood removed at this age has to be replaced (unlike in a healthy adult who can lose one pint or more with no ill effects). A syringe-full at a time of the baby's blood is removed and an equal volume of blood is replaced. The aim isn't to replace all the baby's blood but just enough to allow him to function normally until his body replaces the affected blood cells. **Related topics** Blood groups; blood transfusion.

Exercise Children need exercise as much for psychological and emotional reasons as for physical ones. Unlike many adults who lead largely sedentary lives, most children are constantly on the move and most get as much exercise as they need during the normal course of their day. Running, walking, climbing, crawling, skipping and cycling are just some of the activities that children do when playing. Swimming is an enjoyable form of exercise and many people are within reach of a public swimming bath.

Children often use more energy than adults when doing the same thing. On a walk to the shops, for example, a child may cover twice the distance if you count all his detours and running ahead and then back.

If you live in a flat or a house with no garden and no easy access to a play area you'll have to make a special effort to ensure that your child gets enough exercise. Some plump or naturally inactive children have to be chivvied into being physically active.

It's well known now that physical activity releases morphine-like substances into the bloodstream which increase a person's feeling of well-being. Everyone knows that the tiredness following exertion is pleasant when compared with that following boredom and inactivity. Perhaps a young child's grumpiness and grizzling might be improved if you took him for a walk or played with him in the garden, preferably encouraging some rough and tumble play. Many children also sleep better when they're physically tired.

A lot of the winter months are cold and wet in this country so you'll then have to encourage play indoors that allows the children to let off their physical high spirits. It's easy to make obstacle courses with chairs, and tents and other make-believe structures. Balloon games are good because the potential for damage is small yet the children can have fun and exercise in a small area. **Related topic** Dancing; swimming.

Expressing breast milk

Expressing breast milk, or hand-milking of the breast, is a useful technique for the breast-feeding mother to know about. A low birth weight baby may not be able to suck and so may have to be tube-fed with expressed breast milk obtained by hand or by electric pumping. A baby who isn't sucking well (most often in the newborn period, though this can happen at any time) won't empty the breast properly and to avoid breast engorgement milk will have to be expressed. Even if breast-feeding is going well, the breasts may become tense and overfull when the milk first comes in or even afterwards from time to time. If this happens, or if a tender lump due to a blocked milk duct appears at any time, expression will save the day. Working mothers can continue breast-feeding if they express milk for their baby to be given while they're out and if they express milk while at work both to collect it for the baby and to relieve the pressure of their unemptied breasts when the baby isn't there to suck. Some mothers express breast milk so as to give it to other women's babies via a milk bank. If for some reason a baby is too ill to be allowed any milk, then expression can keep the milk supply going until he's able to drink it again. There are thus many times when expression comes in handy both to relieve the mother and to provide milk for the baby.

To express your milk, put one hand to the breast with the thumb on one side of the breast and the fingers on the other. Press gently but firmly down towards your chest wall and with a firm stroking action slide your thumb and fingers towards the areola and nipple. You'll need to move your hand round the breast systematically to empty each part of the breast and you'll find that it helps to use the other hand as well to empty all the breast. Expressing takes a long time because the milk isn't all available at first – it has to be let down just as when a baby is sucking and hand expression isn't such a strong stimulus to let down the milk as is a baby at the breast. Encourage your let-down by making sure you're warm, unhurried, relaxed and happy. Massage your breasts gently. Women have all sorts of tricks to encourage their milk to flow. Practice until you learn the knack. If you're expressing just to relieve the tension in your breasts you need only take off a little milk. If you're expressing to get milk for your baby, don't be surprised by the small amount you can express. The amount a baby takes at the breast is anyway much smaller than a bottle-fed baby's feed, and hand expressing isn't as productive as a baby's sucking. Remember to do it frequently if you want to collect a large amount, and start a couple of days before (and keep it in the fridge) if you're expressing after each feed in order to collect enough to leave for your baby for a whole feed when you're out.

Collection of milk to be given to your baby must be carefully and hygienically done. If it's to go to a milk bank, your hygiene precautions should be even stricter because other babies won't be used to your normal body bacteria as is your baby. Breast milk, once expressed, will keep for up to 72 hours in the fridge. If layers separate out don't worry: these will go as you warm and shake the milk before giving it to your baby. **Related topics** Breast-feeding problems; milk banks. **Useful organizations** La Leche League of Great Britain; The National Childbirth Trust.

Extended family

Extended family Members of the family other than the children and their parents. In many cultures around the world both historically and today, several generations of people live either under one roof or very close by indeed. This provides all kinds of benefits to each member of the family and perhaps especially to young parents, who don't have the full responsibility of child care on their shoulders. In our society's typical 'nuclear' family today, many parents feel they have too much pressure on them. Human babies are unique in the animal kingdom in being dependent on their parents for many years until maturity is reached. For two adults (or often one) to be able to provide this, with the mother of an under-five living an isolated life in her own home and with the father out at work for much of the day, is often asking too much. Most parents need both practical help and emotional support if they and their family are to stay happy.

While friends and neighbours can often help a family with young children, many are too busy looking after their own families to offer much time. A newly-isolated mother looking after her first child needs to be a fairly confident, outgoing person to make enough friends and acquaintances soon enough to prevent her from feeling lonely, and this loneliness can pave the way to depression.

Unfortunately, the chances of returning to a system of close family ties seems remote, partly because things change so fast in our society that some young couples do not see their parents as being a meaningful source of advice or even of help any more and partly because with the present housing and job situation, families tend to split up, albeit unwillingly.

While few parents want their relatives living on top of them (and vice versa), there's a lot to be said for the extended family living close by, so that mutual help and support through the various stages of life can be easily given.

Children benefit from contact with adult relatives because they provide extra adult 'models' and – hopefully – a warm interest in the child as he grows. Similarly, children with cousins and other young relatives usually enjoy the feeling of belonging to a large family.

Eyes A baby's eyes are relatively large for his size – in fact they are two-thirds of the size of adult eyes – and this is one of the things that makes babies so appealing.

The eyes are filled with fluid and have a light-sensitive inner coating – the retina – from which messages are transmitted to the 'vision' part of the brain at the back of the head.

In the front of the eye there is a hole in the middle of the iris (the coloured part) called the pupil. The size of the pupil can change just like the diaphragm of a camera to let more or less light through. It opens up in dim light and closes down in the sun.

The eyes are moved by small muscles attached to their thick outer coating. Anything wrong with these muscles can produce a squint.

The eye is protected by the eyelids. The under surfaces of these and the visible surface of the eye are covered with a delicate membrane called the conjunctiva. Fluid produced by the tear glands lubricates the conjunctiva and washes any tiny particles of dust and dirt into a drainage channel which drains into the nose itself. ***Related topics*** Blindness; vision; vision testing; visual problems.

Failure to thrive A medical term used to describe babies or children who fail to gain as much weight as they should over a period of several weeks or months, depending on the age of the child. In a looser sense, a thriving child is one that is healthy, eating well, putting on weight and happy.

There are numerous reasons why a baby may not thrive and a shortage of breast milk because of a poor breast-feeding technique is a common one. Unless a baby is breast-fed on an unrestricted basis whenever he needs to be and for as long as he wants at each feed, there is a chance that he won't get enough milk and so won't thrive. If a breast-fed baby is not putting on weight at all, or not as much as he should, the answer is not to switch to the bottle but to investigate the possible reasons behind his slow gain. In many mothers the breast milk supply is insufficient but this can always be increased. Some babies gain very slowly however they are fed, whether by breast or bottle, and so would do no better when put on to the bottle. A few healthy babies take up to two months to regain their birthweight on breast milk alone but there is no reason to put them on to cows' milk formula unless they are unhappy and obviously wanting more milk, which their mother can't provide by increasing her milk supply. A few babies, though, don't get (or take) enough breast milk for their needs, and don't complain: they seem happy to starve. Expert observation and assessment of each baby is therefore necessary.

The decision as to whether to go on solely breast-feeding or whether to give the baby bottles as well (or instead) can be a difficult one to make for the slow-gaining but apparently healthy baby whose mother is already feeding on an unrestricted basis (and offering the breast more than the baby asks for it), and who seems happy. The conventional decision to introduce bottles is by no means necessarily the best for the baby who is simply a slow gainer, but may be right for the very few babies whose mothers cannot produce enough milk even when taking all the many measures available to increase their milk supply.

Some low birth weight babies don't thrive as they should partly because they have a poor start in life in an incubator with a relative loss of emotional and physical affection and partly because breast-feeding isn't established. These problems can be minimized or avoided in those special care baby units whose staff are aware of such problems and do their best to help the mother overcome them.

Some otherwise normal babies and children fail to thrive because they are neglected or emotionally or even physically abused. A baby or child who has a depressed, otherwise disturbed, or disinterested mother or who has a frequently changing procession of mother substitutes, can become depressed and apathetic and eventually – if the situation doesn't improve – may fail to thrive.

Some children who aren't thriving have an underlying physical disease rather than a feeding or environmental problem. Examples of such medical conditions are chromosome disorders, a chronic infection, galactosaemia, kidney disease, cystic fibrosis, coeliac disease, or rarely, a cancer.

Any child who has no obvious cause for his failure to thrive may have to be admitted to hospital for observation and investigation. As with any hospitalized child, it is best for his mother to go into hospital and stay there with him. *Related topics* Breast-feeding problems; complementary feeds; development–physical; emotional deprivation; low birth weight; thin child; underfeeding; weight loss.

Fainting Temporary loss of consciousness caused by too poor a flow of blood to the brain. It is uncommon in the under-fives and if repeated, needs medical investigation, just in case it is really a type of epilepsy.

If your child should faint, lie him down flat, or at least with his head lower than his body (for example, sitting with his head between his knees). Loosen any tight clothing and let him rest. Don't give any drinks or food till he's fully conscious. Fainting isn't dangerous and doesn't permanently damage the brain. The only cause of fainting that is at all common in the under-fives is breath holding, which most often occurs as part of a temper tantrum. *Related topics* Breath holding; convulsions; epilepsy.

Fairy stories A wonderful source of entertainment for children of all ages. You may notice that even a young baby seems to be listening as you read to your older children, even though he can't understand. The sense of wonder, the power of good triumphing over evil, the sheer horror and the other-worldliness of fairy stories makes them compelling reading and listening and most children want to hear them time and again. If this annoys you, remember that as the months and years go by the same story takes on entirely different meanings as the child builds his own life's experiences into it. In effect, the story you read is a sort of scaffolding around which his imagination builds. Also, children take in the pictures often in far more detail than we adults do and this adds to their enjoyment.

Listening to a story is a very good way to relax children before they go to sleep. Watching TV or doing other more creative pastimes may leave them restless, listless or excited. Gearing down these mental and physical activities in a way that shows that you care enough to spend time with them works wonders for the under-fives.

Don't worry about the frightening aspects of fairy stories – these are an integral part of their interest and value. Children have to learn that there are bad people in the world as well as good, and fairy stories are one way of introducing this concept. If a particular story gives your child nightmares or bothers him during the daytime, put it aside for a few months. **Related topic** Books for children.

Falls Once your child is up off his hands and knees and learning to walk, some falls are inevitable. A crawling child is stable, but a child learning to balance on two legs has to learn stability. Some perfectly normal toddlers fall over much more often than others: you'll probably have noticed that some of your friends' children are always covered in bruises, while others never seem to hurt themselves at all. Muscular strength and coordination from practice at walking make some difference, but personality plays an important role as well. Naturally timid and careful children fall less than those who are eager for new experiences.

What should you as a parent do to protect your child from hurting himself at this vulnerable stage? The answer is simply to use your common sense. For a start, you can't possibly prevent every fall or bump unless you stay close to your child every second and follow him around everywhere he goes. That's not a good idea partly because you have other things to do and also because he's got to learn how to stop himself from falling. What you can do is to make your home as safe as possible and keep a watchful eye on him as much as possible. When you're out of your own home you'll have to be more vigilant because you won't be familiar with all the possible hazards.

Childproofing your home is relatively easy. If you have slippery floors, don't let your toddler walk around with socks or tights on, or in soft shoes with slippery soles. Instead, let him walk barefoot or in shoes with non-slip soles. Secure loose rugs on slippery floors, or put a non-slip backing on them, for the sake of other people as well.

Remove ornaments or objects on low surfaces that your child might pick up and drop: they might hurt him as they fall or, if breakable, might cut him. Secure loose electrical flexes so your toddler can't trip over them. Perhaps most important, decide what you're going to do about the stairs. It's no good saying that if your child is allowed free access to stairs, he'll get used to them quicker and will find his own way of getting up and down safely. Many parents have tried that and have discovered that their child is safe ninety nine times out of a hundred but falls and hurts himself – perhaps badly – on the hundredth time. Stairs can be slippery and a child can fall a long way down them, so buy or make a stair gate and use it at the top or bottom of the stairs, depending on where your child is. Don't let this stop you from letting your child practice going up and down stairs under your supervision, otherwise he'll never learn. Try not to leave things lying on the stairs, for everyone's sake. Windows are a difficult matter when inquisitive toddlers are around. Unless you want to put safety catches on all the windows, make sure your young child isn't left alone to play for long, and never leave him by an open window if there's any chance at all that he might climb up.

Check that your furniture is safe for a child who is pulling himself up on it to stand, who is walking round it while holding on, or who is walking between bits of furniture and throwing himself at the one that is his goal. Light occasional tables can be a hazard unless they have well-spaced legs. Chairs can easily be pulled over from behind. Remove what you can that's dangerous and try to stay with your child in a room where there's dangerous furniture that you can't move out. Tables, chairs, fireguards, fenders, cupboards, all these can have sharp corners or edges which you can do nothing about. However, when your baby is at the stage of experimenting with walking and standing, he'll be with you most of the time and you'll be able to protect him by staying close. A more adventurous and able toddler will be that much more stable and won't be so likely to pull things over by hanging on to them for security.

What if your child does fall? You'll soon learn to ignore the bruises and cope with minor grazes and cuts, but it's surprising how difficult it can be to tell if a child is more seriously hurt. Children can hurt themselves badly by falling awkwardly, though luckily most children of this age fall 'well', relaxing as they hit the floor. They don't have to fall from a great height in order to damage themselves, so don't let the circumstances of the accident stop you from getting medical advice if you are all concerned.

Perhaps one of the most common things worrying parents is a *head injury*. If your child has fallen on to his head, ask for medical help if there is a head wound; if there is any bleeding from the nose, mouth or ears, (or any yellowish, watery discharge, though this isn't always easy to recognize); if he is sick or off his food for any time; if he is still pale after some time; or if he loses consciousness. Loss of consciousness is important but often difficult to recognize because a child who has hit his head will exhaust himself from crying more often than not, and then is highly likely to go to sleep. If the accident happens just before bedtime, try waking your child twice in the night just to make sure he is just sleeping. Whenever the accident happens, listen to your sleeping child's breathing because unconscious children tend to breathe noisily. Also, watch his colour: any pallor from the shock of the fall should disappear relatively soon. After a serious head injury an older child might complain of a headache or trouble with his eyesight, but your toddler won't be able to.

The doctor may recommend that your child has a skull x-ray after his accident, or that he is kept in hospital overnight so that he can be watched expertly. You'll probably be able to stay with him if you ask, and with any luck he'll be home the next day.

As for *other fractures*, it can be very difficult to tell the difference between an arm or a leg that is fractured and one that is simply bruised or sprained. The pain from a fracture tends to get worse, and a child avoids using a broken arm or leg. As it's far better to be safe than sorry, ask for medical advice if you're at all worried. An x-ray can give the answer immediately and may save your child a lot of pain and you a lot of worry.

One last word, in some areas a health visitor comes to see the parents of any child who has attended the local casualty department with an injury, to assess the circumstances of the injury. This is routine and is meant to find out whether the child might have been injured on purpose. If so, the parents would then be given as much help as possible to prevent it happening again. *Related topics* Accident prevention; bruises; coordination; cuts; fractures; head injuries; stairs.

Family income supplement

Family income supplement A state benefit for parents in full-time work who have at least one dependent child and whose total weekly income is very low. Single parents can claim, provided they work for at least twenty-four hours a week. Anyone else working less than thirty hours a week or the self-employed should claim supplementary benefit instead.

You can claim FIS on Form FIS1 available from post offices, your local social services office or the local offices of the DHSS.

Family planning – age gaps

Family planning – age gaps No one can advise you on the ideal gap between children because so much depends on your personality, expectations, age and the amount of help you have, together with the personalities of your children, their health and how much you enjoy looking after them. If you ask around you'll hear different stories according to the experiences of the people you ask. Jealousy, for instance, can affect children born two years apart just as much as those born four years apart. Whether or not it's a problem depends to some extent on how you handle it. It's worth bearing in mind that with nature's own method of contraception, unrestricted breast-feeding, (the most widely used method worldwide, even today), babies come at roughly two- to three-year intervals.

Having a very short space between children means that you'll have two babies to look after at once. Unless you continually remind yourself, it's difficult not to expect too much of the older one and he may inevitably be pushed out of your arms rather too quickly for his (and your) liking. You'll also find that you have much less time for the older child once your baby arrives, because inevitably a lot of your time and energy, both emotional and physical, will go to the baby. A very short age gap can mean that you as a couple don't get as much enjoyment out of your children when they are young as you might otherwise have done, simply because you're tired out by the sheer hard work of looking after several very young children.

A large gap means that the older children will not only be a help with the baby, but will learn from the experience of having a baby in the family.

One fact to consider is that children born close together may enjoy each other's company more, simply because they can play similar games as they grow up. Even a four-year gap can mean that the younger child is always too babyish to join in with his older sibling who'll already have a set of friends of his own age. **Related topics** Contraception; firstborn children; jealousy. **Useful organization** Family Planning Information Service.

Fantasy An idea in a child's imagination which often shows up in make-believe or pretend play. Any parent who watches his or her child play 'mummies and daddies' or 'schools' will see the child's fantasy world being acted out. He's experimenting with his interpretations of the world and seeing how they work out in practice. You'll often hear the worst side of yourself being acted out as a child mimics what you say, often in exactly the same tone of voice. By changing roles in games like this they learn to put themselves in other peoples' shoes. After all, how else can a four-year-old learn what it is like to be 'teacher' if she is always a 'pupil' in real life?

When children act out their fantasies they are often subconsciously exploring how to create and maintain relationships. If one has power over the other and then they change sides in the fantasy world, they see both sides of the coin and grow from this. All of this is done in the safe and unthreatening atmosphere of knowing that they don't really have to be good at what they are fantasizing about. They can do it within their limitations yet know that there are real teachers, doctors, TV cops or whoever, who really *can* do things.

But fantasies don't always have to be acted out. They can also be painted, drawn or modelled. The results of such fantasies may be poor by adult standards but this doesn't make them any the less valuable and enjoyable to the child.

When fantasies are being explored the best thing to do is to leave the children alone. The only time you shouldn't do so is if their play involved dangerous situations with 'goodies' punishing the 'baddies' severely, for example. Also if one child always seems to be getting the rough end of the deal it makes sense to step in if only because he may not be able to protect himself from the others. Bullying and setting on one child in a group must be stopped for that child's sake. It's all very well letting children play in a fantasy world but the whole group should be able to share in the fantasy and enjoy it. *Related topics* Copying; creativity; development – social; fairy stories; games; imagination; play.

Father The structure of the family is changing and one of the greatest changes for a long time is that the father is taking a more active and interested role in family life than he has done for decades. This change has partly been thrust upon men because their wives want to work out of the home more than they did but we also see evidence of today's young fathers really being more interested in their young families than was the case up until recently. The concept of the stereotyped mother as the only one who *can* change a nappy, cook, or run the home is thankfully dying in many areas of the country. There are probably more equal partnership marriages today than there have been for a long time and children are getting the benefit.

Just how you share out the care of really young babies depends largely on how you feed them. Breast-feeding can only be done by the woman but anything else can be done by the father if he wants to. There's no reason for a father to feel left out simply because he's not feeding his baby.

Whether you're at home looking after children or out at work both jobs have their pleasures and rewards, their pains and their boredom. Neither the mother's nor the father's life is a bed of roses, though each may think the other's is. If you work on the principle that before father leaves for work and when he comes back any chores remaining are shared out equally, you won't go far wrong. This is the only fair way to run a modern family. Some men enjoy being at home so much that they would like to reverse roles and let their wives go out to work. This is usually unattractive financially though as most women don't earn as much as their husbands.

A father's job continues at work as he earns a living for his family. It may be in *his* best career interests to keep moving his job and home but he needs to consider if he should really go for promotion if it means long periods away from home and family. Does more work and more responsibility amount to anything in real terms if you're so tired that your relationship as a couple and your relationship with your family suffer? These are all questions that need careful discussion between a couple. Today's father has to provide for his family but it's not only money that he provides. The pursuit of money and career alone cannot make for happy family relationships today simply because it throws too much of a burden of responsibility and loneliness on the woman. *Related topics* Fatherless children; parents' relationship; unmarried mothers.

Fatherless children Ideally in our society children should grow up in the care of two adults, one of each sex. Today, with divorce being so commonplace and children from broken homes being left in the custody of their mothers, many are fatherless. The problem is complicated by the fact that such a child may also suffer from the fact that his mother is lonely and unhappy.

Any child needs some male adult company. A man well known to the child becomes a model for the child's impressions and concepts of men in general. After the age of three for a child of either sex a relationship with a man becomes even more important because after this age they are aware not only of their own sexual identity but also of the fact that the rest of the world is made up of two sexes. There are alternatives to having a father, though they can never be the same. Uncles and family friends and even friendly acquaintances can all influence a young child's views of men. Relatives and friends may be prepared to act as a substitute father occasionally.

It's worth encouraging your children to relate to men if you are single because you don't want them growing up fearful and resentful of men through regarding them as alien beings. Make a real effort not to 'over-mother' your son or to allow him to become too deeply involved in your hobbies and pursuits. There is a real (though subconscious) temptation to take over the boy as a kind of substitute partner but this is unfair to him and he'll grow up precocious and interested only in adult pursuits. Striking the balance often isn't easy *Related topics* Divorce; father; one-parent families; psychosexual development; separation of parents; unmarried mothers. *Useful organizations* Gingerbread; One Parent Families.

Fats Food of plant or animal origin and high in calories. The most commonly eaten fatty foods are butter, milk, cheese, margarine, cooking oils and fat in meat (even lean meat has fat in it). Most people in the West consume too many calories as fat and it has been estimated that about forty per cent of the calories in the average person's food comes from fat, yet research shows that we'd be a lot healthier if this were nearer twenty-five per cent.

Although there has been a lot of publicity against saturated fatty foods such as butter, there is no firm evidence that such foods are necessarily harmful at any stage of life. Man has been herding cows for countless thousands of years and has undoubtedly become acclimatized to eating saturated fats. In fact there is research that suggests that too large a proportion of unsaturated fats is harmful.

The main danger for children when it comes to eating fats, is that they'll consume too much and become overweight. There is little doubt that obesity in the under-fives predisposes to fatness later in life so it's worth keeping a fat child's consumption down even at this early age. This can be achieved by three simple measures. First, if your child is on a good mixed diet, either give him skimmed milk or cut his milk intake down to half a pint or so a day; second, keep butter or margarine at room temperature before use and spread it for your child so that it doesn't go on in slabs; and third, cut visible fat from his meat. *Related topic* Food.

Fears Children under five have many fears, which are often fed by their lively imaginations, especially in three, four and five-year-olds. Common fears among young children are of death, animals, the dark, fairy stories, injury, going into hospital, constipation, losing their parents, school, strangers, swimming and many others.

Even young babies can be frightened by noisy or disturbing things such as barking dogs, trains, jet planes or a fire engine's siren. A baby left alone to cry when he's hungry or lonely becomes very frightened. Babies have no concept of time and a minute can seem like an hour to them. They may also be frightened if their mother leaves them in a room with another person. If you know that certain things upset your baby it is unkind to expose him to them to 'try to get him used to them'. He won't be able to reason things out and will continue to be frightened. Some young children are afraid of the bath in case they slip and get water over their heads. Fear of soap getting into their eyes can be very real too, so be gentle and considerate rather than trying to make them be brave. A non-slip mat in the bath makes it actually safer as well as seeming to be so for the child.

Many of the fears outlined above are covered elsewhere in the book but in general the principle that works best is to take the fears seriously and to consider them through the child's eyes and not through your adult eyes. No child under five should have to brave things out if he is really afraid of them. He may appear to cope but will probably simply suppress his fear which will then come out as a sleep or behaviour disturbance. Children who are afraid need reassurance. Indeed, many fears are probably unconscious desires for you to reassure and love him. Children who feel secure and loved don't fear things nearly as much as those who for some reason feel insecure and unloved. *Related topics* Anxiety; behaviour problems; fairy stories; insecurity; night terrors.

Feeding equipment The breast-feeding mother needs to buy no feeding equipment at all. In the unlikely event that she needs to pump her milk, an electric pump can be hired from the local hospital or from the National Childbirth Trust. Most hand pumps are inefficient, though there is a cylindrical one which many mothers have found works well. Though not exactly equipment, bra pads are useful in the early days of breast-feeding especially to stop milk leaking through a mother's bra on to her clothes. They should be changed frequently so the nipples aren't bathed in milk between feeds as this encourages nipple soreness. Some mothers make do with pieces of towelling or handkerchiefs folded inside their bras.

The bottle-feeding mother will need at least one bottle and teat. If she is going to make up several feeds at a time and leave them refrigerated, she'll need several bottles and teats. Even if you have just one bottle you should always have a standby teat in case your regular one becomes damaged or the hole gets too big or too small. If you don't have a reserve teat you could be in trouble at night or weekends. Sterilizing can be done by boiling, though this reduces the life of the teat. If it's done with sterilizing solution, then a special sterilizing unit is useful, though not essential. Get a bottle brush to remove milk residues before sterilizing.

Older babies spill less if they drink from a baby's feeding cup (teacher beaker). Bibs are essential for babies and young children if you want to save on washing. Unbreakable bowls are useful, especially when the baby has charge of his own bowl. Several are available with a suction pad on the bottom, which is helpful, and one has a high, inward curving rim so that the baby starting to use a spoon can more easily manage to get some food on to the spoon. A high chair makes mealtimes easier for the mother and most babies enjoy sitting at the same level as the rest of the family.

As the child starts using cutlery he can either use small knives, forks and spoons or special children's ones. Children often enjoy having their own, especially if they have their favourite cartoon characters on them. Because at first a young child holds his spoon in his fist, he'll find it difficult to feed himself because he has to make larger movements with his arm than if he used a finger-grip (which he can't till he's older). You can buy children's spoons and forks with handles specially made to be easy and comfortable in the early days, or you might prefer your child to get used to normal cutlery from the beginning. For a long time most children alternate between fingers and cutlery to feed themselves. Some children are much more independent than others and want to feed themselves from the start of mixed feeding, while others are happy to be spoon-fed way past a year old. Let your child do what he is happiest doing and he'll become independent at mealtimes sooner than if you battle with him. By two, and sometimes much earlier, a child can use a spoon well. When you let him have a knife and fork is up to you. You'll have to cut up his food for a long time to come, but by four he's quite capable of attempting to cut up much of his food.

A special place mat, bowl, plate and mug are attractive to a child and it's a good idea to have spare ones for visiting children to make them feel at home. When you visit other people or eat out, remember to take your child's feeding equipment with you if his own things at mealtimes are important to him. *Related topics* Cups; eating habits; high chair; mealtimes.

Feeding schedules A term used to describe the timing of the frequency of feeds necessary for babies. It is tempting to imagine that babies would want to eat at roughly the same times as the rest of the family. However, this doesn't work out in practice because when their stomachs are empty their hunger makes them so uncomfortable that they cry until they are fed.

It helps to undertand a baby's needs for frequent feeds if you think back to the way he was nourished before he was born. There was a continuous supply of nutrients from his mother's bloodstream across the placenta and into his bloodstream, albeit with rises in the levels of some nutrients corresponding with their levels in her bloodstream following digestion from her stomach and intestines after a meal. Suddenly, after birth, he has to get accustomed to taking in nourishment at intervals. The smaller and less mature the baby – for instance if he is of low birth weight and especially if he is premature – the more frequent his feeds have to be in order to provide him with enough nourishment. He can only take a very little at a time (because of his small stomach) to sustain his blood sugar levels and to allay his hunger. Very immature babies who are fed with milk down a nasogastric tube are fed hourly; as they grow more mature and bigger they can cope with two-hourly feeds. When they reach the age approximating to when they should have been born, they can often manage with less frequent feeds if they are being bottle-fed.

You can successfully bottle-feed a baby according to an arbitrarily laid-down feeding schedule as long as you are prepared to be flexible if he sometimes wants a feed sooner than the scheduled time. Cows' milk formula stays in the stomach for longer than breast milk and so satisfies a baby for longer. It is an empty stomach that causes hunger pangs. Earlier this century bottle-fed babies were noticed to wake approximately four-hourly for a feed and this observation led to the widespread advice that all babies should be fed four-hourly, whether they were bottle- or breast-fed. However, we now know that breast milk is digested so quickly and completely that breast-fed babies have an empty stomach sooner than bottle-fed babies do, and so need feeding more often. A bottle-fed baby gets used to taking a relatively large volume of milk infrequently, whereas a breast-fed one prefers a smaller amount but more often. (Bottle-fed babies also need to take a greater volume of milk overall because it is not as completely digested as breast milk and so extra volume is required to compensate for this.)

Doctors and other health and babycare advisers have always been eager to give mothers advice on feeding schedules. If you look at commonly suggested schedules even from before the turn of the century, you can see how this advice has changed over the years. Before 1900 schedules recommended for breast-feeding mothers advised far more closely spaced feeds, and far more of them. With the coming of widespread bottle-feeding, and with bottle-fed babies tolerating fewer feeds quite happily, the advice to breast-feeding mothers changed because it was wrongly thought that all babies were able to last as long between feeds as were bottle-fed ones: no one knew that this was quite unphysiological and impossible for most babies.

Rapidly, more and more women turned to bottle-feeding even if they started off by breast-feeding, because with four-hourly breast-feeding, their milk supply dried up over the course of a few weeks. Four-hourly stimulation and emptying of the breasts is simply not enough for the average woman to produce enough milk, she needs what nature intended she should have – much more frequent stimulation as a result of the baby feeding more often. Hand in hand with this concept goes the length of feeds. The stimulation of the breast depends upon the total length of time a baby is at the breast, and this is altered by the length of the feed as well as by the frequency of feeds. Mothers who cut their feeds to ten minutes at each breast (and less than this in the first week or so) notice that their milk supply can be increased if they allow their babies to remain at the breast for longer at each feed. It seems sensible, within reason, to let a baby be the guide as to the number and length of feeds he needs, provided he is thriving. If he isn't it may be that he is too tired, unwell, or apathetic to ask for enough feeds and that you'll have to put him to the breast more to stimulate your milk supply even though he doesn't seem to 'need' this many feeds. The concept of ten minutes a side as the length of a breast feed came about because it was noticed that most babies had finished their feed in that time. However, most is not all, and a baby may sometimes want much longer at the breast than at other times. Timing a breast-feed is unhelpful and worrying if the baby doesn't conform to what is said to be average. Each baby is an individual and should be treated accordingly.

The same goes for bottle-fed babies, many of whom may wake before four hours is up and for whom even the 'flexible' concept of three- to five-hourly feeds may not be flexible enough. Many is the mother who has paced the floor with her baby because he seems to want a feed before the experts say he should. Experts are by no means infallible in this field. Indeed, over the years they have proved themselves wrong time and time again, and you are best guided by your own baby and what he seems to need. If you have any problems you can't sort out, consult your health visitor, local National Childbirth Trust breast-feeding counsellor, or La Leche League leader for help.

Some babies tend to fall into a feeding routine of their own during the first few weeks. Others don't until they are well and truly established on a mixed diet and are eating meals with the family, and even then they may want breast-feeds at unpredictable times. Some babies adopt a fairly regular pattern for a time, then change their pattern completely or feed quite haphazardly for a while.

Most babies gradually adopt a daily pattern of feeds with a predictable and (to the mother) easy routine in the first part of the day. This routine may be more haphazard in the late afternoon and evening. Many babies want a feed in the morning when they hear the family getting up. The noise of the milkman or postman is a regular signal to some. Lots of babies have a long sleep in the morning after the family has had breakfast and this, surprisingly enough, is one of the last naps to be given up as the child grows. Mid to late morning, after a nap – if there has been one – is time for another feed, and from then on he'll often want to feed when food is being prepared or is on the table. Either they smell the food and find it attractive or they miss being in their mother's arms and want the breast for comfort rather than because of hunger, or they may have become so used to the mother's rhythmical surges of nutrients in her bloodstream which corresponded to her mealtimes that their body clock tells them that her mealtime is also theirs. This isn't a bad thing – although sometimes a nuisance early on – as a baby will sooner or later join the family for meals and if feeds at mealtimes become incorporated into his daily scheme of things, it'll help him with the transition of weaning on to a mixed diet.

As your unpredictable baby grows you'll slowly find the elements of an emerging pattern. The days of unpredictability don't last for ever.

If your temperament is such that you find it difficult to cope with unpredictable feed times, you can try to encourage your baby into some sort of routine and you may be lucky, especially if you're bottle-feeding or if your baby has a natural tendency to regularity. However, if he just doesn't want to be guided into a routine – even a flexible one – then you'll have to try to relax and learn to live with the irregular rhythms of his day, fitting in other things you want to do when he's asleep, and being prepared rarely to finish a job in one attempt. This may be hard, especially if it's your first baby and you've previously held down a busy and exacting job that required punctuality and speed, never starting one job until another was finished. It *is* possible to learn to adjust to your baby though and you may find it helpful to talk to other women who have experienced similar difficulties in the transition from being a working woman to being a mother. If you are breast-feeding, simply belonging to a group of women who understand or want to learn what breast-feeding is all about will encourage and support you. You'll feel less peculiar having a baby who is not only feeding on an unrestricted basis but who is quite unpredictable in his needs if you belong to a group of women such as a La Leche League group, many of whom have had similar experiences and have learnt to accept and enjoy their baby as he is. If your only friends are those whose babies' feeds conform to a schedule, you can feel very out on a limb.

Remember that the ultimate success (apart from nourishing a baby adequately) is to make him happy about feeding, not to conform to someone else's idea of a schedule. *Related topics* Bottle-feeding; breast feeding; breast-feeding problems; demand feeding; mealtimes; under-feeding.

Feelings The greatest mistake that many parents make is to assume that their children, because they are immature as human beings, have no feelings. Nothing could be further from the truth and even tiny babies when deprived of their mothers, for example, can show signs of feeling bad. Children's feelings are very real to them and can't be ignored without paying a price. Some children are more perceptive and sensitive to other people than are some adults and such children can easily be hurt by thoughtless adult behaviour.

The way to get the best out of a young child is never to forget that he or she has feelings, right from the earliest days and that these feelings are enormously dependent on you, the parents. A basic principle of handling the under-fives is that a child is more willing to do things that are followed by good consequences or make him feel good and less likely to do things that give him no reward or make him feel bad. If a child makes a model or a sandcastle and shows it to his parents, what he's seeking is interest and approval from parents. Encouragement comes from the parents' interest and this is reward enough. No sweets or treats have passed hands but the child is undoubtedly just as thrilled as if they had done.

But feelings don't just flow one way. Parents have feelings too, though often they're much too complex for an under-five to understand. He can't be blamed for this but has to be encouraged to understand and respect his parents' and others' feelings. No child should be allowed to reach the age of five without realizing that other people's feelings matter too and that he may have to modify his actions to take them into account. There is little point in trying to instil this in children younger than four or so because the concept is too difficult and they are too self-centred to know what you're talking about.

The way we feel rules our lives whether we are parents or children. Unfortunately sometimes for children, the way adults feel often rules their lives and not always in their favour. If you work on the principle that your child didn't ask to be born and only has to put up with your moods because he has no one else to look after him, it may help you not to take out your feelings on him. Children's extreme sensitivity to people's feelings about them and others shouldn't be underestimated.

Feelings are often infectious and moods of joy or sadness, worry or fear, for example, can spread from parent to child or sometimes from child to parent. Children brought up in homes in which the overriding emotions are those of happiness, confidence and love are lucky and will reap benefits from these early feelings for the rest of their lives. *Related topics* Development – emotional; development – social.

Feet A child's feet need care right from the beginning. A baby is born with pads of fat on the soles of his feet so making him seem flat-footed, but he isn't and the shape of his feet will automatically change as he grows. Keep a baby out of shoes for as long as possible and be sure that sleep suits, socks, tights or whatever is on his feet are big enough so as not to cramp his growing feet. Even a walking baby doesn't need shoes indoors. A pair of warm, large bootees will enable his feet to develop as they should without the unnatural and inevitable restriction of shoes but make sure he doesn't stand or walk on slippery surfaces in them.

Always keep a child's toenails short. In the first few months of life they are so soft that you can bite them off. Later you can trim them straight across with blunt-ended scissors. Once your child starts wearing shoes, always go to a shoe shop that will measure his feet properly.

If ever you are worried about your child's feet, take him to a chiropodist or your doctor. Never attempt to cut off hard skin or to treat verrucae yourself because you could damage good skin and cause infection.

Crooked or webbed toes are common congenital abnormalities but surgery is rarely necessary for either. *Related topics* Curly toes; flat feet; footwear; pigeon toes.

Felt-tip pens Children love these easy-to-use pens but need supervision if they're not to cover their clothes and the furniture with marks. Some pens are made with water-soluble ink which is a good idea. Don't forget that the ink from felt-tip pens bleeds through paper and marks what's underneath so protect whatever the child's paper is resting on from being coloured accidentally. Ink remover is easily available. Most felt-tip pens have ink which is non-toxic but it's worth checking just to be sure because they often get sucked or licked.

Foetal development Caring for your baby starts as soon as he starts developing, that is, at conception. Over the next 38 weeks or so the microscopically tiny two-celled creature formed by the meeting of the sperm and egg will develop into the complex being that is your baby. Your womb is a safe, warm, comfortable environment to which your blood-stream can bring oxygen and food and from which it can take any waste products.

If anything major goes wrong with your baby's development due to an abnormality in the chromosomes carried by the sperm or the egg or due to an infection or other insult, either the baby will be aborted spontaneously, or it's possible that he'll be born with something wrong. Genetic abnor-malities can sometimes occur as spontaneous mutations or they may be passed down by a parent with the disease or carrying the disease. If the baby started off all right but is damaged inside the uterus by German measles, for example, then the type of damage will depend on the developmental stage the baby is at when the infection occurs.

If you want to know how your baby develops, there are several beauti-fully produced books of photographs and diagrams showing foetal development stage by stage. If you have another child old enough to be interested, you might like to show them to him as well. **Related topics** Amniocentesis; antenatal care; genetic counselling; inherited disor-ders; miscarriage; pre-conceptual care; ultrasound.

Fever A rise in a child's normal body temperature. The average body temperature stays remarkably constant at 98.6°F (37°C) but can become raised for many reasons. In young children a fever is usually the result of an infection.

The temperature-regulating mechanisms of children are less effective than those of adults and an ill child can have a large swing in body temperature and soon be better again. A child who is very ill with a fever of 104°F (40°C) one day can be climbing trees the next.

Taking a child's temperature is easily done at home and is probably worth doing if you're not sure whether your child has a fever. Knowing the temperature enables you to lower it if it is very high and so perhaps prevent a fit (see below) and enables you to tell the doctor over the phone so that he can more accurately assess at that stage what might be wrong. Infants have to have their temperatures taken rectally (via their back passage) because they might break off the thermometer in their mouths. Older children can usually keep it under the tongue, where it should be left for the recommended time. We feel that whatever the recommended time it should be kept in place for about three minutes to ensure accuracy. Temperatures taken under the armpit or in the groin are 1°F (0.6°C) lower than the temperature taken in the mouth or back passage. Remember not to take a child's temperature after he's just had a hot or cold drink or food or within an hour of having a bath.

A child with a fever feels ill (especially if it is over 101°F (38.3°C), goes off his food, may sleep fitfully, may have a headache or pain behind the eyes and may have a convulsion if his temperature is very high. In spite of this list of symptoms most children are perfectly happy to be out of bed with temperatures well over 100°F (37.8°C) and should not be made to stay in bed unless the doctor says so, or unless they are keen to rest themselves. A fever is not a very good way of telling how ill your child is. A baby can have a serious illness yet have a normal or low temperature, so don't be a slave to the thermometer but be guided by common sense and your feelings about your child. Parents usually know whether or not their children are ill, whatever the thermometer says.

If your child has a high fever of 103°F (39.4°C) or more, strip all his clothes off, lie him on a bed in a room with no heating and get a bowl of warm water and sponge him down with it. Cool his feet, trunk and limbs and leave a wet, warm flannel in his groin and around his neck, checking his temperature every ten minutes until it comes down below 100°F (37.8°C). Paracetamol reduces body temperature and can be given in the recommended dose. Simply reducing a child's temperature like this makes him feel much better and will do no harm.

A fever makes a child lose lots of fluid as sweat, so give plenty of water, very dilute fruit juice or other fluids as soon as he can be coaxed to drink them. Don't pile on too many covers or bedclothes – a light sheet is enough. The dangers of overheating are far greater than those of overcooling. A child with a fever this high must be seen by a doctor, and if ever you are at all worried by your child's temperature, call him for advice. **Related topics** Convulsions; illness; temperature.

Fifth disease A strangely named 'disease' that may not even be a disease at all. It is so called because it was the fifth illness described with a somewhat similar rash (the others being German measles, measles, scarlet fever, and an atypical form of scarlet fever). The incubation period is, on average, sixteen days (with a range of seven to twenty-eight days) and it is thought to be viral in origin, though there is little evidence for this.

The child with fifth disease has a 'slapped cheek' appearance caused by a bright pink rash on his face. A blotchy rash may be present on the trunk, hands and feet. The rash of fifth disease lasts on average eleven days (with a range of two to thirty-nine days). The rash may be itchy and tends to flare up when the skin is hot. Other symptoms can include a cold, sore throat, headache and diarrhoea. No treatment or isolation is necessary. *Related topics* Itching; rashes; viruses.

Fighting   Between two and five many children start to fight other children. The problem is in knowing how to handle such fights. In general you can't and shouldn't get too deeply involved. Children don't usually take their fights too seriously, and nor should you. Some children persistently fight each other whenever they're together and yet seem to enjoy each other's company. Others, though, fight because they dislike each other and they shouldn't be allowed to play with each other until they get on better.

A few children are bullies and terrorize others at play-group or wherever they are playing. If your child is bullied, either keep him away from the bully, tell the play-group leader who can therefore keep a special eye on the child, tackle the parents of the child, or intervene yourself, explaining to the child how you expect him to behave when with your child. Make sure that your child plays near you or another responsible adult. If it's your child who is always the aggressor, tell him each time how you expect him to behave and prevent him from terrorizing other children by staying near him or asking the play-group leader or any other adult looking after him to keep an eye on him. Some children may be naturally more aggressive than other children and have to learn to control themselves, or, more likely, there may be a problem at home (such as marital instability or a new baby of which they are jealous) which is unconsciously making them behave this way. Don't make him feel that you don't love him because of his behaviour and encourage and praise him when he behaves well.

Basically it's best to let children slug it out themselves as long as no one is getting hurt or upset. If you interfere, do so lovingly and thoughtfully, blaming each as necessary and then distracting their attention to something they can agree on. Peace reigns in minutes this way. Obviously as children grow they get stronger and real physical damage can be done. Toys are thrown, hair pulled out and sometimes blood flows, especially when larger boys are involved. Children who are fighting to hurt the other child can be spotted by the expressions on their faces and their gritted teeth. Puppy fighting, done for fun, is quite different with the children rolling around and enjoying themselves, but even this can turn into a real fight if one child gets hurt and wants to defend himself. Children shouldn't be allowed to harm each other physically whatever the provocation because they simply don't realize how dangerous a momentary lashing out with a sharp toy, for instance, can be. They must also learn that fighting is an unreasonable way of behaving and not acceptable in our society today.

Real fights have to be handled firmly. The 'do as you would be done by' philosophy works well for the fours and fives but isn't as powerful as personal example. Parents often forget that if they are physically aggressive and spend a lot of time fighting with each other (physically or verbally), this rubs off on the children who tend to behave similarly to their friends. If the only way you are seen to be able to get your own way is to hit people (your spouse or your children) your children can only be expected to copy you. If a fight seems imminent, set a good example by resolving the agreement peacefully by discussion. Children have to learn that they can't have things all their own way in life and that some give and take is inevitable. *Related topics* Aggression; behaviour problems.

Finger foods Lots of babies enjoy eating with their fingers because it's much more fun than being spoon-fed by their mothers and if they use a spoon themselves they probably get as much down their bibs as they do into their mouths in the early days. Children of all ages appreciate the informality of eating with their fingers, though a few are so fastidious that they don't like to get their fingers grubby.

Suitable finger foods for babies include toast 'soldiers' (fingers of toast thinly spread with butter); rusks of baked wholemeal bread; washed or peeled carrots; and pieces of peeled and cored apple or pear. Older babies enjoy chips, bread and butter, chunks of meat and fruit of all kinds, peeled and depipped. It's essential to be with a baby while he's eating such foods as a small piece may break off when he bites with his gums and make him choke. Rusks dissolve slowly in a baby's mouth but even so small fragments may break off. If your baby does choke, hook the piece of food out of his mouth with your finger. If it doesn't come out, turn him upside down and pat him firmly on the back to bring up the offending chunk.

Once the danger of choking is past (when a baby's chewing and swallowing mechanisms are properly coordinated), any food can be eaten with the fingers. Bananas, biscuits and tomatoes are just a few of the many suitable foods. Peanuts, small round sweets and sultanas can fairly easily be choked upon if a young child is laughing or talking excitedly as he eats them. They should never be eaten as he runs around and should never be given to young babies. Ideally, save them for when your child is older and more sensible. *Related topics* Baby foods; food.

Finger painting A lovely messy pastime for young children which allows them to enjoy all kinds of new sensations. Not only are the fingers used to apply the paint but also the palms, the backs of the hands and even the arms. Commercial finger paints are available but you can make your own much more cheaply. Take two cups of liquid starch, six cups of water and half a cup of soap pieces or flakes. Dissolve the soap in the water, mix well with the starch, and then add coloured powder paint.

Whatever the surface – plain paper, newspaper, models made from cereal packets, waxed paper and so on – make sure that the child is well protected with an apron (waterproof if possible) and then let him get at it. You can buy or make waterproof plastic cuffs about ten inches (25 cm) long with elastic at both ends to fit over your child's sleeves. These save lots of washing because even rolled-up sleeves often get covered with paint by young children.

Have a paint brush, an old, soft baby's hairbrush, a piece of sponge, old, soft make-up brushes or applicators, shaped pastry cutters and anything else that comes to mind close by, so that your child can learn how to put paint on to paper with something other than his fingers. Don't be afraid to get messy!

Cleaning up after painting takes far longer than the painting itself. Clean the child first, then give him something to do while you clean everything else up. Save the pictures – however primitive – and stick them on the wall when dry so they can be admired. **Related topics** Creativity; painting.

Fire The fire brigade should be called to any fire, no matter how small. If your home catches fire, get everyone out of the house to safety, closing windows, fan lights, doors and so on so that draughts don't feed the fire. Don't assume that someone else has called the fire brigade but call it yourself. Dial 999 and ask for fire. When everyone is safely outside the house you can try to tackle the fire but only if you can do so safely. Use your fire extinguisher if you have one. If you are afraid to go back in the house, or it isn't safe to do so wait for the fire brigade.

If you are trapped by fire, close the door of the room you're in and seal up the cracks with rags, sheets or whatever you have to hand. A draught through the room from the window to the door or from one window to another will fan the fire and will bring smoke into the room. Attract attention at the window by waving something and shouting. If the room fills with smoke, go to the window, open it and lean out to breathe. If you can't do this, lie flat on the floor face down (as there is less smoke low down) until help arrives. If the room begins to burn, tie sheets or other fabric together, secure one end to a heavy piece of furniture and lower yourself down from the window.

If your child's clothes catch fire; push him to the ground *at once* and roll him over repeatedly until the fire is out. If you have a rug, blanket, coat or towel handy, smother the flames with that. Never try to remove burned or charred clothes from a person but leave this to the experts.

Should your frying or chip pan catch fire, put a lid on it or cover it with something such as a damp tea towel that will exclude air and so put the fire out. Never walk across the kitchen with it – the flames will come back at you and you'll drop the lot and set the house on fire.

Every home should have a domestic fire extinguisher, kept where everyone knows where it is, preferably in the hall or somewhere else that is central. Keep an eye on the date that it's due to expire because the contents don't last for ever.

No child under five should be allowed to strike a match, or to play with a lighted candle. Keep matches out of sight and out of reach.

Bonfires must be strictly supervised by an adult and fireworks should never be thrown into a fire. Don't put closed bottles, unopened tins, atomizers or spray cans into a fire and beware of burning plastics which can produce poisonous fumes as they burn. *Related topics* Accident prevention; fires; first aid. *Useful organization* The Royal Society for the Prevention of Accidents.

Fires All fires should be guarded at all times because a moment's lack of vigilance can end in tragedy. It is *illegal* to leave a child under the age of twelve in a room with an unguarded fire. Young children cannot be responsible for their safety. A fireguard for an open or gas fire should be of the cage type that has a roof so that the child can't throw toys over the top of it into the hearth. It should be fixed to the fire surround by clips so that an enterprising toddler can't push it out of the way.

Electric fires should always be unplugged when not in use and should never be used to dry clothes. Convector heaters must have their air intake holes left clear at all times, tempting though it is to use a heater to dry off a small garment or nappy. Fix electric fires so that they can't be knocked over and beware of little hands going through a grille that would be perfectly safe for an adult. Remember that a child under two is too young to understand the danger of fire.

Paraffin heaters should be well fixed to a wall so that they can't be kicked over. Modern ones have a special cut-out which operates when they are knocked over. Paraffin fires need ventilation both to provide oxygen for them to burn and also to get rid of the large amounts of water vapour produced when the paraffin burns.

No child under five should be allowed to operate a domestic fire of any kind. *Related topics* Accident prevention; fire; first aid. *Useful organization* The Royal Society for the Prevention of Accidents.

First aid First aid is exactly what it says it is and nothing more. There are nine main rules. **1.** Look after yourself – don't do anything hazardous that could add you to the casualty list. Get the child and yourself away from the hazard as soon as possible if it is safe to move him. **2.** Check casualties first for breathing, choking, bleeding and unconsciousness. These are really important. **3.** Once you have seen that life is not in danger, get help. Professionals are trained to take risks and responsibilities. **4.** Reassure the injured child and stay with him all the time. **5.** Organize bystanders to help if necessary and especially to ring for an ambulance. **6.** If there are several casualties, decide who needs attention most urgently. **7.** Don't be too afraid to do anything and so do nothing. **8.** Once you have done the basic, simple first aid procedures do nothing else but wait for help. **9.** Always stop when you see an accident. You might be able to help and even save someone's life. One day it could be yours or your child's. *Related topics* Accidents; artificial respiration; bleeding; burns; choking; convulsions; dislocation; drowning; electric shock; fire; first aid kit; foreign bodies; fractures; heart massage; poisoning; shock; suffocation; swallowing dangerous substances.

First aid kit Every home should have a first aid kit and preferably one for the car too. This should be kept in a metal or plastic box, well sealed and in a clean, dry place (not in the steamy bathroom). Make sure everyone in the house knows where the kit is and see that things are topped up as they are used. The box should contain: **1.** A triangular bandage and several large safety pins. **2.** Cotton wool (for cleaning but not for putting on wounds or burns). **3.** White gauze in rolls and/or pads. **4.** Paper tissues (white preferably) in small unopened packs. **5.** Gauze bandages; one 2 in (5 cm) and one 3 in (7.5 cm) wide. **6.** Crêpe bandages; two for putting round bulky dressings or for applying pressure over a pad of gauze on a severely bleeding area. (Beware of applying too tightly). **7.** Some small sizes of tubular gauze bandage – useful for fingers (the packs have an applicator). **8.** Absorbent, non-adhesive dressings. These have gauze on one side and plastic film on the other. The shiny side of the film is placed over a wound or burn and does not stick. The dressings are held in place with a gauze bandage. **9.** Adhesive dressings (sticking plasters) of various sizes. **10.** A pre-packed burns dressing. **11.** Adhesive strapping. **12.** Tweezers for removing splinters. **13.** Scissors for cutting bandages and other dressings. **14.** Pain-relieving tablets (soluble aspirin or paracetamol). Don't keep aspirin for more than a year unless it is foil wrapped. Keep a dosage chart or the original instructions on the packet in the first aid box so that you can give the correct dose. If there is any chance that an ill child may have to have an operation, don't give him any tablets or medicine (or anything else to eat or drink). **15.** Thermometer. **16.** Calamine lotion. **17.** Indigestion tablets. **18.** Travel sickness tablets. **19.** An eye bath. **20.** Inside the lid of the box write your GP's name, address and telephone number and also the address and telephone number of the local accident department of your hospital.

Of course, you don't have to make up your own first aid kit: there are many commercial kits available at a reasonable price.

Firstborn children It is well known as a result of many studies that firstborn children behave differently from later borns. Until the next child is born the firstborn is treated as an only child with all that this entails. He'll probably see himself as special for the rest of his life and it's an interesting fact that there are more 'successful' firstborns (in terms of jobs) than later borns, even allowing for their greater numbers.

Firstborn children have a slightly higher risk of developing emotional problems than have later borns. One reason may date back to their being displaced as the only child in the family when number two comes along. Parents talk to, play with and generally interact more with firstborns (partly because they have more time and also because of the novelty of having a child), so a firstborn has had a lot of adult attention which he suddenly has to share. Most firstborns become clinging after the birth of the next baby and try desperately to regain the attention they have lost. Because many newborn babies sleep a lot, the firstborn may not be aware that his position has changed at first. Some newly-delivered mothers, though, feel tired and weighed down by the labour and by having to look after two children, and tend to be annoyed even by the child's normal demands for attention. Once the baby is awake for much of the time and more alert and demanding of attention himself, the firstborn realizes that he's going to have to start competing for his mother's time and affection. Sometimes it's not until the secondborn can actually crawl over to where the elder child is playing and interfere with what he's doing that the firstborn feels threatened.

Unless you make a special effort to show your first child that you haven't given him up in favour of the new baby you could be in for some aggressive behaviour towards you or the baby. Often a firstborn will turn to his father at this stage and this is an ideal opportunity for a father to forge a good relationship with his child.

If your first child is old enough to understand, explain to him about the new baby plenty of time in advance, involve him in the pregnancy, get him interested and excited and buy a present for the new baby to 'give' him when they first see each other. This usually helps to get things off to a good start. Be sensitive to any quite natural and normal feelings of resentment or jealousy he has and talk about them with him to show him you understand.

When feeding your baby, let your other child have a cuddle too or use the time to play with him quietly or to read to him. If you let the firstborn help with the baby it'll make life a lot easier for him, mainly because he'll have something useful to do that makes him feel wanted and important.

It's always difficult to know how long a gap to leave between babies so as to make it easier for a firstborn but experience shows that a gap of four years or more often makes for greater jealousy. If the new baby is born when the firstborn is less than eighteen months there is often no problem, except for the sometimes exhausted mother.

A gap of eighteen months to two years often produces a jealous reaction in the firstborn. Perhaps 'nature's' gap of two to three years (which happens on average when unrestricted breast-feeding is practised) is ideal from the firstborn's point of view. *Related topics* Family planning – age gaps; jealousy; sibling rivalry.

Five-year-olds – a profile The often frustrating and frustrated four-year-old becomes the sensible five. He is usually curious, enjoys singing, performing and acting and chats happily to anyone. He teases other children readily but hates to be teased back. The problem is that many parents forget that their five-year-old is still a child, so adult and sensible is he. He usually needs lots of sleep because of his active life and begins to want answers to his questions about phenomena such as gravity, rain and pregnancy. His talents become sharper every month and you'll already be able to see roughly where his talents and abilities will lie.

His powers of concentration and staying power have improved enormously by this age and he will want to finish things he starts. He can dress and wash himself on a daily routine basis (or can learn to) and is usually ready for school and all it has to offer. He can (or can learn to) hop, skip, move well to music, climb, swing, dig and has some coordination when throwing, catching or kicking a ball. Most five-year-olds can (or can learn to) thread a needle, sew, read and write letters spontaneously, draw people and animals that are recognizable and have parts, say rhymes, understand stories, say their full name, address, telephone number and birthday, use a knife and fork well, and choose friends to play with. Five-year-olds are also sensitive to other people's feelings including their discomfort or suffering.

Five-year-olds are just worldly enough to enjoy life yet are untainted by the world. They'll never be quite the same again.

Flat feet A condition in which the foot sits flat on the floor over its whole lower surface instead of having an arch along its inner side. All babies feet appear to be flat because of the pads of fat they have on the inner sides of their soles. Even when these pads of fat disappear many young children still have feet that look flat but this is nothing to worry about. Most such children do not become flat-footed adults. If when your child stands on tip toe his feet arch there is no cause for concern.

If you are worried about your child's feet, see your doctor who may send your child to an orthopaedic surgeon for an opinion. Foot exercises for flat-footed children are of no proven value but many doctors think they are worth doing just in case.

A child who has flat feet that are painful on exercise will need help from your family doctor or an orthopaedic surgeon. He may prescribe a shoe with a specially-extended heel. ***Related topic*** Feet.

Fleas Small wingless insect parasites of mammals. In this country dog, cat and human fleas are the commonest.

Fleas usually live in the coats of domestic pets. These may jump on to a person and bite him but only a human flea will live on a person for long. Although most people link fleas with filth, this is unfair because any furry animal can harbour fleas, even if it is well cared for. Fleas can be eradicated (ask your vet or pet shop for advice) but are rarely cleared for long and your pet will need re-treating from time to time.

Flea bites cause small, red, itchy pimples. Some people have an allergic reaction to flea bites in which the area around the bite itself shows up as a wheal. Bites can occur in the absence of the pet that is affected. Carpets, beds and upholstery can harbour fleas but a suitable insecticide powder can be used to get rid of them. Call a pest control company or your local authority environmental health department if you cannot seem to control fleas in your house.

Local treatment for flea bites consists of using a bland lotion such as calamine and an antihistamine medicine if the allergic reaction to the bites is severe.

Keep the insecticides you are using to kill off the fleas well away from babies, young children and pregnant mums. ***Related topics*** Itching; pets.

Floppy baby A 'floppy' baby is one who feels limp when you hold him, rather like a rag doll. This is because his muscles offer little or no resistance when they are moved. When lying on his back a floppy baby tends to lie with his thighs splayed wide apart and if you pick up one of his limbs, it'll drop back down again, unlike that of a normal baby who's awake.

There are a number of reasons for floppiness in a newborn baby, among them a form of cerebral palsy; mental retardation (Down's babies, for example are usually floppy to some degree; and various disorders of the brain, spinal cord, muscles and nerves. If necessary tests will be done to try to make a diagnosis but parents of some of these babies will be told that there is no known cause for the condition and that it is likely to improve spontaneously in time. Such babies will be slow to gain head control, to sit up, to roll over, to crawl and to walk but will catch up completely, or almost completely, eventually.

You'll soon get used to handling your baby who is abnormally floppy even though you may have had a baby with normal muscular resistance before. It makes sense to be extra careful not to 'overbend' or 'overstretch' your baby's joints because he'll lack the normal protective muscular resistance. Make sure that all his clothing is easy to put on and take off and remember that you'll have to continue to protect his head from lolling back and forth.

All of this assumes that you are aware that your baby is 'floppy'. If you find your baby suddenly floppy, tell your doctor urgently.

Fluoride A naturally-occurring mineral present in varying amounts in drinking water and also added to it in certain areas where the natural level is low. It is added to some toothpastes and used in drops and tablets for children to help prevent tooth decay. Because dental caries (decay) is so widespread and costs such a fortune to treat and control, it makes sense to try to prevent it. In areas with little natural fluoride in the water, increasing the level of fluoride in the water or in the diet of young children reduces dental decay by at least half – a protection which seems to last into adult life.

There is, however, considerable debate on the subject of added fluoride, especially on its inclusion in drinking water, which many see as an infringement of personal liberty and a hazard to those who consume very large quantities of tap water.

It makes sense to use fluoride toothpaste as the fluoride acts directly on the teeth but make sure that your young child spits it out and doesn't swallow much of it or he could get fluoride toxicity, (which will cause white mottling of his teeth). If he persistently swallows the toothpaste it is probably better to use one without fluoride.

Parents have to decide for themselves whether or not to give additional fluoride to their children but the evidence is in favour of babies and children living in low fluoride drinking water areas having it as drops or tablets until they are twelve years old as well as brushing with a fluoride toothpaste.

Giving too much fluoride can result in the teeth becoming mottled. **Related topics** Dental caries; teeth; toothpaste.

Fontanelles (soft spots) Spaces between the bones of a baby's skull
that enable them to slide over each other as his head is compressed coming down the birth canal and to grow as his brain grows. All the fontanelles gradually close over with bone but the last one to close (in the centre line near the front of the skull) may remain open until about fifteen months. It is usually completely closed by eighteen months.

This fontanelle may sometimes bulge or be sunken, but such changes are normal in a healthy baby. Pulsation is also quite normal. If your baby is unwell and the fontanelle is bulging or sunken, ask your doctor to see him. There is no need to treat your baby's soft spot any differently from the rest of his head. You can wash over it or brush the hair over it just as you treat the rest of his head.

Food Children need a diet made up of a balance of the main food groups
(proteins, carbohydrates, fats, vitamins, minerals etc.) just as adults do in order to stay healthy.

Babies rely totally on milk for their nutritional needs and breast milk is without doubt the best. Research from all over the world points to the fact that for ideal health and growth a baby should be given breast milk exclusively for at least the first three to six months of life. Cows' milk formulae are convenient substitutes for breast milk but are nowhere near as good in many ways. When a mother cannot (which is rare) or – much more likely – chooses not to breast-feed, then cows' milk formulae are life-saving. That is not to say that donated milk from another mother (or actual wet-nursing) is not superior, and in this country many premature babies are nowadays given donated breast milk because doctors agree that it is better for them than formula feeding.

From six months on, babies should be gently accustomed to the foods the rest of the family eats. There is no reason to treat children differently from the rest of the family when it comes to food. Just give them a little of whatever you are eating and they'll do well – provided, of course, that what you eat is nutritious. It's sensible to give your baby only one new food at a time so that in the unlikely event of a food allergy reaction, you'll know what caused it.

There's little doubt that most people's diets today are not nutritionally good, tend to make them fat, and encourage tooth decay and constipation. This is totally unnecessary and is a bad start for a child. A child's growing body is vulnerable to all of these hazards and especially to tooth decay. The answer then is to eat healthily as a family. This involves cutting out all added sugar; cutting down on all products containing sugar; eating high-fibre foods and avoiding foods made from white flour; and cutting down greatly on the amount of fat, salt and foods containing additives and preservatives that you eat. All of these subjects are covered elsewhere in the book in more detail.

Any family who eats like this will be very unlikely to have fat children, will almost never have dental decay (especially if they're also using a fluoride toothpaste) and will never be constipated. That's not a bad start.

Vitamins are a cause of concern to many parents who assume that their children should necessarily be given vitamin supplements. This is not necessary if the children are eating a balance of healthy foods but if you want to give your child extra vitamins they won't do him any harm in the recommended dose.

A most important way to create a healthy diet for your children is to keep to a minimum the amounts of food additives you feed them. Get used to reading labels on everything and keep away from foods which have artificial colours, flavours, preservatives, emulsifiers and so on. Some of these chemicals haven't been sufficiently well tested – indeed some that are permitted in this country are banned in others. There are almost always fresh, additive-free products around and often they don't cost any more. The insidious build-up of such chemicals in our children's bodies is far too poorly understood to be dismissed as unimportant so, if at all possible, use fresh foods and when you can't, go for those with the absolute minimum of additives. **Related topics** Baby foods; breast milk; dietary fibre; food allergy; milk; salt; sugar; vegetarian diet; vitamins; weaning.

Food allergy Although today's parents could be forgiven for thinking that food allergy is a new medical fashion, this isn't the case. Hippocrates described allergy to cows' milk in 400 BC and the treatment of many ailments by dietary manipulation and exclusion was common until a century ago. With the coming of research-based medicine doctors were frustrated by the fact that there were no reliable tests to prove that some people were allergic to foods and they suggested that many food allergy symptoms were 'all in the mind'. Over the past few years our understanding of the body's immune system has come a long way and we can now measure antibodies to foods.

There is no doubt that food allergy is a real entity and can play a part in conditions as seemingly different as eczema, urticaria (nettlerash), migraine and several others. In fact many diffuse and ill-defined symptoms are now being cured by dietary manipulation.

Research in newborn animals has found that the lining of their intestines lets through certain proteins from their food into their bloodstream. This leakage induces the formation of protective antibodies and the animal builds up a resistance to these proteins in its diet. In a human baby fed on breast milk, the permeability of the intestine is reduced in such a way as to let very few foreign protein molecules from a mixed diet through into the bloodstream. He slowly builds up a tolerance to foods and so is later not affected by them. Bottle-fed babies on the other hand have no protective breast milk to reduce their intestinal permeability and foreign proteins (at first, cows' milk protein) may leak through in large amounts.

It is well known that bottle-fed infants are four times as likely to suffer from gastro-intestinal disturbances as breast-fed ones; and that respiratory syncytial virus infections and otitis media are much less common in breast-feds. Studies have proven that completely and solely breast-feeding a baby can reduce his likelihood of suffering from eczema to one seventh of that of bottle-fed babies. Research in Finland has found that six months of exclusive breast-feeding can nullify the effects of even the worst family histories of allergy. So exclusive breast-feeding for six months or so is the best start in protecting your child against food allergies.

The commonest foods to which Western children are allergic are wheat, milk, eggs, pork, peanuts, cheese, tomatoes, coffee and chocolate. Artificial colours and preservatives can also cause allergic reactions. Certain skin tests may be helpful but the best test of all is to remove the suspected food from the diet and see if the child gets better. It takes a couple of weeks before you can be sure that the results are reliable. If on re-introducing the food the trouble recurs you can be sure that the food is at fault and can thereafter exclude it from the child's diet completely.

Medical knowledge about food allergy is still in its early stages, but more is being clarified each year. It is no longer a 'cranky' diagnosis and can undoubtedly help countless thousands of anguished parents who have children with allergic symptoms. Unfortunately, there are few doctors in the UK who are well versed on the latest findings on food allergy, so getting medical help can be difficult. Try excluding likely culprits from your child's diet (always making sure though that the excluded food is replaced in terms of nourishment by other foods) and if there is no improvement, see your family doctor. *Related topics* Allergy; breast milk; eczema; milk intolerance; rashes; urticaria.

Food poisoning

Food poisoning An infection of the intestines caused by consuming infected food or drink. There is usually diarrhoea and there may also be vomiting and a fever. Food poisoning can be caused either by bacteria or by the poisonous toxins they produce. Most cases of food poisoning are caused by types of the Salmonella organism: typhoid is one of the most serious of these diseases. Most food poisoning (now the second most common infectious illness in Europe) is caused by other, less harmful strains of Salmonella.

Salmonella food poisoning produces fever, colicky abdominal pain, nausea and vomiting, aching limbs and diarrhoea – all of which come on between eight and twenty-four hours after eating the contaminated food. The illness lasts only a few days. In young babies, infections such as these can cause such severe dehydration that the baby can become seriously ill or even die if not treated quickly. It is this type of Salmonella food poisoning that goes around schools and institutions, especially during the summer months when the bacteria breed very quickly in unrefrigerated food.

Food poisoning can almost always be prevented by taking care with hygiene and in the storage and preparation of food. Your and your children's hands should always be washed before and after handling food (especially meat and poultry). Utensils should also be kept scrupulously clean. Meat and poultry are especially at risk of infection and these should be kept in a refrigerater at all times and if reheated, should be thoroughly cooked and not just warmed up. Frozen food, especially poultry, must be thoroughly thawed before cooking.

Staphylococcal food poisoning comes on a lot quicker (two to six hours) than Salmonella poisoning. The whole disease is shorter-lived but can be very violent with severe diarrhoea and vomiting. Processed peas and canned meats have been implicated in this sort of food poisoning.

If your child gets food poisoning the main thing is to encourage him to drink. He may vomit even after water but will absorb some as long as he isn't sick as soon as he has drunk it. Should the child be so severely ill that he can't or won't take fluid by mouth he may have to go to hospital to have fluids intravenously. The younger he is, the more likely this is. If ever your child vomits for more than six hours, call your doctor for his advice. A vomiting baby may need professional attention sooner. There is no need to stop breast-feeding a baby who gets food poisoning whilst on a mixed diet as long as he wants to suck. When it comes to the bottle-fed baby, though, you may have to stop giving him his usual bottle and if he is severely dehydrated it's best to give half-strength milk formula or even a special solution suggested by your doctor. Discuss this with your doctor if you are at all worried.

A child with food poisoning should be kept at home until he is completely well again. **Related topics** Bed – ill child in; dehydration; diarrhoea; illness; vomiting.

Footwear The two most basic reasons for wearing anything on our feet are to protect them from whatever we are walking on, be it sharp, rough, hot, cold, dirty or whatever, and to keep them warm and dry. Less important in practical terms, footwear can be decorative.

A commonly asked question is at what age should a child first have shoes. The answer isn't straightforward. Even a young baby *can* have shoes if you like the look of babies in shoes. These are obviously mainly for decoration at this age, though they'll keep his feet warm to some extent. However, shoes are completely unnecessary early on and may even be harmful if the movements of the feet and toes are restricted in any way. When a baby starts putting weight on his feet (which is often from a very early age), you'll notice that his feet and toes curl up and almost seem to grip whatever they're standing on. Shoes are bound to restrict this movement to some extent.

When a baby first stands alone, his foot muscles work hard to help him balance. The same applies when he walks. Ideally, he is best left without shoes unless his feet need to be protected from whatever he is walking on. You'll have to use your common sense about this. A baby's first pair of shoes is sometimes something of a status symbol among a group of mothers with children of about the same age. Ideally though, the longer you can keep your child out of shoes, the better.

Separate knitted or fabric booties or the booties incorporated into all-in-one stretch suits, dungarees and so on all keep a baby's feet warm effectively. Separate booties usually have a ribbon or a knitted cord slotted and tied round the ankle and it's all too easy to tie these up too tightly in an effort to get them to stay on. A danger with these, but especially with stretch suit feet, is that they can cramp the toes if they are at all tight. Unless the feet of a stretch suit are really loose, put your baby into the next size or, if the rest of the suit fits, cut the fabric off at the ankles or across the toes. Some mothers sew on a pair of socks of the right size instead. When your baby is walking, unless he needs shoes to protect his feet, you'll find that booties (specially large knitted ones made out of thicker wool than for non-walking babies) will stay on far more reliably than socks. Socks have a habit of slowly coming off and babies frequently stand on the trailing bit and trip themselves up.

Whatever age your child is, his socks should be loose enough for his toes to wiggle easily. Small stretch nylon socks can restrict the toes almost as much as poorly fitting shoes. Socks keep the feet drier and more pleasant smelling if they are made at least partly of cotton or wool. At any age you'll have to be sure that your baby or young child wearing socks or booties only, stays off polished or shiny floors. A baby can't learn to walk if his booties make him slip and slide all over the place. It's best to let him go barefoot if possible or, if not, he should wear non-slip shoes or slippers.

You'll find your child's feet will grow rapidly during his second and third years especially and you'll need to have them checked. Shoes that are too small can not only make the toes or heels sore where they rub but can also cramp the toes and make them grow in a bad position and may even cause ingrowing toenails.

A good shoe shop will be only too pleased to measure your child's feet and will tell you whether new shoes are advisable or whether his feet still have room for growth inside the old ones. The amount of space allowed for growth in a pair of newly-fitted shoes is generally the equivalent of half a shoe size. If your child has feet of different sizes, you'll obviously have to buy shoes to fit the larger foot. If the size difference is large, one shoe company will supply shoes of different sizes. If the difference is not too much – for instance, half a size, the child will come to little harm with one foot in a shoe too big for it. If it is uncomfortably large though and the foot seems to slip around, ask the shop assistant if she can supply a foam cushion to go at the back of the shoe. Shoes must fit not only in length but also in width and depth. Straps and buckles should be comfortable too and easy to do up and undo, especially if a child is old enough to want to do this himself. Beware of the shaped edge of the upper of the shoe which may cut into a child's plump foot when he has been wearing it for some time.

Increasing numbers of children's shoes are being sold with quite a raised heel on them. This is not a good idea as the alignment of the joints in the child's ankle, knee and spine are altered from their normal position to compensate for this raise. Choose shoes which are as flat as possible and put the foot into a position which resembles being barefoot as closely as possible.

It is often said that it is preferable to buy shoes made of leather. In fact it is difficult to find shoes nowadays that have leather soles: most are of a composition material which is synthetic. However, you can buy shoes with leather uppers and it is worth doing this because the sweat from your child's feet won't be trapped next to his skin as it is in shoes with synthetic uppers. Trapped sweat encourages athlete's foot and soreness between the toes. If your child does have a pair of shoes made totally from synthetic material, at least put him in cotton socks to absorb some of the sweat.

Wellington boots are only sold in full sizes, (not in half sizes) but are usually fairly large for their size compared with shoes. Make sure that your child is measured for his boots in the socks he'll be wearing with his boots if they are thicker than those he usually wears. The higher the boot comes up the leg, within reason, the better, so that your child is less likely to get wet when he walks in puddles.

Slippers too are sold in full sizes. When your child's feet grow enough for him to need new shoes, remember to get his slippers and boots and other footwear checked too. Because slippers sometimes stretch, new ones may not be needed quite so often. Choose slippers that don't come off too easily or your child could have an accident running or going up or down stairs in them. Sew in bands of elastic across the top of the foot if necessary.

It's not only a nuisance but is also potentially dangerous if a child's shoes come off easily or if he has to make an effort to keep them on. Shoes with laces or straps, or sandals allow him to forget about his feet as he runs around. Some young children manage very well with clogs and flip-flops but clogs can be difficult to run in and heavy to wear, while flip-flops make some children's toes sore where the thong goes between them.

Should you pass footwear on from child to child? The shoe trade says 'no' because a child moulds the shoe to the shape of his own foot, which might not be the same as that of the next child even if it is the same size. Also, some children distort their shoes to some extent, for example by wearing the heel down at one side or by making the back of the shoe round the ankle sloppy. (Growing ankles don't need support. Millions of children in the past have managed perfectly well without shoes and still do today.)Whatever the shoe trade says, lots of parents do pass shoes on, partly because they are so expensive to buy new for each child. Passing on applies particularly to young children's shoes which are often hardly worn by one child compared with those of older children who are rougher on their feet. Older children really do wear their shoes out so the question doesn't often arise. If you do intend to pass shoes on, at least make quite sure that they are the right size by getting the child's feet measured. They shoukd be the right width as well as the right length. If the heel is worn down on one side, get it repaired. Boots and slippers can be passed on without qualms, as can flip-flops, sandals, ballet shoes and plimsolls. *Related topic* Feet.

Forceps delivery A pair of forceps may be used to help a baby out of the womb during the second stage of labour.

Forceps deliveries are done for a variety of reasons including to shorten the labour for the mother who has, for example, high blood pressure or heart disease; for foetal distress; to protect the soft head of a premature baby; and to help out a baby who is stuck during the second stage of labour. Women who choose to have an epidural anaesthetic are more likely to need a forceps delivery. They are only used if the cervix is fully dilated (open) and if the obstetrician is sure that there is room for the baby to come out. If there is any doubt a Caesarean section is done instead.

Usually an episiotomy is needed to make enough room for the forceps blades to be put into the birth canal. One blade is put on each side of the baby's head then the two blades are connected and the obstetrician skilfully pulls the baby out. It takes only a minute or so for this to be done. Pain relief can be obtained with any of the usual methods, though very occasionally a general anaesthetic is necessary.

Babies delivered by forceps sometimes have marks on their skins at the sides of their head for a few days only. Occasionally a nerve may be squeezed by the blades and you'll notice a weakness of one side of your baby's face. This too will disappear quickly. If your baby's head seems to be a strange, squashed shape, don't worry because the soft skull bones are easily and safely distorted yet will return to normal soon enough. Babies born with the aid of forceps suffer no long term effects from them. *Useful organizations* Association for Improvements in the Maternity Services; The National Childbirth Trust; The Birth Centre.

Foreign body Splinters are undoubtedly the commonest of foreign bodies but are usually not a problem. Wash the area gently and then dislodge the splinter with a sterilized needle tip before pulling it out with fine tweezers or washed fingernails. To sterilize a needle, pass it through a flame and then let it cool, or boil it for ten minutes instead. If the splinter has gone deeply or is of glass, don't try to do anything yourself but go straight to a hospital casualty department.

Another common foreign body is grit in a wound after a fall on to a road. This has to be removed or the wound could go septic. Severe grazes with gravel or dirt must be cleaned well and again may need professional attention. Badly cleaned, deep grazes can become infected and produce an unsightly scar so it's worth taking trouble.

Grit in the eye is a common complaint. Small pieces are usually washed away by the excess tears that are formed. If your child gets something in his eye, ask him if he can tell you where it is. Don't let him rub his eye or he could scratch the delicate surface. If the foreign body doesn't come out in the tears in a few minutes, pull down the lower lid and remove the grit with the corner of a clean handkerchief or a wisp of cotton wool. If the speck of grit isn't visible it could be under the upper lid. Place a matchstick on the upper lid and pull the lid upwards over it so that you can see its underside. Remove the grit as already suggested.

If ever your child sticks anything into his nose or ears, unless it's very superficial, don't attempt to remove it but take your child to a doctor. Remember that a nosebleed or a pussy discharge from a nostril can be caused by a foreign body there.

Children sometimes swallow things they shouldn't but most pass through the stomach and bowels uneventfully. Always keep small objects out of the reach of babies and toddlers, especially safety and other pins, which are extremely dangerous. A foreign body stuck in the gullet or the windpipe needs very urgent attention, so call an ambulance. More rarely, a child will inhale something right down into his lung. Although this is serious, surgeons can nowadays look down into the lungs with a special instrument and remove a foreign body, often quite easily, without an operation.

Foreskin The loose skin at the end of a boy's penis. At birth it usually covers the tip but as the boy gets older it becomes free from the tip and can be pulled back.

At birth a baby's foreskin sticks to the tip of the penis and only becomes separated as he grows. It has usually separated by the third or fourth year and there is no need to consult a doctor unless the foreskin can't be pulled back at the age of five.

The ideal way to look after your baby's foreskin is to leave it alone except to wash gently under it as and when it will pull back easily. If matter is allowed to collect under the foreskin, the penis can become inflamed. Never force the foreskin back though because you could cause permanent scarring and this may mean the boy will have to have a circumcision later.

Circumcision is the removal of the foreskin from the end of the penis. Circumcision is not a common operation today but is still done occasionally for religious or medical reasons. Until ten to fifteen years ago the operation was much demanded by parents and the medical profession was happy to perform routine circumcisions. This has now changed because it is known that circumcision can lead to infection, bleeding and scar tissue formation and there are always dangers, however small, in having a general anaesthetic. Circumcision at birth or very soon after is sometimes carried out without an anaesthetic but this is less commonly done today because it is obviously very painful. Jewish boys are still circumcised on the eighth day and Muslim boys between their third and fifteenth year.

Having a boy circumcised simply so that he looks like his circumcised father is not a good reason for having the operation and few doctors today would agree to it. *Related topics* Hypospadias; phimosis; smegma.

Foster care A form of child care in which a child is looked after by a family other than its own. There are several different types of fostering ranging from day fostering (a sort of child-minding) to permanent arrangements which are nearly as final as adoption except that the foster parents aren't legally the parents of the child.

Foster care is more complex and probably less satisfactory in some ways than adoption because the foster parents never have absolute responsibility for the child in their care – the real parents still have considerable rights. Foster parents often see themselves as substitute parents but the child care agencies see them as caretakers or therapists. This can be confusing because the child is cared for by a three-way system: the child care agency, his own parents and the foster parents and this can be confusing for him too.

Children who need fostering are of all ages from babies (who often need only very short term care before going back to their mothers) to teenagers who may stay with their foster families for years. Foster parents are paid an allowance to cover the cost of looking after the child and the rates vary with where you live, the age of the child, and the type of problem (if any) that the child presents to the foster parents. Most foster parents already have a family of their own and feel that they can offer something to another, less fortunate, child for a variable period of time.

Fostering can be especially difficult when it comes to the natural parents visiting the child because it is difficult for them and can have an upsetting effect on the child's new relationship with his foster parents. Having said this, the future looks fairly bright for fostering as a part of a system of care for children who don't have parents able to look after them. Fostering is increasingly being done by childless couples who then enjoy a family life that they otherwise would not have. *Related topic* Adoption. *Useful organization* British Agencies for Adoption and Fostering.

Four-year-old – a profile The four-year-old child is rapidly becoming more and more independent and is usually happy to go away from his mother to a familiar place and familiar people for a few hours at a time. He can climb, jump, hop, skip and ride a tricycle and is deft with his hands, using scissors and brushes skilfully. He has a wide vocabulary and talks a lot, trying out new phrases and words and sometimes even making them up. He loves imaginative games, especially those involving dressing up, as well as board games; enjoys a joke; makes up stories and likes to listen to them; can sing or say several nursery rhymes; begins to understand abstract concepts like time; and asks lots of questions. He's a busy and fascinating child to be with and is much less frustrating than in the past because he's so cooperative and enthusiastic. At the same time, he sometimes quickly reverts to babyhood and becomes maddeningly unreasonable, especially when tired. Four-year-olds are easily bored and although increasingly self-motivated still need a lot of your attention.

Your four-year-old can probably kick a ball, catch it, throw it and bounce it, and hit it with a bat. He can go upstairs with one foot per step and is increasingly agile, running round corners and on tiptoe. He can handle tiny objects such as beads very accurately but still hasn't enough coordination (or patience) to thread a needle. He knows his colours, can give his name and address, can count up to twenty (if he's been taught) from his head or can count up to five things. He holds a pencil like an adult and can draw a recognizable man with head, body, legs and probably arms too. If he's interested in letters he'll copy several of them and he'll be able to draw a cross.

As for looking after himself, the four-year-old can feed himself well, using either a knife and fork or a fork and spoon (or sometimes just a spoon). He can clean his teeth, although you may want to do them again afterwards to make sure they are well brushed. He can dress and undress himself but needs help with difficult sleeve buttons, back zips, and stiff shoe fastenings.

He's an attractive child in that he recognizes when others are feeling sad and tries to cheer them up. He also looks after younger brothers or sisters, though you can't rely on him to look after a young baby without supervision. You mustn't let him near a road because he has little, if any, traffic sense. Four-year-olds are often rude and answer back sometimes as though to test themselves against you. Respond gently and firmly and make it clear that it's neither kind nor attractive to be rude. Watch how you speak to your child because he'll copy the way you do things accurately, right down to the tone of voice you use when telling him to do something.

The four-year-old is sociable and increasingly plays with other children, sometimes developing complex games. He has strong likes and dislikes for his playmates but these often change and are fickle – today's enemy can become tomorrow's friend. He enjoys having a friend to tea and being invited back but is usually happier only to be away for half the day at most. Four-year-olds are so busy that they're very tired at the end of the day, so you mustn't expect too much of them.

Fractures A break in a bone. Children often fall and so are more prone to fractures than are adults. Fortunately, their young bones aren't brittle and bend considerably when stressed. They also heal much quicker than adult bones when they fracture.

It's often difficult (or impossible) to tell the difference between a fracture and a bad sprain without the help of x-rays and a medical opinion is always wise if a damaged area seems to be getting more painful and not less so as the hours go by. You can often tell if a child has a fracture by the following signs. There is usually pain over the fracture; there may be swelling or bruising there; there is a loss or severe restriction of movement of the affected area; and there may be an obvious deformity (bending, angularity or even floppiness) of the affected part.

The best thing to do if you suspect a fracture is to get medical help. Don't move the child at all if you think he might have fractured anything other than an arm because you could do more harm than good.

An x-ray will confirm the fracture which then may have to be re-aligned and held in the proper position until it has healed. The majority of common fractures in children involve the long bones which bend and crack (a greenstick fracture) rather than actually break clean across. A plaster of Paris cast around such a simple fracture will see it healed in a few weeks. More serious fractures, such as those produced by a car accident, will have to be set under a general anaesthetic and then held in a plaster for several weeks.

A life-threatening fracture that needs immediate emergency care in children is a skull fracture. If ever your child hits his head and loses consciousness, even for a short time, it's wise to get him to an accident and emergency department at a hospital. A child can fracture his head without an obvious wound and conversely serious head wounds don't necessarily mean there's a fracture underneath. If ever your child becomes drowsy, vomits, becomes pale, or has colourless or blood-stained fluid coming from his nose or ears after a fall, get medical help at once. *Related topic* Falls.

Fresh air A lot of nonsense has been talked about the value of fresh air to children, as if the average home contained air that was in some way unhealthy. The reasons for getting children out of doors today have nothing to do with the air.

A child will enjoy being out of doors to play in a more vigorous and unrestricted way than is possible indoors and this is what he likes so much. Running, jumping and climbing have to be restricted indoors and so must be done outside.

The only other advantage (apart from getting out from under their parents' feet, which can be very beneficial to the parents as well as to the children!) is to get some sunshine. When the sun shines the ultraviolet light acts on a naturally-occurring chemical in the skin to produce vitamin D which is essential for healthy bone growth. Children who don't get enough sun can develop rickets from this lack of vitamin D. Research has found that in this country the average white child getting out into the sun during the summer builds up enough vitamin D to last him through the winter even in the climate of the UK. This goes for babies too especially if they are totally breast-fed by mothers who in turn have had their fair share of sunshine. A certain amount of vitamin D-producing ultraviolet light filters through the clouds even on a dull day.

In the summer, if the house is hot and stuffy, it can be pleasant for a baby to be placed in the shade in his pram outside to get cooler.

Another reason for getting your baby or young child into the fresh air is if it means that you enjoy doing something with him, for example taking him for a walk in his pram. There is undoubtedly some psychological benefit from doing things out of doors especially in a climate such as ours in northwest Europe which keeps us indoors for so much of the year. **Related topic** Exercise; rickets; vitamins.

Fretful baby A baby who is unsettled, whines or cries a lot and just doesn't seem happy a lot of the time.

You could treat two babies the same way and yet one could be a contented baby and the other fretful. However, this is not to say that treating a fretful child differently might not improve him. Babies are different right from birth – which is scarcely surprising as each one has a completely different genetic make-up (except for identical twins and triplets). Unfairly, perhaps, some babies are simply more contented than others.

If your baby is fretful, don't compare what you are doing with what any other mother is doing to her baby but concentrate on *your* baby and on what you might be able to do to make him happier. Most important, make sure he is well. This means checking with your family doctor or the doctor at the baby clinic. If he is healthy, consider whether your feeding technique might be troubling him. If he's not thriving, then you may need to increase your milk supply. If he is thriving, then perhaps more frequent feeds would make him more comfortable than spaced-out ones. Think about what you are eating. Sometimes certain foods can upset breast fed babies. Wind-producing foods such as cabbage and baked beans may be the culprits, as may onions, alcohol, chocolate and unfamiliar spicey or Chinese food. Some babies need to spend a lot of time at the breast and you may decide to let him suck as much as he likes and spend much more of your day sitting with him. Once you've decided to do this you'll relax. If you keep fighting off accepting that this is what your baby wants and trying to make him do without it, you'll continue to have a fretful baby on your hands. Some mothers try to get round having their baby at the breast for what may sometimes seem like a lot of the day by giving a dummy. As long as the baby is getting enough milk, then this may help the situation. If he is still fretful in spite of having a dummy, then it's probably you that he wants, not the dummy.

Frequently, a fretful baby is trying to tell his mother that he wants to be with her more, though not necessarily at her breast. Babies are often thought to need more sleep than they actually do and are put in their cots when they could manage quite happily awake with the rest of the family. Be guided by your baby on this and don't leave him unhappy at any time. If he is awake and fretful, he may just want to be held or carried. Babies have been carried around by their mothers since time immemorial, so why not try carrying yours? Buy or make a sling as you can do a lot with a baby in a sling and there's no need to be idle while your jobs for the day mount up.

Colic is a cause of fretfulness or downright discomfort and crying. Teething is a well-known reason for babies being whiney. Illnesses such as a cold or earache or any of the childhood infections can make a baby miserable. Often fretfulness is the first sign of one of these and may continue for a day or two before you realize that he is sickening for something.

Temporary fretfulness can be caused by a dirty or wet nappy or by being too hot or too cold. Uncomfortable clothing can irritate a baby too. Every mother knows that sometimes a sleepy or tired baby gets fretful. Young breast-fed babies will nearly always drop off to sleep at the breast if they need sleep. If your baby is unaccustomed to going to sleep at the breast, you may need to walk around with him or rock him. Lots of parents have discovered the trick of taking their baby for a car ride or a ride in the pram to get him off to sleep. Smoke is irritating to lots of babies, so avoid smoky rooms and don't let anyone blow smoke near your baby.

We all feel grouchy sometimes and babies are no exception. They often sense the family's mood and are happy or miserable accordingly. Usually, with a bit of intuition, thought, common sense or experimenting, you'll be able to meet your baby's needs and make him happier. Your baby's disposition can affect the whole family for good or bad and can alter your feelings towards him, so any way of keeping him happy is worth considering, quite apart from how much better it is for him. If ever you feel you can't cope with your fretful baby, get help at once. **Related topics** Child abuse; colic; crying; feeding schedules.

Friendships – children's

Babies and one- and two-year-olds by and large tend to play alongside other children, doing their own thing, rather than with them in any cooperative way. Not till three or four do most children start to play in groups or pairs, or to join in games which are not entirely self-centred. However, right from early babyhood, babies are fascinated by other children, often preferring to watch them rather than adults. This is probably because they move faster and speak in higher pitched voices. Babies can become very fond of other children, recognizing them and getting excited when they appear. They are fairly indiscriminate though and another child can easily win their affection with a bit of effort.

Young children play with other children who live nearby, whose mothers are friends of their mothers, or who attend the same toddler group, play-group or crêche. Children who go to a minder or a day nursery class play with other children there. Because their regular playmates are familiar, they single them out in a group situation with lots of strange children, but this doesn't necessarily mean that they are 'friends' in the accepted sense of the word. Sometimes though, strong bonds of affection do form between regular playmates and such friendships can be longlasting. It's obvious that even quite young children know who they like and who they dislike, but these feelings are very fickle and the favoured child can fall out of favour very quickly.

Friendships are formed for complex reasons: a child may be attracted by how another child looks; what he says; what toys he has; whether or not the other child likes him and makes overtures towards him; and by a much more indeterminate feeling of simply being drawn towards him. If your child takes a liking towards another child, make an effort to ensure that they have a chance to play together. This is particularly important for an only child. Perhaps invite the child round to your house, with or without his mother, or take him with you somewhere on an outing.

When one child in a family has a friend round, there's a distinct possibility that he may be 'stolen' by a brother or sister. As this will inevitably cause tears of rage or unhappiness, you'll have to step in and suggest ways for them all to play together. Threesomes often end up squabbling and you'll find that it may pay to invite a friend for each child.

What happens if you don't like the friends your child chooses? It would be glib to say that this shouldn't make any difference to how you behave, but in human terms it shouldn't. If you find the friend rude or unpleasant, let your child play with him and invite him round as you would any other child, but every so often gently point out to your child (privately) what it is in that child that you don't want him to copy. Praise his good points as well so as not to be destructively critical towards the friend. To a certain extent if you criticize your child's friend, you are criticizing your child's choice, and that won't go unnoticed. With tact and loving care, your child's friend may be influenced by your family to lose some of his unpleasant traits, though if his background is full of problems you probably won't have much effect. While he is with you, treat him as you would your own child. If he behaves badly, tell him so and tell him how you expect him to behave.

By coping with this potentially fraught situation in this way, no one will lose out and everyone will gain. If you aren't happy with the friend's parents and how they behave, you have a much more difficult situation because sooner or later your child may be invited back to their house. A series of excuses, plus lots of invitations to the friend to come to your house may be the most tactful way out. Certainly you shouldn't let your young child go to a friend's house unless you are quite certain that he will be looked after well.

Thankfully today people are far less snobbish than they used to be and the way people speak or how much money they earn is accepted by most of us as being unimportant in terms of friendships for our children.

Having a friend, or at least an acquaintance, to go to play-group or school with, makes a potentially awesome situation much less so and can even make the whole thing possible for a child who otherwise might not go at all. Find out which children will be attending your child's play-group or school with him and if you don't already know any of them, try to get to know some of the mothers so you can arrange for your child to meet their children. *Related topics* Development – social; loneliness; only child.

Friendships – mother's A mother's friendships serve many purposes when she has a young family. They can give her a real interest at a time when she could otherwise become lonely and bored if she is cooped up at home with only the children for company. They can also help her

understand her own children and what they need and what they do. If her friends have children of roughly the same ages as hers, they can be playmates for each other. She can take part in various exchange systems for children's clothing, maternity wear, babysitting, baby- or child-minding for odd occasions, more serious minding on a regular basis if she goes out to work, and so on. They can also support her through times of trouble by simply listening to her or by helping out in practical ways with shopping, housework, child care and so on. Conversely, by helping and supporting her friends, a mother can get a lot of pleasure and feel useful in society. Though mutual help and support networks flourish among mothers in any community, they are often overlooked by new mothers who may have worked until their babies were born. This is one contributory reason for the post-natal depression that is so prevalent. Both you and your children will benefit from your network of friends and when you have young children is probably the easiest time in your life to make friends.

For some mothers, however, it is difficult to make friends. There are lots of organizations which young mothers can join so there's no need to be lonely. The National Childbirth Trust, mother and toddler groups, babysitting circles and so on are good places to meet other mothers with young children. Your health visitor will also be happy to put you in touch with other mothers. *Related topic* Loneliness.

Frozen foods Many parents worry about using frozen foods for children but there is probably little harm in it. Several studies have found that freezing certain foods reduces their nutritional value though it leaves the vast majority of nutrients intact. Whether or not this bothers you is very much a personal decision. The average Western child is fed well and can certainly get along without the small percentage of vitamins and minerals that are lost in freezing. However, there's little doubt that fresh foods are best and should be used whenever possible. Freezers also cost money to buy and to maintain so unless you have a productive garden (and most of us do not) or unless you have a large freezer and can bulk buy, there's no financial argument for having one at all. If you're prepared to pay for the convenience and enjoy batch cooking, fine, but many people find they eat more healthily if they get rid of their freezer, simply because they eat more fresh foods and look forward to things when they're in season rather than being able to have them all year round. It's very much a matter of personal choice and the health argument is rather marginal.

When it comes to feeding toddlers and young children feeding small portions of their favourite foods can be a real boon because you can produce ready-made meals fairly instantaneously. This can be particularly helpful if your young child is going through a stage of faddy eating or if you are out at work and need to produce meals swiftly. *Related topic* Food.

Frustration The condition of being hindered or prevented from doing something one wants, is planning or is trying to do. It is a universally experienced emotion and one which we hopefully learn to rationalize and come to terms with as we grow up. If we don't, it can at worst ruin our lives with bitterness and crushed hopes and at best the stress it causes can lead to some degree of physical or mental illness.

Frustration begins at birth for some babies whose needs are not met by their caretakers – most often their mothers. The only obvious way a baby has of communicating his needs is by crying (though experienced and sensitive mothers can often pick up signals that precede crying such as a general unease and certain body movements). If he is hungry, thirsty, lonely, frightened, unhappy, too hot, too cold, unwell, uncomfortable or bored, he can't do anything about it for himself and has to signal to his mother for help. If she ignores the signal at first, all he can do is to signal louder and if that doesn't work, he's stumped. After working himself into a frenzy of crying he'll probably eventually stop and may even go to sleep. Later he'll try again. Each attempt to get attention will tire him so his first efforts will be the strongest. Just imagine what such a frustrated baby must be learning about his world, certainly not that it is a kind and generous place. Yet this is the way millions of babies have been brought up in recent years, not being fed until the recommended time, not being picked up at night, being automatically put in their cot for a sleep after each feed and so on.

Older babies suffer from a different form of frustration – that of not being able to achieve what they want to. This is usually because their physical skills are not well enough developed. A six-month-old baby, for instance, may want to grasp a toy that is just out of his reach and despite all his efforts to stretch for it, it is unattainable. A baby who has just learnt to crawl may find himself crawling backwards, much to his dismay. A walking baby may continually fall over and hurt himself. All these are significant frustrations.

Older children find their desires being frustrated from time to time by their parents. They have to learn that they can't always do what they want and this is a hard lesson. However, whereas with a tiny baby yelling for milk the kindest thing is to feed him, with an older child who wants to do something which would either be dangerous (such as going downstairs by himself, emptying the knife drawer, or crossing the road without holding hands), or an unnecessary nuisance to his parents (such as tipping a bag of flour all over the floor, playing with his mother's make-up, or doing a 'wee-wee' on the carpet), the only reasonable thing to do is to stop him. If possible divert his attention. Children don't understand for a long time why they can't do everything they want, but sooner or later your explanations will sink in and one day you'll smile to yourself as you overhear them playing with their dolls or with each other and explaining carefully why something mustn't be done. **Related topics** Anxiety; aggression; crying; development – emotional; fretful baby; whining.

Galactosaemia A condition in which the sugar galactose is present in the blood at an abnormally high level. Galactose is produced largely from the milk sugar lactose by the action of the enzyme lactase in the baby's gut.

In babies with the disease, there is little or none of one or other of the enzymes that metabolize galactose, so it builds up. If the baby receives no treatment he may fail to thrive, develop cataracts, liver damage with jaundice and mental retardation. The worst affected and undiagnosed children die. Symptoms usually start soon after milk feeds have been started. They include listlessness, feeding difficulties, vomiting and weight loss.

Treatment involves stopping breast or bottle milk and replacing it with specially made lactose- and galactose-free milk. This cures the symptoms if the diagnosis has been made early enough. If cataracts have developed they can be operated on later. When the child is weaned on to a mixed diet it's essential to ensure that he doesn't have any milk-containing foods, which would make him ill.

Your doctor can give you a list of dangerous foods but this needs periodic review because food manufacturers change their constituents from time to time.

Galactosaemia is an inherited condition so if it is suspected from the family history a baby can be tested soon after birth so that any symptoms developing after being given milk can be treated straight away before they have a chance to do any permanent damage. *Related topic* Failure to thrive.

Games Children under five sometimes play for long periods on their own and often generate their own games, usually on a very informal basis. Most children over two like to play organized games from time to time, partly because these involve an adult who is close to them.

Games should be looked upon first and foremost as fun and secondarily as educational. The playing of games can encourage a child to recognize shapes, words, colours and sequences and as he learns numbers games are a painless way of learning what these really mean in practical terms. The well tried and tested games such as Ludo, snakes and ladders, dominoes, and snap are still favourites with children and their parents. Electronic games are increasingly available but show no signs of replacing simpler, cheaper games that can be played by very young children.

But games don't need any equipment or formality at all to be successful. A common game parents play with babies is to hold them facing them and then to smile at them and jiggle them about. The baby likes this and soon realizes that he is producing pleasure by making his response. This is at the root of all games.

As the baby gets to a few months old he'll love the element of surprise, and variations of peek-a-boo become enormously entertaining for him. Parents quite unconsciously change their games to keep their baby interested as he grows older. Familiarity is an important part of games and most children love to play them again and again. Gradually a child wants to play more and more complex games, will play with outsiders and starts to take a pleasure in rules and other things that constrain the situation.

Physical games and the pleasure babies and young children get from being physically handled are also important. In the West Indies such games are a part of a baby's everyday experience. He'll be washed and then massaged. His body is bent and stretched and he is swung around and tossed in the air and caught several times. Research in Europe and the US has shown that fathers are more likely to play such physical games with their children and that mothers play more talking and smiling games. All play with babies and young children is a good starting point for interaction with the world and is yet another preparation for it. A baby who is played with a lot not only enjoys it at the time but develops all kinds of skills sooner. *Related topics* Cheating; play; sibling rivalry; smell.

Gamma globulin An antibody fraction of blood that can be isolated and used to treat certain diseases. This antibody is prepared from the blood of someone who has suffered from the disease in question. It can be given to certain children at risk to prevent or reduce the severity of an attack of an infectious condition such as measles. Children usually build up natural specific immunity to diseases either because they have suffered from them or because they have been immunized against them. If a child gets or has been in contact with an infection which would be dangerous for him, and if he has no immunity of his own, he can be protected to some extent with an injection of gamma globulin. It is expensive and in short supply and is generally only used in the UK for children whose resistance to infection is lowered by certain other diseases or treatments they are receiving (such as children with chronic kidney disease, those with a defective bone marrow and those receiving anti-cancer or steroid therapy). *Related topic* Immunization.

Garage, dangers in Children under five shouldn't be allowed to play in most garages as there are too many dangers and they are too young to be able to foresee them. Here are a few helpful tips. Never leave the car unattended in the garage with the engine running as you might forget it and a child could be poisoned by the exhaust fumes. Always put the handbrake on just in case the car could run away with children in it or squash a child against a garage wall. When repairing your car always use proper ramps, not piles of bricks, or the car could fall on a child. Never store petrol or other poisonous fluids in old lemonade bottles because a child could drink them in error. Keep children away when you're working in your garage or workshop – one third of DIY accidents involve a watching child. Keep petrol in metal cans (plastic degenerates and leaks) and never keep more than the legal limit of four gallons at home. Watch that children don't play in the car unsupervised because they can catch each others' fingers in the doors. *Related topic* Car safety. *Useful organization* The Royal Society for the Prevention of Accidents.

Gas Domestic gas is now free of the poisonous carbon monoxide it used to contain and so is no longer a poison hazard. It has a smell put into it so that you can detect it when it leaks. However, it is still possible to be killed by a gas leak in an airtight room because the gas displaces the oxygen which gets used up as the person breathes. Also, if an appliance isn't burning properly it can produce poisonous carbon monoxide.

To be really safe with gas, here are a few tips. Always report any smell of gas to the Gas Board. Make sure that all your gas appliances are reviewed by a professional at least once a year and never meddle with them yourself. Never block up ventilators (especially in bathrooms with a gas water heater) because natural gas needs plenty of air to burn safely.

Gas fires are just as dangerous as open or electric radiant fires when it comes to a child catching his clothes on fire so take all the necessary precautions and remember that under-fives are too young to understand the danger of fire. *Related topics* Fire; fires. *Useful organization* The Royal Society for the Prevention of Accidents.

Gastroenteritis An inflammation of the stomach and intestine causing diarrhoea, with or without vomiting and other symptoms including abdominal cramps and a fever. Blood in the diarrhoea is uncommon but if it is profuse it should be reported to your doctor. Sometimes there are tiny flecks of blood in the child's vomit and if the vomiting is severe tiny red blood spots in the skin of his face may develop. Gastroenteritis can be caused by many things but is commonly caused by viral or bacterial infections. The infection can come from anywhere in the body or can be primarily in the intestine itself. Infections of the ears and the urinary tract can cause gastroenteritis as the bacteria travel from the infected areas in the blood to the intestines. It can last anything from a day to a week.

Gastroenteritis is spread from person to person by droplets or by infected food and drink due to careless hygiene. The incubation period is about one to four days. The diagnosis is often difficult to make because tonsillitis, urine infections, middle ear infections and, in babies, intussusception, can all mimic the condition. Some doctors think it wise to isolate the affected child in a room of his own if there is a young baby in the house because the disease can be so unpleasant and even potentially dangerous for babies. It isn't a serious disease, except in very young babies, but one attack seems to provide very little or even no immunity against similar attacks with the same infecting organism. There is no connection between 'flu and gastroenteritis.

Breast-fed babies are much less likely to suffer from gastroenteritis than are bottle-fed babies because breast milk has natural anti-infective properties. Gastroenteritis in babies is taken seriously because the dehydration that results from the diarrhoea can kill them if untreated. About five in a hundred babies with the most common type of gastroenteritis die from dehydration and the resulting disturbance of body salts if left untreated. Prompt treatment of babies with diarrhoea is therefore absolutely essential.

Because gastroenteritis can be lethal, it makes sense to take every step possible to prevent your baby getting it. This can be done by breast-feeding exclusively for at least three to six months; by ensuring that anyone dealing with a baby's food is extremely careful about hygiene; by keeping your baby away from people with diarrhoea or houses in which there is a person with diarrhoea; and by reporting diarrhoea, especially in a very young baby, to your doctor at once.

A young child with diarrhoea should stay at home to avoid infecting other people. Disposable nappies make life easier when it comes to doing the laundry. Wrap each soiled nappy in a plastic bag before throwing it away. Disinfect the lavatory seat or potty regularly, as well as the wash-basin; wash your child's glass or mug and eating utensils and plates thoroughly and separately in water as hot as possible and wash your hands well after dealing with his nappies or wiping his bottom. Treatment of older children with gastroenteritis is quite straightforward. Limit food intake to clear fluids and don't make the child eat if he doesn't want to. Ensure that he drinks plenty even if he only fancies drinks you usually wouldn't want him to have. If any signs of dehydration occur, tell your doctor. This is especially important in young babies who can go downhill very quickly. **Related topics** Abdominal pain; appendicitis; blood in motions; blood in vomit; dehydration; diarrhoea; food poisoning; hygiene; vomiting.

General practitioner (family doctor)

General practitioner (family doctor) For the vast majority of people in the UK their family doctor is their first port of call if anything goes wrong with their children's health that they can't cope with themselves or with advice from family or friends. Whilst few general practitioners are trained paediatricians, they do have a good general understanding of illness in babies and young children and are able to handle the majority of conditions that commonly arise. If your general practitioner can't handle your child's illness himself then he can refer the child to a specialist (a paediatrician) for an expert opinion. Some conditions will possibly require expert surgical advice so you may be asked to see a surgeon. This could be a surgeon who operates on children and adults or a specialist paediatric surgeon.

There is no doubt that if your child is ill, the best place to start getting help is with your general practitioner. He knows your family, knows about any local epidemics and is used to dealing with commonplace conditions with the minimum of fuss. With the growth of group practices there is often one member of the group who takes a special interest in children's diseases. Many general practitioners today also have ancillary medical staff working with them, such as social workers, health visitors and midwives. This can provide a very good all-round service to a family with a problem that needs more than straightforward medical treatment.

If you are worried about a sudden-onset medical condition, phone the surgery first and see if one of the doctors could come at once. If none can, they may suggest that you phone for an ambulance or take your child direct to the hospital accident and emergency department yourself by car. If the need isn't really urgent the doctor will decide whether to come to your home or ask you to take the child to the surgery. Home visits take up a lot of time (mainly because of the time spent driving from place to place through traffic) so many doctors discourage them unless the child is really ill or has something contagious they want to keep out of their waiting room. If you are really worried and your doctor cannot or will not come, don't wait until the child is desperately ill but take him by car or taxi to the hospital at once.

In the vast majority of cases your child will be able to go to the surgery. Most practices now have an appointments system so you'll need to book ahead. This is easily done on the phone and you'll almost always get an appointment the same or the next day, especially if you say it's for a baby or young child. Most efficient practices keep a couple of appointments open each day for last minute emergencies and so can easily slot people in who need to be seen quickly. If you think your child has an infectious illness ask the receptionist what they'd like you to do. It's unkind and dangerous to go into a waiting room full of young mothers (any of whom could be pregnant) if your child has German measles, for example.

When asking your general practitioner to see your child, make the decision early in the day: don't wait until late afternoon or evening when he'll be doing an evening surgery or going home himself. It's easy after having watched the child all day to decide at six or seven o'clock to do something before the night, but the doctor will be tired himself and you may have to wait for him to come round if he is seeing several other people. Also, after a certain time in the evening many doctors pass their calls on to a medical service that sends out their own doctors and your child could be seen by someone who neither knows him nor will ever see him again.

If you use the system properly your general practitioner and his team should be able to answer ninety per cent of your health needs quickly and easily. When things become complicated he'll have to send you for a second opinion, don't be afraid to ask if you're not happy with the way things are going.

Generosity As children grow older it becomes apparent that all the members of the family pull in slightly different directions according to what they think and what they want to do. How the family gets on with each other and with other people depends very much on how generous they are to each other and this doesn't just mean generosity with material things. A successful and enjoyable family life involves a lot of giving and it's an important part of a child's development to learn to be generous and giving.

This means that even a child as young as two to three can be shown how to make little presents for people, for example someone who's just had a baby, is sick or has a birthday, or a new neighbour. Children can get great pleasure from giving. Generosity is almost more important in the way a child behaves. You may think that tolerance and sympathy are qualities of children older than five but it's amazing how generous an under-five can be to a handicapped, sick or otherwise disadvantaged person. This generosity of spirit to be kindly to and accepting of everyone, is well worth encouraging. *Related topic* Gifts.

Genetic counselling

Advice given to parents who run the risk of having a child with an inherited illness or malformation, especially if they have had one affected child already. Sometimes such advice can be given by your general practitioner or paediatrician but there are also special centres where full-time genetic counsellors work. A counsellor will take a detailed family history and will then, possibly with the help of special tests, be able to assess how likely it is that an affected family will have an affected baby.

Many inherited conditions can be detected early in pregnancy by examining the amniotic fluid around the baby in the womb (amniocentesis). Should a foetus be affected in a way which could be life-threatening or detrimental to its future health the parents are then given the option of having the pregnancy terminated as soon as possible. Sometimes amniocentesis is just used to find out whether the unborn baby is a boy or girl, because certain inherited conditions are 'sex-linked' – that is they affect only boys, though girls may grow up to be symptomless carriers of the condition and pass it on to their sons.

Extremely difficult and painful decisions have to be made by a couple who are told that there is a risk of their child being affected and often they can't be told with certainty. Usually only couples who know that abortion would be acceptable to them embark on such antenatal testing, though some do so so that if the baby is found to be normal, the rest of the pregnancy is worry-free.

Genetic counselling can also be useful before a couple marries if there is likely to be a particular risk of genetic abnormality in their children. A few people decide against marriage for this reason. Others decide not to have children at all, while yet others are prepared to take the risk of having a baby and accept the fact that it might be abnormal. *Related topics* Amniocentesis; congenital malformations.

German measles (rubella)

An infectious disease caused by a virus. It is mild in young children but can kill or handicap an unborn baby. The symptoms begin after an incubation period of two to three weeks and include a runny nose, reddening of the throat and the whites of the eyes, a mild loss of appetite, swelling and tenderness of the lymph nodes at the back of the neck and behind the ears and, twenty-four hours later, a rash behind the ears and over the forehead. This then spreads over the body but spares the feet and ankles and the area around the mouth.

The rash is composed of flat, pink spots that may converge to make the skin look red. It may be itchy and the temperature is usually normal. It lasts for three days and may be accompanied by a low grade fever.

There is no specific treatment and the condition cures itself in young children. Paracetamol can be used to bring the fever down if it is making the child unwell. Keep the child at home away from other children and their mothers until he is better and for at least four days after the rash has appeared.

A child who has been in contact with German measles starts being infectious to others seven days before the rash appears.

Nowadays children are no longer always put into quarantine (kept away from others if they have been in contact with the illness). However, if you know your child has been in contact with German measles, it makes sense to work out when he will be infectious if he does get it. Because the incubation period is anything from between fourteen and twenty-one days after contact, and because your child will start to be infectious seven days before the rash appears (about a day or so after the initial symptoms), it makes sense to keep him away from people who don't want or shouldn't get German measles from eight to twenty-one days after contact. If he hasn't become obviously unwell by then, you can assume he hasn't got it.

The timing brings its own difficulties: by the time the mother of the child from whom your child got the infection knows that her child has it (usually not until eight days after he starts being infectious – that is, when the rash appears), your child may be starting to be infectious already. Infants born with rubella may be contagious for as long as a year.

The most important person to keep him away from is any pregnant woman you know because German measles can cause a miscarriage or a baby to be born with deafness, cataracts, or a congenital heart deformity. This includes keeping your child away from the children of a woman who might be pregnant and who could pass it on to her. If a woman knows that she has been exposed to German measles, antibody tests should be done at once to see whether or not she is already immune to the disease. If she is not, an injection of gammaglobulin may help reduce the severity and the effects of the infection.

One attack of German measles usually provides life-long protection so do remember if your daughters have it so that later on in life you'll be able to reassure them if they come into contact with an infected child when they are pregnant. However, it's often difficult to know if your daughter has had German measles so it's always best to have her immunized at the age of twelve, when the immunization is routinely offered in schools.

A baby is protected for the first five to six months of life by his mother's antibodies (if she has had German measles herself). Rubella vaccination is now offered routinely to all schoolgirls and is worth having whether they have had the illness or not just as a preventive measure. A woman should not become pregnant within two months of being vaccinated or of having the disease herself.

The diagnosis of German measles is not always easy to make and the illness can sometimes be confused with other viral infections causing a rash. Usually though the combination of the rash and the particular swollen lymph nodes clinches the diagnosis. *Related topics* Fever; incubation period; itching; lymph nodes; measles; rashes; roseola infantum; viruses. *Useful organization* The National Association of Deaf/Blind and Rubella Handicapped.

Germs A lay word for bacteria, viruses and other infective agents.

Gifted children A term used to describe children with very high intelligence (usually an IQ of over 160) as measured by tests. It is not used for those with physical or artistic talents, though gifted children are sometimes very talented in some of these ways too.

As a group, gifted children are more self-sufficient, less neurotic, and less submissive compared with other children, but they may have problems too. Many are easily bored at home and at school and so turn to mischief, and others deliberately under-achieve so as to be accepted by their friends. Many such children have difficulty in finding friends of their own age with whom they can play because of their superior level of intelligence. As a result they can develop behaviour problems. Such children often need less sleep than their peers and have insatiable curiosity and unflagging energy – all of which can be very difficult for their parents. The company and support of other parents with similar problems can be a great help and can also benefit the child. The address of the National Association for Gifted Children can be found on page 772. *Related topic* Behaviour problems. *Useful organization* The National Association for Gifted Children.

Gifts Some parents shower their children with gifts at Christmas and on birthdays. Others give their children small things throughout the year, with perhaps one big present at Christmas and on birthdays. What you do is up to you and will depend on your own experience as a child to some extent and, of course, on what you can afford. Remember that a young child can be so overwhelmed with presents that he doesn't really enjoy any of them. It's better for him perhaps to have one or two at a time so that he can make the most of them. Sometimes people give in order to be thanked. The presents may be totally unsuitable but look grand or attractive to them. Really the child would have liked something quite different. Before you spend money on presents, find out if you can what the child likes playing with and what stage he is at if he isn't your child. It's no good buying a train set for a one-year-old. If he plays with it now he'll break it and if he doesn't use it he'll have nothing. Ideally, parents and grandparents should liaise with each other before Christmas and birthdays, so that the child doesn't get duplicated presents and so that the grandparents can be guided (if they need guiding) as to what to buy.

Gifts don't have to be bought, of course. They can be made or they can be passed on. Some grandparents give their grandchildren heirlooms that are to be kept as valuables. Some gifts require a big investment of time, and it is these that children like most. The book that the parents will read, the sewing cards that their mother will help them do, the plaster moulds that need an adult's helping hand: children like all of these unless they don't get the help, in which case the present is wasted. If you know you haven't the time to spend doing things with your child, buy him something he can enjoy by himself.

Most people will buy your baby soft toys but many babies don't like them much. If your child has accumulated lots of unplayed-with soft toys, he'll be reluctant for you to give them away but you could put most of them into a box in the loft and bring them out one at a time so that they seem more interesting. Toys that make a noise or do something are often much better received, even by a young baby.

Your child will hopefully soon get the message that gifts are not only to receive but also to give. If you help him make cards and presents for other people he'll thoroughly enjoy it, though he may be reluctant to part with them when he's two or three. Encourage him to consider what would really please the recipient and teach him how to give the gift graciously. He'll enjoy thinking what gifts to give when people are unwell or unhappy, just to cheer them up. A young child's gift may be something he has made, something he has bought with his pocket money, or something he has found, like a bird's egg or some wild flowers.

When it comes to parties, some children are lucky enough to receive a present from each guest. This can cause problems for the mother who would like her child to thank each giver if the child opens them all in an excited muddle then and there, as people arrive. Some parents encourage their children to say thank you as the wrapped gifts are given, and then keep them aside till the guests have gone, when the opening can be watched carefully and the gifts and givers matched up by the mother. This can be hard on the giver though. The mother can then ensure that the givers are thanked personally as soon as possible for the gift. This system also prevents jealousy from other children who may find it hard to accept that someone else is having all the presents.

Going home gifts for guests at a party are always welcomed and can be extremely cheap and simple. A small piece of birthday cake, a balloon and perhaps a small item such as a prettily coloured marble cost very little and it's exciting to take home several things. If your child is a party guest, make sure that he thanks the hostess warmly for both the party and the going home gift. **Related topics** Generosity; jealousy; toys.

Gingivitis Inflammation of the gums.

Normal gums are pink, firm and finely stippled but diseased gums are swollen, reddish-blue, spongy and may bleed. If ever your child's gums bleed you should tell your dentist because bleeding gums are not healthy.

The cause of gum disease is the same as that of tooth decay. Plaque on the teeth destroys the fine fibres that tether the teeth to the bone of the jaw, and eventually the teeth fall out. Such gum disease isn't common in under-fives but does exist hand-in-hand with severe dental decay. Daily brushing with a good nylon brush is the best preventive.

One anti-epilepsy drug, phenytoin (Epanutin), can cause swollen gums. *Related topic* Teeth.

Glands
Groups of cells in the body that produce secretions (fluids). There are two main kinds. The first (exocrine) produce secretions that are delivered right to where they are needed. Milk, sweat and salivary glands are of this type. The other (endocrine) pour out their secretions into the bloodstream to be distributed all over the body. These secretions are called hormones.

The word 'glands' is also used by the public (but not by doctors) to describe the nodes that lie along various parts of the lymphatic system, for example in the neck, armpits and groins, where they can be felt if swollen.

All kinds of diseases are wrongly ascribed to 'gland trouble' whereas in fact few conditions in early childhood have anything to do with a child's glands. Children who are fat almost never have gland trouble – it is usually that they are eating too much of the wrong sorts of foods. *Related topics* Hormones; lymph nodes.

Glans
The swollen tip of the penis, usually hidden by the prepuce (foreskin) in a young boy but visible all the time in the circumcised boy. It has the opening of the urethra (the passage from the bladder) at its tip but in a few boys this opening is on the underside. This condition is called hypospadias.

Inflammation of the glans is called balanitis. *Related topics* Balanitis; foreskin; hypospadias.

Glasses (spectacles)
A child's sight can be tested from the age of three or even younger, and should especially be tested if his parents suspect abnormalities or if there is a family history of defective vision. Look out for the following warning signs: watery or inflamed eyes; headaches; dizziness; screwed up eyes; crossed eyes when the child is tired; frequent styes; sensitivity to bright light; frowning; excessive blinking; rubbing the eyes and holding things very close to look at them.

A free NHS examination is available at your local optician under the general ophthalmic services or by the hospital eye service.

Parents of five-year-olds may discover that their child is suspected of having a visual defect following his first school medical. They can either make their own arrangements for sight testing by their optician or at a hospital via the family or school doctor.

If it is suggested that your child needs his sight tested don't worry that he'll automatically require spectacles – fewer than twenty-five per cent of all children seen in either private practice or hospital require glasses. Even if your child is advised to wear them they may only be required for a short period of his life. This is especially so when there are problems with the muscles of the eye or when the sight of one eye is not being used.

Children of this age, however, who are myopic (short-sighted) are much more likely to need spectacles permanently.

A range of frames is available on the NHS and these are entirely free. Very young children would normally be fitted with frames having curl sides or special sides allowing an elastic headband to be fitted for extra security.

Spectacles for this age group have a rough life so unbreakable lenses of plastic or toughened glass are often supplied. If spectacles have been supplied under the NHS an NHS repair service enables parents to get free or low cost replacements in case of breakage.

Contact lenses can also be supplied to the under-fives but are normally only suggested for those children who require them on strong medical grounds such as progressive myopia (short-sight) or congenital aphakia (no lenses in the eyes). *Related topics* Long sight; short sight; vision; vision testing.

Glucose A simple sugar which is one of the basic building blocks of all carbohydrate foods. It is not the same as sucrose which is the sugar known as table sugar. Sugars of all kinds and starches, which are both carbohydrates, are man's main sources of food energy the world over, and are built of multiple units of glucose and other simple sugars. Most carbohydrates are converted to glucose in the body by the action of enzymes in the stomach and intestine.

Because glucose is so rich a source of energy for the body many parents feel it must be valuable as a food supplement and so feed their children glucose tablets, or drinks to 'give them more energy.' This is a complete waste of money as there are many cheaper sources of carbohydrates which would be broken down into glucose at a fraction of the cost and would also provide other useful nutrients.

Even today, normal healthy babies in many maternity units are routinely given glucose water in the first few days of life. This is quite unnecessary unless the baby's blood glucose level is dangerously low (hypoglycaemia). By unnecessarily giving a baby a food other than breast milk he is less likely to want the breast because he won't be so hungry. There is also no doubt that a slug of glucose is totally unnatural and unphysiological. The best way to maintain a baby's blood sugar level and thus to prevent hypoglycaemia is to put him to the breast (or to give him breast milk on a spoon or via a tube down his throat into his stomach if he is too ill or too premature to swallow or suck). Breast milk contains lots of the sugar lactose – taste some for yourself and you'll see how sweet it is. When digested, lactose yields glucose as well as galactose (another simple sugar). All babies should either be put to the breast soon after birth or should be given breast milk by tube or spoon and then should have breast milk frequently throughout the day and night for the first few days. This will prevent the vast majority of babies from ever having a low blood sugar. Routine glucose for babies should be barred altogether and frequent breastfeeding right from birth substituted instead. If you only breast-feed on a three to five hourly schedule for a limited time at each breast and perhaps once or twice only (or even not at all) at night, your milk will take longer to come in and your colostrum alone may not be enough to prevent your baby developing a low level of blood sugar.

Babies and young children, just like adults, need frequent, fairly evenly spaced meals to supply the body with the glucose it needs. If a child misses a meal he may feel faint or even actually faint because his blood sugar has fallen very low. This can easily be overcome by giving him a spoonful of jam or a couple of sugar lumps but don't do this if he is unconscious – call a doctor at once in this case. Normal, healthy children rarely faint from too low a blood glucose level but diabetic children who have had too much insulin, too much exercise or too little food can do so.

Many children who eat little or no breakfast become irritable or tired during the morning because of their low blood sugar level. The remedy for this is to try giving them a proper breakfast. If this doesn't work, discuss the matter with your doctor. *Related topics* Breast milk; diabetes; milk; sugar.

Glue ear A condition in which sticky fluid builds up in the middle ear as a result of a poor drainage down the Eustachian tubes usually after infection. The fluid is a poor conductor of sound and the child becomes partially deaf.

One cause of glue ear is enlarged adenoids which block the Eustachian tube openings at the back of the nose. This prevents fluid produced in the middle ear from escaping into the throat as usual. Viral infections, a cleft palate, allergy or sinusitis can all block off this drainage too by making the lining of the Eustachian tubes swell. Both ears are usually affected.

A glue ear can cause earache, some loss of hearing and eventually, in a young child still learning to speak, speech problems because of the hearing loss. The child may complain of a sensation of fullness in the ear and his ear may click when he swallows or moves his jaw.

Treatment is a matter of medical controversy. Many doctors believe that glue ear can lead to permanent hearing loss and so advise treatment with antibiotics (to cure any infection), decongestant medicines (to shrink the lining of the Eustachian tubes and allow drainage) and nose drops (again to shrink the lining of the Eustachian tubes). If this treatment has no effect in six weeks or so an operation may be recommended to drain the fluid from the middle ear. Other specialists don't agree with this approach except in the treatment of recurrent or chronic glue ears.

If an operation is decided upon the ENT (ear, nose and throat) surgeon sucks out the fluid in the ear through a hole made in the eardrum and then inserts a tiny plastic drain (a grommet) so as to allow any remaining fluid to drain out. The grommet falls out of its own accord in the next few months (it can take up to two years) as the hole in the drum heals. If the child's adenoids are enlarged they are removed. A child with a grommet can't swim without very well-fitting earplugs or water will get into the middle ear and cause inflammation. *Related topics* Adenoids; deafness; earache; otitis media.

Godparents The usual number of godparents for a child baptized into the Christian faith is three: two godfathers and one godmother for a boy and two godmothers and one godfather for a girl. However, you can choose more if you want to. Not all Christian denominations call for godparents – in some the whole church family (the local congregation, in effect) is supposed to fulfil their role in praying for the child and steering his development in the Christian faith.

It would obviously be hypocritical to choose godparents who weren't Christians themselves. If you don't know anyone whom you would like to do the job, you could ask your local vicar who would be only too pleased to advise you. He may suggest you take on the role yourselves. It is necessary for a godparent to have been baptized himself. Some people have their children baptized because it is the socially accepted thing to do and because they feel their children will be pleased to have been baptized later, especially if they ever want to be confirmed.

A good godparent takes his responsibilities seriously and makes sure he stays in touch with the family even though a long distance may separate them. He takes the trouble to get to know the child as he grows up and they may even enjoy outings together. Only by forming a real relationship can the godparent hope to be an example and an influence on the child. Whether or not you give your godchild presents for his birthday and Christmas is a personal affair, though many do. The real job though is to steer the child as he grows so that he knows about Christ and hopefully eventually becomes a committed Christian himself when he is old enough to make the decision. *Related topic* Religion.

Goitre An enlargement of the thyroid gland in the neck. A baby can be born with a goitre caused by his mother taking antithyroid drugs or medicines containing iodides (certain cough and asthma remedies) during pregnancy. This type of goitre usually resolves spontaneously.

In older children the thyroid may swell as part of a condition called lymphocytic thyroiditis. Girls are affected between four and seven times as often as boys but it is hardly ever seen before the age of six since most of the causes of goitre in older children and adults are extremely rare in this age group.

If ever your baby or young child has a swelling in his neck, seek medical advice because there are other causes which are nothing to do with goitre. *Related topic* Glands.

Gonorrhoea A type of venereal disease caused by bacteria called gonococci. Clearly babies and young children don't catch it by sexual intercourse but they can catch it coming down an infected birth canal (it is one of the possible causes of sticky eyes in newborn babies) and from contact with infected parents, towels and bedding. Gonorrhoea is the fastest growing epidemic of infectious disease ever known and unfortunately many women who have it don't even know they do. They can thus spread it to their babies or to their sex partners without realizing it. In an infected person there is a discharge from the penis or vagina, painful urination, itching of the genitals and possibly inflammation of the vagina in women and girls. Fifteen to thirty per cent of women with gonorrhoea are free of symptoms and can easily infect their child without knowing.

If you, your partner, or your child ever have any of these symptoms see your doctor at once to arrange treatment.

Grandparents It's perhaps stating the obvious to say that a child who has four grandparents alive and well is lucky. Because grandchildren represent a stake in the future and because they are their children's children, grandparents almost invariably have a deep and abiding interest in and love for them.

Grandparents can enjoy their grandchildren without having to carry out all the humdrum and tiring duties that parents do. Grandchildren visiting their grandparents are with luck clean, tidy, polite and well behaved. The relationship is a special one and close ties are often formed between the old and the young. Part of the attraction for both is the lack of discipline necessary. The grandchildren are not usually with their grandparents for long enough to need more than a smattering of it, and the grandparents are only too pleased to leave this responsibility to the parents and so spoil the children in a way that would be unwise or undesirable in everyday life. This does the children no harm. Of course, in some families where the grandparent has a hand in the child's day-to-day care, the story is different, but this isn't common today.

For children to see their parents caring for elderly or unwell grandparents is a good example of the loving, caring attitudes that most parents hope to instil in their children. Many grandparents get on better with their grandchildren than they did with their own children and many say how they enjoy their grandchildren in a way they never felt free to with their own children.

Having other adults to love them and to be concerned for them is in turn very pleasant for the grandchildren. Knowing their grandparents gives them a real sense of the continuity of the family and teaches them about their family background. Sometimes if things have gone wrong for a child, it's helpful to be able to talk or play with an uncritical grandparent.

Now that divorce is common, grandparents on the side without custody are all too often forgotten. They care just as much for their grandchildren as the other set of grandparents and if at all possible some sort of relationship should be maintained.

Unfortunately, not all relationships with grandparents are so rosy. Many modern parents have great difficulty pursuading grandparents that the world is a different place now and that their methods of child upbringing aren't applicable any more. Interference from grandparents can be confusing for a child who is torn between the two sets of apparently loving and caring adults and their differing behaviour. The way round this is to make your views about child care and upbringing very plain to your parents so that they know where they stand. The children are after all yours, not theirs. They have had their chance to bring up their children and you know the results because you have to live with them daily. Make the rules firmly and live amicably within them. You'll have to relax the rules now and again because grandparents will always tend to spoil the children. Handle the situation tactfully and explain to the children that their grandparents have different ideas on some things. If you feel really strongly about particular things try to avoid the situations in which trouble can occur and play down friction when it does.

Grasping If you put your thumb into the palm of a newborn baby's hand, you'll be surprised at the strength of his grip. If both his hands grip a thumb each, you can pull him up from a lying to a sitting position. You could even hold him in the air, hanging on to your thumbs with his hands, though this is perhaps not wise. Over the next few days and weeks, this firm reflex grasp weakens somewhat, but the baby's fingers will still curl tightly round anything put against the palm of the hand and will tighten still more if whatever he is clenching is pulled away. Often during a feed your baby will tightly grip your finger, only loosening his hold when his eager swallowing lessens or when he falls asleep.

After about eight to ten weeks, a baby's hands – previously curled into fists for much of the time – are open more and more and he'll start to play with them. He'll enjoy grasping things you give him but has no control over how long he can hold them, and so tends to drop them every so often. When he is holding something, he'll get so excited that he'll wave his arms around, possibly dropping whatever he's holding and so spoiling his fun. If he's holding a rattle or a bell, he'll love the noise his movements make. There are lots of attractive toys around suitable for a baby of this age to hold.

Round about two to three months a baby will begin to discover that he can move his hands and arms to touch whatever is held near him. Sometimes this discovery is made when one of his excited and random wavings accidentally touches something and moves it or causes it to make a sound. Once he realizes what he is capable of doing he'll try his hardest to do it again. Gradually over the weeks his hand-eye coordination will improve so that he can eventually look at something, decide he wants to touch or hold it, then move his hand towards it to do just that. By six months, he'll have good control over his hands and will be able to pick up anything of a suitable size within his reach, using his whole hand to grasp it.

Somewhere between nine months and a year old, your baby will begin to grasp things with his finger and thumb instead of with his whole hand. By a year he'll be able to pick up small crumbs or beads accurately. Letting go of something held in the hand is a different and more complex skill from grasping it in the first place and is one which comes later than grasping, so don't be annoyed if your one year old won't let go of something you want.

A useful trick if you want your baby to release something he's holding (such as a spoon), is to offer him something else. At around the same age that he learns to put his finger and thumb together he'll start learning to let things go and you'll be into games of 'give and take'. In this stage toys are dropped out of the pram and food dropped at the side of the high chair! A stage further on is when he learns to throw. This often happens at the same stage as learning to put things exactly where he wants them.

Once your baby has learnt to pick up small objects, you must be watchful about what lies within his reach, because every little thing will be put into his mouth to be sucked and possibly swallowed, with potentially dangerous results. Once he is mobile, the floor needs to be checked thoroughly for buttons, coins, pins, needles and small toys. Even fluff will find its way into his mouth, so this is the one time when housework should favour keeping the floors clean and hoovered. *Related topics* Coordination; development – physical; spoon-feeding.

Grazes Superficial damage to the skin, usually caused by rubbing it against a rough surface. Grazes are simple to treat and almost never cause problems. Simply wash the area well with plain, warm water to remove all the dirt. If dirt is ingrained, take your child to a doctor, who will clean the area thoroughly. Once the area is cleaned, dab it dry with a freshly-laundered handkerchief and put on a dry sticking plaster. Don't use antiseptics to wash the area and don't use antiseptic cream unless the graze is still red and pussy after a couple of days. Most grazes heal within a few days and will not scar unless they become infected as a result of poor cleaning. *Related topic* Cuts.

Growing pains Young children often complain of vague aches and pains in the legs and because a cause is almost never found they are called growing pains. The term is, of course, meaningless because growth is painless.

Such aching pains usually start in the evening but they can wake a child at night. They always disappear by morning. They are not made worse by movement. The child is otherwise perfectly well and massaging the affected muscles and applying local warmth may help.

No one knows what causes these pains. It could be the result of exercise that day – a type of delayed muscle fatigue. Whatever the cause they always go eventually, so don't worry.

Guardians Some parents take the precaution of asking certain friends or relatives to be the legal guardians of their children in the event of their both dying. Having guardians agreed on beforehand obviously makes a dreadful situation easier for all concerned. Once you have both decided whom you would like to ask, talk to them or ask them in writing whether they would be prepared to take on the responsibility of bringing up your children. Then tell your respective solicitors and have an agreement in writing between you either as part of your Wills or separately.

It's usual to make some sort of provision for your children in your Will and in certain circumstances guardians can use the children's inheritance for their (the children's) good. Some parents make a specific bequest to the guardians to help provide for their children's care. For example, they'll probably need a lump sum to help towards the cost of moving to a larger house if this is necessary.

Although many parents think it is morbid to think about such things, nothing could be further from the truth. You invest an enormous amount of time, love and money in your children yet if you both die unexpectedly what would become of them? Just look at it as a way of ensuring that people *you* choose will end up looking after your children. What peace of mind that can give. **Related topics** Guardian's allowance; legal rights of children.

Guardian's allowance A state benefit paid to the person who looks after an orphaned child. It can also sometimes be paid in other circumstances: when the child's parents are divorced and only one parent is dead; when one parent is missing at the time the other dies; when the child is illegitimate and the mother dead; or when the remaining parent is serving a long term in prison.

The claim must be made before the child has been with the family for three months or the benefit will be reduced. Further information is available from your local Social Security office. **Related topic** Guardians.

Guilt in children Guilt is a normal human emotion but psychologists and psychiatrists are agreed that an excess of guilt can cause permanent problems for a child as he grows up to adulthood. It's a feeling that exists if a child believes he has done something wrong and it tends to persist until his wrongdoing has been acknowledged and forgiven, or disproved.

Sometimes a child can believe that something is his fault even though in reality it has nothing to do with him. This sort of guilt is potentially dangerous because it's likely that his parents won't realize what it is that's worrying him yet he won't be able to explain unless he makes a confession. Half-forgotten or suppressed guilt can make a child feel very unhappy, so if there is no obvious reason for your child's unhappiness, spend some time talking to him quietly to try to get to the bottom of it. Don't bully, nag, or threaten him though, because if you do you're paving the way for him to clam up not only now but in future too. If you spend a long time with a four- or five-year-old, for instance, gently finding out what it is that is worrying him, and if it turns out to be something very 'naughty', don't react in a furious way because that'll make him scared to tell you if he ever does anything that bad again. Instead, praise him for telling you and then discuss why he did it, why it was wrong and why he shouldn't do it again. This will help him behave in the way you expect far more than a harsh telling-off would do. Children who feel guilty are usually children who badly want to be good and to please their parents and other authority figures. They don't need verbal or physical punishment but just loving guidance as to how to avoid it next time. This is the basis of good discipline.

The children to be really worried about are the ones who have no guilt and aren't concerned about or sorry for their wrongdoings. Something somewhere has gone wrong and though their upbringing won't be entirely to blame, it must have played a part in the development of their character. Harsh and over-authoritarian discipline or a lack of love and attention from their mother or mother-figure may be at the root of such behaviour.

Sometimes a young child feels guilty because of what he thinks rather than what he does. When a new baby is born, for example, he may feel resentful that his share of his mother's time has gone down. If she is not careful, he may also believe that his share of her love has diminished too. His feelings towards the new baby include jealousy and even frank hate for what he thinks the baby has done to him. Some children want to hurt the baby and, while few actually do cause a new baby physical harm, simply wanting to is enough to cause intense guilt because they know deep down that this is wrong. Children can also feel guilty about their angry feelings towards their parents if they believe they've been wrongly told off or – sometimes – even if they know they've been justifiably told off. Children need different handling according to their personalities, and some very much resent parental wrath and instead of feeling sorry for what they have done to cause the wrath, feel furious at their parents. Some wish that their parents were dead or gone. In the unlikely situation that something bad eventually happens to one of their parents, such a child may really believe that in some semi-magical way he has been the cause of this happening, simply because he wished it. The guilt all this engenders can be very deep and it is by no means an unusual occurrence. The same can happen if a brother or sister is very ill or actually dies because most children wish their siblings dead and gone from time to time. Because they may have wished this in the past, when it happens they easily believe that in some way it was their fault. Some children then start behaving extra well as an attempt to bring back the life or health of their brother or sister. Others may wish that their parents realized what their feelings were, so they need feel guilty no more. They may behave badly in an attempt to produce understanding and punishment.

If you constantly criticize your child in a negative way and forget to praise him, he'll grow up with a low sense of self-esteem. This is closely bound up with his feelings of guilt at having failed to come up to your expectations, which is particularly sad if in fact he hasn't failed, but you have failed to let him know he has a good side. The image of themselves that children grow up with is largely determined by the reflection they see of themselves in other people. You as parents are the ones who most often reflect to your child what kind of person he is. If you want him to grow up confident and happy, by all means discipline him (lovingly guide him) but take care also to comment when he behaves and does things well, when he looks well-turned out, when he's kind, when he tries hard and so on. It's no good helping him to grow up behaving perfectly yet believing inside that he is inherently bad and worthless because he never seems able to please you.

Some parents behave in the opposite way and underdiscipline their children, giving them no guidelines as to how to behave or what their limits are. These children at first enjoy behaving wildly but sooner or later, unless they're completely insensitive, they'll realize that their behaviour is different from that of other children and that it obviously doesn't please other people. Because they haven't grown up with a strong framework of how to behave, they'll have little idea of what to do and they'll feel resentful at their parents for having let them down. At the same time they'll know that they're at fault for behaving in such a way and they'll end up with a confused batch of feelings of guilt and discontent at behaving badly, resentment and anger at their parents for not controlling and guiding them, and guilt at their feelings towards their parents.

Some forms of punishment can make a child feel guilty for a long time. If you punish your child by preventing him from doing or having something he likes, such as watching a favourite television programme, or having his customary sweet at the end of the day, he'll stew over his guilt and his wrongdoing, his resentment at you for punishing him in this way, and his unhappiness at not being able to do or have whatever it is for much longer than if you had immediately reproved him by the expression on your face or a telling-off as soon as he had done wrong. While this form of punishment is sometimes sensible, if you do it too often it'll make the child too inward looking and the subsequent low opinion he has of himself and of you will eventually embed itself in his unconscious mind. Always remember that the real aim of discipline is to help a child gain self-discipline. Making him feel guilty may be a part of this but helping him to an understanding of what was done wrong and a desire not to do it again is far more important.

Feeling guilty about something and feeling sorry are two quite different things. Knowing that he is to blame doesn't necessarily fill a child with sorrow. This is why as he grows older, it's sensible to explain why it is that his wrongdoing has hurt or upset you or whoever. If he breaks a cup, just losing your temper and getting him to say sorry will make him feel guilty but won't necessarily make him feel sorry. In order to feel sorry he has to know *why* it is that you're concerned about his breaking the cup. Take care not to blow up the incident out of proportion though because one cup here or there is certainly not of earth-shattering importance, but the principle is important.

Guilt about masturbation can be the beginning of a lifetime of sexual hang-ups. It's not easy always to know how to cope with your child if he plays with his genitals or openly masturbates, but the last thing you want to do is to make him think that his behaviour is bad, peculiar, or dirty. You probably won't be able to stop him from doing it once he has discovered that it is pleasant anyway. What he needs to learn is that it's

not acceptable in front of other people, including you. **Related topics**
Anger; anxiety; discipline; jealousy.

Guilt in parents Parents need a good helping of common sense to

overcome the inevitable feelings of guilt that bringing up children can
cause, particularly in our society where so many people express their
opinions about how it should be done. Inevitably there will be conflicts of
interest between parents and children and when the interests of the parents
win, they may feel guilty. In all of this it helps to understand children's
needs because understanding brings the ability to sort out what is really
important and to weigh up the relative needs of children and parents.

Working mothers of children under five often feel some sense of guilt at
leaving their children with someone else. In order to come to terms with
their guilt they must take a straight, honest look at what their priorities are.

Some parents realize in retrospect that they should have brought up their
children differently. It's no use feeling guilty about this because you can
only ever do your best at the time and if you've done this, within the limits
of your knowledge and circumstances at that time, then you've no cause to
reproach yourself. Lots of parents feel that they were too strict with their
babies and young children and envy the way in which so many mothers
today feed their babies on an unrestricted basis, keep them by them all the
time, and enjoy much greater freedom with their young children than when
rules and regulations about child care were rigidly imposed.

Discipline is another area of parental guilt. It's something that every
parent has to know about yet it's rarely discussed. It's often difficult and
parents get little support from other people, except criticism if their
children are badly behaved. Some parents feel guilty about being too strict,
others about not being strict enough. How a parent disciplines depends on
how he or she was brought up, on his personality and expectations, on the
child's personality and age, and on the example of relatives, friends and
neighbours. Discussing other people's views together with your own helps
you to arrive at a commonsense approach to discipline so that you can react
to your child's misdemeanours with confidence and not constantly be
reproaching yourself.

Having a miscarriage, a stillborn baby or a handicapped one arouses
feelings of guilt in many mothers who brood over whether the event could
somehow have been their fault through doing something wrong while they
were pregnant. This is a perfectly normal response but sometimes it is
taken to excess and a mother can become depressed as a result, especially
in combination with her natural mourning of the loss of her baby or of the
loss of her hoped-for normal baby.

Some mothers are shocked to find that they feel no surge of motherly
love towards their newborn baby. Sometimes they even have strong
negative feelings towards the new baby, especially if he is not the expected
sex, or if they don't like his looks, or if he was not wanted in the first place.
Their guilt over such feelings may hamper the development of the natural

bond that eventually forms between almost every mother and her baby but which is often delayed until they get to know each other. Mothers who know in advance that bonding often takes time cope with their feelings better.

Guilt is a destructive emotion – it eats into you and often you can do nothing to reverse the situation that is making you guilty in the first place. If you feel really badly about something to do with your children, first discuss it with your partner, if you can, and then get the subject out in the open with a trusted friend or your general practitioner or health visitor. *Related topics* Behaviour problems; discipline; mothering; stillbirth; working mothers.

Gumboil A lay term for a condition in which there is a collection of pus (a boil) at the tip of the root of a tooth. In some cases the boil may 'point' into the mouth. Such gumboils discharge their pus spontaneously and will then heal with no need for medical or dental treatment. The tooth itself, however, may need treating to prevent a recurrence of the condition. A gumboil is unpleasant because not only is there pain in the gum but also because pressure on and temperature changes of the tooth produce pain. Fever is rare. Gumboils are more common in teeth that have been damaged or filled and this makes the diagnosis easy. The tooth may be tender on tapping and can be slightly loose.

Superficial treatments are not much help; the only thing is for a dentist to let the pus out either by removing the tooth (if it is a baby tooth) or by treating the root canal. In the latter he drills up into the tooth to make a channel down which the pus can flow. This channel is then plugged with an antiseptic filling. While awaiting these treatments a pain-relieving drug such as paracetamol can be used and warm salt water rinses are helpful too.

Thankfully, this is an uncommon condition in children under five but when it does occur the tooth is often soon to be lost. Loss or removal of the tooth allows the pus to drain and cures the condition.

Dentists will always try to save teeth in this condition, even if they are baby teeth, because the loss of certain teeth can produce orthodontic problems later. *Related topics* Orthodontist; toothache.

Gum cysts Some babies have one or more tiny pearl-white cysts on the sharp edge of their gums. These look as if they are teeth about to break through but are round and soft to the touch, unlike teeth. They are completely harmless and disappear on their own. *Related topics* Gum boils; teething.

Gums The pink, firm, slightly stippled parts of the mouth into which the teeth are embedded. Each tooth is tethered into the bone of the jaw by tiny fibres which, if the gums become diseased, weaken and cause the tooth to loosen. Gum disease causes the loss of more teeth than does dental decay in adults but in the under-fives decay is the main problem. However, gum disease can occur. This is unpleasant for the child and can make his teeth fall out.

Gums should never bleed. If they do you should take your child to a doctor or a dentist. The commonest cause of gum bleeding is probably too rough brushing in the under-fives, but gum disease comes next. Very much more rarely gum bleeding is caused by bleeding diseases such as leukaemia.

A painful swelling in a gum is called a gumboil.

Painful or irritating gum edges between six months and two years are almost always caused by teething though by no means all babies have unpleasant symptoms when teething. Soothing gels applied to the gums or – even better – simply rubbing the gums firmly with your finger or thumb seems to help such babies and nothing else is usually necessary. A baby or toddler who really seems distressed by teething may benefit from a correct dose of paracetamol especially at night, as long as you are quite sure he has nothing else wrong with him that is making him ill or upset. Teething powders are now never used, partly because they are almost certainly ineffective and also because of the harmful reputation they gained when they used to contain mercury. *Related topics* Gumboils; gum cysts; teething.

Guthrie test A blood test performed on a tiny drop of a baby's blood on the sixth day of life to exclude a condition called phenylketonuria, a rare but preventable cause of mental handicap. *Related topic* phenylketonuria.

Habits A habit may start off as a result of boredom, because it is pleasant, because the child finds it comforting when he is lonely or upset, or from copying other children (or adults). Thumb sucking, nail biting, head banging, rocking, masturbation and picking the nose are all examples of habits that are common among young children.

A cough can become a habit and this usually carries on after a child has recovered from an infection such as whooping cough or tracheo-bronchitis. Though the cough is no longer necessary, the child has become so accustomed to doing it while he was ill that he forgets to stop. This sort of cough shouldn't be confused with the cough that so many catarrhal children have at night which is caused by a 'post-nasal' drip – catarrh trickling down the back of the throat. Sniffing is another example of a habit that probably had a good cause when it first began, as is the screwing up of the nose that many children with persistent catarrh or hay fever get into the habit of doing.

Some children repeatedly toss their heads to one side because their hair otherwise obscures their vision; cutting the hair or, if it is being grown, keeping it away from the eyes with a secure slide will stop this habit if it is a recent one. However, if it has been going on for long, the child may continue to do it simply because it's become a habit.

Repeated blinking is another thing that annoys a lot of parents and in common with other habits, the more the child is told to stop doing it, the more likely he will be to continue.

Habits are not meant to be annoying to other people. Many of the children who have them are unaware of what they are doing and seem surprised when told to stop. If there is any chance that your child's habit may be the result of preventable boredom, loneliness, worry, fear or illness, then try – with help from your health visitor or doctor if necessary – to put the problems right. Unless the habit is a remnant from an explicable condition (such as the persistent cough after whooping cough) always look for an emotional cause and get professional help if you are at all worried. *Related topics* Behaviour problems; nervousness.

Haemangioma A type of birthmark that can be large or small. There are two sorts of these marks. One, the cavernous haemangioma (strawberry naevus) is a red or purplish-red raised mark caused by a collection of distended veins deep in the skin. The other is the capillary haemangioma (port wine stain) which is flatter and more purple and contains capillaries.

A strawberry naevus may not appear until the baby is a few weeks old. It may enlarge rapidly (out of proportion to general growth) which worries many parents. It is highly likely that a strawberry naevus will disappear completely in time, even though it might leave a permanent white mark, so there is no need to seek a second opinion when your doctor advises no treatment.

A port wine stain is present at birth and will be there for life. It can be covered with make-up when the child is older if necessary. New treatment with a laser beam is proving helpful in skilled hands.

Some haemangiomas have elements of both a strawberry birthmark and a port wine stain and are unlikely to disappear completely.

Both types of haemangioma, because they are made of blood vessels, can bleed a lot if scratched or cut. If bleeding does occur, press over the area with a clean handkerchief until the bleeding stops. If there is still bleeding in 20 minutes, see a doctor. You should also see a doctor if a strawberry mark has a discharge or smells foul, or if redness develops on the surrounding skin. These are all signs of infection and need professional treatment. Apart from this problem strawberry marks are best left entirely alone unless they are in places where skin and mucous membrane meet, for example around the lips. *Related topic* Birthmarks.

Haemophilia An inherited disorder of blood clotting that affects 5,000 people in the UK. Girls are unaffected clinically but 'carry' the disease, which is almost exclusive to boys.

Children who have haemophilia tend to bleed very easily. The first sign is often abnormally severe bruising as they learn to walk. One of the most unpleasant features of the disease is the tendency to bleed into joints which causes pain, reduces movement and possibly even causes longterm damage to the joint if the bleeding is repeated and treatment of the joint is delayed.

Treatment consists of giving blood containing the missing clotting factors or even giving the clotting factor itself.

Parents of such children are naturally fearful and there is a danger that an unprotected child will grow up suffering as a result. The answer must be to strike a balance between being sensible and yet allowing the child to behave as normally as possible. Baby's cots can be padded, older children can have knee pads sewn inside their trousers and, later still, thick protective clothing can be worn to prevent grazes. Dental care is important because the removal of a bad tooth can cause severe bleeding from the socket. There is a tendency towards spontaneous improvement – the child bleeds less readily as he gets older. Many of today's children with the disease are in regular contact with a specialist haemophilia centre. Ask your doctor about one near you. **Related topic** Bleeding. **Useful organization** The Haemophilia Society.

Hair care A newborn baby's hair is sometimes matted with vernix (the thick white substance found on the skin after birth) and blood, and may need a wash with soap or mild shampoo. After this it's up to you how often you wash your baby's hair, if at all. Many people in the world never wash hair but instead brush it, polish it, or oil it to keep it attractive-looking and clean. In the West it is customary to wash hair with shampoo and water regularly and to brush it daily. When you bathe your baby, it's easy to wash his hair at the same time using a mild soap or shampoo. If he has a lot of hair, shampoo is better because soap can leave a dulling film on the hair. Rinse the head well and pat dry. There's no need to wash your baby's hair frequently unless he's in the habit of regurgitating and then lying in a pool of brought-up milk in his cot. The hair has a naturally pleasant smell which comes from the sebum (oil) secreted into the hair follicles by the sebaceous glands. Some parents dislike the oily appearance which comes when a baby produces a lot of sebum, and so wash their baby's hair more often.

During the first six weeks or so many babies get a thick, hardish, adherent, yellowish-white layer of matter on their scalp called cradle cap. There are various ways of getting rid of this – a common one is to soften it by oiling it well before washing. Another is to use a proprietary application as a softening rub and then as a shampoo some hours later.

As your child's hair grows longer, regular brushing is essential. Plaits and bunches are good ways of keeping girls' hair tangle-free and if you plait the hair before bed time, there won't be any fuss in the morning when you attempt to get the clits out. Plaits also give straight hair a wavy appearance. Rubber bands used to secure plaits or bunches may damage the cuticle of the hair and make it break, so use covered elastic bands instead. Ribbon won't stay put for long. Be careful not to pull your daughter's hair too tightly into a pony tail, plaits or bunches because you could make it fall out and cause a bald patch or thinning of the hair line.

Hair washing can be difficult with toddlers and three- and four-year-olds, most of whom hate getting shampoo or water in their eyes and won't keep still enough to prevent it. Some mothers wash their children's hair in the bath, getting the child to lie back in the water to wet the hair, then shampoo it with the child half sitting, and using clean water from a basin to rinse the hair with the child's head tipped backwards but with the hair out of the bath water. You can buy a plastic halo which stops water from running into the child's eyes to some extent and which may help at shampoo time. Other mothers try to wash their children's hair in a wash basin by standing the child on a chair, but this isn't usually very successful. Another method is simply to tip warm water right over the child's head in the bath, then shampoo, then rinse by tipping clean water again. This can be very frightening for a young child and is best avoided. A good way but one which needs two adults to do it is to hold the child in your arms at a basin and to put his head into the water backwards. The other adult can then wash the hair and make sure that no water goes in the child's eyes. Perhaps the easiest way is to put the ironing board up at right angles to the kitchen sink or wash basin in the bathroom and on a level with the draining board. The child lies on a towel on the ironing board (or on a plastic changing mat on the ironing board) and by wriggling up the board a bit can put his head backwards into a basin in the sink. This method needs only one adult and is so comfortable for the child that you can take as much time as you like to wash the hair well. It's a good idea to put a conditioner on long hair as it helps make it tangle-free.

Hair cutting is something you can easily do at home if you have the confidence. You need to have a good eye for judging length and style in order to get professional results, and you also need a really sharp pair of high quality scissors. You may find it easier to cut your child's hair in the morning when he isn't tired and is most likely to keep his head still in the position you put it. It's also a good idea to have another person there to distract a young child who finds it difficult to keep still while having his fringe cut, for example. Choose a style for your child which stays looking good for as long as possible and which doesn't leave stray ends tickling his face or going in his eyes. The occasional trip to the hairdressers can be great fun but is expensive. *Related topics* Cradle cap; nits.

Hair colour Some babies are born with hair of quite a different colour from what it will eventually be. The hair changes colour as it grows, usually from dark to fair. Hair that starts off fair may go dark but this usually happens later in childhood. Hair colour tends to run in families but in no definitely predictable fashion. Similarly, blue eyes tend to be associated with fair hair and brown with dark, but there are many exceptions to this. Overall, most dark-haired children have olive or dark complexions, while most fair-haired children are fair-skinned. Redheads are usually fair-skinned and some have a lot of freckles.

Hair eating A few children – often emotionally disturbed or mentally handicapped – put hair into their mouths, chew it and swallow it. It then collects in the stomach and can form a ball which can cause tummy ache.

Sometimes hair goes into the intestine and may cause a blockage. Surgery is then necessary. Other similar substances such as wool or fur may also be eaten. Some children chew their hair ends and even eat quite a lot without ever coming to any medical harm from it, though.

Such children need more time spent with them to prevent them being bored or lonely and the parents need help to sort out any underlying emotional problems. Get professional help if you need it. *Related topics* Behaviour problems; hair eating.

Hair on body Except on the palms and soles, everyone is covered with body hair which is obvious to a greater or lesser extent depending on race, hair and skin colour and individual characteristics.

Some children have a heavy growth of hair on their backs and especially over their spine. Others have dark hair above their upper lips. If your child develops hair under the armpits, on the chest or in the pubic area, ask for your doctor's advice as soon as possible – it could be a sign of precocious puberty.

Hair twiddling Lots of young children get into the habit of twiddling with a strand of hair, often to the annoyance of their parents. As with other habits, it often starts off as a result of copying someone else, or the child may just discover that it whiles away the time when he or she is bored. However, it can begin because the child is worried, lonely, or afraid. Under these circumstances it becomes a comfort habit. Watch when your child does it to find out if it is usually when he is upset for any reason. If you tell him not to do it or even get cross or punish him, it's likely to go on for much longer than if you correct the basic cause. Some children stop twiddling their hair when told to but replace this habit with another. *Related topics* Behaviour problems; habits.

Hair type European hair tends to be finer than that of the African races, and fair hair tends to be finer than dark. Whether or not a child has curly or straight hair is determined by heredity and depends on the cross-sectional shape of the hair follicles (the shafts in the scalp containing the root of the hair): round follicles produce straight hair; waves are produced if the follicles are kidney-shaped; and curls if the follicles are oval in cross section.

How much hair a young child appears to have depends partly on the density of the hair follicles on his scalp (which can't be altered) and on how long each hair stays on the head – both these factors together determine how many hairs he has on his head at any one time – and partly on the average thickness of each hair (also genetically determined) together with whether or not it is straight. Wavy or curly hair always looks more bulky than straight hair.

The direction in which your child's hair grows depends on the direction of the hair follicles. It's easy to see on the head of a baby without much hair that each hair grows in a certain direction and that there is a pattern to the hair growth. Some children have one crown on the top of their head from which the direction in which the hair grows radiates outwards, while others have two – a double crown. With a double crown the crowns may be at the same level or one above the other; the latter often causes problems with hair styling when the hair grows longer. The side of the head the crown is on determines how the hair falls and on which side the parting wants to lie.

Sebaceous glands empty into the hair follicles and produce an oily secretion called sebum. Some children produce more than others and some dark-haired, dark-skinned children in particular have a lot of sebum which makes their hair oilier than that of others.

The cells of the hair root are the only live parts of the hair and they are nourished by nutrients from blood brought by small blood vessels (capillaries). As the cells age they die and are pushed upwards (by the growth of the new ones in the root) to form the visible hair above the scalp. Each hair has a period of growth after which it enters a rest phase. During this it gradually loosens and either falls out or is pushed out by a new hair growing in its place. Up to 100 hairs are lost on average each day. When you brush your child's hair there will always be some hair on the brush afterwards, because at any one time some are ready to be shed and brushing is enough to dislodge them. In all children there is a constant loss and replacement of hair. Hairs in the eyebrows last for three to five months, for example, while those of the head last for between two and five years. Baldness results when replacement doesn't keep up with loss. The potential length of your child's hair will depend on the average life of each hair together with the rate of growth. The average rate of growth is half an inch a month.

Hair growth is influenced by the season of the year (it tends to be faster in warm weather and therefore in the summer); by the age of the child (it is sometimes extremely slow in babies and may not speed up until around two); and by the health of the child, growing slower if he is unwell.

The first hair a baby has is there even before he is born and is called lanugo. This is fine, soft, colourless hair found especially on the shoulders and back which forms some time between the second and fifth month of pregnancy and usually disappears by the seventh or eight month, which is why it is generally only seen on pre-term babies.

The second sort of hair a baby has is called vellus hair and this is the first sort of hair found on the scalp. It is soft and downy and may or may not be coloured. The colour may bear no relation to the child's permanent hair colour. It rarely grows over an inch long and is followed at a variable time by coarser, permanent, coloured hair. *Related topic* Lanugo.

Halitosis (bad breath)

There is only one common cause of bad breath in children – severe dental decay – although foreign bodies stuck in noses are also a fairly common cause. Pneumonia or tonsillitis and even appendicitis *can* cause bad breath but these conditions are rare compared with rotting teeth and anyway the child will be obviously ill in other ways with these conditions. Constipation is not a cause of bad breath. Some children have bad breath for no apparent reason and others have it as a result of eating certain sweets or foods.

Never use mouthwashes or any other preparations to disguise bad breath in a child. There is usually a treatable cause which needs attention. *Related topics* Constipation; teeth.

Hallucinations
False sensations that have no reality in the environment. These usually take the form of visions, smells or sounds. When a magician performs a trick he fools the senses – his audience doesn't have hallucinations – but when a child has an hallucination there is no basis in reality for it. Any child who persistently hears, sees, smells or otherwise senses things that aren't there needs medical help. Young children often hallucinate during a very high fever or just as they are going off to sleep. This is perfectly normal.

Handedness
The subject of left- and right- handedness is confused and emotive. Because most people are right-handed many parents are over-sensitive as to which hand their baby uses, fearing that he will become one of the ten per cent of children who are left-handed. Many babies use both hands from birth but some seem to prefer to use one hand from an early age. Others use one hand for months and then change to the opposite hand.

There is controversy over whether handedness is inborn or acquired after birth and there seems to be evidence for both arguments. We feel that parents shouldn't get upset about handedness but should use as much common sense about it as possible. If your baby shows an obvious preference for one hand, give things to that hand. If it's his left hand, don't worry. After all, being left-handed is only a nuisance (and then only from time to time), not a serious handicap. Most children will not have become definitely right- or left-handed until toddlerhood. Delay can be a warning sign of late learning difficulties and early recognition leading to special treatment can prevent future problems at school.

About one boy in ten and slightly fewer girls are left-handed once they settle down to a dominant hand but apart from learning to write, which can be difficult because the writing is hidden by the child's hand, they aren't too bothered by their difference.

Today there are many aids for the left-handed and some of these are suitable for left-handed children.

Hands, use of
Most newborn babies have a strong grasp reflex which tends to keep their hands tightly closed. As this reflex weakens they open them more and during the third month the hand is open most of the time. A baby's hands are the first things he sucks, other than his mother's breast, often trying to cram all his fingers into his mouth. Just because your baby

does this, don't think he's teething, because this is usually not the case. Babies simply like the sensation of sucking things and their hands are readily controllable, provide feedback of information (unlike a dummy) and are always there.

A baby also likes to watch his hands and by three or four months he'll be ready to hold something you give him, but can't yet pick it up for himself. He starts to coordinate his eye and hand movements, realizing that he can reach out for something and touch it. He has to be able to get this right before he can pick things up for himself.

At about five months he can reach out and grasp things using both hands. His eventual dominant hand may not be apparent until the second half of his first year or even later and some children are three years old before they are completely right- or left-handed. A baby's first coarse hand movements gradually become coordinated and more precise movements using the thumb and individual fingers appear during the second half of the first year. By six months he'll be able to hold something and will chew it with his gums. At this age too he can bang things on to a surface and can transfer things from hand to hand.

The next big stage in hand control is learning to let go of something. This occurs at about eight to twelve months and is the start of the phase of dropping and throwing things all over the place. Up until about eight months a child who drops a toy will forget that it exists until it is returned to him but by eight or ten months he'll look for a fallen object.

As he becomes more dextrous he can amuse himself for long periods just by handling, banging and chewing things. As he gets better at handling things he tends to spend less time putting them in his mouth. By one year he'll be mouthing things very little as he gains more information from his other senses. Even before this age he'll use his hands surely, to wave goodbye, for example. By the age of fifteen months he'll be able to place one brick on another and will build a tower of four bricks by eighteen months. An average three-year-old can copy a circle with a pencil. At four or soon after he'll be able to learn how to do up his buttons and so may be able to dress himself unaided.

All the ages given here are very flexible, varying considerably from child to child. You can encourage a child to use his hands early on and once he starts to learn you can help him learn more quickly. Babies who receive a lot of stimulation seem to progress faster. Don't force your baby's development at all – it really doesn't matter if he isn't up to what the baby books say, so long as he's not far behind. Be guided by what the child seems to enjoy doing and do more of it with him to encourage his development.

The only abnormality that is at all common in a baby's hands is an extra finger or a tag of skin and even this is easily treated unless there is bone there in which case slightly more serious action may be required. *Related topics* Grasping; handedness; nails.

Harness A useful piece of baby equipment made of nylon or leather straps which is buckled in place round the child's chest. It is then used for safety to keep a child in his high chair, a low baby chair, a car or pram seat or his pram or carrycot. Reins can be attached to the harness if your child is reluctant to hold your hand and is likely to run off when you are out in the street with him. Most children enjoy walking with reins. Car seats come with their own special harnesses but otherwise one harness can be used for everything. You might like to buy several sets of anchorage straps which can be left attached to their own piece of equipment to make the changeover easy. The harness can then be simply and quickly clipped into place when you put the child somewhere else.

Start using a harness before your child is likely to tip himself out of his pram, high chair, or whatever, otherwise you run the risk of him damaging himself. Nylon harnesses can easily be scrubbed clean after a meal, though it's easier to cover them well up with a bib. Don't use your child's immobility in his harness as an excuse to leave him sitting bored and lonely. It is meant only as a safety aid, not as a prison. If he associates his harness with being kept somewhere he doesn't want to be, he'll protest noisily every time you put it on him. *Related topics* Baby carrier; baby chairs; carrycots; car safety; prams.

Hay fever (allergic rhinitis) An allergic condition of the nose and

eyes usually caused by an allergy to certain pollens. When these pollens react in the tissues of the nose and eyes they cause catarrh and inflammation respectively. Attacks are commonest in the summer (especially from May to July) and the condition tends to run in families. Some children suffer from hay fever all the year round. They may be sensitive to house dust, foods, medications, dogs, cats, horses, feathers, certain carpet underlays, guinea pigs, hamsters, gerbils or mice.

The child's nose itches, he sneezes a lot, his nose becomes blocked, his eyes are red and watery and he may have a headache. Some children have painful ears and have temporary reduced hearing. An attack lasts for hours or days and some severely affected children are not without symptoms for months. Such children can become very tired with the condition and secondary bacterial infections are not uncommon. If ever your hay-feverish child has a fever, moderate to severe earache, swollen glands in the neck or a coloured nasal discharge he may have a secondary infection and should see a doctor.

Children with persistent hay fever often have a crease in the skin across the bridge of their noses caused by the often-repeated upward rubbing of the nose (the 'allergic salute') to relieve the itching and irritation.

Treatment involves preventing the child from coming into contact with known sources of allergy if at all possible. A course of desensitizing injections may also be effective. Drugs are helpful in many cases. Sodium cromoglycate prevents hay fever in many children and antihistamines can be useful during attacks. Decongestant nose drops and tablets are also available but the nose drops shouldn't be used indiscriminately over long periods.

Some children with hay fever also have asthma and other allergic conditions.

Attacks of hay fever can be prevented to some extent by noting the pollen counts which are published at bad times of the year and taking medication when the count is high. *Related topics* Allergy; asthma; desensitization.

Headaches Young children hardly ever complain of headaches and if they do they should be taken seriously. Fevers, common in children, can produce headaches (possibly by causing dehydration) and meningitis (an inflammation of the coverings of the brain) can do so too. The chances of a child with a headache having meningitis are very small, though if your child has a headache together with a sudden change in mood, a fever, vomiting, a stiff neck or a bulging soft spot in a baby, tell your doctor at once as this could be meningitis.

Children who have epileptic fits may have a headache before or after a fit and depressed children and those who have fallen and hit their heads often have headaches.

The worry that many parents have when their child has persistent headaches is that he may have a brain tumour. As a tumour grows inside the rigid skull the pressure rises, causing a headache and other neurological signs and symptoms. Such a headache is usually worst in the morning and on changing the position of the head. Any child with a headache on waking should see a doctor. To put it into perspective, only one child in 40,000 is found to have a tumour of the brain or nervous system.

It's sensible to try simple cures before seeking medical advice unless the headache is persistent or repeated, when medical help should be sought at once. Reassure your child, let him lie down in a darkened room if necessary and give him paracetamol in the recommended dose. If this doesn't relieve the headache within an hour or so, tell your doctor at once. It's helpful to remember that decongestant and antihistamine medications can themselves cause headaches in children.

Any sudden, severe headache demands immediate medical attention, as does a headache with any signs of nerve involvement (stiff neck, lethargy, irritability, visual problems or repeated vomiting).

Unfortunately, increasing numbers of children aged as young as five have stress-related headaches. This, and indeed any other cause of persistent headaches will have to be professionally sorted out. Any headache lasting for more than three days must be discussed with your doctor. *Related topics* Analgesic; concussion; migraine.

Head banging A behaviour disorder seen in some children between the ages of six months and one year. It starts off as a sign of boredom or unhappiness and soon becomes a habit. Unfortunately, the child can really hurt himself causing bruising, a patch of hard skin, or even a bald patch. More serious injuries than these are rare. Head banging doesn't cause mental retardation but is relatively often seen in mentally retarded children, especially if they are neglected.

The answer to this disturbing habit is to prevent it in the first place. Never leave your child alone in his cot for long periods unless you know he is asleep and be sure to give him plenty of love and attention. Put bumpers around the cot so that if he does bang his head accidentally he'll come to no harm.

Head banging is one of many behaviour problems seen in babies and young children – the vast majority of which can be prevented and cured by more love, contact with the mother, attention and stimulation. *Related topic* Behaviour problems.

Head control When your baby is born you'll soon find – perhaps to your surprise if it is your first baby – that his head is floppy and needs to be supported all the time he is not lying down. His neck muscles are not yet strong enough or coordinated enough to keep his head up, to move it where he wants, or to keep it still. If you let his head drop back, you'll see that his arms and legs stretch and then the arms are immediately drawn inwards to the chest as if to clutch something. This is known as the Moro reflex.

Over the next few months he'll gradually gain control over his neck muscles and they'll become stronger and able to keep his head where he wants it. You'll notice that as he lies on his tummy he won't be able to lift his head up at all at first, even to move it from side to side. One day he'll manage to lift it up to look to the other side and by around three months he'll be able to look straight ahead with his chin raised for a few seconds before his muscles tire. When he's on his back it won't be until he's about six months that he'll be able to raise his head to see what's going on. As he sits supported on your lap, his head will be quite floppy at first and then as he gains head control you won't need to support it all the time, though it'll still be wobbly, especially when he's tired. If you use a sling you'll need to take care to keep your baby's head supported well, especially if you lean forwards. Some slings have adjustable inner pouches which can be lowered as the baby grows in order to give his head continued support. Others have padded snap on 'head supports' but these don't in fact give any support worth talking about.

If you put your baby in a buggy before he has good head control, support his head with a small folded blanket or a pillow on either side to stop it from lolling about. Sleeping with your head flopped to one side is uncomfortable, as anyone who has fallen asleep in this position will know.

Head injuries Children under five, especially toddlers, are forever banging their heads by accident, usually with no ill effects. As children get older they climb higher and fall harder and serious head injuries can occur. If ever your child has a fit after a fall, cannot remember the injury, or loses consciousness no matter for how short a time, always tell a doctor. Many children fall quite hard and don't cut their scalps but if ever your child does have a scalp wound it's best to get medical help. This is advisable because any bang hard enough to cut the skin could have done other damage and because scalp wounds usually need stitching as they bleed so profusely.

Another important sign to watch for is vomiting. Any child who vomits after a fall needs urgent medical help. The loss of blood or clear, watery fluid from the nose or the ears, persistent vomiting, visual problems, black eyes or blackness behind the ears, continuing paleness, strange behaviour, slow breathing or unequal pupils all need medical attention. A child who has fallen and hit his head should be watched for at least twelve hours after the fall. He may suddenly become drowsy or his breathing may become shallow. If either of these happen, seek medical help at once.

Any of these signs could mean that your child will have to go into hospital for observation for twenty-four hours, just in case something serious happens. If at all possible, stay with your child all the time.

Most falls aren't this serious. The child falls, hits his head, cries, may vomit once or twice, has equal sized pupils, doesn't lose consciousness, and has a lump on his head. Within a few hours such a child is back to normal apart from the lump on his head.

If ever you are worried about your child after a head injury always play it safe and tell a doctor. *Related topics* Falls; unconsciousness.

Health visitor A nurse who has some training in midwifery and in the health needs of the community. Health visitors are usually attached either to a child health clinic or to a family doctor's practice. They are assigned families on either an area basis or according to a doctor's list. One of their main roles is to answer parents' questions about their young children's health – both physical and emotional – and to give advice on the prevention of disease. Some health visitors carry out developmental assessments to check whether babies and young children are progressing as would be expected. If they are concerned, the child can be referred to the family doctor or clinic doctor for a more thorough examination. They are increasingly involved in the care of mothers and are happy to help with social, health, marital and many other problems. Some health visitors are becoming involved in mother and toddler groups, self-help groups and in community work generally.

Health visitors have an important task when it comes to babies and young children in particular: though there is no statutory requirement for them to visit, ninety-nine per cent of all new mothers do in fact get a visit. The hospital maternity department (or the district midwife if the baby was born at home) liaises with the health visitor so that she knows when to call. She will take the time to answer a new mother's questions, will ask about her baby's feeding, and possibly about his bowels and umbilicus, and will make sure the mother knows where the child health clinic is and when it is open. Usually she'll give you a telephone number on which she can be contacted if you are concerned about your baby. A few health visitors are happy to be rung at any time (even at home) but most work only during office hours.

Most mothers in the UK regularly take their babies and young children to a child health clinic for general advice, support and development assessment. The health visitor will see each mother, in some clinics on an appointment system. If necessary, she'll ask the clinic doctor to see the mother and baby to give further advice. During the first year the health visitor will see most mothers and their babies several times although this varies enormously from area to area and depends on how receptive any given mother is and on what her individual needs are.

Remember that health visitors have no 'policing' role and there is no need to regard them with suspicion. Many mothers quite naturally feel over-sensitive soon after the birth of a baby and it's all too easy to take offence at what a health visitor suggests. Don't be afraid to discuss anything with her, however trivial it may seem – she's heard it all before.

Hearing testing In the UK children are offered routine hearing testing. You may think that this is unnecessary for your child but many a family has not realized until after just such a routine test that a baby or child has a hearing deficit in one or both ears. The hearing loss may be very small, but even a small loss in the high frequency range of hearing, for example, can cause problems for the child. The sound made by many parts of speech, such as by some consonants, is of a high frequency and the child may simply miss these sounds altogether. This means that not only does he not learn to speak properly, because he can't imitate what he can't hear, but also that he may not understand what is said very well because he doesn't hear enough consonants to distinguish words with similar-sounding vowels.

A hearing loss may date from before birth or it may begin later as a result of an ear infection, for example. Any ear infection makes a child temporarily deaf but repeated ear infections or a chronic infection can cause some degree of constant, and even sometimes permanent, deafness. A hearing test with a poor result should alert both parents and doctor to the fact that the child has an ear complaint which could be treatable, besides suggesting that he'll need help with listening.

Babies have a routine developmental and medical examination soon after birth and their hearing is tested at this time by watching to see if they quieten when a sound such as a bell ringing is made nearby. This is obviously not a particularly accurate test but it gives some indication as to whether they can hear with both ears together. As your baby grows, take care to watch him respond to sounds from time to time. You'll be able to form a fairly reliable opinion yourself as to whether he can hear adequately or not by whether he turns when a sound is made behind him or to one side or whether he relies on vision alone to know that a sound is being made. If you are at all concerned, ask for your health visitor's or doctor's advice about how to get his hearing tested formally.

Between seven and eight months your baby will be given a hearing test at home or at the child health clinic by the health visitor or doctor. Sounds are made at a certain distance from the baby's ear by one person while another distracts the baby from in front. His responses to these sounds of different frequencies and volumes are carefully watched. Each ear is tested in turn and if there is any reason to suppose that he can't hear, either the test is repeated later, when he is more alert, less tired, or whatever, or he is referred for further advice to your family doctor, clinic doctor or ear nose and throat specialist.

During the toddler and pre-school years various tests are carried out at routine intervals in the child health clinic to test the child's hearing. They are chosen according to the child's age and ability and all involve watching a child's response to sound. They are designed to be like a game and most children partake quite happily. If an otherwise happy child cooperates in everything except his hearing test, this must arouse suspicion that he can't hear. Usually, though, an uncooperative child is simply bored or tired and will perform well another day.

More accurate forms of hearing testing and measurement are available for use with children and are usually used in ENT (Ear, Nose and Throat) out-patient departments or by audiologists in special clinics if it is thought that a child has a hearing problem. *Related topics* Audiometry; deafness; glue ears. *Useful organization* The National Deaf Children's Society.

Heart diseases and abnormalities
Because of the many dramatic and well-publicized advances in the treatment of heart diseases in children parents could be forgiven for thinking that heart diseases are common in children, but they are not. Heart murmurs are common but the majority are not serious and certainly do not mean that the child has a heart disease.

Every newborn baby has his heart listened to as part of his routine examination immediately after birth. Clinic and family doctors will also listen to your child's heart just in case anything has developed since birth. This is worthwhile because many abnormalities of the heart are correctable (unlike those of adulthood), enabling the child to lead a normal or near-normal life.

The commonest abnormalities present at birth are narrowing of the heart valves, and holes between the two sides of the heart that allow the mixing of otherwise separate streams of blood. Some perfectly normal babies are born with their heart in the right side of the chest instead of the left.

Severe heart conditions produce rapid breathing, poor colour and even swelling of the limbs from birth but most children with heart conditions aren't this ill. Any child with a known congenital heart problem should have antibiotics on the day he has to have a tooth out because dislodged bacteria could settle in the heart and set up an infection there. This rarely happens in children with normal hearts.

Even children with quite severe congenital heart abnormalities do very well with today's treatment and can often play games and do the things other children expect to do. They themselves tend to know when to stop and take a rest. Parents should resist the natural temptation to interfere by insisting on limiting their child's activity. Having said this, however, a buggy is an essential piece of equipment in making life easier for the child.

Rheumatic fever, once a common cause of heart troubles in children, is now very rare thanks to improved living conditions and antibiotics.

German measles in a pregnant woman is a serious, though uncommon, cause of heart disease in babies. German measles caught by the mother in the first month of pregnancy means there is a fifty per cent chance of her baby being born with one or more of several abnormalities, including heart disease. This risk falls to ten per cent if she is infected in the third month of pregnancy. Unless you know for certain that you've had German measles it makes sense to talk to your doctor about immunization well before you start trying for a family. *Related topics* Blue babies; heart murmurs; rheumatic fever.

Heart massage A procedure performed on a child who has no heartbeat. Because it is dangerous to do heart massage on a heart that is still beating, here are some tips on how to tell.

A child with no heartbeat: 1 will be unconscious; 2 will look pale or grey/blue; 3 will have large pupils (the black part at the centre of the eye); 4 will have no pulse at the sides of the Adam's apple area of the throat.

Should a child be like this, lie him on the ground on his back and give one sharp blow with the side of your hand to the breastbone. This can sometimes shock the heart into restarting. If it doesn't, send someone for an ambulance and start heart massage yourself.

Kneel on the child's right side and put the heel of one hand over the middle of his breastbone. Keep your hand in this position all the time and rock your body backwards and forwards using the weight of your body to depress the child's breastbone by an inch or so at a rate of 100 times a minute. In a baby do this at 120 times a minute, and use two fingers only to depress the chest. While you are doing this get someone else to do the kiss of life because the child won't be breathing if his heart has stopped.

Continue with this massage until the child recovers his colour, his pupils look normal or a pulse returns. Never do heart massage on a child whose heartbeat has returned. Hopefully, professional help will by then have arrived and you can hand over to them. *Related topic* Artificial respiration.

Heart murmurs Noises in the heart in addition to the normal sounds made when the heart beats. When a doctor listens to a person's heart he's listening for lots of things: the rhythm of the heart; its rate; the quality of the sounds normally produced as the heart contracts; and for added sounds or murmurs which may mean that its structure is abnormal. He'll also listen over other parts of the chest and over the large blood vessels in the neck.

Murmurs are of many different kinds and can often tell a doctor exactly what the trouble is in the heart, even before he does any tests. Many such murmurs in early childhood are innocent ('benign' or 'functional') – they aren't a sign of heart disease at all. Even if a doctor thinks a murmur is harmless he'll ask you to bring your child back every few months so that he can reassess the murmur. Because nearly half of all newborn babies have a murmur of some kind there are lots of babies being followed up in this way. The vast majority have normal hearts.

Some children develop a heart murmur when they have an infectious illness but this goes as they get better and doesn't mean that their heart is affected in any way. *Related topics* Blue baby; heart diseases and abnormalities.

Heating There has been a lot of nonsense written about the ideal temperature of a baby's room. A newborn baby or an ill baby shouldn't breathe very cold air but this doesn't mean to say that you need to keep the temperature in your house up to 70 or 75°F (21 or 24°C). Take the chill off the room with some form of heating by both day and night and keep your baby warm by choosing his clothes and bed covers using your common sense. Remember that if you keep your baby with you for much of the time by day and night (and perhaps in your bed at night) you'll know at once whether he's too hot or cold. A young baby will be comfortable if his room is kept at around 60–65°F (15–18°C). The air temperature is less important for an older baby provided he is warmly clothed.

How you heat the room is up to you. If you are using gas, oil or paraffin heaters be sure to have a window open to supply enough air and in the case of paraffin to let out the water vapour produced when it burns. Heaters around the home should be guarded and fixed so that young children can't pull them over.

Overheating babies is much more likely than keeping them too cold and is more harmful too. Electric over- and under-blankets shouldn't be used for babies but can be used for older children who are dry at night. We feel that no young child should get into a bed with an electric blanket switched on.

Don't gauge how warm to keep the room by how warm you feel yourself, because an inactive baby doesn't generate the body heat that you do as you move around doing things. As a rough guide, make sure that your baby has one more layer of clothing on than you. Several layers of thin clothes will keep your baby warmer than one layer of something thick. It's far cheaper to put on more clothes than to turn the heating up.

Many parents find it difficult to judge whether their baby is warm enough. Feeling his hands or feet is not a good way because they can feel cold yet the baby can still be warm enough. Always slip your hand inside his clothes (and preferably feel his chest). This will give you a much better idea. In a normal domestic situation in the UK it's far easier (and more dangerous because of possible dehydration) to overheat a baby than to hurt him by being too cold. *Related topics* Electric blanket; fever; heat rash; temperature.

Heat rash
A rash produced by being too hot and sweaty. It is probably the commonest rash of all. Young babies are sometimes wrapped too warmly and kept in overheated rooms. Especially if they are dressed in clothes made from man-made fibres, they may get a faint rash on their face, in the skin creases and on the neck and shoulders. The rash consists of hundreds of tiny pinhead eruptions, each surrounding a skin pore. There can be pink or red bumps or even tiny blisters. They are moderately itchy and may have scratch marks. Unfortunately many mothers think the child's cries of discomfort are a sign that he is cold, so they heap more clothes on him and make him even more itchy and rashy.

The problem with the UK is that the weather is so unpredictable that a child dressed in exactly the same clothes can be too hot one day and too cold the next. Ideally, don't put wool next to the skin but use a cotton vest first. Also, keep man-made materials away from the skin because many of them trap sweat.

The treatment of a heat rash involves cooling the child and, if necessary, applying calamine lotion to stop the itching. Baby powder helps too. If the itching is really bad, antihistamines can be used. Detergents and bleaches incompletely washed out of bed clothes and clothing can make a heat rash worse and it makes sense to avoid the use of bubble baths, water softeners and oily cosmetics while the rash is present. When abroad in a hot climate do bear in mind that babies and young children can't stand the heat as well as adults and should be kept in the shade. *Related topics* Heatstroke; itching; nappy rash; prickly heat; sunburn.

Heatstroke
A condition that occurs when a person is exposed to excessive heat for a long time. It rarely occurs in the UK because we don't have sufficiently hot summers but many families travel far afield on their holidays and many experience it in hot countries.

When a baby or young child is exposed to intense heat the sweat glands seem to turn off temporarily and the body can't cool itself down. The child looks red and feels hot. His temperature rises (up to 108°F/42.2°C) and this can cause brain damage. He may be confused, have a rapid pulse, convulsions and incoordinated movements and without treatment will eventually go into a coma. In serious cases a child can die from heatstroke.

Treatment involves cooling the child *slowly* by removing all his clothes, sponging him with tepid water (not cold) and fanning him. If you suspect your child has heatstroke, do these simple things and call the doctor.

Of course a child should never get this badly overheated. If your child is ill with an infectious fever don't cover him up or dress him in lots of clothes, but cover him with a lightweight garment of some kind and lay him on top of his bed or cot. Some children are made worse by their parents' well-intentioned over-dressing during a febrile illness. In hot climates cover your child with something to keep the sun off but make sure that it's lightweight and light in colour to reflect the sun's rays. Choose cotton for your child's clothes because this will keep him cooler than man-made material. Keep babies and toddlers in the shade for most of the time and put a hat on them to shade them from the sun. Older children will want to go into the shade when it's hot but young ones need you to think for them. Make sure your child drinks plenty of fluids, wears a sunscreening cream and gets used to the sun slowly. Half an hour on the first day or two of your holiday is more than enough. Remember too never to leave your child in a closed car on a hot sunny day because the inside will be like an oven and he can get heatstroke very easily. *Related topics* Dehydration; heat rash; sunburn.

Height Because a baby can't stand up his height is usually referred to as his length. It can be measured most accurately by lying him on a board with one person attempting to hold his legs straight and still and the other measuring. A baby's length depends on his own genetic make-up and so reflects the heights of his parents and other relatives. It is also influenced by the duration of the pregnancy, his mother's nutrition and health during her pregnancy, and on whether he is a single baby or one of twins or triplets (in which case he'll be shorter at first than if he'd been a single baby).

During childhood a child's height can be plotted on a chart to give the doctor and parents some idea of his rate of development and of his height in relation to other children of the same age. The rate of growth varies according to the season of the year (more in the summer) and the child's state of health, as well as with his age. It is faster during early childhood than it is in middle childhood.

Rarely, a child is abnormally short because of a deficiency of growth hormone. This can now sometimes be corrected by giving this hormone as a medicine, though its use is strictly controlled because it is so expensive and in such short supply. If you are worried that your child is going to be abnormally short or tall, consult your doctor who will probably put your mind at rest or may refer you to a specialist who will arrange for bone x-rays which can predict the child's final height fairly accurately.

Many parents wonder how tall their child will be when he is a fully grown adult. It has been found from several studies that for children of average height parents and relatives a girl will be about half her final adult height at eighteen months and a boy half his final height at two years.

Henoch-Schonlein purpura An uncommon condition characterized by a skin rash (red-purple spots or patches which fade) with or without abnormalities in the joints, intestines and kidneys. It occurs most commonly between the ages of two and eight and twice as many boys are affected as girls. No one knows the cause but it is probably an allergy to a drug or other substance. Two out of three affected children have painful joints, especially the knees and ankles, and two out of three have abdominal pain or vomiting.

The condition lasts for up to six weeks but mild cases last only a few days. There is no specific treatment except to treat the symptoms. *Related topic* Arthritis.

Hepatitis Inflammation of the liver caused by a viral infection. The child may be yellow (jaundiced) and the liver enlarged. Serious acute complications and chronic, progressive liver disease can occur with this condition.

A baby can get hepatitis whilst still in his mother's womb if she has the disease but this can be prevented to some degree by giving the mother an injection of gamma globulin. A mother who has hepatitis can give her baby the disease but it is now known that the risks are not high so the baby need not be taken away from her. Though expert opinion is divided, it is probably best to breast-feed your baby if you have hepatitis, because your baby will then receive antibodies to the disease produced by your body and transmitted in the milk.

In older children hepatitis occurs along much the same lines as that in adults. There are two main types. Infectious hepatitis (Hepatitis A), spread by contamination of water or food with bowel motions from an infected person and serum hepatitis (Hepatitis B), transferred by the use of contaminated syringes or needles or by very close contact. For a few days before the jaundice appears he usually doesn't want to eat. He may have abdominal pain (and even a tender liver), foul breath and be generally unwell. His urine goes dark with the bile it contains, his stools are pale and as the jaundice appears he feels better. The jaundiced stage can last for up to a month after the end of the acute stage of hepatitis. Hepatitis B is generally milder and more gradual in its onset and is sometimes accompanied by arthritis and rashes in addition to the other signs.

As some children have hepatitis but are not jaundiced the diagnosis can be difficult to make and appendicitis may be suggested. Some doctors recommend that the whole family of an infected child be given gamma globulin to protect them but this practice is not widespread.

There is no specific treatment for hepatitis. Bed rest is valuable if the child is very ill and a diet rich in protein and calories seems to help. Some children will be ill enough to have to be treated in hospital but this is not usually necessary. *Related topic* Jaundice.

Hernia (rupture) A weakness in the muscles of the abdominal wall which allows the abdominal contents (intestines and fat) to bulge out in a lump. There are two fairly common types of hernia in children – an umbilical hernia at the umbilicus (tummy button) and an inguinal hernia in the groin (where the tummy joins the leg).

Umbilical hernias are seen in babies because when the umbilical cord detaches itself from the abdominal wall it leaves a temporarily slightly weakened area. Such hernias are much more common in Negro children.

When a child with a hernia cries or coughs the lump bulges even more. Such a hernia is never painful unless a serious complication is setting in.

Almost all umbilical hernias disappear spontaneously by the age of five years without treatment. A coin over the hernia held in place by strapping or special binders used to be popular on the principle that the piece of bowel is better restrained within the abdominal cavity but they have been shown to be useless and even sometimes harmful if a piece of bowel is trapped underneath. If an umbilical hernia doesn't close over spontaneously a minor operation cures the condition permanently.

Inguinal hernias are much less common and are seen almost exclusively in boys. As the testes develop before a baby is born, they are inside the abdomen. They come down two canals in the lower part of the abdominal wall to enter the scrotum. Each side, at the point where the testis emerges from the abdomen during its development is a relatively weak area and it is here that a hernia can occur. Just as with an umbilical hernia, the first sign is usually a swelling which gets bigger on coughing or crying. Unfortunately, the mouth of this type of hernia can be narrow and can trap a piece of bowel. This needs emergency treatment to free the bowel. Because of this, inguinal hernias once discovered must be treated surgically to repair the defect in the abdominal wall. The operation is short and simple and the child is cured permanently as a result.

If your child has a hernia of any sort and the lump becomes a different colour (dark red, blue or purple) or swollen and tense, or if you can't gently push it back through its hole (the hernial opening) your child must be seen by a doctor straight away as these are signs that the hernia is being 'strangulated'. This means that its blood supply is being cut off by pressure from the edges of its hole, and if the doctor can't put it back ('reduce the hernia') then an emergency operation will be necessary.

Hiccups A short, in-breathing noise caused by repeated, uncontrollable contractions of the diaphragm. Some babies hiccup in the womb and may hiccup a lot early in life especially after a feed. Small amounts of milk are sometimes regurgitated with each hiccup. Older children hiccup with indigestion, an overful stomach and even the 'flu. In the under-fives hiccuping is almost never a sign of any underlying disease but if your child doesn't stop within a day see your doctor.

High chair A chair on legs high enough for a baby or young child to sit at the table with the family. The chair usually has a tray fixed to the arms so that the child's food can be put in front of him, though some high chairs are simply ordinary chairs with long legs.

Some high chairs are made of wood and some consist of a plastic seat on a removable stand made of chrome-coated metal legs. Traditional wooden ones (and now some of the modern chrome ones) are hinged in the middle to convert to a push-along seat on wheels with a table in front of the child. The chair also may be detachable from the legs to make a small child's chair. There are usually anchorage points for a safety harness. To make a high chair extra safe, the legs are splayed out for stability. This has the disadvantage, particularly with some of the metal leg chairs, of tripping people up!

A high chair is a useful piece of baby equipment because it leaves the mother's lap free at mealtimes so that she can eat her own meal at the same time as feeding her baby.

A baby can sit in a highchair as soon as he can sit steadily. Although most babies enjoy sitting in their highchair because they associate it with the pleasure of family mealtimes and food, others are not happy to be left in it for long and try their best, even with a harness on, to climb out, or else cry as soon as their meal is over. It's always best to take your child out as soon as he's unhappy, otherwise you may be laying up trouble for the next time you try and put him in. It is best to harness a baby in a high chair or he could fall out. *Related topic* Mealtimes.

Highly strung child

Highly strung child A non-medical term used to describe a child who seems to be temperamentally edgy, cries easily, is more anxious and more moody than other children and reacts strongly to things around him. Children are all of very different temperaments, just like adults, and there is usually little they (or we as parents) can do about it. Even within a family children can be very different, some being introverted, quiet and easy going and others being the opposite.

The highly-strung child is hard work for his parents because he seems to be affected adversely by so many things in life that don't concern other members of the family. He usually thrives on reassurance and with love and an understanding that he is different, he'll grow up to be a normal (if highly strung) adult. This is no tragedy because it takes all sorts to make the world the way it is. So long as the child isn't so nervous that he can't function properly at home or with his friends he'll turn out perfectly all right. If you are really worried about his being so highly strung then see your family doctor who may refer him to a child psychiatrist or psychologist if necessary.

Some previously calm children become temporarily highly-strung because of something that is worrying them. Try, if you can, to discuss the problem and put it right. Reacting with exasperation will be unhelpful to both your child and you.

Hip dislocation

Hip dislocation A congenital condition occurring in between 4 and 11 in every 1,000 babies in which the head of the thigh bone doesn't remain in the socket in the pelvis where it should be. Four times as many girls are affected as boys and it is slightly more common in firstborns and in winter babies. Breech babies are ten times more likely to have dislocated hips. Even more babies (between 8 and 20 in every 1,000) don't actually have a dislocation but have an unstable hip which may dislocate when they start to walk.

Every baby's hips should be examined by a doctor several times during the first year of life at routine medical examinations to detect a dislocated or unstable hip as soon as possible. If when playing with your baby, changing his nappy, or otherwise handling him you feel a click in one of his hips, ask the clinic doctor or family doctor to examine his hips, as sometimes such clicking is a sign that there is some instability in the hip joint.

If a dislocated hip is left untreated, the child grows up with one leg shorter than the other, has a limp, and may be late in walking. Treatment for a dislocated hip is now very effective. The baby has his hips splinted for six to twelve weeks and has check-ups regularly until he is five. A dislocated hip that isn't detected until after a child starts walking can still be treated though the methods are more complex. A hip that is unstable may cure itself within a few weeks of birth with the help of a firm double nappy, but medical advice is essential.

Hirschsprung's disease (megacolon) A congenital condition of
the large bowel that becomes apparent in the first month of life. A defect in the nerve supply to a part of the bowel causes a damming up of gas and bowel motions and the abdomen becomes distended. Operations can be done to remove the affected segment of bowel and these cure the condition.

Occasionally, the condition is confused with constipation but a special x-ray of the large bowel clinches the diagnosis. Babies with the condition are usually constipated from birth but there may be some normal motions early on so causing the diagnosis to be missed until the baby shows signs of intestinal obstruction, weight loss and dehydration. Less dramatic cases come on slowly but the only way such babies can be made to empty their bowels is with the help of an enema. The motions when passed consists of small pellets or are ribbon-like. *Related topics* Constipation; intestinal obstruction.

Hoarseness Any condition that affects the vocal cords can produce
hoarseness which, if extreme, can result in a complete loss of voice. In young children the commonest cause of hoarseness is using their voice too much (usually by screaming or crying) and this produces a swelling of the vocal cords and hoarseness. If the child often becomes hoarse he can develop small, benign (non-cancerous) growths on his vocal cords called 'screamer's nodes'. Other causes of hoarseness in children are croup, laryngitis and allergies. Rarer causes include diphtheria, inhaled foreign bodies stuck in the larynx (voice box) and injuries to the larynx.

Some babies are born with a soft voice box that partially collapses with each inhalation. This produces an intermittent crowing sound which can make a baby's cry seem hoarse. It cures itself within a year or two.

Treatment for hoarseness involves removing or treating the cause and getting the child to rest his voice. Warm fluids to drink are helpful and a warm application to the neck and humidifying the air in the room can be useful too. If your child's hoarseness gets worse day by day or is still there a week later, tell your doctor.

Any hoarse child of less than three months old or any child with difficult breathing, difficult swallowing or drooling should see a doctor at once. **Related topics** Croup; laryngitis.

Holidays Holidays mean very different things to different people, but to the under-fives they have a different meaning still. The vast majority of under-fives see a holiday as a special sort of family outing and nothing more. They may look forward to and talk about a holiday as though it were very important to them but often the bit they like most is coming home. Because of this, short holidays are often better with the under-fives and all need to be planned with them in mind. Family hotels abound and there are even specialist holidays for those with young children. But wherever you go and whatever you do, your under-five won't want to see buildings and views, won't like long periods of driving and sightseeing, and will very soon become bored if you are sunbathing for long. Holidays with the under-fives are pretty selfless affairs for the adults and it's not a bad idea to take along someone who can help you with the children. A granny, aunt or au pair can be helpful if the children get on well with them. It gives them a break and let's you off the hook of twenty-four-hour-a-day child care on holiday

For many fathers their annual holiday gives them a chance to enjoy being with their children all day and to get to know them better.

It's ironic that when taking holidays is so easy (under-fives have no ties to school holidays) and when it's possible to take advantage of off-peak rates, children are too young really to take advantage of holidays yet are old enough to alter ones' holiday plans considerably. Quite a lot of families decide against expensive hotel holidays abroad or in the UK with the under-fives. They decide instead to go camping or for other self-catering holidays or to have several weekends away.

Self-catering holidays are now more popular than ever and can be excellent with a young family. Unfortunately, this means doing most of the cooking but this is no bad thing for young children who usually prefer familiar food. You can eat out a lot and the under-fives love this. Holidays with small children can be had on farms, at holiday camps, under canvas at home or abroad, in a caravan or chalet, or in hotels that have self-catering facilities and nearby villas or chalets. Swapping houses with another family can be a good way of seeing another part of the country, or indeed of the world, and is cheap.

Holidays away with another family can be successful if you know them very well indeed. When doing this be sure to agree on all the details such as who is going to cook, a baby-sitting rota and so on before you go. It's best not to share a car as this throws you too much together and cramps your own family's freedom. Also, it makes sense to arrange outings on your own with your family. This sort of arrangement works well with grandparents if you all get on with each other.

Going on holiday is often a considerable strain for a father. He isn't used to the children all day and can easily get irritable, especially if he sees the holiday as his only chance to get a bit of peace away from work. Normal home routines are disrupted, young children's sleep patterns take time to settle down again and it can all be too much for some parents. The answer is to be flexible. Don't forget you're on holiday. Cast aside your normal routines and be happy to do so. Let the children have a good time but not at the expense of your enjoyment.

Parents sometimes need a holiday away from their young children. Once your child is old enough to be left *happily* with a relative (we feel that this is unlikely before the age of three at least), take the opportunity to get away together. The joy of a day or two away without the children is often as good as a week on a family holiday in some exotic place. Just being together again with no little voices demanding things and interrupted nights can be a real tonic to a flagging relationship. It doesn't have to be expensive to be successful. **Related topics** Camping; hotels.

Honesty A valuable social attribute but one which can be an embarrassment to parents of the under-fives. We'd all like our children to grow up honest, in that they don't steal, or tell lies. A child can learn this by example from his parents. He'll learn to be honest if you don't tell him lies and if he can see that you are willing to admit to mistakes. When your child takes something that isn't his, or tells a lie, gently and calmly, but firmly, explain why he mustn't do it. Don't give him the impression he's wicked but make sure he understands how you (and society) want him to behave. If your child goes through a phase of lying or stealing, you'll have to be very patient in your repetition of why he mustn't do it. Don't make a great fuss about it or talk about his behaviour in front of other people. If you think there is some underlying reason for his behaviour, you may need some professional help from your doctor or health visitor to get to the bottom of it.

Young children have to learn to understand what is right and wrong and we as parents are the main teachers in the early years.

Honesty can become embarrassing when the socially unsophisticated under-five tells people outside the family things that you (and they) would rather not hear – even though they are completely true. A certain amount of tact – not telling the whole truth – especially in interpersonal matters, is desirable and helps the world tick smoothly. Your loquacious five-year-old, however, won't know when to tell the socially acceptable 'white lie' to save someone else's feelings and will often put his foot in it. Simply understand that he can't be blamed for such behaviour and teach him that in certain circumstances the whole truth can be hurtful to other people. It's a difficult concept and he won't grasp it fully at first but this is just one of the many conflicts he'll have to come to terms with as he becomes socially aware.

When it comes to being honest with your children about things in their (and your) lives, be guided by common sense. Most under-fives are much more perceptive than their parents give them credit for and will understand a simple explanation better than you think. By basing your family life on lies you're doing yourself as a parent and your children untold harm. Living with lies in a family is also very destructive if the lie is discovered by the child. Often he's not fooled anyway. Children have a degree of honesty that is refreshing and we adults can learn in turn from them. *Related topic* Lying.

Hormones Naturally-occurring chemicals produced by the endocrine glands of the body. Once produced, they circulate in the blood around the body to control various vital cellular functions. The pituitary gland lies at the base of the brain and acts as a master control for the other endocrine glands (the ovaries, testes, adrenals and thyroid). Too much or too little of any one hormone can produce disease. A well known example is diabetes caused by the production of too little of the hormone insulin. Specialists who deal with hormone problems are called endocrinologists.

Hospitals Children may need to go into hospital for the investigation of an illness or when they are too ill to be nursed at home. Even though serious disease is rare in the under-fives, half of all children under seven will be admitted to hospital at some stage.

Most hospitals have a special children's ward but some do not. The UK Department of Health has recommended that parents should be allowed to visit their young children in hospital on an unrestricted basis and many hospitals make it easy for them to do so. It has been found from several studies that most children under five are better off if they have a parent with them most of the time and especially at night. More enlightened hospitals provide a bed for a parent either in their child's room or ward or close by but the availability of such facilities is very patchy.

Young children need their mothers, especially when they're ill. If hospitalized alone they can feel betrayed or rejected and it may take weeks or months before they get back to normal once home again. Research studies have found that after a single hospital admission of young children of less than a week there are no identifiable or measurable long-term effects on their psychological development. However, recurrent hospital stays can be associated with long-term psychological problems, particularly if there is a family background of psycho-social disadvantage.

It makes sense to start talking about hospitals from a very early age so that a child thinks of them as helpful and relatively pleasant places. Talking about hospitals and reading books about them helps a child to come to terms with the day when he may have to go into one. Then when he gets there it'll seem familiar to some degree. It helps if you point out the local hospital and tell him what happens there as you go about your daily travels in the town. Take every available opportunity to visit friends or relatives in hospital so that your child can see the inside and so become less in awe of it.

Children in long-stay hospitals have very different problems and ideally need a particular nurse or other health professional with whom they can relate over a long period. Some enlightened short-stay hospitals arrange for this kind of 'mother figure' too.

Babies sometimes have to be kept in hospital in a special care baby unit after birth. Such babies are often unintentionally relatively neglected by their mothers (usually through the mistaken belief that a sick or premature newborn baby isn't influenced one way or the other by his mother's presence). This is a great shame for both mother and baby. Mothers miss their babies terribly at this stage and want to be with them and any baby, however sick or small, should be allowed to be in contact with his mother and – if he's well enough to digest milk – should receive his nourishment from her. Even a baby who is too ill to feed properly can be given expressed or pumped breast milk by the mother down a tube. There is evidence that a baby separated from his mother sleeps badly, is more irritable and doesn't feed or thrive as well as when she is there, and also that bonding may be impaired, which may have long term repercussions for both mother and baby. *Useful organization* The National Association for the Welfare of Children in Hospital is a successful and valuable organization that can give you much more information. For further details see page 773.

Hotels There's no doubt that most hotels and young children don't mix very well! Mealtimes in restaurants are the main problem, because children seldom want to sit still for the time it takes to eat in a restaurant, yet letting them get up to play disturbs other diners. Few hotels have high chairs, plastic bowls or bibs, or suitable chairs or cushions for toddlers to bring them up to the right height at the table. Sleeping arrangements can also bring problems, though it's usually possible to be supplied with a cot for a baby and some hotels have communicating rooms so that children aren't down a corridor from their parents at night.

However, increasing numbers of hotels are being equipped to cope with babies and children and such family hotels can provide parents with all the amenities they'd have at home such as a washing machine, nappy buckets, cots, high chairs and so on. Baby-sitting facilities are often provided or you can make use of a baby alarm system so that if your young children wake up in the bedroom they can be heard in the hotel reception area and the parents told at once, or a member of the staff sent upstairs.

If you stay with a baby in a hotel it's much easier if you are breast-feeding so that you don't have to rely on the hotel to provide you with boiled water throughout the day. If you prefer not to use ready-prepared baby foods for young babies, ask the hotel in advance if they will serve alternative meals when the menu has nothing suitable or if they will provide puréed meals. Also, you are far less likely to wake up other guests at night if you are breast-feeding because you can feed the baby at once instead of having to make up a bottle while he cries. Remember to dress in such a way that you can feed without being an embarrassment to the other guests. Although there is nothing to be ashamed of, you may find it easier to relax if you sit with your back to the other tables in a restaurant so that if your baby needs a feed you can feed him out of the full view of other people. A young baby in a carrycot on the floor by your table may get in the way of the waiter or waitress so you may have to have your baby on your lap or put the carrycot within earshot yet out of the way. Many a young baby has slept on his mother's lap under the tablecloth for a whole meal, to the surprise of everyone around.

If you take your young children to a hotel which doesn't cater for families, take care that they are reasonably well behaved and don't upset other people. Take them out during the day so they can let off steam, even if it is raining. However, if you are neurotically worried all the time about what the children will do, they'll sense it and not only won't enjoy themselves so much but may also act out your worst fears. If you confidently expect them to behave well and enjoy themselves, they're more likely to but don't make the mistake of taking children half-way round the world and expecting them to cope straight away with the time zone differences. Some babies cope extremely well but older children will still be on their old 'clocks' for several days. This can be a real nuisance in a hotel which is organized for people to eat and sleep at fairly well-regulated times. **Related topic** Eating out with a baby.

Hot water bottles A hot water bottle is worth its place in any family. It can be used on cold nights to warm the sheets of a cot or a bed before you put your baby or child to sleep. If the bedding is well tucked in or if you are using a duvet, some of the warmth will be retained even if you take the hot water bottle away. Some parents are well-organized enough to fill a hot water bottle at night so that when they take their baby out of his cot for a feed, they can keep the bedding warm with a hot water bottle so that he doesn't awake with a fright from the coldness of his cot when he is put back in to sleep. If ever you leave a hot water bottle in with the child, you must make sure firstly that the stopper is screwed in properly and fits well; secondly, that there is a cover on the hot water bottle so that the bottle is never in direct contact with the child's skin; thirdly, that you check that the child doesn't get overheated (which can be very dangerous for a young baby or for any child with a fever) with a bottle and lots of bedding; and fourthly, that you never use a hot water bottle anywhere near an electric blanket. To avoid any danger of burns, never use boiling water to fill a hot water bottle but use very hot water instead.

A hot water bottle is not only a source of warmth but is also emotionally comforting to many children. To some extent it takes the place of a parent's or brother's or sister's warm body to cuddle up to. Babies and children who sleep with their parents or another sibling won't want or need a hot water bottle. Children like fancy covers for their bottles such as furry animal ones or ones knitted with pretty coloured wool. In this way they double as a cuddly as well as a source of warmth.

A hot water bottle can be very comforting if a child has earache, before any medicine has a chance to work. Put a covered hot water bottle filled with hot but not boiling water against the child's ear or let him lie with his ear on top of it. Similarly, a hot water bottle may help a tummy ache or an aching muscle. *Related topic* Scalds.

Humidifiers Pieces of equipment designed to increase the amount of water vapour in the air we breathe. Many homes and buildings today are kept very warm and very dry throughout much of the winter. There is a body of medical opinion that suggests that such drying produces a reduced resistance of the nasal passages to infection with the common cold and other respiratory viruses. If you keep the temperature of your home just below 70°F (21°C) there shouldn't be a problem with excessively dry, hot air but if you'd still like to humidify your home there are many commercially produced gadgets available, from pans of water that hang over radiators to sophisticated electric moist air producers.

If a child gets croup, or indeed any upper respiratory infection, humidifying the air seems to give real relief. In the US several different types of cold and steam humidifiers are popular with parents but very few parents in the UK have them. There's very little point going to the expense of buying one simply for when your child is ill, because a domestic kettle boiling away in a safe corner of the room is just as effective. In an emergency with croup, carry the child into a warm bathroom, fill the bath with hot water and shut the door. This generates plenty of steam which helps the child's breathing a lot.

Hydrocele A collection of fluid around the testis on one or both sides which makes the testis look and feel bigger than it is. If you hold a torch behind the swollen part of your baby's scrotum and darken the room, you'll see that the light shines through the fluid in a hydrocele.

Sometimes a hydrocele is present at birth. In the most common sort, the fluid gradually disappears on its own, usually in the baby's first year, and does no damage.

With the less common type of hydrocele the swelling round the testis may seem larger at the end of a busy day. This sort is often associated with an inguinal hernia.

If a hydrocele hasn't disappeared by the age of four or five a small operation can be done to remove it. *Related topic* Hernia.

Hydrocephalus (water on the brain) Fluid is produced within the brain to bathe its surfaces, its interior cavities and the spinal cord. This cerebrospinal fluid carries nutrients to the brain and spinal cord and also acts as a hydraulic buffer to cushion the effect of knocks on the head and the movements of the brain inside the skull as we move our heads in daily life.

Hydrocephalus can be caused by several conditions. The commonest today is a congenital malformation of the brain that blocks off the flow of cerebrospinal fluid. When it comes on later in childhood the cause is usually meningitis or a tumour. Hydrocephalus can be seen alone or with spina bifida.

Although some babies can be diagnosed as having the condition while still in the womb, this is uncommon – normally the signs don't show up until the child is a few weeks or even months old. Routine measurements of the baby's head may baffle you but they're essential if early hydrocephalus is to be detected and treated. A baby with hydrocephalus has a bulging fontanelle (soft spot) and in severe cases the baby's head can enlarge at a rate of one inch (2.5cm) a month. This produces a very distressing appearance. The forehead bulges, the whites of the eyes are clearly visible above the iris and the scalp thins and becomes shiny. If this state isn't treated, permanent brain damage can occur.

Treatment is surgical. Tiny drainage tubes can be inserted to get around the blockage in the brain and the fluid re-routed usually into the heart. Until such operations were invented two-thirds of these children died. Now, two-thirds live. *Useful organization* Association for Spina Bifida and Hydrocephalus.

Hygiene Domestic hygiene is a subject of considerable controversy. Some people believe that a home containing young children and babies should be spotless so that they don't pick up infections and others seem to have perfectly healthy children with dirty homes.

Personal hygiene There's little doubt that personal hygiene is worthwhile. Teaching a child to wash himself is essential or he'll start getting infections in his creases and a sore bottom. Fresh-smelling, clean babies are much more pleasant to have around than babies who smell of vomit or stale milk and this can really only come about if you wash them frequently. Girls left unbathed get irritation and reddening of their vulvas and boys can get inflamed foreskins.

In addition to keeping your children clean their teeth should be cleaned using a good nylon brush and a fluoride toothpaste at least once a day, preferably before they go to bed. An after-breakfast clean is also worthwhile. All children should be taught to wash their hands after going to the lavatory, even if they haven't wiped their own bottoms. Of course, remember to wash your own hands after helping a young child with the lavatory. It also makes sense to wash hands before meals, especially if the child has been playing out in the street or with pets.

Hygiene in the home In the kitchen it's important to keep food refrigerated and to be scrupuously careful about hand washing, especially when dealing with raw meat or poultry. Be sure to keep cuts and sores covered with waterproof dressings. If you do your clothes washing in the kitchen sink be careful to wash everything down afterwards before preparing food on the same surfaces. Keep tea towels well laundered or leave dishes to dry on their own. Don't let dish cloths get smelly but wash them regularly or use kitchen paper instead. Keep food covered, especially if there are pets in the family.

Rubbish isn't usually a source of disease in this country because it is regularly collected. Even so it's sensible to wrap up rubbish in polythene bags or newspaper before putting it in the dustbin. This is especially sensible in hot weather or flies will breed on your rubbish and transfer infections to your food. If you have infestations of mice, rats, cockroaches, fleas or any other pest your local pest control officer at the town hall will help.

Pets are a real source of hygiene hazards and should be kept clean and healthy all the time. It makes sense not to allow animals to lick children's faces and mouths because certain diseases can be transmitted to them. It is probably not sensible to get a new puppy if you have a young baby crawling on the floor. Wait until he's mobile, then get your pup and ensure that he is regularly wormed.

No home is sterile and there's no reason why it should be. Children and adults learn to live with the bacteria that normally live in their house and in the water supply.

On balance the chances of catching a serious infection at home as a result of poor hygiene are very small and there's certainly no need to keep scouring the house with disinfectant solutions. Children pick up more infections in the first year at school than they ever will from your home provided you stick to the simple measures outlined above.

Hyperactive child Hyperactivity is a controversial subject. Hyperactive means 'more active than normal' but straight away we come up against the problem of knowing what 'normal' is. All young children are hyperactive compared with middle-aged people but does this make them abnormal? Any one 'child varies from another in his level of activity and excitement, which depends on his age, health, happiness, how much sleep he's getting, his level of stimulation, the time of day and many other factors. Hyperactivity can only be judged in comparison with other children of the same age or the same stage of development.

Hyperactivity isn't a disease but can be a symptom. Most normal children under the age of five are hyperactive at times; older children who are intellectually bright and imaginative are also sometimes over-active, as are some children with domestic stress, and some with hearing and visual defects. A very few 'medical' conditions can cause it, notably over-activity of the thyroid gland, some cases of retardation, and certain psychiatric disorders. All of these are pretty uncommon though. There is evidence which suggests that some children become hyperactive as a reaction to certain foods or food additives. Often no cause is found.

Although such children can be difficult to control and are very wearing to have around, at the moment the medical profession is none too helpful in sorting out the problem except for prescribing mild tranquillizers. The Hyperactive Children's Support Group (see page 769 for address) will give details of a special diet which has proved useful for many children.

If ever your child becomes unusually active after receiving any medication, take him to the doctor at once. *Useful organization* Hyperactive Children's Support Group.

Hypospadias A congenital condition in which the urinary opening (normally found on the tip of a boy's penis) opens underneath the tip or even way back along the shaft. If your child has this condition he should see a doctor. He should not be circumcised. Some boys with hypospadias will need an operation to cure the condition but if the opening is only a little displaced and wide enough for a good stream of urine, no treatment is needed. When the opening is far back there are often other abnormalities and complicated surgical treatment may be necessary. *Related topics* Circumcision; foreskin.

Hypothermia A condition in which a baby's temperature falls too low, usually because of being exposed to cold conditions.

Babies have poor temperature control mechanisms compared with older children and adults and must be kept warm. Don't judge your baby's temperature by his hands or feet. They can feel cold if he isn't wearing mittens even though his body temperature (feel his chest) is fine. It's really only for the first six to eight weeks that you need to worry about the air temperature around your baby and if you keep this between 60 and 65°F (15 and 18°C) you won't go far wrong. After this age just keep him warm as you would yourself. Dress him up to go out and at night and add more clothing if he feels cold to the touch. A sheepskin placed in a cot or pram for a baby to lie on directly will help keep him warm, especially if you tuck his covers around it. A hat too prevents such heat loss. *Related topics* Fever; temperature.

Ice cream A very popular food among children but one which has little nutritionally to recommend it. Ice creams have large numbers of additives of several different kinds and a high fat content. Because they contain artificial colours and flavours children shouldn't eat too much of them, though there is nothing particularly harmful about ice cream taken in small amounts.

With a freezer in so many homes it's important to remember to keep ice cream fully frozen and not to let it thaw to a semi-liquid and then to re-freeze it. This promotes the growth of food poisoning bacteria. As soon as you have dished out ice cream from a container put the whole lot back in the freezer at once. If you have a freezer it's very easy to make your own ice cream out of more wholesome ingredients.

Illness When children are ill they want love and sympathy and there's no harm letting the child have his own way and enjoy being waited on during the worst part of his illness. The most difficult thing for a parent is to hide his or her own anxieties about the child. Often even a very young child will be more alarmed by his parents' reaction to his condition than he himself ever would have been. Giving a child lots of attention during an acute illness does no harm at all but you may have to have a period of re-adjustment to normality as he gets better. Such spoiling doesn't work well for children with long-term illnesses and both adults and child have to settle down to a very different lifestyle compared with that of a family with an acutely ill child.

When a child is sick he'll probably go off his food. Be guided by what your child wants to eat and pander to what he wants while he's not feeling well. Never force an ill child to eat but do ensure that he gets plenty to drink. Any fluids he likes are acceptable even if you usually wouldn't allow sugar-rich colas and similar 'junk' drinks. An ill child can be tempted to eat something once the acute phase of the illness is over by prettying it up in some way. Hundreds and thousands sprinkled over puddings or little dishes of something made especially for him can get him on the path to eating again. Quite often a child will suddenly start eating a lot at the end of his illness as if to make up for the food he has missed out.

One of the most taxing problems when your child is ill is keeping him amused and entertained. Older children will enjoy watching TV some of the time but even this can be boring after a while because most of the programmes during the day aren't for children of this age. A video cassette recorder comes into its own at a time like this as you can play back your child's favourite programmes time and again. When it comes to toys, bear in mind that your child won't be able to cope with as difficult things as usual because of how he feels. A new toy is a good idea for a sick child because it makes him feel special and takes his mind off feeling rotten for a while. Don't worry about tidiness around a sick child: let him have a mess of familiar things around him and clean up once a day, perhaps before he goes to sleep. Galt Toys 30/31 Great Marlborough Street, London will send you their leaflet on 'Toys & Ideas for Children when Ill' if you send them a stamped addressed envelope.

If your child has a fever, he'll need more drinks than usual to make up for the fluid loss caused by sweating. A covered beaker or a glass with a bendy straw may be useful if he can't sit up comfortably. It doesn't matter for a few days if he doesn't want to eat much, but it *does* matter if he doesn't drink, so be sure to help him take a few sips every so often.

It often surprises parents just how ill their child can seem yet how quickly he can be back to normal. Children do seem to swing from 'death's door' to miraculous recovery much more quickly than do adults. If ever you are worried about your child when he's ill, don't hesitate to phone your doctor. He may put your mind at rest over the phone or come around to see the child if he's at all worried. *Related topics* Bed – ill child in; fever.

Imagination Our minds are wonderful things and besides accepting and correlating information we can make up stories, think up new ideas, have visions of situations, new or old, and dream – by night or day. We can use our imagination in a controlled way or we can let it run riot. It is a fantastic tool and a source of both pleasure and fear to a child.

Fairy stories fuel children's imagination with ideas and pictures they might otherwise not have imagined. However, even children who aren't told such stories can always find something to wonder at or be afraid of, though it might not be cast as a fairy godmother, the treasure at the rainbow's end, a witch, a dragon, or a wolf.

We don't know when a child starts using his imagination but it becomes apparent that he is when he starts making up stories which he hasn't heard before; suggests new games; pretends to be someone else while dressing-up; or lives through a situation he is looking forward to. The powers of a child's imagination can be encouraged by listening to his stories and enjoying them; by making up stories for him; by playing imaginative games with him or suggesting ones to him and his friends; by talking about a pleasurable future event; and by describing past events in vivid detail. 'Let's pretend' is a game that children delight in, especially if a parent participates, or even initiates it.

Sometimes the things a child imagines become difficult to separate in his mind from reality. He may believe that there *is* a witch behind a curtain in his bedroom at night, for example, and be really terrified as a result. He may start thinking about burglars and then be convinced that there is one outside his bedroom. Some children in their half-sleep imagine or dream that they have been to the lavatory then actually wet the bed because in their mind they were actually sitting on the lavatory.

If a child doesn't fully understand a situation, he may imagine that he has had more of an influence on it than he actually has. A child whose brother, sister, or parent is ill or has died, for example, may imagine that because he once ever wished they were ill or dead that somehow he has been the cause of that illness or death. He is so convinced by what he imagines to be the case that he can become emotionally disturbed unless someone fathoms out what he is thinking and helps him sort out fantasy from fact. *Related topics* Creativity; drama; fantasy; guilt in children; imagination.

Immigrant children

Children are children the world over and most of the problems parents have are the same the world over. One of the greatest differences that immigrant parents may face is the loss of their extended family. Such a loss in an alien culture coupled with a real sense of loneliness can be very stressful for immigrant mothers and their children. Financial and housing problems may affect some families too. If you feel all this is getting you down do talk to your doctor or health visitor. Many recent immigrants to this country don't realize at the start that they'll have to re-think their roles. A man might have taken little interest in domestic affairs back home, which was quite acceptable when child-rearing was shared between many women. Now his wife is alone with this task he may have to change his behaviour so as to help her more.

With all this as a background and with all the language problems, immigrants want very much to do the best for their children. Undoubtedly learning English must come high on the list of priorities and many local authorities provide free daytime classes to enable you to do this. Without a good command of English, the immigrant parent can't hope to be integrated into local society and cannot provide the best for his children. Some such families rely on their bilingual children to act as interpreters but this has many drawbacks.

If you have children it really is important to go for regular check-ups at the baby clinic or with your doctor. This ensures that any illnesses are picked up early. A shortage of vitamin D can be a problem for dark-skinned children who need to be exposed to more sunlight than white children if they are to make enough of the vitamin in their skin. Rickets, the disease caused by too little vitamin D, causes bent bones, poor teeth and weakness. A breast-fed baby can get low on vitamin D if his mother rarely goes out of doors and so produces little vitamin D in her skin. In many parts of the country vitamin drops are given to dark-skinned immigrant children to overcome this problem.

There is a lot of help available for immigrant parents and their children and information can be found at your local citizens' advice bureau (number in the telephone book); your local Department of Health and Social Security office; and from your health visitor, and child health clinic. Many of these places have helpful leaflets and booklets written in several Indian dialects and other languages and in most areas with large immigrant populations there are local officials (as well as doctors) who speak your language.

A major decision for immigrant parents with children is choosing which language to teach them. Children brought up speaking their parents' language develop a stronger feeling for their cultural background and experts say that such a child, if fluent in his own language, will have no difficulties learning English. On the other side of the argument the child who starts school at five with no English will have considerable problems in coping with a new environment and a new language at the same time. A child brought up to speak English right from the start gets on quickly and will start school feeling equal to the other children but can have the disadvantage of being regarded as a foreigner by his school friends who hear his strange accent and by some of his family who may not be able to understand him at all. The accent soon disappears at school.

In some areas there are play-groups especially run for immigrant children. It is up to immigrant parents to decide whether they want to integrate their children with the local children right from the start. We feel this is a good idea because at five the child will go to a multi-racial school and so might as well be prepared for it.

Children of immigrant parents may start off with a disadvantage because they can all too easily lose any sense of who they are. They know they are different because they speak differently and may look different but often they have no real roots in their parents' culture because they were born here. It's a tough job for immigrant parents to retain their social differences with dignity yet integrate their children into a new society. **Related topics** Bilingual child; rickets; vitamins.

Immunization There are two ways in which a person can become immune to a disease. He can either have an attack of it, in which case his body produces natural antibodies to it, or he can have his immunity built up by active or passive immunization. Passive immunization involves the giving of antibodies which have been produced in another person or animal. Active immunization involves the injection of weakened forms or extracts of the organisms themselves which trigger off the person's own antibody production.

A baby is born with some antibodies to certain diseases because he gets them from his mother across the placenta. She, of course, must have had the disease or been immunized against it herself or she won't have the antibodies in her blood. Just because a mother has suffered from a particular infection, it doesn't necessarily mean that her baby will be completely (or even partially) protected from it. A breast-fed baby continues to receive valuable antibodies, some of which perform a crucial protective role in the intestine. Colostrum, the earliest breast milk, is especially rich in antibodies. Breast milk also contains other anti-infective factors which a bottle-fed baby misses out on. This is why bottle-fed babies are liable to have more infections (especially of the intestine) than breast-fed babies.

As a baby matures he starts to produce his own antibodies but this takes about three to six months.

All children under five in this country are offered routine immunization against diphtheria, whooping cough, tetanus, polio and measles. Routine vaccination against smallpox is no longer necessary. The timing of these immunizations has varied considerably over the years but the most commonly used schedule today is for a baby to have the first dose of his triple vaccine (diphtheria, tetanus and whooping cough) together with oral polio vaccine at about three months followed by a second dose six to eight weeks later and a third dose six months after that. Measles vaccine is usually given in the second year. If you have your baby immunized according to this schedule he'll either never get these diseases at all or will only get them very mildly.

It's a good idea to keep a record of your child's immunizations just in case another doctor or clinic needs to refer to it. When it comes to the day of your child's injection do tell the doctor if he's at all unwell. The common cold is no reason for putting off immunizing a child but it should not be done if he has anything more serious. The last in the series of routine immunizations will be given in your child's first year at school when he'll receive an injection against diphtheria, tetanus and polio but not whooping cough because the dangers of this disease to a child of five are negligible. If you are taking your child abroad you should enquire whether any special immunizations are advisable or even required in the countries you are visiting. Your travel agent will know. *Related topics* Diphtheria; smallpox; tetanus; whooping cough.

Impetigo A highly infectious bacterial disease of the skin which usually affects the face, scalp or hands. It is most often seen in school children among whom outbreaks can occur. It can also be seen as a complication of eczema, cold sores, scabies and urticaria that has been scratched.

Skin affected with impetigo has weeping, yellow/brown crusts which follow small red spots. Healing starts at the centre, leaving rings of reddened skin. As the area heals there may be a slight loss of skin colour but this returns to normal. Antibiotic ointment is the only effective treatment but antibiotic tablets may also be necessary. If the area is covered with a loose, dry dressing, your child can play with others or go to play-school or nursery. Don't feel ashamed if your child gets impetigo. It's no fault of yours and certainly doesn't mean that your home is dirty. Be sure to wash your hands well after washing or dressing your child's skin, to prevent the spread of infection.

Impetigo has only one serious complication and that rarely occurs. It is a special type of nephritis that can occur in epidemics. It makes the urine go dark brown and there may be a headache and raised blood pressure too. The condition is short-lived and heals completely in the majority of children. ***Related topic*** Nephritis.

Incest Sexual relations between two people in the same family who are prohibited by law from having intercourse. Although it is very common in some degree (intercourse itself is not common but the stages leading up to it certainly are) throughout the world, nowhere is incest considered normal and acceptable behaviour. It has been described by experts in psychosexual medicine as the last taboo. It is rare according to official statistics which record only the few cases that actually get to the courts. Child sexual abuse on the other hand is probably quite common.

It is very common for young brothers and sisters to play with each other sexually, and they may do so with other children too. This sort of sexual discovery virtually never results in any attempt at intercourse. There is no harm in this type of childish play unless there is guilt about it at the time or afterwards. When true incest occurs between brother and sister the brother is often much older. This is the commonest form of incest.

The commonest form of adult-child incest is between fathers and daughters. How much harm is done by such incestuous relationships is difficult to assess but undoubtedly many girls are severely affected psychologically for the rest of their lives. Many feel guilty that they were at fault in leading their fathers on but the responsibility for what happened must lie squarely with the parent who, with his superior experience and wisdom, should not have let things get out of hand.

It may come as a surprise to learn that mothers often know of the incestuous relationship and connive at it for several reasons. No one knows why some men turn to their daughters for sexual gratification but studies have found that many such men are mentally unstable, have alcohol or aggression problems or have a poor relationship with their wives.

Incest with children under five isn't common but certainly does occur. There is no way that a child of this age could lead her father on and anyone who has a sexual relationship with a child so young needs urgent psychiatric help. Unfortunately the damage has been done before the father goes for help and a child can be scarred for life by such an experience. Jailing the father may break up the family and anyway, research shows that once out of jail he often goes back to his old pursuits.

Deciding what to do if you suspect incest in the family can be extremely difficult. It is probably best to start with your GP who may well be able to tackle the problem 'sideways' rather than by direct confrontation. The social services department of your local town hall will also be able to help and will have special knowledge of how to cope with the problem. Although there are no easy answers in such cases, it's probably best to air the problem and get it sorted out sooner rather than later. *Related topics* Child abuse; gonorrhoea.

Incubation period The time that elapses between a child coming into contact with a disease and starting to show signs of having it himself. These times vary from child to child, even within a family, but the following figures are averages: chickenpox 13–17 days; diphtheria 1–5 days; german measles 14–21 days; measles 10 days; mumps 14–28 days; scarlet fever 2–5 days; whooping cough 8–14 days; gastroenteritis 0–24 hours; bacterial meningitis 1–10 days; viral meningitis 0–7 days; coughs and colds 0–48 hours; rheumatic fever 1–6 weeks; polio 10–12 days; roseola 7–17 days. *Related topics* Isolation periods; quarantine.

Incubator A purpose built chamber in which to keep babies that are too ill, too small or too immature to be nursed in a cot. The main purpose of an incubator is to keep babies warm. Premature babies are more likely to get cold than full-term babies, possibly because they don't have as much body fat. Also, if they are kept at an optimum temperature and not allowed to get too cold, their energy reserves (calories from food) can be used for growth rather than for the maintenance of body temperature.

A useful but often forgotten place for a baby to be kept warm is against his mother's body, where he'll benefit not only physically from her body heat but also emotionally by the reassurance of her familiar smell, sound and sight. A sling with ample head support is an ideal way of keeping a newborn premature baby warm, provided he is not too ill to be with his mother. This has the additional advantage that his mother can offer him the breast very frequently as she is with him all the time. An incubator sometimes seems to produce a psychological barrier against the frequent breast-feeding which is so essential for small babies. The majority of babies who need to be nursed in an incubator are premature.

Most incubators are box-shaped containers on wheels or on a trolley that stands at waist height. There is a transparent plastic dome over the top of a surface which acts as a bed for the baby. A thermostatically controlled heater keeps the temperature to the optimum level and air is circulated to keep it pure and fresh. The inside of the dome is a controlled environment shut off from the outside world but is accessible through the port-holes into which parents', doctors' and nurses' hands can be inserted to cuddle or perform procedures on the baby. This controlled environment is designed to overcome the major problems suffered by premature babies – a tendency to a low body temperature and an increased likelihood of getting an infection. Such incubators undoubtedly help save the lives of thousands of babies each year.

Having said this, many hospitals behave as though a baby who needs to be in an incubator doesn't need his mother any more. Nothing could be further from the truth. Research has shown that the separation of mothers from their babies harms both of them and can even have long-term effects on the baby. Because of this we believe that mothers and babies in incubators should be given every possible opportunity to be together right from birth. You will be able to cuddle your baby out of the incubator for short periods if he isn't desperately ill and certainly you can put your hands inside and stroke and hold him. Some enlightened hospitals give mothers a photograph of their baby to take home so that even when they are not with the child they can feel some closeness. It's unpleasant enough going home without your baby, so do all you can to stay close to him whenever you can. *Related topic* Bonding; low birth weight.

Independence One of the basic tasks parents have is to help their child become independent. Only when this has happened is their most important job done, though the average parent will continue to support his grown-up child emotionally and, if possible, practically for much of his life.

In our society, children rely on their parents for shelter, warmth, clothing and food until they are capable of earning a living themselves. During the first five years, they are at first completely dependent on their parents (and usually on their mother in particular) for all their needs, and gradually become increasingly less so. They learn to walk, talk, dress, feed, wash, use the lavatory and amuse themselves. Some children learn certain skills of independence faster than others, and some may be delayed or even prevented from becoming completely independent by problems such as physical or mental handicap or ill health.

Emotional independence is as important as physical independence and it is regularly observed that children allowed to be as dependent on their mothers as they want to be for the first few years are the ones who become more independent and self-confident later. Children go on needing emotional support from their parents throughout their childhood and often later as well.

Apart from not allowing a young child to be sufficiently dependent, the development of independence can also be hampered by smothering him with attention and care and by doing things for him that he could (or would prefer to) do for himself. However much you might enjoy looking after a child, you'll only be doing your best for him if you allow and gently encourage him to learn how to cope with life by himself. If you're there to give a helping hand when he needs it, you'll be doing the best for him in the long term. *Related topic* Dependence.

Indigestion A rather woolly concept in children under five and especially in babies. Undoubtedly tummy ache and discomfort after food can occur in young children who gorge themselves on too much of one food or who bolt their food down quickly, swallowing a lot of air as they do, but indigestion is probably not a helpful concept in this age group. Colic is a much more familiar term. *Related topics* Abdominal pain; colic.

Infanticide The killing of an infant (a child in the first year of life). Fortunately this is an uncommon crime in our society. In the last few years we have become more aware of the number of babies who are dangerously neglected or actually assaulted. The law takes into account the fact that some women are emotionally and psychologically disturbed in the year following the birth of a child and some have severe post-natal depression. Under the Infanticide Act of 1938 a mother can't be found guilty of murdering her child within twelve months of the birth provided that 'the balance of her mind was disturbed by reason of her not having fully recovered from the effects of giving birth'. *Related topic* Child abuse.

Infant mortality The infant mortality rate is defined as the number of babies under one year of age dying out of every thousand babies born alive. In England and Wales in 1980 this figure was twelve. The total number of babies born alive who died before their first birthday was 7,019 in 1981.

The commonest causes of death in this age group are conditions arising in the perinatal period: before, during and after the birth. Over three thousand babies died in 1980 as a result of the respiratory distress syndrome; being of low birth weight; having various other respiratory conditions; being short of oxygen before or during labour; bleeding; or various related conditions.

Over 2,000 babies died because of a congenital abnormality, with spina bifida the worst offender and just over 1,000 babies died from a cot death. Respiratory conditions claimed the lives of about 800 babies, 400 dying from pneumonia or influenza.

The statistics are horrifying in terms of human suffering and misery, but it's important to remember that they have improved tremendously over the last century with the help of modern obstetrics, surgery and medicine. The most dangerous time though is still the first week of life. Once a baby is past this his prospects immediately improve and once he is past a year old, they improve again.

The loss of a much looked-forward-to and much loved baby is a tragic blow to a family and it's important for them to mourn their loss just as they would mourn the loss of an older child or an adult. It seems to make no difference to the extent of their suffering that they have only known the baby for a short time, though sometimes outsiders try to lessen the burden of the loss by suggesting that this is so. Patient, skilled and sympathetic counselling may help to get the parents back on their feet again, and some parents find it helps to talk to other parents who have experienced a similar loss. *Related topics* Bereavement; cot death; dying child; perinatal mortality; stillbirth. *Useful organizations* The Compassionate Friends; The Foundation for the Study of Infant Deaths; The Sudden Infant Death Association.

Influenza ('flu) A general infection usually affecting the upper respiratory system, caused by viruses. 'Flu often occurs in epidemics though the acute stage lasts only a few days in any one person. Unfortunately the immunity conferred by one attack doesn't last very long and the strains of 'flu virus are constantly changing from year to year, which is why we can get repeated attacks of 'flu.

In young children the symptoms may be those of a cold with possibly a sore throat too. There is a high fever, sweating, and the child may have generalized aches and pains, especially in the limbs and back. Painful eyes and a cough are not uncommon and diarrhoea, vomiting and croup or even nosebleeds are sometimes seen too. There is no effective anti-viral treatment for 'flu and rest (though probably not in bed as few children like to rest alone) is the best treatment available. Plenty of fluid is necessary to replace that lost because of the sweating and the diarrhoea but many young children with 'flu don't want to eat. This doesn't usually matter because it is a short-lived infection and they'll come to no harm.

Your doctor may suggest treatment with antibiotics if a bacterial infection occurs as well but otherwise they aren't necessary or even desirable. Young children with 'flu can get pneumonia, middle ear infections, sinusitis or mastoiditis and these will, of course, have to be treated seriously.

Most children recover after three or four days with 'flu but many feel weak or even depressed for some weeks after. This will show up as listlessness and general irritability. If a child is irritable or lethargic at the time of the 'flu you should contact a doctor at once, as you should if there is rapid breathing or earache. *Related topics* Colds; dehydration; fever; virus.

Inherited diseases Some diseases which run in families, such as diabetes and allergic disorders, are inherited as a *tendency* to get the disease under certain conditions and others are inherited as a disease proper.

Although nature rejects most of her mistakes by aborting the affected foetus early in pregnancy, many defective foetuses are born alive. Having said this, only about two in every hundred live births have any abnormality at all and many of these are not inherited.

Some inherited conditions are brought about by an abnormal genetic structure in one parent only and others are caused by abnormalities in both parents even though the parents may be apparently quite well and normal. Some conditions are the result of disordered metabolism in the body, sometimes because of the complete absence of a particular enzyme.

Examples of inherited conditions are galactosaemia, phenylketonuria, colour blindness, albinism and haemophilia and there are many more.

The study of genetics is now so advanced that a great deal of help can be given to parents of a child with an inherited disorder to help them decide whether to have any more children. Many inherited conditions can be detected before the baby is born and, if the condition is severe and parents are willing, such foetuses can be aborted. Genetic counselling is widely available. Most areas of the country have centres where such specialists can be seen. Because certain inherited diseases are carried from generation to generation by seemingly normal people (called carriers) the whole subject can become very complex, especially when it comes to marrying another carrier. If two carriers have children they have a one in four chance of having an abnormal baby and the other three children will either be normal or be carriers themselves. Certain inherited conditions are called sex-linked recessive, that is, they affect boys only (haemophilia is a well-known example). An unaffected woman married to an affected man, who is carrying a boy foetus, has a fifty per cent chance of his being affected with such a condition and so may want to seek an abortion.

There is hope that in the future genetic engineering could provide some of the answers to these unpleasant inherited disorders, which at the moment are mostly unpreventable. Unfortunately, meddling with people's genetic structure is politically a very sensitive subject because of the potential for abuse, so progress is not likely to be very fast. *Related topics* Albinism; colour blindness; galactosaemia; genetic counselling; haemophilia; phenylketonuria.

Insect bites and stings

We are fortunate in the UK in not having many insects which bite people. Most children when stung or bitten by an insect aren't greatly harmed but such stings can be dangerous if they involve the mouth or throat or if the child is over-sensitive to the injected poison. Such children can become very distressed and may have difficulty in breathing. In either of these cases get medical help as an emergency.

A bee leaves its sting in the flesh but it can easily be removed with tweezers or clean finger nails. You can also 'wipe' it out of the skin with a pin or a needle held flat to the skin. Be careful when removing the sting not to squeeze the poison sac. If you grip the sting very low down near the skin you should have no trouble. Once the sting is out, apply a little calamine lotion or hold the area under cold water.

A wasp leaves no sting in the skin. Place some lemon juice or vinegar on the area. If a child should accidentally eat a piece of food with a wasp on it, a sting in the throat can be dangerous. Get immediate medical help and give the child cold drinks or get him to hold ice in his mouth.

Horseflies, mosquitoes, gnats, fleas, bedbugs and sandflies are all possible sources of insect bites in the UK but none produce any problems except in highly susceptible individuals who may even go into shock. Soothing lotions are helpful, ice or saliva is calming and antihistamine tablets are useful if stings or bites are keeping the child awake at night.

Insect repellent creams and insect sprays may be useful in some situations. In some countries nets around the bed at night and insect screens at the doors and windows are used.

Interestingly, some people are much more likely to be stung or bitten than others, perhaps because their individual body smell is more attractive to insects.

Always contact a doctor at once if a child has wheezing; difficulty in breathing; severe urticaria (nettlerash); or abdominal pains after an insect bite. *Related topics* Fleas; insect repellent creams and sprays.

Insect repellent creams and sprays Creams or sprays which if applied to the skin help stop insects from biting you. They have to be applied all over exposed skin and then reapplied frequently in areas where bites are likely because children soon rub the cream off as they play. The degree of protection afforded by a cream or spray depends upon things such as sweating, bathing and being wiped off. They should never be used on the eyelids or the lips and should be kept away from tiny babies.

Don't leave aerosol sprays of insect repellent around where children could get at them. *Related topic* Insect bites and stings.

Insecurity An insecure child is one who is anxious, afraid, unconfident, uncertain, or feels he is not adequately protected. Western, separatist methods of baby and child care must be responsible for many such feelings of insecurity and separation anxiety.

A child can be perfectly confident in his parents' love for him and yet be afraid when his imagination runs riot at night. The insecurity shown by a child who is frightened of being left alone in bed is a direct descendant of the separation anxiety he felt as a young baby when his mother left him crying in his cot. Human babies like to be with their mothers and not just in the same house. They don't feel adequately protected from all the dangers their imaginations can produce unless their mothers are right there by them. However much you love your baby, he may still feel insecure if you expect him to behave as though he were grown-up and brave when he is dependent and scared of being alone. The crying of a baby whose mother insists on making him wait for a specified time between feeds has a good cause. It is designed to worry his mother and to alert her to the fact that her baby needs her. When the system goes wrong because the mother fails to respond to the cry, the baby is naturally worried and insecure because his source of food and drink has vanished, along with his place of comfort.

Separation anxiety can cause feelings of insecurity in toddlers and pre-school children too.

Children can also feel insecure if their parents row and fight. Even young children know that their safety and protection depends on having parents. When they see their parents looking angry and hear them saying terrible things to each other, it naturally makes the child think that his world may be about to break up. It's very important after a row to let your child know that you have made up and forgiven each other, otherwise he might worry for days after you have forgotten the whole incident. Money and housing worries are best kept from young children who haven't the experience to put them into perspective but may worry themselves sick instead. It's understandable that a child will feel terribly insecure if his parents break up and live apart. Such insecurity is all too obvious and can have a lasting effect on a child. Loss of a parent in early childhood through death, separation, long term illness or divorce has been found to be a relatively common occurrence among adults who are seriously depressed.

A common threat to a child who has been misbehaving or annoying his tired and impatient mother is that she will go away from him or send him away. Though *she* knows she won't do either, a young child may easily believe her and worry to himself for a long time in case she might carry out her threat. Try never to make such threats and try also not to let your child go to sleep knowing that you are cross or unhappy with him. Under-fives are much more sensitive than most adults give them credit for yet they don't have the maturity to be able to sort out threats from what you really mean.

It's easy to make your child insecure if you undermine his confidence as he grows up by constantly criticizing his behaviour, his friends, his appearance, his ideas, or what he wants to do or to have. You may not realize that so many of your remarks are negative. It often takes an outsider to remark on it – if they know you well enough to do so. Really make an effort to tell your child about his strong points and never miss an opportunity to boost his self-esteem. No child will know instinctively what you feel about him – he must be told. So take care to balance what you say if you want your child to feel secure. Some parents have the knack of never being negative to their child (or to other people) but instead find ways to influence them which aren't obviously critical in a negative way. Such people also take great care to praise their child when he does well, so letting him grow up thinking he is a good person who pleases them. Such a child is highly likely to grow up to be a confident and happy person with a good self-image and few insecurities. **Related topics** Anxiety; dependence; fear; separation anxiety; separation of parents.

Insurance Many young families never think about insurance because, they argue, they are young and healthy and will worry about that sort of thing in the future. This is a bad policy because you never know when problems will arise.

There are five main areas of insurance that are important for a family with young children. If you own your own home and have a mortgage you'll have to have some kind of insurance to cover your life so that, should you die, the mortgage will be paid off.

As well as a mortgage-linked life insurance it makes sense to have an ordinary life insurance policy if you can afford it. This can take the form of a lump sum payable to the surviving spouse or can be arranged to produce a tax-free income every year until the children are off your hands. Neither is expensive if you take out the policy when you are young and you'll have peace of mind that your family will not suffer financially after your death. By using both these types of insurance policy, if a man dies his home will be paid for, his wife will be able to continue to live much as she did before and she won't have to go out to work.

Something many couples forget is to insure the woman. Everyone worries – quite understandably – about the death of the breadwinner but most ignore the enormous cost of having to replace the mother of young children. For a few pounds a month you can have life cover for the mother of a family. In the event of her death, it may be that a family member steps in to take care of the family. However, things often don't work out so easily and the father may be faced with having to provide not only substitute care for his children, but also someone to cook, clean, shop, mend, take the children around to their various activities and so on. Lots of widowed fathers wear themselves out trying to take on a lot of this burden as well as earning a living. If there is insurance money available in the form of a lump sum or an income, it can make the practicalities of everyday living much easier.

Almost all families are underinsured when it comes to their home contents, and health insurance is something a lot of people forget about, often to their peril, when travelling abroad on holiday.

There are lots of other ways you can insure yourself, your property, your family and even your income so the best thing is to see a good insurance broker who will advise you. Insurance is often overlooked or deliberately ignored by young families but this is almost certainly foolish because when you have young children the pressures on you as parents are great and the unexpected loss of one of you, your belongings, or your home is especially difficult to cope with. When you think of it in this way, it makes a lot of sense to invest in insurance.

Intelligence The capacity a person has to understand and his ability to benefit from experience, especially in new situations. The definition of intelligence is bound to be inadequate because the concepts involved are so abstract. Many parents think of intelligence purely as an academic commodity but this is too restricting as many highly intelligent children are not necessarily academic. We like to consider the intelligent child as one who can cope well with new situations, drawing on his past experiences and learning when he does so. This means that in practice he can manipulate his environment to suit himself and his purpose at the time.

Parents have become accustomed to thinking of intelligence in terms of intelligence tests but such tests are very limited and all they really prove is that the child is good (or bad) at them. They do have a useful function though because such IQ (intelligence quotient) tests can be used to find out how well a child is doing at school. The trouble is that two children with exactly similar IQs could fare very differently in real life situations, so clearly these tests have to be interpreted with caution.

The average IQ by definition has been set at 100. Very gifted children may have an IQ of 160 or more and at the other end of the scale a severely educationally subnormal child could have an IQ of below 30.

Although many parents prize intelligence in their children, there are so many other important virtues and abilities in life that overemphasis on such test results can have unfortunate effects for parent and child alike. Even seemingly dull (in IQ terms) children have human qualities and abilities that both they and others can enjoy.

One of the great problems with the under-fives is the difficulty that arises with children who have a physical or developmental handicap. Very often such children are of perfectly normal intelligence yet are treated as if they were mentally retarded, sometimes even by those close to them. There is a general tendency for many adults to underestimate the intelligence of young children anyway though many a sharp three or four year old can outwit an adult in all kinds of ways.

Finally, remember that the younger the child, the poorer a predictor is his IQ of how intelligent he'll be later in life. **Related topic** Slowness.

Intertrigo A skin condition characterized by red, soggy cracks, in the folds of the body. It comes about as a direct result of trapped sweat and poor personal hygiene and is most often seen in the body folds of obese children or babies who are not washed sufficiently frequently or thoroughly. The commonest sites to be affected are the groin, behind the ears, under the arms, at the base of the neck, and in the fold of the buttocks.

The condition is cured by careful and frequent washing, adequate drying and the application of a barrier cream. Leaving the air to get at the area helps, as does making sure that clothing isn't too tight.

Talcum powder used very sparingly can help prevent soreness in the skin folds by keeping them dry but if too much is used, it can clog up and irritate the skin by being rubbed between the folds.

Unless this treatment doesn't clear the condition up in a few days or unless there are any signs of infection (increased reddening, pus and irritation) there's no need to consult your doctor.

Intestinal obstruction A condition in which the intestines stop passing their contents along. In children this can occur in two types of condition. The first is called paralytic ileus. In this the intestine is affected by an acute infection (especially pneumonia and peritonitis) or by a change in certain vital chemicals in the blood with kidney failure or even with severe diarrhoea and vomiting. The child's tummy is distended and there is little, if any, pain. If ever your child is ill and has a swollen tummy, tell your doctor at once.

The second group of causes of intestinal obstruction is mechanical. A twisted inguinal hernia or an intussusception are the commonest causes but it can also occur after an abdominal operation or after peritonitis, both of which can cause bands of fibrous tissue around the intestines. More rarely a child's intestine is blocked after swallowing something large. Some children with cystic fibrosis can become obstructed as can those with large numbers of roundworms.

As with paralytic ileus, the child's tummy is distended but with these causes there may be pain too. Because all of these need hospital investigation and treatment, often urgently, lose no time in telling your doctor if your child is ill and has a distended tummy or if he vomits brown or green fluid. *Related topics* Cystic fibrosis; hernia; intussusception; roundworms.

Intravenous drip A procedure in which a fluid is run into a vein to supply a child with blood or other vital substances. Blood (or plasma) is given intravenously after a serious accident with blood loss or during a major operation, and other fluids are given if a child has prolonged vomiting and diarrhoea. Very uncommonly a child will be kept alive by 'feeding' him intravenously with nutrients. Quite often, a child who needs blood or some other therapeutic fluid will be started off on a drip of glucose and saline while the definitive treatment is being prepared.

Today's intravenous drip needles are disposable and are thus very sharp and easily inserted. In babies, there are few veins large enough to use for such infusions so the fluid is given via a scalp vein or even sometimes into a large vein in the neck. Special tiny bore needles are available for this purpose. Older children can have a drip into a vein (usually in the arm or hand) that enables them to move about to some degree even though the arm to which the drip is attached is splinted and relatively immobile.

If ever you are with your child in hospital and you notice that his drip has stopped flowing, tell the nursing staff. *Related topic* Blood transfusion.

Intussusception A mechanical abnormality of the intestine of a young baby in which the intestine telescopes into the part in front of it, rather like a sock being turned inside out. It occurs in a previously well baby, usually between the ages of three and twelve months and can be dangerous because the blood supply of the affected part can become obstructed causing gangrene of the tissue.

A baby with this condition will have a sudden attack of screaming, straining as if to open his bowels, and pain. The attacks sometimes recur at very short intervals and the child may be completely well in between. During the first few hours he passes normal bowel motions but later he has 'red current jelly' stools mainly consisting of blood and mucus. Other symptoms include repeated vomiting (sometimes of green bile).

An emergency operation may be vital to save the child's life but some babies get better with medical treatment before surgery is needed.

Invalidism More than nine out of ten children's illnesses are over within a few days and the child is soon back to normal.

There are several potential problems with a child who is ill for a long time. First, he'll get used to being the centre of attention and can become very spoilt. Second, he'll realize that he can manipulate the adults around him. This isn't necessarily healthy for him or the adults. Third, he'll need lots of entertaining. All of this calls for considerable effort on behalf of the parents or other adults looking after him but the secret is to behave as normally as possible. If he senses that you are anxiously playing into his hands all the time even the nicest child will cash in on it and you'll soon get fed up.

When buying toys and games for the child who is not acutely ill, ensure that they will tax his ingenuity and patience. Simple games that would normally have kept him happy are useless for prolonged stays in bed.

Get in touch with your local Red Cross branch if you need helpful equipment such as rubber rings, bed tables, bed pans and so on. They can lend them to you to save you having to buy such things yourself. If the child has a well-known condition there may be a self-help group that could also come up with useful practical hints. See the list at the back of the book.

Under-fives won't need teaching as older children will if they're ill for a long period but they'll need company. Be sure to give them more human company than endless TV can offer and provided the illness doesn't preclude it, invite special friends around in small groups. Remember not to overtire the child. Try to organize your day so that you can be with him at definite pre-planned times that he can look forward to.

Lastly, bear in mind that under-fives are a lot brighter than you imagine. Never discuss the illness in front of them with a doctor or even a friend. Explain to the child in language he can understand exactly what's going on but don't get involved in discussion about his present or future state as though he weren't there. His immature mind will have plenty of time to come to false conclusions and this could delay his recovery and make his life unhappy. **Related topics** Bed – keeping a child in when ill; illness. **Useful organizations** The Disabled Living Foundation; Invalid Children's Aid Association.

Iron An essential element in the body necessary for the formation of blood. Foods rich in iron are liver, kidney, heart, apricots, wholemeal bread, beef, figs, black treacle, spinach, parsley, cockles, black pudding and certain breakfast cereals.

A child who eats too few foods containing iron may become deficient (see Anaemia) and so need to have iron by mouth in the form of tablets. Be guided by your doctor on this.

Iron in excess is a powerful poison to young children and it's essential to keep any iron tablets you may have around the home well out of the reach of children. Even a few tablets (that look just like sweets) can be dangerous and a lot can be lethal. *Related topic* Anaemia.

Irritability If your child is unusually irritable, think whether he might be sickening for something. The early stages of most childhood infections can make a child feel irritable and off-colour yet not cause any obvious symptoms. It is then that he will often be at his most infectious, so if there is any likelihood that he may have caught something, keep him away from other children at this time unless their mothers don't mind them risking getting the illness. When recovering from an illness many children feel irritable for some time.

The commonest cause for a child to be snappy, easily bored and near to tears is tiredness. Children sometimes flop very suddenly and their mood can change from one minute to another. A child will almost always deny that he is tired, but if he seems tired during the day (and this often happens in young children who have only recently given up their daytime nap), then sit him down with you and read to him or let him play quietly or watch television. After a quiet time like this he'll probably soon perk up again. Even long after a child has stopped sleeping during the day he may become irritable at a regular time each day. Many adults find just the same: they have a low period when they feel more and more tired and irritable and for lots of people this is towards the end of the afternoon. Irritability can be caused by being hungry, so give your child something to eat and drink, especially if it's some time since his last meal or if the last meal was high in refined carbohydrate. This would have left his stomach quickly and caused an early peak in the blood sugar followed by a swift dip, which is often associated with a feeling of irritability.

Children are sometimes tetchy, tired and whiney when they first start going to play-group. It is as though they find the excitement of the new surroundings and playmates too much to cope with. Keep the rest of the day as quiet as you can and cut down on other activities until your child has got used to it.

Some babies are irritable as each tooth comes through. If you look at their gums you may see a red, swollen area over the erupting tooth. Sometimes a cyst forms and then disappears before the tooth comes through. If you can remember when your wisdom teeth came through, you may remember that your gum felt itchy and that you wanted to bite it to relieve the sensation. Babies are sometimes very obviously bothered when they are teething and as it takes nearly two years for all the teeth to come through, this state of irritability whenever a new tooth is erupting may go on for some time.

If your child is actually unhappy about something he may react by being irritable and it can often take a lot of detective work to find out the true cause. A new baby in the family who is taking up too much of his mother's time, or marital problems between his parents are likely to be too much for some children to take in their stride and being irritable is simply their way of handling their unease. If you are irritable for some reason, don't forget that your child will probably copy you. Moods are very catching and irritability is no different from any other. **Related topics** Jealousy; teething; whining.

Isolation period Times during which a child with an infectious illness should be kept away from other children (and sometimes even from adults as well) unless they have had the illness or have been immunized against it. Opinions differ on some of these times, partly because it's very difficult in any one child to be sure whether or not he is still infectious. Here are some acceptable guidelines to follow.

A child with chickenpox should be kept in the home until all the spots are dry and scabbed over; for German measles, isolation (except from women who might be pregnant) is not necessary; a child with measles is officially non-infectious by ten days after the appearance of the rash; a child with mumps should be kept away from men and youths who haven't had the disease but is non-infectious once the swelling has gone; a child with scarlet fever should be isolated for about twelve days if you want to be really safe but if he's on antibiotics there's probably no risk to others; and the child with whooping cough can be infectious for up to a month from the start of the coughing or until he has been on erythromycin for seven days. If anyone has gastroenteritis they should stay away from infants (especially bottle-fed ones); children with meningitis should stay away from others until they are recovered; polio sufferers should be isolated for six weeks and polio contacts for three weeks; and a child with diphtheria should be isolated until he is well.

True isolation, with your child kept away from the rest of the family, the sterilization of his plates, laundry and so on is rarely necessary. If a child has been immunized against the infection in question, the chances are that even if he were to catch it from an infectious child (who in the past would have been isolated) he'll only get a mild attack.

What often makes a nonsense of any isolation at all is the fact that many of the common infectious illnesses are at their most infectious on the first and second days (with chickenpox the day *before* the outbreak of the spots is the most infectious), so the child has obviously passed it on before his parents realize he is ill with something other than a cough or a cold. Colds are also at their most infectious the day before symptoms break out. Some infections such as scarlet fever now respond well to treatment so again isolation isn't really necessary.

The extent to which parents isolate their children with infections such as these depends greatly on their outlook on life generally but most modern parents are quite happy for the under-fives to get all the common childhood ailments out of the way while they're young (when the attacks are generally less severe, except for whooping cough in infancy) so they won't miss school later. Some parents go out of their way to get their child infected with a common condition on the basis that they'll otherwise get it at an inconvenient time, probably over Christmas or just before the family holiday. **Related topics** Incubation periods; quarantine.

Itching An irritation of the skin with many causes. One of the commonest in young children is dry skin caused by too much washing, especially with detergents (found in no-soap cleaners marketed for bathing children) and bubble baths. Drugs too can cause itching if the child is over-sensitive to them as can some household chemicals, hair dyes, cosmetics, certain plants and many other things.

Any skin condition or affliction that causes a release of histamine from special cells in the skin causes itching. Urticaria, eczema and other forms of dermatitis are the best known of these but flea and insect bites can do so too. Even being too hot (prickly heat) can produce itching.

Some skin diseases are itchy but by no means all are. Athlete's foot and other fungal infections are itchy and children can itch with generalized whole-body conditions such as jaundice, kidney failure, diabetes and chickenpox.

Itching can occur in particular places so giving a clue to what the cause is. Itching on the scalp is likely to be ringworm; around the anus, inadequate hygiene or threadworms; on the hands and wrists, scabies, and so on.

One neurotic condition can cause itching too. In neurodermatitis (an uncommon condition), the child scratches incessantly, even though there is no apparent physical cause. Such children usually scratch their knees, ankles and elbows and can be very difficult to treat unless the causes of their underlying worry or anxiety are sorted out.

Normally there is a perfectly obvious cause for the itching and your doctor will help cure it quickly. **Related topics** Allergy; athlete's foot; dermatitis; eczema; insect bites and stings; prickly heat; rashes; ringworm; scabies; threadworms; urticaria; vaginal discharge.

Jaundice A yellow coloration of the skin and the whites of the eyes caused by staining of the tissues with an abnormally high level of bilirubin, a substance produced from the breakdown of red blood cells. There are three main causes for jaundice. First, there may be too many red cells being broken down (so producing too much bilirubin); second, there may be failure of the enzymes in the liver to metabolize quite normal amounts of bilirubin; or third, there may be an obstruction to the flow of bile from the liver to the intestine (causing a damming up of bilirubin in the bile).

Some babies (some surveys show as many as sixty per cent) are jaundiced in the first few days of life. This is called physiological jaundice and comes about because their immature liver enzyme systems can't cope with the billirubin load caused by the normal increase in red blood cell breakdown after birth. Premature babies are more likely to have this sort of jaundice – about eighty per cent in some surveys. Such jaundice is first noticed on the second or third day after birth and disappears spontaneously by about a week (a little later in premature babies).

One of the most serious types of jaundice in babies is thankfully becoming much less common – that caused by rhesus incompatibility. Such jaundice is either present at birth or comes on during the first day and will need treating if severe, or the baby's brain can be damaged. Certain drugs, some congenital abnormalities of the bile system, thyroid deficiency and internal bleeding can all cause jaundice in the newborn but these are rare. 'Breast-milk jaundice' begins on the third day in a very few breast-fed babies but the bilirubin level is rarely very high and breast-feeding should only be stopped temporarily in order to make the diagnosis.

If a baby has a high bilirubin level (as judged by blood tests), it can be lowered by placing him in sunlight or under light from a fluorescent tube. Very high levels may need an exchange transfusion.

A perfectly normal baby with none of these conditions can (rarely) become yellow with almost any infection (which seems to damage liver function) and a child with hepatitis, a viral infection of the liver itself, can also be jaundiced. Some drugs cause jaundice. Discuss the possibility with your doctor if your child is taking any medication at all.

If ever your child seems yellow (especially the whites of his eyes), get medical advice at once. It can be more difficult to decide whether your child is jaundiced or not than you'd imagine and you'll need good natural light to be able to see well. The whites of the eyes are often the first areas to go yellow. **Related topics** Blood groups; sleepy baby.

Jealousy The emotions of jealousy are all unpleasant – envy, resentment, fear and suspicion are all feelings that detract from a child's sense of well-being and happiness and interfere with his normal relationship with the person of whom he's jealous. The word jealousy can also be used to denote possessiveness.

Probably everybody reading this will have experienced jealousy to some degree at some time and will know what a destructive emotion it is. A person who is jealous can think of little else, especially when in the company of the person in question. Children can be jealous of other children, adults and even things but a surprising number are also jealous of activities which keep their parents away from them or which make them too preoccupied to give them attention.

Jealousy of a new baby in the family is so widespread as to be considered normal. In fact, it has been said that if a child isn't jealous of his new brother or sister at some time, there must be something wrong with him. It's easy to understand that such a child may envy the time, interest and attention spent on the baby by his parents, friends, relatives and neighbours, not to mention by the various health professionals both in hospital and at home. Almost all young children are naturally egocentric and enjoy being the centre of the stage. They are loathe to give up this position – which has been theirs ever since they were born – to one they consider an imposter. At first, they may be able to feel generous. They've probably realized for some time that a new baby is coming and are interested in what it'll be like. They've also probably been warned that mummy will have to spend a lot of time looking after the baby. What they don't realize, though, is the real amount of time she'll have to spend, or that it will go on not only for day after day, but also for week after week, month after month and year after year! This is a bitter pill for many young children and one that some really never manage to swallow. This is why the obvious signs of jealousy often don't show up for some time, until the child realizes that the baby really is there to stay and that his mother will never again have as much time to spend with him as before the baby arrived.

Jealousy of a new baby may show up in many different ways. The most obvious is extra attention-seeking. You'll never have so many demands for a story, a drink, the potty, to play, or for a cuddle. Sometimes it is virtually non-stop and the child seems almost obsessed with his resentment towards the baby, watching him out of the corner of his eye all the time even when he is with his mother and the baby is asleep. Occasionally, a child may physically hurt a new baby, which is why you have to be so careful not to leave the two together alone. Even a child who doesn't seem very obviously jealous may give the baby's hand a quick hard squeeze, or pinch him just a bit too roughly. Some children are quite open about their desire to hurt the baby, while other older ones only do it when there is no one else around. Yet others bring out their jealousy on other quite unrelated people or things. The two-year-old who starts pushing toddlers over at the mother and toddler group and the three-year-old who smacks her dolls may both be showing signs of suppressed jealousy of their new baby.

Other children revert to wetting their pants or soiling, even though they were already potty trained. Some children who were well on the way to being potty trained go right back to messing their nappies even though they had been asking for the potty before and were almost ready to be out of nappies. A few, knowing that cleaning them takes time, mess their pants or nappy when their mother is in the middle of feeding the baby, knowing that this is the best way to get her attention. Some children damage the baby's toys, clothes, or welcome cards, while others blame anything that goes wrong in the house on the new baby. Older, more sensible children often keep their feelings of jealousy to themselves, recognizing them for what they are and coping with them. Children of any age may react by becoming quiet, sad, moody, rude or tearful, exchanging their previously happy expressions for miserable ones. Of course, no one child will be affected by his jealousy all the time and some may scarcely ever show signs of it. Others however exhibit it in various ways for much of the time.

Jealousy is a perfectly normal, reasonable, but irrational emotion in the circumstances in which young children find themselves with a new baby in the house. The attention-seeking is a very obvious, deliberate and under-standable ploy to get back what they have lost, and it is pointless to be cross with your child for continuing to want and fighting to regain what you were once so happy to give him. His anger at and resentment of the new baby are mixed with feelings of interest and love but this serves only to muddle him.

His thought is a mixture of 'I'm angry with him so I can't love him' and 'I love him so I can't be angry with him'. He is too young as yet to realize that such powerful feelings can coexist. You'll probably be feeling tired with broken nights and an extra person in the family to look after, and much as you may sympathize with and understand your older child's feelings, you may be at a loss to know what to do about them.

Some mothers, with much thought, unselfishness, tact and understanding, are able to help their older children cope with their feelings of jealousy in such a way that they are not a problem to anyone, let alone to themselves. More children are now being breast-fed throughout their mother's next pregnancy. When the baby is born, such mothers give their babies all the time at the breast they need, but also let their older children go to the breast. Most children of more than a year old are eating a mixed diet and drinking other fluids as well as breast milk, so they see their time at the breast as a time for comfort and pleasure as much as for getting the sweet-tasting milk that means so much to them because it comes from their mother. Being allowed to carry on with what they enjoy so much prevents to a great extent the feeling that the new baby has supplanted them. They feel generous at allowing the new baby to share their mother's breasts and so feel warm towards the baby instead of resentful, as they would if their mother forbade them her breasts. Breast-feeding an older child and a baby is known as tandem nursing.

Letting your older child know that you understand his feelings and think they are reasonable helps him to come to terms with them. It also helps him not to think of himself as bad or naughty because of his feelings of jealousy.

Jealousy of other children having possessions your child wants is a much easier sort of jealousy to manage. Over the years you can teach your children that possessions, whilst pleasant, are not the most important things. Point out to your child that being part of a loving family is much more important and that the love he gives and receives will stand him in better stead in the future than things ever will. This isn't an easy concept for a young child to understand or accept, though, especially if other children he knows have many more things than he does. If you are short of money and yet you think he would benefit by having more toys and games, consider joining a toy library (ask your health visitor if there is one in your area), visit jumble sales, join a mother and toddler group or a play-group, and learn how to make toys yourself. Even a battered old toy can come to life if you help your child get some fun out of it by using imaginative games. If your child has set his heart on something another child has and you break the bank to get it for him, it won't be long before he's crazy to have something else, so don't be led up that path.

Resentment of the time you spend with other people or doing something other than with your child, be it working, cooking, or being on the telephone, needs careful consideration. Try working out how much of your child's waking time you spend doing something which means you can't give him your full attention, or indeed any attention at all. It's not fair to let a young child play around your skirts with no response from you for much of the day, and you'll end up with a frustrated, whining child and yourself annoyed, flustered and grumbling that you can never get anything done. Intersperse your jobs with giving your child some time and attention, though there's no need to formalize this. Similarly, when you're with friends of yours, have the courtesy (and that is what it is) not to ignore your child – who may be at a loss to know how to amuse himself in a strange place – but to talk to him every so often and to make him feel important as well as your friend. If you work at home, consider having someone to look after your child if you find that you can't really cope with him as well as the pressure of your work. *Related topics* Attention seeking; firstborn children; new baby – preparing other children for; quarrels; sibling rivalry.

Jellyfish stings If jellyfish are around in the sea where you are swimming be sure to keep a lookout and stay away from them. If a child is stung, get him to the shore, cover your hands with sand and then pick off any adherent pieces of jellyfish. Apply a soothing lotion, cream or both (calamine is good). It's probably wise to tell a doctor if your young child is stung by a jellyfish because there is one poisonous type – the Portuguese man-of-war. This can be identified by its 'sail' that it erects and by its very long tentacles that can stretch for 45 metres behind its body. Always keep away from the back of jellyfish for this reason.

Jumble sales Jumble sales are a good source of dressing-up clothes, second-hand baby equipment that may need some sprucing up, clothes for the family, second-hand nappies that still have a lot of wear in them, toys and many other things. Someone's cast-off is someone else's good find and there is no stigma in sorting through the various stalls at a jumble sale. Your local paper will publish details of jumble sales or you can find out about them from notice boards outside shops and so on.

Organizing a jumble sale is a good way of raising funds for a mother and toddler group or a play-group, for example. Advertise widely and start collecting the jumble in good time. If you are prepared to collect it from people's homes, you'll probably be more successful.

Another way of disposing of or buying baby equipment and baby's and children's clothes is from a second-hand table at a mother and toddler group's or a play-group's meeting place. Sometimes a proportion of the money collected from any one item goes to the group funds and the rest to the seller. *Related topic* Second-hand equipment.

Knock knees A condition in which the knees of a child are close together and the lower legs splayed apart so that there is a larger than normal gap between the ankles.

Many three-year-olds have knock knees. About three out of four children of this age will have some splaying of the lower legs but this is usually a normal phase of development and is nothing to worry about. If when your child is standing with his knees together and his legs straight he has a gap of more than 2in (5cm) between his ankles, he should be seen by a doctor who will observe him regularly. He may recommend that the child's shoes be modified. The vast majority of such children have normal legs at the age of six.

Fat children are more likely to have knock knees than thin ones but as they slim their condition improves and usually disappears altogether.

Obesity is by far the commonest cause of knock knees but, rarely, rickets can be a cause. A child with one-sided knock knee will definitely need medical attention as will a child with knock knees that aren't getting better.

Koplik's spots Small, white spots on red bases found on the inside of the cheeks (in the mouth opposite the molar teeth) in some children with measles. No treatment is needed other than to rinse out the mouth if it is sore. They are simply another manifestation of measles and disappear as the skin rash appears. *Related topic* Measles.

Language The development of language in a young child is fascinating to watch. Soon after birth, a newborn baby responds to his mother by listening to her voice, watching her facial expressions, and enjoying her touch and body movements. One day he'll make a noise (such as a coo) and she'll look delighted and perhaps coo back at him, nodding her head as she does so. Soon he'll understand that she likes him to make a sound and that she'll make one back at him if he does so. Before too long there'll be a conversation of coos going on, much to the delight of both mother and baby. This is an important part of a baby's language development: learning to listen, wanting to respond in order to please the other person, and being able to make an appropriate remark which the other person in turn listens to.

During a child's first year or so, he gradually learns not only that things and people have names, but also what some of those names are. Parents quite spontaneously point things out to their children by name, or name something such as a spoon or a toy as they pass it to him. The realization that any one word is always associated with one particular thing is an important stage in a child's language development. For the first time he knows that words have a meaning and purpose. There's no point in naming things repeatedly for your three-month-old and expecting him to remember or copy, but if you are in the habit of talking to your baby and using simple label words a lot then he'll be used to hearing you and from about eight months or so he'll learn to associate things with the labels you give them. He won't be able to say the words for some time but his delight and obvious recognition when you say them will convince you that he understands them.

At first, he'll only associate an object with its name if it's there in front of him but later if you ask him where his spoon is, for example, he'll look for it. In his mind he understands what the word 'spoon' represents and knows it isn't there at first. Once he can carry a word in his mind like this, he's on his way past his first simple understanding of the labelling of things to thinking about what he wants to say or how he wants to express himself. This happens around about fifteen to eighteen months in many children and it is not until now that words are used in their correct context.

It goes without saying that a child's language development will be slow if he can't listen to people speaking. This can happen if he's deaf and no one has realized, or if he simply isn't spoken to very much. Babies and young children listen best if someone has a one-to-one conversation with them, looks at them directly and involves them emotionally by being pleased when they respond with sounds, words, appropriate facial expressions and body movements. If they are one of several children being spoken to, they soon realize that their response isn't paid as much attention to as if they were the only child being looked after and so they become less interested in listening. This explains why later-born children in a family are often later in talking than firstborns, who benefit from much more exclusive adult conversation and attention in their early years. If their early attempts at making conversational sounds aren't applauded immediately and regularly, they'll be less interested in making them – encouragement and praise are a great help to anyone learning anything, even if it's something that comes naturally. Babies and young children learn faster by listening to a familiar voice. Even if a stranger says the same words as their mother, they may mentally switch off and be unable to understand words they supposedly know.

Talk to and with your baby a lot but take care not to talk too much yourself. Your baby needs a chance to take in what you've said and to associate it with what you're doing or showing him, or what he's doing. A flood of conversation with no pauses will overwhelm him and if you always talk very fast he'll be unable to pick out, recognize or memorize any individual words. Remember to name common everyday objects in your child's life frequently in your conversation. It's the same as if you were learning a foreign language without the help of the written word – you'd need patient repetition of simple and useful words and sentences at first, and would want to go at your own pace. If you were rushed, you'd tend to lose confidence and might even be frightened off continuing with your studies. If a baby or young child is bullied, he may simply turn off and only come back to listening and learning again when the pressure is off him.

What your child says is a relatively unimportant part of his language development. A dumb person is in many ways better off than a stone deaf one! Listening is far more important. Most of your child's first year is spent in listening and learning his language and it's this that you should concentrate on if you want to help him learn. When he says his first word, how many words he can say, and how well he can say them don't matter at all to a child whose language development is progressing well because he is learning to understand what other people say.

During his first year your baby will progress from making cooing sounds to more complex babbling which begins some time after he is six months old. It doesn't matter at all if it doesn't start till much later in the first year and this bears little relation to intelligence. Some children are late in every stage of speech development and yet end up talking perfectly well. The sounds of a babbling baby are repetitive syllables such as 'mamama' or 'dadada' or 'wawawa'. The sounds may progress to 'ama' or 'ada' or 'awa' and are almost always said with an expression of delight, though some babies use babbling when they feel like grumbling, if their teeth are troubling them, for example. Babies sometimes wake up babbling.

Babbling isn't used with any meaning – it may be used to express happiness but the individual sounds don't mean anything. Parents often interpret babble as being meaningful, because they are so keen for their babies to talk. This is quite harmless, and if a father interprets 'dadada' as meaning daddy, and praises his baby and says 'yes daddy', the baby will be delighted, babble some more, and everyone will be happy. Over the next few months the meaningless 'dadada' will in fact become the meaningful 'dada', but when that point actually comes is often unknown. Using words with meaning is often a gradual progression of association and realization rather than one actual moment of changeover from meaningless to meaningful. The more often a baby's mother says delightedly, 'yes, dada', and points to his father, when he baby babbles 'dadada', the sooner he will use the label 'dada' for his father.

As the baby grows older, his vocalizations separate from a string of repetitive syllables into separate syllables, often different, which are said in a conversational rhythm with pauses, intonations and cadences. From his months of listening to you talking to him he has learnt how talking should sound and can give a pretty fair imitation of what he hears. The fact that neither you nor he can understand any of what he says doesn't matter. Many of us have at times pretended to be speaking a foreign language by making a jumble of sounds and this is what the baby is in effect doing. Such talking is known as 'jargon' to psychologists. Some babies carry on using jargon or 'scribble talk' for some months and even well into their second year, but most give it up at round about a year old when they discover that they can actually use words themselves to communicate with other people.

Some people at this stage of their child's language development concentrate on trying hard and patiently to teach their baby to say adult words. Even if a baby does imitate, parrot-like copying won't help his language development. He has to understand the meaning of something in its right context before he can assimilate the word into his vocabulary and use it properly himself. Anyway, until he's ready to pronounce words, he won't be able to, whether by copying or not.

You'll probably never be sure exactly when your child says his first words with meaning. Friends and relatives will enquire as to whether he is 'talking' yet and what they mean is whether he is saying anything that is at all meaningful. There'll probably be some good supportive evidence for the occasion you decide he has said his first meaningful word but remember that you may be foxed by what he says because he may have his own word for something that isn't at all like what you call it. He may have been calling his spoon a 'baa' for several weeks before you realize that 'baa' means spoon. He is, of course, using this word meaningfully even if it isn't English!

Continue to listen and respond with praise and encouragement to whatever your baby says as he tries out his new labelling ability. At first he'll only have one or two words in his vocabulary but he'll understand very many more – perhaps a dozen or so. It helps if you repeat what he says so that if he says 'mi', for example, as he points to his milk, you say 'yes, milk', with a smile on your face and a nod of encouragement. You're not trying to teach him how to say it properly because that really doesn't matter at this stage but you are reinforcing what he has said so that he realizes that you know what he means. This will make him feel that his first attempts at using meaningful words are successful and he'll be more likely to try some more.

When your child begins to use words, you can concentrate on helping him learn new labels for things by patiently repeating the names of things he sees in his daily life. It's more fun though if you simply emphasize any word you want him to learn as you carry on your usual conversation. For instance, while you're playing with him, if you want him to learn the word teddy, keep mentioning the teddy as you play with him. 'Put teddy on your lap. Let's give teddy a drink. Oh, poor teddy, he's spilt it. Dear teddy': all these phrases will implant the label in his mind and over the course of time if you remember to talk about teddy, he'll learn the word and eventually use it himself. There is no need to emphasise single words like this – even if you carry on talking as you would to an adult, he'll learn to talk in his own time, but you will probably encourage his experimentation and his speed of learning to use words if he has some success early on. Talk about what you are doing, what your child is doing, what he can see as you go for walks and what there is to see in picture books or on television.

As your one-year-old can say more and more labels for things, so he's learning not only more labels but also more complex forms of speech. Some time late in his second year or in his third year he'll put two words together and from then on he'll progress in leaps and bounds. Never worry about his grammar – if you and the other adults and older children he meets speak grammatical English, he will too in time. Lots of parents repeat what their child has said but with the grammar right. It's unnecessary to worry a child by correcting him at this stage – all you'll do is put him off telling you something else and it's much more important for him to become confident and to enjoy talking than it is to get some nicety of language correct. However, if he says, for instance, 'Daddy gone', you could say 'Yes, Daddy's gone'. That is repeating the essence of what he's said and without making him feel that he has said anything wrong, you've given him the idea perhaps for next time (or ten times ahead).

All too soon the precious early years of speech development have gone and your child will be chatting away nineteen to the dozen to everyone if he is fairly outgoing by nature, or just quietly to you when you're alone if he is more reserved and shy. Spoken language will have been added to his repertoire of touching, facial expression, and body language as an important and complex form of communication.

Your child will be well on the way to having a good grasp of spoken language before he turns his mind to written language. Written words are just another way of outwardly symbolizing labels and concepts present in the child's mind, just as spoken words are. *Related topics* Baby talk; slowness; talking.

Lanugo The medical name for the fine, soft hair that covers many parts of a baby's body whilst in the uterus. It usually disappears by the seventh or eighth month of pregnancy but is still present in some babies at birth. This unpigmented hair is then replaced by vellus hair which may also be unpigmented. Vellus hair is followed on the head and other parts by coarse, longer hair which becomes pigmented.

A baby that is born prematurely is more likely to be covered with lanugo than a full-term one. *Related topic* Hair type.

Large families With increasing financial and social pressures and improvements in the reliability of contraception, large families are very uncommon today. In many ways this is a shame because the large family (with more than four children) has a lot to offer. Children in such a family often grow up to be more tolerant of others and seem to be very flexible as teenagers and adults. They have been brought up in a community with all its joys and problems and are often more rounded as a result. Certainly there are considerable advantages to having a large family if the age gaps are not too small because the parents have plenty of help with babies and child care and the children in turn learn how to be parents. In the standard nuclear Western family with two children born close together, neither has the opportunity of learning parenting skills at first hand and we think this is a real loss to society because someone else has to teach these skills. The odd lesson on parentcraft at school can't possibly come anywhere near the kind of experiences a child will have while actively helping to care for a real baby within a family.

Strange as it may seem, unless a couple is determined to educate their children privately, large families often cost very little more than smaller ones. Clothes can be passed down, as can equipment and toys. Just think how many things the average family throws or gives away hardly used as their children outgrow them. Just because you have a large family doesn't necessarily mean that you have to move house. Children are quite happy sharing rooms (or even beds when they are young) and provided there isn't any squalid overcrowding this can be a virtue and not the terrible problem so many make it out to be. Perhaps the biggest financial strain is the likelihood of several more years worth of the mother's potential earnings being lost while she stays home to look after another child.

With the world becoming a smaller place, parents find their children move away either temporarily or permanently and this leaves them alone and lonely in their old age. With a large family not only is there a greater degree of 'clan' feeling and a stronger desire to get together but there is also more chance that at least some of the children will be around, albeit different ones at different times.

The main problem for the parents of a large family is to ensure that everybody gets enough time and attention and this can be difficult in these busy times we live in. But parents who are aware of this do very well with large families and reap enormous benefits from having both their own children and their friends as companions for *all* the family. **Related topic** Family planning – age gaps.

Laryngitis An inflammation of the vocal cords. This can be especially serious in babies and young children because the larynx is narrow at this age and if narrowed further by inflammation, can cause breathing difficulties. Laryngitis is more common in the winter. It is related to croup but unlike croup laryngitis produces no breathing problems.

Most cases of laryngitis are caused by a viral infection and it can occur with a cold, 'flu and other childhood infections. The child is hoarse, may have a sore throat, a fever, a dry cough or even croup. In young children the larynx is rarely affected alone and the infection often extends down the trachea (windpipe) into the lungs. Pneumonia or middle ear infection can complicate laryngitis.

The treatment is simple. The air around the child should be made humid and the child kept comfortable. Antibiotics are not routinely used but can be valuable if there is a secondary bacterial infection on top of the viral one causing the laryngitis. If your child seems to be having difficulty in breathing, call your doctor at once. It's also essential to call the doctor if he has a rising fever, difficulty in breathing, or a cough. These can be caused by an inflammation of the epiglottis which is a serious emergency. **Related topics** Croup; hoarseness.

Laughing Although many babies smile from early in life they rarely laugh out loud before about four months. It is lovely when they do laugh. Some enjoy being tickled to make them laugh.

Some families seem much more lighthearted and laugh a lot more than others. Laughter makes the world a more pleasant place to be in and there is even a form of therapy called laughter therapy. There's usually something to laugh about, however much is going wrong.

Laughing with someone is not the same as laughing *at* them. Help your child to understand that it is unkind to laugh at a person in trouble or to laugh behind someone's back.

Laundry Unless you love laundering or have help in the house, choose clothes that can be washed in a washing machine (as opposed to being dry cleaned or hand washed) at an all-purpose temperature and make sure that they are dye-fast. Some washing instruction labels specifically advise separate washing and if you ignore this you can end up with a whole load of washing all the same colour and patchy too. Increasing numbers of children's clothes need little or no ironing. Some towelling or velour clothes are particularly good in this respect, as is much modern knitwear, terylene-cotton mixture shirts, blouses and dresses and jersey trousers. If you have a tumble drier, consider using it regularly to dry things that would otherwise need to be ironed. Often tumble drying gets rid of creases, especially if you hang up the clothes quickly afterwards. Children's vests and pants really don't have to be ironed unless you like doing it. If you fold them neatly when dry, the few remaining creases will be gone in a moment or two when worn by a warm little body. Things that almost always need ironing include most cotton or wool mixture dresses, shirts and blouses, some woollen knitwear, and corduroy.

Second, you'll find every time that it pays to buy the best quality washing or drying machine you can afford. If you invest in an automatic washing machine and a tumble drier from the beginning, the laundry will be much easier to do than if you have a twin tub and a spin drier. The faster your automatic washing machine spins, the drier it will get the clothes and the easier it'll be to finish off drying. Clothes dried outside are no 'fresher' than those dried inside, though sunshine has a slight bleaching effect on white material such as terry nappies. A conventional clothes line takes up more space than a roundabout one but is cheaper and gets things drier quicker. If you dry things outside you'll spend quite a lot of time pegging and unpegging, not to mention bringing everything in when it pours with rain. You may choose to hang some washing, especially large things like sheets, inside on the banister to dry, or you may rig up a wooden clothes rack on a pulley which can be raised and lowered as necessary. A clothes horse (the modern, plastic-coated wire sort) is light and easy to store, can be put over the bath to drip if you're short of space and can also be put outside on a fine day. A tumble drier has the advantage of speed and reliability even on a wet day but is very expensive to run, especially for thick clothes, towels and nappies. However, it's very useful to have such a drier for occasional use or for drying certain things so as to avoid having to iron them. The top of the central heating boiler is a good place for getting things really dry, especially if they've been ironed damp in order to get the creases out. The airing cupboard is useful for this too if you keep it clear of dry things so that air can circulate. If you put damp clothes on top of the boiler, make sure it's on so that they dry quickly, otherwise the clothes may get spots of mould on them. Piles of damp clothing left in a cold airing cupboard soon smell foul and musty. Spread them out neatly, once ironed, to dry them as quickly as possible.

Third, an important decision is where to site your laundry equipment. You may think there's no choice — unless you have a laundry room, which most households don't. You may think there's only the kitchen or perhaps an outside passage or the garage. However, the bathroom is also a good idea because it means that you don't spend ages carting piles of dirty washing and clean, ironed washing up and downstairs. When the washing is done, you can use any of the usual methods to dry the clothes, though it rather defeats the object if you have to trail downstairs to put washing on a line! You could also do hand washing in the bathroom and keep nappy buckets, iron and ironing board upstairs as well and iron in a bedroom.

This problem is important because with two or more children the washing assumes large proportions, and anything that makes it easier is worth considering. Where the airing cupboard and boiler are will influence how much time you spend trailing around with piles of washing. Work out your laundry's journey from people to dirty washing basket to washing machine (or sink) to tumbledrier/clothes horse/clothes line/drying rack to ironing board to airing cupboard/boiler to drawers/wardrobes. Be your own time and motion expert and you could save yourself a lot of running about.

Fourth, if you've decided to use terry nappies and you're going to wash them in the washing machine (which does give good results, especially if you use the highest temperature setting), then think what else you can put in with them so that the nappies don't hang around for several days while you're collecting enough for a machine loadful. White towels, perhaps, or white vests, pants and handkerchiefs; anything that can be washed at a high temperature is suitable. In the early days of having a new baby, you'll be tired and any free time when the baby is asleep is better spent resting than doing useless jobs like folding clean nappies. They may look nice folded but that's all and the ten minutes spent folding them are valuable.

When it comes to repairing clothes, try to put things aside for mending before they are washed, otherwise the tendency is for them to be washed, ironed and put away still torn or buttonless.

Lastly, if your baby or young child has a sensitive skin, use as few laundry products as possible on his clothes. Soap powder is enough for most things, though nappies are best laundered after being soaked in a proprietary antiseptic/bleaching solution. Fabric softener is rarely necessary. However you wash be sure to rinse all the detergent out of the clothes really thoroughly because skin reactions to detergents in baby clothes are a fairly common cause of skin trouble in susceptible babies.

Family laundry is no longer a once-a-week event as it used to be and this is especially true if you have babies and young children. You'll find that you'll be washing something by hand or in a machine most days of the week and this is probably the best way to do it rather than saving things up for a once-a-week wash.

Lavatory Your baby or toddler will be interested in the lavatory a long time before he starts using it, not only because he sees other people sitting on it, flushing it, or cleaning it, but also because once he's noticed the water inside, he'll be fascinated by it. He may also take a fancy to playing with the seat or the lid, or to putting anything under the sun down it. Safeguard his interests by making sure the lavatory is kept clean and is always flushed after use by other young children. If anyone in the family has diarrhoea or suffers a bout of vomiting, take extra care to clean the lavatory and wipe it down afterwards with a solution of suitable household disinfectant. Remember to clean the seat, lid, bowl and handle, and the floor if there has been any slight accident, and don't forget the basin and taps. Remind the whole family to wash their hands after going to the lavatory and before eating or drinking, and don't forget to wash *your* hands well before feeding your baby, whether by breast or bottle. If your baby has diarrhoea, wash your hands after changing his nappy and keep the lavatory especially clean if you use it to flush away soiled disposable nappies or nappy liners.

Keep all lavatory cleaners, bleaches, disinfectants, and so on well out of reach and never, of course, decant chemicals into large lemonade bottles or the like that could be mistaken by a child for a soft drink. If you use a lavatory brush, keep it well cleaned (soak it every so often in disinfectant) and if your child takes a liking to playing with it, put it out of reach.

Because valuable things can be lost down a lavatory, keep the bathroom or lavatory door closed if your toddler likes to put things down it, and discourage him firmly from doing it. The trouble is that at the age of one or so babies and toddlers tend to react with a delighted grin and do it again as fast as possible when told not to do something. Constant supervision and having eyes in the back of your head will help during this stage of development.

It's sensible to remove the bolt or key from the lavatory door so that an enterprising toddler or older child can't lock himself in. Some keyless locks can be undone from the outside. If you want to be able to secure the door, put a hook or bolt high up on the inside. If a pre-school child does manage to lock himself in, remember that if you stay quite calm and try to treat the situation as a game, he'll find it easier to accept instructions from you as to how to turn the key or release the bolt. Try to think whether there are any special tricks for opening the door such as pushing it as you turn the key, and explain what to do as clearly and patiently as you can. If the worst comes to the worst and there is no-one else to help you, the fire brigade will come to his rescue or you could break the lock by forcing the door.

You may decide to buy or to make a stand for your child so that he can get on to the lavatory unaided. Such a stand is most useful if it is really high (in which case two steps might be better than one), so that the child can rest his feet on it as he sits. The more flexed his hips are as he opens his bowels, the easier it will be for him to do it, as the position he is sitting in then resembles a squatting position more closely. The plastic stands you can buy are really only useful as a step to get up, not as an aid to sitting comfortably, because they are too low and too small.

You may find that for a long time after achieving bowel control, your child prefers you to wipe his bottom. If he is a fastidious child and you have ever criticized the way he wiped his bottom, he'll be all the more likely to want your help. It's better for the pre-school child if he can wipe his own bottom, so that he can manage away from home without you and doesn't have to put off opening his bowels or ask another adult to do it which might make him feel embarrassed or shy. Teach a girl how to wipe her bottom from front to back so as not to get any motions near the opening of her urethra (the passage to her bladder). It doesn't matter how a boy does it. Show the child how to fold two pieces of soft paper so as to keep his hands clean, and watch him doing it a few times until you are satisfied that he's doing it fairly thoroughly. If his pants are at all stained at the end of the day, tactfully mention that he might wipe his bottom more thoroughly next time.

Small boys first use the lavatory to pass water by sitting on it as a girl does or as they do when opening their bowels. There'll come a time when they'll want to copy their fathers or other boys and stand up to do it. Help them to aim at first and show them how to lift the seat up beforehand. A stand or box to get them to the right height is a must. When they can cope well, buy trousers with a fly and pants with a front opening. Until then, pulling down their clothes is easier and means they get less wet in the practice phase.

The transition from potty to lavatory is made more easily if you have a child's plastic seat on top of the ordinary lavatory seat. This makes it more comfortable for the child and also stops him from actually sinking into the lavatory pan! If your child is used to such a seat, remember to take it with you when you go out.

Most children are delighted to start using the lavatory once they are reliably out of nappies and you may find that the potty isn't needed for long. An older child may want to revert to using the potty when a younger brother or sister starts using one and it's wisest to let him, to avoid jealousy. He'll soon want to use the lavatory again as he realizes that a potty is babyish. *Related topics* Bladder control; hygiene; potty training.

Laxatives Substances that encourage the bowel to empty. They are also called aperients, cathartics or purgatives.

Laxatives should never be necessary for babies or children and can actually be harmful. There is no need to worry if your baby doesn't open his bowels every day – this is quite normal. A totally breast-fed baby can go for days with no bowel action and be perfectly well.

Once a child is taking solids make sure you give him wholemeal bread, foods made with wholemeal flour, unrefined cereals, brown rice and wholemeal pasta. He should have fruit and vegetables (puréed if necessary) right from the start. Children brought up to eat a high-fibre diet are virtually never constipated and so never need laxatives.

Some parents get into the habit of giving regular laxatives to their children to encourage the daily opening of their bowels. This is harmful because the chemicals in the laxatives can do permanent damage to the bowels and make increased doses necessary to have any effect. The child's bowel can thus become addicted to the laxative and eventually will not work without it.

Any child that complains of extreme pain on opening his bowels may have an anal fissure with constipation. See your doctor.

Lastly, never give a laxative to a child with abdominal pain because this could be dangerous. **Related topics** Constipation; dietary fibre.

Layette Clothes for a newborn baby. Reams have been written about what a new mother *needs* for her baby and by the time the average mother has a second baby she'll have so many clothes she won't need any guidelines any more. There really isn't a set of rules about what your baby should wear and you're likely to be given lots of clothes as presents when he's born, so don't be too worried about what to buy. If you're given clothes that aren't suitable, change them, or else change ones you have already bought if they are duplicated by ones you like better. What clothes you should aim at collecting will depend on the season of the year your baby will be born in. Summer babies need only light vests or all-in-one vests and pants with one layer of clothing on top, while winter babies need several layers to keep them warm. The easier it is to take the clothing off your baby to change him or bath him the better he (and you) will like it, which is an important thing to take into consideration. Babies can't sit up, so dressing them is often rather difficult and if you buy clothes with lots of fastenings you'll find you're all fingers and thumbs, especially if he starts crying while you're in the middle of dressing him.

Leaving aside nappies (which are obviously essential in one form or another), you'll need several sets of underwear. Vests with an envelope neck are best. Ones that tie up are fiddly and the ribbons can get entangled. Those that are all-in-one with pants and do up by a row of poppers at the baby's bottom keep him warm and tidy but if his nappy leaks, it means that you have to take them off as well, which can mean a total strip of everything he's wearing. You can buy a similar garment that ties up with ribbon but this again is fiddly. If you're confident that your baby's nappy system is going to be leakproof (and this is most likely with terry nappies and well-fitting plastic pants or a shaped plastic tie-on nappy cover), then all-in-one poppered 'vestipants' are the most attractive buy. You'll need three or more if your baby is going to wear them for much of the time, to allow for one being dirty and one in the wash or drying.

Some mothers keep their newborn babies in stretch towelling suits day and night. With this outfit all you need is a vest (if it's cold) plus or minus a cardigan or matinée jacket (which is a knitted garment like a cardigan which does up with buttons or a ribbon at the neck only) for your baby to be quite adequately dressed and easy to undo for nappy changing. The more one piece stretch suits you have, the better, and the same goes for matinée jackets which tend to be sicked on quite a lot in the early days. Some mothers choose a dress together with a cardigan or jacket for their daughters, but a dress is scarcely shown off at this age and can be uncomfortable when it gets rumpled up. Also, if it's cold, the baby needs something other than socks on her legs. Tights are one answer, though they're fiddly to put on and have to be taken off for changing the nappy.

In the summer legless rompers or angel tops are cool and attractive for boys and girls, and a cardigan can be added if necessary, together with a sunhat if it's really sunny and bright. A hat that doesn't need to be tied under the chin is the most comfortable and rarely needs washing because it doesn't get messed with regurgitated milk.

Bootees and mittens are only necessary in really cold weather and if you wrap your baby up well in his pram he won't need them at all. However, if your baby travels in a sling, make sure his hands and feet are kept warm. Some makes of stretch suit have mittens incorporated into the cuffs. Even if your baby's feet are covered by the stretch suit, bootees will give him extra warmth. The only reason you might want more than one pair of bootees and mittens is that they have a habit of getting lost!

For a cold day, some warmer outerwear is essential, especially if your baby is travelling in a sling. If you're using a pram, extra covers are not always enough and a hat is certainly essential. There are various sorts of all-in-one boiler suits which zip up the front but be careful which you choose as many are fairly stiff or else leave little spare room to get the baby's arms and legs in. Choose a roomy one with a zip that goes right down to the bottom or even down one leg. A knitted jacket and trousers is an easier garment to put on and if you need to change your baby, you need only take the trousers off and undo the stretch suit. Make sure the trouser elastic is not too tight round the waist. A warm hat is essential unless a hood is incorporated into the jacket or boiler suit, and even then it may be a sensible extra because some hoods let the wind in. Always check that your baby's neck is warm before you go out – this area often gets forgotten.

One snag with dressing a baby warmly on a cold day is that he is likely to get too hot and so complain. If you know you're going somewhere where it will be warm, try to organize his clothing so that some of it is readily removable. If your baby is going in a sling, an outer purpose-made cover can be removed to make sure he doesn't get too hot. If he's in a pram, remember to take off at least one cover.

A good rule when deciding what to dress your baby in is to look at what you've got on and dress him in at least the same number of layers, remembering that you keep warm by being busy and that he may need an extra layer because he's immobile.

If you can't decide how many of each garment to have for your new baby, buy what you think is the minimum number and then add to it later if necessary. Lots of things are nice to have but are inessential. In this category are nightdresses, for there's really no need to change a baby from day into night clothes because he doesn't get his daytime clothes dirty. However, if it pleases you to do it, then nightdresses are cheaply bought or easily made. Your baby could stay in one all day as well because they are an easy and sensible garment and you need only pull them up to change the nappy.

On balance then, buy the minimum of clothes you think you can get away with – you may be given plenty of things and can always add to your collection as and when you find you need something. *Related topics* Bedding; clothes.

Laziness The concept of laziness is not really appropriate in the under-fives yet sometimes people say that their child of this age is 'lazy'. A child who is a late crawler or walker is often misguidedly labelled as being lazy. No child under five should have such burdens in life that he could be called lazy. He may be tired (for which there is often a cause), ill or sickening for something, or he may have poor vision or hearing. Any of these conditions can make a child seem apathetic and the cause must be looked for. Some children seem lazy when they are in fact unhappy or even truly depressed. Normal, healthy children under the age of five are rarely lazy in the adult sense of the word without a cause. It's up to us, the adults, to find out what it is and to help the child.

If your child is branded as lazy simply because he doesn't clear up his toys, you're doing him a great disservice and teaching him that he *is* lazy. He will probably end up living up to his label. Children – with some exceptions – aren't naturally tidy, and need to be set an uncomplaining example when it comes to tidying up. Making it into a game and always doing the lion's share yourself will encourage him to some extent. You may be surprised one day to find he's done a complete about turn. Don't forget to praise him. *Related topic* Depression in children.

Lead poisoning A condition that occurs when excessive amounts of lead accumulate in the body. This can occur if a child swallows lead-containing paint or inhales lead-laden air from exhaust fumes. Lead from exhaust fumes can settle in the soil and get into foods too.

Older houses that have lead water pipes and lead-containing paints are a special hazard and the answer here is to ensure that your toddler doesn't eat paint flakes. Also be sure to run the water for a long time (especially for the first drink in the morning) before using it to drink. This clears the lead-containing water from the pipes and reduces the risk of lead toxicity. Other sources of lead around the house are red lead in putty, lead-containing cosmetics such as surma and an Asian baby tonic which is imported into Britain.

In young children lead poisoning is characterized by stomach pains, sporadic vomiting, a loss of appetite and constipation. The nervous system can also be affected with hyperactivity, aggressive behaviour, irritability, lethargy and a loss of recently-acquired developmental skills. Many of these symptoms aren't present until the lead poisoning is quite severe. In the worst cases the child ends up with fits, vomiting or even in a coma.

The diagnosis is made by analysing the child's urine and blood for lead levels, and tests can be made of the environment too. Treatment involves removing the environmental source of the lead, treating the anaemia it causes and using drugs to bind the lead in the body.

There is a lot of debate on the subject of lead toxicity and exhaust fumes and whether much of the aggressive and anti-social behaviour seen in some urban children could be caused by chronic, low-level lead poisoning.

Leaving a baby or child For most mothers there are very few occasions – if any – when they really *have* to leave their babies with someone else, even temporarily. However, if a baby is already very familiar with someone else and if he is used to being held and cared for occasionally by that person, it won't be frightening for him to find himself in her arms when his mother leaves him. If she's breast-feeding then she won't want to leave him for long because she's the only person who can comfort and feed him at the breast. She can try leaving some expressed milk for him (though not all babies like taking it from a spoon or a bottle), or she could even leave him with a familiar breast-feeding mother who will wet nurse him. The person who looks after a baby may find a way of stopping him crying (when he's not hungry) by walking around with him, jiggling or rocking him, or showing him things and talking to him.

The difficulty for most mothers is that even if they do want to go somewhere without the baby, they haven't anyone with whom he is familiar enough to be left happily, unless the father is there, and even then many babies don't know their fathers well.

Lots of mothers prefer to take their babies with them wherever they go, especially if they are breast-feeding. The baby becomes an extension of them and not an encumbrance, so instead of being resentful of him having to come with them, they feel strangely incomplete without him and worry if they're alone. This is perfectly natural.

A baby can go to other people's houses with you for an evening out: feed him discreetly in company or else sit somewhere else. (The trouble with going somewhere alone to feed him is that if he wants to go on nursing for much of the evening, you'll be pretty lonely!) You can take him to an informal concert or play if you sit near the back where you can slip out if he creates a disturbance. You can't take him to a formal concert, play, ballet or opera, or to the cinema, so forget such amusements until he's older. Choose the shopping centre you go to so that you know there's somewhere you can sit down with your baby to feed him. Most cafes and informal restaurants are suitable as long as you're discreet. If you have a car, you can return to it to feed or change your baby. Many's the mother who has sat at the back (or front) of her church with her baby. No one is bothered by a baby there unless he's noisy but if he can't be calmed at the breast, take him out promptly. Babies who go everywhere with their mothers are mostly happy and secure and never have to suffer from feelings of anxiety at being separated. The mothers feel good too because they know exactly what's happening to their baby all the time and enjoy being with him.

Some parents in our society find the idea of staying so close to their baby difficult to come to terms with because it is unfamiliar. They believe that a little bit of unhappiness and separation anxiety won't hurt a baby in the long run. There is some truth in this. Parents who are resentful at never going out will be less good at parenting. However, as we've explained, there's no need *not* to go out just because you have a baby; you just have to be thoughtful about where you go.

With a stable happy home life, and loving parents, the occasional evening of crying inconsolably when his mother goes out may not make any impression on a baby's overall personality development. In any case, no one can ever prove that it does or does not because only gross degrees of maternal deprivation have been or are capable of being studied. However, given that crying isn't only a signal of a need but is also obviously associated with unhappiness, it must be more pleasant for a baby not to be left. A touch of separation anxiety may not do any permanent harm but is not the best way of making a baby feel secure and loved. Some babies who wake up to find their mother gone and someone else there develop problems with sleeping for some time afterwards.

If you decide that you will leave your baby behind, but you haven't anyone obvious to leave him with, then you'll have to choose a baby-sitter who is kind and competent, if not familiar and loved. You'll know then that your baby will be as well cared for as possible, even though he may miss the familiar comfort of his mother. He may not even wake up if he usually has a long period of sleep at the time you're out. If he does, then a feed and some rocking may be enough to settle him. A lot of how he responds to a stranger or semi-stranger will depend on his personality and a few babies make no protest. What everyone – parents and baby-sitters alike – dreads is the baby who can't be calmed and comforted whatever the sitter does. This happens often enough to put some parents off going out again without their baby. It takes a thick-skinned sitter to leave a baby crying in his own room and yet it is as bad to have a crying baby in your arms and have no means of comforting him.

A decision you'll have to make is whether to let your baby meet the sitter or whether to get him to sleep after a feed before the sitter comes. There's no one right answer to this and a lot depends on the baby's age – a young baby is happier to be left awake with a stranger than a baby of six to nine months or so, who is naturally at a suspicious stage and prefers his mother to anyone else, even if the other person is familiar. If your baby is awake, it makes sense to stay with him and the sitter and talk to her for a bit so that at least the baby has seen that you know and accept her. It must be very startling to wake up to see a completely strange face above you peering into your cot.

Because you may one day have to leave your baby, it's a good insurance policy to familiarize him with a potential sitter. There may be someone obvious like a relative, a good friend or a neighbour with whom you and your baby enjoy spending a lot of time. Explain that you'd like her to get to know the baby so that she can take the time to cuddle him and talk to him during your times together. If you are going to work either away from your home or at home, then arrange to spend some time with your chosen minder or nanny so as to get your baby accustomed to her in your presence. Try never to have an abrupt changeover of caretaker – whether familiar or unfamiliar – but organize a time when both of you are there with the baby before you go and when you come back.

If a baby cries with a familiar person his unhappiness is not so much a demonstration of his feelings towards her but rather of his unhappiness and frustration at the absence of his mother. A young baby can't understand why his mother isn't there and has no idea that she will be coming back. All he knows is that the person he wants is not responding to his signal. As soon as she comes back and he is comforted, he'll smile happily at the sitter from the safety of his mother's arms.

Some people say that if your baby cries or protests when you are about to go out, you should just disappear because so often he'll calm down once you've gone. There is some truth in this and if you've definitely decided to go out by yourself, there's little point in delaying your departure – your baby could be unhappy at any time when you've gone anyway. However, it makes for a very upset parent to leave a crying baby or young child and some mothers are so unhappy at doing it that they prefer to stay until he is happy or asleep, or even not to go out at all. The resentment you may feel at being 'kept in' by your baby may alter your relationship with him, though, so be careful. Someone else has only to sow the seed in your mind that you are being manipulated by your baby, or that he is being spoilt by getting his own way, for you to doubt your decision not to leave him crying. There isn't really an easy answer to any of this and you'll have to decide for yourself what to do, weighing up all the pros and cons.

When it comes to an older baby, it isn't always so easy to take him with you if you go out in the evening because he's not so likely to go to sleep readily or to stay asleep in a strange place. Also, he won't be happy to lie on your lap when he is awake but will want to be amused. This is all right in some company but not in all! By this time though, you will probably have familiarized him with someone with whom he is happy to be left when you go out. Some parents simply never go out without their children until they are much older and can cope easily with being left. If you leave your baby the best thing to hope for is that he will sleep well and if he does wake will be easily amused and settled by the sitter. If he doesn't usually sleep much in the evenings, a well-known sitter will be able to cope easily unless he is one of the not so few babies or young children who are inconsolable if left without their mother. In that case, either take him out with you, entertain or make your amusement at home until he's older, or else decide that he must get used to being left sometimes and that since you've chosen someone kind and well-known, you've done your best.

The same remarks apply to toddlers and pre-school children. However, three-, four- or five-year-olds are beginning to think rationally and can understand that their absent parents will in fact come back. They may prefer not to be left, but they can accept that sometimes their parents want to or have to go out without them. What's easy to accept in the daytime is not always easy to accept in the evening when they're tired, so don't be surprised if your child is happy to be left in the day but not when you go out at night. Overall, babies and most young children – at night particularly – prefer their parents to be their caretakers, however well they know the substitute. *Related topics* Baby-sitter; mother substitute; separation anxiety.

Legal rights of children Like all human beings, children have both rights and duties. The law, however, recognizes that children need more rights than adults, and conversely, that they can have fewer duties.

A child, for example, has a right to be maintained by its parents – and even where the state takes away their rights in other respects, the parents are expected to contribute financially towards the child's maintenance. A child is, of course, protected by the criminal law far more than an adult. An adult can consent when playing sport or undergoing an operation, to what would otherwise be an assault, whereas a child cannot foresee the consequences of its 'consent' – and so cannot give it. This is why parents' consent is required for an operation on a child. On the other hand a child under ten cannot be guilty of any offence under English law.

A child can sometimes have a liability in tort, that is, for damage or civil wrongdoing, but it is usually fruitless to sue a child who usually has no assets. A parent has no responsibility, directly, for the errant child. There may, however, be an indirect responsibility – for a parent could have been negligent. An example is if we give our five year old the unsupervised use of an airgun, and he shoots our neighbour's cat.

A child can enter into a contract but only for 'necessities' and then only if he is old enough to know what he is doing. You needn't worry, therefore, if he tells you he's bought a Ferrari – but if he buys a pair of plimsoles which drop to bits, he can sue the shopkeeper. A parent would, in litigation, act as his representative or 'next friend' as the quaint legal phrase puts it.

In English law a child cannot own land, although he can own personal goods. Land, and some other assets like shares, have to be held 'in trust' for the infant, which is why when making wills, parents should choose trustees carefully.

Finally, as medical science advances so the law too scrambles to keep up. The tragic thalidomide cases demonstrate how children can (after their birth) sue for injuries received when they were as yet unborn. There have been cases, though not yet in England, where parents, after an unsuccessful sterilization operation, have sued the doctors for the maintenance of the resulting child, and yet more bizarre cases when the child has tried to do so.

Let-down reflex When a woman's breasts are producing milk the milk is made continuously and stored in the breasts ready for the baby to drink.

Some milk (the foremilk) is stored in the distended milk ducts and in the reservoirs under the areolae until the baby sucks at the nipple.

As the baby stimulates the nipple and its surrounding skin by sucking he triggers off a nervous pathway (the let-down reflex) that produces the hormone oxytocin. This acts on the breasts to force milk from the milk glands themselves into the milk ducts (by muscle contraction). This can occur very quickly and many women are aware it is happening. Milk released by the let-down reflex is called hindmilk and is of a different composition to foremilk.

' Many women fail to breast-feed successfully because their let-down reflex isn't working properly. It is often a delicately-balanced mechanism, especially in the early days and can be inhibited by pain, embarrassment, mental and emotional upsets and many other things.

Once a baby is put to the breast the let-down usually works within a minute but it can take several minutes in some women. There are several let-downs during a feed if it is long enough.

Many things can trigger the let-down. Some women let down as they prepare their baby for a feed; some when they hear their baby cry (especially if they haven't fed for some time); and others let down at the time they usually feed their baby. Further let-downs can be encouraged by changing the baby from side to side.

Because oxytocin is released as a result of nipple stimulation many women (but not all) notice other bodily sensations as this hormone acts on their body. Not only do the breasts tingle and feel tense with a pleasant feeling that has been called something half-way between a sneeze and an orgasm but the uterus may also contract rhythmically. This is the cause of the so-called 'after pains' that many breast-feeding women notice in the first few days after birth, and which are a good sign because they help the uterus to get back to normal quickly.

As the milk is let down the skin of the breasts feels warmer too. In the early days all these breast sensations may be especially noticeable but as the weeks go by you may hardly notice them even though your let-down is working perfectly well. Some women have different let-down sensations at different stages of their lactation. If you aren't letting down your milk a good breast-feeding adviser will help you find out why.

As milk is being let-down, it can be seen to spray or trickle from the nipple. Sometimes fine jets come from several duct openings at once. If you have a spontaneous let-down and want to keep your clothes dry, press your nipple in firmly with the ball of your thumb. **Related topics** Breast-feeding; breast-feeding problems. **Useful organizations** La Leche League of Great Britain; National Childbirth Trust.

Leukaemia A cancer of the white blood cells. It usually shows itself as paleness of the skin, with or without a tendency to bruise easily. Having said this, just because you have a pale child who happens to have a bruise, don't jump to conclusions. The chances of his having leukaemia are remote. If bleeding does occur it often does so from the gums and mucous membranes. There can also be an unexplained fever or pains in the limbs.

Leukaemia is a very emotive subject and many parents fear that their child will die very quickly once the condition has been diagnosed. Today's leukaemic child will live for longer than he would have done as recently as ten years ago. One survey found that seventy per cent of those children surviving for four years had a normal life span. So great have the advances been that five year survival rates are up to fifty per cent in some studies and as many as a third of children with leukaemia can actually be cured.

The treatments are often complex and time-consuming and repeated visits to the clinic become part of the child's way of life. Methods that are used with success are drug treatments, radiotherapy (x-ray therapy) and blood transfusions. Most clinics will want to follow the child up very carefully for years, even if he appears to be cured.

Some mothers worry that having the occasional x-ray in pregnancy might produce leukaemia in the child. Certainly it's true that large doses of antenatal x-rays increase a baby's risk of leukaemia but precautions today are so strict that you should never receive a dose anywhere near this dangerous level. Always be sure to tell your doctor or dentist if you could be pregnant before he takes any x-rays. He may put off doing it altogether or will ensure that you are covered with a lead apron to protect your body and that of your unborn baby.

If ever you are worried that your child might have leukaemia don't put off going to the doctor. A simple blood test will enable him to give you the answer. **Useful organization** The Leukaemia Society.

Lifting a child at night

To avoid a wet bed or a wet nappy at night, some parents decide to lift their child out of bed and on to a potty or the lavatory to pee just before they go to bed themselves. Sometimes the child wakes up and will walk to the lavatory or potty and at other times he'll be virtually asleep while he is carried there. Many children get so used to this procedure that they pee straight away and go back to bed to sleep quite easily. Some others dislike it and wake up and make a fuss. If this happens, it's best to stop doing it because giving your child an unbroken sleep and keeping him happy is more important that a wet nappy.

Even if he has already wet his nappy, lifting him may prevent him soaking the bed when he pees again later. If you can do it without disturbing him too much, change his nappy to keep him warm and comfortable.

Lifting is most often done when a child has just come out of nappies. Do put a plastic sheet under the bottom sheet as an additional safeguard though, because a whole night is a long time to last out when he has only recently come out of nappies.

You may decide that it is kinder not to disturb your child at all in which case he'll have to stay in nappies until he can last the night without wetting them. Get him to go to the loo just before bedtime, after his story and cuddle, and put a potty by his bed if necessary so he can pee in it as soon as he wakes up. *Related topics* Bedwetting; potty training.

Limping A condition in which a child walks with an uneven step. The commonest cause is an injury to the foot which makes it painful for the child to put his foot to the ground. The bad foot only takes the body weight for a short time before the good leg takes over for longer than would normally be the case. This gives the child's walk a dip towards the side of the injury.

Other causes of limping include badly fitting shoes, a verruca on the sole of the foot, an infection of the hip joint, Perthes' disease and an undiagnosed or poorly treated congenital dislocation of the hip.

Never ignore a limp – always seek medical help. *Related topics* Footwear; hip dislocation; Perthe's disease.

Lisping A minor speech problem, the commonest form of which is the pronounciation of 'S's and 'Z's as 'Th's. Some children lisp temporarily, others when they lose their front teeth and some lisp because of dental deformities. Serious causes include partial deafness and a cleft palate.

Treatable causes can be seen to and most others disappear with time. Speech therapy may be a help for some children. *Related topic* Cleft lip and palate *Useful organization* Association for All Speech Impaired Children.

Listening Listening is a very important tool in learning and in everyday life. We listen three times as much as we read. Listening is the key to much learning in the under-fives and the child's ability to understand verbal language is essential.

The child's physical condition (whether he's hungry, tired, ill or badly affected by his environment) will affect his ability to listen and as parents we should try to create an atmosphere at home that encourages listening. Children should be helped to express themselves freely in the knowledge that what they say is important and accepted. In other words, children need to know that you will listen to them.

A child (or indeed an adult) listens at very different levels throughout any given day and even if he doesn't seem to be deeply involved in what's going on around him, he can easily be taking things in. As a child gets older he can devote more of his concentration and intellect to listening to anything from music and birdsong to people's conversation but in the early years he's easily distracted.

A four- or five-year-old will sometimes have to be reminded to listen as part of learning social skills. Conversation can't occur if the child doesn't listen carefully. Of course, it isn't just the spoken word that one should be encouraging our children to listen to. Noises of all kinds, and music of course, give young children enormous pleasure. Some of the earliest things a baby enjoys are noises.

All this means that a baby or young child has to be given sounds to listen to and needs to be listened to when he makes noises. This takes time on behalf of the parents, older children and other adults. Because listening is such a basic tool in learning about and enjoying the world it's well worth spending time in helping your child's listening powers to develop. It's also a lot of fun. *Related topics* Language; rhythm and music; songs; story telling; talking.

Loneliness Human beings – and young human beings in particular – are sociable creatures who prefer to have company. Babies like to be with their mothers and in many parts of the world they stay with their mothers day and night and are never alone. In our society we are accustomed to separating our babies from ourselves from birth onwards for much of the time, so that some young babies spend as much as three quarters of the day alone. During that eighteen hours, they'll be asleep for some of the time – perhaps even for most of it – but for the rest of the time they'll be awake. Looking at patterns of light and shade, mobiles, toys and pictures will occupy increasingly more time as the baby matures, as will listening to household noises, bird songs and other things around him. He'll also learn to amuse himself by moving his body; he'll watch his fingers moving and eventually manage to bring his hands together to play with his fingers; he'll kick; he'll wriggle; and he'll discover that he can move his bedding and his toys as well. However, all these forms of amusement will only keep him happy for a while before they become boring and he wants human company.

Some babies are never left alone even when they are asleep, and they certainly seem happy and cry rarely. There's no need ever to leave your baby alone – it certainly won't do him any positive good. You may prefer to put him in another room by himself when he is asleep, but when he wakes, go and get him as soon as he lets you know he's awake.

When it comes to bedtime, if you put your baby or young child in his cot or bed before he is asleep and then leave him to go to sleep on his own, you'll probably be disappointed unless he's been made to accept that you won't come back even if he cries from loneliness. Loneliness has a lot to do with fear as well. Fear of the dark, of bogeymen, of shadows and strange noises are never so bad if someone is with you. Consider letting your baby or young child sleep in company – either in your bedroom (or downstairs with you during the day) or in a brother's or sister's bedroom. If he knows that someone else is there, even if they're asleep, he won't be so lonely. Of course, if he can actually cuddle up in bed with someone else, all the better.

Second or later-born children are often lonely if their elder brother or sister is playing somewhere else or when they go to school, because they've become so used to being together. Give them more time and attention than usual to make up for their loss, and try to arrange for other children to come and play.

Loneliness is also linked to boredom. Being at a loss to know what to do is never as likely if someone else is there to think up games and other amusements. Firstborn children are better at amusing themselves simply because they had some practice before the next one came along. It's useful for a child to know how to amuse himself sometimes, so rather than always doing something with your children, or making sure they always have playmates, it's worth encouraging them to play alone on occasions, though this applies only to pre-school children and toddlers and not to babies. Developing inner resources of interest and amusement comes with time and practice and depends to a large extent on the child's personality and the example he is set by other people. If your child watches you amusing yourself by reading, making something or even just watching something, he's likely to think it's a good idea and will copy it.

Many mothers feel lonely when they are at home looking after young children. They miss adult contact and conversation and though they don't miss out on physical contact, they crave mental stimulation. Such loneliness is not good for them or their children and is best avoided. *Related topic* Boredom. *Useful organization* Meet-A-Mum Association.

Longsightedness The inability to see nearby objects clearly. When a baby is born his eyes have a fixed focus of about eight inches (20 cm). Many will follow a moving face if it's held eight inches (20 cm) away. As a baby grows older he becomes able to focus more and more easily on objects at varying distances. If your child habitually tilts his head, looks out of the corner of his eyes, screws up his eyes, or seems excessively sensitive to bright lights, he could have an eyesight problem. Any child who can't see close things as well as you think he should, may be longsighted. If you are at all worried, see your family doctor or clinic doctor who may refer your child to an ophthalmic optician or to an ophthalmologist. *Related topics* Vision; vision testing.

Love Many sorts of loving relationship are important to a child: the love of his father, mother, grandparents, brothers, sisters, other relations and anyone else who has a deep and affectionate attachment to him; his love for each of these people; the love of his parents for each other; their love for others; and his love for himself. He learns how to love by the example of others. The love that seems most important to him in his early days is that of his mother (or whoever has the most sensitive and affectionate interaction with him). A child can be attached to his mother even if she treats him badly physically and emotionally. He won't leave her or criticize her (even when he is old enough) but clings to her desperately because she is the one he knows. However, if he doesn't get the chance to form a close and loving relationship with her, he may find it difficult to make loving relationships with other people, possibly for the rest of his life. Her love is his template for love.

A parent's love for children in the family will influence the way a child will one day parent his own children lovingly. Emotional and physical battering are to some extent repeated by the next generation partly because they haven't learnt by example to develop the inner strength to cope with various situations.

Just as important from the psychological point of view is that if he is encouraged to think well of himself and is not continually put down and made to think he is naughty or silly, then he'll learn to love himself.

The child who is brought up within a secure framework of a loving family is likely to be capable of forming loving relationships with other people in later years. He grows up to be at ease with himself and has little need to 'get himself together' during his teens and twenties. The family that demonstrates warm, positive feelings towards others, whether friends or strangers, teaches its young members a basic trust of humanity.

Mothers and fathers can all too easily miss out on loving their children if they are too preoccupied with bringing them up in the 'right way'. As long as the physical care of a child is adequate, his parents' love for him is infinitely more valuable and it's important that it should be demonstrated. Psychologists and psychiatrists may say that one stable and continuing relationship with a caretaker is the main thing a child needs to grow up emotionally secure, but lots of adults would agree that their perception of the love their parents had for them was the most important thing. A lot of 'mistakes' in upbringing can be harmless if they are motivated by love or are compensated for by a loving atmosphere. *Related topics* Attachment; mother; trust.

Lovemaking Making love is often one of the things that suffers most in a couple with young children when the woman may be tired out looking after the children single-handed, and often lonely and isolated. None of this makes her feel very sexy.

The biggest single disruption to a couple's sex life is the arrival of a new baby. The most common sex problems presented to marriage guidance counsellors are those following the birth of a first child. Most men today are helpful during the latter stages of pregnancy and at birth and many are willing to help in the early days that follow. Very quickly though they want to get back to 'normal' and that usually means back to normal sexually as well.

The new mother on the other hand is coming to terms with being a different sort of person from what she was previously and has very mixed emotions. This is especially so if it is her first baby. Her hormone levels are altered and she may feel so content with her relationship with her baby that she simply doesn't need to be particularly loving or sexy to her husband. Many women are tired because of being awoken at night by the baby and prefer to go straight to sleep at night rather than to make love. Episiotomies (done routinely in too many hospitals) and Caesarean sections (performed in increasing numbers of births) can both add to a woman's lack of interest in or frank discomfort on having intercourse.

There really are no simple answers in a monogamous society. The man can, and probably should, masturbate or get his wife to masturbate him as they cuddle together, if she doesn't feel like having sex. Women often say that they want a lot of cuddling and physical contact rather than intercourse alone but men usually want intercourse more than just physical closeness. It's not easy to discuss such matters calmly unless you have a mature, loving relationship and all too often if the relationship suffers the baby is blamed.

Talk over the problem with each other and if necessary go to a marriage guidance counsellor or a doctor who has a special interest in the subject. The problems are usually short-lived and with consideration on both sides need never cause a serious rift in the marriage.

Some couples worry about making love with a baby or young child sleeping in the room. If having to keep quiet is inhibiting, then it's better to make love elsewhere or to move the baby out to another room. However, many couples find it quite possible to make love quietly and not to disturb the baby. Unfortunately, as some couples have discovered, babies seem to have a sixth sense about their parents' lovemaking and often wake up at the wrong moment. Perhaps pheromones (natural hormomes with a particular smell produced by the skin) have something to do with this phenomenon.

If your young child happens to come into the room when you are making love, ask him to go away and play. If he is too young to do this, you may just have to stop. Don't be cross with him or obviously embarrassed or he may get the idea that you (or he) is doing something wrong.

Low birth weight

A baby is officially a low birth weight baby if he weighs less than 5½ pounds (2,500g) when he is born. He may either be premature – born before he has reached thirty-seven weeks – or light for the length of the pregnancy, which may be full term. A premature baby can be relatively light for the dates as well as being light because he has been born early. About seven per cent of all newborn babies are of low birth weight, of which two-thirds are premature, so it is a fairly common condition.

There are many causes for babies being born prematurely and/or being lighter than expected for the length of the pregnancy. Some mothers sometimes or always have their babies before their pregnancy has lasted for thirty-seven weeks. Toxaemia, multiple births, bleeding, and diabetes can all make a woman go into labour early spontaneously or may make the obstetrician induce labour early or perform a Caesarean section for safety. Mothers who smoke are more likely to have light babies as are those whose placentas aren't working as well as they should or which start to deteriorate towards the end of the pregnancy.

You may or may not have any warning that you're going to have a low birth weight baby. If you don't know it'll be something of a shock as you find your new baby whisked away from you to the special care baby unit. Because so many low birth weight babies have problems with breathing, feeding, jaundice, infection and temperature control, most are taken away for special care straight away. However, some hospitals are only too well aware that mothers and babies do best if they are together, and try hard to prevent or reduce this separation. Babies who are near the top end of the range of low birth weight may be kept by their mothers, perhaps in an incubator, under a radiant heater, or just warmly wrapped in a cot by her bed. If they are actually next to their mother's bodies, they'll be warmer than if they're left by themselves and if they do feel cold, this is noticed and remedied sooner. If the baby has to go to the special care baby unit (SCBU or 'prem baby unit'), then in some hospitals the mother can go too, to a special room just off the nursery. This is by far the best way of managing newborn low birth weight babies, but in most hospitals the facilities just aren't there and there is no choice but for the mother to be in the post-natal ward and her baby in the SCBU, often some distance away. If this does happen, the nursing staff should encourage the mother to spend as much time as possible with her baby by his incubator and to do as many routine nursing jobs such as changing nappies, cleaning and feeding him (even by tube) as she wants to and can. Even a tiny baby does better with lots of attention, including being spoken to lovingly and being stroked and handled by someone whose voice and smell are familiar.

Low birth weight babies mostly thrive better on breast milk than on cows' milk formula, even though many such babies have done well with bottles of formula. One advantage of breast milk is that if the baby gets an infection, the anti-infective properties of breast milk will help him overcome it. It is also easily digestible and contains the nutrients and other ingredients in the right proportions. The milk of mothers who have premature babies is different in make-up from that of mothers of full-term babies, and is more suitable for their immature bodies. Breast milk can be given by a dropper direct into the baby's mouth or by a fine naso-gastric ('gavage') tube which leads via one nostril through his nose, down the back of his throat, into his gullet and hence to his stomach. The tube is taped into position all the time. Babies weighing less than two or three pounds won't have a sucking reflex at all and so can't be fed direct from the breast or by bottle. As they mature, their sucking reflex will gradually appear. The milk is best not given by bottle, though it is in fact often done so, because a baby who gets used to sucking from a teat finds it difficult to change to the different sucking mechanism necessary for getting milk straight from the breast. The alternatives are to feed with a spoon but this needs a lot of patience. There are now special bottle teats available which overcome the problems with normal teats. Ask the nurses for their help in putting your baby to the breast frequently right from the beginning so he is used to being there, and gradually over the days and weeks introduce him to the feel of your nipple in his mouth – you'll have to put it in for him. When he is mature enough for his rooting reflex (see page 511) to appear, stroking the corner of his mouth will make him turn to the breast and open his mouth, reaching for the nipple. One day he'll be ready to suck on it instead of just licking and mouthing it. The first sucks will be useless from the point of view of getting your milk and there'll only be a few fluttering attempts – he may even go to sleep for twenty minutes or so in between bouts of two or three sucks, but as he grows more mature and more experienced, his suck will become stronger and he'll be able to draw the nipple and areola into his mouth and 'milk' it. He'll also suck for longer and longer. Often premature babies only start to suck really well at the time corresponding to the original expected date of delivery. If you always express a drop or two of milk on to your nipple before you put it into your baby's mouth, he'll get the taste of it even though he hasn't sucked it out himself. This will encourage him to associate being at the breast with what is a very pleasant and attractive taste to him. If he has never had your milk from a bottle, it'll also be a new taste to him, because he gets no milk in his mouth from a gavage tube – it goes straight into his stomach. Change your baby from breast to breast every so often during a feed to stimulate your milk to let-down, and be prepared for these early sessions at the breast to last a long time. Just enjoy having your tiny baby with you and forget completely any useless notion of ten minutes a side! Don't be afraid or embarrassed to experiment with holding him in different positions until you are both comfortable and the nipple and areola are well-positioned in his mouth.

At first your baby will get all his milk from the tube, but as he starts sucking he'll start getting some direct from you. Over the next few weeks he'll become more and more adept at sucking and you'll have to express or pump less and less milk to be given to him by tube. One day he'll be able to do without the tube completely. It's much easier – once a baby is ready to start sucking – to give him a bottle than to teach him to take the breast. Though he'll have to take to the bottle gradually as well and won't give up the tube straight away, he'll have to work far less hard at the rubber teat than he would at your breast. However, in the long run this method is shortsighted because it causes such problems when changing over from the bottle to the breast that many mothers never manage it and as a result fail to breast-feed their babies at the breast at all. You can make his work easier at the breast by encouraging your let-down reflex to work before he starts sucking. All the time you are expressing, pumping, or breast feeding your low birth weight baby direct, remember that not only does he need very frequent feeds because of his immaturity (hourly is not too often for a very light baby) but also that, in general, the more often and longer you spend doing any of these methods of milking, the more milk you'll make. Expression and pumping are not as strong a stimulation to the milk supply as is a baby sucking, but the suck of a low birth weight baby is not nearly as strong as that of a mature one anyway, so the frequency and length of the milking become even more important than usual with a young baby. Don't give up at night because if your breasts are unstimulated for long they won't make so much milk. Rest whenever you can, day and night, and console yourself for interrupted nights by remembering that no one else could give your baby such a good start in life.

You'll find that attempting to nourish your low birth weight baby on breast milk only, whether expressed or pumped or given direct, is not always easy, and you'll need lots of patient and sympathetic help and support from those around you. If you have to send breast milk in from home (if you can't stay with your baby in hospital), liaise with the nurses to find out how much they are giving him down the tube or by dropper or spoon at each feed. Amounts of half a fluid ounce (10–15 ml) are quite normal for a baby of just over two pounds (900g), for example. Label the bag of milk with your name and date just in case it goes astray, and store it under suitable conditions, such as in the fridge, for a maximum of forty-eight to seventy-two hours.

Some babies who are 'light for dates' are not premature and may have a sucking reflex in spite of weighing so little. It's worth putting your baby to the breast whatever his weight unless you know that he was definitely born weeks before the expected date, just in case he is one of these. Some light for dates babies suck poorly in spite of being mature, and have a poorly coordinated swallowing reflex. All this, combined with a relatively large amount of mucus, makes them gag and spit. They need frequent feeds in order to keep their blood sugar level up.

Some very tiny or very ill babies have to be nourished by intravenous fluids. When they are bigger and healthier, breast milk can eventually be substituted. If you have decided not to give your baby your breast milk, or if for some reason you can't (which is unlikely with skilled help), then he may be given donated breast milk from a milk bank.

Babies who were of low birth weight tend to cry more during the early months. This may be because they receive relatively little mothering in the early days and is yet another reason for spending as much time as you can with your baby.

Premature babies take time to catch up with full-term babies in their milestones. They have the weeks they should have stayed in their mother's womb to make up for, as well as any coincidental illness which might delay them. By a year your baby will have caught up in many areas of development and by two you'll notice little difference, if any, from what you would expect of an average full-term baby born on the same birthday.

The respiratory distress syndrome is one of the problems that a low birth weight baby may face. Some are relatively short of iron because of the short pregnancy – they have missed out on the last few weeks when a full-term baby will have absorbed iron from his mother's liver. Breast milk contains more easily-absorbable iron than does cows' milk formula, and some premature babies are given extra iron if necessary.

When your low birth weight baby is well, feeding well and you feel you can happily manage him at home, he'll be allowed home. Some hospitals keep such babies until they weigh more than five pounds (2,250g) but this is just a guide. Remember that your baby will continue to need frequent feeds by day and night, and that you may have to wake him sometimes in order to get enough nourishment into him and to stimulate your milk supply.

If at any time you find that hand expressing breast milk is too tedious or produces too little a volume for your baby you can hire an electric pump from your local National Childbirth Trust group (see page 774).

Though you're bound to worry and perhaps to be extra-protective toward your low birth weight baby when you get him home, it won't be long before you forget his initial setback and just think of him as the normal, healthy baby he is. *Related topics* Breast-feeding problems; bonding; sleepy baby; special care baby units; weighing. *Useful organization* National Childbirth Trust.

Lying To lie is to speak untruthfully with the intent to mislead or deceive. One- and two-year-olds haven't the verbal ability to lie even if they wanted to. Some bright two-year-olds and three-year-olds though are capable of replying 'no' when asked if they've done something which they know their mother would be cross about, even though they have in fact done it. This ready lie is an attempt to avoid maternal displeasure. Children of this age are so straightforward that even if they attempt this sort of lie, it is usually done with such an obviously guilty expression that no one is deceived for a minute. It's best to start off teaching your children that it's almost always wrong to lie, so explain gently that he should tell you the truth. If you promise not to be cross, he should tell you, but then you must stick to your word and not be cross. Your being cross was what he was trying to avoid in the first place and he didn't realize at the time that his lying might make you even more cross! Whatever he's done, it's not helpful if he is so afraid of your reaction that he feels he can't tell you something, so consider whether your sort of discipline is too strict or your punishments too harsh. Remember that discipline needn't be punitive. Loving guidance is the essence, and any punishment you think necessary must be geared to the child's age, personality, and the nature of the offence, among other things, and shouldn't be so severe that he's frightened to own up.

Sometimes a child is confused by little white lies you use with other people in an attempt not to hurt their feelings. If he asks you why you say something he knows isn't right, explain as clearly as you can, otherwise he'll think that if you can tell lies, so can he. At this stage he won't be able to distinguish between telling lies to save himself from trouble and telling them to spare other people's feelings. There are some people who prefer never to tell white lies, but they can leave a trail of hurt behind them if they're not careful.

Older pre-school children are often given to telling fantastic lies about what they have at home, what their parents do or own, what they are allowed to do and so on. The lying is really a form of boasting, only the thing boasted about is imagined or blown up beyond reality. Occasionally such fantasies are made up because the child feels hard done by for some reason or because his confidence needs to be boosted and he gets fun from his tales, and the reactions he gets from other people make him feel more important. If someone tells you (perhaps a play-group leader or another child) what your child has been saying, make the time to discuss things with him quietly and gently. Don't tell him off or ridicule him because then he won't tell you anything. If he honestly believes that people will think better of him because he says he has tremendously expensive toys or that his father is a pop-star, explain that these are not important and that anyway possessions and position don't make for lasting happiness. He won't understand it all, but it would be a shame to let him base his judgements of people on what they have and who they are, and so distort what he has and his position in the world so as to make others think more of him. *Related topics* Boasting; discipline; fantasy; honesty; punishment.

Lymph nodes (lymph glands) Small (¼–⅛ inch in diameter), firm
but fleshy structures found throughout the body and easily felt in the following areas: just in front of the ears; just behind the ears; under the angle of the jaw and down the neck to the collarbone; under the chin in the midline; at the base of the skull on both sides; in the armpits; in the folds of the elbows; in the groins; and just below the creases of the groins. There are lots of lymph nodes in the chest, abdomen and the rest of the body but they can't be felt.

All these nodes are part of the lymphatic system. Lymph is a colourless fluid found in the tissue spaces and passed back into the bloodstream after being collected up by the lymphatic system of channels. Lymph nodes are found along the major lymph channels and can occur singly or in clusters. Nodes act as filters for circulating lymph, so preventing foreign substances being taken further around the body. This is why when a child gets a sore throat the lymph nodes in the neck swell up and become tender. They are producing millions of tiny cells which not only eat up the bacteria by engulfing them but also produce antibodies to them.

Children have a lot of lymphatic tissue outside the lymph glands. The thymus gland (present only in young children), the spleen and the liver are all rich in lymphatic tissue, as are the tonsils, adenoids, and the wall of the small intestine. Swelling of this latter tissue can cause quite severe abdominal pain – sometimes bad enough to mimic appendicitis. This condition is called mesenteric adenitis.

Under normal circumstances lymph nodes aren't tender unless they're squeezed or infected. Large, swollen lymph nodes though can be very tender when touched and painful even if not touched. When a node or cluster of nodes swells, look for obvious local causes such as an infection and if you think treatment is necessary, see your doctor. If there is no obvious cause for the swollen nodes make an appointment for your child to see the doctor soon anyway. Common childhood infections and chickenpox especially, often cause a generalized enlargement of all the lymphatic tissue in the body. Leukaemia produces a generalized enlargement too. German measles produces enlargement of the nodes in front of and behind the ears and also often affects those at the base of the skull. This is a helpful diagnostic clue if your child has a generalized rash but there is little else to go on.

If ever your child has nodes that are very swollen, extremely tender, adherent to the skin, or red, tell your doctor. **Related topics** Hormones; leukaemia.

Maintenance Money paid by a man towards the upkeep of his former wife and children. The amount to be paid is decided by a court. Even if you aren't married you can claim maintenance from the father of your child and if he refuses you can take out 'affiliation proceedings' against him. You'll have to go to a court to prove that he is the father. You can apply while you are pregnant or within three months of the child's birth.

The amount you receive can be altered if you become poorer for some reason or if your ex-husband appears well off. Even if you didn't press for maintenance at the time of your separation you can do so later by appealing to the court.

If your husband doesn't pay the maintenance he will have to appear in court to explain why and will usually be ordered to pay. In certain situations you can have the money taken from your husband's pay packet or salary before he gets it.

Because the subject of maintenance is so vexed and because it is open to abuse and ill feeling on the part of both parties, the law is currently under review. At the time of going to press Scotland has introduced new laws to limit to three years the time for which a man pays personal maintenance for his ex-wife and there are pressures afoot to introduce similar legislation in the rest of the UK. Most men don't mind supporting their ex-wives as long as they are acting as mother to their children but certainly do mind keeping their own living standards artificially low when their ex-wife could earn money or get officially re-married herself. There are countless thousands of men who are unnecessarily badly off because of prolonged maintenance payments to their ex-wives and quite rightly the law is beginning to recognize this. **Useful organization** One Parent Families.

Malabsorption A condition in which the intestines don't take up as much of the nourishment from food as they should. It can be caused by many conditions and produces symptoms not only because of the shortage in the body of things that haven't been absorbed but also because of the excess of substances in the bowel that should have been absorbed.

Coeliac disease, cystic fibrosis, sugar intolerance, cows' milk allergy, infestation with intestinal parasites and the absence of a part of the bowel after an operation are all possible causes. Sorting out what is causing malabsorption can be difficult and may involve some hospital tests. The treatment needed will depend on the cause that is found. **Related topics** Malnutrition; small children.

Malnutrition A medical term meaning bad nutrition. It's a sad fact that two-thirds of the world's children are malnourished because they have too little to eat and that a substantial proportion of the rest are malnourished because they have too much. Both are equally unhealthy and take their toll in reducing life expectancy.

A child, like an adult, needs a well-balanced diet and one with any major deficiency or imbalance will produce malnutrition. Very few children in the UK are malnourished in the way that Third World children are but some (especially of Asian immigrant parents) can become very short of vitamin D and get rickets as a result. This occurs because they need a lot more of our weak sunshine than they would in Asia because their dark skin filters off a lot of valuable rays) and they don't get it because they live indoors a lot of the time or in cities with polluted air which shields off the effective rays. Such children need vitamin D supplements to their diet.

A small number of children are malnourished because their parents have them on cranky diets. *Related topic* Food.

Manners The manner in which a child does something or says something has an effect on those around him. As he grows he'll learn to control what he does or says by copying your example and that of others; by observing other people's reactions to his behaviour and modifying it if necessary; and by listening to what you teach him about 'good' and 'bad' manners. Be careful not to encourage good manners solely in order to make other people like your child. The more important reason is to make other people feel at ease and happy in your child's company. If the way he acts and talks doesn't fit in with the sort of behaviour which the society in which you move finds acceptable, then he'll be unhappy in the long run because he'll be criticized by everyone he meets – even those whose manners are as bad or worse. Most children can sense when their behaviour isn't pleasing and feel awkward, not necessarily knowing what it is that they've done wrong, but just knowing that it wasn't right.

Today there are few absolutes when considering manners and most of today's children (even the well-mannered ones) would be considered thoroughly ill-mannered by Victorian standards. Few children wait to be spoken to, almost no one knocks on doors or call their father 'sir', yet all these were considered to be the very essence of good manners a century ago. Be guided by the society in which you live as to what is considered good manners – it varies from country to country and even within areas of any one country.

To help your child fit in and be liked and accepted by others so that he doesn't feel uncomfortable when he doesn't know what to do or how to behave, you'll have to start teaching him good manners from early on. It doesn't matter that he doesn't always behave as you want him to. The important thing is that he knows how to behave and realizes that society has rules about social behaviour.

As with teaching a young child anything, it's not formal teaching he'll need but patient, repetitive example from you and those around him. When you've been out to tea, for example, don't ridicule your child by making an issue about insisting on him saying 'thank you', but say 'thank you' graciously yourself in your child's hearing. As you say 'goodbye', get down to your child's level or take him in your arms and encourage him to say 'thank you', smile and wave goodbye by doing it with him. Depending on his age, you could smilingly say to him 'say thank you for tea', then turn to the hostess, smile and say 'thank you' again yourself. After a few farewells like this, he'll get the message and one day will turn to the hostess with a smile and say 'thank you' either spontaneously or, more likely, when you encourage or remind him. If he's too young to say 'thank you' or if he's feeling tired out and wants to get home, say it for him but never let him see you forget it.

A lot about bad manners at this age is simply a matter of forgetting: forgetting to say 'please' or 'thank you'; forgetting to hold the door open for someone carrying something heavy; forgetting to smile or reply when someone smiles at you or talks to you; forgetting to apologize; forgetting that other people have to be considered as well as you. It's all too easy to forget your own manners and then to wonder why your child seems slow to learn his. Unless you remember to treat him as you would treat a visitor in your house, saying 'please' or 'thank you' instead of ordering him about, you can't expect him to behave any better.

Teaching a child good manners is a form of discipline in the loving guidance sense of the word. You are lovingly guiding your child to behave well. A guide doesn't bully, nag or cajole, but teaches by patient example and points out what to do, time and time again. What you teach your child now he'll remember all his life, so it's worth making a real effort to help him learn good manners. *Related topics* Development-social; discipline; table manners.

Massage Most people find being massaged very pleasant and babies and young children are no exception. You have only to see the pleasure on a child's face as he lies on his tummy and has his back muscles massaged to realize that he is enjoying it. You can start with a newborn baby. Do it in a really warm room and warm some baby oil by putting the bottle into a basin of hot water for ten minutes or so. Put a towel or terry nappy on your lap and undress the baby, then put some oil on your hands and start massaging his muscles gently, rhythmically and with small circular kneading movements or a gentle stroking movement. You'll soon know whether he likes it or not. If he obviously doesn't like it, it may be because he's cold or wasn't in a good mood to start with – it's best to wait until after a feed so he hasn't got an empty tummy, but choose a time when he's not ready to go to sleep immediately. There's usually at least one suitable time in the day in which the baby is not hungry but is awake and quietly alert.

It doesn't matter where you start on your baby. You don't need to do every bit of him, nor do you even have to bother to use oil unless you have time – a little bit of massage at any time is pleasurable for most babies. Lots of mothers massage their babies when they have them undressed for a bath – before or after. Turn the baby on his tummy on your lap or on a flat surface (the floor or bed) and spend some time on his back, including the muscles of his neck, either side of his spine, and his buttocks. Massage his arms and legs, always gently, and don't forget to talk to him and smile at him lovingly as you do so.

Gently massaging your baby is just one more way of communicating with him and carressing him. Opportunities for touching are often sadly lacking in our busy lives but massage gives us the excuse some of us need to spend some time just enjoying being with our babies. *Related topic* Body contact.

Mastoiditis Inflammation of the mastoid bone and sinuses behind the ear. Before antibiotics were available infections of the middle ear (which are common in young children) often used to spread to the mastoid bone. Today this is uncommon but a chronic infection of this bone can still occur as a result of longstanding middle ear infection.

Infections of the mastoid bone are dangerous and must be treated thoroughly because they can spread to involve the brain and nerves nearby in the skull. If the infection can't be controlled adequately with antibiotics a mastoidectomy operation may have to be performed. At this operation the surgeon not only tries to produce a safe, uninfected ear but also tries to save or even improve the hearing by some sort of repair procedure. It is a safe operation and the child is home within a week.

Masturbation Manipulation of the genitals to give sexual pleasure or even a climax (orgasm). The word masturbation is usually used when the person stimulates himself to obtain pleasure but strictly speaking one person can masturbate another.

People of all ages masturbate – it is almost universal. In spite of old wives' tales to the contrary, there is no possible harm in masturbating unless it takes over as the preferred form of sexual pastime in adulthood and ruins a relationship as a result. Children start to masturbate in earnest at around puberty but even quite young babies and under-fives play with their genitals in order to produce pleasant sensations.

The vast majority of parents feel guilty and ill at ease when they know their young children masturbate but this is almost always the result of their repressed upbringing and their guilt about their own masturbation. Almost all babies and young children touch their genitals at some time, boys more than girls, simply because there's something easy to touch. A boy who does this may then get an erection (especially if his bladder if full). Some babies rock themselves rhythmically, look into the distance, their eyes glaze over, they puff or go red in the face, then relax and go to sleep. This disturbs lots of parents who fear they have a potential sex maniac on their hands! This is, of course, complete nonsense. A young boy doesn't ejaculate when he masturbates.

If you don't want your child to masturbate in front of you or others, tell him so pleasantly, but not harshly, and divert his attention to something else. Don't let him see if you are shocked because this will make him grow up thinking that his genitals are nasty in some way. The best thing to do is not to worry about genital play – it'll do no harm. Some parents think that there's a magic age at which genital pleasure becomes allowable but how they arrive at such an age we don't know. Certainly a child who masturbates a lot of the time needs help because it could be a sign of serious family stress. It has been found that if parents repeatedly prevent a child from handling his genitals he can become obsessed with masturbation. *Related topics* Guilt in children; sex education.

Maternal deprivation

Maternal deprivation There are varying degrees of maternal deprivation because so many factors can influence the situation in which a child grows up. Many a child is neither physically thwarted nor slow with his developmental progress, but may be inwardly unhappy because of poor and inadequate mothering for much of the time, even though he has a mother figure to look after him. Simply having a mother figure there doesn't mean that a child isn't deprived of the sort of relationship that would bring out his full potential in every sphere. Even a natural mother can be an inadequate mother. Child battering, which we hear so much about, is not only about physical damage but is also about emotional damage, which isn't by any means always as obvious, except to the trained observer. A child who is deprived of love, abused verbally, neglected physically, and whose mother doesn't respond to his efforts to communicate with her or please her is certainly deprived of good (or even adequate) mothering, even if his mother is there all the time. In really bad circumstances social workers can arrange for a deprived child to go into care if they can't help the mother in other ways. An inadequate mother may be a depressed mother and there are hundreds of babies and young children in the UK today with depressed mothers who are not mothering them as they might if they were happy. This is an example of maternal deprivation which may be unnoticed by those who might be able to offer help. This is why it's so important to let people know when you're depressed.

A mother substitute may similarly be poor at mothering either all of the time or perhaps just from time to time. Before you engage a nanny or make an arrangement with a minder, watch her in action with your child or with someone else's child and spend as much time as you can with her and the child together. With any luck you'll spot any clues which might make you think that she's not going to mother your child adequately.

Occasional lapses of good mothering such as happen in thousands of homes every day won't harm a child permanently either physically or emotionally but a continual lack of affection and interest will affect his personality. If you feel that this applies to you, discuss it with your family doctor or clinic doctor. Perhaps your health visitor might be able to suggest something. Having plenty of adult company is probably the best way of insuring that the situation doesn't arise in the first place. Watch how other mothers behave with their children and encourage your children to play with theirs. This will make up for what you aren't able to offer at least to some extent.

A child benefits from forming more than one close adult relationship in his first few years but he needs one special person to whom he can turn to be mothered. This person is usually his mother, but sometimes a mother substitute takes her place for all or part of the time. Provided a child has a lasting and stable relationship with a caring and loving mother figure he'll thrive emotionally and physically. Children like to have someone who is 'theirs' and most children have that in their mother. If she is ill, dies, leaves her family, or goes out to work, then it's important to arrange for a suitable mother substitute to look after the child. Some fathers take over the mothering role when necessary nowadays, but the majority of single-handed fathers responsible for their children prefer to go out to work and leave their children with someone else. A nanny or a minder can score over a crêche or a nursery because they are able to give a child one-to-one attention and to form a relationship with him. Knowledgeable and eager to do the right thing though nursery or crêche staff may be, they have work shifts, time off, holidays and staff changeovers to cope with, and it is virtually impossible for them to arrange for each child to have a mother figure who is anything like permanent.

Mothers who work sometimes feel they don't want their natural position usurped by anyone else, and so choose a crêche or nursery in preference to a minder or nanny. This may do their child a disservice. He's likely to prefer a mother-figure of his own during the day and though he may grow closer to and even really fond of this person, his relationship with his mother will always remain, though it may not be as close if she isn't there all day. Lots of working mothers try to give their children a special time in the evening when they lavish them with attention and love. The trouble with this is that so often both are tired and the mother has a lot to do, so it's not always successful.

Some children deprived of adequate mothering develop neurotic personality traits as they grow. Because children learn by example, if they are deprived of the chance to form a close relationship with a mother figure, they may find it difficult to love anyone else later in their lives, whether it's their partner or their own child. Conversely, they may form clinging or smothering relationships in a desperate attempt to make someone theirs. The first love a child has for his mother (or her substitute) is usually the base on which he builds all his future relationships. If a child has a constantly changing procession of mother figures or caretakers, he may become so disappointed by them constantly disappearing just as he is getting to know them that he eventually won't allow himself to form a close relationship with any of them at all. Inadequately mothered children may be slow to walk, talk and to reach all the various milestones such as being potty trained. A caretaker with only one young child to look after and to form a relationship with is that much more encouraging, interested and full of praise when he achieves something new than if he is one of many. If she keeps switching from one child to another, she'll forget what each can do and will never be sure what is new and what he has done many times before. The child will be much less likely to want to please, impress, interest and amuse her because he'll be unsure of her reaction and because she won't always be there to encourage or praise him at just the right moment.

Deprivation of a stable mother-figure can even make a child fail to thrive in the physical sense. A baby deprived of love and attention may not grow as he should and may not recover quickly after an illness. It has recently been found that such children have low levels of growth hormone, so clearly this deprivation has profound bodily as well as psychological effects. Restore a mother figure to such a child and he starts growing and becomes strong and healthy. The same can happen to some extent with children who suffer with emotional problems, but even though they may be restored to happiness, the roots of their early insecurity are sometimes never pulled up and may spring up at any time in their lives when they are under stress. Having said this, children's personalities are very adaptable and a poor early start which is subsequently made good may have no permanent effects. A lack of good mothering is unfortunately often associated in our society with other drawbacks, such as a hostile relationship between parents and poor housing, and it may be difficult to put everything right. *Related topics* Behaviour problems; child abuse; depression in mothers; failure to thrive; love; mothering; mother substitutes.

Maternity benefit (allowance)

A state benefit paid (whether you are married or single) each week for a total of eighteen weeks before and after the baby is born. It is paid subject to various conditions which should be checked with your local Social Security office or child health clinic. You must claim not earlier than the fourteenth week and not later than the eleventh week before the baby is due. If you claim after the baby is born it is only payable for the week of confinement and six weeks after that. This allowance is based on the woman's National Insurance contributions (which must be Class 1 or Class 2) and is based on the tax year about twelve months before the year in which you claim. You can still claim maternity benefit even if you are getting maternity pay from your employer but you can't if you're actually working. If you claim maternity benefit you can also claim the maternity grant.

There are new reciprocal arrangements with some other countries (especially in the EEC) so if you have your baby abroad you may qualify for maternity benefits if you have paid contributions in one of these countries. *Related topic* Maternity grant.

Maternity grant

A lump sum paid on the birth of a baby. If a woman is unmarried the grant still is paid. The only condition for payment is that the woman is resident in the UK. Multiple births qualify for multiple grants if the babies live for more than twelve hours. The grant is also payable after a miscarriage or stillbirth if the pregnancy lasted longer than twenty-eight weeks.

The majority of women are eligible for this grant, which should be claimed between eleven weeks before and three months after the birth. Get a form from your local Department of Social Security office. *Related topic* Maternity allowance.

Maternity pay If you have been in your job for two years or more and were working for sixteen hours a week or more when you became pregnant, under the terms of the Employment Protection Act, your employer must allow you to return to your old job (or an equivalent job) within twenty-nine weeks of the baby's birth. If he refuses, you can go to an industrial tribunal. Your employer is also bound to pay you a proportion of your salary for the first six weeks of your maternity leave, whether or not you go back to work. All these rights are set out in a leaflet (No.4) available from the Department of Employment, Jobcentres, employment offices and Unemployment Benefit offices. *Maternity Rights of Working Women* is a cheap, helpful publication which can be obtained from the National Council of Civil Liberties, 186 King's Cross Road, London WC1X 9DE. *Related topic* Maternity rights.

Maternity rights The law has become much more enlightened in recent years about women who find themselves pregnant in various circumstances and today pregnant women, whether married or single, have many rights, some of which are not widely known.

First, you cannot be automatically dismissed from your job because you are pregnant. Second, if you have worked for your employer for two years, you now have the right to your job back (subject to some simple but essential rules) up to twenty-nine weeks after the baby's birth. Third, you have the right to six weeks' maternity pay.

The only reasons you can be dismissed from your job on the grounds of being pregnant are if the pregnancy makes you incapable of doing the job properly or if it is illegal or dangerous for the job to be done by a pregnant woman. In either case your employer is bound to try to offer you an alternative job. If you feel you have been unfairly dismissed you can appeal through an industrial tribunal. You must claim within three months.

When it comes to having more babies, you don't have to work for a further two years, provided you are still working for the same employer. As long as you work up to the eleventh week before the birth you can take up to twenty-nine weeks off after the birth of each child. *Related topic* Maternity pay.

Mealtimes When your baby is feeding purely on milk, timing his feeds and your own can be complicated and we have dealt with this under Feeding schedules. When he starts having foods other than milk, usually at around six months or so, include him in family mealtimes by sitting him on your lap at first and then, when he is capable of sitting, in a high chair at the table. If no one else but the baby is at home, sit down with him to feed him and try to make the mealtime into a sociable occasion, rather than rushing around trying to get other things done and shoving a spoonful of food into his mouth every so often. Babies are usually quite happy to eat at normal family mealtimes, but they may want a snack or at least a drink of breast milk or something else in between meals. Lots of breast-fed babies never fall into any particular routine but can be given their meals at regular intervals even if they want the breast for comfort or pleasure (as well as for a drink) at various unpredictable times in between.

When you're sitting amidst a sea of food thrown on the floor, with a smeary-faced baby with food in his hair crying to be taken from his high chair and on to your lap for a feed, try to look on the bright side of it all and enjoy his company. He'll pass through this stage all too quickly. Don't wish this time away, however much drudgery there sometimes is, but smile at your baby and his grubby face, talk to him and tell him you love him in spite of the mess.

Young children sometimes refuse everything on the table, then pronounce themselves hungry half an hour later. If you've spent time cooking something this can be annoying to say the least. You'll probably feel torn between always preparing a meal that you know from experience your child likes, and cooking the variety of things you're used to and that you had hoped your child would grow up to be accustomed to. However, whatever your hopes of producing a child with a sophisticated palate, you may have to compromise by usually offering familiar food. It's important to let your child know, though, that you expect him to eat at mealtimes, unless he really doesn't like the food. Some parents make their child eat whatever the family is eating, but this treatment can cause all sorts of eating problems either at the time or later. If your child won't eat at mealtimes but will eat the same food half an hour later, then next time he refuses, don't give him anything until his next mealtime if you feel like making a point. If, like many parents, you're too soft-hearted to do that, then only give him something to eat which is easy to prepare.

Even young children like it when the meal table looks attractive. If you usually eat without a tablecloth, try occasionally prettying the table up with one. Table mats can be bought or made in all shapes, colours and sizes. You could make one for your child with his name appliquéd on. A small bunch of flowers makes any table look special and if the children help you choose and pick the flowers, then arrange them, they'll enjoy them even more. Spending five minutes on laying the table and making each person's place look nice is well worthwhile.

Children are unlikely to behave well at mealtimes or to enjoy their food if they're uncomfortable. You wouldn't feel comfortable kneeling on your chair to get to the right height to eat, so don't expect your child to – buy him a high chair (without a tray so it can go right up to the table), or put something on his chair to raise him higher. Cushions often slip off but you can buy or make a special toddler seat to secure to an ordinary chair.

Mealtimes are ideally times to which everyone looks forward. They are times for being with each other and for listening to what everyone's been doing and they are times to get to know each other better. Sometimes you may join other families for a meal, or they could come to your house. This makes a routine meal into a treat and you'll be surprised at the effect it can have on a faddy eater. Children love company and sharing meals with others is pleasant for all the family. *Related topics* Eating habits; feeding schedules; table manners.

Measles A highly infectious disease of childhood. It is probably the most common infectious disease in the world and tends to occur in epidemics.

Measles is caused by a virus infection and starts off like the common cold. It is spread by viruses in the droplets of saliva sprayed when speaking or coughing. The incubation period (before the onset of symptoms) is ten to twelve days from exposure to the infection but the child can be infectious as early as seven days after being exposed to the virus. Officially, he should be isolated from children who haven't had the disease or who haven't been immunized against it from the seventh day after exposure until the tenth day after the rash began, though probably he will be non-infectious after the first three days of the rash. Many parents won't mind you infecting their young child, so ask first before he is allowed into contact with anyone.

Early signs of measles are a slight fever, conjunctivitis, a cough and a cold. There may also be Koplik's spots in the mouth. The rash comes out on the third or fourth day of the illness and is usually first seen on the face, neck and behind the ears. It spreads quickly to involve the body, where it is concentrated mainly on the upper half. The hands and feet are usually not as spotty as the rest of the body. When the rash has erupted fully the fever breaks and the child improves if there are no complications.

The rash is composed of small, flat, red spots which may join up to form red patches. By the red patch stage the child is usually getting better. Measles doesn't itch. As the rash appears the temperature rises sharply (often to 105°F/40°C) and the child goes off his food, has swollen nodes in his neck and pain in the tummy. He may have diarrhoea and vomiting and even earache.

There is no curative treatment for measles but the unpleasant symptoms can be helped. Bring his fever down if it is unacceptably high by using paracetamol or by tepid sponging; if the light hurts his eyes, draw the curtains; don't force food but encourage liquids; and be guided by what the child wants when it comes to lying down in or out of bed. Some children have a cough which is severe enough to warrant a cough medicine and others may need treatment for persistent vomiting.

The acute stage of measles isn't dangerous but uncommonly its complications can cause long-lasting effects if they aren't treated properly. Pneumonia, middle ear infection and bronchitis can occur and encephalitis occurs in one or two cases in a thousand.

Today, serious attacks of measles can be prevented by having an immunizing injection in infancy (given early in the second year). Don't have your child vaccinated if he is ill, has ever had anything wrong with his nervous system (convulsions or meningitis, for example) or is allergic to eggs (as the vaccine is made up in an egg solution). Some children get a fever and a measles-like rash seven to ten days after the vaccination but it's rarely serious. The aim of a vaccination programme is to eradicate measles entirely, as has nearly been achieved in the USA. *Related topics* Earache; encephalitis; immunizations; Koplik's spots; pneumonia; roseola infantum.

Meconium For the first few days after birth a baby's stools are made of a sticky, greenish-black material called meconium. As the 'milk' bowel motions replace meconium, the colour changes quickly to a light brown or yellow colour. Meconium is the normal bowel content of all newborn babies and has to be expelled before the milk motions start to come through. If a baby is born at home, be sure to tell the midwife or doctor if the baby hasn't opened his bowels by the end of the second day. If no bowel motions are passed this could mean that there is an obstruction in the bowel which will need urgent treatment.

If an unborn baby is short of oxygen in the womb, meconium may be passed into the liquor (the amniotic fluid). Meconium-stained liquor seen before labour (during a special investigation called amnioscopy) or during labour after the waters have broken, is a sign that the baby is in trouble, needs to be monitored closely and probably delivered as soon as possible. *Related topic* Bowel motions.

Medical examinations Medical examinations range from the routine developmental tests done at intervals from birth throughout a child's first five years to the special examinations done if your child is unwell.

Well baby clinics exist to give practical support and advice about all aspects of baby and child care and development for the under-fives, as well as to carry out developmental testing and screening for complaints such as congenital dislocation of the hip, deafness, visual problems and so on. They are not there to diagnose illness or to provide treatment and an ill child should be taken to your family's general practitioner. Don't forget to register your new baby with your family doctor (or any other doctor of your choice) as soon as possible: you'll get an NHS medical card with the birth certificate. Lots of parents take children suffering from minor infections and other problems to the baby clinic but this isn't sensible even if a doctor is there because an infection may spread to the other children in the clinic, some of whom may be very young babies; the doctor is not able to prescribe medicines (unless the clinic is run by a general practitioner for the children on his list); and the doctors are there to apply their expertise to problems other than acute illness.

When your child has a medical examination, what he, you and the doctor want is for him to be calm and unprotesting. The doctor will find it extremely difficult, if not impossible, to examine a child who is crying, screaming, whining, wriggling or resisting in any way; the mother will be anxious or even distraught and may not tell the doctor everything he needs to know in order to make his diagnosis; and the child will learn to associate being made to be examined with being miserable and frightened.

If a child is feeling very unwell or is actually in pain, you may not be able to keep him still and quiet. However, if he has any preceding anxiety about doctors and examinations, he's much more likely to be upset whether he's feeling unwell or not. Prepare your well child for medical examinations by talking or reading to him about doctors and hospitals and what they might do to him. Take him with you when you visit the doctor so he can see you're not upset. Also, remember that he'll notice any anxiety on your part, so keep outwardly calm yourself. If you are worried, he'll think there's good reason for him to be worried.

Never threaten your child with the doctor or the hospital. Some parents stupidly do, with the obvious result that the child thinks of them as a punishment for being bad or unwell. Instead, foster the belief that doctors are good, kind, helpful people, and that hospitals are good places. This way your child won't be frightened about going to the doctor or having the doctor visit him at home. It's a good idea to encourage games of doctors and nurses – perhaps even with a pretend stethoscope and other props – to foster a feeling of familiarity with what happens.

Don't forget to tell a child old enough to understand what the doctor might do, so that having his throat looked at with a torch and spatula, his ears looked at with an auriscope, his chest sounded, and his tummy prodded, don't come as a surprise. Tell him that the doctor may want him undressed as well.

When you take your child to a doctor, if there is any chance of him having to be examined, make sure that you dress him in clothes that are easy to undo.

For a full medical examination in hospital, ideally your child will need to be completely stripped. However, if he's going to be upset by being stripped, or if he already is upset, then this isn't a sensible idea: it's no use having his clothes off if he's distraught because little of use can be learnt from an examination done that way. An experienced paediatrician, family or clinic doctor will take heed of any warning signs of anxiety in the child and undress him bit by bit or even not at all. This isn't ideal, as some useful signs which could help in the diagnosis might be missed, but it's better to be able to do some of the examination than none at all, and when a child knows the doctor better, or when he feels a bit better, he may let himself be undressed fully even though he is very upset. If he is screaming with suspected earache, for example, your doctor will *have* to look in his ears and probably his throat as well. Ideally, it's best to calm the child down first but if this is impossible because the doctor is so busy or the child is in too much pain, then you may just have to hold him firmly to keep him still. Whatever the examination, if you keep your child quite still, it'll be over with quicker.

The older a child is, the more likely it is that he'll be cooperative. If he has made a fuss, when he's better and if he can understand, try to help him understand why it was that the doctor had to examine him. If he remains frightened or resentful as a result of being made to be examined, he could have problems next time. *Related topics* General practitioner (family doctor); hospitals.

Medicines The prime rule about medicines and children is never to give them without medical advice. A tablet or medicine that works well for an adult could be very dangerous for an under-five and making a diagnosis from even quite simple symptoms can be very difficult in this age group. Even if your child has symptoms which are exactly like last time he was ill, consult your doctor all the same because unless the condition is a repetitive one (such as hay fever, for example) the cause this time could be totally different and could require quite different treatment.

Adult doses of drugs are quite inappropriate for young children and can even be lethal, so never use left-over tablets you might have in your medicine chest. Especially never use laxatives for stomach ache without first discussing it with your doctor.

Once a medicine has been prescribed it should be given as directed for the full course or it may be ineffective.

Antibiotics, for example, given in too low a dose or for too short a period will produce resistant bacteria which may be difficult to treat with the same (or even another) antibiotic. Urinary infections, for example, can take several weeks to cure even though the symptoms are quickly gone.

When giving medications to children dosage is more important than with adults and is based on their body weight. 'One teaspoonful' of a medicine doesn't mean you can give any size teaspoon – it must be a 5 ml proper measuring teaspoon. If your child vomits within an hour of having any oral medicine you should work on the assumption that it has been lost and give it again.

Timing is also important. Four times a day means that the four doses should be spaced throughout the day. Don't wake the child to give a night-time dose unless the instructions say 'every six hours'.

Getting children to take medicines can be difficult even though today many are pleasantly flavoured. The main rule is not to make a big issue of it as though you were apprehensive in some way (which you may well be). Be matter-of-fact about it and assume that the child will take it.

Use liquid preparations and tablets that can be dissolved or crushed whenever possible and if necessary give the child the medicine mixed in a spoon with something he likes. We have found that many children get to like the taste of the medicine (or its disguising food) so much that they can be tempted to see it as a treat and then want to help themselves when you're not there. Always keep medicines locked away from children and in child-resistant containers whenever possible.

Eye and ear drops can often be put in during sleep but no form of tablet or oral medicine must ever be given when a child is asleep or even very close to sleep or he could choke on it. If you give your child some cough medicine in the night, for instance, make sure it has been swallowed before you leave him to go to sleep.

If a capsule or tablet has to be given whole, put it into a piece of banana or other soft food followed quickly by a spoonful of something the child likes so as to encourage him to gobble it down without thinking.

By the age of about five many children are happy to swallow capsules and tablets whole. Many medicines are available as rectal suppositories. These are useful in the unconscious or severely ill child who can't swallow but aren't as well or as predictably absorbed as are oral medications and shouldn't be used routinely in children who simply aren't keen on tablets and capsules.

Never let children give themselves their medicines.

Keep a look out for side-effects and report anything unexpected to your doctor at once. *Related topics* Analgesics; antibiotics; antihistamines; ear drops; nose drops.

Meningitis Inflammation of the outer coverings of the brain and spinal cord. It is usually caused by a viral or bacterial infection and children rarely catch it from someone known to have the disease. The baby may seem to be getting a minor infection such as a cold but on closer examination he may be pale, lie still, and have a bulging soft spot (fontanelle). Babies also sometimes have a squint or convulsions when they have meningitis.

Children over the age of two have symptoms that are much more like those in an adult. Headache, lethargy, irritability, neck stiffness (the child cannot touch his chest with his chin and keep his mouth closed), vomiting, fever and a dislike of the light are all common with meningitis. He may also be confused and in one sort of meningitis (meningococcal) may have a rash of purplish/red spots over the body. Any child with any combination of these symptoms must be seen by a doctor at once.

The diagnosis of meningitis can be difficult and will probably involve a lumbar puncture. In this procedure a needle is passed in between two vertebrae in the lower back to sample the fluid surrounding the spinal cord. Because this is continuous with that in the brain, changes in it indicate what is going on.

Bacterial meningitis is treated with antibiotics but there is no specific treatment for viral meningitis, which tends to get better on its own.

Bacterial meningitis – especially if not treated – can produce long-term effects including brain damage, blindness and deafness. These problems are less common with viral meningitis. Meningismus is a condition which can look clinically just like meningitis but there is usually no evidence of nervous system involvement. A lumbar puncture may have to be done to be sure that there is no true meningitis. Meningismus is caused by pneumonia or an infection in the upper breathing passages. The signs of the infection are usually obvious and the meningismus goes once the infection is treated. *Related topic* Encephalitis.

Mental handicap Mental handicap is not necessarily the same as mental retardation, though many mentally retarded children are mentally handicapped. Even a child who ends up in an ordinary school and is perhaps average or above average in his mental ability may not be functioning mentally at his full potential: he is – for him – mentally retarded. A condition that causes mental retardation may not necessarily retard a child so much as to push him into the handicapped bracket (in which he can't manage at an ordinary school and may not even be able to cope with living an ordinary life in the outside world later), but may just stop him from being as bright and able as he would otherwise have been. In other words, there are degrees of mental retardation; it is not an all-or-nothing phenomenon.

Anyway, for practical purposes, we shall deal here only with those children who are handicapped enough by their mental retardation to make them obviously dull and unable to cope with normal schooling when they reach school age. About four babies in every thousand born are already severely mentally handicapped and many more are mildly affected. Frequently no cause is ever found, but numerous conditions may be responsible, including those acting even before the baby is born. Genetic disorders such as Down's syndrome (mongolism), hydrocephalus, and phenylktetonuria; maternal infections affecting the foetus as well, such as German measles, toxoplasmosis and cytomegalovirus infection; maternal malnutrition; placental problems; certain drugs or poisons taken by the mother; a deficiency of thyroid hormones; those acting around the time of birth (such as a lack of oxygen during or after the labour, a head injury during labour, and severe jaundice); and those occurring after the birth (such as meningitis, encephalitis, head injuries, poisoning, and the rare damage caused by whooping cough immunization) can all cause a loss of mental functioning in varying degrees.

Real but temporary mental retardation can also be caused by a lack of stimulation in the child's day-to-day life. Unpopular though it may be to have to say it, there are probably many under-fives who under-achieve when compared with their true mental potential simply because they haven't been given the opportunities to learn from being talked to, listened to, encouraged, and played with by someone who is sensitively responsive in his or her interaction with them.

Sometimes it is possible to be reasonably sure that a newborn baby will be mentally retarded to some degree. Most Down's babies, for example, come into this category. It's all too easy for such new parents to get hold of the idea that they have given birth to a condition, instead of to a person, if they are confronted with hard facts too soon. This is why unless they ask for specific information about their child's likely abilities, it's sensible not to try to forecast. It's difficult anyway to forecast accurately, and a few Down's children manage in an ordinary school for a while. As the baby grows, it will be apparent soon enough that he is lagging behind others of his age. Such parents will slowly gather information from many sources about their child's condition and will be able to come to terms slowly and smoothly with their child's probable future capabilities. Some parents describe vividly how they mourned the loss of their expected child after giving birth to a mentally handicapped baby. If they come to realize slowly that their child isn't going to be anywhere near average intellectually, it seems to make the acceptance of the loss of normality easier, partly, perhaps, because they are getting to know the child as a person at the same time as they are learning what his abilities are likely to be.

If a baby has no physical abnormalities, it may be many months before either parents or doctors realize for sure that he is mentally retarded. Such parents are let in on the facts slowly and may enjoy months of getting to know their child, all the time believing him to be quite normal. Again, this is often helpful, as they have a chance to form a good relationship before they know there is anything wrong. Some parents worry a good deal that their child doesn't seem to be doing things as fast as others and are relieved in one sense when a final diagnosis is made. At least then, they think, they can put a label on their child's problem and labels help some people, especially when explaining to friends and relatives why it is that their child seems so slow. For some others, the label is a bombshell. For months they have been hoping against hope that everything will turn out all right, and then their hopes are dashed as their worst fears are confirmed. They need particular help and support at this time.

Some mentally retarded children have other problems as well, such as hearing and visual problems, cerebral palsy, convulsions or a speech disorder. Nowadays all parents should be able to have their mentally retarded child assessed by a team of experts who will advise on the best plan of management and treatment both at the time and following subsequent assessments. The family or clinic doctor or the hospital paediatrician will refer such a child to the nearest assessment centre if necessary.

Looking after a mentally retarded baby is relatively easy because they seem so little different at first from normal children. As the child grows, his lack of mental agility will become apparent and the gap between him and his peers will gradually widen. Intelligence and developmental testing done by psychologists or doctors specially trained in the field can give some idea of the child's mental or developmental 'age' in each area. For instance, a four-year-old child with Down's syndrome may be performing verbally like an average child of eighteen months, socially like a child of two, and in his motor ability like a child of two and a half. There comes a time for each area of ability when a mentally retarded child will progress little further, if at all, but it is not possible to predict what this will be in any one child or indeed for any ability within any one child.

As a child grows older and his mental retardation becomes apparent to strangers, his parents often find it increasingly difficult to cope with their comments and knowing glances. Continued support from friends and other parents in the same position can be of enormous value at this stage. Many parents join a support group in which they feel normal and accepted, can air their problems and can get wise and practical advice from people experienced with bringing up their own mentally retarded children. In some areas health visitors make a special effort to encourage mothers of mentally retarded babies and children to attend mother and toddler groups so that they don't feel too socially isolated. Some play-groups also reserve places for such children. Schools for the educationally subnormal are nowadays divided into two categories: those for the severely subnormal and those for the mildly subnormal. Most of these schools have nursery classes into which three- and four-year-olds can be slotted for part of the week, so giving them plenty of stimulation to encourage them to reach their full potential and also giving their mothers some rest.

Some mentally retarded children are exhausting and difficult to look after while others are just like other children, only slower. They certainly can't all be grouped together into one category. Nowadays, few young retarded children are admitted into long-stay hospitals for the mentally subnormal, though short-stay visits from time to time may give their parents a well-earned break for a holiday or at times of special stress in the family. In some areas there are smaller residential homes for mentally handicapped children to live near their parents if they can't cope with them at home. The children can go home at weekends.

Mentally handicapped children, like other children, thrive on one-to-one mothering. If the mother is able to provide this, then the best place for the child is at home. If she feels she can't – perhaps because the child is extremely retarded, has aggressive tendencies, is wheelchair-bound, or has frequent convulsions – then permanent or short-stay institutional care offers the only practical alternative because so few families are prepared to adopt or foster a mentally handicapped child. With today's awareness of the importance of a mother-figure, the staff in institutions do their best to ensure that each child has someone to turn to whom he knows well.

Parents' reactions to life with a mentally handicapped child differ enormously, as one would expect. Some say that looking after such a child enriches their lives and their relationships with each other. On the other hand, there is a higher rate of marital breakdown among parents of handicapped children, presumably because of the stress involved in caring for them.

Parents of mentally handicapped children deserve more than just sympathy and understanding from their local community. What they often need more than anything is time: time to talk over their problems; time to be friendly with them and not to ostracize them; and time to help them in very practical ways, perhaps by looking after the child when they go out in the evening (babysitters are often hard to find), or during the day so that the mother can have her hair done by herself or go shopping occasionally. Perhaps if each local community took a greater interest in its handicapped children, fewer of them would end up in institutions. *Related topics* Down's syndrome; special schools. *Useful organizations* British Institute of Mental Handicap; Centre on Environment for the Handicapped; Down's

Children's Association; National Society for Mentally Handicapped Children and Adults; Voluntary Council for Handicapped Children – National Children's Bureau.

Mesenteric adenitis A condition in which the lymph nodes in and around the intestine become swollen and tender in a child with an infection elsewhere (usually in the upper respiratory tract). Swallowed bacteria or viruses and those travelling in the bloodstream are trapped by lymph nodes, causing them to swell as they produce infection-fighting antibodies.

The child with mesenteric adenitis has tummy ache. Mesenteric adenitis can mimic all kinds of abdominal conditions including appendicitis but a good doctor examining a child with abdominal pain will hunt for infection elsewhere and then treat the primary cause. *Related topics* Abdominal pain; lymph nodes.

Microcephaly (small head) A congenital condition in which a baby has an abnormally small head although his face size is normal. The head is small because the brain is small and tends to grow very slowly. The brain isn't small because the skull won't let it grow, as the bones of the baby's head are normally jointed and free to expand as the brain grows. A lack of oxygen during delivery, if severe, sometimes results in the death of some brain cells which are not replaced. The brain remains small and so the head is small.

Although most children with microcephaly are of low intelligence this doesn't mean that all children with small heads are mentally handicapped. There is a wide range of normal head size. Head size generally has very little relationship to intelligence. *Related topic* Hydrocephalus.

Migraine A greatly overused word which should really only be applied to a one-sided headache usually preceded by a phenomenon called an aura. With an aura the child may have various visual disturbances including floating lights, patterns in front of the eyes and temporary patchy blindness. There may also be numbness, pins or needles of an arm or leg and, rarely, even complete temporary weakness, paralysis or an inability to speak.

Such true migraine is very uncommon before the age of five but recurrent abdominal pain (sometimes called the periodic syndrome if combined with vomiting) is thought by many experts to be the equivalent of migraine in young children. Indeed, recurrent abdominal pain is often known as abdominal migraine. *Related topics* Headaches; periodic syndrome; recurrent abdominal pain. *Useful organizations* British Migraine Association; The Migraine Trust.

Milestones The word 'milestones' in the context of baby and child development is used to describe specific developmental stages which are usually recognizable and therefore memorable. Because of this, and because of the natural desire that most parents have that their children should develop at least normally and preferably faster than normal, a child's milestones are frequently compared with those of other children. The spirit of competition starts soon after birth, with mothers comparing ages at which their babies first smiled. The next major milestones are sitting up alone; babbling 'mama', or whatever; crawling; standing; walking and talking.

First-time mothers are often interested in other babies' milestones simply because they want to know whether their baby is getting on all right. Babies vary enormously in the ages at which they reach various milestones, and a mother may find that her friends' babies all walk, for instance, before they are one, while hers is still refusing to budge at eighteen months. Six months is a long time at this stage. This is why a visit to the baby clinic can be very reassuring, because the health visitor or doctor will be able to explain the range of normal ages for getting to any one milestone and this, together perhaps with an examination of the baby, will reassure the mother that her baby is quite normal and just a relatively late developer in this particular area. Just because your baby reaches certain milestones early or late doesn't mean that he'll be early or late with all the others. *Related topics* Competition among parents; development – physical (also see profile entries for ages: three months; six months; one year; two year; three year; four year and five year).

Milia Tiny, pearly-white or yellow spots on the skin of newborn babies (usually on or around the nose) caused by blockages in the oil glands of the skin. About half of all newborn babies have milia and in most cases the spots disappear within a few weeks. They shouldn't be squeezed. No treatment is necessary.

Milk A liquid produced by the mammary glands of mammals to feed their young. It consists of a complex mixture of proteins, fats, carbohydrates, minerals, vitamins, hormones, enzymes, live cells and anti-infective substances, all dissolved or suspended in water. Each mammal's milk is unique in composition and is tailored exactly to the needs of its young.

In the West we have become almost obsessed with cows' milk as a food for babies and adults but it should be borne in mind that we are the only species of animal that feeds the milk of another to its young. Whilst cows' milk is a nutritious food for children and adults all the nutrients can easily be obtained from other foods and it is never *essential*.

Cows' milk differs greatly in composition from human milk even after it has been modified by baby milk formula manufacturers to resemble human milk more closely. Ideally babies should have breast milk because it is designed specially for them. There are more than 200 known constituents in breast milk and each has a function. Some of these functions cannot be fulfilled by cows' milk simply because it was meant for calves and not for humans. Dried cows' milk as prepared for babies is, of course, a semi-manufactured product that results from pooling the milk of many cows at different stages of lactation. That's why it always looks much the same colour and consistency. Breast milk, on the other hand, is made by the producer for the consumer on a one-to-one basis and varies enormously in its appearance and content from feed to feed, within a day, and at different stages of lactation. Breast milk can look bluish, thin and watery, or thick and creamy, and all shades in between and still be perfectly normal and healthy.

Breast-fed babies are statistically healthier than bottle-feds, and although babies can and do grow up satisfactorily on cows' milk there is also a price to pay in increased disease and allergy levels. Breast milk contains infection-fighting antibodies to diseases (which cows' milk preparations do not) and there are other anti-infective agents in breast milk too. All of these give a baby protection against a host of diseases early in life before his own immune system is mature.

Another function of antibodies in breast milk is to coat the intestinal wall and prevent large proteins passing into the bloodstream to produce food allergies. Breast-fed babies have fewer allergies than do bottle-fed ones, especially if they are exclusively breast-fed for the first four to six months of life. This makes breast-feeding extremely important for the baby of a family with an allergic background.

Some babies and young children are allergic to cows' milk protein and this is increasingly being recognized as a cause of symptoms as varied as failure to thrive, eczema, nettlerash, runny nose, cough, wheezing, diarrhoea and vomiting. Several studies suggest that up to seven per cent of all babies are allergic to cows' milk. Goats' milk can also cause allergy and affected babies may have to be fed with a suitable plant milk – such as that made from soya bean protein.

We are able to digest the sugar (lactose) in milk because of an enzyme in our intestines called lactase. Many peoples of the world lose this enzyme during childhood and then cannot tolerate milk at all. Many black and oriental children can become quite ill on eating milk or milk products – diarrhoea, a blown-out tummy, dehydration and vomiting within hours of drinking milk are not at all uncommon. If such lactose intolerance is diagnosed, they'll have to cut milk or its products down or even out completely. Lactose intolerance can occur in children who can normally digest lactose after they have had gastroenteritis or with coeliac disease. Such children will have to have a lactose-free milk until their intestines produce lactase again normally. Talk to your doctor about this if your child has any of the symptoms listed above after drinking milk.

As we have seen, breast milk is perfect for a baby. However, cows' milk needs considerable modification if it's to be nutritionally valuable and safe. Breast milk is almost entirely digested in a baby's intestine but cows' milk is relatively poorly digested. This is why breast-fed babies have smaller and more liquid motions than bottle-fed babies. Their motions also smell more pleasant.

Although cows' milk has in the past been given to infants in many forms things are much simpler today. Today, artificial feeds (infant formulae) are manufactured and sold as powders or concentrated liquids, both of which have to be reconstituted with water. Some nutrients are added to infant formulae in amounts which are not found in breast milk. This is done to produce the same biological effect in the baby as breast milk would. For example, iron is added in large amounts to compensate for the fact that babies absorb it less well from cows' milk formula compared with from breast milk. Vitamins too are added to make up for those lost during processing and storage of the formula.

Most infant formulae contain mainly cows' milk but some contain added vegetable oils, animal fats, mineral salts, maltodextrin and vitamins. Infant formulae in the UK fall into three categories. Those made of cows' milk with added carbohydrate; those made of skimmed cows' milk with added carbohydrate and mixed fats; and those made of skimmed cows' milk with demineralized whey and mixed fats. These milks have their advantages and disadvantages but all are safe for infant nutrition as judged by current knowledge and standards. All these groups contain added iron and vitamins A, C and D. Some also have minerals added.

Only a decade ago there was real concern that infant formulae could cause too high a level of salt in a baby under certain circumstances; that there was a risk of low calcium levels in the blood; and that they were more likely to produce obese infants than was breast milk. Modifications have been made to infant formulae to ensure that these risks are now reduced to a minimum, provided the manufacturers' instructions are followed when making up the feeds. Today's formulae need no additives at all (except water) and can be used from birth onwards.

Fresh cows' milk (doorstep milk) shouldn't be given to a baby before six months of age and no dried milk preparations (as used for adding to tea or coffee) other than those specially prepared for babies should be used for infants. Only ever use specially-formulated infant formulae to feed a baby under the age of six months. *Related topics* Breast milk; milk banks; milk intolerance; sugar intolerance.

Milk banks Throughout the UK there is a system of breast milk banking so that donated breast milk can be distributed for low birth weight or ill babies whose own mothers aren't providing milk for them. Most authorities are now agreed that breast milk is nearly always best for very small or ill babies but not all mothers know this and as a result many don't breast-feed but rely instead on the medical and nursing staff to pull their babies through with the help of other mothers' milk if necessary.

Milk from a milk bank is the modern equivalent of wet nursing. It's interesting, though, that wet nursing might in some ways be preferable to a milk bank because it would do away with some of the bacterial contamination of donated milk that occurs during its collection, transport and storage in the hospital. There have always been some mothers who can't (rare) or choose not to (common) breast-feed, so there will always be a need for donated milk.

If you are breast-feeding and would like to give milk for sickly or very small babies in hospital, contact your local maternity unit and ask if they have a milk bank. If they don't they'll be able to direct you to your nearest one. You'll be asked about your present and past state of health and will be told how to collect your milk, store it and get it to the hospital. Follow the instructions carefully because they exist to ensure that the milk is as free from bacterial contamination as possible. Some hospitals arrange for the collection of donated breast milk, which is a great time saver for a busy mother. In some maternity units milk is collected on the wards from recently delivered mothers who are breast-feeding their babies and have milk to spare.

Even small amounts of breast milk are valuable, so don't feel you have to be producing pints of extra milk for it to be of any use. Even a few teaspoonfuls will be appreciated. If you collect the drips from the other breast while your baby is feeding you'll deprive your baby of nothing and won't even have the bother of expressing. Even if you were to express milk specifically to give away, your milk supply would increase to cover your baby's needs.

Donated breast milk is usually pooled with that of other mothers and, if necessary, sterilized, though this impairs its qualities to some extent. *Related topics* Breast milk; low birth weight. *Useful organizations* La Leche League of Great Britain; National Childbirth Trust.

Milk intolerance

Intolerance or allergy to cows' milk protein present in whole milk and in milk formula is what is normally meant by the term milk intolerance. It can produce diverse symptoms in babies and young children including failure to thrive, a chronic cough, wheezing, urticaria, eczema, a runny nose, diarrhoea and vomiting. Some studies have suggested that as many as seven per cent of bottle-fed babies are affected to a greater or lesser extent by milk protein intolerance. Goat's milk may be helpful for these children because it is less likely to cause milk intolerance, but it must be prepared correctly when given to babies.

Children may also develop problems after drinking milk because of an intolerance to the sugar in it. This is a difficult type of problem and is called sugar intolerance.

Soya milks are available on the NHS to babies who have been diagnosed as being milk intolerant. *Related topics* Milk; sugar intolerance.

Milk teeth

The first set of teeth. The average baby's first tooth appears at seven months and he has twenty teeth by 2½ years. The usually erupt in the following order: bottom central incisors, top central incisors, lateral incisors, first molars, canines, then second molars. The second teeth normally begin to come through when the child is six.

Some parents argue that because a child will lose all his milk teeth anyway, it doesn't matter whether they are looked after or not. Nothing could be further from the truth. The milk teeth are necessary to guide the second teeth through in the right places and need to be looked after just like permanent teeth.

If a baby gets a tooth which hurts his mother as she is breast-feeding him, she can help matters by frequently changing the position in which he feeds, so that her areola doesn't always get the tooth in the same place. Bottom teeth are covered by the baby's tongue when he is at the breast and so cause no problem.

If a baby actually bites the breast, take him off at once and put him back a few seconds later. Biting is rarely an insoluble problem, and breast-feeding actually helps the normal development of the jaws and teeth because of the particular sucking and swallowing movements of the breast-fed baby. *Related topic* Teething.

Miscarriage As baby care begins at, or even before conception and as miscarriages are relatively common, this subject is obviously of relevance here. Strictly speaking the term miscarriage is not a medical one – doctors talk of abortions. The first sign of a miscarriage is often bleeding and any blood loss must be taken seriously as it is sometimes possible to prevent a miscarriage and save the baby. Bleeding from the vagina during pregnancy may be serious or not and you won't be able to tell which – this is a job for a gynaecologist.

By definition a miscarriage or abortion is the loss of a foetus before twenty-eight weeks of pregnancy – after that the loss is known as a stillbirth. No one knows why women should lose such a high proportion of their foetuses but about one in five to one in six of all pregnancies ends prematurely in this way. Three quarters of all miscarriages occur in the first twelve weeks. Only a few women miscarry repeatedly. It has been calculated that the risk of miscarrying after one miscarriage is twenty per cent; after two miscarriages, twenty-five per cent; and after three miscarriages, thirty per cent. A woman who loses three or more foetuses at about the same stage of pregnancy is known as an 'habitual aborter' and will receive very special care.

There are several different kinds of miscarriage. A *threatened miscarriage* is one in which there is vaginal bleeding and pain. If ever you have this, go to bed at once and get the doctor to come. The degree of bleeding varies enormously and there may be a dull ache low down in the abdomen. This type of miscarriage usually occurs at the time of the first, second or third missed periods and can also occur at the fourteenth week as the placenta takes over hormone production from the ovaries. Bed rest usually 'cures' this type of miscarriage but be sure not to use tampons and to save every sanitary towel for a doctor to see. It is probably wise not to have intercourse after a threatened miscarriage, at least not until the baby can be felt to move. An increasing number of obstetricians suggest that such a woman should have an ultrasound scan to see if her baby is still alive so that she doesn't spend time in bed resting only to find that she is carrying a dead foetus. This type of miscarriage can go on to become an *inevitable miscarriage*.

This type is associated with pain like a period pain. The bleeding increases in amount and again you should go straight to bed. Your doctor will decide if you should go to hospital. An inevitable miscarriage can occur completely or incompletely. If the loss is complete the uterus will expel the foetus just as in a labour. Keep anything you expel to show the doctor. Hopefully all the uterine contents will have come away but if not medical attention will be required. This will probably involve having a D & C to scrape out the lining of the uterus.

In a 'missed' abortion (miscarriage) the foetus dies in the womb but isn't expelled for some time. There are no other signs of miscarriage but the woman's abdomen stops swelling and she usually doesn't feel pregnant any more. Carrying a dead baby can be very distressing so most women go to hospital for a D & C to remove the foetus.

There are lots of different causes of miscarriage. The commonest cause in the first twelve weeks of pregnancy (and thus the commonest cause of all) is the so-called 'blighted ovum'. The pregnancy starts well but the fertilized ovum doesn't develop into a baby. About a fifth of women who miscarry have a problem with their cervix which can't retain the foetus as the uterus stretches. A simple operation can cure this. Hormone deficiencies are probably very common and some can be treated so as to prevent a miscarriage.

The loss of a foetus is a terrible blow to any couple and whether the loss is over in a few minutes (early in pregnancy) or takes hours like a real labour (later in pregnancy) the woman still knows she has lost what she most wanted. Such a couple are often brushed aside by relatives and friends and even sometimes by the medical profession but their sense of loss can be profound and they need to grieve for their dead baby. Husbands need sympathy too – after all, it's the man's baby as well.

Many women grieve when they've had a miscarriage because they imagine that they might never be able to have another baby. A miscarriage means you've lost *this* baby but doesn't necessarily mean you'll lose another. **Useful organizations** Family Planning Information Service; The National Marriage Guidance Council.

Mobiles Moving objects suspended from the ceiling or from somewhere where a baby can easily see them. If you put a mobile near a window which is sometimes open, or in a through draught, it'll move spontaneously. Lots of parents put a mobile above their baby's cot so that he can watch it before he goes to sleep or when he wakes up. Wherever you put it, take the time to look at it with your baby and he'll enjoy it all the more. If you push it so that it moves and then smile and talk to a three-month-old about the design, the colours and so on, he'll share your enthusiasm and will respond with a delighted smile, chuckle or waving of his arms in an attempt to copy you in making it move. A younger baby may just look interested and smile; while a newborn may be transfixed momentarily by the moving pattern of light and colour that it makes if he is close enough to it to notice it.

Even older children enjoy watching a mobile, so don't think of it as just a baby's thing. They'll like to make it move by blowing it or making a draught by waving their hands. A four- or five-year-old can make a mobile for his baby brother or sister with your guidance. It doesn't have to consist of a delicately-balanced system of thread and fine sticks with cut out card designs suspended from it, though this is perfectly possible to construct at home (use a coathanger, or straws instead of sticks if you like, with cut-outs, milk bottle tops or anything that'll catch the child's attention). It might be just a couple of balloons; a bunch of paper streamers from the Christmas decoration box; a painting or crayonning done on both sides of a cut-out design and hung up by a thread through a small hole; or a three dimensional paper model that your child has made at play-group. If you're short of wall space, hang your child's artistic efforts up for a week or so each so that they can be admired in mid-air rather than being pushed in a drawer.

Leaves on a tree, the hanging fronds of a trailing suspended indoor plant, and even a swinging light can all amuse a baby in the same way that a mobile does. Look around your baby's environment to see what moving things there are for him to be interested in and show them to him.

Modesty In a few decades the average family in the Western world has swung away from Victorian-based ideas on modesty to a much more liberal and open approach. Children are now quite happily allowed to play naked at beaches, swimming pools and in people's gardens. Most under-fives have no qualms about this at all. Trouble with modesty starts later once adult concepts begin to alter their views of their bodies. The concept of modesty in an under-five is really rather silly and puts stress into a situation quite unnecessarily.

When it comes to adult nudity in the presence of young children the story is rather different because the feelings a young child has for his parents (especially of the opposite sex) are very powerful. Child psychiatrists and psychosexual experts talk about the effect that seeing a naked parent can have when one is very young and certainly a child going through the Oedipal stage (of idolizing the parent of the opposite sex) might be influenced by regular parental nudity. It's difficult to be sure what effect such experiences have but certainly locked parental bedrooms or bathrooms are not advisable. Many parents think that letting young children see their father with an erection is unacceptable: this seems to be a relatively common personal limit. Similarly, many parents in our society take care not to let their children see or hear them having sexual intercourse. For one thing, their intrusion would spoil things and for another, they might be afraid – consciously or unconsciously – that their father was hurting their mother. ***Related topic*** Development – psychosexual.

Moles A flat, brown mark, a frondy tag of skin, or a brown swelling on the skin which can be hairy or hairless. A mole is a kind of birthmark and is usually small and trouble-free. They are very common. About two per cent of white babies and twenty per cent of black babies have them.

If ever a mole bleeds, becomes pigmented (darker in colour), tender, itchy or lies in a place where it is subject to repeated rubbing by clothes, it should be seen by a doctor. Such moles, and indeed any moles, can be removed surgically very easily. Very large moles need medical attention because there is a small chance of their becoming cancerous. *Related topic* Birthmarks.

Mongolian blue spot

A flat, bluish-grey patch on or discoloration of the skin at the base of the spine of some babies. It has no known significance and fades spontaneously. Such spots or patches of discoloration are very common around the buttocks, being found in ninety-five per cent of black babies, eighty per cent of oriental babies and ten per cent of white babies.

Moniliasis (candidiasis)

An infection of the mouth (thrush), nails, vagina, or skin (especially of the armpits, groins, umbilicus and buttocks) caused by the fungus or yeast, *Candida albicans*. It usually occurs in healthy babies and young children and thrush and vaginal moniliasis may also occur when a child is on a prolonged course of antibiotics. These kill off the normal bacteria within the mouth and vagina and allow the yeast to grow unchecked.

Moniliasis can be present from birth if the baby's mother has vaginal thrush – he picks it up as he comes down the birth canal. Unsterilized bottle teats are also a source of thrush for babies and this can be the result of a maternal infection.

The signs of thrush are usually fairly typical. The inside of the mouth, the cheeks, and the tongue are most affected. The patches look like milk but, unlike milk, don't wipe off easily, and leave a bleeding base when scraped off. The tongue is often very white and furry. In babies the condition can be so painful that feeding becomes a real problem.

A home remedy for thrush (which is much less messy than using gentian violet, which some people may suggest) is baking soda solution made by dissolving a level teaspoonful of sodium bicarbonate (baking soda) in a cup of water. Swab the inside of the baby's mouth thoroughly after each feed with some clean cotton wool soaked in the solution. Make a new solution each day. If this doesn't work, get some help from your doctor, who may prescribe a drug called nystatin in the form of a suspension. After a feed, wipe the baby's mouth with some cotton wool soaked in warm water, then drip a little (1 ml) of the suspension into his mouth. A baby can be reinfected from anything that has previously been in his mouth, so take care to boil daily for twenty minutes any dummy or bottle teat you may have given him, until he is better. Some doctors suggest that a pessary is sucked by older children with the condition. Such pessaries are usually used for the adult vaginal form of the condition. If you don't treat thrush the yeast gets into the bowel motions and can cause a nappy rash.

Monilia can also cause infection around a nail with redness and swelling of the surrounding skin and horizontal ridging and breaking of the nail. Treatment involves treating the mouth infection as well as the nail infection.

Thrush in the breast-fed baby's mouth may cause a monilial infection of the mother's nipples if her nipples are already sore or cracked. Unless both baby and mother are treated simultaneously they can pass the infection backwards and forwards to each other. *Related topics* Nappy rash; nipple care in mother; paronychia.

Morals Your young child will learn a large part of his moral code from you before he is five, even if you don't realize you're setting him an example. The way you deal with people and talk about them; the way you make decisions; the reasons you give for the way you behave; the way you treat your children; the difference between what you do and what you say you ought to do; the difference between the way you behave when other people can watch you and how you behave when you're alone; and the advice you give your children and others are all examples of your moral code which your child will use as his templates for life. As he grows up and experiences other people with different moral codes, he'll have other examples to compare and contrast with yours, and gradually his own may change. Frank and open discussion at home between parents and children about moral problems both at home and in the outside world will help your child develop his own strong set of morals and will help him decide where his lines of behaviour will eventually be drawn.

Families with a religion will find their moral training is more clear-cut because they have a set of rules to follow. This can be a great strength to young children who see that their parents are bound by a set of rules that seem to be above even them. *Related topics* Development – social; religion.

Moro reflex A reflex movement of a young baby's arms in response to a sudden movement or a shock of some sort. The baby's arms move across his chest in an embracing manner, as though to cling on to something. This movement may represent a very necessary clinging reflex essential in the days when our ancestors clung on to their mothers. Today it no longer has this function. Your baby may give this jerky response if you've handled him too rapidly or if you've let his head fall back in an uncontrolled way which he doesn't like.

Mothering The physical and emotional care needed by all babies and young children which, for most, is provided by their mothers. Because all mothers are different, the ways they mother are different. Their mothering is also influenced by their babies, who are very different in their behaviour and personality from birth. However, all babies do best if they have one person – usually, but not necessarily, their mother – to give them individual and sensitive attention and affection and to respond to their social advances.

The quality of the social and emotional interaction between a baby and his mother is more important than its quantity – one person may physically care for the child for most of the time but if another takes more trouble to talk to and interact with the baby on a one-to-one basis, even if this is only for a short time each day, he'll become more attached to that person. Usually, a mother quickly (or gradually) forms a close bond with her baby, and is the person likely to interact most sensitively with him, giving him the attention and affection he needs. She is therefore the one he becomes most attached to. This doesn't mean to say that she's the *only* one he becomes attached to but she will usually be at the top of the hierarchy.

In many cultures, it's considered important to 'mother the mother'. The new mother and her baby are left very much to themselves in the first few weeks after childbirth so that feeding can be established and the relationship between them cemented. The mother is looked after so that she doesn't have to concern herself with day-to-day domestic duties. Her mothering gets off to a good start if she is mothered herself.

In the UK, some mothers have a rough deal at first. They are sent home from hospital with a brand new baby to look after and with no support from anyone except their husbands when they aren't at work. Mothers who are badly housed (especially if they live in high-rise blocks in inner city areas) and who are in the lower socio-economic groups, are much more likely to suffer from post-natal depression. If there were some way that mothers in isolated, nuclear families could be mothered themselves, their own mothering and their ability to enjoy their babies would be greatly enhanced.

In our culture, preparation for childbirth is better than it ever has been, but preparation for motherhood is sadly lacking. Neither girls nor boys are taught much about mothering and if they are taught anything at all, it is likely to be just about the mechanics of baby care, not the emotional side of the mother-child relationship. The mechanics of baby care, though very necessary, are relatively easily learnt at any time, whereas with our small families in which there is little chance for children to watch their own mothers mother their younger brothers and sisters, and with the isolation of many mothers, what potential mothers so badly need to learn about is the emotional and social side of baby and child care.

Sadly, our society seems to be hung up on the negative aspects of being a mother. Post-natal depression and maternal isolation are much discussed and no one ever seems to talk about the pleasures of motherhood, or the joy of looking after your own baby. Perhaps because of this omission, many women come to believe that looking after a baby is an intrinsically dismal experience. When they have their own baby, they are so concerned with what their teachers have deemed important, that is, the practical care of their babies and young children, that they may not allow themselves to revel in the delights of the good relationship that a mother and baby can enjoy. Certain other societies take a much more obvious pleasure in their children than we do in the UK. Perhaps we should allow ourselves to copy them.

Psychologists have proved to their satisfaction that babies are not permanently psychologically harmed by being looked after by suitable, familiar, well-liked and stable mother substitutes. However, a mother will lose a lot of satisfaction and pleasure for herself if she doesn't care for her own young children. The joys of money and a career don't equate with the rewards of motherhood for most women. Only for a very few is there a choice. Quite apart from the difficulty of getting a stable, good mother substitute the irrational bond of mother-love formed early on with her baby must enrich a mother's day-to-day relationship with him in a way that a mother substitute's affection cannot quite match up to. When a mother looks after another child as well as her own, she's well aware that her feelings towards her own child are different in quality. Adoptive mothers who subsequently have a baby of their own describe the different love they have for their own. Whether this difference in feeling is simply because they have been pregnant with and given birth to their own child who shares their genes, or whether there is an unknown, psychic bond of some sort as well isn't known. It's interesting that adoptive mothers who breast-fed their adopted babies describe how their feelings of motherliness to and bond with that baby are increased. Certainly breast-feeding provides ample opportunity for comforting a baby as well as feeding him.

No one wants the best for their child more than his mother and father, and so his mother is the most obvious person to look after him if his best interests are to be served. A good mother substitute can undoubtedly bring a child up well but will obviously influence his developing personality and behaviour in a different way from the way his mother would. If you want to retain your influence over various aspects of your child's personality and behaviour, you'll have to be there or else he'll follow whoever is looking after him.

But even the best mothers are of course not always good and kind to their children. They have bad moods and get cross just like anyone else. When their mothers get cross with them and then get over it, children learn that such outbursts don't last for ever and it helps prepare them for the anger they'll inevitably meet in themselves and in other people later. Their mothers' changing moods and behaviour act in effect as a set of samples so they can learn to cope with other people's moods and behaviour.

Because the average mother is with her young child more than anyone else, it is she who spends most time disciplining him. She has the job of preparing him to fit into society as well as caring for him physically and emotionally. From her he'll learn his basic behavioural code, how to talk and how to practice all sorts of basic skills such as dressing and washing. What's more, her relationship with her husband acts as a template to the child for his relationship with his partner one day. A mother's personality and the way she runs her home colour the first five years of a child's life:

some homes are happy, laughing ones, full of optimism and love however little money there is and whatever pitfalls beset the family. Others are just the reverse.

Many of us would have far more enjoyment from our babies and young children if we didn't constantly try to separate them from us. As soon as a baby is born, he's put into a cot and often he's taken away to a nursery for several hours or even all night while the mother 'sleeps'. (Actually, few mothers can sleep after giving birth – most are elated, provided the birth went well, and want to be with their babies). They sleep fitfully if at all because every cry they hear they think belongs to their baby. Most mothers would have more rest if their baby were there with them. The four-hourly, ten-minutes-a-side breast-feeding that's been so popular in recent years, or the four-hourly bottle-feeding with no skin contact are just other examples of the separation of mothers and babies.

Our experience shows us that the subject that most concerns parents with babies and young children is sleep. Babies and young children are expected to sleep soundly, preferably for a long time at night, and alone – ideally in their own beds in their own rooms. However, this is a form of separation that also causes problems because most babies and many young children bitterly dislike being made to sleep alone.

Most people claim that a degree of mother–baby/child separation is essential for the mental well-being of the mother. There are times when this may be so and when the baby is best off being cared for by a good substitute. However, for the average mother–child pair, separation simply makes the baby cry more and become unhappy, insecure and anxious. It's a lot more pleasant to have a happy baby around who doesn't cry (or at least, hardly at all). It's said that the average baby in the West spends on average two hours a day crying! Mothers who keep their babies with them for much of the time find that they hardly cry at all and are much happier as babies than those they have previously brought up in a separatist way. It's a good feeling to be able to respond to your baby's signals for attention straight away and to be able to stop him crying. Sometimes a baby may be so demanding that his mother can't keep up with his needs *and* her household and other tasks – something has to give. What that is depends on each individual mother. Research shows that a baby whose needs are generously and quickly met during his early months is likely to be less demanding and more independent when he is older.

Whoever mothers a baby or child, it is likely that a 'non-separatist' upbringing will make the child feel happier and more secure. An early happy existence must affect a child's temperament for the good, though of course lots of other factors are involved as well.

Good mothering does *not* mean that there should be a suffocating, close relationship between a mother and her child. The mother needs to prepare her child for the outside world gradually, lovingly and sensitively, allowing as much dependence on her as he likes. The more people a child learns to know and like, the better. If he learns from his mother how to get on well with people and how to bring out the best in them, she'll have done her job well. If she teaches her child by example how to be a good parent in the future, the parenthood cycle will be complete. *Related topics* Attachment; bonding; crying; dependence; independence; separation anxiety. *Useful organization*   La Leche League of Great Britain.

Mother's help A mother's help is officially a person who is paid to help her in her normal household and child care duties around the house. Though she may from time to time have the sole charge of the children, this is by no means her main task and she isn't there to take over the mothering role, though she'll often support the mother in this. Some mother's helps have had some nursery or nanny training; others are untrained. Generally they'll take on any job a mother would, unlike a domestic help, and may find themselves helping variously with the cooking, driving, taking children to after-school classes, tidying, cleaning and shopping. In some ways a mother's help is an English version of an au pair, but tends to be more highly paid, often does not live in, and usually regards her position as a job rather than a way of learning English, getting free board and lodging and earning a little money towards language school, as an au pair does.

Advertise for a mother's help in your local paper, in a shop window, or in the *Lady* magazine, where many other similar advertisements appear. If you can offer living-in accommodation, the *Lady* is better; if not, the local paper advertisement is more likely to come to the attention of the right local people.

Check on your help's driving licence and insurance before letting her take your children in her car, and check your insurance if she drives your car. Before leaving your children with her, spend a lot of time with them and her together so that they are familiar and happy with her and you know her well enough to trust her. Be sure that she knows all your rules about wearing seat belts, sweets, discipline and so on.

Being a mother's help is a good job in many respects and such a help can make all the difference to a busy mother who has to work at times, does lots of entertaining or who simply wants a hand when life is very busy with young children. *Related topics* Au pairs; nannies.

Mothers-in-law In some parts of the world mothers-in-law are very involved with the care of the new mother and her baby. The young couple may be expected to live in the husband's mother's house and she then rules the roost. In other societies, she comes to live with the new parents to look after both mother and child, or the mother in particular, so as to leave her freer of household tasks and thus more able to mother her new baby.

In every society child-rearing practices are influenced by those of previous generations, not only by the example set to the child's parents by the way their own parents brought them up but also by advice and positive or negative criticism from the parents' parents (and especially the mothers) when their new grandchild is born. Advice, criticism and encouragement may be liked or disliked, but overall it is better to have someone to take an interest than not. In our society in which mothers often live too far away from their grown-up children to be of any particular help or emotional support when the grandchildren are born, new parents – and mothers in particular – often feel very isolated and out on a limb and instead turn to strangers, acquaintances, friends, health professionals or books to help them and tell them what to do.

Some mothers-in-law cannot contain their naturally critical feelings towards their daughters-in-law (who have to some extent taken their sons away from them) and feel they have to put them right when it comes to baby and child care. Other, more mature women understand these feelings and take care to project a balanced attitude, giving positive help, encourage-ment and advice as well as or instead of adverse criticism. Yet others opt only to advise or to help if asked to, for fear of being thought nosey or 'mother-in-lawish'. The variety of behaviour is wide and depends to some extent on the nature of the son and daughter-in-law and how much they want the mother-in-law to be involved in the way they bring up their child.

Of course, an equal number of mothers-in-law are the mothers' mothers and there may be similar feelings from them towards their sons-in-law, and a similar range of behaviour, depending on their personalities. In our society it is the mothers' mothers who are on balance more often involved with the new mother and child, simply because it is accepted that daughters seek advice from their mothers. Provided they are tactful and don't try to usurp the authority of the father, but rather try gently to offer advice and ideas for discussion, and consider the feelings of their sons-in-law as well as their daughters, they can be tremendously supportive not only when the baby is young but during the rest of his childhood.

Some mothers-in-law never went along with the separatist methods of child rearing beloved by so many in the '30s and '40s, and are able to offer advice based on the idea that babies are better off being loved and cared for by their mothers and not made to be independent too early. Others who listened to people telling them that bottle-feeding was as good as breast-feeding, that babies should be allowed to cry between feeds and at night, to sleep alone and to be cared for in crêches while their mother works, are less likely to be listened to in their turn by their sons- and daughters-in-law, who are likely to be reverting to less separatist ways of bringing up their children.

Mothers-in-law have a very valuable role to play in family life. They can set an example as wives, mothers, mothers-in-law, and grannies. The way they are treated by their children sets an example to their grandchildren. If they learn from you that granny is to be loved and listened to (though her advice is not always necessarily adhered to), then that's the way they'll learn to treat their own mothers when they in turn are grannies. And that's you. It's a sobering thought that what we consider to be out of date mother-in-law advice, might just come back into fashion and that when it's our turn to be the grannies and grandpas our children will no doubt feel just the same about us.

A good in-law relationship will be strengthened by the birth of a baby and the tactful mother-in-law will greatly add to the family's richness but for many, bad in-law relationships become disastrously worse as the mother-in-law 'interferes' in her daughter-in-law's mothering. Sometimes a poor in-law relationship can be improved when the older generation are pleased by the arrival of a baby and becoming grandparents. This can be a considerable shot in the arm for many mothers-in-law who are going through a phase in life in which they feel unwanted or at a loose end with all the family gone from the nest. The sensible and mature mother-in-law uses the coming of a new baby to patch up old wounds and indeed it can be the start of a wonderful new life for all concerned. *Related topic* Grandparents.

Mother substitutes A child's mother may not always be able to be with her child or may not always want to be there. A few mothers die when their children are young. In a few divorced or separated couples the children stay with their father. In almost all families there are times in the young children's lives when they are cared for by someone other than their mother.

A mother substitute can be male or female. Such a person is anyone who takes over the mothering of the child and supplies the daily care, attention and affection which every child so vitally needs. Babies and young children can become attached to several people but there is always a hierarchy of these people, with the one the child likes best at the top. Interestingly enough this person isn't necessarily the one who is his main caretaker but certainly *is* the one who has the most loving social interaction with him. A good mother figure will take the trouble not only to look after a child's physical needs but also to care for his emotional needs, giving him lots of sensitive attention and responding to him willingly throughout the day.

If the child's own mother is not usually with him for most of his waking day, it's essential that her substitute should have a secure emotional relationship with the child, because a few minutes at either end of the day with his mother when she is in a hurry or tired and the child is upset that she's going or else tired himself are not conducive to the sensitive interaction so necessary for his happiness. If the mother is with her child most of the time and her substitute is only there temporarily, it is not so essential that he or she and the child form a close relationship, though of course it's desirable.

In our society there are lots of possible mother substitutes. Any family member may become one and this often works well because the child is likely to have formed a close relationship with them already and to feel happy and secure with them. In large families the baby is often mothered for some of the time by an older sister (or even a brother). In some families where both parents work but on different shifts, the father does a lot of mothering. Grannies and aunts are also good mother substitutes, especially if they are familiar to the child. Friends and neighbours may act as mother substitutes when baby-sitting and it's best if they are familiar to your child.

Paid mother substitutes include trained nannies, mothers' helps (who may occasionally be given charge of the child), au pairs and child-minders. When choosing a paid substitute, find out first whether the person knows what's involved in the physical care of the child and is capable of doing it. If she is, find out by questioning her and by watching her with your child what sort of relationship she is likely to form. A warm, loving person is worth a thousand cold, strict ones whose attitude to child care is a mechanical one.

The average mother substitute is likely to form a good relationship with her charge and if she is with the child a lot, he may come to think of her as top of the hierarchy of the people he is attached to. This can be a bitter pill for a mother to swallow when her child runs to her substitute rather than to her when they are both together. In the early days of a mother going back to work, her child will make a fuss when she leaves him with another person because she is his number one favourite and he wants to be with her. This is not to say that he won't enjoy his time with the other person if he or she takes the trouble to mother him well both emotionally and physically. If not, and if his mother is gone for several days, for instance into hospital, he may respond first of all by being very unhappy and withdrawing into himself. When his mother comes back, he may seem not to recognize her or may angrily reject her for deserting him. These emotions are sometimes displayed after a mother's absence even when her child has been looked after well, but they are not nearly so strong. To look at it positively, it's a good thing that the child is drawn towards the person he's with. However, on the other side of the coin, some mothers are so upset that they give up work for this reason.

Remember regularly to re-assess the mother substitute looking after your child if they are together a lot. It's easy to be so eager that the arrangement should work that you unconsciously ignore warning signs that all is not well. Remember that a child is unlikely to tell tales about the person who does most of his mothering. For some reason, children still run to people who look after them even though they may be treated cruelly, physically or emotionally. It's up to you to find out – by asking other people who see them together, if necessary – how things really are going.

If the child's caretaker has her own child or children to look after as well as yours it's possible that your child may feel like a second-class citizen compared with her own children and not get enough attention. That's not pleasant for your young child who needs someone to root for him. You may feel that the pleasure he gets from being with her in other ways, together with the company of the other children, outweigh this negative feature, but remember that the company of other children is relatively unimportant at this age compared with having a mother figure of his own who can offer attention and security as often as he needs it.

Children can develop behavioural and personality problems, finding it difficult to form a close relationship with anyone, if they have so many mother substitutes that they can't form a stable one-to-one relationship with any of them. This sort of situation applies mainly to institutions, where the staff change frequently. However, it could happen to your child if you employ an ever-changing succession of mother substitutes, so be careful.

Given an average mother, who is normally responsive and loving, the average child would probably prefer (if asked and if capable of answering) to be with her virtually all the time during the first two or three years, and most of the time after that until going to school. This is not to say that he wouldn't enjoy and benefit greatly from making other relationships, but just that these would ideally be made in his mother's presence, so that he always had her there to go to when he wanted comfort or encouragement. Because of circumstances and parental wishes, a child can't always have what he wants but we should try to make sure that his mother substitute is the best we can find. *Related topics* Au pairs; child-minders; mothering; mother's help; nannies.

Mouth ulcers The only common type of mouth ulcers in your children are aphthous ulcers – small, acutely painful ulcers often seen on the tongue. It is not known what causes them.

Children can also get painful ulcers on their tongues and cheeks after accidentally biting these areas.

Mouth washes, pain-relieving gels, or even steroid tablets from your doctor can all cure mouth ulcers but the majority get better on their own within a week.

Ulcers with a white, curdy covering are probably caused by thrush (moniliasis) which can be treated. The first ever infection with herpes simplex (cold sores) causes mouth ulcers but these heal on their own. *Related topics* Cold sores; moniliasis.

Moving house Of all the stressful events in life moving house has been found to come very near the top of the list, with only bereavement and divorce ahead. This will come as no surprise to anyone who has moved house. Moving with children is even more stressful because young children especially are thrown into an upheaval over the move and cannot play a meaningful or useful role as older children can.

When choosing a new home it's probably wise not to involve your children until the choice looks like being a final one. Trailing around other people's homes isn't much fun for the under-fives and the parents end up making bad decisions if they are constantly worrying about what the children might be knocking over in someone else's home. It makes sense to go without the children for the first time.

Once you have chosen a new home, talk to the children about it and point out its advantages. If there's room for something indoors or out that they currently don't have, tell them, so that they can see some benefit to *them* from the move. Discuss their new bedrooms and what you could do with them. At this stage, be prepared for endless questions such as 'Will we take the sofa?' and 'Will we take the bath?', which will come out day after day. It is confusing after all, because when you move house you do leave a lot of things that to a child seem to be part of the house (lights, kitchen units, carpets, curtains and so on).

When it comes to packing, let the children pack some of their own things. This isn't easy because you'll both be up to your eyes with things to do and the children will be more demanding and will need more attention than usual. It may be a good idea for the children to stay at a friend's or the grandparents' home for the day of the move because the upheaval can be too disruptive for very young children. The nearer your child is to five, the more he'll enjoy the whole thing and he could even be helpful. Be guided as to whether you keep your children around by their personalities and the complexity of the move.

Once in your new home, get the children's room organized as a priority. This ensures that they aren't in too much of an upheaval for too long and makes them happier, and consequently life easier for you at a very busy time.

'Mucussy baby' A newborn baby who brings up mucus, (perhaps mixed with blood, or milk if he's started feeding), as a result of stomach irritation caused by swallowing blood or amniotic fluid during the birth. Such a baby isn't vomiting because his food disagrees with him or because he's ill but the hospital paediatrician or your general practitioner will have to rule out other possible causes of the vomiting just to be sure. *Related topics* Low birth weight; vomiting.

Mumps An infectious viral illness producing inflammation of the salivary glands, especially those in front of the ears. Serious attacks are rare under the age of five, but mild attacks can occur.

The incubation period from contact with the infection until the first symptoms appear is two to three weeks. The first thing you may notice is that your child will seem irritable and generally off colour. He may have a fever, a headache, and pains in his muscles, especially in his neck. A young child finds it difficult to explain what symptoms he has, however, so you may not realize there is anything really wrong until you notice a swelling of one of his salivary glands – usually the parotid gland which lies in front of the ear at the side of the face. Often the parotid gland on the other side swells a day or two later. Your child may have such large swellings that he looks like a hampster. His mouth will feel dry and talking and eating will both hurt him because of the jaw movement disturbing the swollen glands. If you give him anything sharp or sour to eat or drink, such as lemon juice, this will cause pain by stimulating the inflamed salivary glands.

The swelling usually goes down in three to seven days and there is no specific treatment. You can make your child more comfortable by giving him lots to drink and only soft foods to eat. Keep his mouth and teeth clean with tooth-brushing and mouth washes. One in five children has gingivitis (inflammation of the gums) with mumps. There is no need to put your child to bed unless he is really more comfortable there. He'll probably be happier with a makeshift bed near you downstairs if he does need to lie down.

One in three children with mumps have nothing obvious wrong with them. Babies are temporarily protected by antibodies transferred across the placenta before they are born if their mothers have had mumps.

Mumps is infectious from twenty-four hours before the salivary glands swell until three days after the swelling has gone down. Because it may be difficult to know exactly when the swelling has subsided, isolate your child for seven days from the beginning of the swelling.

Mumps can have unpleasant side effects. About one in five teenage boys or men who get mumps have orchitis (inflammation of the testes). Contrary to what people say, this rarely results in sterility but it is painful, so keep your child away from older boys or men who haven't had it. Similarly, older girls can have abdominal pain with mumps caused by inflammation of their ovaries, though there is no evidence of impairment of fertility afterwards. Mumps can also cause meningitis and encephalitis, as well as other less common conditions such as pancreatitis.

Mumps vaccine is regularly given in the US but is as yet not widely used in the UK.

Muscular dystrophy A degenerative disease affecting the muscles. Which particular muscles are involved depends on the type of the disease. The commonest form is seen in boys under the age of five but even this type only occurs in one boy in 10,000. Half of these boys have a family history of the condition and in the other half the changes have probably come about as a result of a genetic mutation.

Children with this condition are slow to walk, sit and run. They may waddle and have difficulty climbing stairs and in getting up from the ground. The calf muscles may be enlarged. Often these signs are absent and there is no abnormality before the age of three.

There is no specific treatment and many such boys die before the age of twenty. Physiotherapy seems to help but neither strenuous exertion nor bed rest are useful.

Prevention with the help of genetic counselling is possible. Mothers with a family history of the disease can be tested at special centres to see if they are carriers of the abnormal gene. The birth of an affected baby can be prevented if the mother chooses to have an abortion. *Related topics* Amniocentesis; genetic counselling. *Useful organization* Muscular Dystrophy Group of Great Britain.

Nail biting Nail biting always seems to be frowned upon by parents as well as other people the child comes into contact with because not only does it make the child's nails look such an unpleasant mess but it is so often tied up with insecurity or anxiety of some sort. Just frowning and getting cross will have no impact on the child who has got into the habit of biting his nails, though, and you'll have to find out why he does it or what started it off first, then put right anything he might be worrying about or else help him to come to terms with it, understand it and cope with it. If it's done simply because he had discovered (perhaps by copying another child) that he likes doing it, you'll have to find some way of helping him break the habit if you don't like him doing it.

Biting the nails may be just a matter of nibbling off rough or torn edges to make them smooth, or it may be a more fervent and persistent nibbling which can actually shorten the length of the nail bed in time if the nails are constantly bitten down to the quick and beyond. Hangnails are bitten as well and sometimes the fingertips may bleed at the quick or at the sides of the nail. If you look at the nails of a long-term biter, you'll see a sorry sight, with short, stumpy nails which may even be ridged and thick from the persistent trauma, swollen skin around the nails, and even bleeding. Sometimes the nails have vanished completely and the bed is so damaged that they'll never grow again even when the biting is stopped. Of course, few children ever get this bad, but it's a habit that is best avoided simply because of the physical damage it can do.

Keep your child's fingernails well-cared for by checking them at regular intervals and cutting them before they get too long. If your young child accidentally scratches you, get the nail scissors out and trim his nails straight away. If you think that your four- or five-year-old has been biting his nails when you come to cut them, don't get cross but be concerned and ask him gently why he started doing it. If he says it was because his nails were rough, then take more care of them in future. If, however, he's nail biting because of an emotional problem, in order to comfort himself, then he's highly unlikely to have the insight to tell you. You'll have to use your own insight to work out what might be worrying him. Bullying at play-group, insecurity over parental rows or the absence (temporary or permanent) of a parent, and fear of the dark or of being alone are all examples of things that can make a child start to nibble his nails. The cause may not be obvious – a child who is basically insecure as a result of inadequate mothering early on, for instance, or a child who has been through family problems such as the separation of his parents, his mother's depression, or the death of his brother or sister, may start to bite his nails, not necessarily as an immediate result, but perhaps a long time afterwards.

What can start off as something interesting to feel (both with fingers and mouth), useful to keep nails tidy, comforting, or as imitative behaviour, can all too quickly become a habit that the child turns to in any spare moment. Sometimes a special time is chosen – in bed at night, perhaps, or in the car on the way to play-group. Often it is done alone at first because the child is aware of disapproval; later he becomes so used to doing it that his shame or a desire to please others gives way to the sheer need to bite his nails. Nail biting, whenever, wherever, or whyever it is done, can become a compulsion – something beyond a habit – that the child absolutely has to do. He seems driven from within to bite his nails at all costs and whatever ploys you think up to stop him, he'll carry on doing it. If you are to prevent nail biting from becoming a long-term problem, you'll have to catch it before it reaches this stage and, if possible, help him stop doing it.

If his biting is not basically neurotic but has become a habit, then slightly different tactics may be necessary as well. Bribery works if the promise is attractive enough. Suggest, perhaps, a new toy or a visit to the zoo, if he lets his nails grow to the point where you have to cut them. Keep to your promise, though. Hopefully, once the habit is broken once, he won't return to it. If he does, you'll have to think up a cleverer bribe – one that can be taken away if he starts biting, perhaps. This might be a privilege such as watching a favourite television programme that he's usually not allowed to stay up for; a regular swimming session on Saturday mornings; or a special walk with you alone at the weekend. Some parents try bitter aloes or other proprietary substances on the fingertips in an attempt to make the taste so unpleasant that the child can't bear to bite his nails. Teasing sometimes works, but all too often, teasing can turn into unkind taunting and give the child a reason for nail biting for comfort. The habit can be broken if the child is keen enough to stop, but it takes a child with a lot of self-discipline to stop something without a lot of help and support. This type of nail biting is to a child what smoking or eating too much is to an adult, and giving it up is just as hard as slimming or giving up smoking.

What do you do if your child's nail biting has a neurotic basis? If you know what the trouble is and can easily rectify it, then that's easy. More often, you may not have the insight to understand why he does it and you might like to discuss the situation, including any family problems, with an outsider such as your health visitor or doctor. If you know what is causing it (marital problems, perhaps, of which the child is only too well aware) but can't do anything about it at the moment, then you'll just have to give your child as much extra love, attention and security as you are able, and help him to understand that things can go wrong in any family. *Related topics* Behaviour problems; habits; nail care.

Nail care A very young baby's nails can be gently bitten off, possibly while he's sleeping. This is safe and easy to do. As he grows older, his nails become tougher and longer and have to be cut with scissors. Blunt-ended scissors are best just in case he jerks his head or foot and you jab the points into him. Again, cutting nails while a child is asleep works well. Never use nail clippers on a baby or a young child as it is too difficult to be accurate with them and they can split the nails as the curve of a small nail is relatively pronounced. You will always find it easier to cut a child's nails after a bath because they are softened by hot water. Some people advocate cutting toenails straight across but it is also satisfactory to follow the line of the quick.

Sometimes it's difficult to cut a child's nails well, especially if they are shaped oddly. Make sure that you don't leave a spike at the edge of the nail because this can easily inflame the skin, especially if any pressure is put on it by a shoe. Once the skin is inflamed it swells and the spike of nail becomes embedded in it, causing an ingrowing toenail. At this stage you can usually cut the spike of nail off if you use a pair of sharp ended scissors. It'll help if someone else holds the child's foot, even if he's asleep. If you can't easily cut the nail properly, leave the toe alone and it may heal by itself as the nail grows up, provided that no pressure is put on it. However, if it becomes infected, take your child to the family doctor for his advice.

If nails are kept short, cleaning with a nailbrush is only necessary from time to time.

Some newborn babies scratch their faces with their nails, especially if they are left to cry. Scratch mits are not necessary. Instead, bite the nails short and try not to leave your baby to cry.

Names Names can be great fun to choose but they have been known to cause family disputes. If you can't decide between the two of you, make a pact to take it in turns to choose names for your children and toss a coin to decide who has first choice for this baby. It's better to have a name at least one of you really likes than to settle for a name that is neither's favourite. Most parents choose commonplace names and that's probably just as well for the child. There are several paperback books with lists of names and their meanings and you may come across an unexpectedly attractive name by going through such a book together.

It may sound obvious but some parents forget to try saying the baby's whole name out loud to hear if it's easy to say and sounds attractive. Try writing down his initials too to avoid any embarrassing mistakes. A child's name can always be changed at any time but in practice it's unlikely to be done unless he does it himself when he's grown up. A child may be teased unmercifully at school for having a pretentious, unfashionable or ugly name, or a name that can be changed to an embarrassing nickname. While some children can cope with this sort of teasing readily, others can't and there's no way of predicting which sort of child you're going to have. A name which causes a child problems may be quite acceptable to him as an adult, but he's got to live with it for a long time before he grows up.

You can give your child as many names as you like: there is no limit. However, two, three or four names are common and if you give him any more, he'll have difficulty in fitting them on to any legal forms on which he has to put his whole name. Some parents put in an extra surname which may be the mother's maiden name or simply a family name that has been passed down from child to child. Don't forget the 'politics' of what you call your baby. There'll understandably be some family feelings about perpetuating a name that has been around for some time in the family. Think about giving the child a first name of your choice and then another name that would please a relative.

A person can call himself by any Christian (first) name he likes even if it doesn't appear on his birth certificate, but legally his Christian names are always those which were on his birth certificate. However, a surname can be altered by Deed Poll (and a woman's by marriage).

It's sensible to put as your child's first Christian name the name by which you intend calling him because he'll find this easier from the point of view of school and filling in forms.

Although many couples decide upon a name early on in the pregnancy others have no idea what to call their baby even soon after the birth. The hospital staff are used to this, so don't worry. All the documents will say 'Baby Smith' and everyone understands that you may take some days or even weeks to make up your mind. The sooner you do it the better though, because everyone will be asking you. Legally you'll have to have sorted out something in time to get the birth certificate but this gives you some weeks.

Remember that whatever pet names or nicknames you call your child, they're likely to stick for a long time, so choose them carefully. He might not like one which is too soppy when he goes to school, and if it's still used by the family it's unlikely to be kept secret from his schoolfriends for long.

Some people think that a child's name can affect his personality development; whether or not you agree, every child's name is very important to him.

Even after registering your baby you still have an opportunity to change his name (without Deed Poll) and there is a provision on the birth certificate for this. If the name you decide for your child is different at the christening or other naming ceremony you can have the birth certificate altered.

Nannies Trained nannies today are very different creatures from those of fifty to a hundred years ago, who were on the whole concerned very much with routine and discipline in the 'rule and punishment' sense. While there were many good nannies who were subsequently remembered fondly by their grown up charges, some were more occupied with their nursery routines than with getting on well with the children, and some were frankly cruel. Of course, mothers are very variable in their loving kindness too but they hopefully have the advantage of having a closer bond with their children than a nanny could do, which must modify their behaviour to some extent.

Today, nannies are well schooled in child psychology and understand the importance of giving their charges sensitive one-to-one attention. They are even told about the advantages of breast-feeding and although today no nannies act as wet nurses, they are capable of helping a mother to breast-feed. Nannies are expensive to employ and as such are usually employed by working mothers with well paid jobs or by very well-to-do families who may employ other household staff too. They generally do little domestic work, though they usually look after the children's clothes, make their beds, and clean and tidy the nursery and playroom. They'll usually cook for the children but some mothers find that their culinary skills are not all that good and so prefer to cook meals for their children beforehand and leave them in the freezer.

A nanny will look after her charge full time but expects some time off each week. She may live in all week or just Monday to Friday. Some nannies live out. A few are shared between two families, but this arrangement has seldom been found to work well.

When choosing a nanny, look for someone whose ideas on bringing up children correspond as closely as possible with your own, otherwise there'll be clashes. Decide before she comes exactly what will happen in the morning and during the night. Some working mothers find themselves getting their children dressed and breakfasted before they leave for work. They may be seething because they feel the nanny should be doing it; the children probably prefer their mother to do it; and the nanny lies in bed thinking that all is well. At night, similarly, the children may want their mother if they wake up but she may want her sleep more than she wants to comfort her children. The nanny may lie in bed thinking that the children are better off with their mother and unless something is said, the atmosphere can get worse and worse. If your children are not yet at play-group, consider how they will get there if you choose to send them. A nanny who can drive is an asset.

Choose someone with whom you think you'll get on well. Remember that you'll see her in the evenings even if she has a comfortable bed-sitting room, because she'll have to eat. Decide at the start who is going to cook the evening meal and whether she is going to eat with you or not. It's far easier to get the day-to-day mechanics of life with a nanny sorted out before she comes to live with you to avoid hurting her feelings.

Ideally, it's best if a nanny stays with your child until he goes to school at least, and preferably afterwards as well, though this is a counsel of perfection. If you have a nanny whom you and your child like, try to keep her for as long as you can to avoid disrupting the child's life. If he likes her he'll miss her bitterly when she goes and will find it hard to understand why she should choose to desert him. If the nanny can become more like part of the family than an employed person, this is ideal. Your child will watch you and how you behave towards his mother-figure and he'll find it hard to understand if you are cool and business-like with the person who looks after him.

A sensitive and experienced nanny will take care that the child also forms a good relationship with his mother even if she doesn't see much of him. She'll talk about her a lot and will make her seem real to the child. She'll also be tactful in her handling of the situation when the child automatically runs to her rather than to his mother when all are together.

If you want to find a nanny there are good agencies all over the country. They are probably worth their fee because it's very difficult to make good judgements on such a matter if it's your first experience with a nanny and the agency will have a lot of experience for you to draw on. You'll also have some comeback if things don't turn out as you expected, though if you hire a professionally-trained and experienced nanny and take up suitable references you shouldn't go far wrong. *Related topics* Au pairs; mother's help; mother substitute.

Nappy care Supposing you change your baby's nappy on average six times a day, then by the time he's a year old, you'll have had to wash over 2,000 nappies. If you start out with two dozen nappies, each will be washed over ninety times in a year, and your baby will still need them for a long while yet, so it pays to look after your nappies so that they last.

Put nappies into water to soak until you have enough for a wash. If you keep one plastic bucket for dirty nappies and one for wet ones, you'll only have one smelly bucket. A fully breast-fed baby's nappies are inoffensive; early on, most of them will be stained yellow, but over the weeks more and more will be just wet. The cows' milk formula fed baby or the baby on a mixed diet will have both urine and bowel motions that are more smelly, so it's worth rinsing out wet ones before soaking, and flushing, scraping, or quickly washing dirty ones. Pre-soaking makes washing easier, as you'll soon find if you leave a dirty nappy out of water for any time.

Many mothers use a sterilizing solution (such as hypochlorite) for their nappies. This keeps the soaking nappies smelling sweeter and also bleaches them to some extent. The manufacturers of some brands claim that nappies simply need rinsing out well afterwards in cold water, but many mothers find that this isn't enough for soiled nappies, which soon become permanently stained using this method. Washing the soaked nappies once you have enough for a wash removes the yellow stains.

Use soap powder to wash nappies rather than detergent, which is more likely to irritate a baby's skin if any traces are left in the nappy. Most washing powders are detergents but there are those which are soap powders produced specially for front-loading washing machines. A good rinse, and the nappies are ready to dry. Some mothers like to use a fabric softener from time to time, though again some babies' skins react to any remaining traces. If you simply use a sterilizing solution to soak the nappies and then rinse them, be sure to rinse them really well.

As for drying, a washing line in the sun helps keep nappies white (the sun has a bleaching action). A tumble drier makes them soft and fluffy, but is expensive because of the length of time needed to dry wet towelling. If you have a spin drier, or if your washing machine spins, this cuts down the drying time and makes a tumble drier cheaper to run. Mothers without access to a washing line or a machine to dry their nappies have to hang them on a clothes drier or over the banisters to dry. In a small house or in one room this is unsatisfactory as it makes the atmosphere very humid and damp in the winter. If you have to do this, ensure that the windows are open to let the wet air out.

Once the nappies are dry, put them in your airing cupboard or on top of the central heating boiler to keep warm and ready to use.

If you have inadequate drying facilities, if you don't like the idea of washing nappies, or if you want an easier life, you might like to opt for disposable nappies or a nappy service for some or all of the time. **Related topics** Laundry; nappy choosing; nappy services.

Nappy changing There's no mystique about nappy changing, just common sense. It can be done anywhere convenient, warm and easily cleaned. Many mothers have a waterproof changing mat which they put on the floor but this can be put on a bed or table until the baby is old enough to wriggle or roll off. Your lap is an easy place to change your young baby's nappy and babies seem to like being there – perhaps it feels more secure. Before you take the old nappy off, collect together the new nappy plus waterproof pants or nappy cover if the old waterproof pants are dirty; cotton wool swabs, a bowl of warm water if you're not near a basin (if you are, run some warm water) and a towel if you're going to have to clean him up (likely for a young baby) or top and tail him; and cream if you use it. Some mothers use baby lotion and cotton wool swabs to clean their babies' bottoms instead of warm water and cotton wool; actually one can make a pretty good job of the average bottom with a wet corner of the old nappy!

Lay your baby down on a mat, towel or nappy and take off his old nappy and pants or nappy cover. If you can reuse the pants or nappy cover, keep it handy and put the wet or dirty nappy to one side. If you're away from home, it's a good idea to put the nappy into a polythene bag so that you can deal with it later. If the nappy was frankly dirty, or even just stained, clean the baby's bottom and dry his skin well. If there's any sign of a rash, put some suitable cream on. Slide the new nappy under the baby (a disposable one can be put ready on its unpoppered pants or cover beforehand), pin it up and put waterproof pants or a nappy cover over a terry nappy, or do up the sticky tapes of a disposable all-in-one. Don't forget to wash your hands after dealing with the old nappy.

Terry nappies can be folded in a variety of ways and the one you choose will depend on whether you have a boy or a girl, the size of the baby and whether he spends a lot of time lying on his tummy or his back. Three useful ways are the triangle, the kite and the twisted rectangle. The triangle is simple: just fold the square nappy once into a triangle, put the long side uppermost, lay the baby on it, bring the lower point up between his legs and pin all three points together in the crutch. With some deft manipulation you can tuck the two side points down between the two layers of the bottom point and still have six layers to pin together over the baby's tummy. You'll be very ham-fisted at first but practice will make perfect and you'll soon find what suits you and your baby. Make sure the pin doesn't stick into him: it's best to put in the pin so that it lies across his tummy, not up and down it. If you have a small baby, fold the nappy into a triangle, then again into a smaller triangle, and pin as before, only taking fewer layers on to the pin otherwise you won't be able to do it up. You could cut the nappy in half diagonally to make it smaller if you want a less bulky nappy.

For the kite, lay the nappy down with a point towards you. Take each side point to the spot half-way between them to meet each other, then bring the top point down towards the bottom one so the nappy folds along the line where the two side points were drawn across to meet each other. Take the bottom point and fold the nappy away from you so that the bottom point just about touches the top point. You can alter the size of the nappy by adjusting how far you fold up this bottom point. Lay the baby on the nappy and bring the folded bottom part up between his legs. Using two pins, pin one side of this bottom part to the underneath part of the nappy that side, and repeat the other side.

For the twisted rectangle, fold the nappy in half and lay it so that its length is running away from you. Fold the top one third down towards you and lay the baby on it. Bring the bottom part up between the baby's legs, twisting once, then pin each side of this part to each side of the underneath part of the nappy, using a pin each side. If you want the maximum thickness to be on top (for a boy or for any baby who lies on his tummy a lot, instead of folding the top one third down, fold the bottom one third up. This is a good method and gives little bulk between the legs, though there is a lot of absorbency there, so it is comfortable. Unfortunately a baby soon grows out of this sort of nappy.

When pinning a nappy, stick the open safety pin into the carpet or something else handy but don't leave it loose, especially if you have other young children around. Never put the pin in your mouth as this is a very dangerous example to your other children (and even to an older baby). When pins get blunt, throw them away and replace them. Always be sure to have your own hand or fingers under the part you are pinning so that it's impossible to stick the pin into the baby accidentally. There are special nappy safety pins that have a little locking mechanism on their heads which ensures that they can't accidentally pop undone.

Older babies wriggle and protest at nappy-changing times. A small toy to hold will amuse them for long enough to get the job done and anyway it's a phase that doesn't last for long.

Nappy choosing One thing your baby can't do without is nappies. It's worth thinking hard about what sort of nappy system you're going to use because he is going to get through a lot of them! Basically, the choice lies between terry towelling nappies, with or without fabric or paper liners, and disposable nappies. Muslin nappies are not very absorbent and can only really be used for very small babies for whom the bulk of a terry nappy would be too much, or as liners inside terry nappies.

As people's babies needs, their pockets, expectations and available time are so different, a list of the pros and cons for each sort of nappy is perhaps most helpful, because the choice is very much an individual one. Some mothers change their nappy system as their baby grows or from one baby to another, as their circumstances change.

Terry nappies are initially expensive to buy. The more you have, the less often you'll have to wash them. Most people find that two to three dozen is about the right number. If you're going to wash by hand, you'll probably want to wash them daily so that you don't have to wash too many at one go. Washing nappies by hand is hard work because the yellow staining of the bowel motions takes a lot of rubbing to get out, even if they're soaked in a nappy cleansing and sterilizing solution first. If you are going to dry nappies outside or hanging up inside, you'll want more than if you have a tumble drier, because sometimes they won't get dry for a long time with these methods. If you have a washing machine, it's best to wash nappies with the machine on the hottest cycle, and as you'll wash few other things at this cycle, you'll want to accumulate a full load of dirty nappies before running the machine, so you'll need a lot of nappies, especially if you don't have a tumble drier. You'll also have to have a couple of nappy buckets full of cleansing solution so that the nappies don't smell foul while they await their washing.

If you have a very small baby, you can cut terry nappies in half diagonally to reduce the bulk between his legs. Hem the raw edges and use two of these half nappies together when he's bigger. You can make your own nappies out of towelling bought by the yard. They don't have to be white, but if you're going to use nappy cleansing solution or bleach, the colours will fade and go patchy. Some colours fade on boiling as well.

Terry nappies are softer if they're tumble dried and if they're dried on a line they go stiff and hard. A fabric softener in the rinsing water gets over this to some extent, but may irritate some babies' skins. By the time terry nappies have been used for a year or two, they will have lost a lot of their fluffy bulk and will be less absorbent. With careful laundering, best quality terry nappies will last for at least two children though by then they might be a bit holey at the corners where the pin has been through many times.

The time taken to launder terry nappies should be a factor in your decision over what nappies to buy. Buckets of nappy cleansing solution or bleach have to be made up; dirty nappies have to be rinsed or shaken clean before laundering; the washing and drying have to be done; they have to be aired; and many women fold them before they are put away. You could probably make good use of this time playing with your baby or doing other things if you used disposable nappies instead.

Terry nappies virtually *have* to be covered with waterproof pants, or else they just soak whatever is underneath them. Waterproof pants are made of plastic these days and the best ones really are waterproof. If you change your baby often enough and care for his skin well, a nappy rash is unlikely. If the pants aren't tight enough around the tops of the legs, the nappy may leak. Waterproof pants are expensive because they don't last indefinitely and you'll need lots of different sizes as your baby grows. They have to be washed by hand (unless you buy the very best quality ones) and are best dried on the line away from artificial heat. Some plastic pants don't dry very easily and have to be patted dry with a towel. You can use a thin, shaped plastic nappy cover designed to hold nappy pads instead of waterproof pants if you wish.

You can use terry nappies as bibs; as towels; to protect your clothes if you change your baby on your lap, or if your baby is often sick; to protect your bottom sheet from your leaking breast milk at night if you feed your baby lying down in bed; and for a host of other things. When your baby is out of nappies during the day you can even use terry nappies to make trainer pants from.

When terry nappies are wet, the moisture makes them rough against a baby's skin and if he kicks a lot or if he is toddling or crawling this can chafe his skin and cause nappy rash.

Some mothers put their babies' nappies on so that there is a lot of bulk between the legs. When a baby starts walking, this bulk can be very uncomfortable for him and he may develop a trick way of walking in which he throws one leg round the other as he walks, to avoid rubbing his thighs on the bulky nappy. This makes him look bow-legged. Although he'll grow out of it as he gets older and when he comes out of nappies, it's better to avoid it because it'll make him less steady on his feet.

In addition to this collection of equipment you'll also need nappy pins to hold the nappy in place. Keep them closed at all times except when actually putting them in the nappy and never hold them in your mouth – it sets a bad example to older children and an older baby may even try to copy you. When they aren't being used, keep them well away from other children.

As for disposable nappies, if you can find ones which fit your baby so well that they don't leak, they cut right down on your work, are less bulky and annoying for your baby, and are more pleasant to use. There are many sorts of disposable nappy and the more expensive are not always the best. The most expensive all-in-one nappies are basically made of paper and cotton wool padding within a piece of shaped plastic. Sticky tapes join the front and back of the nappy together at the baby's sides. Some of these nappies have quilted paper padding which is supposed to make them more absorbent. They have a stay-dry lining through which urine sinks to be absorbed by the paper padding, leaving little moisture next to the skin. Nowadays, many such brands of nappy are made with elasticated edges for the thighs. They don't cut into the skin because you can adjust the nappy to fit as you do up the sticky tapes.

Cheaper disposable nappies are nappy pads which are like large sanitary towels used either with special plastic pants with pockets into which these paper and cotton wool pads fit, or with thin, shaped pieces of plastic which are tied up with the nappy in position at the baby's sides or else at the front and back. This latter system is cheap, simple and efficient. You can adjust the tightness with which you tie the plastic nappy cover so as to make the nappy leak-free, and the covers wash easily. They do take a long time to dry, and are best patted dry with a towel after being washed. You'll need several special plastic pants or plastic nappy covers to allow for them being washed and they'll need to be replaced fairly often as they go hard or break eventually.

Cheapest of all the disposable nappy systems is nappy roll from which nappy-sized pieces of wadding can be torn off. These are used with special plastic pants or plastic nappy covers as above. It is just as effective as using nappy pads, but not quite as pleasant because the nappy tends to break into little pieces when changing it.

Disposable nappies have some disadvantages. You have to remember to buy them and then have to carry them home. They are bulky, so it's best to take home one packet every time you go shopping, rather than lots less frequently, unless you have help with carrying them. In the US and now in the UK, disposable nappies can be supplied direct to the home, which is a good idea. They are also relatively expensive, though if you use nappy cleansing solution, wash terry nappies in a machine, and dry them with a tumble drier, terry nappies are more expensive, especially if you use the cheapest disposables. They can't be taken off and put on again (unless stapled back on carefully) because removing the adhesive tape tears the plastic outer covering. This means that a slightly damp nappy will have to be thrown away. They also have to be disposed of. Although many are said by their manufacturers to be flushable down the lavatory, thousands of mothers have blocked their drains by doing this, and blocked drains can be very expensive to put right. If you are going to try to flush them away, break them up into little pieces first. Not always the most pleasant of tasks! It's better, perhaps, to put soiled disposables into a small waste bin lined with a bin liner, then to seal it when full before putting it into the dustbin. An alternative is to burn them, but keep away from the fumes from the burning plastic outers of the more expensive nappies. On the whole, many mothers think that disposable nappies are slightly less absorbent than terries, and have to be changed more frequently. Some busy mothers get round this by putting a nappy pad or a piece of nappy roll inside a plastic-covered disposable nappy to make it last longer. You can also use a thick wad of nappy roll or two nappy pads together in an older baby. You could also make a terry nappy last longer by putting a nappy pad or a piece of nappy roll inside it – this is less bulky than using two terry nappies together. *Related topics* Nappy care; nappy liners; trainer pants; waterproof pants.

Nappy liners

These are liners made of a special fabric to go between a baby's bottom and his nappy and are used by some mothers for three reasons. First, a soiled nappy liner can be thrown away, and the nappy itself is then easier and more pleasant to wash. Second, a liner is softer and less likely to chafe the baby's skin when wet than terry towelling. And third, a 'one-way' nappy liner made out of fabric allows the baby's urine to pass through to the nappy beneath, so keeping his skin drier and less liable to develop a rash from being in a wet nappy. Some paper ones act in the same way.

Some mothers use muslin nappies as nappy liners because they are soft and smooth and don't hold the water like towelling ones.

Apart from muslin liners, which are pinned in position with the nappy, other liners are just put on to the nappy before it is pinned up. In an active baby the liner can slip out of position and in a walking or crawling one it may ride up and even sometimes emerge completely from the nappy.

Fabric nappy liners are treated like nappies when laundering. Paper ones can be washed (even in a machine), though eventually after several launderings they shred. Obviously it's only worth laundering them if they're just wet – dirty ones should always be thrown away unless they're perhaps only stained a little, as with a young breast-fed baby. Disposable liners are cheap, but every penny counts if you're trying to save money and unless the baby has gastroenteritis there is no danger from infection.

A few babies are thought to be sensitive to paper nappy liners and develop a rash of the skin touching them. *Related topic* Nappy rash.

Nappy rash The commonest form of nappy rash is caused simply by the irritation of having a wet, chafing nappy against the skin for much of the day. Plastic pants increase the chances of nappy rash simply because they retain the moisture in the nappy. It is now thought that ammonia is not the cause of the rash; it is simply smelt in any nappy that has been wet for a long time. If the skin is already damaged, ammonia can make the inflammation worse.

Nappy rash is more common in babies with sensitive skins and in those prone to seborrhoea (who are likely to have cradle cap or seborrhoeic inflammation of the skin in other areas too). Bowel motions in contact with such sensitive skin may cause a rash around the back passage. Diarrhoea, from whatever cause, can make nappy rash worse. It's unlikely that allergy has much to do with most cases of nappy rash, though it's thought that some babies are allergic to a chemical used in the manufacture of paper nappy liners. Occasionally a nappy rash is an early sign of atopic eczema. Reddening of the skin around the waist or the tops of the thighs where the elastic or plastic pants have been may come about because of sensitivity to the rubber in the elastic; because of friction from elastic which is too tight or from the chemicals in some disposable nappies.

One in two nappy rashes is infected with monilia (the organism that causes thrush in the mouth). In fact if the rash has been there for more than three days, it's highly likely that it will have thrush in it. Monilia can infect a nappy rash caused by a wet, chafing nappy as well as that associated with seborrhoea. Whenever there is a monilial infection of the skin of the nappy area, there is probably thrush in the baby's mouth as well. Any rash may also become infected with bacteria.

A wet, chafing nappy causes an overall reddening of the skin of the nappy area, followed by a tight, papery look with some peeling but the rash tends to skip the creases and folds. A seborrhoeic nappy rash looks red and shiny and extends into the skin creases. A monilial nappy rash may have features of either of these together with some isolated spots. It's possible to have a monilial rash alone, consisting just of isolated spots. In a severe nappy rash, there may be pimples or raised, red patches, which may run into raw areas or shallow ulcers. The baby will feel very uncomfortable when he wets or dirties his nappy but will be soothed temporarily after you have washed, dried, creamed and changed him.

If your baby has nappy rash, take first aid measures straight away, because the quicker you get rid of it, the less likely it is that a monilial infection will occur. Change your baby's nappies very much more frequently – the aim is to leave a wet, and especially a dirty, nappy in contact with the skin as little as possible. If you can leave your baby without a nappy on at all for some of the time, the fresh air and sunlight will help heal the rash and the skin will stay dry provided you don't leave him lying on a wet sheet. Each time you change his nappy, wash his bottom with soap and water (as long as the skin isn't too dry, when soap can make it worse). Dry his skin thoroughly and put some cream on to protect it. Zinc and castor oil or a silicone barrier cream are both suitable as first line measures. An antiseptic cream such as benzalkonium chloride cream is useful if there is much irritation.

Make sure the nappies are washed thoroughly to remove all traces of soap or detergent: some babies are sensitive to the dyes in some detergents. The nappies should also be sterilized adequately to kill any bacteria from the bowel motions which, if still in the nappy, can release irritant ammonia from the baby's urine. A one-way fabric nappy liner may help, but paper ones sometimes seem to make nappy rash worse – when dirty, they often stick to the skin and the bowel motions make the skin even more sore. Plastic pants are said to be best avoided, but it's an unusual mother who is readily prepared to put up with all the extra washing that this would mean. If the nappy is changed really often, as soon as it is wet, within reason, then plastic pants can still be used.

If the rash doesn't clear up and if it is making your baby irritable, ask for your doctor's advice. He may give you a cream containing hydrocortisone in a suitable concentration which won't harm your baby's skin but will probably clear up the rash quickly if it is seborrhoeic. If he thinks that the rash is infected with monilia, he'll prescribe some anti-monilial cream. An antiseptic or antibiotic cream may be necessary. Sometimes a combination cream is most effective. **Related topics** Dermatitis; moniliasis.

Nappy services In most major towns and cities there is a nappy service which collects dirty nappies from your home, launders them, and returns them again, often about three times a week. This time-saving luxury is expensive but helpful. You'll need lots of nappies if you're providing your own but you can usually buy them from the service (either their own or well-known makes). There is usually an enrolment fee and after that you pay on an agreed tariff of charges. Such companies, because they have industrial washing equipment, produce beautiful soft, white nappies time after time so if you don't want to use disposables and can afford a luxury service such a set-up could be right for you – even if you only used it for the first couple of months. With the coming of disposable nappies that are reasonably priced and reliable few mothers now resort to nappy services which, by their very nature, tend to be expensive.

One major UK specialist retail chain runs a disposable nappy service – delivering large quantities (360) to your home at regular intervals. This is a good idea as they are bulky packages to bring home from the shops especially if you have a toddler in tow as well.

Naps Short sleeps that people of all ages take during the day. They are especially common in young children and the elderly.

Children sleep during the day for very different amounts of time and the number and lengths of their naps are likely to change from day to day, let alone as they grow older. Most parents find that it is possible to predict at any one stage of a child's life whether or not he is likely to sleep at all during the day and if so, roughly when and for how long. Among other factors, daytime naps are influenced by the amount of sleep a child has been having at night; by the timing of his last night's sleep; by what he has been doing; by whether or not he is in a familiar environment; by whether there are guests in the house; by how he is feeling physically and emotionally; by what he has eaten and drunk; by the amount of noise in the house; and by how warm he is.

Newborn babies often sleep for some of the time between most of their feeds. Many breast-fed babies fall asleep at the breast, while only a few bottle-fed ones fall asleep at the bottle, because if they go on sucking when their milk is finished, they tend to suck in air unless they keep their seal on the teat airtight, in which case the teat will collapse and won't let in air to the bottle. When a breast-fed baby has fallen asleep, he can be put down somewhere safe and warm to sleep for as long as he wants to. A bottle-fed baby may have to be rocked, cuddled or walked around to help get him off to sleep. On balance bottle-fed babies sleep more than do breast-feds – who are generally more alert.

Some mothers put their babies into a cot before they are asleep, and such a baby can be trained to go to sleep alone but at first, especially, he will probably protest by crying at being left lying in a cot out of his mother's arms. It certainly seems more pleasant for a baby to be able to fall asleep in his mother's arms, but it does mean that if she wants to get something done, she won't be able to put her sleepy but awake baby down without him crying if he isn't used to going to sleep in his cot. Lots of mothers find that they can make the time to get their babies to sleep in their arms and prefer to leave other jobs until the baby is asleep.

As a baby grows older, his frequent daytime naps become fewer. By six months or so he's probably having two or three at most a day; by nine months, one or two a day; and by a year, perhaps only one a day. Children vary in the age at which they give up their remaining daytime nap. Often a first child carries on with it for longer than do subsequent children, because life is quieter for him with no other children around. Most children are through with daytime sleeping by the time they are three or four, but they may have occasional naps when they are especially tired, or perhaps when they're so excited about something that they've worn themselves out with anticipation.

It doesn't matter where a child sleeps during the day, but from adult experience it makes sense to assume that he'd be more comfortable lying down somewhere warm and draught-free. Going to sleep hunched up or awkwardly positioned can make anyone feel uncomfortable when they wake up. Lots of young children and babies go to sleep when they're in a sling, a pram, a pushchair or a car, because the regular motion and noise seems to lull them. The snag with this is if you have to wake them when you get to your destination. A child woken prematurely can be very fractious! It's unsafe ever to leave a child in a car alone and asleep. Similarly, if you're out shopping, it's best to take a child into the shops with you in his pram or pushchair even if he's asleep and it might be quieter outside the shop. A carefully positioned pad of rolled-up blanket or a small pillow can be tucked at the side of a sleeping child's head to stop it from lolling to one side. If you want to do a lot of shopping, it's sensible to time your journey with your young baby so that it's likely to correspond with a nap time. If you feed him first and make him comfortable before you set off, he'll probably sleep for some of the time and will be likely to enjoy himself more when he wakes.

Some children wake up refreshed and raring to go after a nap, however short, whereas others take time to come to and may be crotchety and even sleepy for a while, just like some adults! A nap in the late afternoon or early evening may make a child so refreshed that he doesn't want to go to bed at his usual time. However, it's not always easy (nor is it kind) to keep a sleepy child awake, especially if he's in a car or pram. If you want to go out in the evening and leave your sleeping child with a baby-sitter, try as far as possible to keep his day to its usual routine, so that he has his naps in their usual places and is likely to go to bed at his usual time. Many children don't have a routine of any sort. If this is the case and if, as is often the case, they have two naps, it often works if you can delay the morning sleep and cut out the other one altogether.

Your child's naps will last for however long he needs to sleep, unless he is woken prematurely or has a bad dream which wakes him up. You may be able to predict their length so you can start and finish whatever you want to do while he sleeps. Even if he only sleeps for a short time, he'll probably be happier for his sleep when he has woken properly, and you'll be able to get on with whatever you want to do for a while when he is playing. This goes for babies too. A baby who has had a sleep and a feed is often quite happy to lie in a bouncing-chair near you, watching what you're doing.

Your own naps are important too. Lots of mothers find that they are sleepy during the day when they have a baby or young child to look after, especially if they are up at night a lot. If you can go to sleep when your baby does, you'll wake up refreshed and better able to cope than if you ploughed on doing as much as you could while he was asleep. **Related topics** Rest and relaxation for mothers; resting, children; sleep; sleepy baby.

Nature study

Young children are fascinated by nature and even if you live in a block of flats there are lots of things to show them. Point out birds or build a bird table or a tit house so that they can see birds and squirrels at close quarters. You could even take some photos of birds that come to your table for the children to put into a nature book.

Children love collecting leaves and putting them into patterns once they have been dried between the pages of a heavy book. You can make a simple flower or leaf press from two pieces of hardboard and several sheets of blotting paper held together with a woodworker's clamp. They can also be bought ready made very cheaply. When you go for walks take time to point things out to the children. They won't want to hike for miles at this age but will be interested in collecting conkers, twigs, seedpods, pebbles, flowers or grasses – anything that can be brought home to make a nature collection. As children get nearer five, they enjoy learning to name trees and flowers.

There are lots of pretend games to play in a field or a wood, or even in an urban park. What may be a very ordinary piece of ground is wonderful to an under-five so just because you don't live near the country don't imagine that your children have to miss out on the joys of nature.

If you have a garden, let your children plant seeds there. They'll be thrilled to see flowers or vegetables appearing later in the year and will learn the basis of botany too. A pond stocked with fish will give them pleasure, or you could have a goldfish bowl or tank indoors. Tadpoles are fascinating to children but make sure there is a suitable place for the young frogs to stand on out of the water.

If you take an obvious delight in nature and take the trouble to encourage your children, you'll start them off on what could be a life-long interest. *Related topic* Outings.

Nephritis

Inflammation of any part of the kidney. The commonest type is caused by a sensitivity to an infection with bacteria called streptococci and is called glomerulonephritis. Although streptococcal infection is a common cause of nephritis, only a tiny proportion of all children with a streptococcal sore throat will get nephritis. Twice as many boys are affected as girls and the infection comes on nine to eleven days after a sore throat.

A child with glomerulonephritis isn't usually very ill at first but then becomes ill suddenly. He passes small amounts of brownish-red (bloody) urine and has a slight swelling of his face. There may also be ankle swelling, high blood pressure and headaches, a fever or abdominal pain.

Some children have to go to hospital but your doctor will guide you on this. Most are better within three weeks.

Another sort of kidney infection is called pyelonephritis and arises as a result of infection elsewhere (either in the bladder or in the bloodstream). Children who have an anatomical abnormality of the urinary tract (surprisingly common) are more susceptible to this type of nephritis. Such children may have no symptoms at all.

Often the infection is found by chance when the urine is being treated as part of an investigation of abdominal pain. Many children do have symptoms though with an urgent desire to pass urine frequently, pain on passing it, dribbling of urine, and day or night time wetting in a previously dry child. The urine may smell foul and the child may be ill with a fever, vomiting, tummy ache and a loss of appetite. Girls are three times as likely to have this type of infection as boys (except in infancy) and in babies it can produce jaundice, failure to thrive and apathy.

This type of infection responds well to antibiotics and increased fluid intake but prolonged treatment may be needed.

Urinary infection is always a diagnosis a doctor will think of if your child is ill for no apparent reason. *Related topics* Abdominal pain; urinary infections.

Nervousness A woolly lay term used to describe a child who seems to be edgy, excitable, sensitive or highly-strung. Such children are also often anxious or worried a lot of the time. Just why babies and young children should behave like this isn't known but there is undoubtedly both an inherited and an environmental component. Some children within a family, brought up just like the others, seem to be more nervous and no one ever knows why

Newborn babies startle easily and letting go of a baby quickly (especially letting his head drop backwards sharply in the early months) makes him 'jump' with the Moro reflex. Some babies are unhappy in water, even in a baby bath, and need to be gently taken through this, preferably using play as the way around the anxiety. Some young babies tremble. This is quite normal and is probably nothing to do with nervousness at all. Similarly, twitching, especially during sleep, is nothing to do with nervousness and is quite normal. Babies soon grow out of twitching and trembling as their nervous systems mature.

Some babies rock, bang their heads or bounce rhythmically, sometimes hard enough and long enough to move a cot around the room. This almost always happens when the child is bored, lonely, tired or frustrated and usually represents a need for company and comfort.

Older children may show other signs of nervousness such as nail biting, which is more common in nervous, anxious children.

Tics are nervous habits (such as eye blinking, facial grimacing, shoulder shrugging, nose twitching, throat clearing and dry coughing) that occur more often in highly-strung children. They are more common in children with over-strict and repressive parents and can be signs of tension in the home. Such tics and indeed all nervous habits are almost entirely out of the control of the child – they are the result of a bottling up of the emotions he does not (or cannot) express openly. There is no point in nagging or scolding a child with such nervous habits as this will only make him worse.

One way of minimizing nervousness in children is to give them adequate security right from the very first day. If a child is never left to cry as a baby and is always given plenty of love and affection, he'll be less likely to be nervous as a child. Over-strict parenting and parenting which is based on the needs of the parents rather than on those of the children are sure to increase a child's chances of being nervous and highly-strung. Today's pressures for mothers (and fathers) to separate themselves from their children as often and as soon as possible are simply not in the best interests of the average child's emotional development and are bound to predispose towards nervousness and a sense of insecurity. Many children simply don't have the inborn temperament to cope with this sort of upbringing and show their frustration by unconsciously developing nervous habits.

If a child is very nervous he may need specialist psychiatric help. Talk to your family doctor who may advise you to go to a child (or family) guidance clinic. Drugs are rarely used for nervous children. No amount of parental harshness or insistence will stop a child being nervous: only love, time, security and affection can do so. *Related topics* Anxiety; child guidance; habits; highly strung child; Moro reflex.

New baby – preparing other children for There's no need to
tell your child immediately you know you are pregnant, but let him know as soon as you tell other people otherwise he will hear them talking about the baby and will wonder what is going on. Remember that your child won't necessarily look forward to the baby in the same way that you do. He may even wonder why you want another baby at all when you already have a perfectly good one. It won't be until the baby actually arrives that he discovers that his position in the family has altered. As time passes, he'll realize that the baby is there to stay.

Besides letting your child share in the anticipation and excitement of getting ready for the arrival of a new baby, it's a good idea to give him a realistic idea of what having a brother or sister will mean. If a child is told often enough that the new baby will be someone with whom to play, he'll believe it and will be badly disappointed to find that the much longed-for playmate turns out to be sleeping or feeding for much of the day and not inclined to play at all for many weeks. Even one-year-olds understand a certain amount, and they usually understand far more than you'd think from how much they can say. Two-year-olds won't understand all of what you say, but a certain amount will be absorbed. Three- and four-year-olds are quite able to take in your comments and if you prepare them well, having a baby in the house will come as no shock to them.

It may help your child to accept the baby more easily if you make him realize how clever and big he will be, compared with the baby. Let him know that the baby won't be his equal physically or mentally but instead will be helpless and will need a lot of looking after. Try to make him feel protective and in that way he'll automatically feel less threatened. Talk to a three- or four-year-old about how his status will be improved by being a big brother or sister, and how although there will inevitably be some sharing of toys and sharing of parents' time and energy, he certainly won't be any less important. Tell him that, however many other children you have, he'll always be precious to you. Talk about families and family relationships, your brothers and sisters, aunts, uncles, and cousins. Let him come to understand that what is happening to him is a normal part of family life and is certainly not being done because you want another baby *instead* of him. Some women are obsessed with babies while they are pregnant and their child may think that because he is not a baby, he is no good.

Disappointment at not having a ready playmate, together with a gradual realization that his mother is spending much of her time with the baby and far less time with him than before, naturally makes any child feel let down and neglected to some extent. He doesn't know whether to be cross with his mother for putting him in this situation by having (and wanting) the baby, or cross with the baby for taking his mother away from him and being such a bore. These feelings mingle into a feeling of jealousy of the baby which is often greater when the baby is a few months old and not asleep so much.

To minimize this jealousy, prepare your child for the coming of the baby and try not to cut down his share of demonstrated love and attention when the baby arrives. Talk to him before the baby comes about what family life will be like. Explain that babies have to be looked after all the time and that he can help you change nappies and can talk to you and play quiet games with you while the baby's feeding. Try to keep to these promises when the time comes. If you have friends with babies, spend some time with them so he can see at first hand something of what a young baby is like, and point out that the baby isn't actually talking or even sitting up yet but that he is learning new things all the time so that one day he'll be able to play. Take care never to threaten him, though, by saying something like 'Once the baby's here, you won't be able to have me to yourself all the time.' A child can worry secretly over a statement like that and even though it's true, it can be put more kindly. In simple terms, try to help your child understand that though there is another child, you will still love everyone in the family the same and that you'll have extra love for him.

One of the biggest problems for many a new mother is tiredness. This can make her short-tempered with her older child who isn't old enough to understand the reason for it and will be confused and even more cross with the baby for making his mother like this. You can warn a three- or four-year-old that this might happen. When it does happen, try somehow to take some rest during the day so that you don't get worse and worse towards the evening.

Let your older child join in the practical preparations for the baby. As you collect clothes, nappies, a carrycot and so on, you'll find plenty of opportunities to talk about what it'll be like having a baby at home.

Let your child feel your baby kicking in your tummy and talk about how big he is, how he's growing a little every day, and how when he's big enough he'll come out of your tummy. You may like to show your child some pictures of what your baby looks like and there are one or two beautifully produced books of photographs of unborn babies which you can order from the library. The whole family can have some fun discussing names. The many books of names available can provide hours of amusement and your child will join in your laughter at some of the names, even though he doesn't really understand why you find them funny. By choosing some possible names the baby will become more real to the child.

Some young children who have had little or nothing to do with babies are disappointed by the appearance of their new baby brother or sister. Explain beforehand that babies sometimes have screwed up faces, crooked hands, or even red marks on them, but that all these soon go. Don't forget to say that babies can have very loud yells and can look extremely cross and red-faced when they cry, but that when this happens you will almost always be able to make him feel better by feeding him and cuddling him. Talk about what he was like as a baby and how you love him even more now.

Discuss how you'll all love the new baby, look after him and try to keep him as happy as possible.

If you prepare your child in this way, you'll probably find that his feelings of jealousy are minimal and you may find that he is even more solicitous over the baby than you are.

Don't forget to prepare your child for the practical arrangements you'll have to make for his care at the time of the baby's birth. If he's not used to being left with his father, granny, your friend or neighbour, or whoever will look after him, give them time together without you every so often. Make sure the person knows all the small details of your child's life such as his bedtime routine, how he like his food cooked, whether he needs a special toy at night, and whether he only likes to drink from one special cup. Small differences in his daily life can upset a child who is already feeling disrupted without his mother.

A few weeks before the baby is expected talk about how you'll go into hospital to have the baby and how he'll come to see you there. Read a book about going into hospital or take him with you if you attend an antenatal clinic at the hospital so he's used to the sight, smell and sounds of the place. Don't forget to explain that you'll only be in the hospital for a few days, otherwise he may worry that you and the baby will be there for ever. If you're having your baby at home, let him make friends with the midwife who's likely to deliver you (often difficult because your midwife may be off duty when the time comes).

Although many child care experts would have you believe that a new baby in the family always puts the older children's noses out of joint, don't worry. This can happen, of course, and is perfectly natural when it does but with some careful preparation and your obvious enjoyment of the new baby your other children will love having a baby of their own. Far from being a negative event, a new baby can be tremendous fun for existing children. *Related topics* Hospitals; jealousy.

Nicotine poisoning

Nicotine in cigarettes is, of course, known to be harmful to adults but it is often forgotten how harmful it can be to children. Babies born to mothers who smoke are on average lighter in weight and more likely to be premature than those born to non-smokers. It has been estimated that one or two of every ten babies that die at birth could have been saved if the mother had not smoked during pregnancy. When followed up seven years later, children whose mothers smoked heavily during pregnancy are still undersized for their age and are slower than average on various measurable abilities such as reading.

Babies of parents who smoke have more pneumonia and bronchitis than other babies and are more likely to die from a cot death. Increasing numbers of recent papers are proving the adverse effects of cigarette smoke on those who live with smokers, even if they don't smoke themselves.

More obvious nicotine poisoning occurs if a baby or even a young child eats a cigarette. Even one cigarette can be dangerous to a one-year-old, so keep cigarettes out of the reach of children.

If a breast-feeding mother smokes heavily she may find she has an insufficient milk supply because the nicotine may interfere with her let-down reflex. Heavy smoking can also cause nausea and vomiting in the breast-fed baby. *Related topic* Poisoning.

Nightdresses Today's little girls are happy to wear nightdresses or pyjamas at night and it really doesn't matter which they wear. Pyjamas are probably warmer for the winter.

Nowadays, girls' nightdresses are often made of a flame-resistant material and so are less likely to go up in flames if they stand too close to a fire. However, this is not true of all nighties, and is certainly not true if you make them yourself. Also, even if a fabric melts, rather than goes up in flames, it can still cause burning. If your child is wearing a full-skirted nightie, or a long one, keep her away from the fire. Always keep your fire (whatever sort it is) well guarded; don't put a mirror over the fireplace; and try not to leave a young child alone in a room with a fire. Because there have in the past been so many accidents with children's nighties catching fire, consider pyjamas instead, or else a short nightie. *Related topic* Fires.

Night feeds All young babies wake at night for feeds and many older ones do as well. It's interesting that bottle-fed babies tend to sleep through the night sooner than breast-feds and that by a year, one in five babies is still waking.

The easiest way to get a baby off to sleep at night, whatever his age, is to feed him. Perhaps some people would say that this gets an older baby into the bad habit of waking so that he can be fed, but little seems to influence whether or not a child will wake at night: it's very much an individual matter, and as the only way to get back to sleep yourself is to get your baby to sleep, if feeding works, then it's worth doing it. A variety of ways of getting a baby to sleep other than by feeding him have been and are used. Some parents give their older baby a dummy to suck on at night when he wakes. Children of all ages are given comforters of one sort or another to take to bed with them. Some doctors even prescribe sedatives for children who continue to wake at night.

The biggest single problem reported by parents of the under-fives is waking at night. The easiest solution, yet one which many people try to avoid, is to give the baby a feed and then to cuddle him until he goes to sleep. Some parents have trained their babies to go to sleep alone and so put them down after a feed. If you are breast-feeding, he can suck until he calmly goes off to sleep.

Increasing numbers of parents today are returning to the time-honoured custom of having their babies in bed with them. At the beginning this makes night feeds very much more practical from the parents' points of view. The father needn't be disturbed at all and the mother needs to wake up only enough to put her baby to her breast as they are lying next to each other. She can doze throughout the time the baby is at her breast and he'll probably go to sleep after just one side. If he doesn't, she can roll over with him on her tummy and put him to the other breast. Some babies have to sit up to burp, but they grow out of this and in any case many babies never need to. Many a baby takes a liking to staying at the breast at night for long periods just sucking very gently but not swallowing much. If this bothers you you can stop him when he seems to have stopped swallowing and firmly turn over. If you do this each time, he'll eventually get the message that you don't want him to go on sucking half the night, though he may protest for the first few times. Some mothers feed their babies – by breast or bottle – in bed where they're comfortable (lying down or sitting propped up) and warm, then return them to a cot after a feed. This works well if the baby is accustomed to going to sleep alone and if he is happy to do so. Being able to comfort such a baby at the breast ensures that he stays quiet and the mother can at least have a chance to doze. Breast-feeding certainly does have considerable advantages at night – and especially so if the baby is in bed with you.

Some mothers feed their babies in their baby's own room, sitting in a chair, but they can be cold, lonely and uncomfortable even in the most comfy of chairs. The only person to whom it may appeal is the father, who is relatively undisturbed. However, some fathers prefer to have their babies in their bed or at least in their bedroom because they are less likely to be woken by the baby's cries to signal his mother to wake. A baby actually in the bed has only to wriggle with hunger or for comfort to wake his mother. A baby in a cot near his mother's bed has to make relatively little noise before she wakes too and this can work very well.

If you are bottle-feeding, have a sterilized bottle ready with a sterilized teat upside down in its neck, and a cover on top. Boil some water, let it cool to a suitable temperature, then fill a thermos flask with it. Put the milk powder and a clean spoon nearby, and you're all set to make up a feed at night. Don't forget in your sleepy state to check that the scoop is level, the milk well shaken, and that the feed is at the right temperature. Some mothers have two thermoses of boiled water, one hot and one cold, so that they can adjust the temperature of the feed even more accurately. Others take the made-up feed to the bathroom and shake the bottle under cold running water to cool it, if necessary. On the other hand you could put cooled, boiled water into the bottle ready, then boil an electric kettle of water at night so you can add boiled water to the feed. A kettle takes a long time to boil at night when the baby is screaming for milk, though. Some bottle-fed babies seem quite happy with a bottle of milk (prepared earlier in the day) straight from the fridge at night.

Bottle warmers are no use at night because they take too long. If your baby doesn't finish his feed, the temptation is to give the rest of it to him later when he wakes. This isn't a good idea because not only will it be cold, which he probably won't like, but also bacteria may already have multiplied in the warm milk. Ideally, you should have several bottles ready for the night if your baby wakes frequently.

Try hard not to compete with other mothers as to how soon your baby gives up his night feeds. If you've had several children you'll know that when a child sleeps through the night is up to him, not to what you've done to him. Babies who sleep a lot in their earliest days tend always to sleep a lot. More active ones sleep less altogether and wake at night more. There will come a time when they don't wake up at night but in the meantime all you can do is put up with your broken nights gracefully and try to get a nap during the day if you're tired out. Lots of mothers say that they live on a slightly different plane when they're waking at night a lot, but that they quickly get used to it once they've accepted the fact. It's when they are continually anxious about not getting enough sleep that they'll be snappy during the day and dread the nights.

If your baby wakes up thoroughly at night after a feed and wants to play, you'll have to be very clever in your handling of him if he's not to make this a habit. Try to keep the light off completely (easy if you're breast-feeding in bed but not so easy if you're getting out of bed to feed him, or bottle-feeding him). Otherwise keep the light very dim (have a special low wattage light or put your bedroom light or the baby's bedroom light on a dimmer switch). Talk softly if you have to talk at all, and don't change his nappy unless you absolutely have to (because it's soiled) – many babies can last through the night with a thick terry nappy or an extra nappy pad inside a terry or a disposable nappy.

Some breast-fed babies carry on waking at night until they are weaned from the breast. It's not worth weaning a baby simply to get a night's sleep though, because he may not sleep even when weaned, and then you'll have lost your ability to get him off to sleep at the breast, and he may stay awake longer. It is probably no coincidence that the age at which a baby weans himself from the breast is the age when he's likely to sleep through the night. Some bottle-fed babies carry on wanting a bottle in the middle of the night for several years – night feeds certainly aren't the prerogative of breast-feds, though they are more common in them.

If you possibly can, try to enjoy being awake at night with your baby. These months or years of night waking don't go on for ever. Lots of other societies don't need or get long periods of unbroken sleep like we do and seem perfectly well on it. Many people in our society think they deserve unbroken nights, but they are certainly not essential. You can easily adjust to broken nights if you let yourself, especially if you can catch up during the day on some of the lost sleep. Night feeds can be a special time for you if you want: a time for looking at your baby and smiling and talking to him if you aren't disturbing anyone; a time for enjoying holding and cuddling him; a time for reading; or a time to think your own thoughts or say your prayers undisturbed – a luxury for a busy mother. Think positively about night feeds and stop longing for them to be over, and you'll look forward to going to bed at night. *Related topics* Feeding schedules; sleep.

Night light A small electric light with a very low-powered bulb which gives a dim light at night. Many different designs are available and some children like to have one even if they aren't afraid of the dark. An alternative to buying a night light is to have a dimmer switch on the main light or to leave a light on in an adjacent room all night so that a little of the light floods on to the landing or even into the child's room. The bulb of a night light is usually only twenty or forty watts and this makes it cheaper to run all night than a normal bedroom light. Night lights used to be small, stubby candles but as there is always an element of danger associated with any flame when children are around, they are best avoided.

The fear of the dark shown by needing a light at night is a reflection of the way we bring up our children, separating ourselves from them at night, sometimes from birth. While it can be argued that it's natural for humans to fear the dark, if a young child can reach out at night and feel his parent or sibling lying next to him, he knows he has no need to be afraid. One could say that the security gained from a night light replaces (to some slight extent) the security a young child feels from knowing his family is by him. *Related topics* Nightmares; night terrors; separation anxiety.

Nightmares Unpleasant or frightening dreams that may make the child wake up scared. They are uncommon as far as we know before the age of four, when the child's imagination becomes more active and his interest in fairy tales and other horror-containing stories increases. The child may have dreamed about something unpleasant he saw in a comic, in a film or on TV, or he may have had an unpleasant physical sensation, such as being suffocated (when in fact he has a cold in the nose).

The way to handle nightmares is to comfort the child and to stay with him in his bed until he is all right, or to take him into your bed. Leave his bedside light on if it helps him.

Some children have nightmares after certain foods so if your child has repeated bad dreams it's worth looking for any foods that could be affecting him. If you suspect a food, cut it out of his diet and then if the bad dreams go, re-introduce the food as a final trial. If this produces the dreams you'll know it is at fault and can remove it from his diet permanently.

More rarely, a child may be emotionally disturbed about something and it is this that makes him have bad dreams. Discuss repeated bad dreams with your doctor as they could be a sign that the child is unsettled or unhappy. *Related topics* Behaviour problems; night light; night terrors.

Night terrors Some children cry out or scream in their sleep often about an hour after going to sleep and they may even jump out of bed. A night terror can last as long as twenty minutes. When you go to your child he may tell you he has seen all sorts of strange or frightening things. He may still be able to see them and if so is frankly terrified. He may cling to you or may struggle as if you are the bogeyman of his dream. His eyes may be wide open though he is still asleep, and he looks right through you. Your child's terror may make you feel frightened too but it's sensible not to let him know that. Your child will probably want you with him while he recovers from his frightening experience. Either stay with him until he goes to sleep again or calms down or take him into your bed. You can always carry him back to his bed when he's asleep if your bed is uncomfortably crowded. When he wakes in the morning he probably won't remember anything.

A child who has night terrors may or may not have nightmares as well. About three in every hundred children have night terrors at some time and they may be associated with sleepwalking and sleep talking. They occur during deep, dreamless sleep unlike nightmares, which are dreams occurring during light 'REM' sleep. There may be something worrying him in his everyday life and if gentle discussion doesn't reveal any problems, think hard about every aspect of his life to see if you can spot anything that could be upsetting him. Children are very perceptive and any parental disagreements or rows (which you didn't even realize they knew about) can be extremely upsetting to them. If you can't find anything that might be wrong, even after talking to the play-group leader and anyone else who looks after your child, just try and keep his everyday life as secure and pleasant as possible and try not to read him any frightening tales or let him watch unsuitable programmes on television, especially just before he goes to bed. Make his bedtime routine as pleasant as possible and give him plenty of time to talk to you.

Night terrors are generally shortlived in a child whose home environment is happy. *Related topic* Nightmares.

Night waking It's long been said from the results of a least one survey that one in five babies still wakes at night at one year old. However, our experience is that so many more babies wake at night at this age that night waking can be said to be plum normal for one-year-olds! At a recent conference of about 200 mothers, all of whom had had at least one one-year-old, not one put their hands up when asked whether their one-year-olds had slept through the night. Admittedly, all these babies were still being breast-fed at one-year-old, but that is perfectly natural, though not normal in our society. Most babies who go through the night without crying when a few weeks or months old have either always been bottle-fed but on a restricted basis, or have been taught that even if they wake at night, no one will come, so there's no point in crying. Just because a baby doesn't cry at night doesn't mean to say that he doesn't wake. However, it's not reasonable to assume that a baby who wakes at night and doesn't cry is happy to be awake and alone. This is a possibility but he may also be quiet simply because he's resigned to the idea that no one will come anyway.

Some sleep 'experts' advocate leaving a baby to cry himself to sleep during the first few months to break his habit of night waking. They often say that after three nights of crying his parents will get the night's sleep they need and deserve. Night feeds are seen as evils to be eliminated as soon as possible. This whole way of thinking may, however, be fundamentally wrong and unhelpful. First, parents can usually manage with less sleep than they think they need and, if they can't, then one answer is to go bed earlier themselves while their babies and young children still wake at night. Second, anthropological studies indicate that it's quite normal for children in non-industrialized cultures to wake at night, but that because these children sleep with their parents, their waking doesn't disturb anyone. They simply have a breast-feed while lying at their mother's side, then go back to sleep. Third, it's only comparatively recently, even in our culture, that we have adopted a separatist way of bringing up our children. Not so long ago our babies and young children slept in the family bed too. Fourth, when advocating letting a baby 'cry it out' at night, the experts ignore the feelings of fright, helplessness and anger, not to mention possible hunger, that a baby may feel. Their argument is that this treatment may be the saving grace for the parents who can't cope with night waking. However, if their expectations of their baby's behaviour had been different from the beginning, and if they realized that putting their baby in his own cot in his own room was bound to mean that they woke up thoroughly each time he cried and they had to go to him, then they may have coped differently from the start and not got into trouble at night at all.

Some people may think that because unrestricted breast-feeding seems to go hand in hand with night waking, it's best avoided or just done for a few months. However, not all schedule-fed babies sleep through the night anyway, and at least the breast-feeding mother has a ready and easy way of getting her baby back to sleep again. She may not even have to wake up properly herself if her baby is in bed with her, though this doesn't suit all parents. Also, of course, there are lots of other advantages of continued unrestricted breast-feeding which are nothing to do with comforting a baby at night.

On average, the younger the baby, the more often he'll wake at night but there are lots of exceptions. An ill child, or one who is teething or worried about something, is likely to wake at night, for instance. Some mothers notice that their babies tend to follow roughly the sleep pattern they adopted during pregnancy, waking at roughly the same times at night after birth that they seemed to wake at night for a wriggle before they were born.

Other babies seem to get their day and night muddled up completely after birth but settle down in a few weeks. Some babies quickly adopt a predictable pattern of waking, while others are quite haphazard. One thing parents agree on is that nothing is worse than being woken just after going to sleep. It's sensible to give your baby a feed just before or after you go to bed so that you're likely to have the initial part of your sleep unbroken. It's difficult to generalize, though, and some babies are awake for so long after a feed at bedtime that their parents think it's best not to wake them. It's something each family has to work out for itself.

There's no doubt that most mothers find it easiest at night to breast-feed. If you're bottle-feeding, have everything ready so that you can prepare a bottle quickly and easily without waking everyone else. Lots of babies like to go off to sleep while sucking. This is easy enough at the breast but difficult on an empty bottle, so this is one time when a dummy may come in handy. Some mothers find that their babies go off to sleep quite happily with a dummy in their mouths only to wake when it falls out.

If your baby is near you at night, you'll be able to stop him from waking the rest of the household by feeding him quickly when he wakes. If you put him in another room at night, you might like to have a baby alarm so that you hear him sooner rather than later. A baby who has had to scream hard to be heard may be so anxious and hungry that he swallows a lot of air as he feeds and is uncomfortable afterwards. He may also be so thoroughly awake that he finds it hard to go back to sleep again after his feed.

As your baby grows, his need for food at night may not be so desperate but is none the less real. Some bottle-feeding mothers who are convinced that their babies are ready to start sleeping through the night, but don't want to leave them to cry, try giving their babies a drink of water instead of milk at night. Sometimes a baby will start sleeping through the night at this, perhaps because he doesn't think it's worth waking up for water! The breast-feeding mother can't swap her milk for water if she wants to carry on breast-feeding for long because once she starts cutting down the number of breast-feeds she gives her baby (that is, once she starts breast-feeding on a restricted basis), her milk supply will dwindle. This will only be a problem for younger babies.

If you have to get up at night to tend to your baby, it's quite understandable that you may soon feel that you'd give anything if your baby slept through the night. Taking your older baby into bed with you may not solve the situation because unless he's used to sleeping in your bed, he might be so excited that he wakes up thoroughly and wants to play. He probably links being in bed with you with playing in your bed in the morning when taken from his cot. It's worth thinking about having your baby either in your bed or in a cot right next to your bed from birth onwards, especially if you intend breast-feeding. Even if you don't want to breast-feed or are intending to give it up soon, your baby may be one of those who continues waking past his first birthday, and having him near you at night will mean your nights are less disturbed. Many is the family who have learnt to play musical beds at night just because the parents were so intent on the baby being apart from them at night from the beginning. Often it is the father who puts the pressure on his wife to put the baby in another room.

Giving your young baby food in the evening as well as his milk doesn't seem to make any difference as to whether or not he'll sleep through the night and isn't a good idea. However, it's sensible to ensure that your older baby doesn't go to bed hungry.

As for sleeping medicines, if your doctor suggests one for your baby, by all means try it, but don't expect miracles. Rather than treating night waking as an illness, it's more helpful to remember that it does seem to be the norm, but our customs of keeping mother and baby apart at night simply mean that it can be a very real problem for some parents.

Whatever you do with your baby at night, there will inevitably be some nights when he can't settle, for whatever reason. Rather than feeling resentful, it's better to accept the situation and take the baby downstairs while you have a drink, play with him or listen to the radio. Some mothers use their babies' night feed times as quiet times when they can think, plan, or pray. Others get through more reading than they ever have before. Yet others enjoy night feeds as the only time when they can be alone with their baby. It's worth remembering that your young child won't wake at night for ever. While he does, it's far more sensible to be as constructive as you can about the situation than to be resentful and martyred.

If your baby needs less sleep than you – and these babies aren't as rare as you might think – it's absolutely essential for you to catch up on your sleep during the day. Don't be too proud to ask a relative, neighbour, or friend to take your baby for a walk for a couple of hours so that you can have a rest – you'll soon get used to catnapping even if you were never able to before.

It's a fact of life that some young children go on waking at night for a long time. If only more parents were aware of this, perhaps it wouldn't be seen as such a problem. As it is, the mailbags of magazines on parenthood are full of letters about young children with so-called sleep problems. It's time we all woke up to what babies are really like and not what they have been made out to be. *Related topics* Bedroom sharing; bed sharing; night feeds.

Nipple care in mother It has been shown that antenatal preparation

of the nipples for breast-feeding does nothing to reduce a woman's chances of getting soreness when the baby starts sucking. However, it's a good idea to find out if your nipples are properly shaped for breast-feeding. If the nipple stands out when you squeeze the areola behind it, or if your nipples generally erect when you are sexually excited, then they'll be all right for feeding your baby. If not, it may help to wear breast shells inside your bra for the last few weeks of pregnancy, though many inverted nipples improve spontaneously with pregnancy anyway.

When your baby is born, if your nipples are still inverted, make sure that you avoid engorgement (overfullness) of your breasts and slip a breast shell inside your bra for a few minutes before feeding your baby. This will encourage the nipple to come out for long enough for the baby to take hold and suck. You may have to soften the breast under your areola if it is at all tense before a feed by expressing a little milk.

Soreness of the nipples is a common occurrence and is said to be more frequent in red-haired women. It is made more likely if you feed your baby according to a schedule. Your best chance of avoiding soreness is by feeding on an unrestricted basis by day and night. If your nipples get sore, shorten the length of feeds to the time during which the baby is actually sucking and swallowing. This isn't as easy as it sounds because lots of mothers let down their milk several times during a feed and your baby may stop swallowing for a few minutes, only to start again later. Also, shortening the length of the feeds will reduce the stimulation your breasts receive perhaps so much that your milk supply won't meet your baby's needs.

Sore nipple skin recovers quickest when exposed to light and air and not allowed to get soggy. A piece of one-way nappy liner inside your bra may help keep the nipple skin dry. Leave your bra off as much as possible and if you can, sit in the sun with nothing on! A sun lamp, correctly used, or even the light from an electric light will also help healing. Failing that, change your bra pads very often. Don't use any soap on your nipples – simply splash your breasts with water to wash them and then dry them well. It's most important to change the position in which you feed your baby, both during a feed and from feed to feed, and to make sure he is taking the nipple and areola properly into his mouth and not exerting undue suction on any one part. Make sure that your breasts don't get overfull, because then they will be difficult for the baby to take into his mouth properly and he may chew on the nipples. Always offer the less sore nipple first, to encourage the milk to flow by the time your baby goes to the other one, and try to get your let-down reflex working before you put your baby to the breast so that he doesn't suck too strongly before the bulk of the milk is let down!

Some women find it helpful to cool sore nipples before putting their baby to the breast. This can be done by putting ice cubes into a polythene bag and holding it against the nipple. A successful hint for helping soreness to heal is to express a few drops of milk at the end of a feed, rub it on to the nipples and let it dry before putting your bra on. If you have to stop your baby from feeding, break the suction by putting the top of a finger in the corner of his mouth. Just pulling him off may increase your soreness.

Bad soreness can be an absolute misery and is enough to put some mothers off carrying on with breast-feeding, perhaps because they think it'll always be like that. It does, however, disappear in time and with perseverance!

You may need help from your doctor if nipple soreness persists. Occasionally it is caused by dermatitis from substances in detergents (left in a poorly rinsed bra) or in remedies you've been applying to your nipples to heal them. Hydrocortisone cream may be helpful. Some mothers get a monilial infection of their sore nipple skin (see *Moniliasis*). The source is usually their baby's mouth and both mother and baby must be treated at the same time. Try the home remedy of vinegar solution (one teaspoonful of vinegar to one cup of water) on your nipples after each feed together with sunshine (or light from an ultraviolet lamp or an ordinary electric lamp). If this doesn't help, nystatin ointment after washing and drying your nipples will help. Get this from your doctor.

A few women develop a crack on their nipple, usually because soreness was never cleared up properly. The crack develops where the baby exerts maximum suction and it's essential to change the position in which you feed him regularly throughout the day, besides taking all the other steps for the prevention of sore nipples outlined above. If it doesn't heal, the pain will probably force you to stop breastfeeding for a few days while it heals. Give your expressed or pumped milk to the baby by spoon and when the crack heals, gradually resume feeding, starting twice a day and continuing to express or to pump regularly between these feeds. Some mothers find they can continue to feed by using a nipple shield. *Useful organizations* La Leche League of Great Britain; The National Childbirth Trust.

Nipples and breasts of baby Most babies are born with two nipples but extra, or supernumerary nipples are common in both sexes (more often in boys). When a baby is born it is still under the influence of its mother's hormones that have travelled across in the placental blood supply. Nearly half of all newborn babies have some breast enlargement caused by these maternal hormones. Sometimes the enlarged breasts contain milk – so-called witches' milk – for a few days. Babies who are breast-fed may continue to have swollen breasts for some months – presumably because of breast milk hormones – but most babies, no matter how they are fed, lose their breast swelling within a few weeks at the most. Rarely the breasts of a newborn baby become red and tender as the result of infection. Consult your doctor.

Breast swellings in a baby should be left alone and certainly not squeezed.

Nits The eggs of lice, which are insects that live on the body, are tiny and cigar-shaped. They are laid on hair about half an inch from the scalp. Each nit sticks firmly to the hair and hatches into an adult louse in two weeks or so. At first the eggs are pearly-white but they go darker just before the adult lice hatch. The lice look rather like mosquitoes in the hair and the very sight of them in a child's hair is enough to make anyone feel itchy! The adult lice live on human blood and their bites can cause itching and inflammation of the skin, sometimes with infection. The bites show up as red pimples on the scalp. In severe cases there can be enlargement of the lymph nodes at the back of the neck ('swollen glands').

Children pick up lice from other children by using their combs, brushes or towels, by touching each others' heads, wearing each others' clothes, or by leaning against a place where another child's head has rested. A louse can live for twenty four hours away from a head. Such infestations are extremely common and many schools have regular inspections for nits. Unfortunately, the older insecticides are becoming increasingly ineffective as 'super lice' breed with resistance to them. Today's most widely used treatment is the insecticide malathion which actually combines with the hair to give protection lasting up to five or six weeks. This lotion is rubbed into the hair, usually before bedtime, allowed to dry overnight and then shampooed in the morning (twelve hours later) with ordinary shampoo. Be sure to wear rubber gloves when using the lotion if you are (or might be) pregnant. The wet hair can be combed with a fine toothed comb to remove the nits. They are difficult to remove as each is stuck to the hair with a cement-like glue. Try dipping the comb into hot vinegar as this helps loosen the nits. Even though the insecticide kills the nits within a few days, it's worth removing them if possible so you can tell if reinfestation occurs afterwards from a fresh source. The manufacturers of the lotion recommend that children who have been treated for lice shouldn't swim in a chlorinated pool for several weeks. This is because the chlorine can reduce the efficacy of the malathion in the hair and so allow reinfestation. It's important to find out if possible where the child got the lice from, so you can tell that child's mother and prevent further spread of the lice. As soon as your child has been treated, it's all right for him to mix with other children.

If you see tiny white flakes in your child's hair don't panic and assume they're nits – they could be scurf. Ask your doctor or health visitor if you are in any doubt. *Related topic* Scurf.

Noise The noise of other people's babies crying in hospital can be very upsetting to a new mother who is as yet unable to distinguish her own baby's cry. If her baby is with her, she'll be able to relax and turn off the other cries in her mind. The noise of a cry is designed to be a strong alerting signal and it's not surprising that any person who has been a parent reacts to a baby's cry with unease. It is possible to turn off a sound though, and some people train themselves to ignore their baby as he screams for attention in another room. They rarely feel comfortable doing it but have perhaps been encouraged to believe that crying won't hurt a baby, that he mustn't be 'spoilt', and that a mother shouldn't react at once because she's a free person and her baby mustn't grow up to think that he can dominate her.

When there are several children playing together, as can happen in a large family or when friends are visiting, the noise may be very loud. Children seem immune – they often have the volume control on the television set turned right up so that it is almost painful to an adult's ears.

Sometimes making a loud noise can be very relaxing. At the beginning of a party, when all the children are shy and overexcited, try getting them all to run to the end of the garden shouting as loudly as they can. You'll see a lot of smiling faces when they return and the ice will be broken. It's unfair to expect young children always to play quietly. Shouting will help them to let off steam, and they should have a chance to be noisy sometimes.

A first baby is often disturbed by noise because his life is relatively quiet.

Subsequent babies can usually sleep peacefully through a cacophony of sound. It's all a question of what they're used to.

Nosebleeds Nosebleeds are fairly common in young children who have a cold, pick their noses, stick things into them, or fall over and hit them. Usually there is a simple explanation for a nosebleed but if your child has persistent nosebleeds or bleeds that take more than fifteen minutes to stop, you should seek medical advice.

The best and simplest treatment for a nosebleed is to get the child to sit still at a table with his head slightly forward over a bowl. Get him to hold his nose for ten minutes (you can do it for him if he's too young). The vast majority of nosebleeds stop with this treatment. Once the bleeding has stopped, don't let the child sniff or blow his nose as this could dislodge the newly-formed clot and the bleeding will start all over again.

If ever a child has a nosebleed or a blood-stained watery discharge after a fall on to his head, see a doctor at once.

Some children seem to get nosebleeds as a result of too dry a nose lining. If this seems to be the case with your child, put a little petroleum jelly just inside the nose on the wall of the central dividing wall between the two nostrils.

Nose drops Only one type of nose drop is commonly used in young children – decongestant drops that shrink the lining of the nose to make breathing easier, and to allow mucus and pus to drain more easily. Unfortunately, such drops only have a short duration of action and the nasal lining becomes puffed up again quickly. Long term use of these drops can permanently damage the delicate lining, so never give nose drops without first discussing it with your doctor, and then only give them every four hours at the most.

There are three sorts of condition for which your doctor might suggest the use of nose drops. The first is in a very snuffly baby who cannot breast-feed easily without the nose being unblocked. Usually, however, even if a baby has a cold, he can manage to breast-feed satisfactorily by coming off the breast every so often to breathe through his mouth. The second is in the late stages of a bad cold or sinusitis when the nose is blocked up and the sinuses can't drain. The third is with an ear infection, when the doctor wants the drops to shrink the inflamed lining of the Eustachian tube (opening at the back of the nose) to allow the middle ear to drain.

Antihistamine nose drops are another type of drops which can be useful.

Giving nose drops to very young children can be difficult. The easiest way is to lay the child on a bed with his head hanging over the edge (or you can do the same thing on your lap). Turn the child's head slightly to one side if the idea is to shrink the congested lining of the Eustachian tube, and put the drops in the nostril that side (the side of the earache). Once the drops are in, keep the child still for a couple of minutes if you can, then repeat the process in the other nostril if necessary. Many children won't stay still and it isn't worth having a battle because there are now decongestant tablets that have much the same effect – talk to your doctor.

Nose picking A habit that is usually harmless, though socially unacceptable. Persistent picking can cause nosebleeds – in fact nose picking is the commonest cause of nosebleed. A child may also play with or pick his nose if he has a foreign body in it. This is usually accompanied by a discharge of pus or mucus. If you think your child could have pushed something up his nose, ask your doctor to look with a special instrument.

Numbers Many parents have an innate dislike for, or even fear of mathematics and sums and all too often this comes across to their children. Some children find numbers easy but many don't – the spread is just as great as with any other skill at this age. However, being able to use numbers is really useful to the child and so should be encouraged gently and with fun.

The way to get a child interested is to make numbers part of your everyday conversation and to make them live for him. When you're going out for a walk, for example, count the buses you see. When you're loading the washing machine, say 'let's put in one, two, three pairs of pants'. Sing action songs with numbers in, such as 'One, two, three, four, five, Once I caught a fish alive.' Don't make lessons out of numbers, but incorporate them into your child's play.

The same goes for time. Your child will learn to tell the time only when he's ready, but he'll be better prepared if you have talked about numbers, times and the long and short hand on the clock, as well as if you have given him some idea over his early years of whether an hour or five minutes is a long or a short time. It helps if he has some idea what days, weeks, months and years are as well, and the odd bit of early assimilated information will gradually be pieced together until he eventually has a full understanding of time when he is ready. Similarly, as he plays, tell him about shapes, such as cubes, spheres, triangles, and so on and when you cut a cake or a piece of bread you can use the pieces to show some simple mathematical principle (even if it's as simple as two half apples make one apple). A child under two will enjoy counting simple objects, especially food.

At two a child can recognize that parts are smaller than the whole and will enjoy fitting food and playthings together. He now begins to understand numbers rather than simply repeating them after you and he can understand 'zero' or 'nothing' when he's finished eating his biscuit and it's gone.

A three-year-old is really beginning to get to grips with numbers. He'll be able to recognize a few numbers and may learn how to write the numbers up to ten if you teach him and make the learning fun. Don't expect him to remember how to write a number the first time you show him. He'll need lots of patient repetition and encouragement and praise of his first efforts. It doesn't matter one bit if the numbers aren't well written – he'll perfect them eventually.

At four a child begins to understand how to 'take away' or subtract numbers and enjoys playing games that involve numbers. Encourage playing shops as this involves the counting out of items.

At five the average child is able to learn how to add small numbers confidently and also how to do simple take-away sums. He'll probably enjoy learning tables by rote at this age and can use his new-found patience and understanding to work at simple mathematical problems for several minutes.

Children are, of course, very individual about what they can and cannot cope with at any age but with encouragement during play the average child can be well conversant with numbers and can learn valuable basic mathematical concepts even before he starts school. None of this involves any formal teaching at all

There is a condition call discalculia which is sometimes inherited. Affected children have great difficulty in dealing with numbers and even simple sums.

Nursery classes Nursery classes exist at private nursery schools, at some state first schools and at some private schools. In private schools children are usually taken at three but some may be accepted as young as two and a half. In state schools the children in the nursery class are more often than not four and the age at entry is strictly monitored as there is such a demand for the relatively few available places. A few state first schools have a nursery class which is run as a play-group and is open to children, usually from three onwards. From here they generally enter the school proper at five (or 'rising five', that is, the term in which they're going to be five). Some children attend a nursery class only once or twice a week, while others go regularly for three half days or even every morning.

In most nursery classes, the atmosphere is rather more formal than that in a play-group, which caters for children in the same age range. The children have their own places at tables or desks and there is more sitting down to learn with paper and pencil and less learning through play than there is in a play-group, though informal activities and play still occupy a major part of the child's day. In a nursery class, fewer adults are required than for the same number of children in a play-group, but many establishments are aware that more adults means more contented and interested children, and so increase the teacher-child ratio.

If you decide that you prefer the nursery class, and your child would prefer it – then if you haven't a suitable state class nearby, or if the state class has no places, or if you intend paying for your child's education anyway, then go to see whatever is available in your area. (Your local education authority will have a list.) Make an appointment with the headteacher and make sure that you see the classroom and the teacher that your child would start off with as well. What you should be on the lookout for is an awareness amongst the staff of the particular needs of children this young who are away from their parents. They learn best through play.

enjoy freedom to move around and don't want to sit down for most of the time. Even more important, they need a caring, motherly teacher who will seek to develop a good relationship with each child at the same time as keeping the order that is necessary to look after so many children at once. Watch the teacher, if you are able, as she helps the children and tells them what to do, and take special note of what play and learning materials are around. Ask to see them if they aren't readily visible – if they're stored high up in another room and are covered with dust, they probably aren't ever used! Look at the outdoor space available and at any pets, large play equipment, and interesting things outside.

Is your child really going to benefit from spending his time here, or would he be better off at home with you? If he is old enough to be happy leaving you for a short time every so often, and if you like the look of the teacher and what she does with the children, then he will probably enjoy his experiences in a nursery class. Should you have little time to play with your child, then he will certainly learn more there. Some mothers send their children to a nursery class for other reasons. They themselves want some time alone; they feel that their children will have a head start by going to school early; they are worried that their friend's children who are going to go to the nursery class will get ahead of their child; they want company for an only child; or perhaps they just expect their child to go because they did and it seems natural.

Sometimes a younger brother or sister will miss his older one so much when he goes off to school that he'll want to go too. If there is a nursery class at the school, then he'll probably be delighted to be big like his brother or sister and go to school as well. They'll probably see each other in the playground and will enjoy each other's company.

You won't be alone if you feel that young children are going to have to spend enough of their childhood cooped up inside the four walls of a school, and that it's unfair to start them off any earlier than you have to. This is a somewhat negative and old-fashioned attitude though, because the atmosphere inside many nursery classes is so attractive, friendly, interesting and stimulating for a young child that he'll probably enjoy himself more there than he would at home. What's more, many children of three or four take a delight in playing or working with other children and form close relationships. If the school you have earmarked for your child has a well-used nursery class (or classes) that most of their five-year-olds have attended, your child may be the odd one out if he doesn't join until he's five. Unless he's naturally outgoing or has an attractive personality, he may have problems in fitting in socially in a class where most of the other children already know each other. Some of the mothers will have made friends with each other and their children will have had a chance to get to know each other outside school too. This is just one more factor to consider when deciding whether to send your child to a nursery class at all, whether to send him to a play-group, or just to keep him at home. **Related topics** Play-groups; pre-school education.

Nystagmus A rhythmical involuntary flicking movement of the eyes usually from side to side. There are many causes but one type is perfectly normal – that which occurs when a child looks out of the side window of a moving car or train. Nystagmus can be present from birth in which case there is often poor vision too.

Any child with nystagmus should be seen by a doctor.

Obesity A state of overweight, almost always caused by over-eating. Few obese children have anything wrong with their glands. A child who is twenty per cent or more overweight as compared with the ideal weight for his height and build is defined as obese by medical standards.

Just why some children become obese isn't known but there are certainly inherited as well as environmental factors involved. Some people, children included, put on weight more easily than others: some can burn up excess calories eaten while others store them as fat. This explains why two people of the same height and build can eat the same amount and yet one will grow fat and the other will maintain his ideal weight. For each child there is a balance to be found between the amount of food eaten and the amount of energy expended. If the balance is maintained, then his weight will always be right for his height.

Some families are in the habit of eating too much and children of such families tend to follow the parent's example and are likely to be over-weight.

Obesity can start in babyhood if a mother makes up feeds too strong (with an extra scoop of milk powder) or adds cereal or sugar to them. Neither of these practices is necessary – milk is all a baby needs for at least three to four months and some breast-fed babies thrive on breast milk alone until eight or nine months or more. A totally breast-fed baby can become overweight but research has shown that this fat disappears more easily than does 'cows' milk fat'. There is also evidence that cows' milk has other bad effects on the baby's fat metabolism and that it makes him more likely to have atheroma (hardening of the arteries) at an early age.

The question many parents ask is 'Will my fat baby grow up to be a fat adult?' The evidence on this is confused but what can be said is that fat adults are more likely to have been fat as young children than their thin brothers.

Although parents tend to think of chubby babies and young children as being attractive and healthy, there is no reason for thinking this. On the contrary there is plenty of evidence that fat children (and even more so fat adults) have more diseases and illnesses than do thin children. The extra weight alters the body's metabolic processes and causes mechanical disorders, especially of the hips, legs and feet in obese children.

There is little doubt that the reason children become fat, in the West, is because they eat too much of the *wrong foods* and not because they eat too much *per se*. White bread, white flour products and added sugar in all forms produce a lot of body fat whereas wholemeal bread and flour products and foods free from sugar do not seem to do so nearly as much. Foods rich in dietary fibre including vegetables and fruit are intrinsically 'slimming' because they can't be eaten in such large amounts as refined foods, tend to make the child feel full for longer, are more satisfying to eat and encourage the loss of dietary fat in the stools. Refined foods (for example, white bread and flour products, most breakfast cereals, peeled potatoes and sugar) have the opposite effects and tend to be fattening.

The way to prevent your children becoming unnecessarily obese is to breast-feed them for at least three to six months, then to wean them on to unrefined whole foods. Added-sugar-containing foods can easily be kept to a minimum if this is done from weaning and if sweet cakes and puddings are eaten rarely instead of as a normal part of the diet. Many parents use food to bribe their children but this isn't sensible because not only does it make for problems in the short term but it undoubtedly colours the way they'll think of food for the rest of their lives.

It's certainly unfashionable to be fat today. It's difficult to get attractive clothes; other children tease fat children; and it's not much fun climbing, running and playing with other children either, because the obese child quickly gets out of breath, hot and sweaty. Even among babies there are practical disadvantages to obesity as they can have problems with soreness in their skin creases. One good thing to be said for an under-five carrying excess weight is that if he has an illness which stops him from eating (such as gastroenteritis or whooping cough), his fat stores will help tide him over nutritionally until he is well enough to eat or to keep his food down again.

Preventing obesity is important, just as looking after your children's teeth should be. Not only can you make your child's life more pleasant today but you'll be doing the best for his future too. Fat adults die younger, on average, than thin ones. **Related topics** Dieting; overfeeding.

Objects in the nose and ears
Some young children enjoy stuffing objects into their noses and ears. Bits of paper, beads, small toys, marbles, nuts and so on all find their way into these orifices, often to the amazement of their parents.

The most important thing is to leave the object alone unless it's very superficial. Let a doctor remove it with special instruments. It's all too easy to push the thing further into the nose or ear and so make it even more difficult to get it out.

If ever a child has a discharge (especially a smelly one) from his nose or his ear, take him to a doctor because there may be a foreign body in there which has caused an infection. This is especially likely if the discharge is coming from one nostril only.

A simple first-aid measure that's worth a try is to get the child to blow out through his nose while you close off the other (unblocked) nostril. This can sometimes dislodge the object. Never use this method in really young children though because such a child will sniff in first and this could make matters worse. **Related topic** Foreign body.

Obsessions and compulsions

Obsessions and compulsions Sometimes even quite young children of four or five feel driven to do something quite out of character or unnecessary. Something inside themselves seems to be telling them to tidy their shoes into neat pairs, to put all the books the right way up in the bookcase or just to check once more that the top has been put back on the tube of toothpaste, for example. Even though the job has been done once, or if the child has been told he needn't do it at all, he feels it has to be done and if he doesn't do it, he feels uncomfortable and ill at ease until he does. Compulsive behaviour of one sort or another can become a daily ritual.

In older children or adolescents, this sort of behaviour may be combined with persistent and repetitious thoughts known as obsessions. A child may, for instance, be obsessed with the idea that one of his parents is going to die. Obsessive-compulsive neurotic character traits are commonly found in quite ordinary, normal children and are usually just part of the blend of a child's personality. Obsessional thoughts and compulsive behaviour are a way of preventing repressed and unpleasant feelings from surfacing in a child's mind. Sometimes they can get out of hand and start to be a nuisance, affecting the normal course of daily life, though this is rarely a problem in young children. They may even be seen as part of a psychiatric disorder such as depression, anxiety or schizophrenia.

Signs of compulsive behaviour usually come to light when a child is anxious or upset, perhaps because his life is disrupted in a way he can't fully cope with. Quite often compulsions and obsessional thoughts are unknown to parents because they don't see their child carrying out the tasks and he doesn't necessarily volunteer his thoughts.

In his day-to-day behaviour a child may simply be copying his mother or another adult who cares for him, especially if that person is always tidying up. This is perfectly normal. Most children like routine and some order. The difference between normal and unacceptable behaviour is that with the latter the child isn't in full control of what he does or thinks. A normal tidy child who likes routine isn't compelled to stick to his routine and won't be upset if he can't do so for some reason, whereas the obsessive child will. If this is so, try to find out what is at the bottom of your child's disturbance – it's likely to be a family problem – and do whatever you can to put it right. If you feel you need professional help, see your doctor who might suggest that an expert opinion be sought. *Related topics* Anxiety; behaviour problems; child guidance; child psychiatry; nail biting.

Oedipus complex Between the ages of three and six children begin to relate to the opposite sex – usually a parent – in very well recognized and perfectly harmless ways. The so-called Oedipus complex is a group of emotions (usually totally unconscious) involving the desire of a child to possess (sexually) the parent of the opposite sex and to exclude the parent of the same sex. The term is derived from a mythical Greek who killed his father (while unaware of his identity) and unknowingly married his mother by whom he had four children.

All this may sound rather dramatic for the 1980s but any parent with young children will know the phase that many children go through when Daddy (or Mummy) becomes the most important person in the world and the other parent is shut out for a while.

Children imitate their parents from the beginning and by three they want to be just like their parents. Their play shows this repeatedly as they dress up in their parents' clothes, generally mimic them and mirror their activities in their play. This process is called identification and is normal. But it's not only practical household activities that children copy: they use their parents to model their personalities and behaviour on and even at this early age they're learning how to be parents. Just watch a four-year-old with her doll and see what a powerful influence you have had on her early 'mothering'.

Between three and six girls begin to see themselves as different from boys and they realize that when they grow up they are likely to be mothers with all that this entails. Boys begin to realize that they will become fathers. Children of this age are fascinated by babies and how they are made and they like to care for babies. Sometimes boys talk about having a baby. Identifying with the mother is a normal phase of development that precedes identifying with the father. (Don't forget that some men have very real pregnancy symptoms and even labour-like pains in sympathy with their wives, so it's not that ridiculous a concept.)

By the age of about four a boy's love for his mother starts to be romantic rather than the baby-like dependence he has experienced so far. At this age most boys say they are going to marry their mothers and girls their fathers, which is scarcely surprising since they're the only adults they know really well and the ones they love most. Because a boy becomes so attached to his mother, his father's relationship with his mother annoys him and this produces problems for the child. How can he come to terms with loving and hating his father at the same time? Such thoughts make him feel guilty – an emotion made all the worse by the worry that his father feels equally jealous of him. The same emotions are felt by girls towards their mothers. All of this must be understood by the sensitive parents of children aged four to six. A harsh word from her father can really upset a little girl who sees him as her hero. She can be devastated by the tiniest thoughtless remark he makes. The same happens with mothers and sons.

By six or seven these feelings will have passed and the child's life will be centred around other children, schoolwork and hobbies.

All of this means that when your children are at this age they should not be pandered to in a way that plays down *your* relationship as a couple. Nothing could be more devastating than that your relationship is seen to be faulty. After all, it's their model for married life and it's all they have to cling on to. Go on being just as loving and demonstrative to each other whatever stage of sexual identification your children are going through. There will always be a tendency for a mother to be a bit more loving towards her sons and a father to be less strict with his daughters at this stage of their development and that provides a happy balance.

This web of feelings and emotions is an essential part of a child's development and is certainly not to be ridiculed or played down. For most families there is no connection at all between these feelings and incest as at this age the feelings are purely romantic. *Related topics* Development – psychosexual; guilt in children.

One parent families Today in the UK approximately one in ten children live with only one parent and in 1978 there were about 825,000 single parent families. This is largely because of the massive increase in the divorce rate in this country (currently the highest in Europe), though separation and death also contribute to the numbers considerably. Increasing numbers of young girls who would have had abortions in the 1960s are now choosing to have their baby and look after it single-handed.

The end of a bad marriage can be a great relief to everybody in the family but most people don't see the end of their marriage as a time for celebration, especially if there are children. Most divorced or separated people feel a sense of failure both to themselves and their children and ask themselves what they could have done to save the marriage. Divorce is certainly not something to be entered into lightly: indeed one piece of research has shown that many divorcees are temporarily less happy than while they were still married. Because of all the stresses and strains of being a single parent many become ill either physically or emotionally and this brings the extra worry of 'Who'll look after the children if I'm ill?' It's vitally important to look after yourself both physically and mentally, so do see your doctor as soon as you feel low. Don't wait to get into the depths of depression before going for help.

Help is something a lot of single parent families are often unable to let themselves ask for. However, if you can bring yourself to ask, there are in fact lots of helpful people around, including any friend worth the name, as well as your doctor and special self-help groups for widowed parents as well as other single parents.

Meeting people can be very difficult and it's easy to become isolated, lonely and very tired, especially if you're working to maintain the family too. Contact Gingerbread or the National Council for the Divorced and Separated – they have local branches over most of the country. They can give you very practical information about all your problems because they've seen them all before. They are also very understanding.

To work or not is another burning question. Many single parents, unless they have an active social life, are better off working simply because it will give them something to occupy their minds, boost their confidence and provide some money. Mixing with adults rather than being cooped up with young children at home has its advantages. If you have a baby you may decide not to work unless it's necessary financially or to stop you getting depressed. The single parent of a preschool child may decide that the advantages of staying at home with him outbalance the advantages of returning to work. With a good social support system of friends and relatives, it may be quite possible to stay at home with young children and still have a social life of your own.

About one in eight one parent families is headed by a father. Single fathers are still thought of as being rather odd if they stay at home and look after children. There's no reason why they shouldn't though, and some do so successfully.

One of the most depressing problems for the single parent is housing. Unless you are actually barred from your home by your partner or life is unbearable together, try to stay put. If you don't you could lose some of your legal rights to your home. If you rented a council house, you might have to go to the bottom of the waiting list if you leave your partner. If you want to know about your legal rights to your family home, talk to a solicitor or your local Legal Advice Centre or Citizens Advice Bureau before leaving home.

Some people find that they can live temporarily with parents or friends while they sort out their marriage problems but this is often unsatisfactory as it's so easy to outstay your welcome. If your friends or family live in a council house, check the regulations about overcrowding and find out how strict your local authority is in applying them. Your local health visitor will help you find out answers to such things. It would be terrible if your parents or friends were evicted because of doing you a good turn. Living permanently with another one parent family, sharing all the expenses on a 50/50 basis, is a possibility especially if you have a large enough place for each family to have some privacy and still function as a single unit. Although this can work very well, there are disadvantages. First, you may lose your place on the council house waiting list; second, it can be difficult to back out if things don't work; and third, it can be restricting when trying to form new relationships with the opposite sex.

There are lots of jobs with living-in accommodation provided either cheaply or free which can be ideal for the single parent. The trouble with this is that if you leave or lose your job you also lose your house and you could be wide open to exploitation. Unless you have some pretty watertight arrangements, do get your name down on the local council housing waiting list as soon as possible and keep checking each year that you're still on it. A trip to the housing department of your local authority is well worthwhile. The housing officials may know of local schemes especially designed for people in your position. Many local authorities have started Housing Aid Centres which give free advice. *Related topics* Divorce; maintenance; separation of parents. *Useful organizations* Gingerbread; National Council for the Divorced and Separated; One Parent Families.

The one-year-old child By one year old, your baby seems very much an individual with his own likes and dislikes and his own developing personality. You'll already be well aware of his basic temperament and he'll have formed attachments to all the people who mean anything to him.

You as his mother will probably be his favourite if you're the one who looks after him and if you give him plenty of affectionate and attentive time on a one-to-one basis. If you leave the room, he'll follow you. If he can't he won't be as upset as he would have been a few weeks ago because he understands that a person who goes will come back – they haven't gone for ever. If several people are in the room, you're the one he'll keep coming back to, though he'll slowly become more and more adventurous about going over to other people. He's now starting to explore places and things and will occupy himself for minutes at a time examining toys and the contents of cupboards.

By this age, many babies are mobile. They can crawl, usually on hands and knees but sometimes 'like a bear' on hands and feet, or shuffle along on their bottoms. Many babies are pulling themselves up to stand and some can walk around the furniture, holding on and moving sideways. Many can walk alone (though the average age for walking isn't till thirteen months) and strut along with their hands held out to help them balance, looking extremely pleased with themselves except when they sit down with a bump on their bottoms!

From now on your work will be cut out looking after your baby and making sure he doesn't hurt himself – not to mention keeping him out of mischief.

From now on, your baby's weight gain will slow down a bit, and this is quite normal. Part of the reason this happens is that although he's eating the same amount, he's using much more energy now he's mobile.

The one-year-old is readily amused when you play with him and relatively simple games like watching an object fall to the ground will give him lots of pleasure. This is the age for stacking different size beakers, for posting shapes, putting objects endlessly into containers and taking them out. He enjoys shapes and trying to find out how things work. He'll enjoy playing ball on the floor – if you roll or gently throw a ball to him he'll pick it up and attempt to get it back to you. He'll love playing peep-bo and pat-a-cake and will join in his brothers' and sisters' games with gusto, often to their annoyance. He'll enjoy it if you sing to him or tell him nursery rhymes; even though he doesn't understand them he'll like the interaction with you. He'll look for a hidden object such as a doll under a cushion or a ball that's rolled out of sight. If he's walking round the furniture, he may be steady enough to enjoy a toy animal or other toy on wheels with a handle to push. This sort of toy isn't suitable for some children at one – you'll have to gauge how ready your own child is. The trouble is that they tend to fall over sideways if the child is unsteady. He'll like riding on a push-along train or animal now, if you steady him with one hand and push slowly with the other. Take care that he doesn't fall off and stop as soon as he's had enough.

Many one-year-olds already like to look at pictures with you and listen attentively when you point out things and name them. This is the age when you can go round the house with him in your arms naming things as you go.

During the day, talk to him as you go about your jobs and point out and name things he uses such as his cup or his spoon. Use certain key words a lot, such as names for people and pets. He's slowly building up connections in his mind between things and their verbal labels. The one-year-old can usually recognize his name when called and may understand some simple instructions such as 'give me the spoon', or 'where's Daddy?'. Some babies develop their own nonsense or 'jargon' language around this time and chatter away in a conversational style to the amazement of those around them, who feel they ought to understand what is being said but actually can't. He may be able to say one or two words – usually things that are important to him, but these will probably be his interpretations and may sound nothing like the words you say. He may be able to repeat some words after you, but always make sure that he understands what the word is a label for, otherwise he'll just be imitating you and not learning anything.

The one-year-old is becoming very dextrous and can pick up tiny objects between his finger and thumb. He may be able to put two or three bricks on top of each other to make a castle but will enjoy knocking it over even more. He may even applaud himself afterwards. You may notice that he uses one hand more than the other but don't make an issue about encouraging him to use his right hand if he seems to be favouring his left.

Your baby can now feed himself with his hands if not with a spoon. Spoonfeeding himself will be a messy business. He'll very much enjoy mealtimes as social occasions and will listen to the mealtime talk with interest, joining in when he thinks appropriate! He's good at imitating and will copy other children especially. He'll even help with dressing, pulling his arms out of sleeves you are taking off; stepping out of trousers; and so on.

The second year of a baby's life is a time of rapid advancement especially in the fields of language and mobility. It's also a time when you'll have to teach him the word 'no' for the first time as he begins to do things you don't want him to. As his understanding of why he shouldn't do something is so limited, it's best to keep things you don't want him to touch out of his way if possible. Avoidance of confrontation is the best policy. If you were to get cross with a one-year-old, he'd probably burst into tears at the shock of seeing his beloved mother unhappy. It's quite enough to say 'no' and look crossly at him. Remember that a good way of teaching him how you want him to behave is by praising him when he's good and does things right, rather than by continually saying 'no'. Give him lots of cuddles and affection even if you don't breast-feed him any more. If you do, you'll have lots of opportunities for physical contact and quiet times together which will be appreciated by both of you.

Being one is a time when a child wants his mother there to comfort and reassure him. From this base of dependence he is ready to explore and to begin to assert his independence of choice over what he wants to do. It's an exciting time for him.

Only child The term 'only' child is usually applied to a child who never has a sibling (brother or sister), though all firstborn children are only children for some time and this is one reason why they are so different (and so achieving) compared with later-borns. Though second child infertility is much more common than people suppose, some parents choose to have only one child, partly so that they can lavish on it that much more care, attention and money. A few women dislike the experience of childbirth or caring for a baby and young child so much that they decide to have no more. Other parents choose to limit their family to one because they themselves enjoyed being an only child or perhaps because they disliked being one of a large family.

There are pros and cons to being an only child. Because the child gets so much adult attention, he tends to develop skills such as talking earlier. He'll almost certainly get more time and attention from his parents than if there were other children in the home. His parents may also have relatively more money available for holidays, toys and schooling. However, he may be lonely a lot of the time. All the rough and tumble that goes on when there are several children is great fun and also prepares him for school and for society in the wider sense. Because he lives with his parents only he has no family of his own age group at hand to relate to. This produces a 'them' and 'us' situation, however well the parents handle it. These disadvantages can be overcome to some extent by ensuring that the child has a chance to play with other children.

Strange though it may seem, the fact that an only child gets so much attention may actually be a disadvantage. Such a child often finds himself under parental pressure to do well both in and out of school, partly because the parents have no other children on whom to focus their attention and partly because they have so much invested in him – he's all they have.

Children brought up with other children probably enjoy life more overall; can more easily cope with the pressures of the real world later (after all, a family with its power struggles, moods, troubles and fun is a microcosm of society in general); adapt better to school; and take themselves less seriously. *Related topic* Firstborn children.

Operations If your young child has to have an operation, there are some basic rules worth following to make things as pleasant as possible for him and you.

As soon as you know what's going to be done, explain things to your child at a level you know he can understand without worrying him. Make all the arrangements you possibly can to be with him all the time, even at night and if you have any trouble with this talk to the National Association for the

Welfare of Children in Hospital (see page 773). They'll have a branch near you and have lots of helpful literature. Ideally any child under five should have a parent with him most of the time if he's going to stay in hospital.

If you are there you can cushion your child from what may seem to him to be strange and frightening experiences. No one can help him cope with his anxiety as well as you. If a blood sample has to be taken or a physical examination done your presence will reassure him and your absence (only ever suggested by inexperienced hospital staff) could make him think you've deserted him at his time of need. Press the hospital staff to let you be with him all the time before his operation, right until he goes under the anaesthetic. Some hospitals will let you go to the anaesthetic room to hold his hand as he goes under. Try to be there when he comes round from the anaesthetic and stay with him for at least the rest of the day if you possibly can.

Most operations are simple and straightforward and the child is home within a few days. Increasing numbers of hospitals are trying to do surgery for simple things on a one day basis. This means that the child spends one night in hospital at most and may simply spend one whole day there. More complex operations require longer stays but even major procedures no longer call for weeks in hospital unless something goes wrong. *Related topic* Hospitals. *Useful organizations* The National Association for the Welfare of Children in Hospital.

Orange juice A pleasant drink that can be used as a source of vitamin C (see vitamins) in the diet or just as a thirst quencher.

Normally it's best to wait until your baby is a few months old before starting him on orange juice, and to use vitamin drops to fill any vitamin C gap in the meantime. Start off with fresh orange juice, or pure juice from a can or carton, diluted half and half with cooled boiled water, because the taste of juice alone is too strong for many babies. At first give perhaps just a teaspoonful of orange and a teaspoonful of water, and if your baby likes it then give him a little more each day. Try leaving out the water to see if he likes the juice neat. When he is having as much as two ounces of pure orange juice a day there is no need for him to have vitamin drops. In practice, many mothers carry on giving vitamin drops anyway as a source of vitamin D. The combination of vitamin C in the drops and in the orange juice is quite safe for the baby – he won't get too much.

Never boil orange juice because this will destroy its vitamin C, which is the main reason you're giving it to your baby. Warm the juice by putting the bottle in a bowl of warm water, or add to it boiled water which is warm. If you like you can use a commercial orange drink preparation containing added vitamin C, but read the label and choose one that is pure as it's not a good idea to give anything containing added sugar to a baby because this will accustom him to sweet things. To get really unadulterated orange juice you can squeeze real oranges yourself. Sugar-containing drinks will encourage dental decay when the first teeth come through. There is some debate in dental circles as to whether repeatedly bathing the first teeth with acidic orange juice might rot them. Its natural juice can, it appears, harm the teeth. Give your child orange juice diluted with water and this hazard (if indeed there is one) will be reduced to some extent. Sieve pure juice to stop the bottle teat from getting blocked with pulp.

When giving orange juice to a young baby, remember that you should be just as careful to sterilize the bottle and teat as you are when giving him milk formula. Leave an opened container of orange juice in the fridge, covered.

Orange squash contains little if any orange juice but is just a solution of sugar, artificial sweetener, colouring, flavouring and perhaps some added vitamin C.

Some babies get diarrhoea with orange juice; others vomit, develop a rash, or seem uncomfortable afterwards. In some babies these signs may indicate an allergy to oranges – this is especially likely if they have an allergic family history. Most babies enjoy it though, and develop no side effects at all.

When you start giving a breast-fed baby solids and other drinks as well as breast milk, orange juice can be introduced as part of his normal diet. *Related topic* Vitamins.

Orthodontist A dentist who specializes in the branch of dentistry that deals with crooked teeth. Such problems usually occur because of an imbalance between the growth of the jaws and the teeth, such as occurs if a child inherits a small jaw from one parent and big teeth from the other. This produces an overcrowded mouth with all kinds of problems.

Orthodontists say that breast-fed babies rarely develop orthodontic problems, as the muscular 'pulls' on the developing jaw bones during breast-feeding encourage optimal jaw and tooth development.

Continue to look after your child's mouth by caring for – and teaching him to care for – his milk teeth. If these fall out prematurely or are removed because they are decayed, the direction in which the permanent teeth come through may be altered.

Orthodontists hardly ever start work on a child's mouth under the age of eight or ten, when the permanent teeth are fully developed. *Related topics* Dentist; teeth problems.

Otitis externa An infection of the outer ear caused by bacteria, viruses or fungi. The infection produces inflammation with pain which is worse on moving the jaw, enlargement of the lymph nodes around the ear and in the neck and sometimes also a discharge and itching in the ear canal. Such infections are relatively easy to pick up and parents who screw a towel corner into their child's ears to clean them can cause such an infection easily. Children sometimes poke a small object into their ear and this too can start an infection.

The treatment is simple. The family doctor cleans out the ear canal and if it is not too swollen, checks that there is no infection behind the eardrum in the middle ear. He'll also look to see if there is a foreign body in the ear. He will prescribe some ear drops containing anti-inflammatory, anti-bacterial, or anti-fungal drugs if necessary.

Once the infection is cleared up, be extra careful not to damage your child's ears when cleaning them. Clean the outside of the ears with a soapy flannel and only clean the canal with a cotton wool bud if there is a lot of liquid wax blocking it. Ear canals are usually self-cleaning in young children, partly because of the movement of wax with its antiseptic properties down the canal. Never poke things up the ear canal as it is only too easy to perforate the eardrum if the child moves. *Related topics* Ear drops; objects in nose and ears.

Otitis media An infection of the middle ear that causes earache. It is usually secondary to an infection of the upper respiratory tract or the nose and throat such as tonsillitis, the common cold, 'flu, scarlet fever, whooping cough or measles. Inflammation caused by the infection blocks up the Eustachian tube that joins the middle ear to the back of the throat. This may happen on one or both sides. This traps inflammatory fluid in the middle ear, and the pressure of the fluid builds up and makes the eardrum bulge and sometimes burst. A blockage of the Eustachian tube is especially likely if the child has infected or enlarged tonsils or adenoids. Bottle-fed babies are more likely to suffer from otitis media than are breast-fed ones. The most common age for otitis media is between five and seven but it is often seen in the under-fives as well.

If your child complains of earache when he has another infection, tell your doctor who may prescribe some decongestant nose drops to shrink the inflamed lining of the Eustachian tubes and so open them up and allow drainage. This alone may abort a full-blown attack of otitis media. If it doesn't, the child will develop a fever and increasing pain in his ear. He may cry or scream and pull at his ear. He'll lose his appetite and will temporarily be slightly deaf in the affected ear. Babies and toddlers may go off their food, vomit, cry for no apparent reason, feel irritable, or have loose motions. Even an older child who can talk may not tell you he has earache. A doctor will have to make the diagnosis by looking at the eardrums.

Apart from nose drops to help open the Eustachian tubes, your doctor may suggest painkillers for the earache and antibiotics to clear the infection. The middle ear heals over a few days and the child will feel better quickly. His hearing may take months to return to normal after an attack of otitis media, however it is treated.

If the infection doesn't clear up properly, the child may have a continuing discharge of pus through a perforated eardrum, mastoid infection (rare today), or a hearing loss. *Related topics* Earache; glue ear; nose drops.

Outings When you have children under five it helps enormously to have a structure to the day. The focal point of many days will be going out somewhere. This gives the children something to look forward to which in turn makes life more pleasant for everyone. It doesn't have to be somewhere fascinating to please the under-fives – the smallest outing properly 'sold' will be a thrill. The best outings have a goal but the goal needn't be child-centred. The under-fives can get pleasure out of going anywhere with their parents. Children old enough not to mind leaving their mother (or father) also get pleasure out of outings with people other than their parents. Grandparents, Sunday school teachers, other relatives, neighbourhood teenagers, play-group leaders and so on all have a lot to offer the under-fives and occasional outings with them not only let you off the hook some of the time but also foster your child's developing independence.

For the one-year-old a ride in his buggy will entertain him and expand his horizons. Don't forget to take nappies, food and spare clothes if you're going away for any length of time. As soon as your child can walk he'll want to walk some of the way on his outings, even if he spends most of the time in his buggy or pushchair. The more he walks, the longer the outing will take and the shorter the distance you'll cover. Highly successful outings may take you as little as a hundred yards!

At two your child will enjoy more purposeful outings – to see something or someone. A trip to the ducks on the pond, the bus station, the fire station, a shop, a friend or neighbour and so on are all a great adventure at this age but even now his staying power will be very limited. Outings are more and more interesting though because your child can collect things and will notice things that you have long taken for granted.

A three-year-old is full of curiosity and will be fascinated by almost anything. He may sit through a puppet show but will find it hard to sit still at the cinema. He'll like eating out and will start having ideas of his own for outings.

Four- and five-year-olds are a real joy to take out because they help plan outings and have masses of energy and interest. Fours and fives are reliable on their bicycles or tricycles and outings now take on a new meaning because they can ride while the adults walk. This means you can actually cover some distance which makes a walk more interesting for you. Few young children have the stamina to ride all the way on a walk, so be prepared to push the cycle some of the way without complaining too much!

Organized outings to the beach, zoo, museum and so on are bound to be rare events for most children and it's probably best that they are. They take a lot of organizing, are time-consuming and can be expensive. Most under-fives don't need this sort of outing often in order to have a great deal of fun and adventure.

As we have a lot of cold, wet weather, it makes sense to spend a lot of time out of doors on warm sunny days. If such a day comes unexpectedly, make the most of it and take your child on a spontaneous outing even if you'd planned to do the washing. A makeshift picnic in the park is all the more fun for being unexpected. *Related topic* Nature study.

Overfeeding The most difficult aspect of overfeeding is how to tell if you *are* overfeeding your child. If told by the child health clinic staff that your baby is putting on rather too much weight, it's simpler to cut down his intake if he is bottle-fed than if he's breast-fed. He'll probably still want the same amount of fluid to drink, but you can reduce the number of scoops of milk powder by one in each bottle you prepare, so giving him fewer calories. Don't add sugar or cereal to a baby's bottle in any circumstances because these will be sure to make him fat. If you're breast-feeding and your baby is reluctant to take less milk, you may just have to accept that he's fatter than the clinic staff would like. The only way to cut down his calorie intake is to allow him less time at the breast. It's preferable to have a slightly overweight baby than an unhappy one. You may be able to delay each of his day-time breast-feeds by half an hour or so, which would have the effect of cutting down on their total number. Don't do this at the expense of him crying, only if you can keep him happy in the meantime. Some experts think that it's a good idea anyway for a young baby to be plump, because in times of illness he'll have stores of fat on which to draw. If your breast-fed baby is plump he'll lose it quicker than a similarly-sized bottle-fed baby and is far less likely to end up as a fat adult than is a plump bottle-fed baby.

In an older baby who's having solids as well as milk, the simplest way of avoiding overfeeding is not to feed him high calorie, highly-refined foods. Anything containing fat is especially high in calories and should be cut down or out. Sugar gives calories with no essential nutrients and can be cut out completely. Ask your health visitor to go through your child's diet with you and advise you what to do.

Many one- and two-year-olds are getting most of their nourishment from the family meals and are also often drinking a pint of milk a day or more. This can be cut down if the rest of the diet is balanced. Milk is relatively high in calories and there is nothing in it that can't be supplied by lower calories sources.

Overfeeding your under-five may get him into the habit of overeating and this can stay with him for the rest of his life. Never use food as a bribe and don't praise children who eat up their food or ask for more. Learn about the calorie value of foods and work out well-balanced meals for your child that aren't too fattening but are nutritious. Come down firmly on the side of a high-fibre diet and eat the minimum of refined white flour and its products. A high-fibre diet fills a child up and reduces his appetite for sweet things. **Related topics** Dieting; obesity.

Overlaying It has long been held that having a baby in bed with you at night may lead to its death due to suffocation by overlaying. However, one researcher who followed up lots of reported cases of children being overlain found that none of them were caused by ordinary, healthy parents having ordinary, healthy babies in bed with them and lying on them. When babies or young children do die when sleeping next to one or both parents, it is because one parent is drunk or drugged and unable to respond to the child's wriggling and noises when he is lain on; because one parent is so grossly obese that the child suffocates under some of his body mass and the parent sleeps so soundly that he doesn't wake up; or because the child would anyway have died. It is possible that a baby might die from the sudden infant death syndrome when lying next to his parents, but some experts think that this is less likely than if he was in his own cot, because the wriggling that many babies do when they are short of oxygen after their heart stops would wake his parents lying by him, and they would then pick him up and so stimulate his heart to restart.

If as parents you are neither drunk, drugged nor obese, then it's safe to have your baby in bed with you and the only danger might be if he were to fall out of bed on to a hard, unprotected floor. *Related topic* Cot death.

Pain A mechanism by which the body lets us know that something is wrong. There are many different types of pain: dull, throbbing, aching, stabbing, gnawing, intermittent and so on, but young children rarely describe pains as accurately as this, though older ones can sometimes describe the nature of the pain. This can be very helpful to the doctor who can more easily make a diagnosis if he knows more about the pain. Many under-fives are unable to explain that they have a pain at all. Instead you may notice that they are generally unwell, pale, irritable, off their food, clinging and perhaps crying at the least thing.

Pain is a very difficult symptom in young children because it's hard to know how seriously to take it. (It's difficult enough in adulthood). Certainly young children complaining of headaches (especially first thing in the morning) must be taken seriously and any pain severe enough to make a child vomit or faint must have immediate medical attention. Any really severe pain with no obvious cause must also be investigated professionally as an emergency. Severe pains always have some significance, so don't ignore them.

The answer to the very real dilemma of pain and what to do about it lies in knowing your child. Most parents know when their child is complaining genuinely about something. Some children have periods of complaining of odd aches and pains, especially in the tummy. A physical cause is almost never found and however worried you may be about them, they are usually harmless and self-limiting. Abdominal pains can be of emotional origin in young children and others have repeated pains as a result of psychological or emotional disturbances. Some of these children are depressed and need proper treatment.

Pain can be a very difficult problem to sort out in young children and will always need expert help unless the cause is obvious. *Related topics* Abdominal pain; crying; earache; general practitioner; growing pains; medical examinations.

Painting A baby as young as six months old will enjoy watching others painting. He'll like to look at the bright colours as they go on to the paper.

When he reaches nine months or so, he'll try his hardest to reach for the paints and will put his finger in the paint and make a few splodges on the paper with your guidance. He'll probably put his painty fingers straight to his mouth, so you may justifiably feel that this is too young to start his artistic career!

From one on, you could let him start painting. Dress him suitably in a plastic overall (or undress him completely in summer if it's warm enough) and let him touch the paint. He'll examine his fingers carefully and then he'll go back for more. Show him how to put his whole hand down on the paper to make finger- and hand-prints. He'll like the colour and the texture of the paint and you'll find this finger painting is more successful if you make up the paint by mixing powder paint with water to which some thickener has been added. Use non-toxic wallpaper paste granules or buy a thickener especially made for the job.

As he grows older, he can start using a brush or other suitable implement to make marks on paper with the paint. It doesn't have to be a paintbrush. Try an old dish brush, nailbrush, sponge, feather, or dish mop, for example. Let him do drip painting – letting the paint drip off the brush on to the paper or actually flicking it off. If you fold a piece of paper in half after he's painted on it, you'll get a lovely pattern. This is called a smudge print.

Young children have short attention spans even for something as much fun as painting. You'll find that getting everything ready and clearing up the mess afterwards take far longer than the actual painting. Put newspaper or washable plastic sheeting on top of your table and if the floor isn't easily washable underneath, put it down there too. If you're thoroughly well prepared for any spills, you'll enjoy the painting session more yourself. When your child gets bored, the first thing to do is to take him away from the paints, clean him up and give him something to keep him occupied. Next, put his paintings somewhere to dry. Then take the paints and brushes away and put them in the sink ready to be dealt with when you have time. Lastly, clear away the newspaper or wipe the polythene and clean up any residual paint on the furniture or floor. Children get so excited when painting that the paint tends to go on the backs of the chairs, walls, hair and even sometimes yards away on the floor.

The right equipment will encourage you to let your child paint at home. Non-spill paint pots are cheap to buy or can be made by cutting a washing-up liquid container across two thirds of the way up, taking off the squirter, and replacing the cut off top by turning it upside down, squashing it in to the bottom upside down. Thick, stubby brushes will make bigger marks with the paint and will last longer for young children. As they grow, buy finer ones to give them more satisfaction. Use newspaper for very young children to paint on; save cereal boxes and cardboard boxes from the supermarket; ask around for supplies of old computer print-out; use lining paper or buy cheap white paper in bulk from educational suppliers. Coloured paper is fun but more expensive. Plastic overalls are worth every penny and you can make them yourself if you can find thin plastic by the yard. Older children can cover up with a plastic apron and plastic sleeve covers (tubes with elastic at either end). Four and five year olds will keep clean with a fabric apron or overall, though this will almost certainly have to be washed unless they are very tidy in their painting habits.

Most children enjoy painting. Don't criticize your child's efforts negatively but comment on them with interest and ask him what they are meant to be. If you do some painting too, your child will be enchanted and will enjoy doing it with you more than doing it alone, especially when he sees what it's possible to do with a brush and a certain amount of artistic skill.

Children's emotions are sometimes revealed by their paintings and some find it helpful to be able to paint because to some extent it can help relieve them of any worries or concerns just as painting can in adults. It's interesting to watch a child trying to reproduce a picture of something such as a house, especially if he isn't guided by you to produce a conventional house. Children's abilities to recreate what they have seen improve dramatically once they're three. If you can exhibit your child's paintings around the house he'll feel proud of himself and it'll encourage him to do more. Stick them on the wall with Blu-tack or on the front of the fridge or kitchen units where everyone can see them. *Related topics* Artistic activities; creativity; imagination.

Paralysis A loss of muscle power affecting one or several muscles that can be temporary or permanent. It is caused by one of many conditions affecting the brain, spinal cord or the nerves. Cerebral palsy is a common cause of paralysis in children and brain tumours can also cause paralysis. Polio is thankfully not commonly seen today. Spina bifida can produce paralysis of the legs. A child with a very painful condition may refuse to move a part of his body because of the pain but this isn't real paralysis.

Treatment depends upon the cause but most paralysed children need considerable ongoing care which can be very onerous for the parents. Such children are greatly helped by hand or electrically propelled wheelchairs, calipers, crutches and physiotherapy. With these and other aids many children can lead near-normal lives. There are also domestic aids such as lifts to get a child in and out of the bath and so on. Talk to your health visitor about what can be arranged to convert your home with help from the state and the local authority. An occupational therapist will also have some helpful ideas. *Related topic* Attendance allowance.

Parents' relationship Parenthood can enrich or ruin a couple's relationship and it will inevitably change it in several ways. While the children are very young, the woman becomes primarily a 'mother figure' and secondarily a 'mistress figure'. While her feelings towards her husband may be unchanged or even more loving, she inevitably has less time for him and is often tired. The natural urge to be absorbed in baby care is very basic and, while a woman may regret the fact that there isn't as much time for her husband as there was, her child generally takes priority.

His wife's pregnancy and the early days of having the baby around is a time of major adjustment for a man, especially with a first baby. He probably has to come to terms with the fact that he is solely responsible for the bread-winning now, and many couples have problems with their sexual relationship for the first time. If a woman is exhausted from broken sleep and goes to bed early every night, falling asleep as soon as her head hits the pillow, and if she is reluctant to make love even when she's got over the birth, perhaps because the baby always wakes at the wrong time, or because her episiotomy scar is painful, her husband may honestly believe that she has gone off him. His sleep may be broken at night too. Having and looking after children is an inherent part of a woman's sexuality. During the years when her prime role is being a mother, she gets a lot of physical contact with her children and may not need to cuddle her husband so much. He still needs physical affection though, and even if they still have intercourse as often as before the baby, he may feel deprived of love and basic physical contact. If he is emotionally unprepared for these aspects of parenthood, he may not be able to cope with the change in lifestyle which accompanies the arrival of the baby. It's no wonder that marriages are so often broken within a year after a baby arrives. The stresses are too much for some couples to cope with.

What is often needed is not only someone to help the mother in the early days but also someone to look after the father, because he can all too easily be neglected, both emotionally and practically. Some men react to this neglect by turning away from their families and finding company, friendship, and relaxation outside the home. Help and support for families with young children is often hard to come by in our society, but if both husband and wife are at least aware that each has to make major adjustments to becoming a parent, they can to some extent help and support each other.

Couples tackle their new situation in different ways. Probably the majority try to make their life as much like it used to be as possible. This can work out all right but it can also lead to problems because lots of babies don't need as much sleep – by day or night – as their parents had expected and don't submit readily to being put to bed to give their parents time alone in the evening and at night.

Other parents find it easier to include the baby in their relationship to make a threesome. This gets over the 'problem' of the baby being there most of the time – if you're not trying to stop it, you don't worry about it. This acceptance of the baby as having a perfect right to be there seems to go hand in hand with a greater maturity of parenting and some of the new situations it brings. Because these parents aren't always worried about whether or not the baby is going to wake up and disturb them, they can relax and enjoy each other more, besides taking pleasure in getting to know their baby together.

There are no hard and fast rules about what happens to a couple's feelings for each other when they have children because so much depends on their personalities and expectations. Probably lots of people would benefit from being better prepared for having children though. Many rarely discuss what having children has done to their feelings for each other. Admitting that the children had thrust them apart would be like admitting that having them was a mistake, and people are notoriously reluctant to admit to mistakes, especially over something as basic as having children. Perhaps it would be helpful if, as an adjunct to the normal antenatal relaxation classes, there were discussion groups on parents' feelings as well as what it is really like to be parents. Maybe then some of the myths could be blown up and society's expectations would slowly change.

As children grow past babyhood, most parents find that they are more effective as parents if they pull together, teach their children the same moral code and back each other up when it comes to guiding the children in their behaviour. Inevitably parents have differences in their ideas and it's essential that these are discussed. Many couples have a hard struggle as parents because they allow their opinions to push them apart, not to enrich each other's attitudes.

One criticism of a 'child-centred' approach to child rearing is that the mother inevitably becomes so one-track minded that her relationship with her husband takes a permanent back seat, and fathers can fall into this trap too. It takes two mature, capable and loving people to juggle the needs of everyone in the family so that each has a proper share of attention, love and time, but it is possible. Parents and children all have needs but, overall, children are much more vulnerable. A child-centred approach to child rearing ensures that the children are given as much care and love as they need in order to flourish. At the same time, the parents are well aware that if they too enjoy life, this will reflect on the children and make them happier. Parents with a good relationship try hard to help each other find time to do the things they enjoy.

Having children doesn't mean that you're finished as a person, your only use being to raise the children until they are independent of you, when you can wither away quietly in a corner. The experience, wisdom and maturity you can gain as parents contributes to that gained in other areas to make you a valuable member of society. The parent-child relationship is never quite lost, though it changes with time. If you become so child-centred that you lose sight of yourself, become dull and uninteresting to each other, boring to your children when they are older, and no fun to be with for your friends, you're doing no one a good turn. No one should live their lives through their children. If you find that you have nothing to look forward to when you wake in the morning, nothing that gives you pleasure, then your life needs rethinking. Living unselfishly is fine but not if it's going to turn you into a boring zombie with no fun or interest in life and a deteriorating marriage.

A poor relationship between his parents can not only make a child unhappy but can also cause him to be emotionally disturbed in the long term, especially when other problems arise in his life. Constant rowing, nagging and dissatisfaction with each other even despite good physical care of the children in a family, and lots of sensitive one-to-one attention and affection from parent to child, cannot be good for the emotional security of a child.

Any unhappiness in the parents is bound to reflect on their child to some extent. Most children are well aware of their parents' feelings for each other and are delighted at outward signs of affection. They are correspondingly upset by friction. However quiet parents try to be when arguing, the children almost always know they are doing it and feel unhappy until the air is cleared. It's important for this reason to let your child know that you have made it up after a quarrel.

The way a father treats his wife and vice versa influences to some extent the way their children treat their future partners.

Children of an unhappy marriage are likely to adjust poorly to marriage themselves and are more likely to get divorced, while mutual respect, concern and care for each other teach the children valuable qualities for when it's their turn to be parents.

Happy parents, secure and content in their feelings for each other, provide a secure emotional background for a child's emotional development. The inevitable occasional disharmony is accepted for what it is and the child learns that although people don't always get on with each other, they can find ways of solving their problems. Against this stable background, any problems he encounters are more easily coped with than if he had the additional burden of parental disharmony to bear. It can be a real burden for a young child who may wrongly believe that he or the other children are in some way to blame for his parents' unhappiness.

Research into unhappy or disrupted homes has found that the children are more likely to become teenage mothers; to have illegitimate children; to have unhappy marriages; to get divorced; to have two children born within a year; and to spend less time interacting with their babies.

It has also been found that even though a child is more unhappy and disrupted immediately after the divorce of his parents, two years later he shows significantly less disturbance than those children who remain in intact homes with continuing parental conflict.

However, even with the most terrible parental relationship and the most stressful experiences, some children manage to come through their childhood unscathed and with apparently healthy and stable personalities. This is likely to be due to a combination of their own capable personalities together with perceptive, good parenting. *Related topic* Divorce. *Useful organization* The National Marriage Guidance Council.

Paronychia (whitlow) An infection (usually bacterial) in the skin

around a nail. A paronychia is most commonly seen around an ingrowing toe nail which can happen if the nail has been cut poorly, leaving a spike at the edge, and in children who wear shoes or socks that are too tight. A baby can get an infection if he sleeps on his tummy with his feet turned out or even if his stretch suit is too tight on his feet. The pressure of the feet against the sheets or material pushes the skin on to the nail and infection invades the broken skin. Children who bite their nails or hangnails are more prone to getting a paronychia.

The secret is to catch such an infection early. As soon as the area becomes red and inflamed put a hot, wet pad of cotton wool or something similar on it. Repeat this process several times a day and keep the area clean and dry in between. If this treatment doesn't work, see your doctor who will probably give you an antibiotic cream. A very few of these infections go on to become really deep-seated. Surgical drainage may then be needed and the nail could even have to be removed to let the pus out if it doesn't point to the skin surface.

Monilia (the fungus that causes thrush in the mouth) can also cause a smouldering infection around a nail. There is little pus but the nail may break off and become ridged and misshapen. A child with this condition is usually a finger or thumb sucker and gets it from an inapparent infection in his mouth (see also Moniliasis). It is ideally treated by stopping the child from sucking his thumb or finger and by applying special anti-monilial ointment, but unfortunately it is often very difficult if not impossible to break such a comforting and pleasurable habit and the child sucks the ointment off very quickly, so a monilial paronychia in a thumb sucker is sometimes a long-standing problem. Any mouth infection should be treated, though if the child continues sucking his thumb, the infection may be passed backwards and forwards between mouth and thumb.

If ever your child gets an infection around a nail, see your doctor unless it is really trivial. *Related topics* Moniliasis; nail care.

Patch test A skin test used by doctors to try to find which substances a child is sensitive or allergic to. The suspect substances are applied to the skin on small pieces of blotting paper and held there with sticking plaster. The patch is left there (on the arms, thighs or back) for forty-eight hours unless there is a severe reaction before this, when it is obvious what the result is. If the child is allergic to one or more of these substances the skin will redden or in severe cases blister where it is in contact with the substance.

Patch testing is of limited value because there can be false results and if the result is negative it doesn't rule out the possibility of an allergy to that substance. It is especially unreliable when testing for food allergies. In spite of this the test is widely used and sometimes gives helpful results. The parents can then eliminate the offending substance from the child's environment. *Related topic* Allergy.

Paternity leave Although maternity leave is so widely accepted, time off from work for a father immediately following the birth of a new child is not. Paternity leave isn't a statutory right in Britain but some companies operate a scheme under which new fathers can take off a variable amount of time after a birth. Many other firms have no formal agreement but simply let the man have a few days off and many men just take some holiday. Certain other countries fare rather better. In France, for example, either parent can take up to two years' special leave and be sure of getting their job back.

With the shrinking of family size and the disappearance of the extended family it really is almost essential for a new father to take some time off unless a close relative can come to stay and help. This is especially important as many women do not now stay ten days in hospital and so need a lot of looking after when they get home. Most women spend the first week or ten days after the birth in or around bed and cannot be expected to do household jobs at all during this time. If a woman does overdo it, she'll get very tired, will be more likely to have breast-feeding problems, will take much longer to get back to normal physically and will be more likely to develop a prolapse of the womb later in life.

By being around to help look after his wife, new baby, the home and other children, the father can enjoy playing an active and important role in such a major life event. He'll also have a chance to get to know his new baby better than if he was at work as usual. Because she is given a chance to relax, his wife will be able to spend her time looking after her baby and forming a good relationship with him.

Perinatal mortality A term used to describe the number of babies stillborn after twenty-eight weeks of pregnancy and those dying within the first week of life. The perinatal mortality rate is expressed as the number of babies that die out of every thousand that are born after twenty-eight weeks. In the UK the current figure is thirteen per thousand with considerable social and geographical variations around the country. Babies born to mothers over thirty and all firstborns are at greater risk. The UK has a relatively high perinatal mortality compared with other Westernized countries, mostly because of the higher incidence of spina bifida and anencephaly and partly because of the high rate of babies born too small. Unfortunately it's difficult to compare even within European countries because women in these countries tend to conceive at different ages and therefore are open to different risks. Also, there is more malnutrition in the UK. Undoubtedly improvements could be made with increased antenatal care and vigilance (and even pre-conceptual care), especially in high-risk groups of mothers. Such measures would also reduce the numbers of babies born handicapped, so the time, effort and money would be very well spent in these areas. Even so, it is possible that there are environmental factors in the UK that would keep our perinatal mortality levels above those of many other countries.

Having a baby today is much safer than it was even ten or twenty years ago. The perinatal mortality rate was 13 per 1,000 babies born in 1981 but in 1939 it was 69 per 1,000 births.

Periodic syndrome (cyclical vomiting) A type of stress reaction
seen more often in school age children in which there is vomiting,
sometimes a fever, but always recurring abdominal pains. It is also known
as 'cyclical vomiting'. Children sometimes get tummy aches for emotional
reasons, perhaps because parents in the West are so obsessed with how
much they eat and making sure that their bowels are regular. Potty training
is also a great event in many households. Perhaps all of this makes a young
child focus on his insides, and then when he feels anything there he calls it
pain.

On investigation of these children there is never anything wrong with
them physically but perhaps their normal intestinal movements are
especially strong for some reason which is as yet unmeasurable and
undetectable.

The attacks of the periodic syndrome come on and go away suddenly,
usually within a day or two, and the child is obviously unwell. This means
that he's less likely to be labelled as having an emotional illness than other
children with recurrent abdominal pains alone.

Making the diagnosis can be difficult in the under-fives because there are
lots of causes of fever, vomiting and abdominal pain. Plenty of drinks are
needed to replace the fluid lost by vomiting but little other treatment is
required. As it is generally agreed that this is a condition of emotional
origin it makes sense to look for possible emotional stresses in the child's
life and to reduce them. *Related topics* Abdominal pain; behaviour problems; dehydration; recurrent abdominal pain.

Peritonitis Inflammation of the lining of the peritoneal cavity (in which
the abdominal organs lie). In its acute form peritonitis can be lethal. Babies
can get peritonitis following a twisting or perforation of the bowel or it can
be caused by an infected umbilicus. Older children get it (as do adults) most
usually from an inflamed appendix.

The child with peritonitis is very ill with a high temperature, a rigid,
tender abdomen, vomiting and pallor of the skin. It may be necessary to
open the child's abdomen to find the cause for the peritonitis because if
untreated the child can become severely shocked and even die. If ever your
child has any signs like this, call a doctor at once.

Permissiveness One of the most difficult and confusing problems
many parents with young children face is how strict or permissive to be.
Many of today's parents were brought up fairly strictly by their parents and
some undoubtedly rebel against this when bringing up their own children.
To some extent this is made easier by modern society's easy-going
attitudes, but it throws a lot of decision-making back on to the parents.
When society's rules for children's behaviour were more clear-cut (children
should be seen and not heard, etc.) it must have been a lot easier for most
parents simply to go along with what was expected.

The greatest change over the last twenty years or so has been the realization (or acceptance) that children are people, have rights and ideas and can positively contribute to society (and family life in particular). This is in stark contrast to Victorian and Edwardian times when children were seen as chattels who, whowever much their parents loved them, had little or no say in the family.

This century has seen several changes of fashion in attitudes towards child discipline and no doubt we shall see others but because families are smaller and each child therefore more important, it is unlikely that we'll see children debased in the foreseeable future.

Unfortunately, the 'experts' have produced considerable problems over the years by suggesting, for some quite illogical reason, that it was possible to damage a child's personality by 'spoiling' him. This meant that you let babies cry, fed them on a schedule to suit you and not them, comforted them little, made them sleep alone, had other people to look after them if at all possible and generally made sure they didn't affect *your* life. There is a lot of evidence to show that the opposite type of behaviour makes for happier, more agreeable and less nervous children.

But you can't change society overnight. Most of today's young parents were brought up fairly strictly on matters of manners, sex, sleep, infant feeding, obedience and so on and they find it hard to do a rethink and bring up their children in a way which sometimes seems to go against such conditioning.

However, this is not to say that you should let children do whatever they like, when and how they like. Rather, to try to be more open, more tolerant of your children and more permissive to yourselves as parents. Permit yourself to enjoy your children, especially when they are very young. Discipline is essential, but can be achieved in a loving way. The parent whose only response to a naughty (by his definition) child is to hit him often realizes in his heart that this is a pathetic way of tackling the problem. A child treated like this will be highly likely to behave in exactly the same way as an adult to his own children. The constructive, loving guidance sort of discipline achieves better results and is much more pleasant for all the family.

Being permissive doesn't go hand in hand with letting your children rule you. Children like to have guidelines for their behaviour and like to know that any unacceptable behaviour will be checked. Complete permissiveness of course leads to chaos because young children haven't the breadth of experience to behave in a way that is acceptable to themselves, other members of the family and the society in which they live. However, children do appreciate flexibility and while some rules must never be relaxed (such as not running into the road), others can often be bent a little when applicable.

It's all too easy to get into the habit of saying no to children without properly thinking through why you're saying it. If your child wants to do something and your immediate reaction is to forbid it, take the time to consider the request and to explain why you've refused it. Sometimes on reflection you might change your mind and there's nothing wrong with that. It's better for a child to know that you've thought about his request than for him to think you've dismissed it out of hand.

As children grow they learn their parents' moral code and as they grow older still they adapt this into their own code. Remember though that young children have to learn what is right and wrong – they don't know this instinctively – and that it's senseless to be angry with them for taking something that belongs to someone else, lying, cheating, or being unkind before they really understand what they've done and why it's unacceptable. If he's old enough, the child should have it explained to him why he mustn't behave like that and it should be made clear to a child of any age that such behaviour is unacceptable. Repetition is the order of the day when teaching young children and it may take many attempts at explanation before a child finally realizes what he can and can't do, and the rationale behind this.

Being allowed to find out about the world and to explore goes together with constructive permissiveness. We've probably all known children who were so caged in that they weren't allowed to do anything that children of their age naturally want to do. However much freedom you allow your children, though, it makes sense to help them understand that the world doesn't revolve around them. They ought to grow up learning to consider everyone else's feelings too. Encourage your children in their natural interest and enthusiasm, but don't let them ride rough-shod over others.

Allowing your child a full rein means letting him make some mistakes. Obviously there are many times when you can't let him charge ahead, but often it's possible to let him learn by himself and only to intervene if he is obviously frustrated by his inability to do something or if he is going to hurt himself or someone else. *Related topics* Discipline; provocative behaviour.

Personality The sum total of all the behavioural and mental characteristics by which an individual can be recognized as being unique.

From birth onwards, each baby has his own personality. Anyone experienced with babies (their own or others') comments on their different temperaments and behaviour patterns which show up as differences in feeding, sleeping and even in the amount of physical activity such as kicking. Even before birth a mother may say that her baby feels quite different from others she has carried.

The way a baby responds depends not only on his inborn personality but also on the way he is treated. The way he is treated will in turn affect his developing personality, because personality isn't a stable, unchanging thing – it alters as a child grows, as a result both of his age and his experience. An 'easy' or 'good' baby is commonly accepted as being one who regularly sleeps for a long time between feeds; feeds according to a regular pattern; takes his feeds well; adapts to different circumstances easily; doesn't cry much; and gives up his night feeds early.

However, such a baby is simply showing signs of a different type of personality from one who is irregular in his sleeping and feeding patterns.

carries on wanting night feeds for a long time, is put out by changes in his daily life, has feeding problems and cries a lot. This type of baby isn't 'bad', and even though his parents might consider him difficult it's more helpful to think of him as different, just as adults are different from each other. We all know people who are placid and easygoing, who smile their way through life and get on with people well, who are regular in their ways and yet adaptable in times of upheaval. Similarly, we all know those who are the opposite. We may like people from either group and their personality doesn't make them good or bad, simply different. At first, though, parents (and especially first-time parents) are inexperienced in their role, and a baby who is regular, adaptable and seems to enjoy life is easier to look after and is therefore more attractive to them. This in itself affects the baby's developing personality and a cycle starts to develop: the baby is easy and smiles, so the parents are pleased with him, demonstrate greater affection and smile more. He naturally enjoys the attention, so he smiles more and carries on behaving as he has been. Contrast this with what happens with a 'difficult' baby whose parents are baffled by his irregular, easily disturbed, easy-to-cry behaviour. They treat him perhaps less as a person and more like an object to be coaxed into their idea of what he *should* be doing. They become anxious and feel unconfident in his management; their anxiety and unease are sensed by the baby who reacts by becoming more irregular and crying more.

Rather than expect a baby to behave in a predetermined way, it's best to follow his desires and behaviour patterns, especially in the early days. Let him breast-feed as often and for as long as he likes – the irregularity of his feeding pattern can be coped with easily if it's what you expect. Accept the fact that you'll never know when or for how long he's going to sleep. Give him plenty of one-to-one attention, affection and physical contact even if he isn't always responsive. By doing all this, he'll cry much less and that'll make you feel better towards him. As he grows older, your praise and encouragement will help him feel he's 'good' and even 'easy', though you may not have thought he was as a baby.

You have an important influence on your baby's developing personality from babyhood onwards, but you can't form his personality.

As your child grows, you'll notice personality characteristics emerging and these will affect how you look after him and relate to him. His overall degree of activity, his regularity of habit, his moods and the way he expresses his emotions, his adaptability, levels of persistence, and amount of confidence with new people, situations and things all interplay with each other and make up his own individual personality.

You'll know your child better than anyone else, so you can help him throughout his childhood in a way no one else can. Never apologize for his personality traits or criticize him in front of others, but explain his behaviour if necessary. If your child has personality traits which you think will cause him problems later, such as not relating to people easily, help him by giving him the opportunity to play with and get to know a few children well, and never put him into a situation in which he is made to feel abnormal or a failure.

The relationship you form with your child will be affected to some extent by the way your personalities react with each other's. Some parents know early on that they are going to have a clash of personalities with a child, but given that they are older and more experienced, it's up to them to minimize opportunities for clashes and to cope with them if they do occur. By helping your child fit easily into the family, you'll form a secure base from which he can relate to other people and situations confidently. *Related topic* Personality differences.

Personality differences One of the exciting things about bringing up a family is that one's children are so different from each other. Each has a unique personality from the earliest days. Even though you'd think that because they have the same parents they would be much the same as each other, each child in fact has a unique set of genes (unless he has an identical twin). Something parents also tend to forget is that they change too and as a result their children are actually brought up differently. Parents who had their first child in their late twenties and then a second and third in their thirties notice how differently they behaved towards the latter born children. However much we choose to ignore this, it definitely alters the outcome of our child rearing and will tend to produce children of slightly different character as a result.

Children also differ greatly because of their position within the family. Firstborns are especially different because they are 'only' children for some time and are the ones on whom their parents learn all their lessons, and often have most of their anxieties. Later children, brought up more confidently, and with older siblings, are bound to have different personalities, even if they were born the same to start with, which they aren't.

Unfortunately, some children have personalities that clash with those of their parents and this can be a very real problem. The responsibility to make the situation work must rest on the parents – after all they are the adults, have the experience of the world and life and simply have to make the running. No under-five can modify his personality to suit his parents so they have to meet him with love and affection and overcome the problems. Fortunately, the under-fives are not usually riddled with personality problems – these develop later if they are going to, especially if the parents' behaviour causes existing difficult personality traits to become magnified so that they become a part of the child's normal behaviour. There is little point in trying to impose your personality on that of a young child. You can't do it, and even if you were to succeed, the cost in human terms both then and later in life would be unacceptably great.

Every child has a right to develop to the best of *his* potential and we can't and shouldn't try to force a child into some preconceived mould. *Related topics* Only child; personality.

Perthes' disease A softening of the upper end of the thigh bone (femur) producing pain in the hip and a limp. It is commonest in boys and can occur at any age between three and ten. The cause is not known but often there is a history of hip injury. The pain isn't severe and disappears with bed rest. The child is otherwise perfectly well.

Treatment involves immediate bedrest with traction on the limb and later a plaster or calipers so that the hip does not have to bear any weight for a long period.

Petroleum jelly (petrolatum) A gelatinous, translucent jelly obtained from petrol. As a medical lubricant it can be used on a burn (to prevent a dressing from sticking), on a young child's anus (opening of the back passage) if he is constipated, and on the skin of a baby's bottom to prevent nappy rash. Petroleum jelly has no medical or healing properties but is simply a lubricant and waterproofer. If applied to an already rashy bottom it probably delays healing.

Pets The main thing about buying a pet is to make sure that it is suitable for the situation it will have to live in. The size of the animal and its needs for exercise are two important factors because no under-five can walk dogs or be expected to clean out a guinea-pig cage. This means that pets for the under-fives have to be managed by parents – a reason why many parents with under-fives put off buying a pet. The child will certainly enjoy the pet but he could also tire of it very quickly.

It isn't ideal to get a pet at the same time as a new baby because there'll be quite enough for everyone to do without the extra work of a pet but any time after a baby's first year a pet can be fun for all the family.

Once you have a pet it can be a good source of learning as well as pleasure for a child. He'll learn to have a sense of responsibility for the animal when he sees that it depends on people for its care. Pets also give a young child an opportunity to see mating and birth at close quarters and in so doing to learn about these matters slowly and naturally. Also, when pets die he'll learn a little about life and death. Most of all, though, the child will have something of his own to lavish his affections on and to talk to when upset.

The vast majority of pets don't produce any illnesses in the children who keep them but it makes sense to have an animal checked over by a vet before taking it home.

Fleas are fairly common in cats and dogs, but can be controlled. If your pet scratches himself a lot, take him to the vet.

Don't allow animals to lick your children's mouths or your children to kiss them.

Worms can be passed to children via dogs' or cats' bowel motions. While it's reasonable to assume that virtually all puppies are born with round-worms (Toxocara), by six months only twelve per cent still have worms. Worm eggs passed in the bowel motions can live in earth or dust for a long time. Worm your puppy or kitten regularly, according to your vet's instructions. Don't wait until there are signs of worms (weight loss in spite of a large appetite) but make worming a routine. Your vet will advise frequent worming from a few weeks old. As your dog grows, worming medicines can be given less often. Kittens and adult cats need worming regularly too. Twenty-five per cent of grown cats have worm eggs in their bowel motions. Train your dog to open his bowels in a part of the garden away from where the children play.

Some children are allergic to certain animals, often to the mites in their coats. This can usually be overcome by washing the animal in a suitable solution several times to get rid of the mites..

Toxoplasmosis is a protozoal infection that can produce congenital abnormalities in a baby born to a mother who has the illness in pregnancy. It is spread by infected cats and poorly cooked meat. It's sensible for pregnant women to avoid handling cat's litter and to cook meat thoroughly.

With these few precautions and general common sense the average pet causes few – if any – problems to young children and can be a source of enjoyment for years. *Related topics* Fleas; scabies; toxocariasis, toxoplasmosis.

Phenylketonuria A condition affecting one in 10–15,000 babies caused by a deficiency of the enzyme that converts the aminoacid phenylalanine to tyrosine. Harmful breakdown products of phenylalanine can damage the developing brain if the disorder is not spotted in the first few weeks of life and can cause cataracts and mental retardation.

All newborn babies have a blood test (the Guthrie test) done on blood taken from a heel prick between the sixth and fourteenth days of life. This may need to be repeated, to see if they are suffering from the disease and this helps prevent a vast amount of the damage because a child can be started on treatment before much harm is done.

Treatment involves putting the baby on a diet low in phenylalanine. A special formula baby milk is available and if phenylalanine levels are carefully monitored, some breast-feeding may be permitted as well. The special diet may be able to be relaxed when the child reaches school age, but when an affected girl one day becomes pregnant and breast-feeds, she should resume the special diet to protect her baby. *Related topic* Guthrie test.

Phimosis A medical term for when the foreskin is attached to the head of the penis and thus unable to be pulled back. As it can be normal for a boy's foreskin to be attached to his penis tip until the age of three or so this is a word that can't sensibly be used before that age. A boy whose foreskin can't easily be retracted by the age of four or five may need medical attention for this so-called 'phimosis' but very often this will not mean that circumcision is necessary. Don't worry about your son's unretractable foreskin but simply clean what you can easily get to. Incidentally, a boy will (or won't) play with his penis just as much whether the foreskin can be pulled back or not. *Related topics* Foreskin; masturbation.

Photographing children
Photos are a wonderful way of reliving the past and can be a great source of enjoyment to all the family. Even a two-year-old will love to see photos of himself as a baby and old photos of his parents and grandparents are an endless source of amusement and wonder.

Try to keep a fairly consistent record of your children at all their stages – it's very easy to go over the top with your first and then to ignore the others. This is a pity for all concerned and you'll kick yourself later for it.

Never get children to pose – they hate it and you never get really good pictures. Go around with your camera on a good bright day as they are playing or doing something that is holding their attention. Quietly and unobtrusively click away and you'll get lots of lovely pictures. The secret of taking successful photos of children is to take lots of them – this is especially so if you're looking for something better than a snapshot for a particular purpose. If you reckon on getting one or two really good pictures per roll of film you won't be disappointed. Always take pictures out of doors if possible because the flash indoors is too distracting for little children who then start to behave atypically. Get down to the child's head level when shooting – don't stand up.

You'll never get good pictures if your child doesn't want you to photograph him. Try again another day or you'll waste your money and end up frustrated with the child.

These guidelines apply even more when making cine films or videos of your children because movies are more demanding and expensive.

Physical handicap
Some children are born physically handicapped and others acquire a handicap later. The commonest types to be born with are cerebral palsy and spina bifida. Some cases are inherited and others occur as a result of a mishap during pregnancy or labour.

There has been considerable debate about what should happen to babies who are born physically handicapped. Basically there are two schools of thought, both within and outside the medical profession. The first claims that all life should be preserved at any cost and the second that we should make some judgements (as parents and doctors) to assess the individual child's future life and then decide whether or not to give every available treatment to help the baby to live.

Conditions such as road accidents, encephalitis and meningitis can produce physical handicap in a child who was previously perfectly well and this can be especially difficult for all concerned.

There's a lot that can be done for the physically handicapped today and special homes and schools are available for those who cannot be cared for at home. Many such children also have other handicaps such as hearing, visual, intellectual or emotional problems and these will need specialist care and assessment for diagnosis and treatment.

The care of the physically handicapped under-five is relatively easy because he's light to move and presents few physical problems for the family. As he grows, though, things become a lot more complicated emotionally and physically and the home may have to be modified to make life easier or workable. The Attendance Allowance may be applied for for a two-year-old who needs a lot of care. *Related topic* Attendance allowance; special schools. *Useful organizations* Centre on Environment for the Handicapped; Voluntary Council for Handicapped Children; The Disabled Living Foundation.

Pigeon toes (intoeing) A condition in which a child's toes turn in, and in which he may throw one leg around the other as he walks to stop himself falling over his own toes. It is most commonly seen as a child starts to walk. The commonest cause for this condition is an inturning of the foot and mild cases right themselves in time and with good shoes. A twisting of the lower leg bone (another cause) also rights itself as the child grows. Most children with intoeing get better spontaneously but if ever you are worried, see your doctor.

Play Play takes many forms in the under-fives. Early on parents play with their baby by talking, smiling, playing peek-a-boo and hosts of other games that involve only themselves and their baby. It's a mistake to think of play as having to be structured or having to involve equipment of any kind.

Play is increasingly important during the first few months for a baby as a time of social interaction with parents and other people and as a way of learning how things work, what they feel like, and what he can do with them. 'Learning through play' is an important aspect of a child's first five years (at least) and is the key to preparing your child for school. This sort of learning is enjoyable and makes a child want more. Through playing with someone else, he'll eventually learn to play alone and to occupy and amuse himself. His sense of independence and self-reliance will grow as a result.

Anything can become a plaything to a child who is in the mood to play. Unhappy children tend not to play and unhappy babies certainly don't. Instead, they withdraw into themselves and become apathetic and listless. A background of love and security makes for a happy child who will find endless opportunities to play. Play with things develops later into imaginative play which is fuelled by new and interesting experiences. Lots of play in childhood is imitative of adult behaviour – the child acts out what he sees going on around him and this helps him make sense of and come to terms with what adults do.

A child's play changes as he grows, according to his developmental stage and the experiences and opportunities he has. It's helpful to provide suitable playthings and to help a child develop his skills in play. If you know what to expect your child to be able to do, you'll know what to give him and what to do with him. Having said this though, children take a delight in having their parent or another adult playing with them whatever they do. It is the social interaction with a person to whom they are attached that is such fun. An older child of three or four can enjoy playing with a stranger but a baby of between six to twelve months in particular prefers to play with familiar people. When one- and two-year-olds play in the same room as other children, they tend to play alongside them, watching and perhaps copying, but always jealously guarding their playthings. The three-year-old will gradually learn to play *with* other children and to enjoy games requiring the cooperation of several people. His play becomes less and less self-centred.

Play can be fitted in at any time, while doing household jobs, gardening, even when you're on the telephone. By playing with your child you can show and explain things in a readily acceptable way. Talk as you play and you'll naturally gear your conversation suitably so that he can take out of it what he needs. Simply helping you to do chores is a form of play much enjoyed by young children and you'll find you can get more done in the long run by keeping your child happily amused and occupied like this.

It's interesting to consider several sorts of play. Physical play is much enjoyed at any age and is sometimes sadly neglected as a child grows older. A toddler revels in his new found skills of walking, getting up and down and being independent. During the next year or two he'll learn to run, climb, hop, skip, jump, ride a tricycle and later a bicycle, throw and catch a ball, and become skilful in the playground. He'll enjoy all this even more in your company, particularly if you join him in some of his games. All young children enjoy horseplay and rough and tumble games even at home in the sitting room – if you don't want them jumping on the beds and climbing over the furniture, tell them so from the beginning. Try to go out every day into your garden, the park, the playground, or just for a walk so that your children can get rid of some of their energy without feeling restrained. There is increasing evidence to show that adults are better tempered and less likely to be depressed and miserable when they have plenty of exercise, and children are probably no different.

Imaginative play is increasingly important to a child as he acts out his observations of the world around him and makes up stories of his own. His props vary from 'proper' toys used in his own way to old clothes, cardboard boxes and tents made out of chairs and a blanket.

Manipulative play teaches coordination and is usually combined with imaginative and creative play. Children enjoy toys made specially to put together and take apart (jigsaws, bricks, Lego, screw toys, posting boxes, stacking cups and so on) purely for the thrill of being able to do something themselves, though they easily become frustrated if they attempt something too difficult for them or if they are tired and lack concentration.

Creative play for the threes and under needs help and supervision from an adult, who'll end up doing a lot, not to mention the clearing up. Prepare any tedious stages of making something before your child starts helping you, so that he doesn't get bored, and let him do all the interesting and decorative bits. There are lots of books and other source materials to give you ideas of what to make with your young child and the materials need cost very little, especially if you're in the habit of collecting empty cereal and egg boxes, milk bottle tops and any other potentially useful rubbish (you can store all these bits and pieces in a large cardboard box ready for use), and if you have a well-stocked drawer of glue, brushes, Sellotape, adhesive shapes, split pins, glitter, cotton wool, odd and ends of coloured wool, beads, buttons, and all the other paraphernalia of creative play, not to mention supplies of paper of all colours (including black), crayons and paints, string and scissors. Scissors for children are safer if blunt-ended but you'll also need sharp ones for you to cut cardboard and other tougher materials.

Wherever children are, they need to play. Whether they're in hospital, on an aeroplane, visiting friends, or in the car, prepare yourself by taking suitable playthings. Even books nowadays can be played with: there are books with pictures to feel and pieces to move; pop-up books; books to colour in; puzzle books; and crossword books (useful for four- and five-year-olds if you help with the filling in).

Whatever *you* may thinks of a child's play, bear in mind that to him it is a very important business. Although your baby may seem to be doing very little simply passing a rattle back and forth to you, to him it's all part of learning what he can do and what seems pleasant to him. Children of all ages like simple toys best and you'll find that simple things are the things that get most use. A great mistake that many adults make is to over-complicate a baby's and young children's play. Let young children do their own thing. If they want to paint an orange sky or dress their dolls in strange (to you) assortments of clothes, let them; it's their game, not yours. Slowly a child will become ready developmentally for the toys *you* think he should like and will play with them constructively and in an 'adult' way. The time in between isn't being wasted. **Related topics** Climbing; creativity; dressing-up; painting; playgrounds; swimming; toys. **Useful organizations** Pre-School Playgroups Association; Toy Libraries Association.

Playgrounds Almost all young children enjoy going to a playground. A baby will like the ride in the pram or sling, can watch the trees, the dogs, the sky and the children playing and can listen to the birdsong, the dogs barking and the children shouting. If he gets fed up with sitting or lying down by himself, you can take him out, wrap him warmly if necessary, sit down on a park bench if there is one and sit him on your lap.

An older baby will like being pushed gently in a baby's seat on a swing, or you can hold him and pretend to let him slide down the slide. If you sit on a swing, a rocking horse or a roundabout with him on your lap, he'll thoroughly enjoy himself too. If you hold him firmly and talk to him a lot, he won't be frightened. Babies like it if you stand in front of them as they're slowly swinging on a swing (take care your baby can't possibly fall out though) and smile at them as they come towards you, or catch them, perhaps tickle them, then let them go again. Toddlers also love this sort of game but it can be more vigorous for them. Remember that a toddler will need to be pushed on a swing – he hasn't yet got the coordination to make it swing by himself.

Be careful with your toddler at the playground because he'll be eager to copy the other children but won't yet know his limits. Follow him everywhere to help him on to play equipment and to make sure he doesn't fall and hurt himself. Climb up the slide steps behind him at first and have another adult at the bottom to catch him. Even when he seems safe on slide steps, stand at the bottom just in case and run round to the slide itself as he goes down it to catch him if you are alone. Children sometimes get frightened half-way down the slide and try to catch hold of the side. This can upset their momentum and make them fall backwards or even tip them sideways. If they are wearing rubber-soled shoes and put their feet flat, they can tip forwards. Sometimes if the slide is damp, if they have bare legs, or if they are wearing certain sorts of fabrics, they won't slide down at all, and you may have to mount a rescue operation!

Toddlers like the look of climbing frames but frequently get stuck on ones the size of those in most playgrounds. Stay close to bale them out when necessary. If they climb up one and can't get down, go up after them, hold them firmly, make them let go of the frame and hand them down to another adult. If they're hanging from a frame with their arms and can't move on, tell them to let go and then catch them.

Roundabouts are one of the most dangerous items in a playground. Children can hurt themselves by trying to get off while they are going fast, or by getting their feet stuck underneath the edge while getting on or off. Some children feel dizzy and sick after being on a roundabout. Stay near your child when he's on one, and indeed wherever he is in a playground.

Older children are more adventurous but also have some idea of what they can and can't do, so they tend to be relatively safer than toddlers in a playground. Watch them on the slide because they'll try coming down backwards or forwards on their tummies, backwards sitting up, two at a time, and lots of other ways. Don't allow any children near you to be rough when on playground equipment – what starts off as horseplay on top of the slide steps waiting for the next child to go down can end in a dangerous push. If you are the only adult around, it's up to you to maintain law and order.

The best playgrounds don't have concrete floors, but they are also the dirtiest unless sand – which is expensive to maintain – is used. Grass doesn't stay looking good with lots of children jumping and running on it. All council-run playgrounds should be regularly maintained but do look at the equipment yourself and if you aren't happy with its safety, report it to the appropriate council office.

Many playgrounds, quite rightly, don't allow dogs in because of the hazards from their faeces. If you have a dog either leave him with a friend when you go to the playground or tie him up to the railings of the area and give him a good run before or after the playtime. *Useful organization* Fair Play for Children.

Play-groups Parents differ in their attitudes to play-groups: some feel
that their children get plenty of stimulation through their play at home and
have ample opportunities to play with other children and to relate to other
adults. They may feel that five is early enough to leave home and mother.
Yet others know that they cannot provide the play and social opportunities
provided in a good play-group. They may want their child to get used to
being happy in a group situation so that he doesn't find school too much of a
shock. Of course, going to school is quite different from going to a
play-group – there are different children and different adults and the place
is different, so play-group really only helps accustom him to leaving his
mother. A few mothers want to get on with a job or some other activity
when their child is at play-group and may use it for *their* benefit as a
child-minding service as well as or instead of for the sake of the child.

Many children, but not all, benefit from going to a pre-school play-
group. Some are ready to start at three, while for others this is too soon.
You'll probably have some idea as to whether your child could easily learn
to cope without you in a group situation with strange adults looking after
him. If he's already used to being away from you in the care of a friend or
relative, it may mean he'll find leaving you less traumatic. However, there's
a big difference between being with a familiar person whom he has known
for a long time and with whom he has formed a relationship and being left
with a stranger who has so many other children to watch that she can't give
him the individual attention he might need. A lot will depend on your
child's personality – whether he is naturally outgoing and friendly or shy
and suspicious of people he doesn't know well. Some children already
enjoy playing with others by the time they're three, but many more are still
at the stage of playing alone and are not used to being with a crowd of noisy
children all running around and enjoying themselves. Only you can make
the decision as to whether your child is ready for play-group and it may not
be an easy one. You might also make the wrong decision, so be prepared
for this.

In practice, what many mothers do is put their child's name down on the
waiting list for a play-group of their choice (usually the nearest one) and
then make the decision when a place is offered, which will probably be
around the child's third birthday. If you ask, you'll probably find that you'll
be welcome to stay with your child when he starts at the play-group. Some
mothers are happy to take the gamble of leaving their child the first time.
This works well with the occasional child who is outgoing, independent and
used to being left in such surroundings. It may take weeks or even several
terms before some children settle down to enjoy play-group, and every
play-group leader will recount stories of how some never settle down.
These children are best kept at home with their mothers until they have to
leave to start school, when they'll be that much older and more able to
cope.

If your child is developmentally ready for play-group, you'll find that
he'll gradually venture away from you to play and take part in the various

activities. A good play-group leader will tell one of her helpers to make a special point of looking after the child and trying tactfully to get him involved. It's best for the mother not to join in too much so that her child can get used to relating to the other adults there, though this doesn't always work. Perhaps the next time you go, you could tell your child that you'll stay for twenty minutes or so, then you'll go shopping and come back for him at the end of the morning when he's had some time to play. Don't be later than you promised and preferably come back sooner so that your child doesn't have to go through the agony of watching other mothers collecting their children first.

You may find that you need to stay with your child for a lot longer than one or two sessions. You could force a departure, but if he is too unhappy to enjoy himself while you're gone, there's little point in his going to the play-group at all! Ask the play-group leader how he got on while you were away and, if you can, try and observe him when he thinks you've gone, so you can tell whether he's moping or happily joining in. Most children enjoy going to play-group and are ready for it at some time between the ages of three and four. If your child doesn't seem to want to stay at all, don't be cross with him and certainly don't tease or taunt him. He's only very young and you're expecting a lot of him. The fact that other children manage it is quite beside the point – each child is an individual and if he wants to be with you, then that is right for him. Some mothers are upset at the loss of their longed-for free time from their child, but there'll be plenty of that when he's at school.

Good play-groups offer a lot to the child who is ready for the experience. Many have regular fund-raising activities and this helps provide some interesting toys that are outside the reach of most parents. The leader and her staff will be knowledgeable in all aspects of play and will think up some very creative things for the children to do. There'll probably be outdoor activities in the summer and if the meeting place hasn't a garden, the children may sometimes be taken to one of the mothers' houses or to a park for an outing (with your permission and with plentiful supervision, of course). Some play-groups have visits to interesting places and some even put on a show or take part in the local carnival. Play-group can foster a child's independence and sociability and is a very real benefit for many children and their mothers who would otherwise be very lonely. Mothers are often encouraged to help on a regular basis and can discover all sorts of ideas for play at home as well. Most children start off with a couple of half-days at play-group, but this can be added to as and when they are ready and places become available. A good play-group compares very favourably with a nursery school or nursery class and the 'learning through play' that is so emphasised by the Pre-School Playgroups Association suits many children better than the more formal methods of education offered by a school. *Related topics* Nursery classes; pre-school education; toddler groups. *Useful organization* Pre-School Playgroups Association.

Playing 'doctors and nurses'

Playing 'doctors and nurses' Young children love to do this and should be encouraged to do so because it gets them accustomed to the idea of hospitals should they get ill. They don't need commercially made nurses' or doctors' sets: any dressing-up clothes and equipment will do.

Children like to play doctors and nurses because it gives them an excuse to undress each other and to examine various parts of each others' bodies. It's up to each parent to watch that this doesn't go too far and to stop children digging things into each other's bottoms, ears, noses and so on. Also they have to be told they they mustn't give any tablets or medicines to each other when playing. How much you allow such games to be a voyage of sexual discovery will be up to you but at this age little or no harm can come of it. If you do have to prohibit some activities, do so gently and with a reason because you don't want your children growing up feeling bad or guilty about their natural curiosity over their bodies. *Related topics* Development – psychosexual; guilt in children.

Play in hospital Children who are in hospital for all but the shortest of stays need to have organized play or they'll become bored and will take longer to recover from their illness. Some hospitals have play specialists who are trained to understand a child's feelings as expressed through his play. After all, most under-fives can't express themselves in the ways adults can, especially on matters that are concerning them at such a time.

But play isn't only to keep children occupied and to enable the play specialist to get a feel for what each child needs – it's also a way for the child to relieve his pent-up emotions. After all, unless a child is very ill he'll still want to do many of the things that usually give him pleasure. Some enlightened hospitals have pets and allow boisterous games too. *Related topic* Hospitals. *Useful organization* The National Association for the Welfare of Children in Hospital.

Play-pens Parents have divided feelings about play-pens. Grand-parents, neighbours, friends – anyone who has reared children – seem to react strongly either for or against them. Well, should you or shouldn't you?

Of course, there isn't a pat answer and whether or not they give their money's worth depends entirely on the individual family and the needs of the parents and the baby. Millions of babies have been brought up quite successfully without play-pens so they are certainly not essential. Perhaps it will help to outline their advantages and disadvantages.

A young baby who can't sit alone may enjoy lying or rolling on the floor, or even pulling himself along on his tummy. If you are sitting with him or watching him as you iron, for instance, he'll come to no harm. However, if for some reason you can't watch the baby all the time then there's always the chance that your partially mobile baby may get into mischief. He may gradually move himself over to some small toy, piece of rubbish, or other object left lying on the floor, put it into his mouth and swallow or choke on it. He may move too near an inadequately guarded fire, if there is one. He may wriggle his way to the open back door and fall over the doorstep on to the shoe scraper. A playpen in any of these situations would be a help in protecting him from being hurt.

However, it takes little time to check that there's nothing lying around on the floor that he could hurt himself with; fireguards should be top of your list as new parents; and the back door can always be shut or his passage impeded with a small table in the doorway.

Another so-called advantage is that the mother always knows where her more mobile baby is when he's in the play-pen. However, babies usually prefer to be in the same room as their mothers, and there's nothing to stop her taking him from room to room as she goes round the house and shutting the door of each room they're in. Play-pens are sometimes used as just one more way of separating a mother and her baby, and 'knowing where he is' means 'not wanting him holding on to my skirt'.

Play-pens provide rails at just the right height for the baby learning to walk to hold on to. If he falls, he's unlikely to hurt himself if his mother has put a soft landing flooring in the pen. However, chairs and low tables are helpful for the learner walker as well.

Some play-pens – the lobster-pot types – are raised off the floor and are thus slightly draught-proof. However, warm clothes plus the thickness of a nappy mean that a baby isn't inconvenienced by draughts in most houses.

One advantage of a play-pen is that it gives a baby some protection against dogs who might lick his face or bite him. However, unless you have a pen with walls of netting, a dog can lick a baby's face between wooden bars. A biting dog shouldn't be in a room with a baby anyway, whether he's in or out of a play-pen.

Overall, play-pens are fine as long as the mother doesn't use them as a baby-minder by leaving her baby there with a pile of toys so she can ignore him for hours on end. Any baby showing signs of resentment at being put into a play-pen should be taken out at once, otherwise the play-pen may easily become a prison.

A play-pen should be stable and strong enough to withstand being pulled about, climbed on and swung on. Check the pen for protruding nails, splinters or safety catches which a child might learn to undo. Some play-pens fold flat or collapse for easy storage or transport. A few are on castors so you can push them from room to room. One sturdy metal travelling cot has retractable legs so you can turn it into a play-pen.

If you decide to make one, make sure its sides are high enough to stop a baby or toddler from climbing out and that there are no horizontal footholds such as a bead rail to enable him to do so. Vertical rods or slats should be close enough together so that your baby can't get his head stuck between them. Remember to make the pen with a base so that your child can't walk it along, or else make sure it is well fixed to a wall. A raised base means it can easily be used in the garden.

Pneumonia Inflammation of the lungs caused by bacteria, viruses, irritant fumes, inhaled vomit, a foreign body, or allergy. Bronchiolitis is a type of pneumonia seen in children.

A young child with pneumonia doesn't have the same sort of symptoms as does an adult. Young children may or may not have a fever, there is often shallow, rapid, grunting breathing, a cough (with no sputum coughed up), diarrhoea and vomiting and sometimes a stiff neck or abdominal pain. The diagnosis can be very difficult in children because tonsillitis, appendicitis and meningitis can all produce much the same clinical picture.

Many children with pneumonia can be treated at home with antibiotics alone but propping the child up in bed may be necessary to improve his breathing. Hospital is needed for only the most severely affected children or when conditions make home unsuitable. *Related topic* Bronchiolitis.

Pocket money Although pleasant and valuable for older children who can begin to value money and to look forward to buying things for themselves and other with it, children under five don't need or appreciate pocket money. By all means allow grandparents to give the children presents of money which can then be used for anything they want but most under-fives are too young to appreciate the value of money and so shouldn't have the responsibility for it. *Related topics* Generosity; gifts.

Poisoning The intake of substances which in excess can cause damage to health or even death. Poisons can be liquids, solids or gases and every year thousands of children poison themselves, sometimes fatally. The commonest poisons that children take are household cleaners and medicines. Gas poisoning used to be common but natural gas is non-poisonous, even though it has a smell. Children can die from poisonous fumes when clothes collected from the dry cleaners are left in a closed car, especially in the summer. Always keep a car window open in these circumstances.

Most households have several old containers of tablets and dozens of different toxic chemicals around at any one time so it's not difficult for children to find something poisonous to eat or drink. Many tablets and capsules look like sweets and they see adults swallowing them and think they can too. Obviously they shouldn't as even small doses of adult medicines can be very harmful or even lethal to children and babies.

In practice the average child who takes a poison of some kind ends up in hospital overnight and isn't permanently damaged in any way but the parents feel terribly guilty. Some experts believe that parents who persistently fail to take care that their children are protected from poisons are in effect child abusers in a subtle sort of unconscious way.

Prevention is the best answer. Go around your home and garden looking for trouble, then make some basic rules about how to overcome each trouble spot. Start by looking for poisonous shrubs, trees and plants in the garden. Children should be taught not to eat any berries though poisonous plants in fact rarely cause serious problems. Then go to the garage, laundry room, kitchen, shed and outhouses and look for any chemicals. If possible store them high up where children can't get them or lock them in a safe cupboard. Even bathrooms and bedrooms have potential killers in them because nail varnish remover, lavatory cleaners and some cosmetics can be lethal to a child.

Medicines should be kept locked away at all times and never left by the bedside or on the kitchen table. Any old tablets should be thrown away because they can be dangerous to adults let alone children.

If your child ever consumes any poison it's safest to tell a doctor or to call an ambulance because often you have no idea how much he has taken and a child can go downhill very quickly after poisoning. If the child is still conscious and cooperative ask him what he ate or drank and always take the container along to the hospital with you. If the child has stopped breathing, give the kiss of life and if he's vomiting put him on his side so that he doesn't inhale his vomit. Give nothing by mouth at all unless you are sure that the poison was a corrosive chemical in which case you can give a little milk if he is fully conscious. *Related topics* Lead poisoning; medicines; swallowing dangerous substances.

Polio An infectious disease that affects the brain and spinal cord. It is a viral illness that starts off like 'flu. About two thirds of all those who become infected get better and do not become paralysed. Other children are temporarily paralysed and subsequently recover but a few are permanently paralysed.

In a severe infection the child has a fever, neck stiffness, pains in the back and limbs, muscle tenderness, difficulty in passing urine, and general weakness. Paralysis then comes on with the lower legs being most commonly affected. Breathing can be affected but this isn't common. Without professional care the paralysed limbs can become deformed over the years.

Thanks to immunization polio is rare today in the UK but is still seen in many parts of Europe where British people happily take their families on holiday. All children should be routinely immunized against polio in this country by having three oral doses of vaccine in the first year of life followed by a booster at the age of five and then another on leaving school. If a baby or child is unwell or has diarrhoea he should not have the polio vaccine. *Related topics* Immunization; paralysis. *Useful organization* British Polio Fellowship.

Posture Most children's posture is determined by their genetic make-up but changes can be brought if the child is sufficiently motivated. Nagging a child is no way to do this but encouragement and complimenting him when he does works wonders. Children are good imitators and may well mimic a parent's poor posture, thinking it to be the right way to hold themselves.

Taller children sometimes stoop to make themselves look shorter than they are, and miserable and truly depressed children may stoop as part of their unhappiness. Helping a child stand erect and carry himself well will immediately help his self-esteem but until a child is almost five he won't be too bothered about such lofty concepts.

Potty training Every normal child eventually develops control of his bladder and bowels with or without training, and the only thing he has to learn is where to empty his bladder and open his bowels. Given that children learn by imitation to a great extent, it's quite reasonable to suppose that if a child has the opportunity of seeing other children and adults using the lavatory, then he'll eventually copy them. So, even with his parents doing virtually nothing, a child will become socially acceptable in this respect as soon as *he* is ready. The big drawback to this is that in the West, our babies and toddlers wear nappies, and nappies are difficult to pull down and up easily. This means that even if a young child wants to copy others and use the lavatory or potty, he'll be hindered by his clothing and may give up in frustration. His parents then either have to let him run around (in a warm house or in the garden in summer) with no nappy on, in which case there will probably be lots of puddles and messes on the floor as well as in the potty, or they'll have to intervene actively and start training or helping him use the potty or lavatory.

We've all heard of the mother whose baby was potty trained before he was a year old. We've also all heard of the potty-trained baby who suffered from a prolonged relapse a few months later. It's certainly possible to condition a baby into opening his bowels or emptying his bladder simply by sitting him on a potty, especially if you sit him down after a feed, when he's most likely to perform, and leave him there for a long time if necessary. However, because the baby isn't making a conscious choice and decision about using the potty, but is simply sitting there while his involuntary nervous system acts in a reflex way, he is learning nothing about real control of his bladder and bowels, and his mother will have to wait until he is older before she can really say he is potty trained. Sitting or holding a baby on the potty can lessen the amount of nappy washing you have to do, but that's all. The danger of this type of training is that unless the parents understand that it's not training as such at all, they may be annoyed with the slightly older child who doesn't cooperate when in reality such cooperation shouldn't be expected. Psychiatrists describe the neuroses that can develop in children and adults who were potty trained in a harsh manner, and there are some children who develop chronic constipation and even need hospital treatment because they are nervous about their bowel and bladder functions and their parents' attitudes to them.

Thirty to forty years ago, parents were frequently taught by the 'experts' to potty train early and to make sure that a baby learnt as soon as he possibly could that wetting or messing anywhere other than in the potty or toilet was unacceptable. This is why many parents today have their own parents or grandparents breathing down their necks and tut-tutting if the child is still in nappies at two, or even one! Although a harsh, disciplinarian approach can be harmful in the long term, very many parents do start early, manage well and apparently produce no problems for the child. The emphasis though must be on a calm and relaxed approach, with no pent-up emotions showing if there are accidents, which there inevitably will be.

Perhaps because so many people have heard of the possible damage that strict, early potty training can do, the fashion today is to wait until the child is much older before starting to train. Indeed, many children are still in nappies by day at two or even three, and when their parents do start to train them, they tend to become clean and dry very quickly. One of the reasons why this way of doing it is so popular today is because of the widespread use of disposable nappies and washing machines, which make it so easy to cope with nappies. Many people can also afford the luxury of drying machines, which speed up the process of coping with nappies even more.

However, although many parents may be content to carry on with their child in nappies for as long as seems necessary, it's worth considering that the child himself might actually be happier out of them. Most children are ready to start learning bowel and bladder control from about half-way through their second year – from eighteen to twenty months – and if you give a thought to what it must be like to wear soggy, cold or dirty nappies, you might decide that it's worthwhile starting to train then.

What makes a child not ready one day and ready the next? Of course, it doesn't happen quite like that. A baby or young toddler empties his bowels or opens his bladder automatically, with no conscious effort. His bowels are usually emptied after a meal, because the bowel muscles tend to contract when the stomach contracts to empty its contents into the duodenum (the first part of the bowel). His bladder is opened when it is full. An older child not only has a bigger bladder but can control its opening so that its elastic walls expand to hold more urine. Readiness for potty training depends on the volume and frequency of urine passed – obviously the larger the volume and the less frequently it is passed, the more likely it is that the child will be able to control his bladder between trips to the potty. If he is wet within an hour or so of having his nappy changed, he is almost certainly not ready yet, simply because his bladder is not sufficiently mature.

Readiness also depends on being able to recognize when the bladder is about to be opened or the bowels about to move as well as being able to control both. Only when your child can actually 'squeeze his bottom' by tightening the muscles around the opening of the urethra or back passage is he really ready to start using the potty. If he tries to use it before this stage, he'll have lots of accidents and may be so discouraged that he won't do it at all. As he grows older he'll learn to recognize when his bladder is slightly less than full and not so near to bursting. The urge to open his bowels is easier for a young child to control because it's easier to hold on to something solid than something liquid. (This is why children often have accidents when they have diarrhoea.)

Bowel control is usually (but not always) attained before bladder control. It can be very frustrating for the parents if a child is quite dry but prefers to open his bowels into his nappy, but patience will eventually see him out of nappies. Many children today are constipated because of a highly-refined diet, and if you are having problems with bowel training it's a good idea to check that your child isn't frightened to go because he has difficulty passing unnecessarily hard motions.

Although there are many tried and tested ways of potty training a child, the following way works well in most families and doesn't put undue strains and stresses on parents and children. This involves first introducing the potty as a toy at about eighteen months or occasionally earlier. Play with it and put water in it. Potties make good hats and trains as well. The aim of playing with it is to accustom the child to the look and the name of the potty and to make him like it! The next stage, to be introduced gradually and without undue emphasis, is to play at putting a doll or teddy on the potty and letting him do a 'wee-wee' or a 'pooh' (or whatever your family's names are for opening the bladder and bowels). If your child is used to seeing other members of the family using the lavatory, everything is made easier because you can tell him that the doll is doing a wee-wee just like mummy or daddy. If your child plays with other young children, then it's worth letting him watch them on the potty or lavatory as well, because the desire to imitate is very strong at this age. One day you can casually say to your child that if he likes he can do a wee-wee on the potty, and eventually, with no urging or fussing, he'll take the hint. Many children become frustrated at wearing nappies between eighteen and twenty-four months, and a mention that if they did wee-wees and poohs on the potty instead of in their nappies, they wouldn't have to wear nappies, often works wonders.

Once a child has first passed a bowel motion or urine in the potty his delight in filling the potty plus his joy in having your approval will make him want to repeat his achievement, and potty training is then well away.

This sort of initial training is best done at bath time when the child is undressed, or in the summer (if it's hot), when he can run around outside without a nappy on. If you want to train in the winter, it's worth investing in a few pairs of trainer pants because these are so much easier to pull down if you think you child wants to use the potty. When the plastic covering of the trainer pants eventually becomes hard and brittle, pull it off and you are left with a perfectly serviceable pair of towelling pants.

During the day, if you're lucky, your child will tell you when he wants to use the potty, though as we've said, many children will tell you after the event at first. With some children though, you have to watch carefully for other signs such as a sudden stillness or quietness, holding their crutch, a certain facial expression or signs of discomfort if the nappy is dirty. When you notice the sign, ask if he wants to do something in the potty and produce it quickly but with no fuss for him to sit on. Always keep the potty close at hand during potty training – you may even decide to have one upstairs and one downstairs so that vital seconds aren't lost. Even if he has already wetted or messed his nappy or pants, praise him for sitting on the potty and suggest that next time he could do it in the potty. Repeated and patient suggestions combined with a friendly, optimistic and encouraging approach are the order of the day when starting to potty train. Don't show disapproval when he does it in his pants or nappy – just clean him up in a relaxed way. Don't forget to praise him when he is dry and clean and when he tells you he's ready to go.

If a child shows no signs of telling you he's ready in the second half of the second year, don't worry – he's certainly not unusual. When he's two, try to introduce the potty in the way outlined above. Many children (boys more than girls) are not potty trained until well into their third year, and some take even longer, simply because they haven't enough bladder control.

There is another way of potty training that works – training very fast. If your child is physically ready, if he has good enough bladder control and if he is able to act on instruction, you can use a method that can have a child trained in a day. Many children are ready around about eighteen to twenty months, and the results seem remarkably good. Basically, the method entails concentrating completely on potty training for a period of up to a day. It works because it combines many helpful factors which tend to reinforce each other, such as imitation, lack of distraction, conditioning, repeated and frequent practice and being a pleasant social experience.

Only one child in a hundred is dry at night at a year old. Some children become dry at night before they are dry by day, but most gain night-time control after daytime control, and become dry by night some time between two and three years old. Boys tend to be later in becoming dry at night and accidents must be expected in both boys and girls for a long time, especially if they are ill, over-tired or upset over something. It's often recommended that children should be lifted when their parents go to bed and sat on the potty or lavatory but this doesn't work for lots of families. When a child is ready to be dry at night, he will be and there is no need to interfere. It's not unusual for four- and five-year-olds to wear nappies at night, though they may be totally reliable by day.

Potty training can bring its own minor problems. Any mother with a child recently out of nappies will tell of the accidents that have happened in shops or when out visiting. You'll soon get to know the local public lavatories or quiet patches of grass! Once out of nappies, children are reluctant to go back into them and it's probably wrong to show your lack of confidence by even suggesting a nappy or trainer pants for a trip out. The answer is to get your child to use the potty before every trip from the house and to visit the lavatory at frequent intervals if you're out for the day, in case he doesn't give you enough warning to find a lavatory.

Sometimes an illness or an emotional upset can make a child start wetting and/or dirtying his pants just as he did before he was trained. Patience, love and a lack of disapproval work far better than scolding or punishment here. Put him back in nappies if necessary and when he is better or able to give up acting as though he were younger again (which he probably did unconsciously to gain your love and attention or to attempt to make you like him as much as a younger or untrained sibling), then start training him again. He'll probably remember what to do very quickly.

Sometimes a child starts wetting or messing his pants after the birth of a younger baby, either through jealousy or from a desire to be like the baby in his parents' eyes and so get more attention. There is no reason not to bother to train a child because a baby is soon to arrive. Train him as soon as *he* is ready and then concentrate on making him feel valued, important and clever when the baby arrives, so that he doesn't need to seek attention in this way.

Some children are so pleased with their new-found skill that their trips to the potty become very frequent, which can be wearing for parents. The sooner you can teach your child to pull his clothes up and down alone, the better, though this won't be until around two and a half in most cases.

Many children, once trained, are keen to be completely independent and want to wipe their own bottom long before they can do this competently. Tact is essential here. Let them try, then quickly step in and finish off, otherwise things can soon become messy. Don't forget to wash their hands if they have wiped their own bottoms.

Accustom your child to using various potties and sitting on various lavatories from the word go, otherwise he may baulk at using unfamiliar ones when you're out. Whilst on the subject of potties, anything is suitable, though potties with rounded or flattened rims must be more comfortable than those with narrow ones. Musical potties, though gimmicky, may help, as may those which have seats and covers like proper lavatories. A simple potty is easier for your child or you to empty and easier for you to clean. As for the lavatory, some people buy a child's seat to fit on the adult seat, while others build a special step for the child to clamber up on. A simple but strong box is all that's needed for the child to step on. The average child soon learns to balance on the edge of the lavatory without falling forwards or backwards. The older your child gets, the more likely he'll be to want to copy the older children he meets at home or at play-group, and use the lavatory. Incidentally, many play-groups don't have a potty at all, so it's worth making sure that your three-year-old can use the lavatory competently before he goes. As for boys, a box to stand on will help get them to the right height and they'll soon prefer to pass urine standing up like daddy rather than sitting down, though there's no point in making this an issue.

Finally, remember not to compare your child with any other. Children vary so much as to when they're ready for potty training and it's in no sense 'better' if one child is trained before another. There's no point in causing anxiety trying to train before a child has the necessary control, yet both you and your child will appreciate him being out of nappies when he is ready. Only you know your child, so it's over to you. *Related topics* Bladder control; constipation; lavatory; 'milestones'; soiling; trainer pants; waterproof pants.

Prams A pram is a piece of equipment which provides a mobile place for a baby to be. It is by no means universally used throughout the world – many mothers carry their babies in some form of sling instead until they can get about on their own feet. There are lots of negatives to owning a pram. It needs quite a lot of effort to push a traditional pram and it certainly reduces a mother's freedom to a large extent because there are lots of places that are difficult for her to go to with a baby in a pram, whereas she can go everywhere with a baby in a sling. In department stores, for example, a mother with a pram has to use a lift rather than the stairs or an escalator, and she's likely to get in people's way in crowded areas. Swing doors are a problem (the best solution is to go out backwards yourself and then to pull the pram out after you, unless someone holds the door open for you, of course). You can't take the average pram on a bus or a coach, and it has to go in the luggage compartment of a train. Prams are difficult to take up or down steps and awkward to get through the front door if you have a front door step. They can't be used as a cot upstairs at home. Many babies are happier for longer periods of time in a sling than in a pram, especially in the early months. Having to push a pram means that a mother has only one hand to spare, for example, to hold on to another child.

On the plus side, a pram frees a mother from the weight of her baby, which may be no small factor with an older baby. It can also be used to carry heavy shopping in a special wire basket beneath, in a bag slung over or from the handle or in the end of the pram itself if the baby is very small – pushing a load is always easier than actually carrying it. An older child can sit on a pram seat fixed to the body of the pram (but take great care not to get an inquisitive baby's fingers pinched when folding a seat up or down). Some babies are lulled by the movement of a pram as it is pushed along and others can be rocked to sleep in a stationary pram. A pram is a useful bed for a baby or young child, though any child able to lift himself out must be harnessed in if he is left alone at all, and in it a child can be put near his mother, outside in the sun, in a shaded area, or in another room.

A twin pram is very useful for twins or for babies born with a relatively short gap. A parasol or a pram canopy can be fitted to protect a baby from too much sun, while the hood already attached to it protects him from wind, rain and snow. A hood or a sunshade may make a baby too hot. Most prams have a part of their base which can be pulled up to act as a support for a baby who doesn't want to lie flat.

If you decide to have a pram, first decide whether you will ever need to be able to separate the pram body from its transport mechanism. If so, for instance if you ever want to take it in the car, then buy a pram body with a transporter. This looks very much like a conventional pram except that top and bottom are detachable. Second, decide whether you are likely to want to carry two children at once in the pram. If so, if you want them both to be able to lie down, you'll need either a large ordinary pram or a twin pram with two hoods. If one child can sit up, then a pram seat can be used but you'll need to buy a pram with sturdy enough sides and overall structure to be able to support such a seat. Coach-built prams can certainly do so as can some of the cheaper strong ones. Find out from the shop which pram is suitable. If your children are relatively close in age, you may be able to manage without a pram seat and with one child at either end of the pram, though this can make them rather squashed and you'll have to make sure that the older child doesn't kick or otherwise annoy the younger one. The trouble with pram seats is that they're not very comfortable for a long journey and there is no protection from the rain. The child has to be firmly harnessed in for safety and many children soon get fed up sitting in one. Don't forget to find out whether the pram is easy for you to use. Check that the handle is at the right height, that the hood can be easily put up and down, that the brake is easy to operate, and that (if it is meant to) the top separates from the bottom easily and quickly. If the top (the pram body) is too bulky or heavy for you to lift easily, choose an easier one.

A new version of a baby buggy – the pram buggy – is now available in which the buggy base can be altered to take a carrycot (or light pram body). The top and the bottom are specially made for each other. When you want your baby to ride in an ordinary buggy, you can easily detach the pram top and convert the base into a buggy again. This clever design gives you the option of a carrycot, a carrycot and transporter (in effect, a pram), and a buggy. A twin pram buggy is available to special order. Such pram buggies usually have tiny prams, though, and a baby soon grows out of them. The other problem is that you can't get a shopping tray underneath because of the criss-cross frame.

After considering all these points, the final decision will rest on appearance and cost. On balance, the more expensive the pram, the stronger it will be and the longer it will last, so if you intend having two or more children, this is an important factor. The ride in a more expensive, better-sprung pram with larger wheels is smoother and quieter than in a cheaper pram, especially if it has a transporter base, but whether or not this actually makes any difference to a baby is not known for sure.

If you are buying second hand, you're likely to pick up a bargain, but don't buy the first pram you hear about because prices differ wildly. Some mothers need to get a good price for their old pram while others simply want to get rid of them. A coach-built pram can be painted to look smart again and the metalwork of any pram can be cleaned, derusted and polished as necessary.

Many mothers put a thick mattress into the pram, together with a waterproof sheet which stays smoother if it is fitted. Another sheet for the baby to lie on, plus enough warm, easily washable covers, and you have all your baby needs. Some mothers buy a small sheepskin to use in the pram either on top of the mattress (though that brings the level at which the baby lies rather high) or instead of the mattress. Sheepskins are warm and very comfortable to lie on, and specially treated ones can be washed easily. A pillow is unnecessary for a small baby, though some mothers like to have one in order to prevent their baby's head from rocking from side to side when he is asleep in the moving pram. If you do use one, check that the baby can breathe adequately when lying on it even if he is on his side. With a waterproof apron cover fitted over the bedding when the weather's bad, your baby will be dry and snug.

Once you have your pram ready for use, think about something for the baby to watch or play with if he is old enough. Some mothers stick adhesive pictures on the inside of the pram's hood or linings; others buy a special pram toy such as an elastic string threaded through coloured, plastic, rattling animals suspended between the hood levers. A woolly pom-pom or soft toy animal can be hung from the hood lever. You could make your own version of a mobile to be slung from lever to lever each side of the hood. When your baby is old enough to drop or throw his toys out of the pram, tie them on to the side so they don't get lost or dirty.

Don't forget to look after your pram: dry metal parts after a wetting if you want to keep them rust-free; let the hood dry before folding it down to prevent mould or rustiness; oil squeaks when necessary; check regularly that the brake works; and if you have to store it, do so with the hood up to avoid cracking. From the safety point of view, never let an older child hang from the handle because he'll tip pram plus baby up. A cat net puts some mothers' minds at rest when their baby is alone in his pram anywhere where a cat might jump into it. It's highly unlikely that any physical harm would befall him, but cats do like sleeping by warm babies and your baby might be frightened if he woke to find one very close.

Some mothers go on using a pram for their child until he can walk everywhere himself. Others choose a buggy or pushchair when he no longer needs to lie down and sleep. A pram gives your child the flexibility to be able to sleep in more comfort than is possible in a buggy or a pushchair, but it is bulkier for you to push around, and more babyish for two- or three-year-olds who may still want to ride but may not like the possible teasing from an older brother or sister if he goes in a pram. Most mothers who can afford it opt for the flexibility of having either option – they buy a pram and a pushchair, or the increasingly popular pram buggy which doubles for both. **Related topics** Babycarriers; bedding; carrycots; pushchairs.

Pre-conceptual care

Pre-conceptual care A few years ago if someone had told you to have a medical check-up before you got pregnant you would have thought it very odd indeed but evidence suggests that time and care spent ensuring that a couple are healthy before the woman conceives pays dividends. Today there are several pre-conception clinics up and down the country and the whole concept is no longer considered 'cranky'.

What happens at such a clinic varies considerably with the views of the doctors running it. Some feel that it is enough to talk to the couple about the proven dangers of drugs, x-rays, smoking and drinking during pregnancy, to check the weight and blood pressure of the woman and to discuss her diet during pregnancy. At the other end of the scale are those who feel that it is then that baby care begins and that the couple should be thoroughly examined and specimens of blood, stools, semen and even hair taken.

All this care and attention is important because it's in the very first few weeks of foetal life immediately following conception that a baby's organs develop. Any drug imbalance hanging over from before conception could adversely affect these delicate processes. Research has already found that one group of women (those with a previous baby suffering from spina bifida) benefit from vitamin supplements for a month before conception and new discoveries in this area may prove that other deficiencies could be remedied so as to prevent other foetal wastage, stillbirths, or deformed babies.

Some women become pregnant without knowing whether they've had German measles and then worry in case they come into contact with a child with the disease when they are in early pregnancy. At a pre-conception clinic a woman's immunity to the disease can be assessed and if it is low or non-existent she can have a protective immunization against it. She must then take care not to get pregnant for two months after the injection.

There is only one organization in the UK that devotes itself to pre-conceptual care – it is called Foresight and is based in Godalming, Surrey. It publishes a booklet called *Environmental factors and foetal health – the case for pre-conceptual care* and has started fourteen clinics where pre-conceptual advice can be obtained. Foresight recommends a visit to such a clinic six months before trying to get pregnant so as to allow time to come off the Pill, to establish a regular menstrual cycle, to clear up any reproductive infections and to come off alcohol and tobacco. Some doctors think this is too far in advance and suggest that three months is perfectly safe.

Whatever the pros and cons of early care, if you have a specific disease such as diabetes, high blood pressure, or epilepsy it makes sense to see your doctor before starting a baby. If you have a family history of an inherited disease you should discuss this with your doctor who may refer you to a specialist genetic counselling clinic. If you are over thirty-five your risk of having a baby affected by a particular type of Down's syndrome is increased and you may want to discuss an amniocentesis with your doctor. If you have already had one mongol baby the chances of having another are increased from 1 in 1,000 to 1 in 80. A woman in her early forties has a 1 in 60 chance of having an affected child and in the mid-forties this increases to 1 in 20.

Vaginal infections are not at all uncommon and it is known that such infections can reduce fertility in some couples. It makes sense to clear up venereal disease and other urinary and reproductive infections before conceiving simply because their impact on sperms and eggs is incompletely understood.

With 200 in 10,000 babies being born with malformations it certainly makes sense to ensure that everything that can be done to prevent them *is* done and this starts even before conception occurs. *Related topic* Genetic counselling. *Useful organization* Foresight.

Prescription A simple piece of paper on which a doctor writes the medications he wants you or your child to take. This is taken to the dispensing chemist (pharmacist) at a chemist shop or hospital to be exchanged for the drugs You'll have nothing to pay for the drugs if you are pregnant; are in the first year after giving birth, or if it's for your children.

Whether or not you accept what the doctor is prescribing on a prescription is up to you Hopefully you'll have a degree of trust and a sense of partnership with your family doctor so that if he prescribes a medicine for your child you'll be happy that he really needs it. If ever you're in doubt about whether it's necessary, do discuss the matter with him.

Pre-school education This is a very vexed subject and one on which parents often have very strong views. Some say that their children are going to be away from home for so many years that they want to enjoy them as much as they can in the pre-school years and others can't wait to get rid of them for a part of the day In between are those who feel there might be some positive benefit from some kind of pre-school education.

It's a fact that children are very eager to learn in their pre-school years. However, learning and curiosity can sometimes be encouraged just as well at home as in a formal setting.

One advantage of a nursery school or class is that it encourages the child to play and learn in a setting where there is good equipment and space to enjoy it. Trained leaders or teachers can also be of real value to parents as they can give an outsider's opinion on the child and his behaviour. The child also learns to get on with other children, overcomes shyness and becomes sociable more quickly than he otherwise might. He'll also become more confident.

Nursery schools or classes are for children between the ages of three and five. They are run privately or by the local education authority and have trained teachers who supervise guided play and informal lessons.

Many countries start primary education later than we do and their children are at home with their mothers for longer than ours. It is very rare that a happy, normal child will be ready to leave his mother before three.

Whatever the advantages of formal pre-school education, a child's basic education in every field is given by his parents or other main caretakers, provided, of course, that they take an interest in him.

Large numbers of parents feel that pre-school education should be carried out at home and there are lots of toys, games, TV programmes and even do-it-yourself education kits to help you. When buying educational kits do look carefully because many are overpriced for what they are and frankly can be a complete waste of money. Don't be taken in by advertisements that imply that your child will be backward at school if he doesn't do certain things before he goes – he won't.

Part of pre-school education is preparing your child for the school he'll be going to. To overcome any hesitancy there may be, start introducing your child to the school some months before he has to go. As you pass the building, tell him about it and see if you can take him around the school as a visitor. Never use school as a threat when he's being naughty and only ever put the best ideas about school forward when discussing it in front of the child even if you're not too happy yourself.

Try to find out who else will be starting at the same time and try to arrange for your child to meet others in his class and even possibly strike up some friendship before he starts. This will make the first weeks more pleasant for him.

Before he's five make sure he's ready for school in practical ways. Can he dress himself, cope with the lavatory alone, tie up his shoe laces and so on ? If he can't, ensure that he is wearing clothes he *can* cope with and shoes with buckles rather than laces. If he feels confident on his first day he'll like school a lot better.

When it comes to reading and writing, be guided by what your child seems to want to do. Some parents become obsessed with their children being able to read or write (or even both) before they go to school but there is no point forcing the issue. You could end up teaching a method different from that the school uses and this can confuse the child. If he reads too well he could be so far ahead of the others that he'll be the odd one out and will soon get bored while waiting for the others to catch up. Being able to write his name is a useful attribute when starting school but most children won't be able to write much at this stage and it doesn't matter a bit. *Related topics* Nursery classes; play-groups. *Useful organizations* Advisory Centre for Education; Pre-School Playgroups Association.

Prickly heat An itchy skin condition sometimes seen in babies and young children at the start of hot weather. Patches of tiny pink spots sometimes turn into blisters. The 'rash' is usually over the shoulders and neck and the little pimples are often surrounded by blotchy pink patches. Really bad prickly heat can spread to the chest and face but it is never serious and is often completely prevented by keeping the baby cool.

Prickly heat is caused by excessive sweating so the cure is to keep the baby cool, to soothe the area with calamine, to keep the child out of warm clothing when the weather is hot, to tie back his hair if it encourages sweatiness at the back of the neck, and to bathe him frequently.

Prolapse of the rectum A 'collapse' of the back passage (rectum) so that part of it lies outside the child's body in the crease of his bottom. It can happen in an under-five who strains a lot to pass his bowel motions and is also seen in children with cystic fibrosis. Although it looks alarming, don't worry because it almost always goes back.

The treatment is simple. First, prevent your child ever becoming constipated by ensuring that he eats mainly high-fibre foods and drinks plenty. When your child gets a prolapse lay him down on his bed with the foot end raised with books or blocks to about one foot. To put the rectum back in wrap your finger in a piece of lavatory paper, insert it into the prolapse and push the whole lot back inside. The paper will stay in there when you remove your finger and will be passed with the next bowel motion. If this doesn't work, call your doctor. Encouraging your child to use a lavatory rather than a potty can help prevent the condition in the first place as will giving him foods rich in dietary fibre to keep the bowel motions soft. *Related topics* Constipation; dietary fibre; lavatory.

Provocative behaviour

All children provoke their parents – it's a part of learning how far they are allowed to go and what happens if they go too far. From a year onwards children begin to test their parents by doing things that provoke a negative response. This is the start of a very important phase in the upbringing of your child because it's now that he learns about your ability to control him and the world around him. Many parents make a rod for their own backs by having such an enormous list of prohibited pastimes that the child can hardly move without contravening some domestic bye-law and so being accused of being provocative.

Even if you are being entirely reasonable there are still hundreds of occasions in a week when a young child will provoke you into an annoyed reaction. The main thing is to be firm and not to back down. Once you've decided that Aunty Flo's letter isn't to be torn up you must enforce your decision, perhaps by putting it somewhere out of reach if your child isn't really sensible enough to understand he can't have it. A child who is consistently allowed to wheedle his way around his parents after having first been told he can't is not happy because he can't see what is right and allowable and what isn't. This can make him feel insecure and guilty. Also, we parents have rights too and there's no reason why children should trample over our things and behave in a way that offends us. Being loving and reasonable to children doesn't mean that they're allowed to do as they please at our expense.

No one wants to have an upset, unpleasant, demanding child yet time and again one sees parents rise to their young child's provocation, not realizing that they're doing the child no good at all in the long run by giving in. There may be screams and tantrums for the first few times but pretty soon the child learns that these too don't work. None of this makes you a brute – you simply decide where the line should be drawn and stick to it. If you manage to stick to this for the first three years you're likely to have a pleasant, reasonable child who gets neither pleasure nor reward from provocative behaviour,

Occasionally you may decide that you will yield a little over a decision you've made which is against your child's wishes. There's no harm in this if it's done for the right reason in an attempt to be reasonable and accommodating, and provided it doesn't often happen. *Related topics* Attention seeking; discipline; permissiveness; temper tantrums.

Punishment

When you punish a child you do something unpleasant to him, often because of something he has done wrong. Punishment is universal, carried out in almost every culture and is an essential part of the discipline involved in bringing up a child. It's quite compatible with the 'loving guidance' concept of discipline that we favour and that works so well for young children.

When you bring up a child you are guiding him lovingly so that he learns to behave in a way which is acceptable to you and to the society in which you have to live. He learns how to behave through example from you and from others involved with him. He also learns by you telling him what to do (or what not to do). Sometimes he'll do something which isn't acceptable simply because he doesn't know how to behave. In this case all you should do is tell him or show him how you would like him to behave and no punishment is involved; it is purely a teaching situation.

Babies, once mobile, constantly get into everything and their lives are full of a series of minor misdemeanours such as upsetting a packet of detergent left on the floor, spilling the cat's milk, digging up your newly-planted seedlings and so on. However, simply being told that such behaviour is unacceptable won't teach babies not to do it again. They gradually learn how to behave by repeatedly being told not to do something, being taken away from it, having it taken away from them, by the expression on your face and by the tone of your voice. Most parents make their own lives easier by removing sources of potential trouble from their babies and toddlers, so avoiding the situations that provoke their anger or annoyance until their children are older and more capable of understanding.

It's always more pleasant for a child when you are smiling and pleased with him, so when he realizes that doing something which you consider wrong takes away your usual happy expression, he'll eventually learn that it's better for him not to do it.

As your baby grows older and begins to understand what you say, you can explain what it is that he's done wrong and why it is that you want him to behave in a certain way. The time will come when you'll react automatically to something your child has done wrong, and which you've told him not to do lots of times before, not just with a patient explanation but with a snappy voice and a cross expression. That will probably be the very first form of punishment your toddler has every experienced. And punishment it is, because he will almost certainly be dismayed or even cry.

You may upset yourself by getting annoyed, but accept it for what it is – a normal and spontaneous reaction. Do make sure though that your child understands why it is that you've got cross, otherwise an important teaching situation will have been wasted and your upset and his punishment will have been wasted too. For instance, if your two-year-old empties a packet of flour on the floor when your back is turned, when you've already put it out of reach and told him not to touch it, and if you are busily trying to make some pastry before you have to go out, the temptation is to look cross and to tell him he's a naughty boy, then to clear it up as quickly as you can. However, if you make the time to sit with him and explain gently that you will have to throw away the flour that's been on the floor and that that's a waste both of the flour and of money, then he'll realize that there is an important reason why he shouldn't spill the flour even though he may not fully understand what you are telling him. A four-year-old who's just spilt your expensive nail varnish needs to be told that nail varnish is an expensive luxury for mothers and not a pot of paint for children. If you just get cross, it'll probably be spilt again one day.

As your child reaches three or four, you'll sometimes be quite sure that he is being naughty and that he knows that what he's doing is wrong. The excitement or pleasure at doing whatever it is is probably so great that it overwhelms his conscience and he doesn't remember what he's been told many times before. You may feel that this is a time when looking or sounding cross just isn't enough. Parents react very differently in such situations depending on how they're feeling (perhaps tired, or in a hurry); what sort of a day they've had with the child (is it the morning with everyone feeling bright or is this the last of a series of troubles that day, making this the final straw?); their own personalities (phlegmatic, placid, or easily annoyed, for example); their overall relationship with the child (on the same wave length or often at odds with each other); the personality of the child (usually wanting to do the right thing or often goading his parents beyond the limits of their patience), on the sort of upbringing they had as children themselves (patient, gentle, lovingly guiding parents or quick to anger, impatient, or even harsh parents); and on the example they're set by their friends, family and acquaintances with their own children.

Children know their parents and how they are likely to behave much better than we think they do and they realize they can get away with a lot more when we're feeling fresh and happy – in the morning perhaps – than in the evening when we're tired and frayed. However, they too get tired and frayed sometimes and it's up to us to recognize bad behaviour due to this and to modify our reactions if we possibly can.

How you react in any situation where repeated explanations and your obvious displeasure don't seem to have any affect is up to you but there are some reasonable guidelines. Some parents react verbally, telling the child off in no uncertain terms. This sort of punishment has a variable effect, depending on how often the parent does it. If being shouted at is a common occurrence, the child will probably let it roll off his back, whereas if the parent hardly ever shouts, then he will thoroughly dislike it and it'll have more effect. This also goes for all other forms of punishment. Be careful not to let a telling off go on for hours! Some parents go on talking about the child's misdemeanour even after the child's been quite adequately punished by the initial telling off. Take care also not to shame a child unnecessarily and never belittle him or make him feel worthless. It's surprising how all kinds of unconscious feelings about a child can come out when you tell him off. You may always have thought that he looks like an uncle of yours, for instance, who you think is a cruel man. When your child hits another child, you may overreact because you see your uncle in him and you are partly terrified that your child will turn out like your uncle and partly reacting as though the child were the uncle. A child may have been unwanted and you may tend to bring out your unconscious anger at his being born every time you tell him off for some minor deed. It's also very easy to treat your children differently from each other. Sometimes this is justified if one sort of punishment works for one child and doesn't with another, but sometimes it arises from just such unconscious factors as we've been discussing and certainly isn't fair to the child. Try to work out if there is any reason why one child is treated more strictly or sternly than another. Once you have brought the matter to the surface of your mind, you may be able to understand your behaviour better and so be able to iron out any unfairness. See what your partner thinks about the subject.

Some parents react to their child's repeated wrongdoings by smacking. An immediate smack done in the heat of the moment may relieve your feelings and clear the air, allowing you to find out why your child did it and to repeat why he mustn't. However, you'll find that if you smack your child, he's likely to smack others (you're too big to be smacked, though he may try to if he's cross with you). Smacking is a form of physical aggression which makes a deep impact on a child's mind, partly because most parents – if they do it at all – reserve it for times when they are very cross (or stressed or tired) or when the child has done something very bad.

Punishment in some homes involves sending the child off to another room – usually his bedroom – to cool off alone. Some children are sent to bed, others put outside the door or made to stand in a corner. Parents have even been known to shut their children into cupboards! Faults can be found with any of these punishments: a child's bedroom and bed are his own private places and are best not associated with punishment; standing in a corner or being sent away from the others is a form of humiliation that is unnecessary for this age group; shutting a child in a cupboard is obviously totally unacceptable and could cause permanent psychological damage. Beating a child of any age with any form of implement is unacceptable to most people, and especially when it comes to children in this age group. There is always a better way of teaching a child how he should behave.

Punishment sometimes fails to have its supposed effect – of making the child behave better in future – because it is done without thinking why it is being done. It may be used by parents as a form of revenge – a 'because you've done this, take that' attitude. Revenge isn't a good teaching tool, though sometimes you may think you're justified in using it. Children often use it themselves: when one child is hit he'll often hit back, for example. Sometimes you will be so cross at something your child has done that you'll actually want to hurt him, physically or emotionally. This is something quite different from punishment as a part of discipline. All your child will learn is that you can be just as unthinking, bad, or unkind as he can and worse because you're bigger, older and cleverer and should know better.

Parents, with their greater age, experience and wisdom, should try to understand why they might *ever* want to punish their child and should keep well clear of the various pathways leading away from their overall aim of loving guidance.

Many parents manage very well without ever having to do more to a child than to make it obvious they are upset by his behaviour by their expression, tone of voice and mood, and by telling him off if necessary. If more than this is required, it's worth looking at the basic relationship between a child and his parents to find out why so much punishment seems necessary. Very often the basic love and trust between them is diminished or totally missing for some reason and the child doesn't find it necessary or desirable to try to please them. The more you punish your child the more he'll seem to need it unless the way his personality reacts is never to do anything wrong in a desperate attempt not to provoke parental displeasure. If your child needs a lot of punishment, first ask yourself what you have done wrong. Ten to one it's you who's causing the problem in your child, not him. If you can't work things out for yourself, talk about it with your doctor or health visitor.

Finally, remember that often-repeated punishments lose their effectiveness and that you should never threaten punishment unless you intend to carry it out. Never store up punishments to be dealt with later – always punish a child at the time and leave it at that. Withholding privileges from the child for all but the shortest time is a cruel and over-harsh form of punishment for the under-fives. *Related topics* Child abuse; discipline; emotional deprivation; guilt; permissiveness; smacking; threats.

Pushchairs More and more mothers are buying the buggy sort of pushchair today. A buggy is a very light, collapsible pushchair consisting of a tubular metal frame with wheels and handles and a plastic or fabric seat for the baby to sit in. The simplest form of seat is just a sling of material; others are more structured and padded. There is usually a simple sort of safety strap attached to the buggy and some even have a proper harness. The good things about buggies are their lightness, their collapsibility and their small size. Walking in crowded or cramped spaces is much easier with a buggy than with a pram, carrycot and transporter, or larger pushchair (though not as easy as with the baby in a sling). A mother can hold her baby with one arm while she unfolds or folds up the buggy with the other. A simple flick with a hand and foot operates the folding mechanism and when folded, a buggy takes very little space so it can readily be put in a car boot along with other luggage. It can be carried like a walking stick with the handles (which come together when folded) over one arm, which is helpful for getting in and out of buses and trains. A baby can be put in a buggy early on as long as he is well supported either side of his head and body so that he doesn't slump to one side. You can use a rolled blanket either side to make a young baby comfortable. He won't hurt his back or neck – babies have been carried in slings on their mothers for generations in a similar position without any harm coming to them and they certainly don't need to lie down all the time! You can carry on using a buggy for your child until he literally grows out of it, which may not be until he's three or four.

One problem with a buggy is that because of the way it's balanced and because it's so light, it can easily be tipped over backwards by a child hanging on to the handles or if you hang a heavy bag or basket over the handles. Be absolutely sure to hold on to the buggy all the time until you remove the basket, or else it'll tip backwards and your child could be tipped right out and bang his head, or at least be very frightened. Its wisest not to hang bags on buggies at all. Apart from the safety angle buggies are too light to withstand extra weight and wear and tear with heavy shopping. If you do this it will greatly shorten the life of the buggy, and can pull it out of shape and make it unbalanced. Having said this, most of us do it!

Another problem is that because of the lightweight nature of the seat, it's not very comfortable, warm or draught-free. In the winter, dress your baby warmly and consider buying a small sheepskin to put in the buggy for him to sit on. A sheepskin is lovely and warm, besides being comfortable, and if (after fastening the safety strap) you tuck one or more blankets round the child and under the edges of the sheepskin, he'll be snug and draught-free. Because it's fairly bulky, it gives a small baby more support at the sides too. Special warm-lined fabric bags with leggings are made to slip your baby into if you prefer. The safety strap fits nicely between these leggings. Both the sheepskin and the leggings have to be removed before you can fold the buggy up.

A baby buggy can be bought complete with a removable, (sometimes see-through) plastic cover which keeps the baby dry yet which also allows him to see what's going on. They are fairly expensive, proportionately, and are fiddly to put on, though when folded up they can be left attached to the buggy. A simpler and cheaper solution to keeping your baby dry is a waterproof fabric cover with elastic around the edges which envelopes the whole baby and is fixed with tapes at the sides and round the handles, leaving his face open to the elements. This is easily rolled up out of the way when not in use.

Several varieties of baby buggy can be bought, including a twin buggy (like two single buggies joined together but with three handles and not four), and a pram buggy (which has a carrycot-type pram body on the frame which can be exchanged for a seat when you need it. A twin buggy can be made with one side a pram buggy and the other an ordinary one. Perhaps surprisingly, a twin buggy will go through most shop doors. Yet another version is the lie-back buggy, in which the back of the seat can be tipped back (with the baby in place) to give him a more comfortable position for sleeping. Wheels which can be swivelled right round are to be found on some buggies and really do make pushing easier.

One of the major problems with most available buggies until recently has been that the baby was facing away from his mother, and this isn't a good idea with a young baby who is usually happier if he can at least see his mother, even if he can't be in her arms. Now, though, a buggy is widely available in which the baby can face either way, according to the parents' preference. This buggy can also have a carrycot-type pram body put on the frame, again to be used facing either way, but it loses out on foldability, weight and compactness compared with an ordinary buggy.

Heavier and sturdier pushchairs are still chosen by many mothers in preference or in addition to buggies. They are mostly collapsible, though they take up much more room than a buggy when folded and are heavy to carry. One advantage is that they can be used to carry some shopping – some of them have a special shopping basket in front or behind. You can buy a hood and apron for your pushchair and clip a parasol on to it in bright sunshine. Safety straps are often fitted as standard. Some carry two children sitting (or lying) side by side. In some the child faces forwards; in some, backwards. The seats are usually firmer and better padded than those of buggies, but this is probably not a great advantage, as a buggy seat can be padded. Some pushchairs have a lie-back facility which allows the child to lie flatter than in a lie-back buggy. The biggest single advantage of a heavier pushchair is that they are far longer-lasting than buggies and will easily see several children through, whereas most buggies need frequent repair and all too soon are too weak and battered to use. Many families find that a buggy only lasts for two children, if that and a good one costs a lot of money. These heavier pushchairs are expensive but are sometimes available second-hand. Given that they last well, they are a good investment, like a coach-built pram.

Lighter pushchairs which don't collapse are available and are the cheapest of all the pushchairs because they are so simple.

Out of the wide variety available, how do you decide exactly what sort of buggy or pushchair to buy? Decide what you basically want it for. Is it to use for quick trips from the car to the shops or something sturdier for longer journeys? Does it need to be easily collapsible into a small volume, foldable when occasionally necessary, or won't you ever need to fold it? Is it to carry shopping or not? Do you want it to last for several children or does it matter if it's not much use after one or two? Do you want your child to be able to sleep lying back or down in it? Cost is more of a problem than when buying a pram because second-hand pushchairs and buggies are not so easily available. Make out your list of requirements for your pushchair or buggy, then enlist the help of a knowledgeable shop assistant and make your choice.

As with prams, remember to check your child's buggy or pushchair regularly for signs of wear and tear. Check the brake and oil squeaky wheels. If you dry it after a wetting, it'll stay rust-free for longer, and if you let the hood dry before folding it down, it won't get musty or mouldy. When your child is old enough to attempt to climb out, or to rock or tip the pushchair, put him in a harness clipped on to the pushchair, as well as using the safety straps, unless you are going to be right by him all the time. Safety straps by themselves aren't usually enough to prevent a child from getting out. *Related topic* Prams.

Putting things away This subject is mentioned only because it seems to be a bone of contention among so many parents of young children. It's all too easy to see both sides of the situation. The mother has plenty to do, especially if she has more than one child, and it probably seems to her as though her home is never as she would ideally like it if she didn't have children. She may be depressed by things strewn everywhere and yearn for tidiness, especially when the evening approaches and her husband comes home wondering why the place looks as if a bomb had hit it. If the house is small, she may actually fall over toys left lying around and she'll wonder how the children can possibly enjoy playing with anything when everything seems to be lying in a heap. What's more, she never seems to get any help in putting thing away. The children, when asked, often seem affronted at the very idea that they should put away the things they have been playing with.

On the other hand, young children have no expectations of or desires for tidiness. They know that things always seem to end up in certain places, but this appears to have nothing to do with them and they probably aren't even aware of their mother tidying up half the time. It's much more fun to have all their toys surrounding them, just in case they want to play with them, and of course their mother always puts away the very thing they were just about to play with! Emptying out containers and cupboards full of toys is almost more enjoyable than playing with them, especially if they are playing on their own, when using a toy 'properly' may be too difficult. They don't realize that while their mother can put up with things everywhere most of the time, she may have a low patch at one time of the day during which anything can annoy her, for instance, tripping over a loose toy.

How you feel about tidying up is bound to depend on your personality to a great extent. There are a few tactics though that are worth avoiding. Excessive clearing up may make a child reluctant to play at all in case his mother descends on his toys and puts them away. It'll also encourage a similar neurosis in him. Other children are unlikely to want to come and play if toys are strictly rationed or else disappear when they've only been out for half an hour. It may also discourage your child from his natural curiosity and experimentation with his toys. Most people who've had any experience with children know that children are happy in a calm, relaxed atmosphere in which play is encouraged and the mother is more interested in playing with her children than in spending the same time clearing up. Of course, it's more pleasant to see friends in a tidy house, but not if your children are being prevented from playing. Tidy up by all means before visitors come, but let your children get their things out again when they're ready to play. Older children can be encouraged to play in another room if space is at a premium and you really can't have piles of toys around when the house is full.

Some children are very much more helpful than others, and naturally want to help you in everything you do, especially if you're clever enough to make it into a game. You can throw the toys into their basket, one at a time, collect different sorts of toys together, dress the dolls as they go away and do the jigsaws in their boxes if you have the time. Make tidying up more fun by making sure the storage facilities for toys are easy. Large, open baskets make the job much easier than stuffing them into a small cupboard. It's more fun getting toys out again if they've been put away in an orderly fashion rather than all jumbled up. Shelves for flat toys and games make for easy finding and storage, and empty, large plastic ice-cream boxes or other plastic food containers make good storage places for Lego, doll's shoes, plastic animals, playdough, crayons and so on. Coloured pencils are more easily accessible if kept upturned in a mug and you can see then which need sharpening. The same goes for felt-tip pens. If you ever have time to decorate the various containers and label them with a picture and a word describing the contents, your child may enjoy the game of deciding which box to put which things in.

You'll probably find that you'll have piles of toys and other things to take from room to room at the end of the day. Don't leave piles on the stairs, or someone could have an accident, especially when carrying another pile which is blocking his vision.

There may come a time when you feel aggrieved that your child isn't helping you tidy up because you feel he's quite old enough and you can't let him get away with not helping any more. It's best firmly to insist on help before you get to this stage, but if you haven't you must now because it'll do nobody any good if you feel put-upon and constantly martyred. Gently but firmly explain why you think your four- or five-year-old ought to help you and then put your foot down firmly. Even a two-year-old can understand the principle of helping to tidy up even if he in fact only puts one or two things away. The end of the day isn't a good time to do this if the children are tired out, but you could make your point by expecting them to put *some* things away if not all of them. Help them at the same time and tempers will get less frayed.

Pyloric stenosis A condition seen in babies, in which there is a narrowing of the stomach outlet (the pylorus) into the intestine. It is five times more common in boys than girls and is more common in bottle-fed babies than in breast-feds. The milk curds of bottle-fed babies are bulkier than those of the breast-fed baby. Their bulk may be just enough to cause a partial blockage of the pylorus with consequent accumulation of the stomach contents and vomiting. It's possible even that the muscles of the pylorus may enlarge because they are being overworked by the extra expansion necessary to pass these bulky curds. This is a possible (but unproven) cause of the condition previously thought to be 'congenital.'

The first symptoms usually come on about two to three weeks after birth. Vomiting after feeds is the main feature of the condition even though the child continues to take his feeds well. He may become constipated (because little or no food is getting into the bowel) and his weight gain may slow down or stop for the same reason. The vomiting is unusual in this condition as it is projectile. An affected baby can vomit stomach contents to land several feet away.

The repeated vomiting makes the baby dehydrated and eventually too weak and feeble to suck at the breast or bottle. A doctor examining such a baby can usually feel a lump (in the top right hand part of the abdomen) which hardens and softens while the baby is feeding. Sometimes a barium x-ray is necessary to make the diagnosis. A medicine can be used to help relax the muscular obstruction to the outflow of food from the stomach but many babies need a simple operation to split the pyloric muscle and cure the condition permanently.

The operation is over within an hour and the baby can be fed in a few hours. After a few days the baby can go home. By seven to ten days the wound is completely healed and he can be bathed. There are no after-effects from the operation and the child is well immediately.

Some children have symptoms suggestive of pyloric stenosis but continue to thrive in spite of the vomiting. Eventually it stops without any treatment. The months spent waiting for a child to stop his habitual vomiting can be gruelling for the mother who constantly has to clean up her child, her clothes and her carpets. It's also disconcerting when a child is repeatedly seen by a doctor but no treatment is given. In this case, however, a policy of 'wait and see' is likely to be the best. *Related topics* Dehydration; operations; vomiting.

Quarantine Quarantine is the time that a child who has been in contact with an infectious disease is kept away from others whom he might infect if he is in fact incubating the disease, which is not necessarily so. The term is not widely used today, partly because it's been found that keeping children in quarantine doesn't have much effect on the spread of illness. A child is most infectious towards the end of the incubation period and in the early stages of the illness.

Quarrels All children quarrel and even though other people's children may not do so when they come to visit you, you can be sure they do at home.

Children quarrel for the same reasons that adults do – tiredness, a sense of injustice, ill health and so on. But children also learn quarrelsome behaviour from their parents. If your children are aggressive, quarrelsome and violent it's worth looking at your relationship to see whether they could be picking things up from you.

The problem with quarrels is that once we the parents step in we usually take one side in the dispute and this is bound to annoy someone. Also, once you've done this a few times you'll be bombarded with endless moans and whines whenever there's an argument. Children have to learn about relationships and about testing their will and opinion against that of others. However, they haven't yet got enough experience of life to sort out a quarrel amicably and tend to fight on till one of them gives up in despair unless you step in and show them how to bring common sense, reason and fairness to bear on the situation. If at all possible don't take sides, though sometimes you'll have to if one child's behaviour is clearly outrageous and unfair. It's often best to tell them that they'll have to play alone for a bit if they can't play pleasantly together.

Young children also quarrel with their parents. 'I didn't spill the orange juice'; 'Yes, you did'; 'No, I didn't' is a common type of argument and in this case you should again set an example by bringing reason and common sense to bear, so your child learns from you how to sort out his arguments with other people.

Sometimes children quarrel because one is luckier than another. However, they have to learn that life isn't always fair. The fact that they are loved and wanted gives them a secure background to all life's unfairness. Children have to learn that life isn't all about winning – it's also about losing. In fact teaching and encouraging your children to be winners only does them more of a disservice than you'd imagine. *Related topic* Jealousy.

Questions children ask Children ask questions to find out about themselves and the world around them – they also ask questions to test you out as a source of knowledge. Studies of children's language show that there is a regular order in which children learning English ask questions. This means that the development of questions gives a pretty good guide to the child's progress in learning language. There are four overlapping stages. Stage 1 is a two or three word question such as 'What that?', or 'Where Mummy?' Stage 2 questions are longer but still have several long words missed out, for example 'Me do it?' or 'Mummy take it?' In Stage 3 the sentences sound more adult and there is better construction. 'Can I go there?' 'Why we can't go?' Stage 4 is the final stage when questions are properly formed: 'Where's my teddy?' or 'Why is it raining?'

Most children start off with some version or other of 'What's that?', probably because we all say this quite frequently to our children. The questions asked by children at each stage need quite different answers and you'll soon get the hang of it. At stages 1 and 2 questions don't call for a long or complicated answer. Some parents, especially intelligent ones, tend to feel that such children want or need in-depth answers to a question. Match your answer to the child's level of understanding by trying to put yourself in his place when answering. He wants and deserves an answer but not necessarily the answer you'd give to an adult. Children will soon show you if you've got the level wrong because they'll become easily bored by your answer. Often one or two word answers suffice in the early stages. As children advance through stages 3 and 4 they need more complex answers and have the concentration to cope with them. 'Because I say so' is a common parental put down to the question 'Why?' when things are busy or they can't be bothered with a helpful answer. This does nothing to extend a child's thinking and learning.

Parents are best advised to be totally honest with their answers to their children's questions. If you don't know the answer, say so, and with an older child you can enjoy finding out the answer together from a book. It's not essential or desirable that children grow up thinking that you automatically know everything. It does no harm at all for a child to realize that there are some things adults don't understand or even know about. The types of answers you give will determine what type of questions you get asked and it's helpful to look at your answers to older children to see how far they encourage questions.

Surprising numbers of parents of all levels of intelligence put their children down and stifle questioning by saying that they don't need to know the answer and shouldn't even be asking.

Children's questions can be great fun. They can open up new horizons for us, the parents. if we let them. They make us think afresh about things we've taken for granted for years and formulating an answer can help *us* if we take the trouble to think it out. *Related topics* Curiosity; science.

Rabies A serious, life-threatening disease caught from the bite of an animal suffering from the condition. Dogs are the commonest source but certain other animals can carry the disease too. Rabies is kept out of the UK by strict quarantine laws and the penalties for contravening these laws are considerable. Although the chances of your child being affected by rabies when bitten by a dog in the UK are remote, it's still wise to take a child with any but the most trivial of dog bites to a doctor or casualty department because the wound could become infected, even if not with rabies. Any dog or animal bite occurring abroad, however trivial, should be reported at once to a doctor. *Related topic* Dog bites.

Rashes Different types of eruption on the skin with many causes. Some are composed of flattened, red areas that can't be felt; others of raised, red areas that can be felt; and yet others of blisters with or without pus in them. Many childhood rashes are mixtures of these types.

Rashes occur not only on the skin but also on the body's linings. Koplik's spots occur inside the mouth, for example, in measles. Many rashes are not itchy. Children can get a rash from bites and stings; allergies to food and drugs, plants and fungi; heat; sweating; contact with a wet, chafing nappy; besides, of course, from many of the common childhood infections including bacterial, viral and fungal infections.

If your child has a rash that worries you, phone your doctor first before taking him to the surgery because there may be other children or pregnant women there and they won't want to be infected. Describe the rash and be guided by your doctor.

Rashes are always important but rarely dangerous. They tell us that there's something wrong with the body. Unless you are confident that you know what your child's rash is and can treat it adequately, it's best for your doctor to sort out what's going on. *Related topics* Allergy; chickenpox; fifth disease; German measles; insect bites and stings; itching; measles; milia; prickly heat; ringworm; roseola infantum; scarlet fever.

Rattles From his earliest days your baby will enjoy a rattle even though he can't hold it himself. He'll enjoy it mainly because when you rattle it for him you'll almost certainly do so with a smile on your face, talking to him as you shake it, and when he's awake and alert he'll love such attention from you, with you looking at him and concentrating just on him.

As he grows older he'll watch you moving it and may wave his arms around in an attempt to touch it. At first he'll miss wildly but one day he'll manage to make it rattle and he'll be delighted, especially if you tell him he's a clever boy with a pleased expression and tone of voice. If you have a rattle that's easy for a young baby to hold, such as a hollow basket-weave ball with a bell attached inside, he'll be able to grasp it firmly with his whole hand around one of the strands. Many plastic rattles have slim enough handles for a baby who can hold things in a reflex grasp when he's given them. When he moves his arms in excitement at holding the rattle, he'll shake it (purely by chance) and will be amazed and amused by the noise it makes. After a few similar shakes, he'll connect the fact that his movements are making the rattle make the noise, and from then on he'll know how to shake a rattle.

When a baby has good enough hand-eye coordination to be able to reach out for a rattle, he'll be able to amuse himself for longer than before by picking up toys such as a rattle lying near him.

This early discovery that he can make something happen gives him enormous pleasure and it's something you can make the most of by inventing all sorts of different rattles at home. Remember that they need to be easy for him to hold, so choose small containers such as a Smarties box (with its lid well taped on after it's filled) a toothpaste box, plastic shampoo bottles, or a bag made of scraps of material. Fill the container with dried beans, small pebbles, ends of pencils – anything that will make a noise when shaken – but make quite sure that he can't possibly get at the contents. The only virtue of making your own rattles is that each will interest him afresh. Commercial ones are often attractive and brightly coloured but can get boring after a while. *Related topic* Toys.

Reading There are many ways in which you can prepare your pre-school child for learning to read. Some parents actually tackle reading before their child starts school, though a few schools frown on this, saying that if the child knows too much before he goes, he will soon be bored in class while waiting for the other children to catch up and might not have been taught in the way they'd like. If you know which school your child is going to go to, talk to the head teacher or class teacher about the system (and even the books) they use.

Your child will be well on the way to an interest in reading if he is used to having stories read to him. If you've gone out of your way to provide him with books (bought, or borrowed from the library), he'll already be accustomed to enjoying books and looking at their pictures. Books are associated with sitting down with a parent for a quiet, individual time together.

During the pre-school years, most children learn some or all of the letters of the alphabet even if their parents haven't made a conscious effort to teach them. They'll probably be able to recognize their name when it's written, and they may recognize those of other members of the family too. This early 'reading' is more a recognition of letter patterns which always tends to crop up in the same place – for instance in birthday cards or on gifts for them. Show them a word containing the same letters as their name but arranged differently, and they'd be completely thrown.

Reading readiness is what teachers look for in children during their first year at school. It's a stage during which a child is ready and able to start reading properly and it's a time when reading may take off in a rush, given adequate practice and help. It's a fascinating time and very rewarding for child, teacher and parent. It's also a time that can't be hurried. If you try and push reading before your child is ready, you may put him off for a long time. Once he does show an interest, read with him as often as you can. Research has shown that children who read with their parents make much faster progress in reading. *Related topics* Books for children; pre-school education.

Recurrent abdominal pain Abdominal pain is a difficult diagnostic problem in children because, while it can be a sign that something serious is going on, it can also be of little or no significance. It is especially difficult and frustrating for both parents and doctors if it is recurrent.

Recurrent abdominal pains are common in schoolchildren (about one in ten are said to have them) but are not so common in the under-fives. It is thought that most recurrent abdominal pain is caused by stress, though why children should react in this way no one knows. Perhaps it's because we adults tend to put such importance on the moving of the bowels, eating and potty training. This could make children focus too much on their insides so that when they are under stress they unconsciously produce symptoms of which they know their parents will have to take notice.

Such pains can be carefully and lovingly explained to the child by the doctor or parents once true physical diseases have been ruled out but the treatment must be to make life better for the child.

A specific type of this condition is called the periodic syndrome. *Related topics* Abdominal pain; migraine; periodic syndrome.

Refrigerators Most homes today have a fridge and used sensibly it is a help in keeping foods fresh and safe to eat, especially in hot weather. Meat of all kinds should always be refrigerated, especially once it has been cooked. Be sure when using uncooked meat and poultry from the fridge to cook it thoroughly as partly cooked meats are a potent source of food poisoning.

Apart from keeping the inside of a fridge clean there's really only one other important safety rule. When discarding a fridge never leave it abandoned or in the garage if the door is still on. Children love to play hide and seek in such things and there have been several cases of children hiding themselves in old fridges and suffocating to death. Either remove the door or seal it firmly shut.

Regurgitation The spontaneous bringing up of stomach contents into a baby's mouth. The amount brought up varies enormously from baby to baby and even in any one baby. Usually only a little food comes back. Regurgitation isn't the same as vomiting. Vomiting is accompanied by retching and straining of the abdominal muscles. Regurgitation is a gentle, effortless washing back of stomach content – not the ejection of them. Regurgitation usually occurs soon after a feed and can occur as a child brings up wind. It can also happen hours after a feed and may even be continuous between feeds. Rarely it can be explosive like vomiting but, unlike the vomiting of pyloric stenosis is never projectile. It is rare after the first year.

If your baby regurgitates, don't make the mistake of thinking that he is ill – he may be but this isn't necessarily so. If he is ill he'll be unhappy, may cry, have a temperature, diarrhoea or other signs. Such a baby will keep little food down and will slowly lose weight because he is taking so little food.

Most babies who regurgitate are fit and healthy and even though they may bring up some of each feed this does them no harm.

The problems with regurgitating babies aren't usually medical at all – but social. Such babies often end up smelling horrid because their partially-digested food gets all over their clothes, their mother's clothes, the furniture and the carpets. The secret is to protect the child well – a spare terry nappy is the best thing to have handy. Some mothers lay their regurgitation-prone baby with his head on a terry nappy to sleep so as to reduce the amount of sheet washing. If your baby is likely to regurgitate while asleep, it's safest to lay him on his tummy to sleep. Fully breast-fed babies who regurgitate smell less unpleasant than bottle-fed babies or babies on solid food.

No one knows why babies regurgitate, though it's more likely to happen as wind is brought up. Some babies have a weakness of the junction of the stomach and gullet (oesophagus) which doesn't keep the stomach closed off properly. *Related topics* Rumination; vomiting.

Reins A long nylon or leather strap with clips on each end which can be fastened on to a harness round a toddler's chest to prevent him from straying too far away from you if he objects to having his hand held. Lots of children prefer walking with reins to sitting in a pushchair or buggy, which is the other safe way of taking a would-be independent toddler out. If your child stumbles, you can save him from hurting himself by hoisting him up with his reins. Some children walk in reins rather like some dogs on a lead – straining against them, which can be rather exhausting for you! *Related topic* Harness.

Relatives 'You can choose your friends but you can't choose your relatives' is a cynical saying that ignores the importance of blood ties. Someone may stop being a friend, but an aunt, for instance, will always be an aunt. Most of us are interested and concerned about our relatives and want to help them out in trouble and share their joys. Most relatives take an interest in the children in the family and make a point of sending birthday and Christmas presents.

One of the problems of many parents of young children today is that they live too far away from their relatives to be able to count on them for regular or even occasional help with the children. The children miss out too in not having grandparents, aunts, uncles and cousins around. Visits to relatives who live a long way off often mean an overnight stay and keeping in touch means phone calls and letters rather than popping round for a quick visit. Although many people don't get on well with some of their relatives, overall their loss is a very real one in both practical and human terms. You can help your children keep in touch with the fact that they are part of a family, even though they live far away from their relatives by having lots of photographs.

Belonging to a family – particularly a large extended family whose members keep in close touch with each other wherever they may be – is very pleasant. Children enjoy growing up feeling they belong to their own special club whose members really care for each other and there are also real practical advantages.

Of course, relatives can bring problems. An ageing grandparent, parent or aunt, for example, may need care and the family is the obvious place to which to turn. Having someone, albeit a member of the family, to live in your house needs a lot of patience, tact and love to make it work, especially if there is little space. Though it may be hard work for the parents, young children are usually unaware of such problems and benefit from attention and interest from another adult (if it's forthcoming and the relative is well enough, that is). Parents will find that having a ready baby-sitter available helps them out too.

Religion A belief in God can bring security, joy and strength to children and indeed to family life in general. To deny children a spiritual dimension to their life is to rule out a very positive and, we feel, essential part of them. Man isn't just a collection of anatomical parts and to regard him as such is to debase him.

A religious code not only helps a family spiritually but has enormous practical advantages. An accepted code of conduct and behaviour within a like-thinking cultural group can be a source of considerable strength for all members of the family. Children see that their parents are guided by a set of regulations that seem to be above their individual aims and fancies and this can help a child accept discipline too. There are also benefits from religious institutions that reflect on many a non-believer. The charitable works done for children by church-based groups, the church-based play-groups and so on are all a part of a loving and caring community with their religion in common. Sunday school can be an interesting and enjoyable pastime even for children whose parents aren't religious. Lots of churches will let you send your children to Sunday school even if you don't go to church yourself.

No child should be bribed or brow-beaten into taking the religious views of his parents. A parent with strong religious beliefs should, by his example to his children, encourage them gently and with love in such a way that once they are old enough to make a rational decision they will tend to follow the path they know. Some won't, of course, and will follow another religion or even none at all, but that's each individual's decision.

Our duty as parents is to open as many doors as possible for our children and a chance to learn about and believe in God is the most important door. Whether or not children eventually decide to go through is their decision.
Related topics Baptism; development – spiritual.

Remarriage With one in three marriages in this country a remarriage, a lot of children end up living with another adult who isn't their own parent (a step-parent). Some parents remarry very quickly after a divorce or a death because they feel their children need two parents. Others remarry because they are lonely and many remarry because they want a housekeeper or provider. Many women want to stay at home to bring up their children and some remarry to get financial support to free them to do this. Others remarry to prove that despite their early failure they can still attract and keep a partner. For some people none of these reasons apply – they simply fall in love, just as they did first time around.

Unfortunately, quick remarriage often isn't advisable because it's very easy to marry for the wrong reasons early on in your newly-single life. Settling down after a divorce or a bereavement can take a long time and many divorcees and bereaved parents feel that at least two years need to elapse in order to have enough time to pick up the pieces and sort themselves out again.

One of the greatest problems, especially with young children, is meeting a suitable person to remarry. Children tire you out, especially if you're looking after them single-handed and are working too and baby-sitters can be expensive if you want to start a busy social life. One answer is to join a club or classes so you can meet people who like doing the sorts of things you do. Gingerbread and the National Council for the Divorced and Separated are helpful with ideas for meeting people and marriage bureaux and commercial computer dating companies can – if used with caution and with careful telephone screening of potential partners – work wonders. You may meet people at work too.

It's never easy to find someone with whom you could contemplate spending the rest of your life and it's even more difficult to do this if either of you has children because they too have to be considered. On balance, though, if you are happy and settled the children will be far better off in every way. *Related topics* Divorce; separation of parents. *Useful organizations* Gingerbread; National Council for the Divorced and Separated.

Respect The dictionary defines respect as 'an attitude of deference, esteem, admiration or regard' . . . 'to pay proper attention to one's elders' or 'to show consideration for someone or something and to treat them courteously or kindly'.

This definition is akin to the Old Testament commandment 'Honour thy father and thy mother', which is a moral concept besides being an ideal standard of behaviour. It's easy to grow up learning to respect your parents and others if they are worthy of respect. However, the problems start if they are not! Many of today's young parents no longer see respect as due to them automatically – as their parents did – and anyway the concept of respect is a rather high-flown one for the under-fives.

Respect within a family means treating everybody courteously, kindly and with consideration. We have no right to over-talk our children, to interrupt them when they're absorbed in something, or to ride roughshod over them, and similarly they shouldn't be allowed to behave like this to us. Children brought up with parents who respect them, their talents, their abilities and so on will in turn learn by example to respect other people. Children also need to be helped, by example, to respect things – both their own and other people's.

Our children are not parts of us, they are unique individuals. They have rights as human beings though no more nor less than we do and we must respect that. The world would be a happier and more peaceful place if all children grew up with a real sense of respect – a respect based on courteous kindness and consideration.

Respiratory distress syndrome A condition causing breathing difficulties which affects about ten per cent of all premature babies and up to 50 per cent of those born before thirty-one weeks of pregnancy. Babies born to diabetic mothers are also at risk. Though treatment cures most babies, it is still the commonest cause of death in the first week of life and is responsible for one in ten of all deaths in babies under one year.

The respiratory distress sydrome (RDS) is caused by the lack of a substance called surfactant in the baby's lungs without which the lungs can't pick up oxygen effectively from the air. Breathing becomes difficult, rapid and shallow, and the rib cage is drawn in and upwards instead of expanding on breathing. The baby may need mechanical assistance with breathing, an oxygen-rich air supply, and intravenous fluids to restore the acid balance of his body which becomes deranged because of the lung trouble.

The treatment has to be carried out in a special care baby unit with the baby nursed in an incubator. The aim is to keep him alive until, with time and increasing maturity, his lungs start to make their own surfactant.

It is possible to check the level of surfactant being made before a baby is born by obtaining a sample of amniotic fluid by amniocentesis in late pregnancy. If insufficient is being made and the baby, if born early, would be at risk of suffering from the respiratory distress syndrome, then the obstetricians will try to ensure that he is not born (unless the premature birth cannot be stopped or is necessary for other more urgent reasons) until his lungs are mature.

If your baby develops this condition, you'll have to trust in the medical and nursing staff who will use modern medical techniques to try to pull your baby through. However, you can help your baby by being near him, talking to him, stroking him and carrying out routine care such as changing his nappy. Your breast milk is the best sort of nourishment for him, so get help to learn how to express or pump it if he is too immature or unwell to suck. In order to make enough milk you'll have to do this frequently by day and night. The milk is better given by tube down his nose into his stomach than by bottle, because a baby who gets used to sucking from a bottle may have difficulty in learning to suck from the breast when he's mature enough and well enough. Milk from other mothers may be available for your baby if you decide not to breast-feed or can't produce enough – you need patience and gritty determination to carry on expressing or pumping milk frequently around the clock for what may be several weeks.

Once your baby is well again, there's no need to treat him as though he were more delicate than any other baby. His lung will work quite normally once enough surfactant is made. If all babies were born at full term this condition would not be a problem.

Responsibility Clearly it is the responsibility of parents to look after their children but children too must learn to be responsible. Few children under the age of four can really understand such a concept though and it's often not until a child is five or so that you begin to see a sense of responsibility developing.

Although it's usually a lot easier and quicker to do things yourself you'll do your young child a disservice by not allowing him to share the responsibility for doing some things. A four-year-old can be encouraged to be responsible for cleaning his paint brushes so that they aren't spoiled, for example, and at five a child can feed his hamsters alone and reliably, provided you remember to remind him to do it regularly! Similarly, some basic responsibility for his toys, telling you when they're broken or need replacing and keeping them away from where people are walking, for example, can completely change the way he treats them.

A sense of responsibility for caring for other people comes from following his parents' example. A child learns how to be a responsible parent by copying his mother and father, and learns to care for others by watching them as they do errands for old people, telephone their parents to make sure they're well and happy, and so on.

Be careful not to make your young child anxious about any responsibility you encourage him to take. All you need to do is gently to teach him throughout childhood how to take up the reins of responsibility. He doesn't have to pull a heavy cartload straight away!

Helping children to develop a sense of responsibility is all part of giving them freedom and encouraging their independence. You could easily do everything for them until the day they leave home but your life would be harder and theirs could end up being miserable because they'd never have learned the meaning of responsibility. *Related topic* Independence.

Rest and relaxation for mothers Tiredness is probably one of the most universal feelings of a young mother, especially in the early weeks after having a baby and especially if you have more than one child. Make arrangements for someone to help you at home after the birth and ensure that you get plenty of rest – you'll be a better mother for it and will enjoy your baby more. Be prepared to be tired a lot of the time and to change your lifestyle and expectations in the early months so that your priority is the baby. It's better to let the housework go and simply to keep your home relatively pleasant to live in and the kitchen and bathroom clean than to try to come up to some 'superwoman' image and to be so tired that you can't look after and enjoy your baby.

Try to get into the habit of resting whenever you can. It's all too easy to fill every moment that the baby sleeps with frenzied activity. Use this time only for essential jobs and then rest yourself. If you just have one baby rests are fairly simple to organize because you can take the phone off the hook and rest when the baby sleeps. If you have older children as well as a baby, you can make feeds quiet times for the other children too and read to them or play a quiet game while you feed. If you have a toddler, get some rest by lying down to catnap while he plays. Alternatively, a neighbour, relative or friend might take him out for an hour or so every day.

One of the great joys of breast-feeding is that you can do it lying down or in your bed and drift off to sleep with your baby as he feeds. Even if you don't actually sleep you can rest on and off throughout the day as you feed him and this is Nature's way of making you relax and rest. If you fight your body's real need for rest you'll find it takes a lot longer to get back to normal physically and mentally after the birth. Even a catnap of a few minutes once or twice a day may make you feel a lot better.

If your baby is waking a lot at night you'll find that a daytime nap for you is essential and not a luxury. Cope with each day as it comes. Don't make plans for the first few weeks but allow yourself plenty of time to relax and be alone with your baby and the rest of your family.

Lots of breast-fed babies in particular wake at night well past a year old. If you expect this and don't compare your baby with others who sleep through the night early on, you won't feel hard done by. Carry on resting during the day and getting to bed early to make up for broken nights.

Sometimes boredom or unhappiness makes a mother feel tired. Try to incorporate activities that give you pleasure in your life – looking after a baby should ideally add to the pleasure of life, not detract from it.

Women often get more tired at home all day looking after their children then they did when they went out to work before they had children. The tiring thing is the never-ending demands – some important and many trivial. There is also a lot to do, especially with two or more children. If a mother is going to get through her day without frayed nerves it's a good idea for her to find some time to relax and regain her flagging energy. Some people have a low spot during the day when they always feel tired and droopy and this may be just the time to relax. (It may also be a time to have a snack in case you're going for too long without food.)

Relaxation means different things to different people. For some it is relaxing to go for a run around the garden; some mothers put on a record and dance; while others do exercises. Physical pastimes such as these simply tire some people more and don't release any of their pent-up tension. For them, it may help to lie down somewhere comfortable and read, watch TV or snooze. It's possible to do this even with a young child about, provided he's safe and happy. This can be one time when television can be used as a baby-sitter, just to give you half an hour or so of rest. In the summer you may find that you can get some time to yourself while your child plays in the garden, provided you know he can come to no harm.

Some mothers find that the breathing exercises they learnt at their antenatal classes help them relax with a young baby. They can be used at any time of the day if you feel tense and over-wrought and wherever you are – even if you're standing at the kitchen sink. Deep breathing in particular is useful if you're feeling tired or if you're anxious, cross or in any way upset. Yoga is another way of combining exercise with relaxation and there are several other exercise systems. Some people perfect a method of relaxation whereby they lie down, clear their minds as far as possible, then consciously relax each set of muscles in their body, one at a time. Even after five minutes of this it's possible to feel more relaxed, mentally and physically, if you're practised at it.

If your husband knows how to massage you, you'll find this is extremely relaxing and can really soothe muscular aches in your back and shoulders in particular, besides giving you a feeling of well-being. A scented massage oil makes a massage even more pleasant and for best results do it after a relaxing bath.

There are many more widespread ways of relaxing including: sitting or lying down with your feet raised above the level of your body; having a warm drink (but not one containing a stimulant such as strong tea or coffee); having a bath; or reading or doing some other quiet job such as embroidery or knitting. Talking with a friend can ease away feelings of stress, as can a quiet walk with no purpose other than to show your child things on the way.

So many of us today spend our lives racing from one thing to another, trying to accomplish lots of things that make us feel stressed, wound-up or unhappy, that we end up functioning at a level way below our optimum. If you feel this applies to you, take stock of your life and cut out things which aren't essential or enjoyable in an effort to make your life more pleasant, to make you more relaxed, and to give your family a person who is more pleasant to be with.

Resting, children Babies and young children usually have one or more sleeps during the day and when the last daytime nap is finally given up, a child may be tired and fractious at about the time he used to sleep. Not many years ago it was thought advisable that children should always rest quietly at some time each day. Today, set rest times aren't fashionable for their own sake. If children are tired or mentally or physically exhausted though, they should be encouraged to sit and play quietly or to lie down, perhaps while you read to them. If they're not tired it's quite unnecessary to enforce periods of rest. If your child is tired because he's had an exciting time with new experiences, sit down with him for a quiet time of reading, play or watching television. After a rest and something to eat, he'll perk up later. *Related topics* Naps; sleep.

Resuscitation The medical term for restarting a person's heart and breathing when either or both have stopped. *Related topics* Artificial respiration; asphyxia; heart massage.

Rheumatic fever A rare disease resulting from a sensitivity to a certain type of streptococcal bacterium. Theoretically, any streptococcal infection – be it tonsillitis, scarlet fever, or otitis media – can cause rheumatic fever, though in practice it is a rare complication.

The first signs of rheumatic fever start between one and four weeks after a streptococcal infection. There is a fever with a headache and pains in several big joints (knees, ankles, elbows, or wrists). The painful joints tend to be affected one after another, so giving the impression that the pains are flitting from joint to joint. Movement of the affected joints is painful. The joint involvement is not permanent and does *not* produce lasting damage like rheumatoid arthritis which is a totally different condition.

About a fifth of affected children have a rash consisting of pink irregular circles or crescents, and some get lumps under the skin especially on the knuckles, knees, elbows or spine.

None of these problems produces any lasting damage, though long-term trouble can be caused as a result of rheumatic fever's effects on the heart. Such damage can last into adulthood but today with good treatment rheumatic heart disease is very uncommon. If the brain is involved the child may have jerky and uncoordinated movements of the limbs and face (St Vitus' dance).

Once a child has had rheumatic fever it is sensible for him to take penicillin every day for several years to prevent further attacks and all such children should be 'covered' by antibiotics when having dental treatment or any operation.

If ever your child has a sore throat or an earache and complains of aching joints that don't go by about ten days, see your doctor. **Related topic** Sore throat.

Rheumatoid arthritis A rare condition in childhood but an unpleasant one because it can produce serious joint destruction and even invalidism.

Rheumatoid arthritis is a disease that has many manifestations – it does not simply affect the joints. About one in twenty adults with rheumatoid arthritis had their first symptoms in childhood. In almost half of all children affected by rheumatoid arthritis the main symptom is arthritis (pain) in many joints, including the small joints of the hands. Stiffness, swelling and a loss of range of movement are all features of the disease too. The stiffness is worst after a night's sleep.

In a quarter of affected children the main initial symptoms are a high fever and a rash but arthritis develops eventually, even if it takes months to come on. Three out of four children with rheumatoid arthritis will eventually become free from symptoms but some go on to get crippling joint deformities. Drugs, physiotherapy and expert care need to be supervised by a team of specialists but all but the most severely affected children with rheumatoid arthritis can lead a near-normal life. Various aids and appliances are available to make daily living easier for your child if he has serious joint deformity. Ask your health visitor for details of whom to contact for advice. *Related topic* Invalidism. *Useful organization* The British Rheumatism and Arthritis Association.

Rhythm and music

Children vary greatly in their enjoyment and natural feeling for rhythm and music but there's little doubt that an environment in which these are commonplace is more likely to promote an interest. There is probably an inherited predisposition to a gift for music, just as there is for some other natural skills.

Most children enjoy music, learn to clap and chant and enjoy beating out rhythms on all kinds of simple instruments. Try walking at different speeds with slow, heavy or bouncing steps and then take long steps, on toes or heels, and so on to the rhythm of a drum or to clapping. There are other variations on this sort of game and you can easily make up your own.

Children like to use gestures and to mime to songs. Get them up and about and moving to records and songs, letting them follow your example at first.

When a child shows signs of being interested, give him the opportunity to experiment with rattles, drums (you can make these from tins and containers, you don't have to spend money on them), bells, cymbals, a piano and so on. Pot lids, boxes, combs with old-fashioned shiny toilet tissue, a shoe box with eight or ten rubber bands stretched across to make a harp, wooden blocks to rub on sand paper, and beans in a tin all make a wonderful orchestra for a small amount of money.

At the age of five or even sometimes before, many children are sufficiently interested in real instruments to begin to want to play something. The secret of success lies in selecting a teacher used to dealing with young children and taking the whole thing very gently and with the minimum of persuasion. Make practising the instrument fun rather than a chore and let the child take it at his own pace. Remember that however enthusiastic the child is, his attention span is very short and fifteen-minute sessions will probably be all he can cope with at first. If a young child of this age wants to give up the instrument in a few months, don't worry: he may well come back to it later and anyway will have enjoyed what he has already done with it. Only the most gifted or enthusiastic child will go on from this early a start to a serious interest in or future with the instrument.

Dancing classes for boys and girls encourage an interest in moving to music in a group situation.

Even if you feel your child is too young to attend a children's concert, let him listen to a marching band in the street, a group of Salvation Army singers, carol singers and so on. He'll learn from others the joy of taking part in making music and singing as well as the pleasure of being a spectator. *Related topics* Dancing; songs.

Rickets

An uncommon, but by no means rare disease in the UK today caused by a lack of vitamin D. Although it's essential to have enough of this vitamin at all times of life, this is especially so when the bones are growing because it is a necessary factor for their healthy growth. Because of this, rickets produces particularly unpleasant problems in babies and young children.

In a severely affected child the head is asymmetrical and the soft spots take a long time to close. Teeth appear late and are more likely to decay. The chest has a row of prominences at the sides and the back may be twisted and bent. Knock knees and bow legs are common and the child is constipated, weak and fretful.

Although such serious signs of rickets are uncommon in the UK less dramatic cases do occur, especially in poor urban areas and among some groups of coloured children who spend little or no time in the sunshine and eat a restricted diet. These children are particularly likely to get rickets because their dark skins screen off rays in the sun which are essential for the formation of vitamin D in the skin. Even a few hours' sunshine a day is enough to ensure the production of enough vitamin D and research has shown that enough of the vitamin can be produced and stored during the summer to last a child through the British winter.

No child today need rely solely on sunshine for his vitamin D. Vitamin drops can supply it, as can fish oils, herrings, tinned salmon and sardines, margarine, eggs, butter, liver and cheese. It is now known that exposure to sunlight is more effective a source of vitamin D than dietary sources but it is not essential.

Cows' milk formulae are enriched with vitamin D and breast-fed babies receive it through their mother's milk. If a breast-feeding mother is in any doubt about her vitamin D intake she should spend more time in the sun and eat more vitamin-D containing foods herself to ensure that her baby will get plenty. When giving vitamin D to a child or even to an adult be sure to stick exactly to the dosage recommended as excessive amounts can be dangerous.

Ringworm A fungal infection of the outermost layers of the skin, hair and nails which most commonly affects the scalp, feet (between the toes) and groins. Ringworm between the toes is called athlete's foot.

Ringworm is contagious and can be transferred from infected animals, objects such as combs and scissors, or by the floors of swimming pools and changing rooms. Unfortunately, because the fungus lives in the horny parts of the skin, it can be very difficult to treat using local treatment. This means that a drug by mouth (griseofulvin) will often have to be used. When ringworm affects the body (causing a rash of circular patches of dry skin), an antifungal ointment can be effective. The patches spread from the centre, leaving a central area of healed, normal skin.

On the scalp ringworm causes circular or oval patches of baldness. As each patch spreads, the centre heals, leaving stumps of broken-off hairs. Three weeks' treatment with griseofulvin usually cures the condition and during this time the child should stay away from school or other children. Other members of the family should be watched in case they catch it.

There's nothing to be ashamed of if your child gets ringworm – it can be caught very easily even by the cleanest, best cared-for child.

Rituals Certain patterns or rituals of behaviour are important to children even though they may appear trivial to adults. If they are forgotten or disrupted, a child can be upset seemingly beyond the bounds of reason, especially if other aspects of his life are also not running smoothly or if he is tired.

The bedtime ritual is the commonest of all rituals and is important to many children in our society in which children go to bed before their parents do and sleep in their own beds and often in their own rooms. Such a ritual eases the transition from being part of the family circle to being alone and perhaps even lonely. It's comforting because of its very familiarity. A typical bedtime ritual may consist of telling the child that it's soon bedtime; giving him a snack; going upstairs with him to help him undress; giving him a bath; putting his pyjamas on; cleaning his teeth; getting his clothes ready for the next morning; reading him a story in bed; saying prayers; giving him a kiss and a cuddle; tucking him in with a teddy or hot water bottle; putting the light out; and saying goodnight. Some children always recall their parent for a drink of water or to help them go to the loo again. The pattern is elaborate and always the same for any child.

Sometimes a ritual can become obsessional (overwhelmingly and unreasonably essential) in which case you'll need to use common sense and tact to find out whether anything is worrying your child. *Related topics* Bedtime; obsessions.

Road safety The safest principle to work on is that all under-fives are vulnerable when they are near roads. They should certainly never be allowed on or near roads alone.

Young children are small (and therefore difficult to see); tend to run rather than walk; have no ability to judge the speed and distances of moving vehicles; and are often totally absorbed in what they are doing, which make them absent-minded and oblivious of dangers. All this makes them a very real danger anywhere near roads.

Right from the earliest days when you and your child are out walking it makes sense to start him thinking about road safety but even at the age of five he really can't be expected to master the Green Cross Code or to have any real road sense. Although a child may be perfectly competent on his bicycle on pavements and in the garden, he shouldn't be allowed on to the public roads – they're far too dangerous. *Useful organization* The Royal Society for the Prevention of Accidents.

Rocking Some babies and young children develop the habit of rocking their bodies for minutes on end. Such behaviour usually starts as a result of boredom or loneliness and is the child's attempt to provide himself with a diversion in a temporarily (or permanently) unfriendly world in which he feels neglected. Occasionally, rocking is seen in perfectly normal and happy children who are never left alone unless they are asleep, and who are rarely bored because they are always helped to find something to do. In such children, it is simply a pleasurable activity akin to the nail biting or fiddling with strands of hair in a child who does these things for pleasure and because he's got into the habit of doing it rather than for comfort and consolation.

Always view rocking with suspicion unless you are quite sure that there is nothing to worry about because it may be a sign that your child is spending too much time alone or has too little stimulation.

Older pre-school children may rock rhythmically, go red in the face and puff and pant. This is a sign that they are masturbating. Lots of little girls rock and thereby rub their thighs together because they find it sexually pleasing and rousing. *Related topics* Comfort habits; cot rocking; habits; masturbation.

Rooming-in Rooming-in is a term used to describe a situation in which a newborn baby stays with you in your room or by your bed in hospital by day and night from birth onwards. This allows you to tend to his needs promptly and will probably help you get more sleep because you won't be worried about whether he might be crying in a nursery somewhere and that no one has brought him to you. It gives you more of a chance to look at, to touch and generally to get to know him and all of these things are helpful in encouraging a bond to form between you. We feel that rooming-in is a very important start to any baby's life and should be considered the norm rather than the sort of 'favour' it is today.

Rooming-in gives the breast-feeding mother much more chance of success because she can feed on an unrestricted basis by both day and night. She *can* do this even if her baby's in a nursery if the staff wake her at night, but staff usually try to give mothers as much sleep as possible and only bring a baby to them if it's 'time for a feed', which is not necessarily as soon as he cries. Breast-fed babies sometimes want feeds little (or a lot) and often, and it's difficult to be flexible if they are continually being taken back to the nursery. Mothers can enjoy their bottle-fed babies more too if they room-in, and they can feed on a more flexible basis than if they are just brought for feeds at set times.

If your baby is rooming-in, you can do as much as you want for him. If you're too tired or unwell to look after him all the time, you simply have to ring for help, but you'll enjoy being near your baby even if you aren't doing everything for him. As the days go by you'll be able to do more and more and eventually you'll be completely capable of coping with him on your own. Mothers whose babies spend a lot of time away from them in hospital don't get the opportunity of becoming confident before they go home and often suffer later as a result.

Your husband and other visitors will have a chance to enjoy seeing the baby if he's in your room with you, and you can feed him at visiting time as and when he needs it. In other words, he's already a part of the family.

Unfortunately a lot of hospitals don't encourage or even allow rooming in, so you may have to insist very firmly if you want to have your baby with you, or alternatively go home at the earliest possible opportunity. *Related topic* Bonding.

Rooting reflex If something is stroked against the cheek of a newborn baby, he'll turn towards it and if it touches his lips, he'll take it into his mouth. This reflex behaviour is used in feeding – the baby turns his head towards the nipple or teat when it touches the side of his face and grasps it in his lips. Some babies make a sort of bouncing movement with the rooting reflex – they bounce their heads up and down off the nearest surface in an attempt to find the nipple. They do this most when hungry but also at any time other than when they have just been fed.

A newborn baby is not choosy about where he is when he searches for food in this way. He's just as likely to root when being held by his father or granny as he is when in his mother's arms. As he grows older, the rooting reflex gradually disappears because the baby knows what he's looking for and is more capable of finding it.

The rooting reflex is useful if you're feeding your baby at night lying down in bed, because even though you can't see whether you're aiming your nipple at the baby's mouth, if it's roughly in the right place he will find it. *Related topic* Breast-feeding.

Roseola infantum A mild viral infection occurring in children aged between 6 months and 2 years. The disease has an incubation period of nine to ten days and the child is well until he suddenly gets a very high fever (up to 105°F, 40.6°C) which lasts for three to five days. Convulsions can occur because of the fever and these should be prevented by keeping the temperature down. The child may have a slight cold and a sore throat. Just before or just after the fever drops a rash appears on the chest and back which may spread to the neck and arms, with slight involvement of the face and legs. The rash consists of small, flat, pink spots which remain separate and then disappear within twenty-four hours.

There is no special treatment for the condition except for controlling the fever.

The rash of roseola may be confused with that of German measles, though the high temperature for several days before the rash of roseola appears is usually enough to rule this out. It may also be confused with measles. Though there is a fever before the rash of measles comes out, this fever generally becomes higher when the rash appears and it continues for a couple of days or so, unlike that of roseola, in which the temperature drops to normal as the rash appears. Also, the typical cold, cough, conjunctivitis and Koplik's spots (in the mouth) of measles are absent with roseola.

Sometimes it is difficult to distinguish an allergic rash from roseola, unless you know the timing of the fever and the rash. Usually though, there is no fever with an allergic rash.

When your child gets a high fever with nothing else obviously wrong, your doctor will consider all the other likely causes including otitis media, pyelonephritis (an acute infection of the kidney), pneumonia and meningitis. Until the fever drops and the rash appears, the diagnosis of roseola is chiefly made by excluding these other problems. Occasionally roseola occurs in epidemics but its degree of contagiousness is not known. The incubation period lies between seven and seventeen days. It is most likely to occur in the spring and autumn and most cases are in children between six months and three years old. *Related topics* Allergy; rashes.

Routines A routine is a habitual or regular method of doing something and as such is a part of everyone's daily life. Some babies are naturally regular in their feeding, sleeping and playing habits, while others never conform to any routine. Some parents try to impose a routine on their baby's day even if he is irregular in his habits. This can lead to problems such as the baby not being hungry when it's 'time' for a feed, or not sleepy when it's 'time' for a sleep. It's easier and more humane to follow your baby's natural pattern. Even before birth some babies seem to adopt a daily routine – sometimes being quiet and sometimes kicking. The times when they usually kicked *in utero* may correspond with the times they are most active after birth. Many women comment that their babies kicked a lot when they first lay down in bed at night, and after birth, the mother's bedtime may be a favourite time for a feed. Many mothers find that their newborns naturally adopt sleeping patterns which to some extent fit in with their own, if they are allowed to. It's quite possible to steer babies into sleeping patterns, though it isn't always successful. For instance, if you regularly make a habit of keeping your baby awake in the evening, then bath him with you and feed him as you go to bed, he'll probably have a long sleep for the first few hours of the night, whereas if you had let him sleep all evening, he may wake up for a couple of hours' play just as you are ready for bed!

To a certain extent your baby will adopt the family's daily routine if you include him. By the time he is six months old, he'll almost certainly be sleeping for much of the night and awake for much of the day. Some babies do this even sooner, while others seem to get their days and nights mixed up at first.

It's often said that children thrive on routine. Certainly a routine makes them feel secure simply because they know what to expect. However, lots of children are brought up in unconventional families in which there is little similarity in what happens from day to day, and provided they have a stable, secure relationship with at least one adult (usually their mother), they are quite unaffected by the lack of routine.

A child will find it easier to fit into other situations (such as going out to play with a friend or going to play-group) if he has some idea of what the routine is likely to be. A routine is comforting in its very predictability though he'll enjoy comparing what he does at home with what he does at his friend's house or at play-group.

Mealtimes are important parts of a child's daily routine and because they are social occasions when people sit down together, they are times to be looked forward to quite apart from the food that'll be there. If you're alone with your child during the day, punctuate the day with events such as mealtimes, going shopping, taking the dog for a walk, feeding the rabbit and so on. If you can give your child some idea of the outline of the day to come, he'll enjoy looking forward to it one step at a time.

If you're not there for some reason, explain the details of your child's daily routine to whoever is looking after him. Finding that things are done in much the same way even when you're not there will ease any pangs of separation.

If a child is used to a routine, any change can throw him. A weekend visit to granny may mean that his normal nap time has to be altered because of the travel arrangements, or he may stay up late to see his favourite aunt. While some children cope well with this, others become overexcited and overtired and end up being bad-tempered and whiny the next day. If your child is one of this group, try hard to keep his daily routine the same no matter where you are. *Related topics* Feeding schedules; habits; mealtimes; rituals.

Rules There have to be some rules in every family – even the most easy-going ones. It's up to us as parents to define the way of behaving which are a 'must' and the limits which must never be exceeded. Even a baby can learn to obey some rules, though they'll be unspoken ones. For instance, if every time he tries to pull your hair, you stop and tell him disapprovingly that he mustn't, he'll gradually come to understand that your rule is that he mustn't pull hair. A toddler will come up against more rules because of his developing independence and will. Sooner or later, even though you try to avoid confrontation of any sort by planning ahead and removing sources of trouble or steering him away from them, there'll come a time when you have to enforce a 'no'. It may be for something like squeezing the cat or drinking the water in the lavatory – this sort of rule is to protect him (as well as the cat!). It may be jumping on granny's handbag with her glasses in or for taking a packet of Smarties from the display by the side of the supermarket check-out queue – this sort of rule is to protect other people's things. Or it may be for hitting other children or spitting at them – this sort of rule is to protect them.

It's easiest for both child and parent if a rule is unassailable. The trouble comes if it's rather woolly and is sometimes allowed to be broken. Once it is broken with permission, the child will try his hardest to break it again with permission and his quite reasonable pleas are sometimes difficult to turn down with an adequate explanation (other than that you were weak-willed in the first place) and can be extremely annoying, especially if they turn into whines. If there's to be no arguing or fighting in the car, then if you ever turn a deaf ear to it, the children will do it again without thinking about your 'rule'. If a rule is allowed to be broken (and they say rules are made to be broken), then make sure your child knows why you're letting it be broken, otherwise he'll be confused. Be prepared for the four- or five-year-old to ask 'If *you* let me break the rules, why can't I let myself do it?'

Rules only work if they're enforced and you as parents have the sometimes unpleasant task of enforcing them. Unpleasant because children have to be told lots of times, not just once, and because they may not always want to obey a rule and may fight against cooperating with you. Some parents are better able than others to cope with the continuing stress of keeping law and order in their home. They are the ones who are happy to repeat the rules as often as necessary and then to make sure they are adhered to. Such parents soften their strictness with patient, gentle and helpful explanations of why such rules are necessary so the child learns that they are not just artificially-imposed limits to frustrate him and annoy him in his natural desires, but guidelines to enable him to fit smoothly into the running of the home and of the community in which he lives. If you find your child is constantly breaking rules, it may be because you're not enforcing them consistently, authoritatively, and helpfully enough.

There may be times when a child disobeys and you feel he needs to be punished. There are many sorts of punishment and some are much more helpful than others, but it's surprising how often actual punishment can be avoided if your sort of discipline is based on loving guidance and if you are prepared to help your child with a supporting arm along the difficult path of learning self-discipline and how to behave, rather than to stand behind him 'with a whip'. Rules can make your child's life more pleasant because as he learns to obey them he'll avoid coming up against disapproval from you and others. As he grows older, he'll make some of his own rules besides fitting in with those of school and society. Many rules will become inseparable from parts of his moral code. By teaching him to follow rules and to be guided by someone in authority, you're preparing him by example for leading other people later, whether these are children younger than he at school, or people he works with, or his own children.

Some children naturally kick against rules, partly because of their personality and partly sometimes because of the way the rules are laid down and enforced. If your child is exceptionally wilful and disobedient, he needs help, not punishment, because you'll probably find that his behaviour is the result of factors other than his personality and your way of bringing him up and setting rules. Perhaps there is a new baby, perhaps a lot of parental conflict, perhaps he's not enjoying play-group, or perhaps you've just started a part-time job and his behaviour is his unconscious way of showing his unhappiness.

Once you know the cause, you may be able to rectify things at once but even if you can't change the situation, by understanding the reason for his behaviour you can avoid getting too upset or annoyed by it, and you can help him by talking to him about the situation and showing that you know why he feels the way he does. If you can't get to the bottom of his behaviour on your own, consult your health visitor, clinic doctor, or family doctor. If necessary, they'll refer you and your child for specialist help from a child guidance clinic.

'Rules', 'punishment', 'discipline' – all these words have overtones of harshness because some people have enforced them too strictly in the past (and some always will enforce). There's rarely any reason for harshness though, and most children brought up in the average family home happily accept rules and the loving guidance of good parental discipline and understand only too well that if they go beyond the limits of accepted behaviour, they will be told off. Of course, if you haven't laid down rules in a way that your children know what they are, you can't in all fairness get cross with them if they do something you consider wrong or unacceptable – they must understand what their limits are.

Babies and young children are learning all the time and learning to obey rules is not an easy lesson. Patient repetition and explanation of why a rule is made is essential and it's worth remembering that young children usually disobey because they've forgotten the rule – perhaps because they've been carried away with the excitement of what they're doing. Few young children disobey in order to provoke an adult, though sometimes it can be an attention-seeking mechanism, in which case you should give your child more time and reorganize your daily life so that it doesn't exclude him so much. Sometimes children disobey in order to test you – they want to see what will happen or whether you'll actually carry out the punishment you have threatened them with. *Related topics* Behaviour problems; discipline; permissiveness; provocative behaviour; punishment.

Rumination A rare condition in which a baby brings up food from the stomach which he then chews on. Such children also sometimes chew on their tongues and make themselves choke with it. This 'chewing the cud' can soon become a habit.

Some children who ruminate are thought to do so because their desire to suck is strong yet they are not allowed to suck at the breast for as long as they want and their thumb sucking has been restrained in some way.

Rumination may be initiated by a poor relationship between the child and his mother, with little attention and stimulation being given to him. Rumination is not the same as straightforward regurgitation which almost all babies do from time to time. Mothers of babies who ruminate may need sympathetic and skilled help to form a caring relationship with them. Sometimes the mother has neglected her baby through her own depression or through a coincidental shock such as the death of another child. *Related topics* Mothering; regurgitation; vomiting.

Rusk A type of biscuit often given to babies as one of their first solid foods. Rusks are flour based and usually contain sugar to make them attractive to babies. A rusk dissolves smoothly in the baby's saliva as he bites on it with his gums or (later) with his teeth, and he's unlikely to be able to break off bits which might go down the wrong way or make him choke. Commercially-produced rusks are widely available and those made specially for babies have a low salt content. Some are even available with holes in them through which a piece of ribbon can be threaded and then pinned to the child's clothes.

Rusks can be softened in a bowl with milk or water to be given to a baby by spoon, or he can eat them as finger foods.

Though rusks are so commonly associated with baby foods, many a baby has been perfectly well nourished without them. In fact the commercially produced rusks commonly available are best avoided as they contain white flour and added sugar, neither of which is ideal for your baby.

You can make your own rusks at home by baking bread till it's dry in the oven. Use wholemeal bread as it's best to accustom a baby to its taste from the beginning as it's more nutritious and contains more dietary fibre than does white or brown bread. *Related topic* Baby foods.

Salt A mineral essential for normal health in adults and children but one which taken in excess can be very dangerous, especially for babies. The greatest danger is when making up feeds of cows' milk formula. Many mothers put too much milk powder in the bottle because they feel that it'll do the child good or make him sleep. This is not so and can be dangerous. The content of milk formula powder has been calculated to give the correct balance of protein, carbohydrates, fats and minerals and if you pack the scoop too tightly or heap it up there'll be too much of all of these and the extra salt can make the child really ill. This doesn't often happen but is especially likely if the child vomits or has a fever or diarrhoea, when he'll lose fluid and will be thirsty. The mother, on seeing her child is thirsty gives him more milk and he gets more thirsty because of the salt fluid his body receives and the relatively greater loss of water. This vicious circle can lead to a severely ill baby who is at risk of convulsions, brain damage or even death.

The safest thing to do is to breast-feed your baby. You can't go wrong with this because there is no danger of salt overload with breast milk.

If you are bottle-feeding, never put any cereal or other solids into his milk and never make up the bottle with too much milk powder for the volume of water.

If your bottle-fed baby vomits or has diarrhoea or a fever don't be afraid to give him drinks of cooled, boiled water alone. This will do him no harm at all and will slake his thirst.

When you start giving solid foods don't add salt to them because this puts an added strain on the child's kidneys and they may not be able to cope with such a load. Added salt is in fact unnecessary for any under-fives – they haven't got used to the taste and so don't miss it. Even though they don't eat added salt as such, they still get salt from their food and so don't come to any harm. *Related topic* Dehydration.

Sand pits A sand pit is probably one of the cheapest sources of fun you can buy your children. For all of the summer and some of the spring and autumn they'll love playing in it. There are commercial plastic pits that you can fill with sand but most parents simply dig a hole in the ground, possibly lining it with concrete or heavy duty polythene, and then fill it with sand. A surround of paving stones is a good idea because grass becomes muddy and trampled and with a dirt surround a sand pit gets dirty and unpleasant to play in.

When buying sand for a sandpit always tell the builder's merchant what it's for because there is special playpit sand. This, unlike builder's sand, doesn't stain clothes yellow and so is really worth while looking for. You'll need to top it up occasionally as sand has a habit of wandering all over the garden! Don't forget when constructing a pit that you'll need to have drainage or the sand will become a soggy mess. Children like playing with wet sand but if it is always wet it not only loses its attraction but soaks their clothes and makes them cold too.

Local dogs and cats will think the sand pit is for them to use for their personal needs so it's sensible to keep the surface covered when not in use. Make a simple frame of plastic fencing on wooden battens. It's not very pleasant for the children and can be unhealthy to have cat and dog mess in the sand.

Lastly, try to keep earth out of the pit or the mixture will support plant growth and weeds will take root. Every couple of years it pays to clear out all the sand and replace it with fresh.

In the summer when it's warm, let your children play with water in the sand pit – young ones will spend hours making sand pies, paddling, making ponds, rivers and moats, and floating plastic ducks in the sand pit. A trickle of water from a hose or a bucket of water will give hours of fun. *Related topics* Play; playgrounds.

Scabies An itchy condition caused by mites transferred from person to person by close skin contact or indirectly from clothing or bedding. Animals can also pass on scabies to their owners.

The female mite burrows into the skin mainly between the fingers, on the palms, on the fronts of the wrists and the elbows, in the armpits and around the waist. This causes very bad itching and a rash of little blisters and fine zig-zag lines (the mites' burrows). Some children have an allergic reaction to the mites and get urticaria and others develop a secondary bacterial infection in the skin from all the scratching. Very young babies can get scabies on the front and sides of their upper chest where their infected parents' wrists come into contact with them as they are picked up.

Diagnosis is a skilled job and treatment involves scrubbing the skin in a long, hot bath followed by the application of benzyl benzoate or other special solution all over the body except the eyes. When this is dry a second application is put on and on the next day two more are applied. All clothing, sheets and so on must be washed after the course of treatment.

All the family will need to be treated because scabies can easily and quickly spread. If your dog is the source of your mites, see your vet. *Related topic* Pets.

Scalds Hot fluids are commonplace around the house so scalding is an ever-present danger. Drinks that are too hot can scald the inside of the mouth or throat. Always check the temperature of any food or drink for babies or children too young to test it for themselves. If a child's mouth is scalded, give him an ice cube, some ice cream, or a drink of cold water straight away.

Bath water is a potential danger because it's so easy to forget to check the temperature of the water before putting a child in. One way round the problem is never to have your water supply so hot that it could scald – if it is very hot then the taps too become hot and can burn a child. Always put cold water into the bath first, then add hot to bring it to the right temperature. Remember that your hands are a lot less sensitive to hot water than other parts of your body so your child's bath water should feel on the cool side to your hands. It's a good idea to test the bath water with your elbow, as this is more sensitive to temperature than your hand. Also, if you've used your hand to mix the bath water, it'll be accustomed to the heat and won't be so sensitive.

The second greatest source of scalds are pans of boiling water, and other hot things on the cooker. Chidren love to see what's cooking and will try to look if not told otherwise. In this way saucepans can be emptied all over them with disastrous results. To prevent this, fit a cooker rail around the hob to prevent pans being pulled off and teach your child how dangerous the cooker is. Remember that young children don't learn if they're only told once, but need to have the same warning lots of times. Never leave a pan on the cooker with its handle sticking out towards the child because that's asking for trouble. Whenever you're cooking, keep an eye on your children and try not to leave them alone in the kitchen.

A young baby likes to grab at everything and can easily knock a cup of tea off the table all over himself or you. He'll also try to get a cup that you're holding. Prevention is better than cure – so be warned. Get rid of table cloths for this stage of your life and you'll cut down on spilt drinks and scalds. Check the flex of your electric kettle. It should never be able to hang within reach of a child. It's worth checking kettle flexes in grandparents' houses and other houses that your children regularly visit.

Once a child has scalded himself the best thing to do is to reduce the skin temperature at once. Every second counts. Dowse the area with cold water, plunge the affected part into a bowl of cold water, or run a bath of cold water and throw the child in. If the scald has made the clothes adhere to the skin, leave them alone but if they seem to come away very easily then take them off. Any scald larger than the palm of your hand must be seen by a doctor.

Once the area is dry, cover it with a dry dressing and leave it to heal. Don't apply butter or grease of any sort as it will do no good. If the pain is severe give junior aspirin in the correct dose. Over a few days the scald should heal spontaneously but if it becomes redder, pussy or more painful, see your doctor at once. *Related topics* Accidents; accident prevention; burns. *Useful organization* The Royal Society for the Prevention of Accidents.

Scarlet fever A mild disease, also known as scarlatina, caused by a bacterial infection with a type of streptococcus. Most strains of streptococcus cause only a sore throat but this particular one produces a rash and a sore throat. The incubation period is between two and five days and this is followed by a sudden fever, a headache, swollen lymph nodes (glands) in the neck, a loss of appetite and vomiting. A child often doesn't complain of his sore throat but he may complain of a tummy ache which is caused by a swelling of the lymph nodes around the intestine (mesenteric adenitis). The rash appears the next day and is composed of slightly raised red spots on a flushed skin. It starts on the neck, armpits and groins and spreads to the rest of the body. The child may soon look red all over (hence 'scarlet' fever). Classically the skin around the mouth remains pale. After about a week the skin flakes over the spots, especially in the skin creases and on the fingertips. The tongue which was furred with red projections (like a white strawberry) is now red and shiny (like a red strawberry). Inflammation of the middle ear (otitis media) is a fairly common complication.

Scarlet fever should be treated with a course of antibiotics which will render the child non-infectious within hours if the bacteria are susceptible.

Scarlet fever is not considered a dangerous disease today. *Related topics* Sore throat; nephritis; tonsillitis.

School choice of You'll have to decide on a school well before your child is five and sooner if he's to join a nursery or 'pre-prep' class at three or four. Children are legally required to go to school or to have suitable alternative education from five to sixteen in this country. You may choose a school simply because it's nearest to you (apply to your education authority for information about the local possibilities), especially if you have no transport to take your child to school. It's very pleasant for a child to go to a community school and because he'll probably know so many of the children, he'll feel as though he belongs there very quickly. Also, the children he makes friends with will probably live nearby, making visits easier.

If there are several possible schools for your child, go and see each one to help you choose. Make an appointment with the school secretary (for one or both of you, with or without your child – as you prefer) to see round the school. This will give you an idea of the educational and recreational facilities; the atmosphere produced by the type of building and its decor; the adequacy and cleanliness of the lavatories and washing facilities; the space available; and to meet the headmaster or headmistress and find out about the sort of education provided and whether it would be suitable for your child. It's good, if possible, to meet the teacher with whom your child would start. Ideally it's a good idea to be able to watch him or her teaching. The school secretary will tell you when you should see over the school and when it's necessary to put your child's name down for it. For some schools it's advisable to see over them as early as possible and to get names down quickly, because they tend to be oversubscribed. Others serve a smaller area or are less popular and have places available all the time, so you can take your time.

It's sensible to make lots of enquiries about the school among parents whose children have attended it and to talk to anyone who has had dealings with the school and its pupils. You may know a teacher there who can give you some inside information. It's better to find out beforehand whether your child isn't going to fit in than to have to remove him after he's started, and each school is inevitably different in its approach and its dealings with the children.

Whether you are well-off or can just scrape the money together, if you choose to spend your money on private education your choice of schools is wider because you can opt to send your child to a fee-paying school. Do consider all the schools, because private schools are by no means always better than state ones. You may decide to start your child off at a private school and later to send him to a state one, or vice versa. The system is very flexible and at all times you should choose the school that you think will suit your child best. The school your neighbour or your friend chooses may not be the best choice for your children. Although a headmaster or headmistress can help you decide, ultimately the choice is yours and it can be a difficult one.

Some schools take a special interest in music, others in games, swimming and all sorts of physical education. Some schools encourage early reading and writing; others are very relaxed in their approach to the three Rs. Some at first have a system of family grouping, in which five- and six-year-olds are in a class together, together with vertical streaming, in which children within these classes are grouped according to ability for certain lessons. Others separate the children into classes strictly according to their age, with the classes a year apart (or sometimes six months apart). In some schools children can be put up or down a class (usually at the beginning of an academic year), while in others they always stay with their peer group. Some schools will take children only in September, while others take them at any time, though usually at the beginning of a term. Some schools insist on entrants being five or 'rising five' (that is five in the term in which they start school), while others take them in September only, whether they're five-and-a-half or – less commonly – four-and-a-half. You may have strong feelings about any one of these differences. The school you end up choosing may not be your ideal, but take care that it comes as close as possible.

Remember that a school can gain a very good reputation because of one or two very good teachers. The policy of the school always comes from the top though, so judge it by the headmaster or headmistress and find out if you can what qualities he or she looks for when choosing teachers. There is a wide choice of teachers looking for jobs so the ones chosen reflect the head's priorities.

It may help to make a list of all the things you want to find out about the school. This list will inevitably reflect your background, expectations and knowledge about schooling. You may want to know what is taught and how it is taught, including what reading schemes; how many children can read fluently after two or three years; the size of the classes; any special educational methods; how long the teachers stay at the school on average; which schools the children go to afterwards; what extra subjects are offered; if the school caters for children up to eleven or older; how well the children do in exams; whether there is any facility for extra or individual coaching for a slow child or one who has a difficulty; whether there is one teacher per class or several 'team teachers'; whether the class teacher takes the children for all subjects or not; and, when the children are older, how much homework there is.

You may be interested in things such as whether the school is connected with a church and what form the daily act of worship takes; school rules and their enforcement; school uniform and whether a child must stick to it rigidly (having to buy indoor and outdoor shoes can become expensive: most parents find that one pair of shoes and a pair of wellingtons is adequate); when the school day starts and finishes and whether the children are supervised if they get there early or if you are a bit late in picking them up; and what sort of meals and drinks for break are provided.

Some schools are very good at involving parents in various activities and letting them know how their child is getting on. Ask about reports and also how easy it is to arrange to see your child's teacher at any time.

When you have seen the school, the head, the teachers and some of the other children there, ask yourselves what sort of atmosphere there was in the school. Some schools really do seem happier than others according to people who visit a lot of them. Ask yourselves if you and your child liked the head and the other teachers and whether the children you saw seemed to be enjoying themselves and were well supervised, or whether they looked bored and were playing around. Ask yourselves whether there was plenty of evidence of art and craft work and whether it was well displayed. Was the five-year-old class room in particular cheerful and welcoming, with lots of interesting things in it or were there simply serried rows of desks, bare walls and a blackboard? Ask yourselves if the school seemed well cared for and thriving, with an attractive playground. Ask yourselves whether it was the sort of place where you would want to be for five days a week, for much of the year.

Some parents have no choice over their child's first school, which is satisfactory if they are pleased with it. If they are not, the most important thing to do is to support and encourage your child while he is there, and this includes not criticizing the school in front of him. Get on good terms with his teacher and the head and join the parent-teacher association (if there is one – if not, form a group of interested parents to liaise with the staff) so that you can discuss what could be done to help and improve the school. Remember that however old or poor the school and its surroundings, it is people who count – it is they who have the ability or otherwise to make your child happy and interested. If the staff are well motivated and get on well together, your child stands every chance of enjoying his school days. It's important that he does so, because he'll be spending a third of all his waking hours there from five onwards. *Related topics* Pre-school education; school – preparation for.

School – preparation for Going to school entails a huge change in

your child's life style. From now until he is at least sixteen, he'll be away from home on a regular basis during term time. It's up to you whether you start your child at school before he's five. A nursery class may help ease him gently into full-time school if he only goes for a few half days a week, but this doesn't apply to every child: some are not ready to leave their mothers on a regular basis until at least five. In any case, it's a fallacy that you'll avoid any problems caused by settling in to school if your child starts at three or four. The problems – if any – will simply occur earlier and your child will be less able to cope with them then. Being accustomed to going to a play-group or nursery school often helps a child when he starts school, because at least he's used to being apart from his mother, but it doesn't always work because the adults, children and buildings are all different at school. Some schools allow five-year-olds to attend half-time for the first half term and this can work very well: a full day is very tiring for a child who is having to get used to so many new experiences at once.

Preparation for school starts from birth onwards. By providing a stable, happy home background, you're giving your child a good base from which to go out to school each day and he's more likely to be able to cope with problems if he knows he has the love and support of his parents to help him. By encouraging a liking for and an interest in books, stories and pictures, you'll help him get off to a good start when it comes to reading. By letting him use pencils, crayons, paints, scissors, glue and all the other creative paraphernalia, you're preparing for arts and crafts at school. By letting him play with friends and occasionally leaving him with familiar adults, you're helping him develop the social skills he'll need at school. By teaching him how to dress and undress, wipe his nose and manage in the lavatory, you'll give him confidence in these matters for later. By giving him a variety of meals, you'll pave the way for him to enjoy his school dinners. By encouraging him to talk to you, to tell you what he's been doing, thinking, dreaming, or planning, and to ask you questions, you're helping him not only to build up his verbal skills but also to gain confidence. By teaching him how to behave and how to be considerate to others, you'll help him to be not only acceptable but popular.in class and in the playground. By your obvious enjoyment of reading, writing and making things and all the other skills you learnt at school, he will want to follow your example.

Help your child develop positive, optimistic and enthusiastic feelings about school by talking about how much you enjoyed school (if you did – if you didn't, don't say anything), by talking about his school, the children and the staff you have met, and by arranging for him to meet and hopefully to befriend other children who'll be in his class.

Whether or not your child settles in easily at school at first will depend partly on your preparation, but also to a large extent on his basic personality. Even with the most careful preparation, some children are miserable at school, though usually only temporarily, until they gain confidence there. Conversely, the shyest and most timid of children often surprise everyone by blossoming once they go to school. If your child still seems unhappy after the first couple of weeks or so, try to find out gently and tactfully why. Is it because he's missing you and his home? Is it because he doesn't like the teacher? (Perhaps he can't get used to the fact that he's one of many in her charge or perhaps he's not used to being told what to do and expected to do it.) Is it because he doesn't like one or more of the other children or feels they don't like him? (Children are very sensitive and badly want to be liked and accepted as one of the group. A child who wears glasses, who hasn't got the same uniform as the others, or who is the only one without a biscuit or apple for break may feel very left out.) Is it because he's terrified of the idea that he's got to go on coming to school day in day out for the rest of his childhood? (Some children believe that school is only a temporary interlude and that once they've been there for a while, they can stay at home for good. They are very surprised and some are disappointed to learn that school will last for a long time.) Is it because other children take a toy or something special from home every day and he doesn't? Is it because he wants you to take him to school and not your next door neighbour? There are a myriad of reasons for not liking school. If you can't fathom out why your child is unhappy, have a quiet word with his teacher to see if you can come up with the answer between you. Some teachers offer very sensitive help to unhappy children who've just started school and may come up with suggestions such as that the child goes home early one day a week for the first few weeks, so that he has something to look forward to. Some teachers suggest that you come in to help with artwork or in the playground, to make your child feel more secure.

Almost all children settle down in school at some time during their first year and most enjoy school, or at least many aspects of it. Starting school is a big hurdle, and it's not surprising that some children take to it better than others. If you've prepared your child as well as you can, you can be confident that you have helped him on his way all you can.

Science Just as adults learn about the world around them by experimenting and benefiting from the lessons learned, so can the young child. He'll want to test his theories about what to us adults seem simple or self-evident facts. When a child sorts out toys, beads, cars, dolls, or whatever by size and colour, he is learning about the most basic rudiments of science – classifying things into groups so as to make sense of them.

The world is full of scientific questions for the four and five-year-old. Why do eggs go hard when they're cooked? Why does water flow downhill? These and thousands of others all require a simple scientific answer which you could look up in a book in the library if you don't know the answer. But answering questions is only half the story. How about asking him a few to get him thinking about something that he sees every day. Play is of course the best way to teach children of this age anything and through play he can learn a lot about basic science. Water evaporating from a puddle or a sandpit needs explaining as does the water level in a tumbler when you tip it sideways – and so on.

Growing simple beans or seeds gives a lot of pleasure and enables even a young child to learn how things grow and what they need to grow. He'll enjoy watching the shoots lean towards the sun and move as the sun moves. There are lots of games that will teach him about sound, such as making echoes in a cave or muffling a kitchen timer in a drawer; making a simple parachute with an old handkerchief proves to him that air offers some resistance; an inclined plane to run cars down shows that you store energy in something by lifting it up high.

Today's five-year-old may be hankering after electronic toys and other sophisticated applications of science but it's unlikely that many parents will be able to give more than a fleeting explanation of how these work. A simple encyclopaedia may help you explain many everyday things to your child in a way he can understand.

The under-five of today will be far more technically involved and educated than we, his parents are, as life becomes increasingly electronically based at home and at work, so making an early start to interest him can do no harm at all. *Related topic* Questions.

Scissors Young children love cutting but to do this they need good scissors. Scissors for little children should be sharp (but not razor-edged) and have blunt ends so they don't damage themselves or others. Cutting by two-or three-year-olds should ideally be supervised all the time. All too often experiments with cutting clothes or hair can quickly take the place of paper or card cutting! When learning to cut it's a lot easier learning on thin cardboard than on paper or fabric which is too floppy and frustrating. Plastic scissors are really only useful as toys as they have little cutting ability. *Related topic* Cuts.

Scurf The skin of the scalp is composed of layers of cells. The top layer (the epidermis) sheds cells as they die and these cells, together with oils and sweat, are seen as tiny white flakes on the surface of the scalp between the hairs. A small amount of such scurf is quite normal. If there is an excessive amount, seen as lots of white flakes showering down as you brush your child's hair, it is commonly known as dandruff. Dandruff is associated with seborrhoea (excessive production of scalp oil or sebum). Treatment involves using a medicated shampoo or, if necessary, a shampoo containing coal-tar or other active ingredients. *Related topics* Cradle cap; hair care.

Scurvy A disease caused by a shortage of vitamin C in the diet. The classical type of the disease is rarely seen in older children but babies from six months to two-years-old can suffer from a type of scurvy.

A child short of vitamin C has tender swelling of the bones, painful joints, loosening of the teeth, swollen, bluish gums, delayed healing of cuts and wounds, bruising of the skin, fever, a lack of energy, and delayed growth.

The baby with scurvy cries on being moved because his joints and bones hurt, and many such babies look apprehensive because they know that whatever their parent does, it'll hurt them. The diagnosis is not difficult to make if the child is already ill but there is an increasing body of medical opinion that believes that a less than obvious vitamin C lack can cause health problems in babies. Giving vitamin C makes the child better, often within days.

Prevention is the best cure. A breast-feeding mother should eat foods rich in vitamin C so that her baby gets enough of her milk, and bottle-fed babies should be given supplements because cows' milk formula is low in vitamin C. Vitamin drops containing vitamin C and orange juice (not squash) or tomato juice are good sources for a baby. Commercial sweetened 'vitamin C' drinks and rose hip syrup – although rich in vitamin C – are likely to cause tooth decay and are better avoided.

Second-hand equipment As baby equipment gets more and more expensive many parents buy second-hand things at sales, from small ads in their local papers or corner shop windows and from friends. Very often you can pick up excellent bargains in this way because many baby things are almost as good as new if they have only been used for one or two babies, yet they can be bought for a fraction of the price of the same item new.

The main thing is to be as careful buying second hand as you would be when buying new. Preferably buy equipment that's fairly new rather than very old and done up because newish items will conform to up-to-date safety standards. Really old pieces could be painted with lead paint, for example, which wouldn't be allowed today and old wooden things could have splinters or broken parts. Never buy broken things unless you can mend them to make them safe. For the sake of a few pounds you don't want to put your baby in danger. Many larger items such as prams and cots can be overhauled and new parts bought from the makers.

When you've finished having your babies, if you don't want to pass your equipment on to relatives or friends, you could have a garage sale or something similar. Price all the stuff, advertise among your friends, at the local toddler group and even in the local paper and then have a sale one day. If you don't need the money you can give your baby things to jumble sales or to local charities that look after unmarried mothers: they are always short of things and very grateful. Your health visitor may know of someone who would be hard put to afford equipment herself. *Related topic* Equipment for baby.

Self-confidence A child's belief or trust in himself and his abilities; self-assurance.

Like so many aspects of a child's personality, self-confidence depends partly on his inborn characteristics, partly on how he is brought up and partly on the experience he has of other people and other situations. In other words, his self-confidence can be increased or decreased, though some children start off with more than others.

Self-confidence is closely linked with confidence or trust in other people and a baby brought up to be confident in himself will almost invariably be trustful of other people later.

But how can you increase a baby's inborn level of confidence? You can do it by helping him not to be afraid, worried, or angry. For the first nine months of his life a baby has had a warm and protected environment with a constant supply of nourishment, a constant level of soothing noises from his mother's heart, tummy rumbles and voice, darkness or semi-darkness, and the comfort of being surrounded by fluid and the flexible but resilient walls of his mother's uterus. When he is born, he is assailed by strong stimuli of noise, light, rough handling and strange smells. All these can be minimized and *are* being in a few maternity units and home deliveries.

Many babies today are breast-fed on an unrestricted basis; kept close to their mother's bodies for much of the day and night, perhaps even sleeping next to her in bed at night, and being cuddled, held in one arm, or carried in a sling for much of the waking day; and comforted as soon as they cry by being put to the breast. Bottle-feeding can mimic this degree of security to some extent but doesn't provide quite the same degree of comfort as does breast-feeding, even if combined with a dummy. If you were to make your crying baby wait until it was 'time for a feed', or if you were to leave him awake and screaming in his cot because it was 'time for his sleep', you would be subjecting him to unnecessary levels of anxiety, fear, loneliness and even anger, all of which would tend to reduce his confidence in himself at being able to signal adequately to you that he needed help, and would lessen his basic trust and confidence in you as the person who looks after him.

If a baby is allowed to stay with his favourite person (who is almost always his mother) most of the time during his first year and is then allowed to explore with her nearby as a safe base to which to return, his confidence in himself and in his mother will continue to be built up. He'll feel that his world is safe and that he can conquer anything. Gradually he'll become more adventurous and happy to leave his mother for short periods – perhaps to go out of the room to play alone for a few minutes, but he'll always want to know that she's there. If he is left with someone else, he'll suffer a real blow to his confidence and trust if the separation is frequent or long-term, unless he has an acceptable (to him) mother substitute to whom he can become attached. Babies or children who are separated from their mothers for more than a day first show anxiety, often mixed with anger. When the mother comes back, her child will cling on to her as though never to let go, but may be angry with her as well. If she stays away for longer (the time depends on the individual child), he'll become quiet, less active and downcast. This period of withdrawal may give way to an appearance of normality and the child may start to smile, but if his mother now returns, she may be completely ignored, much to her chagrin. He treats her as an enemy or at any rate as a person of no consequence. If a child is left for long enough, with no adequate substitute care, he eventually makes desperate overtures to all and sundry, seeking the love and attention on a one-to-one basis that he has lost.

In time, a child's feelings about being left disappear though he may always have a basic but hidden fear of being deserted, for that is how young children see their mother's absence. In the meantime, his fear, anger and anxiety may show up in his being very clinging, having sleep problems, bedwetting or daytime 'accidents' although previously dry, or sucking much more often at the breast, bottle, dummy, or other comfort object. Some parents can't put their fingers on the difference in their child's behaviour in any definite way after he has been separated but just feel that he's different. They have to work hard to increase his trust and confidence before they again have the child they knew.

Self-confidence and trust in others are built upon security and stability of personal relationships. On top of this come praise, encouragement and lack of negative criticism, all of which can boost a child's feelings of worth and pride in himself. A child will thrive in his pre-school years on being given gradually increasing responsibility and on being allowed to help in ordinary day-to-day tasks. He'll enjoy the achievement of learning to dress and wash himself, of finding out how things work for himself, of taking the top off an egg, of doing practically anything himself. Of course, he won't be able to do things by himself completely, but you can tactfully help him almost without his being aware of your help. Praise him as though he'd done it himself and encourage him to try again when he's ready. Take care not to give a child tasks which are always a bit too difficult for him. He'll be more confident in trying the next step if he's quite happy and confident about the last one – it always feels good to proceed from a position of strength, however old you are. *Related topics* Development – emotional; development – social; independence; love; mothering; personality; separation anxiety; trust.

Selfishness Children under the age of 2½ really have no sense of selfishness – everything anyone else owns is up for grabs. A tiny child of this age only ever gives things up when he's ready to do so or under extreme duress. He never does it to be unselfish – he can't think that way yet. Children under 2½ take things whether they're theirs or not and sometimes this can lead to bitter conflicts among children, especially those of a similar age. Better to step in and divert their attention altogether than to punish them or to try to make them see reason, because they can't. Making them share things is seen as a great injustice and creates more trouble.

Once a child is about three he's on the way to being able to share things with grace and enjoys others sharing their things with him. Before this age selfishness is normal – so don't worry that your child is developing into a little monster.

If you are always unselfish in your behaviour, your children will tend to follow your example, though they may not do so for years. Being unselfish isn't the same as being a doormat, which would not be a good example to your children any more than selfishness would.

Bringing up the under-fives involves a good deal of unselfishness on the part of the parents, mainly because of the lack of time parents have for themselves at this stage – young self-centred parenting is rarely enjoyable or successful. *Related topic* Generosity.

Separation anxiety As soon as a baby is conceived he is an individual in his own right but so far, even though science today can enable conception to take place in a test tube, the human embryo needs to grow inside the womb for several months before it can mature as a separate person. During the pregnancy a baby is in intimate contact with his mother and shares her oxygen and food supplies, together with her blood supply. She protects him from extremes of temperature and her amniotic fluid around him buffers him from sudden movements. As soon as his hearing system has developed, he hears the sounds of her heart, the blood passing through her blood vessels, the bowel contents being moved along, and her voice. He also hears what she hears, though the sounds are muted by her body to some extent.

The eventual physical separation of mother and baby is inevitable but the relationship·or bond which is begun even before birth remains for ever, even if they are parted permanently and even though it has nothing necessarily to do with love.

After birth a healthy baby can breathe and drink milk but if left to himself would die within hours. He is almost totally dependent on his mother who is nearly always his physical and emotional provider and protector. Though his body is now separate from hers, he remains physically dependent on her for a very long time to come and his need for her is intense. Some mothers find it helpful to think of themselves and their babies as couples or of their babies as extensions of themselves, because the sort of care needed by a baby makes it necessary to keep him close by for twenty-four hours of the day.

The surprise of the abrupt physical separation of birth is made easier for a baby by continued close contact with his mother. The sound of her voice is reassuring in its familiarity to him and her touch and firm hold remind him of being held firmly in her womb. Her breast milk soon becomes very attractive to him and the inevitable physical closeness during breast-feeding (and the ease of access to his mother's breast that accompanies unrestricted breastfeeding) are very comforting. A bottle is frequently used to feed a baby in our society but is just one more way of separating mother and baby. However much medical and nursing care an unwell or immature baby may need, he still benefits from his mother's care and closeness. Just by talking to and stroking her baby in an incubator she can provide some sense of continuity for him.

The role of a mother is to care for her baby while allowing him to develop physically and emotionally at his own rate, so that he can eventually become quite independent of her. In the meantime, he soon makes it obvious that he prefers to be inseparable from her. During the first few months he forms an increasingly close attachment to her and somewhere around the middle of his first year he protests if she so much as leaves him in his father's arms! Babies vary according to how strongly they protest at separation from their mother and a lot depends on their personalities. However, at this age, their protest also depends on the frequency and length of separation, their past experience of being separated and how happy they were to be left, the behaviour and familiarity of the person they're left with, how well they know their surroundings, their emotional stability, their home background and how tired or hungry they are.

Over the next two or three years the growing baby likes to be with his mother and to explore the world from the safety of her as a base. This means that he likes her to be there when he wants her but at the same time wants freedom to go off by himself to try his wings. It's a difficult stage for the mother who is keen to push her child into independence. It's easier by far to accept that your child will learn to cope best if allowed to fly at his own rate. This means that you stay with him unless you are quite sure that he will be happy without you. Leave him once when he's unhappy to be left and you'll set him back in his path to independence.

By around three – sometimes a little earlier, sometimes later – most children cope well for periods of several hours without their mothers (or whoever it is who usually cares for them). By five, the majority can cope with day long separation from mother and home at school.

There are lots of reasons for separation and it's impossible to make any generalizations about how to cope in any one family. Mother and baby may be separated for occasional short times, occasional long times, frequent short times, frequent long times, or even permanently. From the parents' point of view their aim should be to make the time of separation of their baby from his mother as easy and as painless as possible. Obviously both the baby's needs and those of his mother (or other family members) must be considered, but it's worth remembering that babies can suffer when separated from their mothers.

Lots of babies are very often temporarily separated when their mothers leave them alone in their cots or prams so that they can sleep. Some babies take a long time to get used to being left alone and indeed some never do get completely used to it and always protest. They may cry in their cots from loneliness or simply from a feeling of fear of being without their mother. Depending on the age of the baby, only his mother can comfort him. Babies and young children have no concept of time and even though a mother knows that she'll go to her crying baby in a few minutes, he doesn't know when that will be or even if it will be. All he knows is that she isn't there when he wants her and that he's unhappy about it. She may believe that as her baby has the security of being in his own cot in his own room, he ought to be happy there alone until she's ready. However, he cares very little for his cot and his room – inanimate objects have little comfort value to him. All he wants is his mother and he won't be able to understand it when she doesn't respond to his cries. Babies who are seldom left alone to cry are almost always happy and outgoing and they nearly always grow up into confident, independent children.

A baby's or young child's worry or anger at being left alone regularly in his cot may be directed not necessarily at his mother but perhaps at some object, or it may be directed inwardly at the child himself, making him prone to anxiety as he grows. This separation anxiety is a very common problem which doesn't usually become obvious until a baby is over six months or so, when he becomes suspicious of anyone other than his mother and makes it obvious that he prefers to be with her. Babies and young children can learn to cope with their separation anxiety but that doesn't mean to say that it wouldn't be better for them not to suffer from it in the first place. A child who is subsequently exposed to other worrying or fear-provoking situations may not be able to cope with them as well as one who doesn't have a background of separation anxiety to cope with as well. The confidence gained from not being continually separated from his mother throughout babyhood almost certainly makes a child feel more secure throughout his life in the face of new problems.

Thankfully, the loving behaviour of mothers who encourage early separation when they are with their babies and young children usually seems to make up to a great extent for leaving them to cry untended. The reason why most babies can bury their despair at being left to cry alone is because of the love they gradually come to realize their mother feels for them even though she may leave them to cry. Some babies, however, grow up in seemingly loveless families or with parents who have a very poor relationship with each other. Their background of emotional instability may make it more difficult for these babies to come to terms with their separation anxiety. It's quite possible that the insecurity felt by babies and young children separated before they are mature enough to cope stays with some of them to some degree, albeit buried deep in their unconscious minds, for the rest of their lives. This hypothesis is almost impossible to prove, but such babies and young children lead very different and ostensibly far less happy lives overall than those whose mothers don't leave them to cry and who keep them by their side day and night, and it seems unlikely that such unhappiness would leave no scars. Having said this, it's remarkable perhaps that some children manage to weather frequent separation from their mothers together with the most stressful backgrounds and still turn out to have apparently healthy and stable personalities.

Separation is not only a problem if a baby or child is obviously unhappy to be left. Babies and young children can be trained not to cry when left at night, during the day for a sleep in their cot, or with someone else while their mother goes out. The more often a mother does it, the sooner her baby learns not to make a fuss. However, this doesn't mean to say that he is necessarily happy to be left. All it means is that he's learnt to restrain his feelings and to bury his unhappiness. It's easy enough to tell when a baby or child is truly happy to be left. It's when they are quiet, sit there sucking their thumbs, look worried, or watch the door every time there is a noise that it's not so easy to be sure they're content to be without their mother.

Separation anxiety doesn't only affect babies. Even a normally happy two-year-old may be distraught when left by his mother with someone else. Another child may seem apparently happy while she is away then burst into tears when she comes back, demonstrating his pent up anxiety. If a baby or young child has to be left, it's best to leave him with a well-known person, to make the separation easier for him. Instead of trying to encourage him to manage without you as soon as possible, give him the security of your presence for as long as he wants and let him get to know other people with you there too. If you often see your friends, your child will soon get to know them well and is less likely to be clingy than if he only sees them infrequently. Once he is familiar with someone else, then is the time to leave the room for ten minutes or so and thereafter to leave him for gradually increasing periods of time if he is happy to be left. Every child is different and you'll get to know soon enough when your child is really happy to be left with someone else. Babies and young children are most likely to cope with being left with someone else when they are not tired, unwell or hungry. There is nothing to be gained from forcing a child to stay somewhere without you if he doesn't want to. This will only make him feel insecure and unhappy. Never apologize to other people about your child being clingy. Ten to one your child's wanting to be with you is perfectly normal and natural.

Keeping your young child with you for as much as he needs you during the first three years or so is only a nuisance if your expectations are different. It's quite possible to have an active and fulfilling life with your child there all the time. It's not surprising that mothers who live lonely lives cooped up all day with their young child and seeing virtually no one else often get 'cabin fever'. They feel depressed and long to have some time apart from their child. But most mothers can make friends and widen their circle of acquaintances if they really want to. Seeing other people takes the pressure off their relationship with their child and makes them less likely to find his constant presence annoying or frustrating. It's also a tremendous benefit to the child who learns to relate to people other than those in his immediate family.

Sometimes it's essential for a mother to leave her baby or young child, for instance if she has to go into hospital and can't take him with her. A caring, familiar, stable mother substitute makes the separation easier for a child. Of course it helps if he can be taken to see his mother frequently. Even if he cries when he sees her, that doesn't mean he's unhappy to see her, just that his pent-up anxiety at being separated is being released. All the recognized side effects of being separated from his mother may follow, such as anger with her and temporary rejection of her when they are together again, but these would be worse if they didn't see each other at all.

A basically secure child with a stable, happy home life, who has formed a good relationship with his mother, will almost certainly weather her absence well as long as he is cared for by someone he can attach himself to in the meantime. Children with a background of frequent (and perhaps unnecessary) separation, and who have been unhappy to be separated, are much more likely to have emotional problems when left.

Children reared without their mothers in institutions tend to be more clinging than those conventionally brought up. They form more superficial relationships with other people but they're less likely to form close ones. They're also more attention seeking and seemingly over-friendly with strangers. Their behaviour is quite normal considering their circumstances, but if they are taken into a family, they relearn their patterns of interaction.

The behaviour of mothers who choose to have their children brought up by another person has been noticed to be different from that of mothers who are with their children most of the time. Their responses are modified by separation and they may lack an easy relationship with their children, perhaps being over-attentive. Their young children may tend to play up to this and behave quite differently when with their mothers from how they usually behave. *Related topics* Divorce; one parent families; mothering; mother substitute; routines.

Separation of parents With one in four of today's marriages likely to end in divorce, it's probable that even more than this number of couples separate temporarily, if not permanently.

When marital relationships have become so bad that one or both parents want to split up, the child has probably already been exposed to a lot of rowing and bad feeling at home. Even if his parents have tried to keep discussions and quarrels to themselves, it's a rare child who is so insensitive that he doesn't realize that things have gone very wrong. Just the way his parents look at each other or the tone of voice in which quite ordinary, non-aggressive conversations are carried out can be give-aways. The child may spend much of his waking day (including his going to sleep time at night when he may be able to hear raised voices downstairs) worrying about whether his parents are going to make it up or whether there's going to be yet another flare-up. There'll come a time when he'll realize to his horror that they are talking about leaving each other. His emotions are very muddled at this time and include anger at them for disrupting his life and for hurting him and each other; feelings of protectiveness for whoever he feels is the wronged parent; feelings of inadequacy at not being able to mend the situation himself; and feelings of fright and helplessness at the prospect of being left completely: 'if one can go, perhaps both will, and I'll be left behind'.

In the majority of cases of separation, the child stays with his mother.

This is the best that can happen to him if she is the one to whom he is most attached. If she leaves him with his father (or if father and child leave her), however good their relationship is, the child has to endure being rejected by his mother, and that is a very bitter psychological pill to swallow. Such a child will, of course, transfer his main allegiance to his father in time, but he'll feel none the less angry and hurt and may withdraw into himself for a long while. If she comes back soon, he may go to her at once and be extra clinging, but if she's away for long enough, he may reject her in his turn and she'll have to work very hard to win him back. She may feel that their relationship is never quite the same again. This is probably partly because he feels he can never let himself trust her again because she let him down once, and partly because his own self-confidence will have taken a bashing. He sees his mother leaving home as a rejection of him rather than as a rejection of his father. All these feelings occur if the father is the one who leaves the mother and child (or if they leave him), but they are rarely quite so acute if the child has formed his closest attachment to his mother, which is the norm.

There is controversy over whether it's better for unhappily married parents to stay together for the sake of the child or whether it's better for him if they split up. It's rather silly and naïve to generalize on this because each situation is so different. The ideal, of course, is for them to stay together and to attempt to make the marriage work. This is easier said than done without skilled help, and skilled professional help is hard to come by in the UK even if you can afford to pay, which most people can't. Skilled amateur help in the form of trained marriage guidance counsellors is available at a low cost, and such a counsellor may make all the difference to an ailing marriage if allowed to help. Otherwise they may enable the couple to split up amicably and with the best possible arrangements for the children.

It often helps parents to realize that there are common times of stress in families and that they are not unusual in being affected by them. Such stresses include the birth of a baby (especially the first one), the death of a child, unemployment, illness, and bad housing. Even everyday responsibilities can cause stresses and tension so that at the least provocation one or other partner may snap and before long there is permanent disharmony. Many parents today have no shoulders to lean on other than each other's in times of trouble and if they are both feeling put upon by the pressures of everyday life, they may be no support to each other. It is a good insurance policy early in a marriage to join in the community in such a way as to be part of a network of caring friends and acquaintances who will just take a little of the burden off each other when necessary. Even if this is just by talking, it may be enough. Caring families can also help but many couples feel unable to share their marital and relationship problems with close relatives.

Older children whose parents are separated spend hours planning ways of getting them back together again. Younger ones of under-five tend to be more bemused by the situation but almost always believe that everything will turn out all right in the end and that their parents will be reunited. It's important, though difficult for the parent looking after the child, not to impose her feelings of anger, resentment and bitterness at her husband on her child. The child needs to retain an acceptable image of his lost parent and this is all too easily destroyed. If the separation looks like being permanent, arrange times for the other parent to see the child. It's not a question so much of the parent having access to the child as it is of the *child having access to his parent*: the child is the one who is the pawn in the situation and who must be protected.

Inevitably there will be great practical as well as emotional changes in a child's life when his parents separate. One of the most disruptive but most likely is that his mother will have to work. Suitable and permanent substitute care is always difficult to find, and he'll have to put up not only with losing one parent almost completely, but losing the remaining one for a large proportion of the time as well. If work can possibly wait until he goes to school, so much the better. **Related topics** Divorce; separation anxiety. **Useful organizations** Gingerbread; Meet-a-Mum Association; National Council for the Divorced and Separated; One Parent Families.

Sewing Knowing about fabrics and how to cut them out and make things from them is what sewing is all about and under-fives can have hours of fun cutting and sewing and doing simple embroidery. Pieces of fabric make wonderful playthings. They have different colours, patterns, feels and textures; are of different sizes and smells; and can be sewn together to make so many things. Simply taking pieces of fabric and glueing them on to card to make a pattern is great fun and the older child can make a simple patchwork by sewing them together. Don't expect too much too soon though because a young child's coordination and concentration aren't always all that good for such detailed work. As with eating and dressing, children need time to learn control. Most children can cut out well at 3½ if they're sufficiently interested, and four-year-olds can learn to sew simply. Make sure that you use blunt-ended scissors and teach him to cut thin card first (cereal boxes are good) as this is much easier than floppy fabric. Cutting with blunt scissors is no fun for anyone, let alone you as you'll probably end up doing much of it. You can lead up to threading needles by threading other things on to string. Always make sure that needles are put safely away if you have a mobile baby or if people walk about in socks or with bare feet in your house.

Start off real sewing with a large, flat bodkin with a large hole to aim for and thick thread. Always knot the end because it's very annoying for a child if the thread keeps pulling through the material. Once the child has mastered the basic skills get on and make something really useful with him, such as a pair of trousers for teddy or a hat for a doll. If things get tricky, don't be afraid to staple parts together. Children of four and five can have hours of fun making patterns by threading wool through old Christmas or birthday cards if you put some holes in the pictures at strategic places. Use thick wool of different colours and a bodkin and the result can look very attractive. *Related topic* Artistic activities.

Sex awareness Although a lot of research has been done on the differences between the sexes at birth most of the differences (other than the obvious genital ones) are pretty unconvincing. Boys are on average slightly heavier than girls at birth and are born slightly sooner but this isn't thought to be of much significance and the differences are small. The behaviour differences between newborns of either sex have also been shown to be very small.

Hospitals, parents and society 'label' their children according to their sex right from birth and several studies show that male and female babies are handled differently by each sex. There is still a considerable preference in society for male babies, particularly if it is the first baby in a family. Differences in behaviour of people handling babies are manifested in the first few days of life. Boys tend to be treated more physically while girls receive more affectionate contact and talking to. As children age in the first year though their parents tend to treat them more equally. After this age the sex gap widens. Girls start to speak before boys on average – perhaps because they are spoken to more.

Studies among children who, because of rare congenital abnormalities, seem to be of one sex but are in fact of the opposite sex, show that the child grows up thinking itself to be (and behaving like) the sex it is told it is. Sexual identity seems to be the product of the way the child is treated. Research has found that children know which sex they are and have identified with others of that sex by the age of two or three. Well before this age the average child will have realized that there are two groups of people – male and female – and to which he belongs.

Some families have strong feelings about deliberately showing their bodies to their children (or not doing so) but exaggerated behaviour in either direction may perplex him. A child of this age probably won't relate your body to his or hers anyway and child psychologists say that identification and comparison with same-sex parents can make a young child worry about his apparent inadequacy. Many children are amazed and even put off by the hairiness of adults' bodies but the subject can be easily and tactfully handled by telling them that one day they too will be hairy and that everyone has some body hair when they're grown-up. *Related topics* Development – psychosexual; Oedipus complex; sex education; sex identity.

Sex education There's no excuse today for telling children that babies are brought by a stork or are found under gooseberry bushes. Even if said in fun, children may believe it and you'll have lost a golden opportunity for letting your child into the sex education pool at the shallow end.

The first chance most parents have to talk about sex in any form is when the mother is expecting another baby. The young child probably won't notice his mother's expanding tummy until it's pointed out to him, but it's worth talking to him about the baby inside and letting him feel the kicks. Depending on his age, he may ask how it's going to get out. The best way to answer this is to say that the baby will come out the same way that he came out, through a special hole in his mother's bottom. That's usually the end of the first sex education lesson because a young child's mind seldom dwells on anything for long. On another occasion he may ask how the baby got inside his mother's tummy. For a two- or three-year-old, you can elaborate a little, but they don't usually go this far at this age. If a question is asked at an awkward moment, such as in the butcher's shop or in front of a prim relative, you could opt out by saying that you'll tell him later, but this sounds coy and might make the child think there's something secret about it. It's best to be straightforward and to give a brief but truthful answer even if it does embarrass you in front of others.

Another avenue of questioning opens up when a child notices that he or she is different from a brother or sister. The question 'why haven't I got one of those' really is a question girls ask; it wasn't a figment of Freud's imagination! To say tritely that a brother has a penis because he's a boy is unhelpful, if true, so you may think it's a good opportunity to mention as well that his penis can be used to do a wee-wee or when he's grown up to put a seed into a woman's tummy to make a baby. Such a comment may be greeted with delighted laughter – if you think about it, it does sound rather amazing. However, this information will be assimilated alongside such mundane, though interesting, information as why do cows moo or how does water come out of the tap, and the child will be able to build on it later when he asks more questions.

Sex education is a long drawn out process best begun in early childhood as part of a child's general education. It shouldn't be a consciously planned event, though if your child has never asked anything about babies and how they are made you might like to stage a conversation about it when he's four or five, just to give him the opportunity of finding out by asking questions himself. If you leave it till he goes to school, you never know what he'll learn from the other children. Even as young as five children discuss such matters in the playground and some come out with some amazing notions.

Gradually a young child will come to realize why it is that he has a mother and a father and his early sex education lessons will stand him in good stead for the future. It won't be until much later that the more complicated issues of the pleasures (and potential problems) of sex need to be discussed. A good way of getting many of the basic points over is to discuss the goings on among your pets. This lets a young child gently into the whole subject so that he then sees it as perfectly normal. *Related topic* Development – psychosexual.

Sex identity There has been endless argument over encouraging children's sex identity by giving them certain toys and expecting them to behave in specific ways. Whatever one's personal views on this, most children perceive that certain roles in life tend to be filled by men and others by women. This, in its simplest form, means that girls will tend to play nurses and boys firemen, simply because in real life this is what they see. Whether or not it does any good at all to encourage boys to play with dolls and girls with trains is open to debate but it's probably unimportant anyway. Some parents observe that their young sons naturally prefer playing with cars and creative toys whereas their daughters prefer dolls even though both are offered the same play material. It's likely, though, that adults and older children direct young children, albeit unconsciously, to certain forms of play they consider 'suitable' for them. If you take pleasure in playing dressing dolls with your baby son, he'll enjoy copying you just as much as your daughter would, and it certainly won't mean you're teaching him to be a sissy. Similarly, both boys and girls will enjoy playing with trains with you. The way you behave as parents, together with your family's lifestyle, will be much more powerful in forming your children's sex identity than anything else. A mother who can mend a fuse or decorate the home won't be seen as 'male' by her daughter (who'll tend to copy her) but as a female who is competent in certain areas. Similarly, a father who looks after the children won't be seen as feminine by his sons.

By the time children are two not only do they know which sex they are, but sex differences in their behaviour are quite obvious, especially when they are with other children. Given a chance, boys will tend to pick out boys' toys and girls will tend to go for dolls and the Wendy house. They do this just as much to be like the others as to be 'boys' or 'girls' in any abstract sense. Young children have a strong desire to belong and this makes them identify strongly with children of the same sex and age.

However, your daughter, as she gets a bit older, may be a girl who likes to dress as a boy all the time and play adventurous, exciting and dangerous games traditionally associated with boys such as cowboys and indians or anything involving fighting, climbing, or guns; she may be labelled a 'tomboy' and this is a label that will stay with her for a long time.

More often than not, she plays like this simply because these are the games she knows and likes best. She may have older brothers whose play she has imitated and joined in with. She may also have played mostly with friends who are boys. Children copy other children readily and once past a certain age – around two and a half to three – usually prefer playing with other children, whatever they are playing, to playing alone.

Sometimes parents worry because their tomboy daughter says she wishes she were a boy. She may refuse ever to put on a dress and pretend that she really is a boy, even though her sexual identity is in fact developing perfectly normally. There are lots of possible reasons for such behaviour and one is that she believes that boys are intrinsically better or that they get a better deal, perhaps because they are praised more by adults. Her parents may have made it obvious to her that they would have preferred to have had a boy instead of her. They may not realize they've done this but even if she has once overheard them saying it when they thought she was too young to understand or wasn't listening, it may prey on her mind. Most children enjoy active play and boys' toys are often far more conducive to this. Trousers or shorts are easier to put on and warmer than dresses and skirts and even one morning of fiddling with a pair of tights that are too tight or too short can be enough to put a girl off girl's clothes!

If your daughter is a tomboy, don't worry at all unless she really does wish she were a boy. If so, just take time to consider why this is and whether you are unconsciously putting girls down in your attitudes and behaviour. A girl tends to model herself on her mother and identify with her and it's possible that if her mother is constantly being criticized or otherwise treated poorly by her father, she may resent the fact that she's female too. Similarly, if she sees her mother unhappy and discontented with her lot, or hears her grumbling about her life, she may think that by behaving like a boy she can somehow avoid growing up to be like her mother.

The situation is similar with boys who prefer girlish games and pastimes. Unfortunately today many young boys spend very little time with men because in our society fathers are often away from home for much of the child's waking day and then busy at weekends and there may be few, if any, other men closely associated with the family. This means that a boy usually has only his mother as an adult to imitate. While it's quite normal for a child to imitate and identify to some extent with both parents, children of three and over tend more and more to do this with the parent of the same sex. A boy with no adult male around may have little opportunity to pattern himself as a male and has to rely on his mother's direction into traditionally male pastimes and interests. If he has sisters and plays mostly with girls, he'll quite naturally tend to prefer girlish play unless he is encouraged to do otherwise. There's no absolute need to do this because once he's at school he'll be influenced by boys and men teachers, but children are sometimes cruel and a boy who doesn't know how to play boyish games may be teased unmercifully at first and this could hurt a sensitive child a lot. Play-group is a good idea for a child with little or no male company, provided he is ready to be away from his mother.

Lots of boys enjoy dressing up, playing with dolls and dressing them, and playing house. This is quite normal and simply reflects the fact that they are copying their mothers, sisters or girls they play with. Today increasing numbers of fathers share, or at any rate help with, child care, cooking and household tasks, which means that these activities are not seen as exclusively female. A man who looks after his baby is no less masculine than his son who imitates him. Learning to do tasks once associated only with the opposite sex helps children grow up with a wide range of abilities and hence confidence in themselves.

The word 'sissy' is not often used now. If your son is only happy to play with girls and to play girlish games, it is worth considering whether there is some reason – for example, whether you really wanted a girl so badly that you let him know you were disappointed when he was born. In this case he might have come to believe that being a boy is inferior in your eyes and that you would be happier if he were a girl, or at any rate behaved as a girl.

Only if your child really seems to have a problem with 'gender identity' which you can't sort out yourself, do you need to get help via your family doctor or health visitor.

With the current trend towards parents having less stereotyped roles in the family there'll undoubtedly be more opportunity for today's young children to gain much more experience of both sexes at close quarters and as a result to enter childhood with a far greater range of experiences and responses. This is probably valuable in its own right but will certainly be so if society continues to develop in the way it is.

It's a good idea for children brought up in one-parent families to have the opportunity to model themselves on adults of the same sex so as to help them with the development of their sexual identity. *Related topics* Chromosomes; sex awareness.

Shame A powerful emotion which usually results from being aware of having done something wrong. Children feel guilty when they know they've done something they shouldn't even before their parents get to know about it. Shame is closely tied to the feeling of guilt but shame is visible whereas guilt is not. When a child feels ashamed he wants to bury his face or sink into a pit in the ground.

Shaming children into behaving acceptably is a very old practice indeed and many primitive peoples have used shame to train children over the centuries. However, too much shaming can be shown to have adverse affects, resulting as it can in defiant shamelessness or in a deep-seated feeling of unworthiness which can affect the child's developing personality adversely. There is a limit to a child's emotional endurance when it comes to thinking of himself as unworthy, dirty, or bad. Many parents fail to understand this and wonder why shaming their child produces worse behaviour and not better.

We feel that no under-five should be shamed into doing or not doing anything. Such treatment is far too drastic at this age and there are lots of other ways of teaching children to behave acceptably. Shaming someone isn't compatible with loving tolerance and guidance. If you have to tell your child off about something more serious than an on-the-spot misdemeanour, never do it in front of others, especially if the child has a sensitive temperament. Tell the child privately that such behaviour isn't acceptable to you or others and explain why. *Related topics* Guilt; punishment; slowness.

Shock There are several types of shock. Emotional shock can make even a young child feel weak or faint. Such shock can be brought about by any distressing situation. It comes on quickly but the child also recovers quickly from his physical symptoms.

Shock can also be a medical condition that affects the whole body and may even end in death if not adequately and speedily treated.

The causes of medical shock are a severe blood loss (whether externally or internally); a loss of fluid from the body such as occurs with diarrhoea, vomiting, or from the surface of burns; severe bruising (a lot of blood can be lost around a fractured big bone); any condition that stops the heart (for example, electric shock); a severe infection (a burst appendix, for example); and severe allergy.

A shocked child looks pale, feels cold and sweaty to the touch, has shallow breathing and a fast, weak pulse, is restless, anxious and thirsty, and may vomit or become unconscious.

Such a child needs immediate professional help, so get someone to call an ambulance. While waiting for the professional: **1.** Stop any bleeding by pressing on the area; **2.** Remove the child from any serious hazard; **3.** Place him in the recovery position (lying on one side with his top knee drawn up to steady his body and his head bent back); **4.** Loosen tight clothing; **5.** Keep him from getting chilled but do *not* apply heat or lots of blankets; **6.** Do not give anything at all by mouth; **7.** Watch his breathing and if it stops give the kiss of life (page 34); **8.** Feel his pulse at the neck frequently to see if it has stopped. If it has, do heart massage (see page 293).

Except for cases of very severe bleeding, shock takes time to come on. This gives you plenty of time to get professional help.

Shopping Shopping is one of those everyday jobs that can be made into an exciting, interesting and educational journey for a young child, or a boring, dull and unpleasant one, depending on your attitude. Learning and enjoyment don't only come through play: they also come from watching and helping and just enjoying being with a favourite person. However, if that person is too absorbed and anxious to take any notice, the opportunity is lost. So look on shopping as an end in itself rather than something to be got out of the way. Make a shopping trip into an expedition and plan ahead for it, letting your child help with all the preparations. Arrange the trip for a time of the day when he is likely to be awake, alert and happy, and make sure he is not hungry or thirsty and that he has a dry nappy or goes to the lavatory just before you start.

A shopping list is something you may well be able to carry in your head, but if you write it down with your child's help you can help him learn what's involved in deciding what to buy. Plan the family's meals with him and let him tell you what he'd most like to eat. Check whether you have enough staple foods in the fridge and store cupboard, going with him to look unless he's old enough to do it himself. You can ask him all sorts of questions about what's there, such as 'is the marmalade pot empty or full?', or 'how much butter is there in the fridge?', or 'how many tins of baked beans are there in the cupboard?'. All the time he's learning about numbers and quantities.

A supermarket is attractive to a young child because he can ride in the child's seat in the trolley. It's safest to put him in a harness and clip it to the trolley because a moment's lack of vigilance can result in him falling out.

However, there are pros and cons to this sort of shopping and you may choose a small shop instead.

As you go round the shop or supermarket, let your child help you choose, or let him decide himself if you are sure to be happy with his choice. With a younger child, point out to him familiar things you have at home and talk about the various colours and shapes of packets, tins, fruits, vegetables and so on. The younger your child, the shorter will be his attention span and the more likely he'll be to take more of an interest in the ride in the trolley or in trying to hook an interesting-looking packet out of the trolley behind him.

Try to go shopping at a time of the day when the shops aren't too crowded, because children very quickly become bored while waiting for you to pay for the shopping. Never let a child ride on the side of the trolley or hang on to its handle because it may tip over and that can be disastrous if you have a baby in it as well. Some trolleys have special baby carriages on top but if they don't, you can support a baby of around six months in the child's seat if you bring a couple of cot blankets with you. A younger baby is most likely to be contented if you carry him in a sling. If your baby isn't happy in a sling, you would do better to avoid supermarkets and take him in his pram or buggy into smaller shops, unless you leave him with someone else.

Carrying a lot of heavy shopping and a baby, besides watching an older child, is quite a burden. Some supermarkets will get a member of staff to help you to your car if you ask. If you are shopping on foot, it's better to shop little and often if you want your sanity to remain intact. *Related topic* Outings.

Short-sight A child who is short-sighted can see close objects clearly but can't bring distant objects into focus. This is caused by the eyeball being too long and the eyeball's focussing power too strong. Concave correction lenses in spectacles are needed to correct the problem.

Short-sightedness is the commonest eye trouble in young children and can interfere with their reading, writing and close work. It is usually inherited and is rarely present at birth but gets worse as the child grows. It is unusual for a child to have problems before the age of six.

You'll know if your child has something wrong with his vision because he'll tilt his head, look out of the corner of his eyes, may squint, may be sensitive to bright lights, may not want to read, and may not recognize familiar things or people at a distance.

There is nothing you can do as a parent. Take the child to an optician, who will check his vision properly and prescribe glasses if necessary. *Related topics* Glasses; vision; vision testing.

Showing off Usually a child who constantly shows off is craving attention. Some children manage perfectly well with minimal attention from their parents whilst others demand lots. There are undoubtedly personality differences over this and some children seem to need a lot more attention and praise than others.

If a child seems to want a lot more attention than usual, a parent should ask himself why. Is it because he has been too busy, too tired, or is going through a bad marital patch that's making the child feel insecure, or what? Has he got into the habit of fobbing the child off with one word answers so that he's beginning to feel unloved and unwanted? The more we fail to respond to a child's needs, the more demanding he is likely to be and this can set up a disastrous cycle of ill feeling.

If you have a 'showy' child who likes being at the centre of the stage and entertaining people, don't slap him down but praise him and help him to share his gift with others in the family. However, don't let him think that the sun shines out of his eyes only or he'll become unbearable. It's rare for an under-five to show off so much that he is unbearable, provided he's handled sensitively. *Related topics* Attention seeking; boasting.

Shyness It's rare to find a child who isn't shy at some time. Even an outgoing, confident child will be subdued to some extent on starting a new play-group, moving to a new neighbourhood, or on going into a strange social situation. Such shyness doesn't last long, provided the child is allowed to find his own way around it. Most children respond best to being left alone or to very gentle and sympathetic encouragement in these situations. Forcing him to adapt prematurely will put more pressures on him and he may then be unable to cope at all. In these circumstances giving the child something positive to do can work wonders and before you know where you are he'll be outgoing and at ease again.

Some children have basically shy personalities and need more careful handling. Encourage such a child to make friends on his own territory by inviting other children to play (with or without their mothers). If he relies heavily on you in a social situation, let him, and don't force him away from you. Children learn to be independent social beings by first being allowed to be dependent for as long as they, as individuals, need to be. Shyness is especially likely to occur in an only child. A child who is shy because he feels different (because of his race or colour, a speech impediment, a birthmark, or whatever) needs help to think about his good points rather than his so-called bad ones. As he becomes more at ease with what was making him shy, the other children will accept him and the vicious circle will be broken.

Shyness is usually a perfectly normal form of behaviour. The only thing that's wrong with being shy is when it interferes with a child's ability to enjoy and participate in his daily activities, to make friends or to relate to other people. If you think your young child is being hampered by his shyness, you'll have to help him to overcome it.

The traditional advice for shy adults is to think about the other person rather than about themselves. This can work with young children too. Stay with your child and talk to the other child or person. If you start playing a game or making something, your child will eventually be fascinated and will want to join in. Don't make it obvious that you want him to, but don't ignore him either. Certainly don't comment on his shyness or tease him at all.

If your child is too shy to play at someone else's house, ask the other child's mother if you can go too for a chat and a cup of tea. Confide in her and she'll understand that this is a better way of helping your child with his shyness than forcing him to go somewhere by himself if he would be unhappy there. Don't keep on at your child to go off and play – he may not want to until he's quite at ease with the house, the child and the other mother, and this may take several visits.

Don't confuse shyness with dependence on you. Children vary as to the age at which they are ready to go off and play with others. Some prefer to be with their mothers until they are three, four or five and are only really confident with other people when they have the security of their mother there as a familiar base. *Related topics* Dependence; independence.

Sibling rivalry A normal state of affairs in which brothers and sisters in a family compete with each other.

Competition between brothers and sisters is present from a very early age and sometimes even before a baby is born an older brother or sister may feel competitive. The amount of rivalry that goes on will depend on your children's personalities and on the way you handle them.

The root cause for this is that brothers and sisters have to share not only their parents' time but also their approval, attention and worldly goods. Each time another sibling is born, the existing brothers and sisters lose some of their share, and they are very aware of this. However, all is not black. Time can be re-allocated so that less is spent on household chores and the parents' own pursuits and the same amount as before is given to the existing children, with a share to the new baby. Of course, it doesn't work out quite 'fair' because a new baby inevitably takes up more time than an older, more independent child, but the principle is important – the older children want to have the same amount of time spent on them and with them as they had before, and that can be arranged, though at your expense! While you are looking after the new baby, give plenty of attention to your older child as well, involving him in the baby's care and making him feel important. There's no need to feel despondent about your child's feelings when a new baby arrives as long as you handle the situation well. Ten to one he'll gain far more from having a sibling than he'll lose from having to share you.

Problems can arise if you become depressed after the birth of your new baby. All your older child's worries and fears about having a brother or sister will be realized because he'll have lost his 'old' mother. Unconsciously or even on a conscious level he'll blame the baby and be jealous of him and he'll also become much more demanding towards you, trying to win some time from the baby and to get back what he's lost. This sort of situation needs careful handling by your husband or by anyone else who will help. Thankfully, the depression will pass in time, and as you begin to behave more normally, your older child will slowly bury his negative feelings towards his sibling.

Once a baby becomes mobile, he'll be able to interfere with what the other children are doing and this is bound to annoy all but the most patient siblings. Problem times are when they are tired after a morning at playgroup, for example. You'll need to watch what's going on to make sure the baby is handled gently enough. You'll find that the baby will quickly be educated as to what's his and what belongs to the older child or children! Teaching the children to share their things isn't always sensible if the baby is going to spoil or break something precious, so a few rules about what the baby is allowed to have are useful.

When it comes to playing with things that don't belong to anyone in particular, most children have a minor competition going on for much of the time as to who is going to get the best thing (or the most favoured thing of that day). 'It's mine' is a call frequently heard and as soon as the thing in question has been claimed, everyone else will automatically want it. One child, often but not always the eldest (sometimes a younger child has a more dominant personality), will usually come out on top in any competitive situation. He'll probably grow up being the leader in play situations, the one who decides the game, and makes the rules and ensures that the others stick by them. When he gets to school, he'll find his naturally-assumed position will be strongly challenged by other erstwhile 'leaders' and he may have to back down. Once he gets home though, he'll probably assert his position as leader more than before.

A child who has always been sat upon or beaten in competitive situations at home may grow up with an unconscious desire to do better than his siblings. What's more, he may succeed if his determination is strong enough. The quiet one who always came second may be the one who grits his teeth and works hard so that he passes exams, gets into all the teams and so on. Sibling rivalry can go on for a lifetime. It isn't by any means always obvious but is always there to some degree, mingled with all the other perfectly normal feelings towards one's brothers and sisters such as love, protectiveness, pride, a desire to see them do well, and jealousy.

All through childhood children compare themselves with each other, constantly measuring up to see who is biggest, tallest, thinnest, noisiest, cleverest, prettiest, has the longest hair, is strongest, can run fastest and so on. This again is quite normal and is just a part of finding out where he stands in the world in comparison to others. If he didn't do that he'd never know what his strengths and weaknesses were.

Danger can creep in if a child believes that because he's stronger than his brother, for example, he's intrinsically a better person and loved more by his parents as a result. It's important to teach your children that you love them for what they are, warts and all, and always will do. *Never* imply or tell one child that you love him more than another (even if you do). This could stick'in his mind for ever and do him a lot of harm. It's a question you *will* be asked because each child wants to know how much you love him and comparison is a good way of estimating his worth. Tell him that you love each child the same.

Sibling rivalry can make one child feel a failure and another a bully. It's up to you to smooth things over, to help each child accept himself and to show that you love everyone equally. *Related topics* First-born children; jealousy.

Sickle cell disease An inherited condition seen in some people of black African, Indian and Mediterranean origins in whom almost half the blood cells are sickle-shaped (instead of disc-shaped) and live for a much shorter time than normal. Their premature destruction produces anaemia. The blood is also more likely to clot and this can cause painful problems, depending on where the clot is.

Children with sickle cell anaemia are especially prone to infections and many die before the age of twenty because there is no specific treatment.

Sickle cell anaemia can also be inherited as a less serious trait rather than as the disease proper. *Related topic* Anaemia.

Sinusitis An infection of the mucous membranes lining the sinuses which are spaces in the bones of the face that are connected to the inside of the nose. The various sinuses develop at different ages throughout childhood and the frontal sinuses in the bones of the forehead don't develop until the age of ten.

The commonest infection to cause inflammation of the lining of the sinuses is probably the common cold. This produces a watery, mucous discharge which drains into the nose and then out of the nostrils or down the throat. The discharge that goes down the throat is called a post-nasal drip and causes a cough if it tickles the throat (which is especially likely at night). A viral infection like this usually gets better spontaneously and quickly and the sinuses return to normal. In some children and for reasons that are a mystery, bacteria invade the sinuses and cause a secondary infection with a pussy discharge into the nose. The sinuses then become painful (producing so-called 'sinus headaches') and tender; there may be a fever; and a child can become quite ill. Call the doctor immediately.

Under the age of two only two sinuses have so far formed. These are the ethmoids in the bridge of the nose. Inflammation of the ethmoid sinuses (ethmoiditis) is a rare condition but can be serious. It causes a high temperature, pain over the eyes and temples (and possibly at the back of the ear), and swelling around the eye. The infection can spread to the eye and the brain if treatment isn't started quickly.

By the age of four the maxillary sinuses in the cheekbones are formed and so can become infected. Acute bacterial infection here produces fever and pain in the face. Infected tooth roots and a foreign body in the nose can also produce this type of sinusitis.

Treatment of sinusitis consists of pain relief (junior aspirin in the correct dose); antibiotics if necessary; and decongestant nose drops to improve drainage of the infected sinus into the nose. Very rarely an operation is necessary.

Sitting up From his early days in his mother's womb, a baby uses his muscles to move and to keep himself still. By the time he actually manages to sit up momentarily, all the various muscles involved will have been practising for this moment for months. It is not an end point in itself, but simply an obvious stage in the development of his body control. As such, sitting up is one of the commonly recognized milestones and one which family and friends can comment on and compare with other children.

In order to sit up unaided, a baby needs to have adequate head control, which means that his neck muscles must be strong. All the time he was lying down on his tummy or his back, trying to lift his head up and eventually succeeding, his neck muscles were gaining in strength and coordination. All the time you held him on your lap in a sitting position, or he sat propped up in his bouncing chair, pram, or buggy, he was practising holding his wobbly and heavy head in the position he wanted so that he could see what was going on. Along with this, his back muscles were developing, as were those of his shoulders, arms and legs. When a baby is pulled by his hands from his back up into a sitting position, his back will be rounded until he is around five or six months old, when it'll straighten momentarily. Around this age too you'll notice that he braces his shoulders when you pull him up and also that he has good head control, bringing his head up with him as he sits.

You won't harm your baby at all by letting him sit up supported in the early months, provided that you support his head when necessary. As soon as he is ready, he'll sit unsupported, though he won't be able to get himself up into a sitting position from lying down yet awhile. There is a very wide age range for sitting unsupported – the average lies between seven and ten months, but some are earlier and some later. Talk to your health visitor if you think your child is slow in reaching this stage of development.

As he gets stronger and more confident, he'll be able to get into a sitting position himself. He may get stuck in a sitting up position because the knack of lying down again comes later. He'll gradually learn all sorts of new tricks such as reaching forward for a toy and twisting round to look at you. Once he can sit up, his desire to move will increase daily and you may notice the first tentative attempts to move into a crawling position by tucking one foot under the other leg and leaning forward on to his hands and knees. Bottom shufflers somehow avoid learning the trick of leaning forward on to hands and knees and instead learn to get along with an almost crab-like action by moving their tucked-in legs on the floor.

The baby who can sit up has a whole new world opened up to him and is great fun to play with. He can now sit in a high chair comfortably at mealtimes and will enjoy sitting bolt upright harnessed in his pram when his back is strong enough. He'll need to be harnessed into his carrycot in the car or else into a child safety seat – no longer can you leave him lying in a carrycot which is strapped to the car. A baby who can sit up can be put on the floor near you when you're doing things and will amuse himself for longer than before. When he's tired, he'll become less confident and may topple over, so don't leave him anywhere where he could tip forwards or to one side on to something and hurt himself. *Related topics* Back; head control.

Six-month-old baby – a profile

The average six-month-old baby already has a lot of skills. He can sit for a few moments unaided and sits well when supported, with his head held firmly and his back straight. If you hold his hands when he's lying on his back, he'll pull himself up into a sitting position. When lying on his back he can lift his head right off the ground and can bend his legs up and catch hold of his feet. He may be able to roll over (most likely from his tummy to his back). When lying on his tummy, he can push his chest off the floor with his straight outstretched arms, and he'll enjoy being in a baby-walker or in a baby-bouncer.

Your baby will thoroughly enjoy holding interesting things and can pass them from one hand to another, showing no preference for side. He reaches out for things with both hands together and enjoys shaking a rattle. If something drops on to the floor, he won't look for it – as far as he's concerned it's disappeared for good.

Some six-month-old babies make babbling noises such as sing-song vowel sounds and two-syllabled sounds: 'a-a', 'goo-goo' and 'ada'. They listen intently to a voice, particularly their mother's and react to her changing moods. Squeals, giggles and shouts are likely and your baby will be delighted to be tickled or played with actively.

From about this age (or a little later), babies tend to go through a stage of being wary of anyone who isn't their mother (or mother figure), including such familiar people as their father and grandmother. As long as they are with their mother they are happy, but if they are held by someone else, they cry with apparent fear. As soon as they are back in their mother's arms, all is well again and they smile through their tears at the other person.

Babies of this age are ready to start having a mixed diet and enjoy sharing in a family meal while sitting in a high chair. They still have a need to suck and are thrilled when the breast or bottle appears. The six-month-old sometimes takes very short feeds if he sees something that interests him, while when he's tired he's happy to go on sucking for long periods until he falls asleep.

Skin care

By and large, the skin takes care of itself, provided it is not subjected to any irritation or abnormal conditions. In babyhood in particular, some areas of the skin do have to put up with a lot and care is needed to keep them healthy.

The skin of the nappy area is most likely of all to have problems. Nappy rash occurs even in the best cared-for babies from time to time but can usually be prevented, or at least nipped in the bud, with a timely change in the way the skin is looked after. Prompt nappy changing when a nappy is wet or dirty, and particularly when it is wet and dirty, thorough cleansing and a barrier cream will usually prevent any initial redness from developing into a florid nappy rash.

Some babies get dribble eczema on their cheeks, chins or necks. This can usually be alleviated by putting on a barrier cream when the child is sleeping. Breast-feeding reduces the chances of any eczema occurring and reduces the incidence of nappy rash.

Adequate hygiene means that your child's skin will not only look clean but will smell clean. When the weather is hot or if a child is very active, infrequent bathing can mean that his skin creases become sore and smelly. This may eventually become true intertrigo.

Rarely is there a real need for any of the myriad of available skin care preparations but if you like using them because of their smell or because you enjoy touching your child when you put them on, then use them. Soap and water is all that the average child needs for most of the time. *Related topics* Bathing; eczema; intertrigo; nappy rash; rashes; soap; talcum powder.

Sleep One of the biggest disruptions to parents with a young family is the alteration in their sleep patterns. Babies spend much more of their sleeping time (about half, in fact) in a state of REM sleep (rapid eye movement or dreaming sleep) than do adults, who tend to dream about four or five times a night for a total of an hour or so. One-year-old babies spend about one quarter of the night in dreaming sleep. Several times in the night babies surface from their deep sleep, and come up through dreaming sleep to a state of fidgeting and restlessness. They then wake up and soon start to cry if no attention is given them. It is probably no accident that during the last few weeks of pregnancy in particular, many women wake frequently at night. This may be nature's way of preparing them for the disturbed sleep they'll have once their baby is born. The breast-feeding mother is only too pleased that her baby wakes at night because otherwise her breasts would become uncomfortably full and tense. It's interesting that when such a mother wakes at night with full breasts, her baby almost inevitably wakes within a few minutes. There seems to be some unspoken signal between them and it can't be because the noise of the baby wriggling and preparing to wake rouses the mother in the first place because the same thing often happens if the baby is sleeping in a room some way away.

Adults spend on average about eight hours a night sleeping, though there is an enormous range. They tend to need less sleep as they grow older. Babies are just the same as adults – the average baby spends longer than the average adult sleeping, but the range is very wide and they too need less sleep as they grow older. Some babies need less sleep than some adults. It's quite useless and unhelpful to give average sleep times for babies of different ages as once an average is given, parents tend to worry if their child needs less. (They don't worry if he needs more!) A baby will get as much sleep as he needs by napping during the day – hopefully having his longest sleep during his parents' sleeping hours. Some babies naturally have a tendency towards regularity and seem to have learnt a wake and sleep pattern before birth which fits in well with family life. Others seem to get nights and days muddled and take a long time before their longest sleeps coincide with their parents' sleep.

We believe that if babies could choose, they'd prefer to be near the person they're most attached to (usually their mother) at night as well as during the day. Most very young mammals like to snuggle up at night to one or both parents, for warmth, comfort and protection. They also like to be near the mother so she can feed them as and when they need milk. Human babies are no exception and while they can be conditioned into sleeping alone, they are much happier – in that they never have to cry – if they sleep with their parents. Young children too are happier lying with someone at night.

Given that most young children need more sleep than their parents, once they have stopped their daytime naps, this sleep has to be fitted in in the evening and night time. This generally means that they have to go to bed before their parents do, especially if they have to be up the next morning for play-group. This sounds obvious, yet it causes many problems throughout the Western world for children who are reluctant to leave their parents at night for the loneliness of their own beds. Lots of parents overcome this by building up a bedtime ritual which includes cuddling the child in bed until he goes to sleep. This can be time-consuming, but at least means he goes to sleep happy and secure. You needn't worry that you'll always be spending half an hour or so lying down with your child at night. There'll come a time when he's quite happy to be left to read, to talk to his brother or sister, and to think his own thoughts as he goes to sleep.

What happens if your baby or child needs about the same amount of sleep (or even less) than you? Some parents simply let their child stay up with them in the evenings. Others insist on an early bedtime and then have to cope with him waking early in the morning. You can't make children sleep longer than they need and if you consider evenings with just the two of you are essential you'll have to make contingency plans for the morning. Some parents try to snooze while their child plays in or near their bed or in his own room. Others put interesting toys, books, games and even food near their child's bed to keep him occupied in the morning. A few lock their bedroom door and tell the child he can only come in when he hears the alarm clock ring. This last only seems at all humane if you have more than one child. A large number of parents simply make do with too little sleep, not having their long evenings as they used to before their baby arrived, and being woken early in the morning by a fresh and playful child. These are the ones who may fray at the edges mentally because they try to pack too much in to a day fuelled by insufficient sleep.

Babies like to feel secure when they sleep. They often sleep well when wrapped comfortably and firmly in a sheet before being tucked into their cot. A sling keeps them hugged firmly to an adult's chest or back. An arm round them at night while they're lying next to you helps too. A baby lying in bed and going off to sleep next to his mother or father often puts out an exploratory hand or foot just to make sure someone's there. As soon as he makes contact, he settles.

Sleeping is – or should be – a natural and easy way of restoring our tired bodies and minds. The reasons why parents so often have problems with their children's sleep habits and patterns are first and foremost because they have been conditioned into expecting a period when they are separated from their children. This period is divided into an evening alone while they (the parents) are awake and a night alone while they are asleep. However, some families get on extremely well without insisting on this separation. Various groups of pre-industrial people around the world never get unbroken sleep and provided they have enough opportunity for REM sleep, don't appear to suffer. We in the West want all of our sleep at night, whereas it might be more practical for mothers at home with their children to get used to taking some of it in the day when their babies and young children have a nap, if their nights seem too short.

As with so many other aspects of bringing up children, you'll have to make your own decisions about sleeping and children based on your priorities. What suits one family won't necessarily suit another, but sometimes it helps to know that there is more than one way of arranging things. Sleeping patterns and habits change from babyhood onwards and what your baby does at six months may be quite different from what he'll do when he's two. Be flexible and don't be afraid to try new methods; as long as you don't confuse your child by chopping and changing too much, you'll find a method that suits everyone better. *Related topics* Bedtime; bed sharing; naps; night waking; rest and relaxation for mother; sleep problems.

Sleep problems
Sleep problems Sleep problems form a large proportion of the mailbag to any parents' magazine's advice column and any health visitor or doctor working in a child health clinic will agree that young children's sleeping habits worry a good many parents.

As with so many other modern problems, the answer lies in the way our society expects children to be brought up. Young babies are trained from birth onwards to get used to sleeping alone, in their own cots and often in their own rooms. They are expected to be able to go off to sleep when their parents are ready for them to do so, regardless of how tired they are, and they are also expected to sleep for a certain amount of time. Most important of all is the emphasis everyone puts on young children sleeping through the night. If a nine-month-old baby still wakes at night, friends and relatives will sympathize as though this were something peculiar, to be stamped out at all costs, instead of regarding it as the normal habit that it is.

The fact is that it is perfectly normal for babies to wake at night. They wake at night for two main reasons: for food and a need for reassurance. We all have several cycles of deep and shallow sleep during the night and young children have more light sleep than adults, causing them to wake up more often. It's interesting that a breast-feeding mother often wakes just before her baby. Some researchers think this may be connected with the changing levels of hormones circulating in her body. Often her sleep pattern will alter if she stops breast-feeding at night, even though the baby carries on waking.

Much research has been done into sleep patterns in children. One study showed that one in five one-year-olds wakes at night and the proportion at two is the same. Of the one-year-old wakers, forty per cent wake when they are eighteen months old, and forty per cent when they are two. However, the two-year-old wakers are not necessarily the same children as the eighteen-month-old wakers, showing that some children have learnt to sleep through the night while others have started waking. Of the eighteen-month-old wakers, fifty-four per cent wake at two and twenty-three per cent at three.

If your baby or toddler wakes at night and after a cuddle and a drink wants to play, discourage him from the beginning so that he learns that night-time is a time for lying quietly in bed. Make sure he is warm and comfortable and then if he sleeps in your room lie down yourself, put the light out and shut your eyes. You may have to lie down with your baby in your bed to get him off to sleep again. You can transfer him to his cot later if you want to. If he sleeps in his own room he will probably end up crying if you leave him while he's wide awake. If you want to avoid this, either play with him until he's sleepy or take him into your bed. Some parents find that they sometimes have to give in and play for a while in the middle of the night but it's certainly not a good idea to make this a habit.

Many two-year-olds need only ten hours sleep at night and some need even less, so parents putting them to bed at six o'clock will be disappointed if they expect them to sleep through until beyond six the next morning. Parents sometimes feel resentful when their child wakes them up early in the morning but it isn't fair to blame the child if he was put to bed too early that he has had as much sleep as he needs to make him as fresh as a daisy by five thirty. As children grow older they can be encouraged to play alone or with each other so as not to wake you when they wake early, but you can't expect them to do this for long before they are four or five or so.

It's rare for a toddler to be short of sleep: a tired one-year-old will catch up on the sleep he needs by falling asleep at any time – in the pushchair or car, or simply slumped on the floor.

Many British families sleep with their babies in bed with them or at least in the same room, though they may not publicize the fact. When a baby or a young child cries at night, it's a natural human instinct to comfort him by cuddling him and seeing to his needs. Cultures other than ours in which members of the family sleep together have no sleeping problems in their young children. The children can move closer to a parent at night for physical comfort or warmth and security. A breast-feeding baby or toddler can easily suck while his mother dozes. There is no need for him to cry and the whole family sleeps well as a result. Contrast this with our culture in which parents of waking babies or toddlers are so frequently advised by 'experts' to let them 'cry it out'. This rarely works and often makes the child more unhappy at night when he wakes than he was before because of an increased feeling of insecurity.

Our cultural conditioning and small bedrooms with even smaller beds make sleeping with children difficult. Worries about sex, being cramped for space at night, spoiling the child, teaching it a habit that won't easily be broken, and overlaying, are rife and need to be sorted out. However, you may like to consider a change to a more natural way of looking after children at night – keeping them with you. You may feel this is not for you, in which case you may have no easy answer. You may decide on a compromise. *Related topics* Bed sharing; bedtime; keeping children in bed; nightmares; night terrors; night waking; rituals; sleep; sleep talking; sleep walking; sleepy baby.

Sleep talking

Lots of young children talk in their sleep from time to time. It's more common at certain times, including when the child is feverish, worried about something, or excited. It tends to occur when he is dreaming, during periods of REM (rapid eye movement) sleep. It can also occur during deep, dreamless sleep as part of a night terror, when a child cries out in fright and talks fearfully and uncontrollably.

What do you do if your child talks in his sleep? Most parents go to check that he's comfortable – not too hot or cold and not running a fever. If he wakes when you go to him, find out whether he wants to go to the lavatory or have a drink. He may want a cuddle if he's been having a bad dream, or he may want to come into your bed to sleep. If you can't get to sleep because you're unused to having him there, either carry him back when he's well and truly asleep or go to his bed and sleep there yourself.

Occasionally, what a child says in his sleep reveals what he's worrying about. Once you know what it is, you can take steps to put it right. More often what he says is of no particular relevance. He may laugh or talk in a conversational manner – he's probably talking to someone in his dreams. A brother or sister sharing his room may be disturbed by the talking, so it's best then to try to stop it. If he is restless and yet doesn't wake when you go to him, try lying down beside him to cuddle him – not so as to wake him though. He'll probably settle down comforted by this.

If the talking goes on night after night you may have to make other sleeping arrangements for the child sharing his room to avoid broken nights for him.

Never tell a child what he has said the next morning, and certainly never tease him. What he said is best forgotten – unless it helps *you* improve his life in some way. *Related topics* Night terrors; nightmares.

Sleep walking Seeing a child walk in his sleep is a very unsettling business. Contrary to the scenes in children's comics, a sleep-walking child doesn't walk around with his eyes closed and his arms straight out in front of him. He usually walks with his eyes open and looks as if he is awake but isn't aware of anyone else. The walking often seems purposeful, as if he knows where he wants to go. Having gone there, he'll usually turn round by himself and go back to bed.

Sleep-walking children rarely hurt themselves, but because this must remain a possibility, if your child does sleep walk, make sure he *can't* hurt himself. Don't leave things lying on the stairs and leave a light on on the landing and in the hall.

Never try to wake up a sleep-walking child, but lead him gently back to bed perhaps with a gentle and reassuring comment such as 'let's just take you back to your bed'. It's a good idea to lie down by him and cuddle him as you make sure he is sound asleep. We say 'don't wake a sleep-walking child' because it is confusing and upsetting for him to wake up with a jolt. It also draws attention to the problem and this in itself can make him feel bad.

Sleep walking can be a sign that a child is worrying about something but as it's best not to let such a child know what he's been doing, you may have some trouble in finding out the cause of his concern unless it's obvious. You could ask him outright if he's happy. Children are often much more open than adults and with some tactful and gentle questions you may well find out what it's all about. *Related topic* Anxiety.

Sleepy baby If you had pethidine during labour, you may find that your baby seems very sleepy for his first few days or even longer. You'll probably have to wake him to feed him, otherwise he might go on sleeping for hours at a stretch. Don't be lulled into thinking that you have a 'good' baby on your hands, or that because you have decided to demand feed him, you needn't wake him. Your baby needs nourishment and a little fluid and if you're breast-feeding, you don't want him to miss out on the valuable anti-infective and other protective factors in colostrum (the earliest milk you produce).

Wake your sleepy, breast-fed, full-term baby every three hours during the day if he doesn't wake himself. The three hours should be counted from the beginning of one feed to the beginning of the next; if you make the mistake of counting from the end of a feed to the beginning of the next, you'll end up with approximately four-hourly feeds, which probably won't be enough to stimulate an adequate milk supply. Don't muddle up getting full, tense breasts with making too much milk. Everyone gets some degree of fullness but that doesn't mean that they're necessarily going to have enough milk for their babies' gradually increasing needs. Full, tense breasts simply mean that you should wake your baby to let him drink some milk to take away your discomfort, or else you should express a little milk yourself. The combination of a sleepy baby who is having infrequent feeds together with unrelieved fullness of the breasts is a recipe for speedy failure of the milk supply and can also lead to blocked ducts and thence to mastitis.

If you are bottle-feeding, your full-term baby will get enough milk if you wake him for four-hourly feeds.

Of course, however your baby is being fed, feed him if he cries before you had planned to wake him. The suggested feed schedules above are only intended for the baby who isn't naturally waking often enough.

If your baby weighs less than average or if he comes into the low birth weight category, he'll need to be woken more often in order to get enough milk to supply nourishment and to keep his blood sugar level at a satisfactory level. Because his stomach is smaller than that of a full-term baby, he'll need smaller, more frequent feeds. Babies small enough to need hourly feeding are generally being fed with milk (expressed or pumped breast milk, or cows' milk formula) put down a naso-gastric tube. Those needing two-hourly feeding may be having a mixture of tube feeding and breast- or bottle-feeding, with increasing amounts being taken by breast or bottle as the sucking reflex appears and strengthens. Low birth weight babies are likely to sleep a lot quite apart from the effects of any pethidine you may have had, and feeds will inevitably be long drawn-out episodes because they tend to cat-nap throughout the feed, whether at the breast or bottle. Because sucking at the breast is harder work, involving milking the nipple and areola besides sucking (whereas getting the milk from a bottle requires mainly sucking with much less muscular milking effort), small breast-fed babies drop off (both literally, off the breast, and off to sleep) more often and considerable patience is needed by the mother. She also needs support, praise and encouragement from the staff and her family if she is not to be discouraged by her small, sleepy baby.

Jaundice can also make a newborn baby sleepy. Because this condition is more common in low birth weight babies, you may find yourself with a baby who is sleepy because he is small and jaundiced *and* because you had pethidine in labour. One important thing to remember with such babies is not to fill them up and tire them out by giving them water. Milk alone is best and extra water has not been shown to improve their jaundice or their weight gain. You'll need to be especially patient with such a baby, and you may find that the only practicable way to look after him is to let him feed on and off in short bursts throughout the day and night. This especially applies if he's being breast-fed. If you try to make him take his milk in more spaced out 'feeds', he probably won't be able to take enough and before you know where you are he'll be having cows' milk formula complements.

If your baby is well enough to be out of an incubator, instead of letting him lie in a cot most of the time, keep him with you on your lap or by your side in bed and feed him on and off throughout the twenty-four hours, just to make it easier for him to wake up and easier for you than if you were sitting down away from your belongings in the special care baby unit. If a sleepy baby is actually in contact with you, he'll probably wake up more often because of the stimulation of your touch, movements, smell and sounds. There are relatively few stimuli to wake a baby up when he's in an incubator or lying in a cot.

Some babies fall into a pattern of sleeping for a long time at night or even for part of the day. This is fine and gives you a lot of time to get on with other things, as long as he is adequately nourished by the feeds you can fit in when he is awake. If you're breast-feeding and the number of feeds in twenty-four hours drops too low, you could find that your baby fails to gain weight satisfactorily simply because your breasts aren't being stimulated often enough to produce sufficient milk for him. To counteract this, wake him up for extra feeds. Some mothers prefer not to wake their baby but instead express or pump their milk when he's asleep in order to stimulate their breasts and then give a little of this extra milk to their baby after each of his usual feeds. Only a very few women can maintain an adequate milk supply for their fully breast-fed babies if the number of feeds in twenty-four hours drops below five, and most need far more than this to produce enough.

Older sleepy babies sometimes get fractious and find it hard to drop off. This is just a stage they go through and all you can do is help as much as you can. Some of these babies just want to be cuddled and allowed to suck as and when they want. Others fight till the last minute and may take an hour before they 'give in' to sleep. *Related topics* Jaundice; low birth weight.

Slowness The first suspicion you may have of your child's slowness may be when as a baby he doesn't reach his developmental milestones at the same time as other children of his age. Your family doctor, clinic doctor or health visitor may be able to put your mind at rest because there is a wide variation in the time at which any of these milestones are reached. If he is concerned at all, the doctor may refer your baby to a paediatrician for his opinion and an assessment of his development. If necessary, developmental testing will be done, and you'll be given some idea as to whether your baby is a slow developer but is likely to catch up, or whether he is definitely slower than normal for his age.

The same goes for toddlers and pre-school children and their assessment is easier as there's more to go on. Intelligence testing can be done and is carried out by a psychologist or a specially trained doctor. The results will be discussed with you taking into account all the other aspects of the child's development and environment. Hearing and eyesight tests are a must because even a minor hearing impairment or visual problem can make a child appear slow when he in fact has normal potential. In this age group many parents worry if their child's language development is slow. This can be affected by many factors, including the amount of speech a child has the opportunity of hearing, and the interest with which his attempts to talk are greeted. Some bright children are comparatively late in talking, then suddenly start talking very well. Language development tests take into account both language as understood by the child and their own speech as spoken. If a child can understand well for his age, then even if he can't speak too well, he's likely to be able to do so eventually.

If your child is found to be slow, simply treat him as you would treat a child of normal intelligence but take care to speak to him clearly and face to face. He'll probably need to hear things many times over before he remembers them. This goes too, of course, for children who are not slow, but slow ones need even more repetition. The same information doesn't always need to be given in the same way, parrot-fashion, but can be made more interesting by varying it slightly, always trying to help the child understand. Give him playthings and activities to suit his stage of development, not that of other children his own age.

Never make your child feel ashamed of his slowness. It's not his fault – and it's almost certainly not your fault either, unless you are under-stimulating him or depriving him emotionally so much that his intellectual abilities haven't yet had the chance to reach their full potential. Try your best to make him feel proud of what he can do and proud of himself. If he grows up with confidence in what he can do and always does his best, it'll help him in the future. If one child in your family is slower than the others, it helps if they're encouraged to develop a loving tolerance towards him, never teasing him unkindly but always trying to help him and, if necessary, protecting him from others who might poke fun at him.

The cause of a child's slowness is often never discovered. Some slow children go on to become more scholastically capable later, perhaps more by application than by any real increase in intelligence. **Related topics** Deafness; intelligence; language.

Smacking There is always a better alternative to smacking. Most parents smack because they are too busy, anxious, flustered, embarrassed or simply at a loss to know what to do and as a result cannot think of a more appropriate way of stopping their child's unacceptable and annoying behaviour.

Some parents never smack. They are lucky enough to have the combination of a child whose personality and upbringing are such that he tends not to behave in a way that provokes parental rage; a personality of their own which enables them to keep calm even when provoked; a less busy life than many (perhaps with few children or fewer activities crammed into a day); and a determination to avoid physical punishment for their children.

Others may be just as keen to avoid smacking but still find themselves doing it when pushed too hard by a combination of circumstances. If this applies to you, think afterwards what happened to make you smack your child and how you could have avoided that particular set of circumstances. The more you smack without taking stock afterwards, the easier it becomes to smack next time. Some parents seem to smack their children continually, but research has shown that this rarely produces the desired effect.

If a smack is going to work at all, it'll work because it is such a surprising form of behaviour on behalf of the parent that the child takes it very seriously. The more it is done, the less it'll work, and sadly the dangerous situation in which parents smack harder and harder in order to have an effect at all is seen only too often. In its most serious form it can be frank baby battering or child abuse, when the smacking is done out of desperation, or it can be premeditated corporal punishment, which to many seems even worse. Both can have very serious effects on the child's developing personality, quite apart from any damaging physical effects there may be.

Smacking is a quick and easy way of relieving the parents' feelings. However, as with any punishment, it is a very negative way of behaving and does little to inform the child what he has done wrong and why it *is* wrong. Unless you take the time to explain to a child why you smacked him, he may not know what the actual trigger was. If you only smacked him because, for instance, you were tired at the end of the day, your period was just about to begin, everyone seemed to be making demands on you at once, your husband left in a bad mood that morning to go to work, and the child dropped a bottle of milk by accident, you'll have to explain that although dropping the milk was careless, it wasn't wicked (and it's only naughty if you'd warned him not to do it immediately beforehand) but that it was just too much for you to cope with when you had so much else on your plate. The trouble is, of course, that when you're tired at the end of the day, the children will probably be feeling just the same, and tempers and patience are short all round. Children of three and upwards can understand that you react differently at different times of the day and are much more sympathetic than you might give them credit for. However, it's essential to explain your behaviour. You needn't explain at the time – later will do, but do it before the child goes off to sleep. The child will respect you more for having the decency to explain and say sorry than if you just let it go.

The best way to avoid smacking if you feel that any trigger might make you lash out, is to calm down and give yourself some space and time. This isn't always possible, unfortunately, but there's almost always time for a count to ten or even some deep breathing or other relaxation technique (such as you learnt at your antenatal relaxation class). Try to recognize the danger signs and act on them quickly, because you'll often feel far worse after smacking a child than you did before.

In some families, smacking is part of a well thought out scheme of discipline and the children know exactly what sort of behaviour will be followed by a smack. Their parents may give them warnings or threaten them beforehand, such as, 'if you do that again, you'll get a smack', or 'if you don't stop doing that before I count to ten, I'll smack you'. Whether or not this is better than a quick lash out in anger is debatable, but to many people it is and it does at least let the child know where he stands.

Smacking can induce aggressive behaviour in children, who reason that if it's acceptable for you to do it, then it's all right for them to do it too. They may try it on you but when they find that this isn't on, they'll smack their dolls or friends. Smacking can also produce nasty-looking red hand prints on a child's skin which gaze at you reproachfully for several days.

All in all, smacking, slapping, spanking, beating or whatever should not be done because there are other ways of controlling bad behaviour which are always preferable and more effective. Physical punishment can produce long-lasting negative feelings towards the parents and even one smack (or perhaps especially one smack) may be remembered for ever by a very sensitive child.

If you think the occasional smack is acceptable, try only ever to do it as a response to naughtiness, not to a mistake; to do it immediately, so the child can understand at once what he's done to deserve it; and if you find yourself doing it too often, to get professional help. *Related topics* Child abuse; punishment.

Small child A child can be small because he is too light in weight or too short for his age. An underweight child either doesn't eat enough or doesn't absorb enough nourishment from the foods he does eat. Children may not want to eat if they are ill, if they have a chronic disease, or if they are emotionally upset or deprived. The commonest causes for not absorbing food properly are coeliac disease and cystic fibrosis.

A baby or young child who is underweight and not gaining weight adequately over a period of time is said to be failing to thrive and such a child needs to be sorted out in hospital if there's no obvious cause.

Short children are usually short because one or both parents are short (or another close relative) but they may also be short as a result of long-term poor nourishment or a bowel, heart or kidney disease. The pituitary or thyroid gland may be malfunctioning or the skeleton could be affected by rickets or even a kyphosis. Some mentally retarded children are short, sometimes because of feeding difficulties.

Dwarfism in its classical form (achondroplasia) is an inherited disorder of cartilage metabolism. The long limb bones are most affected so the child becomes shorter in relation to his peers as he grows older. The head is relatively larger, the forehead very prominent and the bridge of the nose flattened. There is no cure.

Lastly, some children can be short because of long term treatment with certain drugs and even rarely because of emotional deprivation.

If you are worried because your child seems too small compared with others of his age, see your doctor. He may suggest an expert second opinion. *Related topics* Failure to thrive; height.

Smallpox A serious viral infection with a characteristic rash. It has been declared eradicated from the world by the World Health Organization. This has come about as a result of widespread vaccination and containment programmes and means that the routine vaccination of children against smallpox is no longer necessary. In spite of this a few countries still insist that visitors have a vaccination certificate. If you find this is the case, consult your doctor first.

Smegma The white, curdy material that collects in the vulval region of girls and under the foreskin of uncircumcized boys. It is harmless but will irritate if left. Simple washing removes it in a girl and pushing back the foreskin as far as it will easily go will enable it to be cleaned away in boys. *Related topic* Foreskin.

Smell Like all of our senses, the sense of smell is an essential and enjoyable facet of our lives. Without it we lose a whole dimension of life.

Even newborn babies will turn away from unpleasant smells and have been shown to turn towards pads that have been in contact with their mother's breasts after one week of age. Wet nurses tell the same story too. A baby will take any breast if he is hungry but quite noticeably reacts differently to a strange (non-mother's) breast before drinking from it. Babies can easily recognize a change of 'caretaker' at ten days and it is thought that smell is important in such recognition systems. Pheromones (naturally-produced chemicals that are made by the body and released into the air) may play an important factor in mother-baby interaction and these are probably recognized by the brain as a kind of 'smell'.

It's interesting that many mothers comment on the delightful smell of their newborn baby's head. Even the bowel motions of her baby may smell attractive to the breast-feeding mother. Those of a bottle-fed baby don't have the same effect.

As children grow they love to smell things and it's worth encouraging your child to smell things as part of his growing repertoire of sensations. Smelling games can be fun with a dozen small bottles or containers with things in to be smelled blindfolded. *Related topic* Bonding.

Smiling The age at which a baby is said to smile for the first time depends on the individual baby and his personality, what his parents expect of him, and how he's treated.

For a long time it was thought by experts that babies didn't smile till they were about six weeks old. However, parents know differently. Lots of babies smile when they're very young indeed – even sometimes soon after birth. What is meant by saying they don't smile for six weeks is that it may not be until then that you can be sure they're smiling *at you*, as opposed to just smiling. Even so, many babies certainly seem to smile at a person when they're only a few weeks old.

Babies grow to like faces and at a few weeks old are much more interested in a face than in an inanimate object. Sooner or later, the first 'social smile' will appear – a smile which is a result of being happy to see someone. It needn't necessarily be the person who provides food and care – babies are quite indiscriminate at first and many a mother is somewhat disappointed to find her baby's first smile being bestowed on someone else. Soon, however, he'll come to recognize her as being his main provider of food, warmth, comfort, smiles and sweet talk, and will bestow more of his ready smiles on her than anyone else.

By about six months, a baby has a hierarchy of people to whom he's attached, and will prefer to be with his favourite – usually his mother, if she is the one who gives him most loving attention. As long as he is with her, he'll smile at other people, but take him away from her and he'll be likely to cry. He can be in tears one minute, even with a familiar person such as his granny or father, and the next minute, when he's restored to his mother's arms, will be happy and smiling again, even at the person he's just left.

A smiling baby creates a smiling response and this leads to a cycle of more and more smiling. So it is that babies with a basically more contented personality smile more and more as they grow older, and their pleased and smiling parents say how 'good' they are. It's sensible for parents of a baby who isn't such a natural smiler to spend lots of time being affectionate, responsive and lovingly smiley even though their baby doesn't necessarily join in the fun, otherwise he'll miss out on a lot of what other babies seem to induce unthinkingly.

When going off to sleep, lots of babies produce flickering smiles interspersed with small frowns or grimaces, jerks or squeaks. Within minutes, this stage passes and they go off into a deep sleep. The same thing may occur just as they are about to wake. *Related topics* Attachment; laughing.

Sneezing Young babies sneeze much more often than older children. This is because their nasal passages are small and sensitive to dust in the air and dried mucus in the nostrils. Any obstruction, wet or dry, makes a baby sneeze it away and some babies make terrible snorting noises, much to the amazement and fright of their parents. Most babies who sneeze and snort haven't got a cold but a baby with a cold will sneeze more than older children with a cold.

Soap There's nothing special about soap for washing babies and children – use any ordinary toilet soap that you like. When soaping a baby you may find it's easier and safer if you do it on your lap with the baby on a towel or a terry nappy so that he won't slip out of your hands and under the water. Needless to say, be careful not to let soap get into babies' or older children's eyes because this can put them off bath time for days. When washing hair get the child to hold a folded flannel over his eyes or position him lying back in the bath so that no soapy water runs into his eyes.

Many bath liquids or 'cleansers' in attractive containers are available to make bathtime more enjoyable for children but almost all of these are detergents and cause skin drying and irritation in some children if used every day. The detergent removes the natural skin oils and the child itches a lot. Such detergents should only be used occasionally and ordinary soap for everyday use. Some very allergic children are sensitive to the perfumes in soap, bubble bath or cleanser. Simple soap is a way around this problem as it contains nothing but pure soap.

If you think your child gets a rash when wearing clothes washed with detergent, use soap flakes instead.

Soiling The uncontrolled passage of bowel motions. It can take the form of true defaecation or may simply be a slight staining of the child's pants or knickers. A very young child who soils may not yet be ready to come out of nappies. Young children who have been potty-trained when they were ready and in a relaxed way may still have an occasional accident, especially around a time of special stress or emotion – such as the arrival of a new baby in the family. It's probably best to put the young child who soils back into nappies and to have another try at potty-training once his need to seek attention is over. Some children are so accustomed to their mother's delight and pleasure when they perform on the potty that when a new baby arrives or when she has less time and pays them little attention for some other reason, they find that their efforts don't get the praise they feel they deserve. By remembering to continue making a fuss of your child when he uses the potty and at other times, you'll probably prevent him from soiling.

The older child who suddenly starts soiling is a much more difficult problem but thankfully the commonest cause is constipation, which is treatable. This may at first seem strange but what happens is that the large, hard, bulky stools of the constipated bowel let fluid bowel motions pass round them. These fluid motions leak out of the back passage and cause soiling. Cure the constipation and the child stops soiling.

An older child will be embarrassed by his soiling and this can produce all kinds of behaviour problems. Treat any child who soils with tact, love and patient attention, and never let him wear smelly clothes longer than you can help. If your child ever soils, carry some baby-wipes and soft toilet tissue with you wherever you go, besides a spare pair of pants or knickers and a polythene bag to put the dirty ones in, so you can clean him up and make him comfortable and nice to be with. If you are prepared, you can do this in a public lavatory or at a friend's house as well as at home. If your child goes to play-group, discreetly give the play-group leader a spare pair of pants or knickers in case of an accident.

Mentally retarded children may soil because they're not developmentally ready to be clean, because of poor bowel training, or because of a lack of awareness that their bowels are ready to be opened but almost all of them can be taught to stay clean with persistence. Some children with nerve conditions such as spina bifida cannot control their back passage muscles and so will inevitably soil themselves. ***Related topic*** Potty training.

Songs Songs are traditionally sung to babies and young children to calm them and send them to sleep and later in childhood for enjoyment and play. A lullaby doesn't have to be formalized with set music and words. It can be made up as you go along, with any words and any tune. It needn't even be rhythmical – it can be more of a singing speech, if you can't sing. The important thing about a lullaby from a baby's point of view is that it sounds soft and gentle and that it is sung by you. If you combine it with rocking him in your arms or in his pram or cot, or sitting in a rocking chair with him on your lap, then the rocking motion and the song together will be a help to calm most babies. Lots of mothers sing lullabies to their babies at the breast and there's nothing lovelier than the smile of a baby at the breast in appreciation of your singing, cuddling and milk.

Songs can sometimes take the place of a bedtime story for older children. You can buy small volumes of nursery rhymes, marching songs, dancing songs, action rhymes and so on, many with music written out if you know how to read it.

The songs that children enjoy aren't only those aimed at them. They will love joining in with adults' songs as well. It's the atmosphere of conviviality they like, with everyone enjoying the singing, as much as songs themselves. Christmas carols, songs used in party games, hymns at Sunday school, action songs at play-group, Salvation Army songs in the street, songs to join in with on television and radio; most children experience some of these even if they are growing up in an unmusical family.

Sing to your child when he's sleepy and with him when he's not. Never laugh at how he sings or you may put him off for a long time. Sing while you're washing up or just when you're happy. Songs and music in general have a very relaxing and therapeutic effect on many people and if you can encourage your child to be interested in singing and not embarrassed about his voice, you'll have done him a good turn. *Related topics* Listening; rhythm and music.

Sore throat There are two common conditions that cause a sore throat in children – tonsillitis, which is an infection of the tonsils, and pharyngitis, which is a viral infection of the back of the throat. In young children, except babies under one year who have very small tonsils, the tonsils are usually inflamed in pharyngitis too.

Almost any acute infectious illness of the nose, ears and sinuses can cause pharyngitis and it is a feature of diphtheria and glandular fever.

Children between four and seven are especially prone to pharyngitis and the younger the child the more likely he is to complain of a tummy ache rather than a sore throat. This comes about because of the swelling of the lymph nodes ('glands') around the small intestine. Pain in the ear is a common accompaniment of a sore throat though there may or may not be an infection of the ear. Because of all this a doctor will always look at the throat of a child who is complaining of tummy ache or ear ache.

Four out of five sore throats are caused by viruses and the other one by bacteria. The most common of the bacterial causes is an infection with the streptococcus. This type of infection can occasionally lead on to nephritis, rheumatic fever or scarlet fever and sore throats of this kind are best treated with antibiotics.

However, it's very difficult to distinguish a viral from a bacterial sore throat just by looking and even most doctors can't do so. Both infections cause similar symptoms – a fever, a general feeling of being unwell or irritable, a loss of appetite, tummy ache, hoarseness, a cough, a runny nose and enlarged lymph nodes ('glands') in the neck. A streptococcal sore throat may cause vomiting as well. Young children rarely complain of a sore throat itself.

Because of the difficulty of diagnosis many doctors give antibiotics to all children with bad sore throats while others take a swab from the throat and send it off to be cultured to see which organisms are causing the trouble.

Sore throats are treated with rest (if the child wants to go to bed let him, but otherwise let him play near you); temperature-lowering measures; cool drinks; and a light diet if the child wants to eat anything at all.

Complications aren't at all uncommon. Otitis media, sinusitis, and laryngitis are often seen but serious complications such as rheumatic fever and nephritis are rare.

Sore throats are infectious, especially in the early stages, for several days. However, treatment of a bacterial sore throat with suitable antibiotics (to which the infection responds) renders the child non-infectious within a few hours. *Related topics* Nephritis; rheumatic fever; scarlet fever; tonsillitis.

Special care baby units
These are nurseries attached to many maternity units which are staffed by skilled nurses and supervised by the medical paediatric staff. They contain the modern equipment necessary to give small or sickly babies the best chance of surviving. If a baby is very ill, he'll probably be transferred from his special care baby unit to an intensive care baby unit. There are fewer of these and he may need to be taken to another hospital, but this is worth it for the extra experience, skill and equipment he'll have access to there.

Some babies are taken to the special care baby unit simply for observation and for the guaranteed warmth of an incubator. If you feel strongly that you would prefer to have your baby with you, ask the staff if it would be possible for the incubator to be plugged in by your bed. Some hospitals are happy to do this if a baby is not on the danger list, and it does mean that you get much more of a chance to look at him, look after him and stroke him. If they think it preferable that he should stay put, make sure you spend as much time as possible with him. Low birth weight and sickly babies need one-to-one attention and affection just as much as full-term, healthy babies do. The nurses will probably be aware of the importance of your presence and will actively encourage you to help by teaching you how to cope with the portholes of the incubator, how to change your baby's nappy, how to express or pump your milk, how to put him to the breast frequently even before he's old enough to suck (just to get him used to it and so you don't miss the time when he's ready to start sucking), and how to caress and talk to him.

If you are tactful, you can spend a lot of time in the SCBU and be a real help to the busy nursing staff. Remember that you need rest after having a baby, so don't tire yourself out. If you have had a difficult delivery or if you're unwell, you may not be able to be with your baby as much as you'd like. Some thoughtful hospitals arrange for such mothers to be taken to their babies in the SCBU in a wheelchair or on a trolley every day. If your baby is not in the same hospital as you, the staff may take a Polaroid photograph of the baby for you to have by your bed.

If you are unable to see your baby, ask your husband, a friend or a nurse to tell you about him and to take a photo of him if possible. It's all too easy to forget you've had a baby if he's not with you and this can make it difficult when you are suddenly plunged into looking after him later. It's also more difficult to feel loving towards someone you've virtually never seen, though it's never too late to start up a bond between you and your baby. Talking about him, looking at his photograph and thinking about him will all help, and so will expressing or pumping milk for him, because that will make you feel valuable and important rather than useless and expendable.

The medical and technological care given by these units is often life-saving and it's something of a miracle when a tiny scrap of humanity is nursed over the weeks into a large, healthy baby. Remember, too, that not everyone is so lucky, and try if you can to offer other mothers the support and camaraderie they so badly need when watching over their ill babies.
Related topics Bonding; incubator; low birth weight.

Special schools There are special schools for all sorts of children who wouldn't be able to benefit to the full from an education in an ordinary school. You may be aware from your baby's early days that he'll need special schooling, or it may only become apparent later after careful assessment by a team of experts. Some children start at an ordinary school and it is found later that they would have been better off in a special school and vice versa. The system is thankfully very flexible and in the unlikely situation that you feel your child is wrongly placed in a school, and if discussion with the headteacher doesn't put your mind at rest or result in further assessment from specially trained psychologists, doctors and other specialists, you have the right of appeal to the Department of Education.

The commonest of the special schools are those for mentally handicapped children. The ESN (M) and ESN(S) schools come into this category. ESN stands for educationally subnormal, M stands for mild and S stands for severe. The decision as to which of these two schools a child should go (or, indeed if he should go to an ordinary school) is difficult if he is on the borderline of ability. Formal intelligence, aptitude and developmental testing can help a lot, and this is often done several times over a period of two or three years before the child is due to start school full time, partly to allow for him to have an off day when he is assessed, and partly to see whether certain treatments (for instance, for partial deafness or visual problems) or extra stimulation (for instance in a child who has for some reason been neglected) will improve the child's abilities.

Often these special schools for the mentally handicapped have one or more nursery classes for three- and four-year-olds. Such classes serve several purposes: they give the child the stimulation which his parents, however well-meaning, may be unable to provide at home; they enable the staff to assess the suitability of the child for the school, with the help of visiting experts; they give the parents some time without the often heavy burden of the child; and of course they provide him with company and many different experiences and opportunities.

As with nursery classes for children of normal intelligence, you may feel that you can manage at home just as well, that you don't need any rest, and that you can give him more opportunities, experiences, and company than he'll get at school. In this case, keep him home with you until he's five.

Special schools also exist for physically handicapped children, for obvious reasons. Many of them need lots of time during the day for medical treatment, exercises or physiotherapy; some of them are in wheelchairs and local ordinary schools may simply not be able to accommodate them; a few have problems such as athetosis (involuntary writhing movements of the muscles of their limbs, face and neck) which would make participating in ordinary schooling difficult for them; some are incontinent and need extra staff to help them manage; and some may have lower than average intelligence yet would not get suitable treatment, exercise and so on in an ESN school. If your child is physically handicapped, don't automatically assume he'll need special education. Some parents have collaborated with the staff of ordinary schools to make it possible for such children to be educated there. Sometimes it's possible, for instance, for a mother or other volunteer to go in at break and lunch time to help with incontinence pads, and for a special ramp to be built at key places to enable a child to propel himself (or to be pushed) in his wheelchair from place to place in the school. Although such a child will miss out on sport, he may be able to join a local group of physically handicapped children for games specially arranged for children in wheelchairs. Each child is unique and the best sort of education for him needs to be carefully worked out. You must also consider whether your child would be happier being the odd one out among normal children, or one of a similarly-handicapped group.

There are special schools – mostly boarding schools – for children with severe epilepsy. Such children have such frequent fits that they can't be controlled well enough for them to manage in an ordinary school without disrupting classes. If you feel that boarding is not the answer for your child, you might consider moving to live close to such a school. Only a tiny fraction of all children with epilepsy go to such schools.

Thankfully nowadays the number of children classified as 'delicate' is far smaller than it used to be. Even so, there are some special schools catering for children not robust enough to attend ordinary schools. Their health disorders range from severe asthma to disfiguring skin conditions. A few such children are sent to these schools (which may be boarding schools) because they seem to be more ill when living at home. Others can't cope with the teasing at normal schools.

Another category of special school is that for maladjusted children: healthy children with serious emotional and behavioural problems that can't be adequately catered for in ordinary schools.

If it is thought that a five-year-old child may be able to cope in an ordinary school, then whatever his handicap, he'll be given a chance. However, if he runs into difficulties, special schooling may be the best thing for him.

Speech therapy Speech therapists who work mainly with children are trained in the assessment of speech delay in pre-school children and use special tests to find out how well a child can express himself and how well he can understand. Together with a doctor the speech therapist works out why the child is slow in talking and then plans suitable help for him, both from his parents at home and also perhaps in the clinic, on a group or an individual basis. The object of therapy is to provide a child with lots of experience of listening to people talking to him so that he will hopefully be understanding and talking adequately by the time he goes to school.

Speech therapists can give a lot of help to children with cerebral palsy and can teach the parents how to continue with help at home. Children who have had a cleft palate repair usually need speech therapy, often on a long term basis. Some children speak so indistinctly, missing out some consonants and substituting others, that therapy is helpful if they are to stand a good chance of being understood by the time they go to school. Often these children have only heard indistinct talking (and perhaps little of it) at home. Listening to the television is no way to learn to talk – children need direct communication to do that. Time alone improves the speech of most children, but a little help from the therapist will help them on their way.

Children who stammer generally don't need speech therapy, but their parents may benefit from some counselling from the speech therapist in order to help their children grow out of it faster. *Related topics* Language; slowness; talking. *Useful organization* Association for All Speech Impaired Children.

Spina bifida A defect in one or more of the vertebrae of the spinal column. It is one of the commonest congenital abnormalities in Britain and each year about 3,000 children – more boys than girls – are born with the condition.

There are various degrees of severity of spina bifida and in the least severe form there is simply an absence of bone in one of the vertebrae in the spinal column. At the other end of the scale there is a serious and large defect, often at the lower end of the back, in which the spinal cord within several adjacent vertebrae is exposed to the open air because all the bone, skin and other coverings are absent. Such severely affected children will have paralysed legs, incontinence of urine and bowel motions and possibly other abnormalities of the central nervous system as well. Nine out of ten have hydrocephalus and half of all children with spina bifida are mentally retarded.

The cause isn't known but it is likely to be a combination of genetic and environmental factors. It is certainly more common in some families and in certain geographical areas.

Treatment depends on the degree of damage. In some children an operation will have to be done in the first few days of life if infection is not to affect the spinal cord and thence the brain. Unfortunately, even with good surgery and care early on many children with spina bifida need permanent care for the rest of their lives and some require further operations over the years to correct urinary and orthopaedic problems.

Once a woman has had a child with spina bifida she's statistically more likely to have another, or one with anencephaly or hydrocephalus. Genetic counselling is available to help such families and tests can be done on a pregnant woman's serum and amniotic fluid to find out whether the foetus is affected. If so, an abortion will be offered. Such tests (looking for raised levels of alpha-feto protein) are offered routinely in some hospitals. *Useful organization* Association for Spina Bifida and Hydrocephalus.

Spoiling A spoilt child is one whose upbringing has been such that he is unpleasant to be with in one way or another, both for his parents and for other people. He is also not at ease with himself, realizing that somehow he seems to upset everyone. Spoiling is the fault of the parents, not the child, though sometimes circumstances beyond both parties' control make it more likely.

The first time the issue of spoiling crops up is soon after birth, when a new mother may be unjustifiably criticized for attempting to meet her baby's needs. 'If you pick him up every time he cries, you'll spoil him' is a remark familiar to many mothers and one which tends to come from those women who brought up their own babies according to the clock. However, you can spoil him by making him wait. A baby allowed to cry for long periods from hunger, thirst, loneliness, boredom, or fear may become justifiably suspicious and distrustful of his caretakers. He grows up feeling that in spite of his powerful feelings he's unable to gain other people's attention by letting them know he's in trouble, and so his self-confidence is dashed. Similarly, not allowing an older baby, toddler, or pre-school child to be with his mother as much as he seems to need can cause problems. This child grows up to be more clinging and dependent than the one allowed to be with her and to use her as a base from which to explore and to become confident in other people. This is spoiling.

Giving a baby or child what he needs is not always the same as giving him what he wants. Needs should be satisfied generously and willingly when possible but wants may have to be refused if they are unreasonable, impossible or unsuitable for other people. A child may want to eat a box of chocolates, for example, but you know that if he did, he'd be sick, so you don't let him. He may want a dog, but if you don't want to look after one, or can't have one in a flat, for example, you'll say no. Unfortunately, a few children are given virtually everything they ask for yet little that they really need. Sometimes this is because they are not getting their parents' time, attention and love and the gifts are material substitutes. If you can't spare your child the time and attention he needs, don't waste time feeling guilty about it and trying to make up for it by buying things for him – things are no substitute for the people he loves. Instead, arrange for someone else to spend time with him on a regular basis so that he can form an attachment to him or her and learn to enjoy their company as much – or even more – than yours. By trying guiltily to hold on to your child's affection by giving him things, he'll want more and more things and yet will be increasingly dissatisfied because he's not getting what he really needs. When you do spend time with him he's likely to be bad tempered because he's unconsciously angry that you've neglected him, and in time he may simply forget how to react pleasantly to people. By then you'll have spoiled him.

Giving a child presents isn't intrinsically bad of course. It's only bad if they're guilt offerings. A child knows if he's being given such offerings – he's not fooled for a moment except perhaps during the initial pleasure of having the gift. Every parent enjoys giving their child presents and many wish they could afford to give more, but young children are as delighted to receive your time and attention as they are your presents, and an hour spent helping them in the sandpit or taking them to the common for a discovery walk will more than take their minds off a new tricycle or doll.

Presents don't have to be expensive to be welcomed, and second-hand toys and equipment often represent good value.

The way a child asks for something is important. If he whines, nags, or bullies you for something, it would be foolish to spoil him by letting him have it because you would be teaching him that that was a successful and acceptable way of getting what he wanted. It's better to explain to a pre-school child that you're much more likely to say 'yes' to a reasonable request if he asks nicely and times his request well. (A toddler won't be able to time his request because he has no concept of waiting but wants things when he wants them).

By encouraging and later insisting on good manners, and by showing your child a good example, you'll help him learn how to be good company and how to make other people feel good with him. A child who has never been taught how to say 'thank you' or 'please', or to shut the door when he goes out into the garden to play, or to offer guests food before piling it on his own plate, or to queue for help in a shop or for a bus, or not to get down until he's finished his meal, can make other people annoyed, uncomfortable, or even angry as he grows up. While it's easy to make excuses for a two-, three- or even a four-year-old, people expect more of a child of five or more, and even though they'll blame the child's parents for not showing him how to behave, they'll also think badly of him. The child will realize that his behaviour is having an adverse effect on other people but may not understand why. By not teaching him to be considerate of others you end up spoiling him.

Spoilt children have learnt that they can do what they want or get what they want simply by making a fuss. If their parents try to control them they simply make a bigger fuss and win. Some parents are so worried about not damping down their children's natural high spirits or not wanting to be over-strict that they end up going to the other extreme, allowing high spirits to run wild and the children to have complete freedom. Children don't really like this, however much they might think they want it. Without exception, children like to be given guidelines and limits on their behaviour, especially when other children are around who might goad them into doing or saying things they otherwise might not have done. By all means try not to impose unnecessary rules and certainly allow yourself to be charmed or persuaded to change your mind if it seems quite reasonable to do so on occasions, but explain why you've changed your mind so your child realizes you weren't just saying 'no' for the sake of it.

There's potential for good and bad in every child. You can spoil a child by fostering the bad or at least by not checking it, just as you can by not encouraging and making the most of the good. You certainly don't get a blank slate with a newborn baby because babies are born with certain personality and behavioural traits programmed into them, but you can decide that you'll do your best for him. Being aware of the dangers of spoiling can help you do this. **Related topics** Personality; rules; self-confidence; selfishness; whining.

Spoon-feeding One way of giving your baby his first food is to spoon-feed him. The food should be of a soft, smooth consistency to enable him to swallow it easily. Babies can't cope with lumpy food at all competently until they are around six to eight months when they can chew the lumps with their hard gums instead of gagging while trying to swallow unchewed lumps, as a younger baby does. You can prepare the food by mashing it with a fork, sieving or liquidizing it and you can mix it with some milk, water or gravy to make it softer if necessary. At first your baby will try to suck the food from the spoon but he'll soon learn to transfer it from his tongue to the back of his mouth and then swallow it. Spoon feeding with you holding the spoon is cleaner than finger feeding, but many babies thoroughly enjoy finger feeding, and of course you can try both. The time will come (in some babies from the beginning) when a baby wants to hold the spoon and feed himself, which will be a very messy experience and one which he'll adore. Do let him do this because he'll enjoy it and the earlier you let him use a spoon, the earlier he'll become proficient with it. If you find – as you will at first – that most of the food doesn't go anywhere near his mouth, use two spoons, one for him to try to feed himself with and one for you to feed him with. By fifteen months, most babies make a passable job of feeding themselves with a spoon. Don't forget that your baby will have trouble in giving you back the spoon he's using for you to reload it because the skill of letting go comes later than that of holding. Don't be cross with him for holding on to it – he's not being difficult on purpose. Try resting his hand on the tray of his high chair or on the table and he'll probably be able to let go easily. Otherwise, give him a spoon in his other hand and his grasp will weaken as his attention is transferred. There's no need to put your baby's bowl of food in front of him – if you do he'll probably play with it, stir it with his fingers, and throw it on the floor. Load his spoon with food and give it to him. When he's older and gets hungrier at mealtimes you can put his bowl in front of him and take it away when he's had enough before he starts playing. *Related topic* Feeding equipment.

Sprain The tearing of a ligament – one of the tough, fibrous bands that hold joints together. When a child has a sprain, blood oozes from the torn area of ligament and causes internal bleeding, severe pain and an unwillingness to move the sprained joint. The pain can be so severe that the joint may have to be x-rayed to rule out a fracture. Generally, fracture pain gets worse if left untreated, whereas the pain from a sprain gets better with time.

The treatment is simple. Make the area cold with ice cubes in a polythene bag or a pack of frozen peas from the freezer. Do this at once and most of the swelling and pain will be prevented. Give the child a full dose of painkilling medicine if the pain is so severe that he cannot sleep. After the first day or so as the pain begins to go, encourage him to move the joint. This prevents stiffness and helps a speedy recovery. Immobilizing a sprained joint is the worst thing you can do.

Squint A condition (strabismus, 'lazy eye', cast, crossed eyes) in which the eyes don't look at an object in conjunction. The word 'squint' is also used for when a person screws up his eyes to look at something. This isn't a squint in the medical sense of the word but may indicate that the person has a visual problem of some kind. If your child seems to screw his eyes up to look at things take him for an eye test.

In babies under the age of three months a squint may be quite harmless but over this age you should certainly report a squint to the family or clinic doctor, even though nothing may have to be done. Such squints are more likely to occur if either parent squinted in childhood.

Some squints are serious and if left they can cause blindness in the affected eye because the brain suppresses the image that is out of line with the 'good' (non-squinting) eye. The child who squints on and off is much less likely to lose the vision in his bad eye but should still be seen by a specialist. Never ignore a squint in a child of over three months old.

The simplest treatment for most squints is to cover the good eye so as to encourage the muscles controlling the movements of the squinting eye to work properly. This also encourages the brain to be re-educated into perceiving the image from the squinting eye. If this doesn't work, a surgical operation can be done to alter the length of the muscles that move the eye so as to make both eyes work in unison again. Sometimes several operations at intervals of months or years are necessary to achieve a good result. The eyes aren't bandaged after such operations today and the child is up and about almost immediately after the operation and is pain-free very soon.

There are lots of possible causes for a squint. Short sight, or long sight which is much worse in one eye, measles and meningitis can each be responsible but often there is no apparent cause at all. It makes sense to take children for routine developmental checks so that proper tests for a squint can be done and the eyesight tested. If your child's eyes seem to be slightly 'off centre', don't panic and immediately think he'll need an operation because it could just be tiredness. If you are at all worried or the child has any other signs of a visual problem, see your doctor as soon as possible. Often a parent thinks his child has a squint when there is no actual squint but the folds of skin at the nasal edge of each eye are covering the white of each eye next to the nose to some extent, so giving the impression of a squint. This will disappear as the child grows older. If in doubt consult your doctor. **Related topics** Vision; vision testing.

Stairs As soon as a baby becomes mobile, stairs are a hazard. You'll find it'll save you having to watch him constantly if you have a gate at the bottom for when he is downstairs and at the top for when he is upstairs.

Stairs can also be a hazard for all the family. Never leave piles of things on the treads waiting to be taken upstairs and teach the children not to leave toys there. A small toy can be lethal if caught underfoot coming downstairs, especially if you have a baby in your arms and can't see where you're putting your feet. It's always best to have one hand (nearest the bannisters) free when carrying a baby downstairs. Never carry too much when going up and down stairs: make more trips and be safe.

Worn parts of stair carpet or carpet that isn't properly fitted are also dangerous, so keep the carpet in good order – it gets a lot of traffic.

An enterprising crawler or toddler will be very keen to get on to the stairs and once he is steady and reliable on his feet you can start teaching him how to come downstairs on his own. Some children sit on a stair and come down on their bottoms. The safest way though for a young child is on his tummy, feet first. In this way he can control his speed of descent to some extent and will enjoy it too. As he grows and becomes more confident you can teach him to crawl downstairs backwards. Finally, when he's confident with these methods you can help him learn to walk downstairs himself. At first he'll do this one step at a time.

Never allow children to play on the stairs under the age of five – they may forget where they are and step backwards or get overexcited and push and both of these can have disastrous results.

Stammering (stuttering) A speech disorder in which the speech is interrupted or hesitant. With a stutter the sounds are repeated before the word or sentence finally comes out.

Stammering or stuttering can be a normal part of a child's speech development between 2½ and six and often occurs because the child's brain races ahead of his ability to make the words. Most children grow out of this kind of stammer as long as it is ignored. Never tease or ridicule the child or show signs of impatience, even though this can be difficult when life is busy. It's best not even to comment on the stammer or to let other people do so. It has been suggested that obvious and excessive parental concern and correction over stammering can make it permanent. Such children may even start contorting their bodies, faces and tongues as they try in vain to get the words out.

It isn't known why but stammering seems to occur in families. If ever you get to the stage when you're really concerned about your child's stammering, ask your doctor if he can arrange for you and your child to be seen by a speech therapist. *Related topics* Speech therapist; talking.

Standing The age at which a child can pull himself up to stand, stand holding on to you or to the furniture, and stand alone, varies enormously according to his individual programming by his genes, his experience of taking weight on his legs, his enthusiasm for doing new things and the encouragement he gets for trying. Any illness can slow down a child's progress or even make him go back a stage or two.

At some time from about seven months onwards, (or even earlier in a very few children), your baby will pull himself up to stand. He'll have been taking weight on his legs for a long while before this in a baby-walker, baby-bouncer, on your lap or on the floor with your support. Pulling himself up to stand shows that his arms are strong enough to get him up there and that he likes being on two feet. Some normal, healthy babies don't stand until they are over a year old.

At first a standing baby finds it hard to sit down again and may even get stuck standing up until someone rescues him. From standing holding on to something, he'll learn to stand alone for a while, falling down with a bump on his bottom every so often at first. One day he'll start walking round the furniture and from then it won't be many weeks before he tries to walk alone.

Stealing Children under the age of four or so often take things that don't belong to them but this can't be called stealing because they don't yet really understand what's theirs and what isn't. If they take something belonging to somebody else they do it because they like it and want it and don't realize it has an owner. It's a foolish parent who even thinks of a child of this age 'stealing' in the adult sense of the word. Handle the situation simply and sensibly by telling him that the toy belongs to someone else and then forget it.

Over this age children begin to have a concept of possessions belonging to other people and of other people's things being valuable to them just as theirs are to themselves. An under-five is highly unlikely deliberately or wantonly to 'steal', though he might take something home meaning to bring it back some time. If an under-five does take something deliberately because the power of his desire outweighs that of his conscience, it's best to handle the matter firmly, explaining who the thing belongs to and that he mustn't take something that isn't his. Don't get cross – just be matter of fact and straightforward about it. Never call a child a thief or blow up an isolated incident out of all proportion because you could make him feel guilty and naughty without his being able fully to understand the morality involved. ***Related topics*** Behaviour problems; cheating; lying.

Step-parents With nearly one in three marriages a remarriage and lots of these involving children there are hundreds of thousands of children living in a family with an adult who is not their parent.

If you are separated, divorced, or widowed you'll probably want to remarry eventually, especially if you have children under five years old. Needless to say you'll have plenty of decisions and problems of your own to come to terms with but so too will your children. It's only fair to them to introduce your prospective new partner slowly into the family's life by having him or her home for meals, going on family outings together and so on. If you follow this gentle progression your children will see the new partner as a natural follow-on to the last one and not as an interloper.

Problems can arise if the new partner hasn't had children because he or she will be thrown in at the deep end and may even resent the fact that they take up so much of your time. This can be especially true of a woman with no experience of children who comes straight into a ready-made family. After all, she has had no gentle run-in to the situation, and they're not her children either. Still, it shouldn't be difficult to share the care of the children – after all you'll have been doing it single-handed until now.

There are almost bound to be problems with new step-parents for children of any age. Perhaps under-fives are more tolerant because they haven't established themselves in the outside world yet but even so the step-parent starts off with several disadvantages. The greatest of these is the 'wicked stepmother' syndrome with the stepmother worrying about disciplining the children at all just in case they don't accept her as part of the family. Some step-parents even refuse to discipline their new children (at least early on) on the grounds that they're not theirs and they don't want to risk falling out with them. Sometimes the natural parent becomes stricter because of what he fears the newcomer will think of his children and because he doesn't want to fail in her eyes. The best thing to do is get the subject sorted out between you and then to treat the children in a consistent way so that they know where they stand. Your guidelines and limits for their behaviour are usually best left as they were before. They shouldn't end up playing one adult off against another.

A new baby in a remarriage can be a very real strain to the other children because in addition to all the usual feelings of displacement are those associated with the step-parent's child who is the only natural child of the new couple. Only by creating a meaningful, loving parental relationship with the children can such problems be overcome.

Another problem is that of having three parents. This can be very confusing for the child, who doesn't know whether to be loyal to the departed parent or to his or her replacement. A three-way discussion with the adults can often sort this out, provided of course that they are on speaking terms on such matters. Some step-parents taking over a very young family want the children to change their allegiance and to be 'theirs' but the real parent feels differently, of course. There are no magic answers to this problem because the child will in time see the step-parent as his parent in practice if not in fact, to the personal dismay of the departed parent who knows that this is best for the child but may dislike it all the same.

Research has shown that women don't find it easy to become instant stepmothers and those who haven't had previous close contact with children or haven't talked it all through with their new partners do worst of all. One survey found that more stepmothers have trouble with discipline than do stepfathers and that more stepfathers were called 'Dad' than stepmothers were called 'Mum'. This study found that overall, most such families were 'close' or 'very close' and that in nine out of ten of the families the children had adjusted well to the new situation. The highest satisfaction score came where children were under four when the step-parent came into the home. At least half of the families said that a new baby improved family relationships and stepmothers said that there was a better atmosphere once they had had a child of their own (perhaps because they felt more like mothers in their own right). The study found, perhaps surprisingly, that the greater number of children did *not* produce greater problems. Marital satisfaction it seems is very high too, even in spite of family problems.

Sterilizing bottles Because of the hazard of infection from bacteria or inadequately cleaned bottles and teats, they need to be sterilized between every feed. This is most important for a baby of under six months, who is at special risk from gastro-enteritis, but is also important for a baby of any age sucking from a bottle, because bacteria thrive on any traces of milk left behind. It's worth continuing with your sterilization of bottles even when your child is two or three and still using a bottle, because at least then you'll know that it is as clean and bacteria-free as possible each time you fill it, even if he does drop it on the floor without you noticing, or leaves it lying around on surfaces where bacterial contamination is highly likely, or if another child with a cold, for instance, drinks from it without anyone seeing. A young baby should only ever be given a clean, sterilized bottle, and if the teat does touch the floor or anything which might harbour dangerous germs, another sterilized one should be put in its place. It's probably safe for it to touch your hands if you've washed them before feeding your baby, because he is likely to have built up a resistance to the germs that you normally carry on your skin, and in any case preparing a bottle feed is not an aseptic business, with no bacteria around, though it should be as aseptic as possible.

Before sterilization it's essential that any milk residue is cleaned away from bottles and teats by brushing well with a bottle brush in hot water and soap or detergent. Rinse well when clean to remove traces of soap or detergent. If you want to clean the equipment later, just rinse it out quickly with cold water – hot water makes the milk protein coagulate and more difficult to remove. Turn the teat inside out to clean it thoroughly by pushing it with a spoon handle and rub salt over its inside and outside to get rid of clinging fat. Check that the hole isn't clogged. Cleaning is most easily done before the film of milk has had time to dry.

There are three ways of sterilizing feeding equipment: by immersing it in a special solution; by boiling it; and by boiling the bottle containing the feed. Bottles and teats sterilized by immersion in a sterilizing solution must be left there for the recommended time, making sure they are completely immersed and that there are no air bubbles in the bottle. Take care to make up the sterilizing solution to the correct strength, and make up fresh solution every day, as its life is short. You can put discarded sterilizing solution in a bucket to soak your nappies in because although its antiseptic activity is not enough to sterilize feeding equipment safely, it will do for the nappies which don't need to be sterile. Keep the teat immersed in the solution by putting it under a small upturned jar. You can leave everything soaking for as long as you like except the teat, which will perish faster if you don't remove it after three hours. Keep the sterilized teat in the jar you used to keep it immersed. The jar should be covered. Teats eventually fade but this is not important. You can sterilize the equipment in an ordinary bowl, or you can buy a special unit.

When you're ready to make up a feed, wash your hands, remove the bottle, teat, screw ring and cap from the water, and rinse them to remove traces of the sterilizing solution by pouring cooled boiled water over them as you hold them. The manufacturers say that this is not essential, but it seems wise not to expose a baby to any unnatural chemicals unnecessarily. You're now ready to make up the feed.

You can sterilize the feeding equipment by boiling it for a minimum of ten minutes in plenty of water, taking care to immerse the bottle completely and to remove any air bubbles. Boiling makes the teats go hard in time and tends to alter the colour and opacity of the plastic. You can also see a hard water deposit on the bottle after boiling it in areas where the domestic water is hard, though this can be overcome by filling the saucepan with water which has previously been boiled. The advantages of boiling are that there is no chance of the baby being exposed to unnecessary chemicals, you don't have to remember to buy anything, and it only takes ten minutes. The cost of sterilizing solution in counterbalanced by the cost of fuel to heat the water.

Nowadays few mothers make up lots of feeds at a time because making up a feed is so quick and easy with today's dried cows' milk formula powder. If you are leaving your baby with someone you don't trust to make up feeds correctly or hygienically, you could leave the number of bottles needed ready made up in the fridge. This can be done by making up feeds as usual in ready-sterilized bottles, or – more safely still – you could make up feeds in bottles (which don't have to be sterile, just clean) and then sterilize bottles and milk together by boiling the bottles for 25 minutes. Remember to loosen the screw ring slightly to allow room for expansion of the air inside the bottle. Sterilizing bottle and milk together makes it safer to leave filled bottles in the fridge. Prepared the other way, bacteria can slowly multiply when feeds are left even in a cold place.

If you wash your baby's feeding equipment (bottle, teat, screw ring and cap, if you've used one) after a feed, and put it straight into sterilizing solution, you can get by with one set of equipment, though it makes sense to have another just in case. Extra bottles are always useful to have for outings, to leave for a sitter, or if you are unwell. If you sterilize by boiling, you might like to wait until you've got two or three sets used and washed, so that you save on fuel.

If you have the sort of bottle in which you can put the teat upside down in the bottle with a cap over it before screwing on the screw ring, you'll need to use a sterilized screw ring and cap, because both could contaminate the milk. If you only ever give a feed as soon as you've made up the bottle, the screw ring doesn't need to be sterilized, only cleaned, though many mothers sterilize it anyway as it takes up so little room. The screw ring and cap can be sterilized along with the bottle and teat. The sort of cap that fits right over the bottle with the teat ready to give to the baby doesn't need sterilizing before each use.

There's no point in taking great care over sterilizing equipment if you then leave a bottle of warm milk lying around for a long time before your baby drinks it, or even between feeds. Milk to be drunk on journeys, while out visiting, or at night should be made up at the time by adding boiled water (that has been allowed to cool to the right temperature) from a thermos flask to the milk powder in the bottle. Alternatively, if you make up the feed and cool it at once in the fridge, you can warm it up later when needed. Milk shouldn't be left made up from one day to another, even if kept in the fridge, because of the risk of germs multiplying in the milk. They can do this whether the milk is warm or cold, but bacterial reproduction is much slower when it's cold.

Similarly, you should take care only to handle the scoop for the milk powder with clean, dry hands. Wash your hands with soap, make sure your nails are clean, and dry your hands on a towel kept for this purpose and changed daily. Don't leave the lid off the tin of milk longer than necessary.

If you're using evaporated milk (which is extremely unlikely in the West), you can safely leave the tin opened but covered for twenty-four hours in a cool place – ideally a refrigerator. Buy tins small enough to be used up in twenty-four hours. The inside of the can is lacquered to prevent tin from seeping into its contents. Wash the top well with soap and hot water, before opening by piercing two holes with a tin opener kept just for this, and kept very clean.

If you're using doorstep milk for your older baby, keep it in a cool place and only use milk fresh that day unless you boil it first. Once the bottle is opened, keep it covered. If you boil enough milk at once for a whole day, keep it in a sterilized and covered container in the fridge.

If you're using evaporated or bottled milk, you may use a funnel or jug when making up a bottle for your baby. It's important that this is well washed, sterilized and covered along with the other feeding equipment.

Any bottle that a child sucks needs to be sterilized, whether or not it has contained milk. Bottles and teats used to give your child drinks of fruit juice or water, even if only the very small ones, must be cleaned and sterilized as above, though salt won't be necessary to clean the teats. While bacteria thrive in milk, they can also multiply in other drinks, especially sugary solutions. Even your child's dummy is best sterilized once a day.

Use your common sense about sterilizing feeding equipment. Don't let other babies or toddlers suck from your baby's bottle, but if they do, change the teat. This is especially important the younger your baby is and is particularly so if the other child has a cold or cough. If you're ever unsure about the safety of a bottle of milk, discard it and prepare a new feed in a sterilized bottle. It's always better to be safe than sorry, and with poor hygiene bottle-fed babies are at risk of bowel infection. Whilst such infections no longer kill babies the way they did, you'll be sorry to see your baby ill and he'll possibly end up in hospital if the infection is serious. *Related topics* Bottle feeding; feeding equipment.

Sticky eye A type of conjunctivitis that occurs in babies in the newborn period. The baby has a yellow discharge from one or both eyes which may make the eyelashes stick together. This is usually caused by irritation from amniotic fluid or blood entering the eye during birth. The eye is sometimes, but not usually, infected and swabs may be taken and sent to the laboratory, just in case. Gonococcal conjunctivitis is common in babies whose mothers have gonorrhoea but can be prevented with 1% silver nitrate drops in the eyes after birth.

Treatment is simple. Wipe your baby's eyes with cotton wool swabs soaked in saline and then squeezed out. When wiping with a swab, wipe from the nasal side of the eye to the ear side so as not to transfer any infection from one eye to the other, and use a clean swab for each eye. Some doctors advise that the baby be laid on his side with the discharging eye downwards so that if the discharge is infected, it doesn't run into the unaffected eye.

Itchy, red, discharging eyes occurring after this period are usually infected and will need treatment with an antibiotic eye ointment. They clear up very quickly indeed. If such an infection doesn't clear up or is repeated it could be caused by a blocked tear duct which may need simple surgery to correct it. *Related topics* Blepharitis; blocked tear duct; conjunctivitis; gonorrhoea.

Stillbirth The birth of a dead baby after twenty-eight weeks of pregnancy.

The commonest causes of stillbirth are too early a separation of the placenta, toxaemia of pregnancy and abnormalities of the baby such as severe spina bifida and anencephaly. Infections in pregnancy such as with cytomegalovirus or listeria infection can also cause a baby to be stillborn. Some babies who are in danger before they are born with, for example, a lack of oxygen and nourishment because of a placental problem can be saved by Caesarean section but some are too damaged to live however they are delivered.

The stillbirth rate can be reduced to some extent with meticulous antenatal care, improved living conditions and nutrition, a reduction of the amount a pregnant woman smokes and drinks, and her avoidance of. dangerous (to the foetus) medicines and drugs.

Parents who have a stillborn baby need a lot of support and love. To some extent having a stillborn baby is worse than having an abortion or miscarriage (before twenty-eight weeks) because the nearer a woman gets to the anticipated end of her pregnancy the more difficult is it to accept the loss. Most parents grieve the loss of their baby bitterly, partly because the whole pregnancy seems to have been such a waste of time and effort with nothing to show for it, but also because a potential life has been wasted.

Many parents want to see and hold their dead baby and in some instances having a photograph of him helps them to mourn. If a woman has had a stillborn baby it's quite wrong for everyone to pretend it didn't happen and for the staff simply to take it away. Research has shown that mothers who accept that their baby lived inside them and then died fare much better in coming to terms with their grief later. After all, a mother can't forget the fact that she has had a swelling tummy and a baby moving inside her for several weeks. A relationship is begun months before a baby is born and to try to negate the loss or to get over it too quickly as though it wasn't important because the baby never lived independently would be unreasonable. The hurt always comes out somehow.

If your baby dies in this way you'll need to register the stillbirth with the

Registrar of Births, Marriages and Deaths – the hospital staff or your doctor will tell you about this. Many parents don't make their own arrangements for the baby's burial and in such cases the hospital will arrange for him to be put into a common grave. If you want to have a funeral service for him and his own coffin you can, of course, do so but either way parents say it helps them in their mourning and afterwards if they know where their baby is buried.

Don't expect to get over a stillbirth quickly – it could take months or even years. After all, you've lost a potential member of your family and that's always hard, especially if you have had trouble conceiving or a history of miscarriage or if you've been told you shouldn't get pregnant again. The pain of grieving is lessened by the understanding of friends and relatives but some parents, especially mothers, find that the first few months go past in a sort of numb haze. Most women want to talk about their experience and their feelings over and over again and a listening ear is more helpful than anything else. After that, people tend to forget what has happened and to assume that they're getting over their loss, whereas in fact they're only just then realizing properly the bleakness of what has happened. This is the time when the full force of the loss can hit and depression or marital problems may occur. Remember that your other children will be upset and will need more love and attention than ever. Studies have shown that overall it is better to wait until you have finished mourning the stillborn baby before getting pregnant again. Some women who have started again too soon say they find it hard to relate to the new baby when he is born because they see him as a replacement for the one they lost rather than as an individual in his own right. Waiting till you feel happy and back to normal again mentally will also give your body a well-earned rest. After all, after losing a baby your body has to readjust just as after having a live one. *Related topics* Bereavement; miscarriage; perinatal mortality. *Useful organization* The Compassionate Friends.

Storytelling

Whilst older children obviously enjoy listening to stories, many parents don't realize that a baby as young as a year old also gets pleasure out of listening to them at the same time. He won't understand the story, but if you take the trouble to show him the pictures, he'll enjoy looking at them and will also be interested in the rhythm and sounds of your voice. Don't exclude your baby from storytime with the older children – he'll know something nice is going on and he'll enjoy being a part of it.

Don't bother too much about the level or complexity of the stories you tell your child: he doesn't need to understand them all or remember them afterwards in order to enjoy them. Children have their favourite stories and want to have them read time and again. What they often like most of all is an original story made up by you on the spot. Make such a story pertinent to your child's life and possibly even include members of the family in it. Real life stories about things people in your family have done, things your child has done, the day he was born, and so on are often more fun than make-believe ones. Your stories don't have to be brilliantly composed for your child to love them. This is perhaps partly because you can look at him as you tell your own story, and embroider it with your facial expressions, rather than both of you having your noses buried in the book. If you've been reading too long a story to finish in one go, when you get to a natural break or to an exciting part, stop for that evening and take up the story again the next day.

As your child gets older he'll want to tell you stories he has made up. This can be great fun for you and is often very illuminating about his life, fears, loves and hates. If you listen to a four- or five-year-old's spontaneous stories you'll learn a lot about his life that might not come out in any other way.

Most people's daily conversations contain stories about what they've done, heard or seen. Simply by listening to these a child will learn how to tell stories of his own and how to enrich them with gestures, facial expressions and a variety of tones of voice. *Related topics* Creativity; drama; imagination; listening.

Strangers For the first few months of life a baby will smile at anyone who takes an interest in him if he is in the right mood and the person is used to approaching babies, but he reserves his best smiles and vocalizations for his mother. Round about six months, most babies begin to be disturbed by strangers, unless they are secure in their mother's arms, and even then if a stranger makes overtures to them they tend to nestle in to their mother with a shy smile.

A child who is crawling or walking is old enough to explore and may approach a stranger but will hurry back to his mother who is his fortress. Toddlers and pre-school children become independent and less wary of strangers sooner if allowed to be dependent on their mothers for as long as they need to be. It is children who are forced to stay away from their mothers before they are ready who find it most difficult later to take an interest in other people and to approach them without shyness or fear.

Of course, unsupervised children may unfortunately be at risk from mentally ill or criminal adults. If you allow your under-five to play in the street without you or someone else looking after him, he'll have to be warned to refuse all invitations to go off with strangers. It is difficult to explain to a bright four- or five-year-old that not all people are 'good' and every parent will have to find his or her own way round this problem in the light of their individual child's temperament and personality. It's a sobering thought that more children come to physical, mental, or sexual harm at the hands of someone close to them than from strangers. *Related topics* Independence; shyness.

Stye An infection occurring in one of the sebaceous (oil) glands at the base of an eyelash. Styes sometimes occur in crops if a child re-infects himself by rubbing his eyes. They are also contagious and can be caught by other members of the family and friends.

A stye is simply a boil and behaves just like boils elsewhere. At first an area of redness appears at the edge of the eyelid and this becomes a swelling. After a few days the stye 'points': it produces pus as a 'head' – and is soon ready to burst. Most styes break spontaneously, discharge and heal in a day or two. Sometimes they don't burst but heal from within.

The only thing that a stye can be confused with is a cyst but cysts are usually pale yellow, almost never painful (unlike styes) and never come to a head.

The best treatment for styes is a warm soak (with a face flannel or a pad of cotton wool soaked in hot water) several times a day. Some doctors suggest giving antibiotic eye drops to prevent the formation of other styes but this isn't essential. Cysts need no treatment at home unless they become infected. If this happens, consult the doctor.

As styes can spread around a family keep the child's face flannel and towel separate for his personal use and wash your hands each time after dealing with his eye. Boil his face flannel and towel daily, or soak it in nappy sterilizing solution. Sometimes if the eyelash at the centre of the stye can be pulled out with fingers or tweezers this releases the pus and brings instant relief.

Styes usually occur when a child is tired or run down but quite normal, healthy children get them from time to time, especially if they have dandruff. If your child gets recurrent styes, consult your doctor.

Sucking Newborn babies sometimes make sucking movements even without anything in their mouths to suck on. This automatic sucking is called the sucking reflex and it has been noticed to be at its strongest twenty to thirty minutes after a baby is born. After this it becomes weaker if the baby hasn't been put to the breast in that first half hour or so. After forty hours, it again becomes stronger. This variation in strength applies whether a baby is to be breast or bottle-fed.

Babies get milk in a slightly different way from the breast than from the bottle. Sucking is by no means the only way in which a baby gets milk from the breast. In fact he uses a combination of three methods – sucking, milking, and just allowing let-down milk (or leaking milk from a full breast) to drip or spray into his mouth. Sucking keeps the nipple and areola in the baby's mouth and also draws some milk from the breast. The further the baby can draw the nipple and areola into his mouth by sucking it in, the better he'll be able to empty the reservoirs under the areola, which is why the protractility of the nipples is so important. However, a lot of milk is actually 'milked' from the reservoirs under the areola. The baby sticks the front of his tongue out beneath the nipple as far as his lower lip and curls it up slightly, then he pushes the back of his tongue up against the nipple and areola. The whole tongue moves back into his mouth, pressing against the nipple and areola as it does so, milking the milk out of the reservoirs. The baby's jaws open and close during this milking action to help the tongue compress the nipple and areola. This milking action stimulates the let-down reflex which ejects milk from the nipple in fine jets so that all the baby has to do is swallow it. You'll notice that he'll take several gulps in a row and then rest, keeping the breast in his mouth by a little suction, before taking more gulps. This is because the milk lets down in spurts with a gap between each spurt.

The swallowing reflex is then essential for a baby to get the milk into his stomach.

A bottle-fed baby learns to 'bottle-suck', which is much easier than getting milk from the breast and uses far less of his energy. He applies a little suction to the teat, lets the milk pour into his mouth, and swallows it. There is little up and down or in and out movement of his tongue and less jaw movement.

If a baby who has learnt to bottle-suck is put to the breast, he'll try to use the same technique to get milk from the breast. Unfortunately, it doesn't work very well at the breast and he'll get very little milk. He'll have to learn or re-learn how to milk the breast if he is to get enough. This is possible, but can take a lot of patience. Once a baby has been breast-fed for several weeks, the occasional experience of sucking from a bottle won't make him forget how to milk the breast, but some learn very quickly that milk comes out of a bottle more easily than from the breast and are reluctant to take the breast if there's the slightest chance of getting a bottle.

Because so much more muscular effort is expended in getting milk from the breast, it's not surprising that orthodontists say that they see few orthodontic problems in children who have been breast-fed. The vigorous sucking actually promotes healthy jaw development.

Don't confuse your baby in the early days especially by giving him sometimes the breast and sometimes the bottle. Any milk he has other than your breast milk is best given by spoon (or by naso-gastric tube to a very small or premature baby).

You can spot a baby trying to use the bottle-sucking technique at the breast by the occasional indrawing of his cheeks caused by sucking his tongue, by his tongue thrusting, and by his ineffective (sometimes fluttering) sucking action. Feeds are long in such a confused baby because his poor milking action doesn't encourage his mother's milk to let down. Intervals between bouts of sucking are longer and he doesn't swallow very often.

The sucking reflex may be impaired in babies who are brain damaged, jaundiced, or who have an infection. It is also impaired if the mother has had a lot of painkilling drugs in labour. A cleft lip or palate may interfere with sucking, though some mothers manage with skilled help and lots of patience to breast-feed such a baby.

The sucking reflex first appears when a baby is still in his mother's womb and some babies suck their thumb before they're born. If a baby is born prematurely, and if he weighs less than two or three pounds (1000–1400g), he won't have a sucking reflex at first. With time and when he has grown mature enough, it will appear. Even before it appears, hold your baby at your breast and offer him your nipple and areola every so often. This works best if the areola and nipple are held in such a way as to form a flattened 'biscuit'. Don't force it into his mouth. After some days or weeks of keeping your milk supply going by expression or pumping (and giving this milk to your baby by naso-gastric tube), he'll one day take an interest in your nipple by licking it. Another day he'll suck on the nipple and areola and draw them into his mouth. Sucking makes small babies very tired at first and they often suck a few times then go to sleep for twenty minutes or so, exhausted. Often a small baby will only start to suck really strongly at about the time he was originally expected to be born. Breast-feeds are very long drawn out at first and the changeover from feeding by naso-gastric tube to breast-feeding isn't an abrupt one – he'll continue to be tube-fed and breast-fed until he's old enough, mature enough and strong enough to get all the milk he needs straight from the breast.

Babies like to go on sucking for several years and if they're weaned from the breast or bottle before they're ready to give up sucking, they'll choose something else on which to suck, such as their fingers, thumb, a toy, or a piece of material. Many babies like to spend a lot of time sucking for pleasure and comfort, especially when they're tired or unwell.

Babies' sucking habits and patterns vary a lot. It's been said that a baby writes his signature with his sucking pattern. Not only does the strength of the suck vary from baby to baby, but also the number of sucks in each bout of sucking, the speed of sucking, and the length of time he likes to carry on sucking altogether (which varies according to the time of day, the amount of milk, and whether he wants to suck for milk mainly or for comfort or pleasure). Newborn babies who are apathetic because their mothers have been given painkillers in labour, following a difficult labour, or with jaundice, suck only weakly at first and are easily tired, especially by breast-feeding. Lots of patience is necessary to make sure such babies stimulate the breast often enough and for long enough for their mothers to produce enough milk for them, or even to make sure they get enough milk from a bottle. *Related topics* Breast-feeding; bottle-feeding; dummies; jaundice; let-down reflex; low birth weight; sleepy baby; thumb and finger sucking.

Sugar (sucrose)

Sugar (sucrose) A sweet-tasting carbohydrate extract of sugar beet or cane. Its scientific name is sucrose. Almost all animals seem to like the taste of sweet things and Man is no exception. However, sugar in the form of sucrose is completely unnecessary for health and need never be eaten. Most carbohydrate foods are converted to simple sugars such as glucose by the intestines, so as long as your child is eating a reasonable balance of carbohydrate foods he'll be getting plenty of essential glucose.

Some parents feel they should add extra glucose or sucrose to their children's food 'for energy'. This is totally unnecessary because all food gives energy, but added sugar – especially sucrose – causes tooth decay and is likely to produce fat children.

Unfortunately, eating sugar is habit-forming – the more you have of it, the more you want it. Try weaning a child off sugar and you'll see how difficult it is.

Ideally it's best if your child never gets hooked on sugar in the first place. Start him off as you wean him by never giving him sugar. The natural sugars in fruit and vegetables are delicious. Carrots and onions especially taste very sweet if the child's palate isn't jaded by eating lots of added sugar. Use only tiny amounts of added sugar in your cooking and avoid bought foods containing sugar such as fruit squashes and even some tinned vegetables which have sugar added to them. Get used to reading labels on packets, drinks and so on and you'll be amazed by how many foods have added sugar.

Sweets can easily be avoided in your child's first few years without him feeling at all hard done by.

Added sugar in the form of sucrose isn't a poison but it definitely has some harmful effects. *Related topics* Diabetes; sweets.

Sugar intolerance A condition in which a person lacks certain digestive enzymes which break down complex sugars into simple, absorbable ones.

Lactose intolerance is caused by a lack of the digestive enzyme (lactase) that normally breaks down lactose (milk sugar) into simpler sugars in the child's gut. Rarely, it starts from birth in either breast- or bottle-fed babies. More usually, it develops during adolescence, especially in some black and oriental people, when it causes abdominal pain and distension and diarrhoea within a short time of drinking cows' milk. Another important cause of this sort of sugar intolerance is damage to the gut such as can happen after gastro-enteritis. Instead of recovering from his acute diarrhoea, the child continues to have it, with watery or fatty motions, nausea, tummy rumbling, and abdominal pain and distension which may continue for anything from a few days to a few weeks. If milk is withdrawn from the child's diet, recovery is faster, though sometimes there is also an intolerance to other sugars such as sucrose (table sugar). If your child's diarrhoea doesn't clear up quickly, you may think it worthwhile to try withdrawing both milk and added sugar from his diet for a few weeks. After all, neither is essential and it may produce a cure.

Symptoms caused by intolerance to the sugars sucrose or isomaltose added to cows' milk formula may develop in babies as soon as they are given formula. These problems are caused by an inherited lack of the digestive enzymes sucrase and isomaltase. The baby suffers from watery diarrhoea, abdominal distension and cramps but can be treated by putting him on a formula free from these sugars, or by restarting the mother's breast milk supply. The breast-fed baby with these enzyme deficiencies is protected from suffering symptoms until he is weaned on to foods containing these sugars. Breast milk doesn't contain them.

Another sort of inherited sugar intolerance which develops on drinking breast milk or cows' milk is caused by the poor absorption of glucose and galactose by the gut. This produces watery diarrhoea and treatment involves severe carbohydrate restriction. Glucose-galactose intolerance may develop in a normal child after gastro-enteritis (as can lactose intolerance, see above). Intravenous feeding is necessary in this case until the gut recovers. It's interesting that if your child is intolerant to cows' milk protein, any gut damage caused by the foreign protein overload may also be followed by this sort of sugar intolerance. *Related topics* Galactosaemia; milk intolerance.

Sunburn A heat burn caused by excessive exposure to the sun. Sometimes the sun also produces urticaria (nettle rash). Babies and young children, especially if they have fair complexions, are susceptible to sunburn even when the sun isn't very strong.

Prevention is the best cure. Be sure to take time to get your child acclimatized to the sun and bear in mind that young children and babies take longer than you will to do so. Only let a child go in the direct sun for a few minutes on each of the first few days of exposure and make sure he wears a hat. Afterwards keep him covered up and in the shade as much as possible. Use an effective sun cream or sun screening lotion and when you're on or near water with your children bear in mind that the sun reflects back from water and can burn them very easily. (This goes for beaches too which are very reflective). Creams and lotions wash off very easily so re-apply them liberally after your child has got wet.

If your child does get burnt, try calamine lotion as the first treatment and keep him out of the sun. If you are at all unhappy about your child's skin or his general condition, see a doctor. *Related topics* Burns; heat stroke; prickly heat; sunshine.

Sunshine When the sun shines in this country, or if we go abroad for a sunny holiday, it's very tempting for us to want our children to get as much of it as possible to make up for our long, dark winters. Though some people prefer to keep out of the sun, most of us feel better when we get some sun on our bodies, and we certainly look better with some colour in our skin. If you have a young baby, though, take care. It's difficult enough for an adult to make sure he doesn't get too much sun, and it's even more difficult to assess when someone else has had enough.

It has been shown that the action of the sun's rays on chemicals in the skin produces much more vitamin D than our diet offers. There have been some babies who have been inadvertently given an overdose of vitamin D in the form of vitamin supplements, but there's no chance of producing too much in the skin, however much sunshine we have, so this source is quite safe.

Ultraviolet rays are reduced in their intensity as they travel through our atmosphere, partly because of clouds of mist, and partly as a result of atmospheric pollution from smoke. If you live in a city whose smoke production isn't controlled, or if you live in an area which has relatively few hours of sunshine, then there is some likelihood that your baby won't get enough sunshine on his skin. The same goes if you live further north, as the further you go, the greater the angle of the sun's rays and the less the amount of ultraviolet light that gets to you, as it has more of the atmosphere to penetrate.

If you always tend to keep your baby's skin covered, as happens especially in some Indian and Pakistani immigrant families, or if the only sunshine your baby gets is through a window, then again it is likely that he won't get enough sunshine to ensure that his skin's vitamin D production is adequate. Vitamin D supplements in doses recommended by your baby clinic or doctor can be useful if for any reason your baby doesn't get enough sun.

However, breast-fed babies whose mothers have enough sunshine and eat well will almost certainly get enough vitamin D from breast milk, which contains more of the vitamin than we used to think. Bottle-fed babies whose main food is still milk get enough vitamin D from the milk formula, which is fortified with the vitamin.

Vitamin D produced by the skin in the summer can be stored by the body for the winter months, and the more sun a person has in the summer, the greater the levels of vitamin D in his body the following winter. It therefore makes sense to put your baby out in his pram in the sun provided it is not too fierce.

Don't forget to make sure your baby has plenty to drink when it's hot. The breast-feeding mother should drink more herself to make sure she has enough milk for her baby's increased demands. Not only the baby but the whole family may suffer from sunburn if you forget that the sun's rays are reflected off water, so you can burn in a boat even if the sun isn't directly on you. Salt from dried sea water makes you burn faster as well.

The sun is a good friend but a bad enemy, so treat it with respect. *Related topics* Dehydration; sunburn; vitamins.

Suppositories Drugs or medications designed to be given via the rectum. Such preparations can be useful for a very ill child who can't tolerate oral medications but the absorption of drugs from the rectum is very uncertain and we recommend that you don't use suppositories of any kind unless instructed to do so by a doctor. Certainly the use of soap stick suppositories for constipation is a bad practice because soap can irritate the large bowel severely. *Related topic* Constipation.

Swaddling Wrapping young babies firmly with lengths of material (swaddling) is an age-old custom for helping them to feel secure, warm and comfortable. It seems to help many babies to sleep more soundly and for longer and stops some from crying so much. This may be because it mimics the conditions a baby felt inside his mother's womb, with her uterine walls holding him firmly within the amniotic fluid.

Today in the West, we often swaddle newborn babies by wrapping them in a soft sheet or blanket before putting them down for a sleep. There's a knack of folding such a sheet or blanket so that it doesn't come undone easily – a midwife or nursery nurse will show you how to fold and tuck the material as you wrap your baby in it. Take care that he doesn't get overheated when wrapped in this way, and don't leave him like it all the time – babies like a chance to kick and to move their arms.

Carrying a baby in a sling has much the same effect as swaddling – his body is held firmly by the material of the sling. A length of material tied round baby and mother is used in some countries to hold the baby firmly against his mother's back.

To get the full effect of swaddling, it's important that the baby's arms are wrapped firmly next to his body and his legs are wrapped together. If he can move his arms and legs out of the swaddling material, it does no good other than to keep him warm. *Related topic* Baby carriers.

Swallowing dangerous substances If a child has swallowed dangerous tablets or other poisons lay him over your legs and place a basin under his head to catch the vomit. Then stick your fingers down his throat until he vomits. If this doesn't work, don't give anything else but get him to a doctor or hospital urgently: the child may be given an emetic to make him vomit. Making a child vomit is only useful in this situation if it is done before the swallowed substances have been absorbed into the bloodstream. As significant absorption has usually taken place within half an hour there's no point in trying to bring the drugs back up if they were taken longer ago than this.

If your child has consumed any of the following, *do not make him sick* as vomiting could damage his gullet and the vomit itself could even get into his lungs: petrol, paraffin, furniture polish, dry-cleaning fluids, lighter fuel, turpentine, acids of any kind, bleach, ammonia, washing soda, caustic soda or paint. Any child who has consumed any of these (or similar caustic chemicals) should be given water or milk to coat the lining of his stomach and to neutralize to some extent the effects of the chemical in the intestine, and then should be taken to hospital. *Related topics* Accidents; first aid.

Swearing If you don't want your children to swear, it's hypocritical to swear in front of them, or at them. If you do it, they'll see no reason why they shouldn't do it either, yet few parents want their children using words which are considered by a substantial number of people to be socially taboo for young children in particular.

Both swearing and cursing have for some people become part of their everyday language and are used to illustrate or punctuate the most mundane or emotionless conversation. It's all too easy to accept swear words as ordinary adjectives or inoffensive exclamations, without bothering to consider their derivations. If people who swear and curse a lot were asked if they really meant what they said, most would say that they didn't; swear words and curses have, for them, simply become figures of speech used initially from anger and then, through continued use, from habit.

Some people use swear words when they are feeling frustrated by, contemptuous of, or angry with someone, as a form of verbal abuse. Children are only too well aware that swearing is often associated with anger. If this is directed at them, the swearing can markedly increase the effect of a telling off, especially if the person doesn't usually swear.

Swearing may help relieve your feelings but it can hurt other people's feelings, especially when it's imitated by children. There's almost always another word you can use instead – especially in front of them. *Related topics* Anger in parents; child abuse.

Sweets Although added sugar is quite unnecessary for children, many of them like sweets. Research has shown that they are most harmful to the teeth if eaten repeatedly throughout the day and that the same amount of sweets eaten in one or two 'doses' during the week does little or no harm to teeth, especially if the teeth are cleaned afterwards.

It's easy to keep sweets away from your first child completely for several years. Eventually one day he'll be given them while with another child or parent and he'll probably like them and want them again. Rather than ban them completely (and so make your child even keener to have them), try having a 'sweet day' once a week or a sweet each day after tea. Sweets are, after all, like cakes, a pleasant occasional addition to the diet. Try never to give sweets when your child hurts himself, as a reward for being good, or as a bribe. That way he may turn to sweet things to comfort himself later, and may run the risk of getting fat.

There's nothing intrinsically evil about sweets and if you prohibit them entirely your children will understandably feel unusual and done down if all their friends have them. Remember that lots of foods have added sugar in them – not only sweets – but as sweets are kept in the mouth for long periods the sugar has longer in which to harm the enamel. An excessive sweet intake can not only rot the teeth but can also produce fat children and fill them up with 'empty calories', making them less likely to want to eat nourishing foods. *Related topic* Sugar.

Swimming You and your young child can get a lot of fun out of going into the swimming pool or sea. By helping him to learn confidence in the water you'll teach him not to react to water by panicking, which may save him from drowning one day. Everyone knows that a young child can drown in a few inches of water. If your child is accustomed to water, he's not so likely to scream if he falls in or to thrash around wildly. Never take any risks with your baby or young child. He should be within sight and easy reach of you or another responsible adult at *all* times when he's in the water. If ever your child doesn't want to go into or stay in the water, never make him. Water is for fun, not to make him miserable, and you can't force him to like it, only to put up with it.

There's no need to wait until your baby is six months old to take him into the water at the swimming pool or sea. Start going as early as two weeks or so if you like. The newborn baby placed tummy down in water naturally moves his arms and legs rhythmically. His body twists from side to side too and these two sets of movements are strong enough to propel him through the water. If he goes under the water, he automatically stops breathing. The baby older than four months is well on the way to losing these reflexes. Some parents, usually with the guidance of an experienced baby's swimming teacher, condition their young babies into using these reflexes so they continue to be automatic. These babies grow up virtually 'waterproof' – they are happy under water and bob up happily after being thrown in. Of course, most mothers wouldn't dream of wanting their babies to learn to swim let alone ever letting them go under the water. They simply like to play with their babies in the water and watch their delight, and they hope that this early pleasure in the water will foster a desire to learn to swim later.

Whether you use the sea or a pool, remember that babies and young children can become chilled easily. The water should be at least 85°F and the air temperature should be pleasantly warm as well unless you are only going to have a very quick dip. Take your child out before he gets really cold, with blue lips and chattering teeth. If he's already got a cold, chilling can make him more likely to go down with any other infection he meets, so be extra careful. Ten to one he won't want to come out even though he's cold, but insist that he does for his own sake. If your child is to enjoy the water, try your best to make the whole experience happy, including the undressing, the time in the water and the dressing up again. As for clothes, it's nicest for a child to have nothing on, but if he has to wear something, choose something easy to put on, comfortable and attractive. Don't worry that a baby will dirty the water. Babies in fact don't often open their bowels in water. As for a baby peeing in the swimming pool, it doesn't matter if he does and anyway there's no way of stopping him. The swimming pool chlorination system can cope quite happily and the water is regularly monitored. Children who are out of nappies can be taken to the loo before going into the pool and encouraged to tell you when they want to go when they're in the pool so you can take them to the loo. At the seaside, find out where the public lavatory is or else take your child somewhere deserted. If he wants to open his bowels, dig a hole, and then cover up the contents!

Try and choose a time of the day for your swim when your child is usually alert, awake and happy. Give your baby a feed beforehand, and if he's usually sick afterwards, wait until you're pretty sure he's finished before going into the water.

You mustn't expect a child to like the water straight away if it's his first visit. Accustom him gently to the feel, smell, noise and taste of the water. Hold him close to you at first, so he feels secure and can hear and see you. If you wear a bikini your child will be able to feel your skin and he'll like that better than material. Talk to him and relax so that you can enjoy it yourself. Children have a good idea of their mother's mood and if you feel tense, your child won't be as happy as he could be. If you're smiling, he will think that this experience must be good and worth enjoying.

Play with your child and hold a baby or toddler close all the time. Bob up and down in the water, keeping his head well clear of the water. Let him look around and don't forget some toys. Swimming pools can be rather uninteresting unless you take some brightly-coloured things into the water. At the seaside, show your child the shells, stones and seaweed besides playing with the sand and water.

Hold your baby or young child on his tummy in the water with his face towards you. Hold him confidently but not tightly. Remember to smile as he looks at you and praise him all the time. When he's used to this position, move backwards with his head on your shoulder and his arms over yours. You can kick his legs up and down so he gets used to moving them as he moves through the water. As you kick his legs, say 'kick, kick, kick'.

Your child won't use formal arm movements for a long time – not even the dog paddle – but he can learn to use his arms to maintain his stability. With your hands under his chin and your fingers under his armpits, move back in the water and watch what he does. Floating is another skill that's worth teaching. Hold him in your arms with his back to your chest, then put him into the water feet first until he's lying on his back with his head nearest you. Lean over his head so he can just see you. This means he'll have to keep his neck straight and so will float easily.

From these beginnings, it won't be long before your baby or young child is thoroughly accustomed to the water and enjoys being in it. You may decide to go to mother-and-baby lessons or to wait until your child is old enough for more formal lessons from a swimming teacher, perhaps when he is four or five. Learning to enjoy the water is an important stage of learning to swim, so don't be anxious about how soon he swims but instead have a good time together. Children who have the opportunity to play in water with others frequently and regularly learn to swim by copying them and wanting to keep up with them. Naturally confident, physically strong children may learn to swim earlier than their shy, weaker counterparts, but everyone can learn eventually if they want to. Exercise of any sort, including splashing around in water, is exhilarating and makes people – including children – happier and less affected by stress. After a swim your child will be tired and hungry, so try to remember a snack for the journey home to keep him going until you can give him a meal.

When taking young children swimming don't forget to use inflatable rings or arm bands for any who can't swim. Also it makes sense to have at least one adult supervising every two children under five. *Related topics* Drowning; exercise; play.

Table manners Because mealtimes are so socially important in our society, children are often pressurized from an early age to behave properly when they are eating. However, the concept of table manners only really means anything when a child is old enough to understand that other people are eating, talking and listening at the table, and not just him! For a baby, mealtimes are times either to stuff his food into his tummy, to play with it, to throw it on to the floor, to smear it over himself, or to reject it. He is certainly not concerned with the unselfish pursuit of making the meal pleasant for other people.

Betweeen one and two, your toddler will slowly learn to feed himself and as he gets better at aiming his spoon into his mouth, there will be less and less mess to clear up. Some mothers carry on spoon-feeding their one-year-olds in an attempt to cut down on the work involved in clearing up after the meal. However, it's common experience that the sooner you allow a child to practise new skills himself, the sooner he becomes expert at them, so it's more sensible from the mother's point of view and much more enjoyable from the child's if he feeds himself as soon as he seems to want to. Some babies insist on feeding themselves with a spoon from seven months or so. At first, don't let your baby have his bowl of food near him, but when he is old enough to eat from it in preference to playing with it a plastic bowl rather than a breakable one is sensible, and you may find a suction pad on the undersurface of the bowl a help.

As for cutlery, let your child use a spoon or his fingers at first, then as he grows older, encourage him to use his fingers less and his spoon more. Some time during his second or third year he'll want to copy you and have a knife and fork and from that time on it's practice that'll perfect the way he eats, as well as your example.

It helps create a feeling of a social occasion if the family all eat at the same time. This is often possible at least at breakfast every day if everyone is up early enough. At lunchtime, even if you don't have a meal as such, sit down with your child while he eats. At teatime you may not want anything to eat if you're going to eat later on, but it's still important to sit down at the table and devote your attention to the occasion and your child and not to a book or the television.

If you have an easily cleanable floor under the table, you won't be upset by the amount of food that finds its way on to it. If not, why not cover the carpet with a small piece of cheap carpet that you can scrub, or a sheet of lino or vinyl. Far better that than to worry all through the meal about what's being dropped. Large bibs are a must at this age and many mothers find the plastic pelican type with a tray a real godsend. Once you're relaxed about any possible mess, you can enjoy the meal and your child will enjoy it more too if you're not flustered.

Children learn table manners by copying others. If the rest of the family is considerate and polite, the youngest will one day be the same. Gentle firmness is the order of the day when your one-year-old climbs on the table and kneels in his soup – it's not a tragedy but it isn't to be encouraged either. With time, your child will learn that it's best to take it in turn to talk at the table; not to stretch across and knock things over but to ask someone to pass what he can't reach; not to grab what he wants first but to pass things round (one of the most difficult things to learn); only to put on his plate what he will be able to eat; not to stuff his mouth too full; not to speak with his mouth full; not to rock on his chair; to sit down properly; and not to touch other people and annoy them unnecessarily. It's not surprising that with so much to learn it takes time for a child to become civilized at the table. Interestingly enough, toddlers often imitate other children more than adults, so if you haven't any older children yourself, why not borrow some from time to time for tea?

Some parents who like taking a long time over a meal let their children go off to play between courses, so they don't have to fidget or behave badly in their boredom. If you have something that has to be said to your husband or vice versa, then the children can be asked to be quiet, but otherwise it's good manners on your part to include them in the conversation at the table.

If your child doesn't want to eat, never make him but just think whether you have filled him up with food between meals; whether the food you're offering is appetizing or whether it's unattractive or badly cooked; and whether his rejection of food is his way of making you pay him some attention. There's usually an answer. *Related topics* Copying; feeding equipment; mealtimes; spoon-feeding.

Talcum powder A white, pale green, or grey, soft, greasy mineral (magnesium silicate) used to dry babies' skin and to make it smell pleasant. Talc isn't necessary, of course, but the act of rubbing it into his skin all over is pleasant for both parent and baby. Talc has become an accepted part of some babies' bath time and nappy changing rituals, but many parents never use it at all: they prefer to dry their babies thoroughly with a towel; they enjoy the natural smell of their skin; and they don't need an excuse to touch or stroke their babies. Some medical experts discourage its use at all because of its dangers.

If talc is shaken into skin creases that are wet, it can clog up and irritate the skin where the folds rub together. It shouldn't be used on inflamed skin such as with nappy rash.

The only serious danger with talc is that if it is spilt or if it is shaken in clouds in the air, a child might inhale a lot of it. This could irritate the lungs and might cause breathing difficulties if enough is inhaled.

Talking Talking is only an outward sign of a child's language ability, but it is the sign used by parents and others as an easily recognizable developmental milestone. When a parent is asked 'Can your child talk yet?', what is really meant is not only whether or not the child can say any words, but whether he understands what he is saying. When this is asked of the parent of a child about a year old, it's often a difficult question to answer, because he may well be saying some words but not all of them will be decipherable by strangers – he may have his own word for something which only those close to him know, or he may be trying unsuccessfully to copy what he actually hears. Also, the 'words' may still be a meaningless joining together of syllables – the official term is babbling – and said for pure enjoyment of making conversational-sounding noises which seem to please grown-ups. Lastly, he may be able to say words which are quite clear but uses them in the wrong context, such as 'da-da'. 'Da-da' may first be said as an experiment while babbling, then because his parents applaud him and encourage him to say it time and again, it becomes part of his repertoire of sounds. Over the next few weeks or months, when he says 'da-da' and his father happens to be there, everyone excitedly says 'yes, da-da', pointing to his father. Gradually, depending on his age and level of language development (which doesn't only depend on age, but on inbuilt factors, experience and encouragement as well), he'll associate his babbled sounds with his father and he'll have his first label word. Only then can he be said to be using the word with meaning. It's not an easy point to recognize and may not even be a 'point' at all but simply a gradual realization. In any case, exactly when your baby says his first meaningful word doesn't matter – the fact that he's learning to talk is what counts.

By the time he says his first meaningful word – which could be at any age from ten or eleven months to after two, he'll already be beginning to understand lots more words – usually label words for everyday objects that you have mentioned to him time and time again. This understanding is far more important than whether he can reproduce the words in speech.

If your child starts talking at around a year old, during the next six months he'll probably say only a few new words, though many more are being learnt through constant exposure to them. Words for favourite foods or things connected with meals such as 'spoon' or 'cup' follow closely on people's names, but this order simply reflects the importance given by the mother and father or other caretakers to these labels when accentuating them or repeating them frequently in their speech. By one and a half, your child may have a vocabulary of a dozen words or so, but during the second half of this year he'll speed ahead and may add on a couple of hundred more (and of course he'll understand many more). The words he learns are those connected with his everyday life and those you take the trouble to say to him, teaching him in the course of your ordinary conversation with him by pointing to or otherwise making him aware of what you are naming as you name it.

All these single words can be used in lots of ways, not just as labels. A bright toddler can put all sorts of meaning into a single word, and from the way the word is said you'll know whether he is, for example, pleased, excited, disapproving, sad, apprehensive, or frightened. Because, when he says something, you're likely to respond automatically with a slightly more complicated version of what he's just said, he'll gradually learn to put words together. For instance, if he says 'car', and you answer every time with some variation on 'yes, John's car', one day he'll do the same, only simpler, for example, 'John car'. This will extend to 'John spoon' and 'John shoe' in time.

These two word phrases are followed by more complicated sentences, still missing out all the 'thes' and 'ands' and 'ans' and so on, but using all the necessary words to make what he says a recognizable and useful form of communication. You never need to correct his talking overtly. Just by repeating what he has said but with any necessary additions, he'll gradually learn the grammar of our language without ever needing to be reproved or corrected formally. Some bright children who nevertheless start talking late suddenly talk in three-word sentences, showing that they've been learning during all their quiet months.

From using simple sentences, your two-year-old will gradually progress during the pre-school years until he is speaking much like an adult. He'll learn hundreds of new words. He'll learn with your help how to describe things; how to talk about their shape, size, colour, quantity, weight and height; how to comment on what he thinks and feels; how to ask questions; and how to cure pronouns, though he won't give up the easy way of using people's names (including his own) instead of pronouns completely for a while. Sometimes what he says when he's playing will reflect the way you talk to him and what you say. You'll hear your instructions, soothings and warnings reproduced, sometimes to your chagrin.

Throughout his first five years a child needs feedback in the form of two-way conversation in order to talk more and more fluently. Time spent talking with him is never wasted – it'll help him express himself and make it easier for him when he starts school. A love of words can be encouraged in many different ways – by reading aloud, by making up your own stories with your child, by singing, by chanting jingles you hear on the television, and by saying nursery rhymes. Tongue twisters, riddles and jokes all help your child's grasp of English too. Remember that baby talk and your family's own special words won't be looked upon with such amusement by outsiders, so start teaching your child alternatives to use with other people. Even when he's as young as three, it'll help him at play-group or at another mother's house, for example, if he knows the right words to use when he wants to use the lavatory. When he starts at school he'll feel very silly if he's the only one in the class who uses baby words. It doesn't matter, of course, if you carry on using these words at home – some grown-ups go on using their old family words with their own children years later.

Children like to practise talking a lot. Sometimes their talk seems to be incessant and it takes a lot of willpower not to tell them to be quiet. However, sooner or later each child has to learn that sometimes it is right not to talk at all, let alone quietly. Try your hardest (though it's sometimes difficult) always to explain why it is that your child should keep quiet. If it's because you're in church, for instance (where the temptation for a child to talk loudly is great amidst the silence during a sermon), then tell him firmly that no one else can hear if he talks so much. Similar situations can crop up in a library, when you are trying to listen to the news, when you're talking to someone in hospital, and so on. There are bound to be some situations in which it would have been better not to take a young child who really hasn't got enough control to keep quiet. If you find yourself continually saying 'shhh', then think twice before taking him there again for a while.

Take care not to exclude your child from adult conversation all the time. Children aren't lesser mortals than adults, they're just smaller, younger and have less experience and authority. If you are busy chatting to a friend and your child is at a loose end, include him in your talk every so often. Unpleasant though it may be, you may sometimes decide that you'll talk over the phone to your friend later and give more time and attention to your child now. That's not giving in to him, it's just pragmatic and sensitive. Bored children all too soon start whining. Just think how you would feel if you were with two highly articulate and seemingly intelligent people who talked to each other animatedly and non-stop, leaving you out in the cold completely and with nothing to amuse you.

Being able to talk brings with it the ability to say rude things and unkind things. Your child may not always mean what he says but may not know how to express himself clearly. Take the time to discuss his feelings with him if necessary and to help him understand what he is saying. Let him know that words can hurt just as much as physical blows and help him learn that unkind and rude thoughts are best left unsaid.

Being able to talk also brings with it the ability to say loving things. Your child will tell you all the loving things you've told him in the past, and very pleasant it is too. Help him to learn to praise and encourage others in what he says rather than to run down and criticize. Help him to learn to speak well of people or else to be quiet. All this will come best from your example. *Related topics* Baby talk; language; talking problems.

Talking problems The commonest problem with talking that parents take their children to the doctor with is not talking. A speech delay is usually just a simple delay in a child whose language development is within the normal range. If he's saying any words at all when you take him for advice, then it's highly likely that all will be well and that he's simply a late starter. However, it's worth asking for advice if your child is late or slow in starting because sometimes there is a remediable reason for it. If he is two and can't say anything – no single words and no jargon language (his own talk that sounds like a foreign language) – then go to your clinic doctor or family doctor. The doctor will refer him for specialist help, if necessary. Some of the more serious causes for speech delay are mental retardation (which may or may not have been obvious to you, depending on its degree and on your experience with children); deafness (a relatively common cause; even a minor degree of deafness can make it difficult for a child to hear the spoken voice in all its frequencies, and if he can't hear it, he can't reproduce it); 'word deafness' – an inability to understand what people say – which is associated with dyslexia; autism; and emotional problems –

perhaps due to emotional neglect. Your child may need a thorough assessment at a specialist clinic to get to the bottom of his speech delay.

Less serious and more easily remediable causes of speech delay are simply caused by a lack of opportunity to listen to an adult and to have enough one-to-one attention from him. Many children come into this category: those looked after by someone who talks very little, whether a parent or another caretaker; those with a brother or sister very close to them in age, including twins and triplets; those who are the youngest or among the youngest of a large family; and those looked after by someone who has several other children to look after, for example a child-minder or a nursery nurse in charge of several children in a day nursery. Children who are mainly looked after by an au pair have their own problems: the au pair may have a poor command of English and may use a lot of gestures or even her own language when she's alone with the child; she's likely to go after six months or so, and the child may then be cared for by another au pair whose language ability may be at a different level and who may use her own language which is different from that of the earlier one. Children of bilingual (or multilingual) parents are also sometimes slow to speak, but they catch up eventually.

Helping your child with one of these less serious causes of speech delay usually involves giving him much more one-to-one attention. Talk to him a lot but don't bombard him or talk *at* him: simply talk as you do things with him, whether it's playing, walking, cooking, or having a bath. Talk to him in the car, not trying to force him to say something, but just commenting on what you see. Repeat useful words a lot in the course of your conversation but don't reduce your language to a baby level. The odds are that once he has a chance to learn, he'll catch up quickly.

Lisping is fairly common in babies and young children learning to talk. It may continue out of habit because an older child is copying another. Most children grow out of it by the time they go to school. Some children lisp for the first time when they lose their front teeth, but this is only temporary. Occasionally, lisping is due to faulty tongue action, deafness or a cleft palate, and can be helped by a speech therapist experienced in such problems. Treatment is best started as soon as possible because if it persists until the child starts school, he may be teased for his baby talk.

The mispronunciation of consonants. muddling some up and omitting others completely, usually improves spontaneously as a child has more and more experience of listening to other people talking. It's important that deafness is excluded. Sometimes such a child has had too little opportunity to listen and in his haste to talk has become accustomed to mispronouncing words. He may have had little feedback from his parents – most parents often repeat what their child has said but saying it correctly and with proper grammar, not in an obvious attempt to correct the child, but just spontaneously. If a child can only be understood with difficulty and he has already reached four, then speech therapy may be suggested to help him to speak more clearly by the time he starts school. *Related topics* Deafness;

language; lisping; listening; speech therapist; talking. *Useful organization* Association for All Speech Impaired Children.

Tapes Audio-tapes are yet another way that children can entertain themselves and be entertained. They have the advantage of being small and relatively robust compared with records and a five year old can be relied upon to use a simple cassette player under supervision.

Cassettes really come into their own in the car when pre-recorded (either by yourself or professionally) stories will keep children entertained for long periods. There are also nursery rhyme tapes and you could record their favourite songs too.

Just as photographs record your child's looks for posterity, cassettes can record his first words, his wonderful phrases and so on that would otherwise be lost for ever. Today, of course, with video tapes and video cameras becoming commonplace in the home that facility is increasing further.

Teat A rubber nipple-shaped object that fits on the end of a baby's bottle for him to suck. They come in various shapes and sizes, some more anatomically accurate than others. Comforters have teats on them too.

The most important thing about a bottle teat is its hole size. This should let milk flow at a rapid rate of drops rather than in a stream. Too small a hole means that the baby will fight for the milk because it doesn't come through fast enough, and in so doing may swallow too much air. Too large a hole means he'll swallow air as he tries to cope with the fast-flowing milk by gulping it down. If the hole is too small the effort required to get the milk will be so great that your baby may fall asleep exhausted but still hungry. Too big a hole can make a baby vomit from taking too much milk and air too fast and doesn't give him enough sucking time to enjoy. Sucking on an empty bottle will make him swallow air which will either be burped up or will go down the intestine and perhaps cause colic as well as flatulence. A teat hole may start off the right size but becomes too big with use. Check the flow of milk from time to time and replace the teat when it flows too fast.

A hole that is too small can be enlarged with a red hot needle. Take this gently or you'll easily make it too big.

Most teats suit most babies but you can experiment to find which suits your baby best. Once you find one he gets on with stick to it so as not to confuse him. What suits your baby early on may not suit him so well as he grows. Some babies are best with a small hole when they are little because they can't coordinate their sucking and swallowing well enough to cope with a fast flow of milk. They prefer a faster flow when they are older and more capable so that they can get the milk faster. Don't forget to have a spare teat or two in the house in case one perishes or gets lost or damaged.

You can now get a special Variflow teat with an oval-shaped hole. By rotating the bottle through 90° you can get a fast or slow flow rate according to the baby's preference at the time. There are other special teats to help babies who are normally breast-fed to learn to take a bottle (of expressed breast milk or formula).

When feeding your baby be sure that the teat is full of milk at all times. If you have the wrong tilt on the bottle the teat could be half-full of air which he'll gulp down, giving him wind and making him unhappy.

Teats should be sterilized along with the bottles. *Related topics* Feeding equipment; sterilizing bottles.

Teeth Teeth are made of two main substances – an outer coat of hard, dead enamel and an inner core of softer, living dentine. It is when decay reaches the inner living part that toothache starts.

Babies are sometimes born with a tooth but the average child starts teething between the ages of five and seven months – about the time he becomes interested in foods other than milk. The age variation, as with most developmental milestones in children, is enormous and lots of children, 'normal' in every other way, have no teeth until a year. This has no significance whatsoever. Girls tend to produce teeth earlier than boys and boys tend to lose their milk teeth earlier than girls.

Two sets of teeth are produced in children. The twenty milk teeth are all formed under the gums at birth and by the age of two years they have all come through (erupted). The first permanent teeth to appear are usually the big back teeth (molars) at about six years old.

Unfortunately, milk teeth (especially as they come through) are exceptionally prone to dental decay and it is often at this time that parents are first adding sugar to their child's food or even giving sweetened drinks in a comforter or a bottle. First teeth need looking after because they help the healthy development of jaw and gums and help guide the second teeth through in the right places. This makes it vital to care for your child's milk teeth in just the same way as you would his permanent teeth.

It's a sobering fact that more than a third of the population of the UK over the age of sixteen have *no* teeth of their own and very often the trouble started in early childhood. Good oral hygiene and tooth care starts as soon as your child's first tooth comes through. *Related topics* Dental caries; dentist; dentures; fluoride; sugar; sweets; teething; toothbrush; toothpaste.

Teething The process in which teeth come through the gums. It starts in early infancy (some babies are even born with a tooth) and goes on until a child has all his milk teeth. People rarely think of teething as applying to older children – it is a term usually used only for babies and the appearance of their first teeth.

From the age of about five to six months babies teeth on and off for up to two years or so and it's tempting to put every little ailment and health problem down to this. This is not only misleading but can actually be dangerous because a more serious condition may be overlooked and treatment unnecessarily delayed. There is no medical evidence that teething is responsible for fever, diarrhoea, convulsions, or generalized rashes.

One Finnish paediatrician carefully studied 126 babies throughout their early teething period and found that the eruption of a tooth was not associated at all with infections, diarrhoea, bronchitis, fever, rashes, convulsions, sleeplessness at night, or ear rubbing. Many parents resolutely believe, however, that teething makes their babies more prone to loose, frequent motions and sleeplessness. Many babies do seem to dribble a lot, have red patches on their faces, become restless or irritable, lose their appetite and even lose some sleep when their first four teeth come through but anything other than these relatively minor symptoms should be reported to your doctor.

The teething rash so commonly seen on the face is caused by dribbling (often at night) and can be prevented by using a barrier cream and washing the skin frequently.

A teething child may go off his food temporarily, especially if it's lumpy or hard. Don't make him eat because you think he's crying from hunger. A baby with teeth can carry on breast-feeding as long as you teach him not to bite. There's absolutely no need to wean him when his teeth come through.

Sometimes a blister forms on the gum over a tooth lying just beneath the surface. The gum may look red and swollen and it isn't surprising that the child is annoyed by the inflammation.

The main problem parents have is what to do about any apparent discomfort their baby has. Many babies like to chew on something hard when they are teething and some like to chew on their finger or on you! Try rubbing your baby's gums firmly with your fingertip if they seem to be worrying him. Soothing gels are available and are quite effective; and – as a last resort – a suitable dose of paracetamol can be useful, especially if the irritation is stopping the baby (and you) from getting to sleep. Such painkillers should not become a routine and certainly shouldn't be given for weeks or months.

If you can remember what it felt like when your wisdom teeth came through (if they've erupted, that is), you'll know that teething can make your gums feel itchy so that you want to bite on them all the time. It must be just the same for a baby, who may have several teeth erupting at much the same time, so making it worse.

Television It has been calculated that the average UK family has the TV on for about four hours a day but it's highly unlikely that the under-fives are watching it for much of this time. Television for the under-fives has three main functions. First, it gets them sitting down quietly after lots of running around and outdoor games and this can be good, especially just before bedtime if they are over-excited. Second, it can be entertaining and informative – provided that they watch the sort of programme they can understand and cope with. Third, it can give a busy or tired mother a few minutes to herself to do a household chore or simply to put her feet up to rest or to phone a friend. Unfortunately, far too many people use TV as a 'baby-sitter' to keep young children occupied for hours. This is undoubtedly bad because they can't understand much of what they see and because they have no opportunity for conversation or other interaction – it is a one-way communication medium. Such children become bored and lonely and eventually come to accept TV as a kind of moving wallpaper against which the rest of life is carried on. Few thinking people want to run their homes in this way.

The 'evils' of TV have been much debated but for the under-fives there really shouldn't be a problem because you can choose what they watch and when. By and large we are fortunate in the UK in having excellent children's programmes at suitable times of the day for them. Whether or not you let your child see adult programmes is up to you but even a cowboy film can have an effect on a child. The news too is pretty gory these days. Remember that your child may be alarmed by things you take for granted and take the trouble to explain scenes which might frighten, worry or confuse him. Both BBC and ITV operate the nine o'clock watershed policy whereby all programmes before that time come into the family viewing category.

As with most things in life watching television is a matter of balance and common sense. TV isn't an evil and used properly it can be a real bonus both to parents and children.

With the coming of video playback equipment at a reasonable price (either to rent or buy) the average family can now choose what it wants to see and when. This can be excellent for young children because you can record their favourite TV shows or cartoons and can buy programmes or films they really like. This will amuse them on dark, cold winter days when they can't play outside, you're busy, they're bored and there's nothing suitable on TV.

Though there are guidelines laid down by the Independent Broadcasting Authority, which controls TV advertising, some children are fascinated by adverts for toys and sweets and try to pressurize their parents into buying them.

Some researchers worry that excessive exposure to the radiation from a TV set might affect the growth and development of children but there is no conclusive evidence yet. Young children who tend to sit very close to the set could be told to move further away and lengthy viewing cut down if you are concerned about any possible effect.

If you have a television, check that you're not setting a bad example by glueing yourself to it all day. Discuss, explain and expand on programmes with your children, however young. If your children are shown how to make or do something, collect any necessary materials and help them do it. Most important of all, switch off unless there's a good reason for having it on.

Telling the time Your child almost certainly won't be able to tell the time really well until he's over five, but he can make a start on learning before this. Lots of things are involved in reading a clock face. First of all, he'll have to know his numbers. You can start getting him used to them very early on by mentioning them in your everyday talk and play with him. There are all sorts of games you can play using numbers. First of all he'll learn to understand what the numbers mean as you say them and then he'll learn to recognize them when they're pointed out. You can accustom him to a clock face by drawing it, by buying a large plastic or wooden one with large numbers, or by playing carefully with a real clock or watch (though a watch is rather small.) Let him see the hands moving round and teach him which is the long hand and which the short. Remember that constant repetition is essential and that your child certainly won't learn any of these stages in one sitting – they take weeks or months and the child has to be at the right developmental stage in order to learn them all.

Help your child understand something of what time is about by bringing in lengths of time and ideas about minutes, hours, days, weeks and so on into your conversation during the pre-school years. He'll be more interested in learning to read the clock if he knows that there's some point to it. If he wants to know when you'll be ready to do something, say something like 'When the long hand reaches the five. . . . that's in ten minutes.' Give him some idea of how long times are, such as 'Play-group lasts for two hours', or 'Your bath will be ready in five minutes.'

One pre-school TV programme has a time-telling section and if your child watches it'll help if you use the same sort of teaching outline. When he's ready, start by telling him that when the long hand points upwards, it's 'something o'clock'. Later, you can go on to other times, half hours first, and then you'll have the job of explaining the way the sixty minutes are split up.

Temperament A difficult word to define but generally accepted as being a child's character, disposition and tendencies as revealed in his actions. Temperament isn't the same as personality which includes more mental characteristics than temperament. Personality is that distinctive collection of mental and behavioural features that make a person uniquely individual, but temperament is a word applied more to the outward display of the personality. Children with basically similar personalities can have very different temperaments.

There's no doubt that all babies are different and that the difference depends both on their inherited disposition and on the way they are treated. Parents with several children say how incredibly different they all are. Some are naturally 'easy' and others more 'difficult' with feeding and everything else right from the earliest days. Why this should be isn't known but to some extent it seems to be linked to the parents' age, expectations, level of knowledge and capability at the time when each child is young. It is widely accepted that firstborns are more aggressive, more achieving and more success-orientated than later-borns and many people say that later-borns are softer, easier to get on with, more adaptable and so on than firstborns. Many of these differences probably reflect the difference in parental handling of the child. Firstborns often have a poor start because their parents have unrealistic expectations of family life in general and babies in particular and as a result are more 'uptight' generally. This feeds back to the child who reacts accordingly.

Babies, and even more so young children, react and show their temperament very much along the lines of what we, their parents, expect. A child whose parents behave temperamentally, with dramatic mood swings from hour to hour (let alone from day to day) may mimic this behaviour and will soon be a tiny model of what he sees as normal. So to some extent the temperament of our children will mirror ours, whatever we do. The problem here is to be able to see your own temperament for what it is and to try to protect your children from the worst aspects of it. A delicate and 'nervy' baby who may perhaps have been born prematurely may be overprotected for too long because his parents forget that he won't necessarily always be weak. Normal robust behaviour with rough and tumble games among friends when he's older will help decondition him from your over-protective tendencies.

It's foolish to label children (or indeed adults) when it comes to temperament. We are all complex individuals who change from year to year. To label a young child as 'miserable', 'nervy', 'highly-strung', 'shy' or whatever, gets through to him and he may begin to act up to your labelling of him. Such generalizations aren't helpful and certainly shouldn't be discussed with friends and relatives in front of the child. He is how he is at that time. Things could dramatically change when he goes to play-group or real school. Home life is rather lonely and inward-looking for some children who may become more and more quiet and shy. Playing with other children may work wonders because your child will have to learn not only to give and take but also that other children will take far less notice of his mood changes than do his parents. *Related topics* Personality; personality differences.

Temperature Under normal conditions of health the human body stays at a remarkably constant temperature no matter how hot or cold the surrounding temperature is. But like every other body measurement it is subject to variations between individuals. Some people's normal body temperature is 97°F (36°C) and others 99.5°F (37.5°C) The average is 98.6°F (37°C).

Body temperature is usually measured in the mouth. If measured under the arm it is 1°F lower and in the rectum ½°F higher. Although a normal child's temperature is raised by a hot bath, a big meal, or heavy exercise the average temperature in a child's mouth is 98.6°F, (about 37°C).

Babies and young children seem to have an easily-influenced temperature-regulating mechanism – they have fevers very easily – some of which can be very high. Some doctors feel that households shouldn't have a clinical thermometer because a child's temperature is such a poor indication of his true state of health; a baby or young child can be quite ill yet have a near-normal temperature, which may lull his parents into a false sense of security so that they don't call the doctor even though the child needs attention and would have had it had his health been judged in other ways. Many parents can tell if their child is feverish by touching him but this gives no idea at all of how feverish he actually is.

It can be argued that a thermometer *is* valuable because when your child has a fever you can see if it is very high and reduce it, so preventing the possible occurrence of fits caused by the high body temperature. It also means that you can tell the doctor accurately what your child's temperature is when you phone him.

Babies and very young children can't have their temperature taken in their mouths because they might bite the thermometer and swallow the glass and mercury, so other methods are used.

Before you take your child's temperature shake the mercury well down using jerky, sharp flicks of the wrist until the level is right down. Then you can put it under the child's arm or in his groin. Keep him still to avoid breaking it. Be sure to leave it in place for the recommended time and then add 1°F on to the reading.

To take a rectal temperature, tell an older child what you're going to do, then lubricate the end of the thermometer with petroleum jelly, place the baby or very young child over your knees face down and gently insert the thermometer into his back passage a short way. Don't hold on to it firmly but keep it between your fingers with the palm of your hand flat on his bottom (rather like a cigarette). If he moves he won't then snap off the thermometer.

Older children can keep the bulb of the thermometer under their tongue for the correct amount of time. It's best to leave it in for a full three minutes. If he can breathe through his nose, make sure that he doesn't breathe through his mouth instead and that he hasn't eaten anything for half an hour beforehand as this would give a false reading. You can't get a reliable reading from the mouth in a child who can't keep his mouth shut for the duration of the temperature reading because he is too young or can't breathe through his nose because it is stuffed up.

There are now all kinds of electronic thermometers available for domestic use and paper strips that change colour are becoming popular. None is as cheap and effective as an ordinary clinical thermometer. A stubby bulb, all purpose thermometer that can be used rectally or orally is best.

Lastly, don't treat your child's temperature: treat the child. If he gives you cause for concern even if he only has a low-grade fever, still tell your doctor and let him make the medical decisions no matter what the thermometer says.

Babies can become too cold and serious illness can result if they aren't treated quickly. A temperature below 97.4°F (36.5°C) should be reported to your doctor who will repeat the measurement using a special low-reading thermometer. If ever you want to keep evidence of your baby's temperature for your doctor to see, simply place the thermometer somewhere carefully. The level stays where it is until it is shaken down again no matter how you place the thermometer. **Related topics** Convulsions; fever.

Temperature of baby's room The room temperature advised for a baby varies according to the country in which the question is asked. Babies are brought up in countries with widely differing temperatures quite successfully and there's no need to be unduly cautious about the room temperature.

However, there are some guidelines. Low birth weight babies don't have efficient temperature-regulating mechanisms and are safest if kept in air of a constant, warm temperature. A radiant heater or an incubator can provide this readily in hospital. A healthy but small baby may be kept perfectly warm in a comfortably heated room if he is kept close to his mother so that the warmth of her body keeps him warm too. The incubator is then only used to keep him warm when she isn't holding him.

Babies under about eight pounds (3,600g) in weight aren't as efficient at keeping themselves warm as are larger babies and the temperature of the room they are in is best kept at somewhere around 68–70°F (20–21°C) day and night. You might like to buy a room thermometer if you're not sure how warm this is. It's not sensible to judge whether the room is warm enough for your baby by how warm you feel, because your temperature-regulating mechanism is mature and more efficient than his and you are bound to be keeping warm to some extent as you move around doing things. Never dress your baby in fewer layers of clothing than you have on, but take care too not to overheat him because that can be as dangerous, if taken to extremes, as letting him get too cold. Use your common sense in assessing how warm he is. While many very young babies have blueish feet and hands even though they are warm enough, these same blue hands and feet can be an indication that an older baby in particular is too cold. Feel the baby's body (his chest, for example) in order to decide and don't be complacent – if your hands and feet were blue, you'd feel pretty miserable.

Once a baby passes the eight-pound (3,600g) mark, he is better insulated by his extra fat and can also control his body temperature better. Try not to let the room temperature go below 60°F (16°C) at night, unless he is sleeping next to you and you are quite sure he is warm enough. If a baby has a respiratory infection, breathing in air which is very cold can make his breathing more difficult. Most people feel comfortable in light clothing when the room temperature is around 68–70°F (20–21°C) if they are sitting around doing nothing or lying down in bed. Your baby comes into this category too. If you prefer the temperature lower make sure your baby is warmly dressed with several layers of clothes on, and check regularly to make sure he's warm enough. He'll be quite comfy in a room temperature of 60°F (16°C) if he's got enough clothes and covers on.

Some mothers warm their baby's cot with a hot water bottle so that the bedding is pleasantly warm when they put him into it. Don't leave a hot water bottle in with a baby because not only could it burn him but it could also make him dangerously hot.

Some form of room heating can dry the air excessively and this in turn can dry the mucous membranes lining the nose and other breathing passages. This feels uncomfortable and may hamper breathing if the child has a respiratory infection. Either keep a window open even when you have heating on if you feel the air in your house is very dry or, to avoid heat loss through a window, invest in a humidifier or just put a large container of water in front of the heat source. Paraffin fires put out a certain amount of water into the air as they burn.

When you take your baby out in cold weather, wrap him up warmly and check every so often to make sure he's warm. If you put him in a sling and wrap your coat round the sling, or wear a cape round you and him, he'll breathe in warmed air in his own microclimate inside your coat. This will keep him reliably warm and comfortable. *Related topics* Heating; temperature.

Temper tantrums The majority of young children between the ages of one and three have the occasional temper tantrum. A temper tantrum happens when a child becomes uncontrollably angry or has a fit of rage, usually because of frustration at not being able to do something, not being allowed to do something, or being made to do something he doesn't want to do. He may not be able to do the thing because he's too small (such as reaching a toy on a high shelf), or too weak (such as pushing a cupboard away from the wall to get something that's fallen behind it). His parents are generally the ones who prevent him from doing what he wants to all the time, though older brothers and sisters can lay down the law as well and aren't nearly so tactful about the way in which they do it. Not being able to get his own way is far more frustrating for a child of this age than for an older child or adult, because he won't yet have learnt to accept that he can't always have what he wants.

One- and two-year-olds are enchanted by their new-found ability to control things. It takes them time to learn that they have to fit in with other people and sometimes must be controlled. If ever discipline should take the form of loving guidance, it is now, because there is a natural tendency to balk at any instructions or even to do entirely the opposite. If you know that your child is unlikely to let you brush her hair without a tantrum, for example, instead of telling her that it's time to have her hair brushed and would she please come right now, fetch her doll and the brush and start brushing the doll's hair. She's likely to be delighted with this game and will want to join in. If you do the doll's hair first, then say how nice it would be if they looked the same, you're far more likely to have a smiling acceptance than if you'd made her stand still. Many mothers have neither the time nor the inclination for this sort of persuasion, but there's usually a quick equivalent if you're clever enough to think of one. Try not to tell a child of this age what to do but just get on and do it with him, so that he's bowled along by you but hasn't a verbal request or instruction to counteract.

By thinking ahead you can often avoid situations in which a tantrum is likely. You know your child and you know what sort of things provoke him. If he is quick to anger when he's tired (as are most children), treat him with kid gloves at this time. If he flares up when you have visitors, ask yourself why this is and whether you tend to ignore him when they are there. When he's unwell, take extra care that you help him do anything he finds difficult and spend more time playing with him. Some children tend to be easily frustrated when they're hungry and remain on an even keel if they never go more than a couple of hours without food. If your child has his temper tantrum at a time of the day when *you* are tired, ask yourself if you could prevent the same situation arising again perhaps by having a rest earlier on.

Children not only look alarming when they're having a temper tantrum but also frighten themselves with the force of their feelings. Their rage is rarely taken out on other people but they can hurt themselves by hammering their heels or fists or sometimes even their heads on the floor. Some children race round in a blind fury and others break whatever they're holding by bashing it against the floor. The worst thing you can do is to get angry yourself, because the whole episode can blow up out of all proportion. Your child hasn't got your control and that is why he's having a tantrum. When he has more self-control, he'll be able to get angry in moderation. He needs to know that it is possible to control anger and if you get mad at him, you'll be setting him a bad example. Different parents cope with tantrums in different ways and there is no right or wrong way except that the child shouldn't be punished. He's done nothing wrong as such but is simply the subject of his wildly swinging and out of control emotions, which are quite normal at this age. Some parents quietly go about their business and ignore the tantrum. Others leave the room. Yet others try to soothe the child. Whatever you do, reassure him afterwards that all is well because he'll probably be frightened and upset. If you change your mind and let him do whatever it was that was responsible for the tantrum, or don't do something he kicked up the fuss about, you'll be teaching him that a tantrum is a sensible way to behave because it gets him what he wants. Even if you don't feel very strongly about it, stick to what you said initially. Next time such a situation arises, if you don't feel particularly strongly about something, don't insist on it, especially if you know your child is likely to flare up. Tantrums can take a lot out of you as well as your child.

As a child gets older, temper tantrums become fewer and further between. Encourage him to tell you when he's angry about something because although it's a good thing that the tantrum stage is passing, it's not a good idea for a child to learn to bottle up his rage. *Related topics* Aggression; frustration.

Tetanus A bacterial infection that produces spasm in the muscles, especially in those of the jaw and neck.

It is very uncommon indeed in the under-fives because most children are routinely immunized against the disease. Should an infection occur it does not necessarily have to have been preceded by a serious cut or wound. As the symptoms don't start until several months after the infection was introduced into the body it's often difficult to remember what could have caused it. A sore throat is the first symptom; pain in the neck and muscles follows; then spasm of the jaw and mouth muscles sets in. Slowly the rest of the body's muscles are involved and the child can die if not treated at once.

If your child hasn't been immunized for any reason and sustains a deep wound or skin puncture take him to your doctor or to a hospital at once so that he can receive an immediate-acting anti-tetanus injection.

There are two old wives' tales that need to be dispelled. The first is that you can only get tetanus by cutting yourself between the thumb and the forefinger and the second is that tetanus comes from getting rust in a wound. Neither is true.

Thalassaemia (Mediterranean anaemia) An inherited type of anaemia of varying degree seen in people who come from around the Mediterranean, in which red cells are broken down more quickly than the body can replace them. It can be treated by blood transfusions and sometimes by removal of the spleen.

Growth is impaired and diabetes and heart conditions are common with it.

Thin children Undoubtedly the commonest cause for thinness is a child's genetic make up. He may have thin parents or other close relatives as evidence for this theory. The next commonest cause is not being particularly fond of eating. The child is perfectly healthy and normal in every way but just isn't keen on food. Such children stay thin and grow into thin adults. Don't forget when you're making comparisons of fatness and thinness that you're comparing your child with other so-called 'normal' children, many of whom will be overweight. As far as we know there is no disadvantage or harm in being thin apart from having no fat reserves for times of need, but there are many disadvantages and health hazards to being fat.

However, some thin children have abnormally poor appetites for one of many reasons and are thin as a result. If you are worried about your child's appetite, talk to your doctor. Most children who get thin during an acute illness (and lots do, especially if they are vomiting a lot) soon recover their weight and look normal again in a week or two.

Any loss of weight, particularly if sudden, needs medical attention as does a thin child who suddenly becomes ill, tired or weak for no apparant cause, or a thin child who has put on no weight for a long time. *Related topics* Appetite; failure to thrive.

Thirst A normal drive experienced by us all in order to ensure that our bodies get the fluid they need to stay healthy. When the level of water in the body falls (a long time after fluid intake, after vigorous exercise, and with prolonged diarrhoea, sweating, fever or vomiting), centres in the brain tell us to drink. Older children and adults recognize these sensations and drink to slake their thirst.

Babies on the other hand can be thirsty for just the same reasons yet can only cry to let their parents know what they want. Usually the parent assumes such a child is hungry or thirsty and so gives some milk which quenches the baby's thirst.

In hot weather, if your bottle-fed baby has diarrhoea, vomiting or a fever, or if he has been crying a lot, work on the assumption that you'll need to give him boiled water rather than just more milk in order to prevent or treat dehydration. If he doesn't like water you can give half-and-half boiled water and milk formula feeds while the body rebalances its water over a couple of days. Giving extra fluid or milk formula can dangerously overload the body with salt, especially if the feed is made up too strong by overloading the scoop with milk powder. What the thirsty baby in danger of dehydration needs is more water, not more milk powder.

Breast-fed babies rarely need to be given drinks of water even when they have diarrhoea, vomiting, excessive sweating, a fever, or are overheated in a hot climate – they need more frequent breast-feeds and do very well on them. There is no danger here of overloading the baby with salts as breast milk is perfectly balanced and can do no harm.

If an older child suddenly becomes thirsty for no apparent cause he could be developing diabetes mellitus (sugar diabetes). He will also probably be losing weight and will be passing lots of dilute urine.

See your doctor at once if you suspect this so that he can do blood and urine tests to prove or disprove the diagnosis. Diabetes insipidus (an entirely different condition) is a disease in which the child has a pathological thirst – even drinking flower vase or pond water to slake his insatiable thirst. Always report any such desperate thirst to your doctor at once. *Related topic* Dehydration.

Threadworms (pinworms)
The commonest sorts of worm living in the bowel of Western children. The adults are ¼ – ½ inch (6 – 12 mm) long and look like pieces of white sewing thread. They live in the bowel and the females come out of the anus (back passage) at night to lay thousands of microscopic eggs on the skin around the anus. The eggs are transferred to the child's mouth on his own hands after he has scratched his itchy bottom, and are swallowed. Eggs can be transmitted to other children and to adults who touch surfaces touched by the infested child. Twice as many girls are affected as boys, presumably because girls are more likely to sit on the lavatory seat and thus to get eggs on their hands from it directly or via their bottoms.

Most children with threadworms have no symptoms though they may complain of itching around the back passage. Sometimes the worms find their way into a girl's vagina and urinary passage where they may produce inflammation. Old wives' tales ascribe head banging, nightmares, teeth grinding and fits to threadworms, but these symptoms are no more common in children with worms than in those without them. Threadworms are sometimes found in an inflamed appendix and they have been known to cause vague tummy ache, usually centred around the umbilicus. If a child spends a lot of time scratching at night, his sleep may be disturbed.

You won't necessarily see threadworms in the bowel motions, though it's worth looking for them. By looking at the skin around your child's anus with a torch as he sleeps you may be able to see them. They'll dive back into the anus as soon as you shine the light on them though, so you'll have to be quick. If anything makes you suspect that your child has worms, take him to your doctor, preferably in the morning and without washing or wiping his bottom. The doctor will probably stick a piece of Sellotape by the side of his anus and then examine it under his microscope. He is looking for worm eggs which stick to the Sellotape as the eggs aren't visible to the naked eye.

It's essential for the whole family to be treated with antiworm medicines at once. If a treated child has a recurrent threadworm infestation, it's usually because one of the adults or other children in the family still has them. One of two commonly used medicines will be prescribed and your doctor may suggest that the medicine is given again in two weeks' time to get rid of any eggs that have hatched in the meantime. 'Pripsen' (piperazine phosphate plus senna to speed up bowel movements) acts by making the worms so sleepy that they are expelled with the bowel motions. Side effects include slight tummy ache together with loose bowels. 'Vanquin' kills the worms directly. You may notice that the bowel motions are subsequently stained red because the drug is a red dye.

Threadworm eggs can survive in a room for two to three weeks, so after treatment with the medicine, strip the beds and wait for the dust to settle, then vacuum clean the carpet and damp dust the bedrooms thoroughly. Vacuum clean any other area where anyone has been in their bedclothes too. Wash each person's bedclothes and bedding separately, in case any eggs survive in a warm wash. Cut your child's fingernails and scrub them thoroughly to remove eggs.

If your child goes to a play-group or nursery class and the threadworms come back after treatment, mention this to the leader or teacher. Probably another child is harbouring them and hasn't been treated. The leader or teacher should ensure that the children wash their hands after going to the lavatory. Ideally she should turn the taps on as well, as worm eggs can be transferred by taps. Paper towels instead of communal ones help cut down the spread of threadworms.

It's sensible not to be too shocked or melodramatic if your child has worms because a sensitive four- or five-year-old can be very upset about them. You can probably get away with not letting your child know what's wrong at all if you're careful. *Related topics* Hygiene; worms.

Threats A threat is a declaration of the intention to inflict harm, pain, or misery. It is most usually used by parents as a warning of punishment if a child doesn't do what he is told. With the sort of discipline based on loving guidance it might seem that threats should never be necessary. However, parents are sometimes too busy to give a child the sort of treatment that would make him behave well without threat of punishment, so threats are occasionally inevitable. If you realize that you usually threaten your child frequently throughout the day, take the time to consider whether his behaviour is the result of boredom and too little attention from you.

Most threats are centred around matters of discipline. 'If you don't behave I'll . . .' is the commonest threat of all. Any threat of punishment loses impact with repetition so beware of threatening too much or too often because you may achieve nothing, except getting yourself into a state. It's also dishonest to threaten with lies.

Knowing what to do when your child repeatedly misbehaves is a problem. Appeals to reason work much better than threats. 'If you do that you'll probably break it and you won't get another one' is a warning rather than a threat in the accepted sense of the word but it often works, is based on truth and is much more pleasant to live with than a real threat. If this doesn't work you can try using the threat of punishment by the removal of an indulgence or treat: 'If you do that I won't take you to tea with James on Friday.' This often clinches the situation but for some children on some occasions the third level of threat will have to be resorted to: 'If you do that I'll be very cross with you.'

If you use a threat you must be prepared (and able) to carry it out. And your child must know that. Don't make idle threats or you'll gain nothing and your child will think poorly of you. Ideally, of course, it would be pleasant if threats were never necessary, but children do sometimes behave 'badly' (or other than their parents wish) and if they won't stop doing something dangerous such as walking on an unsafe wall, or unacceptable such as hitting another child, and you can't physically take them away or divert their attention, then a threat may jolt them into obeying you. Children have to learn to obey rules laid down by someone in authority in order to fit into our society. When they grow older and go to school they'll be expected to obey rules and requests and no one will dream of diverting their attention or removing them from the trouble. As adults, really bad behaviour is punishable by fines or even by a prison sentence and if your child has never learnt to obey you or to respond when you have to threaten him, he may find himself in trouble. A dangerous situation and an unresponsive child may need a serious threat. Best of all, however, is to put neither yourself nor your child in a position in which you need to threaten him. Thinking ahead is ninety per cent of the skill of being a successful parent. Your under-five is rarely capable of thinking ahead, so you'll have to do it on his behalf.

Lastly, never threaten a child with authority figures such as policemen, doctors, dentists, teachers, and so on. This can only do harm to his relationships with these people in the future. *Related topics* Discipline; punishment.

Three-month-old baby – a profile When your baby is three
months old, you'll notice that he's developing a distinct personality of his

own. He may have settled into some sort of pattern for at least part of the day and by now you'll be quite used to looking after him and satisfying his needs. His cries aren't usually quite so desperate sounding as those of a newborn baby and he'll warn you when he's hungry or lonely by crying in a fretful way at first rather than in a full-blown yell. You'll probably start feeling that you're getting back to normal. All in all the house with a three-month-old in it is a more settled house than that containing a newborn baby.

By now your baby will have learnt to bring his hands together and will amuse himself for quite long periods when he's lying on his back simply by playing at clasping and unclasping them. His arm and leg movements are becoming more controlled and he'll kick his legs and wave his arms vigorously when lying down. When you lay him on his tummy, he'll prop himself up on his forearms to get a good view. He can control his neck muscles quite well by now but you'll still have to support his head as you lay him down from a sitting position when you're playing with him, or if you bend forwards with him in a sling.

The three-month-old baby is becoming more and more interested in what's going on around him and will watch people's faces intently. He'll smile at anyone who takes the trouble to make a fuss of him and from now on is increasingly likely to look pleased when his mother approaches. He has no fear of strangers yet and is happy to be held by anyone unless he's tired or hungry, when he prefers his mother because he knows she can comfort him and feed him at the breast. If he's bottle-fed, he's content to take a bottle from anyone. Babies of this age show a real interest in their feeds and look at the breast or bottle with excitement when they're hungry. During a feed they stare at your face and kick their legs in sheer delight.

Your baby will briefly manage to hold on to an easily held object such as a rattle but can't sustain his grip. He'll be interested in small things held near him but won't be able to pick them up yet although he may take a swipe at them. He'll also enjoy looking at a mobile or other moving objects and will try to get hold of any interesting looking things close to him by waving his arms at them and perhaps hitting them. At some stage he'll manage to grasp hold of whatever he's swiping at and from then on he'll try over and over again to get it. Over the next three months he'll become adept at controlling his hands and arms so that he can reach out and grasp something accurately.

At this age a baby likes to make cooing and gurgling noises and can carry on a polite conversation of coos and gurgles with you. He'll wait smilingly until you say something to him, then he'll respond while you smile at him, and so it'll go on. Your delight and responsiveness to him are important in encouraging him to make more noises and also in cementing the bond between you. Babies thrive when they have lots of individual care and attention and provided your baby's happy, you can't talk to him or play with him too much. You'll probably find that he'll enjoy sitting in a bouncing-chair while you work.

When you take your baby out, prop him up into a sitting position in the pram so he can see what's going on, or carry him in a sling. He'll be happier for longer in a buggy if it's the kind that faces you.

Three-year-old child – a profile Around the time of their child's third birthday many mothers heave a sigh of relief as they see their troublesome and often annoying two-year-old change into a charming little three-year-old.

The birthday itself, of course, isn't a magic date, but usually early in the fourth year the negativistic traits of the two-year-old are shaken off and replaced by behaviour which seems – to an adult – to be more reasonable. The child has learnt that he can sometimes control a situation by refusing to eat, having a temper tantrum, saying 'no' to everything his mother wants him to do and so on, but realizes that it is more acceptable and enjoyable on the whole to do what he is asked. He is also more capable of talking to his mother to explain what he needs or wants, which often improves their relationship.

The three-year-old is often a remarkably good companion, both for his parents and for children and other adults. He trusts most grown-up people and is affectionate towards them.

Mealtimes gradually become more civilized as he can cope better with his cutlery and stops spilling his food all down his clothes. He can pull his pants up and down, but won't be able to cope with every type of fastening. Most children can wash their hands at this age but not many will dry them as well.

Three-year-olds at play are fascinating to watch because many of them have make-believe friends and playthings and talk to them for hours. They do this with other children as well and will happily share toys with friends, brothers and sisters. Constructional toys really come into their own now and with their help many children play quietly for long periods. Activities such as painting, helping wash up, cutting out, sticking and rolling pastry are much enjoyed by the three-year-old, though you'll have to do the clearing up unless you are inventive enough to make that enjoyable too, so he wants to help. A three-year-old's attention span is increasing all the time and he'll like you to read to him, showing him pictures as you go, or to tell him a simple story in your own words. Many – but not all – three-year-olds are happy to go to a play-group two or three times a week and enjoy the social stimulation they get from playing with other children, new toys and equipment, learning new activities, and relating to other adults. Most of the time, though, they like to be with their mothers and are only happy to be left with someone else who is familiar and well-liked.

During the fourth year most children begin to understand that they may have to wait for some things they want. As well as looking forward to existing events their memory is expanding and they may be able to remember things that happened several months before.

The rate of increase in weight and height slows down now to a steady level that will continue until the adolescent growth spurt. Fairly accurate predictions of eventual adult height can be made at this age with the aid of special charts and a knowledge of the heights of the rest of the family.

By three, all the first teeth are through. Your child should be making his first visit to the dentist for a check-up and should certainly be cleaning his teeth with your help.

The three-year-old is very confident on his feet – he can go upstairs like an adult, although he comes down with two feet to a step. He can climb over things and run round corners without falling over. He can play ball games with a big ball, both kicking and catching it and he can pedal a tricycle. He can also stand on one leg for a short while and stand on tiptoe.

Many children are obviously right- or left-handed by this age, but some are still undecided and it is best not to influence their final decision at all. Whichever hand they prefer they can use to hold a pencil like an adult does and can attempt a picture of a person, usually drawing a head only! They thoroughly enjoy painting with a large brush on a large sheet of paper, and can also cut things up with scissors. As they grow older their finger control becomes better and they learn to thread beads and pick up tiny objects easily and accurately.

Eyesight should be checked at the baby clinic. While some children recognize colours at this age it is too young to test for colour vision yet. Red and yellow are the colours usually recognized first.

Speech is progressing in leaps and bounds now and many three-year-olds chatter non-stop. He still doesn't get all his consonants in the right places but this doesn't matter at this age though he should be using pronouns, prepositions and plurals with relative ease. Contact with other children plus lots of conversation with adults improves his speech tremendously and bedtime stories and nursery rhymes are often learnt by heart as they have to be repeated so many times. Hearing ability should be checked at the clinic because it's possible for a child to be slightly deaf without his parents ever noticing and even a small hearing loss can cause problems with understanding and speech development.

Many children touch themselves in their genital area about now and again this is a perfectly normal phase of development. Discourage him gently from doing it in front of people but don't make an issue out of it.

Although three out of four three-year-olds are dry at night, there's no need to worry if your three-year-old isn't. Often, an unsettling episode around this age – such as going into hospital, the arrival of a new baby, an illness, or moving to a new house – can delay the onset of being dry at night. Many children don't have large enough bladders to hold all the urine produced during the night and can't help wetting themselves if they sleep very soundly or are afraid to get up in the dark.

Active children often wake early in the morning and want their parents to wake up and play with them. The best way round this is to provide toys in the child's bedroom and to tell him that he mustn't wake you. Most children will happily amuse themselves for a while. If not, consider whether you are expecting your child to go to bed too early. You can't expect him to sleep longer than he needs to, and going to bed later will mean – once he's adjusted to the change – sleeping later in the morning. All in all the fourth year is usually a pleasant one – the child enjoys learning all the time and being with other people, and the parents enjoy having him around.

Thumb and finger sucking Early on a baby's thumb, finger or fingers find their way into his mouth more by luck than judgement, but as the months pass and his coordination and control increase he is able to put them into his mouth on purpose whenever he wants. All babies want to suck – in fact sucking is a reflex activity. A baby's sucking reflex appears in the eighth month of pregnancy and some babies suck their thumbs even before they are born. As a baby drifts off to sleep you can sometimes see him making sucking movements with his mouth as though he were dreaming he was still at the breast or bottle. Babies need to suck in order to swallow their milk. One spin-off is that sucking aids the normal development of their jaws and teeth, and another is that it is pleasant and comforting in itself. Lots of babies like to suck as they go to sleep. Babies allowed to stay at the breast when they're sleeping don't need to suck their thumbs. Bottle-fed babies, however, can only fall asleep while sucking at the bottle if there is still some milk there, otherwise they might be sucking in air from an empty bottle and would give themselves wind, so thumb sucking is very useful for them. Babies who don't get enough sucking time at the breast or bottle make up for it by sucking their fingers, thumb or a dummy if one is offered. Babies who are breast-fed on an unrestricted basis don't need to suck their thumbs and some babies never suck their thumbs anyway.

Thumb sucking is generally believed to be harmless in the under-fives except in breast-fed babies who are not gaining weight properly because they are being underfed. These babies should be sucking at the breast much more in order to stimulate their mothers' milk supply and so get more milk. But babies don't only get milk from the breast; they also get comfort and pleasure from sucking. While there's nothing wrong with thumb sucking in a baby, the baby would probably prefer to be at the breast and in his mother's arms than by himself sucking his thumb, and there's a good chance that he'd be talked to more when with her than when lying alone.

Sometimes in older children thumb sucking is done as a form of amusement, just to give them something to do when they are bored. It's also done when they are tired. Most often it's simply a pleasurable and comforting habit that began because they were brought up not allowed to suck at the breast for comfort both during babyhood and in their early years. Older breast-fed children suck at the breast more for comfort and pleasure than for milk – they often like to suck just as much as babies, though they don't spend so much time doing it.

Thumb sucking is in some ways better than sucking a dummy because at least a thumb is warm and relays sensations back to the child. It can't get lost or dirty on the floor either. Babies not allowed to wean themselves from the breast or bottle often go on sucking their fingers or thumbs for an average of two or three years. During this period of time a child feels he needs to and wants to suck and it is quite understandable that he should want to suck his thumb for that time as well. This is only an average time and many children want to go on sucking for longer. As a thumb is always available, sucking it becomes a habit that is very hard to give up. Attempts to deprive a young child of the comfort he gets from sucking his thumb are often fraught with problems because his desire and need to suck are so strong early on. There is no reason why a child shouldn't be allowed to suck his thumb but some parents dislike it, in older children especially.

No medical problems arise from thumb sucking this early in life. Some children get sores or blisters on the skin from prolonged thumb sucking but these need no special treatment and heal themselves. Bandages get soggy and fall off and creams and ointments soon get licked off. First teeth it seems come to no harm from thumb sucking but second teeth can be pushed out of line and may need dental correction. *Related topic* Dummies.

Toddler groups

Toddler groups, toddler clubs and mother and baby clubs are all much the same. They cater for mothers and their babies and young children who are usually aged up to three or so. Older pre-school children are welcome in some groups as well. Your child needn't be toddling in order to go to such a group. Babies are welcome and some club leaders encourage pregnant women to come as well so as to make friends before their baby is born.

These groups serve two main functions. First, they give mothers a chance to get to know other local mothers and to make contacts for friendship, baby-sitting, child-minding and so on. Many a father is seen from time to time in a toddler group, as are grannies, nannies and minders – anyone in fact who has care of a young child. In a welcoming, friendly group, new mothers are made to feel at home and introduced to other people, and mothers who already attend the group keep their eye open for others who may not know about it yet would welcome the chance to have somewhere pleasant to go. Second, these groups provide toys, space and other facilities for young children to play. Many mothers who live in cramped conditions, in a flat, or have little money for big toys find this aspect a real boon.

A toddler group may open for one half-day a week or more often. It is most likely to be run by volunteer mothers, often with young children themselves, and the more help that is offered with getting toys out, making coffee and washing up, and putting toys away, the better. The meeting usually lasts for 1½–2 hours. One o'clock clubs open in the early afternoon and finish in time for mothers to pick up older children from school. In some areas there are 'drop-in' clubs which are open every day for coffee, play and a chat.

That such groups serve a very useful social function is shown by their popularity. Money for toys and coffee is raised by a small entry charge together with fund-raising events such as jumble sales and commissions from the sale of clothes. Toys are sometimes given to the group as well. The choice of toys and equipment for this age group is very important. A collection of dirty, scruffy toys will be ignored completely – toddlers enjoy ride-on vehicles, push carts, a slide, large Lego, a doll's pram with a doll, a Wendy house and bricks, while older babies enjoy the various activity centres, soft balls, musical boxes and stacking sets, to mention but a few. Paints, playdough and sand are also popular. As the children play and watch each other, the mothers can talk, keeping half an eye on their children and helping them when necessary.

Some children go through a phase when they can't bear their mothers to talk to other grown-ups. It's hard for such a mother to have to give her full attention to her child at a social event like this and if both she and her child are made anxious, cross, or unhappy by coming, they should give it a miss until he is older and more able to amuse himself for a bit. Most children are happy to play near their mothers and as they near the three-year stage, they start playing more *with* the other children and tend to leave their mothers for much of the time.

Attending a toddler group is a good prelude to going to play-group. You'll be better able to assess how your child will manage without you at play-group if you've been able to watch him with other children first. If he's still clinging and shy at three, think twice about letting him start play-group – he's probably not ready yet. *Related topic* Play-groups.

Tongue furring This whitish-yellow coating of the tongue is very common and can be quite normal. Lots of children have furred tongues and it is usually nothing to worry about. Dehydration and low grade fevers can produce a furred tongue but constipation does not.

The white, curdy patches seen with thrush and the white coating that milk temporarily causes are easily distinguished from furring. If you gently scrape the tongue with your nail, milk will come off easily but the tongue will bleed slightly if there is thrush. *Related topic* Moniliasis.

Tongue tie A condition in which some of the tissues under the tongue tie its undersurface to the floor of the mouth. It rarely causes a problem even with sucking but if necessary it can be operated on quickly and safely. Tongue tie has nothing to do with stammering, stuttering or any other speech defect. There is always another cause for these speech problems.

Tonsillitis Inflammation of the tonsils usually due to infection. Babies under a year old have very small tonsils so tonsillitis is not usually a problem. The tonsils are usually inflamed when a child has a sore throat or a cold but tonsillitis can also occur alone.

Most infections of the tonsils are caused by viruses but some are caused by bacteria and are treatable with antibiotics. Suitable antibiotics help prevent a child from developing complications such as rheumatic fever, nephritis, or a middle ear infection (otitis media) – which occasionally follow tonsillitis caused by certain strains of streptococci in some children.

The tonsils are masses of tissue at the back of the throat that trap and kill bacteria and viruses. They are designed to stand up to repeated infection. Bacteria that are trapped in this way do less harm than they would if they had got past and settled in the lungs. The fact that tonsils enlarge with an infection causing tonsillitis is good because it means they are actively fighting the bacteria. Damaged, useless tonsils never enlarge.

In most children with tonsillitis the tonsils become very large, red and covered with spots of pus. They may even meet in the middle. Swallowing is difficult because of the size of the tonsils themselves and because they are so tender. The child is irritable, off his food and may have a slight cough and fever but within a day or two is usually better. The whole episode is rather like a sore throat in an adult. Antibiotics aren't usually needed for this type of tonsillitis because they don't kill viruses and such cases are usually caused by viruses.

More severe cases of tonsillitis can cause a child to feel very ill, vomit, have swollen nodes in the side of his neck and a temperature. He may have a tummy ache if the infection involves the lymph nodes around his intestine, making them painful (mesenteric adenitis). You should ask for your doctor's advice if your child has any combination of these symptoms. Few parents ever look at their child's throat when he is ill and even if they do it may be difficult for them to assess what they see.

Young children rarely complain of a sore throat and the news that they have one is often a complete surprise to the parents. Doctors can't tell with any degree of certainty just by looking whether tonsillitis is viral or bacterial, let alone whether it is streptococcal, so many prescribe an antibiotic for a child with tonsillitis in order to be on the safe side. The doctor might send off a throat swab to the local laboratory to find out if the tonsillitis is bacterial and if it is, which antibiotics are most suitable, but this takes several days to produce answers and in the meantime he may start the child on what is likely to be a suitable antibiotic anyway.

As well as the antibiotic, a child with tonsillitis will need plenty of fluids, whatever food he wants, paracetamol if the pain and temperature are unpleasant, and rest if he feels like it. A child may take as long as a week or ten days to get over tonsillitis and may not be completely well for three weeks or so. It's best to keep him away from other children until he starts getting better because even if he is on antibiotics, you can't be sure they are going to be effective and if they are not, he'll still be infectious during the acute stage. If the antibiotics are effective, the child will be non-infectious within twenty-four hours or so of starting them.

The problems come if your child gets repeated tonsillitis. At this stage you may feel his tonsils should be removed but today doctors are loath to operate unless there are good reasons. If the tonsils become so badly deformed from repeated infections that their function is impaired (they are then small, fibrous and obviously infected) they may have to be removed. Tonsils sometimes have to be removed if they are so large that they obstruct the throat and make eating so difficult that the child doesn't eat enough, or if an older child gets very frequent attacks.

Tonsillectomy does nothing to reduce the number of upper respiratory infections your child will have; produces no decrease in the frequency of chest infections or laryngitis; and no decrease in middle ear infections, sinusitis or nasal allergy. Your child will still get sore throats after his tonsils are out but he will feel better in himself, will eat more (because he can swallow more easily), and will probably lose his bad breath.

So unless your child is losing lots of schooling (unlikely to be important in the under-fives), has frequent attacks of tonsillitis over several years, or has difficulty in swallowing, don't bully your doctor into having your child's tonsils removed. Any operation, however small, has its dangers, so don't expose your child to them unless it's absolutely necessary.

Because the adenoids are usually infected at the same time as the tonsils, a child with tonsillitis may get otitis media as well. If tonsillectomy is recommended, the adenoids are often removed at the same time. *Related topics* Glue ear; otitis media; sore throat.

Toothache Pain produced by irritation of the soft, inner, living part of the tooth – the dentine. By far the commonest cause is dental decay (caries). Decay eats through the hard, outer enamel first but this produces no symptoms because enamel is dead. As soon as the decay gets into the living centre of the tooth, pain sets in.

Toothache can be made worse by hot or cold foods and by tapping the tooth. It always seems worst at night.

The only real treatment for toothache is to cure the cause – and this has to be done by a dentist. In the meantime you can give your child paracetamol in the correct dose and place a covered hot water bottle over the part of the face that's affected. Never place an aspirin between the gum and the tooth to soothe the pain as this can ulcerate the lining of the mouth which in itself is a very painful condition. Oil of cloves is probably worth trying in an emergency but is only of any use if the child has a pain in a tooth that has lost a filling or in a really large cavity. If ever your child falls over and breaks a tooth, bathe the edge in alcohol (whisky will do) to deaden the pain while awaiting dental help.

A tooth that is producing pain will almost always need to be filled or removed, so get help from your dentist and take your child to see him regularly so that things don't get this bad again. *Related topic* Dentist.

Toothbrush The counsel of perfection is to start cleaning your child's teeth as soon as the first one has come through to protect them from the building up of food deposits that can harbour decay-producing bacteria. Some parents clean their children's teeth with a soft cloth at first. Others use a toothbrush from the beginning. Cleaning the teeth is even more important if your baby's diet contains sugar or refined carbohydrate. If he eats a diet which is mainly added-sugar free and high in unrefined carbohydrates, cleaning them is not so essential, though it's still advisable.

Try hard to make tooth cleaning fun. If you once hurt your child while cleaning his teeth, he'll be reluctant to cooperate in future, so go gently. If he sees the rest of the family cleaning their teeth regularly, he's likely to want to do it as well. Toothpaste is inadvisable and unnecessary until your child is old enough to spit it out afterwards.

A good toothbrush should have a very small head so that it can easily get to all the corners of a child's mouth; should have nylon bristles; and should be changed at least every six months (or sooner if the bristles are splayed). The shape and angle of the handle is immaterial at this age so just choose one your child can easily manage in his hand. Your child might like a toothbrush with a picture on its handle and a bell inside. He should, of course, have his own brush.

Brush (and teach your child to brush) his teeth from gum to tooth edge using a vertical rolling motion of the brush (not a side-to-side scrubbing motion) and work systematically around his mouth. Don't forget the biting surfaces of the big back teeth in particular and the insides of all of them. Your child won't be able to clean his teeth reliably and systematically until he's about five or six, so let him clean them in his own way first and do them again afterwards, if necessary but don't be too obsessive about it because he could quite easily be put off altogether.

Ideally, teeth should be cleaned after every meal (or drink), the aim being not to let food particles stay on the teeth for too long. Most parents settle for cleaning before bed and after breakfast.

Your child's teeth can be cleaned with an electric toothbrush (which could encourage the reluctant child to clean his teeth) but take care to be gentle. *Related topics* Dental caries; toothpaste.

Toothpaste A finely particulate paste used on a toothbrush to clean teeth.

There is absolutely no doubt that toothbrushing is a vital part of the fight against tooth decay and although you can clean teeth well without using paste the finely abrasive action of the toothpaste seems to do the job better and makes the mouth and gums feel nice.

Research has shown that a toothpaste containing fluoride definitely reduces tooth decay, so it's well worth using. Very young children should be given only a tiny amount of toothpaste on their brush and should be discouraged from swallowing it because it has been found that repeated swallowing can cause fluoride toxicity and mottled teeth.

There are several brands of children's toothpaste but most of them contain colourings and flavourings and some even have sugar in them! It's best just to let your children use the fluoride paste you use.
Related topics Fluoride; toothbrush.

'Topping and tailing' A term used to describe the procedure in which a parent washes his baby's face and bottom instead of giving him a full bath.

There's no need for a baby to be bathed daily but it is a good idea to top and tail him if he doesn't have a bath, just to keep his face and bottom clean, as these are the areas most likely to benefit from a wash. Some mothers like to top and tail in the morning even if they bath their baby every night.

Wash your hands first, then wipe your young baby's face with cotton wool swabs squeezed out after being immersed in warm water. Use one at a time and wipe each eye separately, starting at the nose end of the eye and wiping outwards. Then wipe the rest of the face with another swab, making sure you get the skin around the mouth clean. If your baby regurgitates much milk, clean his neck and behind his ears too. Pat his face dry with a towel or with a clean terry nappy, then take his dirty nappy off and clean his bottom. Wipe the worst of any mess off with a clean part of the nappy. The traditional way of doing this is with several warm moist cotton wool swabs, wiping them from the front backwards for a girl so as to avoid contaminating the urinary entrance with bowel motions. Put all the soiled cotton wool in the loo if you are in the bathroom, or else in a paper or polythene bag. Dry his bottom with a towel or nappy, then put his clean nappy on and do up his clothes. He is now topped and tailed. There is no need for powder and a barrier or antiseptic cream should only be used when necessary.

You can wash your baby's bottom by running a washbasin of warm water and then, holding the baby with your left arm round his body (if you are right-handed), 'sit' him on the edge of the basin and wash his bottom with soap and water or just water with your right hand. This is an effective way of tailing a baby, especially an older one who is likely to get messier. Make sure that the baby doesn't burn himself on the hot tap if it is too hot. Use a bowl instead of the washbasin if in doubt.

Alternatively you can top and tail your baby on your lap – protecting it with an apron, a towel, or a clean nappy, or on a changing mat on the floor. Don't leave him on a mat on a table if there is any chance at all that he'll roll off. If you like to tail your baby like this whenever you change a dirty nappy, take a bowl, some cotton wool and a spare nappy to dry him with whenever you leave the house, and don't forget at least one clean nappy for him. Individual, foil-wrapped, moist, medicated 'baby wipes' make cleaning up a baby's bottom easy when away from home.

Topping and tailing is really quite straightforward and is simply a way of keeping your baby clean and fresh without bathing him if you are short of time or don't believe in frequent baths.

Toxocariasis An infestation with the larvae of cat or dog round-worms (*Toxocara catis* or *canis*). Children are affected when they swallow worm eggs which have been passed in bowel motions from dogs or cats infested with adult worms. These eggs hatch into larvae in the child's intestine and the larvae then migrate all over the body. If the infestation is severe, damage can be caused to the liver, lungs, brain and eyes, which can even be blinded, though this may not necessarily happen till years later. Thankfully such complications are rare.

It is difficult to know when a child has toxocariasis, though blood and skin tests are occasionally helpful. The first symptoms may last for several months and include a slight fever, a cough and, occasionally, wheezing. A definite diagnosis can only be made by a biopsy from an affected part and examining it microscopically for larvae.

Treatment is difficult but most children seem to get better spontaneously over a six to twelve month period if they don't get re-infested. Prevention is the best cure. Because children often put dirty hands to their mouths when playing, try to keep them away from any public play areas where it's obvious that dogs have opened their bowels. Lots of children's play areas in parks are nowadays out of bounds to dogs, which is sensible, as not everyone take the trouble to worm their dogs regularly. Having said this, it's worth keeping a sense of proportion about the possibility of children getting toxocariasis. The risk in fact is very small. Be sure to keep your own pets de-wormed regularly. Roundworm infestation in dogs and cats is common and kittens are especially likely to have worms, which they contract from their mother either across the placenta before birth or from her milk. *Related topic* Pets.

Toxoplasmosis A disease acquired by a baby in the womb (from an infected but symptom-free mother) that is caused by tiny micro-organisms in infected meat or dust. If a newborn baby has a full-blown infestation he has a fever, a rash, jaundice, inflammation of the retina in the eye, encephalitis and subsequently hydrocephalus. Death occurs from convulsions and breathing failure. Many affected infants are stillborn or are born prematurely.

A second type of the disease is acquired after the newborn period and is much milder. In fact it can be so mild that the diagnosis is not made until all other possible causes have been eliminated, by which time the child is better.

Except for the transmission of the disease between a mother and her unborn baby, toxoplasmosis isn't transmitted from person to person. It is usually caught from eating contaminated meat (mutton and beef especially) and from cats. Pregnant women should therefore be extremely careful about eating only very well-cooked meat and should not handle cat litter. *Related topic* Pets.

Toys A toy isn't necessarily a brightly coloured plaything bought from a shop – it can be anything which a child uses to play with. Toys are playthings used for all forms of play: creative, manipulative, imaginative and more active or outdoor play. Children are fascinated by all sorts of objects that adults see as mundane and ordinary. A toddler, for instance, can pick up something such as a plastic mixing bowl and put it on his head as a hat, fill it with smaller bowls, hide something under it when upturned, kick it like a ball, let it drop and watch it rattling from side to side on the floor as it settles, enjoy feeling it and try throwing it. He's learning what it feels like, what it can be made to do and what he can use it for. Give him the same bowl in the bath or in the sandpit and he'll have even more enjoyment out of it.

A commercially made toy should be good value to make it worth your investment. If it's likely to be used once or twice and then ignored, it's a waste of money, Find out from friends with children the same age as yours what toys they have most enjoyed. If you can't decide whether or not to buy a certain toy, try to imagine how your child will play with it. Young children tend to play more often with simple toys which they can play with in their own way. More complicated toys can often only be played with in one way and soon bore young children. This is why toys such as building bricks are perennial favourites and why children return to them again and again, regardless of age. Bricks are fuel for the imagination and as such aren't boring. Remember also that poorly made toys which break quickly are not only a waste of money but are also disappointing for a child. Some toys, of course, are only meant to last a short while. Into this category come paper toys, balloons, cheap clockwork bath toys and so on.

The safety of toys is very important. Avoid toys with eyes that can come off and be inhaled or swallowed; fillings or stuffings that might leak out and be inhaled or swallowed; seams that don't look strong; splinters; small bits that might be swallowed (if the toy is meant for a child under about eighteen months); sharp edges that might cut; and old, flaky paint which might be poisonous. Check toys such as bicycles regularly for their mechanical safety. If you have several children, take care to keep small toys or parts of toys away from a young child who investigates everything with his mouth and might swallow or inhale something.

Commercial toys are often very attractive and good toy firms put a lot of research into finding out what children like and how to make the toy stand up to hard use. Some firms operate a repair service, which is very useful. If ever a toy breaks after little use, complain to the manufacturers, who may replace it.

Take care not to overload your child with toys because if he has too many he won't ever have time to play with them. Children can be happy with very few toys if you have time to play with them. When you play with your child, don't take the toy and show him how to use it, however great the temptation. It's his toy and he wants advice and company only. If you have to demonstrate, do, but don't go on for too long – your demonstration doesn't have to be exhaustive, nor should it become a time for you to revert to childhood and play with the toy selfishly yourself. Your child may not play with the toy as you would play with it, but that doesn't matter at all. Let him do what he wants. As he grows he'll do different things with it and still learn from it in different ways. Remember too that children don't by any means always finish something they've started. Your child may stack two beakers and then divert his attention to another toy. He'll gain staying and finishing power when he's older – few under-fives concentrate as long as their parents think they 'ought' to.

Look around your house for lots of free toys. You can make mobiles and rattles, however unartistic or ham-fisted you are. From the age of two or even earlier children like to copy what you're doing around the house. Take advantage of this to amuse them while you're working: for instance, if you're brushing the kitchen floor, give your child a small brush and dustpan and get him to help. If you're writing a letter, give him some paper (it doesn't have to be your writing paper) and a pencil. An older baby or toddler will enjoy baking tins and saucepans, mixing spoons and other plastic or wooden utensils. Keep cardboard boxes of all sizes for imaginative play; make playdough from the kitchen cupboard; use old cotton reels for building and threading; keep old clothes for dressing up. You'll probably have paper, scissors, glue, pens, paints and scraps of fabric at hand for creative play. String can make cat's cradles. The list is endless and its only limit is your imagination and patience.

More formal games need an adult or older child with an under-five in order to control arguments and explain how to play. Under-fives very much enjoy games such as snap, ludo, dominoes, and snakes and ladders and can learn a lot about matching and counting from them.

Store your child's toys somewhere easily accessible, preferably downstairs if you have the space, because a young child likes to be near his mother and will ignore his toys for much of the time if they're all upstairs. Shelves are a good way of being able to see what there is to play with. A box sounds like a good idea but children always tip everything out each time they play and are sometimes put off by the ensuing jumble. Drawers can be useful but be careful they don't get pulled right out and hurt your child's feet as they fall. A cupboard with shelves inside it is a good way of keeping toys out of sight when they aren't being played with. Keep your child's toys well maintained and encourage him to take care of his things by letting you know if something has broken or if he's lost a vital piece. It's a good idea to have a family rule that each night all toys made of many parts should be collected together. If thirty bricks live in a box make sure that all thirty go back in the box. This seems a nuisance at the time but is a small price to pay for the next day's enjoyment. It's all too easy to end up with a cupboard full of toys none of which is complete.

While certain toys are aimed at certain age groups, children enjoy toys not 'meant' for them even though they may use them in different ways from those intended by the makers. A young child growing up in a family with older brothers or sisters has an advantage over an only or first child because he has the full range of toys for all ages to play with. Some toys can be ruined by the rough handling of an over-enthusiastic toddler – a doll's house is a case in point. Help your older children protect and keep their precious and fragile things from a younger one and don't insist that everything must be shared. Children like to have some things which are their own, even if they pass them on later. Certain large and expensive items must be shared, of course, such as a climbing frame or swing. Others may be passed on when outgrown, such as a tricycle.

The following list is intended as a guide for those whose minds go blank when they walk into a toyshop. There is inevitably a lot of overlap between different ages, depending on the personality, preferences and experience of the child, and younger children invariably find 'older' toys fascinating.

Young babies Mobiles; rattles; small, soft toys; squeaky toys; pram beads; balloons; anything moving near him – perhaps suspended from the ceiling or pram hood; 'activity centres'.

Six to eighteen months Balls of any sort (the soft foam ones are useful for playing with indoors especially and the transparent ball half-filled with water with a floating duck and some beads is very popular; bath toys (including clockwork ones and plastic jugs); baby-bouncer; baby-walker; musical box; bricks; stacking plastic men; stacking cups; push-along truck or animal; push/ride toys; peg-rack and hammer; posting box; hardy books.

Eighteen months to three years Lift-out jigsaw (with knobs on the pieces at first); simple ordinary jigsaws; screw toys; rocking horse; small tricycle; wheelbarrow; dolls and doll's clothes, pram, cot and bedding; toy tea set; toy garage and cars; junior Lego; telephone (an old real one from the Telecom office is enjoyed more than a toy one).

Three to five years Small Lego; farmyard and animals; doll's house and furniture; carpentry set; card and board games; dominoes; larger tricycle or bicycle.

Certain toys are worth having as 'staple' toys, such as all the ingredients for creative play, such as paper, including cheap rolls of lining paper, plain white paper and coloured paper; cardboard; scissors (both blunt ended for young children and sharp for older children); paints – powder paints can be mixed to give water colours or thick finger paints if you have some non-toxic thickener; crayons; pencils and coloured pencils; a pencil sharpener; felt-tip pens; paper doilies; Sellotape; stapler; scrapbook; old magazines to cut up; and a ruler. A box of discarded smaller boxes, plastic containers, tins with lids, egg boxes, old string, yoghurt cartons, plastic washing-up liquid containers, scraps of material, ends of wool, old buttons cut off discarded clothes, bottle tops, cardboard rolls from inside lavatory paper, empty Sellotape rolls, empty foil/cling film/kitchen paper rolls and so on is a useful store when it comes to making things. In the garden children of all ages appreciate a swing, a slide, a climbing frame, a paddling pool and a sandpit, or any combination of these. A rocking horse, a Wendy house, a blackboard and chalk, a dressing-up box, a cheap record player and suitable records, musical instruments such as a xylophone, triangle, recorder or drum, playdough and Plasticine are also popular with most.

Of course your children won't have all these toys but they'll enjoy the ones they haven't got at their friends' houses and at play-group and toddler group, where their novelty will add to their attraction.

You can make your child's play more interesting and more fun if you join in every so often. Your enthusiasm and pleasure are infectious and your company is nearly always welcome. The most expensive toys can be unutterably boring if no one takes any interest in them or shows the child how to enjoy them. Dumping a child on the floor with a whole load of toys is a form of rejection and he will be well aware of this. Help him select and get started with some toys and come back to him from time to time to make sure he's happy.

It's well worth finding out if there is a toy library in your area. Children enjoy playing with unfamiliar things and you'll have access to many more toys from a toy library than you could probably afford yourself, even if you wanted to spend your money on them. There is a nominal charge for borrowing a toy from most toy libraries and a maximum borrowing period. Some of these libraries are run by social services departments, others by various charities. Some mother and toddler groups operate their own toy library, asking only that the toy should be returned in time for the session each week. *Related topics* Bicycles and tricycles; creativity; games; play; rattles. *Useful organization* Toy Libraries Association.

Trainer pants Terry towelling-lined plastic pants used in older babies as they are being trained to become dry.

Today, with the vast amount of baby clothes and equipment available in the shops, parents are choosing what they actually need for their babies very carefully before spending their hard-earned cash. Trainer pants are non-essential items in the older baby's 'layette', and it's worthwhile thinking fairly carefully about whether they'll really be useful to you and your baby before you buy them.

In spite of the fact that one can get by without trainer pants, some mothers swear by them, so let's look at some of the advantages first. First and foremost, they are easier to put on than a nappy, because no folding or safety pins are necessary to keep them up. This can obviously save time unless your baby is wearing trousers or tights, in which case you'll have to take them off before you can put dry pants on.

Second, trainer pants are quick to take off, and this is very useful for the child who needs to get to the potty quickly if he is to avoid a puddle. Most children who are in the process of being potty trained have to wee urgently once they've realized they want to. If using the potty means waiting two minutes for a nappy to be taken off, then that might make all the difference between the child choosing to use the potty or not, so the quicker and easier it is for him to get there the better.

Trainer pants can be a fairly powerful inducement to a child to learn to be dry, provided of course he is ready to learn. They look much more like pants or knickers than does a nappy, and it's surprising how soon the child of eighteen months or so realizes that older children and adults don't wear nappies. Children are born imitators, amd many of them at this age will be proud to wear trainer pants. The clever parent will make trainer pants seem grown up to the child so that he is keen to wear them.

Because so many newly potty-trained children are unreliable at first, if only because of the urgency with which they need a potty, trainer pants are very useful if you are going out shopping or even just for a walk. They at least prevent an obvious puddle! It's also possible to put a piece of nappy roll or a disposable nappy pad inside to soak up more urine if necessary.

Finally, trainer pants look far less bulky than a nappy and are less unpleasant to wear.

The most serious disadvantage of trainer pants is their cost. If your child is still very unreliable, you'll need several pairs to take the place of nappies, and that will be expensive. They are most useful if your child just wets his pants occasionally, or if you intend to use them at home only, when you can be extra vigilant about taking him to the potty regularly, or at least as soon as you think he wants to go.

Also, the plastic coverings of the terry towelling inside tend to become hard with repeated washing, and eventually crack completely. You can cut the plastic away and use the towelling pants separately later, but in that case ordinary pants would have been cheaper.

Trainer pants are all right for the small leak before a child gets to the potty, but they really can't cope with the volume of urine some children pass, and this can prove embarrassing if you're out, though a true puddle is unlikely. Trainer pants are also useful on long car journeys just in case your child sleeps at some stage. The child who is not yet out of nappies at night may well wet his pants while asleep in the car.

Finally, it has been said that trainer pants imply to the child that you don't mind if he wets them as they're a sort of substitute nappy. It is true to say that they do prevent him feeling the trickle down his legs that he would feel with ordinary pants, and this trickle can be a useful teaching tool in potty training. **Related topic** Potty training.

Transporter A metal frame on wheels used to hold a carrycot or larger pram body. Together a carrycot (or pram body) and transporter act as a pram, with the advantage that the carrycot can be taken out of its transporter and used separately. If a baby goes to sleep in the carrycot and transporter when you are out for a walk, or when he is in the garden, for instance, and you want to take him inside but don't want to wake him, you can simply lift the carrycot inside with him undisturbed inside it. Similarly when you use the car, he can be transferred in the carrycot from transporter to car or vice versa undisturbed. You'll also have a ready-made pram at each end of your journey. Don't forget to secure the carrycot safely in the car and if he is sitting up, harness him into it as well.

Most transporters made nowadays are collapsible at the simple flick of the safety catch. This means that they can be put out of the way against a wall or even in a cupboard when not in use. If you leave a transporter outside in the rain or in the garage, it'll rust at the joints eventually. If you want to keep it in really good condition and if you can make the time, wipe it dry when you get home after going out in the rain. Being collapsible also means that you can fold it up and put it in the boot of the car when you need a pram at the other end of your journey, or you can take it in a bus or train in the luggage space. It's none too easy coping with a baby, shopping, a carrycot and a transporter on such journeys and this is one of the times when a helping hand really will make a difference to the speed with which you and your baby can travel around (especially on public transport).

You'll probably find that your baby will sleep better in a carrycot and transporter than he would if he were in a lie-back buggy, and you can also carry shopping, parcels and so on at the end of a carrycot as long as they're not lying on the baby's feet. Bags can be hung from the handle of a transporter safely, because it is well-balanced, whereas with a buggy, any shopping hung on the handles is likely to make the whole thing tip backwards. You can't put a pram seat onto a carrycot and transporter because the sides of the carrycot aren't strong enough. If you use a pram body (which has strong sides) with a transporter, though, you can fix a seat safely.

Before you buy a transporter, check that your carrycot will fit into it easily and that you can lift it in and out without having to force it. Most people buy a carrycot and a transporter at the same time, which makes the choice easier because you'll then buy them specially made for each other.

If you're wondering whether to buy a carrycot and transporter or a more solid, better padded pram base and transporter, there are several factors to take into consideration, the main one being whether you will need to separate the two frequently. If so, choose the lighter and easier carrycot and transporter because a heavy pram body is awkward and heavy to lift into a car and if it is coach-built, impossible to lift into a bus. If you need something in which to carry a baby and a toddler, then a light carrycot won't be strong enough. Buy a heavier pram body and transporter instead, or consider buying a twin buggy. Such a buggy can be adapted in a variety of ways such as by having one side as a simple buggy and the other as a carrycot on the basic buggy base, or as a lie-back buggy. Some clever new buggies start off as a carrycot and transporter yet are readily converted back to a buggy. Some heavier pushchairs can carry two children (a baby lying back and an older child sitting) together with some shopping, and are also collapsible, but they tend to be as expensive as a heavy pram base and a transporter and are heavy and awkward to lift. If you never need to separate the top from the bottom, buy a conventional pram or a large two-child pushchair. If you'll need it only seldom (for instance, when taking the pram in the car to go to stay with granny) then choose a heavy pram body with a transporter. Baby equipment can be very expensive, so choose wisely, taking into account what you will actually be doing with your baby's transport. You can pick up second-hand equipment cheaply and might even consider advertising in a shop window, at a mother and toddler group, or in the local paper.

Choose an unpainted transporter because painted ones get scratched and tatty-looking quickly. Check its brakes regularly and oil it as necessary. Used with care, a transporter can do good service for baby after baby, so pass it on, sell it, or keep it for your children's children when its life in your family is over. *Related topics* Prams; pushchairs.

Travelling It's relatively easy to travel for very long distances today with young children and you'll find it helps a lot if you plan carefully how to travel and what to take with you. As far as possible, stick to your child's usual habits of sleeping and eating but be sensitive to any change in his daily pattern so that you can help him cope with it. If you're staying somewhere overnight, pack things needed for the journey in a travel bag separately from everything else, so you need only to keep this travel bag near you. Other cases or bags can be stored away. There are five groups of things to consider when packing the travel bag: food and drink; extra clothes in case he's sick, wet, dirty, or cold; things to keep him amused; a blanket and pillow to make him comfortable when he sleeps; and nappies, potties and all that goes with them.

Food and drink for a young baby not yet on a mixed diet is simplest if you're breast-feeding. You can breast-feed in the back of a moving car. A seat belt fitted on the back seat for you is a good idea because your baby will be safer on your lap if you are strapped in. There'll be lots of times when travelling by car with a young baby when he will want to be cuddled or put to the breast for food, comfort or pleasure, and if you stopped every time you wouldn't get far. If you are clever you could put a harness round your baby and attach it to your seat belt to prevent him from being thrown out of your arms in case of an abrupt stop. This is also what is suggested by the staff on aeroplanes, and a special baby safety harness is provided to attach to your lap belt. If you're driving, of course, there's no alternative but to stop.

If you're feeding in front of other people in a plane, coach, train or boat, be as discreet as possible in your clothing so you don't offend anyone! Choose a seat that isn't too public so that you can feed without being aware of other people's fascinated (or amazed) gazes all the time.

Don't forget to take bra pads (if you use them) in your handbag, and remember a change of bra for you in your overnight case unless you wash yours out overnight.

Bottle-feeding is quite possible while travelling but is slightly more of a problem. There are three basic ways of preparing feeds from dried milk powder. First, you can prepare however many bottles of milk you think you'll need on the journey before you leave, (always allowing extra in case you break down or the baby is especially hungry or thirsty, or the journey takes longer than you think for some reason). Sterilize the capped bottles with the milk inside them and the teat upside down by boiling them in a pan of water for twenty-five minutes, remembering to unscrew the screw rings slightly to allow for expansion of the air inside the bottle. You can then pack these bottles and use them at any time during the journey. If your baby is used to having cold milk, the bottle needn't be warmed, which makes it easier. If he likes warm milk, you'll either need a thermos flask of very hot water and a bowl in which to put the water and the bottle or you'll need a bottle warmer which plugs into the car's cigarette lighter. On a long journey you can fill up your flask of hot water at a roadside café or restaurant.

Second, you can take sterilized bottles with the teat upside down and firmly covered, together with a can of milk powder and a thermos flask of boiled water. Wash your hands if you can, or else wipe them with a medicated tissue, then prepare the feed as usual. Airline staff are very helpful and will provide you with boiled water or assist you in making up the feed. Half-full bottles shouldn't be left around and given to the child for his next feed. Take as much care about preventing infection as you would at home and work out how you're going to sterilize bottles while you're away before you go. Don't forget to take sterilizing tablets (easier to transport than solution) if you use the hypochlorite soaking method, and make sure you'll have a large enough container at the other end of the journey in which to soak or boil them.

Third, you can prepare a bottle at home in your usual way and put it into a cool box for the journey. Warm the bottle if necessary as above. This is only safe for one bottle – that is, for a short journey, as the cool box won't keep cool for very long.

Young children soon get cross if they don't have something to eat for a long time. Have a snack or a meal every hour or two if you're travelling by car. You can take your own food or a picnic or go to a café or restaurant, or both. Everyone will feel better anyway for stretching their legs from time to time on a long journey. However you are travelling, bear in mind that the food provided on trains, planes and boats may not be what you would ideally like to give your child, not what he's used to, or not to his liking. If your child eats any food you haven't prepared for him, choose it carefully and avoid foods containing cream, salad cream or mayonnaise and cold meats, fish or eggs, as these are the foods most likely to cause infectious diarrhoea or food poisoning. Take some of your own food, including fruit, biscuits (not necessarily sweet ones), sandwiches, pieces of cheese and dried fruit. Take a knife if you need it for cutting up apples, together with something like a polythene bag to put it in afterwards. Another bag for rubbish comes in handy. Many children like crisps but these can make a lot of mess and are also fairly greasy. If it's unlikely that your baby will eat mashed up café or restaurant food, or the food provided on a train or plane, or if you don't want him to, take jars of baby food with you. The staff on a plane will readily warm this up and most café or train kitchen staff would do the same if told what to do. Discard half-eaten jars of food.

If you give your child a drink, give it to him in a beaker with a spout on it unless you're stationary or unless you can steady an ordinary mug or glass for him.

Clean up the children after they've eaten with a damp flannel which you've brought in a polythene bag or washbag, or use disposable moist wipes. Paper tissues are useful but don't get rid of all the stickiness. There's no need to keep your children thoroughly clean but it's more comfortable for them if they're not sticky and greasy and it'll protect your clothes and the car upholstery as well.

It's sensible to have a change of clothing easily available in case it's cold or in case your child is sick, his nappy leaks, or he spills a drink. Tissues, disposable wipes and a moist flannel are helpful and a strong paper bag can be used for him to be sick in if you have enough warning.

If your child has a dirty nappy, you'll be able to clean him up relatively easily on a plane or boat. On a train it's more difficult because of the lack of room in the lavatory – you would be well advised to take a piece of polythene or even a large piece of paper so that you can lie him down on the floor to change him more easily. With soap and water and paper towels at hand, you'll be able to clean him up satisfactorily. If you're travelling by car, you may need to stop to clean your child up, and you'll find this easier if you have either a container of warm water and lots of soft loo paper, or baby lotion and soft paper, or lots of throw-away moist wipes. Don't forget a bag to put all the paper and the dirty nappy in. It's sensible to use disposable nappies while travelling if you can find ones that fit your baby well and don't leak. Take more than you think you'll need with you. Don't forget spare covers or pants if you need them.

For the child out of nappies, take his potty together with a roll of soft loo paper (and a bag to put the paper in) if he's not yet used to sitting on the lavatory. If you're travelling by car and your child can sit on the lavatory, take advantage of meal stops at cafés to encourage him to do so. If you're nowhere near a lavatory, let your child squat in a suitable place (a field or behind a bush at the roadside, though not in a built-up area) to wee. In built-up areas you'll soon become adept at spotting suitable-looking filling stations with adequate lavatories. If you ask nicely, most garage staff will let your young child use the lavatory even if you're not buying any petrol. If your child is used to a special child's clip-on lavatory seat, don't forget to take it with you. If your child is desperate and you're travelling by coach, ask the driver to stop specially. Even if your child has to wee in the gutter, it's better than having an accident on the coach. Some long distance coaches have a lavatory at the back. Put a newly-trained child in a nappy or trainer pants for a coach trip, just in case.

As for things to keep your child amused, be guided by his age and if you're going on a long journey, consider taking some new things as well as his familiar toys. Large toys can get in the way in a small space and will be annoying to carry on to a plane, train or boat. Remember to take your child's favourite toy or cuddly or comforter if he has one. Musical boxes and a rattle for older babies may drive you mad after a while but are popular. Large Lego, paper and pencils, or a magnetic drawing board are well liked by toddlers and pre-school children, but if they tend to feel sick, such close activities aren't suitable. Games such as I-Spy or counting the numbers of, for example, red cars that they see help to pass the time. Songs, stories, tongue twisters and riddles help too. A car radio rarely has anything more suitable than music on it, but the children's programmes can come in handy if you remember when they are. Tape cassettes of children's stories or songs are a real boon and well worth investing in if your car has a cassette player. Don't exhaust all your ideas for amusements in the first half hour of the journey but space them out. Older children will enjoy it if you promise them a surprise from the travel bag every hour. If you're clever, the travel bag can become as exciting as a Christmas stocking for very little expense.

Marked pressure changes are uncommon in aeroplanes used for the public these days but minor fluctuations can occur and these can be upsetting to a young child, particularly if he has an upper respiratory tract infection or any congestion or stuffiness. Let a baby suck at the breast or bottle at times like these and give an older child a sweet or teach him how to equalize the pressure either side of his ear drum by swallowing or making a trick movement with his jaw. On long flights the cabin staff will provide a carrycot for your baby if you book it in advance. Try to book seats with plenty of leg room whatever the age of your children, because the more space they have, the better. There can be long delays when travelling by air, so take plenty of everything you might need and try to make sure your children have a chance to get their usual naps.

When travelling by car, don't smoke if you're carrying children with you. Sitting in smoke is repulsive to many children and upsets quite a lot of babies too. Try to make sure the car is adequately warm and yet well ventilated, but at the same time don't let a young child or baby sit in a draught.

Car safety is essential and a carrycot should be strapped to the back seat by straps attached to special anchorage points. An approved car seat is better for a child who wants to sit up than letting him sit in his carrycot even with a harness on (see car safety).

Take care when travelling by boat or ship not to let your child out of your sight. A toddler might be safest in a harness and reins if he won't stay with you. Trains provide children with more space than cars or coaches but try not to let your children annoy the other passengers by running up and down the carriage too much.

Before you go, think about any transport you might need for your children. A sling is ideal to carry a baby in most situations, but if you find him too heavy or if you want somewhere other than your lap for him to sleep, a carrycot and transporter are helpful. A buggy is easy to fold and carry when not being used and a child can sleep in one (especially if it has a lie-back facility) at a pinch. Most airlines insist on buggies going into the hold of the plane, not into the cabin, but they'll let you keep your baby in his buggy right up till the last minute. You may be able to take your own carrycot into the hold by prior arrangement if there isn't one available on the plane already.

Finally, don't forget travel insurance if you are going abroad. EEC countries have a reciprocal health arrangement which means that you'll get your money back but other countries, especially the USA and Canada, do not have such arrangements. Medical bills in such countries can soon become horrifyingly large, so be prepared. Young children are always falling over and getting childhood infections and there's no reason to suppose that your holiday will be more illness-free than a similar period at home. *Related topic* Travel sickness.

Travel sickness Nausea and vomiting are fairly common when travelling in any transport that rolls about. Planes and ships are probably the worst offenders, but many children are travel-sick in cars and coaches. Anxiety is known to make matters worse. Some children seem to be immune and others highly susceptible.

A motion sick child looks pale and anxious and may sweat and vomit. There is no way that the child can prevent it – he has no control over himself. No one knows what causes it but the inner ear that controls balance is probably highly sensitive to repeated rhythmical motion, and body position has something to do with it because children lying down are less likely to be travel sick. Children as young as six months can suffer from the condition but it's important to bear in mind that children of any age can be sick for lots of reasons other than travel sickness, even though they happen to be in transport of some kind at the time.

Certain things are worth trying when it comes to reducing the likelihood of motion sickness. A large, fatty meal is thought to predispose to sickness and a combination of an empty stomach and motion can produce severe sickness, so give your child a light meal before he travels and small snacks while you're travelling.

Emotion plays a great part, so keep calm, don't work the child up into a state of nervous anticipation about the journey and ensure that he is occupied during it. Audio tapes on the car cassette player are good for this whereas reading and any games requiring looking down, drawing, and looking out of the side windows make travel sickness more likely.

Unfortunately, the safest seats in a car (the back ones) are also the worst from a car sickness point of view. Don't let your child talk you into occupying the front seat because this is the most dangerous place in the car.

Give him an anti-motion sickness tablet half an hour before the journey and take a thick paper bag with you (but don't tell him). Polythene bags aren't a good idea because when full of vomit they look so awful and will make the other children feel sick. Keep a window open near the affected child and stop from time to time to let him walk in the fresh air.

Most children grow out of their motion sickness. *Related topic* Travelling.

Trust When a baby or child trusts someone he has confidence in them and feels he can rely on them. Being confident or trusting in others is closely tied up with a child's own self-confidence. If he feels secure and isn't suspicious that other people will let him down, he'll feel confident that the world is a good place and that he has some control over what is happening. If others neglect his needs in spite of his signals, he feels that whatever he does or however he feels, he can't make things happen. His own opinion of himself drops together with his trust in the people looking after him.

What all this means as far as babies are concerned is that if their needs for milk and comfort, warmth and stimulation are met generously and ungrudgingly, they'll grow up with plenty of self-confidence and trust in their caretakers who are usually, of course, their mothers.

Following on from this, if an older baby or toddler is allowed to be with his mother as much as he needs her, besides having all his other basic needs met, he's likely to become a more independent child than if he were constantly being pushed away from her to stand on his own two feet. Children who are forced away from their mothers before they are ready to enjoy being with someone else, or even just to accept being with someone else, are often found to become as clinging and dependent as two- and three-year-olds. They have been made to lose their basic trust that their mothers will provide them with what they need – in this case, their company as a fortress to return to for comfort and strength whenever necessary. It's no help to the child if his mother knows she'll come back when she's finished her shopping or having her hair done or whatever – he may be told this but if he's unable to understand what she means, because he's too young or because he has no concept of time, he may think she's gone for good. Children left like this often feel angry at their mothers for leaving them and such anger is tied up with a feeling of having been let down. In future if it looks as though they're about to be left again, such children tend to be very clinging and whiney. Children don't have the experience or wisdom to understand the reasons behind their parents' behaviour and some can't cope with the idea that their mother has done something which has made them anxious, sad, angry and frightened. In the end some of them cope with prolonged separation in the only way they know how – by switching off their attachment and warm feelings towards their mother. Their affection thankfully usually comes back with time and considerable effort, provided they aren't left again until they're able to cope with it.

This same response of anxiety and anger followed by withdrawal can be seen in some babies who can't trust their mothers to meet their basic needs for food. A baby breast-fed according to a four-hourly schedule, for instance, may scream after two hours and if no one goes to him, his screams get louder and louder. Eventually he may stop completely as he gives up trying. When the time comes for a feed he may even be uninterested because he has tired himself out with crying so much. This baby is unlikely to thrive at the breast, Also most mothers' milk supply soon fails with inadequate stimulation, and the feed the baby is waiting for quietly is not enough to nourish him anyway. Soon, such a baby is put on to the bottle. His initial trust that his mother would supply his needs is soon broken.

In our society, we seem to have become confused between responding instinctively to a baby or young child's needs and spoiling him. If we stop responding because we're worried about spoiling, we run the risk of losing our child's trust.

There is so much that children trust their parents to do. If this early trust is fostered by parents rising to their children's needs and expectations, then the children are more likely to grow up trusting other people and situations.

Older children trust their parents to teach them to do and say the right things. They look to their parents for guidance in all sorts of situations and it's not until much later that they start to question their parents' opinions. Becoming independent from their parents is a very long drawn-out process, but having a basic trust in them enables many children to let go sooner. *Related topics* Anxiety; independence; self-confidence; whining.

Twins About one in four of all sets of twins are identical, formed by the splitting of one fertilized egg. Identical twins are therefore of the same sex and have the same genetic structure. Identical twins also have similar basic personalities though these can be influenced by differences in upbringing, health and so on. Non-identical twins are formed when two eggs are fertilized and both embed in the uterus. Some women inherit the tendency to shed more than one egg at ovulation.

During pregnancy you'll have a relatively large tummy, relatively more kicks and are more likely to suffer from anaemia and toxaemia if you are carrying twins. Almost all twins are born in hospital nowadays. A twin labour doesn't last any longer than with a single baby.

It's useful to know if you're expecting twins because then you can prepare everything you'll need for when they're born. A few mothers have unexpected twins even with good antenatal care and this can be as much of a shock as a surprise. Twins inevitably mean a lot more work and to give yourself enough time to enjoy them, to prevent yourself from becoming fraught with too much to do, and to make life pleasant for everyone in the family, it's absolutely essential to think of every way possible to cut down on any unnecessary jobs and to make essential ones easier.

The most important thing of all is to make sure you organize plenty of help for after you've had your twins. However you feed them, however easy their temperaments are, and whatever else you have to do, twins take up a lot more time than one child. Many mothers choose to get help with the housework, shopping, or laundry rather than with their new babies, especially if they are breast-feeding, but every mother occasionally needs some help with the babies even if it's just to comfort one crying twin while she bathes the other. Arrange if you can for your husband to have some time off work, for a relative to come and live in for a while, for friends and neighbours to pop in and do odd jobs, or for some paid help.

Breast-feeding is a very good way of feeding twins and the milk supply adapts to fit the needs of two babies simply because of the extra stimulation the breasts get from two babies sucking. If you're worried that you aren't producing enough milk, fit in more feeds and let the babies suck for longer –

the milk supply will rise within two or three days with this extra stimulation. As with breast-feeding one baby, it's folly to be guided by people who encourage you to adhere to schedule feeding and to cut feeds down in length to a prescribed time. Frequent feeds by day and night will get your milk production off to a good start. A few women will find that their babies automatically settle down into a routine of sorts so that they can predict roughly when feeds will be. If you allow both twins to feed on an unrestricted basis, you'll soon find that you're spending most of your day and night with a baby at the breast. Try always feeding both together (with separate feeds kept for an occasional luxury). If both don't wake simultaneously, wake the sleeping twin up. There are lots of ways in which you can breast-feed two babies at once and you'll find your favourites by trial and error. You'll probably feel too shy to experiment in hospital but once you get home, do some acrobatics to find out the best ways for you. Most mothers find that they have to vary the positions they use for their twins in order to avoid nipple soreness, which is more of a problem in the early days in particular than if you had one baby. Don't let your nipples stay under a wet bra pad or bra; expose them to light and air as much as possible; don't use soap; make sure your babies aren't tugging at the nipples but are well positioned; change the position of each baby during a feed at least once in the first few weeks so that even though he stays at the same breast, the force of his sucking and milking action doesn't only hit one part of the nipple. If you come up against soreness or any other breast-feeding problem, don't be discouraged from carrying on but seek help from someone who is committed to helping mothers breast-feed and knows her business. You'll have a quieter life if you breast-feed twins because it's so quick and easy to comfort a crying baby at the breast.

You may be helped with feeding or any matter to do with twins by joining a twins club by post or locally if there is one. Sometimes a health visitor will put a new twin mother in touch with a more experienced one for support, or you can find out the names of other twin mothers from your local toddler group.

Bottle-feeding twins is certainly no easier than breast-feeding them, because of all the sterilization and feed preparation. It's difficult to feed both babies at once, unless you have a helping hand or discover ways of propping one or both babies while you hold the bottle in each hand. Beware of propping the bottle – a baby can choke if he's not supervised, especially if the milk comes out of the teat of its own accord.

When it comes to mixed feeding, spoonfeed both at once using one dish and one spoon or, preferably, encourage both to eat finger foods and to feed themselves with a spoon from the start.

There are positives and negatives to being a twin. A twin has to get used to less individual attention but he has ready-made company all the time. He may talk later because twins so often use sign language or their own made up 'foreign' language with each other that no one else understands, but at least there is always someone to talk to. It's very frustrating for twins as they grow older to be labelled 'the twins' and not to be recognized as the individuals they are. From the point of view of their eventual independence it's essential to treat them emotionally as individuals, so they don't come either to dislike each other or to rely too heavily on each other for support. Whether or not you dress them similarly, give them the same presents, give them their own toys, or make them share is up to you and there are pros and cons to both. Overall, it's your relationship with each twin that is most important, not material things. Being a twin can be fun but it can also be annoying. How you handle your twins can make all the difference as to whether each one enjoys being a twin and you enjoy having them. Try to make sure that each has plenty of love, attention and cuddling. Don't forget that an older or younger non-twin will feel very left out occasionally. If you see this happening a lot, give him extra attention or arrange for him to play with a friend regularly. It's all too easy for a child to think that being a twin is better or more special than being a single child and jealousy can easily spoil the pleasure of having two extra siblings.

Having triplets or quadruplets makes help all the more essential. You may like to insure against having twins. As twins occur in about one pregnancy in eighty in this country, you might think that the relatively small premium (£10 is about the lowest) is worth it. The premium depends on several factors. Twins are more likely if there is a family history of them on either side, though twins on the father's side only makes identical twins more likely. The insurance premium is higher if there are twins on the mother's side. Twins are also more likely if you have already had a set – your chance then is one in ten! Triplets occur once in 6,000 births and quads about once in 500,000. Multiple births are less common in some races (for instance the Chinese) and more common in others (for instance among some people of African origin). A multiple birth is most likely in your thirties and is also more likely with certain fertility drugs. Insuring against having twins has to be done at least six months before the birth, so you have very little time to do it in. You have to sign a form to say that you haven't had a medical opinion as to whether you are having twins or not. The maximum payment is £1000 at the time of writing. Twins can be diagnosed by sixteen weeks of pregnancy by ultrasound and they are often born prematurely. *Related topics* Jealousy; sibling rivalry. *Useful organization* Twins Clubs Association.

Two-year-old child – a profile Helping your two-year-old toddler grow up is at the same time tremendously rewarding and very frustrating. During one day he may throw a temper tantrum in the morning and cling to your skirt and crave affection in the afternoon; he may drop off to sleep for the afternoon and be wide awake to entertain you and your friends at ten o'clock at night. He is changing rapidly as he learns new skills every day and the development of his personality is almost more exciting to watch than his physical development.

The average two-year-old can run around, starting and stopping easily;

he can jump over things with both feet together, attempt to kick or throw a ball and walk on tiptoe. He has boundless energy and loves practising things he has learnt – he will spend hours going up and down stairs one step at a time, opening and closing doors, and pushing and pulling things all over the house.

He is also becoming much more skilful with his hands and will build bricks into towers and trains, put things into containers, unscrew pots and jars and hold a pencil to scribble. Gradually he learns how to cope with buttons, take off his shoes, socks and pants and wash and dry his hands. He may be able to manage going to the lavatory alone except for wiping his bottom.

As for eating, he will enjoy feeding himself independently and does well on his own apart from needing some help with cutting. He should be given a knife and fork as soon as he wants to try using them and has shown that he can manage a spoon easily. The more he is allowed to try to do for himself, the sooner he'll stop making a mess with his food.

The two-year-old child can see everything an adult can see, both close to and in the distance. If you are not sure whether he is seeing properly then take him to the child health clinic where the staff are trained to assess vision in young children. It is worth having his vision checked (at the regular developmental examinations at your health clinic) even if you aren't worried.

Similarly, he should be able to hear perfectly. He'll have routine hearing tests at his regular developmental examinations or you can ask for an extra hearing test if you think he isn't hearing properly.

The average child's speech is developing by leaps and bounds now – he often chatters incessantly and can put several words together into meaningful phrases. The pronouns 'I', 'me', 'you' and so on are used properly, and his vocabulary will increase daily. The more varied the conversation around him, the more words he will learn. The child who has no one to talk to him will inevitably be slow in learning to understand and to talk. Children learn to talk by understanding what the word means first, and then using it and practising it. Some children occasionally echo what is said to them – this is usually a normal part of speech development and should be ignored. Sometimes one syllable is repeated constantly and some people think that if the parents make too much of a fuss about this then stuttering may eventually develop.

The child of two needs the constant love and security that goes with good mothering if he is to be emotionally healthy now and later. It is thought that many people who are unable to be loving or to receive love have been deprived of care and affection when they were children. The child needs most of all to have someone there all the time to comfort and praise him, cuddle and feed him. He also needs someone to imitate and to talk to. If his mother can't be with him, she should make sure that the person looking after him is warm, loving and communicative, not someone who will leave him to his own devices hour after hour.

When he is with other young children the two-year-old often plays on his own and not with the rest of the group. There's no need to worry that he is turning out to be antisocial because it's a perfectly normal stage of development and he will gradually learn to play with the others and eventually to share his·things with them. Sharing develops as the child begins to realize that he is not the centre of the universe as he had previously thought but that there are other people around who are just as important as he is. At the same time he is learning to realize that he can make decisions about what to do or not to do for himself, and this may lead to clashes with his parents if they cross him.

Indeed, you will notice that during the third year a child will frequently do exactly the opposite to what you want him to do, apparently just for the sake of being difficult. This 'negativism' is quite normal and will be replaced by less frustrating behaviour later. The most important thing for parents to do in order to avoid unnecessary stress in their relationship with their child is to try not to fight with him because he'll often get his own way in such a situation, whether by having a temper tantrum or by refusing to eat or sleep.

The most common age for temper tantrums is between fifteen months and two years, and the more active and determined the child, the more likely he is to have them. Tantrums are always worse if a child is tired, bored, hungry, or if he feels insecure for some reason. Sometimes he will hold his breath during a bout of temper, but there is no reason to panic over this – much better to keep calm and to help him get over his rage as quickly as possible.

One of the commonest problems arising with the two-year-old is trouble at mealtimes: the trouble may take the form of hardly eating at all or taking so long over a meal that other people's plates are washed and dried before he has even started eating. Dawdling is understandable at this age because time means nothing to a two-year-old, and there is no reason why it should as he has nothing which has to be done during the day, unlike his mother. If his plate is cleared away after a reasonable time he will soon learn that he has to eat faster if he wants any food at all. The worst thing to do in this situation is to force a child to eat if he doesn't want to. He will eat what he needs to be healthy, provided he is offered the right food, and if he doesn't eat the food given him he probably isn't hungry or else he doesn't like the taste or is unhappy for some other reason. If he has been forced to eat at any stage then he may not eat because he realizes that this is a good way of getting attention – some families go to the utmost lengths to persuade a child to eat, and of course the child loves every minute of it.

Sleeping, like eating, if handled correctly creates no problems. But there are great individual differences in the amount of sleep which children need, and some children of this age can make do with as little as eight hours a night, though this isn't the norm. The best guide to whether your child is getting enough sleep is the absence of tiredness during the day. Many children develop rituals which must be carried out before they go to bed.

often to keep their mothers with them for as long as they can.

During his third year, a child is changing from being a toddler who is adventurous most of the time but still dependent on his mother for much of the day, to a more independent child with an obvious will and personality of his own. Some children are ready towards the end of their third year to leave their mother on a regular basis to savour the delights of a play-group. However, each child develops in every sphere at precisely his own rate, and if your child is not ready to leave you, even for two hours twice a week, then it would be quite wrong to push him away. Forcing him to cope away from you is likely to create dependent and neurotic behaviour based on insecurity, not the reverse.

During the third year some children demonstrate their readiness to move on but they often like to explore within easy reach of their fortress, which is their mother, for a long time. This is the age when your child will be a baby one minute and a child the next and that can be confusing for him as well as you. Give him all the security and encouragement that you can, mixed together, and he'll grow in ability, maturity, and inner strength all the better.

Ultrasound ('scan') A procedure in which very high, inaudible sound frequencies are used to visualize structures inside the body. Ultrasound has many uses but a common application is in pregnancy to visualize the foetus.

The principle behind ultrasonic diagnostic techniques is exactly the same as that used in the echo sounder of a ship. In a sonic echo sounder sound frequencies are bounced off the ocean floor, and collected by an instrument. The time this cycle takes is recorded and the depth of the water under the boat calculated accordingly. In medical ultrasound the principle is much the same. After first wetting the patient's skin with an oily fluid a probe is rubbed gently over the skin. The probe emits high frequency sound waves and picks them up fractions of a second later. The sound wave reflections so produced are fed into an electronic system which converts them into a TV picture which can be 'frozen' by the operator for inspection. These pictures can be photographed at once and kept for record purposes.

In obstetrics, ultrasound can enable doctors to work out the age of the foetus very accurately (to within eight days) and can display several abnormalities likely to lead to a miscarriage. It is helpful in diagnosing multiple births and with some scanners the foetal heart can be seen moving from 7½ weeks onwards. Certain congenital abnormalities such as spina bifida can be picked up early too.

One common application of ultrasound is to locate the pool of amniotic fluid in the womb so that a needle inserted into it can avoid the foetus and the placenta during the procedure known as amniocentesis.

Ultrasound is nothing to do with x-rays, is thought to be safe for the foetus (according to several studies), and is set for an increasingly rosy future as methods become more refined.

Umbilical hernia

Umbilical hernia A hernia (rupture or weakness) of the muscles around the umbilicus (navel) allowing some of the underlying abdominal contents (fat or a part of the small intestine) to push through as a lump. The hernia takes the form of a soft lump under the skin which increases in size on coughing, crying or straining. It can normally be pushed back easily and there is no need to stop a baby crying because of the effect it may have on his hernia.

Such hernias are fairly common in newborn babies (though they may not appear until some time after birth) and are especially common in children of African origin.

Most umbilical hernias disappear spontaneously before a child's first birthday and even very large ones mostly go by the age of five or six years. An operation to close the gap is only necessary if the hernia shows no signs of closing spontaneously by the age of five years, if it enlarges after the age of two years, or if the child has troublesome symptoms from it.

Such hernias used to be strapped (sometimes with a coin underneath) but this is now thought to be potentially harmful because the strapping could trap the delicate bowel that lies so close to the skin and damage it.

Keep a watchful eye on your child's umbilical hernia and if ever it becomes tense, changes colour, or can't easily be pushed back, get medical help as an emergency.

Umbilicus (navel; tummy button)

Umbilicus (navel; tummy button) The scar on the abdomen that occurs where the umbilical cord dropped off. In the uterus a baby is linked to its mother by a cord which carries the arteries and vein that give nutrients and oxygen and take away waste products. This umbilical cord can occasionally become knotted or looped tightly around the baby's neck, so reducing his oxygen supply. If this happens early in labour a Caesarean section may have to be done to save the baby, but if the cervix is fully open, forceps can be used to pull him out.

After birth the cord need not be cut until the placenta has separated from the wall of the uterus. Midwives can recognize this stage by the cessation of pulsation of the cord and by feeling the uterus. Delaying cutting of the cord means that a baby who doesn't breathe at once has the advantage of a few minutes' extra blood supply via the cord from his mother. The cord is clamped in two places fairly close to the baby's abdomen, then cut between the clamps, leaving the long end attached to the placenta (afterbirth). The cut end of the cord left attached to the baby usually dries up and detaches itself within a week or so of the birth but in some babies it takes longer. The raw surface scars over within a week or two. The scar can become infected but this infection can usually be easily cleared up by putting surgical spirit on the area several times a day. If this simple measure doesn't cure it, ask for your doctor's advice.

Whether or not your baby's navel is left with a dressing on or is simply left open to the air will be up to the medical and midwifery staff who are helping you look after your baby. A dressing-free umbilicus seems to heal quicker.

especially if it is dried with a sterile piece of cotton wool or gauze after a bath. It's wise to keep a baby's nappy well clear of the raw area so that it doesn't get wet. In the vast majority of babies the umbilicus heals perfectly well and never gives any trouble.

Apart from being washed along with the rest of his body, a child's umbilicus needs no special attention as he grows. *Related topic* Umbilical hernia.

Unconsciousness There are so many causes of unconsciousness that you probably won't be able to sort them out. Leave the diagnosis to a doctor and in the meantime help the child to stay alive. Any period of unconsciousness, however short, must always be reported at once to a doctor or an ambulance called.

A child is unconscious if he can't be aroused by any external stimulus. If you think your child is unconscious don't slap him vigorously to try to arouse him – try gentle stimulation only.

Once you have decided the child *is* unconscious, here's what to do. **1.** Make sure he is breathing. If he isn't, give the kiss of life (page 34). **2.** Get someone to call an ambulance or a doctor. **3.** If he is breathing lay him in the recovery position. (Lay him on his side; turn his head to one side; and pull the jaw forward to clear his airway.) If he makes gurgling or snorting noises you haven't cleared the airway properly. **4.** Give him absolutely nothing to eat or drink by mouth until he can hold a cup and even then he should take only sips. **5.** Don't leave him alone until professional help comes. **6.** If the child is not your own ask any adults present if they know why the child might have become unconscious and look to see if he carries or wears a Medic-alert medallion which might explain why he became unconscious. *Related topic* Artificial respiration.

Underfeeding Underfeeding in the breast-fed baby is most often caused by insufficient milk being produced because of a lack of stimulation of the milk supply. The amount of stimulation necessary is different for each woman and also depends on her baby's sucking strength. Simply increasing the milk supply by offering the breast more often and for longer periods by day and night usually solves the problem in a few days.

Some bottle-fed babies need more milk than is commonly recommended for their size and are hungry if not given more. Simply make up a bigger volume of milk in the bottle and let him have as many feeds as he wants.

Older babies and children are sometimes underfed because they don't want to eat much at any one meal and aren't offered food between meals. Small, frequent meals are more attractive to them and they take in more calories that way. *Related topics* Appetite; breast-feeding problems; failure to thrive; small child; thin child; weight loss.

Undescended testes When a baby boy is still in the womb his testes move down from inside his abdomen into his scrotum. In some boys this descent is delayed and they are born with no testes in their scrotum. This is especially likely to occur in a boy who is born too early. In such boys the testes often come down within a few days.

It's known that the testes should be down by the age of six years because an undescended testis after this age may have a poor potential for producing sperms. However, if you can't feel your son's testes before this don't worry, because the majority are 'retractile' – that is they can pop up into the canals above the scrotum and seem to disappear, especially in the cold. Your doctor will be able to push them down gently if they are there. If you have ever felt both testes in the scrotum there's no need to worry. Even though they may pop up and down, the canal down which they came will slowly close off and they'll eventually become fixed in the 'down' position.

If your son's testes are still not there by five or six years of age a minor operation can be done to bring them down and tether them to the bottom of the scrotum so that they can't pop up again.

Unmarried mothers Being a mother is difficult enough at the best of times but if you are unmarried there are formidable problems, many of them purely practical. Money is a real problem but the courts can help. You can claim maintenance from the father of the child (if you know who he is) and if he refuses, you can take him to a magistrates' court and take out 'affiliation proceedings' against him. This means you'll have to prove he's the father. You can apply while you are pregnant or within three years of the child's birth. Get advice and forms from the local citizens' advice bureau. The hearings will be in private at the court.

But even if you are all right financially you'll have problems with housing and looking after the two of you. Some areas have hostels for unmarried mothers on a short-term basis and some mothers choose to live at home with their parents for a while.

If your child was the result of an unmarried relationship try to explain as he grows how and why it was that you couldn't have a permanent relationship with his father. By making the child feel a part of your family he'll understand something of a normal family life.

Groups such as Gingerbread will help you but try to take advantage of all the state and local facilities can offer. A good, caring social worker, marriage guidance counsellor or citizens' advice bureau can help you get the best deal possible. *Related topic* One-parent families. *Useful organizations* British Pregnancy Advisory Service; Family Planning Information Service; Gingerbread; One Parent Families; Pregnancy Advisory Service.

Urinary infections Urinary system infections are common in childhood, affecting about 5 per cent of girls and 3 per cent of boys, so about one in twenty girls will have had a urinary infection by the time she reaches puberty. In infancy an abnormality of the urinary tract may be responsible for the infection but after infancy anatomical abnormalities are not a common cause. Girls are more likely to suffer from these infections because their urinary passage is far shorter than a boy's. Most urinary infections are caused by bacteria called *E. coli* which are normally resident in the large bowel and cause no harm there. Infections of the vagina and foreign bodies in the bladder or urinary passage can also cause infections of the urinary system.

Because the urinary system is an intercommunicating collection of tubes and spaces, infection in any one area can easily spread to affect the rest, and as a result it can be difficult to distinguish between cystitis (an infection of the bladder) and infection involving the kidneys (nephritis).

A urinary tract infection may produce no symptoms at all or can produce any combination of: bedwetting; an urgent desire to pass water; a desire to pass water very frequently; pain on passing water; dribbling of urine; daytime wetting in a previously dry child; foul-smelling, cloudy and dark urine; fever; lower abdominal or back pain; and vomiting. Untreated infections may get better only to reappear later. Many of these symptoms are difficult, if not impossible, to detect in infancy for obvious reasons and this can make urinary infections difficult to diagnose, though it's important to try because untreated urinary infection can lead to high blood pressure or kidney failure in adult life. A good doctor will always think of a urinary infection in any child who seems to be ill for no apparent reason. He'll send off a sample of urine for testing at the pathology laboratory and will then be able to prescribe the appropriate antibiotics if necessary. Be sure to complete the recommended course of treatment. Once the acute infection has been treated your doctor may suggest that some x-rays are taken to rule out structural abnormalities of the urinary system, especially if your child is especially prone to these infections. *Related topics* Cystitis; nephritis.

Urticaria (nettlerash; hives) An allergic reaction of the skin
characterized by itchy, raised, red wheals of any size. The condition can affect any area of the body and if it involves the mouth and lips or the genitalia the swelling can be very considerable. The most characteristic thing about urticaria is that it changes its appearance almost hourly.

The vast majority (nine out of ten cases) are caused by eating foods or drugs to which the child is sensitive (allergic). Chocolate, citrus fruits, nuts, fish, shellfish, tomatoes and artificial flavourings are often to blame.

The remaining one in ten cases of urticaria are caused by contact with something to which the child is allergic. Cosmetics, plants, medications, insect bites and stings, sunshine, pollens, moulds and animal fluff can all be causes. Urticaria from these and other causes is sometimes associated with pain in the joints as well.

Thankfully simple treatment works wonders in the vast majority of cases. Oral antihistamines cure the condition within hours but may have to be continued for up to a week to keep it in check. Cold applications of calamine lotion or even water help soothe the angry skin.

If ever a child with urticaria has breathing or swallowing problems, get help as an emergency. Get medical help at once too if antihistamine tablets or medicine don't work. Your doctor has other medications he can use in such cases. *Related topics* Allergy; antihistamines; itching.

Vaginal discharge A colourless or pale mucous discharge from the vagina is normal in young girls and can be quite profuse in a newborn baby in the first couple of weeks of life when her mother's hormones are still acting in her body. It is normally not smelly, nor does it irritate.

A vaginal discharge that smells and irritates the vulval membranes or makes them itchy can be caused by a sensitivity to chemicals in bubble baths, threadworms, a urinary tract infection, or a foreign body in the vagina. True infection of the vagina with bacteria, viruses, VD or monilia (thrush) can also produce such a discharge.

A lack of hygiene or repeated rubbing during masturbation can cause irritation of the mucous membranes lining the vulva, with a discharge.

Any foul-smelling, itchy, and irritating discharge must be seen by your doctor. He'll look for any obvious causes and will take a swab for the pathology laboratory to look for any infective organism.

Many of the simpler causes can be avoided. Only add chemicals to the bath water occasionally; never use vaginal sprays on your daughter; put her in cotton pants; teach her to wipe her bottom from front to back after opening her bowels; and look for threadworms and tell your doctor if there are any. *Related topics* Urinary infections; threadworms.

Vaporizer A humidifier used to produce steam or a cold mist in a room to make a child's breathing easier by liquefying secretions in the breathing passages when a child has a croup or a cough. A cold mist humidifier or vaporizer is preferable because there is no risk of burning although modern models have safety cut-outs and are much safer than the old steaming kettle.

Various medications aimed at helping the child to breathe by shrinking the membranes lining his breathing passages can be put into special vaporizers but probably don't do much to improve on the help given by the mist alone. Some types of vaporizer have no humidification system at all but are simply a way of vaporizing a medicated liquid so that it fills the room and eases the child's breathing. Some of these are candle-powered, so be careful with young children around. *Related topic* Humidifiers.

Vegetarian diet Today with the increasing number of immigrants from the East there are probably more vegetarians in the West than there have ever been. Indeed, many Westerners are tending to question the importance and value of meat and the wholefood movement has helped make vegetarianism fashionable.

As millions of women around the world know, a perfectly healthy child can be raised eating no meat at all. All the nutrients found in meat can be obtained from other foods even though this might mean eating foods which aren't too familiar to the average Westerner (such as fermented foods and seaweed). But very few vegetarians are exclusively plant eaters (vegans) – most eat eggs and dairy products as well as vegetables. Such people not only survive perfectly well provided they have enough to eat but are probably healthier and suffer from certain Western diseases much less than do their meat-eating brothers and sisters.

Provided you feed your baby a sensible, balanced vegetarian diet there'll be no danger to his nutrition at all. Keep away from cranky diets that only allow a restricted number of foods because these could harm a young growing child.

Vernix caseosa Many babies are born with a covering of a creamy-white substance rather like adherent soft cheese. This is called vernix caseosa. Some doctors and midwives think it best to leave it and not to wash it off because it might give some protection against skin infections. Large amounts of it in the main skin folds are usually removed and the baby's face and head are usually washed but often that's all.

Viruses Very small infective agents that live and reproduce only in living cells. They are much smaller than bacteria and stimulate antibody production in the host animal. Immunity to viruses can be obtained by having an infection with them or by being immunized against them.

Most of the common infections of childhood are caused by viruses, including chickenpox, the common cold, polio, 'flu, mumps, cold sores, measles, German measles and many others. Some of the largest viruses behave more like bacteria and can be killed by antibiotics but by and large antibiotics have little or no effect on viruses. This is why they are not used routinely in the above diseases. They are only useful if a secondary bacterial infection occurs *on top* of the viral one, for example when a child with 'flu gets pneumonia.

Antiviral agents are beginning to be produced and are already used for certain localized viral conditions such as cold sores or shingles affecting the eyes but we are some way off an agent that will act in the body against viruses in the way that antibiotics do against bacteria. Because of this there is still no cure for the vast majority of common childhood infections.

Viral infections cause several generalized symptoms irrespective of the actual virus involved. A raised temperature is common, the child often feels generally unwell, there may be a headache and lethargy, tummy ache and vomiting, he may cry a lot and may well have generalized aches and pains in his muscles and back. Viral infections also tend to leave the person feeling unwell, tired and listless for some time after the infection itself has cleared up. This is especially true of viral hepatitis and glandular fever which can leave a child feeling depressed and unwell for months.

Vision A newborn baby can fix his eyes on an object. He is certainly not blind as some old wives say! Many newly-delivered mothers report that their babies spend a lot of time staring them in the eyes as though getting to know them. Very early it can be demonstrated that a baby prefers to look at a face and it's interesting that the focal length (the distance at which things are in focus) of his eyes is equal to the distance from his eyes when he is at his mother's breast to her eyes.

Soon after birth his field of vision as tested is one quarter of that of an adult (he sees things directly in front of him only) but by six weeks he can see things in a 90° range (45° each side of centre when looking forwards). By three months he can see things in a 180° arc, the full adult field of vision. This progress comes about as his eye muscles develop over this period. It is claimed that binocular vision (using both eyes together) isn't present at birth but takes about six weeks to develop.

We adults automatically check everything we see against our bank of experience but babies have no such experience and have to build it up gradually. Perhaps one reason why some newborn babies don't fix their eyes on anything is because it takes time for them to learn what is worth looking at. As soon as they associate their mother's face with her sound, smell, milk, warmth and feel, they'll spend ages staring at her because she is so important to them.

By six months infants can pick out simple forms and shapes. Children can't judge distances reliably in the way adults can until they are ten years old. It seems from tests that colour vision develops at about three months of age.

Depth of vision develops too in the first year. A month-old baby can see a small white ball six to ten inches (14–24 cm) from his face but apparently can't see the same ball on the other side of the room. Babies will search for a nearer, smaller object rather than a larger, more distant one even though they appear to be the same size. By six months a baby can see a one-quarter-inch ball ten feet (3 metres) away. This suggests that a baby of this age can see an object from twenty feet (6 metres) away as clearly as a normal adult would see it if it were 120 feet (36 metres) away. Tests suggest that by one year a baby has a normal, adult-type visual capacity. *Related topics* Blindness; glasses; longsightedness; shortsightedness; squint; vision testing; visual problems.

Vision testing If ever you are worried about your child's vision, the way to get it tested is first to go to your general practitioner or your baby clinic doctor and to ask for an eye test. If further, more detailed tests are thought necessary the child can be sent to a hospital ophthalmologist, or a special form is issued which enables him to be seen by an optician or an ophthalmic medical practitioner (who may work in a hospital or a medical eye centre). Once you have such a form your child can have further tests at any time without having to have another form. It doesn't really matter which kind of expert sees your child and this will anyway depend on what's available locally. By and large, hospital specialists deal with more serious eye conditions and those which require surgery but just because your child sees such a specialist doesn't necessarily mean that he has something seriously wrong.

Ideally, all children should be tested at regular intervals to ensure that their vision is developing normally, but in some areas of the country only children considered 'at risk' can be tested routinely. Such 'at risk' children include those who come from families with a squint or with known defective sight; those with a difficult birth history; and those that are mentally retarded. Routine vision testing in pre-school children not only ensures that long sight, short sight and astigmatism are picked up early, so that such children can see cars, look at pictures and so on, but also prevents the blindness in one eye that can develop very quickly in a squinting child. Since such blindness is eventually permanent it is essential to prevent it if at all possible. Because many squinting children often don't squint very obviously, you can easily miss it in your child.

Children who have poor eyesight are often more clumsy than others, may have obvious problems in seeing things, may rub their eyes, squint, look sideways at things and have other problems that could be corrected by wearing glasses. Even a very young child can have his eyes tested accurately. Such testing must be done very carefully and by expert, patient people because it's all too easy to write off a child with poor vision as 'tired' or 'uncooperative' when in fact he can't see. **Related topics** Blindness; glasses; squint; vision.

Visitors to mother When you've just had a baby, you'll feel rather special, regardless of what sort of delivery you've had, how many stitches, or whatever. It's right that you should be consulted on the matter of visitors to you and your baby. Visitors may want to see the new baby, but it's you who has done all the work of carrying him for nine months and producing him after your labour, and you should decide whether or not you want to see people. Try to arrange for your husband, mother or someone close to be the go-between for you and your visitors, so that they tell that person whether or not they may come to see you in hospital or at home in the first couple of weeks. You may feel quite different after one baby from after another, however outgoing and gregarious, or quiet and shy a person you usually are. One time you may want to have lots of visitors, with champagne flowing and presents and congratulations everywhere, and another time you may want to see only one or two people and stay peacefully in the haven of your room. Cards, letters and flowers are one thing; people are quite another. Decide for yourself and if you feel tired out or weepy, ask your husband to put off a visitor who wants to see you until you feel like receiving him or her warmly.

Some visits may be duty visits from people (perhaps close relatives) you might ideally have preferred not to see but who it's impossible tactfully to put off. It's easy enough to say that you're tired after half an hour or so and everyone should understand that this is perfectly acceptable behaviour from a newly-delivered mum.

Of course, most mothers welcome visits from friends and relatives most of the time. These visits are best kept fairly short and should be limited to only one or two people at a time, and not too many in a day, otherwise however much you enjoy them, you'll soon become exhausted because of waking for your night-time feeds for the baby. Lots of mothers experience a time of feeling low and weepy, often on the fourth day after the birth. Visitors at this time may be surprised to find you bursting into floods of tears for no apparent reason. They may need to have it explained to them that you're not suffering from post-natal depression but are just going through a natural feeling that hits many newly-delivered mothers at this time.

You may sail through the first few weeks with your new baby because of help and support in the house and with other children, but suddenly find yourself exhausted when that help and support leaves you to it. Don't rush round tidying up for visitors or cooking elaborate meals for them – you need to be looking after yourself at this time (especially if there's no one else to look after you) so that *you* can look after your baby. Visitors might be encouraged to put the kettle on to make a cup of tea themselves, to help you with the shopping the next day, or to play with an older child while you have a rest, depending on how well you know them. This is not to suggest that you won't feel well – you probably (and hopefully) will, but all too many mothers find the first couple of months a strain, especially if they have one or more older children and can't snooze easily during the day.

As your children grow up visitors are a great boon if you spend much of your time with your children at home. They can give you a chance for some sensible adult conversation and make you feel a part of the outside world again. Social isolation is a problem for mothers of young children and thankfully this is increasingly being recognized. If you have a circle of friends and neighbours you get on well with, invite them round frequently (or ask them to drop in when they like) if you find it hard work to go out to meet people in the early weeks or months after a baby.

Babies and young children thrive on having people around, provided that their mother is there. Having people to your home will give your children the experience of different ways of talking, behaving, dressing and so on, and if they see them often enough to get to know them it'll help build their confidence in other people. They'll learn about social interaction and getting on with people by watching you talk to and enjoy the company of your visitors too. Visiting children are usually a great hit and if your friends and their children frequently visit you, both sets of children will have the chance to get to know each other well as they grow up. They'll enjoy each other's company while still having their mothers to run back to when necessary, and when they're ready to come and play alone, your house won't seem strange and neither will you. Similarly, your child can become accustomed to other mothers, their children and their houses if you take them visiting. *Related topics* Development– social; strangers.

Visual problems Apart from total blindness, which is very uncommon indeed, children can have three main visual problems, all of which are fairly common. Long sight and short sight are discussed under their respective headings.

Astigmatism is the only other condition at all commonly seen in children. In this the front of the eyeball is irregular in shape and not normally spherical. This is often brought about by a change in the curvature of the lens and cornea. Light rays entering the eye are distorted, causing difficulties with reading, headaches, eye pain, tiredness and redness of the eyes. Glasses can be prescribed to help the child.

Routine attendance at the baby clinic for developmental testing means that your child's visual problem should be picked up as soon as possible. If you are at all concerned about your child's eyesight, ask for advice from the clinic doctor or your family doctor, who will refer your child for specialist help if necessary. **Related topics** Blindness; glasses; longsightedness; short sightedness; squint; vision testing.

Vitamins Essential compounds, most of which can't be produced by the body. Because of this they have to be provided in the diet and, in the case of vitamin D, by exposing the body to sunlight.

By and large parents worry too much about vitamins. There is considerable medical and scientific controversy about the 'optimal' amounts of any one vitamin and while the effect of gross deficiencies *are* known it is also possible that some diseases and illnesses are caused by sub-optimal amounts. Although vitamins are essential for life it's perhaps surprising that we can't be dogmatic about exactly how much of each is needed – but it's a fact.

In the UK there is very little evidence that babies (whether bottle- or breast-fed) suffer from vitamin deficiency or excess. Very little is known about how vitamins get across the placenta, their role in the foetus or the needs of the newborn. As a consequence it's impossible to be sure what infant formulae should contain. It makes sense, however, to ensure that such artificial feeds have the same amounts of vitamins as are available in breast milk but even this can be difficult because the amounts of various vitamins in any given mother's milk vary according to *her* diet from day to day. In the case of vitamin D her body levels will depend on how much sunshine she has had over the past few months. There is no reason to suppose that the breast milk of an adequately nourished mother automatically needs to be supplemented in any way with vitamins (given in the form of vitamin drops or vitamin C-containing drinks). However, a mother with a pigmented skin (one of African or Asian origin, for example) may not produce enough vitamin D in our cloudy climate. Extra vitamin D may have to be given to her baby. This is especially likely if either of them rarely goes into the sunshine.

It is well known that cows' milk loses substantial amounts of its vitamin content in processing and storage to produce infant formula and to compensate for these losses vitamins are added. However, vitamin C cannot be added to cows' milk formula because it would be inactivated when the hot water is added to mix the feed. This means that a bottle-fed baby has to have extra vitamin C in the form of orange juice, tomato juice, rose hip syrup, crushed vitamin C tablets in the recommended dose or vitamin drops.

Vitamin A is exceptionally plentiful in colostrum; in fact it contains three times as much as does mature breast milk. The concentration of vitamin A in a mother's milk depends on her diet. This vitamin is essential for growth, for normal vision in dim light and for keeping the body's lining cells healthy. It is stored in the liver and mobilized when needed. A child who is short of the vitamin will have poor vision in dim light and can eventually become blind. Such deficiences are rarely seen in Western countries but are still seen in developing countries. Vitamin A deficiency has never been reported in breast-fed infants in the UK. It is found in breast milk, egg yolks, liver, fish oils, milk fat, green and yellow vegetables and yellow fruits. It is one of the three vitamins in Children's Vitamin Drops available from child health clinics.

Vitamin B is a group of 8 different vitamins. All of the group are found in cereals, meat, fruit, vegetables, breast milk and cows' milk. Deficiences are extremely rare in bottle- or breast-fed infants and are very rarely seen in older children in the West.

Vitamin C is ascorbic acid. Too little in the diet leads to scurvy. It is not well stored in the body and so needs to be taken almost every day. Fresh fruit and vegetables are a good source but cooking vegetables destroys most of the vitamin. Most animals make their own but primates (and guinea pigs) must have dietary sources or they get scurvy. A breast-fed baby gets vitamin C in his mother's milk. It's probably sensible for a breast-feeding mother to increase her intake of vitamin C-containing foods but even this is debatable if she's eating healthily. If you are at all unsure about your intake of vitamin C when you are breast-feeding, if your baby is bottle-fed, or if your weaned baby doesn't have enough vitamin-C-containing food or drink, err on the safe side and give Children's Vitamin Drops or another source of vitamin C (see above) from the age of one month until the child starts school.

Vitamin D is present in adequate amounts in breast milk in fat soluble and water soluble forms which together provide the same amount of vitamin D as is found in most cows' milk formulae. It is also present in Children's Vitamin Drops. Vitamin D is essential for growth, for the absorption of calcium and the formation of bones. Rickets occurs if there is a deficiency of vitamin D.

The most important source of vitamin D for an older child or an adult is sunshine and a vitamin D-deficient mother can produce a baby whose body calcium level is too low. Infants exposed to bright sunlight need no additional vitamin D but others who rarely go into the sunshine do.

Vitamin E is a group of related compounds whose actions are still ill-understood. It is found in breast milk and cows' milk and recommended amounts for older children are easily obtained from nuts, peas, beans and green leafy vegetables.

Vitamin K is present in smaller amounts in breast milk than cows' milk and is essential for the normal clotting of blood. It occurs in green plants and is actually made by bacteria in the large bowel of humans. Deficiency is extremely rare in bottle or breast-fed babies after the newborn period. In a condition called haemorrhagic disease of the newborn a two-day-old baby becomes short of vitamin K. Such a baby will bleed from the bowel or from the stump of the umbilical cord. To prevent this babies are often given an injection of the vitamin at birth to maintain body levels until their own bacteria can produce sufficient. Rarely, the prolonged use of oral antibiotics in an older child can so destroy the bowel's bacteria that no vitamin K is produced and bleeding can occur.

Once a baby's diet no longer consists mainly of milk additional vitamins are not thought to be necessary but if you want to supplement your child's dietary intake by giving him extra vitamins, you can, provided you stick closely to the recommended doses.

Never give large doses of vitamin preparations not meant for children as this can be very dangerous. The Department of Health in the UK in a report published in 1980 recommended that vitamin supplements should still be available under the Welfare Foods Scheme either free or at reduced cost to expectant and lactating mothers, and to infants and young children up to the age of five years. They recommend that the dose of Children's Vitamin Drops be reduced from a range of two to seven drops to five drops per day and be given from one month until at least two years and preferably five years of age. Children's Vitamin Drops contain vitamins A, C and D only because all of the other vitamins are adequately supplied in cows' and breast milk.

The report recommended that all children should have an adequate vitamin intake, especially low birth weight babies, those who receive doorstep milk, and Asian children (and others who get little sunshine). Not more than one type of supplementary vitamin D should be given at a time because of the dangers of overdose. *Related topics* Immigrant children; orange juice; sunshine.

Vomiting Vomiting is by definition an ejection of stomach contents through the gullet (oesophagus) into the mouth. Regurgitation and chewing the cud are not true vomiting. Although most adults hardly ever bring up stomach contents, many babies regurgitate after every feed and others do so only occasionally. Such mild regurgitation of stomach contents causes no health problems and can be dealt with on a purely practical basis. However, any baby who has persistent or violent vomiting or vomiting with failure to gain weight needs medical attention.

In babies and pre-school children there are many causes of vomiting. They may be intolerant of cows' milk formula, cows' milk, or certain foods. Frequent projectile vomiting (in which the vomit lands some way away) in the first month suggests pyloric stenosis. In older children gastroenteritis or an infectious disease elsewhere can cause vomiting and less common causes are migraine, meningitis, encephalitis, poisoning, appendicitis, emotional shock, jaundice, foreign bodies in the digestive tract, abdominal injuries and travel sickness.

Speak to your doctor if you are at all worried as to why your child is vomiting, especially if he has: a fever; diarrhoea; if his tummy is blown up; if he is dehydrated (not passing much urine or wetting his nappy very little); if he vomits very forcibly; if he vomits repeatedly; or if there are any other worrying symptoms or signs.

Treatment depends on the cause and if your child's vomiting is due to an emergency likely to need surgery such as appendicitis, you should give him nothing to eat or drink at all. If necessary he'll be given fluid in hospital via an intravenous drip. If his vomiting is due to something less serious, he must still be rehydrated, so offer him plenty of drinks, preferably immediately after he has vomited. It doesn't matter if a young child goes off his food for a couple of days with the vomiting but his body needs fluids. He may prefer lots of small sips rather than a glassful at a time. Give any cold, clear liquids (ice cubes are nice to suck) or special solutions supplied by your doctor.

Most babies and young children don't need anti-vomiting medicine but your doctor may suggest some if he thinks it necessary. Never use anti-vomiting pills prescribed for adults because some of these can have serious effects on the nervous system of children.

Many medications can cause vomiting in babies and if your child is taking any prescribed medicine remember that vomiting will interfere with its absorption. Tell the doctor at once so that he can make alternative arrangements if the drug is essential to your child's wellbeing.

Always call your doctor as soon as possible if your child vomits black or bloody vomit, has severe abdominal pain with the vomiting, or if he becomes irritable or lethargic.

Sorting out the cause of vomiting can be a skilful business. By all means look at the list on page 739, but on balance it's wisest to let your doctor take the matter in hand. **Related topic** Recurrent abdominal pain (cyclical vomiting).

Walking The average age for a baby to walk is thirteen months, but the variation is enormous. Most babies walk somewhere between twelve and eighteen months. Some babies walk as early as six months, while others aren't walking until two. Early walkers tend to be those who are accustomed to lots of exercise which has strengthened their muscles (babies who are encouraged to swim very early on or babies who have enjoyed walking round in a baby-walker, for instance). Late walkers may be particularly heavy for their age; placid children who are content with sitting down and playing; or happy to get around fast by shuffling around on their bottoms, or crawling. Babies left alone a lot with little stimulation and encouragement may also walk late. Most, but not all babies crawl or bottom shuffle before they walk. Some learn to get around by crawling at much the same time as they first walk. A few walk first – they go straight from sitting to standing and then walking.

If a baby is happy to put weight on his feet, it's safe for him to do so, so if he likes pushing with his feet on your lap, or being stood up on the floor with you holding him, let him. By six months lots of babies take most of their weight on their feet when supported. Similarly, it's safe to put a young baby in a baby-walker or a baby-bouncer because if he's uncomfortable he simply won't put weight on his legs. Weight bearing won't make him bow-legged or strain his back. One exception to this can occur if your child has a congenital dislocation of his hip which hasn't been spotted. Weight-bearing could push this hip out of its socket, cause the child to limp and to have one leg shorter than the other as he grows older. If he has had the routine hip checks after birth and at the usual intervals (six weeks and three months), you'll have nothing to worry about.

Lots of babies enjoy being stood on the floor and allowed to 'walk' before they are old enough to pull themselves up into a standing position. Your pleasure in what he is doing will be infectious and will make him feel very proud of the fact that he's upright.

When your baby can sit quite steadily, lean forwards and twist round, he'll soon be ready to pull himself up on furniture (or on your hands) into a standing position. He'll sit down again by falling on to his bottom with a bump. When he's steadier on his feet, he'll start to move around the furniture, holding on and moving in a sideways fashion. When he lets go, he'll fall. Over the course of a few weeks, he'll become more and more adventurous and will try again and again to walk without holding on. With practice he'll manage first one step, then several, and soon he'll be walking from one person to another across the room.

When babies first walk, they balance themselves by holding their arms out sideways or in front of them. They tend to look like little drunks with swaying, unsure and staggering steps and huge grins on their faces. Most people are delighted to see a baby walking and the ready smiles that come his way encourage him to try harder and harder.

An illness or a nasty fall can put a baby back when he's learning to walk, but when he's properly recovered he'll soon get back to where he was.

If your baby walks early, he'll be into everything before he has any idea of what 'no' means. Magnetic or other cupboard and drawer locks will save time and patience, though they'll spoil the child's fun. An early walker needs shoes that much earlier.

If your child shows no signs of walking by eighteen months, have a word with the clinic or family doctor. The odds are that there is nothing wrong, but it's worth checking for any possible signs of physical disorder. Most babies who walk later than average are simply programmed to walk at that age. If your baby is pulling himself up to stand and is developing normally apart from the fact that he isn't walking, you can put off seeing the doctor until he's about two.

When a baby first learns to walk, you'll notice that he crawls if he wants to go anywhere fast. You'll have to stay with him when he's walking if you want to be there to protect him from falling against sharp corners but don't be over-protective or you'll make him frustrated and perhaps even reduce his confidence. Over the next few months there'll be a good many tumbles. As he becomes more confident, he'll be able to stop without falling over, then he'll learn to change direction and eventually to bend over to pick up something. Most babies enjoy their new-found skill so much that they walk around a lot when they get good at it. This activity can make them tired at the end of the day.

A walking baby can be very bothered by a bulky nappy between his legs, especially if he is on the plump side. If your baby is fairly slim, you may still be able to fold his nappy into a twisted rectangle, which is more comfortable for him. Don't put two terry nappies on together during the day because the thickness of four layers of towelling between his legs will certainly be too much. Disposable nappies are much less bulky but may need changing more often than terries unless you put some extra nappy roll or a nappy pad inside. Too much nappy between the legs can make a child throw his legs out round each other for the sake of comfort when he walks, giving him a strange-looking gait and making him fall over his own feet from time to time.

Children's feet tend to grip the ground they're walking on to some extent. Watch the toes of your newly-walking toddler and you'll see them curl down as he stands still. He'll be more stable and steady on his feet if he walks barefoot and there's no chance of a barefooted child having his toes cramped by shoes, slippers, boots, or socks which are too tight. To keep his feet warm inside, you may find that knitted bootees are just the job and fall off less often than socks. Both socks and bootees are slippery on wooden floors, ceramic tiles, vinyl, cork or lino, but safe on carpeted areas. When your baby is ready to walk outside on rough ground or in the street, you'll have to buy him shoes to protect his feet. Make quite sure that they are not only long enough and wide enough, but also high enough over the toes. If your child's foot looks at all sore after wearing shoes for the first time, take them back to the shoe shop. Shoes should cause no soreness at all and you mustn't be fobbed off with the excuse that they'll soon become supple as he 'wears them in'. Wearing them in may cause callus formation on his heel, toes or top of his foot or pain or soreness so bad as to cause bleeding. Shoes that are too tight or wrongly shaped can permanently alter the direction of growth of the toes, making them bent or even giving rise to hammer toes. Use your common sense when choosing shoes and take the advice of a fitter trained in measuring children's feet.

When you're out with your newly-walking child, a harness and reins may be safer than nothing if he objects to having his hand held.

When your child is confident on his feet, you can start teaching him how to climb stairs. He'll do this one at a time going upstairs first. He won't be able to come downstairs facing forwards for a long time. Running and walking on tiptoe will come when your child is ready. *Related topics* Bow legs; flat feet; footwear.

Warts Small growths on the skin. They are caused by viruses and can occur anywhere on the body. The commonest kind of wart is rough and yellowish and is found on the hands. They usually disappear spontaneously in months or years – no one knows why. Plane warts are flat, brown and smooth and appear on the face, neck and hands. Plantar warts (verrucae) are flat warts found on the soles of the feet and are painful when the child puts pressure on them when walking or standing. They are often covered with hard skin and so can be difficult to spot.

Verrucae are infectious in that if your child goes barefoot somewhere where a person with a verruca has been barefoot, he is likely to 'catch' a verruca by picking up the viruses. The viruses are particularly easily passed on in moisture, which is why swimming pools and bath mats are sources of infection.

Eight out of ten warts disappear spontaneously, which probably accounts for the 'success' of so many remedies. Some verrucae however, are difficult to eradicate and you may need help from your family doctor or chiropodist if your child's verruca is painful or unsightly. Surgery, liquid nitrogen and several other chemical applications are available on the N.H.S. and various chemical applications can be bought over the chemist's counter. Verrucae are most easily treated in their early stages while they are still small.

If your child has a verruca and wants to go swimming, it's sensible to cover it with a special water-tight plastic sock that can't come off. Ordinary waterproof plasters soon come off in the water.

Dry your child's feet before he gets out of the bath and put his slippers on before he steps on the floor or bathmat. Don't let him go barefoot anywhere until his verruca has disappeared and in the meantime keep it covered with a waterproof plaster so as to prevent reinfection from his own viruses via sweaty socks or other footwear. Have a look at the feet of other people in the family because someone may have an unrecognized verruca.

Washing children Babies don't need a bath every day but they do need regular topping and tailing to remain fresh and to avoid nappy rash and soreness in the skin creases. Many babies around the world are never bathed; they are oiled instead and keep remarkably clean and sweet-smelling. Our society has taken washing to its heart though, and if done sensibly it can be very pleasant for babies and children and is not something to be avoided at all costs.

Don't make the mistake of getting soap or water in a child's eyes, because that'll put him off for ages. Be very gentle when you use a flannel to soap him – it's all too easy to be much rougher than you think you're being, simply in an attempt to get it over with quickly when your child is wriggling. When you're washing his face, start round the mouth with a pleasantly warm flannel, then do round the nose and cheeks and lastly the forehead and eyes. Leave the eyes till last because most children dislike them being covered with a wet flannel and will try to avoid having the rest of their face done if you start there. Boil the flannel regularly or at least put it through the washing machine once a week to keep it sweet-smelling. Rinse it well after use and spread it out to dry so as to avoid it becoming slimy with soap residue.

Obviously the easiest way to wash a child thoroughly is in the bath with soap and water. Soapless cleansers are mostly detergent-based and can dry the skin. Some children are sensitive to them and may come up in a rash, though this is not common. Most children enjoy playing in the bath and a wide variety of bath toys are available. You can bath two or three children together quite easily in the average bath, unless one of the older children likes to stretch out and gets annoyed at being squashed. If you purposely keep the temperature of the bath water only lukewarm because you are bathing your baby together with an older child, take care that neither gets chilled, by heating the bathroom if necessary, not leaving them in the water for too long, and wrapping each up in a large towel afterwards.

Bath time for the children can be a pleasant social occasion. It can even be a time for relaxing if you stretch out on the floor while your children play, though you risk getting wet. Singing is rewarding in the bathroom because of the echo and amplification of the voices. Bathtime is a good prelude to bedtime and forms part of the bedtime ritual in many homes. While it's sensible to wash your child's face, hands, feet and bottom, if he has a bath every day there's usually no need to wash him all over unless he's dirty because he's fallen over or has got paint all over him, for example. Too much washing removes natural oils from the skin and makes it dry.

Make bathtime safe by putting a non-slip mat in the bottom of the bath. If your hot water tap gets scalding hot, a child might easily burn himself on it, so either make sure he stays up the other end or else swaddle the tap with a small towel. Be sure to stay in the bathroom all the time while a baby or young child is in the bath, because they can so very easily slip under the water, inhale some into their lungs, and not be able to cry for help. An older child can't be held responsible for a younger one in the bath – the responsibility is yours. Remember that a child can drown in just a few inches of water, so don't be complacent and don't think that just because your baby can sit alone you can leave him in the bath while you sort out the dirty clothes.

A few children take a violent dislike to having a bath and can be washed while standing up on a bath mat, though getting rid of all traces of soap is difficult. An ill child can be washed by giving him a 'blanket bath' – lay him on a towel in bed with another towel or a sheet over him to keep him warm, then wash him with soap and flannel bit by bit.

Sooner or later your child will want to wash himself. Encourage his desire for independence but make sure that he does it well.

A toddler or pre-school child who wears a nappy at night, or wets the bed occasionally, even though he's dry during the day, should have his bottom washed every morning if possible to keep him smelling fresh, especially if he goes to play-group where other children might notice if he smells at all unpleasant. This is particularly important if your child starts school at three or four.

When you go to the beach, for a picnic, or on long journeys by car, train, or coach, take a soapy flannel or J-cloth in a polythene bag or wash-bag to wash sticky hands on the way. Sachets or canisters of moistened wipes do the job very well but are relatively expensive. *Related topics* 'Topping and tailing'; water play.

Water An essential constituent which makes up two-thirds of our bodies and one which is present in all drinks and most foods your child will eat. Any excess of water he takes in is got rid of by the kidneys as urine, by the bowels in the motions, by the skin as sweat, and from the lungs as invisible water vapour in the breath.

Water is sometimes neglected by parents as a drink in its own right. Accustom your child to plain water and only give him other drinks from time to time. It's cheap and it can't damage the teeth or make a child fat. It's also more thirst-quenching that almost anything else. Whether you are breast- or bottle-feeding, if ever your baby gets thirsty or shows signs of dehydration, plain, boiled, cooled water is the best drink unless your doctor advises a special fluid to rehydrate him.

If the fluoride content of your water supply is low, you might like to give your child extra fluoride – ask your dentist what the concentration is locally and if extra is desirable. *Related topics* Dehydration; fluoride; thirst.

Water play Even during their first three months many babies love being in water. Your baby is most likely to take readily to the water if you hold him on your lap while you are in the bath. Make sure the water is neither too hot nor too cold and that the room temperature is adequate, then get in yourself and get your husband to hand your baby to you. Because he's with you, he's unlikely to be frightened as so many babies are in a baby bath. If he does seem upset by the experience with its echoing sound, steam and so on, hold him closer to you and put him to the breast to see if its familiar comfort will quieten him. You can play some simple water games with even a tiny baby by sliding him up your thighs on to your tummy, for instance, or submerging him up to his neck and then lifting him out of the water. See what pleases him.

As he grows older, he'll enjoy watching you splash the water with your hand, either in the bath with you, his brother or sister, or by himself. The family bath offers more opportunities for fun than a baby bath because there's more space to splash. A bath mat helps him stop slipping, but you must always hold him until he is sitting really steadily, and then you should stay right by him in case he topples under the water accidentally.

Colour, perfume and foam from time to time will all be appreciated and foam keeps many young children amused for ages.

Bath toys are fun for everyone. The ubiquitous yellow plastic duck has given way to ingenious wind-up swimming fish and frogs, spouting elephants and hippos that eat a fish! Plastic jugs, mugs and aprons, empty shampoo bottles (preferably with a little bit of shampoo or bubble bath in them), and even a boring old face flannel, can all be used by a baby to amuse himself, and if you and anyone else in the bathroom have a go too, it'll make bathtime even better.

Older children like to have a doll in the bath to wash thoroughly. Ships, submarines and harbours can all be improvised with a bit of imagination and there are even coloured sticks of soap with which the children can draw or write on their skin before they wash it off.

Water can be played with outside the bath as well. Your young child will like to 'help' you with the washing up because of the bubbles and the feeling of the warm soapy water. Give him a basin of warm frothy water and a washing up brush and let him wash up some plastic bowls, egg cups, mugs or wooden spoons. A colander is good fun to play with as he's washing up, as is a lemon squeezer. Dress your child in a plastic apron with sleeves well rolled up, or if it's warm, take off all his clothes.

The sand pit is a good place for water play in the summer, as is the garden generally, especially if there is a paddling pool with a hose pipe running and watering cans to water the flowers and each other. As long as you don't mind your children getting wet, and they are dressed accordingly, then they'll have the time of their lives. Bring them in to dry and warm up if they show any signs of getting too cold.

Letting young children play with water and containers of different widths and heights teaches them something about volumes – a tall thin container holds the same as a short fat one, and so on. You might like to grow some seeds such as cress or mung beans indoors and let your child water them every day. It's even more interesting doing this if you buy a bean sprouter and watch the roots and shoots being immersed in the dripping water as you water them. Such things teach them that water is essential for life.

Children almost always love playing with water. Painting is often enjoyed mostly because of the coloured water, the spills, the wetting of the paper, and so on.

It goes without saying that the sea and swimming pools are good places for children to enjoy the water. Swimming is only one way in which this can be done, so don't concentrate exclusively on encouraging your child to learn to swim but instead teach him generally to enjoy himself. The seashore offers endless opportunities for play, which is why so many young children are happy to play on a beach all day. Making castles with moats around them, dripper castles (fairy tale palaces made by letting very wet sand run between the fingers to make a spire) and interconnecting rivers and lakes will happily occupy both children and adults. The old fashioned bucket and spade are still the best tools but choose a spade carefully: cheap ones have handles which are sharp and uncomfortable to hold and often break sooner than more expensive ones.

If any of your family enjoy sailing, fishing or just messing about in boats, let your children have a taste of these pastimes if possible too.

Finally, don't forget that when there is any volume of water (even in a shallow bath or paddling pool) there is a danger to babies and toddlers. All children playing near water should be watched *all the time*: a moment's lack of vigilance could spell disaster. Older children who are mobile must wear life-jackets all the time near or on water except at the water's edge on a beach when they should be watched every minute.

Water is a wonderful plaything but has real hazards so think ahead and look for dangers. *Related topics* Sand pits; swimming.

Waterproof pants Waterproof pants save hours of washing of clothes and bedding, not to mention your clothes. Without a waterproof layer of some sort over his terry nappy every time it gets wet it soaks everything next to it, which isn't much fun when it happens several times a day. You can buy waterproof pants in all sizes and they are made from a variety of materials, some of various grades of plastic and some from close knit fabric. Not all are equally as efficient or long-lasting, and you may have to experiment with several sorts before you find the right one for your baby. Some aren't completely waterproof and the wetness leaks straight through the material itself after a while, though they offer some protection so are better than nothing. Some leak at the seams and others leak round the thighs if they aren't just the right fit. Some are made of material which cracks or hardens after several washes. It's best to rinse them through in lukewarm water with as little soap as possible, then to shake them, pat them dry with a towel and hang them up to dry away from direct heat. You'll need several pairs to last you through the many dirty nappy changes but you needn't change the pants unless they are dirty: being next to a nappy which is just damp or one in which the bowel motions haven't actually penetrated right through doesn't mean they have to be washed.

Some pants have fabric covering the elastic at the top of the legs. This makes them useless at night because the fabric gets wet and then wets the bed or pyjamas.

Waterproof pants are available covered in coloured nylon, with frills if you want, or plain. They come in sizes to fit older children as well, though the elastic round the thighs may be too tight for a child who is still in nappies at night at four or more. In such cases you could release the elastic or enquire at the chemist about larger 'incontinence' ones.

If the elastic round the waist touches your child's skin, it may cause an irritating red mark which will disappear when you stop using these pants.

An alternative to plastic pants which is cheaper is the tie-on dumb-bell shaped plastic cover for nappies. You buy these in packets and they can be used over disposable nappies or terry ones. They are folded round the child's bottom and the ends either tied at each side or in front and behind. They harden eventually after several washings but are very cheap to replace.

Some waterproof pants are made with a pocket for a disposable nappy and these fasten with snaps at the side.

Increasing numbers of mothers are using disposable nappies which have plastic outer coverings, so doing away with the need for waterproof pants. *Related topics* Nappy choosing; trainer pants.

Wax in ears Wax is made by the outer ear canal to remove dust and debris from the canal. It is produced in all children but the amount and consistency differ considerably from child to child even within a family.

Never poke anything down the ear canal to clean out your child's wax but simply clean away any wax you can see in the outer ear. This can be done with a cotton wool bud – you should never use a screwed-up corner of a towel or face flannel as this can cause infection of the outer ear and the ear canal. If you poke things into your child's ear he'll be tempted to try the same which could be dangerous.

An older pre-school child may have so much hardened wax that the ear canal is blocked, so causing a degree of hearing loss. If you think your child isn't hearing too well with one or both ears, tell your doctor. He may suggest you use ear drops to soften the wax and may then syringe it out in his surgery.

When a child has otitis media (page 445), the heat from the inflamed eardrum tends to melt any wax which then runs out. This can be confused with a creamy-yellow discharge from a perforated eardrum. Consult your doctor if your child is in pain or has a discharge which you are not entirely sure is wax. Any staining on the child's pillow in the morning may be a sign that there is a perforation. *Related topics* Earache; eardrops.

Weaning Weaning means getting a baby used to foods other than milk (*to wean* comes from the old English word, *weinian,* meaning 'to accustom'). It's generally unnecessary before three months at the earliest and your baby may be quite happy on breast milk alone for very much longer. The foods you give your baby should be well chosen and well prepared as they set the stage for his future health.

Babies have to be weaned because milk alone doesn't provide enough nourishment for them to grow and develop optimally after a certain time. However, giving your baby solids earlier than is recommended won't make him grow better, as milk (and especially breast milk) provides him with all the food and drink he needs in the early months. In fact, it's been shown that giving early solids doesn't affect the rate of gaining weight in young babies. Provided they have enough milk they grow as fast as they should on milk alone.

Mothers often start weaning their babies because they see other babies being given solids, and the spirit of competition among mothers is high. It's far more sensible though to wait until your baby is ready for solids – giving solids before four months has been shown to lead to allergic problems in some susceptible babies.

The latest report of an expert committee of nutritionists who make recommendations to the UK government on infant feeding suggests that solids shouldn't be given before three months. The same committee recommended that all babies should be breast-fed for at least two weeks and preferably for four to six months. Ideally, then, your baby should be fully breast-fed until he is at least three months old, when you can gradually introduce solids, cows' milk and other drinks. Because your baby is taking solids, there's no need to abandon the breast or bottle. Babies and young children enjoy sucking and it is still good for them both physically and emotionally.

Some babies in the UK are weaned before four months because they seem to need more than milk alone. Mothers of bottle-fed babies wean before mothers giving both breast and bottle, who in turn wean before those fully breast-feeding.

As many mothers discover when they're breast-feeding, their milk supply depends to a large extent on the amount of time during the day that the baby spends sucking – the more sucking, the more milk is produced and vice versa. When a baby takes increasingly more nourishment from solid foods and is given other drinks as well, he may spend less time at the breast, so the milk supply fails. This is a shame because breast milk is the ideal food for young babies and provides the right levels of nutrients in the right proportions, so it's worth preserving the milk supply by avoiding solids for at least until three months. Completely breast-fed babies suffer from fewer infections, especially gastro-enteritis and respiratory infections. They are also less likely to develop allergy in infancy or later and less likely to die from a 'cot death'. Early solids interfere with all these protective features of full breast-feeding, as does cows' milk formula, even if given only as complements.

Some mothers worry that babies not given early solids will become short of iron (anaemic). Breast milk has recently been shown to contain iron which is more readily absorbed than that in cows' milk formula, so a breast-fed baby takes more iron into his body than a bottle-fed one. The successfully breast-fed baby of a well-nourished mother has enough iron to last well into the second half of his first year without needing any solids. Because the iron in modified cows' milk isn't so readily absorbed (though there is more of it) solids should be introduced to a bottle-fed baby at some time after three months. If a baby was premature (and thus short of the iron that crosses the placenta into the baby in the last few weeks of pregnancy) regular blood tests may be advised by the doctor to make sure he is getting enough iron from his milk. Iron can be given if necessary.

One reason why early weaning is not recommended is that during the first few months of life a baby doesn't manufacture high enough levels of the protective substance called immunoglobulin A in his bowels and so if susceptible, he may develop allergies to certain protein foods. Once he is about three or four months old, it's thought that he makes enough of this protective factor to guard against food allergy. The breast-fed baby receives immunoglobulin A in his breast milk and this does the job that his own immunoglobulin A will do once he makes it in large enough quantities. The bottle-fed baby receives no immunoglobulin A from cows' milk and is at special risk of developing allergies to solids if given early. He can even become allergic to cows' milk protein and this early development of food allergy can, surprisingly enough, prime his body's immune system so that he is more likely to become allergic to other foods or allergy-producing substances later.

Immunoglobulin A is thought to work by coating the baby's gut lining, so preventing protein molecules from solids or cows' milk formula from passing undigested into the bloodstream. Without immunoglobulin A, these proteins could enter the blood and set up the formation of antibodies in certain susceptible babies, especially those from families with a history of allergy. Later, the protein-antibody complexes can be deposited at various sites in the body and cause the appearance of allergic symptoms such as asthma or eczema. The symptoms don't necessarily appear immediately after the baby has taken the responsible food – they may appear weeks or even years later.

The baby who is fully breast-fed for at least six months stands the best chance of avoiding allergy. The partially breast-fed baby who may be given a drink of cows' milk or some solids hours after his last breast-feed runs some risk of foreign proteins entering the bloodstream and setting up an allergy, simply because the immunoglobulin A coating from the last drink of breast milk may have been washed away.

It's important to stress here that comparatively few babies run the risk of getting food allergy, even if they are bottle-fed and have early solids.

Food allergy may account for more illness than we once thought, according to several leading paediatricians. Besides asthma and eczema, allergy can show itself as a chronic runny nose, diarrhoea, vomiting, colic, anaemia, cough, wheezing and rattling of the chest, irritability, and failure to thrive.

Another reason why early solids are best avoided is the possibility of coeliac disease, in which a baby is intolerant to the protein gluten present in wheat, rye, barley and oats. Babies with this condition don't thrive because the digestion of various foods they eat is impaired by the damage done to the gut lining by gluten. It's possible that the immunoglobulin A mentioned earlier may prevent early damage by this protein, though coeliac disease may develop later. Because it's wise to avoid any degree of malnourishment in the first six months of life when brain growth is at its height, experts advise that cereal shouldn't be given to young babies before three months to avoid the risk of them developing coeliac disease at such a vulnerable time.

How do you decide exactly when to introduce solids? Try to be guided by your baby. If in spite of increased numbers and lengths of feeds a baby of over four months still seems hungry after a breast feed, then the time has probably come to introduce solids. Similarly, try giving a three- or four-month-old, hungry, bottle-fed baby more milk to start off with and if this doesn't satisfy him, try solids. Appetite spurts between four and six months can often be satisfied by milk, so don't be in too much of a hurry to give solids.

Weaning is best done gradually, giving one new food at a time – perhaps one every four or five days – so you'll know if any food disagrees with him.

Satisfy his initial hunger and thirst with some milk, then give him some food. Give him only a tiny amount of food at first. Never force your baby to eat what he doesn't want or you may have trouble for a long time because he'll become tense and anxious about meals. Go at his pace. Show that you're pleased with him when he takes the food, and don't be cross with him if he spits it out and won't have any more. Milk provides his main source of nourishment for most of the first year, so there's certainly no hurry to replace it. By a year, many babies are receiving a good deal of their nourishment from solids but some are still uninterested and prefer their milk. To stop a baby who continues to want milk in a bottle from growing fat, dilute it with water. The baby breast-fed into his second year may get fat if most of his drinks are from the breast and he is also taking a lot of solid food, but this fat will be lost later – it's no longer thought that fatness in infancy (and in breast-fed babies in particular) automatically leads to fatness as an adult.

The easiest way to wean a baby is to let him help by picking up foods with his fingers, putting them to his mouth and finding they taste pleasant. Try letting your baby sit on your lap while you're eating, so he can reach out for the food you're eating. Alternatively, you can sit him in his high chair while you're eating, and put carefully chosen pieces of food on his tray for him to explore. Once he starts experimenting, he'll be keen to try again, and with any luck you'll be well away with weaning. Another way of offering food is by mashing, sieving or blending it and giving it on a spoon. The baby virtually sucks this food into his mouth like milk at first. Some babies are happy to be spoon-fed, while others are quite determined to use the spoon themselves from the beginning.

Remember that even young babies love to be sociable, and mealtimes are social occasions for most families. During the day, especially if the baby is your first child, you may be alone with him when he eats, but try and include him as often as you can when you and your husband eat. Babies often try to copy other children, and if they see older children tucking into their meals and using spoons or other cutlery to eat with, weaning will be easier.

As soon as your baby has shown that he likes his food, and if he is over six months, you can try him with food of increasingly lumpy consistency. He may spit it out at first, but try again, perhaps with slightly less lumpy food. It's been said that if a baby isn't encouraged to chew on lumpy food when he's ready to do so, he may develop the skill of chewing months after he otherwise would have done. However, don't be too concerned about this: some babies are not particularly interested in food at all – lumpy or smooth – till they are nearer a year old than six months, yet they learn to eat soon enough. If you hurry your baby against his will, you may make him anxious about eating.

Many people worry quite unnecessarily about the order in which to give different foods when weaning. The baby of six months is able to digest most foods the family eats, though he may have his own likes and dislikes. Some babies can't take foods such as egg white without being sick and if you find that a certain food makes your child sick, then steer clear of it for a few weeks. You'll soon notice that much of what you give him, especially vegetables and fruit, passes unchanged into his nappy, and this will be more noticeable when you stop mashing his food.

Introduce a variety of foods, one by one, so that he gets used to many different tastes. Babies thrive on all sorts of different diets worldwide, but the more solid food and the less milk your baby has, the more careful you should be to give him a balanced diet with sensible proportions of proteins, fats, carbohydrates, vitamins and minerals. It's interesting that children allowed to pick their own food from a selection put in front of them tend to choose foods which together create a balanced diet, so you can be guided to a certain extent by what your baby likes.

Using commercial foods in tins, packets, or jars is an easy way of feeding your baby but many contain added sugar or refined cereal products or both. It's sensible to give your baby the same fresh food that you eat and to avoid commercially prepared foods which are relatively expensive and some of which contain additives in the form of colourings, flavourings, emulsifiers, stabilizers, preservatives and so on. Though these additives are all 'permitted' some have not been adequately tested as far as side effects go, and some are banned in other countries.

A young baby eats only a very small amount of food at first and most of a jar is wasted until his appetite increases when he's older. You could store a half-used jar in the fridge for a day and give it for several meals running, though. This would mean that you'd be able to pin down any reaction to the food more accurately than if you gave several foods in a day. With dehydrated baby food you can make up just as much as your baby needs.

Even a young child needs dietary fibre – roughage – in his diet to prevent constipation and other problems developing, and the interested mother will give her baby unrefined food from the word go. This means using wholemeal (100 per cent of the grain) flour to cook with; buying or making wholemeal (not wheatmeal) bread; peeling and cooking fruit and vegetable as little as possible; and later buying wholemeal rice and pasta products. Sieving fruit and vegetables removes much of the fibre, so liquidize or mash instead. Don't be alarmed when you see the fibrous residue of fruit and vegetables pass into your baby's nappy – this is what should happen.

It's worth avoiding the addition of sugar and salt to your baby's food. Sugar is an unnecessary addition, providing 'empty' calories with no other useful food value, and causing dental decay. Salt can cause very real illness in a young baby, especially if too much is added, not enough fluids given and the baby also gets diarrhoea or a fever, leading to dehydration. Babies' taste buds don't need all the flavourings adults are accustomed to, so don't sweeten or salt his food to *your* taste.

Carry on giving your baby his breast or bottle feeds, but as you give more solids, give extra drinks of water or well diluted fruit juice to avoid thirst and possible dehydration. If you want to carry on breast-feeding, go easy on the other drinks, because your milk supply will fall in proportion as he satisfies his thirst elsewhere and doesn't want to suck so much from you. If you dilute real fruit juice with lots of water, you'll find that it doesn't work out much more expensive than squash and is far better for your baby. Once a baby is having a well-balanced diet and taking most of his nourishment from solids. there's no need to make him drink cows' milk if he doesn't like it. All the nutrients in cows' milk can be found in other foods.

Consider letting your child give up breast-feeding at his own rate – this is called baby-led weaning. Many babies will choose to be breast-fed for several years, though others give up spontaneously before they are a year old. Some mothers allow their babies to go on breast-feeding for as long as they want to but give them subtle encouragement to lose interest. During the day, for instance, they avoid putting their baby to the breast when he is miserable because he is bored, but play with him instead. It's usually easy to tell when a baby really wants and needs the pleasure or comfort of the breast and when he is simply demanding a feed as the only way he knows of getting your attention.

Your milk supply will last as long as your baby is still being put to the breast. Lactation doesn't last for a fixed time – it is simply dependent on the stimulation received by the breasts. If you wean your baby only to decide that you want to go on breast-feeding, you can get your milk back at any time (days, weeks or months later) by putting him to the breast frequently and by expressing or pumping your breasts as well.

Putting him to the breast is a good way of calming a sick or miserable child or getting a tired one off to sleep, so don't be in too much of a hurry to give it up. Babies also have an instinctive urge to suck and if you stop breast-feeding before your baby is ready, he'll find something else to suck like his thumb or a 'cuddly'. If you decide you want to stop before your baby is ready to give it up spontaneously, cut out a feed at the time of the day when he is least interested in the breast or when you have least milk. By cutting down on the number of feeds slowly, you'll have no trouble with overfull breasts. 'Drying up' pills not only have no effect on established breast-feeding, but they can also lead to unpleasant side effects, so don't take them.

Weighing It's important to weigh a baby at birth because it gives the medical and nursing staff a baseline on which to assess his progress. Most babies, of course, thrive but some don't and a failure to regain the birth weight or to put on sufficient weight may be the way in which a treatable problem, for instance a poor feeding technique, is discovered. Various medical conditions, some potentially serious, can also be picked up by a baby's failure to thrive noticed only by repeated weighing.

A rough guide to a baby's increase in growth is given during the last few weeks of pregnancy by the mother's increase in weight. If she stops gaining weight this, along with other symptoms and signs, might suggest to her doctor that her baby had stopped growing. A cessation of weight gain around the time a baby is due is often an indication that he is soon to be born.

A normal, healthy baby can be weighed any time soon after birth. He's weighed naked and his birth weight is recorded at once. The frequency of weighing in the newborn period depends on the custom of the hospital or the individual midwife, together with the baby's condition and the way he's feeding. Weighing a baby might superficially appear to be an easy task but it's surprising how often mistakes are made. A baby should ideally be weighed naked, but failing that the weight of his clothes needs to be known and deducted in order to arrive at a true weight.

A baby's weight changes throughout the day according to when his bowels and bladder are opened. Weighing a baby with a full bladder and a wet nappy one week and an empty bladder and a dry nappy the next can make a great deal of difference to the supposed weight change in that week. This is why more notice is taken of the weight change over a period of several weeks than from one week to another, unless a baby is obviously ill.

Test weighing (weighing a baby before and after a feed to see how much milk has been taken) is carried out on breast-fed babies in some hospitals that encourage schedule feeding or four-hourly or three-to-five-hourly feeds, with a restriction on the length of feeds and on night feeding. Many babies in such hospitals don't get enough milk, are hungry and don't put on as much weight as they should. Test weighing only serves to underline this point to the staff and the mother by demonstrating that the baby is only getting a very small feed but unless steps are then taken to teach the mother how to increase her milk supply by allowing unrestricted feeding, it's a completely useless procedure and only serves to upset the mother.

More useful is once- or twice-weekly weighing to find out whether a baby is doing well, bearing in mind that some perfectly healthy babies, however they are fed, put on weight only very slowly, while others with a slow weight gain may be in trouble. On balance, babies who are doing well and seem healthy and happy don't need routine weighing.

It is possible to hire scales for home use but it's far better not to because you'll find that you'll become extremely anxious about the whole question of your baby's weight if you have scales in the house and anxiety can make you produce less milk. If you think you're not producing enough milk for your baby, take steps to increase your milk supply and enlist the help and support of someone in whom you feel confident to give you well-informed information.

If you want your baby, toddler or pre-school child weighed regularly, the baby clinic staff will do this for you if you haven't any scales at home. If you or the clinic staff are at all concerned about the child's weight, you can consult the clinic doctor or your family doctor for advice.

Weight loss Most babies lose some weight after birth because the weight they lose by the passing of urine, bowel motions and breathing water vapour is greater than the weight they gain from colostrum. This weight loss continues until they are drinking enough milk to maintain and then gain weight. Larger babies tend to lose more weight than smaller ones (the average being 4–7 oz – 100-200 g), while low birth weight babies may continue losing weight for longer than heavier or more mature ones.

This weight loss is quite natural and is nothing to worry about. Breast-fed babies fed on an unrestricted basis by night and day from birth onwards stop losing weight when their mother's mature milk comes in – usually within a day or two. If a baby is breast-fed according to a schedule more suited to a bottle-fed baby, that is three-to-five-hourly, with few or even no feeds at night, his mother's mature milk will take four or five days to come in and his weight loss will continue for longer. Similarly, if a baby is too tired, apathetic, or weak, for whatever reason, to suck often enough, well enough, or strongly enough at the breast, his mother's milk will be delayed in coming in. Bottle-fed babies tend to stop losing weight on about the second or third day, unless they are tired, apathetic or weak, though even then it is easier for them to take in milk from a bottle than it would be from the breast.

The sooner a baby stops losing weight and starts gaining, the sooner the breast-feeding mother will know that her milk is satisfying him. If the weight loss doesn't stop, she should increase her milk supply by feeding her baby more often, day and night, and let him stay at the breast for as long as he wants. If her nipples get sore by doing this, there are several tips which can help her overcome this problem. Her baby should never go longer than three hours (from the start of one feed to the start of another) between feeds and many feeds will be even closer than that. Bottles of complementary cows' milk formula may stop the weight loss but they'll do nothing to increase her milk supply. Only if two or three days' real effort don't stop it should she consent to bottles being given to her baby. If she can produce enough milk to maintain her baby's weight, albeit at its lower level (than his birth weight), then she must be producing quite a lot of milk and can almost certainly build on this as described above.

If a baby starts losing weight during the first few months in spite of previously successful feeding, this may be due to a decrease in his mother's milk supply by her cutting down the number of feeds she gives him each day. The answer to this is to take steps to increase her milk supply.

Other causes of weight loss are diarrhoea and vomiting; whooping cough, in which most feeds are vomited up with bouts of coughing (try putting the baby to the breast to abort a coughing spasm, and in any case feed the baby – by breast or bottle – immediately after a coughing spasm, when he's most likely to keep milk down); other acute infectious illnesses – even a cold can put a baby off his feeds; and some more serious conditions. Consult your family or clinic doctor if your baby is losing weight unless the diagnosis is obvious and you are confident it's not serious.

Even healthy, thriving babies don't necessarily gain weight in a regular way and from time to time they may lose some weight. It's the average weight gain over a period of several weeks that is important, not the gain or loss in any one week.

Older children may lose weight during the course of an acute illness or a long-term one. Weight lost in this way is generally regained quickly once the child is well again.

Weight gain While the average healthy full-term baby has regained his birth weight by the tenth day after birth, smaller ones take longer and in any case the word 'average' covers a wide range of normals. Don't compare your baby with others but be guided by his general appearance and behaviour. If you are breast-feeding on an unrestricted basis by day and night, he'll regain his birth weight as soon as is right for him. If you're breast-feeding according to a schedule, or if your baby doesn't seem to want feeding very often or doesn't suck strongly, he'll take longer to regain his birth weight and you may have to increase your milk supply by feeding more often and for longer or by expressing or pumping milk after or between feeds. If you are bottle-feeding, he'll regain his birth weight sooner on average than if you are breast-feeding, though this timing is unimportant.

Some babies take several weeks to regain their birth weight and yet are quite healthy. Others taking this long might be failing to thrive. Each baby needs an individual assessment by the health visitor or clinic or family doctor as to whether or not he is doing well in spite of a low weight gain. The decision to put a breast-fed baby on to the bottle simply because of a slow weight gain is nearly always unnecessarily hasty. Experience has shown that such babies almost always thrive if their mothers are taught, encouraged and supported to make the most of their potential milk supply, and stop breast-feeding according to a restricted schedule. Having said this, there *are* a very few babies whose mothers don't make enough milk for them even with the best of help and after trying for several weeks. These are the ones who really do benefit from complements of cows' milk formula. Whatever breast milk they have received and continue to receive will have stood them in good stead.

The average weight gains during the first year are as follows: in the first month, 4-7 oz (106-200 g) per week; in the second to fourth month, 6-8 oz (175-225 g) per week; from six to nine months, 4 oz (100 g) per week; and from nine to twelve months, 2-3 oz (50-75 g) per week. These are only average gains and only one baby in a hundred is midway between the slowest and the fastest gainers. Lots of babies put on far less and yet are healthy and thriving. Again, it's best not to be over-concerned with weight gains but to judge your baby's progress by his general appearance and alertness.

The reason why babies are weighed regularly in some baby clinics is so that the health visitor and doctor can spot any who are failing to thrive. It is the average weight gain over a period of weeks that is being watched, not the individual gain in any one week. Babies don't gain weight regularly week after week – their weight may be static for a week and then show a rise the next. Also, most babies have growth spurts from time to time, during which their appetite suddenly increases and their weight rises correspondingly.

The average child gains about 14 lb (6·4 kg) in his first year, 7 lb (3·2 kg) in his second year, and 5 lb (2·3kg) in his third. After that his weight gain slows down considerably.

Some babies put on what might seem like too much weight. If you're bottle feeding, simply reduce the number of scoops of milk powder in each bottle by one, to give your baby fewer calories and never, of course, add sugar or cereal to the bottle. If you're breast-feeding, you may not easily be able to cut down your baby's sucking time without distressing him, but at least don't offer him feeds unless he seems to want them, and check that you're not putting him to the breast instead of giving him other forms of attention, just as an easy way of keeping him quiet when you're talking to friends or reading. Older babies often need something else, and if they're just put to the breast whatever they want, they can easily become too fat.

If your toddler or pre-school child seems to be putting on too much weight in that he looks fatter and his clothes are rapidly getting too tight, take a close look at his diet and eating habits. *Related topic* Obesity.

Wheezing A high-pitched whistling sound produced by air flowing through a narrowed air passage, usually worst when the child breathes out, though it can also be present on breathing in. It is not like croup which is more of a crowing sound and comes from the voice-box in the neck.

Wheezing is usually caused by a viral infection or an allergy (as in asthma). In children under the age of two years, bronchiolitis can cause wheezing, as can pneumonia in a child of any age. Asthma is the commonest cause of allergic wheezing but an allergic reaction to an insect sting, to a particular food or medicine, or to certain chemicals in the air can also be responsible. Some children wheeze after taking aspirin. Sometimes an inhaled foreign body causes wheezing.

Wheezing should be taken seriously because it always means that there is some underlying breathing difficulty. Wheezing can occur in a child with a respiratory infection *before* shortness of breath is noticeable, so if your child wheezes and has a fever tell your doctor as soon as possible. Any wheezing of sudden onset should be evaluated by your doctor unless you know your child has asthma and you are used to handling it.

The treatment of wheezing is primarily to enlarge the breathing passages and so to relieve the distressing symptoms. If wheezing is caused by a bacterial infection, suitable antibiotics will cure it. Asthmatic wheezing may have an identifiable cause which could be avoided in the future. Unexplained wheezing in a previously healthy child may mean a foreign body has to be found.

The breathing of wheezing children is helped if they are given plenty to drink and if a humidifier (even if only a boiling kettle somewhere safe in the corner of the room) is used to make the air moist. Of course if your child is a known asthmatic you'll give the medications as usual. A child wheezing with pneumonia will be more comfortable not lying flat but propped up.

Some young children are frightened by the noise of their wheezing and by their breathing difficulty. It helps them if you keep calm and stay with them. *Related topics* Asthma; breathing difficulties; bronchitis; foreign body; humidifier; respiratory distress syndrome; vaporizer. *Useful organization* Asthma Society and Friends of the Asthma Research Council.

Whining Unfortunately most children whine or whinge at some time in their first five years, and some do an awful lot of it.

Whining or whinging can start in babyhood, though few parents describe the fretful cries of a young baby or the plaintive 'uh-uh-uhs' of an older baby as either. Sometimes it's obvious what such a baby wants: more cuddling; more milk; more time to suck at the breast even though it's empty; his dummy; his cuddly; his mother ; the list is long. Often babies cry fretfully when they're tired. Sometimes it's when they're uncomfortable with a sore bottom or a tooth coming through. Sometimes they do it when they're bored. Sometimes they do it for no apparent reason and nothing seems to console them. This sort of crying can make a parent distraught very quickly if he or she is tired too. Strangely, it's easier to cope with a fretful baby if it's not your own – the noise doesn't seem to be so distressing. If you can stop a baby from crying or whinging, do, because there's nothing clever or positive to be gained from letting him carry on feeling unhappy, and any child who is making this sort of noise is unhappy, for whatever reason. Sometimes nothing helps but an unhappy baby is usually happier to be with his mother than without her, so even if he still cries in your arms, carry him round with you or sit with him. Simply by being with him, you're doing the best you can for him, which may help you if you're feeling at a complete loss.

As babies grow up into toddlerhood, it's sometimes easier to know how to cope with them because by then you know them well and can often pinpoint what is the matter. The frustration of not being able to communicate by talking fluently sometimes annoys toddlers, but the commonest causes of whining seem to be tiredness and hunger.

As a child becomes more independent and starts asserting his will more and more in family life, there will inevitably be times when he can't get his own way. Because a one- or two-year-old can't always understand explanations of why not (either because they're too complicated or because he's too tired), he may simply decide to whine until he gets what he wants. Children seem able to go on whining for a long time as though by constant repetition they'll wear you down so you say 'yes' to whatever it is they want. If you do give in, they're all the more likely to try the same tactics next time. Parents who mean it when they firmly say 'no' have less trouble than those who can be swayed. Letting your child know where he stands is all part of the loving guidance concept of discipline. If he knows that there are limits imposed on what he can have and do, he'll be happier in the long run.

Of course children get their own way with their parents' blessing sometimes. Because it's useful for children to know how to win people round, encourage them to understand that they're more likely to get what they want if they have a smile on their face and ask nicely (if they're old enough to know what this means) than if they whine incessantly or, indeed, at all. Giving something to a smiling child is much more pleasant for an adult.

Whining pre-school children are often bored, either because they haven't enough to do or because aren't self-motivated enough to amuse themselves. Boredom can all too easily set in when you're too busy doing things to play with your child. The easy answer to this is to involve the child in whatever you're doing or to set him up with something he likes doing. Everyone knows that this takes the patience of a saint sometimes, but it usually works. Whining is sometimes used as a protest when the child feels he's being shabbily treated. When adults spend too much time talking to each other and leave a child out in the cold, his whining may be a very reasonable way of telling you that he'd like some attention too. The older a child is, the more able he is to understand that sometimes adults have to talk to each other seriously and without involving children, and that at these times he must amuse himself. Young ones can't always cope with this, especially if there are no other children to play with or if they're tired or off-colour.

Whining can all too easily become a habit. If he's old enough – and four or five is old enough – explain to him that the noise of his whining is most unpleasant and that it annoys you so much that it doesn't make you want to do what he wants at all. Some parents are infuriated with whining and it's better for them to send their child out of the room or get some adult company to help them look after the child temporarily or just to give them moral support so that no harm is done. It's worth taking stock of the way you talk to your child. Do you ever whine at him? You may find that when you are nagging him or telling him off you tend to use just the same sort of whining tone to your voice as he does to you sometimes. Children learn by example and you may be able to help him stop whining just by acknowledging that you do the same and trying to stop.

Whooping cough An infectious illness which kills nearly half of all affected infants under the age of four months. It is caused by bacteria and is extremely contagious among non-immune children in close contact with the affected child. Spread is by droplet infection from the millions of tiny bacteria-containing droplets of water sprayed out as an infected child coughs, sneezes or talks. Whooping cough usually affects children under the age of four years but older children and adults can be infected, although they'll probably be much less ill with it than young children. Immunity conferred by immunization is, unfortunately, not life-long. This is why some adults get it from their children even though they had it or were immunized as a child.

The incubation period is between eight and fourteen days and the child is infectious in the last four days of this time before symptoms are apparent. The illness itself lasts for several weeks and goes through quite distinct stages.

In the first stage there are symptoms rather like an ordinary cold. In the second stage there is usually a typical, whooping cough (a series of short coughs followed by a 'whoop' as air is breathed in through a partially closed windpipe). Bouts of coughing occur any number of times throughout the day. A classical whoop may not be present in babies under six months. Children who have had whooping cough tend to whoop with ordinary coughs later – they seem to have got into the habit. The most annoying and unpleasant part of this stage is the vomiting that occurs during a bout of coughing. Such repeated vomiting can make the child lose weight because little food is kept down. It's best to feed him immediately after a whoop if you want him to keep food down at all. Some babies have to be treated in hospital if they are so ill that little food or fluid is kept down. Water and nourishment can be given intravenously, if necessary. When a baby whoops he may go blue as he stops breathing for a while and this can be very alarming. Rarely, this can even be accompanied by a convulsion.

The third stage of the disease is the convalescent one which lasts until the cough disappears entirely. Children with the condition should be isolated for twenty-one days from the onset of the coughing so as to be sure not to give it to others, though treatment with erythromycin can shorten the isolation period to seven days from the start of the cough. Cough medicines are useless but putting a breast-fed baby to the breast seems to abort many whooping attacks. Sedation may be necessary to allow the child to sleep at night. Talk to your doctor about this.

Whooping cough is a severe disease and can produce serious complications such as acute and chronic lung disease, otitis media and convulsions. The blood spots in the whites of the eyes caused by coughing disappear later. Most children today recover completely. If a secondary infection occurs then antibiotics are certainly useful. There is no specific treatment for whooping cough but the antibiotic erythromycin seems to shorten the course of the illness, lower the complication rate, and reduce its infectivity. Some children have a very mild form of the illness.

There has been long and heated discussion as to the advisability of having babies immunized against whooping cough. If all children born in Britain each year were immunized with whooping cough vaccine, it's been estimated that two would have a severe reaction to the vaccine with permanent disability (brain damage), a risk calculated at 1 in 310,000 immunizations. The balance of risks and benefits of the vaccine to the individual child can only be considered against a background of how large a proportion of other children is immunized. If this proportion is low, then the risk-benefit balance to the individual child tips strongly in favour of being immunized, because whooping cough will be more common. However, as more children are immunized, whooping cough becomes less common and it may be better for the individual not to run the tiny risk of side effects from the immunization. The dangers of the disease are certainly greatest in the first six months of life but immunization should also be considered for older children (who might not get it so seriously) because they could spread the disease to infants in the family in whom it is very much more serious.

There are five groups of children who should *not* be immunized against whooping cough.

1 Those with a history of fits (convulsions) or irritation of the brain in the newborn period.
2 Those with a personal or family history of epilepsy (fits).
3 Those with a developmental neurological defect.
4 Those who have had a severe local or general reaction to a previous dose of the vaccine.
5 Those with any feverish illness (especially a respiratory one). These children can be immunized when they have fully recovered.

Widowed mothers' allowance A state benefit paid to mothers with a dependent child or children. It is paid in addition to the widow's allowance which is paid for the first twenty-six weeks after the death of her husband. If your husband didn't pay full National Insurance contributions the amount may be reduced. Leaflet NI 13 from your local social security office will give you more details.

Widowhood Most of the problems of widows apply also to widowed men, but a woman bringing up children on her own has a more difficult job in many ways than does a man. Society generally accepts that a man will stay on at work and will provide a full-time nanny or other care for his children when his wife dies but unless a woman has a well-paid job this option rarely occurs when she is widowed. People accept that a man should carry on working and find someone to look after his children but find it more difficult to accept when a woman does the same. Most women are better off financially by leaving their children with a child-minder and going out to work, unless they have a very low earning capacity.

There are, of course, very real problems in finding good mother substitutes but as the remaining partner may *have* to work to support the family (even with state benefits) he or she will have to come to terms with what is available because the family has to survive.

A mother bringing up children alone after the death of her spouse not only has to cope with the actual loss and her mourning early on but also has to fill the roles of two people. On top of all these demands she'll often feel lonely and feel the need for emotional support. The main problem for any woman alone, assuming that she can cope with her family in practical terms, is that she'll find it difficult to make enough time for herself, especially if she is also working. It's also difficult to find the energy to go out.

As time passes the pain of the bereavement lessens, her husband is less idolized and other men stand a chance of matching up to him.

Practical considerations are bound to vary greatly from family to family depending upon the amount of money available. Some men die leaving large company pensions or insurance policies, thus leaving their widow with few or no money worries. Even so many women want to work, if only to meet people and possibly to find a potential partner. Women are rarely insured and so a widowed man can have very real financial problems as he attempts to replace his wife who was also a nanny, a housekeeper, a launderer, a cleaner, a cook and a chauffeur.

Children who lose a parent suffer too, of course, and they are likely to worry unduly about the health and welfare of their remaining parent. The under-fives need careful help in coming to terms with the death of a parent, though the younger the child is the less it seems to affect him. During their childhood both boys and girls need a male and a female figure in their close family experience, so it makes sense for widows to encourage male relatives or ·friends to spend as much time as possible with their children, and vice versa for widowers.

Lots of practical matters arise when you are recently widowed. Talk to your solicitor, citizens' advice bureau, health visitor, or your general practitioner to be sure that you are getting all the help to which you are entitled. *Related topics* Divorce; one-parent families; separation of parents. *Useful organization* The Compassionate Friends.

Working mothers Throughout history some women have always worked, children or no, but women are unusual this century in having to leave home to work. Leaving home is what creates the problems of working with young children, not the working itself.

Mothers of young children have many different reasons for working, including being a single parent; the need to meet other adults; working to earn money to buy extras for the family (or even essentials); working to stay on the career ladder; wanting to keep a valued job; feeling unfulfilled at home with children; and having to replace the earning capacity of an ill or unemployed partner.

Unfortunately in the UK, as in many other industrialized societies, many parents don't have an extended family to call on to help out with child care which means that they have a dilemma on their hands.

If you feel you have to work while you have children at home under five, your first priority will be that your children are well cared for in your absence so that they don't suffer in any way, physically or emotionally. Finding a suitable form of child care is by no means always easy and even if you find something suitable initially, it's unlikely that it'll be permanent, so you'll have to be ready to make alternative arrangements when necessary. You may also have to make contingency plans for what will happen to your child if his mother-substitute is ill and unable to care for him. This can happen if you employ a child minder, an au pair, a mother's help or a nanny, or if a friend or relative looks after him, but won't be a problem if your child goes to a nursery or crêche, except on the rare occasions when the establishment is closed.

Don't assume that just because the person you choose as your child's mother-substitute has opted to work with children, she will necessarily be as good at caring for them as you. The physical and emotional care and attention.

not to mention affection, your child gets from her may not measure up to what you could give. Mother-substitutes are like mothers – some good and some bad. Children are said to be adaptable, but they are not infinitely so, and anyway this adaptability may be at the cost of their optimal wellbeing and happiness. When you are lucky enough to find a warm, motherly, capable substitute, guard her like gold dust.

How children react to the absence of their mother or special person depends to some extent on their age. Many babies under six months or so are capable of being quite happy with someone other than a familiar person, but rely on their mother for breast-feeds unless they've learnt to take milk (expressed breast milk or cows' milk formula) from a bottle. There seems to be a period from around six months when they become suspicious of anyone other than their special person, however familiar that other person may be. Babies of over six months and toddlers like to have this special person with them all their waking hours and become more independent in their pre-school years if they've been allowed to be dependent on this person earlier. However, if that special person goes away from them briefly they don't seem to suffer any permanent emotional damage provided that someone else who is familiar to them, and to whom they are already attached, looks after them.

Children of over three or so are more independent and can manage without their special person for longer and longer periods, though they like to be based with her.

With any child, the effect of his mother's (or other special person's) absence depends not only on his age but on his personality, his relationship with his mother, and his experience of life to date. While most children if they could voice an opinion would probably prefer their mothers to stay with them, some children don't really have a good relationship with their mothers even though she is the person to whom they are most attached. She may actually dislike mothering, and show it, or her personality may clash with that of her child. These children may actually be happier with someone else who enjoys being with young children and relates to them well, once they have got to know and trust her and become attached to her. Other children can be as happy with a mother substitute as with their mother. One factor to bear in mind is that apart from close relatives, few people will be as committed as you are to the wellbeing of your child or will love him as much as you.

The length of the mother's absence is an all important factor. If she is going to be away at work full-time, she may see her child for little or even for none of her waking day. In this case, it's only fair that she realizes that he is going to form a close relationship with, or attachment to, the person who looks after him. Though she may give him plenty of loving attention on an individual basis at the weekend, or at one end of the day, he may come to prefer the one who looks after him. He'll have a conflict of loyalty when both the mother and her substitute are together with him, and that itself is unsatisfactory to some extent. The best solution is if the substitute is accepted as being part of the family and if the child is used to going to her or to his mother, depending on what he wants or needs.

If a mother is to work part-time then in a sense this is even more difficult for her child than if he is looked after by one person most days. His days will be split between two people and he may become confused as to who is his special person and will be unhappy about the situation. His mother may be too tired when she's with him to give him all the attention he needs, and may feel guilty about being away from him. Or she may feel she has to smother him with affection and attention, which is just as bad. Luckily some children cope very well with having two part-time 'mothers'.

Working at home can be an ideal solution as long as the child isn't neglected. Either the work has to be done when the child is asleep or content to amuse himself for longish periods or there has to be someone else there to share child care.

Working mothers often have to settle for less than ideal child care arrangements. The minder or nanny may not be the person they would ideally have chosen. The nursery may not seem to have enough experienced staff. The au pair may speak very little English and seem rather young. Much of this is inevitable, unless you are extremely lucky. The most important thing a mother gives up when she leaves her child with someone else is the ability to bring him up exactly as *she wants,*with her own standards, her own morals and her own ideas to guide him.

If you work, don't be afraid to step in and make changes if your child seems unhappy. Don't be afraid to give up work if you can't make the child care arrangements work either. Your child's emotional stability is worth far more than extra cash or even staying on the career ladder. Having said that, everyone knows at least one child who has a mother who works full-time and yet seems perfectly well-balanced – more so than some children who have their mothers at home. By going out to work you're certainly not automatically sentencing your child to spending his time missing you, but you do run the risk that you might be. And you'll probably miss him.

Some mothers stop work simply for this reason. Looking after her own child often makes a woman more likely to want more children. In countries where children are almost all looked after by nursery staff, mothers are deciding not to have more than one or at the most two. **Related topics** Child-minder; leaving a baby or child; mothering; mother's help; mother substitute; nannies; separation anxiety.

Worms There are several types of worms that can inhabit the human body. Most are found only in tropical parts of the world but some occur in the UK. With the spread of foreign travel and with our large numbers of immigrant families, a variety of worms is increasingly often seen nowadays.

The commonest worms seen in this country are threadworms. 'Human' roundworms and whipworms thrive only in areas where sanitation is poor or where human sewage is used as a fertilizer. For this reason, they are rarely found in the UK. Hookworms are only seen in the UK when brought here from abroad by holidaymakers and immigrant families. Tapeworms are usually the result of eating undercooked pork.

The 'human' roundworm *(Ascaris lumbricoides)* looks like an earthworm. Symptoms from this sort of worm infestation include tummy ache (or even colic or obstruction), fever, wheezing and shortness of breath, and even coughing up of blood. The variety of symptoms is because larval stages of the worm live in the lungs. The worm itself may be vomited up.

Whipworms are the same size as threadworms and the only symptom they are likely to cause is diarrhoea. Hookworms can cause itching where the larvae entered the skin. This is why it's sensible not to go barefoot in hot countries anywhere where there's the slightest danger of the ground or water being contaminated with sewage. They can also cause tummy ache, diarrhoea, and iron deficiency anaemia. Though a tapeworm can cause tummy ache, the first sign is usually seeing pieces of the worm in the bowel motions.

If your doctor has any reason to suspect an infestation with any worms other than threadworms, he will send a sample of your child's bowel motions to be examined at a pathology laboratory. There are effective drugs for most worm infestations nowadays, though whipworms can be difficult to get rid of.

Good hygiene on holiday helps prevent roundworm and whipworm infestations, bearing in mind that worm eggs are passed from one person to another via bowel motions. However, good hygiene on the part of kitchen staff who may themselves be infested is not always to be relied on. *Related topics* Pets; threadworms; toxocariasis.

Writing Learning to write is a very long process and involves many skills. Just being able to hold a pencil or crayon takes months of muscle and nervous system development, with gradually increasing strength, coordination and control. Your baby will naturally want to pick things up and play with them and all you need to do is provide him with encouragement and lots of interesting things to hold – any small objects will do. He'll hold a pen either with his hand in a fist or, when he's older, between his fingertips. If he has lots of opportunity to watch you writing or drawing, he'll want to copy you and will try his hardest to make marks. Let him have paper (even newspaper will do, or old cereal packets – it doesn't have to be good quality writing or drawing paper) and a biro, felt tip, wax crayon, coloured pencil, or ordinary pencil. Don't leave him alone to play because he might dig himself or someone else in the eye with a pen, or start marking his clothes, the walls, the carpet or the furniture.

Sooner or later he'll make a mark on the paper, and from then on he'll become more and more interested in doing more, particularly if he sees you or his older brothers and sisters enjoying writing or drawing. He'll enjoy simply scribbling at first. Then he'll use different colours to scribble, then he'll make less haphazard marks such as single lines and circles. Encourage him by sitting down with him and telling him how clever he is or by doing your own drawing at the same time. He'll enjoy taking over something you're doing and finishing it off in his own way. When he's older he'll become interested in colouring in designs you've drawn – colouring books as such are not as popular as you might think with most children until they're older, perhaps because the pictures are too complicated to be immediately appealing to one- and two-year-olds, who prefer simpler pictures, especially if they represent people and things they are familiar with. During his toddler and pre-school years he'll become better and better at drawing recognizable pictures and he'll put more and more detail into them.

The first word most children show any interest in writing is their own name, especially if they are shown it. As you write your child's name, spell it out as you form each letter. Don't make him try to copy it or put undue emphasis on it. When he is ready to take an interest in doing the same, he will. Whether he tries in pencil, pen, crayon or even in paint with a brush, this is his first real attempt at writing.

There's no need for your child to recognize letters before he starts school at five, but if you want to teach him as part of your play with him, then do, as long as he is interested and not made to feel that this is something terribly serious and important. A few children are so interested that they want to learn to write more than their own name. At this stage no emphasis at all should be put on the way the letters are formed. Your child's writing attempts will blossom under your interest, praise and encouragement and not with your minute criticism of letters formed wrongly. He has years in which to learn to write clearly at school. Now is just the time to foster any interest he has.

Children brought up in homes where letters, reading and writing are much in evidence naturally tend to be more interested in writing because they simply see it as one of the everyday things their parents do which they want to copy, not as something special which has to be taught formally. If you read to your child a lot, he'll already have got the message that words are interesting because they tell interesting stories. You can even point out the occasional letter such as the first letter of his name and say, for example, 'look, a J like J for John'. You can do this with writing anywhere, not just in books but on cereal packets, posters, labels on clothes, trade names on shoes and so on as well. The more experience he has with seeing letters used in various ways and in different situations, the more he'll become accustomed to them and gradually he'll learn to hold the shape of one particular letter in his mind so that when he sees it. he can recognize it.

A letter is simply a shape to a young child and all his previous practice of feeling shapes, drawing them, posting them into a letter-box, doing jigsaws and so on helps him look at a letter, break it down in his mind into its component shapes if necessary and reproduce it. Some children see and reproduce a 'd' as a line and a circle, for instance. Others are helped by pictorial descriptions of letters, such as a 'b' being a man with a fat tummy. With this sort of help you can make what could have been boring marks into friendly and interesting shapes which your child takes a pleasure in recognizing.

If you are thinking of teaching your child to write in any serious way before he starts school it's sensible to talk to the headmistress or the class teacher to see what they'll be doing. It's very confusing for a child who has been taught all capital letters to go to school only to find that his classmates who knew nothing romp ahead with small letters from scratch. Some schools would rather that the children started knowing nothing about writing (except perhaps for writing the child's name) so that they can start everyone off in the same way. *Related topic* Reading.

X-rays X-rays work by casting a shadow on to a photographic film and show up tissues in the body according to their density. A 'gun' shoots a tiny dose of x-rays at the part of the body to be examined after an x-ray-sensitive (photographic) film, has been put behind it. Some x-rays go straight through (where there is little tissue to interrupt them) and others are blocked by more solid tissue. The bones (very dense structures) let very few x-rays through and show up as white areas and the lungs (very 'open' and full of air) show up dark. Other tissues show up as intermediate shades of grey according to their own density.

Once the x-ray film has been exposed it has to be processed just like the film in a camera. After processing, the film is coded and stored for future reference. A radiographer is the person who takes the x-ray and a radiologist is the doctor who specializes in interpreting the findings.

The worry about x-rays has always been about their safety. Today's x-ray methods are extremely safe and deliver the rays only to the part being x-rayed. Even so it's important to put on a lead apron when you are holding your child during an x-ray just in case you could be pregnant. Because there could theoretically be a long-term health hazard from repeated x-rays in young children most doctors keep the number of x-rays done in the under-fives down to the absolute minimum. Similarly, because doctors are so aware of the potential harm excessive doses of x-rays could do to an unborn baby they keep their use to a minimum during pregnancy. The risk to a baby from one abdominal x-ray (to look for twins, for example) is tiny and anyway with the use of ultrasound many such x-rays are now unnecessary.

Having an x-ray isn't at all unpleasant for a child if you are there to explain that the clicking noises made by the equipment are quite normal and completely harmless. Needless to say there is no pain involved in having an x-ray but a young child may need to be told this specifically. A good radiographer will show the child the equipment and even an x-ray film before starting so as to put the child's mind at rest. *Related topics* Hospitals; ultrasound.

SECTION THREE

Medical action chart

If your under-five has something wrong with him go down the list on the next few pages until you find the trouble. The conditions are organized by areas of the body so that you can find them quickly.

This will give you at least one page reference and sometimes more. The first reference will take you further into the medical action chart in this section – the others will lead you to entries in the main part of the book. Any entry with an asterisk (*) is a main heading in Section two: A-Z of topics. Where the condition is almost exclusively seen in the newborn (nb) we have shown this as follows – Pyloric stenosis (nb).

We have tried to give some instructions on how to cope with the problems outlined but more details are usually to be found in the main part of the book. The action terms we have used need some explanation. 'Tell doctor' means see your general practitioner as soon as you can or phone him. 'See doctor urgently' means just that – or you could call an ambulance. 'See doctor at once' means as soon as is possible given the constraints of appointments systems and his availability – these are not life or death conditions but should be seen by a doctor the same or the next day. 'See doctor soon' means as soon as you reasonably can within a few days. *If ever you are seriously concerned, always err on the safe side by getting a medical opinion sooner rather than later as babies and young children can go downhill very quickly.* Except for where we have said 'See doctor urgently', you could consult another health professional such as a health visitor or a baby clinic doctor if you'd be seeing her anyway. Remember that baby clinics are not there to deal with emergencies or acute medical problems but if you mention something that happens to be going on when you take your child in a routine way, they'll be only too happy to tell you what to do. If they feel happy to deal with the condition they will and if not they'll suggest the best course of action to take.

Our experience with parents has taught us that books about child care are often difficult to use simply because most parents see a problem, not a diagnosis and have (understandably) no idea what to look up. They know their child has a red patch on his face but don't know what it could be. In order to be able to use most baby and child care books you need to know what the problem is so that you can look it up. In this unique medical action chart you simply look up the part of the body involved and find the heading that applies to your child. For example, if the child has pain behind his ear you look up Ear, pain behind, and you'll find a list of all the common things it could be. It'll also tell you what to do in broad terms and then you can look up the subjects in more detail in the body of the book. At least you'll know what to look up!

Remember at all times that a do-it-yourself diagnosis such as you'll arrive at can only be a guide. If you are in any doubt or if matters are getting worse, tell your doctor.

Topics covered in the medical action chart

● *Hair*

—Colour of

Usually of no significance – red-haired children more sensitive to sunlight and sunburn. White forelock with other hair normal occurs in albino* children.

—Hair eating* and twiddling

Nervous habit – tell doctor only if worried or large bald patches appearing.

—In abnormal places

Tuft on back – usually harmless. Can be a sign of a defect in the underlying spinal bone.
Tell doctor if worried.

Early development of adult hair pattern – see doctor soon – other signs of precocious puberty might be present.

Body hairy overall – can be normal, especially in hairy families. See doctor soon if worried.

—Loss of

Scalp rubbing in infancy – usually a sign of boredom* or unhappiness. Give more love and attention and don't leave baby alone in cot for long periods even if not actually crying. See doctor soon if still worried. Hair will regrow over bald patch.

Bouncing chairs – bald patch can appear for a few weeks if child uses a bouncing chair. Hair regrows – no problem.

Pulling hair out – part of nervous habit in older child. Child grows out of it. Often does it from boredom* or lack of stimulation.
Try to stop child eating the hair, otherwise no problem.

*Ringworm** – causes patchy hair loss usually with other signs. Patches on scalp oval or circular and enlarge as centre heals.
Patches covered with stumps of broken-off hairs. Needs medical treatment. May also affect feet (athlete's foot*) or groin.

*After a fever** – especially if very high.

After certain medications – (see your doctor soon if there's no other obvious cause and the child has taken medications).

— No hair

Normal – some children take a year or more to grow hair. Such children in fact do have some short hair. If no hair at all, see doctor soon.

— Objects stuck to

Food, sweets, etc – wash hair thoroughly and remove anything remaining with a fine tooth comb.

Nits* – tiny, white, oval, pearly objects. For what to do, see page 428.

Seborrhoea (cradle cap*) – a dry, scaly condition of the scalp producing flakes of scurf. For what to do, see page 153.

— Sparse hair

Can be normal.

Cretinism* – in this rare condition the hair is usually dry, thin, brittle and the baby may also have thin eyebrows. See doctor soon.

● Head and scalp *(See also face; eyes; ear; nose; skin; throat and neck; mouth, tongue and teeth.)*

— Bleeding scalp

After injury – see page 162.

As a result of scratching with nits*.

Itching* – from any cause results in severe scratching which can cause bleeding. Commonest causes of itching are nits; ringworm; dry scalp from too much detergent and shampoo.

— Discoloration

Birthmarks* – especially stork's beak marks and other transient marks immediately after birth. These are often at back of head at hair line, on forehead or on upper eyelid. Report any new discoloration to doctor at once.

— Dizziness/giddiness

Spinning around – no need to worry unless the child gets into the habit of spinning; if so see doctor soon. Dizziness goes soon after spinning stops.

Food allergy* – look for other signs of allergy. More likely if family history of asthma*/eczema*/hay fever*. Try stopping suspected food to see if dizziness goes. Reintroduce food to see if it returns. If yes, avoid food.

Low blood sugar – can occur normally if long time since last meal. Try giving spoonful of jam or sugar lumps. If giddiness goes, make sure child has more frequent meals. If not, see doctor soon. Also seen in diabetic children with too little food or too much insulin. Give jam or sugar to prevent a hypoglycaemic attack. Discuss with doctor why diabetes* is out of control unless cause is obvious (too much exercise, too little food; accidental overdose of insulin).

— Flaking scalp

Cradle cap * (nb).

Dandruff – wash hair more frequently with anti-dandruff shampoo.

Psoriasis – only a serious possibility if there is a strong family history or if there is evidence of psoriasis elsewhere (knees, elbows). Rare in under-fives.

— Headache*

Childhood infections – (especially with throat infections). Look for other signs of illness. Headache may precede the onset of the rash or other signs. Watch child for developments. Give paracetamol* and plenty to drink. Any fever* without obvious cause – see doctor same day.

Migraine * – rare in under-fives but can occur in affected families. One-sided headache with visual disturbances, speech problems or even weakness of the limbs. Rest child in darkened room. See doctor at once; he'll decide what to do according to severity of attack.

After a fit – normal. No treatment needed. Rest child and reassure.

Brain tumour * – rare cause but important.
Pain worst in morning and on changing position. See doctor same day.

After head injury * – usual. Give paracetamol* and report any change in level of consciousness to doctor or hospital urgently. Any sign of clear, watery fluid or blood from nose or ears, contact doctor urgently.

Food allergy * – family history of allergy* (eczema*, asthma*, hay fever*) usual, or reaction to drugs and certain foods known already. Stop suspect food intake. If headaches go, try reintroducing food to see if it was the cause. If headaches recur with the food, omit it in future.

Depression /anxiety* * – depressed and anxious children sometimes complain of headaches. Is the child normally active and happy? If not, see doctor soon.

Meningitis * – rare but important. Any vomiting*, fever*, neck stiffness, irritability, lethargy, or visual disturbance? If any of these, see doctor at once.

After medication – telephone doctor to discuss. Any headache *lasting more than three days* – see doctor soon.

Recurrent headaches – see doctor soon.

— Head banging*

Normal – stage in baby's play.

Neurotic – results from stress in family, neglect and boredom*. Prevent child hurting himself by using cot bumpers. Stimulate him more, play with him and give more affection. If he still bangs head see doctor soon.

— Head injury

Severe injury; any period of unconsciousness*; loss of memory; a fit; visual problems*; bleeding other than from scalp; black eye; problem with breathing or heart rate; persistent vomiting*; clear fluid from ear or nose; sleepy, irritable or lethargic child? If yes to any of these – see doctor at once.

If none of these – watch child carefully for next twenty-four hours and report any changes for the worse to the doctor at once.

— Head pulled back

Meningism – seen especially in children with a high fever caused by pneumonia* or an upper respiratory infection. See doctor at once.

*Meningitis** – often other signs too (vomiting*, lethargy, irritability, visual disturbances, fever*, neck stiffness). If any of these present with head pulled back, see doctor at once.

Injury – can cause certain kinds of brain haemorrhage – if history of injury, see doctor at once.

— Head shape

Lots of odd shapes – perfectly normal.
One side flatter than other – normal.
Flat back to head – normal.
Many children with oddly-shaped heads seem to grow out of the 'problem'; others' abnormalities are hidden by hair and yet others retain odd head shapes into adulthood.

— Head size

Normal – can be large, average or small.

Very large – could be hydrocephalus*. If worried see doctor soon.

Very small – microcephaly*. If worried see doctor soon.

— Itching

See page 713.

— Lump on

Caput* (nb) – at or soon after birth.

Cephalhaematoma* (nb) – at or soon after birth.
Neither of these is serious and both go spontaneously.

Bulging soft spot between skull bones (fontanelle*) – normal from time to time. If persistent, can be sign of raised pressure inside skull. See doctor soon.
If soft spot tense and firm – see doctor urgently.

Injury – normal after a fall. Children can get very large lumps after a fall and still not have a fractured skull. Apply cold compress or ice to area at once and watch child carefully for any signs of lethargy, vomiting*, drowsiness* or unconsciousness*. If any of these occur see doctor at once.

— Rash on

Ringworm*.

Nits* – bites of lice can look like a rash.

Impetigo*.

— Soft spots (fontanelles*)

Normal up to eighteen months. If still present after this, see doctor soon.

● *Ear*

— Boil in

Pain on moving jaw – may be visible in outer ear canal. See doctor soon.

— Deafness*

Hearing loss can be one-sided or affect both ears. If one-sided can be easily missed. If in any doubt see doctor soon.

Wax or foreign body blocking ear canal – see doctor soon to examine ear. Never poke around yourself.

Things that damage the nerves or the brain – German measles* in pregnant mother (risk is greatest in first three months); jaundice* in newborn (has to be quite severe to cause deafness* – see your doctor soon); mumps*; meningitis*; encephalitis*; certain drugs in pregnancy, or cytomegalovirus* infection in pregnancy (you may not know you've had this).

Glue ear* – very common. Child will have history of otitis media* in the past, possibly badly treated. Child may have speech problems* because of hearing loss. The condition may or may not result in permanent deafness*. See doctor soon. He may seek ENT surgeon's opinion.

The common cold* – can cause temporary deafness. No action is necessary. Hearing returns as cold goes.

'Flu (Influenza*) – no action needed. Hearing returns as 'flu goes.

— Discharge from

Wax* – yellow/ golden semi-liquid discharge. Clean out gently with cotton wool buds. Never screw towel corner in. Never poke deeply into canal.

Otitis externa* – crusty, pussy discharge. Leave alone. Ask doctor to clean professionally, then use drops prescribed by him.

Perforated eardrum – caused by otitis media* – pussy discharge down clean ear canal. Other signs of otitis media always present. See doctor soon.

— Earache*

Sore throat* – the commonest cause in this age group. Give aspirin* for earache if severe and see doctor at once.

Otitis externa* – pain is in the outer ear canal. Pain is made worse on moving jaw and there may be swollen lymph nodes* around the ear and in the neck. There may also be itching* and a discharge. See doctor soon.

Otitis media* – bad throbbing earache which keeps child awake at night. Young child may scream, shake his head and pull his ears. He may be ill, have a fever*, lose his appetite* and be slightly deaf. May also have vomiting*, irritability and loose stools. See doctor at once.

Foreign body* in ear. Child may have poked something inside. Look and remove only if it is very superficial. Otherwise see doctor soon.

— Foreign body in*

May be easily visible. Possibly pain on moving jaw or pulling ear. Possibly pus or discharge. Look to see if very superficial. If yes – remove gently. If no – leave well alone and see doctor soon.

— Lump behind

Fibroma – hard, solid-feeling lump underneath skin. Harmless. See doctor soon.

Lymph nodes* – fleshy but firm lumps enlarged with infection locally. Child may have fever and rash of German measles*.

Mastoiditis* – red, tender, swelling behind ear canal caused by infection in mastoid bone. See doctor at once.

— Noises in

Common cold* – transitory only. Go with cold.

Insects trapped in ear canal – clean out with cotton wool bud or see doctor at once.

Otitis media* – other signs of disease present. See doctor at once.

Air pressure changes in aircraft. Disappear after being on the ground for a few minutes.

— Pain behind

Dermatitis* – inflammation, itching and redness of skin but no tenderness. See doctor soon. Cream will cure.

Otitis externa* – other signs of the condition usually present. See doctor soon.

Otitis media* – other signs of the disease usually present. See doctor at once.

Mastoiditis* – other signs usually present. There is tenderness too in this condition. See doctor at once.

— Rash behind

Intertrigo* – skin red and itchy and superficial layers soggy and white. Wash clean and keep dry. Apply drying powder.

Seborrhoea (see also cradle cap*) – see doctor soon.

Measles* – other signs present.

German measles* – other signs present.

Fourth disease – unlike other infectious rashes, this spreads within hours to affect whole body and face. Harmless but tell doctor if worried.

Eczema* – may be the only patch on the baby. See doctor soon.

— Sticking out

Bat ears – normal. See doctor if worried to discuss plastic surgery.

— Wax in*

Normal – only clean with cotton wool buds superficially. In older children with wax blocking ear canal see doctor soon to syringe ear especially if deafness* is a problem.

● *Throat and neck*

—Choking*

Breath-holding attack* – in toddlers. Not really choking but looks like it. Rarely occurs without an audience. Child takes deep breath as if to scream, then holds breath. Face goes red then blue. May have convulsion* and period of unconsciousness*. Get finger over back of tongue early on if possible. If not stay with child while he comes through attack. Prevent attacks by avoiding precipitating situations.

Foreign body* – usually food. Never let children play with food or toss things in air to catch in mouth. Use first aid*. Beware of leaving young babies with small objects they can choke on. If no immediate result with first aid call ambulance.

Mucus in babies – some very mucussy babies choke and can't breathe well. Steam in room from boiling kettle; or fill bath with hot water, close door and sit with child in bathroom: both help. Decongestants from doctor can be helpful. See doctor soon.

Food/drink going down wrong way – usually transitory. Slap child firmly on back with him face down over your knee or lap. Cures at once.

Overflow of tracheo-oesophageal fistula (nb) – baby swallows milk which goes through abnormal opening into windpipe. If newborn baby chokes on feeding stop feeding and see doctor at once. Operation cures condition permanently.

—Cough*

Common colds* *and upper respiratory infections including croup**** – mucus produced trickles down throat from back of nose and causes ticklish cough. Moist heat (from commercial humidifier* or boiling kettle in corner of room) will help. Nasal decongestants from doctor good too especially at night to help child sleep. Cough medicine to be given only at night to allow sleep. Never use in excess. Cough reflex useful – do not suppress.

Tonsillitis* – other signs usually present.

Psychological – a nervous cough is common in highly-strung children. May be copying an older child or adult. Try to get child to stop by keeping him interested in things and by lavishing affection on him. Usually temporary.

Habit* – rather like psychological causes but child now not nervous; he's become used to coughing. Dry cough, as above. Goes on its own but annoying for parents in meantime.

Laryngitis* – other signs of the condition usually present.

Tracheo-bronchitis* – other signs usually present.

Asthma* – other signs usually present.

Foreign body* – could he have inhaled something? If yes, turn upside down, slap on back and see if it comes out. If not, call ambulance or see doctor urgently.

Whooping cough* – a special in-breathing 'whoop'. Can be very serious disease in child under four months and in the unvaccinated. If other features of the disease present see doctor at once.

Measles* – other signs usually present.

Irritant fumes – cause usually obvious. If not better within ten to fifteen minutes see doctor at once.

Pneumonia* – rarely a cause of cough in young children. Is there rapid breathing plus a cough? May follow a cold or 'flu by a few days. Tell doctor if worried.

Any coughing child of less than three months or any child who has been coughing for more than ten days should see a doctor at once.

Any child with rapid breathing, difficulty with breathing, or a fever lasting more than four days should see a doctor at once.

— Difficulty in breathing (See also chest and nose.) —————————

Laryngitis* – usually other signs of the condition present. See doctor soon.

Croup* – characteristic crowing on breathing in. See doctor at once.

Acute lung infections – usually other signs of bronchitis*, bronchiolitis* or pneumonia*. See doctor at once.

Foreign body* *in throat* – look for obvious cause in mouth and throat. If present, pull out with finger. If this can't be done easily turn child upside down and slap on back a few times. If this doesn't work try Heimlich manoeuvre or call ambulance.

Food allergy* – uncommon cause but asthma-like symptoms can be produced by certain foods in susceptible children. Try cutting out possible foods completely. Then if symptoms go, reintroduce the foods one by one to see if symptoms recur. If so, remove culprit for good. If severe in acute stages see doctor urgently.

Irritant fumes – remove child from source of fumes. See doctor urgently or call ambulance* if child doesn't recover at once in clean air.

Respiratory distress syndrome* (nb) – baby will be Caesarean* or premature*. Hospital treatment essential to save life.

Brain damage* – during birth can produce breathing difficulty in newborn. This needs hospital treatment.

Diphtheria* – produces breathing problems in a non-immunized child.

Asthma* – produces recurrent bouts of difficult wheezy breathing. Child panics, cannot breathe out. Reassure child, keep calm yourself. Tell doctor if first attack, otherwise give prescribed treatment. Ensure that child has plenty of oral fluids.

— Difficulty in swallowing

Food refusal – normal infants vary in their readiness to swallow lumps; food held in mouth then spat out. Don't rush solid foods, especially lumpy ones. Wait until baby is ready to cope with them.

Sore throat* – very common cause of child not wanting to eat. Look at throat yourself. Throat lining red; may be covered with tiny blisters; tonsils may be enlarged (red, fleshy masses of tissue at each side of throat) and pussy. If worried, tell doctor.

Cleft palate* – you'll know about this unless the baby is newborn. Get professional advice soon.

Micrognathia – a small, underslung jaw which makes sucking inefficient. If severe, special feeding methods needed. See doctor at once.

Goitre or a branchial cyst – swelling in the neck that can press on the windpipe and gullet. If your child has any neck swellings see doctor soon.

Brain damage* – some cerebral palsied children have swallowing problems and dribble saliva and food. See doctor soon.

— Hoarseness*

Sore throat* – cause usually obvious; tell doctor if necessary.

Laryngitis* – cause usually obvious; tell doctor if necessary.

Papilloma of the larynx – non-cancerous growth on voice box. Diagnosis can't be made by parents. If hoarseness comes on other than with sore throat or laryngitis, see doctor soon.

— Loss of voice

Sore throat* – other signs present.

Laryngitis* – other signs present.

Shouting or screaming – cause usually obvious.

— Lumps in neck

Lymph nodes* – firm, rubbery, tender lumps the size of small marbles are usually a response to local infection somewhere. If infection isn't obvious (sore throat. etc.) see doctor at once.

Goitre* – large, fleshy, soft swelling on front of neck. Can be present at birth. See doctor soon.

— Soreness on neck

Dribbling baby –often around teething* time. Wash area frequently, dry well and apply barrier cream. Keep damp clothes away from sore area.

Inefficient drying – after washing or bathing (especially in newborn).

— Sore throat

Infection – other signs present.

Laryngitis* – other signs present.

Foreign body* may be stuck. If you think this is possible, see doctor at once. Children can get soreness or pain in the throat after swallowing a sharp bone, crusts of bread, etc. This disappears within a day or so.

— Stiff neck

Draughts – cause usually obvious. Keep child well wrapped, especially around head and neck if he has to be left anywhere draughty. Warmth and gentle massage cure.

Acute, short-lived infections – some unidentified infections that come and go within a day or two can produce a stiff neck. Child usually not at all ill but if worried, or any signs of meningitis present (see below) see doctor at once.

Meningitis* – other signs present. If vomiting*, lethargy, irritability, head drawn back, or visual disturbance see doctor at once.

Meningism – meningitis*-like stiffness of neck seen in some children with very high fevers and in some with pneumonia or infections of the upper respiratory system. See doctor at once.

Encephalitis* – other signs usually present. See doctor at once.

— Webbed neck

A fold of skin behind the ear to the shoulder. May be part of general congenital abnormality. See doctor soon.

— Wry neck

Head is held to one side. If sudden onset, usually due to cold or inflammation. See doctor at once. If longstanding, can be habit, damaged muscle, or abnormal neck bones. See doctor soon.

● *Mouth, tongue and teeth*

— Bad breath (halitosis*) – normal in some children —————

*Gingivitis** – swollen, tender, bleeding, infected gums*. Usually caused by tooth decay but can be caused by infection with herpes (cold sore* virus). See dentist* at once.

*Fevers** – many children with fevers have bad breath. Usually a sign of dehydration*. Give plenty of fluids by mouth and reduce fever if high with paracetamol.

*Dental decay** – a common cause. Look at the teeth* yourself – any sign of discoloration or rotting areas, see dentist* soon.

Tonsillitis or enlarged adenoids* – other signs usually present. See doctor at once.

*Diphtheria** – other signs present.

*Bronchiectasis** – permanent lung damage usually caused by cystic fibrosis*. Other signs of cystic fibrosis usually obvious.

*Foreign body in nose** – look for obvious signs. One-sided nasal discharge? Never poke around. See doctor at once.

Sweet-smelling – breath smells of pear drops. This can be caused by dehydration* or starvation*. Lots of children have this during infectious illnesses when they aren't eating much. Give plenty of fluids. If child's breath smells like this and he is otherwise well, see doctor at once. It could be diabetes*.

*Appendicitis** – usually other signs present too.

*Sinusitis** – usually other signs present too.

— Bleeding gums ———————————————————————

Infection (gingivitis*) – swollen, tender, bleeding, infected gums*. Usually caused by tooth decay. See dentist* at once.

Toothbrushing – too vigorous use of toothbrush*. Always brush from gum to tooth – never scour the gums across with the brush.

Mouth breathing – habit, blocked nose, or abnormal jaw formation can all be causes. See doctor to sort out cause if bad enough to cause bleeding gums.

Drugs – some cause swelling of gums which readily bleed. See doctor at once, but don't stop drug until he says.

Blood diseases – a rare but important cause, especially bleeding diseases (such as haemophilia* and leukaemia*). If ever your child's gums bleed very easily see doctor at once.

Scurvy* – other signs usually present.

— Broken teeth

Injury – see dentist* at once. Teeth can sometimes be fixed back on or cosmetic materials used to make them look nice until they fall out naturally.

— Chewing the cud

Habit* – harmless but annoying for parents. Baby may need more love* and attention and less boredom*.

— Cleft palate*

Developmental (nb) – see doctor at once if just discovered.

— Cracks at corners of mouth

Normal – if lips chapped in cold weather. Coat lips with vaseline or clear lip gloss and stop child licking lips.

Vitamin B deficiency – uncommon. No harm trying commercial vitamin B preparation for few weeks. If not better see doctor soon.

— Crooked teeth

Developmental – see dentist* soon.

— Difficulty with speaking

Delayed speech – often caused by a hearing defect, an intellectual defect, cerebral palsy or a lack of stimulation. If you are already stimulating your baby a lot and he still doesn't speak when he should, see doctor soon for full assessment.

Cleft palate* – other signs present.

Stuttering*

Stammering*.

Dribbling

Normal – no problem. Wash skin gently and dry well. Keep skin dry with barrier cream so sores don't develop.

Teething* – from age of teeth appearing. Treat as above.

Cerebral palsy* – some of these children lack control of lips and mouth. Speech therapy may help.

— Foaming at the mouth

Fits – febrile convulsions* (high fever usually obvious) or epilepsy*. No treatment needed to mouth. Prevent child from hurting himself as fits occur. Leave mouth and tongue alone – you could break teeth. If first fit see doctor urgently. If not, deal with fit as usual. If caused by fever*, reduce temperature as on page 233.

— Hare lip

Developmental.

— Inflamed gums

Teething* – normal. Soothe gums by rubbing with finger. Gel also available at chemist. If severe pain, especially at night, give paracetamol* to allow sleep. (This should rarely be necessary.)

Gingivitis* – infection secondary to dental decay. Gums swollen, tender, sometimes bleeding and pussy. See dentist* at once.

Scurvy* – vitamin C shortage. Gums bleed readily around teeth. Other signs of scurvy often present. See dentist* or doctor at once.

— Loose teeth

Normal – first teeth lost after age five.

Gum diseases – usually infection (gingivitis*), see above. See dentist* at once.

— Mouth breathing

Normal – in some children.

Malocclusion – abnormal jaw or teeth formation affect the bite and keep jaw permanently open. See dentist* at once.

Nose blocked – by infection (colds and other upper respiratory infections). Mucus goes with infection cure.

Mucussy baby * – other signs present.

Mental retardation* – some severely retarded children mouth breathe all the time.

— Swallowed object

Accident – if small and not sharp – don't worry. Will come out in two to three days. If pointed or sharp (for example, a kirby grip) – see doctor urgently.

— Teeth discoloured

Normal – some families have darker or yellower teeth than others. There is no treatment.

Drugs – especially the tetracycline family taken in pregnancy or by young children under the age of eight. Yellow/brown discoloration can affect second teeth too. Some drugs cause breakdown of red blood cells in sensitive children. This can cause yellow/green teeth. See doctor soon.

Jaundice* – (especially haemolytic disease of newborn) can cause green/ yellow tooth pigmentation which can then affect the secondary teeth. Tell doctor if worried.

Dental decay causes discoloration. Yellow/brown patches over decayed areas – see dentist* soon.

After injury – a severe blow to a tooth can break the main blood supply so letting blood leak out into the tooth substance. This can eventually make it look darker or even black. Discuss with your dentist*. Action unlikely in an under-five.

White mottling – occurs with too much fluoride intake. Tell your dentist* soon.

— Teeth grinding

Habit – often at night. Can be normal or reflect anxiety. No treatment available. Tell dentist* soon to see if teeth are wearing away.

— Teething delayed

Normal – usually familial. Some families have teeth late. They always appear eventually.

Rickets* – usually other signs present.

Severe malnutrition* – rare in the West.

— Teeth present at birth

Normal – breast-feeding* quite possible.

— Teeth wearing away

Normal.

Abnormal bite (malocclusion) – see dentist* soon for opinion. Some problems can be corrected.

Teeth grinding – see above.

— Tongue coloured

Coated – white/yellow/brown – normal with dehydration* and fever*. Cure cause of fever, reduce fever if necessary and give plenty of fluids. Usually completely harmless.

White – curdy coating can be milk. If concerned, scrape away with finger: if red and raw underneath, this is thrush (moniliasis*). See doctor at once. Possibly thrush present elsewhere in mother (vagina or nipples, for example).

Looks like a strawberry – (white strawberry with red 'pips' or red strawberry with white 'pips'). Either of these is a sign of scarlet fever*. Other signs usually present.

— Tongue furred

Normal – very considerable growth and proliferation of normal surface structure of tongue.

Child dry – with fever or other causes of dehydration* Give fluids to cure and call doctor if underlying cause worries you.

— Tongue 'geographical'

Normal – this tongue has large deep fissures on it like a contour map. No treatment needed. No danger.

— Tongue painful

Food too hot – cure obvious.

*Thrush** – other signs present.

Mouth ulcers.*

— Tongue tie*

Developmental – underside of tongue attached to floor of mouth. No treatment needed.

— Toothache*

Food too hot/too cold – cure obvious.

Dental decay (dental caries*) – see dentist* soon.

— Ulcers in mouth

Aphthous ulcers – most go in a week with no treatment. If present for longer tell doctor.

Herpes simplex (cold sore* virus) – first attack of cold sores in babies and young children produces mouth and tongue ulcers, *not* cold sores around mouth. See doctor at once. He may use antiviral medicine, if the baby is severely ill with virus* in many organs of body.

● *Eyes*

— Blinking of eyelids

Irritation – fumes, smoke, cigarettes, etc. Remove child from source. If no immediate improvement see doctor at once.

*Habit** – harmless but annoying to those around the child. Child grows out of it. What originally made child nervous?

— Crossed eyes

*Squint** – see doctor soon or sight in one eye can be lost.

— Discharge from eye

'Normal' – common in newborns. Sticky eyes* are not really normal because there is irritation and possibly even infection present. Needs no medical treatment. Bathe eyes with saline as directed by doctor.

*Conjunctivitis** – other signs usually present.

Blocked tear duct – tears (pussy when infected) run down cheeks. See doctor at once.

*Eyelash inturned or foreign body** – remove gently if possible or see doctor urgently.

— Droopy eyelid

Congenital – usually harmless and needs no treatment. See doctor soon if worried.

— Eye colour

Grey/blue – normal colour for most newborns. Final colour can take weeks or months to develop.

Each eye different – normal. This usually evens out and eventually both eyes become same colour.

Red pupils – present in albinos* with grey irises.

— 'Flicking' eyes (nystagmus*)

May be present from birth or may develop later. Can be combined with visual problems – see doctor at once.

— Foreign body in

If small and easily visible, remove as on page 248. If not really easy get medical help at once.

— Hand movements in front of eyes

Defective eyesight – baby makes 'rubbing', circular motions with backs of hands in front of eyes but doesn't touch eyes. See doctor soon.

— Injury to

See doctor at once.

— Intolerance to light

Albinos don't like bright sunlight.

Fair complexion/blue-eyed children are often less tolerant to sunlight than others.

Meningitis* – if other key signs present (vomiting*, visual disturbances, lethargy, irritability, or stiff neck) see doctor at once.

Migraine* – other signs usually present.

— Itching

Conjunctivitis* – see doctor at once.

Blepharitis* – see doctor at once.

Measles* – other signs usually present. See doctor if worried.

— Oriental appearance of

Normal – in children of oriental or part oriental parents.

Down's syndrome* (mongolism) – other signs usually present.

— Pain in

Conjunctivitis* – other signs usually present. See doctor at once.

Viral infection – common with influenza* and other viral infections. Pain worst on moving eyes.

*Foreign body** – cause usually obvious. If you can remove it easily, do so; if not, see doctor urgently.

—Poor vision

*Visual problems** – long sightedness*, short sightedness*, astigmatism. Child may screw up eyes, rub eyes, look sideways at things, may obviously not see, squint, hold objects close to him or not be keen to read. See doctor or ophthalmic optician soon.

*Squint** – squinting eye's messages to brain get suppressed and sight may be lost. See doctor at once with any squint.

*Cataracts** – you may be able to see milky opacity of lens through pupil. See doctor at once.

Injury to eye causes temporary poor vision. If vision doesn't return to normal in minutes see doctor urgently.

Drugs in pregnancy.

Retinoblastoma – a rare tumour.

*Toxocariasis** – this dog or cat parasite can affect the eye. If at all likely, see doctor at once.

—Red eye

Normal – with crying*, especially if prolonged.

*Allergy** – often with hay fever, usually in the season. See doctor soon for treatment and advice.

Infection – white of eye usually red with conjunctivitis*. See doctor at once.

Irritation – immediately after birth with blood or amniotic fluid. Bathe eye with saline as directed by doctor. In older children fumes and gases can irritate.

Injury – rubbing eye persistently (for any reason) can make it red. Find cause for rubbing and prevent or cure. Any eye that remains red for more than a day after an injury should be seen by a doctor urgently.

—Red eyelids

*Blepharitis** – other signs usually present.

*Conjunctivitis** – other signs usually present.

Stye* – localized, inflamed, swollen eyelid, often painful and tense. Bathe with cotton wool or flannel soaked in water several times a day. If stye very large, or styes repeated, or if child has fever*, headache*, loss of appetite*, or lethargy, see doctor at once. Beware transfer of infection to others.

Seborrhoea (cradle cap*) – other signs usually present.

— Rubbing eyes

Sleepy baby – normal and only happens when tired and sleepy.

Visual problems* – see doctor at once if other signs present.

Irritation – with infection (conjunctivitis*), fumes, cigarette smoke, etc.

— Sticky eye

Common in newborn – caused by contamination and irritation with blood and amniotic fluid. Clean with saline (tablespoon of salt in tumblerful of warm water) on cotton wool balls. Clears in few days. If it doesn't – see doctor at once.

Infection – conjunctivitis*. Other signs present. See doctor at once for ointment. This cures in few days.

Crying* – some children look as if they have a sticky eye after prolonged crying. Cause obvious – goes within minutes of stopping crying.

— Swelling of eyelid

Stye* (see above).

Crying* – normal and short-lived.

— Watering

'Normal' in newborns. Disappears spontaneously over a few days.

Blocked tear duct at inner corner of eye. Tears or pus run down cheek when baby isn't crying. See doctor at once if you suspect this.

Allergy* in older children. Especially as part of hay fever*. Seasonal difference is best clue. Child may be known to be allergic (may have eczema*, or asthma*).

Irritant fumes/gases – especially cigarette smoke.

Crying* – cause usually apparent. Find cause and deal with it lovingly.

— White centre to eye

Congenital cataract* – see doctor soon.

● *Chest*

— Breast enlargement* ——————————————————

Neonatal (nb) – occurs in about half of all babies. May also have 'witches' milk' caused by mother's hormones. Always goes spontaneously and lasts longer in breast-feds.

*Abscess** – rare. Hot, tender, swollen lump in breast. See doctor at once.

Precocious puberty – may also have other signs of adult development (pubic and armpit hair, etc) – see doctor at once.

— Breath-holding* ——————————————————

*Anger** – after being corrected and/or a sign of frustration*. Try to abort attack by hooking finger over back of tongue. Be kind to child, show more love* and don't let him get frustrated. Ignore attacks: they're self-limiting and the child grows out of them.

After sudden fright – comfort and cuddle child.

After overbreathing – normal.

— Breathlessness ——————————————————

After running or playing – normal.

*Croup** – difficulty breathing in and other signs usually present. See doctor at once.

Obstruction to airway – difficult breathing, gasping, drooling, breathing with head forward – call ambulance at once.

*Wheezing** – difficulty breathing out. Asthma* is commonest cause. Treat as usual or tell doctor if worried.

Normal – infants breathe rapidly (fifty to sixty times a minute). At one year rate is twenty-five to thirty-five times a minute.

*Fever** – very common to have rapid breathing. Treat fever and condition causing it.

*Pneumonia** – other signs usually present. If after bringing fever down child's respiratory. rate is still high think of pneumonia and see doctor at once.

*Aspirin** overdose causes breathlessness.

Diabetes, severe diarrhoea*, and vomiting** – can cause metabolic changes that produce breathlessness.

The majority of breathless children need medical attention. If ever in any doubt – see doctor at once.

— Cough

See throat and neck section, page 695.

— Deformity of

Asymmetrical chest – can be normal but can also be caused by spinal deformity, especially twisting of spine (scoliosis). Tell doctor if in any doubt.

Funnel chest – usually congenital. Breast bone greatly depressed. May cause breathlessness. If so see doctor soon.

Pigeon chest – breast bone protrudes. Can be normal or follow coughing or wheezing* attacks in infancy. See doctor soon.

Projecting lower ribs – normal. No treatment needed.

Bulging over heart on left side of chest. Sign of congenital heart disease. See doctor soon.

— Difficult breathing

See page 696.

— Difficult swallowing

See page 697.

— Heart beating too fast

Exercise or emotion – normal.

Just before going to sleep – if under 120, no need to worry. If over this, see doctor soon.

Overbreathing – can also cause a fast heartbeat in children.

There is normally a small increase or decrease of the heart rate on breathing – this does no harm. With other irregularities of the heartbeat or if a fast heart is accompanied by shortness of breath, see doctor urgently.

— Injury to

Any other than the most superficial cuts* and bruises* should be seen by a doctor.

— Nipple discharge

Normal in newborns – at any other time, see doctor soon.

— Nipples (extra)

More common in boys. No treatment needed.

— Painful breathing

Injury to chest – broken ribs can produce restricted breathing due to pain. See doctor at once if you suspect such an injury.

Pleurisy – infection of the lung coverings. Usually complicates pneumonia* or the bursting of a bubble on the lung's surface, allowing air to escape into the chest cavity so collapsing the lung. See doctor urgently.

*Early pneumonia** – other signs usually present.

Any child with painful breathing needs medical attention at once.

— Pain in

Rarely serious in children.

Stitch – a stabbing pain on exercise (usually on the left), goes with rest. Harmless.

Behind breastbone – common with bronchitis* and colds*. See doctor at once.

At rib margins – common with hard coughing. Harmless.

One-sided chest pain – pleurisy or shingles. See doctor at once.

Injuries – muscle strains, bruises* and fractured ribs all cause pain, worse on breathing and chest movement. Local heat and painkillers help. Tell doctor if not better in a few days or if any new symptoms appear.

Hernia of the diaphragm* – pain worse on lying down (absent or improved on sitting up or standing). See doctor soon.

Any chest pain with shortness of breath, high fever*, cough* with blood in spit, or with severe illness needs immediate medical attention. Any pain under the armpit made worse by breathing – see doctor at once.

— Rash on

See page 714.

— Stopped breathing

See page 34 for diagnosis and action.

— Wheezing* (noisy breathing)

*Bronchitis** – other signs usually present. Keep room warm and humid with kettle boiling in corner. Keep child's fluid intake up. See doctor at once.

Bronchiolitis* – treat as bronchitis*. See doctor at once. In both bronchitis and bronchiolitis wheezing may occur before shortness of breath caused by the infection.

Asthma* – if first attack see doctor urgently. If repeated attacks do what you have been advised. Keep calm. Reassure child.

Foreign body* – could it be caused by an inhaled foreign body? If so, very unlikely to be able to do anything yourself. Get child to hospital or doctor urgently.

Emotion – some children wheeze when they're excited or upset. This is usually temporary and is of little significance. It could mean that they are potential asthmatics.

Laryngeal stridor – some babies are born with a soft larynx and wheeze or crow on breathing in. Goes by three or four years. See doctor soon.

● *Skin*

—Birthmarks*

Stork's beak marks* – on back of neck, mid-forehead and upper eyelids. Harmless, salmon pink patches. Disappear in a few months.

Salmon patches – salmon pink or red, at centre of forehead or almost anywhere. Disappear within a few months. Harmless.

Discoloration around buttocks or lower back – especially seen in Mediterranean, black or Oriental babies. Disappears, always by adolescence. Harmless. Sometimes called 'Mongolian spot'.

Strawberry marks* – rarely visible at birth. Fleshy, red lumps enlarge before disappearing. Harmless, but if around lips or anus can bleed – see doctor soon.

Port wine stains* – flat, purple marks anywhere on body. Permanent.

Moles* – hairy/non-hairy. Permanent but usually harmless. Large moles, those in prominent places or those that rub against clothes should be removed surgically – see doctor soon.

No medical intervention is necessary for most birthmarks but always tell your doctor if worried or if any birthmark other than a strawberry mark* enlarges.

—Bleeding from

Blood diseases – tiny pin-point bleeding capillaries. See doctor at once.

Injury – grazes* and cuts*.

— Blisters*

Rubbing – against a piece of clothing or a shoe, for example. Protect area at back of heel with sticking plaster. Keep clean and it will heal within a few days.

Burns* and scalds* – treat as on page 104. If in doubt always go to a hospital*. Any burn or scald bigger than the palm of the child's hand *must* be seen by a doctor.

Impetigo* – starts as a fragile blister* which breaks leaving an open sore. Yellow crusts or scabs are characteristic. Often starts with insect bite*, injury, eczema*, scrape or nose-picking. Remove crusts by softening with soap and water. Apply ointment from doctor. Highly infectious so keep sores covered.

Eczema* – other signs present too but eczema often starts as itchy blisters*. See doctor at once.

Plant contact – primula family especially, but some other plants may cause blistering. Prompt bathing of child and laundering of clothes removes most of the offending plant chemicals. See doctor at once if at all severe. Apply calamine to soothe.

Scabies* – other evidence of the condition usually present. Small blisters* between fingers and in front of armpits in babies not uncommon. See doctor at once. Only contagious for close contacts.

— Blood blisters

Injury – harmless – goes in a few days as blood is absorbed. No treatment necessary.

— Boils

See page 83.

— Bruise*

Injury – collection of blood in tissue. Harmless. Goes spontaneously within ten days. Cold applications help prevent them if applied at once after injury. After twenty-four hours hot applications help bruise disperse. If around eyes or in small of back after injury see doctor urgently. Always report spontaneous bruising to doctor at once.

All over body – see doctor at once.

Fracture* – other signs of fracture usually, but not always, present. Large tender bruise* may have fracture underneath. See doctor at once if you suspect fracture.

—Burn

See page 104.

—Dry

Too much washing – cause and remedy obvious. Use moisturizer if necessary.

Detergent – especially in form of baby bath or foam bath products. Use sparingly and only occasionally. Good moisturizer will help.

Sun – often with other signs of sunburn* or over-exposure. Keep skin well covered with screening cream and repeat applications to children frequently because they rub it off. Any good moisturizer will do to rehydrate the skin.

—Flaky

Psoriasis – silver, shiny flakes on affected areas (elbows, knees and scalp mainly but can be anywhere). Tiny bleeding points when flakes picked off. See doctor soon.

*Sunburn** – skin flakes off leaving red underneath. Don't pick it off: let it fall off. Soothing creams useful. Warm baths help too. Prevent sunburn.

After scarlet fever – other signs of condition present.

*Eczema** – other signs of condition present.

—Itching

Dry skin – from any of the above causes. Treat as above.

*Eczema** – other signs present. To treat eczema see doctor soon.

*Scabies** – other signs of the condition usually present but itching* can be first sign. If any scabies in family or intimate contacts, or any of the signs on page 517, see doctor at once.

*Sunburn** – soothing lotions (for example calamine). Warm baths. Keep out of sun for few days until healed.

*Bites and stings** – soothing lotions (calamine) or special bite and sting preparations are helpful. Prevent when possible. See doctor at once if bite or sting in mouth affects breathing or with any other over-reaction.

Drugs – see doctor at once if itching* follows taking of any medicines.

Fungal infections – especially ringworm* of scalp or athlete's foot*. Treat ringworm with drugs from doctor. See doctor at once. Beware of infecting rest of family.

Chickenpox* – other signs of the condition present. Put mittens or gloves on tiny babies. Cut finger nails of older children to reduce damage done by scratching. Soothing calamine lotion. Warm baths. Don't tell doctor unless worried.

Head lice – nits* may be present in hair. See doctor at once for special shampoo or go to pharmacist.

Urticaria* (nettle rash) – allergic reaction to many things. Itchy, red, raised wheals. Can be enormous (several inches across). Mostly caused by eating foods or drugs, or by skin contact with things to which child is allergic. Calamine soothes locally. Cold applications also help. If urticaria affects the tongue, causes a cough or difficulty in breathing and swallowing, see doctor urgently. If antihistamines don't work – see doctor at once.

Prickly heat* – other signs of the condition present.

— Peeling

Normal – in newborn for first two weeks.

Seborrhoea* – other signs usually present.

Eczema* – other signs always present.

Ringworm* – other signs always present.

— Rash

Can be localized or all over body.

Local rashes

Nappy rash* – treat as on page 410.

Ringworm* – between toes, in groin, on scalp. Ring-shaped, red, centre heals as rash spreads. Itchy, cracks and peels. See doctor at once.

Urticaria* – very itchy, swollen lumps on skin: scratching produces white wheals. Can occur anywhere. Usually after eating certain foods or less commonly from contact with plants, (nettles). Give antihistamines* if child distressed and apply soothing lotion (calamine).

Impetigo* – yellow/gold crusts; healing occurs from centre leaving reddened rings of skin. Usually on face, scalp or hands. See doctor soon for antibiotic ointment.

Eczema* – itchy and red with small blisters, anywhere on body. Dries and cracks with or without bleeding. Goes scaly and then heals. See doctor soon.

Psoriasis – silver scales on red areas over knees, elbows or scalp. Brushing off scales with finger nail produces tiny bleeding points underneath. See doctor soon for advice.

Seborrhoea (cradle cap*) – usually on scalp. Browny-yellow crusts all over, often worst over soft spots. May also spread to ears, forehead, nose, eyelids, and folds at top of thighs. Sometimes difficult to distinguish from eczema*. Responds to shampooing with special shampoo from chemist.

*Intertrigo** – seen only in folds (groins, buttocks, under arms, neck folds). Skin looks wet and soggy. Wash well. Dry well, using drying powder (available from chemist) and keep baby dry at all times.

Generalized rashes are much more difficult to diagnose sometimes even for doctors. The best thing is to read up the entries on each of the following – see which most fits and act accordingly. Consult doctor if worried.

Heat rash.*

Milia.*

Chickenpox.*

German measles.*

Measles.*

Scarlet fever.*

Roseola.*

Drug intake – relationship to drug intake often obvious. If not, discuss with doctor.

Purpura – multiple tiny specks of blood within the skin. Tell doctor at once.

— Red —————————————————————————

*Sunburn** – keep out of sun. Apply soothing calamine.

Sitting in front of fire – can produce red skin even through clothes if child is too close. Goes in few minutes away from heat.

*Scarlet fever** – whole body can look red but other signs usually present.

*Localized dermatitis** – red patch of eczema*.

*Measles** – other signs usually present.

*German measles** – other signs usually present.

*Urticaria** – other signs present and very itchy blotches.

Scalds and burns** – cause usually obvious.

*Birthmarks** – usually characteristic (see page 72).

Many rashes – see page 714.

— Splinters in

See page 248.

— Warts on

See page 655.

● *Face*

— Blushing*

Normal – in older children. No treatment.

*Masturbation** – some young children become very flushed as they rock to and fro and have a climax.

— Chapped lips

Normal – in cold weather. Stop child licking lips if possible. Apply cream, petroleum jelly or lip gloss.

— Cold sores*

Herpes simplex – virus infection around lips. Small blisters then crusts. Tell doctor if severe. Antibiotic ointment can be helpful and special antiviral solutions are available.

— Flaking skin on

*Cradle cap** – usually other signs present but not necessarily.

Skin too dry – see page 713.

— Hairiness

Familial – some families have lots of body hair. If your family is not hairy then see doctor soon about hair on your child's face.

— Lumps on

Spots and boils.*

*Mumps** – swelling in front of and below ears.

Injury – after falls and hits – large bruises*.

Asymmetrical face – some children have a lopsided face. Many become more even as they grow.

Bites and stings.*

— Puffiness of

Normal - after crying and screaming.

Hay fever* – intense itching, irritation and eye watering too. See doctor at once.

Kidney disease – if puffiness with no redness or discharge, see doctor at once with urine specimen in clean bottle.

— Rash on

See page 714 – almost any of these rashes* can occur on the face.

— Swelling of

Mumps* – swelling in front of and below ears. Other signs usually present. See doctor at once.

Boils* – may cause generalized swelling around the boil. See doctor at once if this occurs. Can be dangerous on face.

After prolonged crying* – some children get a puffy face.

Allergy* – often to something the child has eaten. Hay fever* can also make face puffy if severe.

Bites and stings* – cause usually obvious.

● *Nose*

— Bleeding*

Picking – can be just a habit. Try to stop it by keeping child occupied or distracted. Nose lining can be dry. Smear petroleum jelly* into nostrils (don't block them up). Stops irritation and child stops picking.

Injury – a hit or a fall, cause usually obvious. For treatment, see page 430.

Foreign body* – never poke around. See doctor at once.

Blood disorders – such as haemophilia* and leukaemia* sometimes first show up as repeated, difficult-to-stop nosebleeds. See doctor at once if your child falls into this category. These are rare causes of nosebleeds.

Acute fevers – such as measles*, scarlet fever*, chickenpox*, diphtheria* and influenza* can cause bleeding*.

Hay fever* – other signs usually present.

Enteric fevers – gastro-enteritis.* Other signs usually present.

Vulnerable blood vessels in nose – some children have very easily damaged blood vessels on the dividing part between the two nostrils. These may have to be cauterized to stop the bleeding.

— Broken

Injury – may be obvious deformity but always pain, swelling and tenderness that gets worse with time. May also be bruising around nose and eyes. See doctor urgently if in doubt.

— Discharge from

Watery – colds* and mucus in babies. Treat accordingly.

Pussy – colds*, influenza* and other upper respiratory infections with secondary bacterial infection. See doctor at once if child unwell. Most get better spontaneously with no antibiotics*. Humidify air and keep child warm.

*Foreign body** – foul-smelling discharge from one nostril possibly caused by something stuck up nose some time before. See doctor at once.

— Food coming back through

Normal – if baby splutters and coughs on feed.

*Cleft palate** – may be other signs too. If not sure, always see doctor at once.

— Foreign body* in

In child over five try closing other nostril and getting child to blow out. If no success see doctor at once. Child under five – take to doctor at once. Do nothing yourself.

— Picking

*Habit** – stop by distracting child and keeping him busy.

Dry nose lining. Smear with petroleum jelly* to reduce irritation.

— Running

Common cold.*

*Hay fever** – seasonal (most of summer). Other signs present.

Childhood infections – measles*, chickenpox*, etc.

Foreign body in* – often runny before pus (sometimes bloodstained) develops.

*Sinusitis** – other signs present.

*Skull fracture** – pale, watery fluid (not mucus) after head injury in otherwise well child. See doctor urgently.

—Sneezing*

Hay fever* – other signs usually present.

Foreign body* – if this is the only sign see doctor at once.

Common cold* – treat yourself.

Measles * – other signs usually present.

—Snoring

Normal – can be positional.

Enlarged adenoids – see doctor soon. You may be able to see large swellings at the back of your child's throat in a good light.

—Snuffling

Normal.

After crying*.

'Mucussy' baby*.

● Girl's sex organs

—Bruising

From falls – see doctor at once if severe.

Sexual abuse or other non-accidental injury must be considered. Contact doctor, health visitor, social worker, or NSPCC at once.

—Bleeding from

Normal during first two weeks of life. Caused by mother's hormones still present in baby after birth having crossed placenta.

Precocious puberty – bleeding can begin at five. This is really a very early period. See doctor at once.

Injury – foreign body* stuck in vagina. Wounds heal well. Tell doctor only if bleeding persistent.

Girls whose mothers received diethylstilboestrol during pregnancy may have a deformity of the vagina that causes bleeding.

—Discharge from

Normal – small amount of clear or pale mucussy fluid.

Foreign body* – girls sometimes put things into their vaginas either when alone or playing with others. Can go for weeks unnoticed and forgotten. If you suspect a foreign body ask the child and see doctor at once.

Thrush* – white, curdy substance like cheese on red base. Causing itching. See doctor at once.

Gonorrhoea* – other signs usually present. See doctor at once especially if you or your partner has the condition. Young girls can contract it from their parents via an infected towel, if not from sexual contact.

— Itching*

Poor hygiene – a girl's vulva needs washing regularly. Apply bland cream (zinc and castor oil) before nappy or pants.

Thrush* – white, curdy discharge. See doctor at once.

Threadworms* – sometimes visible around back passage at night or in early morning. See doctor at once.

— Nappy rash

Can extend from the buttocks behind to involve the vulval area in front.

Poorly washed nappies – detergent irritates and causes rash. Cure obvious.

Chafing nappy – child left in nappy too long.

Thrush*/eczema*/psoriasis/seborrhoea.

— Too big

'Constitutional' – some normal girls have a large vulva.

Cretinism* – a feature of this condition. Other signs always present.

Tumours of adrenal gland – produce sex hormones at the wrong time of life. See doctor at once.

● *Boy's sex organs*

— Penis caught in zip

Accidental – cut bottom of zip and undo from bottom. Any other approach painful and dangerous.

— Erections*

Normal – especially with full bladder, even in babies. Ignore.

— Inflammation

Balanitis* Improve hygiene. Wash penis frequently. Pull back foreskin as far as it will *easily* go. Wash well and apply bland cream (zinc and castor oil). See doctor at once if this doesn't cure within a few days.

— Nappy rash* (see above)

— No testes

On one or both sides.

Absent – see doctor at once.

Pop up and down – don't worry. Perfectly normal.

— Pain in testes

Injury – cause usually obvious.

*Mumps** – other signs present.

*Chickenpox** – other signs present.

*Scarlet fever** – other signs present.

— Penis bent

*Hypospadias** – baby passes urine from under-side of penis and not end. See doctor soon.

— Tight foreskin*

Normal – leave alone unless it balloons out when passing water. If so, see doctor soon. If foreskin won't go back after being pulled back, see doctor urgently.

Pin hole opening – see doctor at once.

— Too big scrotum

Temporarily swollen immediately after birth – normal. Subsides quickly.

*Hydrocele** – one-sided swelling. Usually subsides untreated.

Hernia in groin* – usually groin swelling obvious. See doctor at once.

— Too small scrotum

Very rare – see doctor if worried.

— Urine coming from wrong place

*Hypospadias** – see doctor at once.

● *Nails*

—Absent

Developmental – discuss with doctor soon.

—Bitten

Nervousness*/boredom* – try to remedy reasons.

Too long/annoying – cut regularly. Keep short.

Habit.

—Ingrowing

Poor nail care* – see page 400.

Bad shoes* – ensure shoes plenty big enough not to cramp toes.

—Malformed

Developmental – many babies have odd-looking nails* which become quite normal over the first year or so of life. See doctor soon if worried.

—Ridged

Fevers* – ridges correspond to high fevers. Ridges grow out slowly. Harmless.

—Splinters* under

Accidental – get doctor to remove unless there's a big and easily-grasped piece to pull on with tweezers.

—White flecks in

Probably nutritional – no one knows what causes them but a shortage of foods containing zinc has been suggested. Get child to eat more herrings, bran, oatmeal, pork, liver, milk, nuts and wheat germ, all of which are rich in zinc.

Injury.

● *Back*

—Defects of

Spina bifida* – other signs present.

—Hair on

Normal – in hairy families.

Vertebral abnormality – a tuft of hair at the base of the spine may be the only outward sign. See doctor soon.

—Pain in

Viral infections – commonly cause an aching back: influenza* and the common cold* especially. Treat accordingly.

Spinal disease – rare. If you suspect this see doctor at once.

Injury – usually self-limiting and goes quickly in under-fives. If still present after three days tell doctor at once. Any serious back pain after injury should be notified to a doctor as an emergency.

Kidney infections – pain high up in back on one or both sides of spine. See doctor at once. Child may have signs of nephritis*.

—Rash on

See page 714.

—Round shoulders

Poor posture*.

—Twisted

Postural – see doctor soon to discuss.

One leg shorter than other – don't bother measuring. See doctor at once.

*After poliomyelitis** – you'll know that your child has had the condition.

A very asymmetrical chest – this can be a developmental abnormality that causes little other trouble. See doctor soon to discuss.

● *Urinary system*

—Abnormal coloured urine

Pale – dilute – drinking plenty of fluids. Diabetes* produces lots of pale urine. See doctor at once if you suspect diabetes. If child is always thirsty and losing weight too, see doctor at once.

Dark – concentrated because of drinking too little or with a fever.
May contain blood (see blood in urine, below).
May stain nappy pink if urine contains lots of phosphates. Harmless. Do nothing.

Orange – can be caused by bile pigments, senna in laxatives* or rhubarb. See doctor at once.

Red – after beetroot or blackberries and some dye-containing sweets*. Normal. No treatment needed.

— Bedwetting* (or wetting clothes in day) —

Control not yet developed – normal at certain ages.

Emotional stress – can cause wetting even in a usually dry child.

*Petit mal epilepsy** – other signs usually present.

*Urinary infections** – other signs usually present.

Abnormalities of the urinary system – can produce constant dribbling rather than involuntary release of urine. See doctor soon to discuss.

— Blood in urine

*Ulcers with nappy rash** – change nappy more often. Wash well and keep bottom as dry as possible. Use barrier cream.

*Nephritis** – other signs usually present. Blood mixed with urine.

Bleeding diseases – blood appears as part of a disease such as haemophilia*.

Injury to urethra caused by poking things into it or to kidney after serious accident.

— Not passing urine

Holding back urine – dislike of lavatory * when away from familiar one at home.

Post-operatively – common, especially after an abdominal operation.

After serious injury – see doctor urgently.

*After a blood transfusion** – see doctor urgently.

At onset of nephritis.*

— Pain in loin (small of back)

Kidney stone – rare under five. Pain comes and goes in waves. Very severe. May travel to groin. See doctor urgently.

*Urinary infection** – other signs present. See doctor at once.

— Pain on passing urine

Urethritis – usually caused by gonorrhoea* caught from parent. Mother may not know she has it – see doctor at once.

Any discharge from urinary passage or persistent pain or irritation – see doctor at once.

Ulcer at opening of urethra – see doctor at once.

Always see doctor at once if a child cries or complains on passing water. See if crying is before, during or after passing water. Many babies cry just before as a signal. Sometimes the pain is caused by local inflammation of the vulva or penis caused by poor hygiene. Wash regularly and apply bland cream to cure.

— Passing too much urine

Diabetes* – child also thirsty and losing weight. See doctor at once. Child passes urine in large volumes and too often.

Longstanding kidney disease – you'll know if your child has one of these.

Compulsive drinking – usually needs no treatment but discuss with doctor if worried.

— Passing urine too often

Cold weather – normal.

Anxiety* – normal.

Nervousness*.

Urinary infections including cystitis* – other signs present. See doctor at once.

Diabetes* – child passes too much urine too often. Child also loses weight and drinks too much. See doctor at once.

Papilloma (wart) of bladder – may also produce urine. See doctor at once.

Appendicitis* – other signs usually present. See doctor urgently.

Compulsive drinking – see doctor soon if worried.

— Smelly urine

Strong, concentrated urine – can smell nasty. Give child lots to drink. This can occur especially with fevers* or diarrhoea* when child loses lots of water and isn't drinking enough.

Normal urine has a faint smell which is normal. Some children have smelly urine after certain foods.

Ammonia – produced by bacterial action in nappies. Can be very strong and make your eyes water. Change nappies more frequently and keep baby's bottom clean, washed and covered with barrier cream to prevent rash.

Fishy smell – tells you there may be infection in urine from kidney or bladder. See doctor with urine specimen in clean bottle soon, or urgently if child feverish or ill.

— Urine coming from wrong place

Hypospadias* – in boy with urine coming from under-side of penis. See doctor at once.

● *Arm and hand*

— Blue fingers

Cold weather – cure obvious.

Congenital heart disease* – you may already know about this. If child short of breath with blue fingers see doctor at once.

— Extra fingers

Developmental – see doctor soon. Easily removed, sometimes without an operation.

— Fingers swollen at ends (like drumsticks)

Congenital heart disease* – you'll know if your child has one.

Endocarditis – inflammation of lining of heart. Child ill with high fever, abdominal pain*, blood in urine*, paralysis*, or may just be vaguely ill with fever*, weight loss*, pallor, loss of appetite and tiny haemorrhages in skin. See doctor at once.

Familial

Chronic lung disease – you'll know if your child has this.

If ever you notice this change in your child's fingers tell your doctor soon.

Single finger swollen – cause usually obvious. Sucking, injury or an infection. If no obvious sucking or injury see doctor at once to treat infection.

— Injury to

Always tell your doctor if you are at all worried or if cuts* or puncture wounds affect hand deeply.

— Paralysis*

Cerebral palsy* – other signs usually present. See doctor at once.

Poliomyelitis* – other signs usually present. See doctor urgently.

Cut nerve in an accident – see doctor urgently.

Severe pain* – can make child reluctant to use limbs and so appear paralysed. This can occur with scurvy* or fractures*. Other signs usually present.

—Rash on

See rash, page 714.

—Swelling of

Normal – bluish colour of hands and swelling sometimes present in infancy. Cause unknown. Seems to be self-limiting. See doctor soon if worried.

Whole arm and hand swelling – is abnormal. See doctor urgently.

—Thumb sucking*

Normal – source of comfort from soon after birth.

—Weakness in

*Floppy baby** – some normal babies are rather floppy but muscular or nervous disease is possible – see doctor soon.

*Cerebral palsy** – baby usually weak and stiff with other signs present. See doctor at once.

*Poliomyelitis** – baby usually weak and floppy with other signs usually present. See doctor urgently.

—Webbed fingers

Developmental – harmless. See doctor soon.

● *Leg and foot*

—Bow legs*

Normal in young babies and toddlers. Disappears before five years old.

*Rickets** – other features usually present.

*Bulky nappy** between legs can exaggerate normal bow-legged appearance.

—Clicking hip

*Congenital dislocation of hip** – a click may be noticed as you change newborn baby's nappy. See doctor at once if you feel your baby's hip click.

—Cramps

Over-exertion – cure obvious.

*With acute fever** – ensure child is drinking plenty.

Spontaneous – rub affected part; stretch muscle by firm pressure upwards on foot (push sole towards face with leg straight); place covered hot water bottle on area.

— Deformity of foot

Positional – persistence of position in the womb for a few weeks. Rights itself but tell doctor.

Club foot* – see doctor at once. High arch to foot can be congenital or caused by cerebral palsy*. Other signs will usually be present with latter.

Paralysis* – usually after polio*.

— Flat feet

Normal – in babies.

Normal – in older children but if arch forms on standing on tip toe, don't worry.

Developmental – if not either of above. See doctor soon.

— Injury to

See doctor if worried and always if injury has damaged or penetrated sole of foot.

— Itching*

See list on page 713 but *ringworm** commonest cause. Itching between toes and other signs of condition present. See doctor at once.

— Knock knees*

Normal – stage in development for some children.

Obesity* – condition disappears unless extreme as child slims and grows. See doctor soon if worried.

One-sided – see doctor at once.

— Limp*

Injury to leg or foot – you'll probably know about this already.

Badly-fitting shoes* – go to a good shoe shop that measures children's feet properly.

Congenital dislocation of hip * – may have been diagnosed by time child is walking but not necessarily. See doctor at once if in doubt.

Perthes' disease * – other signs may be present. See doctor at once.

Irritable hip – child refuses to stand or walks with pain in hip or knee from infection or mild injury. Rest child and see doctor at once.

Warts * – on sole of foot. Cure these verrucae* and limp goes.

— Muscles too big

Muscular dystrophy* – almost always in calves in boys and then rarely before age five. Difficulty climbing stairs and getting up from ground. See doctor at once.

— Not walking and delayed walking

Normal – very large variation in normal age of walking (ten to twenty months). If in doubt discuss with doctor. Being able to walk with support is the test – not walking alone.

No practice – child needs to be stimulated and encouraged or he won't walk.

Congenital dislocation of hip * – other signs may be present.

If your child isn't walking when you think he should be, even with plenty of help and encouragement, see your family doctor or clinic doctor soon.

— Swelling of feet

Chilblains – don't let child sit too close to fire.

Heart or kidney disease – excess tissue fluid accumulates. You'll probably know if your child has one of these conditions. Always report such swelling to doctor at once.

— Swollen joints

Injury – cause usually obvious. Tell doctor if not better in forty-eight hours or if pain very severe or any signs of fracture*

Infection – joint may be hot, red, tender and painful to move. See doctor at once. If several joints are swollen the child may have rheumatic fever* or another rheumatic condition – see doctor at once.

— Walking difficulties

Intoeing.*

Overtired when learning – take things more slowly and don't expect too much too soon.

Legs of unequal length – could be hip dislocation or old polio*.

— Weakness or paralysis*

Birth injuries – some of these weaknesses may be self-limiting. Others are life-long. Tell your doctor if worried.

*Meningocele and spina bifida** – other signs of these conditions are usually present too. Tell your doctor if at all worried.

*Poliomyelitis** – usually other signs of the disease, or child is known to have been effected. Tell your doctor if at all worried.

*Apparent paralysis in scurvy** – because of pain involved in using joints. Other signs usually present.

Apparent paralysis with fractures * – because of pain in moving fractured part. Other signs (deformity, pain, swelling, tenderness, bruising) usually present.

— Won't use hip

Irritable hip – see limp, page 728.

Perthes' disease – other signs may be present.

Always see doctor soon if your child won't use his hip.

● *Back passage*

— Bleeding from

*Anal fissure** – cure constipation* and fissure heals. Blood appears as streaks on stool. If further help needed see doctor soon.

Injury – will have been obvious. Tell doctor if bleeding doesn't stop quickly.

*Acute summer diarrhoea** *in infants* – blood mixed with very loose stool. Discuss with doctor at once.

*Overdose of laxatives** – goes when drugs stopped.

*Intussusception** *in infants* – periodic severe pain. Child passes material like redcurrant jelly. An emergency – see doctor urgently.

Polyps – within bowel cause periodic small bleeds without pain. Internal examination required. See doctor soon.

Ulcers in the stomach or intestine – can cause a loss of blood that makes the stools black or very dark. Always report such stools to your doctor at once.

— Coloured bowel motions ——————————

Pale – seen in conditions producing obstruction to bile outflow, and with jaundice* from other causes (for example, hepatitis*). Such stools may float. Report to doctor at once. Urine may be very dark. Pale stools can also be normal. In such cases surface is white but inside is coloured.

Redcurrant jelly stools – caused by intussusception*. See doctor urgently.

Red – after eating beetroot, rose-hip syrup. Harmless.

Black – loss of blood from intestine. See doctor at once. Normal meconium*, the very first stools a baby passes, can be blackish-green. Iron-containing medicines. Normal and harmless. Stops when medicines are stopped.

Green – normal in all babies on first day or so as meconium* clears from bowel.

'Scrambled egg' appearance – normal in breast-fed babies.

Greeny-brown – normal as meconium* changes to normal motions as milk is introduced.

Orangey-yellow – normal for breast-fed babies.

— Constipation* ——————————————

Poor diet – low in high-fibre foods. Change diet to one containing plenty of dietary fibre* to cure condition for ever.

Withholding stools – especially in an unfamiliar place. Gradually get child confident about opening bowels away from home. Take potty with you. Long-term withholding of stools is one form of behaviour problem* – see doctor soon.

*Hirschsprung's disease** (nb) – an enlargement and inactivity of the large bowel. Can cause obstruction soon after birth and may need an operation. See doctor urgently. Sometimes runs in families.

Post-operative – especially after abdominal operation when bowel opening may be difficult. See doctor at once.

*Anal fissure** – pain puts child off opening bowels. Cure constipation*: fissure heals and circuit is broken.

Insufficient time allowed to open bowels in family routine. Get child into habit of going.

— Diarrhoea* ——————————————

Babies fed too much sugar/fruit juice* – cut down or out to cure.

Normal breast-feds pass unformed motions at variable frequencies.

Infection – salmonella food poisoning*, dysentery, gastroenteritis*: other signs often present too.

Absence of sugar-splitting enzyme in intestine – especially common in black races. May have to cut milk consumption down or out. Get advice from doctor.

*Constipation** – loose stools leak around craggy masses in back passage causing soiling*.

*Cystic fibrosis** – other signs of the condition usually present, especially foul-smelling stools. See doctor at once.

*Weaning** – many children have increased numbers of loose stools as new foods are introduced. Food residues can often be recognized undigested: don't worry.

*Food allergy** – try to isolate culprit, remove from diet for a week or two, then if diarrhoea cured, reintroduce food to produce it. Then eliminate food from diet for good. May be other signs of allergy* too.

Drugs – antibiotics* and iron* especially.

— Eating bowel motions —

Normal – in young baby; harmless unless persistent. If worried see doctor soon.

— Floating bowel motions —

Normal – if child on high-fibre diet. Colour normal.

Fatty stools – seen in certain types of jaundice*. May also be pale and foul-smelling. See doctor at once.

— Itching* —

*Nappy rash** – change nappy frequently; wash bottom several times a day; use barrier cream.

*Thrush** – other signs of the condition usually present. See doctor at once.

*Threadworms** – worms when visible appear as pieces of white cotton which move. Itching bad at night. See doctor at once.

— Pain on opening bowels —

*Constipation** – cured by going on to diet rich in dietary fibre*.

*Anal fissure** – caused by constipation. May also be bleeding with pain. See doctor soon if diet change to high fibre doesn't cure in two weeks.

Withholding motions – especially in strange surroundings, child says it is painful. Encouragement and getting child to open bowels at home while at vulnerable stage cures the condition.

—Prolapse of *

Constipation* – cure constipation and condition won't recur.

—Smearing bowel motions

Normal – some infants and toddlers smear over their cots or on walls. This appears to be normal rather than a behaviour disturbance. Discourage firmly rather than be angry. Discuss with your health visitor* or doctor.

—Soiling*

Constipation* – loose, fluid stools leak around hard masses of stool in back passage. Cure constipation to cure leaking.

Behaviour disorder – emotionally upset child or one with other behaviour problems* may also soil his pants. Can be difficult to treat. See doctor at once who may refer to specialist.

Emotion and fear* – can cause soiling in a normally clean child.

Mental retardation* – some severely retarded children can't learn to keep clean. They may need training by experts. See doctor soon.

Spina bifida* – children who have nerve problems also have constipation* with soiling*. Specialist help is needed. See doctor at once.

—Soreness at anus

Dirty bottom – wash bottom twice daily at least and be especially sure to wash after dirty nappy. Apply bland barrier cream (zinc and castor oil). Goes in a day or two.

Nappy rash* – may be other signs of nappy rash elsewhere, or may not. Red, raw areas of skin improve with frequent, gentle washing of bottom and more frequent nappy changing. Use special nappy rash cream or ordinary barrier cream (zinc and castor oil is cheap and effective).

Reaction to foods – some children get a sore anus after passing food residues that contain particular foods to which they are sensitive. Hot (spicy) foods are a common cause. Look out for links between specific foods and sore bottom and cut out offending foods.

Diarrhoea* – can produce red, sore anus. See your doctor soon if you don't know what's causing diarrhoea.

On taking antibiotics* – some children have a sore anus on taking oral antibiotics. Try giving live yoghurt to eat – this replaces essential bacteria in the bowel killed off by the drugs, Soreness goes when drugs stopped.

Threadworms* – worms* can often be seen at night when itching is worst. Any persistent itching/soreness of anus suggests that worms may be the cause. See doctor at once. Medicines cure quickly.

—Worms*

Any sign of worms or segments in stools: see doctor at once. One dose of medicine kills most worms.

● *Abdomen*

—Abnormal appetite

Appetite poor – see page 27.

Food refusal – see page 65.

Overeating – see page 434.

Eats unusual things – see dirt eating*(pica).

—Colic*

In bottle-fed babies – often because teat has too large or too small a hole and baby gulps down air with feed. Try different teat or wind* baby afterwards.

Fractious evening baby – mother busy, too little time for baby – irritability wrongly labelled as colic. Babies are often fretful* and crying because they are lonely, tired, bored or hungry. 'Colic' has become an accepted label. Breast-feed your baby exclusively and keep him with you all the time and he'll have less trouble with 'colic'. Breast-feeding mothers should eat frequently and regularly.

—Hiccups*

Normal – some babies hiccup (even in the womb) quite normally. If it lasts for more than one day see doctor at once.

Pneumonia* – other signs usually present.

Meningitis*, brain tumour*, and acute infectious fevers* can all produce brain irritation and thence hiccups. Signs of these conditions always are present as well as hiccups.

— Lumps in

Enlarged liver (right side) and spleen (left side) – see doctor at once if you can feel large lumps at the top of your child's abdomen.

Kidney tumour – medical examination needed to detect this if small. Later on, abdomen is enlarged. See doctor at once with urine specimen in clean bottle.

Hernia* – around navel or in groin. Tell doctor at once. You can tell it's a hernia because the lump increases in sizes or bulges on coughing or straining.

Lymph nodes* in groin – firm, rubbery, separate lumps. Tell doctor at once.

Any mass or lump in your child's tummy must be seen by a doctor at once. The commonest unimportant cause is probably constipation.

— Nausea (feeling sick)

Exhausted child – very tired children sometimes say they feel sick.

Emotion, nervousness*, and fright – normal response.

After repeated unpleasant motion – as on roller coaster, travel sickness, etc. Stop the motion and nausea goes.

Uraemia – too high a level of urea in the blood caused by kidney disease. A diagnosis only possible after a blood test.

After an anaesthetic.

Onset of acute infections.

Severe pains* of any type.

Dietary indiscretion – especially in children who gorge themselves on one food.

Drugs –discuss prescribed drugs with your doctor to see if they could be causing it.

Horrible smells.

Migraine*.

Anything that makes a child feel sick can also produce actual vomiting*.

— Navel discharge

Infection – often accompanied by bleeding* in young baby. See doctor soon.

— Pain in —————————————————————————
Acute pains

Pains that come on suddenly and demand urgent medical attention and can even be dangerous. Any such pains should be reported at once to your doctor as should any which seem to fit the descriptions of the conditions outlined in this section.

Appendicitis* – see doctor urgently.

Cystitis* – see doctor at once.

Foreign body swallowed* – see doctor urgently.

Meningitis* – see doctor urgently.

Swallowed dangerous substances* – see doctor or go to hospital* urgently.

Intestinal obstruction* – child will also be vomiting*, have constipation* and a swollen abdomen. See doctor urgently.

Hernia* obstruction – as intestinal obstruction, but hernia may be very tense and extremely tender. See doctor urgently.

Gastroenteritis* – treat as outlined on page 260.

Intussusception – see doctor urgently.

Mesenteric adenitis* – other signs of infection present. Tell doctor if worried.

Volvulus* – see doctor urgently.

Measles* – see doctor at once but this is not serious.

Mumps* – see doctor at once.

Tonsillitis* – see doctor at once.

Sickle cell crisis – disease may be recognized already. See doctor urgently.

Drugs – ask doctor if pain comes on after taking particular drug.

Torsion of testes – if there is any pain or tenderness in the testes (testicles), see doctor urgently.

Peritonitis* – abdomen rigid, with pain as you take hand away, fever*, child ill, see doctor urgently.

Lung conditions – especially pneumonia* and asthma*. Other signs usually present. See doctor urgently.

—Recurrent pains

Uncomfortable, rather than severe pains, child otherwise well but pains often frightening for parents and doctors. With recurrent pains the pain comes and goes and the child is completely normal in between. There is often stress somewhere in these children's lives.

Emotional – child needs more love* and attention. Discuss with doctor if not happy about how to cope with this.

*Cystitis** – see doctor at once.

*Periodic syndrome** – see doctor at once.

*Worms** – may be signs of worms or segments in stools. See doctor at once.

*Colic**.

Food intolerance and allergy** – culprit food can usually be pinpointed and eliminated.

—Chronic pains

Child has these on and off all the time or even continuously. Rarely serious enough to provoke admission to hospital but are annoying for parents and equally for child.

*Indigestion** – poor chewing of food, eating too quickly, eating wrong foods. Cure obvious.

*Hydronephrosis** (a blown-up kidney) – may be signs of urinary infection. See doctor at once.

*Lead poisoning** – may be other signs of the disease. See doctor at once.

*Hirschsprung's disease** – chronic constipation*, tummy bloated. See doctor at once.

*Constipation** – only if severe and longlasting. See doctor at once.

*Cystic fibrosis** – other signs present. See doctor at once.

*Diabetes** – other signs present. See doctor at once.

Meckel's diverticulum – may cause a pain like acute appendicitis*. See doctor urgently.

Abdominal tumours – rare in childhood. If ever you see or feel any lumps in your child's tummy see doctor at once.

—Poor appetite

Normal – from time to time. Even an adult's appetite varies.

Slowing down in growth – appetite* reduces naturally. Harmless. Often seen in second year of life.

Child unwell with any disease. Consult doctor if worried.

Doesn't like food as presented.

Childhood infections – child may go off food even before infection is obvious.

Emotional stress – anxiety* about disharmony at home or elsewhere. Get professional help if you can't cope.

Serious diseases – such as liver, kidney, thyroid disease. Rare causes. Will have to be sorted out by your doctor or even in hospital.

Allergic to specific foods and so refuses them. Commonly eggs, milk, fish and nuts. Never force a child to eat something he doesn't like. Give something else and try again a few months later. Food refusal is an increasingly accepted sign of food allergy*.

Introduction of new foods – not just at weaning. Many children very conservative about what they eat and don't take to new foods easily. Some children eat only a very few foods. If they are good foods don't worry. Substitute new ones as child seems interested.

Food dawdling up to 2½ years – very common. A toddler likes to play with food and eats very slowly. Don't worry. He'll eat if and when hungry. Don't make a scene. Could be due to too many snacks (or sweets) between meals. Try cutting them out.

Thirsty not hungry – always give drink with food and let child drink rather than eat if he wants to.

Uncomfortable – chair at wrong height – needs cushion. Look for other causes of discomfort.

Tired – as with adults, tired children eat little. Don't worry; let child sleep, then he'll eat well.

Bored children often eat poorly. Stimulate more. Make food and mealtimes fun. Give him foods he likes.

— Rigid

Nervousness* – common, especially if child worried because parents seem concerned.

Cold hand – of doctor (or parent) – makes child contract abdominal muscles involuntarily.

Abdominal infection – usually appendicitis* but not always.

Peritonitis* – other signs usually present.

Pleurisy* – other signs usually present.

If when you have got your child to relax and using warm hands his tummy seems rigid, see doctor urgently.

— Swelling

Obesity* – some fat children appear to have swollen tummies.

Hernias* – cause a localized swelling around navel or in groin. See doctor at once.

Intestinal obstruction* – other signs include vomiting*, ill child and constipation*. See doctor urgently.

Chronic constipation – Hirschsprung's disease* in newborn baby. See doctor at once.

Enlarged abdominal organs – spleen or liver or a swelling of a kidney. See doctor at once.

Fluid – caused by heart disease or kidney failure. See doctor at once.

Lymph nodes* – firm, rubbery, separate lumps in groin(s). See doctor at once.

— Tenderness

Normal – many children dislike having their tummy touched because it is ticklish. If it is tender to the touch or on pressure see your doctor at once.

— Vomiting* (being sick)

Children vomit very readily compared with adults. They are also much more likely to become seriously dehydrated, especially in the first year of life. See your doctor at once if your child has been vomiting for six hours or more. Any of the following can cause vomiting. See main entry for further discussion.

After an anaesthetic.

Diabetes*.

Onset of acute infections.

Recurrent (cyclical) vomiting (periodic syndrome*).

Food poisoning*.

Pyloric stenosis*.

Intestinal obstruction*.

Appendicitis*.

Whooping cough*.

Shock*.

Offensive smells.

Concussion*.

Brain tumour*.

Meningitis*.

Hydrocephalus*.

Epilepsy*.

Motion sickness*.

Emotion.

Prolonged crying* in baby.

— Wind

Baby needs burping* often and cries because of air bubble in stomach.

Normal – some babies swallow a lot of air even when breast-feeding*. Burp frequently and then switch to other breast.

Wrong-sized bottle teat* hole – too large – baby guzzles air with milk. Too small – baby fights to suck enough milk and swallows air.

Poor bottle-feeding* technique – see page 87.

Prolonged crying* – child gulps down air in distressed state and is made worse by air swallowing and the discomfort it causes. Never leave a baby to cry and you'll never have this problem.

● *General conditions affecting the whole body*

— Aches and pains

Growing pains* – in muscles, between joints. Not serious. With warmth to area and more love and attention they should go spontaneously.

After injury – warm, rest and massage area. If pain severe see doctor urgently – may be a fracture*.

No cause found – fairly common. Harmless. If continuous or longlasting, discuss with doctor. Could be depressed or unhappy child who'd benefit from professional help.

Viral illnesses – commonly produce backache and aching in limbs. Keep fluid intake up.

After exercise – common in young children – no one knows why. Harmless.

Lead poisoning* – other evidence of disease usually present. Discuss possibility with doctor.

Rheumatic fever* – other signs usually present. See doctor at once if you feel this could be possible.

Leukaemia* – a very rare cause.

— Aggression*

Normal.

Child being bullied himself – ask at play-group* or nursery school*. Watch when playing with friends.

Copying parents – many parents are very aggressive verbally, emotionally or even physically to each other. Child copies. May need outside help if parents can't help.

Too much parental restriction too many 'Nos' and child rebels with aggression*. Children need more freedom especially if of a free-spirited temperament.

— Anger*

Normal – in certain situations, as with adults.

Too much parental restriction – too many 'Nos' and child rebels by being angry. Give child more freedom.

At specific things – often understandable. Talk it over with child and be understanding – he's still a baby. Remove frustrations* from his life as far as possible.

At being punished – lots of children resent being punished harshly. Treat such children with kid gloves – they don't need harsh treatment to achieve results. Be guided by temperament of child.

Temper tantrums* – a normal reaction to frustration which usually goes before the age of four years. Treat sympathetically and only see doctor if worried.

— Anxiety*

Babies whose needs aren't met – babies need to be loved and their needs met at once. They don't understand waiting and should never have to cry for more than a few moments to tell their mothers they need something. Learn your baby's cries and answer his call at once. Life becomes a lot easier and produces a happy, contented baby, rarely anxious or upset. A baby or young child can also become anxious at night, about sex, about death, about not living up to his parents' expectations and for many other reasons. All of these are discussed in Section two.

— Blue

*Breath holding** attacks in toddlers.

Certain congenital abnormalities of the heart – in which blood is wrongly channelled through the heart. You'll probably know about the underlying condition already.

*During fits**.

Serious lung disease.

*Poisoning**.

*Shock**.

— Bone swelling

Intra-uterine fracture – (occurs before birth). Seen any time from birth to three years. If other signs of fracture (reluctant to move, obvious deformity, swelling or tenderness) see doctor urgently.

*Traumatic fracture** – signs as above but usually after obvious trauma. If you suspect a fracture, gather together all the details of how it happened and tell your doctor. He will want to know.

*Rickets** – especially swollen wrists and joints on the sides of the ribs. See doctor at once.

Bone tumours – very rare. Hard, bony swelling. Not tender. See doctor at once.

— Bruises* easily

Normal – some children are prone to bruises on the legs yet are perfectly well. Bruises elsewhere need an explanation.

Bleeding diseases – such as haemophilia* and leukaemia*. Rare. If you are at all worried or if there is a family history of either of them see doctor at once.

— Burns*

Cause usually obvious, see page 104.

— Clicking joints

Usually normal and harmless except in hip.

Clicking hip (nb) – see doctor at once.

— Clinging*

See page 127.

—Clumsiness*

See page 131.

—Crying*

Sorting out the cause of crying* is often not easy but a few things cause ninety per cent of crying. Remember that a baby will communicate mainly by crying if he wants something. Check through the following things quickly if your baby cries.

Hungry – if in doubt, give a feed, even if you have recently fed him. If hungry he'll eat, if not you'll know it's something else. With very young babies hunger is the commonest cause of crying.

Thirsty – as above. If bottle-fed baby vomits, has a fever*, or diarrhoea*, give water or half-strength milk to replace fluid. Breast-feed thirsty breast-fed child more often – don't give water if possible.

*Dirty or wet nappy** – if at all wet or dirty change to see if this stops the crying.

Wind – put baby upright on your lap or over shoulder. Massage (rub) back and wind will come up within a minute or so if it is the cause.

Bored or lonely* – keep baby with you and involve him in what you and the family are doing. Never leave babies alone when awake – always have them with you where the action is.

Frightened – cause usually obvious. Console and feed to calm.

*Pain** – an uncommon cause. If at all worried, see doctor at once.

Too hot, too cold – cause usually obvious. Don't judge baby's temperature* by hands and feet but feel chest.

*Lack of body contact** – many babies stop crying when held. There is nothing wrong with them but they simply want body contact.

Difficult breathing – especially snuffly and 'mucussy' baby. See doctor at once for nose drops. Steam in room helps too.

*'Colic'**.

Overstimulation – if a baby has been passed around other people in a noisy room, even a 'sunny' baby may react badly and cry. Give him peace, calm, and a feed.

—Depression*

See page 176.

— Enlarged lymph nodes* (glands)

Normal – some children's lymph nodes are easily felt even when not enlarged. Nodes are 'palpable' under the skin which moves easily over them.

Infections – nodes tender, enlarged and may even be visible. Generalized infections can involve all the body's nodes but a few only are involved near a localized infection.

*Leukaemia** – causes generalized lymph node enlargement. If there is no sign of an infection and your child has enlarged nodes in several places, see a doctor at once.

In front of and behind ears – classical sign of German measles*.

— Faints

Too hot and stuffy – cure obvious. Fresh air, lay child down flat and unbutton clothing.

*Breath-holding attacks** – with toddlers.

*Diabetes** – low blood sugar attack – with too little food or too much insulin. See doctor at once to rebalance insulin unless cause is obvious. For treatment, see low blood sugar (below).

*Severe anaemia** – see doctor at once.

Standing up too long.

Low blood sugar – a long time after a meal or after exercise*. Give child sugar lump or spoonful of jam or honey but only if still conscious.
Never give anything by mouth to an unconscious child.

— Falling over

Normal – learning to walk.

*Accident proneness** – other signs usually present.

Ambitious exploration.

*Visual problems** – a child who can't see properly will fall over things.

— Fatness (obesity*)

Wrong food – too many highly-refined, low-fibre foods rich in sugar. Give only unrefined, high-fibre foods and no added sugar. Keep sweets* to a minimum.

Too much food – too much of even the right food can cause obesity. Some children overeat because they are unhappy. Emotional deprivation is a common cause of overeating. Get professional help if this is your child's problem.

Familial – some families are fat even when eating the right foods in sensible amounts.

Too little exercise.

Normal in some breast-fed babies. Some get quite fat. As soon as they are mobile they lose it quicker than do bottle-fed babies.

—Fever* (high body temperature)

Specific childhood infections – mumps*, measles*, etc.

Viral infections – can produce very high fevers.

Tonsillitis * – other signs usually present.

Urinary infections * – other signs may be absent and the diagnosis difficult to make except by laboratory tests on urine. See doctor at once if child has abdominal pain*, passes urine frequently, has loin pain (in middle of back on either side), passes dark (blood-stained) urine, has pain on passing urine or suddenly becomes wet when previously dry.

Otitis media * – other signs usually present.

Food poisoning * – other signs usually present.

Pus somewhere – place may be obvious or may need medical help to find. See doctor at once anyway.

Prolonged coughing*, crying*, or exertion – can all cause a fever.

—Fits* (convulsions*)

'Febrile convulsions' * – in infants. Any really high fever can cause a fit. Treat as on page 233. Tell doctor urgently. Seen with otitis media*, pneumonia*, whooping cough*, gastroenteritis*, and urinary infections*, for example, as well as with childhood infectious diseases.

Epilepsy*. Other signs also present.

Birth injuries. Fits come on months or years after birth. See doctor urgently.

Meningitis*/encephalitis * – other signs usually present.

Months or years after encephalitis*.

Infantile spasms – fits in which the baby doubles up, cries out and repeats this many times (perhaps a hundred or more) a day. See doctor at once.

Lead poisoning * – other signs usually present.

Brain tumour * – a rare cause.

Suffocation or anoxia at birth and suffocation* at any age.

Hysteria – a few children have no organic (bodily) cause for fits yet seem to produce them, sometimes at will.

—Habits*

See page 279.

—Hairiness

Familial – some families are unusually hairy and yet are quite normal.

Adrenal gland overactivity – a rare but important cause. This produces signs of precocious puberty. Other signs of puberty may be present even in an under-five. If your child becomes hairy see your doctor at once.

—Hallucinations*

*Fevers** – a common cause. No treatment needed except to reduce the temperature.

On going off to sleep – normal in some children.

Mental illness – rare in under-fives.

—Hyperactivity*

Normal – a busy child who won't settle to anything for long is in danger of being called hyperactive. If his behaviour worries you, see your doctor soon.

*Food allergy** – some children show their allergy to a food by being uncontrollably active. Try removing foods that seem to be causing it and then if the overactivity stops keep child off that food for good. Re-introduce food carefully: if symptoms return, avoid food for good.

Food additives – some children are sensitive to certain food additives (for example, colourings, flavourings and preservatives). Keep him off food that provokes overactive behaviour.

—Itching*

See page 713.

—Jealousy*

See page 329.

—Nightmares*

See page 422.

— Not talking

Normal – before a certain stage of development.

Deafness* – usually other evidence of deafness. See doctor at once if you think your baby or child is deaf or even partially deaf. There may be simple, treatable causes.

Cerebral palsy* – other signs usually present.

Mental retardation* – other signs usually present.

Insufficient stimulation – children left to themselves and not stimulated won't talk as soon as they should.

— Painful joints

Viral illnesses – including many of the common childhood infectious illnesses. No treatment necessary except pain relief with analgesics*. Warmth may help.

Injury – sprains and strains of ligaments common when children play. Can be extremely painful. First aid* – apply cold (ice packs) and rest joint. One day later mobilize joint and apply heat. See doctor at once if not improving in twenty-four hours: may be a fracture*.

Rheumatic diseases – actual arthritis* rare in children. Rheumatic fever* rare today, and other signs of the disease usually present.

Poliomyelitis* – a rare cause today and unlikely after immunization. Have you been in an endemic area? See doctor urgently.

Drug sensitivities – lots of medicines* can cause joint pains in susceptible people. Check with your doctor if pains come on after prescribed (or other) medicines.

— Pale

Normal – some children look very pale, (especially redheads) and yet are perfectly healthy. Pale cheeks usually have no significance medically. Pale lips or pale insides to the eyelids can be a sign something is wrong. Tell your doctor.

Shock* – emotion/fear/fright. True 'medical' shock* with other signs, see page 539.

Anaemia* of any cause. See doctor at once if worried.

Leukaemia* – there is no way of telling whether your child's pallor is serious or not. Usually pallor of face alone is of little significance but to be sure see doctor soon: he'll do blood tests if he's concerned.

— Poisoning*

See page 472.

— Poor weight gain

Remember that advice on weight gain is often based on data from bottle-fed babies.
See also page 666.

Poor breast-feeding technique* – feed more often and for longer, waking baby if necessary. Forget schedules: demand feed*, and more often if you feel you need to.

Poor bottle-feeding technique* – milk too dilute or insufficient taken.

Too little breast milk – as a result of mother's failure to stimulate supply because of poor technique. See above.

Food fads – see doctor if worried.

Poor quality diet – rare in UK, but child eating small quantities of junk food only can be undernourished.

Vomiting/regurgitation** – most foods brought back up and therefore not absorbed. Especially true of pyloric stenosis* in infancy.

*Prolonged diarrhoea** – see pages 731–2 for causes. This can cause poor absorption of food.

*Emotional deprivation** – mechanism not completely understood but emotionally deprived children have low growth hormone levels.

Infections – especially those which go on for a long time. Even common infections such as whooping cough* can produce loss of weight or poor weight gain.

*Mental retardation** – if severe child won't eat properly or even at all.

Malabsorption.*

— Rash

See page 714.

— Redness of skin

See page 715.

— Rudeness

Normal to some extent as child tries himself out against adults.

Copying* contemporaries.

Parents rude to each other or others – child learns from them.

Wrong type of discipline* – too many prohibitions; child feels over-controlled. Loosen up. Be more loving and less rigid, yet firm.

Illness* – a normally happy and pleasant child can become rude and unbearable if he is ill or tired. Be patient: it'll pass. No point having battles – no one wins.

—Shyness*

Normal – in some children and in certain situations (new school, new adults, etc.)

Shy parents – tend to have shy children.

Sensitive personality – Beware of being too tough on such a child. Let him find his feet socially at his own pace.

Ridicule – Never humiliate a child in front of others: it can produce long-term shyness and a low self-esteem that can persist into adulthood.

Overprotective parents – especially with only children. Let child be as outgoing as he wants to be. You can't tie him to you and if you do the price you pay could be that he's terribly shy and unable to cope with social situations.

Tiredness/boredom* –not shy normally.

Poor opportunities to mix and make friends at home on his own ground where he feels secure.

—Sleep problems*

See page 550.

—Speech problems*

See page 595.

—Sweating

Exercise – normal.

Normal – some children sweat very readily.

Too many bedclothes or clothes.

Hot weather.

*Fevers** – take temperature* to be sure if this is the cause.

*Rickets** – other signs of disease usually present.

*Overdose of aspirin** – tell doctor urgently.

— Temper tantrums*

See page 605.

— Thirst*

Too little to drink.

Excessive sweating with fevers.*

Diarrhoea.*

Hot weather and sweating.

Diabetes mellitus and diabetes insipidus.* In sugar diabetes (mellitus) child drinks a lot and passes lots of urine. In diabetes insipidus child drinks a lot and may even drink peculiar things such as bathwater and flower vase water so desperate is his thirst. If you suspect either of these, always see a doctor at once.

— Tics

See page 279.

— Tiredness*

Normal – after lack of sleep or exercise*. Especially found in young child trying to stay up with older siblings or in day trying to keep up with their physical activities.

Unhappiness – depressed and unhappy children often seem tired.

Bored children seem tired – until they are stimulated and involved in things, when they take on a new lease of life.

*Severe anaemia** – can produce real tiredness.

*Malnutrition** – other signs usually present.

Severe chronic illnesses – you'll know if your child has one of these.

Children have variations in natural energy at various times of their lives. This is normal, as in adults. A change to tiredness in a previously energetic child should be reported to your doctor at once.

— Too short

Familial – short parents usually produce short children.

Emotional deprivation* and rejection – cause a lowering of growth hormone levels.

Chromosome disorders.

Malnutrition* – other signs usually present.

Malabsorption* – other signs usually present.

Serious infections.

Cystic fibrosis* – other signs usually present.

Coeliac disease* – other signs usually present.

Chronic kidney disease – other signs usually present.

Congenital bone defects – such as achondroplasia* and others.

Congenital heart disease* with cyanosis.

Cretinism*.

Mental retardation*.

Poor pituitary gland function.

Other signs of these diseases are usually more obvious and compelling than the shortness. But if your child is short yet seems otherwise well, see doctor soon. If he is short (and you are both of usual height) and has anything else wrong with him – see doctor at once.

— Too tall

Familial – tall parents usually produce tall children. Very tall children (especially girls) can feel very isolated from their peers and this can produce behaviour problems.

Pituitary gland tumours.

Precocious puberty – other signs of puberty (muscles, breasts, hair growth, body shape, voice changes, etc.) also present. If you are both of normal height and your child is exceptionally tall, see doctor soon.

— Twitching

Normal – before/during/after sleep.

Habit tics.

Autism* – other signs usually present.

Mild epilepsy* – other signs may not be present. See doctor if worried.

After breath-holding* attack.

Fatigue – disappears when child is rested.

— Unconsciousness* —————————————————————

Normal – during sleep.

Injury/concussion – after an accident, a knock or a fall. Tell doctor urgently.

Drug overdose.

After epileptic or other fit.

Meningitis.*

Diabetic coma – child will probably be known to have diabetes*.

*Severe lead poisoning** – other signs will be present.

*Shock** – other signs will be present. See page 539.

If ever your child is unconscious, put him into the recovery position*, check his heart and breathing (pages 108 and 34 respectively) and get an ambulance at once. Start artificial respiration* if necessary and continue until professional help arrives.

Any child who has been unconscious for however short a time should see a doctor and ideally should be observed in hospital for the next twenty-four hours.

Never give an unconscious child anything to eat or drink.

— Weight loss ——————————————————————
With normal food intake

Emotional deprivation/anxiety*.*

Very active child.

Worms.*

*Diabetes mellitus** (sugar diabetes) – child may also drink a lot and pass a lot of urine.

Misuse of laxatives – food not absorbed properly.

Malabsorption.*

Overactive thyroid gland – child will also be edgy, sweaty and have a fast pulse.

Chronic infections.

With poor food intake

Depression.*

Lead poisoning.*

Food fads.

Food intolerance.

Longstanding heart disease.

See page 737 for other causes of poor appetite which might also cause weight loss because of poor food intake.

── Yellow skin (jaundice) ────────────────
(with or without yellow whites of eyes)

Common in normal babies in the first few days of life.

Normal – in Oriental babies and children.

Certain drugs – discuss with your doctor if any drugs have been taken.

Thyroid deficiency – see cretinism, page 156.

Hepatitis* – other signs usually present.

Any childhood infection can cause temporary jaundice*.

Breast milk jaundice (nb).

Congenital obstruction of the bile system (nb).

Internal bleeding – usually after obvious injury.

Rhesus incompatibility (nb) – see blood groups on page 79.

If ever you notice your child is yellow (the whites of his eyes are often the first to go yellow) see your doctor at once.

SECTION FOUR

A-Z of useful organizations

Throughout the UK and the old Commonwealth there are many organizations offering helpful advice (and often much more) to parents and their children – especially those families with special problems and needs. In this section we outline all the main ones in the UK and many others in Australia, New Zealand and South Africa.

The information you can find about each organization is:

1 its name, address and telephone number (if they want to be contacted by telephone);
2 when it was founded;
3 what its aims are;
4 how big the membership is;
5 how much it costs to join and how to do so;
6 what you have to do to be able to join;
7 how to contact it;
8 what services it offers you;
9 some brief details of what periodicals, publications, films, etc. are available.

If you want to know more, contact the organization direct.

Organizations listed

UK

Throughout the UK and the old Commonwealth there are many organizations offering helpful advice (and often much more) to parents and their children – especially those families with special problems and needs. In this section we outline all the main ones in the UK and many others in Australia, New Zealand and South Africa.

The information you can find about each organization is:

1 its name, address and telephone number (if they want to be contacted by telephone);
2 when it was founded;
3 what its aims are;
4 how big the membership is;
5 how much it costs to join and how to do so;
6 what you have to do to be able to join;
7 how to contact it;
8 what services it offers you;
9 some brief details of what periodicals, publications, films, etc. are available.

If you want to know more, contact the organization direct.

Organizations listed

UK

Other useful addresses

British Tourist Authority, 64 St James's Street, London SW1A 1NF.
Camping Club of Great Britain and Ireland, 11 Lower Grosvenor Place,
   London SW1W 0EY.
Canvas Holidays, 7 Bull Plain, Hertford SG14 1DY.
Centre for the Teaching of Reading, University of Reading, School of
   Education, 29 Eastern Avenue, Reading, Berks.

The Children's Book Centre, 229 Kensington High Street, London W8. An excellent children's book shop with worldwide mail order service. Publishes a quarterly newsletter.

Childsplay, 112 Tooting High Street, London SW17. A shop offering a mail order service of everything for children's art – paper, drawing equipment, modelling, cutting, sticking. etc.

Clarks Shoes, Street, Somerset. Makers of strong, stylish and well-fitting shoes. Trained staff available in shops selling their products to ensure that child gets a proper fit.

Disability Design Research Group, Middlesex Polytechnic, Trent Park, Cockfosters, Herts.

Early Learning Centre, 25 King's Road, Reading. A monthly system of pre-school education for children.

Galt Toys, 30–31 Great Marlborough Street, London W1. Creative, well-made toys. On sale elsewhere. Useful leaflet ('Choosing Good Toys for Young Children').

Hamleys, 188 Regent Street, London W1R 6BT. The biggest toy shop in Britain.

Mothercare, Cherry Tree Road, Watford WD2 5SH, will supply baby equipment and accessories by mail order.

Nanny and mother's help agencies

Au pair Bureau, 87 Regent Street, London W1.

Baxter's Agency, PO Box 12, Peterborough.

Occasional and Permanent Nannies, 11 Beauchamp Place, London SW3.

Universal Aunts, 36 Walpole Street, London SW3. Temporary help after having a baby, for example.

Advisory Centre for Education (ACE)

18 Victoria Park Square, Bethnal Green, London E2 9PB (01 980 4596). Founded in 1960 as an independent, non-profit-making educational charity to provide information and advice for both the users and providers of the education service; to encourage greater contact between homes and schools; to promote a wider discussion of educational issues, both at local and national level; and to press for greater consideration of parents' and students' points of view in educational decision making.

There is no membership but the public is encouraged to contact ACE by letter or telephone to help with complaints and conflicts with schools, local education authorities, etc. ACE provides information on a wide range of education topics, for example, legal duties of LEAs, appeals procedures, education law, etc. ACE publications are available – order form on request, and a bi-monthly magazine *Bulletin*, published to provide more information about education, on subscription only, at present £7.50 (overseas additional £2.70).

Association for All Speech Impaired children

347 Central Markets, Smithfields, London EC1A 9NH. (01 236 3632/ 6487). Formed in 1968 to help children with specific speech and language disorders. Membership is approximately 1,500 and open to anyone on submission of a completed application form and subscription. Minimum subscription £5. For information write to the above address or telephone. The Association provides an advice and information service; fund raises for mobile speech therapy clinics; organizes activity weeks for children; campaigns for more language units attached to ordinary schools; runs courses, symposia and training courses for teaching of language-disordered children. Information leaflets and list of publications available.

Association for Improvements in the Maternity Services

Hon. Sec. Elizabeth Cockerell, 21 Franklin Gardens, Hitchin, Herts, SG4 0NE. Founded in 1960 and aimed at those who believe that childbearing couples ought to be regarded as normal, reasonable adults. capable of making their own decisions in matters relating to childbirth, and that these choices should be respected.

Membership is open to anyone – subscriptions £5 p.a.; £4 for subscription to newsletter only; £7 for institutions. Write to the treasurer for membership details. Members' support is valued more than the fees and the Society are happy to accept less if the fee is too high. To contact the Society write with sae or telephone Chairman Beverley Beech, 21 Iver Lane, Iver, Bucks. (0753 652781) or Vice Chairman Christine Burley, Tudor Lodge, St Monica's Road, Kingswood, Surrey (07373 58147). Pressure group campaigning. The newsletter is the best form of advertisement and most important service. Other leaflets are available.

Association for Post-natal illness

Queen Charlotte's Hospital, Goldhawk Road, London W6. Founded in 1979 to support and advise women who are currently ill. To educate women about the illness so that they can seek treatment early. To raise money and support research into the illness. There are about 650 members. To become a member write to the secretary formally requesting membership which is free. Members of the public should write to the secretary who assures a prompt reply. The Association can offer advice on all aspects of the treatment and management of the illness. There is also a network of volunteers who support women who are currently ill. Literature is supplied to area health authorities, doctors and other health workers. Pamphlets are available on the illness.

Association for Spina Bifida and Hydrocephalus (ASBAH)

22 Upper Woburn Place, London WC2H 0EP (01 388 1382). Founded in 1966 to give every support and help possible to those who are born with spina bifida and/or hydrocephalus, to their families, and those who care for them. Membership is approximately 12,000. There is no national

membership fee but a fee which varies from one local association to another, and in order to belong one has to approach the appropriate local association. The public should contact ASBAH direct, either at head office or at the appropriate local association. The public is offered support through social work and welfare grants, and information and advice on the provision of aids and equipment, adaptation to property, accommodation, education, social development and independence training, leisure, occupation and employment. There are thirty-one field workers in different parts of England and Wales who help families. There are more than eighty local associations in Britain for parents and children and meetings are held for the exchange of information and to plan events and projects. There is a list of publications, a fact sheet and a magazine, *Link*, available to members.

Asthma Society and Friends of the Asthma Research Council

300 Upper Street, London N1 2XX (01 226 2260).   Founded in 1927 to provide mutual aid and assistance for those with asthma and for their families, to spread knowledge about asthma and its treatment and to raise funds for research. Membership is open to anyone, at a minimum subscription of £2 p.a. or at the discretion of the treasurer, to join one of the one hundred branches throughout the country. For details of the nearest branch write to head office, or ask your doctor or local Citizens' Advice Bureau. Branches hold regular meetings to provide mutual aid and assistance for those with asthma and for their families, show films, have talks or panel discussions, provide a library of books on asthma and related subjects and make sure that the public, particularly in schools and industry are aware that asthmatics can lead normal lives provided they take their medicine correctly.

There is a list of books and pamphlets available from various sources and the Society has produced a comprehensive series of pamphlets covering all aspects of asthma.

British Agencies for Adoption and Fostering

11 Southwark Street, London SE1 1RQ (01 407 8800).   Founded in 1980 to promote good standards of practice in adoption, fostering and social work with children and families.

Membership is open to adoption and fostering agencies, organizations, individuals with a special interest in adoption and fostering, legal advisers and medical advisers, and applications are accepted at the discretion of the management committee. Enquiries are welcome by phone or letter.

The organization maintains and extends a range of services including advice, information, consultancy, acts as an exchange for families for children with special needs, training schemes, has a research programme and a wide range of publications for professional workers and provides information for the public through booklets and leaflets. Publishes a quarterly journal *Adoption and Fostering*.

British Diabetic Association

10 Queen Anne Street, London W1M 0BD (01 323 1531). Founded in 1934 to give counsel and confidence to diabetics. Membership stands at 70,000 and it costs only £5 a year to join, or a single payment of £105, or £15 a year for seven years under covenant. There is also a pensioner membership at £1 annually and overseas annual payment of £10 or £150 for overseas life membership. Application for membership forms are attached to the information sheet available on request. BDA supplies a wide and continuing range of free advice and help for diabetics on diet, employment, education, insurance, travel and care of diabetic children, takes up cases of hardship with government bodies and voluntary organizations, runs a holiday camp for the young diabetic, organizes conferences for professional people concerned with diabetes, and campaigns incessantly to wipe out prejudice and ignorance about diabetes. Members receive six free copies of the Association's newpaper *Balance* annually. Over fifty publications are available on subjects from childhood, marriage and old age, to insurance, holidays and jam-making.

British Epilepsy Association

Anstey House, 40 Hanover Square, Leeds LS3 1BE (0532 439393). Founded in 1950 to provide services of various kinds to represent the interests and well-being of those with epilepsy in the UK. Anyone interested in epilepsy may join the BEA and the membership at present stands at 4,500. Subscription is £5 per year which includes an accident insurance policy. Details of how to become a member are supplied on application. In addition to the research fund, the services include social work and family services, catering for the needs of people with epilepsy themselves and their familes; an education programme for professional groups and an Action Campaign department which organizes a network of voluntary self-help groups throughout the UK. A selection of leaflets is freely available providing details of the services available.

British Institute of Mental Handicap

Wolverhampton Road, Kidderminster, Worcestershire DY10 3PP (0562 850251). Founded in 1972 to raise standards of treatment, care and management of the mentally handicapped, both in hospital and in the community. There are four categories of membership available on application, completion of membership form, and payment of the subscription applicable. Membership is open to anyone interested in the mentally handicapped. The Institute provides an up-to-date information service to all staff working in the many professions involved with the mentally handicapped, provides education and training for parents and relatives of the mentally handicapped, stimulates general interest in mental handicap, provides specialized services, conducts research and has established an information and resources centre to answer specific queries. There are many publications and leaflets available.

British Migraine Association
178A High Road, Byfleet, Weybridge, Surrey KT14 7ED (Byfleet 52468). Founded in 1958 to press for the wider use of preventive treatments for migraine; to organize and conduct a national appeal for the endowment of more specialized facilities for migraine; to introduce more intensive and coordinated research; to keep members informed of new advances in treatment and to endeavour to secure an accurate census of the number of migraine sufferers in the UK. Membership stands at 6,500 and is available to anyone on completion of a membership application form and submission of the subscription. Correspondence should be addressed to the secretary at the above address. A newsletter, fact sheet and various leaflets are available.

British Polio Fellowship
Bell Close, West End Road, Middlesex HA4 5LP (Ruislip 75515). Founded in January 1939 to give help and encouragement in the development of interests and abilities of sufferers; to alleviate loneliness and to bring those in need into contact with available sources of help; and to arouse the social conscience on the problems and difficulties encountered by the paralysed. At present there are 10,000 members, roughly fifty per cent disabled and fifty per cent able-bodied. Membership subscription is £1 per annum or £10 for life membership and would-be members should make a formal application to the central office. Contact should be made initially by telephone or letter. The Fellowship exists to help the disabled person and provides a personal welfare service to all polio-disabled people in the UK; social, recreational and cultural activities through its branches and regions; annual competitions in the form of inter-branch, inter-regional swimming and sports; holiday accommodation; and an informative quarterly newspaper *The Bulletin*. Publicity material is available, leaflets, films, etc.

British Pregnancy Advisory Service
Austy Manor, Wootton Wawen, Solihull, West Midlands B95 6DA (021 643 1461). Formed in 1968 to provide advice, treatment and assistance for women who are suffering from any physical or mental illness or distress as a result of or during pregnancy. It is a non-profit making charitable trust and provides the services of trained counsellors and qualified medical staff at its thirteen full-time and eleven part-time branches for any problem connected with pregnancy, contraception and sexuality. Contact can be made by letter, telephone or personal call. Fees are charged for consultation services, treatment and infertility services. Pregnancy testing is available at all branches (£3). Funds come from patients' fees and a limited amount is set aside to help women who are in real financial difficulties to pay for an abortion. There is a comprehensive range of leaflets available from the Information Officer at BPAS head office.

The British Red Cross Society
9 Grosvenor Crescent, London SW1X 7EJ (01 235 5454). Founded in 1879 to furnish aid to the sick and wounded in time of war, and to foster the improvement of health, the prevention of disease and the mitigation of suffering throughout the world. Anyone who wishes to volunteer his or her services should contact the nearest Red Cross Office, the address of which can be found in the telephone directory under 'B' for British or 'R' for Red Cross. There are some 200 million members among the 126 National Societies who are bound in their work by seven principles: humanity; impartiality; neutrality; independence; voluntary service; unity; and universality. In peacetime its principle tasks are to train members and the public to alleviate suffering among the sick, the handicapped and the frail elderly. To carry out this work through unpaid voluntary members, it relies on donations from the public.

Brittle Bone Society
112 City Road, Dundee DD2 2PW (0382 67603). Formed in October 1972 to promote research into the causes and inheritance of brittle bone disease and the best ways of treating it. The Society has more than 800 members in all parts of the UK. Complete an application form to become a full or free associate member. Full members £3 p.a., life members £24, or £12 if over sixty years of age. Through the society affected families can get in touch with each other and share ideas on how to cope with the disorder. Letters and telephone calls reassure hard-pressed families that they are not alone. A regular newsletter is issued with advice on ways of living with brittle bones. Advice on grants and allowances, schooling, equipment and genetics is also given. The Society has fourteen active branches in different parts of the country but in addition holds local meetings in major centres every year to allow members to share ideas for coping with brittle bones. Society provides equipment not obtainable through statutory sources.

Centre on Environment for the Handicapped
35 Great Smith Street, London SW1P 3BJ (01 222 7980). Founded in 1969 to make the environment of handicapped people better so that handicapped people can as individuals make the most of their potential for living and contribute their best to the world about them. Membership is currently 300. To become one fill in a membership form and enclose £15 for an individual member or £30 for a corporate body. All enquiries are welcome either in writing or by telephone. CEH is concerned not only with environment, but with opportunities for the handicapped and facilities in public buildings. It holds seminars on topics of current concern and provides an information service. There is a comprehensive library concerned with the environment for the handicapped, publications on design, design sheets and design sheets on gardens and grounds for the handicapped.

Church of England Children's Society
Edward Rudolph House, Margery Street, London WC1X 0JL (01 837 4299). Founded in 1881 and then known as the 'Waifs and Strays'. The Society's aims are: to work with teenagers; to give them a purpose in life; to reduce juvenile crime and provide an alternative to deliquency; to work with the handicapped so that they can achieve an independent life; to work within the community so that those vulnerable to the pressures of society can learn to help themselves and cease to become dependent upon the state; and to work with children and their families to reduce the incidence of children received into residential care. The Society does not have a membership, but 300,000 supporters from all over the country help with donations and fund-raising events and receive a copy of the quarterly magazine *Gateway*. Contact the Society's headquarters to receive a copy. For details of fund-raising work or for information about the society contact the headquarters at the address or telephone number above. The Society helps over 10,000 children and their families every year through its residential homes and special schools for the handicapped, teenage units and family, community and day centres. Also has an adoption and fostering agency and a network of social work support teams throughout England and Wales. Information leaflets and a colour slide/film strip and cassette programme on the problems of the handicapped with full background notes for teachers and group leaders are available in request.

The Coeliac Society
PO Box 220, High Wycombe, Bucks HP11 2HX (High Wycombe 37278). Formed in 1968 in order to help coeliacs and those with dermatitis herpetiformis to follow the gluten-free diet. It is run by voluntary workers and relies solely on donations for its income. There are 23,000 coeliacs on the mailing list. Anyone with a coeliac condition or dermatitis herpetiformis who would like to be on the Society's mailing list should write to the above address. There are sixty local groups in the UK which arrange visits to newly-diagnosed coeliacs and give advice and immediate help with the management of a gluten-free diet. Meetings are arranged to demonstrate gluten-free cookery with talks and question and answer sessions. There is one main publication, the *Coeliac Handbook*, and also a booklet on gluten-free products. In addition there is a magazine every spring and autumn.

The Compassionate Friends
Gill Hodder, 6 Denmark Street, Bristol BS1 5DQ (0272 29778). Founded in 1969, this is an organization of bereaved parents who have themselves experienced heartbreak, loneliness and social isolation and who seek to help other bereaved parents. There are about 2,500 members who each receive a newsletter quarterly. The national secretary, above, will be able to put you in touch with a local branch; the chief service to the public is to provide a willing ear to bereaved parents who need to talk about the

child they have loved and lost, to someone who has also lost a child. As there are no membership fees, administrative costs for running expenses come from donations and fund-raising activities by the members. Any parent who has suffered the loss would be a child is welcome to become a member irrespective of the age the child would be now. The Compassionate Friends have accumulated many books on child bereavement and there is a list available to members who may borrow any book on application to the librarian.

The Cystic Fibrosis Research Trust
5 Blyth Road, Bromley, Kent BR1 3RS (01 464 7211).   Founded in 1964 to finance research to find a complete cure for cystic fibrosis; to establish branches and groups throughout the UK for the purpose of helping and advising parents of those affected with cystic fibrosis and to educate the public about the disease. Membership is free and open only to a person with cystic fibrosis or one who has it in the family, or to those who signify their willingness to enter into the fund-raising or research activities of the Trust. The public are asked to contact the above address by letter or telephone, or to contact members of local branches and groups, or to make an approach via the medical or para-medical professions. A booklet and general information is available, together with an application form to join a local group or to help raise funds.

The Disabled Living Foundation
380–384 Harrow Road, London W9 2HU (01 289 6111).   Established in 1970, its aims are to collate and distribute information on all matters to do with the daily living problems caused by disability. There are various types of subscriptions available on request, either by telephone, letter, or visiting the aids centre. The information collated is distributed to those either professionally or personally concerned in the most appropriate manner to the particular problem. The majority of the professionally concerned receive bi-monthly printed information which consists of twenty-one information sheets on different subjects.

Dr Barnardo's
Tanners Lane, Barkingside, Ilford, Essex (01 550 8822).   Founded by Dr Barnardo in 1866 when the first 'Ragged School' was started in the Stepney area of East London and was registered as a 'company' on 4th April 1899. The present day aim of Barnardo's is to provide and develop in consultation with statutory authorities and other agencies selected services for children in need and for their families on a regional basis. There is no membership and the services provided are broadly of two kinds: services whereby specialized residential, educational or day care is offered for sponsored use by local authority, social services and education departments; and services, provided by voluntary contributions, which are often experimental in nature and method and which concentrate on

preventive work. Field work projects include efforts to find homes for the 'hard to place child'; programmes for training of social work volunteers; support projects for the bereaved and for one-parent families; day care centres for pre-school children and for non-school attenders and unemployed youths; and holiday play schemes and holiday placements for mentally handicapped children. Information booklets are available telling all about the work of Barnardo's and how the public can help raise funds.

Down's Children's Association
4 Oxford Street, London W1N 9FL.   Founded in 1970 to promote the care, nurture and education of people with Down's syndrome, particularly in the early years of life and to promote research into the causes and effects of the condition and into the care, nurture and education of people with Down's syndrome. There are 4,000 members and full membership costs £5 p.a. (associate membership £2.50). Anyone can join. Contact the Association by letter preferably, though telephone advice is available either from the above address or at ten regional centres throughout the UK.
   The Association offers leaflets and a series of free parent guides covering the first five years of life. There is also a newsletter about three times per year.

Fair Play for Children Safety Committee
248 Kentish Town Road, London NW5.   Formed in 1975 to campaign for better playground equipment. Membership and advice is free to anyone concerned about the dangers of playgrounds. Written or phone enquiries are answered about outdated, faulty or unsafe equipment and tenants' associations and other groups are advised about which equipment to install. Fair Play for Children issues an excellent booklet, *Danger on the Playground*, giving detailed information on all aspects of equipment.

Family Planning Information Service
27–35 Mortimer Street, London W1N 7RJ (01 636 7866).   Set up in 1977 and run jointly by the Family Planning Association and the Health Education Council to provide information and enquiry services to ensure that people know about and use the free National Health family planning facilities. Membership consists of 850 people and the fee is £6.50. If you would like to join, write or fill in a form in the annual report and details will be supplied. The public may contact the Service by telephone or personal visit. The services offered to the public are wide-ranging from giving free literature on all methods of birth control and fertility, to information about the nearest family planning clinic, advice on all aspects of fertility control, personal relationships, population and related topics. There is an abundance of literature available and a book list of publications that can be sent by mail order from the Book Centre 27/35 Mortimer Street, London W1N 7RJ from Monday to Friday.

Foresight . . . The Association for the Promotion of Pre-conceptual Care

The Old Vicarage, Church Lane, Witley, Surrey (0428 794500). Founded in 1978 to try to prevent congenital disorders by pre-conceptual care. There are about 400 members who pay the annual subscription of £3 and another 500 or so professional contacts who do not pay membership. Anyone can join by paying £3. The public can contact Foresight by post (preferably) and an sae would be welcome.

There is a booklet for parents 'Guidelines for Future Parents' (£1.20), a booklet for health professionals ('Environmental Factors and Foetal Health – the case for pre-conceptual care,' £1.20) and a booklet for those interested in starting a Foresight Clinic in their area called 'Running a Foresight Clinic' (£2.50). There are local meetings and major symposia once or twice a year. They run a library of literature on causes of congentital damage, the promotion of health and so on.

The Foundation for the Study of Infant Deaths

15 Belgrave Square, London SW1X 8PS (01 235 0965). Registered as a charity in 1971 with three aims: 1 to promote and sponsor research into unexpected deaths for no obvious cause of infants aged between one week and two years; 2 to encourage, support and counsel bereaved parents, and 3 to act as a centre for information and the exchange of knowledge. The Foundation is a company limited by guarantee; at 31st March 1980 the company had thirty-nine members, the number of members at present is limited to fifty. Each member has a liability to contribute to the assets of the company the sum of £1. Anyone who wishes to be kept in touch can be put on the mailing list – write to the above address or telephone the secretary in office hours. Any parent who contacts the Foundation for personal reassurance and information is offered to be put in touch with other formerly bereaved parents if they wish. Newsletters, information leaflets and a reference list are available.

Gingerbread

35 Wellington Street, London WC2 (01 240 0953). Founded in 1970 to provide support and friendship, practical help and advice, information and counselling to single parents about all kinds of problems connected with single parenthood. Gingerbread has about 20,000 members, and the membership fee is £1.25. Anyone can belong as long as they are a single parent. Phone or write for further information about joining. They also offer advice about helpful organizations on related problems and publish a quarterly magazine and a number of leaflets.

The Haemophilia Society

123 Westminster Bridge Road, London SE1. Founded in 1950 to provide fellowship for haemophiliacs and their families; to give advice on their problems; to provide financial help in cases of hardship; to publish

and distribute information useful to haemophiliacs; to give financial and other help to those in hospital, and to do all it can to enable a haemophiliac to be a useful and productive member of society. Membership is approximately 5,000 with a subscription of £5, but free for those haemophiliacs who cannot pay, and just needs completion of an application form to join. The Society is best contacted by telephone or letter. They provide a comprehensive care system, as well as education, employment, self-treatment and financial help. Many booklets are available.

Hyperactive Children's Support Group
Sally Bundy, 59 Meadowside, Angmering, Sussex BN16 4BW.   Formed in 1977 to help and support hyper-active children and their parents and to conduct research and promote investigation into the incidence of hyper-activity in the UK. Membership stands at 2,500 parents and 400 plus professional members. Subscriptions are: family membership plus diet sheet £5; diet sheet only £2. The public usually contact the Group by letter after reading articles or being advised by doctors, health visitors, schools, etc. Local contacts and groups (of which there are 114 throughout the UK) are able to cope with telephone calls. Local groups of mothers may get together for mutual support and help and aid is given to hyper-active children and their families. There is a special food programme and information leaflets are available.

Invalid Children's Aid Association
126 Buckingham Palace Road, London SW1 9SB (01 730 9891).   Founded in 1888 to work with handicapped children and their families to enable them to live as full a life as possible. Membership is limited by constitution and consists of members of various committees and other people proposed by the Executive Committee because of their expertise or past connections with the Association. For details of membership and subscriptions apply direct. The public are asked to contact the above address in the first instance where staff will deal with all enquiries on all aspects of handicap and refer to specialist agencies where appropriate. The Social Work Service helps handicapped children and their families in London and parts of the Home Counties. There are five special residential schools for children from all over the UK and a worldwide information and advisory service is available to parents, social workers and other professionals and organizations. There are books on various aspects of the Association's work, a publication, *Specialist Research,* and films are available for hire, as are speakers on a number of subjects.

La Leche League of Great Britain
BM 3424 London WC1V 6XX (01 242 1278).   This organization was founded in Chicago in 1956 by a group of mothers keen to help others breast-feed successfully and to improve their enjoyment of motherhood. There are 4,331 groups in forty-one countries worldwide and there are

12,752 group leaders. Of these, 65 groups are in Great Britain and there are 120 UK leaders. The UK organization started in 1980 although groups had been functioning for several years in an *ad hoc* way. Membership costs £8 and anyone can join. To be a counsellor, though, involves training and certain other prerequisites. Contact La Leche on the above telephone number or at the address in London. You'll be told where your local groups are. La Leche League publishes an extensive booklist and has over 100 publications available in the areas of mothering and breast-feeding. Please send an sae when requesting information. Local groups hold meetings to which anyone interested can go, and each group has a free lending library of books on breast-feeding and related subjects.

This highly professional and worldwide organization is advised by a panel of thirty-four doctors and nutrition experts and holds international conferences for health professionals and lay people.

The Leukaemia Society
Hamlyns View, St Andrews Road, Exeter, Devon EX4 2AF (0392 218514) (secretary). Formed in December 1967 with the object of doing all within their power to help other parents in the same position. Membership is now approximately 1,500. No membership fee is payable. To become a member one has to be either a sufferer, or have a very close relative with the disease. Associate members are those people who are interested in the aims of the Society. The medical profession usually recommends the Society to the family directly the disease is diagnosed; area secretaries are in constant touch with the hospitals and social workers in contact with area secretaries. Otherwise the address to contact is available from the local social services office or citizens' advice bureau. Donations are welcome to help the patients. Packs of literature are available.

Meet-a-Mum Association (MAMA)
Mrs Mary Whitlock, 26a Cumnor Hill, Oxford OX2 9HA. Founded in 1979 to provide friendship, practical help, and moral support for any mother with a new baby or small children, and particularly those suffering from post-natal depression. Membership is approximately 1,500 and there is no membership fee. If you wish to belong write to Mrs Mary Whitlock as above and enclose an sae. She will provide a local contact where possible. New mums with new babies get together to beat everything from loneliness and depression to anxiety and the fear that can blight a mother's first few months with a baby. A MAMA booklet is available from Mrs Whitlock, price 25p.

The Migraine Trust
45 Gt Ormond Street, London WC1N 3HD. Founded in 1965 to provide assistance for the furthering of research into the causes, alleviation and treatment of migraine; the promotion, assistance and encouragement of

schemes of research, education, technical training and treatment having as their basis the improvement of diagnosing, alleviating and curing migraine; the promotion of and the exchange and propagation of information relating to migraine; and the making of grants for research into the causes and treatment of migraine at universities and research institutions anywhere in the world. Donations are welcomed. The public are asked to make contact either by telephone or letter. The main purpose of the Trust is to fund research; it also offers an information service. A booklet called 'Understanding Migraine' is available together with *Migraine News*.

Muscular Dystrophy Group of Great Britain and Northern Ireland
Nattrass House, 35 Macaulay Road, London SW4 0QP (01 720 8055). Formed in 1955 as part of the Central Council for the Care of Cripples, it became independent in 1959 and was registered as a charity in 1961. The group's aims are threefold: to find out through medical research both the cause and cure of muscular dystrophy and to raise funds to further that research; to act by means of a network of branches as a friendly and supportive link between affected people and their families; and to promote knowledge about the range of diseases covered by the Group by means of an educational programme. There are 450 branches with 138 representatives scattered through the UK. However, anybody from anywhere in the world who has muscular dystrophy or neuromuscular diseases is welcome as a member and there is no membership fee. Anyone interested in promoting the aims of the group, whether they are a sufferer or related to one or not, is also welcome. Contact can be made through Headquarters or a local contact. Information leaflets and booklets are available on request.

The National Association for Gifted Children
1 South Audley Street, London W1Y 5DG (01 499 1188). Founded in 1966 to assist by all possible means children with outstanding gifts and talents to fulfil their potential, and to give support to parents, teachers and others professionally concerned with their development, thus to ensure that these children develop naturally. Membership currently runs at about 3,000 and is open to any adult on completion of the appropriate form and payment of the subscription for the class of membership they require. Individual membership fee £7.50 p.a., family membership £12 p.a., corporate membership £15 p.a. Parents of gifted children are often referred by teachers, doctors, educational psychologists, health visitors and social workers. Application forms are sent on request to headquarters. The NAGC offers counselling services, children's activities, residential courses and publicity material – film and video tapes – all of which are available from headquarters. The main publication is a twice yearly newsletter which goes to all members.

National Association for Maternal and Child Welfare

1 South Audley Street, London W1Y 6JS (01 491 2772).   Founded in 1938 to assist health education in its widest sense by producing leaflets on home management, child care and family health mainly for sale to mothers but also to promote discussion amongst interested groups. Membership is open (upon payment of an annual fee) to four categories, mainly organizations. It works in association with all health. education and service authorities, community health councils, teaching hospitals, university departments, and any organization concerned with the welfare of mothers and children and is concerned with all aspects of human relationships, homemaking, preparation for parenthood and child development and management (including teenagers). Basic courses are offered to secondary schools and colleges, and there is a list of publications and many information booklets.

National Association for Mental Health (MIND)

22 Harley Street, London W1N 2ED (01 637 0741).   Formed in 1946 to improve and develop services for people who are mentally ill or mentally handicapped and to encourage discussion of mental health issues throughout the community. There are approximately 5,000 full members and 10,000 affiliated members. Full membership costs £5.50, which includes a subscription to the monthly magazine *Mind Out*, and is open to anyone. Contact is made via the central MIND office or via one of the five regional offices. MIND's advice and information workers deal with thousands of enquiries each year from families and professionals; it has training programmes aimed to give mental health workers access to specialist skills; runs courses, conferences and workshops for professionals and volunteers; and has a legal and welfare rights department which fights discrimination against people who have a history of mental disability. Mind's mental health review tribunal offers a representation service to patients who want to leave psychiatric hospitals. MIND publishes books, reports and leaflets as well as the monthly magazine *Mind Out*.

The National Association for the Welfare of Children in Hospital

Argyle House, 29–34 Euston Road, London N1 (01 833 2041).   Began in 1961 to raise standards of care for all children in hospital. Membership stands at 800. Subscriptions: £5 for individual members or a lower subscription to become an active group member. Membership is open to anyone concerned with the welfare of children in hospital. Contact head office at above address for national information service, details of publications, membership and active local groups.

NAWCH groups aim to persuade local hospitals to improve children's services, give practical help, visit lonely children, give equipment or arrange transport or baby sitting, help to teach children about hospital care by visiting local schools and speak to many parent and student meetings. There is a list of available publications.

The National Autistic Society
276 Willesden lane, London NW2 5RB (01 451 3844).   Founded in 1962 to provide help and encouragement to autistic children and their parents, to encourage research and to stimulate understanding among doctors, teachers and the general public. Subscription stands at £1 p.a. for parents and professionals. (£35 life membership for parents). Membership is open to parents of autistic children, interested friends and relatives, and to professionals interested in the problems of autism. Contact can be made by telephone, letter, personal interview at the above offices or through a doctor or social worker. The services offered are advisory for parents, information for professionally interested people on teaching methods, special schools or classes, adult communities and training units. Booklets, a newsletter, and a list of available publications may be obtained from the above address.

National Children's Bureau
8 Wakeley Street, Islington, London EC1V 7QE.   Founded in 1963 and has a membership around 2,000. Individual membership is available to anyone completing the application form and returning it to the registered office with the subscription of £12.50 and not only individuals are welcomed but all organizations, professional workers and anyone concerned with the betterment of children whether normal or handicapped, whether they live with their own families or are cared for elsewhere. The bureau has an unrivalled storehouse of information about children's special needs, as well as their normal growth and runs an information service supported by a specialist library, carries out research, monitors practice in the field, sets up working parties and special enquiries and reviews, and evaluates and summarises other people's research. It has a quarterly journal, *Concern,* and produces books and journals, lists of which are available on application.

National Children's Homes
85 Highbury Park, London N5 1UD (01 226 2033).   Founded in 1869 to care for children and their families in need through a variety of provisions in homes, hostels or schools, or in the community-based centres and projects. In 1980 membership consisted of 6,500 children and 2,000 staff. Contact is made through the regional social work officer. There is also a family network service which is a phone-in service for people with family cares. It has a bank of information on local and national facilities and services for the family; provides residential homes for different ages and needs and a variety of day care in the community for families at risk. Leaflets on the services provided are available.

The National Childbirth Trust
9 Queensborough Terrace, Bayswater, London W2 3TB (01 221 3833). Founded in 1956 when a number of women joined together to improve

women's experience of birth and to relieve the fear with which many women approached birth. The aim is to improve women's knowledge about childbirth and to promote the teaching of relaxation and breathing for labour; to help women to have babies happily and without fear; and to prepare young families for the experience of childbirth and parenthood. There are over 10,000 national members. Membership fees are: £10 individual; £15 couples and £20 overseas. To become a member of the Trust it is necessary to pay an annual subscription fee. For those needing immediate support and advice contact the national office by telephoning the number above. The services offered include antenatal classes, breast-feeding counselling, post-natal support, training for antenatal teachers, and education in schools. A series of leaflets is available and the NCT sells a range of books on preparation for birth and breast-feeding. The NCT also markets a nursing brassiere, nightdresses, baby nests, baby slings, etc.

The National Child-minding Association
8 Mason's Hill, Bromley, Kent BR2 9EY (01 464 6164). Founded in 1977 by a group of child-minders, parents and other interested people. There are now over 5,000 members, many of whom are child-minders belonging to increasing numbers of local groups and associations all over the country.

The aims of the Association are: to foster and promote the provision of educational, happy, secure and stimulating day care facilities for young children; to encourage the recognition of child-minding as a positive part of this provision; to encourage contact and communication between child-minders (mainly through the quarterly newsletter); to encourage the setting up of local groups; and to provide help and advice to those looking after other people's children so that the quality of the service to the children can be improved.

Annual membership costs £5.00 for individuals and there are various group memberships.

The Association organizes National Child-minding Week, publishes a book on child-minding, looks into programmes for training child-minders, has a block insurance scheme available to members and publishes *Who Minds?* quarterly and other free leaflets for would-be child-minders or those needing a minder. Various other publications are available. Send sae.

National Council for the Divorced and Separated
41 Summit Avenue, Kingsbury, London NW9 OT4 (01 205 8316). Founded in 1974, the aims of the council are 'to identify and promote the interests and welfare of all persons whose marriages have ended in divorce or separation'. This is done by providing a forum for discussion of matters of general concern and common interest. It also aims to develop services for the welfare and benefit of all divorced and separated people and their children, to develop counselling services in various parts of the country

and to review existing and proposed legislation that is of relevance. It has over 100 branches all over the British Isles, and help and advice are freely given by the council's welfare consultant irrespective of whether the applicant is a member. There are 8,500 branch members and 200 individual members. Applications for corporate membership will be considered (an annual fee of 50p per head is payable) and the individual membership fee is £2 annually. The council distributes a quarterly newssheet. If you are interested in joining, write, enclosing a stamped, self-addressed envelope, to the secretary at the above address.

National Council for Voluntary Organizations
The Information Department, NCVO, 26 Bedford Square, London WC1B 3HU. Founded in 1919 to promote the systematic organization of voluntary social work, both nationally and socially. There are various categories of membership and a booklet 'Guide to NCVO Services – an aid for users', is available which explains this. NCVO works with 187 councils for voluntary services, 43 rural community councils, 628 community associations and many other local groups, has a large membership of national organizations, works with international governmental and non-governmental organizations and at least six million people help the work of charities and voluntary organizations either as volunteers or as professional staff. NCVO's principal task is to provide support to the voluntary organizations who provide many of the vital welfare services in this country. It provides training courses and has a library of 5,000 books and pamphlets, and 400 periodicals – all relevant to voluntary organizations.

National Deaf/Blind and Rubella Association (SENSE)
311 Grays Inn Road, London WC1X 8PT (01 278 1005). Founded in 1965 to provide direct financial or material help to the deaf/blind and rubella handicapped or those who care for them; to collect and spread useful information and to encourage and initiate research in all aspects of the handicaps and their treatment; and to campaign for an effective vaccination programme. Membership is 750 and includes 300 parents of handicapped children. Subscription is £2.50 p.a. Membership is open to deaf/blind and/or rubella handicapped people, a relation, or someone having a personal or professional interest in the aims and philosophy of the Association. Write, telephone, or pay a personal visit. Information booklets and leaflets containing information on deaf/blindness and education and training are available.

The National Deaf Children's Society
45 Hereford Road, London W2 5AH (01 229 9272). Founded in 1945 to make the public aware of the problems of deaf children and to help them and their parents obtain maximum benefits from education and welfare and to give support to all parents of deaf children. Membership is open to

anyone and the public usually telephone or write to headquarters for general information – an sae is helpful. The Society tries to inform the public about the problem of deaf children by leaflets; and talks are arranged by people from the head office and from regions and branches but the main part of the service is to parents of deaf children. Several helpful booklets are available, the main publication being the magazine *Talk* issued to members.

National Eczema Society
Tavistock House North, Tavistock Square, London WC1H 9SR. Formed in 1975 to act as a channel of information for eczema sufferers and those oncerned with their welfare, and to fund research into the condi tion. Membership at the end of 1980 was approximately 3,400. To become a member enclose the subscription with the completed application form and return to Head Office. Subscription £7 p.a. For help and information contact the head office or a local branch by letter or telephone. The Society runs meetings for people with the problem so as to gain mutual support and exchange information. There are also talks by experts and discussions among patients and parents. Information leaflets, advice on self-help and treatment, and a mail order service for cotton clothing for eczema sufferers is available.

The National Marriage Guidance Council
Herbert Gray College, Little Church Street, Rugby CV21 3AP. A self-help organization founded in 1937 to offer people in marital conflict a rational alternative to the dilemma of either ending the partnership by divorce or perpetuating unchanged the marriage with its barriers and tensions. There are 140 local groups throughout the country whose job is to organize support and to raise money to provide a marriage counselling service in their area. To arrange a talk ring the number listed in the local telephone directory; advice is free but a contribution to the cost of the work is welcome, a suggested figure is between £1.50 and £3 per hour. As well as personal counselling services, many local MGCs contribute towards education for marriage and family life by providing speakers for schools, youth clubs, parents' associations and local organizations. Courses are run for professionals who are called upon to help people who are in personal difficulty, and leaflets are available on many subjects.

National Society for the Prevention of Cruelty to Children
67 Saffron Hill, London EC1N 8RS. Founded in 1884 to alleviate the suffering of children and to help when problems are small before matters are allowed to get out of hand. The NSPCC has a force of 235 men and women Inspectors in thirty-one groups in Great Britain and Scotland. The Society is run on voluntary contributions and has 5,000 voluntary district committees in 217 branches who work with the inspectors and help to raise funds. The inspectors are on call twenty-four hours a day, seven days

a week on a telephone number found in the local directory and with voluntary helpers investigate cases involving children and help parents or relatives who ask them for assistance. NSPCC provides skilled treatment through special units for families in which children are considered to be seriously at risk, provides care and stimulation for pre-school children from disturbed family backgrounds, trains new inspectors and provides courses for caring professionals. The Society's supporters are kept informed through publications and also help with the distribution of publicity leaflets.

One Parent Families
255 Kentish Town Road, London NW5 2LX (01 267 1361). Founded in · 1918 to improve the position of lone parents and their children. For details of subscription scheme apply direct. Contact the information office, telephone number above. The Council offers help and advice to individual parents and single pregnant women and helps in cases of poverty, employment, housing, legal problems and stress. Its library acquires the latest books, pamphlets, periodicals, press cuttings and official publications relating to one-parent families and social policy and produces leaflets and information sheets for parents on social security, tax, legal aid and children in care.

Parents Anonymous
6 Manor Gardens, off Holloway Road, Islington, London N7 (01 263 8918). Founded in 1976 as a voluntary organization designed to help parents who are likely to abuse their children. There are at present 100 volunteer members who must be a parent and must attend a twelve-hour preparation course spread over six weeks, and be 'passed' by the committee. Contact should be made initially by telephone, although some people write. The volunteers offer telephone counselling and befriending by visits and have a back-up team of social workers, doctors and administrators who will help with individual cases. The volunteer's main task is to offer sympathetic and positive aid to callers who have need of a friend. Users may remain anonymous if they wish and all information given by callers remains confidential. See local telephone directories for telephone number or call the number above (twenty-four-hour service).

The Patients' Association
Room 33, 18 Charing Cross Road, London WC2. Started in 1963 to represent and further the interests of patients; to give help and advice to individuals and to promote understanding and goodwill between patients and everyone in medical practice and related activities. Membership is between 8–900 and the membership fee is £3 p.a. Any individual may join but corporate bodies are not accepted. The Association prefers to deal with the public by correspondence or telephone and gives advice on: using the NHS; getting information; sorting out difficulties; making suggestions;

making complaints; and patients' rights. An application for membership form, pamphlets and a newsletter are available. A self-help directory of organizations is also published at a charge of £3.00.

Pregnancy Advisory Service
11–13 Charlotte Street, London W1P 1HD.   Set up in 1968 to provide advice and assistance for women in distress because of an unwanted pregnancy; to help those with lawful grounds for termination to obtain treatment; and to promote education and research into the subject of pregnancy and abortion. Fees are paid by patients for consultation and operations and contribute towards cost of the advisory service. A charitable fund is available for women who cannot afford to pay for treatment. There is a separate advisory service for women from overseas. It provides a caring and flexible service to women which is responsive to the emerging needs of women. Advisory leaflets are available.

Pre-School Playgroups Association
61–63 Kings Cross Road, London WC1X 9LL (01 833 0991).   Founded in 1962 to promote community situations in which parents can with growing enjoyment and confidence make the best use of their knowledge and resources in the development of their children and themselves. Membership stands at 16,500 with a fee of £10 for individual members and £19.50 p.a. for a play-group. Membership application forms just need to be filled in and sent to head office together with the subscription. Contact can be made either at the above address or through local organizations. Membership is open to all and aims at providing play opportunities for pre-school children and to encourage parent involvement, offering children time and space, activity and rest, talk and listening, companionship, etc. Parents become involved in planning and setting up equipment and materials. Many leaflets on every type of play are available together with a list of publications.

The Psoriasis Association
7 Milton Street, Northampton NN2 7JG.   Founded in 1968 to promote and fund research; to set up branches and groups in various parts of the country to provide social contact; to inform sufferers and the general public, about psoriasis. Membership stands at almost 9,500 with subscriptions of £7 p.a. (ordinary) or £4 (senior citizens and those of low income) on completion of an application form or by writing a letter with the appropriate membership fee. Contact is mostly made by correspondence or telephone and the Association provides moral support and general information about all aspects of psoriasis. Helpful information leaflets are available.

Royal National Institute for the Blind

224 Great Portland Street, London W1N 6AA.   Founded in 1868 to help blind people in the UK. It depends on funds from donations, covenants and legacies to continue and expand its services to the 120,000 blind people in the UK. Contact can be made through regional offices or local authorities in the first place and a very wide variety of services are offered including education advice, residential grammar schools, training for employment, employment, rehabilitation for newly-blind people, recreation, homes, hostels and hotels and financial help. All types of literature and music are available in braille and there is a talking library. Items of games and apparatus are available especially for the blind. The Institute is also active in funding and supporting research. Many free leaflets are available as well as general leaflets, prospectuses for RNIB establishments, and books.

The Royal National Institute for the Deaf

105 Gower Street, London WC1 6AH.   Founded in 1911 to promote and encourage the prevention and alleviation of deafness and generally to promote, safeguard and protect the interests and welfare of deaf people. The Institute is limited to 500 members only. An application form is available on request, but services are available to anyone who seeks advice by letter or telephone. It offers a wide range of services: library and information services; training in manual communication; research and development; special training centres and residential homes; and deals with many personal problems. A book, *Into The 80s,* gives a general idea of the services available. There is a wide selection of publicity and information material as well as a list of publications and aids.

Royal Society for Mentally Handicapped Children and Adults (MENCAP)

Mencap National Centre, 123 Golden Lane, London EC1Y 0BT.   Founded in 1946 to provide help and support for families of the handicapped, to increase the understanding of mental handicap by the general public and to obtain provision for all mentally handicapped people commensurate with their needs. The Society has 55,000 members in local societies and affiliated members from forty other associations.

The central office at Golden Lane is open daily from 9.30 a.m. – 5.30 p.m. where professional staff deal with enquiries from parents and professionals on all aspects of mental handicap. It provides special advice and help through both central and regional offices, education in three residential centres for young adults and appropriate educational programmes in four other residential homes for younger children. Books, reports, handbooks and pamphlets are available for both parents and professionals. A general price list is available.

The Royal Society for the Prevention of Accidents

Cannon House, The Priory, Queensway, Birmingham B4 6BS. Founded in 1916 to prevent accidents at home, on the road, at work or school, in agriculture, in water and at leisure. It is Europe's largest safety organization. The Society is divided into three divisions each with a membership scheme and scales of charges for the various schemes, open to Government agencies, the British Standards Institution, trade associations and other voluntary bodies who serve on the various committees. There are about 20,000 subscribers at present. There is also the Tufty Club for children (formed in 1961) and membership is around the three million mark. This Society offers publicity, training, education, improvements in the environment, improved medical care and legislation for safer practices to prevent accidents. Publicity material is available on all aspects of safety. Films and posters are also supplied.

The Samaritans

17 Uxbridge Road, Slough SL1 1SN. Founded in 1953 to help the suicidal and despairing, this is a worldwide fellowship of volunteers dedicated to the prevention of suicide and the alleviation of loneliness and depression. Contact by telephone, personal call to centres, or by letter. The Samaritans offer friendship, a round-the-clock service to the suicidal and despairing, absolute confidentiality, no evangelizing, a free service, and listening without strings. Factual leaflets are available.

The Spastics Society

12 Park Crescent, London W1N 4EQ. Founded in 1952 for the care, welfare, interest, treatment, education and advancement of those suffering from any form of cerebral palsy. There are approximately 250 members of whom about 200 are nominee members of local groups. There is no membership fee, but individuals, apart from a few in special categories, cannot become voting members of the Society. They can become associate members on payment of £3 per annum which entitles them to a copy of the annual report and *Spastics News* and to attend the Society's AGM. Contact by writing or telephone. The Society offers accommodation and care, holidays, employment, personal social services, research programmes and many leaflets. Books and films are also available.

Spinal Injuries Association

Yeoman's House, 76 St James' Lane, London NW10 3DF. Founded in 1974 to help individuals achieve their own goals, to bring about the best medical care and rehabilitation and to stimulate scientific research into paraplegia. Membership is some 4,500 full (spinal cord injured), associates (all other individuals) and affiliates (groups, companies, etc.). Membership £5 p.a. for individuals and £10 p.a. affiliate membership. To join complete a membership form and return. The public can contact SIA by telephone or letter. SIA offer information on living with a spinal cord injury; how and why the environment needs to be modified to enable disabled people to live normal, everyday lives; information on rehabilitation, housing, employment, mobility, etc.; information about spinal injuries in this country and abroad; sports for disabled people and sports and recreational facilities. Of particular interest to the general public is the publication *So You're Paralysed and Able to Work* and other publications which may be purchased through the post. Information leaflets are also available.

Toy Libraries Association
Seabrook House, Wyllyotts Manor, Darkes Lane, Potters Bar, Herts EN6 2HL.   Established in 1972 to act as the parent body for toy libraries; to test and assess toys and play equipment and to publish the findings for the benefit of the general public and groups; and to produce design worksheets of toys, leisure aids and communication aids for severely handicapped children and adults. Membership is around 800. Application by completion of form – individuals £4.50; active groups, toy libraries or other groups £6.50; corporate £50; and overseas £18 p.a. Toy Libraries may be contacted at the above address by letter or telephone during office hours from Monday to Friday. Toy Libraries offers contact with the nearest toy library or local active group, publications, advice on setting up a toy library or local active group, and advice on buying toys. Available on request are lists of publications, articles and the *Journal of the Toy Libraries*.

Twins Clubs Association
Judi Linney, 198 Woodham Lane, New Haw, Weybridge.   Started in 1978 to give encouragement and support to parents of twins, triplets or more; to publish a national register of twins clubs; to promote and establish future clubs; to produce and disseminate helpful information and literature to members; to increase public and commercial awareness of the special needs of twins and their families; to promote greater appreciation within the medical profession of the problems of multiple births; and to raise funds to promote the above aims. The annual subscription of £1 covers newsletters and allows members access to all information and special membership cards to facilitate shopping discounts. For information contact the chairman (Judi Linney) enclosing an sae. Twins Clubs members meet to hold discussions, coffee mornings, speakers, outings, etc. Available through the TCA are leaflets on the general management of twins, the Register of Twins Clubs, stationery and a 'Guide for Mothers with Twins', all available at a small charge.

Voluntary Council for Handicapped Children – National Children's Bureau
8 Wakeley Street, Islington, London EC1V 7QE.   Established in 1975 to draw attention to the gaps, overlaps and general lack of coordination in

services for handicapped children and their families. The Voluntary Council has no individual membership fee but charges £15 for organizations. Its present day overall purpose is to promote coordination between organizations concerned with handicapped children. Contact is made directly by telephone or letter. The Council offers information to both parents and professionals, workshop seminars and community residential homes. Many publications and fact sheets are published.

Australia

The Asthma Foundation of New South Wales
Wingello House, 1–12 Angel Place, Sydney 2000. Founded in December 1961 to acquire and utilize information concerning the cause, management and ultimate cure of asthma and related respiratory ailments. Membership currently runs at approx. 200. The Foundation is a public company limited by guarantee. There is no membership fee for the Foundation but a subsidiary body – The Asthma Welfare Society – welcomes members at an annual subscription of $A10. Membership of the Foundation is by invitation. Membership of the Welfare Society is by application and payment of subscription. Contact can be made by mail or telephone. The Society offers general advice, informative literature, special swimming classes, annual holday camps, mothers' meetings, seminars, etc. and will supply information leaflets on request.

Autistic Children's Association of New South Wales
Head Office: 545 Pacific Highway, Artarmon, NSW 2064. All correspondence should be addressed to Box 607, PO Chatswood, NSW 2067. Founded in July 1966 to provide and promote day and residential centres for the care and education of autistic children; to help parents, particularly by arranging meetings between them where they can exchange information; to encourage research into the problems of these children; to stimulate more understanding amongst the medical and lay public of these children's problems; and to tell them what can and must be done to help them lead normal lives. The present membership is approximately 650, the fee for which is $A10 p.a. To become a member send a completed application form together with subscription to the correspondence address above. Services are offered through the professional services which include a diagnostic teaching centre, schools, counselling, encouragement of research and the advancement of public awareness and understanding.

Challenge Foundation of New South Wales
Box 229, PO Ryde 2112; Central office – 8 Junction St, Ryde, NSW 2112. Founded in 1951 to promote the welfare of the intellectually handicapped in the moderately and severely handicapped range through education, training, ensuring that they receive maximum opportunities to

allow them to reach their full potential, and to guarantee that those in the Association's care will be adequately cared for during their lifetime. Membership stands at approximately 3,800 at $A15 family membership p.a. and $A10 single person p.a. One can join either through the central office or through one of the sixty-two branches throughout New South Wales. Contact can be made by the public through the central office. Members are offered an information service, a library service from central office and branch members are entitled to use whatever facilities the branch may run. A 'Challenge Advocate' Newsletter is published quarterly.

Childbirth Education Association of Australia (NSW) Ltd
PO Box 413, Hurstville, NSW 2220. Founded in 1964 to advise and prepare couples for childbirth and parenting. Membership consists of 2,500 couples who pay a subscription of $A10 per annum. Most couples become members as a result of attending classes, fill out a membership form and pay the fee. The public can contact CEA at Childbirth Education Association (NSW) Ltd, 127 Forest Road, Hurstville, NSW 2220. Ph: 574927. CEA offer preparation for childbirth and parenting, post-natal support, Caesarean support and Caesarean preparation classes, unexpected outcomes support, film nights for expectant couples, childbirth education classes for school children, sales of lambskins, baby slings and books on childbirth; library facilities are available to all people attending classes. Several publications are available. Video hire service available to public.

The Coeliac Society of New South Wales
PO Box 271, Wahroonga, NSW 2076. Founded in 1974 to assist people who have been diagnosed as coeliacs. There are approximately 800 members in NSW with branches in all other states of Australia. Membership fee is $A7 p.a. On completion of the diagnosis, patients are referred to the Society, contact being made by letter or telephone; ninety-nine percent of members come to the Society through the dietary department of public hospitals after diagnosis by gastro-enterologists. They are offered dietary advice, medical lectures, recipes, etc.

Cystic Fibrosis Foundation of NSW
40 Milton Street, Ashfield, PO Box 241, NSW 2131 (Burwood 2134). Founded in 1967 to provide funding for research; to educate by providing information on cystic fibrosis; to ensure early diagnosis; and to create public awareness of cystic fibrosis. Further objectives are to promote the welfare of cystic fibrosis children and adults by providing help with equipment costs and support to the family through social work and welfare services.

Membership is approximately 750 which include families with a cystic fibrosis member as well as interested parties not suffering from the disease. The membership fee is $A10. To join, an intending member simply fills out an application form which is obtainable from the office or cystic fibrosis clinic. The public may contact the Association by telephone, letter or personal call to the office. Members are offered a Family Support Scheme and a social work and youth work service. Speakers can be arranged to address groups such as child care trainees. Literature is available on request.

Diabetic Association of New South Wales
9th Floor, National Building, 250 Pitt St, Sydney NSW 2000. Founded in 1937 to educate the public in the needs of the diabetic, and to give counselling for the diabetic, relatives, friends and employers of the diabetic. Membership is approximately 8,000 and is open to diabetics and non-diabetics – full member (diabetic) $A24, associate (non-diabetic) $A24, pensioner $A16, junior $A20 and family members $30 – who agree to abide by the rules of the Memorandum and By-Laws of the Association as incorporated in 1961. The public may contact the Association by correspondence or telephone. The aim is to try to educate diabetics, families of diabetics, medical and para-medical groups, employers and unions, Government bodies and the public at large regarding the needs of diabetics, to provide counselling and welfare assistance to diabetics and their families and to provide literature and medical supplies for the diabetic.

Epilepsy Association of NSW
468 Pennant Hills Road, (PO Box 521), Pennant Hills 2120. Founded in 1952 to break down the barriers relating to epilepsy and to educate the public. This is an ongoing project. The only nursing home for people with epilepsy in the southern hemisphere is conducted by the Association and they aim to build more. Another aim is to provide a hostel for country people who have to come to the city for specialized treatment. Membership consists of 720 families throughout NSW with a membership fee of $A15 per family. To join, telephone or call personally then complete a printed membership form. The public is welcome to contact the Association by phone, letter or through any country branch. Services offered: a specially trained welfare/counsellor, and an honorary medical panel which members can visit for consultation by referral from their own doctor. A specially printed newsletter is distributed regularly to branch office and support groups advising of happenings within the association. Public meetings are conducted and there is a speaking panel to promote the work through service clubs.

The Muscular Dystrophy Association of New South Wales
Cnr Chalmers and Bedford Streets, PO Box 10, Strawberry Hills 2012. Established in 1957 to supply wheelchairs and other orthopaedic aids to muscular dystrophy patients and funding for research into the cause of

muscular dystrophy. Membership consists of approximately 370 patients of various types who pay $A2 per person or family annually. A handbook is supplied on request by telephone or letter to assist families and patients in their search for available services. The Association offers genetic counselling and blood analysis for carrier detection. Helpful leaflets are available on request. Family support group meets every 6–8 weeks to help patients and their families.

The Royal New South Wales Institute for Deaf and Blind Children
361–365 North Rocks Road, North Rocks 2151.   Founded in 1860 to care for deaf, blind, deaf/blind and multi-handicapped blind children from all parts of the State of NSW. A fund-raising volunteer support group with members of thirty clubs and eleven different committees and auxiliaries raise money for the institute each year. The services are available only to parents and children living in NSW and ACT. The institute offers everything deaf and blind children need, the most advanced technological equipment and every possible amenity for learning, sporting and leisure activities is provided. The children also receive the care and compassionate guidance of highly specialized, trained and qualified staff. It provides a career education programme and has a computerized braille production department which supplies the institute's own requirements and offers a braille transcription service to clients throughout Australia. The institute is Australia's major braille publisher.

The Spastic Centre of New South Wales
6 Queen Street, Mosman, NSW 2088.   Started in 1945 to investigate and ascertain particulars of cerebral palsied children, educate, transport, give vocational training guidance and set up workshops, farms, hostels, etc. Membership is composed of the parents of cerebral palsied children and adults who are admitted to the Centre on a permanent basis for treatment and training and disabled people over age of 18. The membership fee is $A10 for adults, but the Spastic Centre does not make any charge for the service it renders to those in its permanent care. Honorary memberships may be appointed from time to time for those persons who have performed outstanding voluntary services to the centre and its children, limited to 20 at any one time. Contact should be made with the Medical Director at the address above or alternatively contact the Spastic Centre of NSW, 189 Allambie Road, Allambie Heights, 2100, Australia. The Spastic Centre is constituted for providing the specialized treatment, training, education, work training, employment and residential care of the cerebral palsied who live within the state of New South Wales. Printed matter regarding facilities and services is available on request.

The Spina Bifida Group of New South Wales
PO Box 15, Carlingford 2118.   Founded in 1972 by a group of parents to solve some of the many problems faced by these families. The Association

is essentially a self-help organization and the constitution demands that not less than three-quarters of the management committee be either parents or people who themselves have spina bifida. There are about 600 known families and membership is $A15 per family per year. Membership is open to anyone interested in spina bifida. The Association pays fifty per cent of costs of the following: orthopaedic boots; boys' urinal equipment; catheters; major buggies; wheelchairs for home use; disposable nappies and incontinence pants. A magazine, *Torque,* is published to keep members informed. Counselling, physiotherapy, occupational therapy, vocational training and employment advice, and schooling services are also available through the Association.

The Sudden Infant Death Association
Box 172, St Ives, 2075 NSW. Founded in 1977 to provide support for parents who have lost a baby to cot death (SIDS); to educate the public on the known facts about SIDS; and to promote research into the causes and prevention of SIDS. There are now about 1,000 families that belong to the Association in New South Wales and each state in Australia has its own Association. Membership costs $A4 p.a. and anyone who has lost a baby or who is a close relative of someone who has can belong. Friends and professional health care workers can belong too. Contact the Association by mail or at public meetings.

Services include those of a team at Sydney Children's Hospital offering advice and investigation of 'subsequent' babies in an SIDS family or of babies thought to be 'at risk'. The Association also provides finance for the home monitoring of 'at risk' babies and regional support groups for parents to attend. There is also a regular newsletter.

New Zealand

National Children's Health Research Foundation Cot Death Division
5 Clonbern Road, PO Box 28–177, Auckland (Tel 548597). The division was formed in 1979 to combat cot death, with the following stated aims: to spread true information; to help bereaved parents; to establish nationwide cot death support groups; to safeguard infants 'at risk' from cot death; and to maintain contact with workers and developments in other countries. There are thirty support groups throughout NZ and while there is no membership fee, donations are welcomed.

New Zealand Asthma Foundation
PO Box 1459, Wellington. Formed in 1983, the Foundation is the central body of the thirty local Asthma Societies which are found throughout New Zealand. The Foundation is involved with the education of asthmatics and health care professionals, and research, welfare and liaison. Membership of the local societies is approaching 10,000 and is open to anyone. The Societies offer summer camps for asthmatic children,

swimming and exercise classes, advice on drugs and medical treatment. and general support. The Foundation has published several pamphlets about asthma in a series which will eventually have at least twenty titles – more than 300,000 copies have already been printed. The Foundation's national journal 'Timohu' (Maori for wheezing) is published quarterly and contains news, medical and other treatment articles, book reviews, letters, etc. All society members and all NZ GPs receive copies. The Foundation's funding is entirely from public donations.

New Zealand Asthma Society (Inc.)

PO Box 40-333, Upper Butt.   Founded in 1958 to assist the welfare of asthmatics by promoting research and providing welfare. There are sixteen branches throughout New Zealand, each with a panel of doctors in an advisory capacity. Membership is approximately 4,000 and is open to anyone on payment of an annual subscription of $NZ5. The public is encouraged to contact the Society by publishing notices in the newspapers of functions held. The Society offers summer camps for asthmatic children, swimming classes, advice on drugs and medical treatment and general support. A leaflet is available on understanding asthma and a journal is published containing branch news, book reviews, letters and a membership application form.

The New Zealand Crippled Children Society (Inc.)

PO Box 6349, Te Aro, Wellington.   Te Aro was founded in 1935 and is concerned with the care of all crippled children in New Zealand. There are currently 8,500 under the Society's care with 23,000 members supporting the Society, the fee for which varies from branch to branch but is approximately $NZ5 with a range of options for family, corporate, and life membership. To join one pays the fee to a branch office. The public can contact the Society in person, by telephone or by letter. Services vary from branch to branch but offer direct welfare assistance, ensure that every child has the earliest possible treatment, help the immediate family understand the child's problems and needs, ensure that the child has a sound vocational training and help promote an attitude among employers which will bring suitable work. There is a recreational programme and they also offer architectural and mobility advisory services as a complement to the State Welfare programme. Many booklets and leaflets are published.

New Zealand Federation for Deaf Children

PO Box 2914, Wellington.   The Federation serves as a parent group for regional associations for deaf children; there are fourteen member groups and five associate member groups throughout the country, which charge an annual subscription fee of $NZ10. The Federation is committed to the education, health and welfare of deaf children, and is involved with such activities as lobbying government to promote the interests of their members.

The New Zealand Society for the Intellectually Handicapped (Inc.)
Private Bay, Wellington. Registered in 1949 to promote physical, educational, economic and social welfare of the intellectually handicapped. Supported by donations, fund-raising and legacies. There is no membership as such and paid staff run the services in thirty-two branches, which may be contacted by the public. It assists parents and guardians to provide care and welfare for any intellectually handicapped person; promotes and assists in the establishment and maintenance of schools, classes, centres, homes, hostels, clinics, camps, etc. and enlists the support of the Government and other bodies to help in all aspects of service needed for the handicapped. Many leaflets, books, etc. are available.

Royal New Zealand Plunket Society
New Zealand Headquarters, PO Box 6042, Dunedin North. Formed in 1907 to provide the best opportunity for parents to learn the routine and accepted procedure of infant care. The services provided are free but contributions are welcomed. There are 121 branches and nearly 700 sub-branches but individual membership is difficult to assess. Contact is usually made with mothers through the Plunket nurse at or just prior to the birth of her infant. The Society has 400 full-time and part-time nurses who see nearly all newborn babies in New Zealand, offers accident prevention, immunization campaigns, baby-sitting services, health information and gives sound, reliable instructions, advice and assistance on all matters affecting the health and well-being of babies and children. Leaflets are available on many aspects of child care.

The Spina Bifida Association of New Zealand
PO Box 68454, Newton, Auckland. Founded in 1973 because a group of interested people, not only parents, wanted to offer extra help and assistance over and above that already provided by various organizations to people with spina bifida.

The aims of the Association are to assist those with spina bifida to adapt to their environment and to endeavour to assist in the prevention of the condition.

The Association provides many beneficial services and holds functions such as panel discussion evenings; picnics; Christmas parties and social evenings for parents and friends. Membership is open to anyone interested in the welfare, education and happiness of those with spina bifida.

South Africa

Child Welfare Society
PO Box 2539, Johannesburg 2000. Founded in 1909 to protect children from abuse and to be champion of children's rights. Membership extends

to approximately 260. The membership fee is R5 and to belong one has to be affiliated by one's work or interest/fund-raising/committee member and to pay a membership fee. The public should report any suspicious case or act relating to the welfare of a child through the Society's social workers. Services range from professional services in family counselling, casework, (including foster care, adoption, care of unmarried mothers), to group and community work. The Society runs five children's family homes, four crêches and one after school care centre, the latter to alleviate the problem of latch-key children. Information leaflets are limited at present but there is a newsletter, *Today's Children*, available.

The National Council for the Care of Cripples in South Africa
10173 Johannesburg 2000.   Established in 1939. Its aims are to ensure a national service for cripples by coordinating and correlating the activities and work of the various societies, departments and institutions concerned with or interested in the problems of crippled people of all ages and population groups through the Republic of South Africa; to formulate policies and supporting measures and schemes for the total rehabilitation and general welfare of cripples; and to be the official channel for communication in matters of general policy between constituent bodies, the government and provincial authorities. Also aims to cooperate with national organizations in South Africa and in other countries and is generally concerned with all matters and questions relating to the care and rehabilitation of cripples and the prevention and research into crippling conditions. Membership consists of four representatives from eight autonomous regions which cover the entire country. The membership of each region runs into thousands as they have local associations and branches in each area. Members of Regional Cripple Care Associations pay a nominal subscription. Any person prepared to pay the membership fee may join a Cripple Care Association. Members of the public may contact the Council through the above address and directories of names and addresses of regional secretaries are published. The services offered include social work, arranging attendance of cripples at clinics, establishment and maintenance of institutions such as special schools, care centres, etc., employment projects and assistance to crippled persons by way of transport aids and materials needs. Many printed leaflets are available.

The South African National Council for the Blind
PO Box 11149, Brooklyn 0011.   Founded in 1929 and constituted from people who are representatives of affiliated societies (schools, societies, etc.). The Council acts as a consultative body to the government on matters of policy and as a reviewing authority concerning activities or developments in work with blind and partially sighted persons. It acts as a channel for information; as a liaison between societies and agencies; promotes and provides financial assistance for education, training and employment; provides eye care; promotes welfare projects; supports or

promotes legislation; and manufactures or commissions appliances and articles for the visually handicapped. A bimonthly magazine is published reporting local and international developments in the field. There are also various pamphlets on available services and biennial reports.

South African National Council for the Deaf
PO Box 31663, Johannesburg.   Founded in 1929 and constituted of affiliate and associate members, operating on a national basis to coordinate services for the deaf. Eleven societies and nineteen schools for the deaf are affiliated to the Council whilst some thirty other organizations dealing among other things with the deaf are associate members of the Council. No membership fee is applicable to member organizations. Normal people are not allowed to become members of the Council except such people who, because of their special knowledge of, or interest in, the deaf have been invited to become special members. The Council is responsible for the provision of a professional welfare service to the deaf; provides recreational services; ensures that the public develops an understanding of the world of the deaf and their welfare problems; and has made an incalculable contribution to the integration of the deaf into society as happy and productive citizens. Brochures are available.

South African National Tuberculosis Association (SANTA)
621 Leisk House, Cor. Bree and Rissik Streets, Johannesburg 2001, PO Box 10501, Johannesburg 2000.   Founded in 1947 to involve themselves in the prevention, cure and control of tuberculosis in South Africa and to create an awareness of the disease and methods of combating it among the general public. The Association comprises 275 voluntary committee branches, care groups and small anti-TB associations in rural areas as members. No membership is payable. The only criteria for membership of the Association and its branches are a caring for humanity and a willingness to work for the combating of TB among the population groups in South Africa. Any interested members of the public may write for further information. Functions are detailed in the annual report and the Association offers a wide variety of pamphlets, posters, films and slides dealing with TB, its symptoms, control and cure.

South African Speech and Hearing Association
PO Box 31782, Braamfontein, 2017, South Africa.   An association representing qualified and student speech therapists and audiologists in the Republic of South Africa. Speech therapists and audiologists only may be members and the only service offered to the public is an information leaflet to aid scholars interested in following the degree in Speech Pathology and Audiology.

Index

Where reference is made to the **medical action chart**, see list of contents on pp. 683–7.
When looking up any medical complaint, also check medical action chart's list of contents.